Collins
School
Thesaurus

Collins

HarperCollins Publishers
Westerhill Road
Bishopbriggs
Glasgow
G64 2QT
Great Britain

Fourth edition 2009

Reprint 10 9 8 7 6 5 4 3 2 1

© HarperCollins Publishers 1999, 2002,
2006, 2009

UK paperback
ISBN 978-0-00-728983-7

UK hardback
ISBN 978-0-00-728984-4

Australian edition
ISBN 978-0-7322-8905-8

Collins ® is a registered trademark of
HarperCollins Publishers Limited

www.collinslanguage.com

A catalogue record for this book is
available from the British Library

Designed by Wolfgang Homola

Typeset by Davidson Pre-Press, Glasgow

Printed and bound in China
by South China Printing Co Ltd

Acknowledgements
We would like to thank those authors and
publishers who kindly gave permission
for copyright material to be used in the
Collins Word Web. We would also like to
thank Times Newspapers Ltd for providing
valuable data.

When you buy a Collins dictionary or
thesaurus and register on
www.collinslanguage.com for the free
online and digital services, you will not be
charged by HarperCollins for access to
Collins free Online Dictionary content or
Collins free Online Thesaurus content on
that website. However, your operator's
charges for using the internet on your
computer will apply. Costs vary from
operator to operator. HarperCollins is not
responsible for any charges levied by online
service providers for accessing Collins free
Online Dictionary or Collins free Online
Thesaurus on **www.collinslanguage.com**
using these services.

HarperCollins does not warrant
that the functions contained in
www.collinslanguage.com content
will be uninterrupted or error free, that
defects will be corrected, or that
www.collinslanguage.com or the server
that makes it available are free of viruses or
bugs. HarperCollins is not responsible for
any access difficulties that may be
experienced due to problems with network,
web, online or mobile phone connections.

Contents

Editorial Staff

Introduction

Since its first publication, **Collins School Thesaurus** has proved itself to be a vital language and literacy tool for today's students. It was created to meet their needs and aspirations through research among teachers. Many samples were tested so Collins could establish exactly what features would be considered most helpful, and all those identified were incorporated into its text. This new edition has been revised and expanded to give students even more language and study help.

Collins' unique approach ensures that each entry word is followed by a short explanation of its meaning, which is then followed by an example of real English showing the context in which the word may be used. Furthermore, each synonym given for the entry word is also accompanied by an example showing context. This makes it easier for students to see which synonyms can be directly substituted for the entry word, and which involve a slight shift in sense.

Collins School Thesaurus has even more ways to help. It provides:

- Panels containing more advanced synonyms for the preceding entry word, a suitable antonym where appropriate, and related words

- Themed lists relevant to the entry word, such as *shades of red* at **red**, to expand students' vocabulary and enhance their creative writing skills

- A **Word Studies** supplement with advice on how to avoid the most over-used words, offering detailed groups of alternatives for every context and shade of meaning

- A **Subject Lists** supplement providing students with the essential vocabulary relevant to key school subjects

- A detailed index listing all the synonyms which appear in the thesaurus and showing which headwords each synonym appears under, so that students can see at a glance whether a word is a synonym for more than one entry word

Collins School Thesaurus is even more relevant, accessible, and student-friendly than before, and it's an indispensable companion to the *Collins School Dictionary*.

How To Use The Thesaurus

Collins School Thesaurus is easy to use and understand. On the outer edge of
each page there is a marker highlighting the letter of the alphabet featured on
that page. At the top of each page, the first and last words entered on the page
are clearly shown. Below are some entries showing the thesaurus's main
features, along with an explanation of what they are.

The entry word ●   **horse** NOUN   ● The word's part
of speech

an animal kept for riding • *a fall
from a horse*

brumby (AUSTRALIAN AND NEW
ZEALAND) • *There's a mob of about
30 brumbies up there.*

equine • *the history and uses of
equines*

● Coverage of
World English

moke (AUSTRALIAN AND NEW
ZEALAND; SLANG) • *a tired old moke*

nag (INFORMAL) • *He unhitched his
sorry-looking nag from a nearby
post.*

Advice on when to ●
use the synonym

pony • *Peter trotted about on the
fat pony he had been given.*

MORE SYNONYMS
- mount
- steed

● More advanced
synonyms

RELATED WORDS
- ADJECTIVES: equestrian, equine,
horsey
- NOUN: equitation
- MALE: stallion
- FEMALE: mare
- YOUNG: foal, colt, filly

Words related to ●
the entry word

vain ② ADJECTIVE

Each sense of a word is shown as a separate entry

not successful in achieving what was intended • *He made a vain effort to cheer her up.*

An example of the entry word being used

abortive • *the abortive coup attempt*
fruitless • *It was a fruitless search.*
futile • *their futile attempts to avoid publicity*
unproductive • *an unproductive strategy*
useless • *a useless punishment which fails to stop crime*

Synonyms

ANTONYM

Antonym

● successful

valley NOUN

TYPES OF VALLEY

canyon	dingle
chasm	glen
coomb	gorge
cwm (WELSH)	gulch
dale	gully
defile	hollow
dell	ravine
depression	strath (SCOTTISH)

Themed list of words connected with the entry word

nice ADJECTIVE

What the word means

attractive or enjoyable • *Did you have a nice time, dear?*
▷ *see Word Study* **nice***, page 697*

Cross-reference to expanded Word Study panel in the supplement

How To Use The Index

The index helps you find any word in the thesaurus. Below is a section showing how the index is arranged.

Look up a word here to find which entry word it appears under as a synonym

absorbing → interesting
abstain → decline
abstain → refuse
abstruse → mysterious
abstruse → obscure

The arrow directs you to the entry word

absurd → impossible
absurd → incredible
absurd → irrational
absurd → ridiculous
absurd → silly
absurd → stupid
absurdity → stupidity
abundance → a **lot** *or* **lots**
abundance → wealth

If a word appears as a synonym in more than one entry, there is an index reference for each place where it can be found

abundant → ample
abundant → generous
abundant → plentiful
abundant → rich

If a phrase is given as the synonym's target, you should look under the word shown in bold to find the entry it appears under

abuse → **impose** on
abuse → harm
abuse → insult
abuse → mistreat
abuse → wrong
abused → oppressed
abusive → offensive
abutment → support
abysmal → awful
abysmal → terrible
abyss → hell

Aa

abandon ❶ VERB
to leave someone or something
• *His parents had abandoned him.*
desert • *Medical staff have deserted the city's main hospital.*
jilt • *She was jilted by her first fiancé.*
leave • *My husband has left me.*
leave behind • *He walked out and left behind a wife and two young children.*

MORE SYNONYMS
● forsake
● leave in the lurch

abandon ❷ NOUN
lack of restraint • *He began to laugh with abandon.*
recklessness • *the headstrong recklessness of youth*
wildness • *Her wildness just needed to be channelled properly.*

ANTONYM
● control

abate VERB
to become less • *The four-day flood at last abated.*
decrease • *The pain had decreased considerably.*
diminish • *The attacks on the village did not diminish.*
ebb • *Her strength was ebbing fast.*
lessen • *After a while, the cramps lessened.*
subside • *Their enthusiasm was beginning to subside.*

wane • *His popularity shows no sign of waning.*

ability NOUN
the skill needed to do something
• *the ability to get on with others*
capability • *We have the capability of going out and winning.*
competence • *They have a high level of competence.*
expertise • *legal expertise*
skill • *the skill to play at a higher level*
talent • *a talent for music*

MORE SYNONYMS
● aptitude
● dexterity
● proficiency

ANTONYM
● inability

able ADJECTIVE
good at doing something
• *He proved himself to be an able politician.*
accomplished • *an accomplished pianist*
capable • *a very capable manager*
efficient • *a team of efficient workers*
expert • *My mother was an expert baker.*
first-rate • *This run is only suitable for first-rate skiers.*
skilled • *a skilled craftsman*
talented • *a talented actor*

Can't find the word you're looking for? Try the index.

A

B C D E F G H I J K L M N O P Q R S T U V W X Y Z

abolish

MORE SYNONYMS
- competent
- proficient

abolish VERB

to do away with something • *Their objective was to abolish capital gains tax.*

annul • *The marriage was annulled last month.*

do away with • *the proposal to do away with nuclear weapons*

overturn • *criminals seeking to overturn their convictions*

put an end to • *efforts to put an end to the traffic in drugs*

MORE SYNONYMS
- quash
- rescind
- revoke

about ❶ PREPOSITION

of or concerning • *anxiety about his sick son*

concerning • *documents concerning the estate*

on • *his book on Picasso*

regarding • *strict rules regarding the disposal of food*

relating to • *the rules relating to transfer fees*

about ❷ ADVERB

not exactly • *The procedure takes about thirty minutes.*

almost • *Their wages have almost doubled.*

approximately • *It was approximately three times the size of a domestic cat.*

around • *The crowd here is around 12,000.*

nearly • *a tradition going back nearly 20 centuries*

roughly • *One unit is roughly equivalent to half a pint of beer.*

above ❶ PREPOSITION

over or higher than something • *above the clouds*

higher than • *There are no hotels higher than four storeys.*

over • *the picture over the fireplace*

ANTONYM
- below

RELATED WORDS
- PREFIXES: super-, supra-, sur-

above ❷ PREPOSITION

greater than a certain level or amount • *The death toll will rise above 50.*

beyond • *I expect to live way beyond 100.*

exceeding • *a floor area exceeding 50,000 square feet*

abrupt ❶ ADJECTIVE

sudden or unexpected • *the abrupt resignation of the prime minister*

sudden • *this week's sudden thaw*

unexpected • *His career came to an unexpected end.*

unforeseen • *unforeseen difficulties*

MORE SYNONYMS
- precipitate
- unanticipated

abrupt ❷ ADJECTIVE

unfriendly and impolite • *He was a taken aback by her abrupt manner.*

curt • *"The matter is closed," was the curt reply.*

rude • *He was frequently rude to waiters and servants.*

short • *She seemed tense and was definitely short with me.*

terse • *He received a terse one-line rejection from the Ministry.*

MORE SYNONYMS
- brusque
- unceremonious

Can't find the word you're looking for? Try the index.

ANTONYM
- polite

absent ADJECTIVE
not present • *absent from work*
away • *She is away on a business trip.*
elsewhere • *Four witnesses can prove he was elsewhere at the time.*
gone • *I'll only be gone for ten minutes.*
missing • *Another 44 passengers are still missing.*

ANTONYM
- present

absent-minded ADJECTIVE
forgetful or not paying attention
• *Her absent-minded stepfather left the camera under the carriage seat.*
distracted • *He seems distracted, giving the impression of being elsewhere.*
forgetful • *She's getting rather forgetful, and living mostly in the past.*
random (NEW ZEALAND) • *I'm sorry, I'm a bit random these days.*

absolute ❶ ADJECTIVE
total and complete • *He is talking absolute nonsense.*
complete • *The operation was a complete success.*
downright • *That's a downright lie!*
pure • *a work of pure genius*
sheer • *It would be sheer madness to carry on after this.*
thorough • *He has a thorough knowledge of the subject.*
total • *the total destruction of the city*
utter • *He stared at me in utter disbelief.*

MORE SYNONYMS
- unmitigated
- unqualified

absolute ❷ ADJECTIVE
having total power • *an absolute ruler*
dictatorial • *a dictatorial system of government*
supreme • *humble subjects of her supreme rule*
tyrannical • *popular uprisings against tyrannical rulers*

absorb VERB
to soak up or take in something
• *Plants absorb carbon dioxide.*
digest • *Fats are hard to digest.*
soak up • *Stir until the wheat has soaked up all the water.*
take in • *A growing tree takes in light and processes it for food.*

abstain VERB
to choose not to do something
• *The patients had to abstain from alcohol.*
avoid • *Heartburn sufferers should try to avoid fatty foods.*
deny oneself • *I won't deny myself some celebration tonight.*
forgo • *My wife and I have to forgo holidays now.*
give up • *She gave up smoking last year.*
refrain • *He appealed to all factions to refrain from violence.*

MORE SYNONYMS
- desist
- forbear
- renounce

absurd ADJECTIVE
ridiculous or nonsensical • *an absurd waste of money*
crazy (INFORMAL) • *It would be crazy to tinker with a winning team.*
illogical • *his completely illogical arguments*
ludicrous • *It was ludicrous to*

Can't find the word you're looking for? Try the index.

suggest that the visit could be kept secret.
nonsensical • *He says many diets are harmful and nonsensical.*
ridiculous • *The programme is too ridiculous to take seriously.*

MORE SYNONYMS
- incongruous
- preposterous

abundance NOUN
a great amount of something • *an abundance of wildlife*
affluence • *Pockets of affluence coexist with poverty.*
bounty • *autumn's bounty of fruit, seeds, and berries*
plenty • *Allow plenty of time to get home.*

MORE SYNONYMS
- cornucopia
- plethora

ANTONYM
- shortage

abundant ADJECTIVE
present in large quantities • *an abundant supply of cheap labour*
ample • *ample space for a good-sized kitchen*
copious • *copious amounts of red wine*
full • *a full tank of petrol*
plentiful • *a plentiful supply of vegetables*

ANTONYM
- scarce

abuse ❶ NOUN
cruel treatment of someone • *child abuse*
exploitation • *Most human life involves the exploitation of animals.*
harm • *the harm smokers willingly do to their own health*

hurt • *The victims suffer mental scars as well as physical hurt.*
ill-treatment • *the ill-treatment of political prisoners*
oppression • *the oppression of black people throughout history*

abuse ❷ NOUN
unkind remarks directed towards someone • *I was left shouting abuse as the car sped off.*
censure • *a controversial policy which has attracted international censure*
derision • *He was greeted with shouts of derision.*
insults • *They shouted insults at each other.*
invective • *A woman had hurled racist invective at the family.*

abuse ❸ VERB
to speak insultingly to someone • *He was verbally abused by other soldiers.*
curse • *We started cursing them under our breath.*
insult • *I did not mean to insult you.*
scold • *Later she scolded her daughter for having talked to her father like that.*
slate (BRITISH; INFORMAL) • *Willis's acting skills have been slated, yet again.*

abusive ADJECTIVE
rude and unkind • *abusive language*
disparaging • *He made some disparaging remarks about the team.*
insulting • *She was charged with insulting behaviour to a police officer.*
offensive • *The book was seen by many Muslims as being deeply offensive to Islam.*
rude • *He is rude to her friends.*

Can't find the word you're looking for? Try the index.

scathing • *He made some particularly scathing comments about the design.*

MORE SYNONYMS
- censorious
- vituperative

abyss NOUN
a very deep hole • *He crawled to peer over the edge of the abyss.*
chasm • *The climbers strung a rope across the chasm and crawled along it.*
fissure • *The earthquake opened large fissures in the ground.*
gorge • *The valley narrowed to a gorge with cascading crags.*
pit • *Eric lost his footing and began to slide into the pit.*
void • *His feet dangled in the void.*

accelerate VERB
to go faster • *She accelerated away from the kerb.*
hurry • *He shouted at me to hurry.*
quicken • *Her pulse quickened in alarm.*
speed up • *It is designed to speed up credit-card transactions.*

ANTONYM
- decelerate

accept VERB
to receive or agree to something • *All those invited to next week's conference have accepted.*
acknowledge • *He was willing to acknowledge her as his child.*
agree to • *Hours before the deadline, the Chinese agreed to the conditions.*
concur with • *I concur with her opinion.*
consent to • *The Russians consented to the peace treaty.*
take • *He took the job.*

ANTONYM
- refuse

acceptable ADJECTIVE
good enough to be accepted • *an acceptable standard of living*
adequate • *a lack of adequate facilities*
all right • *The meal was all right for the price.*
fair • *He is a fair player, but not outstanding.*
good enough • *I'm afraid that excuse just isn't good enough.*
passable • *She can speak fluent Spanish and passable French.*
satisfactory • *The workmen have done a satisfactory job.*
tolerable • *a tolerable level of noise*

accidental ADJECTIVE
happening by chance • *The fire was accidental.*
casual • *a casual remark*
chance • *a chance meeting*
inadvertent • *She giggled at the inadvertent pun.*
random • *the random nature of death in war*

ANTONYM
- deliberate

accommodate VERB
to provide someone with a place to stay • *a hotel built to accommodate guests for the wedding*
house • *The building will house 12 boys.*
put up • *I wanted to know if she could put me up for a few days.*
shelter • *There were no facilities for sheltering the refugees.*

accommodating ADJECTIVE
willing to help • *his polite, accommodating manner*

a
b
c
d
e
f
g
h
i
j
k
l
m
n
o
p
q
r
s
t
u
v
w
x
y
z

Can't find the word you're looking for? Try the index.

A
B
C
D
E
F
G
H
I
J
K
L
M
N
O
P
Q
R
S
T
U
V
W
X
Y
Z

considerate • *I try to be considerate to non-smokers.*
helpful • *The staff in the Newcastle office are very helpful.*
hospitable • *He was very hospitable to me when I came to New York.*
kind • *It was very kind of you to come.*
obliging • *an extremely pleasant and obliging man*

accommodation NOUN

a house or room for living in
• *Travel and overnight accommodation are included.*
digs (BRITISH; INFORMAL) • *I was studying and living in digs all round the country.*
house • *He sold his house in London and moved to the country.*
housing • *a serious housing shortage*
lodgings • *At the moment the house provides lodgings for Oxford students.*
quarters • *the officers' quarters*

accompany ❶ VERB

to go somewhere with someone
• *Children must be accompanied by an adult.*
conduct (FORMAL) • *He asked if he might conduct us to the ball.*
escort • *They were escorted by police to their plane.*
go with • *I haven't asked my friend to go with me yet.*
usher • *I ushered him into the office.*

accompany ❷ VERB

to occur with something • *severe pain accompanied by fever*
come with • *Stress comes with this job.*
go together with • *Poverty and illiteracy go together with high birth rates.*

accomplish VERB

to manage to do something • *If we'd all work together, I think we'd accomplish our goal.*
achieve • *Achieving our aims makes us feel good.*
bring about • *the only way to bring about political change*
complete • *She has just completed her first novel.*
do • *Have you done it yet?*
fulfil • *All the necessary conditions were fulfilled.*
manage • *40% of children managed the required standard in reading.*

MORE SYNONYMS

● effect
● execute
● realize

accurate ADJECTIVE

correct to a detailed level • *Quartz watches are very accurate.*
correct • *The correct answers can be found at the bottom of the page.*
exact • *an exact copy*
faithful • *a faithful translation*
precise • *precise sales figures*
right • *That clock never tells the right time.*
strict • *He has never been a playboy in the strict sense of the word.*
true • *a true account of what happened*

ANTONYM

● inaccurate

accuse VERB

to charge someone with doing something wrong • *He accused her of having an affair.*
blame • *The police blamed the explosion on terrorists.*
censure • *The Stock Exchange took*

the unusual step of censuring him in public.

charge • Police have charged Mr Smith with murder.

cite • He was banned for 30 days after being cited for foul play.

denounce • He publicly denounced government nuclear policy.

MORE SYNONYMS
- impeach
- incriminate
- indict

accustomed ADJECTIVE

used to something • The manager has become accustomed to abuse of late.

adapted • The camel's feet, well adapted for dry sand, are useless on mud.

familiar • He was very familiar with contemporary music.

used • I'm used to having my sleep interrupted.

ANTONYM
- unaccustomed

achieve VERB

to gain by hard work or ability • She has achieved her best tournament result for years.

accomplish • halfway towards accomplishing an important career goal

carry out • debate about how such reforms should be carried out

complete • The commission completed this task in March.

do • I have done what I came here to do.

fulfil • The army has fulfilled its objective.

perform • He has not performed his administrative duties properly.

achievement NOUN

something which someone has succeeded in doing • His presence here is an achievement in itself.

accomplishment • The list of her accomplishments is staggering.

deed • His heroic deeds were celebrated in every corner of India.

exploit • His wartime exploits were later made into a TV series.

feat • A racing car is an extraordinary feat of engineering.

acquire VERB

to get something • I have recently acquired a digital camera.

attain • students who attain the required grades

gain • He gained valuable experience from the job.

get • My video's broken - I'll have to get a new one.

obtain • I couldn't obtain a ticket at any price.

pick up • You can pick up some real bargains at the January sales.

procure • It was still difficult to procure food and fuel.

secure • The team have secured a place in the semi-finals.

act ❶ VERB

to do something • The bank acted properly in the best interests of the depositors.

function • All the computer systems functioned properly.

operate • In the first half he operated effectively in defence.

perform • He performed well in a World Cup match last summer.

work • All sides will work towards a political solution.

act ❷ VERB

to perform in a play or film • He acted in 91 films altogether.

a
b
c
d
e
f
g
h
i
j
k
l
m
n
o
p
q
r
s
t
u
v
w
x
y
z

Can't find the word you're looking for? Try the index.

act out • *It was made using real people to act out the scene.*
perform • *She performed the role on television twice more.*
play • *He plays agent Lillian Scully in a spoof of The X-Files.*
play the part of • *She agreed to play the part of Evita.*
portray • *His mean, moody looks are perfect for the cynical anti-hero he portrays.*

MORE SYNONYMS
- characterize
- personify

act ❸ NOUN
a single thing someone does
• *an act of disloyalty to the King*
accomplishment • *Winning the tournament would be an incredible accomplishment.*
achievement • *She was honoured for her achievements as a film-maker.*
deed • *forgotten deeds of heroism*
feat • *an outstanding feat of athleticism*
undertaking • *Organizing the show has been a massive undertaking.*

action ❶ NOUN
the process of doing something
• *He had to take evasive action to avoid being hit.*
activity • *the electrical activity of the brain*
operation • *It is quite a tricky operation.*
process • *the peace process*

action ❷ NOUN
something that is done • *He did not like his actions questioned.*
accomplishment • *sporting accomplishments*
achievement • *If we can win the*

league it will be a great achievement for me.
deed • *daring and heroic deeds*
exploit • *the stories of his wartime exploits*
feat • *prodigious feats of engineering*

active ❶ ADJECTIVE
full of energy • *Having an active child around the house can be exhausting.*
energetic • *an energetic, happy young girl*
lively • *a lively and attractive teenager*
restless • *On Christmas Eve the kids are too restless to sleep.*
sprightly • *a small, sprightly 60-year-old*
vivacious • *He was very vivacious and great fun to work with.*

MORE SYNONYMS
- dynamic
- indefatigable

active ❷ ADJECTIVE
busy and hardworking • *people who are active in local politics*
busy • *My husband lived a full and busy life.*
engaged • *The contenders are now fully engaged in their campaigns.*
enthusiastic • *As a student he was an enthusiastic member of the Communist party.*
hardworking • *a team of hardworking and dedicated volunteers*
industrious • *It is a happy and industrious community.*
involved • *She is heavily involved in local fundraising projects.*
occupied • *A busy social life will keep you fully occupied in February.*

Can't find the word you're looking for? Try the index.

activity ❶ NOUN
a situation in which lots of things are happening • There is an extraordinary level of activity in the office.
action • a film full of action and excitement
bustle • the hustle and bustle of a busy hospital
energy • I love the energy you find in big cities.
liveliness • a restaurant with a wonderful atmosphere of liveliness

activity ❷ NOUN
something you do for pleasure • sports and other leisure activities
hobby • My hobby is birdwatching.
interest • Amongst his many interests are angling and painting.
pastime • You need a more active pastime than playing computer games.
pursuit • I like art, cooking and outdoor pursuits.

actual ADJECTIVE
real, rather than imaginary or guessed at • That is the official figure: the actual figure is much higher.
authentic • music played on authentic medieval instruments
genuine • a store selling genuine army clothing
realistic • a realistic picture of Dublin life
true • The film is based on a true story.
verified • verified reports of serious human rights violations

acute ❶ ADJECTIVE
severe or intense • an acute shortage of supplies
critical • suffering from a critical illness

extreme • a crippling disease which causes extreme pain
grave • His country faces grave problems.
great • He died in great agony.
intense • I felt an intense loneliness.
serious • It increases the risk of serious injuries.
severe • Nuts can trigger off a severe allergic reaction.

acute ❷ ADJECTIVE
very intelligent • an acute mind
alert • He is old, but he has a very quick and alert mind.
astute • He has a remarkably astute brain.
bright • You don't need a bright mind to figure that one out.
keen • a competent economist with a keen intellect
perceptive • a perceptive analysis of the situation
quick • a child with an enquiring mind and a quick intelligence
sharp • His gentle manner disguised a sharp mind.
shrewd • He demonstrated a shrewd understanding of human nature.

MORE SYNONYMS
● discriminating
● discerning
● perspicacious

adapt VERB
to alter for a new use • Shelves were built to adapt the library for use as an office.
adjust • He had to adjust the driver's seat.
alter • The government has altered the rules.
change • The law needs to be changed.
convert • a table that converts into an ironing board

Can't find the word you're looking for? Try the index.

A
B
C
D
E
F
G
H
I
J
K
L
M
N
O
P
Q
R
S
T
U
V
W
X
Y
Z

modify • *Our workshop is busy modifying the tanks for desert conditions.*

add ❶ VERB
to put something with something else • *Add the grated cheese to the sauce.*
attach • *Don't forget to attach the completed entry form.*
augment • *a way to augment the family income*
supplement • *I suggest supplementing your diet with vitamin A.*

MORE SYNONYMS
● adjoin
● affix
● append

add ❷ VERB
to combine numbers or quantities • *Banks add all the interest and other charges together.*
add up • *adding up calories on a calculator*
count up • *They counted up all the hours the villagers worked.*
total • *They will compete for prizes totalling nearly £300.*

ANTONYM
● subtract

addition NOUN
something that has been added to something else • *recent additions to their range of cars*
increase • *a substantial increase in workload*
supplement • *a supplement to their basic pension*

MORE SYNONYMS
● addendum
● adjunct
● appendage

adequate ADJECTIVE
enough in amount or quality for a purpose • *an adequate diet*
acceptable • *a company which offers an acceptable benefits package*
ample • *You've had ample time to discuss this matter.*
enough • *enough money to live on*
satisfactory • *a satisfactory bid for the company*
sufficient • *One teaspoon of salt should be sufficient.*

ANTONYM
● insufficient

administer ❶ VERB
to be responsible for managing something • *people who administer large companies*
be in charge of • *Who is in charge of this division?*
command • *Who would command the troops in the event of war?*
control • *He controls the largest publishing house in the country.*
direct • *Christopher will direct day-to-day operations.*
manage • *Within two years he was managing the shop.*
run • *This is no way to run a business.*
supervise • *the men who supervised the project*

administer ❷ VERB
to inflict or impose something on someone • *He administered most of the blows.*
carry out • *You are not authorized to carry out disciplinary action.*
deal • *His attacker dealt him a severe blow to the face.*
dispense • *They have set up military courts to dispense swift justice.*
execute • *She leapt up and executed a spinning kick to his head.*

Can't find the word you're looking for? Try the index.

impose • *The judge had no choice but to impose a death sentence.*
inflict • *Inflicting punishment to stop crime is not the answer.*
perform • *He had to perform emergency surgery.*

MORE SYNONYMS
- mete out

admiration NOUN

a feeling of great liking and respect • *I have always had the greatest admiration for him.*
appreciation • *gifts presented to them in appreciation of their work*
approval • *His son had an obsessive drive to gain his father's approval.*
esteem • *Their public esteem has never been lower.*
regard • *He has always been held in high regard.*
respect • *We all have so much respect for her.*

admire VERB

to like and respect someone or something • *All those who knew him will admire him for his work.*
appreciate • *the need for children to appreciate their mother tongue*
look up to • *A lot of the younger girls look up to you.*
respect • *I want him to respect me as a career woman.*
value • *She genuinely values his opinion.*

MORE SYNONYMS
- esteem
- venerate

ANTONYM
- scorn

admit ❶ VERB

to agree that something is true

• *The driver admitted to falling asleep at the wheel.*
accept • *I accepted the truth of all that Nicola had told me.*
acknowledge • *Belatedly the government has acknowledged the problem.*
grant • *The magistrates granted that the RSPCA was justified in bringing the action.*

ANTONYM
- deny

admit ❷ VERB

to allow to enter • *He was admitted to university after the war.*
accept • *Stephen was accepted into the family.*
let in • *Turnstile operators were accused of letting in fans without tickets.*
receive • *He was received into the priesthood.*
take in • *The monastery has taken in 26 refugees.*

ANTONYM
- exclude

adult NOUN

a grown-up person • *Becoming a father signified he was now an adult.*
grown-up • *Las Vegas is the ultimate playground for grown-ups.*
man • *He is now a man of 42.*
woman • *a woman of child-bearing age*

ANTONYM
- child

advance ❶ VERB

to move forward or develop • *Rebel forces are advancing on the capital.*
make inroads • *They have made impressive inroads in the movie business.*

Can't find the word you're looking for? Try the index.

a
b
c
d
e
f
g
h
i
j
k
l
m
n
o
p
q
r
s
t
u
v
w
x
y
z

press on • *Poland pressed on with economic reform.*
proceed • *He proceeded down the spiral stairway.*
progress • *the ability to progress from one step to the next*

advance ❷ NOUN
progress in something • *scientific advance*
breakthrough • *a breakthrough in cancer treatment*
development • *the development of the car*
gain • *a gain of nearly 10%*
progress • *signs of progress in his reading*
step • *the first step towards peace*

advantage NOUN
a more favourable position or state • *We have a competitive advantage.*
ascendancy • *The extremists are gaining ascendancy.*
benefit • *For maximum benefit use your treatment every day.*
dominance • *the battle for high-street dominance*
superiority • *military superiority*

ANTONYM
● disadvantage

advertise VERB
to present something to the public in order to sell it • *Bookmakers cannot advertise on television.*
plug (INFORMAL) • *If I hear another actor plugging his latest book I will scream.*
promote • *What are you doing to promote your new film?*
publicize • *He never publicized his plans.*
push • *a publisher who knows how to push a product*

MORE SYNONYMS
● blazon
● promulgate

advertisement NOUN
a public announcement to sell or publicize something • *She recently placed an advertisement in the local newspaper.*
ad (INFORMAL) • *an ad for a minicab company*
advert (BRITISH; INFORMAL) • *She appeared in a coffee advert.*
commercial • *She has turned down a small fortune to do TV commercials.*
notice • *The request is published in notices in today's national newspapers.*
plug (INFORMAL) • *a shameless plug for his new film*

advice NOUN
a suggestion as to what to do • *Take my advice and stay away from him!*
counsel (FORMAL) • *He had always been able to count on her wise counsel.*
drum (AUSTRALIAN; INFORMAL) • *What's the drum on this?*
guidance • *The nation looks to them for guidance.*
opinion • *You should seek a medical opinion.*
suggestion • *She made suggestions as to how I could improve my diet.*

advise ❶ VERB
to offer advice to someone • *The minister advised him to leave as soon as possible.*
caution • *The researchers caution against drawing general conclusions from this study.*
counsel • *My advisers counselled*

A
B
C
D
E
F
G
H
I
J
K
L
M
N
O
P
Q
R
S
T
U
V
W
X
Y
Z

me to do nothing.

recommend • *We strongly recommend reporting the incident to the police.*

suggest • *He suggested a visit to the Cézanne exhibition.*

urge • *We urge that vigorous action be taken immediately.*

MORE SYNONYMS

- commend
- enjoin
- prescribe

advise ❷ VERB

to notify someone • *I think it best that I advise you of my decision to retire.*

inform • *My daughter informed me that she was pregnant.*

make known • *The details will be made known by the end of August.*

notify • *The skipper notified the coastguard of the tragedy.*

adviser NOUN

a person whose job is to give advice • *The President and his advisers spent the day in meetings.*

aide • *a former aide to Ronald Reagan*

consultant • *a management consultant*

guru • *He became Britain's modern design guru after launching Habitat in 1964.*

mentor • *He is my friend and musical mentor.*

tutor • *my college tutor*

advocate VERB

to publicly support a plan or course of action • *Mr Smith advocates corporal punishment for young offenders.*

back • *The newspaper is backing the residents' campaign.*

champion • *He passionately champions our cause.*

endorse • *We are reluctant to endorse such drastic measures.*

favour • *judges who favour the death penalty*

promote • *He promoted the idea of Scottish independence.*

recommend • *I can't recommend such a course of action.*

support • *people who supported his policies*

uphold • *We uphold the capitalist free economy.*

affair ❶ NOUN

an event or series of events • *The funeral was a sad affair.*

business • *This business has really upset me.*

event • *A wedding should be a joyous event.*

issue • *a major political issue*

matter • *I never interfere in these business matters.*

question • *the difficult question of unemployment*

situation • *The whole situation is now under control.*

subject • *a subject which had worried him for some time*

affair ❷ NOUN

a secret and romantic relationship • *He had an affair with someone he met on holiday.*

fling • *We had a brief fling, but it was nothing serious.*

liaison • *He denied that he had had a sexual liaison with his secretary.*

relationship • *She went public on her relationship with a Hollywood star.*

romance • *Our company discourages office romances.*

affect VERB

to influence something or

a
b
c
d
e
f
g
h
i
j
k
l
m
n
o
p
q
r
s
t
u
v
w
x
y
z

someone • *More than 7 million people have been affected by the drought.*

act on • *This drug acts very fast on the central nervous system.*

alter • *The earth's climate appears to have been altered by pollution.*

change • *It was to change the course of my life.*

impinge on • *My private life does not impinge on my professional life.*

affection NOUN
a feeling of fondness for someone or something • *She thought of him with affection.*

attachment • *Mother and child form a close attachment.*

fondness • *his fondness for cats*

liking • *a liking for flashy cars*

love • *My love for all my children is unconditional.*

warmth • *He greeted us both with warmth and affection.*

ANTONYM
- dislike

affectionate ADJECTIVE
full of fondness for someone • *She gave me a long and affectionate hug.*

caring • *a loving, caring husband*

fond • *She gave him a fond smile.*

loving • *The children were very loving to me.*

tender • *a tender kiss*

ANTONYM
- cold

afraid ADJECTIVE
scared of something unpleasant happening • *I was afraid of the other boys.*

apprehensive • *People are still terribly apprehensive about the future.*

fearful • *Bankers were fearful of a world banking crisis.*

frightened • *She was frightened of flying.*

nervous • *Emotionally, he left me a wreck, nervous of everyone.*

scared • *I was too scared to move.*

ANTONYM
- unafraid

after ADVERB
at a later time • *Shortly after, police arrested five suspects.*

afterwards • *He was taken to hospital but died soon afterwards.*

following • *We shared so much, not only during the war, but in the many years following.*

later • *He resigned ten years later.*

subsequently • *She subsequently became honorary secretary.*

ANTONYM
- before

RELATED WORD
- PREFIX: post-

again ADVERB
happening one more time • *He kissed her again.*

afresh • *The couple moved abroad to start life afresh.*

anew • *She's ready to start anew.*

once more • *Rage overcame him once more.*

against ❶ PREPOSITION
in opposition to • *I am against animal cruelty.*

averse to • *He's not averse to a drink.*

hostile to • *countries that were once hostile to South Africa*

in opposition to • *radio stations set up in opposition to the BBC*

versus • *Portugal versus England*

RELATED WORDS
- PREFIXES: anti-, contra-, counter-

against ❷ PREPOSITION
in preparation for or in case of
something • *precautions against fire*
in anticipation of • *His school
was one of several which closed in
anticipation of Arctic conditions.*
in expectation of • *The hotel was
being renovated in expectation of a
tourist boom.*
in preparation for • *The army
massed troops and guns in
preparation for a counter-attack.*

aggressive ADJECTIVE
full of hostility and violence
• *These fish are very aggressive.*
hostile • *The prisoner eyed him in a
hostile silence.*
quarrelsome • *He had been a wild
boy and a quarrelsome young man.*

MORE SYNONYMS
● belligerent
● pugnacious

ANTONYM
● peaceful

agile ADJECTIVE
able to move quickly and easily
• *He is as agile as a cat.*
lithe • *a lithe young gymnast*
nimble • *He built his career around
quick reflexes and nimble footwork.*
sprightly • *She is alert and
sprightly despite her 85 years.*
supple • *She is as supple as a dancer.*

MORE SYNONYMS
● limber
● lissom *or* lissome

ANTONYM
● clumsy

agitate ❶ VERB
to campaign energetically for
something • *The women had begun
to agitate for better conditions.*

campaign • *an organization which
campaigns for better consumer
rights*
demonstrate • *marchers
demonstrating for political reform*
protest • *country dwellers who
were protesting for the right to hunt*
push • *Some board members are
pushing for the merger.*

agitate ❷ VERB
to worry or distress someone
• *Everything she said was beginning
to agitate me.*
bother • *It really bothers me when
you talk like that.*
distress • *sudden noises which
distressed the animals*
disturb • *These dreams disturb me
for days afterwards.*
trouble • *Are you troubled by
thoughts of the future?*
upset • *The whole incident upset
me dreadfully.*
worry • *I didn't want to worry you
with my own problems.*

MORE SYNONYMS
● discompose
● faze
● perturb

agree ❶ VERB
to have the same opinion as
someone • *So we both agree there's
a problem?*
assent • *I assented to the request of
the publishers to write this book.*
be of the same opinion • *All the
other players are of the same opinion.*
concur • *Four other judges concurred.*
see eye to eye • *He has not
always seen eye to eye with his
brother.*

ANTONYM
● disagree

Can't find the word you're looking for? Try the index.

a b c d e f g h i j k l m n o p q r s t u v w x y z

agree ❷ VERB

to match or be the same as something • *His second statement agrees with facts as stated by the other witnesses.*

accord • *I cannot support policies that no longer accord with my principles.*

conform • *It doesn't conform with current building regulations.*

match • *Attendances do not match the ticket sales.*

square • *Does that explanation square with the facts?*

tally • *The figures don't seem to tally.*

agreeable ❶ ADJECTIVE

pleasant or enjoyable • *I found it a most agreeable experience.*

delightful • *I've had a delightful time.*

enjoyable • *an enjoyable meal*

lovely • *I hope you have a lovely holiday.*

nice • *It would be very nice to get away from it all for a few days.*

pleasant • *This restaurant offers good food in pleasant surroundings.*

pleasurable • *the pleasurable task of deciding where to go on holiday*

ANTONYM

- disagreeable

agreeable ❷ ADJECTIVE

willing to allow or do something • *She said she was agreeable to this plan.*

game • *Are you game to try something a little bit different?*

happy • *I'm happy to go along with what everyone else thinks.*

prepared • *Would you be prepared to queue for hours for a ticket?*

ready • *I'm ready to take over if he resigns.*

willing • *Are you willing to take part in a survey?*

MORE SYNONYMS

- amenable
- compliant

agreement NOUN

a decision reached by two or more people • *The two countries have signed agreements on fishing and oil.*

arrangement • *Eventually we came to an arrangement that suited us both.*

contract • *She has signed an exclusive solo-album contract.*

deal (INFORMAL) • *The company recently won a five-year deal to build runways.*

pact • *He ruled out any formal pact with the government.*

settlement • *She accepted an out-of-court settlement of £4000.*

treaty • *negotiations over a 1992 treaty on global warming*

MORE SYNONYMS

- compact
- covenant

aim ❶ VERB

to plan to do something • *The company aims to sign 1 million customers within five years.*

aspire • *people who aspire to public office*

attempt • *He will attempt to win the title for the second year running.*

intend • *I intend to remarry.*

plan • *Mr Beach was planning to sue over injuries he received.*

propose • *And where do you propose building such a huge thing?*

strive • *He strives hard to keep himself very fit.*

Can't find the word you're looking for? Try the index.

aim ❷ NOUN
what someone intends to achieve
• *Our main aim is to offer a superior product.*
ambition • *His ambition is to sail round the world.*
goal • *I have to keep setting goals for myself.*
intention • *It was always my intention to stay in Italy.*
objective • *His objective was to play golf and win.*
plan • *His plan was to acquire paintings by the best artists in Italy.*
target • *his target of 20 goals this season*

alarm ❶ NOUN
a feeling of fear • *The cat sprang back in alarm.*
anxiety • *anxiety about crime*
apprehension • *I tensed every muscle in my body in apprehension.*
fright • *The birds smashed into the top of their cages in fright.*
nervousness • *I smiled warmly so he wouldn't see my nervousness.*
panic • *There was panic in the streets of the capital.*
scare • *Despite the scare there are no plans to withdraw the drug.*

MORE SYNONYMS
● consternation
● trepidation

ANTONYM
● calm

alarm ❷ NOUN
a device used to warn people of something • *a burglar alarm*
distress signal • *The pilot was trying to send a distress signal when the aircraft crashed.*
siren • *a police siren*
warning • *A second air raid warning sounded over the capital.*

alarm ❸ VERB
to fill with fear • *We could not see what had alarmed him.*
distress • *He is very distressed by what happened.*
frighten • *The future frightens me.*
panic • *He was panicked by his wife's behaviour.*
scare • *Horses scare me.*
startle • *startled by a gunshot*
unnerve • *Investors had been unnerved by the country's ailing stockmarket.*

ANTONYM
● calm

alcohol NOUN
a drink that can make you drunk
• *There wasn't even any alcohol at the party.*
booze (INFORMAL) • *clutching a bottle of booze*
drink • *Too much drink is bad for you.*
grog (AUSTRALIAN AND NEW ZEALAND; INFORMAL) • *They demanded a bottle of grog.*
liquor • *I could smell liquor on his breath.*
spirits • *a voluntary ban on advertising spirits on TV*

RELATED WORD
● LIKE: dipsomania

alert ❶ ADJECTIVE
paying full attention • *apprehended by alert security staff*
attentive • *an attentive audience*
observant • *an observant policeman*
on guard • *on guard against the threat of invasion*
vigilant • *letter bombs intercepted by vigilant post office staff*

a
b
c
d
e
f
g
h
i
j
k
l
m
n
o
p
q
r
s
t
u
v
w
x
y
z

Can't find the word you're looking for? Try the index.

wary • *He kept a wary eye on the dog as he passed the gate.*

ANTONYM
● unaware

alert ❷ VERB
to warn of danger • *I was hoping he'd alert the police.*
forewarn • *The guide had forewarned me what to expect.*
inform • *The patient was not properly informed of the risks.*
notify • *The passengers were notified of the bomb threat.*
warn • *They warned him of the dangers of sailing alone.*

alike ❶ ADJECTIVE
similar in some way • *You and your father are so alike.*
analogous • *a ritual analogous to those of primitive cultures*
close • *a creature close in appearance to a panther*
identical • *Nearly all the houses were identical.*
similar • *These two wines are very similar in taste.*
the same • *products which are almost the same in every respect*

ANTONYM
● different

alike ❷ ADVERB
in a similar way • *I punish all my pupils alike if they misbehave.*
equally • *Democracy calls for all people to be treated equally.*
in the same way • *He speaks in the same way to his boss as to his own employees.*
similarly • *All the children were dressed similarly.*
uniformly • *The rules apply uniformly to everyone.*

alive ❶ ADJECTIVE
having life • *They kept her alive on a life support machine.*
animate • *animate beings*
breathing • *Not only is he still breathing, but he lives right here in New York.*
living • *The blue whale is the largest living thing on the planet.*

ANTONYM
● dead

alive ❷ ADJECTIVE
lively and active • *I never expected to feel so alive in my life again.*
active • *Half an hour's physical activity, five times a week, will keep you active.*
alert • *A brisk walk will make you feel more alert.*
animated • *He becomes animated when talking about his work.*
energetic • *a vital and energetic man*
full of life • *She was so chatty and full of life.*
lively • *Cheryl was a very lively and attractive girl.*
vivacious • *a vivacious personality*

ANTONYM
● dull

all PRONOUN
the whole of something • *Why did you have to go and say all that?*
each • *Each of us received a free gift.*
every one • *Every one of you must take a share of the blame.*
everything • *Sit down and tell me everything.*
the whole amount • *Have you paid the whole amount of the fine?*
the (whole) lot • *The whole lot of you are under arrest.*

A
B
C
D
E
F
G
H
I
J
K
L
M
N
O
P
Q
R
S
T
U
V
W
X
Y
Z

RELATED WORDS
- PREFIXES: pan-, panto-

allow ❶ VERB
to permit someone to do
something • *Smoking will not be
allowed.*
approve • *The Housing Minister
approved the building of the flats.*
authorize • *authorized to carry
weapons*
let • *They won't let her leave the
country.*
permit • *Unauthorized personnel
are not permitted to enter.*
stand for • *We won't stand for it
any more.*
tolerate • *I won't tolerate
sloppiness.*

MORE SYNONYMS
- brook
- give leave
- sanction

ANTONYM
- forbid

allow ❷ VERB
to set aside for a particular purpose
• *Allow four hours for the paint to dry.*
allocate • *an efficient method of
allocating resources*
allot • *We were allotted just 15
minutes.*
assign • *the full amount of
economic aid assigned for the year*
grant • *Funding had been granted
for the project.*
set aside • *money set aside for
education*

all right ADJECTIVE
acceptable • *It was all right but
nothing special.*
acceptable • *We've made an
acceptable start, but it could have
been better.*

adequate • *Our accommodation
was adequate.*
average • *I was only average
academically.*
fair • *The overall standard of the
entries was fair.*
okay or **OK** (INFORMAL) • *The prices
here are okay.*

almost ADVERB
very nearly • *Over the past decade
their wages have almost doubled.*
about • *I was about nine at the time.*
approximately • *The family owns
approximately 8% of the company.*
close to • *He spent close to 30
years in prison.*
nearly • *The beach was very nearly
empty.*
not quite • *It's more than a hill but
not quite a mountain.*
practically • *I've known him
practically all my life.*

alone ADJECTIVE
not with other people or things
• *He was all alone in the middle of
the hall.*
detached • *a 'counter-culture'
detached from the rest of the world*
isolated • *Talking things over in a
group meant none of us felt isolated.*
separate • *They were kept separate
from the other prisoners.*
single • *I get depressed on
Valentine's Day because I'm still
single.*

aloud ADVERB
out loud • *Our father read aloud to us.*
audibly • *Hugh sighed audibly.*
out loud • *I tried not to laugh out
loud.*

also ADVERB
in addition • *He is also an army
doctor.*

Can't find the word you're looking for? Try the index.

as well • *She published historical novels as well.*

besides • *You get to sample lots of baked things and take home masses of cookies besides.*

furthermore • *Furthermore, they claim that any such interference is completely ineffective.*

into the bargain • *The machine can play ordinary cassettes into the bargain.*

moreover • *They have accused the government of corruption. Moreover, they have named names.*

too • *I was there too.*

always ADVERB

all the time or forever • *She's always moaning.*

continually • *Malcolm was continually changing his mind.*

every time • *You can't get it right every time.*

forever • *He was forever attempting to arrange deals.*

invariably • *Their teamwork was invariably good.*

perpetually • *The two groups are perpetually at loggerheads.*

amaze VERB

to surprise greatly • *He amazed us by his knowledge of Welsh history.*

astonish • *I was astonished by his stupidity.*

astound • *I am astounded at the comments made by the Chief Superintendant.*

shock • *She was shocked by the appalling news.*

stagger • *He was staggered by the sheer size of the crowd.*

stun • *Many cinema-goers were stunned by the film's tragic end.*

surprise • *We'll solve the case ourselves and surprise everyone.*

MORE SYNONYMS
- dumbfound
- flabbergast
- stupefy

amazement NOUN

complete surprise • *Much to my amazement, he arrived on time.*

astonishment • *They looked at each other in astonishment.*

shock • *I am still getting over the shock of winning.*

surprise • *To my surprise, I found I liked it.*

wonder • *Cross shook his head in wonder.*

MORE SYNONYMS
- perplexity
- stupefaction

amazing ADJECTIVE

very surprising or remarkable • *some of the most amazing stunts you're ever likely to see*

astonishing • *an astonishing display of physical strength*

astounding • *The results are quite astounding.*

staggering • *a staggering 17% leap in sales*

startling • *startling new evidence*

stunning • *a stunning piece of news*

surprising • *A surprising number of customers order the same sandwich every day.*

among ❶ PREPOSITION

surrounded by • *The bike lay among piles of chains and pedals.*

amid • *a tiny bungalow amid clusters of trees*

amidst • *His parents were found dead amidst the wreckage of the plane.*

in the middle of • *a tiny island in*

the middle of the Pacific
in the thick of • *a restaurant built on stilts in the thick of a vast mangrove swamp*
surrounded by • *surrounded by bodyguards*

among ❷ PREPOSITION
between more than two • *The money will be divided among seven charities.*
between • *Proceeds from the auction will be shared between the artists.*
to each of • *£2,000 to each of the five winners*

amount NOUN
how much there is of something • *I still do a certain amount of work for them.*
expanse • *a vast expanse of grassland*
quantity • *vast quantities of food*
volume • *the sheer volume of traffic and accidents*

ample ADJECTIVE
of an amount: more than enough • *There is ample space for a good-sized kitchen.*
abundant • *providing abundant food for local wildlife*
enough • *Do you have enough money for a taxi home?*
plenty of • *You've had plenty of time to make up your mind.*
sufficient • *The police have sufficient evidence to charge him.*

ancestor NOUN
a person from whom someone is descended • *He could trace his ancestors back 700 years.*
forebear • *our Victorian forebears*
forefather • *the land of their forefathers*

MORE SYNONYMS
● precursor
● progenitor

anger ❶ NOUN
extreme annoyance • *She vented her anger at the umpire.*
fury • *She screamed, her face distorted in fury.*
outrage • *The decisions provoked outrage from human rights groups.*
rage • *An intense rage was burning inside her.*
wrath • *He incurred the wrath of the referee.*

MORE SYNONYMS
● choler
● ire
● pique
● spleen
● vexation

anger ❷ VERB
to make someone angry • *remarks which will anger his critics*
enrage • *He enraged the government by renouncing the agreement.*
infuriate • *Peter's presence had infuriated Gordon.*
outrage • *Customers are outraged by the bank's soaring profits.*

ANTONYM
● calm

angry ADJECTIVE
very annoyed • *He gets angry with me if I'm late.*
cross • *She was rather cross about having to trail across London.*
enraged • *The enraged crowd stoned the car, then set it on fire.*
furious • *He is furious at the way his wife has been treated.*
mad (INFORMAL) • *I'm pretty mad about it, I can tell you.*

Can't find the word you're looking for? Try the index.

animal NOUN

a living creature • *He was attacked by wild animals.*
beast • *the threat our ancestors faced from wild beasts*
creature • *sea creatures*

RELATED WORD
● PREFIX: ZOO-

animosity NOUN

a feeling of strong dislike towards someone • *There is no animosity between these two players.*
antagonism • *a history of antagonism between the two sides*
antipathy • *our growing antipathy towards our manager*
dislike • *She looked at him with dislike.*
hatred • *He didn't bother to conceal his hatred towards my mother.*
hostility • *unacceptable hostility toward minority groups*
ill will • *He didn't bear anyone any ill will.*
malice • *There was no malice in her voice.*
resentment • *There is growing resentment towards newcomers.*

announce VERB

to make known something publicly • *He will announce tonight that he is resigning from office.*
advertise • *He did not want to advertise his presence in the town.*
make known • *Details will be made known tomorrow.*
proclaim • *He loudly proclaimed his innocence.*
reveal • *They were now free to reveal the truth.*
tell • *She was relieved that she'd finally told the full story.*

MORE SYNONYMS
● promulgate
● propound

announcement NOUN

a statement giving information about something • *There has been no formal announcement by either government.*
advertisement • *an advertisement placed in the local newspaper*
broadcast • *In a broadcast on state radio the government announced its plans.*
bulletin • *At 3.30pm a bulletin was released announcing the decision.*
declaration • *a public declaration of support*
report • *Local press reports estimate that at least sixteen people have died.*
statement • *a short statement by her solicitors*

annoy VERB

to irritate or displease someone • *Try making a note of the things which annoy you.*
bother • *I didn't think it would bother me so much to see Brian again.*
displease • *Not wishing to displease her, he avoided answering the question.*
get on someone's nerves (INFORMAL) • *That song gets on my nerves.*
hack off (BRITISH AND NEW ZEALAND; SLANG) • *This will just hack people off more.*
hassle (INFORMAL) • *Then my husband started hassling me.*
irritate • *The flippancy in her voice seemed to irritate him.*
plague • *We were plagued by mosquitoes.*

vex • *Cassandra was vexed at not having noticed it herself.*

annoyance ❶ NOUN

a feeling of irritation • *He made no secret of his annoyance.*
displeasure • *She voiced her displeasure at her treatment.*
irritation • *He tried not to let his irritation show.*

annoyance ❷ NOUN

something that causes irritation • *Snoring can be more than an annoyance.*
bore • *It's a bore to be off sick.*
drag (INFORMAL) • *A dry sandwich is a drag to eat.*
nuisance • *He could be a bit of a nuisance when he was drunk.*
pain (INFORMAL) • *The peacocks are a pain - beautiful but noisy.*
pain in the neck (INFORMAL) • *Traffic jams are a pain in the neck.*
pest • *He climbed on the table, pulled my hair, and was generally a pest.*

answer ❶ VERB

to reply to someone • *I knew Ben was lying when he answered me.*
reply • *He replied that this was absolutely impossible.*
respond • *"Mind your manners, lady!" I responded.*
retort • *"Was he afraid?", he was asked. "Afraid of what?" he retorted.*

ANTONYM
- ask

answer ❷ NOUN

a reply given to someone • *Without waiting for an answer, he turned and went in through the door.*
reply • *I called out a challenge but there was no reply.*
response • *There has been no response to his remarks from the government.*
retort • *His sharp retort clearly made an impact.*

MORE SYNONYMS
- rejoinder
- riposte

ANTONYM
- question

anxiety NOUN

nervousness or worry • *our growing anxiety about their safety*
apprehension • *a feeling of apprehension about the future*
concern • *growing concern about the environment*
fear • *His fears might be groundless.*
misgiving • *She had some misgivings about what she had been asked to do.*
nervousness • *I smiled, trying to hide my nervousness.*
unease • *a deep sense of unease about the coming interview*
worry • *a major source of worry to us all*

MORE SYNONYMS
- perturbation
- trepidation

anxious NOUN

nervous or worried • *He admitted he was still anxious about the situation.*
apprehensive • *Their families are apprehensive about the trip.*
bothered • *I'm still bothered about what she's going to say.*
concerned • *a phone call from a concerned neighbour*
fearful • *We are all fearful for the security of our jobs.*
nervous • *I still get nervous before*

a
b
c
d
e
f
g
h
i
j
k
l
m
n
o
p
q
r
s
t
u
v
w
x
y
z

Can't find the word you're looking for? Try the index.

a visit to the dentist's.
troubled • *He was troubled about his son's lifestyle.*
uneasy • *an uneasy feeling that something was wrong*
worried • *His parents are worried about his lack of progress.*

apathetic ADJECTIVE

not interested in anything
• *apathetic about politics*
cool • *The idea met with a cool response.*
indifferent • *People have become indifferent to the sufferings of others.*
passive • *His passive attitude made things easier for me.*
uninterested • *unhelpful and uninterested shop staff*

ANTONYM
● enthusiastic

apologize VERB

to say sorry for something
• *I apologize for being late.*
ask forgiveness • *He fell to his knees asking for forgiveness.*
beg someone's pardon • *I was impolite and I do beg your pardon.*
express regret • *Mr Galloway expressed regret that he had caused any offence.*
say sorry • *I wanted to say sorry to her.*

appeal ❶ VERB

to make an urgent request for something • *The police appealed for witnesses to come forward.*
beg • *I begged him to leave me alone.*
call upon • *Frequently he was called upon to resolve conflicts.*
plead • *I pleaded to be allowed to go.*
request • *She had requested that the door to her room be left open.*

MORE SYNONYMS
● entreat
● implore
● pray

appeal ❷ VERB

to attract or interest • *The idea appealed to him.*
attract • *What attracted you to research work?*
fascinate • *Classical music had fascinated him since the age of three.*
interest • *It was the garden that really interested me.*
please • *It pleased him to talk to her.*

appeal ❸ NOUN

a formal request for something
• *an appeal for peace*
petition • *The court rejected their petition.*
plea • *his emotional plea for help in solving the killing*
request • *France had agreed to his request for political asylum.*

MORE SYNONYMS
● entreaty
● supplication

appear ❶ VERB

to become visible or present
• *A woman appeared at the far end of the street.*
come into view • *Nearly fifty gliders came into view to the south of the plateau.*
crop up (INFORMAL) • *Problems will crop up and hit you before you are ready.*
emerge • *The postman emerged from his van soaked to the skin.*
show up (INFORMAL) • *He failed to show up at the ceremony.*
surface • *The same old problems would surface again.*

Can't find the word you're looking for? Try the index.

turn up • *This is like waiting for a bus that never turns up.*

ANTONYM
● disappear

appear ❷ VERB

to begin to exist • *small white flowers which appear in early summer*
become available • *In 1950, legal aid became available in Britain.*
be invented • *The lawn mower was invented in 1830.*
come into being • *Fireworks first came into being with the invention of gunpowder.*
come into existence • *before our solar system came into existence*
come out • *This book first came out in 1992.*

appear ❸ VERB

to take part in a show or play • *He is soon to appear in two more films.*
act • *She has also been acting in a sitcom.*
perform • *He is currently performing in the West End show 'Grease'.*
play • *He played Hamlet to packed houses.*
play a part • *His ambition is to play the part of Dracula.*

appearance ❶ NOUN

the time when something begins to exist • *the appearance of computer technology*
advent • *the advent of satellite and cable channels*
arrival • *the arrival of modern technologies*
coming • *the coming of the railways*
debut • *the debut of the new channel*

emergence • *the emergence of pay-per-view TV*
introduction • *the introduction of the minimum wage*

appearance ❷ NOUN

the way that a person looks • *She used to be so fussy about her appearance.*
bearing • *a man of iron will and military bearing*
image • *He urged the rest of the band to update their image.*
look • *She is so much happier with her new look.*
looks • *a young woman with wholesome good looks*

MORE SYNONYMS
● demeanour
● mien

appointment ❶ NOUN

an arrangement to meet someone • *She has an appointment with her accountant.*
date • *I have a date with Wendy.*
interview • *a job interview*
meeting • *Can we have a meeting to discuss that?*
rendezvous • *I had almost decided to keep my rendezvous with Tony.*

appointment ❷ NOUN

the choosing of a person to do a job • *his appointment as manager*
election • *the election of the government in 1997*
naming • *the naming of the new captain*
nomination • *They opposed the nomination of a junior officer to the position.*
selection • *his selection as a parliamentary candidate*

appointment ❸ NOUN

a job • *He applied for an*

Can't find the word you're looking for? Try the index.

appointment in Russia.
assignment • *my first assignment for The New York Times*
job • *He's trying for a job in the Civil Service.*
place • *All the candidates won places on the ruling council.*
position • *She took up a position at the Arts Council.*
post • *He has held several senior military posts.*

appreciate ❶ VERB
to value something highly
• *He appreciates fine wines.*
admire • *All those who knew him will admire him for his work.*
prize • *Military figures made out of lead are prized by collectors.*
rate highly • *The four-year-old mare is rated highly by her trainer.*
respect • *I respect his talent as a pianist.*
treasure • *She treasures her memories of those joyous days.*
value • *I value the work he gives me.*

ANTONYM
● scorn

appreciate ❷ VERB
to understand a situation or problem • *I didn't appreciate the seriousness of it at the time.*
be aware of • *I am well aware of the arguments on the other side.*
perceive • *to get pupils to perceive for themselves the relationship between success and effort*
realize • *People don't realize how serious this is.*
recognize • *They have been slow to recognize it as a problem.*
understand • *They are too young to understand what is going on.*

appropriate ADJECTIVE
suitable or acceptable for a given situation • *Jeans are not appropriate wear for work.*
apt • *an apt title for his memoirs*
correct • *the importance of correct behaviour and social niceties*
fitting • *a fitting tribute to a great man*
proper • *the proper course for the court to take*
suitable • *a suitable location*

MORE SYNONYMS
● apposite
● appurtenant
● congruous
● germane

ANTONYM
● inappropriate

approval ❶ NOUN
agreement given to something
• *The plan will require approval from the local authority.*
agreement • *The clubs are seeking agreement for a provisional deal.*
authorization • *We didn't have authorization to go.*
blessing • *Mr Ryabov appeared to give his blessing to Mr Yeltsin's plan.*
endorsement • *His endorsement has been fervently sought by all the main presidential candidates.*
permission • *They cannot leave the country without permission.*
sanction • *The King cannot enact laws without the sanction of Parliament.*

MORE SYNONYMS
● assent
● imprimatur
● mandate
● ratification

Can't find the word you're looking for? Try the index.

A
B
C
D
E
F
G
H
I
J
K
L
M
N
O
P
Q
R
S
T
U
V
W
X
Y
Z

approval ❷ NOUN
liking and admiration of a person
or thing • *He wanted to gain his
father's approval.*
admiration • *a strategy that is
winning admiration from around the
world*
esteem • *Their public esteem has
never been lower.*
favour • *He has won favour with a
wide range of groups.*
praise • *She is full of praise for the
range of excellent services available.*
respect • *We all have so much
respect for her.*

ANTONYM
● disapproval

approve ❶ VERB
to think something or someone is
good • *Not everyone approves of the
festival.*
admire • *I admire him for his work.*
favour • *The opposition parties
favour constitutional reform.*
praise • *He praised the fans for
their continued support.*
respect • *I want him to respect me
as a career woman.*
think highly of • *He thought
highly of his brother.*

ANTONYM
● disapprove

approve ❷ VERB
to agree formally to something
• *The court approved the
compensation plan.*
authorize • *to authorize the use of
military force*
consent to • *His parents consented
to an autopsy.*
endorse • *I can endorse their
opinion wholeheartedly.*
permit • *The doorman is not

allowed to permit them entry to the
film.*
sanction • *He may now be ready to
sanction the use of force.*

ANTONYM
● veto

approximate ADJECTIVE
close but not exact • *We believe
that an approximate figure of 20% is
nearer the mark.*
estimated • *Our estimated time of
arrival is 3.30.*
inexact • *Forecasting is an inexact
science.*
loose • *a loose translation*
rough • *a rough estimate*

ANTONYM
● exact

ardent ADJECTIVE
full of enthusiasm and passion
• *an ardent supporter of capital
punishment*
avid • *an avid follower of the team*
devoted • *surrounded by devoted
fans*
enthusiastic • *enthusiastic
collectors of Elvis memorabilia*
fervent • *a fervent admirer of his*
intense • *his intense love of
football*
keen • *a keen supporter of the
cause*
passionate • *He developed a
passionate interest in motor racing.*

ANOTHER SYNONYM
● zealous

ANTONYM
● apathetic

area ❶ NOUN
a particular part of a place
• *a built-up area of the city*
district • *I drove around the*

Can't find the word you're looking for? Try the index.

business district.

locality • *All other factories in the locality went on strike in sympathy.*

neighbourhood • *She no longer takes evening strolls around her neighbourhood.*

region • *a remote mountainous region of Afghanistan*

zone • *a war zone*

area ❷ NOUN

the size of a two-dimensional surface • *The islands cover a total area of 625 square kilometres.*

expanse • *a huge expanse of blue-green sea*

extent • *the extent of the rain forest*

range • *a driver's range of vision*

size • *a country nearly three times the size of ours*

argue ❶ VERB

to disagree with someone in an angry way • *They argued over the cost of the taxi fare.*

bicker • *They bickered endlessly about procedure.*

disagree • *They can communicate even when they strongly disagree.*

fall out (INFORMAL) • *Mum and I used to fall out a lot.*

feud • *feuding neighbours*

fight • *We're always fighting about money.*

quarrel • *My brother quarrelled with my father.*

row • *We started rowing about whose turn it was next.*

squabble • *The children were squabbling over the remote control.*

wrangle • *Delegates wrangled over the future of the organization.*

argue ❷ VERB

to try to prove • *She argued that her client had been wrongly accused.*

assert • *The defendants continue to assert their innocence.*

claim • *Statisticians claim that the book contains inaccuracies.*

debate • *Parliament will debate the issue today.*

maintain • *He had always maintained his innocence.*

reason • *I reasoned that if he could do it, so could I.*

MORE SYNONYMS

- controvert
- expostulate
- remonstrate

argument ❶ NOUN

an angry disagreement • *She got into an argument with one of the marchers.*

barney (BRITISH, AUSTRALIAN AND NEW ZEALAND; INFORMAL) • *We had such a barney that we nearly split up.*

blue (AUSTRALIAN; SLANG) • *He gets into more blues with authority than I do.*

clash • *clashes between police and demonstrators*

dispute • *a dispute over ticket allocation*

feud • *a two-year feud between neighbours*

fight • *We had another fight about money.*

row • *Maxine and I had a terrible row.*

squabble • *a family squabble over Sunday lunch*

argument ❷ NOUN

a set of reasons presented for something • *There's a strong argument for lowering the price.*

case • *the case for his defence*

grounds • *facts providing grounds for an unfair dismissal complaint*

Can't find the word you're looking for? Try the index.

logic • *The logic is that, without more growth, the deficit will rise.*
reasoning • *the reasoning behind the decision*

arrange ❶ VERB

to make plans to do something • *Why don't you arrange to meet him later?*
fix up • *I fixed up an appointment to see her.*
organize • *She organized the trip to the museum.*
plan • *She planned to leave in August.*
schedule • *Our appointment is scheduled for Tuesday.*

arrange ❷ VERB

to set things out in a particular order • *He started to arrange the books in piles.*
classify • *Weathermen classify clouds into several different groups.*
group • *The fact sheet is grouped into seven sections.*
order • *The French order things differently.*
organize • *He began to organize his materials.*
sort • *The students are sorted into three ability groups.*

MORE SYNONYMS

● array
● systematize

arrest ❶ VERB

to take someone into custody • *Police arrested five men in connection with the attack.*
apprehend • *Police have not apprehended her killer.*
capture • *Her accomplice was captured by Dutch police.*
nick (BRITISH; SLANG) • *Keep quiet or we'll all get nicked.*

seize • *Two military observers were seized by rebels yesterday.*
take prisoner • *He was taken prisoner in 1940 at the fall of Dunkirk.*

arrest ❷ NOUN

the act of arresting someone • *The police made two arrests.*
apprehension • *information leading to the apprehension of the killer*
capture • *He was trying to evade capture by security forces.*
seizure • *the mass seizure of terrorists*

article ❶ NOUN

a piece of writing in a newspaper or magazine • *There's an article about it in today's paper.*
feature • *a feature about Gulf War syndrome*
item • *I read an item about this only last week.*
piece • *I disagree with your recent piece about Australia.*
story • *Most newspapers had a story about the film's premiere.*

article ❷ NOUN

a particular item • *household articles*
item • *Various items have gone missing from my desk.*
object • *everyday objects such as wooden spoons*
thing • *I have a few things to buy for the trip.*

ashamed ADJECTIVE

feeling embarrassed or guilty • *He was not even ashamed of what he had done.*
embarrassed • *I'm not embarrassed to admit I cried.*
guilty • *When she realized I was*

a
b
c
d
e
f
g
h
i
j
k
l
m
n
o
p
q
r
s
t
u
v
w
x
y
z

watching, she looked guilty.
humiliated • *I felt humiliated at the scene he was causing.*
sheepish • *"I'm afraid it was my idea," he admitted, looking sheepish.*
sorry • *She's really sorry for all the trouble she's caused.*

MORE SYNONYMS
- chagrined
- mortified

ANTONYM
- proud

ask ❶ VERB
to put a question to someone
• *She asked me if I'd enjoyed my dinner.*
inquire • *I rang up to inquire about train times.*
interrogate • *I interrogated everyone even slightly involved.*
query • *He queried whether it could have been sabotage.*
question • *He was questioned by police.*
quiz • *He was quizzed about his eligibility for benefits.*

ANTONYM
- answer

ask ❷ VERB
to make a request to someone
• *We had to ask him to leave.*
appeal • *The police appealed for witnesses to come forward.*
beg • *I begged him to leave me alone.*
demand • *I demanded an explanation from him.*
implore • *I implored him not to give it up.*
plead • *She pleaded to be allowed to go.*
seek • *Always seek legal advice before entering into any agreement.*

MORE SYNONYMS
- beseech
- entreat

ask ❸ VERB
to invite someone • *Not everybody had been asked to the wedding.*
bid (LITERARY) • *They all smiled at him and bade him eat.*
invite • *She invited him to her 26th birthday party.*

aspect NOUN
a feature of something • *Exam results are only one aspect of a school's success.*
consideration • *The cost involved will be a chief consideration in our choice.*
element • *Fitness is now an important element in our lives.*
factor • *an important factor in a child's development*
feature • *the most significant feature of his childhood*
part • *Respect is an important part of any relationship.*
point • *There is another point to remember when making your decision.*
side • *He had a darker side to his character.*

assemble ❶ VERB
to gather together in a group
• *a convenient place for students to assemble between classes*
collect • *We all collected round him to listen.*
come together • *a common room where we can come together and relax*
congregate • *Youngsters love to congregate here in the evenings.*
convene • *A grand jury has convened to gather evidence.*
gather • *We all gathered in the board room.*

Can't find the word you're looking for? Try the index.

mass • *Troops were massing on both sides of the border.*

assemble ❷ VERB

to fit the parts of something together • *Workers were assembling planes.*

build • *A carpenter built the shelves for us.*

construct • *He had constructed a crude explosive device.*

erect • *Stagehands are employed to erect the scenery.*

make • *I like making model aeroplanes.*

put together • *You can buy the parts and put it together yourself.*

assistant NOUN

a person who helps someone • *His assistant took over while he went out.*

aide • *a presidential aide*

ally • *her political allies*

colleague • *a business colleague*

helper • *volunteer helpers*

right-hand man • *the resignation of the manager's right-hand man*

associate ❶ VERB

to connect one thing with another • *Poverty is associated with old age.*

connect • *a common problem directly connected with stress*

couple • *The papers coupled the Gulf crisis with the problems facing the former Soviet Union.*

identify • *Candidates want to identify themselves with reform.*

link • *Liver cancer is linked to the hepatitis B virus.*

associate ❷ VERB

to spend time with a person • *I began associating with different crowds of people.*

hang out (INFORMAL) • *People want to hang out with you for the wrong reasons.*

mingle • *reporters who mingled freely with the crowd*

mix • *local youths who want to mix with the foreign tourists*

run around (INFORMAL) • *What's he doing running around with a teenager?*

socialize • *She made little effort to socialize with other staff.*

MORE SYNONYMS

● consort
● fraternize

associate ❸ NOUN

a person known through work • *the restaurant owner's business associates*

colleague • *learning from more experienced colleagues*

co-worker • *Their Chinese co-workers often worked seven days a week.*

workmate • *employees who expose dishonest workmates*

association ❶ NOUN

an organization • *a research association*

body • *the chairman of the policemen's representative body*

club • *the local Young Conservatives' club*

company • *a major motor company*

confederation • *the Confederation of British Industry*

group • *an environmental group*

institution • *a member of various financial institutions*

league • *the World Muslim League*

society • *the Royal Society for the Protection of Birds*

syndicate • *a syndicate of international banks*

a
b
c
d
e
f
g
h
i
j
k
l
m
n
o
p
q
r
s
t
u
v
w
x
y
z

Can't find the word you're looking for? Try the index.

A
B
C
D
E
F
G
H
I
J
K
L
M
N
O
P
Q
R
S
T
U
V
W
X
Y
Z

ANOTHER SYNONYM
● fraternity

association ❷ NOUN
a connection or involvement with
a person or group • *his association
with a terrorist group*
affiliation • *He has no affiliation
with any political party.*
attachment • *Mother and child
form a close attachment.*
bond • *There is a special bond
between us.*
connection • *He has denied any
connection with the organization.*
relationship • *Ours was strictly a
professional relationship.*
tie • *I had very close ties with the
family.*

MORE SYNONYMS
● affinity
● liaison

assume ❶ VERB
to accept that something is true
• *I assumed that he would turn up.*
believe • *I believe she'll be back
next week.*
guess (INFORMAL) • *I guess she
thought that was pretty smart.*
imagine • *You tend to imagine that
you cannot put a foot wrong.*
suppose • *I see no reason to
suppose that it isn't working.*
think • *They thought that they had
the match won.*

assume ❷ VERB
to take responsibility for
something • *Mr Cross will assume
the role of Chief Executive.*
accept • *He accepted the role of
player-captain.*
shoulder • *He has had to shoulder
the responsibility of his father's
mistakes.*

take on • *Don't take on more
responsibilities than you can handle.*
undertake • *He undertook to edit
the text himself.*

astute ADJECTIVE
very intelligent or perceptive
• *an astute judge of character*
alert • *He is old, but he has a very
quick and alert mind.*
clever • *a clever business move*
keen • *a keen understanding of
politics*
perceptive • *his perceptive
analysis of the situation*
quick • *He has an enquiring mind
and a quick intelligence.*
sharp • *His gentle manner
disguised a sharp mind.*
shrewd • *He demonstrated a
shrewd understanding of human
nature.*
smart • *a very smart move*

ANOTHER SYNONYM
● discerning

attach VERB
to join or fasten things together
• *The gadget can be attached to any
surface.*
affix • *His name was affixed to the
wall of his cubicle.*
connect • *Connect the pipe to the
tap.*
couple • *The engine is coupled to a
gearbox.*
fasten • *The shelves are fastened to
the wall with screws.*
join • *two sticks joined together by
a chain*
link • *tree houses linked by ropes*
tie • *He tied the dog to a post with
its leash.*

ANTONYM
● separate

Can't find the word you're looking for? Try the index.

attachment ❶ NOUN

a feeling of love and affection
• *Mother and child form a close attachment.*

affection • *the affection between a pet and its owner*
bond • *There has always been a strong bond between us.*
fondness • *I have a great fondness for all animals.*
liking • *He has never shown any liking for his colleagues.*
love • *A deep love gradually developed between them.*

attachment ❷ NOUN

a part attached to something else
• *The drill comes with a wide range of attachments.*

accessory • *a range of accessories for your mobile phone*
component • *Additional components are available as listed.*
fitting • *bathroom fittings*
fixture • *The box can be adapted to take a light fixture.*
part • *Extra parts can be added later.*
unit • *The unit plugs into any TV set.*

attack ❶ VERB

to use violence against someone or something • *I thought he was going to attack me.*

assault • *The gang assaulted him with iron bars.*
charge • *He ordered us to charge.*
invade • *The allies invaded the Italian mainland at Anzio.*
raid • *He was found guilty of raiding a bank.*
set upon • *As the lorry drove east it was set upon by bandits.*
storm • *The refugees decided to storm the embassy.*

attack ❷ VERB

to criticize someone strongly • *She attacked the government's economic policies.*

blast • *He blasted the referee for his inconsistency.*
censure • *The bank has been censured and fined by the authority.*
criticize • *The regime has been harshly criticized.*
have a go at (BRITISH; INFORMAL) • *If they made a mistake the crowd would have a go at them.*
put down (INFORMAL) • *He was always putting me down.*
vilify (FORMAL) • *He was vilified, hounded, and forced into exile.*

MORE SYNONYMS

● berate
● lambast *or* lambaste
● revile

attack ❸ NOUN

violent physical action against someone or something • *a vicious attack on an unarmed man*

assault • *The rebels are poised for a new assault.*
charge • *a bayonet charge*
invasion • *the Roman invasion of Britain*
offensive • *the government's military offensive against the rebels*
onslaught • *civilians trying to flee from the military onslaught*
raid • *a raid on a house by armed police*

attempt ❶ VERB

to try to do something • *They attempted to escape.*

endeavour • *I will endeavour to arrange it.*
seek • *We have never sought to impose our views.*
strive • *The school strives to treat*

Can't find the word you're looking for? Try the index.

pupils as individuals.
try • I tried hard to persuade him to stay.
try your hand at • He'd always wanted to try his hand at writing.

attempt ② NOUN
an act of trying to do something • one of his rare attempts at humour
bid • a bid to save the newspaper
crack (INFORMAL) • his third crack at the world heavyweight title
go (INFORMAL) • My mum suggested I should have a go at becoming a jockey.
shot (INFORMAL) • We'd like a shot at winning the league.
stab (INFORMAL) • Several tennis stars have had a stab at acting.
try • That makes the scheme worth a try.

attitude NOUN
someone's way of thinking and behaving • negative attitudes to work
outlook • behaviour that seems contrary to his whole outlook
perspective • It gave me a new perspective on life.
point of view • Try to look at this from my point of view.
position • What's your position on this issue?
stance • the Church's stance on contraception

attract VERB
to appeal to or interest • The trials have attracted many leading riders.
appeal to • The idea appealed to him.
draw • The match drew a large crowd.
entice • She resisted attempts to entice her into politics.
lure • They were being lured into a trap.

pull (INFORMAL) • They have to employ performers to pull a crowd.
tempt • Can I tempt you with some wine?

ANTONYM
● repel

attractive ADJECTIVE
pleasant, especially to look at • an attractive woman
appealing • a sense of humour that I found very appealing
charming • a charming little village
fetching • a fetching outfit
handsome • a handsome man
lovely • a lovely island
pretty • a shy, pretty girl

MORE SYNONYMS
● comely
● prepossessing
● winsome

ANTONYM
● unattractive

attribute NOUN
a quality or feature • a normal attribute of human behaviour
characteristic • their physical characteristics
feature • the most striking feature of his music
property • the magnetic properties of iron
quality • His humility is one of his most endearing qualities.
trait • personality traits

MORE SYNONYMS
● idiosyncrasy
● peculiarity

augment VERB
to add something to something else • a good way to augment your basic wage

Can't find the word you're looking for? Try the index.

add to • *A fitted kitchen adds to the value of your house.*

boost • *people who boost their earnings by working part-time from home*

complement • *an in-work benefit that complements earnings*

increase • *He is eager to increase his income by any means.*

reinforce • *measures which will reinforce their current strengths*

supplement • *I suggest supplementing your diet with vitamin A.*

top up • *compulsory contributions to top up pension schemes*

authentic ADJECTIVE
real and genuine • *an authentic French recipe*

bona fide • *We are happy to donate to bona fide charities.*

dinkum (AUSTRALIAN AND NEW ZEALAND; INFORMAL) • *a place which serves dinkum Aussie tucker*

genuine • *Experts are convinced the manuscript is genuine.*

real • *It's a real Rembrandt.*

true • *Of course she's not a true blonde.*

ANTONYM
● fake

automatic ❶ ADJECTIVE
operating mechanically by itself • *Modern trains have automatic doors.*

automated • *highly automated production lines*

mechanical • *the oldest working mechanical clock in the world*

robot • *a robot telescope*

self-propelled • *self-propelled artillery*

automatic ❷ ADJECTIVE
without conscious thought

• *automatic body functions*

instinctive • *an instinctive reaction*

involuntary • *involuntary muscle movements*

natural • *the insect's natural instinct to feed*

reflex • *Blushing is a reflex action linked to the nervous system.*

automobile NOUN (AMERICAN)
a vehicle for carrying a few people • *the Japanese automobile manufacturer*

car • *My dad's promised me a car if I pass my finals.*

motor • *He's bought himself a flash new motor.*

vehicle • *A child ran straight out in front of the vehicle.*

available ADJECTIVE
ready for use • *There are three small boats available for hire.*

accessible • *This information is accessible on the Internet.*

at hand • *Having the right equipment at hand will be enormously useful.*

at someone's disposal • *Do you have all the facts at your disposal?*

free • *There was only one seat free on the train.*

handy • *Keep your keys handy so you can get into your car quickly.*

to hand • *Keep your insurance details to hand when driving.*

ANTONYM
● unavailable

average ❶ ADJECTIVE
standard or normal • *the average American teenager*

normal • *I am now back to leading a perfectly normal life.*

regular • *He's just a regular guy.*

standard • *the standard price of a CD*

a
b
c
d
e
f
g
h
i
j
k
l
m
n
o
p
q
r
s
t
u
v
w
x
y
z

Can't find the word you're looking for? Try the index.

typical • *A typical day begins at 8.30.*

usual • *This isn't the usual kind of mail-order catalogue.*

average ②, on average
ADVERB

for the most part • *Men are, on average, taller than women.*

as a rule • *As a rule, the fee is roughly equal to the savings you have made.*

generally • *A glass of fine wine generally costs about £4.*

normally • *Normally, the transport system carries 50,000 passengers a day.*

typically • *In America, estate agents typically charge 5–6% of the sale price.*

usually • *In good condition, these models usually fetch up to 300 dollars at auction.*

avoid ① VERB

to make an effort not to do something • *We economists always try to avoid giving a straight answer.*

dodge • *dodging military service by feigning illness*

duck out of (INFORMAL) • *ducking out of the post-match press conference*

fight shy of • *She fought shy of confronting her critics.*

refrain from • *Mrs Hardie refrained from making any comment.*

shirk • *We won't shirk our responsibility.*

MORE SYNONYMS
● circumvent
● give a wide berth to

avoid ② VERB

to keep away from someone or something • *She thought he was trying to avoid her.*

dodge • *He refuses to dodge his critics.*

elude • *an attempt to elude photographers*

eschew (FORMAL) • *He eschewed publicity and avoided nightclubs.*

evade • *He managed to evade the police.*

shun • *Everybody shunned him.*

sidestep • *Rarely does he sidestep a question.*

steer clear of • *It would be best to steer clear of her.*

aware ①, aware of ADJECTIVE

conscious of something • *She was acutely aware of the noise of the city.*

acquainted with • *He was well acquainted with American literature.*

conscious of • *She was very conscious of Max studying her.*

familiar with • *I am not familiar with your work.*

mindful of • *Everyone should be mindful of the dangers.*

ANTONYM
● unaware

aware ② ADJECTIVE

knowing about something • *Keep me aware of any developments.*

informed • *the importance of keeping the public properly informed*

in the picture • *He's always kept me in the picture.*

knowledgeable • *He's very knowledgeable about new technology.*

MORE SYNONYMS
● au courant
● in the loop

awful ADJECTIVE

very unpleasant or very bad • *the*

same *awful* jokes
appalling • *living under the most appalling conditions*
dreadful • *They told us the dreadful news.*
frightful • *a frightful ordeal*
ghastly • *a mother accompanied by her ghastly unruly child*
horrendous • *The violence used was horrendous.*
terrible • *Her French is terrible.*

MORE SYNONYMS
● abysmal
● deplorable

Bb

babble VERB
to talk in an excited way
• *He babbled on and on.*
burble • *He burbles on about the goals he has scored.*
chatter • *Jane chattered about the children.*
gabble • *I started to gabble in the interview.*
prattle • *Alan is prattling on again.*

baby NOUN
a very young child • *I've had this birthmark since I was a baby.*
ankle-biter (AUSTRALIAN AND NEW ZEALAND; SLANG) • *I knew him when he was just an ankle-biter.*
bairn (SCOTTISH) • *My wife's expecting a bairn.*
child • *They celebrated the birth of their first child.*
infant • *young mums with infants in prams*

back ❶ NOUN
the part that is behind the front
• *the back of a postcard*
end • *the end of the corridor*
rear • *the rear of the building*
reverse • *the reverse of the sheet*
stern • *the stern of a boat*

ANTONYM
● front

back ❷ VERB
to support a person or organization
• *His friends are backing him.*
advocate • *Mr Jones advocates longer school days.*
encourage • *The government is encouraging better child care.*
endorse • *Do you endorse his opinion?*
favour • *I favour a different approach.*
promote • *She promoted his ideas.*
support • *We supported his political campaign.*

MORE SYNONYMS
● champion
● espouse
● second

ANTONYM
● oppose

background NOUN
where you come from • *a rich background*
culture • *people from different cultures*
environment • *the environment I grew up in*
history • *She has an interesting history.*
upbringing • *a strict upbringing*

bad ❶ ADJECTIVE
harmful, unpleasant, or upsetting
• *I have some bad news.*
▷ see Word Study **bad**, pages 667–8

ANTONYM
● good

bad ❷ ADJECTIVE
of poor quality • *bad roads*
▷ see Word Study **bad**, pages 667–8

Can't find the word you're looking for? Try the index.

ANTONYM
- satisfactory

bad ❸ ADJECTIVE
evil in character • *a bad person*
▷ see Word Study **bad**, pages 667–8

ANTONYM
- good

badly ❶ ADVERB
in an inferior way • *This essay is badly written.*
▷ see Word Study **badly**, page 668

ANTONYM
- well

badly ❷ ADVERB
seriously • *She was badly hurt in a fall.*
▷ see Word Study **badly**, page 668

ANTONYM
- slightly

badly ❸ ADVERB
in a cruel manner • *He treated his dog badly.*
▷ see Word Study **badly**, page 668

ANTONYM
- well

bait NOUN
something used to tempt someone • *Charles isn't taking the bait.*
bribe • *a politician who took bribes*
decoy • *He acted as a decoy to trap the murderer.*
inducement • *financial inducements to talk to the newspapers*
lure • *the lure of a huge salary*
temptation • *the temptation of easy money*

balance ❶ VERB
to make or remain steady • *Balancing on one leg is difficult.*
level • *He got two goals to level the score.*
stabilize • *attempts to stabilize the economy*
steady • *He steadied himself and shot at goal.*

balance ❷ NOUN
a stable relationship between things • *the chemical balance of the brain*
equilibrium • *the political equilibrium of Europe*
equity • *plans for greater equity of incomes*
equivalence • *the lack of equivalence between film and radio*
parity • *She won pay parity with male colleagues.*

ball NOUN
a round object • *a ball of wool*
drop • *a drop of blood*
globe • *the globe of the eyeball*
pellet • *an airgun pellet*
sphere • *a sphere the size of the Earth*

MORE SYNONYMS
- globule
- orb
- spheroid

ban ❶ VERB
to disallow something • *I am banned from taking part.*
bar • *The press will be barred from the talks.*
disqualify • *He was disqualified from driving.*
exclude • *They were excluded from the maths class.*
forbid • *The rules forbid the use of force.*
outlaw • *regulations outlawing child labour*
prohibit • *a law that prohibits alcohol*

a b c d e f g h i j k l m n o p q r s t u v w x y z

Can't find the word you're looking for? Try the index.

A
B
C
D
E
F
G
H
I
J
K
L
M
N
O
P
Q
R
S
T
U
V
W
X
Y
Z

ban | 40

MORE SYNONYMS
- banish
- proscribe
- suppress

ANTONYM
- permit

ban ② NOUN
a rule disallowing something
• *a ban on smoking*
disqualification • *a four-year disqualification from athletics*
embargo • *an embargo on trade with the country*
prohibition • *a prohibition on tobacco*
suppression • *the suppression of anti-government protests*

ANTONYM
- permit

band ① NOUN
a group of musicians who play together • *a singer in a rock and roll band*
group • *They formed the group while they were still at school.*
orchestra • *the National Youth Orchestra*

MORE SYNONYMS
- combo
- ensemble

band ② NOUN
a group of people who share a common purpose • *a band of rebels*
bunch • *A bunch of protesters were picketing the factory.*
company • *a company of actors*
crowd • *A small crowd of onlookers had gathered.*
gang • *a gang of criminals*
party • *a party of sightseers*
troupe • *She toured with a professional dance troupe.*

bang ① VERB
to hit or put something down hard, with a loud noise • *a toddler banging a saucepan with a wooden spoon*
beat • *They sat in a circle, beating small drums.*
hammer • *The supporters hammered on the windows of the bus.*
hit • *They were hitting the sides of the van with sticks.*
knock • *I knocked on the door for ages, but no-one answered.*
pound • *We pounded on the walls.*
slam • *I slammed down the receiver.*
thump • *The children cheered and thumped on their desks.*

bang ② NOUN
a sudden, short, loud noise • *The TV exploded with a bang.*
blast • *the ear-splitting blast of a cannon*
boom • *There was a boom and a cloud of smoke.*
crack • *the crack of a pistol shot*
detonation • *We heard several loud detonations coming from the building.*
explosion • *the deafening explosion of gunshots*
thump • *She dropped her case to the floor with a loud thump.*

bang ③ NOUN
a hard or painful bump against something • *I got a nasty bang on the elbow.*
blow • *a blow to the side of the head*
clout (INFORMAL) • *She gave him a swift clout on the ear.*
knock • *Knocks like this can cause damage to the spine.*

Can't find the word you're looking for? Try the index.

thump • *Ralph got a thump on the chest.*
whack • *She gave the horse a whack on the rump.*

banish ❶ VERB

to exile someone • *She banished him from the house.*
deport • *Many fans are being deported from Italy.*
eject • *He was ejected from the club.*
evict • *Police evicted ten families from the building.*
exile • *He was exiled from Russia.*
expel • *patients expelled from hospitals*
transport • *He was transported to a prison camp.*

banish ❷ VERB

to get rid of something or someone • *to banish illness*
discard • *Read the instructions before discarding the box.*
dismiss • *I dismissed the idea from my mind.*
dispel • *The myths are being dispelled.*
eliminate • *They eliminated him from their enquiries.*
eradicate • *projects to eradicate certain diseases*
remove • *talks to remove the last obstacles to the deal*

bank ❶ NOUN

a store of something • *a blood bank*
fund • *a pension fund*
hoard • *a hoard of treasure*
reserve • *the world's oil reserves*
stock • *stocks of paper and ink*
store • *a secret store of sweets*

MORE SYNONYMS

● reservoir
● stockpile

bank ❷ NOUN

the edge of a river or lake • *He sat fishing on the bank.*
brink • *orchards near the brink of the sea cliffs*
edge • *She stood too close to the edge and fell in.*
shore • *He swam towards the shore.*
side • *a picnic by the side of the river*

bar ❶ NOUN

a piece of metal • *bars across the windows*
pole • *He was tied to a pole.*
rail • *a curtain rail*
rod • *a fishing rod*
shaft • *the shaft of a spear*

bar ❷ VERB

to stop someone • *His bodyguards barred the way.*
obstruct • *Vehicles have obstructed the entrance.*
prevent • *A fence prevents people from entering.*

bare ❶ ADJECTIVE

not covered • *bare legs*
exposed • *His whole back is exposed.*
naked • *a naked body*
nude • *a nude model*
stripped • *I got stripped to have a shower.*
uncovered • *His arms were uncovered.*
undressed • *She got undressed in the bathroom.*

ANTONYM

● covered

bare ❷ ADJECTIVE

with nothing on top or inside • *a small bare office*
empty • *an empty room*

Can't find the word you're looking for? Try the index.

a
b
c
d
e
f
g
h
i
j
k
l
m
n
o
p
q
r
s
t
u
v
w
x
y
z

open • *open country*
spartan • *spartan accommodation*
vacant • *a vacant chair*

barely ADVERB
only just • *She is barely sixteen.*
almost • *I almost didn't make it.*
hardly • *I could hardly believe it.*
just • *They only just won.*
scarcely • *I can scarcely hear her.*

barren ❶ ADJECTIVE
with nothing growing on it
• *a barren desert*
arid • *the arid lands of Botswana*
desert • *desert regions*
desolate • *a desolate place*
dry • *poor, dry countries*
empty • *the empty desert*
waste • *waste land*

MORE SYNONYMS
● unfruitful
● unproductive

ANTONYM
● fertile

barren ❷ ADJECTIVE
unable to produce babies • *women who are barren*
childless • *childless couples*
infertile • *infertile women*
sterile • *sterile females*

ANTONYM
● fertile

barrier ❶ NOUN
something preventing entry
• *Demonstrators broke through the barriers.*
barricade • *a barricade of vehicles*
fence • *a garden fence*
obstruction • *Check the exhaust pipe is clear of obstructions.*
wall • *the huge city walls*

MORE SYNONYMS
● fortification
● obstacle
● rampart

barrier ❷ NOUN
something that prevents progress
• *plans to reduce the barriers to trade*
handicap • *It is a handicap not knowing a foreign language.*
hindrance • *a potential hindrance to the peace process*
hurdle • *the first hurdle in a job search*
impediment • *a serious impediment to free trade*
obstacle • *the main obstacle to the takeover*

base ❶ NOUN
the lowest part of something
• *the base of the cliffs*
bed • *the river bed*
bottom • *the bottom of the lake*
foot • *the foot of the mountain*
foundation • *They have laid the foundations for the new building.*
pedestal • *The statue is back on its pedestal.*
stand • *a microphone stand*

ANTONYM
● top

base ❷ NOUN
the place you work from
• *a military base*
camp • *refugee camps*
centre • *a health centre*
headquarters • *army headquarters in Colombo*
post • *a military post in the capital*
station • *the police station*

base ❸ VERB
to use as a foundation • *The film is based on a true story.*

Can't find the word you're looking for? Try the index.

build • *a reputation built on lies*
derive • *The name is derived from a Greek word.*
found • *My hopes were founded on a mistake.*
ground • *I like a film to be grounded in reality.*
hinge • *The whole play hinges on one character.*

basic ADJECTIVE
most necessary • *the basic requirements for the job*
elementary • *elementary computer training*
essential • *essential reading and writing skills*
fundamental • *fundamental rights*
key • *key skills such as communication and teamwork*
necessary • *They lack the necessary resources.*
vital • *vital supplies*

MORE SYNONYMS
○ central
○ indispensable
○ primary

basis NOUN
the main principle of something • *The same theme is the basis of several poems.*
core • *the core of Asia's problems*
fundamental • *the fundamentals of road safety*
heart • *the heart of the matter*
premise • *the premise of his argument*
principle • *the principles of Buddhism*

bay ❶ NOUN
a curve in a coastline • *the Bay of Biscay*
cove • *a sandy cove with white cliffs*

gulf • *the Gulf of Mexico*
inlet • *a deep inlet on the west coast*
sound • *streams that run into the sound*

bay ❷ VERB
to make a howling noise • *wolves baying in the moonlight*
bark • *a small dog barking at a seagull*
cry • *I heard animals cry in the forest.*
howl • *distant coyotes howling in the night*
yelp • *A dog snapped and yelped at them.*

beach NOUN
an area beside the sea • *making sandcastles on the beach*
coast • *a day at the coast*
sands • *the long white sands of Goa*
seashore • *walks along the seashore*
seaside • *trips to the seaside*
shore • *He swam out from the shore.*
strand • *collecting shells on the strand*

bear ❶ VERB
to carry something • *The ice wasn't thick enough to bear their weight.*
carry • *He always carried a gun.*
convey • *The taxi conveyed us to the centre.*
shoulder • *He had to shoulder the blame for the mistake.*
support • *Thick wooden posts support the ceiling.*
take • *You'd better take an umbrella.*

bear ❷ VERB
to have or show something • *The room bore the signs of a violent struggle.*

a
b
c
d
e
f
g
h
i
j
k
l
m
n
o
p
q
r
s
t
u
v
w
x
y
z

Can't find the word you're looking for? Try the index.

exhibit • *He began to exhibit symptoms of the disease.*
harbour • *She still harbours feelings of resentment.*
have • *I have a grudge against her.*

bear ❸ VERB
to accept something • *He can't bear to talk about it.*
abide • *I can't abide arrogant people.*
endure • *The pain was hard to endure.*
stomach • *He could not stomach violence.*
suffer • *I had to suffer his company all day.*
tolerate • *Women tolerate pain better than men.*

beat ❶ VERB
to hit someone or something hard • *He threatened to beat her.*
batter • *The waves kept battering the life raft.*
buffet • *Their plane was buffeted by storms.*
hit • *He hit me on the head.*
pound • *Someone was pounding on the door.*
strike • *She struck him across the mouth.*
thrash • *He was thrashed by his father.*

beat ❷ VERB
to defeat • *She was easily beaten in the race.*
defeat • *The team hasn't been defeated all year.*
outdo • *One man was trying to outdo the other.*
outstrip • *The company is outstripping its rivals.*
overcome • *Molly had overcome her fear of flying.*
overwhelm • *One attack could overwhelm the enemy.*
vanquish • *the man who helped vanquish Napoleon*

MORE SYNONYMS
● conquer
● master
● surpass

beat ❸ NOUN
a rhythm • *the thumping beat of rock music*
cadence • *the pulsing cadences of his music*
metre • *the strict metre of the poem*
rhythm • *His foot tapped a rhythm on the floor.*
stress • *differences of stress in speech*
time • *a song written in waltz time*

beautiful ADJECTIVE
attractive or pleasing • *beautiful music*
attractive • *an attractive woman*
delightful • *The perfume is delightful.*
fine • *a fine summer's day*
gorgeous • *a gorgeous man*
lovely • *You look lovely.*
pleasing • *a pleasing appearance*

MORE SYNONYMS
● exquisite
● fair

ANTONYM
● ugly

beauty ❶ NOUN
the quality of being beautiful • *an area of outstanding beauty*
attractiveness • *the attractiveness of the region*
charm • *a woman of great charm*
elegance • *the elegance of the overall design*

Can't find the word you're looking for? Try the index.

loveliness • *the loveliness of the scene*

ANTONYM
● ugliness

beauty ❷ NOUN
a good-looking person • *a dark-haired beauty*
hunk (INFORMAL) • *The Swedish hunk is back again.*
stunner (INFORMAL) • *the 23-year-old stunner*

beauty ❸ NOUN
an attractive feature • *The beauty of the fund is its simplicity.*
advantage • *the advantages of the new system over the old one*
asset • *The one asset the job provided was contacts.*
attraction • *The main attraction of the place is the monument.*
benefit • *Every age has its benefits.*

because CONJUNCTION
for the reason that • *I went home because I was tired.*
as • *Don't cook for me as I'll be home late.*
since • *Since you didn't listen, I'll repeat that.*

MORE SYNONYMS
● in that
● on account of
● owing to

before ADVERB
at a previous time • *Have you been to Greece before?*
earlier • *Here is a cake I made earlier.*
formerly • *He had formerly been in the army.*
in advance • *We booked the room well in advance.*
previously • *Previously she had*

little time to work.
sooner • *I wish I'd arrived sooner.*

ANTONYM
● after

RELATED WORDS
● PREFIXES: ante-, fore-, pre-

beg VERB
to ask anxiously for something
• *I begged him to leave me alone.*
beseech • *Her eyes beseeched him to show mercy.*
implore • *I implore you not to say anything.*
petition • *He petitioned the Court to let him go free.*
plead • *She was pleading with me to stay.*

MORE SYNONYMS
● entreat
● importune
● solicit

begin VERB
to start or cause to start • *She began to move around the room.*
commence (FORMAL) • *He commenced his journey.*
inaugurate • *The committee was inaugurated ten days ago.*
initiate • *They wanted to initiate a discussion.*
originate • *Mankind may have originated in Africa.*
set about • *He set about tackling his problems.*
start • *The meeting starts at 10 o'clock.*

MORE SYNONYMS
● instigate
● institute

ANTONYM
● end

a
b
c
d
e
f
g
h
i
j
k
l
m
n
o
p
q
r
s
t
u
v
w
x
y
z

Can't find the word you're looking for? Try the index.

A
B
C
D
E
F
G
H
I
J
K
L
M
N
O
P
Q
R
S
T
U
V
W
X
Y
Z

beginner NOUN
someone learning to do something
• *a beginner's course*
apprentice • *an apprentice in a law firm*
learner • *young learners of French*
novice • *Many of us are novices on the computer.*
starter • *new starters at school*
trainee • *a trainee in a newspaper office*

ANTONYM
● expert

beginning NOUN
where something starts • *the beginning of the city*
birth • *the birth of modern art*
commencement (FORMAL) • *a date for the commencement of talks*
opening • *the opening of the trial*
origin • *the origins of civilization*
outset • *There were lots of problems from the outset.*
start • *the start of all the trouble*

MORE SYNONYMS
● inauguration
● initiation
● onset

ANTONYM
● end

behave VERB
to act in a certain way • *They were behaving like animals.*
act • *He is acting like a spoilt child.*
function • *They are functioning as a team.*
operate • *I know how Graham operates.*
work • *My mind is working well today.*

belief ❶ NOUN
the certainty something is true

• *belief in reincarnation*
confidence • *I have every confidence that you'll do well.*
conviction • *She speaks with conviction.*
judgment • *My judgment is that he should leave.*
opinion • *Robert has strong opinions.*
trust • *She has complete trust that you'll help her.*
view • *In my view, he is wrong.*

belief ❷ NOUN
a principle of a religion or system
• *the culture and beliefs of ancient times*
creed • *people of every race and creed*
doctrine • *Christian doctrine*
dogma • *religious dogma*
faith • *Do you practise any faith?*
ideology • *different political ideologies*
principle • *the principles of Jewish faith*
tenet • *the fundamental tenets of Islam*

believable ADJECTIVE
possible or likely to be the case
• *The book is full of believable characters.*
credible • *credible witnesses*
imaginable • *It is scarcely imaginable that it happened here.*
likely • *It's more likely that she forgot.*
plausible • *a plausible explanation*
possible • *It's quite possible that I'm wrong.*
probable • *the most probable outcome*

ANTONYM
● unbelievable

Can't find the word you're looking for? Try the index.

believe VERB

to accept something is true
• *Don't believe everything you read in the papers.*
accept • *He can't accept that he is wrong.*
assume • *I assume these eggs are fresh.*
presume • *The missing person is presumed to be dead.*
swallow (INFORMAL) • *I found their story hard to swallow.*
trust • *I trust that you will manage.*

ANTONYM
○ doubt

belittle VERB

to make someone or something seem less important • *He belittles my opinions.*
deride • *He is derided as weak and incompetent.*
detract from • *Her sour comments detracted from Meg's happiness.*
downgrade • *I fear failure, but I downgrade my successes.*
scorn • *Eleanor scorns the work of others.*
undervalue • *We must never undervalue freedom.*

MORE SYNONYMS
○ denigrate
○ disparage
○ minimize

ANTONYM
○ praise

beloved ADJECTIVE

dearly loved • *He lost his beloved wife last year.*
adored • *an adored father*
cherished • *his most cherished possession*
darling • *our darling child*
dearest • *my dearest Maria*

precious • *I love my precious cat.*
treasured • *treasured memories*

ANTONYM
○ despised

below PREPOSITION or ADVERB

lower down • *six centimetres below soil level*
beneath • *She hid the letter beneath her mattress.*
down • *I fell down to the bottom.*
lower • *The price will fall lower than this.*
under • *tunnels under the ground*
underneath • *He crawled underneath the table.*

ANTONYM
○ above

bend ➊ VERB

to make or become curved • *Bend the bar into a horseshoe.*
buckle • *A wave buckled the ship's deck.*
curve • *The wall curves to the left.*
turn • *The road turns right at the end.*
twist • *glass twisted into elaborate patterns*
warp • *The wood had started to warp.*

bend ➋ VERB

to move forwards and downwards • *I bent over and kissed her cheek.*
arch • *Don't arch your back!*
bow • *He turned and bowed to her.*
crouch • *We were crouching in the bushes.*
incline • *The woman inclined her head to one side.*
lean • *She leant out of the window.*
stoop • *Stooping down, he picked up a stone.*

bend ➌ NOUN

a curve in something • *a bend in the road*

a
b
c
d
e
f
g
h
i
j
k
l
m
n
o
p
q
r
s
t
u
v
w
x
y
z

Can't find the word you're looking for? Try the index.

A
B
C
D
E
F
G
H
I
J
K
L
M
N
O
P
Q
R
S
T
U
V
W
X
Y
Z

arc • *the full arc of a rainbow*
corner • *He drove round the corner.*
curve • *the curve of the stream*
loop • *The river curves in a loop.*
turn • *a turn in the path*

MORE SYNONYMS
● angle
● arch
● twist

beneficial ADJECTIVE
giving some benefit • *Wine in moderation is beneficial to the health.*
advantageous • *an advantageous arrangement*
good for you • *Regular exercise is good for you.*
healthy • *trying to switch to a healthy lifestyle*
helpful • *This treatment is particularly helpful to hay fever sufferers.*
useful • *a useful addition to your first aid kit*
wholesome • *food made with good, wholesome ingredients*

benefit ❶ NOUN
an advantage • *the benefits of relaxation*
advantage • *The advantages of the new system far outweigh its disadvantages.*
asset • *A second language is an asset in this job.*
boon • *a great boon for busy housewives*
gain • *He used the knowledge for his personal gain.*
good • *Study for your own good!*
help • *It's no help to know I was right.*
profit • *the profits of working hard*
use • *His training was of no use to him.*

ANTONYM
● disadvantage

benefit ❷ VERB
to help in something • *The experience will benefit you.*
aid • *measures to aid working mothers*
assist • *The extra money will assist you.*
enhance • *His injury does not enhance our chances.*
further • *His support will further our cause.*
help • *The new laws won't help the environment.*
profit • *It won't profit us to complain.*

ANTONYM
● harm

benevolent ADJECTIVE
kind and helpful • *a benevolent ruler*
benign • *a benign and loveable man*
charitable • *charitable organizations*
compassionate • *my compassionate friends*
humane • *humane treatment of prisoners*
kind • *You have been kind and helpful to us.*

MORE SYNONYMS
● altruistic
● beneficent
● philanthropic

beside PREPOSITION
next to • *I stood beside my father and my uncle.*
adjacent to • *a hotel adjacent to the beach*
alongside • *a house alongside the river*

Can't find the word you're looking for? Try the index.

close to • *The restaurant is close to their home.*
near • *He stood very near the front door.*
next to • *She sat down next to him.*

best ➊ ADJECTIVE
of the highest standard • *the best film I have seen in a long time*
▷ see Word Study **best**, page 669

ANTONYM
● worst

best ➋ ADJECTIVE
most desirable • *the best thing you could have said*
▷ see Word Study **best**, page 669

ANTONYM
● worst

best ➌ NOUN
the preferred thing • *Of all my presents, this is the best.*
▷ see Word Study **best**, page 669

ANTONYM
● worst

betray ➊ VERB
to do someone harm • *I was betrayed by someone I had thought a friend.*
be unfaithful • *He's been unfaithful to his wife.*
break your promise • *I broke my promise to help her.*
double-cross (INFORMAL) • *I was angry that he double-crossed me.*
inform on • *people who inform on their colleagues*

betray ➋ VERB
to show feelings • *Jeremy's voice betrayed little emotion.*
expose • *She never exposed her hostile feelings.*
manifest • *Fear can manifest itself*

in many ways.
reveal • *Her expression revealed nothing.*
show • *His eyes showed his unhappiness.*

better ➊ ADJECTIVE
of more worth than another
• *Today was much better than yesterday.*
▷ see Word Study **better**, page 670

ANTONYM
● inferior

better ➋ ADJECTIVE
well after being ill • *I hope you feel better soon.*
▷ see Word Study **better**, page 670

ANTONYM
● worse

beware VERB
to be cautious • *Beware of the dog.*
be careful • *Be careful what you say to him.*
be cautious • *Doctors are cautious about using the treatment.*
be wary • *Michelle is wary of marriage.*
guard against • *We have to guard against thieves.*
look out • *Look out, there's a train coming.*
watch out • *Watch out for fog and ice.*

bias NOUN
prejudice for or against a person or group • *bias against women*
bigotry • *religious bigotry*
favouritism • *His promotion was due to favouritism.*
prejudice • *racial prejudice*

biased ADJECTIVE
showing prejudice • *biased attitudes*

a
b
c
d
e
f
g
h
i
j
k
l
m
n
o
p
q
r
s
t
u
v
w
x
y
z

Can't find the word you're looking for? Try the index.

A B C D E F G H I J K L M N O P Q R S T U V W X Y Z

one-eyed (AUSTRALIAN AND NEW ZEALAND) • *I may be a bit one-eyed because of the family connection.*
one-sided • *a one-sided argument*
partial • *a very partial view of the situation*
prejudiced • *Don't be prejudiced by what you read.*
slanted • *a slanted newspaper article*
weighted • *a scheme weighted towards those in need*

ANTONYM
- neutral

big ❶ ADJECTIVE
of a large size • *a big house*
▷ see Word Study **big**, page 671

ANTONYM
- small

big ❷ ADJECTIVE
of great importance • *a big name*
▷ see Word Study **big**, page 671

ANTONYM
- unimportant

bill NOUN
a statement of how much is owed • *a huge restaurant bill*
account • *Please charge it to my account.*
charges • *charges for eye tests*
invoice • *They sent an invoice for the damage.*
statement • *a credit card statement*

bit NOUN
a small amount • *a bit of coal*
crumb • *a crumb of comfort*
fragment • *glittering fragments of broken glass*
grain • *His story contains a grain of truth.*
part • *part of the problem*

piece • *The vase was smashed to pieces.*
scrap • *a scrap of evidence*

MORE SYNONYMS
- iota
- jot
- speck

bite VERB
to cut into something with your teeth • *His cat bit me when I tried to pat it.*
chew • *a video of a man having his leg chewed off by a bear*
gnaw • *The bones had been gnawed by wild animals.*
nibble • *She nibbled a biscuit.*
nip • *There were blotches where the mosquitoes had nipped him.*

bitter ❶ ADJECTIVE
angry and resentful • *a bitter row*
acrimonious • *an acrimonious discussion*
begrudging • *He gave me begrudging thanks.*
embittered • *an embittered old lady*
rancorous • *the issue that has led to rancorous disputes*
resentful • *She is resentful of others' success.*
sour • *a sour expression*

bitter ❷ ADJECTIVE
tasting or smelling sharp • *bitter lemons*
acid • *the acid smell of sweat*
acrid • *clouds of acrid smoke*
astringent • *astringent disinfectant*
sharp • *a clean, sharp taste*
sour • *a rich, sour stew*
tart • *the tart qualities of citrus fruit*

ANTONYM
- sweet

Can't find the word you're looking for? Try the index.

bizarre ADJECTIVE
very strange or eccentric • *He has some bizarre ideas about women.*
curious • *a curious mixture of ancient and modern*
eccentric • *Her eccentric behaviour was beginning to attract attention.*
extraordinary • *What an extraordinary character he is!*
odd • *a series of very odd coincidences*
outlandish • *her outlandish style of dressing*
peculiar • *a peculiar combination of flavours*
queer • *A very queer thing happened to me tonight.*
strange • *She's been behaving in a very strange way lately.*
weird • *his weird theories about UFOs*

ANTONYM
- ordinary

black NOUN or ADJECTIVE

SHADES OF BLACK	
coal-black	jet-black
ebony	pitch-black
inky	raven
jet	sable

blame ❶ VERB
to believe someone caused something • *Don't blame me for this trouble.*
accuse • *She accused him of causing the fire.*
charge • *He will be charged with murder.*
hold responsible • *I hold you responsible for this mess.*

blame ❷ NOUN
the responsibility for something bad • *I'm not going to take the blame for that!*

accountability • *He escaped accountability for his crimes.*
fault • *The fault was all yours.*
guilt • *the sole guilt for the outbreak of war*
liability • *He admitted liability for the crash.*
rap (SLANG) • *A maid took the rap for stealing the letters.*
responsibility • *responsibility for the murder*

MORE SYNONYMS
- culpability
- incrimination

blank ❶ ADJECTIVE
with nothing on it • *a blank sheet of paper*
bare • *bare walls*
clean • *a clean sheet of paper*
clear • *a clear patch of floor*
empty • *an empty page*
plain • *a plain envelope*
unmarked • *an unmarked board*

blank ❷ ADJECTIVE
showing no feeling • *John just looked blank.*
deadpan • *a deadpan expression*
dull • *a dull stare*
empty • *She saw the empty look in his eyes.*
impassive • *her impassive smile*
vacant • *the vacant expression on his face*

blend ❶ VERB
to mix things so as to form a single item or substance • *Blend the butter with the sugar.*
combine • *Combine the ingredients in a large bowl.*
merge • *how to merge the graphics with the text*
mingle • *the mingled smells of flowers and cigar smoke*

a
b
c
d
e
f
g
h
i
j
k
l
m
n
o
p
q
r
s
t
u
v
w
x
y
z

A
B
C
D
E
F
G
H
I
J
K
L
M
N
O
P
Q
R
S
T
U
V
W
X
Y
Z

mix • *Mix the two liquids together with a whisk.*

ANTONYM
- separate

blend ② VERB
to combine in a pleasing way • *The colours blend with the rest of the decor.*
complement • *The flavours complement each other perfectly.*
co-ordinate • *Choose accessories which co-ordinate with your outfit.*
go well • *a wine which goes well with fish*
harmonize • *shades which harmonize with most skin tones*
match • *Those shoes don't match that dress.*
suit • *glasses which suit the shape of your face*

blend ③ NOUN
a mixture or combination of things • *a blend of wine and sparkling water*
alloy • *an alloy of copper and tin*
amalgamation • *Bartók's rich amalgamation of musical styles*
combination • *a fantastic combination of colours*
compound • *a compound of water, sugar and enzymes*
fusion • *a fusion of cooking styles*
mix • *a delicious mix of exotic spices*
mixture • *a sticky mixture of flour and water*

bless VERB
to ask God's protection • *The bishop blessed the congregation.*
anoint • *The priest anointed the child with oil.*
consecrate • *ground that has been consecrated*
dedicate • *The well was dedicated to saints.*

hallow • *A building could be hallowed by prayer.*

ANTONYM
- curse

blessing ① NOUN
something good • *Good health is a blessing.*
benefit • *the benefits of technology*
boon • *This service is a boon to the elderly.*
gift • *A cheerful nature is a gift.*
godsend • *The extra twenty dollars was a godsend.*
help • *My computer is a real help in my work.*

ANTONYM
- disadvantage

blessing ② NOUN
approval or permission to do something • *She got married with her parents' blessing.*
approval • *Does this plan have your approval?*
backing • *We can't do anything without his backing.*
consent • *He gave his consent to the article.*
leave • *She gave us leave to start.*
permission • *You have my permission to go.*
support • *My manager has given his full support to my project.*

MORE SYNONYMS
- approbation
- sanction

ANTONYM
- disapproval

blob NOUN
a small amount of a thick or sticky substance • *He had a blob of chocolate mousse on his tie.*
bead • *Beads of blood spattered*

the counter.
dab • *You've got a dab of glue on your nose.*
drop • *a few thick drops of fluid*
droplet • *droplets of congealed fat*

block ❶ NOUN
a large piece • *a block of wood*
bar • *a bar of soap*
brick • *concrete bricks*
chunk • *chunks of meat*
ingot • *a gold ingot*
lump • *lumps of metal*
piece • *a big piece of cake*

block ❷ VERB
to close by putting something across • *Mud blocked the river.*
choke • *The town was choked with cars.*
clog • *Dishes clogged the sink.*
obstruct • *The crash obstructed the road.*
plug • *Have you plugged the leaks?*

ANTONYM
● unblock

block ❸ VERB
to prevent something happening • *The council blocked his plans.*
bar • *He was barred from entering.*
check • *a policy to check population growth*
halt • *attempts to halt the spread of disease*
obstruct • *Lack of funds obstructed our progress.*
stop • *measures to stop the rising crime rate*
thwart • *My plans were thwarted by Taylor.*

blockage NOUN
a thing that clogs something • *a blockage in the pipe*
block • *a block in the blood vessel*
obstruction • *an obstruction on the track*
stoppage • *We have to clear the stoppage.*

blot out VERB
to cover and prevent from being seen • *The smoke blotted out the sky.*
eclipse • *The moon eclipsed the sun.*
obliterate • *Our view was obliterated by mist.*
obscure • *My way was obscured by fog.*
shadow • *Her veil shadowed her face.*

blow ❶ VERB
to move or cause to move in the wind • *The wind blew his papers away.*
buffet • *The ship was buffeted by gales.*
drive • *The strong wind drove us forward.*
flutter • *The flags are fluttering.*
sweep • *A sudden blast swept away the cloth.*
waft • *His hair wafted in the breeze.*
whirl • *The fallen leaves whirled around.*

blow ❷ NOUN
a hit from something • *a blow to the head*
bang • *He suffered some bangs and bumps.*
clout (INFORMAL) • *a clout on the head*
knock • *Knocks can cause damage to the spine.*
smack • *She gave the child a smack.*
thump • *Ralph got a thump on the chest.*
whack • *The horse got a whack from its rider.*

a b c d e f g h i j k l m n o p q r s t u v w x y z

Can't find the word you're looking for? Try the index.

blow ❸ NOUN
something disappointing or upsetting • *Marc's death was a terrible blow.*
bombshell • *His departure was a bombshell for the team.*
disappointment • *My exam results were a real disappointment.*
misfortune • *a series of misfortunes*
setback • *We faced many setbacks before we got the house.*
shock • *The news came as a shock.*
upset • *The defeat caused an upset.*

MORE SYNONYMS
- calamity
- catastrophe
- jolt

blue NOUN OR ADJECTIVE

SHADES OF BLUE

aqua	navy
aquamarine	Nile blue
azure	peacock blue
cerulean	periwinkle
cobalt	petrol blue
cyan	royal blue
duck-egg blue	sapphire
electric blue	saxe blue
gentian	sky-blue
indigo	teal
lapis lazuli	turquoise
midnight blue	ultramarine

blunt ❶ ADJECTIVE
having rounded edges • *blunt scissors*
dull • *a dull knife*
rounded • *rounded edges*
unsharpened • *an unsharpened pencil*

ANTONYM
- sharp

blunt ❷ ADJECTIVE
saying what you think • *a blunt speaker*
bluff • *a bluff old man*
brusque • *His response was brusque.*
forthright • *a forthright reply*
frank • *I'll be frank with you.*
outspoken • *an outspoken critic*
straightforward • *She has a straightforward manner.*

MORE SYNONYMS
- explicit
- tactless
- trenchant

ANTONYM
- tactful

blush ❶ VERB
to go red in the face • *I felt myself blushing.*
colour • *I found myself colouring as I spoke.*
crimson • *He looked at her and she crimsoned.*
flush • *I saw her face flush.*
go red • *His face went red as a beetroot.*
turn red • *He turned red with embarrassment.*
turn scarlet • *She turned scarlet with humiliation.*

blush ❷ NOUN
a red colour • *Ann took the gift with a blush.*
colour • *The walk will bring colour to your cheeks.*
flush • *A slow flush spread over the man's face.*
glow • *a healthy glow*

boast VERB
to talk proudly • *Carol boasted about her costume.*
brag • *I don't mind bragging about my talents.*

Can't find the word you're looking for? Try the index.

crow • *Stop crowing about your success.*
skite (AUSTRALIAN AND NEW ZEALAND; INFORMAL) • *That's nothing to skite about.*

boastful ADJECTIVE
tending to brag about things
• *a boastful liar*
bragging • *bragging stories about his time in the navy*
cocky • *The boxer is cocky and brash.*
conceited • *Young men tend to be conceited.*
crowing • *crowing remarks*
egotistical • *egotistical fibs*
swaggering • *He has a swaggering arrogance.*

ANTONYM
● modest

body ❶ NOUN
all your physical parts • *My whole body hurt.*
build • *He is of medium build.*
figure • *Janet has a nice figure.*
form • *clothes that flatter your form*
frame • *their bony frames*
physique • *a powerful physique*
shape • *his trim shape*

RELATED WORDS
● ADJECTIVES: corporal, physical

body ❷ NOUN
a dead body • *Police found a body hidden in the forest.*
carcass • *a sheep's carcass*
corpse • *They found the corpse of a young man.*
dead body • *He'd never seen a dead body.*
remains • *human remains*

body ❸ NOUN
an organized group of people
• *local voluntary bodies*

association • *the Football Association*
band • *a band of rebels*
company • *the Royal Shakespeare Company*
confederation • *a confederation of workers*
organization • *student organizations*
society • *I joined the local opera society.*

MORE SYNONYMS
● bloc
● collection

boil ❶ VERB
to bubble • *The water is boiling.*
bubble • *Potatoes bubbled in the pot.*
fizz • *The liquid fizzed and bubbled.*
foam • *When the butter foams, add the onions.*
froth • *The milk frothed over in the pan.*

MORE SYNONYMS
● effervesce
● seethe

boil ❷ NOUN
a swelling on the skin • *five boils on his face*
blister • *a blister on my index finger*
swelling • *a swelling under the eye*
tumour • *The tumours had all disappeared.*

MORE SYNONYMS
● blain
● carbuncle
● pustule

bold ❶ ADJECTIVE
confident and not shy • *a bold question*
brash • *a brash young sergeant*
brazen • *a brazen young woman*

a
b
c
d
e
f
g
h
i
j
k
l
m
n
o
p
q
r
s
t
u
v
w
x
y
z

Can't find the word you're looking for? Try the index.

cheeky • *a cheeky grin*
confident • *I felt confident confronting him.*
forward • *It was forward of you to ask him.*
impudent • *an impudent child*

MORE SYNONYMS
- barefaced
- pert
- saucy

ANTONYM
- shy

bold ❷ ADJECTIVE
unafraid of risk or danger • *a bold attempt*
adventurous • *an adventurous spirit*
brave • *a brave woman*
courageous • *courageous firefighters*
daring • *daring feats*
fearless • *a fearless warrior*
intrepid • *an intrepid explorer*

MORE SYNONYMS
- audacious
- heroic
- valiant

ANTONYM
- cowardly

bold ❸ ADJECTIVE
clear and noticeable • *bold colours*
bright • *bright light*
flashy • *flashy clothes*
loud • *a loud tie*
striking • *a striking tartan pattern*
strong • *dressed in strong reds and yellows*
vivid • *vivid green and purple*

MORE SYNONYMS
- conspicuous
- prominent
- pronounced

ANTONYM
- dull

bolt VERB
to escape or run away • *I bolted towards the exit.*
dash • *He dashed out of the room in a panic.*
escape • *They escaped across the frontier.*
flee • *We fled before the police arrived.*
fly • *She flew down the stairs with her attacker in hot pursuit.*
run away • *I called to him but he just ran away.*
run off • *The children ran off when they spotted me.*
rush • *They all rushed away as we approached.*

bomb ❶ NOUN
an explosive device • *The bomb exploded in the centre of the city.*
device • *Experts defused the device.*
explosive • *a block of plastic explosive*
missile • *long-range missiles*
rocket • *a rocket launcher*
shell • *Shells began to fall.*
torpedo • *The torpedo struck the ship.*

MORE SYNONYMS
- grenade
- mine
- projectile

bomb ❷ VERB
to attack with bombs • *His house was bombed.*
attack • *We are being attacked!*
blow up • *He attempted to blow up the building.*
bombard • *Warships began to bombard the coast.*
destroy • *Helicopters destroyed his village.*

Can't find the word you're looking for? Try the index.

A
B
C
D
E
F
G
H
I
J
K
L
M
N
O
P
Q
R
S
T
U
V
W
X
Y
Z

shell • *They shelled the troops heavily.*
torpedo • *His ship was torpedoed in the Channel.*

bond ❶ NOUN
a close relationship • *a special bond between us*
attachment • *Mother and child form a close attachment.*
connection • *a family connection*
link • *the links of friendship*
relation • *the relation between husband and wife*
tie • *the ties of blood*
union • *the union of father and son*

MORE SYNONYMS
● affiliation
● affinity

bond ❷ NOUN
an obligation to do something • *the social bonds of community*
agreement • *He has broken our agreement.*
contract • *He signed a two-year contract.*
obligation • *your obligation to your father*
pledge • *a pledge of support*
promise • *You must keep your promises.*
word • *I give you my word.*

MORE SYNONYMS
● compact
● covenant
● guarantee

bond ❸ VERB
to attach separate things • *Strips of wood are bonded together.*
bind • *Tape was used to bind the files.*
fasten • *I fastened the picture to the wall.*
fuse • *The pieces to be joined are melted and fused together.*

glue • *Glue the pieces together.*
paste • *He pasted posters to the wall.*

book ❶ NOUN
a number of pages in a cover
• *I'm reading a great book just now.*
publication • *publications about job hunting*
textbook • *He wrote a textbook on law.*
title • *We publish a range of titles.*
tome • *a heavy tome*
volume • *small volumes of poetry*
work • *my favourite work by this author*

TYPES OF BOOK

anthology	gazetteer
atlas	glossary
autobiography	guidebook
biography	manual
dictionary	novel
directory	phrasebook
encyclopedia	thesaurus

PARTS OF A BOOK

appendix	heading
bibliography	illustration
blurb	index
caption	introduction
chapter	jacket
contents	layout
cover	line
footnote	page
foreword	preface
glossary	title

RELIGIOUS BOOKS

Bible (*Christianity*)
Book of Mormon (*Mormonism*)
Diamond Scriptures (*Zen Buddhism*)
Guru Granth *or* Adi Granth (*Sikhism*)
I Ching (*Confucianism and Taoism*)

a
b
c
d
e
f
g
h
i
j
k
l
m
n
o
p
q
r
s
t
u
v
w
x
y
z

Can't find the word you're looking for? Try the index.

A
B
C

Mahabharata (*Hinduism*)
Qu'ran or Koran (*Islam*)
Ramayana (*Hinduism*)
Sutras (*Buddhism and Hinduism*)
Talmud (*Judaism*)
Tao-te-Ching (*Taoism*)
Torah (*Judaism*)
Tripitaka (*Buddhism*)
Veda (*Hinduism*)

D
E
F
G
H
I
J
K
L
M
N
O
P
Q
R
S
T
U
V
W
X
Y
Z

book ❷ VERB
to arrange to have or use
• *The tickets are booked.*
charter • *A plane was chartered for them.*
engage • *We engaged the services of a plumber.*
organize • *I have organized our flights.*
reserve • *Hotel rooms have been reserved.*
schedule • *A meeting is scheduled for Monday.*

border ❶ NOUN
a dividing line between things or places • *the border between two countries*
borderline • *the borderline between health and sickness*
boundary • *national boundaries*
frontier • *the American frontier*
line • *the line between fact and fiction*

border ❷ NOUN
an edge of something • *plain tiles with a bright border*
bounds • *the bounds of good taste*
edge • *the edge of town*
limits • *the city limits*
margin • *the western margins of the island*
rim • *the rim of the lake*

border ❸ VERB
to form an edge • *Tall trees*

bordered the fields.
edge • *the woods that edge the lake*
fringe • *Street lights fringe the bay.*
hem • *dresses hemmed with feathers*
rim • *the restaurants rimming the harbour*
trim • *coats trimmed with fur collars*

bored ADJECTIVE
impatient and not interested in something • *I am bored with this business.*
fed up • *He is fed up with this country.*
tired • *I am tired of this music.*
uninterested • *He seems uninterested in politics.*
wearied • *He spoke in a wearied voice.*

ANTONYM
● interested

boredom NOUN
a lack of interest • *the boredom of long trips*
apathy • *political apathy*
dullness • *a period of dullness*
flatness • *a feeling of flatness*
monotony • *the monotony of winter*
tedium • *the tedium of unemployment*
weariness • *a sense of weariness*

ANTONYM
● interest

boring ADJECTIVE
dull and uninteresting • *a boring job*
dull • *dull tasks*
flat • *a flat performance*
humdrum • *humdrum lives*
monotonous • *the monotonous prison routine*
tedious • *The work is tedious.*
tiresome • *a tiresome old man*

Can't find the word you're looking for? Try the index.

MORE SYNONYMS
- insipid
- repetitious
- stale

ANTONYM
- interesting

boss NOUN

a person in charge of something
• *He can't stand his boss.*
chief • *the police chief*
director • *the directors of the bank*
employer • *He was sent to Rome by his employer.*
head • *Heads of government met in New York.*
leader • *The party's leader has resigned.*
manager • *the company's marketing manager*

bossy ADJECTIVE

telling people what to do • *a rather bossy little girl*
arrogant • *arrogant behaviour*
authoritarian • *He has an authoritarian approach to parenthood.*
dictatorial • *a dictatorial management style*
domineering • *She is domineering and ruthless.*
imperious • *He has an imperious manner.*
overbearing • *an overbearing mother*

botch VERB

to do something badly • *a botched operation*
bungle • *inefficient people who bungled the job*
mar • *She marred her exit by twisting her ankle.*
mess up • *He manages to mess up his life.*

bother ❶ VERB

to cause worry or concern • *His lack of money bothers him.*
annoy • *the things that annoy me*
concern • *The future concerns me.*
disturb • *It disturbs me to see you unhappy.*
get on someone's nerves (INFORMAL) • *This place gets on my nerves.*
trouble • *Are you troubled by nightmares?*
worry • *I'm worried by the amount he is drinking.*

MORE SYNONYMS
- harass
- inconvenience

bother ❷ NOUN

trouble and difficulty • *I hate the bother of shopping.*
annoyance • *Snoring can be an annoyance.*
difficulty • *The strikes are causing difficulties for commuters.*
inconvenience • *a minor inconvenience*
irritation • *Noise is an irritation.*
trouble • *You've caused me a lot of trouble.*
worry • *It was a time of worry for us.*

MORE SYNONYMS
- nuisance
- strain

bottom ❶ NOUN

the lowest part of something
• *the bottom of the stairs*
base • *the base of the spine*
bed • *the river bed*
depths • *the depths of the earth*
floor • *the ocean floor*
foot • *the foot of the bed*

ANTONYM
- top

a
b
c
d
e
f
g
h
i
j
k
l
m
n
o
p
q
r
s
t
u
v
w
x
y
z

Can't find the word you're looking for? Try the index.

A
B
C
D
E
F
G
H
I
J
K
L
M
N
O
P
Q
R
S
T
U
V
W
X
Y
Z

bottom ➋ NOUN
the part of the body you sit on
• *Sit on your bottom!*
backside (INFORMAL) • *the muscles in your backside*
behind (INFORMAL) • *He kicked me on the behind.*
buttocks • *exercises for your buttocks*
posterior (HUMOROUS) • *He fell on his posterior.*
rear • *I was thrown out on my rear.*

bottom ➌ ADJECTIVE
in the lowest place or position
• *the bottom drawer*
base • *the base edge of the curtain*
basement • *a basement flat*
ground • *ground level*
lowest • *the lowest part of the brain*

ANTONYM
● highest

bounce ➊ VERB
to spring back • *I bounced a ball against the wall.*
bump • *My bicycle bumped along the rough ground.*
ricochet • *The bullets ricocheted off the jeep.*

MORE SYNONYMS
● rebound
● recoil

bounce ➋ VERB
to move up and down • *He bounced across the floor.*
bob • *The raft bobbed along.*
bound • *He bounded up the stairway.*
jump • *They jumped up and down to keep warm.*

box NOUN
a container with a firm base and sides • *All her possessions were packed in boxes.*

carton • *cartons full of books*
case • *It is still in its original case.*
chest • *She kept her heirlooms in a carved wooden chest.*
container • *substances kept in heavy metal containers*
trunk • *a trunk full of toys*

boy NOUN
a male child • *I knew him when he was a boy.*
fellow • *a fine little fellow*
lad • *I remember being a lad his age.*
schoolboy • *a group of schoolboys*
youngster • *I was only a youngster in 1970.*
youth • *gangs of youths who cause trouble*

boycott VERB
to refuse to have anything to do with • *Some parties are boycotting the elections.*
blacklist • *He has been blacklisted by various societies.*
embargo • *Imports of fruit were embargoed.*
exclude • *I exclude animal products from my diet.*
reject • *She rejected her parents' religion.*
spurn • *You spurned his last offer.*

MORE SYNONYMS
● proscribe
● refrain from

brag VERB
to boast about something • *I hate people who brag about their achievements.*
boast • *She kept boasting about how many guys she'd been out with.*
crow • *Stop crowing about your victory.*
skite (AUSTRALIAN AND NEW

Can't find the word you're looking for? Try the index.

ZEALAND; INFORMAL) • *That's nothing to skite about.*

braggart NOUN
a person who boasts • *He was a braggart and a liar.*
bigmouth (SLANG) • *He's nothing but a bigmouth.*
boaster • *an idle boaster looking for the main chance*
bragger • *He was quite a bragger.*
show-off • *I've always been a show-off.*
skite *or* **skiter** (AUSTRALIAN AND NEW ZEALAND; INFORMAL) • *a bit of a skite*

brave ❶ ADJECTIVE
willing to do dangerous things • *a brave attempt to stop the attack*
bold • *Amrita became a bold rebel.*
courageous • *a courageous decision*
fearless • *his fearless campaigning for justice*
heroic • *The heroic sergeant risked his life.*
plucky • *The plucky schoolgirl amazed the doctors.*
valiant • *a valiant attempt to keep going*

MORE SYNONYMS
- daring
- intrepid
- valorous

ANTONYM
- cowardly

brave ❷ VERB
to face something without fear • *Fans braved the rain to hear him sing.*
face • *I can't face another three years of this.*
stand up to • *I have tried to stand up to the bullies.*

bravery NOUN
the quality of being courageous • *He deserves praise for his bravery.*
boldness • *an outward display of boldness*
courage • *They do not have the courage to apologize.*
fortitude • *He suffered with tremendous fortitude.*
heroism • *acts of heroism*
pluck • *He has pluck and presence of mind.*
valour • *He won a medal for valour.*

MORE SYNONYMS
- fearlessness
- gallantry
- mettle

ANTONYM
- cowardice

breach ❶ NOUN
a breaking of an agreement or law • *a breach of contract*
infringement • *an infringement of the rules*
offence • *criminal offences*
trespass • *a campaign of trespasses and demonstrations*
violation • *a violation of the peace agreement*

MORE SYNONYMS
- contravention
- transgression

breach ❷ NOUN
a gap in something • *the breach in the Berlin Wall*
crack • *a large crack in the ice*
gap • *a narrow gap in the curtains*
hole • *We cut holes in the fabric.*
opening • *an opening in the fence*
rift • *The earthquake caused a deep rift.*
split • *There's a split in my mattress.*

a
b
c
d
e
f
g
h
i
j
k
l
m
n
o
p
q
r
s
t
u
v
w
x
y
z

Can't find the word you're looking for? Try the index.

A
B
C
D
E
F
G
H
I
J
K
L
M
N
O
P
Q
R
S
T
U
V
W
X
Y
Z

MORE SYNONYMS
- chasm
- fissure
- rupture

break ❶ VERB
to separate into pieces • *I broke a plate.*
▷ see Word Study **break**, page 672

break ❷ VERB
to fail to keep a rule or promise • *He broke his promise to attend.*
breach • *breaches of discipline*
contravene • *His behaviour contravenes our code of conduct.*
infringe • *The judge ruled that he had infringed no rules.*
violate • *They violated the peace agreement.*

break ❸ NOUN
a short period of rest or change • *I took a five-minute break from work.*
interlude • *a happy interlude in my life*
interval • *a long interval when no-one spoke*
pause • *After a pause Alex spoke.*
recess • *The court adjourned for a recess.*
respite • *They have had no respite from bombing.*
rest • *I'll start again after a rest.*

breed ❶ NOUN
a type of animal • *rare breeds of cattle*
kind • *What kind of horse is that?*
species • *Pandas are an endangered species.*
stock • *cattle of Highland stock*
strain • *a special strain of rat*
type • *What type of dog should we get?*
variety • *many varieties of birds*

breed ❷ VERB
to produce and look after • *He breeds dogs for the police.*
cultivate • *She cultivates fruit and vegetables.*
develop • *A new variety of potato is being developed.*
keep • *He keeps guinea pigs.*
nurture • *trimming and nurturing plants and saplings*
raise • *He raises birds of prey as a hobby.*
rear • *the difficulties of rearing children*

breed ❸ VERB
to produce offspring • *Frogs can breed in most ponds.*
multiply • *Rats multiply quickly.*
produce • *She produced a son.*
propagate • *This plant is difficult to propagate.*
reproduce • *the natural desire to reproduce*

MORE SYNONYMS
- engender
- procreate

brief ❶ ADJECTIVE
lasting for a short time • *a brief appearance on television*
fleeting • *a fleeting glimpse*
momentary • *There was a momentary silence.*
quick • *a quick look at the newspaper*
short • *a short holiday*
swift • *a swift glance at John's face*

MORE SYNONYMS
- ephemeral
- temporary
- transitory

ANTONYM
- long

Can't find the word you're looking for? Try the index.

brief ② VERB

to give necessary information
• *A spokesman briefed reporters.*
advise • *I must advise you of my decision to retire.*
fill in (INFORMAL) • *Can you fill me in on Wilbur's visit?*
inform • *They would inform him of their progress.*
instruct • *He instructed us in first aid.*
prepare • *I will prepare you for this exam.*
prime • *Arnold primed him for his duties.*

bright ① ADJECTIVE

strong and startling • *a bright light*
brilliant • *brilliant green eyes*
dazzling • *a dazzling white shirt*
glowing • *the glowing windows of the Cathedral*
luminous • *a luminous star*
radiant • *eyes as radiant as sapphires*
vivid • *strong, vivid colours*

MORE SYNONYMS

● blazing
● illuminated
● resplendent

ANTONYM

● dull

bright ② ADJECTIVE

clever and alert • *my brightest student*
brainy (INFORMAL) • *I don't consider myself brainy.*
brilliant • *She has a brilliant mind.*
clever • *a clever child*
ingenious • *an ingenious idea*
intelligent • *Dolphins are an intelligent species.*
smart • *He thinks he's as smart as Sarah.*

MORE SYNONYMS

● acute
● astute
● sharp

ANTONYM

● dim

bright ③ ADJECTIVE

cheerful and lively • *a bright smile*
cheerful • *Jack sounded quite cheerful about the idea.*
happy • *a confident, happy child*
jolly • *a jolly nature*
light-hearted • *They are light-hearted and enjoy life.*
lively • *He has a lively personality.*
merry • *bursts of merry laughter*

brilliant ① ADJECTIVE

very bright • *a brilliant light*
bright • *a bright star*
dazzling • *a dazzling white shirt*
gleaming • *gleaming headlights*
glowing • *glowing colours*
luminous • *luminous orange paint*
radiant • *a figure surrounded by a radiant glow*
sparkling • *a choker of sparkling jewels*
vivid • *the vivid hues of tropical flowers*

ANTONYM

● dull

brilliant ② ADJECTIVE

very clever • *a brilliant pupil*
acute • *His relaxed exterior hides an acute mind.*
brainy (INFORMAL) • *You don't have to be too brainy to work that one out.*
bright • *an exceptionally bright child*
clever • *What a clever idea!*
intelligent • *a lively and extremely intelligent woman*
perceptive • *a perceptive analysis of the situation*

a
b
c
d
e
f
g
h
i
j
k
l
m
n
o
p
q
r
s
t
u
v
w
x
y
z

Can't find the word you're looking for? Try the index.

sharp • *a sharp intellect*
smart • *He's the smartest student we've ever had.*

ANTONYM
● stupid

brilliant ❸ ADJECTIVE
wonderful or superb • *It's a brilliant film.*
first-class • *a first-class violinist*
great • *one of the greatest novels of the century*
magnificent • *a magnificent display*
marvellous • *I've had a marvellous time.*
outstanding • *He's an outstanding actor.*
superb • *a superb artist*
tremendous • *a tremendous performance*
wonderful • *the most wonderful music I've ever heard*

ANTONYM
● terrible

bring ❶ VERB
to take somewhere • *Bring a friend to the party.*
bear • *They bore the box into the kitchen.*
carry • *She carried her son to the car.*
convey • *Emergency supplies were conveyed by truck.*
lead • *She led him into the house.*
take • *He took cakes to the party.*
transport • *The troops were transported to Moscow.*

bring ❷ VERB
to cause to happen • *Bring the vegetables to the boil.*
cause • *My mistake caused me some worry.*
create • *The new factory will create more jobs.*

inflict • *The attack inflicted heavy casualties.*
produce • *The drug produces side effects.*
result in • *Many accidents result in serious injuries.*
wreak • *Violent storms wreaked havoc.*

MORE SYNONYMS
● effect
● occasion

bring about VERB
to cause something to happen • *It was his arrogance which brought about his downfall.*
cause • *This may cause delays.*
create • *The new scheme will create even more confusion.*
generate • *the excitement generated by this film*
make happen • *If you want change, you have to make it happen yourself.*
produce • *His comments produced a furious response.*
provoke • *a move that has provoked a storm of protest*

broad ❶ ADJECTIVE
large, especially from side to side • *His shoulders were broad and his waist narrow.*
expansive • *There are also several swing sets and an expansive grassy play area.*
extensive • *The palace grounds were more extensive than the town itself.*
large • *He was a large man with a thick square head.*
thick • *a finger as thick as a sausage*
vast • *rich families who own vast stretches of land*
wide • *a sunhat with a wide brim*

Can't find the word you're looking for? Try the index.

MORE SYNONYMS
- ample
- spacious

ANTONYM
- narrow

broad ② ADJECTIVE
including or affecting many different things or people • *A broad range of issues was discussed.*
comprehensive • *This book is a comprehensive guide to the region.*
extensive • *extensive research into public attitudes to science*
general • *The project should raise general awareness about bullying.*
sweeping • *sweeping economic reforms*
universal • *the universal problem of pollution*
wide • *a major event which brought together a wide range of interest groups*
wide-ranging • *The aims of our campaign are wide-ranging but simple.*

broad ③ ADJECTIVE
general rather than detailed • *These documents provided a broad outline of the Society's development.*
approximate • *They did not have even an approximate idea of what the word meant.*
general • *The figures represent a general decline in employment.*
non-specific • *I intend to use these terms in a deliberately non-specific way.*
rough • *I've got a rough idea of what he looks like.*
sweeping • *a sweeping statement about women drivers*
vague • *They have only a vague idea of the amount of water available.*

broken ① ADJECTIVE
in pieces • *a broken window*
burst • *a burst pipe*
demolished • *a demolished house*
fractured • *He suffered a fractured skull.*
fragmented • *fragmented images*
shattered • *shattered glass*
smashed • *smashed windows*

broken ② ADJECTIVE
not kept • *a broken promise*
infringed • *a case of infringed human rights*
violated • *a series of violated agreements*

MORE SYNONYMS
- disobeyed
- traduced
- transgressed

brown NOUN or ADJECTIVE

SHADES OF BROWN	
auburn	ginger
bay	hazel
beige	khaki
bronze	mahogany
brunette	mocha
buff	oatmeal
burnt sienna	ochre
burnt umber	putty
café au lait	russet
camel	rust
chestnut	sandy
chocolate	sepia
cinnamon	tan
coffee	taupe
dun	tawny
fawn	terracotta

build ① VERB
to make something • *The house was built last year.*
assemble • *Workers were assembling planes.*

a
b
c
d
e
f
g
h
i
j
k
l
m
n
o
p
q
r
s
t
u
v
w
x
y
z

Can't find the word you're looking for? Try the index.

A
B
C
D
E
F
G
H
I
J
K
L
M
N
O
P
Q
R
S
T
U
V
W
X
Y
Z

construct • *plans to construct a temple on the site*
erect • *The building was erected in 1900.*
fabricate • *All the tools are fabricated from steel.*
form • *hotels formed from cheap cement*
make • *a wall made of bricks*

ANTONYM
● dismantle

build ❷ VERB
to develop gradually • *I want to build a relationship with them.*
develop • *These battles could develop into war.*
extend • *Three new products extend the range.*
increase • *The population continues to increase.*
intensify • *The conflict is bound to intensify.*
strengthen • *Cycling strengthens the muscles.*

MORE SYNONYMS
● augment
● enlarge
● escalate

build ❸ NOUN
the size of a body • *He is of medium build.*
body • *a body of average size*
figure • *Janet has a nice figure.*
form • *clothes that flatter your form*
frame • *their bony frames*
physique • *a powerful physique*
shape • *his trim shape*

building NOUN
a structure with walls • *a glass building*
edifice • *historic edifices in the area*
structure • *The museum is an impressive structure.*

bulge ❶ VERB
to swell out • *He bulges out of his black T-shirt.*
expand • *The pipes expanded in the heat.*
protrude • *His blue eyes protruded from his head.*
stick out • *His stomach stuck out under his jacket.*
swell • *My ankles swelled.*

bulge ❷ NOUN
a lump in something • *My purse made a bulge in my pocket.*
bump • *a bump in the road*
hump • *a camel's hump*
lump • *itchy red lumps on the skin*
protrusion • *a strange protrusion on his forehead*
swelling • *a swelling on my foot*

bully ❶ NOUN
someone who deliberately frightens or hurts others • *I fell victim to the class bully.*
oppressor • *They were powerless against their oppressors.*
persecutor • *Eventually he stood up to his persecutors.*

bully ❷ VERB
to frighten or hurt someone deliberately and repeatedly • *I wasn't going to let him bully me.*
intimidate • *Jones had set out to intimidate and dominate Paul.*
oppress • *men who try to dominate and oppress women*
persecute • *Tom was persecuted by his sisters.*
pick on • *I don't like to see you pick on younger children.*
tease • *The boys in the village had set on him, teasing him.*
torment • *My older brother and sister used to torment me.*

Can't find the word you're looking for? Try the index.

bully ❸ VERB

to make someone do something by using force • *She used to bully me into doing my schoolwork.*
force • *I cannot force you in this. You must decide.*
intimidate • *attempts to intimidate people into voting for the governing party*
pressurize • *Do not be pressurized into making your decision immediately.*

MORE SYNONYMS

- coerce
- dragoon

bump ❶ VERB

to hit something • *He bumped his head on the wall.*
bang • *I banged my shin on the edge of the table.*
collide • *The car collided with a tree.*
hit • *She hit the last barrier and fell.*
jolt • *He jolted my elbow.*
knock • *He knocked on the door.*
strike • *His head struck the windscreen.*

bump ❷ NOUN

a dull noise • *He heard a bump outside.*
bang • *I heard four or five loud bangs.*
knock • *They heard a knock at the door.*
thud • *She tripped and fell with a thud.*
thump • *There was a loud thump against the house.*

bump ❸ NOUN

a raised part of something • *a bump in the road*
bulge • *My purse made a bulge in my pocket.*
hump • *a camel's hump*

knob • *a door with a brass knob*
lump • *itchy red lumps on the skin*
swelling • *a swelling on my foot*

MORE SYNONYMS

- contusion
- node
- protuberance

bunch ❶ NOUN

a group of people • *The players were a great bunch.*
band • *Bands of criminals have been roaming some neighbourhoods.*
crowd • *All the old crowd have come out for this occasion.*
gaggle • *A gaggle of journalists sit in a hotel foyer waiting impatiently.*
gang • *Come on over - we've got lots of the old gang here.*
group • *The trouble involved a small group of football supporters.*
lot • *Future generations are going to think that we were a pretty boring lot.*
multitude • *surrounded by a noisy multitude*

bunch ❷ NOUN

several cut flowers held together • *He had left a huge bunch of flowers in her hotel room.*
bouquet • *She laid a bouquet on his grave.*
posy • *a posy of wild flowers*
spray • *a small spray of freesias*

bunch ❸ NOUN

a group of things • *George took out a bunch of keys and went to work on the lock.*
batch • *She brought a large batch of newspaper cuttings.*
bundle • *a bundle of sticks tied together with string*
cluster • *a cluster of shops, cabins and motels*

a b c d e f g h i j k l m n o p q r s t u v w x y z

Can't find the word you're looking for? Try the index.

heap • *a heap of old boxes for the bonfire*
load • *His people came up with a load of embarrassing stories.*
pile • *I've got a pile of questions afterwards for you.*
set • *Only she and Mr Cohen had complete sets of keys to the shop.*

burden ❶ NOUN
a load that is carried • *My wet clothes were an added burden.*
load • *a big load of hay*
weight • *straining to lift heavy weights*

burden ❷ NOUN
something that worries you • *the burden of looking after a sick parent*
anxiety • *He expressed his anxieties to me.*
care • *Forget all the cares of the day.*
strain • *I find the travelling a strain.*
stress • *the stress of exams*
trouble • *The Sullivans have money troubles.*
worry • *My son is a worry to me.*

MORE SYNONYMS
- affliction
- millstone
- trial

RELATED WORD
- ADJECTIVE: onerous

bureaucracy NOUN
complex rules and procedures • *Is there too much bureaucracy in government?*
administration • *high administration costs*
officialdom • *Officialdom is against us.*
red tape • *Our application was delayed by red tape.*
regulations • *absurd regulations about opening hours*

burn ❶ VERB
to be on fire • *a fire burning in the fireplace*
be ablaze • *The houses were ablaze.*
be on fire • *The ship was on fire.*
blaze • *The wreckage blazed.*
flame • *We watched as the house flamed.*
flare • *The match flared in the dark.*
flicker • *The fire flickered and crackled.*

burn ❷ VERB
to destroy with fire • *They burned the house down.*
char • *charred bodies*
incinerate • *Hospitals incinerate waste.*
scorch • *The bonfire scorched the grass.*
shrivel • *The papers shrivelled in the flames.*
singe • *Her hair was singed and her coat burnt.*

burst ❶ VERB
to split apart • *The balloon burst.*
break • *He broke the box open.*
crack • *A water pipe had cracked.*
explode • *The glass exploded.*
puncture • *The nail punctured the tyre.*
rupture • *His appendix ruptured.*
split • *The seam of my dress split.*

burst ❷ VERB
to happen or appear suddenly • *to burst into flames*
barge • *He barged into the room.*
break • *Her face broke into a smile.*
erupt • *Violence could erupt soon.*
rush • *Water rushed out of the hole.*

burst ❸ NOUN
a short period of something • *a burst of energy*

Can't find the word you're looking for? Try the index.

fit • *a fit of rage*
outbreak • *an outbreak of violence*
rush • *a sudden rush of excitement*
spate • *a spate of attacks on horses*
surge • *a surge of emotion*
torrent • *a torrent of words*

business ❶ NOUN

the buying and selling of goods
• *a career in business*
commerce • *commerce between Europe and South America*
dealings • *All dealings with the company were suspended.*
industry • *the American car industry*
trade • *French trade with the West Indies*
trading • *trading between the two countries*
transaction • *We settled the transaction over lunch.*

business ❷ NOUN

an organization selling goods or services • *a family business*
company • *the Ford Motor Company*
corporation • *international corporations*
enterprise • *small industrial enterprises*
establishment • *shops and other commercial establishments*
firm • *a firm of engineers*
organization • *a well-run organization*

MORE SYNONYMS
● concern
● conglomerate
● venture

business ❸ NOUN

any event or situation • *This business has upset me.*
affair • *He handled the affair badly.*

issue • *What is your view on this issue?*
matter • *This is a matter for the police.*
problem • *solutions to the drug problem*
question • *the whole question of TV censorship*
subject • *He raised the subject of money.*

bustle ❶ VERB

to move hurriedly • *My mother bustled about the room.*
dash • *We dashed about purposefully.*
fuss • *Waiters were fussing round the table.*
hurry • *Claire hurried along the road.*
rush • *I'm rushing to finish the cooking.*
scurry • *rats scurrying around*
scuttle • *Crabs scuttle along the bank.*

bustle ❷ NOUN

busy and noisy activity • *the bustle of modern life*
activity • *a burst of activity in the building*
commotion • *He heard a commotion outside.*
excitement • *The news created great excitement.*
flurry • *a flurry of activity*
fuss • *He works without any fuss.*
hurry • *the hurry and excitement of the city*

ANTONYM
● peace

busy ❶ ADJECTIVE

doing something • *What is it? I'm busy.*
active • *He is active in local politics.*

Can't find the word you're looking for? Try the index.

A
B
C
D
E
F
G
H
I
J
K
L
M
N
O
P
Q
R
S
T
U
V
W
X
Y
Z

employed • *He was employed helping me.*
engaged • *He was engaged in conversation.*
engrossed • *She is engrossed in her work.*
occupied • *He is occupied with the packing.*
working • *I am working on a novel.*

ANTONYM
● idle

busy ❷ ADJECTIVE
full of activity • *a busy tourist resort*
active • *an active, independent country*
full • *a full life*
hectic • *my hectic work schedule*
lively • *a lively restaurant*
restless • *a restless mind*

busy ❸ VERB
to occupy or keep busy • *Kathryn busied herself in the kitchen.*
absorb • *Her career absorbed her completely.*
employ • *You'd be better employed helping me.*
engage • *He was engaged in a meeting when I called.*
immerse • *She immersed herself in her book.*
occupy • *Try to occupy yourself with something.*

but ❶ CONJUNCTION
although • *Heat the cider until it is very hot but not boiling.*
although • *He was in love with*

her, although he had not yet admitted it to himself.
though • *He's very attractive, though not exactly handsome.*
while • *The first two services are free, while the third costs £35.*
yet • *It is completely waterproof, yet light and comfortable.*

but ❷ PREPOSITION
with the exception of • *The crew gave them nothing but bread to eat.*
except • *I don't take any drugs except aspirin.*
except for • *No-one has complained except for you.*
other than • *This route is not recommended to anyone other than the most experienced cyclist.*
save • *The people had no water at all save that brought up from bore holes.*

buy VERB
to obtain with money • *I'd like to buy him lunch.*
acquire • *I have acquired a new car.*
invest in • *I invested in a house.*
obtain • *She went to obtain a ticket.*
pay for • *He let me pay for his drink.*
procure • *attempts to procure more food*
purchase • *He purchased a sandwich for lunch.*

ANTONYM
● sell

Cc

calculate VERB
to work out a number or amount
• *how to calculate the total cost*
count • *Shareholders are counting the cost of the slump.*
determine • *calculations to determine the rate of tax*
reckon • *an amount reckoned at 140 billion marks*
work out • *Work out the distance of the journey.*

calculated ADJECTIVE
deliberately planned • *Everything they said was calculated to wound.*
aimed • *The restructuring is aimed at reducing costs.*
designed • *a scheme designed to help poorer families*
intended • *the intended effect of the revised guidelines*
planned • *a carefully planned campaign*

ANTONYM
● unplanned

call ❶ VERB
to give a name • *a man called Jeffrey*
▷ *see Word Study* **call***, page 673*

call ❷ VERB
to telephone • *He called me at my office.*
▷ *see Word Study* **call***, page 673*

call ❸ VERB
to say loudly • *I heard someone calling my name.*
▷ *see Word Study* **call***, page 673*

call ❹ NOUN
an instance of someone shouting out • *a call for help*
cry • *the cry of a seagull*
shout • *I heard a distant shout.*
yell • *He let out a yell.*

callous ADJECTIVE
not concerned about other people • *his callous disregard for human life*
cold • *What a cold, unfeeling woman she was.*
heartless • *It was a heartless thing to do.*
indifferent • *indifferent to the suffering of others*
insensitive • *insensitive remarks*

MORE SYNONYMS
● hard-bitten
● hardhearted
● obdurate
● unsympathetic

ANTONYM
● caring

calm ❶ ADJECTIVE
not worried or excited • *Try to keep calm.*
collected • *She was cool and collected during her interrogation.*
composed • *a very composed, business-like woman*
cool • *We have to keep a cool head in this situation.*
impassive • *He remained impassive as his sentence was passed.*

Can't find the word you're looking for? Try the index.

relaxed • *a relaxed manner*

MORE SYNONYMS
- imperturbable
- unemotional
- unruffled

ANTONYM
- worried

calm ❷ ADJECTIVE

still because there is no wind
• *Tuesday was a fine, clear and calm day.*
balmy • *balmy summer evenings*
mild • *a mild winter climate*
still • *The air was still.*
tranquil • *a tranquil lake*

ANTONYM
- rough

calm ❸ NOUN

the state of being peaceful
• *He liked the calm of the evening.*
calmness • *an aura of calmness*
peace • *a wonderful feeling of peace*
peacefulness • *the peacefulness of the gardens*
quiet • *I need quiet to work*
serenity • *the peace and serenity of a tropical sunset*
stillness • *the stillness of the summer night*

calm ❹ VERB

to make less upset or excited
• *We were trying to calm him.*
quieten • *trying to quieten the restless horses*
relax • *This music is supposed to relax you.*
soothe • *I think a bath may soothe me.*

MORE SYNONYMS
- mollify
- placate

campaign NOUN

actions planned to get a certain result • *a campaign to educate people*
crusade • *the crusade for feminism*
movement • *the human rights movement*
operation • *a full-scale military operation*
push • *an all-out push to promote the show*

cancel ❶ VERB

to stop something from happening
• *We're going to have to cancel our picnic.*
abandon • *He had to abandon his holiday plans.*
call off • *The union has called off the strike.*

cancel ❷ VERB

to stop something from being valid
• *They were forced to cancel their contract.*
annul • *The marriage was annulled.*
quash • *His jail sentence was quashed when new evidence came to light.*
repeal • *The new law was repealed within the year.*
revoke • *His licence was immediately revoked.*

MORE SYNONYMS
- abrogate
- countermand
- rescind

candid ADJECTIVE

honest and frank • *a candid interview*
blunt • *She is blunt about his faults.*
frank • *They had a frank discussion about the issue.*

Can't find the word you're looking for? Try the index.

honest • *What is your honest opinion?*
open • *He had always been open with her and she would know if he lied.*
straightforward • *I was impressed by his straightforward manner.*
truthful • *We've all learnt to be fairly truthful about our personal lives.*

candidate NOUN
a person being considered for a position • *a candidate for the presidency*
applicant • *one of thirty applicants for the manager's post*
competitor • *several competitors for the contract*
contender • *a strong contender for the chairmanship*

MORE SYNONYMS
● nominee
● possibility
● runner

capable ADJECTIVE
able to do something well • *a capable leader*
able • *a very able businessman*
accomplished • *an accomplished painter*
adept • *an adept diplomat*
competent • *a competent and careful driver*
efficient • *efficient administration*
proficient • *proficient with computers*
skilful • *the country's most skilful politician*

ANTONYM
● incompetent

capacity ❶ NOUN
the maximum amount that something holds or produces

• *the vehicle's fuel capacity*
dimensions • *a car of compact dimensions*
room • *There wasn't enough room in the baggage compartment for all the gear.*
size • *My bedroom is half the size of yours.*
space • *There is space in the back for two people.*
volume • *a container with a volume of two litres*

capacity ❷ NOUN
a person's power or ability to do something • *Our capacity for giving care, love and attention is limited.*
ability • *The public never had faith in his ability to handle the job.*
capability • *a country with the capability of launching a nuclear attack*
facility • *Humans have lost the facility to use their sense of smell properly.*
gift • *As a youth he discovered a gift for making people laugh.*
potential • *the economic potentials of Eastern and Western Europe*
power • *Human societies have the power to solve the problems confronting them.*

capture ❶ VERB
to take prisoner • *He was captured by rebels.*
apprehend • *Police have not yet apprehended the killer.*
arrest • *Seven people were arrested.*
catch • *The thief was caught and the money was returned.*
seize • *seized by armed police*
take • *An army unit took the town.*

ANTONYM
● release

Can't find the word you're looking for? Try the index.

A
B
C
D
E
F
G
H
I
J
K
L
M
N
O
P
Q
R
S
T
U
V
W
X
Y
Z

capture ❷ NOUN

the act of capturing • *He evaded capture for eight years.*
arrest • *Police made two arrests.*
seizure • *the seizure of territory*
taking • *the taking of hostages*
trapping • *The trapping of these animals is illegal.*

car NOUN

a vehicle for carrying a few people • *I finally left the car at the garage.*
automobile (AMERICAN; FORMAL) • *the Japanese automobile manufacturer, Nissan*
motor
vehicle • *She managed to scramble out of the vehicle.*

care ❶ VERB

to be concerned about something • *a company that cares about the environment*
be bothered • *I am not bothered what others think about me.*
be concerned • *We are concerned about the problem.*
be interested • *He's not interested in what anyone else says.*
mind • *I do not mind who wins.*

care ❷ NOUN

something that causes you to worry • *without a care in the world*
anxiety • *anxieties about money*
concern • *Their main concern is unemployment.*
trouble • *She has had her share of troubles.*
woe • *They blame the government for all their woes.*
worry • *My biggest worry is how I will cope on my own.*

MORE SYNONYMS

- tribulation
- vexation

care ❸ NOUN

close attention when doing something • *We took great care in choosing a location.*
attention • *medical attention*
caution • *Proceed with caution.*
pains • *She takes great pains with her appearance.*

MORE SYNONYMS

- circumspection
- forethought

careful ❶ ADJECTIVE

acting with care • *Be careful what you say to him.*
cautious • *a cautious approach*
prudent • *prudent management*

MORE SYNONYMS

- chary
- circumspect
- punctilious
- scrupulous

ANTONYM

- careless

careful ❷ ADJECTIVE

complete and well done • *It needs careful planning.*
meticulous • *meticulous attention to detail*
painstaking • *a painstaking search*
precise • *precise instructions*
thorough • *a thorough examination*

ANTONYM

- careless

careless ❶ ADJECTIVE

not taking enough care • *careless driving*
irresponsible • *an irresponsible attitude*
neglectful • *neglectful parents*
sloppy (INFORMAL) • *sloppy work*

Can't find the word you're looking for? Try the index.

MORE SYNONYMS
- cavalier
- lackadaisical
- slapdash
- slipshod

ANTONYM
- careful

careless ② ADJECTIVE
relaxed and unconcerned • *careless laughter*
casual • *a casual remark*
nonchalant • *a nonchalant attitude*
offhand • *his usual offhand way*

carry VERB
to hold and take something somewhere • *He was carrying a briefcase.*
bear • *He arrived bearing gifts.*
convey (FORMAL) • *The minibus conveyed us to the station.*
lug • *lugging boxes of books around*
take • *Don't forget to take your camera.*
transport • *goods being transported abroad*

carry out VERB
to do and complete something • *the surgeon who carried out the operation*
accomplish • *the desire to accomplish a task*
achieve • *We have achieved our objective.*
fulfil • *to fulfil a promise*
perform • *people who have performed acts of bravery*

MORE SYNONYMS
- execute
- implement

carve VERB
to make something by cutting

• *He carves his figures from pine.*
chisel • *the mason chiselling his stone*
cut • *a figure cut from marble*
engrave • *an engraved crystal goblet*
inscribe • *the words inscribed on his monument*
sculpt • *a sculpted clay figure*

MORE SYNONYMS
- hew
- whittle

case ① NOUN
a particular situation or example • *a case of mistaken identity*
example • *an example of what can go wrong*
illustration • *a clear illustration of this point*
instance • *a serious instance of corruption*
occasion • *the last occasion on which he appeared*
occurrence • *a frequent occurrence*

case ② NOUN
a container for holding something • *a spectacle case*
box • *a chocolate box*
container • *a huge plastic container*

MORE SYNONYMS
- holder
- receptacle

case ③ NOUN
a trial or inquiry • *a libel case*
action • *a civil action for damages*
lawsuit • *the rising cost of defending a lawsuit*
proceedings • *criminal proceedings against the former leader*
trial • *Police lied at the trial.*

a b **c** d e f g h i j k l m n o p q r s t u v w x y z

Can't find the word you're looking for? Try the index.

casual ❶ ADJECTIVE
happening by chance • *a casual remark*
accidental • *a verdict of accidental death*
chance • *a chance meeting*
incidental • *an incidental effect*

MORE SYNONYMS
● fortuitous
● serendipitous
● unintentional
● unpremeditated

ANTONYM
● deliberate

casual ❷ ADJECTIVE
showing no concern or interest • *a casual look over his shoulder*
careless • *careless remarks*
cursory • *a cursory glance*
nonchalant • *his nonchalant attitude to life*
offhand • *a deceptively offhand style*
relaxed • *a relaxed manner*

MORE SYNONYMS
● blasé
● insouciant
● lackadaisical
● perfunctory

ANTONYM
● concerned

cat NOUN
a small animal kept as a pet • *sharing his flat with four cats*
feline • *Even the most cuddly feline has claws.*
kitty • *a kitty stuck up a tree*
moggy or **moggie** (BRITISH AND NEW ZEALAND; SLANG) • *a grey, long-haired moggy*
pussy, **puss** or **pussycat** (INFORMAL) • *a fluffy little pussycat*

RELATED WORDS
● ADJECTIVE: feline
● MALE: tom
● FEMALE: queen, tabby
● YOUNG: kitten

catch ❶ VERB
to capture an animal or fish • *We still haven't caught any tuna.*
capture • *Poachers had captured a gorilla.*
snare • *He'd snared a rabbit.*
trap • *Their aim was to trap a tiger.*

catch ❷ VERB
to capture a person • *another technique for catching criminals*
apprehend • *the force necessary to apprehend a suspect*
arrest • *Police arrested the gunman.*

catch ❸ NOUN
a device that fastens something • *windows fitted with safety catches*
bolt • *the sound of a bolt being slid open*
clasp • *the clasp of her handbag*
clip • *She took the clip out of her hair.*
latch • *You left the latch off the gate.*

catch ❹ NOUN
a hidden difficulty • *The catch is that you have to fly via Paris.*
disadvantage • *The disadvantage is that this plant needs frequent watering.*
drawback • *The flat's only drawback was its size.*
snag • *The snag is that you have to pay in advance.*

MORE SYNONYMS
● fly in the ointment
● stumbling block

Can't find the word you're looking for? Try the index.

category NOUN
a set of things with something in common • *The items were organized into six different categories.*
class • *dividing the stars into six classes of brightness*
classification • *There are various classifications of genres or types of book.*
group • *She is one of the most promising players in her age group.*
set • *Pupils are divided into sets according to ability.*
sort • *What sort of school did you go to?*
type • *The majority of complaints received are of this type.*

cause ❶ NOUN
what makes something happen • *the most common cause of back pain*
origin • *the origin of the present war*
root • *We need to get to the root of the problem.*
source • *the source of the leak*

cause ❷ NOUN
an aim supported by a group • *dedication to the cause of peace*
aim • *political aims*
ideal • *socialist ideals*
movement • *the women's movement*

cause ❸ NOUN
the reason for something • *They gave us no cause to believe that.*
basis • *There is no basis for this assumption.*
grounds • *discrimination on the grounds of race or religion*
justification • *There was no justification for what he was doing.*
motivation • *the motivation for his actions*
motive • *Police have ruled out robbery as a motive.*

reason • *You have every reason to be upset.*

cause ❹ VERB
to make something happen • *This may cause delays.*
bring about • *We must try to bring about a better world.*
create • *The scheme may create even more confusion.*
generate • *the excitement generated by this film*
produce • *His comments produced a furious response.*
provoke • *a move that has provoked a storm of protest*

MORE SYNONYMS
● effect
● engender
● give rise to
● lead to
● result in

caution ❶ NOUN
great care taken in order to avoid danger • *Drivers are urged to exercise extreme caution in icy weather.*
care • *Scissors can be safe for young children if used with care.*
prudence • *A lack of prudence may lead to problems.*

MORE SYNONYMS
● forethought
● circumspection

caution ❷ VERB
to scold or warn someone against doing something • *The two men were cautioned but police say they will not be charged.*
reprimand • *He was reprimanded by a teacher for talking in the corridor.*
tick off (INFORMAL) • *Traffic police ticked off a pensioner for jumping a red light.*

a
b
c
d
e
f
g
h
i
j
k
l
m
n
o
p
q
r
s
t
u
v
w
x
y
z

Can't find the word you're looking for? Try the index.

A
B
C
D
E
F
G
H
I
J
K
L
M
N
O
P
Q
R
S
T
U
V
W
X
Y
Z

warn • *My mother warned me not to talk to strangers.*

cautious ADJECTIVE
acting very carefully to avoid danger • *a cautious approach*
careful • *Be extremely careful when on holiday abroad.*
guarded • *a guarded response*
tentative • *a tentative approach*
wary • *small firms remain wary of committing themselves to debt*

ANOTHER SYNONYM
● prudent

ANTONYM
● daring

cease ❶ VERB
to stop happening • *Almost miraculously, the noise ceased.*
be over • *The captured planes will be kept until the war is over.*
come to an end • *The strike came to an end.*
die away • *The sound died away and silence reigned.*
end • *The college year ends in March.*
finish • *The teaching day finished at around four o'clock.*
stop • *The rain had stopped.*

ANTONYM
● begin

cease ❷ VERB
to stop doing something • *A small number of firms have ceased trading.*
desist from • *His wife never desisted from trying to change his mind.*
discontinue • *Do not discontinue the treatment without consulting your doctor.*
finish • *As soon as he'd finished eating, he excused himself.*

give up • *smokers who give up before the age of 30*
stop • *Stop throwing those stones!*
suspend • *The union suspended strike action this week.*

ANTONYM
● start

celebrate VERB
to do something special to mark an event • *I was in a mood to celebrate.*
commemorate • *The anniversary of the composer's death was commemorated with a concert.*
party • *It's your birthday - let's party!*
rejoice • *My family rejoiced at the happy outcome to events.*

ANTONYM
● mourn

celebration NOUN
an event in honour of a special occasion • *his eightieth birthday celebrations*
festival • *a religious festival*
festivity • *the wedding festivities*
gala • *the Olympics' opening gala*
party • *a housewarming party*

MORE SYNONYMS
● merrymaking
● revelry

celebrity NOUN
a famous person • *At the age of twelve, he was already a celebrity.*
big name • *all the big names in rock and pop*
name • *some of the most famous names in modelling and show business*
personality • *a well-known radio and television personality*
star • *Not all football stars are ill-behaved louts.*
superstar • *a Hollywood superstar*

Can't find the word you're looking for? Try the index.

VIP • *such VIPs as Prince Charles and the former US President*

censure ❶ NOUN
strong disapproval • *a controversial policy which has attracted international censure*
blame • *I'm the one who'll get the blame if things go wrong.*
condemnation • *There was widespread condemnation of Saturday's killings.*
criticism • *This policy had repeatedly come under strong criticism.*
disapproval • *His action had been greeted with almost universal disapproval.*
reproach • *Those in public life should be beyond reproach.*

censure ❷ VERB
to criticize severely • *I would not presume to censure him for his views.*
condemn • *He condemned the players for lack of ability and application.*
criticize • *The regime has been harshly criticized for its human rights violations.*
denounce • *The letter called for civil rights, but did not openly denounce the regime.*
reproach • *She had not even reproached him for breaking his promise.*

MORE SYNONYMS
- berate
- castigate

centre ❶ NOUN
the middle of something • *the centre of the room*
core • *the earth's core*
focus • *Her children are the main focus of her life.*

heart • *the heart of the problem*
hub • *The kitchen is the hub of most households.*
middle • *in the middle of the back row*

ANTONYM
- edge

centre ❷ VERB
to have as the main subject • *All his thoughts were centred around himself.*
concentrate • *Scientists are concentrating their efforts on finding a cure.*
focus • *Attention is likely to focus on sales growth.*
revolve • *Since childhood, her life has revolved around tennis.*

ceremony ❶ NOUN
formal actions done for a special occasion • *his recent coronation ceremony*
observance • *a Memorial Day observance*
pomp • *His departure was celebrated with suitable pomp.*
rite • *a fertility rite*
ritual • *a Summer Solstice ritual*
service • *The President attended the morning service.*

ceremony ❷ NOUN
formal and polite behaviour • *He hung up without ceremony.*
decorum • *a responsibility to behave with decorum*
etiquette • *the rules of diplomatic etiquette*
formality • *his lack of stuffy formality*
niceties • *social niceties*
protocol • *minor breaches of protocol*

certain ❶ ADJECTIVE
definite or reliable • *One thing is*

a
b
c
d
e
f
g
h
i
j
k
l
m
n
o
p
q
r
s
t
u
v
w
x
y
z

Can't find the word you're looking for? Try the index.

A
B
C
D
E
F
G
H
I
J
K
L
M
N
O
P
Q
R
S
T
U
V
W
X
Y
Z

certain - they respect each other.
definite • It's too soon to give a definite answer.
established • an established medical fact
guaranteed • Success is not guaranteed.
inevitable • If she wins her case, it is inevitable that other people will sue the company.
known • It is not known when the bomb was planted.
sure • Sharpe's leg began to ache, a sure sign of rain.
undeniable • undeniable proof of guilt

ANTONYM
● uncertain

certain ➋ ADJECTIVE
having no doubt in your mind
• She's absolutely certain she's going to succeed.
clear • It is important to be clear about what you are doing.
confident • I am confident that everything will come out right.
convinced • He was convinced that I was part of the problem.
definite • Mary is very definite about this fact.
positive • I'm as positive as I can be about it.
satisfied • People must be satisfied that the treatment is safe.
sure • She was no longer sure how she felt about him.

ANTONYM
● uncertain

certainly ADVERB
without any doubt • I'll certainly do all I can to help.
definitely • Something should definitely be done.

undeniably • Bringing up a baby is undeniably hard work.
undoubtedly • He is undoubtedly a great player.
unquestionably • He is unquestionably a star.
without doubt • The refugees are, without doubt, extremely vulnerable.

challenge ➊ NOUN
a suggestion to try something
• They issued a challenge to their rivals.
dare • He'd do almost anything for a dare.

challenge ➋ VERB
to give someone a challenge
• He challenged his rival to a duel.
dare • I dare you to ask him.
defy • He looked at me as if he was defying me to argue.

challenge ➌ VERB
to question the truth or value of something • challenging the authority of the state
dispute • He disputed the charge.
question • questioning the jury's verdict

champion ➊ NOUN
a person who wins a competition
• Kasparov became a world chess champion.
hero • the goalscoring hero of the British hockey team
title holder • He became the youngest world title holder at the age of 22.
victor • the British Grand Prix victors
winner • The winner was a horse called Baby Face.

champion ➋ NOUN
someone who supports a group, cause, or principle • He received

acclaim as a champion of the
oppressed.
advocate • *He was a staunch
advocate of free trade.*
defender • *a strong defender of
human rights*
guardian • *The party wants to be
seen as a guardian of traditional
values.*
protector • *She sees him as a
protector and provider.*

champion ❸ VERB
to support a group, cause, or
principle • *He passionately
championed the poor.*
defend • *his courage in defending
religious and civil rights*
fight for • *Our Government should
be fighting for an end to child
poverty.*
promote • *You don't have to
sacrifice the environment to promote
economic growth.*
stick up for (INFORMAL) • *He has
shown courage in sticking up for civil
liberties.*
support • *The vice president has
always supported the people of New
York.*
uphold • *upholding the artist's
right to creative freedom*

MORE SYNONYMS
● advocate
● espouse

chance ❶ NOUN
a possibility of something
happening • *a good chance of
success*
likelihood • *the likelihood of
infection*
odds • *What are the odds of that
happening?*
possibility • *the possibility of pay
cuts*

probability • *a probability of
victory*
prospect • *There is little prospect
of peace.*

chance ❷ NOUN
an opportunity to do something
• *He didn't give me a chance to
explain.*
occasion • *I had no occasion to
speak to her that day.*
opening • *an opening for finding a
peaceful outcome to the conflict*
opportunity • *an opportunity to go
abroad to study*
time • *There was no time to think.*

chance ❸ NOUN
the way things happen without
being planned • *events which were
merely the result of chance*
accident • *a strange accident of
fate*
coincidence • *It was no
coincidence that she arrived just then.*
fortune • *a change of fortune*
luck • *His injury was just bad luck.*

RELATED WORD
● ADJECTIVE: fortuitous

change ❶ NOUN
an alteration in something
• *a change in her attitude*
alteration • *some alterations in
your diet*
difference • *a noticeable
difference in his behaviour*
modification • *Some minor
modifications were required.*
transformation • *the transformation
of a wilderness into a garden*

MORE SYNONYMS
● metamorphosis
● mutation
● transition
● transmutation

a
b
c
d
e
f
g
h
i
j
k
l
m
n
o
p
q
r
s
t
u
v
w
x
y
z

Can't find the word you're looking for? Try the index.

change ❷ VERB

to make or become different • *Her views have changed since her husband's death.*

alter • *There is no prospect of the decision being altered.*

convert • *a plan to convert his spare room into an office*

moderate • *They persuaded him to moderate his views.*

modify • *He refused to modify his behaviour.*

reform • *his plans to reform the economy*

transform • *The landscape has been transformed.*

MORE SYNONYMS

- metamorphose
- mutate
- transmute

change ❸ VERB

to exchange one thing for another • *Can I change this sweater for one a size bigger?*

barter • *bartering wheat for cotton and timber*

exchange • *the chance to sell back or exchange goods*

interchange • *Meat can be interchanged with pulses as a source of protein.*

replace • *His smile was replaced by a frown.*

substitute • *You can substitute honey for the sugar.*

swap • *Let's swap places.*

trade • *They traded land for goods and money.*

changeable ADJECTIVE

likely to change all the time • *changeable weather*

erratic • *erratic driving*

fickle • *Fashion is a fickle business.*

irregular • *an irregular heartbeat*

unpredictable • *unpredictable behaviour*

unstable • *The political situation is unstable.*

variable • *a variable rate of interest*

volatile • *a volatile atmosphere*

MORE SYNONYMS

- mercurial
- mutable
- protean

ANTONYM

- constant

character ❶ NOUN

the qualities of a person • *He has a dark side to his character.*

make-up • *Determination has always been a part of his make-up.*

nature • *a sunny nature*

personality • *an outgoing personality*

temperament • *his impulsive temperament*

MORE SYNONYMS

- disposition
- quality
- temper

character ❷ NOUN

an honourable nature • *She showed real character in her attempt to win over the crowd.*

honour • *He has acted with honour.*

integrity • *a man of integrity*

strength • *He had the strength to turn down the offer.*

characteristic ❶ NOUN

a typical quality • *His chief characteristic is honesty.*

attribute • *a normal attribute of human behaviour*

feature • *a feature of the local culture*

Can't find the word you're looking for? Try the index.

property • *This liquid has many unique properties.*
quality • *leadership qualities*
trait • *personality traits*

MORE SYNONYMS
- idiosyncrasy
- peculiarity
- quirk

characteristic ➋ ADJECTIVE

typical of a person or thing • *He responded with characteristic generosity.*
distinctive • *a distinctive voice*
distinguishing • *no distinguishing marks*
typical • *his typical British modesty*

MORE SYNONYMS
- idiosyncratic
- peculiar
- singular
- symptomatic

ANTONYM
- uncharacteristic

charge ➊ VERB

to ask someone for money as a payment • *The majority of producers charged a fair price.*
ask (for) • *The artist was asking £6,000 for each painting.*
bill • *Are you going to bill me for this?*
levy • *Taxes should not be levied without the authority of Parliament.*

charge ➋ VERB

to rush forward, often to attack someone • *He charged into the room.*
dash • *She dashed in from the garden.*
rush • *A schoolgirl rushed into the burning flat to help an old man.*
stampede • *The crowd stampeded.*

storm • *He stormed into the shop, demanding to see the manager.*

charge ➌ NOUN

the price you have to pay for something • *We can arrange this for a small charge.*
cost • *Badges are available at a cost of £2.50.*
fee • *Pay your solicitor's fees.*
payment • *I'll do it in return for a small payment.*
price • *We negotiated a price for the service.*

charm ➊ NOUN

an attractive quality • *a man of great personal charm*
allure • *the allure of Egypt*
appeal • *confident of his appeal to women*
attraction • *the attractions of living by the sea*
fascination • *It is hard to explain the fascination of this place.*
magnetism • *a man of enormous magnetism*

charm ➋ VERB

to use charm to please someone • *He charmed his 2,000-strong audience.*
bewitch • *bewitched by her beauty*
captivate • *The crowd was captivated by her honesty.*
delight • *a style of music that has delighted audiences*
entrance • *entranced by her smile*

MORE SYNONYMS
- beguile
- enchant
- enrapture

chase ➊ VERB

to try to catch someone or something • *She chased the thief for a hundred yards.*

a
b
c
d
e
f
g
h
i
j
k
l
m
n
o
p
q
r
s
t
u
v
w
x
y
z

Can't find the word you're looking for? Try the index.

A
B
C
D
E
F
G
H
I
J
K
L
M
N
O
P
Q
R
S
T
U
V
W
X
Y
Z

hunt • *He fled to Portugal after being hunted by police.*
pursue • *She pursued the man who had snatched her bag.*

chase ❷ VERB
to force to go somewhere • *Angry demonstrators chased him away.*
drive • *The troops drove the rebels into the jungle.*
hound • *He was hounded out of his job.*

MORE SYNONYMS
- expel
- put to flight

chat ❶ NOUN
a friendly talk • *We sat around and had a chat.*
conversation • *a telephone conversation*
gossip • *Don't you enjoy a good gossip?*
natter (INFORMAL) • *Let's get together for a natter some time.*
talk • *We will have a talk about it later.*

chat ❷ VERB
to chat in a friendly way • *He was chatting to his father.*
gossip • *We gossiped into the night.*
natter (INFORMAL) • *His mother would natter to anyone.*
talk • *She's very easy to talk to.*

cheap ❶ ADJECTIVE
costing very little • *Cheap flights are available.*
bargain • *selling at bargain prices*
economical • *These cars are very economical to run.*
inexpensive • *an inexpensive wine*
reasonable • *His fees were quite reasonable.*

MORE SYNONYMS
- cut-price
- low-cost
- low-priced

ANTONYM
- expensive

cheap ❷ ADJECTIVE
inexpensive but of poor quality • *a suit made of some cheap material*
inferior • *an inferior imitation*
second-rate • *second-rate equipment*
tawdry • *tawdry souvenirs*

cheat VERB
to get something from someone dishonestly • *the people he cheated out of their life savings*
con (INFORMAL) • *He conned his way into a job.*
deceive • *Investors were deceived by a scam.*
defraud • *charges of conspiracy to defraud the government*
dupe • *Stamp collectors were duped into buying fakes.*
fleece • *He fleeced her out of thousands of pounds.*
rip off (SLANG) • *ticket touts ripping off soccer fans*
swindle • *two executives who swindled their employer*

MORE SYNONYMS
- bilk
- hoodwink

check ❶ VERB
to examine something • *Check all the details first.*
check out (INFORMAL) • *Check out the financial figures.*
examine • *He examined her passport and stamped it.*
inspect • *the right to inspect company files*

test • *The drug must be tested in clinical trials.*

MORE SYNONYMS
- inquire into
- look over
- scrutinize

check ➋ VERB
to reduce or stop something • *a policy to check fast population growth*
control • *a measure to control illegal mining*
curb • *reforms which aim to curb spending*
halt • *an attempt to halt the spread of the disease*
inhibit • *factors which inhibit growth*
restrain • *the need to restrain wage rises*
stop • *measures to stop the trade in ivory*

check ➌ NOUN
an examination • *a thorough check of the equipment*
examination • *a medical examination*
inspection • *a routine inspection of the premises*
test • *a test for cancer*

cheek NOUN
speech or behaviour that is rude or disrespectful • *I'm amazed they had the cheek to ask in the first place.*
audacity • *I was shocked at the audacity of the gangsters.*
gall • *She had the gall to claim she had been victimized.*
impudence • *My sister had the impudence to go out wearing my clothes.*
insolence • *The pupil was excluded for insolence.*

nerve • *He had the nerve to ask me to prove who I was.*
rudeness • *Mother was cross at Tom's rudeness.*

MORE SYNONYMS
- effrontery
- temerity

cheeky ADJECTIVE
rude and disrespectful • *cheeky teenagers*
impertinent • *an impertinent question*
impudent • *his rude and impudent behaviour*
insolent • *a defiant, almost insolent look*
rude • *She was often rude to her mother.*

ANTONYM
- polite

cheerful ADJECTIVE
in a happy mood • *She was very cheerful despite her illness.*
bright • *"May I help you?" said a bright voice.*
buoyant • *in a buoyant mood*
cheery • *a cheery nature*
happy • *a confident, happy child*
jaunty • *a jaunty tune*
jolly • *a jolly, easy-going man*
light-hearted • *They were light-hearted and enjoyed life.*
merry • *a burst of merry laughter*

ANTONYM
- miserable

cheery ADJECTIVE
happy and cheerful • *He is loved by everyone for his cheery disposition.*
cheerful • *They are both very cheerful in spite of their circumstances.*
chirpy • *She sounded quite chirpy on the phone.*

Can't find the word you're looking for? Try the index.

A
B
C
D
E
F
G
H
I
J
K
L
M
N
O
P
Q
R
S
T
U
V
W
X
Y
Z

good-humoured • *Charles was brave and remarkably good-humoured.*
happy • *Marina was a confident, happy child.*
jolly • *She was a jolly, kind-hearted woman.*
sunny • *a nice lad with a sunny disposition*
upbeat • *Neil's colleagues said he was in a joking, upbeat mood.*

MORE SYNONYMS
● genial
● jovial

ANTONYM
● gloomy

chew VERB
to break food up with the teeth
• *Eat slowly and chew your food properly.*
crunch • *She crunched the ice cube loudly.*
gnaw • *He sat and gnawed at an apple.*
munch • *Sheep were munching the leaves.*

MORE SYNONYMS
● champ
● chomp
● masticate

chief ❶ NOUN
the leader of a group or organization • *the deputy chief of the territory's defence force*
boss • *He cannot stand his boss.*
chieftain • *the legendary British chieftain, King Arthur*
director • *the financial director of the company*
governor • *The incident was reported to the prison governor.*
head • *heads of government from 100 countries*

leader • *the leader of the Conservative Party*
manager • *a retired bank manager*

chief ❷ ADJECTIVE
most important • *The job went to one of his chief rivals.*
foremost • *one of the world's foremost scholars of ancient Indian culture*
key • *He is expected to be the key witness at the trial.*
main • *one of the main tourist areas of Amsterdam*
prevailing • *the prevailing attitude towards women in this society*
primary • *His language difficulties were the primary cause of his other problems.*
prime • *The police will see me as the prime suspect!*
principal • *The principal reason for my change of mind is this.*

MORE SYNONYMS
● pre-eminent
● premier

child NOUN
a young person • *I lived in France as a child.*
ankle-biter (AUSTRALIAN AND NEW ZEALAND; SLANG) • *I knew him when he was just an ankle-biter.*
baby • *She took care of me when I was a baby.*
bairn (SCOTTISH) • *a two-year-old bairn*
infant • *young mums with infants in prams*
juvenile • *a prison for juveniles*
kid (INFORMAL) • *They've got three kids.*
minor • *charged with selling cigarettes to minors*
offspring • *parents choosing shoes for their offspring*

Can't find the word you're looking for? Try the index.

toddler • *a toddler in a pushchair*
tot • *The tot was too young to know what was happening.*
youngster • *I was only a youngster in 1965.*

ANTONYM
- adult

RELATED WORDS
- ADJECTIVE: filial
- PREFIX: paedo-

childish ADJECTIVE
immature and foolish • *I don't have time for this childish behaviour.*
immature • *She is emotionally immature.*
infantile • *infantile jokes*
juvenile • *juvenile behaviour*
puerile • *a puerile sense of humour*

ANTONYM
- mature

china NOUN (SOUTH AFRICAN; INFORMAL)
a friend • *How are you, my old china?*
buddy (INFORMAL) • *We've been buddies since we were kids.*
chum (INFORMAL) • *He went on holiday with his two best chums.*
crony (OLD-FASHIONED) • *She is always surrounded by her cronies.*
friend • *lifelong friends*
mate (BRITISH; INFORMAL) • *Come on mate, things aren't that bad.*
pal (INFORMAL) • *He'd never let a pal down.*

choice ❶ NOUN
a range of things to choose from • *available in a choice of colours*
range • *a range of sun-care products*
selection • *an interesting selection of recipes*

variety • *a variety of candidates from which to choose*

choice ❷ NOUN
the power to choose • *They had little choice in the matter.*
alternative • *He said he could not see any alternative.*
option • *He was given the option of going to jail or paying a fine.*
say • *We don't have a say in the company's decisions.*

choose VERB
to decide to have or do something • *a number of foods to choose from*
opt for • *He opted for early retirement.*
pick • *She was picked for the debating team.*
select • *She paused to select another cookie from the box.*
take • *She took the option he offered her.*

MORE SYNONYMS
- elect
- fix on
- settle on

chop VERB
to cut down or into pieces • *I heard him chopping wood in the yard.*
cut • *Cut the vegetables up.*
fell • *43,000 square miles of tropical forest are felled each year.*
hack • *They hacked away at the undergrowth.*
lop • *Somebody had lopped the heads off our tulips.*

MORE SYNONYMS
- cleave
- hew

circulate VERB
to pass around • *He circulated rumours about everyone.*

a b **c** d e f g h i j k l m n o p q r s t u v w x y z

Can't find the word you're looking for? Try the index.

A
B
C
D
E
F
G
H
I
J
K
L
M
N
O
P
Q
R
S
T
U
V
W
X
Y
Z

distribute • *distributing leaflets*
propagate • *They propagated their political ideas.*
spread • *spreading malicious gossip*

MORE SYNONYMS
● disseminate
● promulgate

city NOUN

a large town • *the city of London*
metropolis • *a busy metropolis*
town • *the oldest town in Europe*

MORE SYNONYMS
● conurbation
● municipality

RELATED WORD
● ADJECTIVE: civic

civilized ADJECTIVE

having an advanced society
• *a highly civilized country*
cultured • *a mature and cultured nation*
enlightened • *this enlightened century*

claim ❶ VERB

to say something is the case • *He claims to have lived here all his life.*
allege • *He is alleged to have killed a man.*
assert • *The defendants continued to assert their innocence.*
hold • *She holds that these measures are unnecessary.*
insist • *They insisted that they had no money.*
maintain • *I still maintain that I am not guilty.*
profess • *She professed to hate her nickname.*

claim ❷ NOUN

a statement that something is the case • *He rejected claims that he*

had taken bribes.
allegation • *allegations of theft*
assertion • *his assertion that he did not plan to remarry*

MORE SYNONYMS
● pretension
● protestation

clash ❶ VERB

to fight or argue with another person • *A group of 400 demonstrators clashed with police.*
battle • *In one town thousands of people battled with police officers.*
fight • *two rival gangs fighting in the streets*
quarrel • *My brother quarrelled with my father.*
wrangle • *Delegates wrangled over the future of the organization.*

clash ❷ VERB

of two things: to be so different that they do not go together
• *Don't make policy decisions which clash with company thinking.*
conflict • *He held opinions which sometimes conflicted with my own.*
contradict • *Cut-backs like these surely contradict the Government's commitment to education.*
differ • *The two leaders differed on several issues.*
disagree • *Our managers disagreed on several policy issues.*
go against • *Changes are being made which go against my principles.*
jar • *They had always been good together and their temperaments seldom jarred.*

clash ❸ NOUN

a fight or argument • *a number of clashes between rival parties*
battle • *a gun battle between*

police and drug traffickers
conflict • attempts to prevent a conflict between workers and management
confrontation • This issue could lead to a military confrontation.
fight • He had had a fight with Smith and bloodied his nose.
skirmish (INFORMAL) • Border skirmishes between the two countries were common.
squabble • There have been minor squabbles about phone bills.
struggle • a struggle between competing political factions

clasp ❶ VERB
to hold something tightly • Mary clasped the children to her desperately.
clutch • She was clutching a photograph.
embrace • People were crying for joy and embracing each other.
grip • She gripped the rope.
hold • He held the pistol in his right hand.
hug • She hugged her legs tight to her chest.
press • I pressed the child closer to my heart and prayed.
squeeze • He longed to just scoop her up and squeeze her.

clasp ❷ NOUN
a fastening such as a hook or catch • She undid the clasp of her hooded cloak.
buckle • He wore a belt with a large brass buckle.
catch • She fiddled with the catch of her bag.
clip • She took the clip out of her hair.
fastener • a product range which includes nails, woodscrews, and fasteners

fastening • The sundress has a neat back zip fastening.

class ❶ NOUN
a group of a particular type • a new class of vehicle
category • different categories of taxpayer
genre • films of the horror genre
grade • the lowest grade of staff
group • a plan to help people in this group
kind • the biggest prize of its kind in the world
set • The fashionable set all go to this club.
sort • several articles of this sort
type • various types of vegetable

class ❷ VERB
to regard as being in a particular group • They are officially classed as visitors.
categorize • His films are hard to categorize.
classify • Carrots are also classified as a fruit.
designate • The house is designated as a national monument.
grade • This ski-run is graded as easy.
rank • She is ranked in the world's top 50 players.
rate • He rates the film highly.

classify VERB
to arrange similar things in groups • We can classify the differences into three groups.
arrange • Arrange the books in neat piles.
categorize • This film is hard to categorize.
grade • musical pieces graded according to difficulty
rank • He was ranked among Britain's best-known millionaires.

a
c
d
e
f
g
h
i
j
k
l
m
n
o
p
q
r
s
t
u
v
w
x
y
z

Can't find the word you're looking for? Try the index.

sort • *sorting the material into folders*

MORE SYNONYMS
- pigeonhole
- systematize
- tabulate

clean ❶ ADJECTIVE
free from dirt or marks • *clean shoes*
immaculate • *immaculate white flannels*
impeccable • *dressed in an impeccable trouser suit*
laundered • *freshly laundered shirts*
spotless • *The kitchen was spotless.*
washed • *newly washed hair*

ANTONYM
- dirty

clean ❷ ADJECTIVE
free from germs or infection • *a lack of clean water and sanitation*
antiseptic • *an antiseptic hospital room*
hygienic • *a hygienic kitchen*
purified • *Only purified water is used.*
sterilized • *sterilized milk*
uncontaminated • *uncontaminated air*
unpolluted • *unpolluted beaches*

ANTONYM
- contaminated

clean ❸ VERB
to remove dirt from • *She cleaned the house from top to bottom.*
cleanse • *a lotion to cleanse the skin*
dust • *I vacuumed, dusted and polished the living room.*
scour • *He scoured the sink.*

scrub • *I started to scrub off the dirt.*
sponge • *Sponge your face and body.*
swab • *an old man swabbing the floor*
wash • *He got a job washing dishes in a restaurant.*
wipe • *He wiped the sweat from his face.*

ANTONYM
- soil

clear ❶ ADJECTIVE
easy to see or understand • *He made it clear he did not want to talk.*
apparent • *There is no apparent reason for the crime.*
blatant • *a blatant piece of cheating*
conspicuous • *one conspicuous difference*
definite • *a definite advantage*
evident • *He ate with evident enjoyment.*
explicit • *He was very explicit about his intentions.*
obvious • *There are obvious dangers.*
plain • *The results are plain to see.*

MORE SYNONYMS
- incontrovertible
- manifest
- palpable
- patent
- unequivocal

clear ❷ ADJECTIVE
easy to see through • *a clear liquid*
crystalline • *crystalline green waters*
glassy • *The water was a deep glassy blue.*
translucent • *translucent stones*
transparent • *transparent glass walls*

Can't find the word you're looking for? Try the index.

MORE SYNONYMS
- limpid
- pellucid
- see-through

ANTONYM
- cloudy

clear ❸ VERB
to prove someone is not guilty
• *She was cleared of murder.*
absolve • *He was absolved of all charges.*
acquit • *acquitted of disorderly conduct*

ANTONYM
- convict

clever ADJECTIVE
very intelligent • *My sister was always a lot cleverer than I was.*
brainy (INFORMAL) • *I don't consider myself to be especially brainy.*
bright • *an exceptionally bright child*
intelligent • *a lively and intelligent woman*
shrewd • *a shrewd businessman*
smart • *a very smart move*

MORE SYNONYMS
- astute
- quick-witted
- sagacious

ANTONYM
- stupid

climb VERB
to move upwards over something
• *Climbing the first hill took half an hour.*
ascend • *He ascended the ladder into the loft.*
clamber • *They clambered up the stone walls.*
mount • *He mounted the steps.*
scale • *the first British woman to scale Everest*

close ❶ VERB
to shut something • *Close the gate behind you.*
secure • *The shed was secured by a padlock.*
shut • *Someone had forgotten to shut the door.*

ANTONYM
- open

close ❷ VERB
to block so that nothing can pass
• *All the roads out are closed.*
bar • *Protesters barred the way to his car.*
block • *The road was blocked by debris.*
obstruct • *buskers obstructing the pavement*
seal • *Soldiers had sealed the border.*

close ❸ ADJECTIVE
near to something • *a restaurant close to their home*
▷ see Word Study **close**, page 674

ANTONYM
- distant

close ❹ ADJECTIVE
friendly and loving • *We became close friends.*
▷ see Word Study **close**, page 674

ANTONYM
- distant

cloth NOUN
woven or knitted fabric • *a piece of red cloth*
fabric • *waterproof fabric*
material • *This material shrinks badly.*
textiles • *a trader in clothes and textiles*

clothes PLURAL NOUN
the things people wear • *She*

a
b
c
d
e
f
g
h
i
j
k
l
m
n
o
p
q
r
s
t
u
v
w
x
y
z

Can't find the word you're looking for? Try the index.

A
B
C
D
E
F
G
H
I
J
K
L
M
N
O
P
Q
R
S
T
U
V
W
X
Y
Z

spends all her money on clothes.
attire (FORMAL) • *suitable attire*
clothing • *men's clothing*
costume • *national costume*
dress • *traditional dress*
garments • *winter garments*
gear (INFORMAL) • *trendy gear*
outfit • *a stunning scarlet outfit*
wardrobe • *next summer's wardrobe*
wear • *evening wear*

MORE SYNONYMS
● apparel
● garb
● raiment

cloud ❶ NOUN
a mass of vapour or smoke
• *The sky was dark with clouds.*
billow • *billows of smoke*
fog • *a fog of cigar smoke*
haze • *a haze of exhaust fumes*
mist • *The valley was wrapped in thick mist.*
vapour • *warm vapour rising from the ground*

cloud ❷ VERB
to make something confusing
• *Anger has clouded her judgement.*
confuse • *You're just confusing the matter by bringing politics into it.*
distort • *a distorted memory*
muddle • *The question muddles two separate issues.*

cloudy ❶ ADJECTIVE
full of clouds • *a cloudy sky*
dull • *It's always dull and wet here.*
gloomy • *gloomy weather*
leaden • *leaden skies*
overcast • *a damp, overcast morning*

ANTONYM
● clear

cloudy ❷ ADJECTIVE
difficult to see through • *a glass of*

cloudy liquid
muddy • *a muddy duck pond*
murky • *murky waters*
opaque • *an opaque glass jar*

ANTONYM
● clear

club ❶ NOUN
an organization for people with a special interest • *a swimming club*
association • *the Women's Tennis Association*
circle • *a local painting circle*
group • *an environmental group*
guild • *the Screen Writers' Guild*
society • *a historical society*
union • *the International Astronomical Union*

club ❷ NOUN
a heavy stick • *armed with knives and clubs*
bat • *a baseball bat*
stick • *a crowd carrying sticks and stones*
truncheon • *a policeman's truncheon*

club ❸ VERB
to hit with a heavy object • *Two thugs clubbed him with baseball bats.*
bash • *They bashed his head with a spade.*
batter • *battered to death*
beat • *beaten with rifle butts*
bludgeon • *bludgeoning his wife with a hammer*

clumsiness NOUN
awkwardness of movement • *The accident was entirely the result of his own clumsiness.*
awkwardness • *They moved with the awkwardness of mechanical dolls.*
ungainliness • *his physical ungainliness*

clumsy ADJECTIVE

moving awkwardly • *He is big and clumsy in his movements.*
awkward • *an awkward gesture*
gauche • *He makes me feel stupid and gauche.*
lumbering • *a big, lumbering man*
uncoordinated • *an uncoordinated dancer*
ungainly • *As a youth he was lanky and ungainly.*

MORE SYNONYMS

- accident-prone
- bumbling
- gawky
- maladroit

ANTONYM

- graceful

coast NOUN

the land next to the sea • *a holiday by the coast*
beach • *a beautiful sandy beach*
border • *the border of the Black Sea*
coastline • *the stunning Caribbean coastline*
seaside • *a day at the seaside*
shore • *a bleak and rocky shore*
strand • *boats fishing from the strand*

coat NOUN

an animal's fur or hair • *She gave the dog's coat a brush.*
fleece • *a blanket of lamb's fleece*
fur • *a kitten with black fur*
hair • *He's allergic to cat hair.*
hide • *rhino hide*
pelt • *a wolf pelt*
skin • *convicted of attempting to sell the skin of a Siberian tiger*
wool • *Lanolin comes from sheep's wool.*

coating NOUN

a layer of something • *a thin coating of ice*
coat • *a coat of paint*
covering • *a covering of dust*
layer • *a layer of dead leaves*

coax VERB

to persuade gently • *We coaxed her into coming with us.*
cajole • *Her sister cajoled her into playing.*
persuade • *My husband persuaded me to come.*
talk into • *They've talked him into getting a new car.*

MORE SYNONYMS

- inveigle
- prevail upon
- wheedle

cocky ❶ ADJECTIVE

cheeky or too self-confident • *He was a bit cocky because he was winning all the time.*
arrogant • *an air of arrogant indifference*
brash • *On stage she seems hard and brash.*
conceited • *I thought him conceited.*
overconfident • *She couldn't cope with this new generation of noisy, overconfident teenage girls.*

MORE SYNONYMS

- egotistical
- swaggering

cocky ❷ NOUN (AUSTRALIAN AND NEW ZEALAND)

a farmer, especially one whose farm is small • *He got some work with the cane cockies on Maroochy River.*
crofter (SCOTTISH) • *the financial plight of crofters in the islands*
farmer • *He was a simple farmer scratching a living from the soil.*

a
b
c
d
e
f
g
h
i
j
k
l
m
n
o
p
q
r
s
t
u
v
w
x
y
z

Can't find the word you're looking for? Try the index.

coil VERB
to wind in loops • *a coiled spring*
curl • *dark, curling hair*
loop • *A rope was looped between his hands.*
spiral • *vines spiralling up towards the roof*
twine • *This lily produces twining stems.*
twist • *She twisted her hair into a bun.*
wind • *a rope wound round her waist*

cold ❶ ADJECTIVE
having a low temperature
• *the coldest winter for ten years*
arctic • *arctic conditions*
biting • *a biting wind*
bitter • *driven inside by the bitter cold*
bleak • *The weather can be bleak on the coast.*
chilly • *It's chilly for June.*
freezing • *This house is freezing.*
icy • *the icy north wind*
raw • *a raw December morning*
wintry • *wintry showers*

ANTONYM
● hot

cold ❷ ADJECTIVE
not showing affection • *a cold, unfeeling woman*
aloof • *He seemed aloof and detached.*
distant • *She was polite but distant.*
frigid • *a frigid smile*
lukewarm • *a lukewarm response*
reserved • *emotionally reserved*
stony • *He gave me a stony look.*

MORE SYNONYMS
● standoffish
● undemonstrative

ANTONYM
● warm

collapse ❶ VERB
to fall down • *The whole building is about to collapse.*
fall down • *The ceiling fell down.*
give way • *The bridge gave way beneath him.*

collapse ❷ VERB
to fail • *50,000 small businesses collapsed last year.*
fail • *His hotel business has failed.*
fold • *We were laid off when the company folded.*
founder • *a foundering radio station*

collapse ❸ NOUN
the failure of something
• *the collapse of his marriage*
downfall • *the downfall of the government*
failure • *the failure of his business empire*

colleague NOUN
a person someone works with
• *I'll have to consult my colleagues.*
associate • *business associates*
fellow worker • *She started going out with a fellow worker.*
partner • *her business partner*
workmate • *the nickname his workmates gave him*

collect VERB
to gather together • *collecting signatures for a petition*
accumulate • *Most children enjoy accumulating knowledge.*
assemble • *trying to assemble a team*
gather • *gathering information*
raise • *They've raised over £100 for charity.*

Can't find the word you're looking for? Try the index.

MORE SYNONYMS
- aggregate
- amass

ANTONYM
- scatter

collection NOUN
a group of things collected together • *a collection of paintings*
assortment • *an assortment of pets*
group • *a group of songs*
store • *a vast store of knowledge*

colloquial ADJECTIVE
used in conversation • *a colloquial expression*
conversational • *a conversational style*
everyday • *He used plain, everyday English.*
informal • *an informal expression*

MORE SYNONYMS
- demotic
- idiomatic
- vernacular

colony ❶ NOUN
a country controlled by another country • *an American colony*
dependency • *the tiny British dependency of Montserrat*
dominion • *The Republic is a dominion of Brazil.*
territory • *territories under Israeli control*

colony ❷ NOUN
a group of settlers in a place • *a colony of Scots*
community • *the Sikh community in Britain*
outpost • *a remote outpost*
settlement • *a Muslim settlement*

colossal ADJECTIVE
very large indeed • *a colossal statue*

enormous • *The main bedroom is enormous.*
gigantic • *a gigantic task*
huge • *They are making huge profits.*
immense • *an immense cloud of smoke*
mammoth • *This mammoth undertaking was completed in 18 months.*
massive • *a massive steam boat*
vast • *farmers who own vast stretches of land*

ANTONYM
- tiny

colour ❶ NOUN
a shade or hue • *Her favourite colour is blue.*
hue • *delicate pastel hues*
pigmentation • *skin pigmentation*
shade • *walls painted in two shades of green*
tint • *a distinct orange tint*

colour ❷ NOUN
a substance used to give colour • *food colour*
dye • *hair dye*
paint • *a pot of red paint*
pigment • *a layer of blue pigment*

colour ❸ VERB
to give something a colour • *Many women colour their hair.*
dye • *Only dye clean garments.*
paint • *She paints her toenails red.*
stain • *Some foods can stain the teeth.*
tint • *tinted glass*

colour ❹ VERB
to affect the way you think • *Her upbringing has coloured her opinion of marriage.*
bias • *a biased opinion*
distort • *The shock of the accident distorted my judgement.*

a
b
c
d
e
f
g
h
i
j
k
l
m
n
o
p
q
r
s
t
u
v
w
x
y
z

Can't find the word you're looking for? Try the index.

A B C D E F G H I J K L M N O P Q R S T U V W X Y Z

prejudice • *Criticism will prejudice the Government's decision.*
slant • *deliberately slanted news coverage*

colourful ❶ ADJECTIVE
full of colour • *colourful clothes*
bright • *a bright green dress*
brilliant • *The garden has burst into brilliant flower.*
intense • *an intense shade of blue*
jazzy (INFORMAL) • *a jazzy tie*
rich • *a rich blue glass bowl*
vibrant • *vibrant orange shades*
vivid • *vivid hues*

MORE SYNONYMS
● kaleidoscopic
● multicoloured
● psychedelic

ANTONYM
● dull

colourful ❷ ADJECTIVE
interesting or exciting • *a colourful character*
graphic • *a graphic account of his career*
interesting • *He has had an interesting life.*
lively • *a lively imagination*
rich • *the rich history of the island*
vivid • *a vivid description*

ANTONYM
● dull

combination NOUN
a mixture of things • *a combination of charm and skill*
amalgamation • *an amalgamation of two organizations*
blend • *a blend of wine and spring water*
mix • *a mix of fantasy and reality*
mixture • *a mixture of horror, envy and awe*

MORE SYNONYMS
● amalgam
● coalescence
● composite
● meld

combine VERB
to join or mix together • *trying to combine motherhood with work*
amalgamate • *a plan to amalgamate the two parties*
blend • *The band blends jazz and folk music.*
fuse • *a performer who fuses magic and dance*
integrate • *integrating various styles of art*
merge • *The two countries have merged into one.*
mix • *mixing business with pleasure*
unite • *people uniting to fight racism*

MORE SYNONYMS
● meld
● synthesize

ANTONYM
● separate

come ❶ VERB
to move or arrive somewhere • *Two men came into the room.*
appear • *He appeared at about 9 o'clock.*
arrive • *My brother has just arrived.*
enter • *The class fell silent as the teacher entered.*
materialize • *The car just materialized from nowhere.*
show up (INFORMAL) • *He showed up over an hour late.*
turn up (INFORMAL) • *I'll call you when she turns up.*

come ❷ VERB
to happen or take place

Can't find the word you're looking for? Try the index.

• *Christmas only comes once a year.*
happen • *Nothing ever happens on a Sunday.*
occur • *How did the accident occur?*
take place • *The meeting never took place.*

comfort ❶ NOUN
a state of ease • *He settled back in comfort.*
ease • *a life of ease*
luxury • *brought up in an atmosphere of luxury*
wellbeing • *a wonderful sense of wellbeing*

comfort ❷ NOUN
relief from worry or unhappiness
• *Her words gave him some comfort.*
consolation • *He knew he was right, but it was no consolation.*
help • *Just talking to you has been a great help.*
relief • *temporary relief from the pain*
satisfaction • *At least I have the satisfaction of knowing I tried.*
support • *His family were a great support to him.*

comfort ❸ VERB
to give someone comfort • *trying to comfort the screaming child*
cheer • *The thought did nothing to cheer him.*
console • *"Never mind," he consoled me.*
reassure • *He did his best to reassure her.*
soothe • *She took him in his arms and soothed him.*

comfortable ❶ ADJECTIVE
physically relaxing • *a comfortable chair*
cosy • *a cosy living room*
easy • *You've had an easy time of it.*

homely • *a homely atmosphere*
relaxing • *a relaxing holiday*
restful • *a restful scene*

ANTONYM
● uncomfortable

comfortable ❷ ADJECTIVE
feeling at ease • *I don't feel comfortable around him.*
at ease • *He is not at ease in female company.*
at home • *We soon felt quite at home.*
contented • *a contented life*
happy • *I'm not very happy with that idea.*
relaxed • *a relaxed attitude*

ANTONYM
● uneasy

command ❶ VERB
to order someone to do something
• *She commanded me to lie down.*
bid • *The soldiers bade us turn and go back.*
demand • *They demanded that he leave.*
direct • *His doctor has directed him to rest.*
order • *He ordered his men to cease fire.*

MORE SYNONYMS
● charge
● enjoin

command ❷ VERB
to be in charge of • *the general who commanded the UN troops*
control • *He now controls the whole company.*
head • *Who heads the firm?*
lead • *He led the country between 1949 and 1984.*
manage • *I manage a small team of workers.*

a b c d e f g h i j k l m n o p q r s t u v w x y z

Can't find the word you're looking for? Try the index.

A
B
C
D
E
F
G
H
I
J
K
L
M
N
O
P
Q
R
S
T
U
V
W
X
Y
Z

supervise • *He supervised more than 400 volunteers.*

command ❸ NOUN

an order to do something • *The execution was carried out at his command.*

bidding • *They refused to leave at his bidding.*

decree • *a presidential decree*

directive • *a government directive*

injunction • *He left her with the injunction to go to sleep.*

instruction • *They were just following instructions.*

order • *I don't take orders from you.*

MORE SYNONYMS
- behest
- edict

command ❹ NOUN

knowledge and ability • *a good command of English*

grasp • *a good grasp of foreign languages*

knowledge • *He has no knowledge of law.*

mastery • *a mastery of grammar*

commemorate VERB

to do something in memory of • *concerts to commemorate the anniversary of his death*

celebrate • *celebrating their golden wedding*

honour • *celebrations to honour his memory*

MORE SYNONYMS
- memorialize
- pay tribute to

comment ❶ VERB

to make a remark • *He refused to comment on the rumours.*

mention • *I mentioned that I didn't like jazz.*

note • *He noted that some issues remained to be settled.*

observe • *"You're very pale," he observed.*

point out • *I should point out that these figures are approximate.*

remark • *Everyone had remarked on her new hairstyle.*

say • *"Well done," he said.*

MORE SYNONYMS
- interpose
- opine

comment ❷ NOUN

something you say • *sarcastic comments*

observation • *a few general observations*

remark • *snide remarks*

statement • *That statement puzzled me.*

commit VERB

to do something • *A crime has been committed.*

carry out • *attacks carried out by terrorists*

do • *They have done a lot of damage.*

perform • *people who have performed acts of bravery*

perpetrate • *A fraud has been perpetrated.*

common ❶ ADJECTIVE

of many people • *a common complaint*

general • *the general opinion*

popular • *a popular belief*

prevailing • *the prevailing atmosphere*

prevalent • *Smoking is becoming more prevalent among girls.*

universal • *The desire to look attractive is universal.*

widespread • *widespread support*

Can't find the word you're looking for? Try the index.

ANTONYM
- rare

common ❷ ADJECTIVE
not special • *the common man*
average • *the average teenager*
commonplace • *a commonplace observation*
everyday • *your everyday routine*
ordinary • *an ordinary day*
plain • *My parents were just plain ordinary folks.*
standard • *standard practice*
usual • *In a usual week I watch about 15 hours of television.*

MORE SYNONYMS
- humdrum
- run-of-the-mill
- workaday

ANTONYM
- special

common ❸ ADJECTIVE
having bad taste or manners
• *a common, rude woman*
coarse • *coarse humour*
rude • *It's rude to stare.*
vulgar • *vulgar remarks*

ANTONYM
- refined

common sense NOUN
the ability to make good judgments • *Use your common sense.*
good sense • *He had the good sense to call me at once.*
judgment • *I respect your judgment.*
level-headedness • *He prides himself on his level-headedness.*
prudence • *His lack of prudence led to financial problems.*
wit • *They don't have the wit to realize what's happening.*

communicate ❶ VERB
to be in touch with someone
• *We communicate mainly by email.*
be in contact • *I'll be in contact with him next week.*
be in touch • *He hasn't been in touch with me yet.*
correspond • *We correspond regularly.*

communicate ❷ VERB
to pass on information • *The results will be communicated by post.*
convey • *They have conveyed their views to the government.*
impart • *the ability to impart knowledge*
inform • *Will you inform me of any changes?*
pass on • *I'll pass on your good wishes.*
spread • *She has spread the news to everyone.*
transmit • *He transmitted his enjoyment to the audience.*

MORE SYNONYMS
- disseminate
- make known

companion NOUN
someone you travel with or spend time with • *He has been her constant companion for the last six years.*
comrade • *Unlike so many of his comrades he survived the war.*
crony (OLD-FASHIONED) • *a round of golf with his business cronies*
friend • *Sara's old friend, Charles*
mate • *A mate of mine used to play soccer for Liverpool.*
pal (INFORMAL) • *We've been pals for years.*
partner • *a partner in crime*

Can't find the word you're looking for? Try the index.

A B C D E F G H I J K L M N O P Q R S T U V W X Y Z

company ❶ NOUN
a business • *a publishing company*
business • *a family business*
corporation • *multi-national corporations*
establishment • *a commercial establishment*
firm • *a firm of engineers*
house • *a top fashion house*

company ❷ NOUN
a group of people • *the Royal Shakespeare Company*
assembly • *an assembly of citizens*
band • *bands of rebels*
circle • *a large circle of friends*
community • *a community of believers*
crowd • *I don't go around with that crowd.*
ensemble • *an ensemble of young musicians*
group • *an environmental group*
party • *a party of sightseers*
troupe • *a troupe of actors*

MORE SYNONYMS
- concourse
- coterie

company ❸ NOUN
the act of spending time with someone • *I could do with some company.*
companionship • *He keeps a dog for companionship.*
presence • *Your presence is not welcome here.*

compare VERB
to look at things for similarities or differences • *Compare these two illustrations.*
contrast • *In this section we contrast four possible approaches.*
juxtapose • *art juxtaposed with reality*

weigh • *She weighed her options.*

compartment ❶ NOUN
a section of a railway carriage • *We shared our compartment with a group of businessmen.*
carriage • *Our carriage was full of drunken football fans.*

compartment ❷ NOUN
one of the separate parts of an object • *the freezer compartment of the fridge*
bay • *the cargo bays of the aircraft*
chamber • *the chambers of the heart*
division • *Each was further split into several divisions.*
section • *a toolbox with sections for various items*

compassionate ADJECTIVE
feeling or showing sympathy and pity for others • *My father was a deeply compassionate man.*
caring • *He is a lovely boy, very gentle and caring.*
humane • *She began to campaign for humane treatment of prisoners and their families.*
kind • *I must thank you for being so kind to me.*
kind-hearted • *He was a warm, generous and kind-hearted man.*
merciful • *a merciful God*
sympathetic • *She was very sympathetic to their problems.*
tender • *Her voice was tender, full of pity.*

MORE SYNONYMS
- benevolent
- humanitarian
- lenient

compatible ADJECTIVE
going together • *Lifelong partners should be compatible.*

Can't find the word you're looking for? Try the index.

congenial • *congenial company*
consistent • *injuries consistent with a car crash*
harmonious • *a harmonious partnership*
in keeping • *This behaviour was in keeping with his character.*

MORE SYNONYMS
- accordant
- congruent
- congruous
- consonant

ANTONYM
- incompatible

compensate ❶ VERB
to repay someone for loss or damage • *You will be properly compensated for your loss.*
atone • *He felt he had atoned for what he had done.*
refund • *The company will refund the full cost.*
repay • *collateral with which to repay swindled investors*
reward • *Their patience was finally rewarded.*

MORE SYNONYMS
- make amends
- make restitution
- recompense
- reimburse
- remunerate

compensate ❷ VERB
to cancel out • *His lack of skill was compensated for by his enthusiasm.*
balance • *The pros balance the cons.*
cancel out • *The two influences cancel each other out.*
counteract • *pills to counteract high blood pressure*
make up for • *I'll make up for what I've done.*

offset • *The loss is being offset by a new tax.*

MORE SYNONYMS
- counterbalance
- countervail
- redress

compensation NOUN
something that makes up for loss or damage • *compensation for his injuries*
amends • *an attempt to make amends for his crime*
atonement • *an act of atonement for our sins*
damages • *damages for libel*
payment • *a redundancy payment*

MORE SYNONYMS
- recompense
- reimbursement
- remuneration
- reparation
- restitution

compete VERB
to try to win • *companies competing for business*
contend • *two groups contending for power*
contest • *the candidates contesting in the election*
fight • *rivals fighting for supremacy*
vie • *The contestants vied to finish first.*

competition ❶ NOUN
an attempt to win • *There's a lot of competition for places.*
contention • *contention for the gold medal*
contest • *the contest between capitalism and socialism*
opposition • *They are in direct opposition for the job.*
rivalry • *the rivalry between the two leaders*

a
b
c
d
e
f
g
h
i
j
k
l
m
n
o
p
q
r
s
t
u
v
w
x
y
z

Can't find the word you're looking for? Try the index.

A
B
C
D
E
F
G
H
I
J
K
L
M
N
O
P
Q
R
S
T
U
V
W
X
Y
Z

struggle • *a power struggle*

competition 2 NOUN
a contest to find the winner in
something • *a surfing competition*
championship • *a swimming
championship*
contest • *a beauty contest*
event • *major sporting events*
tournament • *a judo tournament*

competitor NOUN
a person who competes for
something • *one of the youngest
competitors in the event*
adversary • *his political
adversaries*
challenger • *20 seconds faster
than the nearest challenger*
competition • *staying ahead of
the competition*
contestant • *contestants in the
Miss World pageant*
opponent • *the best opponent I've
played all season*
opposition • *They can outplay the
opposition.*
rival • *a business rival*

complain VERB
to express dissatisfaction • *He
came round to complain about the
noise.*
carp • *She is constantly carping at
him.*
find fault • *He's always finding
fault with my work.*
grouse • *You're always grousing
about something.*
grumble • *It's not in her nature to
grumble.*
kick up a fuss (INFORMAL) • *He
kicks up a fuss whenever she goes out.*
moan • *moaning about the
weather*
whine • *whining children*
whinge (INFORMAL) • *Stop*

whingeing and get on with it.

MORE SYNONYMS
● bemoan
● bewail

complaint NOUN
an instance of complaining about
something • *There have been a
number of complaints about the
standard of service.*
criticism • *The criticism that we do
not try hard enough to learn other
languages was voiced.*
grievance • *They had a legitimate
grievance against the company.*
grumble • *Her main grumble is
over the long hours she has to work.*
objection • *I have no objections
about the way I have been treated.*
protest • *Despite our protests, they
went ahead anyway.*

complete 1 ADJECTIVE
to the greatest degree possible
• *a complete transformation*
absolute • *absolute nonsense*
consummate • *a consummate
professional*
outright • *an outright victory*
perfect • *a perfect stranger*
thorough • *a thorough snob*
total • *a total failure*
utter • *an utter shambles*

complete 2 ADJECTIVE
with nothing missing • *a complete
set of tools*
entire • *the entire plot*
full • *a full report*
intact • *the few buildings which
have survived intact*
undivided • *I want your undivided
attention.*
whole • *I told him the whole story.*

ANTONYM
● incomplete

Can't find the word you're looking for? Try the index.

complete ❸ VERB
to finish • *He has just completed his first novel.*
conclude • *The judge concluded his summing-up.*
end • *The crowd was in tears as he ended his speech.*
finish • *I'll finish my report this week.*

complex ❶ ADJECTIVE
having many different parts • *complex issues*
complicated • *a very complicated voting system*
difficult • *the laborious and difficult process of adopting a child*
intricate • *intricate patterns*
involved • *a long, involved explanation*
tangled • *His personal life has become more tangled than ever.*

MORE SYNONYMS
● convoluted
● tortuous

ANTONYM
● simple

complex ❷ NOUN
an emotional problem • *I have never had a complex about my weight.*
fixation • *She has a fixation about men with beards.*
obsession • *95% of patients know their obsessions are irrational.*
phobia • *The man had a phobia about flying.*
preoccupation • *his total preoccupation with neatness*
problem • *an eating problem*
thing • *He's got this thing about women's shoes.*

complicated ADJECTIVE
complex and difficult • *a complicated situation*
complex • *a complex issue*
convoluted • *a convoluted plot*
elaborate • *an elaborate theory*
intricate • *an intricate process*
involved • *a long, involved explanation*

MORE SYNONYMS
● Byzantine
● labyrinthine
● perplexing

ANTONYM
● simple

compose VERB
to create or write • *He has composed a symphony.*
create • *He has created a new ballet.*
devise • *a play devised by the drama company*
invent • *the man who invented gangsta rap*
produce • *He has produced a book about the city.*
write • *I've never been able to write poetry.*

comprehend VERB
to understand or appreciate something • *I just cannot comprehend your attitude.*
appreciate • *She has never really appreciated the scale of the problem.*
fathom • *I really couldn't fathom what Steiner was talking about.*
grasp • *The Government has not yet grasped the seriousness of the crisis.*
see • *I don't see why you're complaining.*
take in • *I try to explain, but you can tell she's not taking it in.*
understand • *They are too young to understand what's going on.*

a
b
c
d
e
f
g
h
i
j
k
l
m
n
o
p
q
r
s
t
u
v
w
x
y
z

Can't find the word you're looking for? Try the index.

A
B
C
D
E
F
G
H
I
J
K
L
M
N
O
P
Q
R
S
T
U
V
W
X
Y
Z

work out • *It took me some time to work out what was causing the problem.*

compulsory ADJECTIVE

required by law • *School attendance is compulsory.*

mandatory • *the mandatory retirement age*

obligatory • *an obligatory medical examination*

required • *the required reading for this course*

requisite • *the requisite documents*

ANTONYM
- voluntary

con ❶ VERB

to trick someone into doing or believing something • *He claimed that the salesman had conned him out of his life savings.*

cheat • *a deliberate attempt to cheat employees out of their pensions*

deceive • *She deceived us into giving her a job.*

mislead • *Ministers must not knowingly mislead the public.*

swindle • *A City businessman swindled investors out of millions of pounds.*

trick • *They tricked him into parting with his life savings.*

MORE SYNONYMS
- defraud
- dupe

con ❷ NOUN

a trick intended to mislead or disadvantage someone • *Slimming snacks that offer miraculous weight loss are a con.*

bluff • *The letter was a bluff.*

deception • *You've been the victim of a rather cruel deception.*

fraud • *an investigation into frauds*

in the world of horseracing

swindle • *a tax swindle*

trick • *a cheap trick to encourage people to switch energy suppliers*

conceit NOUN

excessive pride • *his insufferable conceit*

egotism • *typical showbiz egotism*

pride • *a blow to his pride*

self-importance • *his bad manners and self-importance*

vanity • *her vanity about her long hair*

MORE SYNONYMS
- amour-propre
- narcissism
- vainglory

conceited ADJECTIVE

too proud • *a conceited young idiot*

bigheaded (INFORMAL) • *an arrogant, bigheaded man*

cocky • *I was very cocky as a youngster.*

egotistical • *an egotistical show-off*

self-important • *self-important pop stars*

vain • *a shallow, vain woman*

MORE SYNONYMS
- narcissistic
- swollen-headed
- vainglorious

ANTONYM
- modest

concentrate ❶ VERB

to give something all your attention • *Concentrate on your studies.*

be engrossed in • *He was engrossed in his work.*

focus your attention on • *focusing his attention on the race*

give your attention to • *I gave*

my attention to the question.
put your mind to • *You could do it if you put your mind to it.*

concentrate ❷ VERB
to be found in one place • *They are mostly concentrated in the urban areas.*
accumulate • *Cholesterol accumulates in the arteries.*
collect • *dust collecting in the corners*
gather • *residents gathered in huddles*

concern ❶ NOUN
a feeling of worry • *public concern about violence*
anxiety • *anxiety about the economy*
apprehension • *apprehension about the future*
disquiet • *a growing sense of disquiet*
worry • *She has no worries about his health.*

concern ❷ NOUN
someone's duty or responsibility • *His private life is not my concern.*
affair • *If you want to go, that's your affair.*
business • *This is none of my business.*
responsibility • *He's not my responsibility.*

concern ❸ VERB
to make someone worried • *It concerns me that he doesn't want to go.*
bother • *Nothing bothers me.*
distress • *They are distressed by the accusations.*
disturb • *disturbed by the news*
trouble • *Is anything troubling you?*
worry • *an issue that had worried him for some time*

MORE SYNONYMS
● disquiet
● perturb

concern ❹ VERB
to affect or involve • *This concerns both of us.*
affect • *the ways in which computers affect our lives*
apply to • *This rule does not apply to us.*
be relevant to • *These documents are relevant to the case.*
involve • *meetings which involve most of the staff*

MORE SYNONYMS
● bear on
● pertain to
● touch

concise ADJECTIVE
using no unnecessary words • *a concise guide*
brief • *a brief description*
short • *a short speech*
succinct • *a succinct explanation*
terse • *a terse statement*

MORE SYNONYMS
● epigrammatic
● laconic
● pithy

ANTONYM
● long

conclude ❶ VERB
to decide something • *He concluded that she had been right.*
decide • *I decided he must be ill.*
deduce • *She deduced that I had written the letter.*
infer • *His feelings were easily inferred from his reply.*
judge • *The doctor judged that he was not fit enough to play.*
reckon (INFORMAL) • *I reckon we*

a
b
c
d
e
f
g
h
i
j
k
l
m
n
o
p
q
r
s
t
u
v
w
x
y
z

Can't find the word you're looking for? Try the index.

should wait a while.
suppose • *There's no reason to suppose he'll be there.*
surmise • *It is surmised that he must have known.*

conclude ❷ verb

to finish something • *He concluded the letter with a postscript.*
close • *They closed the show with a song.*
end • *His speech ended with a prayer for peace.*
finish • *We finished the evening with a walk on the beach.*
round off • *This rounded the afternoon off perfectly.*
wind up • *She quickly wound up her conversation.*

ANTONYM
● begin

conclusion ❶ noun

a decision made after thinking carefully about something • *I've come to the conclusion that she was lying.*
deduction • *a shrewd deduction about what was going on*
inference • *There were two inferences to be drawn from her letter.*
judgment • *My judgment is that things are going to get worse.*
verdict • *The doctor's verdict was that he was fine.*

conclusion ❷ noun

the finish or ending of something • *the conclusion of the programme*
close • *bringing the talks to a close*
end • *The war is coming to an end.*
ending • *a dramatic ending*
finish • *the finish of the race*
termination • *the termination of their marriage*

ANTONYM
● beginning

condemn ❶ verb

to say that something is bad or unacceptable • *He was condemned for his arrogance.*
blame • *I blame television for the rise in violence.*
censure • *a motion censuring the government*
criticize • *He was criticized for his failure to act.*
damn • *The report damns the government's handling of the affair.*
denounce • *He was denounced as a traitor.*

condemn ❷ verb

to give a punishment • *condemned to death*
damn • *sinners damned to eternal torment*
doom • *doomed to die for his crime*
sentence • *sentenced to ten years in prison*

condition ❶ noun

the state of something • *The house is in good condition.*
form • *The team are not in good form this season.*
shape • *He's in great shape for his age.*
state • *Look at the state of my car!*

condition ❷ noun

something required for something else to be possible • *terms and conditions of the contract*
prerequisite • *A science background is a prerequisite for the job.*
provision • *a provision in his will forbidding the sale of the house*
proviso • *The answer is yes, with one proviso.*

Can't find the word you're looking for? Try the index.

qualification • *He agreed, but with some qualifications.*
requirement • *The product meets all legal requirements.*
requisite • *the main requisite for membership*
stipulation • *The only dress stipulation was "no jeans".*
terms • *the terms of the agreement*

conduct ❶ VERB

to carry out an activity or task
• *to conduct an experiment*
carry out • *to carry out a survey*
direct • *Christopher will direct day-to-day operations.*
do • *I'm doing a piece of important research right now.*
manage • *his ability to manage the business*
organize • *The initial mobilization was well organized.*
perform • *Several grafts were performed during the operation.*
run • *Each teacher will run a different workshop.*

MORE SYNONYMS
- execute
- implement
- orchestrate

conduct ❷ NOUN

the way someone behaves • *Other people judge you by your conduct.*
attitude • *His attitude made me angry.*
behaviour • *Make sure that good behaviour is rewarded.*
manners • *He dressed well and had impeccable manners.*
ways • *I urged him to alter his ways.*

MORE SYNONYMS
- comportment
- demeanour

conduct yourself VERB

to behave in a particular way • *The way he conducts himself reflects on the school.*
act • *a gang of youths who were acting suspiciously*
behave • *He'd behaved badly.*

ANOTHER SYNONYM
- acquit yourself

conference NOUN

a meeting for discussion
• *a conference on education*
congress • *a congress of coal miners*
convention • *the Geneva convention*
discussion • *a round of formal discussions*
forum • *a forum for trade negotiations*
meeting • *a meeting of shareholders*

MORE SYNONYMS
- colloquium
- convocation
- symposium

confess VERB

to admit to something • *Your son has confessed to his crimes.*
acknowledge • *He acknowledged that he was a drug addict.*
admit • *I admit to feeling jealous.*
own up • *The headmaster is waiting for someone to own up.*

ANTONYM
- deny

confession NOUN

the act of confessing • *a confession of adultery*
acknowledgment • *an acknowledgment of his mistakes*
admission • *an admission of guilt*

a
b
c
d
e
f
g
h
i
j
k
l
m
n
o
p
q
r
s
t
u
v
w
x
y
z

Can't find the word you're looking for? Try the index.

A
B
C
D
E
F
G
H
I
J
K
L
M
N
O
P
Q
R
S
T
U
V
W
X
Y
Z

confidence ❶ NOUN
a feeling of trust • *I have complete confidence in you.*
belief • *his belief in his partner*
faith • *He has great faith in her judgment.*
reliance • *I don't put much reliance on that idea.*
trust • *He destroyed my trust in people.*

ANTONYM
- distrust

confidence ❷ NOUN
sureness of yourself • *I've never had much confidence.*
aplomb • *She handled the interview with aplomb.*
assurance • *He led the orchestra with great assurance.*
self-assurance • *his supreme self-assurance*
self-possession • *an air of self-possession*

ANTONYM
- shyness

confident ❶ ADJECTIVE
sure about something • *confident of success*
certain • *certain of getting a place on the team*
convinced • *He is convinced it's your fault.*
positive • *I'm positive it will happen.*
satisfied • *We must be satisfied that the treatment is safe.*
secure • *secure about his job prospects*
sure • *I'm not sure I understand.*

ANTONYM
- uncertain

confident ❷ ADJECTIVE
sure of yourself • *a confident attitude*
assured • *His playing became more assured.*
self-assured • *a self-assured young man*
self-possessed • *a self-possessed career woman*

ANTONYM
- shy

confine ❶ VERB
to limit to something specified • *They confined themselves to talking about the weather.*
limit • *Limit yourself to six units of alcohol a week.*
restrict • *The patient was restricted to a meagre diet.*

confine ❷ VERB
to prevent from leaving • *confined to bed for two days*
hem in • *hemmed in by spectators*
imprison • *imprisoned in a tiny cell*
restrict • *We were restricted to the building.*
shut up • *He can't stand being shut up in the house.*

MORE SYNONYMS
- immure
- incarcerate
- intern

confirm ❶ VERB
to say or show that something is true • *Police confirmed that they had received a call.*
bear out • *The figures bear out his words.*
endorse • *This theory has been endorsed by research.*
prove • *The results prove his point.*
substantiate • *no evidence to substantiate the claims*
validate • *It is difficult to validate this belief.*

Can't find the word you're looking for? Try the index.

verify • *I was asked to verify this statement.*

MORE SYNONYMS
- authenticate
- corroborate

confirm ② VERB
to make something definite • *Can we confirm the arrangements for tomorrow?*
fix • *The date for the election was fixed.*
settle • *I've settled a time to see him.*

conflict ① NOUN
disagreement and argument • *conflict between workers and management*
antagonism • *antagonism within the team*
disagreement • *The meeting ended in disagreement.*
discord • *public discord*
friction • *friction between him and his father*
hostility • *hostility between parents and teachers*
opposition • *a wave of opposition*
strife • *a cause of strife in many marriages*

conflict ② NOUN
a war or battle • *the conflict in the Gulf*
battle • *a battle between two gangs*
combat • *men who died in combat*
fighting • *Villagers have left their homes to avoid the fighting.*
strife • *civil strife*
war • *the war between Israel and Egypt*

conflict ③ VERB
to differ or disagree • *conflicting ideas*

be at variance • *His statements are at variance with the facts.*
be incompatible • *These two principles are incompatible.*
clash • *a decision which clashes with official policy*
differ • *The two leaders differ on several issues.*
disagree • *Governments disagree over the need for action.*

confuse ① VERB
to mix two things up • *confusing fact with fiction*
mistake • *I mistook you for someone else.*
mix up • *He sometimes mixes up his words.*
muddle up • *I keep muddling him up with his brother.*

confuse ② VERB
to puzzle or bewilder • *Politics confuse me.*
baffle • *Police are baffled by the murder.*
bewilder • *His silence bewildered her.*
mystify • *I was mystified by his attitude.*
puzzle • *One thing still puzzles me.*

MORE SYNONYMS
- bemuse
- faze
- nonplus
- perplex

confused ① ADJECTIVE
puzzled or bewildered • *confused about health risks*
baffled • *He stared in baffled amazement.*
bewildered • *bewildered holidaymakers*
muddled • *She was muddled about the date.*

a
b
c
d
e
f
g
h
i
j
k
l
m
n
o
p
q
r
s
t
u
v
w
x
y
z

Can't find the word you're looking for? Try the index.

A
B
C
D
E
F
G
H
I
J
K
L
M
N
O
P
Q
R
S
T
U
V
W
X
Y
Z

perplexed • *perplexed by recent events*
puzzled • *a puzzled expression*

MORE SYNONYMS
- at a loss
- at sea
- flummoxed
- nonplussed

confused ❷ ADJECTIVE
in an untidy mess • *They lay in a confused heap.*
chaotic • *the chaotic mess on his desk*
disordered • *a disordered pile of papers*
disorganized • *a disorganized lifestyle*
untidy • *an untidy room*

ANTONYM
- tidy

confusing ADJECTIVE
puzzling or bewildering
• *a confusing situation*
baffling • *a baffling statement*
bewildering • *a bewildering choice of products*
complicated • *a complicated voting system*
puzzling • *a puzzling problem*

confusion NOUN
an untidy mess • *My life is in confusion.*
chaos • *economic chaos*
disarray • *The nation is in disarray.*
disorder • *The emergency room was in disorder.*
disorganization • *scenes of chaos and disorganization*
mess • *He always leaves the bathroom in a mess.*

ANTONYM
- order

connect ❶ VERB
to join together • *Connect the pipe to the tap.*
affix • *His name was affixed to his cubicle.*
attach • *Attach the curtains to the rods with hooks.*
couple • *The engine is coupled to a gearbox.*
fasten • *A hatchet was fastened to his belt.*
join • *two springs joined together*
link • *the Channel Tunnel linking Britain with France*

ANTONYM
- separate

connect ❷ VERB
to associate one thing with another • *evidence connecting him with the robberies*
ally • *The new government is allied with the military.*
associate • *symptoms associated with migraine headaches*
link • *research which links smoking with cancer*
relate • *the denial that unemployment is related to crime*

connection ❶ NOUN
a link or relationship • *a connection between drinking and liver disease*
affiliation • *He has no affiliation with any political party.*
association • *the association between the two companies*
bond • *the bond between a mother and child*
correlation • *the correlation between unemployment and crime*
correspondence • *the correspondence between Eastern and Western religions*
link • *a link between smoking and lung cancer*

Can't find the word you're looking for? Try the index.

relation • *This theory bears no relation to reality.*
relationship • *the relationship between humans and their environment*

connection ❷ NOUN
a point where things are joined • *The fault was just a loose connection.*
coupling • *The coupling between the railway carriages snapped.*
fastening • *a zip fastening*
junction • *the junction between nerve and muscle*
link • *a link between the city and the motorway*

conscience NOUN
a sense of right and wrong • *He had a guilty conscience.*
principles • *It's against my principles to eat meat.*
scruples • *a man with no moral scruples*
sense of right and wrong • *children with no sense of right and wrong*

conservative ADJECTIVE
unwilling to change • *People get more conservative as they grow older.*
conventional • *conventional tastes*
traditional • *a traditional school*

MORE SYNONYMS
- hidebound
- reactionary

ANTONYM
- radical

consider ❶ VERB
to think of someone or something as • *They do not consider him a suitable candidate.*

believe • *I believe him to be innocent.*
judge • *His work was judged unsatisfactory.*
rate • *The film was rated excellent.*
regard as • *They regard the tax as unfair.*
think • *Many people think him arrogant.*

MORE SYNONYMS
- deem
- hold to be

consider ❷ VERB
to think carefully • *I will consider your offer.*
contemplate • *He contemplated his fate.*
deliberate • *The jury deliberated for three days.*
meditate • *He meditated on the problem.*
muse • *She sat musing on how unfair life was.*
ponder • *pondering how to improve the team*
reflect • *I reflected on the child's future.*
think about • *I've been thinking about what you said.*

MORE SYNONYMS
- cogitate
- mull over
- ruminate

consider ❸ VERB
to take into account • *We should consider her feelings.*
bear in mind • *There are a few points to bear in mind.*
make allowances for • *Remember to make allowances for delays.*
respect • *We will respect your wishes.*

a
b
c
d
e
f
g
h
i
j
k
l
m
n
o
p
q
r
s
t
u
v
w
x
y
z

Can't find the word you're looking for? Try the index.

A
B
C
D
E
F
G
H
I
J
K
L
M
N
O
P
Q
R
S
T
U
V
W
X
Y
Z

take into account • *another factor to be taken into account*
think about • *more important things to think about*

consideration ❶ NOUN
careful thought about something • *a decision requiring careful consideration*
attention • *I gave the question all my attention.*
contemplation • *The problem deserves serious contemplation.*
deliberation • *After much deliberation, he called the police.*
study • *The proposals need careful study.*
thought • *I've given the matter a great deal of thought.*

consideration ❷ NOUN
concern for someone • *Show some consideration for other passengers.*
concern • *concern for the homeless*
kindness • *We have been treated with great kindness.*
respect • *no respect for wildlife*
tact • *a master of tact and diplomacy*

consideration ❸ NOUN
something to be taken into account • *Safety is a major consideration.*
factor • *an important factor in buying a house*
issue • *Price is not the only issue.*
point • *There is another point to remember.*

consist, consist of VERB
to be made up of • *The brain consists of millions of nerve cells.*
be composed of • *The committee is composed of ten people.*
be made up of • *The bouquet was made up of roses and carnations.*

comprise • *The show comprises 50 paintings and sketches.*

conspicuous ADJECTIVE
easy to see or notice • *Her conspicuous lack of warmth confirmed her disapproval.*
apparent • *It has been apparent that someone has been stealing.*
blatant • *a blatant disregard for rules*
evident • *He spoke with evident emotion about his ordeal.*
noticeable • *the most noticeable effect of these changes*
obvious • *an obvious injustice*
perceptible • *a perceptible air of neglect*

MORE SYNONYMS
● patent
● manifest

constant ❶ ADJECTIVE
going on all the time • *a city under constant attack*
continual • *continual pain*
continuous • *continuous gunfire*
eternal • *an eternal hum in the background*
nonstop • *nonstop music*
perpetual • *her perpetual complaints*
relentless • *relentless pressure*

MORE SYNONYMS
● incessant
● interminable
● sustained
● unremitting

ANTONYM
● periodic

constant ❷ ADJECTIVE
staying the same • *a constant temperature*
even • *an even level of sound*

Can't find the word you're looking for? Try the index.

fixed • *a fixed salary*
regular • *a regular beat*
stable • *a stable condition*
steady • *travelling at a steady 50 miles per hour*
uniform • *a uniform thickness*

MORE SYNONYMS
○ immutable
○ invariable

ANTONYM
○ changeable

construct VERB
to build or make something • *The boxes are constructed from rough-sawn timber.*
assemble • *She had been trying to assemble the bomb when it went off.*
build • *Workers at the plant build the F-16 jet fighter.*
create • *We created a makeshift platform for him to stand on.*
erect • *The building was erected in 1900.*
make • *The company now makes cars at two plants in Europe.*
put together • *the mechanic whose job was to put together looms within the plant*
put up • *He was putting up a new fence.*

consult VERB
to go to for advice • *Consult your doctor before undertaking exercise.*
ask for advice • *Ask your bank manager for advice on mortgages.*
confer with • *He is conferring with his lawyers.*
refer to • *I had to refer to the manual.*

contact ❶ NOUN
the state of being in touch with someone • *We must keep in contact.*

communication • *The leaders were in constant communication.*
touch • *I've lost touch with her over the years.*

contact ❷ NOUN
someone you know • *a contact in the music business*
acquaintance • *We met through a mutual acquaintance.*
connection • *She had a connection in England.*

contact ❸ VERB
to get in touch with • *We contacted the company to complain.*
approach • *A journalist has approached me for a story.*
communicate with • *We communicate mostly by email.*
get hold of • *I've been trying to get hold of you all week.*
get in touch with • *I will get in touch with my solicitors.*
reach • *Where can I reach you in an emergency?*

contain ❶ VERB
to include as a part of • *Alcohol contains sugar.*
comprise • *The band comprises two singers and two guitarists.*
include • *The price includes VAT.*

contain ❷ VERB
to keep under control • *efforts to contain the disease*
control • *He could hardly control his rage.*
curb • *measures to curb inflation*
repress • *people who repress their emotions*
restrain • *unable to restrain her anger*
stifle • *stifling the urge to scream*

container NOUN
something which holds things

a
b
c
d
e
f
g
h
i
j
k
l
m
n
o
p
q
r
s
t
u
v
w
x
y
z

Can't find the word you're looking for? Try the index.

• *a plastic container for food*
holder • *a cigarette holder*
vessel • *storage vessels*

MORE SYNONYMS
● receptacle
● repository

contemplate ❶ VERB
to think carefully about something
• *He cried as he contemplated his future.*
consider • *She paused to consider her options.*
examine • *I have examined all the possible alternatives.*
muse on • *Many of the papers muse on the fate of the President.*
ponder • *He didn't waste time pondering the question.*
reflect on • *I reflected on the child's future.*
think about • *Think about how you can improve the situation.*

contemplate ❷ VERB
to consider doing something • *He contemplated a career as a doctor.*
consider • *Watersports enthusiasts should consider hiring a wetsuit.*
envisage • *He had never envisaged spending the whole of his life in that job.*
plan • *I had been planning a trip to the West Coast.*
think of • *Martin was thinking of taking legal action against his employers.*

contempt NOUN
complete lack of respect • *I shall treat that remark with the contempt it deserves.*
derision • *He was greeted with shouts of derision.*
disdain • *Janet looked at him with disdain.*

disregard • *total disregard for the safety of the public*
disrespect • *complete disrespect for authority*
scorn • *They greeted the proposal with scorn.*

ANTONYM
● respect

contest ❶ NOUN
a competition or game • *Few contests in the history of boxing have been as thrilling.*
competition • *a surfing competition*
game • *the first game of the season*
match • *He was watching a football match.*
tournament • *Here is a player capable of winning a world tournament.*

contest ❷ NOUN
a struggle for power • *a bitter contest over who should control the state's future*
battle • *the eternal battle between good and evil*
fight • *the fight for the US Presidency*
struggle • *locked in a power struggle with his Prime Minister*

contest ❸ VERB
to object formally to a statement or decision • *Your former employer has 14 days to contest the case.*
challenge • *The move was immediately challenged.*
dispute • *He disputed the allegations.*
oppose • *Many parents oppose bilingual education in schools.*
question • *It never occurs to them to question the doctor's decisions.*

ANTONYM
● accept

Can't find the word you're looking for? Try the index.

continual ❶ ADJECTIVE

happening all the time without stopping • *Despite continual pain, he refused all drugs.*

constant • *She suggests that women are under constant pressure to be abnormally thin.*

continuous • *a continuous stream of phone calls*

endless • *her endless demands for attention*

eternal • *In the background was that eternal hum.*

nagging • *a nagging pain between his shoulder blades*

perpetual • *the perpetual thump of music from the flat downstairs*

uninterrupted • *five years of uninterrupted growth*

MORE SYNONYMS

- incessant
- interminable
- unremitting

continual ❷ ADJECTIVE

happening again and again • *She suffered continual police harassment.*

frequent • *He is prone to frequent bouts of depression.*

recurrent • *buildings in which staff suffer recurrent illness*

regular • *He is a regular visitor to our house.*

repeated • *Mr Smith did not return the money, despite repeated reminders.*

ANTONYM

- occasional

continue ❶ VERB

to keep doing something • *Will you continue working after you're married?*

carry on • *The assistant carried on talking.*

go on • *Unemployment is likely to go on rising.*

keep on • *He kept on trying.*

persist • *She persists in using his nickname.*

continue ❷ VERB

to go on existing • *The fighting continued after they'd left.*

carry on • *My work will carry on after I'm gone.*

endure • *Their friendship has endured for 30 years.*

last • *Nothing lasts forever.*

persist • *The problem persists.*

remain • *The building remains to this day.*

survive • *companies which survived after the recession*

continue ❸ VERB

to start doing again • *After a moment, she continued speaking.*

carry on • *He took a deep breath, then carried on.*

recommence • *He recommenced work on his novel.*

resume • *Police will resume the search today.*

continuous ADJECTIVE

going on without stopping
• *continuous growth*

constant • *under constant pressure*

continued • *a continued improvement*

extended • *conflict over an extended period*

prolonged • *a prolonged drought*

uninterrupted • *uninterrupted rule*

ANTONYM

- periodic

control ❶ NOUN

power over something • *He was forced to give up control of the company.*

a b **c** d e f g h i j k l m n o p q r s t u v w x y z

Can't find the word you're looking for? Try the index.

A
B
C
D
E
F
G
H
I
J
K
L
M
N
O
P
Q
R
S
T
U
V
W
X
Y
Z

authority • *You have no authority here.*
command • *He was in command of the ceremony.*
direction • *The team worked well under his direction.*
government • *The entire country is under the government of one man.*
management • *the day-to-day management of the business*
power • *a position of great power*
rule • *15 years of Communist rule*
supremacy • *The party has re-established its supremacy.*

MORE SYNONYMS
● jurisdiction
● mastery
● superintendence

control ❷ VERB
to be in charge of • *companies fighting to control the Internet*
administer • *the authorities who administer the island*
be in charge of • *She is in charge of the project.*
command • *the general who commanded the troops*
direct • *He will direct day-to-day operations.*
govern • *his ability to govern France*
have power over • *Her husband has total power over her.*
manage • *the government's ability to manage the economy*
rule • *the dynasty which ruled China*

convenient ADJECTIVE
helpful or easy to use • *a convenient mode of transport*
handy • *Credit cards can be handy.*
helpful • *a helpful fact sheet*
useful • *a useful invention*

MORE SYNONYMS
● labour-saving
● serviceable

ANTONYM
● inconvenient

convention ❶ NOUN
an accepted way of behaving or doing something • *It's just a social convention that men don't wear skirts.*
code • *the code of the Shaolin monks*
custom • *The custom of lighting the Olympic flame goes back centuries.*
etiquette • *the rules of diplomatic etiquette*
practice • *It is normal practice not to reveal the sex of the baby.*
tradition • *different cultural traditions from ours*

MORE SYNONYMS
● propriety
● protocol

convention ❷ NOUN
a large meeting of an organization or group • *the annual convention of the Parapsychological Association*
assembly • *an assembly of women Olympic gold-medal winners*
conference • *a conference attended by 450 delegates*
congress • *A lot changed after the party congress.*
meeting • *the annual meeting of company shareholders*

conventional ❶ ADJECTIVE
having or relating to a very ordinary lifestyle • *a respectable married woman with conventional opinions*
conformist • *He may have to become more conformist if he is to prosper.*

Can't find the word you're looking for? Try the index.

conservative • *The girl was well dressed in a rather conservative style.*
unadventurous • *He was a strong player, but rather unadventurous.*

MORE SYNONYMS
● bourgeois
● staid

conventional ❷ ADJECTIVE
familiar, or usually used • *These discs hold 400 times as much information as a conventional floppy disk.*
customary • *the customary one minute's silence*
ordinary • *It has 25 per cent less fat than ordinary ice cream.*
orthodox • *Many of these ideas are being incorporated into orthodox medical treatment.*
regular • *This product looks and tastes like regular margarine.*
standard • *It was standard practice for untrained clerks to deal with serious cases.*
traditional • *traditional teaching methods*

convey VERB
to cause information or ideas to be known • *I tried to convey the wonder of the experience to my husband.*
communicate • *They successfully communicate their knowledge to others.*
express • *She did her best to express wordless disapproval by scowling.*
get across • *I wanted to get my message across.*
impart • *the ability to impart knowledge*

convince VERB
to persuade that something is true • *I convinced him of my innocence.*

assure • *She assured me that there was nothing wrong.*
persuade • *I had to persuade him of the advantages.*
satisfy • *He had to satisfy the doctors that he was fit to play.*

convincing ADJECTIVE
persuasive • *a convincing argument*
conclusive • *conclusive proof*
effective • *an effective speaker*
persuasive • *persuasive reasons*
plausible • *a plausible explanation*
powerful • *a powerful speech*
telling • *a telling criticism*

MORE SYNONYMS
● cogent
● incontrovertible

ANTONYM
● unconvincing

cook VERB
to prepare food for eating by heating it in some way • *I enjoy cooking for friends.*
bake • *a machine for baking bread*
barbecue • *a Korean method of barbecuing meat*
boil • *Boil the fruit and syrup together for half an hour.*
fry • *Garnish the rice with thinly sliced fried onion.*
grill • *Grill the fish for five minutes.*
microwave • *Microwaved vegetables have a fresher flavour.*
poach • *I had ordered poached eggs on toast for breakfast.*
roast • *Roast the aubergine in the oven for about one hour until soft.*
steam • *mussels on a bed of steamed cabbage*
stew • *You can stew the vegetables in oil.*
toast • *This currant loaf is delicious either fresh or toasted.*

a
b
c
d
e
f
g
h
i
j
k
l
m
n
o
p
q
r
s
t
u
v
w
x
y
z

Can't find the word you're looking for? Try the index.

cool ❶ ADJECTIVE

having a low temperature • *a gust of cool air*
chilled • *a chilled bottle of wine*
chilly • *a chilly afternoon*
cold • *Your dinner's getting cold.*
refreshing • *a refreshing breeze*

ANTONYM
- warm

cool ❷ ADJECTIVE

staying calm • *He kept cool through the whole thing.*
calm • *Try to stay calm.*
collected • *She was cool and collected throughout the interview.*
composed • *a composed player*
level-headed • *Simon is level-headed and practical.*
relaxed • *a relaxed manner*
serene • *a serene smile*

MORE SYNONYMS
- dispassionate
- imperturbable
- unemotional
- unexcited
- unruffled

ANTONYM
- nervous

cool ❸ VERB

to make or become cool • *Put the cookies on a wire rack to cool.*
chill • *a glass of chilled champagne*
cool off • *Dip the carrots in water to cool them off.*
freeze • *Make double the quantity and freeze half for later.*
refrigerate • *Refrigerate the dough overnight.*

ANTONYM
- heat

cooperate VERB

to work together • *The family cooperated with the author of the book.*
collaborate • *They collaborated on an album.*
join forces • *The two political parties are joining forces.*
pull together • *The staff and management pull together.*
work together • *industry and government working together*

copy ❶ NOUN

something made to look like something else • *He had kept a copy of the letter.*
counterfeit • *This credit card is a counterfeit.*
duplicate • *I lost my key and had to get a duplicate made.*
fake • *How do I know this painting isn't a fake?*
forgery • *The letter was a forgery.*
imitation • *Beware of cheap imitations.*
replica • *a replica of the Statue of Liberty*
reproduction • *a reproduction of a famous painting*

MORE SYNONYMS
- facsimile
- likeness
- replication

copy ❷ VERB

to do the same thing as someone else • *My little brother copies everything I do.*
ape • *Generations of women have aped her style and looks.*
emulate • *Sons are expected to emulate their fathers.*
follow • *Where America goes, Britain will surely follow.*
imitate • *Children imitate what they see on TV.*
mimic • *He mimicked her accent.*

Can't find the word you're looking for? Try the index.

MORE SYNONYMS
● follow suit
● parrot
● simulate

copy ❸ VERB
to make a copy of • *documents copied by hand*
counterfeit • *These banknotes are very easy to counterfeit.*
duplicate • *Videos are being illicitly duplicated all over the country.*
reproduce • *a new method of reproducing oil paintings*

corny ADJECTIVE
unoriginal or sentimental • *corny old love songs*
banal • *banal dialogue*
hackneyed • *a hackneyed plot*
maudlin • *a maudlin film*
sentimental • *a sentimental ballad*
stale • *stale ideas*
stereotyped • *a stereotyped image of Britain*
trite • *a trite ending*

MORE SYNONYMS
● mawkish
● old hat
● unoriginal

correct ❶ ADJECTIVE
without mistakes • *a correct diagnosis*
accurate • *an accurate description*
exact • *an exact copy*
faultless • *Hans's English was faultless.*
flawless • *a flawless performance*
precise • *precise calculations*
right • *That clock never shows the right time.*
true • *a true account*

correct ❷ ADJECTIVE
socially acceptable • *correct behaviour*
acceptable • *It is becoming more acceptable for women to drink.*
appropriate • *appropriate dress*
fitting • *behaving in a manner not fitting for a lady*
okay or **OK** (INFORMAL) • *Is it okay if I bring a friend with me?*
proper • *In those days it was not proper for women to go on the stage.*
seemly • *It is not seemly to joke about such things.*

ANTONYM
● wrong

correct ❸ VERB
to make right • *trying to correct his faults*
amend • *They want to amend the current system.*
cure • *an operation to cure his limp*
improve • *We must improve the situation.*
rectify • *attempts to rectify the problem*
reform • *He promised to reform his wicked ways.*
remedy • *What is needed to remedy these deficiencies?*
right • *I intend to right these wrongs.*

MORE SYNONYMS
● emend
● redress

correction NOUN
the act of making something right • *the correction of obvious mistakes*
adjustment • *My car needs a brake adjustment.*
amendment • *He has made lots of amendments to the script.*
righting • *the righting of the country's domestic troubles*

a
b
c
d
e
f
g
h
i
j
k
l
m
n
o
p
q
r
s
t
u
v
w
x
y
z

Can't find the word you're looking for? Try the index.

A
B
C
D
E
F
G
H
I
J
K
L
M
N
O
P
Q
R
S
T
U
V
W
X
Y
Z

MORE SYNONYMS
- emendation
- rectification

correspond VERB
to be similar or connected to
something else • *The two maps
correspond closely.*
agree • *His statement agrees with
those of other witnesses.*
be related • *These philosophical
problems are closely related.*
coincide • *He was delighted to find
that her feelings coincided with his
own.*
correlate • *Obesity correlates with
increased risk for diabetes.*
fit • *The punishment must always
fit the crime.*
match • *Our value system does not
match with theirs.*
tally • *This description did not tally
with what we saw.*

corrupt ❶ ADJECTIVE
acting dishonestly or illegally
• *corrupt politicians*
crooked • *a crooked cop*
dishonest • *a dishonest scheme*
fraudulent • *fraudulent trading*
shady (INFORMAL) • *shady deals*
unscrupulous • *unscrupulous
landlords*

MORE SYNONYMS
- unethical
- unprincipled
- venal

ANTONYM
- honest

corrupt ❷ VERB
to make dishonest • *Organized
crime has corrupted local
government.*
bribe • *accused of bribing officials*
buy off • *Police were bought off by*

drugs dealers.
fix (INFORMAL) • *He fixed the match
by bribing the players.*

corrupt ❸ VERB
to make immoral • *TV is corrupting
our children.*
deprave • *material likely to
deprave those who watch it*
pervert • *perverted by their contact
with criminals*

corruption NOUN
dishonest and illegal behaviour
• *charges of corruption*
bribery • *on trial for bribery*
dishonesty • *She accused the
government of dishonesty and
incompetence.*
fraud • *jailed for fraud*

MORE SYNONYMS
- extortion
- profiteering
- venality

cost ❶ NOUN
the amount of money needed
• *The cost of petrol has increased.*
charge • *We can arrange this for a
small charge.*
expense • *household expenses*
outlay • *Buying wine in bulk is well
worth the outlay.*
payment • *an initial payment of
just $100*
price • *House prices are expected to
rise.*
rate • *specially reduced rates*

cost ❷ NOUN
loss or damage • *the total cost in
human misery*
detriment • *These changes are to
the detriment of staff morale.*
expense • *I supported my
husband's career at the expense of
my own.*

Can't find the word you're looking for? Try the index.

penalty • *paying the penalty for someone else's mistakes*

cost ❸ VERB
to involve a cost of • *The air fares were going to cost a lot.*
come to • *Lunch came to nearly £15.*
sell at • *The books are selling at £1 per copy.*
set someone back (INFORMAL) • *This wedding will set us back thousands of pounds.*

cosy ❶ ADJECTIVE
warm and comfortable • *Guests can relax in the cosy bar.*
comfortable • *a comfortable fireside chair*
snug • *a snug log cabin*
warm • *warm blankets*

cosy ❷ ADJECTIVE
pleasant and friendly • *a cosy chat between friends*
friendly • *a friendly little get-together*
informal • *The house has an informal atmosphere.*
intimate • *an intimate candlelit dinner for two*
relaxed • *a relaxed evening in*

council NOUN
a governing group of people • *the city council*
assembly • *the National Assembly*
board • *the Pakistan Cricket Board*
committee • *the management committee*
panel • *a panel of judges*

MORE SYNONYMS
- conclave
- convocation
- quango
- synod

count ❶ VERB
to add up • *I counted the money.*
add up • *Add up the sales figures.*
calculate • *First, calculate your monthly living expenses.*
tally • *Computers now tally the votes.*

MORE SYNONYMS
- compute
- enumerate
- tot up

count ❷ VERB
to be important • *Our opinions don't count.*
carry weight • *a politician whose words carry weight*
matter • *It doesn't matter what she thinks.*
rate • *This does not rate as one of my main concerns.*
signify • *His absence does not signify much.*
weigh • *This evidence did not weigh with the jury.*

count ❸ NOUN
a counting or number counted • *The count revealed that our party had the majority.*
calculation • *I did a quick calculation in my head.*
reckoning • *By my reckoning we were about two miles from camp.*
sum • *I've never been good at sums.*
tally • *They keep a tally of visitors to the castle.*

MORE SYNONYMS
- computation
- enumeration

counteract VERB
to reduce the effect of something • *pills to counteract high blood pressure*
act against • *The immune system*

Can't find the word you're looking for? Try the index.

A
B
C
D
E
F
G
H
I
J
K
L
M
N
O
P
Q
R
S
T
U
V
W
X
Y
Z

acts against infection.
offset • *The slump was offset by a surge in exports.*

MORE SYNONYMS
- counterbalance
- countervail
- negate
- neutralize

countless ADJECTIVE
too many to count • *the star of countless films*
infinite • *an infinite number of atoms*
innumerable • *innumerable problems*
myriad • *pop music in all its myriad forms*
untold • *untold wealth*

MORE SYNONYMS
- incalculable
- limitless
- measureless
- multitudinous

country ❶ NOUN
a political area • *the boundary between the two countries*
kingdom • *The kingdom's power declined.*
land • *America, land of opportunity*
state • *a communist state*

country ❷ NOUN
land away from towns and cities • *He lives right out in the country.*
bush (NEW ZEALAND AND SOUTH AFRICAN) • *a trip out to the bush*
countryside • *surrounded by beautiful countryside*
outback (AUSTRALIAN AND NEW ZEALAND) • *nostalgic paintings of the outback*
outdoors • *He loves the great outdoors.*

RELATED WORDS
- ADJECTIVES: pastoral, rural

courage NOUN
lack of fear • *His courage impressed everyone.*
bravery • *an act of bravery*
daring • *tales of daring and adventure*
guts (INFORMAL) • *He didn't have the guts to admit he was wrong.*
heroism • *the young soldier's heroism*
nerve • *I didn't have the nerve to complain.*
pluck • *You have to admire her pluck.*
valour • *He was decorated for valour in the war.*

MORE SYNONYMS
- dauntlessness
- fearlessness
- grit
- intrepidity

ANTONYM
- fear

course ❶ NOUN
a series of lessons • *a course in computing*
classes • *I go to dance classes.*
curriculum • *the history curriculum*

course ❷ NOUN
a policy of action • *He took the only course left open to him.*
plan • *Your best plan is to see your doctor.*
policy • *She decided the best policy was to wait.*
procedure • *He did not follow the correct procedure.*

course ❸ NOUN
a way taken to get somewhere

Can't find the word you're looking for? Try the index.

• *She sensed the plane had changed course.*
direction • *He went off in the opposite direction.*
line • *the birds' line of flight*
path • *the path of an oncoming car*
route • *the most direct route*
trajectory • *the trajectory of the missile*
way • *What way do you go home?*

court ❶ NOUN
a place where legal matters are decided • *He ended up in court for theft.*
bench • *He was brought before the bench.*
law court • *prisoners tried by a law court*
tribunal • *The claim was thrown out by a European tribunal.*

court ❷ VERB (OLD-FASHIONED)
to intend to marry • *I was courting Billy at 19 and married him at 21.*
go steady • *They've been going steady for six months now.*
woo • *He wooed and married his first love.*

courtesy NOUN
polite and considerate behaviour • *a lack of courtesy to other drivers*
civility • *Handle customers with tact and civility.*
courteousness • *his courteousness and kindness*
gallantry • *He treated me with old-fashioned gallantry.*
good manners • *the rules of good manners*
grace • *He didn't even have the grace to apologize.*
graciousness • *The team displayed graciousness in defeat.*
politeness • *basic standards of politeness*

cover ❶ VERB
to protect or hide • *He covered his face.*
cloak • *a land cloaked in mist*
conceal • *The hat concealed her hair.*
cover up • *I covered him up with a blanket.*
hide • *His sunglasses hid his eyes.*
mask • *A cloud masked the sun.*
obscure • *One wall was obscured by a huge banner.*
screen • *The road was screened by a block of flats.*
shade • *shading his eyes from the glare*

ANTONYM
● reveal

cover ❷ VERB
to form a layer over • *Tears covered his face.*
coat • *Coat the fish with batter.*
overlay • *The floor was overlaid with rugs.*

cover ❸ NOUN
something which protects or hides • *a duvet cover*
case • *a spectacle case*
coating • *steel covered with a coating of zinc*
covering • *a plastic covering*
jacket • *the jacket of a book*
mask • *a surgical mask*
screen • *They put a screen round me.*
wrapper • *Take the product from its sealed wrapper.*

cow NOUN
a farm animal kept for milk or meat • *a herd of dairy cows*
bovine • *a herd of deranged bovines*
cattle • *fields where cattle graze*

a b **c** d e f g h i j k l m n o p q r s t u v w x y z

Can't find the word you're looking for? Try the index.

coward NOUN
someone who is easily scared
• *He's too much of a coward to fight.*
chicken (SLANG) • *We called him a chicken.*
wimp (INFORMAL) • *He seems like a wimp to me.*

cowardly ADJECTIVE
easily scared • *too cowardly to tell the truth*
chicken (SLANG) • *I was too chicken to complain.*
faint-hearted • *This is no time to be faint-hearted.*
gutless (INFORMAL) • *a gutless coward*
sookie (NEW ZEALAND) • *a sookie thing to do*

MORE SYNONYMS
- craven
- lily-livered
- pusillanimous
- spineless
- timorous

ANTONYM
- brave

cower VERB
to bend down with fear • *The hostages cowered in their seats.*
cringe • *I cringed in horror.*
quail • *She quailed at the sight.*
shrink • *He shrank back in terror.*

crack ❶ VERB
to become damaged, with lines on the surface • *A gas main has cracked.*
break • *She broke her leg playing rounders.*
fracture • *You've fractured a rib.*
snap • *The mast snapped like a dry twig.*

crack ❷ VERB
to find the answer to something

• *We've managed to crack the problem.*
decipher • *trying to decipher the code*
solve • *attempts to solve the mystery*
work out • *I've worked out where I'm going wrong.*

crack ❸ NOUN
a line or gap caused by damage
• *a large crack in the wall*
break • *a train crash caused by a break in the rails*
cleft • *a cleft in the rocks*
crevice • *a crevice in the cliff-face*
fracture • *a hip fracture*

MORE SYNONYMS
- fissure
- interstice

crafty ADJECTIVE
clever and rather dishonest • *That crafty old devil has taken us for a ride.*
artful • *the smiles and schemes of an artful woman*
cunning • *I have a cunning plan to get us out of this mess.*
devious • *By devious means she obtained the address.*
scheming • *You're a scheming little devil, aren't you?*
slippery • *a slippery customer*
sly • *He is a sly old beggar if ever there was one.*
wily • *the wily manoeuvring of the President*

cram VERB
to stuff something into a container or place • *She crammed her mouth with nuts.*
jam • *The place was jammed with people.*
pack • *The drawers were packed with clothes.*

Can't find the word you're looking for? Try the index.

squeeze • *The two of us were squeezed into one seat.*
stuff • *wallets stuffed with dollars*

crash ❶ NOUN
an accident involving a moving vehicle • *a plane crash*
accident • *a serious car accident*
bump • *I had a bump in the car park.*
collision • *a head-on collision*
pile-up (INFORMAL) • *a 54-car pile-up*
smash • *He nearly died in a car smash.*

crash ❷ NOUN
a loud noise • *There was a sudden crash outside.*
bang • *The door slammed with a bang.*
clash • *the clash of cymbals*
din • *the din of battle*
smash • *the smash of falling crockery*

crash ❸ NOUN
the failure of a business • *a stock market crash*
bankruptcy • *Many firms are now facing bankruptcy.*
collapse • *The economy is on the edge of collapse.*
depression • *the Great Depression of the 1930s*
failure • *a major cause of business failure*
ruin • *Inflation has driven them to the brink of ruin.*

crash ❹ VERB
to have an accident • *His car crashed into the rear of a van.*
bump • *I've just bumped my car.*
collide • *Two trains collided in London today.*
drive into • *He drove his car into a tree.*

have an accident • *My brother's had an accident on his moped.*
hurtle into • *The racing car hurtled into the spectator enclosure.*
plough into • *The plane had ploughed into the mountainside.*
wreck • *He's wrecked his van.*

crawl VERB
to be full of • *The place is crawling with drunks.*
be alive with • *The river was alive with frogs.*
be full of • *The place was full of insects.*
be overrun (SLANG) • *The area is overrun with tourists.*
swarm • *The wood was swarming with police officers.*
teem • *ponds teeming with fish*

craze NOUN
a brief enthusiasm for something • *the latest fitness craze*
fad • *a new-age fad*
fashion • *the fashion for Seventies toys*
trend • *the latest trend among film stars*
vogue • *a vogue for so-called health drinks*

crazy ❶ ADJECTIVE (INFORMAL)
very strange or foolish • *People thought we were crazy when we told them our plans.*
foolish • *It is foolish to risk skin cancer for the sake of a tan.*
insane • *If you want my opinion, I think your idea is completely insane.*
mad • *You'd be mad to work with him again.*
ridiculous • *It was an absolutely ridiculous decision.*
wild • *all sorts of wild ideas*
zany • *zany humour*

Can't find the word you're looking for? Try the index.

A
B
C
D
E
F
G
H
I
J
K
L
M
N
O
P
Q
R
S
T
U
V
W
X
Y
Z

ANTONYM
- sensible

crazy ❷ ADJECTIVE (INFORMAL)
very keen on something • *He's crazy about football.*
fanatical • *fanatical about computer games*
mad • *She's not as mad about sport as I am.*
obsessed • *He was obsessed with American gangster movies.*
passionate • *He is passionate about the project.*
smitten • *They were totally smitten with each other.*
wild • *I'm just wild about Peter.*

MORE SYNONYMS
- enamoured
- zealous

create ❶ VERB
to make something happen • *His reaction created a bad atmosphere.*
bring about • *helping to bring about peace*
cause • *Sugar causes dental decay.*
lead to • *The takeover led to widespread redundancies.*
occasion • *the distress occasioned by her dismissal*

create ❷ VERB
to invent something • *creating a new style of painting*
coin • *the man who coined the term 'virtual reality'*
compose • *Vivaldi composed many concertos.*
devise • *We devised a scheme to help him.*
formulate • *He formulated his plan for escape.*
invent • *He invented the first electric clock.*
originate • *the designer who*

originated platform shoes

creative ADJECTIVE
able to invent • *her creative talents*
fertile • *a fertile imagination*
imaginative • *an imaginative writer*
inspired • *his inspired use of colour*
inventive • *an inventive storyline*

credit NOUN
praise for something • *He took all the credit for my idea.*
commendation • *Both teams deserve commendation.*
glory • *basking in reflected glory*
praise • *Praise is due to all concerned.*
recognition • *She got no recognition for her work.*
thanks • *He received no thanks for his efforts.*

MORE SYNONYMS
- acclaim
- Brownie points
- kudos

ANTONYM
- disgrace

creepy ADJECTIVE (INFORMAL)
strange and frightening • *This place is really creepy at night.*
disturbing • *There was something about him she found disturbing.*
eerie • *I walked down the eerie dark path.*
macabre • *macabre stories*
scary (INFORMAL) • *We watched scary movies.*
sinister • *There was something sinister about him.*
spooky • *The whole place has a slightly spooky atmosphere.*
unnatural • *The altered landscape looks unnatural and weird.*

Can't find the word you're looking for? Try the index.

crime NOUN
an act that breaks the law • *the problem of organized crime*
misdemeanour • *a financial misdemeanour*
offence • *a serious offence*
violation • *tax law violations*
wrong • *I intend to right that wrong.*

MORE SYNONYMS
- felony
- malfeasance
- misdeed
- transgression

criminal ❶ NOUN
someone who has committed a crime • *the country's most dangerous criminals*
crook (INFORMAL) • *The man is a crook and a liar.*
culprit • *the true culprit's identity*
delinquent • *juvenile delinquents*
offender • *a first-time offender*
skelm (SOUTH AFRICAN) • *a skelm from the city*
villain • *He tackled an armed villain single-handed.*

MORE SYNONYMS
- evildoer
- felon
- lawbreaker
- malefactor

criminal ❷ ADJECTIVE
involving crime • *criminal activities*
corrupt • *corrupt practices*
crooked • *crooked business deals*
illegal • *an illegal action*
illicit • *illicit dealings*
unlawful • *unlawful entry*

MORE SYNONYMS
- culpable
- felonious
- indictable

- iniquitous
- nefarious

ANTONYM
- legal

cripple ❶ VERB
to injure severely • *crippled in a car accident*
disable • *disabled by polio*
lame • *He was lamed for life.*
maim • *mines maiming and killing civilians*
paralyse • *paralysed in a riding accident*

cripple ❷ VERB
to prevent from working • *The crisis may cripple the Irish economy.*
bring to a standstill • *The strike brought France to a standstill.*
impair • *Their actions will impair France's national interests.*
put out of action • *The port has been put out of action.*

critical ❶ ADJECTIVE
very important • *a critical point in history*
crucial • *a crucial election campaign*
deciding • *Price was a deciding factor.*
decisive • *a decisive moment in my life*
momentous • *a momentous decision*
pivotal • *He played a pivotal role in the match.*
vital • *vital information*

ANTONYM
- unimportant

critical ❷ ADJECTIVE
very serious • *a critical illness*
grave • *grave danger*
precarious • *a precarious financial situation*

a
b
c
d
e
f
g
h
i
j
k
l
m
n
o
p
q
r
s
t
u
v
w
x
y
z

Can't find the word you're looking for? Try the index.

A
B
C
D
E
F
G
H
I
J
K
L
M
N
O
P
Q
R
S
T
U
V
W
X
Y
Z

serious • *His condition is said to be serious.*

critical ❸ ADJECTIVE
finding fault with something or someone • *critical remarks*
carping • *carping comments*
derogatory • *derogatory references to women*
disapproving • *a disapproving look*
disparaging • *He spoke in disparaging tones.*
scathing • *a scathing attack*

MORE SYNONYMS
- captious
- cavilling
- censorious
- fault-finding

ANTONYM
- complimentary

criticism NOUN
expression of disapproval • *public criticism of his actions*
censure • *They deserve praise rather than censure.*
disapproval • *a chorus of disapproval*
disparagement • *their disparagement of this book*
fault-finding • *her husband's constant fault-finding*
flak (INFORMAL) • *I got a lot of flak for that idea.*
panning (INFORMAL) • *a panning from the critics*

MORE SYNONYMS
- animadversion
- denigration
- stricture

ANTONYM
- praise

criticize VERB
to find fault • *The regime has been harshly criticized.*
censure • *a decision for which she was censured*
condemn • *He refused to condemn their behaviour.*
find fault with • *She keeps finding fault with my work.*
knock (INFORMAL) • *Don't knock it till you've tried it.*
pan (INFORMAL) • *Critics panned the show.*
put down • *She's always putting him down in front of the kids.*

MORE SYNONYMS
- disparage
- excoriate
- lambast *or* lambaste

ANTONYM
- praise

crook ❶ NOUN (INFORMAL)
a criminal • *The man is a crook and a liar.*
cheat • *a rotten cheat*
rogue • *Mr Scott wasn't a rogue at all.*
scoundrel (OLD-FASHIONED) • *He is a lying scoundrel!*
shark • *Beware the sharks when you are deciding how to invest.*
swindler • *Swindlers have cheated investors out of £12 million.*
thief • *The thieves snatched the camera.*
villain • *As a copper, I've spent my life putting villains behind bars.*

crook ❷ ADJECTIVE (AUSTRALIAN AND NEW ZEALAND; INFORMAL)
ill • *He admitted to feeling a bit crook.*
ill • *I was feeling ill.*
nauseous • *The drugs may make*

Can't find the word you're looking for? Try the index.

the patient feel nauseous.
poorly • *Julie's still poorly.*
queasy • *He was very prone to seasickness and already felt queasy.*
sick • *The very thought of food made him feel sick.*
under the weather • *I was still feeling a bit under the weather.*
unwell • *He felt unwell as he was travelling home this afternoon.*

crooked ❶ ADJECTIVE
bent or twisted • *a crooked tree*
bent • *a bent back*
deformed • *born with a deformed right leg*
distorted • *a distorted image*
irregular • *irregular and discoloured teeth*
out of shape • *The wires were bent out of shape.*
twisted • *bits of twisted metal*
warped • *warped wooden shutters*

ANTONYM
- straight

crooked ❷ ADJECTIVE
dishonest or illegal • *crooked business practices*
corrupt • *corrupt police officers*
criminal • *criminal activities*
dishonest • *dishonest salespeople*
fraudulent • *a fraudulent claim*
illegal • *illegal trading*
shady (INFORMAL) • *shady deals*

MORE SYNONYMS
- dishonourable
- nefarious
- unprincipled

ANTONYM
- honest

cross ❶ VERB
to go across • *the bridge which crosses the river*

ford • *trying to find a safe place to ford the stream*
go across • *going across the road*
span • *the iron bridge spanning the railway*
traverse • *a valley traversed by streams*

cross ❷ VERB
to meet and go across • *the intersection where the roads cross*
crisscross • *Phone wires criss-cross the street.*
intersect • *The circles intersect in two places.*

cross ❸ NOUN
a mixture of two things • *a cross between a collie and a retriever*
blend • *a blend of the old and the new*
combination • *a combination of fear and anger*
mixture • *a mixture of two factors*

cross ❹ ADJECTIVE
rather angry • *I'm very cross with him.*
angry • *Are you angry with me?*
annoyed • *I'm annoyed with myself for being so stupid.*
fractious • *The children were getting fractious.*
fretful • *the fretful expression on her face*
grumpy • *a grumpy old man*
in a bad mood • *He's in a bad mood about something.*
irritable • *She had been restless and irritable all day.*

MORE SYNONYMS
- irascible
- peevish
- splenetic
- testy
- tetchy

a
b
c
d
e
f
g
h
i
j
k
l
m
n
o
p
q
r
s
t
u
v
w
x
y
z

Can't find the word you're looking for? Try the index.

crouch VERB

to squat down • *A man was crouching behind the car.*
bend down • *I bent down and touched the grass.*
squat • *He squatted on his heels to talk to the children.*

crowd ❶ NOUN

a large group of people • *A huge crowd gathered in the square.*
horde • *hordes of tourists*
host • *a host of fans*
mass • *a heaving mass of people*
mob • *a mob of demonstrators*
multitude • *surrounded by a noisy multitude*
swarm • *swarms of visitors*
throng • *An official pushed through the throng.*

crowd ❷ VERB

to gather close together
• *Hundreds of fans crowded into the hall.*
congregate • *A large crowd congregated outside the stadium.*
gather • *Dozens of people gathered to watch.*
swarm • *Police swarmed into the area.*
throng • *The crowds thronged into the mall.*

crowded ADJECTIVE

full of people • *a crowded room*
congested • *congested cities*
full • *The train was full.*
overflowing • *buildings overflowing with students*
packed • *By 10.30 the shop was packed.*

crucial ADJECTIVE

very important • *a crucial moment in his career*
central • *central to the whole process*

critical • *a critical point in the campaign*
decisive • *ready to strike at the decisive moment*
momentous • *a momentous event*
pivotal • *He played a pivotal role in the match.*
vital • *vital information*

crude ❶ ADJECTIVE

rough and simple • *a crude weapon*
primitive • *They managed to make a primitive harness.*
rough • *a rough sketch*
rudimentary • *some form of rudimentary heating*
simple • *a simple stringed instrument*

crude ❷ ADJECTIVE

rude and offensive • *a crude sense of humour*
coarse • *coarse speech*
dirty • *a dirty joke*
indecent • *indecent lyrics*
obscene • *obscene language*
tasteless • *a tasteless remark*
vulgar • *a vulgar phrase*

MORE SYNONYMS

● boorish
● crass
● smutty

ANTONYM

● refined

cruel ADJECTIVE

deliberately causing hurt • *I hate people who are cruel to animals.*
barbarous • *a barbarous attack*
brutal • *a brutal murder*
callous • *callous treatment*
cold-blooded • *a cold-blooded killer*
heartless • *It was a heartless thing to do.*
inhumane • *He was kept under*

Can't find the word you're looking for? Try the index.

inhumane conditions.
sadistic • *mistreated by sadistic guards*
vicious • *a vicious blow*

ANTONYM
● kind

cruelty NOUN
cruel behaviour • *an act of unbelievable cruelty*
barbarity • *the barbarity of war*
brutality • *police brutality*
callousness • *the callousness of his murder*
inhumanity • *man's inhumanity to man*
savagery • *scenes of unimaginable savagery*
viciousness • *the viciousness of the attacks*

ANTONYM
● kindness

crumple VERB
to squash and wrinkle • *She crumpled the paper in her hand.*
crease • *Don't crease the material.*
crush • *Andrew crushed his empty can.*
screw up • *He screwed the letter up in anger.*
wrinkle • *trying not to wrinkle her silk skirt*

crush ❶ VERB
to destroy the shape of by squeezing • *Their car was crushed by an army tank.*
crumble • *Crumble the stock cubes into a jar.*
crumple • *She crumpled the note up and threw it away.*
mash • *Mash the bananas with a fork.*
squash • *She squashed the wasp under her heel.*

crush ❷ VERB
to defeat completely • *his bid to crush the uprising*
overcome • *working to overcome the enemy forces*
put down • *Soldiers moved in to put down the rebellion.*
quell • *Troops eventually quelled the unrest.*
stamp out • *steps to stamp out bullying in schools*
vanquish • *his vanquished foe*

cry ❶ VERB
to have tears coming from your eyes • *Stop crying and tell me what's wrong.*
▷ see Word Study **cry**, page 675

cry ❷ VERB
to call out loudly • *"See you soon!" they cried.*
▷ see Word Study **cry**, page 675

cry ❸ NOUN
a loud or high shout • *a cry of pain*
call • *the call of a seagull*
exclamation • *an exclamation of surprise*
shout • *I heard a distant shout.*
yell • *Bob let out a yell.*

cunning ❶ ADJECTIVE
clever and deceitful • *a cunning and ruthless businessman*
artful • *an artful old woman*
crafty • *a crafty plan*
devious • *a devious mind*
sly • *a sly trick*
wily • *a wily politician*

MORE SYNONYMS
● foxy
● Machiavellian

ANTONYM
● open

a
b
c
d
e
f
g
h
i
j
k
l
m
n
o
p
q
r
s
t
u
v
w
x
y
z

Can't find the word you're looking for? Try the index.

A
B
C
D
E
F
G
H
I
J
K
L
M
N
O
P
Q
R
S
T
U
V
W
X
Y
Z

cunning ➋ NOUN
cleverness and deceit • *the cunning of today's criminals*
deviousness • *the deviousness of drug traffickers*
guile • *She was without guile or pretence.*

curb ➊ VERB
to keep something within limits • *He must learn to curb that temper of his.*
check • *an attempt to check the spread of the disease*
contain • *A hundred firefighters are still trying to contain the fire.*
control • *the need to control environmental pollution*
limit • *He limited payments on the country's foreign debt.*
restrain • *efforts to restrain corruption*
suppress • *The Government is suppressing inflation by devastating the economy.*

curb ➋ NOUN
an attempt to keep something within limits • *He called for stricter curbs on immigration.*
brake • *Illness had put a brake on his progress.*
control • *price controls*
limit • *limits on government spending*
limitation • *We need a limitation on the powers of the government.*
restraint • *new restraints on trade unions*

cure ➊ VERB
to make well • *a treatment which cures eczema*
heal • *plants used to heal wounds*
remedy • *an operation to remedy a blood clot on his brain*

cure ➋ NOUN
something that makes an illness better • *a cure for cancer*
medicine • *herbal medicines*
remedy • *a remedy for colds and flu*
treatment • *the most effective treatment for malaria*

curiosity ➊ NOUN
the desire to know • *a curiosity about the past*
inquisitiveness • *the inquisitiveness of children*
interest • *a lively interest in current affairs*

curiosity ➋ NOUN
something unusual • *a museum displaying relics and curiosities*
freak • *a freak of nature*
marvel • *a marvel of science*
novelty • *in the days when a motor car was a novelty*
oddity • *Tourists are still something of an oddity here.*
rarity • *Mexican restaurants are a rarity here.*

curious ➊ ADJECTIVE
wanting to know • *He was curious about my family.*
inquiring • *He gave me an inquiring look.*
inquisitive • *Cats are very inquisitive.*
interested • *A crowd of interested villagers gathered.*
nosy (INFORMAL) • *nosy neighbours*

ANTONYM
● incurious

curious ➋ ADJECTIVE
strange and unusual • *a curious mixture of the old and the new*
bizarre • *his bizarre behaviour*
extraordinary • *an extraordinary story*

Can't find the word you're looking for? Try the index.

odd • *an odd coincidence*
peculiar • *a peculiar smell*
singular • *a singular talent*
strange • *a strange taste*
unusual • *an unusual name*

ANTONYM
● ordinary

current ❶ NOUN
a strong continuous movement of water • *swept away by the strong current*
flow • *the quiet flow of the olive-green water*
tide • *We will sail with the tide.*
undertow • *Dangerous undertows make swimming unsafe along the coastline.*

current ❷ ADJECTIVE
happening, being done, or being used now • *current trends*
contemporary • *He has adopted a more contemporary style.*
fashionable • *the fashionable theory about this issue*
ongoing • *an ongoing debate on inner city problems*
present • *skilfully renovated by the present owners*
present-day • *Even by present-day standards these are large aircraft.*
today's • *In today's America, health care is big business.*
up-to-the-minute • *up-to-the-minute information on sales and stocks*

ANTONYM
● past

curve ❶ NOUN
a bending line • *a curve in the road*
arc • *The ball rose in an arc.*
bend • *a bend in the river*
trajectory • *the trajectory of an artillery shell*

turn • *every turn in the road*

RELATED WORD
● ADJECTIVE: sinuous

curve ❷ VERB
to move in a curve • *The road curved sharply to the left.*
arc • *A rainbow arced over the town.*
arch • *a domed ceiling arching overhead*
bend • *The path bent to the right.*
swerve • *His car swerved off the road.*

custom ❶ NOUN
a traditional activity • *an ancient Chinese custom*
convention • *the conventions of Western art*
practice • *an old Jewish practice*
ritual • *an ancient Shintoist ritual*
tradition • *different cultural traditions*

custom ❷ NOUN
something a person always does • *It was his custom to start work at 8.30.*
habit • *his habit of making tactless remarks*
practice • *her usual practice of attending church*
routine • *his daily routine*
wont • *Paul woke early, as was his wont.*

customer NOUN
someone who buys something • *The shop was filled with customers.*
buyer • *show homes to tempt potential buyers*
client • *a solicitor and his client*
consumer • *the increasing demands of consumers*
patron • *the restaurant's patrons*
purchaser • *a prospective purchaser*

a
b
c
d
e
f
g
h
i
j
k
l
m
n
o
p
q
r
s
t
u
v
w
x
y
z

Can't find the word you're looking for? Try the index.

A
B
C
D
E
F
G
H
I
J
K
L
M
N
O
P
Q
R
S
T
U
V
W
X
Y
Z

shopper • *late-night shoppers on their way home*

cut ❶ VERB
to mark, injure, or remove part of (something or someone) with something sharp • *The thieves cut a hole in the fence.*
▷ see Word Study **cut**, pages 672–3

cut ❷ VERB
to reduce something • *The department's first priority is to cut costs.*
cut back • *The Government has decided to cut back on defence spending.*
decrease • *calls to decrease income tax*
lower • *The Central Bank has lowered interest rates.*
reduce • *Gradually reduce the dosage.*
slash • *Holiday prices have been slashed.*

MORE SYNONYMS
● abridge
● downsize
● rationalize

ANTONYM
● increase

cut ❸ NOUN
a mark or injury made by cutting • *a cut on his left eyebrow*
gash • *There was a deep gash across his forehead.*
incision • *a tiny incision in the skin*
slash • *jeans with slashes in the knees*

slit • *Make a slit along the stem.*

cut ❹ NOUN
a reduction in something • *another cut in interest rates*
cutback • *cutbacks in funding*
decrease • *a decrease in foreign investment*
lowering • *the lowering of taxes*
reduction • *reductions in staff*
saving • *household savings on energy use*

ANTONYM
● increase

cute ADJECTIVE
pretty or attractive • *You were such a cute baby!*
appealing • *an appealing kitten*
attractive • *I thought he was very attractive.*
charming • *a charming little cottage*
dear • *Look at their dear little faces!*
good-looking • *Cassandra noticed him because he was so good-looking.*
gorgeous • *All the girls think Ryan's gorgeous.*
pretty • *She's a very pretty girl.*

ANTONYM
● ugly

cynical ADJECTIVE
always thinking the worst of people • *a cynical attitude*
distrustful • *distrustful of all politicians*
sceptical • *a sceptical response*

Can't find the word you're looking for? Try the index.

Dd

daft ADJECTIVE
extremely silly • *Now there's a daft suggestion!*
crazy • *He has this crazy idea about his neighbours.*
foolish • *It would be foolish to raise his hopes unnecessarily.*
ludicrous • *It was ludicrous to suggest that the visit could be kept a secret.*
preposterous • *their preposterous claim that they had discovered a plot*
ridiculous • *It was an absolutely ridiculous decision.*
silly • *That's a silly question.*
stupid • *I made a stupid mistake.*

ANTONYM
● sensible

damage ❶ VERB
to cause harm to something • *A fire had severely damaged the school.*
harm • *a warning that the product may harm the environment*
hurt • *He had hurt his back in an accident.*
injure • *Several policemen were injured in the clashes.*

damage ❷ NOUN
harm that is done to something • *The bomb caused extensive damage to the restaurant.*
harm • *All dogs are capable of doing harm to human beings.*
injury • *He escaped without injury.*

damp ❶ ADJECTIVE
slightly wet • *a damp towel*
clammy • *clammy hands*
dank • *The kitchen was dank and cheerless.*
humid • *Visitors can expect hot and humid conditions.*
moist • *The soil is reasonably moist after the September rain.*
sodden • *We stripped off our sodden clothes.*
soggy • *soggy cheese sandwiches*
wet • *My hair was still wet.*

damp ❷ NOUN
slight wetness • *There was damp all over the walls.*
dampness • *I could see big circles of dampness under each arm.*
humidity • *The heat and humidity were intolerable.*
moisture • *Compost helps the soil retain moisture.*

MORE SYNONYMS
● clamminess
● dankness

danger NOUN
the possibility of harm • *Your life is in danger.*
hazard • *a health hazard*
jeopardy • *A series of setbacks have put the whole project in jeopardy.*
menace • *In my view you are a menace to the public.*
peril • *the perils of the sea*
risk • *There is a small risk of brain damage.*

Can't find the word you're looking for? Try the index.

A
B
C
D
E
F
G
H
I
J
K
L
M
N
O
P
Q
R
S
T
U
V
W
X
Y
Z

threat • *Some couples see single women as a threat to their relationship.*

ANTONYM
● safety

dangerous ADJECTIVE
likely to cause harm • *It's dangerous to drive when you're tired.*
hazardous • *They have no way to dispose of the hazardous waste they produce.*
perilous • *a perilous journey across the war-zone*
risky • *Investing is risky.*
treacherous • *Blizzards had made the roads treacherous.*

ANTONYM
● safe

dare ❶ VERB
to challenge someone to do something • *I dare you to ask him his name.*
challenge • *He left a note at the scene of the crime, challenging detectives to catch him.*
defy • *I defy you to watch it on your own.*
throw down the gauntlet
• *Jaguar has thrown down the gauntlet to competitors by giving the best guarantee on the market.*

dare ❷ VERB
to have the courage to do something • *Nobody dared to complain.*
risk • *The skipper was not willing to risk taking his ship through the straits.*
venture • *the few Europeans who had ventured beyond the Himalayas*

daring ❶ ADJECTIVE
willing to take risks • *a daring escape by helicopter*

adventurous • *an adventurous skier*
audacious • *an audacious plan to win the presidency*
bold • *bold economic reforms*
brave • *He was not brave enough to report the loss of the documents.*
fearless • *They were young and strong and fearless.*

MORE SYNONYMS
● intrepid
● valiant

ANTONYM
● cautious

daring ❷ NOUN
the courage to take risks • *His daring may have cost him his life.*
audacity • *He had the audacity to make a 200-1 bet on himself to win.*
boldness • *the boldness of his economic programme*
bravery • *He deserves the highest praise for his bravery.*
courage • *He impressed everyone with his personal courage.*
guts (INFORMAL) • *I haven't got the guts to tell him.*
nerve (INFORMAL) • *He didn't have the nerve to meet me.*

MORE SYNONYMS
● fearlessness
● intrepidity
● temerity

ANTONYM
● caution

dark ❶ ADJECTIVE
lacking light • *It was too dark to see what was happening.*
cloudy • *a cloudy sky*
dim • *the dim outline of a small boat*
dingy • *a dingy bedsit*
murky • *the murky waters of the loch*

Can't find the word you're looking for? Try the index.

overcast • *a cold, windy, overcast afternoon*
shadowy • *a shadowy corner*

ANTONYM
● light

dark ❷ ADJECTIVE
dull in colour • *a dark suit*
black • *a black leather coat*
swarthy • *a broad swarthy face*

dark ❸ NOUN
lack of light • *I've always been afraid of the dark.*
darkness • *The room was plunged into darkness.*
dimness • *I squinted to adjust my eyes to the dimness.*
dusk • *She disappeared into the dusk.*
gloom • *the gloom of a foggy November morning*

MORE SYNONYMS
● murk
● murkiness

ANTONYM
● light

dash ❶ VERB
to rush somewhere • *Suddenly she dashed out into the garden.*
bolt • *I bolted for the exit.*
fly • *She flew downstairs.*
race • *The hares raced away out of sight.*
run • *The gunmen ran off into the woods.*
rush • *Someone rushed out of the building.*
sprint • *Sergeant Greene sprinted to the car.*
tear • *He tore off down the road.*

MORE SYNONYMS
● make haste
● hasten

dash ❷ VERB
to throw or be thrown violently against something • *The waves dashed against the rocks.*
break • *Danny listened to the waves breaking against the shore.*
crash • *The door swung inwards and crashed against a cupboard behind it.*
hurl • *He hurled the vase to the ground in rage.*
slam • *They slammed me on to the ground.*
smash • *smashing the bottle against a wall*

dash ❸ VERB
to ruin or frustrate someone's hopes or ambitions • *They had their hopes raised and then dashed.*
crush • *My dreams of becoming an actor have been crushed.*
destroy • *Even the most gifted can have their confidence destroyed by the wrong teacher.*
disappoint • *His hopes have been disappointed many times before.*
foil • *Our idea of building a water garden was foiled by the planning authorities.*
frustrate • *The government has deliberately frustrated his efforts.*
shatter • *A failure would shatter all our hopes.*
thwart • *Her ambition to be an artist was thwarted by failing eyesight.*

MORE SYNONYMS
● confound
● quash

dash ❹ NOUN
a sudden movement or rush • *a 160-mile dash to the hospital*
bolt • *He made a bolt for the door.*
race • *a race for the finishing line*

a
b
c
d
e
f
g
h
i
j
k
l
m
n
o
p
q
r
s
t
u
v
w
x
y
z

Can't find the word you're looking for? Try the index.

run • *One of the gang made a run for it.*
rush • *the mad rush not to be late for school*
sprint • *a last-minute sprint to catch the bus*
stampede • *There was a stampede for the exit.*

dash ⑤ NOUN
a small quantity of something • *a dash of wine vinegar*
drop • *I'll have a drop of that milk in my tea.*
pinch • *a pinch of salt*
splash • *add a splash of lemon juice*
sprinkling • *a light sprinkling of sugar*

daydream ① NOUN
a series of pleasant thoughts • *He learnt to escape into daydreams.*
dream • *My dream is to have a house in the country.*
fantasy • *fantasies of romance and true love*

MORE SYNONYMS
- castle in Spain
- castle in the air
- pipe dream
- reverie

daydream ② VERB
to think about pleasant things • *He daydreams of being a famous journalist.*
dream • *She used to dream of becoming an actress.*
fantasize • *I fantasized about writing music.*

dazed ADJECTIVE
unable to think clearly • *At the end of the interview I was dazed and exhausted.*
bewildered • *Some shoppers looked bewildered by the sheer variety.*
confused • *Things were happening too quickly and Brian was confused.*
dizzy • *Her head hurt and she felt dizzy.*
light-headed • *If you miss breakfast, you may feel light-headed.*
numbed • *I'm so numbed with shock that I can hardly think.*
stunned • *a stunned silence*

MORE SYNONYMS
- disorientated
- punch-drunk
- stupefied

dead ① ADJECTIVE
no longer alive • *My husband's been dead a year now.*
deceased • *his recently deceased mother*
departed • *my dear departed father*
extinct • *the bones of extinct animals*
late • *my late husband*

ANTONYM
- alive

dead ② ADJECTIVE
no longer functioning • *a dead language*
defunct • *the now defunct Social Democratic Party*
not working • *The radio is not working.*

deadly ADJECTIVE
causing death • *a deadly disease*
destructive • *the destructive power of nuclear weapons*
fatal • *a fatal heart attack*
lethal • *a lethal dose of sleeping pills*
mortal • *Our lives were in mortal danger.*

deal VERB
to cope successfully with

Can't find the word you're looking for? Try the index.

something • *He must learn to deal with stress.*
attend to • *We have business to attend to first.*
cope with • *She has had to cope with losing all her money.*
handle • *I have learned how to handle pressure.*
manage • *As time passed I learned to manage my grief.*
see to • *Sarah saw to the packing while Jim fetched the car.*
take care of • *Malcolm took care of all the arrangements.*

dear ❶ NOUN
a person for whom you have affection • *What's the matter, dear?*
angel • *Be an angel and fetch my bag.*
beloved (OLD-FASHIONED)
• *He took his beloved into his arms.*
darling • *Thank you, darling.*
treasure (INFORMAL) • *Charlie? Oh, he's a treasure.*

dear ❷ ADJECTIVE
much loved • *a dear friend of mine*
beloved • *He lost his beloved wife last year.*
cherished • *his most cherished possession*
darling • *his darling daughter*
esteemed • *my esteemed colleagues*
precious • *Her family's support is very precious to her.*
prized • *one of the gallery's most prized possessions*
treasured • *one of my most treasured memories*

dear ❸ ADJECTIVE
costing a lot • *They're too dear.*
costly • *Having curtains professionally made can be costly.*
expensive • *Wine's so expensive in*

this country.
pricey (INFORMAL) • *Medical insurance is very pricey.*

deceive VERB
to make someone believe something untrue • *I was really hurt that he had deceived me.*
con (INFORMAL) • *The British motorist has been conned by the government.*
double-cross • *They were frightened of being double-crossed.*
dupe • *a plot to dupe stamp collectors into buying fake rarities*
fool • *They tried to fool you into coming after us.*
mislead • *He was furious with his doctors for having misled him.*
take in • *I wasn't taken in for one moment.*
trick • *His family tricked him into going to Pakistan.*

MORE SYNONYMS
● bamboozle
● beguile
● hoodwink

decent ❶ ADJECTIVE
of an acceptable standard
• *He gets a decent pension.*
adequate • *an adequate diet*
passable • *She speaks passable French.*
reasonable • *He couldn't make a reasonable living from his writing.*
respectable • *investments that offer respectable rates of return*
satisfactory • *I never got a satisfactory answer.*
tolerable • *to make life more tolerable*

decent ❷ ADJECTIVE
correct and respectable • *the decent thing to do*

a
b
c
d
e
f
g
h
i
j
k
l
m
n
o
p
q
r
s
t
u
v
w
x
y
z

Can't find the word you're looking for? Try the index.

A
B
C
D
E
F
G
H
I
J
K
L
M
N
O
P
Q
R
S
T
U
V
W
X
Y
Z

proper • *It is right and proper to do this.*

respectable • *He came from a perfectly respectable middle-class family.*

ANTONYM
- improper

deceptive ADJECTIVE

likely to make people believe something untrue • *First impressions can be deceptive.*

false • *"Thank you," she said with false enthusiasm.*

fraudulent • *fraudulent claims about being a nurse*

illusory • *They argue that freedom is illusory.*

misleading • *It would be misleading to say that we were friends.*

unreliable • *His account is quite unreliable.*

MORE SYNONYMS
- delusive
- specious

decide VERB

to choose to do something • *She decided to do a secretarial course.*

choose • *The council chose to inform the public about the risks.*

come to a decision • *Have you come to a decision about where you're going tonight?*

determine (FORMAL) • *He determined to rescue his two countrymen.*

elect (FORMAL) • *I have elected to stay.*

make up your mind • *He simply can't make his mind up whether he should stay.*

reach a decision • *He demanded to know all the facts before reaching any decision.*

resolve (FORMAL) • *She resolved to report the matter to the authorities.*

decision NOUN

a judgment about something • *The editor's decision is final.*

conclusion • *I've come to the conclusion that she's a great musician.*

finding • *It is the finding of this court that you are guilty.*

judgment • *a landmark judgment by the Court of Appeal*

resolution • *a resolution condemning violence*

ruling • *He tried to have the court ruling overturned.*

verdict • *The judges will deliver their verdict in October.*

declaration NOUN

a forceful or official announcement • *a declaration of war*

affirmation • *her first public affirmation of her decision*

protestation (FORMAL) • *his protestations of innocence*

statement • *He made a formal statement to the police.*

testimony • *His testimony was an important element in the case.*

MORE SYNONYMS
- assertion
- avowal

declare VERB

to state something forcefully or officially • *He declared that he was going to be famous.*

affirm • *a speech in which he affirmed a commitment to lower taxes*

announce • *She was planning to announce her engagement.*

assert • *He asserted his innocence.*

certify • *The president certified that*

the project would receive $650m.
proclaim • He still proclaims himself a believer in the Revolution.
profess (FORMAL) • Why do organisations profess that they care?
pronounce • The authorities took time to pronounce their verdict.
state • Please state your name.

MORE SYNONYMS
- attest
- aver
- avow

decline ❶ VERB

to become smaller or weaker • a declining birth rate
decrease • The number of independent firms decreased from 198 to 96.
diminish • The threat of nuclear war has diminished.
drop • His blood pressure had dropped.
fall • Output will fall by six per cent.
go down • Crime has gone down 70 per cent.
plummet • The Prime Minister's popularity has plummeted to an all-time low.
reduce • The number of students fluent in Latin has been steadily reducing.

MORE SYNONYMS
- dwindle
- wane

ANTONYM
- increase

decline ❷ VERB

to refuse politely to accept or do something • He declined their invitation.
abstain • I will abstain from voting in the ballot.
excuse yourself • I was invited,

but I excused myself.
refuse • He refused to comment after the trial.
turn down • I thanked him for the offer but turned it down.

ANTONYM
- accept

decline ❸ NOUN

a gradual weakening or decrease • economic decline
decrease • a decrease in the number of young people out of work
downturn • a sharp downturn in the industry
drop • a drop in support for the Conservatives
fall • a sharp fall in the value of the pound
recession • pull the economy out of recession
shrinkage • a shrinkage in industrial output
slump • a slump in property prices

ANTONYM
- increase

decorate ❶ VERB

to make more attractive • He decorated his room with pictures.
adorn • Several oil paintings adorn the walls.
deck • The house was decked with flowers.
ornament • a high ceiling, ornamented with plaster fruits and flowers

MORE SYNONYMS
- beautify
- bedeck
- embellish
- festoon

decorate ❷ VERB

to put paint or wallpaper on

a b c **d** e f g h i j k l m n o p q r s t u v w x y z

A
B
C
D
E
F
G
H
I
J
K
L
M
N
O
P
Q
R
S
T
U
V
W
X
Y
Z

• when they came to decorate the bedroom

do up (INFORMAL) • *He spent the summer doing up the barn.*

renovate • *The couple spent thousands renovating the house.*

decrease ❶ VERB

to become or make less
• *Population growth is decreasing by 1.4% each year.*

cut down • *He cut down his coffee intake.*

decline • *The number of staff has declined.*

diminish • *The threat of nuclear war has diminished.*

drop • *Temperatures can drop to freezing at night.*

dwindle • *his dwindling authority*

lessen • *changes to their diet that would lessen the risk of disease*

lower • *The Central Bank has lowered interest rates.*

reduce • *It reduces the risk of heart disease.*

shrink • *The forests have shrunk to half their size.*

MORE SYNONYMS

● abate
● curtail
● subside
● wane

ANTONYM

● increase

decrease ❷ NOUN

a lessening in the amount of something • *a decrease in the number of unemployed*

cutback • *cutbacks in defence spending*

decline • *the rate of decline in tobacco consumption*

drop • *a drop in temperature*

lessening • *a lessening of tension*

reduction • *dramatic reductions in staff*

MORE SYNONYMS

● abatement
● curtailment
● diminution

ANTONYM

● increase

deep ❶ ADJECTIVE

having a long way to the bottom
• *a deep hole*

bottomless • *a bottomless pit*

yawning • *a yawning chasm*

ANTONYM

● shallow

deep ❷ ADJECTIVE

great or intense • *his deep love of Israel*

extreme • *extreme poverty*

grave • *a grave crisis*

great • *the great gulf between the two teams*

intense • *The pain was intense.*

profound • *discoveries which had a profound effect on medicine*

serious • *a serious problem*

deep ❸ ADJECTIVE

low in sound • *a deep voice*

bass • *a beautiful bass voice*

low • *Her voice was so low she was sometimes mistaken for a man.*

MORE SYNONYMS

● resonant
● sonorous

ANTONYM

● high

defeat ❶ VERB

to win a victory over someone
• *His guerrillas defeated the colonial army in 1954.*

Can't find the word you're looking for? Try the index.

beat • *the team that beat us in the final*
conquer • *During 1936, Mussolini conquered Abyssinia.*
crush • *in his bid to crush the rebels*
rout • *the battle at which the Norman army routed the English*
trounce • *Australia trounced France by 60 points to 4.*
vanquish (FORMAL) • *after the hero had vanquished the dragon*

defeat ❷ NOUN

a failure to win • *a 2-1 defeat by Sweden*
conquest • *He had led the conquest of southern Poland.*
debacle (FORMAL) • *It will be hard for them to recover from this debacle.*
rout • *The retreat turned into a rout.*
trouncing • *after a 6-2 trouncing on Sunday*

ANTONYM
● victory

defect NOUN

a fault or flaw • *A defect in the aircraft caused the crash.*
deficiency • *the most serious deficiency in NATO's air defence*
failing • *She blamed the country's failings on its culture of greed.*
fault • *a minor technical fault*
flaw • *The only flaw in his character is a short temper.*
imperfection • *my physical imperfections*
shortcoming • *The book has its shortcomings.*
weakness • *His only weakness is his laziness.*

defence ❶ NOUN

action to protect something • *The flat land offered no scope for defence.*

cover • *They could not provide adequate air cover for ground operations.*
protection • *Such a diet is believed to offer protection against cancer.*
resistance • *Most people have a natural resistance to the disease.*
safeguard • *legislation that offers safeguards against discrimination*
security • *Airport security was tightened.*

defence ❷ NOUN

an argument in support of something • *Chomsky's defence of his approach*
argument • *There's a strong argument for lowering the price.*
excuse • *There's no excuse for behaviour like that.*
explanation • *The authorities have given no explanation for his arrest.*
justification • *The only justification for a zoo is educational.*
plea • *a plea of insanity*

defend ❶ VERB

to protect from harm • *They would have killed him if he hadn't defended himself.*
cover • *travel insurance covering you against theft*
guard • *A few men were left outside to guard her.*
protect • *What can women do to protect themselves from heart disease?*
safeguard • *action to safeguard the ozone layer*
shelter • *a wooden house, sheltered by a low roof*
shield • *He shielded his head from the sun with an old sack.*

defend ❷ VERB

to argue in support of • *I can't defend what he did.*

a
b
c
d
e
f
g
h
i
j
k
l
m
n
o
p
q
r
s
t
u
v
w
x
y
z

Can't find the word you're looking for? Try the index.

A
B
C
D
E
F
G
H
I
J
K
L
M
N
O
P
Q
R
S
T
U
V
W
X
Y
Z

endorse • *I can endorse their opinion wholeheartedly.*
justify • *No argument can justify a war.*
stick up for (INFORMAL) • *Why do you always stick up for her?*
support • *Would you support such a move?*
uphold • *upholding the artist's right to creative freedom*

defender NOUN
a person who argues in support of something • *a committed defender of human rights*
advocate • *a strong advocate of free market policies*
champion • *a champion of women's causes*
supporter • *a major supporter of the tax reform*

deficiency NOUN
a lack of something • *signs of vitamin deficiency*
deficit • *a staffing deficit*
deprivation • *sleep deprivation*
inadequacy • *the inadequacies of the current system*
lack • *a lack of people wanting to start new businesses*
want (FORMAL) • *a want of manners and charm*

ANTONYM
● abundance

deficient ADJECTIVE
lacking in something • *a diet deficient in vitamins*
inadequate • *inadequate staffing*
lacking • *Why was military intelligence so lacking?*
poor • *soil that is poor in zinc*
short • *The proposals were short on detail.*
wanting • *He analysed his game*

and found it wanting.

definite ❶ ADJECTIVE
unlikely to be changed • *It's too soon to give a definite answer.*
assured • *Victory was still not assured.*
certain • *Very little in life is certain.*
decided • *Is anything decided yet?*
fixed • *a world without fixed laws*
guaranteed • *Success is not guaranteed.*
settled • *Nothing is settled yet.*

definite ❷ ADJECTIVE
certainly true • *The police had nothing definite against her.*
clear • *It was a clear case of homicide.*
positive • *We have positive proof that he was a blackmailer.*

MORE SYNONYMS
● black-and-white
● clear-cut
● cut-and-dried

deformed ADJECTIVE
abnormally shaped • *a deformed right leg*
disfigured • *the scarred, disfigured face*
distorted • *the distorted image caused by the projector*

degrade VERB
to humiliate someone • *the notion that pornography degrades women*
demean • *I wasn't going to demean myself by acting like a suspicious wife.*
humiliate • *He enjoyed humiliating me.*

delay ❶ VERB
to put something off until later • *the decision to delay the launch until tomorrow*

Can't find the word you're looking for? Try the index.

defer • *Customers often defer payment for as long as possible.*
postpone • *The visit has been postponed indefinitely.*
put off • *women who put off having a baby*
shelve • *The project has now been shelved.*
suspend • *Relief convoys will be suspended until the fighting stops.*

delay ❷ VERB
to slow or hinder something • *Various setbacks delayed production.*
check • *a policy to check fast population growth*
hinder • *Further investigation was hindered by the loss of all documentation.*
impede • *Fallen rocks are impeding the progress of rescue workers.*
obstruct • *The authorities are obstructing a UN investigation.*
set back • *public protests that could set back reforms*

MORE SYNONYMS
- hold up
- retard

ANTONYM
- hurry

delay ❸ NOUN
a time when something is delayed • *a 7-hour stoppage that caused delays on most flights*
interruption • *interruptions in the supply of food*
obstruction • *Obstruction of justice is a criminal offence.*
setback • *a setback for the peace process*

delete VERB
to remove something written • *The word 'exploded' had been deleted.*

cross out • *He crossed out the first sentence and wrote it again.*
erase • *It was unfortunate that she had erased the message.*
rub out • *She rubbed out the marks in the margin.*

MORE SYNONYMS
- blue-pencil
- cancel
- edit out
- strike out

deliberate ❶ ADJECTIVE
done on purpose • *a deliberate act of sabotage*
calculated • *a calculated attempt to cover up her crime*
conscious • *I made a conscious decision not to hide.*
intentional • *The kick was intentional.*
premeditated • *a premeditated attack*
studied • *"It's an interesting match," he said with studied understatement.*

ANTONYM
- accidental

deliberate ❷ ADJECTIVE
careful and not hurried • *His movements were gentle and deliberate.*
careful • *The trip needs careful planning.*
cautious • *a cautious approach*
measured • *walking at the same measured pace*
methodical • *Da Vinci was methodical in his research.*

ANTONYM
- casual

deliberate ❸ VERB
to think carefully about something

a
b
c
d
e
f
g
h
i
j
k
l
m
n
o
p
q
r
s
t
u
v
w
x
y
z

Can't find the word you're looking for? Try the index.

• The jury deliberated for five days before reaching a verdict.

debate • He was debating whether or not he should tell her.

meditate • She meditated on the uncertainties of his future.

mull over • McLaren had been mulling over an idea to make a movie.

ponder • He was pondering the problem when Phillipson drove up.

reflect • I reflected on the child's future.

delicious ADJECTIVE

tasting very nice • a wide selection of delicious meals

appetizing • the appetizing smell of freshly baked bread

delectable • delectable wine

luscious • luscious fruit

tasty • The food was very tasty.

MORE SYNONYMS
- ambrosial
- mouthwatering
- scrumptious

delight ❶ NOUN

great pleasure or joy • To my great delight, it worked.

glee • His victory was greeted with glee by his supporters.

happiness • Our happiness at being reunited knew no bounds.

joy • the joys of being a parent

pleasure • the pleasure of seeing her face

rapture • gasps of rapture

satisfaction • I felt a glow of satisfaction at my achievement.

delight ❷ VERB

to give someone great pleasure • The report has delighted environmentalists.

amuse • a selection of toys to amuse your baby

captivate • captivated the world with her radiant looks

charm • He charmed his landlady, chatting and flirting with her.

enchant • Dena was enchanted by the house.

please • It pleased him to talk to her.

thrill • The electric atmosphere thrilled him.

demand VERB

to need or require something • This situation demands hard work.

involve • Running a kitchen involves a great deal of discipline.

need • a problem that needs careful handling

require • Then he'll know what's required of him.

take • Walking across the room took all her strength.

want • The windows wanted cleaning.

MORE SYNONYMS
- call for
- entail
- necessitate

deny ❶ VERB

to say that something is untrue • She denied both accusations.

contradict • Her version contradicted the Government's claim.

refute • He angrily refutes the charge.

MORE SYNONYMS
- abjure
- disavow
- disclaim
- gainsay
- rebut
- repudiate

Can't find the word you're looking for? Try the index.

ANTONYM
- admit

deny ❷ VERB

to refuse to believe something
• *He denied the existence of God.*
reject • *children who rejected their parents' religious beliefs*
renounce • *after she renounced terrorism*

deny ❸ VERB

to refuse to give something • *His ex-partner denies him access to the children.*
refuse • *The council had refused permission for the march.*
withhold • *Financial aid for Russia has been withheld.*

department NOUN

a section of an organization • *the marketing department*
division • *the bank's Latin American division*
office • *Contact your local tax office.*
section • *a top-secret section of the Foreign Office*
unit • *the health services research unit*

depend ❶ VERB

to rely on • *You can depend on me.*
bank on • *The government is banking on the Olympics to save the city money.*
count on • *I can always count on you to cheer me up.*
rely on • *They can always be relied on to turn up.*
trust • *I knew I could trust him to meet a tight deadline.*

depend ❷ VERB

to be affected by • *Success depends on the quality of the workforce.*
be determined by • *Social status is largely determined by occupation.*
hinge on • *Victory or defeat hinged on her final putt.*

MORE SYNONYMS
- be subject to
- hang on
- rest on

deposit VERB

to put down or leave somewhere
• *The barman deposited a bottle in front of him.*
drop • *He dropped me outside the hotel.*
lay • *The table was spread with a cloth, and the box was laid on top.*
leave • *Leave your key with a neighbour.*
place • *I placed the book on the counter.*
put down • *Mishka put down her heavy shopping bag.*

derelict ADJECTIVE

abandoned and in poor condition
• *a derelict warehouse*
abandoned • *a network of abandoned mines*
dilapidated • *a dilapidated castle*
neglected • *a neglected garden*
ruined • *a ruined church*

descend VERB

to move downwards • *as we descend to the cellar*
dip • *The sun dipped below the horizon.*
dive • *The shark dived down and under the boat.*
fall • *Bombs fell in the town.*
go down • *after the sun has gone down*
plummet • *as the plane plummeted through the air*
sink • *A fresh egg will sink and an old egg will float.*

a b c **d** e f g h i j k l m n o p q r s t u v w x y z

Can't find the word you're looking for? Try the index.

A
B
C
D
E
F
G
H
I
J
K
L
M
N
O
P
Q
R
S
T
U
V
W
X
Y
Z

ANTONYM
- ascend

describe VERB
to give an account of something
• We asked her to describe what she did in her spare time.
define • Culture can be defined in many ways.
depict • a novel depicting a gloomy, futuristic America
portray • a writer who accurately portrays provincial life

MORE SYNONYMS
- characterize
- detail

deserve VERB
to have a right to something
• He deserves a rest.
be entitled to • She is entitled to feel proud.
be worthy of • The bank might think you're worthy of a loan.
earn • You've earned this holiday.
justify • The decision was fully justified by economic conditions.
merit • Such ideas merit careful consideration.
warrant • no evidence to warrant a murder investigation

design ❶ VERB
to make a plan of something
• They wanted to design a machine that was both attractive and practical.
draft • The legislation was drafted by Democrats.
draw up • a working party to draw up a formal agreement
plan • when we plan road construction

design ❷ NOUN
a plan or drawing • his design for a new office

model • an architect's model of a wooden house
plan • when you have drawn a plan of the garden

MORE SYNONYMS
- blueprint
- schema

design ❸ NOUN
the shape or style of something
• a new design of clock
form • the form of the human body
pattern • a pattern of coloured dots
shape • a kidney shape
style • Several styles of hat were available.

desire ❶ VERB
to want something • We can stay longer if you desire.
crave • I crave her approval.
fancy • She fancied living in Canada.
long for • He longed for the winter to be over.
want • I want a drink.
wish • We wished to return.
yearn • He yearned to sleep.

MORE SYNONYMS
- ache for
- covet

desire ❷ NOUN
a feeling of wanting something
• I had a strong desire to help people
appetite • She had lost her appetite for air travel.
craving • a craving for sugar
hankering • a hankering to be an actress
longing • her longing to return home
wish • Her wish is to be in films.
yearning • a yearning for a child or my own

Can't find the word you're looking for? Try the index.

yen (INFORMAL) • *Mike had a yen to try cycling.*

despair ❶ NOUN
a loss of hope • *feelings of despair*
dejection • *There was an air of dejection about her.*
despondency • *There's a mood of despondency in the country.*
gloom • *the deepening gloom over the economy*
hopelessness • *She had a feeling of hopelessness about the future.*

despair ❷ VERB
to lose hope • *I despair at the attitude with which their work is received.*
feel dejected • *Everyone has days when they feel dejected.*
feel despondent • *John often felt despondent after visiting the job centre.*
lose heart • *He appealed to his countrymen not to lose heart.*
lose hope • *You mustn't lose hope.*

despite PREPOSITION
in spite of • *He fell asleep despite all the coffee he'd drunk.*
in spite of • *In spite of all the gossip, Virginia stayed behind.*
notwithstanding (FORMAL) • *Notwithstanding his age, Sikorski had an important job.*
regardless of • *He led from the front, regardless of the danger.*

destroy VERB
to ruin something completely • *The building was completely destroyed.*
annihilate • *The lava annihilates everything in its path.*
demolish • *A storm moved over the island, demolishing buildings.*
devastate • *A fire had devastated*

large parts of Windsor castle.
obliterate • *Whole villages were obliterated by fire.*
raze • *The town was razed to the ground during the occupation.*
ruin • *My wife was ruining her health through worry.*
wreck • *the injuries which nearly wrecked his career*

destruction NOUN
the act of destroying something • *the destruction of the ozone layer*
annihilation • *Leaders fear the annihilation of their people.*
demolition • *the demolition of an old bridge*
devastation • *A huge bomb blast brought chaos and devastation.*
obliteration • *the obliteration of three rainforests*

detail NOUN
an individual feature of something • *We discussed every detail of the performance.*
aspect • *Climate affects every aspect of our lives.*
element • *one of the key elements of the peace plan*
particular • *You will find all the particulars in Chapter 9.*
point • *Many of the points in the report are correct.*
respect • *At least in this respect we are equals.*

MORE SYNONYMS
● fine point
● nicety

determination NOUN
a firm decision to do something • *the government's determination to beat inflation*
perseverance • *Adam's perseverance proved worthwhile.*

Can't find the word you're looking for? Try the index.

a b c **d** e f g h i j k l m n o p q r s t u v w x y z

A
B
C
D
E
F
G
H
I
J
K
L
M
N
O
P
Q
R
S
T
U
V
W
X
Y
Z

persistence • *She was determined to be a doctor and her persistence paid off.*
resolution • *She acted with resolution and courage.*
resolve (FORMAL) • *the American public's resolve to go to war if necessary*
tenacity • *Hard work and sheer tenacity are crucial to career success.*

MORE SYNONYMS
- doggedness
- single-mindedness
- steadfastness
- willpower

determine ❶ VERB
to cause or control a situation or result • *The size of the chicken pieces will determine the cooking time.*
control • *Scientists may soon be able to control the ageing process.*
decide • *The results will decide if he will win a place on the course.*
dictate • *A number of factors will dictate how long the tree will survive.*
govern • *the rules governing eligibility for unemployment benefit*
shape • *the role of key leaders in shaping the future of Europe*

determine ❷ VERB
to decide or settle something firmly • *The final wording had not yet been determined.*
arrange • *It was arranged that the party would gather in the Royal Garden Hotel.*
choose • *Houston was chosen as the site for the convention.*
decide • *Her age would be taken into account when deciding her sentence.*
fix • *The date of the election was fixed.*
resolve • *She resolved to report the matter to the authorities.*

settle • *That's settled then. We'll do it tomorrow.*

determine ❸ VERB
to find out the facts about something • *The investigation will determine what really happened.*
ascertain (FORMAL) • *We need to ascertain the true facts.*
confirm • *X-rays have confirmed that he has not broken any bones.*
discover • *It was difficult for us to discover the reason for the decision.*
establish • *an autopsy to establish the cause of death*
find out • *one family's campaign to find out the truth*
verify • *A clerk verifies that the payment and invoice amount match.*

determined ADJECTIVE
firmly decided • *She was determined not to repeat her error.*
bent on • *They seem bent on destroying the city.*
dogged • *dogged persistence*
intent on • *He is intent on repeating his victory.*
persistent • *He phoned again this morning. He's very persistent.*
purposeful • *She had a purposeful air.*
resolute (FORMAL) • *a decisive and resolute leader*
single-minded • *a single-minded determination to win*
tenacious • *a tenacious and persistent interviewer*

MORE SYNONYMS
- steadfast
- unflinching
- unwavering

develop ❶ VERB
to grow or become more advanced • *Children develop at different rates.*

advance • *tracing how medical technology has advanced to its present state*
evolve • *As scientific knowledge evolves, beliefs change.*
grow • *The boys grew into men.*
mature • *Other changes occur as the child matures physically.*
progress • *His disease progressed quickly.*
result • *Ignore the warnings and illness could result.*
spring • *His anger sprang from his childhood suffering.*

develop ② VERB
to become affected by an illness or fault • *He developed pneumonia.*
catch • *to catch a cold*
contract (FORMAL) • *He contracted AIDS from a blood transfusion.*
fall ill • *She fell ill with measles.*
get • *When I was five I got mumps.*
go down with • *Three members of the band went down with flu.*
pick up • *They've picked up an infection from something they've eaten.*
succumb • *I was determined not to succumb to the virus.*

devious ADJECTIVE
getting what you want by sly methods • *a devious politician*
calculating • *a calculating businessman*
scheming • *He was branded a "scheming liar".*
underhand • *He used underhand tactics to win the election.*
wily • *a wily old statesman*

devoted ADJECTIVE
very loving and loyal • *a devoted father*
constant • *her constant companion*
dedicated • *dedicated followers of classical music*

doting • *His doting parents bought him a racing bike.*
faithful • *I'm very faithful when I love someone.*
loving • *Jim was a loving husband.*
loyal • *a loyal friend*
true • *David was true to his wife.*

dictionary NOUN

PARTS OF A DICTIONARY OR THESAURUS	
antonym	homophone
definition	pronunciation
entry	root word
example	synonym
homonym	word derivation

die ① VERB
to stop living • *My mother died of cancer.*
cark it (AUSTRALIAN AND NEW ZEALAND; INFORMAL) • *You think you're about to cark it.*
expire (FORMAL) • *before he finally expired*
pass away • *He passed away last year.*
pass on • *My mother passed on four years ago.*
perish (FORMAL) • *the ferry disaster in which 193 passengers perished*

die ② VERB
to fade away • *My love for you will never die.*
fade away • *With time, they said, the pain will fade away.*
fade out • *Thanks to supermarkets, the corner shop is gradually fading out.*
peter out • *The six-month strike seemed to be petering out.*

die out VERB
to cease to exist • *That custom has died out now.*

a
b
c
d
e
f
g
h
i
j
k
l
m
n
o
p
q
r
s
t
u
v
w
x
y
z

Can't find the word you're looking for? Try the index.

A
B
C
D
E
F
G
H
I
J
K
L
M
N
O
P
Q
R
S
T
U
V
W
X
Y
Z

disappear • *Huge areas of the countryside are disappearing.*
fade • *Prospects for peace had already started to fade.*
vanish • *those species which have vanished*

difference ❶ NOUN
a lack of similarity between things • *the vast difference in size*
contrast • *the real contrast between the two poems*
discrepancy • *discrepancies between their statements*
disparity • *disparities between poor and wealthy districts*
distinction • *a distinction between the body and the soul*
divergence • *There's a substantial divergence of opinion within the party.*
variation • *a wide variation in the prices charged*

ANTONYM
● similarity

difference ❷ NOUN
the amount by which two quantities differ • *The difference is 8532.*
balance • *They were due to pay the balance on delivery.*
remainder • *They own a 75% stake. The remainder is owned by the bank.*

different ❶ ADJECTIVE
unlike something else • *We have totally different views.*
contrasting • *painted in contrasting colours*
disparate (FORMAL) • *The republics are very disparate in size and wealth.*
dissimilar • *His methods were not dissimilar to those used by Freud.*
divergent (FORMAL) • *divergent opinions*
opposed • *two opposed ideologies*

unlike • *This was a foreign country, so unlike San Jose.*

MORE SYNONYMS
● at odds
● at variance

ANTONYM
● similar

different ❷ ADJECTIVE
unusual and out of the ordinary • *The result is interesting and different.*
special • *a special variety of strawberry*
unique • *Each person's signature is unique.*

different ❸ ADJECTIVE
distinct and separate • *The lunch supports a different charity each year.*
another • *Her doctor referred her to another therapist.*
discrete (FORMAL) • *two discrete sets of nerves*
distinct • *A word may have two quite distinct meanings.*
individual • *Each family needs individual attention.*
separate • *The word 'quarter' has two completely separate meanings.*

difficult ❶ ADJECTIVE
not easy to do or solve • *a difficult decision to make*
arduous • *a long, arduous journey*
demanding • *a demanding job*
hard • *He found it hard to get work.*
intractable (FORMAL) • *an intractable problem*
laborious • *a laborious task*
uphill • *an uphill battle*

MORE SYNONYMS
● knotty
● problematic
● thorny

Can't find the word you're looking for? Try the index.

ANTONYM
- easy

difficult ❷ ADJECTIVE
not easy to deal with • *I hope she isn't going to be difficult.*
demanding • *a demanding child*
troublesome • *a troublesome teenager*
trying • *The whole business has been very trying.*

MORE SYNONYMS
- obstreperous
- refractory
- unmanageable

difficulty ❶ NOUN
a problem • *The central difficulty is his drinking.*
complication • *An added complication is the growing concern for the environment.*
hassle (INFORMAL) • *all the usual hassles at the airport*
hurdle • *preparing a CV, the first hurdle in a job search*
obstacle • *To succeed, you must learn to overcome obstacles.*
pitfall • *the pitfalls of working abroad*
problem • *He left home because of family problems.*
snag • *The only snag was that he had no transport.*
trouble • *What seems to be the trouble?*

MORE SYNONYMS
- impediment
- stumbling block

difficulty ❷ NOUN
the quality of being difficult • *the difficulty of the problem*
hardship • *economic hardship*
strain • *the stresses and strains of a busy career*
tribulation (FORMAL) • *the trials*

and tribulations of everyday life

MORE SYNONYMS
- arduousness
- laboriousness

dig ❶ VERB
to break up soil or sand • *He dug a hole in the ground.*
burrow • *The larvae burrow into cracks in the floor.*
excavate • *A contractor was hired to excavate soil from the area.*
gouge • *quarries which have gouged great holes in the hills*
hollow out • *They hollowed out crude dwellings from the soft rock.*
quarry • *The caves are quarried for cement.*
till • *freshly tilled fields*
tunnel • *The rebels tunnelled out of jail.*

dig ❷ VERB
to push something in • *He could feel the beads digging into his palm.*
jab • *A needle was jabbed into the baby's arm.*
poke • *She poked a fork into the turkey skin.*
thrust • *She thrust her hand into the sticky mess.*

dig ❸ NOUN
a push or poke • *She silenced him with a dig in the ribs.*
jab • *a swift jab in the stomach*
poke • *a playful poke in the arm*
prod • *He gave the donkey a prod in the backside.*
thrust • *knife thrusts*

dim ❶ ADJECTIVE
not bright or well-lit • *a dim outline of a small boat*
dark • *a dark corridor*
dull • *The stamp was a dark, dull blue.*

Can't find the word you're looking for? Try the index.

a b c **d** e f g h i j k l m n o p q r s t u v w x y z

grey • *a grey, wet, April Sunday*
murky • *one murky November afternoon*
poorly lit • *a poorly lit road*
shadowy • *a shadowy corner*

dim ➋ ADJECTIVE

vague or unclear • *a dim memory*
faint • *a faint recollection*
hazy • *Many details remain hazy.*
indistinct • *the indistinct murmur of voices*
obscure • *The origin of the custom is obscure.*
shadowy • *the shadowy world of spies*
vague • *I have a vague memory of shots being fired.*

MORE SYNONYMS

- fuzzy
- ill-defined
- indistinguishable

ANTONYM

- clear

dim ➌ ADJECTIVE (INFORMAL)

slow to understand • *He is rather dim.*
dumb (INFORMAL) • *I've met a lot of dumb people.*
obtuse • *I've really been very obtuse.*
slow • *He got hit on the head and he's been a bit slow since.*
stupid • *How could I have been so stupid?*
thick (INFORMAL) • *I must have seemed incredibly thick.*

ANTONYM

- bright

diminish VERB

to reduce or become reduced • *The threat of war has diminished.*
contract • *Output fell last year and is expected to contract further.*
decrease • *Gradually decrease the amount of vitamin C you are taking.*
lessen • *The attention he gets will lessen when the new baby is born.*
lower • *This drug lowers cholesterol levels.*
reduce • *It reduces the risk of heart disease.*
shrink • *the entertainment giant's intention to shrink its interest in the venture*
weaken • *The Prime Minister's authority has been fatally weakened.*

dinkum ADJECTIVE (AUSTRALIAN AND NEW ZEALAND; INFORMAL)

genuine or right • *a fair dinkum bloke with no pretensions*
genuine • *If this offer is genuine I will gladly accept.*
guileless • *She was so guileless that he had to believe her.*
honest • *My dad was the most honest man I ever met.*
sincere • *a sincere desire to reform*

direct ➊ ADJECTIVE

in a straight line or with nothing in between • *the direct route*
first-hand • *She has little first-hand knowledge of Quebec.*
immediate • *his immediate superior*
personal • *I have no personal experience of this.*
straight • *Keep the boat in a straight line.*
uninterrupted • *an uninterrupted view*

ANTONYM

- indirect

direct ➋ ADJECTIVE

open and honest • *He can be very direct sometimes.*

Can't find the word you're looking for? Try the index.

blunt • *She is blunt about her personal life.*
candid • *I haven't been completely candid with you.*
forthright • *forthright language*
frank • *She is always very frank.*
straight • *He never gives you a straight answer.*
straightforward • *his straightforward manner*

ANTONYM
● devious

direct ❸ VERB
to control and guide something • *Christopher will direct day-to-day operations.*
control • *He now controls the entire company.*
guide • *He should have let his instinct guide him.*
lead • *He led the country between 1949 and 1984.*
manage • *Within two years he was managing the store.*
oversee • *an architect to oversee the work*
run • *Is this any way to run a country?*
supervise • *I supervise the packing of all mail orders.*

direction ❶ NOUN
the line in which something is moving • *ten miles in the opposite direction*
course • *The captain altered course.*
path • *He stepped into the path of a reversing car.*
route • *We took the wrong route.*
way • *Does anybody know the way to the bathroom?*

direction ❷ NOUN
control and guidance of something • *He was chopping vegetables under the chef's direction.*
charge • *A few years ago he took charge of the company.*
command • *In 1942 he took command of 108 Squadron.*
control • *The restructuring involves Ronson giving up control of the company.*
guidance • *the reports which were produced under his guidance*
leadership • *The agency doubled in size under her leadership.*
management • *The zoo needed better management.*

dirt ❶ NOUN
dust or mud • *I started to scrub off the dirt.*
dust • *The furniture was covered in dust.*
filth • *tons of filth and sewage*
grime • *Kelly got the grime off his hands.*
muck • *This congealed muck was interfering with the filter.*
mud • *Their lorry got stuck in the mud.*

dirt ❷ NOUN
earth or soil • *He drew a circle in the dirt with the stick.*
earth • *a huge pile of earth*
soil • *an area with very good soil*

dirty ❶ ADJECTIVE
marked with dirt • *The kids have got their clothes dirty.*
filthy • *a pair of filthy jeans*
grimy • *a grimy industrial city*
grubby • *kids with grubby faces*
mucky • *a mucky floor*
muddy • *his muddy boots*
soiled • *a soiled white apron*
unclean • *unclean water*

ANTONYM
● clean

a
b
c
d
e
f
g
h
i
j
k
l
m
n
o
p
q
r
s
t
u
v
w
x
y
z

Can't find the word you're looking for? Try the index.

A
B
C
D
E
F
G
H
I
J
K
L
M
N
O
P
Q
R
S
T
U
V
W
X
Y
Z

dirty ❷ ADJECTIVE
unfair or dishonest • *a dirty fight*
corrupt • *corrupt practices*
crooked • *crooked business deals*

ANTONYM
● honest

dirty ❸ ADJECTIVE
sexually explicit • *a dirty joke*
blue • *a blue movie*
filthy • *a filthy book*
pornographic • *pornographic videos*
rude • *a rude joke*

MORE SYNONYMS
● risqué
● salacious
● smutty

disadvantage NOUN
an unfavourable circumstance
• *the advantages and disadvantages of allowing their soldiers to marry*
drawback • *The apartment's only drawback was that it was too small.*
handicap • *The tax issue was undoubtedly a handicap to Labour.*
minus • *The plusses and minuses were about equal.*
weakness • *the strengths and weaknesses of the argument*

MORE SYNONYMS
● downside
● hindrance

ANTONYM
● advantage

disagree ❶ VERB
to have a different opinion • *They can communicate even when they disagree.*
differ • *They differ on lots of issues.*
dispute • *Nobody disputed that Davey was clever.*
dissent • *dissenting views*

ANTONYM
● agree

disagree ❷ VERB
to think that something is wrong
• *I disagree with drug laws in general.*
object • *We objected strongly but were outvoted.*
oppose • *protesters opposing nuclear tests*
take issue with • *I take issue with much of what he said.*

disagreeable ADJECTIVE
unpleasant in some way • *a disagreeable odour*
horrible • *a horrible small boy*
horrid • *What a horrid smell!*
nasty • *What a nasty little snob you are!*
objectionable • *an objectionable, stuck-up young woman*
obnoxious • *One of the parents was a most obnoxious character.*
unfriendly • *She spoke in a loud, rather unfriendly voice.*
unpleasant • *The side-effects can be unpleasant.*

ANTONYM
● agreeable

disagreement ❶ NOUN
a dispute about something • *My driving instructor and I had a brief disagreement.*
altercation (FORMAL) • *an altercation with the referee*
argument • *an argument about money*
difference • *We have our differences but we get along.*
dispute • *a pay dispute*
quarrel • *I had a terrible quarrel with my brother.*
row • *a major diplomatic row*

Can't find the word you're looking for? Try the index.

squabble · *minor squabbles about phone bills*
tiff · *a lovers' tiff*

ANTONYM
● agreement

disagreement ❷ NOUN
an objection to something
· *Britain and France have expressed some disagreement with the proposal.*
dissent · *voices of dissent*
objection · *I have no objection to banks making money.*
opposition · *their opposition to the scheme*

disappear ❶ VERB
to go out of sight · *The aircraft disappeared off the radar.*
be lost to view · *They observed the comet for 70 days before it was lost to view.*
drop out of sight · *After his first film he dropped out of sight.*
fade · *We watched the harbour fade into the mist.*
recede · *Luke receded into the distance.*
vanish · *Anne vanished from outside her home the Wednesday before last.*

ANTONYM
● appear

disappear ❷ VERB
to stop existing · *The pain has finally disappeared.*
cease (FORMAL) · *At 1 o'clock the rain ceased.*
die out · *How did the dinosaurs die out?*
go away · *All she wanted was for the pain to go away.*
melt away · *His anger melted away.*

pass · *He told her the fear would pass.*
vanish · *species which have vanished*

disappointed ADJECTIVE
sad because something has not happened · *I was disappointed that Kluge was not there.*
dejected · *Her refusal left him feeling dejected.*
despondent · *After the interview John was despondent.*
disenchanted · *She has become very disenchanted with the marriage.*
disillusioned · *I've become very disillusioned with politics.*
downcast · *After his defeat Mr Rabin looked downcast.*
saddened · *He is saddened that they did not win anything.*

MORE SYNONYMS
● disheartened
● let down

ANTONYM
● satisfied

disappointment ❶ NOUN
a feeling of being disappointed
· *Book early to avoid disappointment.*
dejection · *There was an air of dejection about her.*
despondency · *a mood of gloom and despondency*
regret · *my one great regret in life*

MORE SYNONYMS
● disenchantment
● disillusionment

disappointment ❷ NOUN
something that disappoints you
· *The reunion was a bitter disappointment.*
blow · *It was a terrible blow when*

a
b
c
d
e
f
g
h
i
j
k
l
m
n
o
p
q
r
s
t
u
v
w
x
y
z

Can't find the word you're looking for? Try the index.

A
B
C
D
E
F
G
H
I
J
K
L
M
N
O
P
Q
R
S
T
U
V
W
X
Y
Z

he was made redundant.
setback • *a setback for the peace process*

disapproval NOUN
the belief that something is wrong • *his mother's disapproval of his marriage*
censure • *He deserves support, not censure.*
condemnation • *the universal condemnation of French nuclear tests*
criticism • *actions which have attracted fierce criticism*

ANTONYM
● approval

disapprove VERB
to think that something is wrong • *Everyone disapproved of their marrying so young.*
condemn • *Political leaders condemned the speech.*
deplore (FORMAL) • *He deplores violence.*
dislike • *Her father seemed to dislike all her boyfriends.*
find unacceptable • *I find such behaviour totally unacceptable.*
take a dim view of • *They took a dim view of local trade unionists.*

MORE SYNONYMS
● frown on
● take exception to

ANTONYM
● approve

disaster NOUN
a very bad accident • *another air disaster*
calamity (FORMAL) • *It could only end in calamity.*
catastrophe • *War would be a catastrophe.*

misfortune • *She seemed to enjoy the misfortunes of others.*
tragedy • *They have suffered an enormous personal tragedy.*

discard VERB
to get rid of something • *Read the instructions before discarding the box.*
cast aside • *In America we seem to cast aside our elderly people.*
dispose of • *how he disposed of the murder weapon*
dump (INFORMAL) • *The getaway car was dumped near the motorway.*
jettison • *The crew jettisoned excess fuel.*
shed • *a snake that has shed its skin*
throw away • *I never throw anything away.*
throw out • *Why don't you throw out all those old magazines?*

discern VERB (FORMAL)
to notice or understand something clearly • *trying to discern a pattern in his behaviour*
detect • *Arnold could detect a certain sadness in the old man's face.*
make out • *I could just make out a shadowy figure through the mist.*
notice • *Mrs Shedden noticed a bird sitting on the garage roof.*
observe • *In 1664 Hooke observed a reddish spot on the planet's surface.*
perceive • *Get pupils to perceive the relationship between success and effort.*
see • *Supporters saw in him a champion of the oppressed.*
spot • *I've spotted an error in your calculations.*

discharge ❶ VERB
to send something out • *The resulting salty water will be*

discharged at sea.

emit • *the amount of greenhouse gases emitted*

empty • *companies which empty toxic by-products into rivers*

expel • *Poisonous gas is expelled into the atmosphere.*

flush • *Flush out all the sewage.*

give off • *natural gas, which gives off less carbon dioxide than coal*

release • *a weapon which releases toxic nerve gas*

discharge ② VERB
to allow someone to leave hospital or prison • *He has a broken nose but may be discharged today.*

free • *The country is set to free more prisoners.*

let go • *They held him for three hours and then let him go.*

liberate • *They promised to liberate prisoners held in detention camps.*

release • *He was released on bail.*

set free • *More than ninety prisoners have been set free.*

discharge ③ VERB
to dismiss someone from a job • *He was discharged from the military.*

dismiss • *The military commander has been dismissed.*

eject • *He was ejected from his first job for persistent latecoming.*

fire (INFORMAL) • *If he wasn't so good at his job, I'd fire him.*

sack (INFORMAL) • *The teacher was sacked for slapping a schoolboy.*

discharge ④ NOUN
a sending away from a job or institution • *They face a dishonourable discharge from the Army.*

dismissal • *shock at the director's dismissal from his post*

ejection • *These actions led to his ejection from office.*

expulsion • *his expulsion from the party in 1955*

the sack (INFORMAL) • *People who make mistakes can be given the sack.*

discourage VERB
to make someone lose enthusiasm • *Don't let these problems discourage you.*

daunt • *He was not the type of man to be daunted by adversity.*

deter • *Tougher sentences would do nothing to deter crime.*

dissuade • *He considered emigrating, but his family managed to dissuade him.*

put off • *I wouldn't let it put you off applying.*

MORE SYNONYMS
● demoralize
● dishearten

ANTONYM
● encourage

discover VERB
to find something or find out about something • *He discovered that she had a brilliant mind.*

come across • *He came across the jawbone of a carnivorous dinosaur.*

find • *The police also found a pistol.*

find out • *Watch the next episode to find out what happens.*

learn • *The Admiral, on learning who I was, wanted to meet me.*

realize • *As soon as we realized something was wrong, we took action.*

stumble on or **stumble across** • *They stumbled on a magnificent waterfall.*

unearth • *Researchers have unearthed documents implicating her in the crime.*

discuss VERB

to talk about something • *I will be discussing the situation with colleagues tomorrow.*

debate • *The UN Security Council will debate the issue today.*

exchange views on • *They exchanged views on a wide range of subjects.*

go into • *We didn't go into that.*

talk about • *What did you talk about?*

discussion NOUN

a talk about something • *informal discussions*

consultation • *consultations between lawyers*

conversation • *I struck up a conversation with him.*

debate • *There has been a lot of debate among scholars about this.*

dialogue • *a direct dialogue between the two nations*

discourse • *a long tradition of political discourse*

talk • *We had a long talk about it.*

disgrace ❶ NOUN

lack of respect • *She has brought disgrace upon the whole team.*

scandal • *They often abandoned their children because of fear of scandal.*

shame • *I don't want to bring shame on the family name.*

MORE SYNONYMS
- discredit
- dishonour

ANTONYM
- credit

disgrace ❷ VERB

to bring shame upon • *I have disgraced my family's name.*

discredit • *He said such methods discredited the communist fight worldwide.*

shame • *I wouldn't shame my father by doing that.*

disgraceful ADJECTIVE

deserving of shame • *disgraceful behaviour*

scandalous • *a scandalous waste of money*

shameful • *the most shameful episode in US naval history*

shocking • *a shocking invasion of privacy*

MORE SYNONYMS
- discreditable
- dishonourable

disgust ❶ NOUN

a strong feeling of dislike • *his disgust at the incident*

nausea • *I was overcome with a feeling of nausea.*

repulsion • *a shudder of repulsion*

revulsion • *They expressed their shock and revulsion at his death.*

disgust ❷ VERB

to cause someone to feel disgust • *He disgusted many with his behaviour.*

repel • *a violent excitement that frightened and repelled her*

revolt • *The smell revolted him.*

sicken • *What he saw there sickened him.*

MORE SYNONYMS
- nauseate
- turn your stomach

disgusting ADJECTIVE

very unpleasant or unacceptable • *one of the most disgusting sights I had ever seen*

foul • *a foul stench*

gross • *Don't be so gross!*

Can't find the word you're looking for? Try the index.

obnoxious • *a most obnoxious character*
repellent • *a very large, repellent toad*
revolting • *The smell was revolting.*
sickening • *a sickening attack on a pregnant woman*
vile • *a vile odour*

MORE SYNONYMS
● nauseating
● repugnant

dishonest ADJECTIVE
not truthful • *It would be dishonest to mislead people.*
corrupt • *corrupt police officers*
crooked • *crooked business deals*
deceitful • *The ambassador called the report deceitful and misleading.*
fraudulent • *fraudulent claims about being a nurse*
lying • *He called her "a lying little twit".*

MORE SYNONYMS
● mendacious
● untruthful

ANTONYM
● honest

dishonesty NOUN
dishonest behaviour • *She accused the government of dishonesty.*
cheating • *He was accused of cheating.*
corruption • *The President faces 54 charges of corruption.*
deceit • *the deceit and lies of the past*
trickery • *They resorted to trickery in order to impress their clients.*

MORE SYNONYMS
● duplicity
● fraudulence
● mendacity

ANTONYM
● honesty

disintegrate VERB
to break into many pieces • *At 420 mph the windscreen disintegrated.*
break up • *There was a danger of the ship breaking up completely.*
crumble • *The flint crumbled into fragments.*
fall apart • *Bit by bit the building fell apart.*
fall to pieces • *The radio handset fell to pieces.*
fragment • *The clouds fragmented and out came the sun.*

dislike ❶ VERB
to consider something unpleasant • *We don't serve it often because many people dislike it.*
abhor (FORMAL) • *a man who abhorred violence*
be averse to • *He's not averse to a little publicity.*
detest • *Jean detested being photographed.*
hate • *Most people hate him.*
loathe • *a play loathed by the critics*
not be able to abide • *I can't abide liars.*
not be able to bear • *I can't bear people who speak like that.*
not be able to stand • *He can't stand the sound of her voice.*

ANTONYM
● like

dislike ❷ NOUN
a feeling of not liking something • *She looked at him with dislike.*
animosity • *The animosity between the two men grew.*
antipathy • *their antipathy to my smoking*

a
b
c
d
e
f
g
h
i
j
k
l
m
n
o
p
q
r
s
t
u
v
w
x
y
z

Can't find the word you're looking for? Try the index.

A
B
C
D
E
F
G
H
I
J
K
L
M
N
O
P
Q
R
S
T
U
V
W
X
Y
Z

aversion • *I've always had an aversion to being part of a group.*
distaste • *Roger looked at her with distaste.*
hatred • *her hatred of authority*
hostility • *hostility to ethnic groups*
loathing • *He made no secret of his loathing of her.*

ANTONYM
● liking

disobey VERB
to deliberately refuse to follow instructions • *He was forever disobeying the rules.*
break • *drivers breaking speed limits*
defy • *the first time that I dared to defy my mother*
flout • *illegal campers who persist in flouting the law*
infringe • *He was adamant that he had infringed no rules.*
violate • *They violated the ceasefire agreement.*

MORE SYNONYMS
● contravene (FORMAL)
● transgress

ANTONYM
● obey

disorder ❶ NOUN
a state of untidiness • *Inside, all was disorder.*
clutter • *She prefers the worktop to be free of clutter.*
disarray • *Her clothes were in disarray.*
muddle • *a general muddle of pencils and boxes*

ANTONYM
● order

disorder ❷ NOUN
a lack of organization • *The men fled in disorder.*

chaos • *Their concerts often ended in chaos.*
confusion • *There was confusion when a man fired shots.*
disarray • *The nation is in disarray following rioting.*
turmoil • *the political turmoil of 1989*

disorder ❸ NOUN
a disease or illness • *a rare nerve disorder*
affliction • *an affliction which can ruin a young man's life*
complaint • *a common skin complaint*
condition • *a heart condition*
disease • *heart disease*
illness • *mental illness*

dispose of VERB
to get rid of something • *Fold up the nappy and dispose of it.*
discard • *Read the instructions before discarding the box.*
dispense with • *We got a CD-player and dispensed with our old-fashioned record-player.*
dump • *The government declared that it did not dump radioactive waste at sea.*
get rid of • *The owner needs to get rid of the car for financial reasons.*
jettison • *The crew jettisoned excess fuel and made an emergency landing.*
throw away • *I never throw anything away.*

disprove VERB
to show that something is not true • *the statistics that will prove or disprove the hypothesis*
discredit • *There would be difficulties in discrediting the evidence.*
give the lie to • *This survey gives*

Can't find the word you're looking for? Try the index.

the lie to the idea that the economy is recovering.
invalidate • *Some of the other criticisms were invalidated years ago.*
prove false • *It is hard to prove such claims false.*
refute • *the kind of rumour that is impossible to refute*

ANTONYM
- prove

dispute ❶ NOUN
an argument • *The dispute between them is settled.*
argument • *a heated argument*
clash • *the clash between trade union leaders and the government*
conflict • *Avoid any conflict between yourself and your ex-partner.*
disagreement • *disagreements among the member states*
feud • *a bitter feud between the state government and the villagers*
row • *a major diplomatic row with France*
wrangle • *a legal wrangle*

dispute ❷ VERB
to question something's truth or wisdom • *He disputed the allegations.*
challenge • *I challenge the wisdom of this decision.*
contest • *Your former employer wants to contest the case.*
contradict • *Her version contradicted the Government's claim.*
deny • *She denied both accusations.*
query • *No one queried my decision.*
question • *It never occurred to me to question the doctor's diagnosis.*

ANTONYM
- accept

distant ❶ ADJECTIVE
far away in space or time
• *a distant land*
far • *Is it very far?*
outlying • *outlying districts*
out-of-the-way • *an out-of-the-way spot*
remote • *a remote village*

MORE SYNONYMS
- faraway
- far-flung
- far-off

ANTONYM
- close

distant ❷ ADJECTIVE
cold and unfriendly • *He is polite but distant.*
aloof • *He seemed aloof and detached.*
detached • *He observed me with a detached curiosity.*
reserved • *She's quite a reserved person.*
withdrawn • *Her husband had become withdrawn and moody.*

MORE SYNONYMS
- standoffish
- unapproachable

ANTONYM
- friendly

distinguish ❶ VERB
to see the difference between things • *Could he distinguish right from wrong?*
differentiate • *At this age your baby cannot differentiate one person from another.*
discriminate • *He is unable to discriminate a good idea from a terrible one.*

a
b
c
d
e
f
g
h
i
j
k
l
m
n
o
p
q
r
s
t
u
v
w
x
y
z

Can't find the word you're looking for? Try the index.

A
B
C
D
E
F
G
H
I
J
K
L
M
N
O
P
Q
R
S
T
U
V
W
X
Y
Z

tell • *How do you tell one from another?*
tell apart • *I can only tell them apart by the colour of their shoes.*
tell the difference • *I can't tell the difference between their policies and ours.*

distinguish ❷ VERB
to recognize something • *I heard shouting but was unable to distinguish the words.*
discern • *We could just discern a narrow ditch.*
make out • *He couldn't make out what she was saying.*
pick out • *Through my binoculars I picked out a group of figures.*
recognize • *He did not think she could recognize his car in the snow.*

distract VERB
to stop someone from concentrating • *Playing video games distracts him from his homework.*
divert • *They want to divert our attention from the real issues.*
draw away • *to draw attention away from the crime*

MORE SYNONYMS
● sidetrack
● turn aside

distress ❶ NOUN
great suffering • *Jealousy causes distress and painful emotions.*
heartache • *the heartache of her divorce*
pain • *eyes that seemed filled with pain*
sorrow • *a time of great sorrow*
suffering • *to put an end to his suffering*

distress ❷ NOUN
the state of needing help • *The ship might be in distress.*

difficulty • *rumours about banks being in difficulty*
need • *When you were in need, I loaned you money.*
straits • *The company's closure left them in desperate financial straits.*
trouble • *a charity that helps women in trouble*

distress ❸ VERB
to cause someone unhappiness • *Her death had profoundly distressed me.*
bother • *It bothered me that boys weren't interested in me.*
disturb • *dreams so vivid that they disturb me for days*
grieve • *It grieved her to be separated from her son.*
pain • *It pains me to think of you struggling all alone.*
sadden • *The cruelty in the world saddens me deeply.*
trouble • *He was troubled by the lifestyle of his son.*
upset • *I'm sorry if I've upset you.*
worry • *I didn't want to worry you.*

distribute ❶ VERB
to hand something out • *They publish and distribute brochures.*
circulate • *He has circulated a discussion document.*
hand out • *One of my jobs was to hand out the prizes.*
pass around • *Sweets were being passed around.*
pass round • *She passed her holiday photos round.*

distribute ❷ VERB
to spread something through an area • *Distribute the topping evenly over the fruit.*
diffuse • *Interest in books is more widely diffused than ever.*
disperse • *The leaflets were*

dispersed throughout the country.
scatter • *She scattered the petals over the grave.*
spread • *A thick layer of wax was spread over the surface.*

distribute ❸ VERB
to divide and share something • *Distribute chores evenly among all family members.*
allocate • *funds allocated for nursery education*
allot • *The seats are allotted to the candidates who have won the most votes.*
dispense (FORMAL) • *The Union had already dispensed £400 in grants.*
divide • *Paul divides his spare time between the bedroom and the study.*
dole out • *I got out my wallet and began to dole out the money.*
share out • *You could share out the food a bit more equally.*

MORE SYNONYMS
● apportion
● mete out

disturb ❶ VERB
to intrude on someone's peace • *She slept in a separate room so as not to disturb him.*
bother • *I'm sorry to bother you.*
disrupt • *Protesters disrupted the debate.*
intrude on • *I don't want to intrude on your parents.*

disturb ❷ VERB
to upset or worry someone • *Some scenes may disturb you.*
agitate • *The thought agitated her.*
distress • *Her death had profoundly distressed me.*
shake • *Well, it shook me quite a bit.*

trouble • *He was troubled by the lifestyle of his son.*
unsettle • *The presence of the two policemen unsettled her.*
upset • *I'm sorry if I've upset you.*
worry • *I didn't want to worry you.*

dive VERB
to jump or fall into water • *She was standing by the pool, about to dive in.*
jump • *He ran along the board and jumped in.*
leap • *as she leapt into the water*
submerge • *Hippos are unable to submerge in the few remaining water holes.*

divide ❶ VERB
to split something up • *The idea is to divide the country into four sectors.*
cut up • *Halve the tomatoes, then cut them up.*
partition • *a plan to partition the country*
segregate • *Police were used to segregate the two rival camps.*
separate • *Fluff the rice with a fork to separate the grains.*
split • *Split the chicken in half.*
split up • *He split up the company.*

ANTONYM
● join

divide ❷ VERB
to form a barrier between things • *the frontier dividing Mexico from the USA*
bisect • *The main street bisects the town.*
separate • *the fence that separated the yard from the paddock*

divide ❸ VERB
to cause people to disagree • *the enormous differences that still divide them*

Can't find the word you're looking for? Try the index.

a b c **d** e f g h i j k l m n o p q r s t u v w x y z

come between • *It's difficult to imagine anything coming between them.*
set against one another • *The case has set neighbours against one another in the village.*
split • *Women priests are accused of splitting the church.*

division ❶ NOUN
separation into parts • *the unification of Germany after its division into two states*
partition • *fighting which followed the partition of India*
separation • *the separation of church and state*

division ❷ NOUN
a disagreement • *There were divisions in the Party on economic policy.*
breach • *a serious breach in relations between the two countries*
difference of opinion • *Was there a difference of opinion over what to do with the money?*
rupture • *a rupture of the family unit*
split • *They accused both sides of trying to provoke a split in the party.*

division ❸ NOUN
a section of something • *the Research Division*
department • *the company's chemicals department*
section • *a top-secret section of the Foreign Office*
sector • *the nation's manufacturing sector*

dizzy ADJECTIVE
about to lose your balance • *He kept getting dizzy spells.*
giddy • *She felt slightly giddy.*
light-headed • *If you skip breakfast, you may feel light-headed.*

do ❶ VERB
to carry out a task • *He just didn't want to do any work.*
carry out • *Police believe the attacks were carried out by nationalists.*
execute (FORMAL) • *The landing was skilfully executed.*
perform • *people who have performed outstanding acts of bravery*
undertake • *She undertook the arduous task of monitoring the elections.*

do ❷ VERB
to be sufficient • *Home-made stock is best, but cubes will do.*
be adequate • *The western diet should be perfectly adequate for most people.*
be sufficient • *One teaspoon of sugar should be sufficient.*
suffice (FORMAL) • *Often a far shorter letter will suffice.*

do ❸ VERB
to perform well or badly • *Connie did well at school.*
fare • *Some later expeditions fared better.*
get on • *I asked him how he had got on.*
manage • *How did your mother manage after your father died?*

dodge ❶ VERB
to move out of the way • *We dodged behind a pillar out of sight of the tourists.*
duck • *I wanted to duck down and slip past but they saw me.*
swerve • *He swerved to avoid a truck.*

dodge ❷ VERB
to avoid doing something • *dodging military service by feigning illness*

Can't find the word you're looking for? Try the index.

A B C **D** E F G H I J K L M N O P Q R S T U V W X Y Z

avoid • *They managed to avoid paying their fares.*
elude • *He eluded the police for 13 years.*
evade • *by evading taxes*
get out of • *He'll do almost anything to get out of paying his share.*
shirk • *We can't shirk our responsibility.*
sidestep • *Rarely, if ever, does he sidestep a question.*

dog NOUN
an animal often kept as a pet
• *a children's book about dogs*
brak (SOUTH AFRICAN) • *a rabid brak*
canine • *a new canine was needed*
mongrel • *a rescued mongrel called Chips*
mutt (SLANG) • *the most famous mutts in the western world*
pooch (SLANG) • *Julian's pet pooch*

RELATED WORDS
● ADJECTIVE: canine
● FEMALE: bitch
● YOUNG: pup, puppy

doomed ADJECTIVE
certain to fail • *a doomed attempt to rescue the children*
condemned • *Many women are condemned to poverty.*
hopeless • *I don't believe your situation is as hopeless as you think.*
ill-fated • *his ill-fated attempt on the world record*

double ❶ ADJECTIVE
twice the usual size • *a double whisky*
twice • *Unemployment in Northern Ireland is twice the national average.*
twofold • *a twofold risk*

double ❷ ADJECTIVE
consisting of two parts • *a double album*

dual • *dual nationality*
twin • *twin beds*
twofold • *Their concern was twofold: personal and political.*

doubt ❶ NOUN
a feeling of uncertainty • *This raises doubts about the point of advertising.*
misgiving • *I had misgivings about his methods.*
qualm • *I have no qualms about recommending this approach.*
scepticism • *The report has been greeted with scepticism.*
uncertainty • *the uncertainties regarding the future funding of the company*

ANTONYM
● certainty

doubt ❷ VERB
to feel uncertain about something
• *No one doubted his ability.*
be dubious • *I was dubious about the entire proposition.*
be sceptical • *Other archaeologists are sceptical about his findings.*
query • *No one queried my decision.*
question • *It never occurs to them to question the doctor's decisions.*

ANTONYM
● believe

doubtful ADJECTIVE
unlikely or uncertain • *It is doubtful whether he will appear again.*
debatable • *Whether the Bank of England would do any better is highly debatable.*
dubious • *This claim seems to us rather dubious.*
questionable • *It is questionable whether the expenditure is justified.*

a b c d e f g h i j k l m n o p q r s t u v w x y z

uncertain • *It's uncertain whether they will accept the plan.*

ANTONYM
- certain

down ❶ ADVERB
towards the ground, or in a lower place • *We went down in the lift.*
downwards • *She gazed downwards.*
downstairs • *Denise went downstairs and made some tea.*

ANTONYM
- up

down ❷ ADJECTIVE
depressed • *He sounded really down.*
dejected • *Everyone has days when they feel dejected.*
depressed • *She's been very depressed about this situation.*
dispirited • *I left feeling utterly dispirited.*
fed up (INFORMAL) • *I'm just fed up and I don't know what to do.*
glum • *She was very glum and was missing her children.*
melancholy • *It was in the afternoon that Tom felt most melancholy.*
miserable • *My work was making me really miserable.*

MORE SYNONYMS
- despondent
- morose
- pessimistic

downfall NOUN
the failure of a person or thing • *His lack of experience had led to his downfall.*
collapse • *The medical system is facing collapse.*
fall • *the fall of the military dictator*

ruin • *Inflation has driven them to the brink of ruin.*

drab ADJECTIVE
dull and unattractive • *the same drab grey dress*
dingy • *his rather dingy office*
dismal • *a dark dismal day*
dreary • *a dreary little town*
gloomy • *the gloomy days of winter*
grey • *a New Year that will be grey and cheerless*
sombre • *a worried official in sombre black*

MORE SYNONYMS
- cheerless
- lacklustre

ANTONYM
- bright

drag VERB
to pull something along the ground • *He dragged his chair towards the table.*
draw • *He drew his chair nearer the fire.*
haul • *A crane was used to haul the car out of the stream.*
lug • *Nobody wants to lug around huge suitcases.*
tow • *They threatened to tow away my car.*
trail • *She came down the stairs slowly, trailing the coat behind her.*

drain ❶ VERB
to cause a liquid to flow somewhere • *Miners built the tunnel to drain water out of the lakes.*
draw off • *The fluid can be drawn off with a syringe.*
pump • *to get rid of raw sewage by pumping it out to sea*

drain ❷ VERB
to flow somewhere • *rivers that*

drain into lakes
discharge • *Blood was discharging from its nostrils.*
empty • *The Washougal empties into the Columbia River.*
flow • *The waters of Lake Erie now flow into the Niagara River.*
seep • *Radioactive water has seeped into underground reservoirs.*

drain ❸ VERB
to use something up • *The prolonged boardroom battle drained him of energy and money.*
consume • *plans which will consume hours of time*
exhaust • *People are now living longer and exhausting natural resources.*
sap • *The illness sapped his strength.*
tax • *Overcrowding has taxed the city's ability to deal with waste.*
use up • *They aren't the ones who use up the world's resources.*

drastic ADJECTIVE
severe and urgent • *It's time for drastic action.*
extreme • *I would rather die than do anything so extreme.*
harsh • *harsh new measures to combat drink-driving*
radical • *radical economic reforms*
severe • *a severe shortage of drinking water*

draw ❶ VERB
to make a picture • *He starts a drawing by painting simplified shapes.*
paint • *He is painting a huge volcano.*
sketch • *He sketched a map on the back of a menu.*
trace • *She learned to draw by tracing pictures out of old storybooks.*

draw ❷ VERB
to move somewhere • *as the car drew away*
move • *She moved away from the window.*
pull • *He pulled into the driveway.*

draw ❸ VERB
to pull something • *He drew his chair nearer the fire.*
drag • *He dragged his chair towards the table.*
haul • *A crane was used to haul the car out of the stream.*
pull • *a freight train pulling waggons*

drawback NOUN
a problem that makes something less than perfect • *The only drawback was that the apartment was too small.*
difficulty • *There is only one difficulty - I don't have the key.*
hitch • *It's a great idea but I can see a serious hitch.*
problem • *The main problem with the house is its inaccessibility.*
snag • *It's a great school - the snag is the fees are £9,000 a year.*
trouble • *The trouble is that he might not agree with our plans.*

dreadful ADJECTIVE
very bad or unpleasant • *He told us the dreadful news*
appalling • *living under the most appalling conditions*
atrocious • *The food here is atrocious.*
awful • *Jeans look awful on me.*
frightful • *The war had been so frightful he couldn't talk about it.*
ghastly • *a ghastly pair of shoes*
horrendous • *the most horrendous experience of his life*
terrible • *Thousands more people suffered terrible injuries.*

a
b
c
d
e
f
g
h
i
j
k
l
m
n
o
p
q
r
s
t
u
v
w
x
y
z

Can't find the word you're looking for? Try the index.

ANTONYM
- wonderful

dream ❶ NOUN
mental pictures while sleeping
• *He had a dream about Claire.*
hallucination • *The drug induces hallucinations at high doses.*
trance • *She seemed to be in a trance.*
vision • *seeing the Virgin Mary in a vision*

MORE SYNONYMS
- delusion
- reverie

dream ❷ NOUN
something that you want very much • *his dream of winning the lottery*
ambition • *His ambition is to sail round the world.*
aspiration • *one of his greatest aspirations*
daydream • *He learned to escape into daydreams of becoming a writer.*
fantasy • *fantasies of romance and true love*

MORE SYNONYMS
- Holy Grail
- pipe dream

dreary ADJECTIVE
dull or boring • *the dreary winter months*
boring • *a boring job*
drab • *The rest of the day's activities often seem drab.*
dull • *There was scarcely a dull moment.*
humdrum • *The new government seemed rather humdrum.*
monotonous • *It's monotonous work, like most factory jobs.*
tedious • *Such lists are tedious to read.*

uneventful • *her dull, uneventful life*

ANTONYM
- exciting

dress ❶ NOUN
a piece of clothing • *a black dress*
frock • *a party frock*
gown • *wedding gowns*
robe • *a fur-lined robe*

dress ❷ NOUN
clothing in general • *evening dress*
attire (FORMAL) • *women dressed in their finest attire*
clothes • *casual clothes*
clothing • *protective clothing*
costume • *women in traditional costume*
garb (FORMAL) • *his usual garb of a dark suit*

MORE SYNONYMS
- apparel
- raiment

dress ❸ VERB
to put on clothes • *a tall woman dressed in black*
attire (FORMAL) • *He was attired in a smart blue suit.*
clothe • *He lay down on the bed fully clothed.*
garb (FORMAL) • *He was garbed in sweater, jacket and boots.*

ANTONYM
- undress

drink ❶ VERB
to swallow liquid • *He drank some tea.*
gulp • *She quickly gulped her coffee.*
guzzle • *She guzzled gin and tonics like they were lemonade.*
sip • *She sipped from her coffee mug.*
swig (INFORMAL) • *I swigged down two white wines.*

Can't find the word you're looking for? Try the index.

A B C **D** E F G H I J K L M N O P Q R S T U V W X Y Z

MORE SYNONYMS
- imbibe
- quaff
- sup

drink ❷ VERB

to drink alcohol • *He drinks little and eats carefully.*

booze (INFORMAL) • *drunken businessmen who had been boozing all afternoon*

tipple • *We saw a woman tippling from the sherry bottle.*

drip ❶ VERB

to fall in small drops • *Rain dripped from the brim of his cap.*

dribble • *Sweat dribbled down his face.*

splash • *Tears splashed into her hands.*

trickle • *A tear trickled down the old man's cheek.*

drip ❷ NOUN

a small amount of a liquid • *drips of water*

bead • *beads of sweat*

drop • *a drop of blue ink*

droplet • *water droplets*

MORE SYNONYMS
- dribble
- globule

drive ❶ VERB

to operate or power a machine or vehicle • *Don't drive a car or operate heavy machinery after taking this medication.*

operate • *A rock fall trapped the men as they operated a tunnelling machine.*

pilot • *He piloted his own plane to Washington.*

power • *The flywheel's battery could be used to power an electric car.*

propel • *Attached is a tiny rocket designed to propel the spacecraft towards Mars.*

run • *I ran a Rover 100 from 1977 until 1983.*

steer • *What is it like to steer a ship this size?*

work • *I learned how to work the forklift.*

drive ❷ VERB

to force someone to do something • *Depression drove him to self-harm.*

compel • *He felt compelled to speak out against their actions.*

force • *A back injury forced her to withdraw from the tournament.*

lead • *His abhorrence of racism led him to write his first book.*

motivate • *What motivates people to behave like this?*

prompt • *The recession has prompted consumers to cut back on spending.*

push • *James did not push her into stealing the money.*

spur • *It's the money that spurs these fishermen to take such risks.*

drive ❸ VERB

to force something pointed into a surface • *I used the sledgehammer to drive the pegs in.*

hammer • *Hammer a wooden peg into the hole.*

knock • *He knocked a couple of nails into the wall.*

ram • *He rammed the stake with all his strength into the creature's heart.*

sink • *He sinks the needle into my arm.*

thrust • *thrusting a knife into his ribs*

drive ❹ NOUN

a journey in a vehicle • *We might go for a drive on Sunday.*

a b c **d** e f g h i j k l m n o p q r s t u v w x y z

Can't find the word you're looking for? Try the index.

excursion • *an excursion to a local vineyard*

jaunt • *Let's take a jaunt down to the beach.*

journey • *The journey from Manchester to Plymouth took a few hours.*

ride • *We took some friends for a ride in the family car.*

run • *We went for a run in the new car to try it out.*

spin • *I was thinking about going for a spin.*

trip • *We went on a coach trip to the seaside.*

drive ❺ NOUN

energy and determination • *He is best remembered for his drive and enthusiasm.*

ambition • *When I was young I never had any ambition.*

determination • *her natural determination to succeed*

energy • *At 54 years old, her energy is magnificent.*

enterprise • *the group's lack of enterprise*

initiative • *We were disappointed by his lack of initiative.*

motivation • *His poor performance may be attributed to lack of motivation.*

vigour • *He played with great vigour.*

drop ❶ VERB

to fall downwards • *She let her head drop.*

descend • *as the aircraft descended*

fall • *Bombs fell in the town.*

plummet • *His parachute failed to open and he plummeted to the ground.*

sink • *She sank to her knees.*

tumble • *The gun tumbled out of his hand.*

drop ❷ VERB

to become less • *Temperatures can drop to freezing at night.*

decline • *The number of staff has declined.*

decrease • *Population growth is decreasing by 1.4% each year.*

diminish • *diminishing resources*

fall • *Her weight fell to under seven stone.*

plummet • *Share prices have plummeted.*

sink • *Pay increases have sunk to around 7%.*

slump • *Net profits slumped by 41%.*

tumble • *House prices have tumbled by almost 30%.*

ANTONYM

● rise

drop ❸ NOUN

a small amount of a liquid • *a drop of blue ink*

bead • *beads of sweat*

drip • *drips of water*

droplet • *water droplets*

MORE SYNONYMS

● dribble
● globule

drug ❶ NOUN

a treatment for disease • *a new drug in the fight against AIDS*

medication • *She is not on any medication.*

medicine • *herbal medicines*

RELATED WORD

● COMBINING FORM: pharmaco-

drug ❷ NOUN

an illegal substance • *She was sure Leo was taking drugs.*

Can't find the word you're looking for? Try the index.

narcotic • *He was indicted for dealing in narcotics.*
stimulant • *the use of stimulants in sport*

drunk ❶ ADJECTIVE
having consumed too much alcohol • *I got drunk.*
babalas (SOUTH AFRICAN) • *He was babalas again last night.*
intoxicated (FORMAL) • *He appeared intoxicated.*
tipsy • *I'm feeling a bit tipsy.*

MORE SYNONYMS
● bacchic
● inebriated

ANTONYM
● sober

drunk ❷ NOUN
someone who consumes too much alcohol • *A drunk lay in the alley.*
alcoholic • *after admitting that he was an alcoholic*
boozer (INFORMAL) • *He's a bit of a boozer.*

dry ❶ ADJECTIVE
without any liquid • *The path was dry after the sunshine.*
arid • *arid conditions*
dried-up • *a dried-up river bed*
parched • *parched brown grass*

ANTONYM
● wet

dry ❷ VERB
to remove liquid from something • *Wash and dry the lettuce.*
dehydrate • *Avoid alcohol, which dehydrates the body.*
drain • *The authorities have mobilized vast numbers of people to drain flooded land.*

MORE SYNONYMS
● dehumidify
● desiccate

ANTONYM
● moisten

dubious ❶ ADJECTIVE
not entirely honest or reliable • *a rather dubious claim*
crooked • *expose his crooked business deals*
dishonest • *He had become rich by dishonest means.*
questionable • *allegations of questionable business practices*
suspect • *The whole affair is highly suspect.*
suspicious • *two characters who looked suspicious*
unreliable • *a notoriously unreliable source of information*

dubious ❷ ADJECTIVE
doubtful about something • *My parents were a bit dubious about it all.*
doubtful • *I was still very doubtful about our chances for success.*
nervous • *The party has become nervous about its prospects of winning.*
sceptical • *Other archaeologists are sceptical about his findings.*
suspicious • *I'm a little suspicious about his motives.*
unconvinced • *Most consumers seem unconvinced that the recession is over.*
undecided • *After university she was still undecided as to what career she wanted.*
unsure • *Fifty-two per cent were unsure about the idea.*

dull ❶ ADJECTIVE
not interesting • *I found him rather dull.*

Can't find the word you're looking for? Try the index.

a
b
c
d
e
f
g
h
i
j
k
l
m
n
o
p
q
r
s
t
u
v
w
x
y
z

boring • *a boring job*
drab • *The rest of the day's activities often seem drab.*
humdrum • *The new government seemed rather humdrum.*
monotonous • *It's monotonous work, like most factory jobs.*
tedious • *Such lists are tedious to read.*
uninteresting • *Their media has a reputation for being dull and uninteresting.*

ANTONYM
● interesting

dull ❷ ADJECTIVE
not bright or clear • *a dark, dull blue colour*
drab • *the same drab grey dress*
gloomy • *Inside it's gloomy after all that sunshine.*
muted • *He likes sombre, muted colours.*
sombre • *an official in sombre black*
subdued • *subdued lighting*

ANTONYM
● bright

dull ❸ ADJECTIVE
covered with clouds • *It's always dull and raining.*
cloudy • *In the morning it was cloudy.*
leaden • *a leaden sky*
murky • *one murky November afternoon*
overcast • *For three days it was overcast.*

ANTONYM
● bright

dumb ❶ ADJECTIVE
unable to speak • *We were all struck dumb for a minute.*

mute • *a mute look of appeal*
silent • *Suddenly they both fell silent.*
speechless • *Alex was almost speechless with rage.*

dumb ❷ ADJECTIVE (INFORMAL)
slow to understand • *I've met a lot of pretty dumb people.*
dim • *He is rather dim.*
obtuse (FORMAL) • *I've really been very obtuse.*
stupid • *How could I have been so stupid?*
thick (INFORMAL) • *I must have seemed incredibly thick.*

ANTONYM
● smart

dump ❶ VERB
to get rid of something • *The getaway car was dumped near the motorway.*
discharge • *The resulting salty water will eventually be discharged at sea.*
dispose of • *how he disposed of the murder weapon*
get rid of • *The cat had kittens, which they got rid of.*
jettison • *The crew jettisoned their excess fuel.*
throw away • *You should have thrown the letter away.*
throw out • *You ought to throw out those empty bottles.*

dump ❷ VERB
to put something down • *We dumped our bags at the hotel and went for a walk.*
deposit • *Imagine if you were suddenly deposited on a desert island.*
drop • *Many children had been dropped outside the stadium by their parents.*

Can't find the word you're looking for? Try the index.

dupe VERB

to trick someone • *Some of the offenders duped the psychologists.*
cheat • *Many brokers were charged with cheating customers.*
con (INFORMAL) • *The British people have been conned by the government.*
deceive • *He has deceived us all.*
delude • *Television deludes you into thinking you are experiencing reality.*
fool • *Art dealers fool a lot of people.*
play a trick on • *She realized he had played a trick on her.*
trick • *He'll be upset when he finds out you tricked him.*

duty ❶ NOUN

something that you ought to do • *We have a duty as adults to listen to children.*
obligation • *He had not felt an obligation to help save his old friend.*
responsibility • *work and family responsibilities*

duty ❷ NOUN

a task associated with a job • *My main duty as librarian was the acquisition of books.*
assignment • *dangerous assignments*

job • *One of my jobs was to make the tea.*
responsibility • *He handled his responsibilities as a counsellor very well.*
role • *Both sides had important roles to play.*

duty ❸ NOUN

tax paid to the government • *customs duties*
excise • *These products are excused VAT and excise.*
levy (FORMAL) • *An annual motorway levy is imposed on all drivers.*
tariff • *America wants to eliminate tariffs on such items as electronics.*
tax • *the tax on new cars and motorcycles*

dying, be dying for VERB

to want something very much • *I'm dying for a breath of fresh air.*
ache for • *She still ached for the lost intimacy of marriage.*
hunger for • *Jules hungered for adventure.*
long for • *He longed for the winter to be over.*
pine for • *I pine for the countryside.*
yearn for • *He yearned for freedom.*

a
b
c
d
e
f
g
h
i
j
k
l
m
n
o
p
q
r
s
t
u
v
w
x
y
z

Ee

eager ADJECTIVE
wanting very much to do or have
something • *Robert is eager to earn
some extra money.*
anxious • *She was anxious to leave
early.*
ardent • *one of the government's
most ardent supporters*
avid • *He's always been an avid
reader.*
enthusiastic • *Tom usually seems
very enthusiastic.*
keen • *Kirsty has always been a
keen swimmer.*
raring to go (INFORMAL) • *They're
all ready and raring to go.*

MORE SYNONYMS
- fervent
- hungry
- zealous

early ❶ ADJECTIVE
before the arranged or expected
time • *You're not late – I'm early!*
advance • *We got an advance copy
of her new book.*
premature • *The injury put a
premature end to his sporting career.*
untimely • *her untimely death in a
car crash at the age of 21*

ANTONYM
- late

early ❷ ADJECTIVE
near the beginning of a period of
time • *the early 1970's*
primeval • *These insects first

appeared in the primeval forests of
Europe.*
primitive • *We found a fossil of a
primitive bird-like creature.*

early ❸ ADVERB
before the arranged or expected
time • *We left early so we wouldn't
have to queue.*
ahead of time • *The bus always
arrives ahead of time.*
beforehand • *If you'd let me know
beforehand, you could have come
with us.*
in advance • *You need to book in
advance to get a good seat.*
in good time • *We arrived at the
airport in good time.*
prematurely • *men who go
prematurely bald*

earn ❶ VERB
to get money in return for doing
work • *He earns a lot more than I
do.*
bring in • *My job brings in just
enough to pay the bills.*
draw • *I draw a salary, so I can
afford to run a car.*
get • *How much do you get if you're
a lorry driver?*
make • *She makes a lot of money.*
obtain • *the profits obtained from
buying and selling shares*

MORE SYNONYMS
- net
- procure
- reap

Can't find the word you're looking for? Try the index.

earn ➋ VERB

to receive something that you deserve • *He earned the respect of his troops.*

acquire • *She has acquired a reputation as a liar and a cheat.*

attain (FORMAL) • *He finally attained his pilot's licence.*

win • *She won the admiration of all her colleagues.*

earth ➊ NOUN

the planet on which we live • *the tallest mountain on earth*

globe • *from every corner of the globe*

planet • *the effects of pollution on the atmosphere of our planet*

world • *the first person to cycle round the world*

RELATED WORD

- ADJECTIVE: terrestrial

earth ➋ NOUN

soil from the ground • *He filled a pot with earth and popped the seeds in it.*

clay • *lumps of clay that stuck to his boots*

dirt • *kneeling in the dirt*

ground • *digging potatoes out of the ground*

soil • *We planted some bulbs in the soil around the pond.*

MORE SYNONYMS

- loam
- topsoil
- turf

ease ➊ NOUN

lack of difficulty or worry • *He passed his driving test with ease.*

leisure • *living a life of leisure*

relaxation • *The town has a feeling of relaxation and tranquillity about it.*

simplicity • *The simplicity of the new scheme has made it popular with motorists.*

ease ➋ VERB

to make or become less severe or intense • *The doctor gave him another injection to ease the pain.*

abate • *By morning the storms had abated.*

calm • *The government is taking steps to calm the situation.*

relax • *He relaxed his grip on the axe and smiled.*

relieve • *The pills will help relieve the pain for a while.*

slacken • *Her grip on the rope slackened and she fell back.*

MORE SYNONYMS

- allay
- alleviate
- assuage

ease ➌ VERB

to move slowly or carefully • *He eased the door open and peered outside.*

creep • *The car crept down the ramp.*

edge • *I edged the van slowly back into the garage.*

guide • *Bob guided the plane out onto the tarmac.*

inch • *The ambulance inched its way through the crowds of shoppers.*

lower • *He lowered himself into the armchair.*

manoeuvre • *We attempted to manoeuvre his canoe towards the shore.*

squeeze • *They squeezed him into his seat and strapped him in.*

easy ➊ ADJECTIVE

able to be done without difficulty • *The software is very easy to install.*

a
b
c
d
e
f
g
h
i
j
k
l
m
n
o
p
q
r
s
t
u
v
w
x
y
z

Can't find the word you're looking for? Try the index.

A
B
C
D
E
F
G
H
I
J
K
L
M
N
O
P
Q
R
S
T
U
V
W
X
Y
Z

light • *a few light exercises to warm up*
painless • *Finding somewhere to stay was pretty painless in the end.*
simple • *All you have to do is answer a few simple questions.*
smooth • *a smooth changeover to the new system*
straightforward • *The route is fairly straightforward so you shouldn't need a map.*

ANTONYM
● hard

easy ❷ ADJECTIVE
comfortable and without worries • *He has not had an easy life.*
carefree • *a carefree summer spent on the beach*
comfortable • *a comfortable teaching job at a small private school*
leisurely • *a leisurely weekend spent with a few close friends*
quiet • *a quiet weekend in the sun*
relaxed • *It's very relaxed here, you can do what you like.*

eat ❶ VERB
to chew and swallow food • *For lunch he ate a cheese sandwich.*
▷ see Word Study **eat**, page 678

eat ❷ VERB
to have a meal • *We like to eat early.*
breakfast (FORMAL) • *The ladies like to breakfast in their rooms.*
dine • *We usually dine at about six.*
feed • *Leopards only feed when they are hungry.*
have a meal • *We could have a meal at Pizza Palace after the film.*
lunch (FORMAL) • *We lunched at El Greco's.*
picnic • *After our walk, we picnicked by the river.*

eat away VERB
to destroy something slowly • *The front of the car had been eaten away by rust.*
corrode • *buildings corroded by acid rain*
destroy • *Areas of the coast are being destroyed by the sea.*
dissolve • *Chemicals in the water are dissolving the bridge.*
erode • *the floods that erode the dry, loose soil*
rot • *Too many sweets will rot your teeth.*
wear away • *The weather soon wears away the paintwork.*

eccentric ❶ ADJECTIVE
regarded as odd or peculiar • *His maths teacher was considered a bit eccentric.*
bizarre • *He's quite a bizarre character.*
outlandish • *His outlandish behaviour sometimes put people off.*
quirky • *a quirky, delightful film that is full of surprises*
strange • *his strange views about UFOs*
weird • *His taste in music is a bit weird.*
whimsical • *a whimsical old gentleman*

eccentric ❷ NOUN
someone who is regarded as odd or peculiar • *He's always been regarded as a bit of an eccentric.*
character (INFORMAL) • *a well-known character who lived in Johnson Street*
crank • *People regarded vegetarians as cranks in those days.*

economic ❶ ADJECTIVE
concerning the way money is managed • *the need for economic reforms*

budgetary • *a summit meeting to discuss various budgetary matters*
commercial • *a purely commercial decision*
financial • *The financial pressures on the government are mounting.*

MORE SYNONYMS
- fiscal
- monetary

economic ② ADJECTIVE

making a profit • *goods that happen to be economic to produce*
productive • *the need to make these industries more productive*
profitable • *a new venture that has proved highly profitable*
viable • *businesses that are no longer viable*

MORE SYNONYMS
- money-making
- profit-making
- remunerative

economical ① ADJECTIVE

cheap to use and saving you money • *Our car may not be fast, but it's very economical.*
cheap • *This isn't a very cheap way of buying stationery.*
cost-effective • *the most cost-effective way of shopping*
economic • *the most economic way to see the museum*
inexpensive • *There are several good inexpensive restaurants in town.*

economical ② ADJECTIVE

careful and sensible with money or materials • *He's never been very economical about housekeeping.*
careful • *She's very careful with her pocket money.*
frugal • *his frugal lifestyle*
prudent • *the prudent use of*
precious natural resources
thrifty • *My mother was very thrifty because she had so little spare cash.*

economy NOUN

the careful use of things to save money • *improvements in the fuel economy of new cars*
frugality (FORMAL) • *We must live with strict frugality if we are to survive.*
prudence • *A lack of prudence could seriously affect his finances.*
restraint • *We need to exercise some restraint in our spending.*
thrift • *He was widely praised for his thrift and imagination.*

ecstasy NOUN

extreme happiness • *his feeling of ecstasy after winning the medal*
bliss • *husband and wife living together in bliss and harmony*
delight • *He squealed with delight when we told him.*
elation • *His supporters reacted to the news with elation.*
euphoria • *There was a sense of euphoria after our election victory.*
exaltation • *the mood of exaltation that affected everyone*
joy • *her joy at finding him after so long*
rapture • *His speech was received with rapture by a huge crowd.*

edge ① NOUN

the place where something ends or meets something else • *on the edge of the forest*
border • *a pillowcase with a lace border*
boundary • *The area beyond the western boundary belongs to Denmark.*
brim • *He kept climbing until he reached the brim of the crater.*

a b c d **e** f g h i j k l m n o p q r s t u v w x y z

Can't find the word you're looking for? Try the index.

A B C D **E** F G H I J K L M N O P Q R S T U V W X Y Z

fringe • *the rundown areas on the fringes of the city*
lip • *The lip of the jug was badly cracked.*
margin • *standing on the margin of the land where it met the water*
rim • *a large round mirror with a gold rim*

MORE SYNONYMS
● perimeter
● periphery

ANTONYM
● centre

edge ❷ VERB
to move somewhere slowly • *He edged towards the phone, ready to grab it if it rang.*
creep • *The car crept forward a few feet, then stopped.*
inch • *The ambulance inched its way through the crowds.*
sidle • *A man sidled up to him and tried to sell him a ticket.*

educated ADJECTIVE
having a high standard of learning • *He is an educated, tolerant and reasonable man.*
cultivated • *His mother was an elegant, cultivated woman.*
cultured • *a cultured man with a wide circle of friends*
intellectual • *He is the intellectual type.*
learned • *He was a scholar, a very learned man.*

MORE SYNONYMS
● erudite
● well-educated

education NOUN
the process of learning or teaching • *the importance of a good education*
coaching • *extra coaching to help* him pass his exams
instruction • *All instruction is provided by qualified experts.*
schooling • *He began to wish he'd paid more attention to his schooling.*
training • *His military training was no use to him here.*
tuition • *personal tuition in the basics of photography*

effect NOUN
a direct result of something • *the effect that divorce has on children*
consequence • *aware of the consequences of their actions*
end result • *The end result of this process is still unclear.*
fruit • *The new software is the fruit of three years' hard work.*
result • *The result of all this uncertainty is that no-one is happy.*
upshot • *The upshot is that we have a very unhappy workforce.*

efficient ADJECTIVE
able to work well without wasting time or energy • *The new hatchback has a much more efficient engine.*
businesslike • *a highly businesslike approach that impressed everyone*
competent • *an extremely competent piece of work*
economic • *The new system is much more economic, and will save millions.*
effective • *effective use of the time we have left*
organized • *Tony seemed very organized, and completely in control of the situation.*
productive • *the need to make farmers much more productive*

ANTONYM
● inefficient

Can't find the word you're looking for? Try the index.

effort ❶ NOUN

physical or mental energy • *It took a lot of effort, but we managed in the end.*

application • *His talent, application and energy are a credit to the school.*

energy • *He decided to devote his energy to writing another book.*

exertion • *Is it really worth all the exertion?*

trouble • *It's not worth the trouble.*

work • *All the work I put in has now been wasted!*

effort ❷ NOUN

an attempt or struggle • *an unsuccessful effort to ban Sunday shopping*

attempt • *an attempt to obtain an interview with the President*

bid • *a last-minute bid to stop the trial going ahead*

stab (INFORMAL) • *his latest stab at acting*

struggle • *his struggle to clear his name*

elaborate ❶ ADJECTIVE

having many different parts • *an elaborate research project*

complex • *a complex explanation*

complicated • *a complicated plan of the building's security system*

detailed • *the detailed plans that have been drawn up*

intricate • *an intricate system of levers and pulleys*

involved • *a very involved operation, lasting many hours*

ANTONYM
● simple

elaborate ❷ ADJECTIVE

highly decorated • *elaborate wooden carvings*

fancy • *the fancy plasterwork on the ceiling*

fussy • *a rather fussy design*

ornate • *an ornate wrought-iron staircase*

elaborate ❸ VERB

to add more information about something • *He promised to elaborate on what had been said last night.*

develop • *Maybe we should develop this idea.*

enlarge • *He was enlarging on proposals made earlier.*

expand • *a view that I will expand on later*

eliminate ❶ VERB

to get rid of someone or something • *We've eliminated two of the four options so far.*

cut out • *His guilty plea cut out the need for a long, costly trial.*

do away with • *the attempt to do away with nuclear weapons altogether*

eradicate • *Efforts to eradicate malaria seem to be failing.*

get rid of • *Why don't we just get rid of the middlemen altogether?*

remove • *You should try and remove these fatty foods from your diet.*

stamp out • *We need to stamp out this disgusting practice.*

eliminate ❷ VERB

to beat someone in a competition • *His team was eliminated in the first round.*

knock out • *We were knocked out by the Dutch champions.*

put out • *Decker finally put her fellow American out in the quarter final.*

a
b
c
d
e
f
g
h
i
j
k
l
m
n
o
p
q
r
s
t
u
v
w
x
y
z

Can't find the word you're looking for? Try the index.

A
B
C
D
E
F
G
H
I
J
K
L
M
N
O
P
Q
R
S
T
U
V
W
X
Y
Z

embarrass VERB

to make someone feel ashamed or
awkward • *You always embarrass
me in front of my friends!*
disconcert • *The way Anderson
was smirking disconcerted her.*
fluster • *Nothing could fluster him.*
humiliate • *How dare you
humiliate me like that!*
shame • *Her son's behaviour had
upset and shamed her.*

MORE SYNONYMS
- discomfit
- faze
- mortify

embarrassed ADJECTIVE

ashamed and awkward • *I'm not
embarrassed about taking my
clothes off.*
ashamed • *I felt so ashamed I
wanted to die.*
awkward • *It was a very awkward
occasion.*
humiliated • *A humiliated Mr
Stevens admitted that the concert
had been cancelled.*
red-faced • *Red-faced executives
had to explain this fact.*
self-conscious • *I always feel self-
conscious when I'm having my
picture taken.*
sheepish • *He looked very sheepish
when he finally appeared.*

MORE SYNONYMS
- abashed
- bashful
- discomfited
- mortified

embarrassment NOUN

shame and awkwardness
• *I laughed loudly to cover my
embarrassment.*
awkwardness • *the awkwardness*

of our first meeting
bashfulness • *Overcome with
bashfulness, he lowered his voice.*
humiliation • *the humiliation of
having to ask for money*
self-consciousness • *her painful
self-consciousness*
shame • *the shame he felt at
having let her down*

MORE SYNONYMS
- chagrin
- discomfiture
- mortification

emergency NOUN

an unexpected and difficult
situation • *This is an emergency!*
crisis • *the economic crisis affecting
parts of Africa*
pinch • *I don't mind working late in
a pinch.*

emit VERB

to give out or release something
• *Polly blinked and emitted a long
sigh.*
exude • *a plant that exudes an
extremely unpleasant smell*
give off • *The fumes it gives off are
poisonous, so watch out.*
give out • *The alarm gave out a
series of bleeps, then stopped.*
release • *The factory is still
releasing toxic fumes.*
send out • *The volcano has been
sending out smoke for weeks.*
utter • *He uttered a loud snort and
continued eating.*

MORE SYNONYMS
- produce
- radiate
- send forth

emphasis NOUN

special or extra importance • *too
much emphasis on commercialism*

Can't find the word you're looking for? Try the index.

accent • *In the new government the accent will be on co-operation.*
importance • *There's not enough importance being given to environmental issues.*
prominence • *Crime prevention has to be given more prominence.*
weight • *This adds more weight to the government's case.*

emphasize VERB
to make something seem specially important or obvious • *He emphasized the need for everyone to remain calm.*
accent • *a white dress accented by a coloured scarf*
accentuate • *His shaven head accentuates his round face.*
highlight • *This disaster has highlighted the difficulty faced by the government.*
play up • *He played up his bad-boy image.*
stress • *I would like to stress that we are in complete agreement.*
underline • *This underlines how important the new trade deal really is.*

MORE SYNONYMS
● foreground
● prioritize
● underscore

employ ❶ VERB
to pay someone to work for you • *Mollison was employed by Mr Darnley as a bodyguard.*
appoint • *We need to appoint a successor to Mr Stevens.*
commission • *He has been commissioned to design a new bridge.*
engage (FORMAL) • *They have finally engaged a suitable nanny.*
hire • *I was hired as a gardener on*
the estate.
take on • *the need to take on more workers for the summer*

employ ❷ VERB
to use something • *the tactics employed by the police*
bring to bear • *We can bring two very different techniques to bear on this.*
make use of • *He makes use of several highly offensive terms to describe them.*
use • *the methods used in the investigation*
utilize • *Engineers will utilize a range of techniques to improve the signal.*

employee NOUN
someone who is paid to work for someone else • *the way they look after their employees*
hand • *He's been working as a farm hand down south.*
worker • *Workers at the plant have been laid off.*
workman • *A council workman finally arrived to fix the door.*

employer NOUN
someone that other people work for • *a meeting with her employer to discuss the issue*
boss • *My boss has always been very fair.*
gaffer (INFORMAL) • *You'll need to speak to the gaffer about that.*

employment NOUN
the fact of employing people • *the employment of children to work in shops*
engagement • *the engagement of suitable staff*
enlistment • *Enlistment in the armed forces is falling.*

a
b
c
d
e
f
g
h
i
j
k
l
m
n
o
p
q
r
s
t
u
v
w
x
y
z

Can't find the word you're looking for? Try the index.

A
B
C
D
E
F
G
H
I
J
K
L
M
N
O
P
Q
R
S
T
U
V
W
X
Y
Z

hiring • *The hiring of new staff is our top priority.*
recruitment • *new policies on recruitment and training*
taking on • *Taking on extra staff would make life a lot easier.*

empty ➊ ADJECTIVE

having no people or things in it
• *The roads were empty.*
bare • *When she got there, the cupboard was bare.*
blank • *all the blank pages in his diary*
clear • *The runway must be kept clear at all times.*
deserted • *By nightfall, the square was deserted.*
unfurnished • *The flat was unfurnished when we moved in.*
uninhabited • *The house has remained uninhabited since she moved out.*
vacant • *two vacant lots on the industrial estate*

ANTONYM
● full

empty ➋ ADJECTIVE

boring or without value or meaning
• *My life is empty without him.*
inane • *a series of inane remarks*
meaningless • *the feeling that his existence was meaningless*
worthless • *a worthless film with nothing to say about anything*

empty ➌ VERB

to remove people or things • *He emptied all the cupboards before Tony arrived.*
clear • *The police cleared the building just in time.*
drain • *She drained the bottles and washed them out.*
evacuate • *Fortunately the*

building had been evacuated.
unload • *It only took twenty minutes to unload the van.*

ANTONYM
● fill

enclose VERB

to surround a thing or place completely • *The book arrived enclosed in a red plastic bag.*
encircle • *The area had been encircled by barbed wire.*
fence off • *We decided to fence off the land.*
hem in • *We were hemmed in by walls and hedges.*
surround • *the low wall that surrounded the rose garden*
wrap • *Wrap the chicken in foil and bake it in a medium oven.*

encourage ➊ VERB

to give someone confidence
• *We were very encouraged by the response.*
cheer • *This news cheered us all and helped us keep going.*
hearten • *I am heartened to hear that.*
reassure • *He always reassures me when I'm feeling down.*

ANTONYM
● discourage

encourage ➋ VERB

to support a person or activity
• *the need to encourage people to be sensible*
aid • *I tried to aid his creative efforts.*
boost • *Efforts to boost investment seem to be succeeding.*
favour • *conditions which favour growth in the economy*
help • *policies aimed at helping small businesses*

Can't find the word you're looking for? Try the index.

incite • *He incited his followers to attack the police station.*
support • *Rowe will support me in this campaign.*

MORE SYNONYMS
- foster
- further
- promote
- strengthen

end ❶ NOUN
the last part of a period or event
• *the end of the 20th century*
▷ *see Word Study end, page 679*

ANTONYM
- beginning

RELATED WORDS
- ADJECTIVES: final, terminal,
- ultimate

end ❷ NOUN
the furthest point of something
• *the room at the end of the corridor*
▷ *see Word Study end, page 679*

end ❸ NOUN
the purpose for which something is done • *The army is being used for political ends.*
▷ *see Word Study end, page 679*

end ❹ VERB
to come or bring to a finish • *talks being held to end the fighting*
bring to an end • *The treaty brought to an end fifty years of conflict.*
cease • *By one o'clock the storm had ceased.*
conclude • *The evening concluded with the usual speeches.*
finish • *waiting for the film to finish*
stop • *When is it all going to stop?*
terminate • *the decision to terminate their contract*

ANTONYM
- begin

endanger VERB
to put someone or something in danger • *a dispute that could endanger the peace talks*
compromise • *We will not allow safety to be compromised.*
jeopardize • *a scandal that could jeopardize his government*
put at risk • *those who were put at risk by her stupidity*
risk • *He is risking the lives of others.*
threaten • *A breakdown in this system could threaten the whole project.*

endure ❶ VERB
to experience something difficult
• *He had to endure hours of discomfort.*
cope with • *We've had a lot to cope with in the last few weeks.*
experience • *The company has experienced heavy financial losses.*
go through • *having to go through the public humiliation of a court case*
stand • *I don't know how he stood it for so long.*
suffer • *Steven has suffered years of pain from arthritis.*

endure ❷ VERB
to continue to exist • *Our friendship has endured through everything.*
last • *a car that is built to last*
live on • *His name will live on as an inspiration to others.*
remain • *When all the rest is forgotten, this fact will remain.*
survive • *the few traces of their civilization that have survived*

enemy NOUN
someone who is against you • *She*

a
b
c
d
e
f
g
h
i
j
k
l
m
n
o
p
q
r
s
t
u
v
w
x
y
z

Can't find the word you're looking for? Try the index.

A
B
C
D
E
F
G
H
I
J
K
L
M
N
O
P
Q
R
S
T
U
V
W
X
Y
Z

has many enemies in the
government.
adversary • *face to face with his
old adversary*
antagonist • *He killed his
antagonist in a duel.*
foe • *He plays Dracula's foe, Dr.
Van Helsing.*
opponent • *Her political
opponents will be delighted at this
news.*

ANTONYM
- friend

energetic ADJECTIVE
full of energy • *an able, energetic
and very determined politician*
animated • *an animated
conversation about politics and sport*
dynamic • *a dynamic and
ambitious businessman*
indefatigable • *trying to keep up
with their indefatigable boss*
spirited • *a spirited defence of his
new tax proposals*
tireless • *a tireless campaigner for
the homeless*
vigorous • *a vigorous campaign*

energy NOUN
the ability and strength to do
things • *I'm saving my energy for
tomorrow.*
drive • *a man with immense drive
and enthusiasm*
life • *At 96, she's still as full of life
as ever.*
spirit • *Despite trailing 6-2, they
played with a lot of spirit.*
strength • *She put all her strength
into finding a new job.*
vigour • *They returned to their
work with renewed vigour.*
vitality • *a woman with
considerable charm and endless
vitality*

MORE SYNONYMS
- élan
- verve
- zeal
- zest

enjoy VERB
to find pleasure in something
• *I haven't enjoyed a film as much as
that in ages!*
appreciate • *people who don't
appreciate Satie's music*
delight in • *He delights in playing
practical jokes.*
like • *Kirsty likes shopping.*
love • *He loves skiing.*
relish • *She relished the opportunity
to get back at him.*
revel in • *Stevens was revelling in
the attention.*
take pleasure from • *He took no
pleasure from the knowledge that he
had won.*
take pleasure in • *She seemed to
take pleasure in my discomfort.*

enlarge VERB
to make something larger • *plans
to enlarge the 30,000 seat stadium*
add to • *We've decided to add to
this house rather than move again.*
expand • *If we want to stay in
business, we need to expand.*
extend • *They extended the house
by adding a conservatory.*
increase • *They have increased the
peace-keeping force to 2000.*
magnify • *A more powerful lens
will magnify the image.*

MORE SYNONYMS
- augment
- broaden
- distend
- elongate
- lengthen
- widen

Can't find the word you're looking for? Try the index.

enlarge on VERB

to give more information about
something • *I'd like you to enlarge
on that last point.*
develop • *Maybe I should develop
this idea a little bit further.*
elaborate on • *He refused to
elaborate on what he had said
earlier.*
expand on • *an idea that I will
expand on later*

enormous ADJECTIVE

very large in size or amount
• *an enormous dust cloud*
colossal • *a colossal waste of
public money*
gigantic • *The road is bordered by
gigantic rocks.*
huge • *Several painters were
working on a huge piece of canvas.*
immense • *an immense cloud of
smoke*
massive • *The scale of the problem
is massive.*
tremendous • *I felt a tremendous
pressure on my chest.*
vast • *vast stretches of land*

ANTONYM
● tiny

ensure VERB

to make sure about something
• *We must ensure that this never
happens again.*
guarantee • *Further investment
should guarantee that profits will
rise.*
make certain • *to make certain
that he'll get there*
make sure • *I will personally make
sure that the job gets done.*

enterprise ❶ NOUN

a business or company • *a small
enterprise with a high turnover*
business • *a medium-sized
business*
company • *a company that was
doing very well*
concern • *It's not a large concern,
but it makes a profit.*
establishment • *a modest
establishment dedicated to sailing*
firm • *a clothing firm*
operation • *a one-man operation*

enterprise ❷ NOUN

a project or task • *a risky enterprise
such as horse breeding*
effort • *her latest fund-raising
effort for cancer research*
endeavour • *an endeavour that
was bound to end in failure*
operation • *He'd set up a small
mining operation.*
project • *a project that will attract
a lot of media attention*
undertaking • *This undertaking
will rely on the hard work of our
volunteers.*
venture • *a venture that few were
willing to invest in*

entertain VERB

to keep people amused or
interested • *things that might
entertain children in the school
holidays*
amuse • *He amused us all evening,
singing and telling jokes.*
charm • *He charmed Mrs Nisbet
with his tales of life on the road.*
delight • *a routine that will delight
everyone*
enthral • *He enthralled audiences
all over Europe.*
please • *He certainly knows how to
please a crowd.*

entertainment NOUN

enjoyable activities • *Their main
form of entertainment is the TV.*

a
b
c
d
e
f
g
h
i
j
k
l
m
n
o
p
q
r
s
t
u
v
w
x
y
z

Can't find the word you're looking for? Try the index.

A
B
C
D
E
F
G
H
I
J
K
L
M
N
O
P
Q
R
S
T
U
V
W
X
Y
Z

amusement • *looking for some amusement on a Saturday night*
enjoyment • *We need a bit of enjoyment to cheer us up.*
fun • *It's not really my idea of family fun.*
pleasure • *Hours of pleasure can be had with a pack of cards.*
recreation • *a healthy and enjoyable form of recreation*

enthusiasm NOUN
eagerness and enjoyment in something • *We were disappointed by their lack of enthusiasm.*
eagerness • *He could barely contain his eagerness.*
excitement • *Her excitement got the better of her.*
interest • *He doesn't show much interest in football.*
keenness • *I don't doubt his keenness, it's his ability that worries me.*
warmth • *He greeted us with his usual warmth and affection.*

MORE SYNONYMS
- ardour
- fervour
- relish
- zeal

enthusiastic ADJECTIVE
showing great excitement and eagerness for something • *He was very enthusiastic about the new scheme.*
ardent • *one of the government's most ardent supporters*
avid • *an avid reader*
devoted • *a devoted Star Trek fan*
eager • *He is eager to learn more about computers.*
excited • *We are very excited about getting a new dog.*
keen • *Dave is an keen angler.*

passionate • *a passionate opponent of the government*

MORE SYNONYMS
- fervent
- wholehearted
- zealous

ANTONYM
- apathetic

entrance ❶ NOUN
the way into a particular place • *I met Barry at the entrance to the station.*
door • *She was waiting by the front door.*
doorway • *the mass of people blocking the doorway*
entry • *Kevin had been hanging round the back entry for hours.*
gate • *the security guard at the main gate*
way in • *Is this the way in?*

entrance ❷ NOUN
a person's arrival somewhere • *She had failed to notice her father's entrance.*
appearance • *She had timed her appearance at the dinner to perfection.*
arrival • *journalists awaiting the arrival of the team*
entry • *He was arrested on his entry into Mexico.*

entrance ❸ NOUN
the right to enter somewhere • *He gained entrance to the hotel where the band were staying.*
access • *We were denied access to the stadium.*
admission • *no admission without a ticket*
entry • *I was unable to gain entry to the meeting.*

Can't find the word you're looking for? Try the index.

entrance ❹ VERB
to amaze and delight someone
• *The audience was entranced by her voice.*
bewitch • *Young Gordon's smile bewitched everyone.*
captivate • *I was captivated by her piercing blue eyes.*
charm • *He charmed Mr Darnley and made him feel young again.*
delight • *a CD that will delight her many fans*
enthral • *Audiences were enthralled by his spectacular stage act.*
fascinate • *She never failed to fascinate him.*

MORE SYNONYMS
- enchant
- enrapture
- spellbind

entry ❶ NOUN
a person's arrival somewhere • *her dramatic entry*
appearance • *She made her appearance to tumultuous applause.*
arrival • *He apologized for his late arrival.*
entrance • *My entrance was spoiled when I tripped over the carpet.*

entry ❷ NOUN
the way into a particular place • *He was hanging around at the entry to the station.*
door • *I'll meet you at the front door.*
doorway • *A bicycle was blocking the doorway.*
entrance • *The bomb had been left outside the entrance to the building.*
gate • *Guards were posted at the main gate.*
way in • *I can't find the way in.*

entry ❸ NOUN
something that has been written down • *the final entry in his journal*
item • *A number of interesting items appear in his diary.*
note • *He grunted and made a note in his pocket book.*
record • *There is no record for 13 October in the log book.*

envy ❶ NOUN
a feeling of resentment about what someone else has • *his feelings of envy towards Kevin*
jealousy • *the jealousy people felt towards him because of his money*
resentment • *All the anger, bitterness and resentment suddenly melted away.*

envy ❷ VERB
to want something that someone else has • *I don't envy you one bit.*
be envious • *people who were envious of her good fortune*
begrudge • *Surely you don't begrudge me one night out.*
be jealous • *I couldn't help being jealous when I knew he had won.*
covet • *She coveted his job.*
resent • *Anyone with money was resented and ignored.*

equal ❶ ADJECTIVE
the same in size, amount, or value • *equal numbers of men and women*
equivalent • *A kilogram is equivalent to 2.2 pounds.*
identical • *glasses containing identical amounts of water*
the same • *different areas of research that have the same importance*

equal ❷, equal to ADJECTIVE
having the necessary ability for

a b c d e f g h i j k l m n o p q r s t u v w x y z

A
B
C
D
E
F
G
H
I
J
K
L
M
N
O
P
Q
R
S
T
U
V
W
X
Y
Z

something • *She was equal to any task they gave her.*
capable of • *I'm no longer capable of this kind of work.*
up to • *He said he wasn't up to a long walk.*

equal ❸ VERB

to be as good as something else • *a time that equalled the European record*
be equal to • *The final score is equal to his personal best.*
match • *able to match her previous time for the 100m*

equip VERB

to supply someone with something • *The boat was equipped with an outboard motor.*
arm • *The children arrived armed with a range of gardening tools.*
endow • *The male bird is endowed with a vicious-looking beak.*
fit out • *the amount spent on fitting out their offices*
provide • *We provided them with waterproofs and sandwiches.*
supply • *They supplied us with camping gear and a stove.*

equipment NOUN

the things you need for a particular job • *a shed full of gardening equipment*
apparatus • *All the firemen were wearing breathing apparatus.*
gear • *Police in riot gear have sealed off the area.*
paraphernalia • *ashtrays, lighters and other paraphernalia associated with smoking*
stuff • *The builders had left all their stuff in the garden.*
tackle • *Martin kept all his fishing tackle in the spare room.*

MORE SYNONYMS
● accoutrements
● appurtenances

erode VERB

to wear something away and destroy it • *The cliffs were being eroded by the constant pounding of the sea.*
corrode • *buildings corroded by acid rain*
destroy • *ancient monuments destroyed by pollution*
deteriorate • *The tapestry had deteriorated badly where the roof was leaking.*
disintegrate • *Once they were exposed to light the documents rapidly disintegrated.*
eat away • *The chemicals in the water had eaten away the cables.*
wear away • *rocks worn away by the action of the wind*
wear down • *Some of her teeth were worn down with gnawing on the bars.*

err VERB

to make a mistake • *The builders had erred considerably in their original estimate.*
blunder • *Fletcher had obviously blundered.*
go wrong • *We must have gone wrong somewhere in our calculations.*
make a mistake • *Okay, I made a mistake, I'm only human.*
miscalculate • *They miscalculated, and now they're in deep trouble.*

error NOUN

a mistake • *a mathematical error*
blunder • *He made a tactical blunder by announcing his intentions.*

fault • *It is a fault to think you can learn how to manage people in business school.*

lapse • *a serious security lapse*

mistake • *spelling mistakes*

slip • *We must be careful - we can't afford any slips.*

escape ❶ VERB

to manage to get away • *Three prisoners who escaped have given themselves up.*

break free • *He was handcuffed to his bed, but somehow managed to break free.*

break out • *two prisoners who broke out of the maximum security wing*

get away • *She got away from her guards.*

make your escape • *We made our escape down a drainpipe using knotted sheets.*

run away • *I called him but he just ran away.*

run off • *The children ran off when they spotted me.*

MORE SYNONYMS

- abscond
- bolt

escape ❷ VERB

to manage to avoid something • *He was lucky to escape injury.*

avoid • *She has managed to avoid arrest so far.*

dodge • *He dodged his military service by pretending to be ill.*

duck • *a pathetic attempt to duck her responsibilities*

elude • *He managed to elude the police for 13 years.*

evade • *He has now been charged with evading tax.*

escape ❸ NOUN

something that distracts you from

something unpleasant • *Cycling gives me an escape from the routine of work.*

distraction • *a distraction from his troubles*

diversion • *a pleasant diversion from my studies*

relief • *The piano provides relief from all the stress.*

essence ❶ NOUN

the most basic and important part of something • *The essence of good management is the ability to listen.*

core • *the need to get to the core of the problem*

heart • *a problem that reaches to the very heart of the party*

nature • *the nature of what it is to be European*

soul • *a song that captures the soul of this proud nation*

spirit • *the spirit of modern manhood*

MORE SYNONYMS

- crux
- kernel
- quintessence
- substance

essence ❷ NOUN

a concentrated liquid • *vanilla essence*

concentrate • *orange concentrate*

extract • *lemon extract*

essential ❶ ADJECTIVE

extremely important • *Good ventilation is essential in a greenhouse.*

crucial • *Her speech was a crucial part of the campaign.*

indispensable • *She has become indispensable to the department.*

vital • *a vital aspect of the plans that everyone has overlooked*

a b c d e f g h i j k l m n o p q r s t u v w x y z

essential ❷ ADJECTIVE

basic and important • *an essential part of any child's development*
basic • *the basic laws of physics*
cardinal • *He had broken one of the cardinal rules of business.*
fundamental • *the fundamental principles of democracy*
key • *Mollison had a key role to play in the negotiations.*
main • *an attempt to analyse the main points of his theory*
principal • *the principal idea that underpins their argument*

essentials PLURAL NOUN

the things that are most important • *We only had enough money for the essentials.*
basics • *We need to get back to basics.*
fundamentals • *the fundamentals of road safety*
necessities • *Water, food, and shelter are the necessities of life.*
prerequisites • *Self-confidence is one of the prerequisites for a happy life.*
rudiments • *teaching him the rudiments of car maintenance*

esteem NOUN

admiration and respect for another person • *He is held in high esteem by his colleagues.*
admiration • *I have always had the greatest admiration for him.*
estimation • *He has gone down in my estimation.*
regard • *I had a very high regard for him and his work.*
respect • *I have tremendous respect for Dean.*
reverence • *He is still spoken of with reverence by those who knew him.*

MORE SYNONYMS
● honour
● veneration (FORMAL)

estimate NOUN

a guess at an amount, quantity, or outcome • *This figure is five times the original estimate.*
appraisal • *an appraisal of your financial standing*
assessment • *assessments of mortgaged property*
estimation • *The first group were correct in their estimation of the man's height.*
guess • *He examined her and made a guess at her temperature.*
quote • *Never agree to a job without getting a quote first.*
reckoning • *By my reckoning we were seven kilometres from the town.*
valuation • *The valuations reflect prices at the end of the fiscal year.*

eternal ADJECTIVE

lasting forever • *the secret of eternal life*
everlasting • *everlasting love*
immortal • *your immortal soul*
unchanging • *the unchanging laws of the cosmos*

even ❶ ADJECTIVE

flat and level • *I need an even surface to write on.*
flat • *a small hut with a flat roof*
horizontal • *He drew a series of horizontal lines on the paper.*
level • *checking the floor to make sure it was level*
smooth • *the smooth marble floor tiles*

ANTONYM
● uneven

even ❷ ADJECTIVE

without changing or varying • *an*

A
B
C
D
E
F
G
H
I
J
K
L
M
N
O
P
Q
R
S
T
U
V
W
X
Y
Z

even flow of liquid
constant • *The temperature remained more or less constant.*
regular • *her quiet, regular breathing*
smooth • *He caught the ball and passed it in one smooth motion.*
steady • *a steady stream of people*
uniform • *The prices rises are not uniform across the country.*

even ❸ ADJECTIVE
the same • *At halftime the scores were still even.*
equal • *The two teams shared equal points into the second round.*
identical • *At the end of the contest, our scores were identical.*
level • *The scores were level at halftime.*
neck and neck • *They're still neck and neck with two minutes to go.*

event ❶ NOUN
something that happens • *still amazed at the events of last week*
affair • *He preferred to forget the whole affair.*
business • *Do you remember that business with Jim?*
circumstance • *due to circumstances beyond our control*
episode • *a rather embarrassing episode at Yvonne's wedding*
experience • *an experience that changed his mind about going to university*
incident • *the incident in the restaurant*
matter • *She doesn't seem to be taking this matter seriously.*

event ❷ NOUN
a competition • *The next event is the long jump.*
bout • *This is his fifth heavyweight bout in three months.*
competition • *the first competition of the afternoon*
contest • *She's out of the contest for good.*

everyday ADJECTIVE
usual or ordinary • *the drudgery of everyday life*
common • *a common occurrence*
daily • *In our daily life we follow predictable patterns of behaviour.*
day-to-day • *I use a lot of spices in my day-to-day cooking.*
mundane • *the mundane realities of life*
ordinary • *ordinary tableware*
routine • *routine maintenance of the machine*

MORE SYNONYMS
● banal
● unexceptional

evident ADJECTIVE
easily noticed or understood • *He spoke with evident emotion about his ordeal.*
apparent • *He spoke with apparent nonchalance about his experience.*
clear • *It became clear that I hadn't convinced Mike.*
noticeable • *a noticeable effect*
obvious • *It's obvious that he doesn't like me.*
palpable • *The tension between Jim and Amy is palpable.*
plain • *It was plain to him that she was having a nervous breakdown.*
visible • *the most visible sign of her distress*

MORE SYNONYMS
● conspicuous
● manifest
● patent

evil ❶ NOUN
the force that causes bad things to

a
b
c
d
e
f
g
h
i
j
k
l
m
n
o
p
q
r
s
t
u
v
w
x
y
z

Can't find the word you're looking for? Try the index.

A
B
C
D
E
F
G
H
I
J
K
L
M
N
O
P
Q
R
S
T
U
V
W
X
Y
Z

happen • *the conflict between good and evil*
badness • *behaving that way out of sheer badness*
immorality • *the immorality that is typical of the arms trade*
sin • *The whole town is a den of sin and corruption.*
vice • *a place long associated with vice and immorality*
wickedness • *the wickedness of his behaviour*

MORE SYNONYMS
- baseness
- depravity
- sinfulness

ANTONYM
- good

evil ❷ NOUN
something unpleasant or harmful • *a lecture on the evils of alcohol*
affliction • *Hay fever is an affliction that affects thousands.*
ill • *Many of the nation's ills are his responsibility.*
misery • *the misery of drug addiction*
sorrow • *the joys and sorrows of family life*

evil ❸ ADJECTIVE
morally wrong or bad • *an utterly evil man*
bad • *He's not a bad man, he's just very unhappy.*
depraved • *a throughly depraved film*
malevolent • *a malevolent influence on the whole school*
sinful • *He is a good person in a sinful world.*
vile • *vile acts of brutality*
wicked • *a wicked attack on a helpless child*

ANTONYM
- good

exact ❶ ADJECTIVE
correct in every detail • *It's an exact reproduction of the first steam engine.*
accurate • *an accurate description of the man*
authentic • *authentic Elizabethan costumes*
faithful • *faithful copies of ancient stone tools*
faultless • *She spoke with a faultless French accent.*
precise • *It's difficult to give a precise date for the painting.*
true • *Is this a true picture of life in the Middle Ages?*

ANTONYM
- approximate

exact ❷ VERB (FORMAL)
to demand and obtain something • *They are certain to exact a high price for their cooperation.*
command • *an excellent surgeon who commanded the respect of all his colleagues*
extract • *to extract the maximum political advantage from this situation*
impose • *the first council to impose a fine for dropping litter*
insist on • *She insisted on conducting all the interviews herself.*
insist upon • *He insists upon good service.*
wring • *attempts to wring concessions from the government*

exactly ❶ ADVERB
with complete accuracy and precision • *He arrived at exactly five o'clock.*
accurately • *We cannot accurately predict where the missile will land.*

Can't find the word you're looking for? Try the index.

faithfully • *I translated the play as faithfully as I could.*

just • *There are no statistics about just how many people won't vote.*

on the dot • *At nine o'clock on the dot, they have breakfast.*

precisely • *No-one knows precisely how many people are in the camp.*

quite • *That wasn't quite what I meant.*

ANTONYM
○ approximately

exactly ❷ INTERJECTION
an expression implying total agreement • *"We'll never know the answer." - "Exactly. So let's stop speculating."*

absolutely • *"It's worrying, isn't it?" - "Absolutely."*

indeed • *"That's a topic that's getting a lot of media coverage." - "Indeed."*

precisely • *"So, you're suggesting we do away with these laws?" - "Precisely."*

quite • *"It's your choice, isn't it?" - "Quite."*

exaggerate VERB
to make things seem worse than they are • *He thinks I'm exaggerating, but I'm not!*

overdo • *I think he's overdoing it a bit when he complains like that.*

overestimate • *I think we're over-estimating their desire to cooperate.*

overstate • *It's impossible to overstate the seriousness of this situation.*

exam NOUN
a test to find out how much you know • *a maths exam*

examination • *a three-hour written examination*

oral • *I got good marks for my French oral.*

test • *I failed my history test again.*

examination ❶ NOUN
a careful inspection of something • *The Navy is carrying out an examination of the wreck.*

analysis • *An analysis of the ash revealed traces of lead oxide.*

inspection • *The police inspection of the vehicle found no fingerprints.*

study • *A study of the wreckage has thrown new light on the crash.*

examination ❷ NOUN
a check carried out on someone by a doctor • *The doctor suggested an immediate examination of his ear.*

check • *a quick check just to make sure everything's working properly*

checkup • *my annual checkup at the clinic*

medical • *He had a medical before leaving England.*

examine ❶ VERB
to look at something very carefully • *Police scientists are examining the scene of the crash.*

analyse • *We haven't had time to analyse all the samples yet.*

go over • *I'll go over your report tomorrow.*

go through • *We went through his belongings and found a notebook.*

inspect • *Customs officials inspected the vehicle.*

look over • *Once we've looked the house over we should know what caused the fire.*

study • *Experts are studying the frozen remains of a mammoth.*

MORE SYNONYMS
○ peruse
○ scrutinize

a
b
c
d
e
f
g
h
i
j
k
l
m
n
o
p
q
r
s
t
u
v
w
x
y
z

Can't find the word you're looking for? Try the index.

examine ❷ NOUN
to give someone a medical
examination • *I was examined by
several specialists.*
check • *Dr Mollison checked my
nose and throat.*
inspect • *I was inspected twice by
Dr Stevens.*
look at • *He said he wanted to look
at my chest again just to make sure.*
test • *They tested my eyes but my
vision was fine.*

example ❶ NOUN
something that represents a group
of things • *some examples of
medieval wood carving*
illustration • *Lo's success is an
illustration of how well China is
doing.*
sample • *This drawing is a sample
of his early work.*
specimen • *I had to submit a
specimen of my handwriting for
analysis.*

example ❷ NOUN
something that people can imitate
• *His dedication is an example to us
all.*
ideal • *a woman who was the
American ideal of beauty*
model • *His conduct at the talks
was a model of dignity.*
paragon • *She is a paragon of
neatness and efficiency.*
prototype • *He was the prototype
of the English gentleman.*

MORE SYNONYMS
● archetype
● exemplar
● paradigm

excellent ADJECTIVE
extremely good • *It's an excellent
book, one of my favourites.*

beaut (AUSTRALIAN AND NEW
ZEALAND; INFORMAL) • *a beaut spot
to live*
brilliant • *What a brilliant film!*
cracking (BRITISH, AUSTRALIAN
AND NEW ZEALAND; INFORMAL)
• *You've done a cracking job in the
garden!*
fine • *There's a fine view from the
bedroom window.*
first-class • *a first-class effort*
great • *He's a great player and
we'll be sorry to lose him.*
outstanding • *an outstanding
performance*
superb • *a superb craftsman*

ANTONYM
● terrible

except PREPOSITION
apart from • *I don't drink, except for
the occasional glass of wine.*
apart from • *The room was empty
apart from one man seated by the
fire.*
but • *He didn't speak anything but
Greek.*
other than • *She makes no
reference to any research other than
her own.*
save (FORMAL) • *We had almost
nothing to eat, save the few berries
and nuts we could find.*
with the exception of
• *Yesterday was a day off for
everybody, with the exception of
Tom.*

exceptional ❶ ADJECTIVE
unusually excellent, talented, or
clever • *His piano playing is
exceptional.*
excellent • *The recording quality is
excellent.*
extraordinary • *He is an
extraordinary musician.*

Can't find the word you're looking for? Try the index.

outstanding • *an outstanding athlete*
phenomenal • *The performances have been absolutely phenomenal.*
remarkable • *a remarkable achievement*
talented • *He is a talented violinist.*

ANOTHER SYNONYM
● extraordinary

ANTONYM
● mediocre

exceptional ❷ ADJECTIVE
unusual and likely to happen very rarely • *The courts hold that this case is exceptional.*
isolated • *They said the allegations related to an isolated case.*
out of the ordinary • *I've noticed nothing out of the ordinary.*
rare • *those rare occasions when he did eat alone*
special • *In special cases, an exception to this rule may be made.*
unheard-of • *buying rum at the unheard-of rate of $2 per bottle*
unusual • *To be appreciated as a parent is unusual.*

ANOTHER SYNONYM
● unprecedented (FORMAL)

ANTONYM
● common

excess ❶ NOUN
behaviour that goes beyond what is acceptable • *a life of excess*
extravagance • *Examples of her extravagance were everywhere.*
indulgence • *a moment of sheer indulgence*

MORE SYNONYMS
● debauchery
● dissipation

● intemperance
● overindulgence

excess ❷ NOUN
a larger amount than necessary • *An excess of houseplants made the room look like a jungle.*
glut • *the current glut of dairy products in Europe*
overdose • *An overdose of sun can lead to skin problems later.*
surfeit • *A surfeit of rich food did not help his digestive system.*
surplus • *Germany suffers from a surplus of teachers at the moment.*

MORE SYNONYMS
● overabundance
● plethora
● superabundance
● superfluity

ANTONYM
● shortage

excess ❸ ADJECTIVE
more than is needed • *problems associated with excess weight*
extra • *Pour any extra liquid into a bowl and set aside.*
superfluous • *all our superfluous belongings, things we don't need*
surplus • *Farmers have to sell off their surplus stock cheap.*

excessive ADJECTIVE
too great • *an excessive reliance on government funding*
enormous • *She spent an enormous amount on clothes.*
exaggerated • *the exaggerated claims made by their supporters*
needless • *a film that is full of needless violence*
undue • *the need to avoid undue expense*
unreasonable • *unreasonable increases in the price of petrol*

a
b
c
d
e
f
g
h
i
j
k
l
m
n
o
p
q
r
s
t
u
v
w
x
y
z

Can't find the word you're looking for? Try the index.

A
B
C
D
E
F
G
H
I
J
K
L
M
N
O
P
Q
R
S
T
U
V
W
X
Y
Z

MORE SYNONYMS
- disproportionate
- exorbitant
- immoderate
- inordinate
- profligate

exchange ❶ VERB
to give something in return for something else • *We exchanged phone numbers.*
barter • *Traders came from everywhere to barter in the markets.*
change • *Can you change pesetas for pounds?*
swap • *I wouldn't swap places with her for anything!*
switch • *They switched cars and were away before the alarm was raised.*
trade • *a secret deal to trade arms for hostages*

exchange ❷ NOUN
the act of giving something for something else • *a ceasefire to allow the exchange of prisoners*
interchange • *a meeting at which the interchange of ideas was encouraged*
swap • *They agreed to a swap and made the necessary arrangements.*
switch • *The switch went ahead as planned.*
trade • *I am willing to make a trade with you.*

excite ❶ VERB
to make someone feel enthusiastic or nervous • *The idea of visiting America really excited the kids.*
agitate • *I've no idea what has agitated him.*
animate • *There was plenty about this match to animate the capacity crowd.*
thrill • *The reception he got at the*

meeting thrilled him.
titillate • *a meal that will titillate the taste buds of every gourmet*

excite ❷ VERB
to cause a particular feeling or reaction • *The meeting failed to excite strong feelings in anyone.*
arouse • *a move that has aroused deep public anger*
elicit • *His proposal elicited a storm of protest.*
evoke • *The film has evoked a sense of nostalgia in many older people.*
incite • *a crude attempt to incite racial hatred*
inspire • *The handling of the new car quickly inspires confidence.*
provoke • *The suggestion has provoked anger.*
stir up • *He's just trying to stir up trouble.*

MORE SYNONYMS
- fire
- foment
- inflame
- kindle
- rouse

excited ADJECTIVE
happy and unable to relax • *We are very excited about getting a new dog.*
agitated • *in an excited and agitated state*
enthusiastic • *Tom usually seems very enthusiastic.*
feverish • *a state of feverish anticipation*
high (INFORMAL) • *I was feeling really high after Lorraine's party.*
thrilled • *The children were thrilled when the snow came.*

ANTONYM
- bored

Can't find the word you're looking for? Try the index.

excitement NOUN
interest and enthusiasm • *The release of his latest film has caused great excitement.*
activity • *a scene of frenzied activity*
adventure • *setting off in search of adventure*
agitation • *He reacted to the news with considerable agitation.*
commotion • *We decided to find out what all the commotion was about.*
enthusiasm • *They greeted our arrival with enthusiasm.*
thrill • *the thrill of scuba diving*

MORE SYNONYMS
- animation
- elation
- furore
- tumult

exciting ADJECTIVE
making you feel happy and enthusiastic • *the most exciting race I've ever seen*
dramatic • *Their arrival was dramatic and exciting.*
electrifying • *It was an electrifying performance.*
exhilarating • *an exhilarating walk along the cliff tops*
rousing • *a rousing speech*
stimulating • *It's a stimulating book, full of ideas.*
thrilling • *a thrilling opportunity to watch the lions as they feed*

MORE SYNONYMS
- intoxicating
- sensational
- stirring

ANTONYM
- boring

exclude ❶ VERB
to decide not to include something

• *We cannot exclude this possibility altogether.*
eliminate • *We can eliminate Mr Darnley from our list of suspects.*
ignore • *We cannot afford to ignore this option.*
leave out • *We can narrow it down by leaving out everywhere that's too expensive.*
omit • *His name seems to have been omitted from the list.*
rule out • *The police have already ruled out a retrial.*

ANTONYM
- include

exclude ❷ VERB
to stop someone going somewhere or doing something • *The university used to exclude women from all lectures.*
ban • *Tony was banned from driving for three years.*
bar • *She was barred from the tennis club.*
forbid • *Carver was forbidden to attend any of the society's meetings.*
keep out • *We need to keep out troublemakers.*

MORE SYNONYMS
- blackball
- debar

exclusive ADJECTIVE
available only to a few rich people • *one of Britain's most exclusive golf clubs*
chic • *a chic nightclub in Monaco*
classy • *a very classy restaurant*
posh (INFORMAL) • *She took me to a posh hotel to celebrate.*
select • *a very lavish and very select party*
up-market • *The area is much more up-market than it used to be.*

Can't find the word you're looking for? Try the index.

excuse ❶ NOUN

a reason or explanation • *Stop making excuses and get on with it!*
explanation • *You'd better have a good explanation for your conduct.*
justification • *What possible justification can there be for this?*
pretext • *His pretext for leaving early was an upset stomach.*
reason • *This gave me the perfect reason for visiting London.*

excuse ❷ VERB

to forgive someone or someone's behaviour • *Please excuse my late arrival.*
forgive • *Forgive me, I'm so sorry.*
overlook • *the need to overlook each other's failings*
pardon • *Pardon my ignorance, but who is Cliff Hanley?*
turn a blind eye to • *We can't be expected to turn a blind eye to this behaviour.*

exempt ADJECTIVE

excused from a duty or rule • *Teachers were exempt from military service.*
excused • *Some MPs will have been officially excused attendance.*
immune • *Members of the parliament are immune from prosecution.*
not liable • *They are not liable to pay income tax.*

exercise NOUN

activity that keeps you fit • *I need to get more exercise.*
activity • *a bit of physical activity to get the heart going*
exertion • *I'm tired out by all this exertion.*
training • *He needs to do a bit more training before the match.*
work • *I'm doing a lot more work at the gym now I'm feeling better.*

exhaust ❶ VERB

to make very tired • *I mustn't exhaust myself as I did last time.*
drain • *My emotional turmoil had drained me.*
fatigue • *He is easily fatigued.*
tire out • *a great new job that tires me out*
wear out • *Living out of a suitcase wears you out.*

exhaust ❷ VERB

to use something up completely • *She has exhausted all my patience.*
consume • *plans which will consume hours of time*
deplete • *chemicals that deplete the earth's protective ozone shield*
run through • *The project ran through its funds in months.*
use up • *The gas has all been used up.*

expand VERB

to make or become larger • *The rails expanded and buckled in the fierce heat.*
develop • *We need to develop the company's engineering division.*
enlarge • *Plans to enlarge the stadium have been approved.*
extend • *We're trying to extend our range of sports wear.*
fill out • *The balloon had filled out and was already almost airborne.*
grow • *The Japanese share of the market has grown dramatically.*
increase • *We will need to increase our overseas operations.*
swell • *The river had swollen rapidly.*

ANTONYM
- decrease

A B C D **E** F G H I J K L M N O P Q R S T U V W X Y Z

Can't find the word you're looking for? Try the index.

expand on VERB

to give more information about something • *an idea that I will expand on later*
develop • *You should develop this theme a little bit further.*
elaborate on • *He refused to elaborate on what he had said earlier.*
enlarge on • *I'd like you to enlarge on that last point.*

expect ❶ VERB

to believe that something is going to happen • *The trial is expected to last several weeks.*
anticipate • *We do not anticipate any problems.*
assume • *He assumed that they would wait for him.*
believe • *Experts believe the comet will pass close to the earth.*
imagine • *The meal cost more than we had imagined.*
presume • *I presume they'll be along shortly.*
reckon • *We reckon it'll be a fairly quick journey.*
think • *I thought the concert would be cancelled.*

MORE SYNONYMS
● envisage
● forecast
● foresee
● predict

expect ❷ VERB

to believe that something is your right • *I was expecting to have a bit of time to myself.*
demand • *a job that demands a lot of time and money*
rely on • *I'm relying on you to help me.*
require • *They require a lot of her, maybe too much.*

expensive ADJECTIVE

costing a lot of money • *a very expensive Italian suit*
costly • *a costly court case*
dear • *Those trainers are far too dear.*
pricey • *Medical insurance can be very pricey.*

MORE SYNONYMS
● exorbitant
● overpriced

ANTONYM
● cheap

experience ❶ NOUN

knowledge or skill in a particular activity • *We're looking for someone with engineering experience.*
expertise • *They lack the expertise to deal with such a complex case.*
know-how • *Her technical know-how was invaluable.*
knowledge • *We need someone with knowledge of computing.*
training • *His military training made the difference between life and death.*
understanding • *someone with considerable understanding of the law*

experience ❷ NOUN

something that happens to you • *a terrifying experience that she still talks about*
adventure • *a series of hair-raising adventures during the war*
affair • *He seemed keen to forget the affair and never discussed it.*
encounter • *his first encounter with alcohol*
episode • *The episode has proved deeply embarrassing for her.*
incident • *an incident he would rather forget*

a
b
c
d
e
f
g
h
i
j
k
l
m
n
o
p
q
r
s
t
u
v
w
x
y
z

Can't find the word you're looking for? Try the index.

ordeal • *a painful ordeal that is now over*

experience ❸ VERB
to have something happen to you
• *We are experiencing a few technical problems.*
encounter • *The storms were the worst they had ever encountered.*
have • *We're having a few difficulties with the computer.*
meet • *The next time you meet a situation like this, be careful.*
undergo • *The market is now undergoing a severe recession.*

experienced ADJECTIVE
very skilful as a result of practice
• *an experienced diver*
expert • *an expert pilot*
knowledgeable • *He's very knowledgeable in this field.*
practised • *a practised and accomplished surgeon*
seasoned • *a seasoned climber*
well-versed • *He is well-versed in many styles of jazz.*

ANTONYM
● inexperienced

expert ❶ NOUN
a skilled or knowledgeable person
• *A team of experts will be on hand to offer advice.*
ace (INFORMAL) • *former motor-racing ace Stirling Moss*
authority • *an authority on ancient Egypt*
buff (INFORMAL) • *Cliff is a bit of a film buff.*
guru • *fashion gurus who predicted a 70's revival*
master • *He is a master in the art of office politics.*
professional • *He's widely respected in the theatre as a true professional.*

specialist • *a specialist in tropical diseases*
wizard • *a financial wizard who made millions in the early 80's*

ANTONYM
● beginner

expert ❷ ADJECTIVE
skilled and knowledgeable
• *Mollison's expert approach impressed everyone.*
able • *an able and dedicated surgeon*
adept • *He's an adept guitar player.*
experienced • *He was an experienced traveller and knew the area well.*
knowledgeable • *He's very knowledgeable about Chinese pottery.*
proficient • *Jackson is proficient in several European languages.*
skilful • *the skilful use of light in his early paintings*
skilled • *Ian is a highly skilled photographer.*

MORE SYNONYMS
● adroit
● dexterous
● masterly
● practised

explain VERB
to give extra information about something • *He explained to us how the system worked.*
define • *Can you define what you mean by "excessive"?*
describe • *an attempt to describe the whole process*
illustrate • *Let me illustrate this point with an example.*

MORE SYNONYMS
● elucidate
● expound

explanation NOUN

a helpful or clear description • *his lucid explanation of Einstein's theories*

clarification • *Her clarification has done little to help matters.*

definition • *a definition of what we actually mean by 'symbolism'*

description • *a fascinating description of how the pyramids were built*

exposition • *the fullest available exposition of Coleridge's ideas*

explode ❶ VERB

to burst or cause to burst loudly • *the sound of a bomb exploding nearby*

blow up • *Their boat blew up as they slept.*

burst • *Joey blew up the balloon until it burst.*

detonate • *Troops managed to detonate the mine safely.*

go off • *The bomb went off without any warning.*

set off • *No-one knows who planted the bomb, or how it was set off.*

explode ❷ VERB

to become angry suddenly • *I asked him if he'd finished and he just exploded.*

blow up • *When she finally told him, he blew up and walked out.*

go berserk • *He'll go berserk if he ever finds out.*

go mad • *He went mad when I mentioned the kids.*

explode ❸ VERB

to increase suddenly and rapidly • *Sales of computer games have exploded in recent years.*

rocket • *Inflation has rocketed in the last few months.*

shoot up • *Prices shot up and the shelves were soon empty.*

soar • *Demand for shares in his new company has soared.*

explosion NOUN

a violent burst of energy • *The explosion shattered windows all along the street.*

bang • *A loud bang made me run for cover.*

blast • *Three people were killed in the blast.*

expose ❶ VERB

to make something visible • *The wreck was exposed by the action of the tide.*

reveal • *His shirt was open, revealing his tattooed chest.*

show • *a short skirt which showed too much of her legs*

uncover • *She removed her scarf and uncovered her head.*

expose ❷ VERB

to tell the truth about someone or something • *He has been exposed as a liar and a cheat.*

bring to light • *The truth will be brought to light eventually.*

reveal • *an investigation that revealed widespread corruption*

show up • *She was finally shown up as a hypocrite.*

uncover • *We uncovered evidence of fraud.*

unearth • *Investigators have unearthed new evidence.*

express ❶ VERB

to say what you think • *She expressed interest in the plans for the new dam.*

communicate • *People must learn to communicate their feelings.*

couch • *Their demands, though*

a b c d **e** f g h i j k l m n o p q r s t u v w x y z

A B C D **E** F G H I J K L M N O P Q R S T U V W X Y Z

extreme, are couched in moderate language.
phrase • *It sounds fine, but I would have phrased it differently.*
put • *Absolutely – I couldn't have put it better.*
put across • *the need to put across your message without offending anyone*
voice • *Local people have voiced their concern over plans for a bypass.*

MORE SYNONYMS
● articulate
● enunciate
● utter
● verbalize

express ② ADJECTIVE
very fast • *a special express delivery service*
direct • *There's also a direct train.*
fast • *delays due to an accident in the fast lane*
high-speed • *the high-speed rail link between London and Paris*
nonstop • *the new nonstop service to New York*

expression ① NOUN
the look on your face that shows your feelings • *an aggrieved expression*
countenance • *the beaming countenance of the prime minister*
face • *Why are you all wearing such long faces?*

MORE SYNONYMS
● aspect
● mien

expression ② NOUN
a word or phrase used to communicate • *a good old American expression*
idiom • *talking in the idiom of the Home Counties*

phrase • *What is the origin of the phrase?*
remark • *her passing remark to the camera*
term • *a derogatory term for an Arab*

extend ① VERB
to have a particular size or position • *The region will extend way beyond the capital.*
continue • *The caves continue for miles beneath the hills.*
hang • *The branches hang down to the ground.*
reach • *a long shirt that reached to her knees*
stretch • *an area of forest stretching as far as the eye could see*

extend ② VERB
to stick out • *a brass peg that extended from the end of the mast*
jut out • *The tip of the island juts out like a finger into the sea.*
project • *the ruins of a fort which projected from the mud*
protrude (FORMAL) • *a huge rock protruding from the surface of the lake*
stick out • *pieces of rough metal that stuck out like spikes*

extend ③ VERB
to make something larger • *We'd like to extend the house and build a conservatory.*
add to • *They will be adding to their range of children's wear.*
develop • *He developed the US arm of the company.*
enlarge • *plans to enlarge the conference centre*
expand • *an unsuccessful attempt to expand the store's range of footwear*
widen • *the need to widen the appeal of the scheme*

Can't find the word you're looking for? Try the index.

MORE SYNONYMS
- augment
- broaden
- supplement

extensive ❶ ADJECTIVE
covering a large area • *a manor house set in extensive grounds*
broad • *a broad expanse of green lawn*
expansive • *an expansive grassy play area*
large • *a large country estate*
spacious • *a spacious dining area*
sweeping • *the sweeping curve of the bay*
vast • *vast stretches of land*
wide • *Worktops should be wide enough to allow food preparation.*

extensive ❷ ADJECTIVE
very great in effect • *The blast caused extensive damage.*
comprehensive • *comprehensive television coverage of last week's events*
considerable • *He has considerable powers within the party.*
far-reaching • *a decision with far-reaching consequences*
great • *great changes in British society*
pervasive • *the pervasive influence of the army in national life*
untold • *This might do untold damage to her health.*
widespread • *There is widespread support for the proposals.*

extent NOUN
the length, area, or size of something • *The full extent of the losses was revealed yesterday.*
degree • *To what degree were you in control of these events?*
level • *the level of public concern*

over this issue
measure • *The full measure of the government's dilemma has become apparent.*
scale • *He underestimates the scale of the problem.*
size • *the size of the task*

MORE SYNONYMS
- expanse
- magnitude

extra ❶ ADJECTIVE
more than is usual or expected • *The company is taking on extra staff for the summer.*
added • *The Tandoori Cottage has the added advantage of being cheap.*
additional • *the need for additional funding*
excess • *If there's any excess sauce, you can freeze it.*
further • *the introduction of further restrictions*
more • *We need three more places at the table.*
new • *the burden of new legislation on top of all the recent changes*
spare • *There are spare blankets in the cupboard.*

MORE SYNONYMS
- ancillary
- auxiliary
- supplementary

extra ❷ NOUN
something that is not included with other things • *Air conditioning is an optional extra.*
accessory • *the accessories you have to buy to make the place look good*
addition • *the latest addition to the team*
bonus • *The view from the hotel was an added bonus.*

a b c d e f g h i j k l m n o p q r s t u v w x y z

Can't find the word you're looking for? Try the index.

extract ➊ VERB

to take or get something out of somewhere • *Citric acid can be extracted from orange juice.*

draw • *Villagers still have to draw their water from wells.*

mine • *the finest gems, mined from all corners of the world*

obtain • *Opium is obtained from poppies.*

pull out • *I can pull that information out of the database for you.*

remove • *Three bullets were removed from his wounds.*

take out • *I got an abscess so he took the tooth out.*

extract ➋ VERB

to get information from someone • *He tried to extract further information from the witness.*

draw • *They finally drew a confession from him.*

elicit (FORMAL) • *the question of how far police should go to elicit a confession*

get • *How did you get an admission like that out of her?*

glean • *We're gleaning information from all sources.*

obtain • *Police have obtained statements from several witnesses.*

extract ➌ NOUN

a small section of music or writing • *an extract from his latest novel*

excerpt • *an excerpt from Tchaikovsky's Nutcracker*

passage • *He read out a passage from Milton.*

reading • *The author treated us to a reading from his latest novel.*

section • *Let's study a section of the text in more detail.*

snatch • *We played them a snatch of a violin concerto.*

snippet • *snippets of popular classical music*

extraordinary ADJECTIVE

unusual or surprising • *He really is an extraordinary man.*

amazing • *What an amazing coincidence!*

bizarre • *It's such a bizarre thing to happen.*

odd • *It's an odd combination of colours.*

singular • *Cathy gave me a smile of singular sweetness.*

strange • *It's a strange piece of music.*

surprising • *A surprising number of women prefer to wear trousers to work.*

unusual • *It's a most unusual way to spend your holiday.*

ANTONYM

● ordinary

extreme ➊ ADJECTIVE

very great in degree or intensity • *those people living in extreme poverty*

acute • *a mistake that caused acute embarrassment for everyone concerned*

deep • *a decision that caused deep resentment*

dire • *He is in dire need of hospital treatment.*

great • *a change in the law that could cause many people great hardship*

intense • *A number of people collapsed in the intense heat that day.*

profound • *feelings of profound shock and anger*

severe • *a business with severe financial problems*

A B C D E F G H I J K L M N O P Q R S T U V W X Y Z

extreme ❷ ADJECTIVE

unusual or unreasonable • *I think that's rather an extreme reaction.*
drastic • *Let's not do anything too drastic.*
exceptional • *I think this is an exceptional case.*
excessive • *a newspaper feature about the use of excessive force by the police*
extravagant • *All that money being spent on hospitality seemed a bit extravagant.*
radical • *The government is introducing a series of radical economic reforms.*
unreasonable • *I don't think she's being the least bit unreasonable.*

extreme ❸ NOUN

the highest or furthest degree or point • *We're just going from one extreme to the other.*
boundary • *the boundaries of artistic freedom*
depth • *the beauty of the countryside in the depths of winter*
end • *There are extremist groups at both ends of the political spectrum.*
height • *His behaviour was the height of bad manners.*
limit • *The ordeal tested the limits of their endurance.*
ultimate • *A Rolls-Royce is the ultimate in luxury.*

MORE SYNONYMS
- acme
- apex
- nadir
- pinnacle
- zenith

a
b
c
d
e
f
g
h
i
j
k
l
m
n
o
p
q
r
s
t
u
v
w
x
y
z

Can't find the word you're looking for? Try the index.

Ff

face ❶ NOUN
the front part of the head • *A strong wind was blowing in my face.*
countenance • *He met each enquiry with an impassive countenance.*
features • *Her features were strongly defined.*
mug (SLANG) • *He managed to get his ugly mug on the telly.*

MORE SYNONYMS
● lineaments
● physiognomy

face ❷ NOUN
a surface or side of something
• *the north face of Everest*
aspect • *The house had a south-west aspect.*
exterior • *The exterior of the building was made of brick.*
front • *There was a large veranda at the front of the house.*
side • *narrow valleys with steep sides*
surface • *tiny waves on the surface of the water*

face ❸ VERB
to look towards something or someone • *a room that faces on to the street*
be opposite • *I was opposite her at the breakfast table.*
look at • *She turned to look at the person who was speaking.*
overlook • *The pretty room overlooks a beautiful garden.*

fact NOUN
a piece of information that is true
• *a statement of verifiable fact*
certainty • *A general election became a certainty three weeks ago.*
reality • *Fiction and reality became increasingly blurred.*
truth • *In the town, very few know the whole truth.*

ANTONYM
● lie

factor NOUN
something that helps to cause a result • *Physical activity is an important factor in maintaining fitness.*
aspect • *Exam results illustrate only one aspect of a school's success.*
cause • *Smoking is the biggest preventable cause of death and disease.*
consideration • *Money was also a consideration.*
element • *Fitness has now become an important element in our lives.*
influence • *Van Gogh was a major influence on the development of modern painting.*
part • *Respect is a very important part of any relationship.*

MORE SYNONYMS
● circumstance
● determinant

factory NOUN
a building where goods are made

Can't find the word you're looking for? Try the index.

• He owned furniture factories in several areas.
mill • a textile mill
plant • The plant produces most of the company's output.
works • the steel works

fade VERB
to make or become less intense • The fabric had faded in the bright sunlight.
die away • The sound died away gradually.
dim • The house lights dimmed.
discolour • Exposure to bright light can cause wallpaper to discolour.
dull • Repeated washing had dulled the bright finish.
wash out • This dye won't wash out.

fail ❶ VERB
to be unsuccessful • He failed in his attempt to take over the company.
be defeated • The vote to change the law was defeated.
be in vain • It became clear that his efforts had been in vain.
be unsuccessful • My job application was unsuccessful.
come to grief • Many marriages have come to grief over lack of money.
fall through • Negotiations with business leaders fell through last night.
flunk (INFORMAL) • He flunked all his exams.

ANTONYM
● succeed

fail ❷ VERB
to omit to do something • They failed to phone her.
neglect • They never neglect their duties.

omit • He had omitted to tell her of the change in his plans.

fail ❸ VERB
to become less effective • His eyesight began to fail.
cease • The secrecy about his condition had ceased to matter.
decline • His power declined as he grew older.
give out • All machines give out eventually.
sink • Her spirits sank lower and lower.
stop working • The boat came to a halt when the engine stopped working.
wane • her mother's waning strength

failure ❶ NOUN
a lack of success • to end in failure
breakdown • a breakdown of the talks between the parties
defeat • It is important not to admit defeat.
downfall • people wishing to see the downfall of the government
fiasco • The evening was a total fiasco.
miscarriage • a miscarriage of justice

ANTONYM
● success

failure ❷ NOUN
an unsuccessful person or thing • The venture was a complete failure.
disappointment • a disappointment to his family
flop (INFORMAL) • The play turned out to be a flop.
loser • He had always been a loser.
no-hoper (AUSTRALIAN AND NEW ZEALAND) • hanging around a group of no-hopers

a
b
c
d
e
f
g
h
i
j
k
l
m
n
o
p
q
r
s
t
u
v
w
x
y
z

MORE SYNONYMS
- incompetent
- ne'er-do-well

failure ❸ NOUN
a weakness in something • *a failure in the insurance system*
deficiency • *a serious deficiency in their defence system*
shortcoming • *The book has many shortcomings.*

faint ❶ ADJECTIVE
lacking in intensity • *a faint smell of tobacco*
dim • *dim lighting*
faded • *a faded sign on the side of the building*
indistinct • *The lettering was worn and indistinct.*
low • *She spoke in a low voice.*
muted • *some muted cheers from the gallery*
vague • *a vague memory*

ANTONYM
- strong

faint ❷ ADJECTIVE
feeling dizzy and unsteady • *Feeling faint is one of the symptoms.*
dizzy • *suffering from dizzy spells*
giddy • *He felt giddy after the ride.*
light-headed • *She felt light-headed because she hadn't eaten.*

MORE SYNONYMS
- enervated
- vertiginous

faint ❸ VERB
to lose consciousness temporarily • *to faint from shock*
black out • *The blood drained from his head and he blacked out.*
collapse • *I collapsed when I heard the news.*
pass out • *to pass out with pain*

swoon (LITERARY) • *Women in the '20s swooned over Valentino.*

fair ❶ ADJECTIVE
reasonable and just • *a fair trial*
equal • *the commitment to equal opportunities*
equitable • *an equitable allocation of resources*
impartial • *an impartial observer*
legitimate • *a legitimate claim to the money*
proper • *It's right and proper that he should be here.*
upright • *an upright and trustworthy man*

MORE SYNONYMS
- disinterested
- dispassionate
- unbiased

ANTONYM
- unfair

fair ❷ ADJECTIVE
having light-coloured hair or pale skin • *long fair hair*
blonde or **blond** • *she had blonde tresses*
light • *He had a light complexion and blue eyes.*

ANTONYM
- dark

fair ❸ NOUN
an outdoor entertainment • *a country fair*
bazaar • *a fundraising bazaar*
carnival • *the annual Antigua Carnival*
exhibition • *an international trade exhibition*
festival • *a rock festival*
fete • *The church fete was a popular attraction.*
show • *an agricultural show*

Can't find the word you're looking for? Try the index.

faith ❶ NOUN

trust in a thing or a person
• *to have great faith in something*
confidence • *They had no confidence in the police.*
trust • *His trust in them was misplaced.*

faith ❷ NOUN

a person's or community's religion
• *They believed in the old faith.*
belief • *united by belief*
creed • *open to all, regardless of creed*
persuasion • *people of all religious persuasions*
religion • *the Christian religion*

faithful ❶ ADJECTIVE

loyal to someone or something
• *a faithful dog*
devoted • *They are devoted to each other.*
loyal • *a sign of true and loyal friendship*
staunch • *a staunch member of the party*
true • *a true believer*

MORE SYNONYMS
⬤ steadfast
⬤ unwavering

ANTONYM
⬤ unfaithful

faithful ❷ ADJECTIVE

accurate and truthful • *The film was faithful to the novel.*
accurate • *an accurate description of the event*
exact • *an exact copy of the original*
strict • *We demand strict adherence to the rules.*
true • *The film was quite true to life.*

fake ❶ NOUN

a deceitful imitation of a thing or person • *These paintings are fakes.*
copy • *It wasn't real, just a copy.*
forgery • *The signature was a forgery.*
fraud • *Many psychics are frauds.*
imitation • *The 'antique' chair is in fact a clever imitation.*
reproduction • *a reproduction of a famous painting*
sham • *The election was denounced as a sham.*

fake ❷ ADJECTIVE

imitation and not genuine • *fake fur*
artificial • *It's made with artificial sweeteners.*
counterfeit • *a large number of counterfeit documents*
false • *a false passport*
imitation • *bound in imitation leather*
phoney or **phony** (INFORMAL)
• *He used a phoney accent.*

ANOTHER SYNONYM
⬤ assumed

ANTONYM
⬤ real

RELATED WORD
⬤ PREFIX: pseudo-

fake ❸ VERB

to pretend to experience something • *He faked his own death.*
feign • *to feign illness*
pretend • *Todd shrugged with pretended indifference.*
simulate • *writhing around in simulated agony*

fall ❶ VERB

to descend towards the ground
• *The tile fell from the roof.*

a
b
c
d
e
f
g
h
i
j
k
l
m
n
o
p
q
r
s
t
u
v
w
x
y
z

Can't find the word you're looking for? Try the index.

A B C D E F G H I J K L M N O P Q R S T U V W X Y Z

collapse • *The bridge collapsed on to the road.*
drop • *bombs dropping from the sky*
plunge • *A bus plunged into the river.*
topple • *He toppled slowly backwards.*
trip • *She tripped and broke her leg.*

ANTONYM
● rise

fall ❷ VERB
to become lower or less • *Output fell by more than half.*
decline • *a declining birth rate*
decrease • *The number of bankruptcies decreased last year.*
diminish • *Resources are diminishing steadily.*
dwindle • *his dwindling authority*
plummet • *plummeting share prices*
subside • *The flood waters have subsided.*

MORE SYNONYMS
● abate
● depreciate
● ebb

ANTONYM
● increase

fall ❸ NOUN
a reduction in amount • *a fall in the exchange rate*
decline • *signs of economic decline*
decrease • *an overall decrease of 10%*
drop • *the sharp drop in export sales*
reduction • *The bank announced a reduction in interest rates.*
slump • *a slump in property prices*

ANTONYM
● rise

false ❶ ADJECTIVE
not true or correct • *He gave a false name and address.*
erroneous • *to arrive at an erroneous conclusion*
fictitious • *the source of the fictitious rumours*
incorrect • *a decision based on incorrect information*
mistaken • *I had a mistaken view of what had happened.*
untrue • *The remarks were completely untrue.*

ANTONYM
● true

false ❷ ADJECTIVE
not genuine but intended to seem so • *false hair*
artificial • *an artificial limb*
bogus • *their bogus insurance claim*
fake • *a fake tan*
forged • *They crossed the frontier using forged documents.*
simulated • *a simulated display of affection*

MORE SYNONYMS
● ersatz
● spurious

ANTONYM
● genuine

RELATED WORD
● PREFIX: pseudo-

false ❸ ADJECTIVE
unfaithful and deceitful • *They turned out to be false friends.*
deceitful • *deceitful and misleading remarks*
disloyal • *He was accused of being disloyal to the company.*
insincere • *A lot of actors are insincere.*

Can't find the word you're looking for? Try the index.

unfaithful • *left alone by her unfaithful husband*

MORE SYNONYMS
- duplicitous
- perfidious

fame NOUN
the state of being very well-known • *The film brought him international fame.*
eminence • *to achieve eminence as a politician*
glory • *my moment of glory*
prominence • *He came to prominence with his bestselling novel.*
renown • *a singer of great renown*
reputation • *the city's reputation as a place of romance*

familiar ADJECTIVE
knowing something well • *Most children are familiar with the stories.*
acquainted with • *Peter was well acquainted with Wordsworth.*
aware of • *aware of the dangers of smoking*
knowledgeable about • *They were very knowledgeable about gardening.*
versed in • *She was well versed in company law.*

ANTONYM
- unfamiliar

family ❶ NOUN
a group of relatives • *My family are always supportive of me.*
descendants • *Their descendants lived there for centuries.*
relations • *friends and relations*
relatives • *She had relatives in many countries.*

RELATED WORD
- ADJECTIVE: familial

family ❷ NOUN
a group of related species • *Tigers are members of the cat family.*
class • *several classes of butterflies*
classification • *The classification includes conifers.*
kind • *different kinds of roses*

famous ADJECTIVE
very well-known • *the most famous woman of her time*
celebrated • *his most celebrated film*
distinguished • *a distinguished academic family*
illustrious • *the most illustrious scientists of the century*
legendary • *His skills are legendary.*
noted • *He is noted for his generosity.*
renowned • *The area is renowned for its cuisine.*

MORE SYNONYMS
- lionized
- signal

ANTONYM
- unknown

fan NOUN
an enthusiast about something or someone • *a fan of the new band*
adherent • *The movement was gaining adherents everywhere.*
admirer • *one of her many admirers*
devotee • *a devotee of chamber music*
lover • *an art lover*
supporter • *rival football supporters*
zealot • *a religious zealot*

MORE SYNONYMS
- aficionado
- buff
- enthusiast

Can't find the word you're looking for? Try the index.

fanatic NOUN
someone who is extremely
enthusiastic about something
• *a football fanatic*
activist • *political activists*
devotee • *a devotee of the movement*
extremist • *groups of religious
extremists*
militant • *The militants took over
the organization.*
zealot • *He was a supporter but
not a zealot.*

fanatical ADJECTIVE
showing extreme support for
something • *a fanatical patriot*
fervent • *a fervent supporter*
obsessive • *obsessive about motor
racing*
passionate • *a passionate interest*
rabid • *a rabid racist group*
wild • *I am wild about this band.*

MORE SYNONYMS
● immoderate
● zealous

fancy ❶ VERB
to want to have or do something
• *He fancied a drink.*
be attracted to • *I am attracted to
the idea of emigrating.*
hanker after • *to hanker after a
bigger car*
have a yen for • *She had a yen for
some new clothes.*
would like • *I would really like
some ice cream.*

fancy ❷ ADJECTIVE
special and elaborate • *dressed up
in fancy clothes*
decorated • *She preferred
decorated surfaces to plain ones.*
elaborate • *his elaborate costume
ideas*
extravagant • *the extravagant*

frescoes in the upper church
intricate • *covered with intricate
patterns*
ornate • *an ornate picture frame*

MORE SYNONYMS
● baroque
● embellished
● ornamented

ANTONYM
● plain

far ❶ ADVERB
at a great distance from something
• *The sea was far below us.*
afar • *seen from afar*
a great distance • *They travelled
a great distance.*
a long way • *The guy's lonely and
a long way from home.*
deep • *deep into the jungle*
miles • *He lived miles away.*

far ❷ ADVERB
to a great extent or degree • *far
better than the others*
considerably • *The dinners were
considerably less formal than before.*
incomparably • *South Africa
seems incomparably richer than the
rest of Africa.*
much • *I feel much better now.*
very much • *Things got very much
worse.*

far ❸ ADJECTIVE
very distant • *in the far south of the
country*
distant • *the distant horizon*
long • *a long distance from here*
outlying • *The outlying areas are
accessible only by air.*
remote • *a cottage in a remote
village*

ANTONYM
● near

Can't find the word you're looking for? Try the index.

A
B
C
D
E
F
G
H
I
J
K
L
M
N
O
P
Q
R
S
T
U
V
W
X
Y
Z

fascinate VERB

to be of intense interest to someone • *He was fascinated by the new discovery.*
absorb • *totally absorbed by her career*
bewitch • *Bill was bewitched by her charm.*
captivate • *Her looks captivated the whole world.*
enthral • *She sat enthralled by the actors.*
intrigue • *Her story intrigued them.*

MORE SYNONYMS

- beguile
- enchant
- spellbind
- transfix

fashion ❶ NOUN

a popular style of dress or behaviour • *changing fashions in clothing*
craze • *the latest health craze*
fad • *just a passing fad*
style • *a revival of an old style*
trend • *the current trend in footwear*
vogue • *a vogue for fitness training*

fashion ❷ NOUN

a manner or way of doing something • *It works in a similar fashion.*
manner • *in a friendly manner*
method • *He did it by his usual method.*
mode • *a different mode of life*
way • *in her usual resourceful way*

fashion ❸ VERB

to make and shape something • *fashioned from rough wood*
construct • *an inner frame constructed from timber*
create • *It was created from odds and ends.*

make • *a doll made from fabric*
mould • *They moulded the cups from clay.*
shape • *Shape the dough into a loaf.*
work • *a machine for working the stone*

fashionable ADJECTIVE

very popular • *a fashionable restaurant*
current • *the current thinking on the subject*
in (INFORMAL) • *Jogging was the in thing.*
latest • *all the latest hairstyles*
popular • *the most popular movie*
prevailing • *contrary to prevailing attitudes*

MORE SYNONYMS

- chic
- in vogue
- trendsetting

ANTONYM

- old-fashioned

fast ❶ ADJECTIVE

moving at great speed • *a fast train*
accelerated • *at an accelerated pace*
hurried • *He ate a hurried breakfast.*
quick • *a quick learner*
rapid • *a rapid rise through the company*
speedy • *best wishes for a speedy recovery*
swift • *as swift as an arrow*

MORE SYNONYMS

- fleet
- mercurial
- winged

ANTONYM

- slow

a
b
c
d
e
f
g
h
i
j
k
l
m
n
o
p
q
r
s
t
u
v
w
x
y
z

Can't find the word you're looking for? Try the index.

A
B
C
D
E
F
G
H
I
J
K
L
M
N
O
P
Q
R
S
T
U
V
W
X
Y
Z

fast ❷ ADVERB
quickly and without delay • *You'll have to move fast.*
hastily • *sheltering in hastily erected tents*
hurriedly • *students hurriedly taking notes*
quickly • *She worked quickly and methodically.*
rapidly • *moving rapidly across the field*
swiftly • *They had to act swiftly to save him.*

ANTONYM
● slowly

fast ❸ ADVERB
firmly and strongly • *She held fast to the rail.*
firmly • *with windows firmly shut*
securely • *The door was securely locked and bolted.*
tightly • *held tightly in his arms*

fasten VERB
to close or attach something • *Fasten your seat belts.*
attach • *He attached a label to the plant.*
fix • *It was fixed on the wall.*
join • *joined together by string*
lock • *a locked door*
secure • *The chest was secured with a lock and chain.*
tie • *Tie your shoelaces.*

fat ADJECTIVE
weighing too much • *a fat man*
▷ see Word Study **fat**, page 680

ANTONYM
● thin

fatal ❶ ADJECTIVE
causing death • *fatal injuries*
deadly • *a deadly disease*
incurable • *It was regarded as an*

incurable illness.
lethal • *a lethal dose of sleeping pills*
mortal • *They were in mortal danger.*
terminal • *terminal cancer*

fatal ❷ ADJECTIVE
having an undesirable effect • *The mistake was fatal to my plans.*
calamitous • *a calamitous air crash*
catastrophic • *The water shortage is potentially catastrophic.*
disastrous • *This could have disastrous consequences for industry.*
lethal • *a lethal left hook*

fate NOUN
a power believed to control events • *the fickleness of fate*
chance • *a victim of chance*
destiny • *We are masters of our own destiny.*
fortune • *Remember, fortune favours the brave.*
providence • *His death was an act of providence.*

MORE SYNONYMS
● kismet
● nemesis
● predestination

fault ❶ NOUN
something for which someone is responsible • *It was all my fault.*
blame • *They put the blame on her.*
liability • *The company was forced to admit liability.*
responsibility • *He accepted full responsibility for the error.*

fault ❷ NOUN
a defective quality in something • *a minor technical fault*
blemish • *a blemish on an otherwise outstanding career*

defect • *a manufacturing defect*
deficiency • *serious deficiencies in the system*
drawback • *The plan had one major drawback.*
failing • *the country's many failings*
flaw • *serious character flaws*
imperfection • *small imperfections on the surface*
weakness • *his one weakness*

ANTONYM
- strength

fault ❸ VERB
to find reasons to be critical of someone • *Her conduct cannot be faulted.*
blame • *I don't blame him.*
censure • *He was censured by the committee.*
criticize • *The minister criticized the police.*

faulty ADJECTIVE
containing flaws or errors • *Faulty goods should be sent back.*
defective • *a lorry with defective brakes*
flawed • *The test results were seriously flawed.*
imperfect • *an imperfect specimen*
invalid • *That's an invalid argument.*
unsound • *a building that is structurally unsound*

MORE SYNONYMS
- fallacious
- imprecise
- malfunctioning

favour ❶ NOUN
a liking or approval of something • *The proposals met with favour.*
approval • *to gain his father's approval*
esteem • *in high esteem*

grace • *to fall from grace*
support • *They gave us their full support.*

ANTONYM
- disapproval

favour ❷ NOUN
a kind and helpful action • *Can you do me a favour?*
courtesy • *the courtesy of a personal response*
good turn • *to do someone a good turn*
kindness • *She did me the kindness of calling.*
service • *a service to your country*

ANTONYM
- wrong

favour ❸ VERB
to prefer something or someone • *They favoured the eldest child.*
prefer • *the preferred candidate*
single out • *He is always being singled out for special treatment.*

favourable ❶ ADJECTIVE
of advantage and benefit to someone • *favourable conditions*
advantageous • *the most advantageous course of action*
beneficial • *a beneficial effect on our health*
good • *He got a very good deal.*
opportune • *an opportune moment to attack*
suitable • *Conditions were not suitable for life to flourish.*

MORE SYNONYMS
- auspicious
- propitious
- timely

ANTONYM
- unfavourable

a
b
c
d
e
f
g
h
i
j
k
l
m
n
o
p
q
r
s
t
u
v
w
x
y
z

Can't find the word you're looking for? Try the index.

A
B
C
D
E
F
G
H
I
J
K
L
M
N
O
P
Q
R
S
T
U
V
W
X
Y
Z

favourable ❷ ADJECTIVE
positive and expressing approval
• *a favourable response*
affirmative • *to give an affirmative answer*
amicable • *amicable discussions*
approving • *a warm, approving glance*
friendly • *The proposal was given a friendly reception.*
positive • *a positive effect on the situation*
sympathetic • *He got a sympathetic hearing.*
welcoming • *a welcoming atmosphere*

ANTONYM
● unfavourable

favourite ❶ ADJECTIVE
being someone's best-liked person or thing • *my favourite hotel*
best-loved • *our best-loved music*
dearest • *Her dearest wish was fulfilled.*
favoured • *the favoured child of elderly parents*
preferred • *his preferred method of exercise*

favourite ❷ NOUN
the thing or person someone likes best • *The youngest was always her favourite.*
darling • *the darling of the family*
idol • *the idol of his fans*
pet • *the teacher's pet*
pick • *the pick of the bunch*

favouritism NOUN
unfair favour shown to a person or group • *There was never a hint of favouritism.*
bias • *political bias in broadcasting*
one-sidedness • *The committee must show no one-sidedness.*

MORE SYNONYMS
● nepotism
● partiality
● partisanship

ANTONYM
● impartiality

fear ❶ NOUN
an unpleasant feeling of danger
• *shivering with fear*
alarm • *I looked at him with growing alarm.*
awe • *in awe of his great powers*
dread • *She thought with dread of the coming storm.*
fright • *He jumped with fright at the noise.*
panic • *a moment of panic*
terror • *to shake with terror*

MORE SYNONYMS
● apprehensiveness
● cravenness
● trepidation

fear ❷ VERB
to feel frightened of something
• *There is nothing to fear.*
be afraid • *The dog was afraid of him.*
be frightened • *I am frightened of thunder.*
be scared • *Are you scared of snakes?*
dread • *He dreaded angry scenes.*
take fright • *The horse took fright at the sudden noise.*

feature ❶ NOUN
a particular characteristic of something • *an unusual feature of the room*
aspect • *every aspect of our lives*
attribute • *a normal attribute of human behaviour*
characteristic • *their physical characteristics*
mark • *distinguishing marks*

Can't find the word you're looking for? Try the index.

property • *the magnetic properties of iron*
quality • *skills and personal qualities*

feature ❷ NOUN
a special article or programme
• *a news feature*
article • *a travel article*
column • *the advice column*
item • *an item about chemical waste*
piece • *a specially-written piece*
report • *a film report on the scandal*
story • *front-page news stories*

feature ❸ VERB
to include and draw attention to something • *featuring an interview with the president*
emphasize • *to emphasize their differences*
give prominence to • *The Times is alone in giving prominence to the visit.*
spotlight • *a book spotlighting female singers*
star • *starring a major Australian actor*

feel ❶ VERB
to experience emotionally • *I felt enormous happiness.*
experience • *They seem to experience more distress than the others.*
suffer • *suffering from pangs of conscience*
undergo • *to undergo a change of heart*

feel ❷ VERB
to believe that something is the case • *She feels she is in control of her life.*
believe • *I believe they are right.*

consider • *We consider them to be our friends.*
deem • *I deemed it best to cancel the party.*
judge • *She was judged to be capable of anything.*
think • *I think I am very lucky.*

feel ❸ VERB
to touch something physically
• *Feel this lovely material!*
finger • *He was fingering the coins in his pocket.*
fondle • *She fondled the dog's ears.*
stroke • *I stroked the smooth wooden surface.*
touch • *He touched my face.*

feeling ❶ NOUN
the experiencing of an emotion
• *feelings of envy*
emotion • *trembling with emotion*
fervour • *religious fervour*
heat • *He spoke with some heat about his experiences.*
passion • *She argued with great passion.*
sentiment • *I'm afraid I don't share your sentiments.*

feeling ❷ NOUN
a physical sensation • *a feeling of pain*
sensation • *a very pleasant sensation*
sense • *a slight sense of heat at the back of my throat*

feeling ❸ NOUN
an opinion on something • *strong feelings on politics*
inclination • *neither the time nor the inclination*
opinion • *a consensus of opinion*
point of view • *an unusual point of view on the subject*
view • *You should make your views known to your local MP.*

a
b
c
d
e
f
g
h
i
j
k
l
m
n
o
p
q
r
s
t
u
v
w
x
y
z

Can't find the word you're looking for? Try the index.

fellowship ❶ NOUN
a feeling of friendliness within a group • *a sense of community and fellowship*
brotherhood • *a symbolic act of brotherhood*
camaraderie • *the camaraderie among soldiers*
companionship • *the companionship between old friends*

fellowship ❷ NOUN
a group of people with a common interest • *a fellowship of writers*
association • *a trade association*
brotherhood • *a secret international brotherhood*
club • *a youth club*
league • *the League of Nations*
society • *the historical society*

female ❶ NOUN
a person or animal which can have babies • *Hay fever affects males more than females.*
girl • *a girls' school*
lady • *a nice young lady*
sheila (AUSTRALIAN AND NEW ZEALAND; INFORMAL) • *his role as a sheila in his own play*
woman • *the number of women in the police force*

ANTONYM
● male

female ❷ ADJECTIVE
relating to females • *the world's greatest female distance runner*
feminine • *the traditional feminine role*
girlish • *She gave a girlish giggle.*
womanly • *a womanly shape*

ANTONYM
● male

fertile ADJECTIVE
capable of producing plants or offspring • *fertile soil*
fruitful • *The fruitful earth gave forth its treasures.*
productive • *the most productive vineyards*
prolific • *Chinchillas are prolific breeders.*
rich • *This plant grows in moist rich ground.*

MORE SYNONYMS
● fecund
● generative

ANTONYM
● barren

fervent ADJECTIVE
showing sincere and enthusiastic feeling • *a fervent admirer of her work*
ardent • *one of the most ardent supporters of the policy*
committed • *a committed socialist*
devout • *She was a devout Christian.*
enthusiastic • *a huge and enthusiastic crowd*
impassioned • *an impassioned appeal for peace*
passionate • *I'm a passionate believer in public art.*
zealous • *He was a recent convert, and very zealous.*

festival ❶ NOUN
an organized series of events • *an arts festival*
carnival • *The carnival lasted for three days.*
entertainment • *theatrical entertainments*
fair • *The book fair attracted many visitors.*
fete • *a church fete*
gala • *the May Day gala*

festival ❷ NOUN

a day or period of religious celebration • *open except on days of religious festivals*
anniversary • *The anniversary is celebrated each spring.*
holiday • *the Easter holiday*

CHRISTIAN FESTIVALS

Advent
Ascension Day
Ash Wednesday
Candlemas
Christmas
Corpus Christi
Easter
Epiphany
Good Friday
Lent
Maundy Thursday
Michaelmas
Palm Sunday
Pentecost
Quadragesima
Shrove Tuesday
Trinity
Whitsun

JEWISH FESTIVALS

Feast of Tabernacles
Hanukkah, Hanukah or Chanukah
Passover or Pesach
Purim
Rosh Hashanah
Shavuot, Shabuoth or Pentecost
Sukkoth or Succoth
Yom Kippur or Day of Atonement

HINDU FESTIVALS

Diwali
Durga-puja
Dussehra
Ganesh Chaturthi
Holi
Janmashtami
Navaratri
Raksha Bandhan
Ramanavami
Sarasvati-puja

MUSLIM FESTIVALS

Al Hijrah
Ashura
Eid-ul-Adha or Id-ul-Adha
Eid-ul-Fitr or Id-ul-Fitr
Lailat-ul-Isra' wa'l Mi'raj
Lailat-ul-Qadr
Mawlid al-Nabi
Ramadan

SIKH FESTIVALS

Baisakhi Mela
Diwali Mela
Hola Mohalla Mela
the Gurpurabs

BUDDHIST FESTIVALS

Wesak

few ADJECTIVE

small in number • *a few moments ago*
infrequent • *at infrequent intervals*
meagre • *a society with meagre resources*
not many • *Not many people attended the meeting.*
scanty • *scanty memories of his childhood*
scarce • *Resources are scarce.*
sparse • *a bare landscape with sparse trees*

ANTONYM
● many

fidget VERB

to move and change position restlessly • *fidgeting in his seat*
fiddle (INFORMAL) • *She fiddled with her pencil.*
jiggle • *He's jiggling his keys.*

a
b
c
d
e
f
g
h
i
j
k
l
m
n
o
p
q
r
s
t
u
v
w
x
y
z

Can't find the word you're looking for? Try the index.

squirm • *He squirmed and wriggled with impatience.*
twitch • *Everybody twitched in their seats.*

field ❶ NOUN

an area of farm land • *a field full of sheep*
green • *on the village green*
meadow • *a grassy meadow*
pasture • *cows grazing in the pasture*

field ❷ NOUN

a particular subject or interest • *a breakthrough in the field of physics*
area • *a politically sensitive area*
department • *Health care isn't my department.*
domain • *in the domain of art*
province • *This is the province of a different section.*
speciality • *His speciality was mythology.*
territory • *an expert in his own territory of history*

MORE SYNONYMS

● bailiwick
● discipline
● metier

fierce ❶ ADJECTIVE

wild and aggressive • *a fierce lion*
aggressive • *encouraging aggressive behaviour in later life*
dangerous • *These birds are dangerous.*
ferocious • *two and a half days of ferocious violence*
murderous • *a murderous attack*

MORE SYNONYMS

● barbarous
● fell
● feral

ANTONYM

● gentle

fierce ❷ ADJECTIVE

very intense • *a fierce contest*
intense • *We found ourselves standing in intense heat.*
keen • *a keen interest in cars*
relentless • *The pressure was relentless.*
strong • *a strong dislike*

fight ❶ VERB

to take part in a battle or contest • *He fought the world champion.*
battle • *The gang battled with the police.*
brawl • *men brawling drunkenly in the street*
grapple • *grappling with an alligator*
struggle • *He was struggling with police outside the club.*

fight ❷ NOUN

an aggressive struggle • *a fight to the death*
action • *wounded in action*
battle • *a gun battle*
bout • *a wrestling bout*
combat • *the end of a long combat*
duel • *He was killed in a duel.*
skirmish • *a minor border skirmish*

fight ❸ NOUN

an angry disagreement • *a fight with my mother*
argument • *an argument over a boyfriend*
blue (AUSTRALIAN; SLANG) • *a bloke I'd had a blue with years ago*
dispute • *a dispute over ticket allocation*
row • *Maxine and I had a terrible row.*
squabble • *a family squabble over Sunday lunch*

fighter NOUN

someone who physically fights another person • *a tough street fighter*

Can't find the word you're looking for? Try the index.

soldier • *well-equipped soldiers*
warrior • *a brave warrior*

figure ❶ NOUN

a number, or amount represented by a number • *No one really knows the true figures.*
amount • *Postal money orders are available in amounts up to $700.*
digit • *a code made up of letters and digits*
number • *A lot of marriages end in divorce, but we don't know the exact number.*
numeral • *the numeral six*
statistic • *Official statistics show wages declining by 24%.*
total • *Then he added everything together to arrive at the final total.*

figure ❷ NOUN

a shape, or the shape of someone's body • *A figure appeared in the doorway.*
body • *She's got nice hair and a great body.*
build • *a tall woman with a naturally slim build*
form • *The shadowy form receded into the darkness.*
physique • *He has the physique and energy of a man half his age.*
shape • *tall, dark shapes moving in the mist*
silhouette • *Tuck the shirt in to give yourself a streamlined silhouette.*

figure ❸ NOUN

a person • *international political figures*
character • *What a sad character that Nigel is.*
dignitary • *a visiting dignitary of great importance*
person • *My grandfather was a person of some influence.*

personality • *The event was attended by many showbiz personalities.*
player • *a key player in the negotiations*

figure ❹ VERB (INFORMAL)

to guess or conclude something • *I figure I'll learn from experience.*
expect • *I expect you're just tired.*
guess • *I guess he's right.*
reckon (INFORMAL) • *Toni reckoned that it must be about three o'clock.*
suppose • *What do you suppose he's up to?*

fill VERB

to make something full • *Fill it up with water.*
cram • *Mourners crammed the small church.*
gorge • *gorged with food*
pack • *a lorry packed with explosives*
stock • *a lake stocked with carp*
stuff • *Stuff the pillow with feathers.*

ANTONYM
● empty

final ❶ ADJECTIVE

being the last one in a series • *the fifth and final day*
closing • *in the closing stages of the race*
concluding • *the concluding part of the serial*
eventual • *the eventual aim of their policies*
last • *his last chance*
ultimate • *The ultimate outcome will be different.*

ANTONYM
● first

final ❷ ADJECTIVE

unable to be changed or questioned • *The judges' decision is final.*

a b c d e **f** g h i j k l m n o p q r s t u v w x y z

Can't find the word you're looking for? Try the index.

absolute • *absolute authority*
conclusive • *conclusive proof*
definite • *too soon to give a definite answer*
definitive • *the definitive account of the war*

finally ❶ ADVERB

happening after a long time
• *It finally arrived.*
at last • *He came at last.*
at the last moment • *They changed their minds at the last moment.*
eventually • *The flight eventually left.*
in the end • *It all turned out right in the end.*
in the long run • *a success in the long run*

finally ❷ ADVERB

in conclusion of something
• *Finally, I'd like to talk about safety measures.*
in conclusion • *In conclusion, we have to agree.*
in summary • *It was, in summary, a satisfactory outcome.*
lastly • *Lastly, I would like to thank my agent.*

finance ❶ VERB

to provide the money for something
• *financed by the government*
back • *a fund backed by local businesses*
fund • *The scheme is funded by the banks.*
pay for • *He paid for his trip out of his savings.*
support • *She supported herself through university.*

finance ❷ NOUN

the managing of money and investments • *the world of high finance*

banking • *the international banking system*
budgeting • *We must exercise caution in our budgeting this year.*
commerce • *industry and commerce*
economics • *the economics of the third world*
investment • *tax incentives to encourage investment*

financial ADJECTIVE

relating to money • *financial difficulties*
economic • *an economic crisis*
fiscal • *the long-term fiscal policy of this country*
money • *on the money markets*

MORE SYNONYMS

● budgetary
● monetary
● pecuniary

find ❶ VERB

to discover something • *I can't find my notes.*
come across • *He came across the book by chance.*
discover • *They discovered the body in the bushes.*
locate • *locating the position of the gene*
track down • *to track down her parents*
turn up • *They failed to turn up any evidence.*
unearth • *to unearth the missing copy*

MORE SYNONYMS

● descry
● espy
● ferret out

ANTONYM

● lose

Can't find the word you're looking for? Try the index.

find ❷ VERB

to realize or learn something • *We found that we got on well.*

become aware • *I became aware of his work last year.*

detect • *I detected a note of envy in her voice.*

discover • *It was discovered that the goods were missing.*

learn • *I flew from New York on learning of his death.*

realize • *They realized too late that it was wrong.*

fine ❶ ADJECTIVE

very good and admirable • *fine clothes*

admirable • *with many admirable qualities*

beautiful • *a beautiful view of the river*

excellent • *inns with excellent cuisine*

magnificent • *his magnificent country house*

outstanding • *an area of outstanding natural beauty*

splendid • *a splendid collection of cartoons*

fine ❷ ADJECTIVE

small in size or thickness • *powder with very fine particles*

delicate • *delicate curtains to let in the light*

lightweight • *certain lightweight fabrics*

powdery • *soft powdery dust*

sheer • *a sheer chiffon shirt*

small • *netting with a small mesh*

MORE SYNONYMS

- diaphanous
- gauzy
- gossamer

fine ❸ ADJECTIVE

subtle and precise • *the fine details*

fastidious • *fastidious attention to detail*

keen • *a keen eye for a bargain*

precise • *a gauge with precise adjustment*

refined • *a woman of refined tastes*

sensitive • *The radio had very sensitive tuning.*

subtle • *a very subtle distinction*

finish ❶ VERB

to complete something • *to finish a report*

close • *They have closed the deal.*

complete • *She completed her first novel.*

conclude • *He concluded his speech.*

end • *That ended our discussion.*

finalize • *to finalize an agreement*

ANTONYM

- start

finish ❷ NOUN

the last part of something • *to see it through to the finish*

close • *to bring to a close*

completion • *The project is nearing completion.*

conclusion • *at the conclusion of the programme*

end • *the end of the race*

ending • *The film had an unexpected ending.*

finale • *the grand finale of the evening*

MORE SYNONYMS

- culmination
- denouement
- termination

ANTONYM

- start

a
b
c
d
e
f
g
h
i
j
k
l
m
n
o
p
q
r
s
t
u
v
w
x
y
z

Can't find the word you're looking for? Try the index.

A
B
C
D
E
F
G
H
I
J
K
L
M
N
O
P
Q
R
S
T
U
V
W
X
Y
Z

finish ❸ NOUN

the surface appearance of
something • *a glossy finish*
grain • *the smooth grain of the wood*
lustre • *a similar lustre to silk*
polish • *The bodywork had a high
polish.*
shine • *It gives a beautiful shine to
the hair.*
surface • *a polished surface*
texture • *paper with a linen-like
texture*

fire ❶ NOUN

the flames produced when
something burns • *a ball of fire*
blaze • *The firemen were hurt in
the blaze.*
combustion • *Energy is released
by combustion.*
flames • *rescued from the flames*
inferno • *The building was an inferno.*

fire ❷ VERB

to shoot or detonate something
• *to fire a cannon*
detonate • *to detonate an
explosive device*
explode • *They exploded a bomb.*
launch • *The protesters launched
the missile from a boat.*
set off • *the largest nuclear
explosion ever set off on Earth*
shoot • *people shooting guns in all
directions*

fire ❸ VERB (INFORMAL)

to dismiss someone from a job
• *She was fired yesterday.*
discharge • *A trooper has been
discharged from the army.*
dismiss • *He was dismissed by the
bank.*
make redundant • *Many people
were made redundant.*
sack (INFORMAL) • *Jones was sacked
for disciplinary reasons.*

firm ❶ ADJECTIVE

solid and not soft • *Leave the ice
cream until it is firm.*
compressed • *compressed wood
pulp made into cardboard*
congealed • *a bowl of congealed
grease*
hard • *The snow was hard and
slippery.*
rigid • *Pour the mixture into a rigid
plastic container.*
set • *The glue wasn't completely
set.*
solid • *a block of solid wax*
stiff • *egg whites beaten until stiff*

ANTONYM
● soft

firm ❷ ADJECTIVE

resolute and determined • *The
department needs a firm manager.*
adamant • *He was adamant that
he would not resign.*
determined • *She was determined
to finish the game.*
inflexible • *his inflexible routine*
resolute • *a willingness to take
resolute action*
staunch • *many staunch
supporters*
unshakable • *an unshakable belief
in democracy*

MORE SYNONYMS
● obdurate
● steadfast
● unwavering

firm ❸ NOUN

a commercial organization • *a firm
of builders*
business • *a stockbroking business*
company • *his software
development company*
corporation • *one of the leading
banking corporations*

Can't find the word you're looking for? Try the index.

enterprise • *small business enterprises*
organization • *a multinational organization*

first ❶ ADJECTIVE
done or in existence before anything else • *the first moon landing*
earliest • *The earliest settlers lived there.*
initial • *our initial meeting*
opening • *There was a standing ovation on opening night.*
original • *She was one of the original cast.*
primeval • *the primeval forests of Europe*

ANTONYM
● last

first ❷ ADVERB
done or occurring before anything else • *You must do that first.*
beforehand • *Bill had prepared beforehand.*
earlier • *I did that one earlier.*
firstly • *Firstly, I'd like to thank you all for coming.*
initially • *not as bad as they initially predicted*
to begin with • *To begin with, we must prepare the soil.*

first ❸ ADJECTIVE
more important than anything else • *our first responsibility*
chief • *the chief pilot*
foremost • *one of our foremost thinkers*
leading • *the team's leading scorer*
prime • *He was the prime suspect.*
principal • *the principal reason*

first-rate ADJECTIVE
excellent • *They were dealing with a first-rate professional.*
excellent • *She does an excellent job as Fred's personal assistant.*
exceptional • *His piano playing is exceptional.*
first-class • *The food was first-class.*
marvellous • *He certainly is a marvellous actor.*
outstanding • *an outstanding athlete*
splendid • *We had a splendid meal.*
superb • *a superb 18-hole golf course*

MORE SYNONYMS
● superlative (FORMAL)
● unparalleled

fissure NOUN
a deep crack in rock or the ground • *There was a rumbling, and a fissure opened up.*
cleft • *a narrow cleft in the rocks*
crack • *The building developed large cracks in walls and ceilings.*
crevice • *a huge boulder with ferns growing in every crevice*
fault • *the San Andreas Fault*
rift • *In the open bog are many rifts and potholes.*
split • *The slate has a few small splits around the edges.*

fit ❶ VERB
to be the right shape or size • *made to fit a child*
belong • *I just didn't belong there.*
correspond • *The two angles didn't correspond exactly.*
dovetail • *The movement's interests dovetailed with her own.*
go • *small enough to go in your pocket*
match • *Match the pegs with the holes.*

a
b
c
d
e
f
g
h
i
j
k
l
m
n
o
p
q
r
s
t
u
v
w
x
y
z

Can't find the word you're looking for? Try the index.

fit ❷ VERB
to place something in position
• *a fitted carpet*
adapt • *shelves adapted to suit the smaller books*
arrange • *Arrange the pieces to form a picture.*
place • *Place the card in the slots.*
position • *plants which are carefully positioned in the alcove*

fit ❸ ADJECTIVE
in good physical condition
• *a reasonably fit person*
healthy • *a healthy mind in a healthy body*
in good condition • *in good condition for his age*
robust • *a strong, robust man*
trim • *a trim figure*
well • *Alison was looking well.*

ANTONYM
● unfit

fitting ❶ ADJECTIVE
appropriate and suitable for something • *a fitting end*
appropriate • *an appropriate outfit for the occasion*
correct • *the correct thing to say*
proper • *It isn't proper that she should be here.*
right • *He always said just the right thing.*
suitable • *some hymns suitable for a wedding*

MORE SYNONYMS
● apposite
● decorous

fitting ❷ NOUN
a part attached to something else
• *fixtures and fittings*
accessory • *bathroom accessories*
attachment • *a wide range of attachments*

component • *special components*
part • *Extra parts can be added later.*
unit • *The unit plugs into any TV set.*

fix ❶ VERB
to attach or secure something
• *fixed to the wall*
attach • *The label was attached with glue.*
bind • *sticks bound together with string*
fasten • *Fasten the two parts securely.*
secure • *firmly secured by strong nails*
stick • *She stuck the pictures into the book.*

fix ❷ VERB
to repair something broken
• *The bike is fixed now.*
correct • *He may need surgery to correct the problem.*
mend • *They finally got round to mending the roof.*
patch up • *Patch up those holes.*
repair • *I had my shoes repaired.*

fix ❸ NOUN (INFORMAL)
a difficult situation • *in a bit of a fix*
difficulty • *He was in real difficulties with money.*
mess • *Their economy was in a mess.*
predicament • *a tricky predicament*
quandary • *in a quandary about what to do*

flabby ADJECTIVE
fat and with loose flesh • *a flabby stomach*
floppy • *the floppy bodies in tracksuits*
sagging • *a sagging double chin*
slack • *The skin around her eyelids is now slack and baggy.*

MORE SYNONYMS
- flaccid
- pendulous

ANTONYM
- taut

flash ❶ NOUN
a sudden short burst of light
• *a flash of lightning*
burst • *a burst of fire*
flare • *the sudden flare of a match*
sparkle • *sparkles from her sequinned dress*

flash ❷ VERB
to shine briefly and often repeatedly • *They signalled by flashing a light.*
flare • *matches flaring in the darkness*
glint • *the low sun glinting off the windscreens*
glitter • *the glittering crown on his head*
sparkle • *Diamonds sparkled on her wrists.*
twinkle • *stars twinkling in the night sky*

flashy ADJECTIVE
showy in a vulgar way • *flashy clothes*
flamboyant • *an unsuitably flamboyant outfit*
garish • *curtains in garish colours*
showy • *an expensive and showy watch*
tacky (INFORMAL) • *tacky red sunglasses*
tasteless • *a house with tasteless decor*

MORE SYNONYMS
- meretricious
- ostentatious

ANTONYM
- modest

flat ❶ NOUN
a set of rooms for living in • *a two-bedroomed flat*
apartment • *a huge apartment overlooking the park*
rooms • *We shared rooms while we were students.*

flat ❷ ADJECTIVE
level and smooth • *a flat surface*
horizontal • *horizontal with the ground*
level • *a completely level base*
levelled • *The floor must be levelled before you start.*
smooth • *a smooth marble top*
unbroken • *the unbroken surface of the sea*

ANTONYM
- uneven

flat ❸ ADJECTIVE
without emotion or interest • *a dreadfully flat speech*
boring • *a boring menu*
dull • *He told some really dull stories.*
insipid • *an insipid performance*
monotonous • *an interesting story expressed in a monotonous voice*
weak • *A weak ending spoiled the story.*

flatter ❶ VERB
to praise someone insincerely • *flattering remarks*
compliment • *She was often complimented for her looks.*
fawn • *surrounded by fawning attendants*

flatter ❷ VERB
to make more attractive • *clothes that flatter your figure*
enhance • *an enhancing neckline*
set off • *Blue sets off the colour of your eyes.*

a b c d e **f** g h i j k l m n o p q r s t u v w x y z

Can't find the word you're looking for? Try the index.

A
B
C
D
E
F
G
H
I
J
K
L
M
N
O
P
Q
R
S
T
U
V
W
X
Y
Z

suit • *That shade really suits your skin tone.*

flattery NOUN
flattering words and behaviour
• *susceptible to flattery*
adulation • *received with adulation by the critics*
fawning • *the constant fawning of her courtiers*

MORE SYNONYMS
● blandishment
● obsequiousness
● sycophancy

flaw NOUN
an imperfection in something
• *The program contained serious flaws.*
blemish • *A small blemish spoiled the surface.*
defect • *a manufacturing defect*
fault • *a fault in the engine*
imperfection • *slight imperfections in the weave*

flee VERB
to run away from something
• *to flee the country*
bolt • *He bolted for the exit.*
escape • *They escaped across the frontier.*
fly • *to fly from war*
leave • *to leave the scene of the crime*
run away • *to run away from the police*
take flight • *250,000 took flight from the floods.*

flexible ❶ ADJECTIVE
able to bend or be bent easily
• *long flexible bristles*
elastic • *an elastic rope*
lithe • *lithe and graceful movements*
pliable • *baskets made from pliable cane*

supple • *exercises to keep you supple*

MORE SYNONYMS
● ductile
● lissom *or* lissome
● pliant

flexible ❷ ADJECTIVE
able to adapt or change • *flexible working hours*
adaptable • *an adaptable attitude to work*
discretionary • *the discretionary powers of the courts*
open • *an open mind*

flinch VERB
to move suddenly with fear or pain
• *The sharp pain made her flinch.*
cringe • *to cringe in terror*
shrink • *She shrank from the flames.*
start • *They started at the sudden noise.*
wince • *I could see him wincing with pain.*

float ❶ VERB
to be supported by water • *leaves floating on the river*
be on the surface • *The oil is on the surface of the sea.*
bob • *toys bobbing in the bath*
drift • *to drift in on the tide*
lie on the surface • *The boat lay on the surface of the lake.*
stay afloat • *They could stay afloat without swimming.*

ANTONYM
● sink

float ❷ VERB
to be carried on the air • *floating on the breeze*
drift • *The music drifted in through the window.*

Can't find the word you're looking for? Try the index.

glide • *eagles gliding above us*
hang • *A haze of perfume hung in the room.*
hover • *Butterflies hovered above the flowers.*

flood ❶ NOUN
a large amount of water coming suddenly • *Many people were drowned in the floods.*
deluge • *houses overwhelmed by the deluge*
downpour • *a downpour of torrential rain*
spate • *The river was in spate.*
torrent • *Torrents of water gushed into the reservoir.*

flood ❷ NOUN
a large amount of something • *a flood of angry letters*
rush • *a sudden rush of panic*
stream • *a stream of bad language*
torrent • *He replied with a torrent of abuse.*

flood ❸ VERB
to overflow with water • *The river flooded its banks.*
deluge • *Heavy rain deluged the capital.*
drown • *a drowned village*
overflow • *an overflowing bath*
submerge • *to prevent water submerging the cobbled streets*
swamp • *His small boat was swamped by the waves.*

flourish ❶ VERB
to develop or function successfully or healthily • *Business was flourishing.*
bloom • *Not many economies bloomed during that period.*
boom • *Sales are booming.*
come on • *He is coming on very well at his new school.*

do well • *Out-of-town superstores are doing well.*
prosper • *The high street banks continue to prosper.*
succeed • *the qualities needed in small businesses to succeed*
thrive • *Today the company continues to thrive.*

ANTONYM
● fail

flourish ❷ VERB
to wave or display something • *He flourished his glass.*
brandish (LITERARY) • *He appeared brandishing a sword.*
display • *She proudly displayed the letter and began to read.*
hold aloft • *He held the cup aloft.*
wave • *Crowds were waving flags and applauding.*

flourish ❸ NOUN
a bold sweeping or waving movement • *with a flourish of his hand*
flick • *a flick of the whip*
sweep • *With one sweep of her hand she threw back the sheets.*
wave • *Steve stopped him with a wave of the hand.*

flow ❶ VERB
to move or happen in a continuous stream • *a river flowing gently down into the valley*
circulate • *to circulate round the entire house*
glide • *models gliding down the catwalk*
roll • *rolling gently to the sea*
run • *A stream ran beside the road.*
slide • *Tears slid down her cheeks.*

flow ❷ NOUN
a continuous movement of something • *traffic flow*

a
b
c
d
e
f
g
h
i
j
k
l
m
n
o
p
q
r
s
t
u
v
w
x
y
z

Can't find the word you're looking for? Try the index.

A
B
C
D
E
F
G
H
I
J
K
L
M
N
O
P
Q
R
S
T
U
V
W
X
Y
Z

current • *currents of air*
drift • *the drift towards the cities*
flood • *a flood of complaints*
stream • *a constant stream of visitors*
tide • *to slow the tide of change*

fluent ADJECTIVE
expressing yourself easily and without hesitation • *a fluent speaker of French*
articulate • *an articulate young woman*
easy • *the easy flow of his argument*
effortless • *He spoke with effortless ease.*
flowing • *a smooth, flowing presentation*
ready • *a ready answer*

ANTONYM
● hesitant

fly ❶ VERB
to move through the air • *to fly to Paris*
flit • *butterflies flitting among the flowers*
flutter • *The birds fluttered on to the feeder.*
sail • *a kite sailing above the trees*
soar • *eagles soaring in the sky*

fly ❷ VERB
to move very quickly • *She flew down the stairs.*
dart • *She darted to the window.*
dash • *We had to dash.*
hurry • *They hurried to catch the train.*
race • *I had to race round the shops.*
rush • *rushing off to work*
speed • *The car sped off.*
tear • *He tore off down the road.*

foam ❶ NOUN
a mass of tiny bubbles • *waves tipped with foam*

bubbles • *She liked to have bubbles in the bath.*
froth • *Yeast swells up to form a froth.*
head • *the foamy head on beer*
lather • *It took a lot of shampoo to get a good lather.*

foam ❷ VERB
to swell and form bubbles • *a foaming river*
bubble • *The boiling liquid bubbled up.*
fizz • *a drink fizzing in the glass*
froth • *It frothed up over the top.*

focus ❶ VERB
to concentrate your vision on something • *His eyes began to focus.*
aim • *Astronomers aimed optical telescopes in their direction.*
concentrate • *concentrating his gaze on a line of ants*
direct • *He directed the light on to the roof.*
fix • *Their radar was fixed on the enemy ship.*

focus ❷ NOUN
the centre of attention • *the focus of the conversation*
centre • *She was the centre of an admiring crowd.*
focal point • *the focal point of the whole room*
hub • *the hub of the financial world*
target • *the target of the attack*

foil ❶ VERB
to prevent something from happening • *The police foiled an armed robbery.*
check • *to check the rise in crime*
counter • *countering the threat of strike action*
defeat • *an important role in defeating the rebellion*

Can't find the word you're looking for? Try the index.

frustrate • *a frustrated attempt*
thwart • *to thwart someone's plans*

MORE SYNONYMS
● circumvent
● nullify

foil ② NOUN
a contrast to something • *a perfect foil for his temperament*
antithesis • *the antithesis of his crooked brother*
background • *a fitting background for her beauty*
complement • *the perfect complement to the antique furniture*
contrast • *The green woodwork is a stunning contrast to the black walls.*

fold ① VERB
to bend something • *He folded the paper carefully.*
bend • *Bend the top towards you.*
crease • *Crease along the dotted line.*
crumple • *He crumpled the note and put it in his pocket.*
tuck • *Tuck in the top and bottom.*
turn under • *The end was turned under.*

fold ② NOUN
a crease in something • *hanging in folds*
bend • *There was a bend in the photograph.*
crease • *sharp creases in his shirt*
pleat • *a skirt with pleats*
wrinkle • *all the little wrinkles on Paul's face*

follow ① VERB
to pursue someone • *We were being followed.*
hound • *constantly hounded by photographers*
pursue • *He was pursued across several countries.*

stalk • *Her former husband was stalking her.*
track • *They tracked him to his home.*

follow ② VERB
to come after someone or something • *Night follows day.*
come after • *Summer comes after spring.*
succeed • *He was succeeded by his son.*
supersede • *Horses were superseded by cars.*

ANTONYM
● precede

follow ③ VERB
to act in accordance with something • *Follow the instructions carefully.*
comply • *in order to comply with EC regulations*
conform • *conforming to the new safety requirements*
obey • *You must obey the law.*
observe • *The army was observing a ceasefire.*

follower NOUN
a supporter of a person or belief • *a loyal follower of the movement*
believer • *many devout believers in the faith*
disciple • *one of his disciples*
fan • *football fans*
henchman • *always surrounded by his henchmen*
supporter • *He was a major supporter of the plan.*

MORE SYNONYMS
● adherent
● protagonist

ANTONYM
● leader

a
b
c
d
e
f
g
h
i
j
k
l
m
n
o
p
q
r
s
t
u
v
w
x
y
z

Can't find the word you're looking for? Try the index.

fond ❶ ADJECTIVE

feeling affection or liking • *a fond father*

adoring • *an adoring husband*
affectionate • *an affectionate smile*
devoted • *a devoted couple*
doting • *doting grandparents*
having a liking for • *She had a great liking for chocolate.*
loving • *a loving son*

fond ❷ ADJECTIVE

unlikely to happen or be fulfilled • *fond wishes for a better life*

deluded • *a deluded belief in future improvement*
empty • *empty promises of full employment*
foolish • *What foolish dreams we have!*
naive • *her naive belief in others' goodness*
vain • *the vain hope that he might lose weight*

MORE SYNONYMS

● delusory
● overoptimistic

food NOUN

things eaten to provide nourishment • *our favourite food*

diet • *a healthy balanced diet*
fare • *traditional regional fare*
foodstuffs • *basic foodstuffs*
kai (AUSTRALIAN AND NEW ZEALAND; INFORMAL) • *There's no kai in the house.*
nourishment • *unable to take nourishment*
provisions • *provisions for two weeks*
refreshment • *Refreshments will be provided.*
tucker (AUSTRALIAN AND NEW ZEALAND; INFORMAL) • *some of the cheapest pub tucker in town*

MORE SYNONYMS

● provender
● subsistence
● victuals

RELATED WORDS

● ADJECTIVE: alimentary
● NOUN: gastronomy

fool ❶ NOUN

an unintelligent person • *What a stupid fool he is!*

dope (INFORMAL) • *He felt such a dope.*
dunce • *I was a complete dunce at chemistry.*
idiot • *acting like an idiot*
ignoramus • *the ignoramus of the group*
moron • *They treated him like a moron.*

fool ❷ VERB

to trick someone • *Don't let him fool you.*

con (INFORMAL) • *conned out of all his money*
deceive • *deceiving the audience*
dupe • *in order to dupe the medical staff*
mislead • *a deliberately misleading statement*
trick • *They tricked him into believing it.*

MORE SYNONYMS

● bamboozle
● hoodwink

foolish ADJECTIVE

silly and unwise • *feeling foolish*

inane • *an inane remark*
nonsensical • *a nonsensical thing to say*
senseless • *It would be senseless to stop her.*
silly • *a silly thing to say*
unintelligent • *a weak and*

Can't find the word you're looking for? Try the index.

A B C D E F G H I J K L M N O P Q R S T U V W X Y Z

unintelligent man
unwise • *He had made some unwise investments.*

ANTONYM
- wise

forbid VERB
to order someone not to do something • *forbidden to go out*
ban • *banned from driving*
exclude • *Women were excluded from the classes.*
outlaw • *the outlawed political parties*
prohibit • *Fishing is prohibited.*
veto • *Their application was vetoed.*

ANTONYM
- allow

force ❶ VERB
to compel someone to do something • *We were forced to turn right.*
compel • *I felt compelled to act.*
drive • *They are driving the company into bankruptcy.*
make • *They made me do it.*
oblige • *We were obliged to abandon the car.*
pressurize • *trying to pressurize them*

MORE SYNONYMS
- coerce
- impel
- obligate

force ❷ NOUN
a pressure to do something • *They made him agree by force.*
compulsion • *a compulsion to write*
duress • *carried out under duress*
pressure • *under pressure to resign*

force ❸ NOUN
the strength of something • *the force of the explosion*
impact • *the impact of the blast*
might • *the full might of the army*
power • *massive computing power*
pressure • *the pressure of work*
strength • *The storm was gaining strength.*

foreign ADJECTIVE
relating to other countries • *foreign travel*
distant • *in that distant land*
exotic • *filmed in an exotic location*
overseas • *a long overseas trip*

foremost ADJECTIVE
most important or best • *one of the world's foremost scholars*
best • *He was the best player in the world throughout the 1950s.*
chief • *my chief reason for objecting to the plan*
first • *The first priority is to defeat inflation.*
greatest • *one of the West Indies' greatest cricketers*
leading • *the leading researchers in this area*
most important • *the country's most important politicians and philosophers*
prime • *I regard this as my prime duty.*
principal • *one of the country's principal publishing houses*
top • *The President met with his top military advisers.*

forest NOUN

TYPES OF FOREST	
bush	jungle
coppice	spinney
copse	thicket
grove	wood

a b c d e f g h i j k l m n o p q r s t u v w x y z

Can't find the word you're looking for? Try the index.

A
B
C
D
E
F
G
H
I
J
K
L
M
N
O
P
Q
R
S
T
U
V
W
X
Y
Z

forget VERB

to fail to remember something
• *I forgot to lock the door.*
fail to remember • *He failed to remember my name.*
omit • *omitting to mention the details*
overlook • *to overlook an important fact*

ANTONYM
- remember

forgive VERB

to stop blaming someone for something • *Can you ever forgive me?*
absolve • *The verdict absolved him from blame.*
condone • *We cannot condone violence.*
excuse • *Please excuse our bad behaviour.*
pardon • *Relatives had begged authorities to pardon him.*

ANTONYM
- blame

forgiveness NOUN

the act of forgiving • *I ask for your forgiveness.*
acquittal • *The jury voted for acquittal.*
mercy • *to beg for mercy*
pardon • *a presidential pardon*
remission • *with remission for good behaviour*

MORE SYNONYMS
- absolution
- exoneration

form ❶ NOUN

a type or kind • *He contracted a rare form of cancer.*
class • *a new class of nuclear-powered submarine*
kind • *a new kind of leadership*

sort • *Try to do some sort of exercise every day.*
type • *There are various types of this disease.*
variant • *The quagga was a beautiful variant of the zebra.*
variety • *an unusual variety of this common garden flower*

form ❷ NOUN

the shape or pattern of something
• *Valleys often take the form of deep canyons.*
contours • *the contours of the body*
layout • *He tried to recall the layout of the farmhouse.*
outline • *I could just see the outline of a building in the mist.*
shape • *little pens in the shape of baseball bats*
structure • *the chemical structure of this molecule*

form ❸ VERB

to be the elements that something consists of • *the articles that formed the basis of his book*
compose • *The force would be composed of troops from NATO countries.*
constitute • *The country's ethnic minorities constitute about 7% of its total population.*
make up • *Women officers make up 13 per cent of the police force.*
serve as • *an arrangement of bricks and planks that served as a bookshelf*

form ❹ VERB

to organize, create, or come into existence • *The bowl was formed out of clay.*
assemble • *a model assembled entirely from matchsticks*
create • *These patterns were created by the action of water.*

Can't find the word you're looking for? Try the index.

develop • *We must develop closer ties with Germany.*

draw up • *We've drawn up a plan of action.*

establish • *The school was established in 1989 by an Italian professor.*

fashion • *Stone Age settlers fashioned necklaces from animals' teeth.*

make • *The organic waste decomposes to make compost.*

formal ❶ ADJECTIVE

in accordance with convention • *a formal dinner*

conventional • *a conventional style of dress*

correct • *polite and correct behaviour*

precise • *They spoke very precise English.*

stiff • *his stiff manner and lack of humour*

ANTONYM
● informal

formal ❷ ADJECTIVE

official and publicly recognized • *No formal announcement has been made.*

approved • *a legally approved method of dealing with these*

legal • *They have a legal responsibility.*

official • *according to the official figures*

prescribed • *There is a prescribed procedure for situations like this.*

regular • *through the regular channels*

former ADJECTIVE

existing in the past • *a former tennis champion*

ancient • *the ancient civilizations*

bygone • *memories of a bygone age*

old • *our old school*

past • *a long list of past winners*

formidable ADJECTIVE

difficult to overcome • *They faced formidable obstacles.*

challenging • *a more challenging job*

daunting • *a daunting prospect*

difficult • *A difficult task lay ahead.*

intimidating • *She was an intimidating opponent.*

mammoth • *a mammoth undertaking*

onerous • *onerous responsibilities*

fort NOUN

a building for defence and shelter • *They had to abandon the fort.*

castle • *a heavily-guarded castle*

citadel • *The citadel towered above the river.*

fortification • *fortifications along the border*

fortress • *an ancient fortress*

fossick VERB (AUSTRALIAN AND NEW ZEALAND)

to search for something • *If you fossick around in some specialist music stores, you may find a copy.*

forage • *They were forced to forage for clothing and fuel.*

hunt • *A forensic team was hunting for clues.*

look • *I've looked through all my drawers and I can't find it anywhere.*

rummage • *He rummaged around the post room and found the document.*

search • *We've searched through the whole house for the keys.*

a
b
c
d
e
f
g
h
i
j
k
l
m
n
o
p
q
r
s
t
u
v
w
x
y
z

fragile ADJECTIVE
easily broken or damaged • *fragile china*
breakable • *Anything breakable or sharp had to be removed.*
dainty • *a dainty Japanese tea service*
delicate • *a delicate instrument*
flimsy • *packed in a flimsy box*
frail • *a frail shell*

MORE SYNONYMS
● frangible
● infirm

ANTONYM
● tough

fragrance NOUN
a pleasant smell • *the fragrance of the roses*
aroma • *the aroma of fresh bread*
bouquet • *a wine with a lively fruit bouquet*
perfume • *enjoying the perfume of the lemon trees*
scent • *flowers chosen for their scent*
smell • *a sweet smell of pine*

fragrant ADJECTIVE
having a pleasant smell • *fragrant oils*
aromatic • *a plant with aromatic leaves*
perfumed • *perfumed body cream*
sweet-smelling • *posies of sweet-smelling flowers*

ANTONYM
● smelly

frank ADJECTIVE
open and straightforward • *a frank discussion*
blunt • *his blunt approach*
candid • *She was completely candid with me.*

honest • *my honest opinion*
open • *an open, trusting nature*
plain • *plain talking*
straightforward • *spoken in a straightforward manner*

fraud ❶ NOUN
the act of deceiving someone • *electoral fraud*
deceit • *deliberate deceit*
deception • *obtaining money by deception*
guile • *children's lack of guile*
hoax • *a bomb hoax*
trickery • *They had to resort to trickery.*

MORE SYNONYMS
● chicanery
● duplicity
● spuriousness

fraud ❷ NOUN
someone or something that deceives you • *Many psychics are frauds.*
charlatan • *exposed as a charlatan*
cheat • *Cheats will be disqualified.*
fake • *The painting was a fake.*
forgery • *just a clever forgery*
imposter • *an imposter with false documents*
quack • *He tried all sorts of quacks.*

free ❶ ADJECTIVE
not being held prisoner • *a free man*
at large • *Three prisoners are at large.*
at liberty • *the last top Nazi still at liberty*
liberated • *newly liberated slaves*
loose • *He broke loose from his bonds.*

ANTONYM
● captive

free ❷ ADJECTIVE
available without payment • *a free brochure*
complimentary • *complimentary tickets*
gratis • *The meal was gratis.*
unpaid • *unpaid voluntary work*
without charge • *They mended it without charge.*

free ❸ VERB
to release from captivity • *to free the slaves*
discharge • *discharged from prison*
liberate • *liberated under the terms of the amnesty*
release • *The hostages were soon released.*
set at liberty • *He was set at liberty after ten years.*
set loose • *The animals were set loose after treatment.*

MORE SYNONYMS
● emancipate
● unfetter

ANTONYM
● imprison

freedom ❶ NOUN
the ability to choose • *freedom of action*
discretion • *Use your own discretion.*
latitude • *There is more latitude for personal opinions.*
leeway • *granted more leeway to pass reforms*
licence • *a licence to kill*
scope • *plenty of scope for improvement*

freedom ❷ NOUN
the state of being free or being set free • *gaining their freedom after months of captivity*
emancipation • *the emancipation of the slaves*

liberty • *three months' loss of liberty*
release • *the immediate release of the captives*

MORE SYNONYMS
● deliverance
● manumission

ANTONYM
● captivity

freedom ❸ NOUN
the absence of something unpleasant • *freedom from pain*
exemption • *granted exemption from all taxes*
immunity • *information in exchange for immunity from prosecution*

frenzy NOUN
wild and uncontrolled behaviour • *gripped by a frenzy of nationalism*
agitation • *in a state of intense agitation*
fury • *She stalked out in a fury.*
hysteria • *mass hysteria*
madness • *a moment of madness*
rage • *She flew into a rage.*

MORE SYNONYMS
● delirium
● paroxysm

frequent ❶ ADJECTIVE
happening often • *his frequent visits*
common • *a common occurrence*
continual • *continual demands for money*
everyday • *an everyday event*
habitual • *a habitual daydreamer*
recurrent • *a recurrent theme in her work*
repeated • *His parents made repeated attempts to visit.*

a
b
c
d
e
f
g
h
i
j
k
l
m
n
o
p
q
r
s
t
u
v
w
x
y
z

Can't find the word you're looking for? Try the index.

A
B
C
D
E
F
G
H
I
J
K
L
M
N
O
P
Q
R
S
T
U
V
W
X
Y
Z

ANTONYM
- rare

frequent ❷ VERB
to go somewhere often • *a restaurant which he frequents*
attend • *He often attends their meetings.*
haunt • *She haunted their house.*
patronize • *to patronize a hotel*
visit • *a place we often visit*

ANTONYM
- avoid

friend NOUN
a person you know and like • *lifelong friends*
china (SOUTH AFRICAN; INFORMAL) • *a drinking session with his chinas*
companion • *my constant companion*
confidant or **confidante** • *her only confidant*
crony • *surrounded by her cronies*
mate (INFORMAL) • *going out with his mates*
pal • *We are great pals.*

MORE SYNONYMS
- alter ego
- soul mate

ANTONYM
- enemy

friendly ADJECTIVE
kind and pleasant • *a very friendly crowd*
affectionate • *on affectionate terms*
amiable • *He was very amiable company.*
close • *The two were very close.*
cordial • *a most cordial welcome*
genial • *a genial host*
welcoming • *a welcoming house*

MORE SYNONYMS
- companionable
- comradely
- convivial

ANTONYM
- unfriendly

friendship NOUN
a state of being friendly with someone • *I value our friendship.*
affection • *to win their affection*
attachment • *the deep attachment between them*
closeness • *her closeness to her sister*
goodwill • *as a gesture of goodwill*

ANTONYM
- hostility

frighten VERB
to make someone afraid • *trying to frighten us*
alarm • *alarmed by the noise*
intimidate • *She is intimidated by her boss.*
scare • *You aren't scared of mice, are you?*
startle • *I didn't mean to startle you.*
terrify • *Heights terrified her.*
terrorize • *The gunmen terrorized the villagers.*
unnerve • *an unnerving silence*

frightened ADJECTIVE
having feelings of fear about something • *frightened of thunder*
afraid • *Jane was afraid of the other children.*
alarmed • *Don't be alarmed.*
petrified • *petrified of wasps*
scared • *scared of being alone in the house*
startled • *a startled animal*
terrified • *a terrified look*

MORE SYNONYMS

● cowed
● panicky
● terror-stricken

frightening ADJECTIVE

causing someone to feel fear • *a frightening experience*
alarming • *an alarming increase*
hair-raising • *at hair-raising speed*
intimidating • *threatening and intimidating behaviour*
menacing • *a menacing glance*
terrifying • *one of the most terrifying diseases*

frivolous ADJECTIVE

not serious or sensible • *a frivolous young person*
flippant • *a flippant comment*
foolish • *saying foolish and inappropriate things*
juvenile • *juvenile behaviour*
puerile • *your puerile schoolboy humour*
silly • *making silly jokes*

ANTONYM

● serious

front ❶ NOUN

the part that faces forward • *the front wall of the house*
face • *the face of the building*
frontage • *a restaurant with a river frontage*

ANTONYM

● back

front ❷ NOUN

the outward appearance of something • *a respectable front*
appearance • *the appearance of fair treatment*
exterior • *his tough exterior*
face • *a brave face*
show • *a convincing show of affection*

front ❸, in front PREPOSITION

further forward • *too close to the car in front*
ahead • *ahead of the rest of the field*
before • *I'm before you.*
leading • *the leading rider*

frown VERB

to draw the eyebrows together • *She frowned in concentration.*
glare • *The woman glared angrily at him.*
glower • *She glowered but said nothing.*
knit your brows • *He knitted his brows in concentration.*
scowl • *He scowled at the waiter.*

frozen ADJECTIVE

extremely cold • *frozen to the bone*
arctic • *arctic weather conditions*
chilled • *chilled to the marrow*
frigid • *frigid temperatures*
icy • *an icy wind*
numb • *numb with cold*

frustrate VERB

to prevent something from happening • *His efforts were frustrated.*
block • *They are blocking the peace process.*
check • *to check the spread of the virus*
foil • *They foiled all my plans.*
thwart • *his way to thwart your club's ambitions*

MORE SYNONYMS

● forestall
● nullify

fulfil VERB

to carry out or achieve something • *He decided to fulfil his dream and go to college.*

a
b
c
d
f
g
h
i
j
k
l
m
n
o
p
q
r
s
t
u
v
w
x
y
z

Can't find the word you're looking for? Try the index.

A
B
C
D
E
F
G
H
I
J
K
L
M
N
O
P
Q
R
S
T
U
V
W
X
Y
Z

accomplish • *If they all work together they can accomplish their goal.*
achieve • *We will strive to achieve these goals.*
carry out • *They seem to have very little intention of carrying out their commitments.*
perform • *Each component performs a different function.*
realize • *The question is, will our hopes ever be realized?*
satisfy • *The procedures should satisfy certain basic requirements.*

full ❶ ADJECTIVE
filled with something • *full of books*
filled • *filled up to the top*
loaded • *The van was loaded with furniture.*
packed • *The train was packed.*
saturated • *completely saturated with liquid*

ANTONYM
● empty

full ❷ ADJECTIVE
missing nothing out • *I want a full account of what happened.*
comprehensive • *a comprehensive guide to the area*
detailed • *a detailed description*
exhaustive • *an exhaustive treatment of the subject*
extensive • *extensive coverage of the earthquake*
maximum • *the way to take maximum advantage of pay TV*
thorough • *a thorough search*

full ❸ ADJECTIVE
loose-fitting • *a full skirt*
baggy • *a baggy sweater*
loose • *hidden under his loose shirt*
voluminous • *voluminous sleeves*

fun ❶ NOUN
an enjoyable activity • *It was great fun.*
amusement • *There is no amusement for teenagers in this village.*
enjoyment • *It gave us much enjoyment.*
entertainment • *little opportunity for entertainment*
pleasure • *to mix business and pleasure*
recreation • *time for recreation*

fun ❷, make fun of VERB
to tease someone • *Don't make fun of him.*
deride • *This theory is widely derided.*
laugh at • *They laughed at his hat.*
mock • *He was often mocked by his classmates.*
ridicule • *She allowed them to ridicule her.*
taunt • *a fellow pupil who had taunted him about his height*

MORE SYNONYMS
● lampoon
● rib
● satirize

function ❶ NOUN
the useful thing that something or someone does • *The main function of merchant banks is to raise capital.*
duty • *My duty is to look after the animals.*
job • *Their main job is to keep us healthy.*
purpose • *The purpose of the occasion was to raise money for charity.*
remit • *The centre's remit is to advise businesses.*
responsibility • *He handled his responsibilities as a counsellor in an intelligent fashion.*

Can't find the word you're looking for? Try the index.

role • *information about the drug's role in preventing infection*

function ② NOUN

a large formal dinner, reception, or party • *We were going down to a function in London.*
dinner • *a series of official dinners*
gathering • *I'm always shy at formal gatherings like that.*
party • *They met at a party.*
reception • *At the reception they served smoked salmon.*

function ③ VERB

to operate or work • *The heater was not functioning properly.*
go • *My car won't go in fog.*
operate • *Ceiling and wall lights can operate independently.*
perform • *When there's snow, how is this car going to perform?*
run • *The system is now running smoothly.*
work • *Is the telephone working today?*

fund ① NOUN

an amount of money • *the pension fund*
capital • *difficulty in raising capital*
foundation • *money from a research foundation*
pool • *a reserve pool of cash*
reserve • *a drain on the cash reserves*
supply • *to curb money supply and inflation*

fund ② NOUN

a large amount of something • *an extraordinary fund of energy*
hoard • *his hoard of supplies*
mine • *a mine of information*
reserve • *oil reserves*
reservoir • *the body's short-term reservoir of energy*
store • *a store of fuel*

fund ③ VERB

to provide the money for something • *to raise money to fund research into breast cancer*
finance • *big projects financed by foreign aid*
pay for • *His parents paid for his holiday.*
subsidize • *heavily subsidized by the government*
support • *He is supporting himself through college.*

fundi NOUN (SOUTH AFRICAN)

an expert • *The local fundis are wonderfully adept and have created a car for hunting.*
expert • *our team of experts*
guru • *Fashion gurus dictate some crazy ideas.*
master • *a master of the English language*
specialist • *a specialist in diseases of the nervous system*
virtuoso • *He was gaining a reputation as a piano virtuoso.*

funny ① ADJECTIVE

being strange or odd • *They heard a funny noise.*
mysterious • *in mysterious circumstances*
odd • *There was something odd about her.*
peculiar • *It tasted very peculiar.*
puzzling • *a puzzling development*
strange • *A strange thing happened.*
unusual • *a most unusual man*

funny ② ADJECTIVE

causing amusement • *a funny story*
amusing • *a most amusing lecturer*
comic • *comic moments*
comical • *the comical expression on his face*

a b c d e f g h i j k l m n o p q r s t u v w x y z

Can't find the word you're looking for? Try the index.

A
B
C
D
E
F
G
H
I
J
K
L
M
N
O
P
Q
R
S
T
U
V
W
X
Y
Z

hilarious • *We thought it was hilarious.*
humorous • *a humorous magazine*
witty • *a very witty speech*

MORE SYNONYMS
- droll
- jocular
- risible

ANTONYM
- serious

furious ❶ ADJECTIVE
extremely angry • *He is furious at the way his wife has been treated.*
enraged • *I got more and more enraged at my father.*
fuming • *He was still fuming over the remark.*
infuriated • *He knew how infuriated the conversation had made me.*
livid • *She was absolutely livid about it.*
mad • *I'm pretty mad about this, I can tell you.*
raging • *Inside, Sally was raging.*

MORE SYNONYMS
- frenzied
- incensed
- tumultuous

furious ❷ ADJECTIVE
involving great energy, effort, or speed • *a furious gunbattle*
breakneck • *Jack drove to Mayfair at breakneck speed.*
fierce • *Competition has been fierce between the rival groups.*
frantic • *There was frantic activity behind the scenes.*
frenzied • *the frenzied run-up to the general election*
intense • *The military on both sides are involved in intense activity.*

manic • *Preparations continued at a manic pace.*

ANOTHER SYNONYM
- frenetic

fuss ❶ NOUN
anxious or excited behaviour • *What's all the fuss about?*
agitation • *in a state of intense agitation*
bother • *I don't want any bother.*
commotion • *a commotion in the market*
confusion • *in the confusion after an ammunition dump blew up*
stir • *The play caused a stir here.*
to-do • *a big to-do*

MORE SYNONYMS
- ado
- fluster
- palaver

fuss ❷ VERB
to behave in a nervous or restless way • *Waiters fussed around the table.*
bustle • *shoppers bustling around the store*
fidget • *He was fidgeting with his tie.*
fret • *Stop fretting about the details.*

fussy ADJECTIVE
difficult to please • *fussy about his food*
choosy (INFORMAL) • *Cats can be choosy about what they eat.*
discriminating • *a discriminating visitor*
exacting • *She failed to meet his exacting standards.*
fastidious • *Disney was also fastidious about cleanliness.*
particular • *very particular about the colours he used*

Can't find the word you're looking for? Try the index.

MORE SYNONYMS
- faddish
- finicky
- pernickety

futile ADJECTIVE
having no chance of success • *a futile effort to run away*
abortive • *the abortive coup attempt*
forlorn • *forlorn hopes of future improvement*
unsuccessful • *an unsuccessful bid for independence*
useless • *It was useless to even try.*
vain • *in the vain hope of success*

ANTONYM
- successful

future ADJECTIVE
relating to a time after the present • *to predict future growth*
approaching • *concerned about the approaching winter*
coming • *in the coming months*
forthcoming • *candidates for the forthcoming elections*
impending • *her impending marriage*
later • *We'll discuss it at a later date.*
prospective • *my prospective employers*

ANTONYM
- past

a
b
c
d
e
f
g
h
i
j
k
l
m
n
o
p
q
r
s
t
u
v
w
x
y
z

Gg

gadget NOUN

a small machine or tool • *kitchen gadgets such as toasters and kettles*
appliance • *Switch off all electrical appliances when they're not in use.*
device • *a device that warns you when the batteries need changing*
machine • *a machine for slicing vegetables*
tool • *a tool for cutting wood, metal or plastic*

MORE SYNONYMS

- implement
- instrument
- utensil

gain ❶ VERB

to get something gradually • *Students can gain valuable experience by working.*
achieve • *Achieving our goals makes us feel good.*
acquire • *Companies should reward workers for acquiring more skills.*
earn • *She has earned the respect of the world's top women cyclists.*
obtain • *You would need to obtain permission to copy the design.*
secure • *He failed to secure enough votes for outright victory.*
win • *The long-term aim is to win promotion.*

MORE SYNONYMS

- attain
- capture
- reap

gain ❷ VERB

to get an advantage • *Areas of the world would actually gain from global warming.*
benefit • *Both sides have benefited from the talks.*
profit • *Frankie is now profiting from his crimes.*

gain ❸ NOUN

an increase or improvement in something • *The Party has made substantial gains in local elections.*
advance • *advances in computer technology*
growth • *The area has seen a rapid population growth.*
improvement • *a major improvement in standards*
increase • *an increase of 7% in visitors to the UK*
rise • *a 3% rise in electricity prices*

gamble ❶ VERB

to bet money on something • *John gambled heavily on the horses.*
back • *I backed Germany to win 1–0.*
bet • *He bet them 500 pounds they would lose.*

gamble ❷ VERB

to take a risk • *Few firms will be willing to gamble on new products.*
chance • *Armstrong chanced a gallop to the water.*
risk • *One of his daughters risked everything to join him in exile.*
stake • *He has staked his reputation on the outcome.*

Can't find the word you're looking for? Try the index.

MORE SYNONYMS
- hazard
- take a chance
- venture

gamble ❸ NOUN

a risk that someone takes • *We are taking a gamble on a young player.*
chance • *You take a chance on the weather when you holiday in the UK.*
lottery • *Robinson described the final as a bit of a lottery.*
risk • *How much risk are you prepared to take?*

game NOUN

an occasion on which people compete • *South Africa's first game of the season*
clash • *the clash between Australia and the West Indies*
contest • *The rain spoiled a good contest.*
match • *a football match*

gap ❶ NOUN

a space or a hole in something • *They squeezed through a gap in the fence.*
break • *stars twinkling between the breaks in the clouds*
chink • *All the walls have wide chinks in them.*
crack • *a crack in the curtains*
hole • *a hole in the wall*
opening • *an opening in the trees*
space • *the space between their car and the one in front*

MORE SYNONYMS
- cleft
- cranny
- crevice

gap ❷ NOUN

a period of time • *After a gap of nearly a decade, Manley was back.*
hiatus (FORMAL) • *The shop is open again after a two-year hiatus.*
interlude • *a happy interlude in the Kents' life*
interval • *There was a long interval of silence.*
lull • *a lull in the conversation*
pause • *Then, after a pause, he goes on.*

gap ❸ NOUN

a difference between people or things • *the gap between rich and poor*
difference • *He denied there were any major differences between them.*
disparity (FORMAL) • *disparities between poor and wealthy school districts*
inconsistency • *There were major inconsistencies in his evidence.*

garbage ❶ NOUN

things that people do not want • *piles of garbage*
debris • *screws, bolts and other debris from a scrapyard*
junk (INFORMAL) • *What are you going to do with all that junk?*
litter • *If you see litter in the corridor, pick it up.*
refuse (FORMAL) • *refuse collection and street cleaning*
rubbish • *household rubbish*
trash • *I forgot to take out the trash.*
waste • *industrial waste*

garbage ❷ NOUN (INFORMAL)

ideas and opinions that are untrue or unimportant • *I personally think this is complete garbage.*
drivel • *What absolute drivel!*
gibberish • *a politician talking gibberish*
nonsense • *all that poetic nonsense about love*
rubbish • *He's talking rubbish.*

Can't find the word you're looking for? Try the index.

A B C D E F **G** H I J K L M N O P Q R S T U V W X Y Z

garbled ADJECTIVE

confused or incorrect • *A garbled message awaited us at the desk.*
confused • *the latest twist in a murky and confused story*
distorted • *a distorted version of what was said*
incomprehensible • *Her speech was incomprehensible.*
jumbled • *his jumbled account of how Jack had been hired*
unintelligible • *He muttered something unintelligible.*

gasp ❶ VERB

to breathe in quickly through your mouth • *She gasped for air.*
choke • *People began to choke as smoke filled the air.*
gulp • *She gulped air into her lungs.*
pant • *Amy climbed rapidly until she was panting with the effort.*
puff • *I could see he was unfit because he was puffing.*

MORE SYNONYMS
● catch your breath
● fight for breath

gasp ❷ NOUN

a short quick breath of air • *An audible gasp went round the court.*
gulp • *I took in a large gulp of air.*
pant • *Her breath came in pants.*
puff • *He blew out a little puff of air.*

gather ❶ VERB

to come together in a group • *We gathered around the fireplace.*
assemble • *a place for students to assemble between classes*
congregate • *Youngsters love to congregate here in the evenings.*
flock • *The criticisms will not stop people flocking to see the film.*

mass • *The General was massing his troops for a counterattack.*
round up • *The police rounded up a number of suspects.*

MORE SYNONYMS
● convene
● marshal
● muster

ANTONYM
● scatter

gather ❷ VERB

to bring things together • *I suggest we gather enough firewood to last the night.*
accumulate • *In five years it has accumulated a huge debt.*
amass • *She has amassed a personal fortune of $38 million.*
collect • *1.5 million signatures have been collected.*
hoard • *They've begun to hoard food and gasoline.*
stockpile • *People are stockpiling food for the coming winter.*

gather ❸ VERB

to learn or believe something • *"He speaks English." "I gathered that."*
assume • *I assume the eggs are fresh.*
conclude • *He concluded that Oswald was somewhat abnormal.*
hear • *I heard that he was forced to resign.*
learn • *She wasn't surprised to learn that he was involved.*
understand • *I understand that he's just taken early retirement.*

gathering NOUN

a meeting with a purpose • *polite social gatherings*
assembly • *an assembly of party members*
congregation • *The congregation*

sang hymns and said prayers.
get-together (INFORMAL) • *family get-togethers*
meeting • *Can we have a meeting to discuss that?*
rally • *a pre-election rally*

MORE SYNONYMS
- conference
- congress
- convention

gaudy ADJECTIVE

colourful in a vulgar way • *gaudy fake jewellery*
bright • *fake fur, dyed in bright colours*
flashy • *women in flashy satin suits*
garish • *They climbed the garish purple-carpeted stairs.*
loud • *a loud checked shirt*
showy • *He favoured large showy flowers.*
tacky (INFORMAL) • *tacky red sunglasses*
vulgar • *I think it's a very vulgar house.*

MORE SYNONYMS
- jazzy
- ostentatious
- tasteless
- tawdry

general ❶ ADJECTIVE

relating to the whole of something • *a general decline in employment*
broad • *a broad outline of the Society's development*
comprehensive • *a comprehensive guide to the region*
overall • *The overall quality of pupils' work had shown a marked improvement.*

MORE SYNONYMS
- generic
- indiscriminate

- panoramic
- sweeping

ANTONYM
- specific

general ❷ ADJECTIVE

widely true, suitable or relevant • *The project should raise general awareness about bullying.*
accepted • *the accepted version of events*
broad • *a film with broad appeal*
common • *Such behaviour is common to all young people.*
universal • *Music and sports programmes have a universal appeal.*
widespread • *The proposals have attracted widespread support.*

ANTONYM
- special

generosity NOUN

willingness to give money, time or help • *She is well known for her generosity.*
benevolence • *Banks are not known for their benevolence.*
charity • *private acts of charity*
kindness • *We have been treated with such kindness by everybody.*

MORE SYNONYMS
- bounty
- liberality
- munificence
- open-handedness

ANTONYM
- meanness

generous ❶ ADJECTIVE

willing to give money, time or help • *The gift is generous by any standards.*
charitable • *Individuals can be charitable and help their neighbours.*

Can't find the word you're looking for? Try the index.

hospitable • *He was very hospitable to me when I came to New York.*

kind • *She is warm-hearted and kind to everyone.*

lavish • *The Princess received a number of lavish gifts from her hosts.*

liberal • *Don't be too liberal with your spending.*

MORE SYNONYMS
- munificent
- open-handed
- prodigal
- unstinting

ANTONYM
- mean

generous ❷ ADJECTIVE
very large • *a generous portion of spaghetti*

abundant • *an abundant supply of hot food*

ample • *There is ample space for a good-sized kitchen.*

plentiful • *a plentiful supply of beer*

ANTONYM
- meagre

genius ❶ NOUN
a very clever or talented person • *a mathematical genius*

brain • *the financial brain behind the company*

master • *Spiro Rosakis is a master of his craft.*

mastermind • *the mastermind of the plot to kill the ex-prime minister*

virtuoso • *The man is a virtuoso of pop music.*

genius ❷ NOUN
extraordinary ability or talent • *a poet of genius*

brains • *She has brains as well as beauty.*

brilliance • *his brilliance as a director*

intellect • *people of great intellect*

gentle ADJECTIVE
not violent or rough • *a quiet and gentle man*

benign • *a good-looking chap with a benign expression*

kind • *I fell in love with him because of his kind nature.*

kindly • *a kindly old gentleman*

meek • *He was a meek, mild-mannered fellow.*

mild • *Alexis was quiet, mild and happy-go-lucky.*

placid • *a look of impatience on her normally placid face*

soft • *She had a very soft heart.*

tender • *Her voice was tender.*

MORE SYNONYMS
- compassionate
- humane
- lenient
- sweet-tempered

ANTONYM
- cruel

genuine ADJECTIVE
not false or pretend • *They're convinced the picture is genuine.*

authentic • *an authentic French recipe*

bona fide • *We are happy to donate to bona fide charities.*

dinkum (AUSTRALIAN AND NEW ZEALAND; INFORMAL) • *They are all dinkum stolen bank notes.*

real • *a real Rembrandt*

ANTONYM
- fake

get ❶ VERB
to fetch or receive something • *I'll get us all a cup of coffee.*

Can't find the word you're looking for? Try the index.

acquire • *I have recently acquired a new camera.*
fetch • *Sylvia fetched a towel from the bathroom.*
obtain • *Evans was trying to obtain a false passport.*
procure (FORMAL) • *It remained very difficult to procure food.*
receive • *I received your letter of November 7.*
secure (FORMAL) • *He failed to secure enough votes for outright victory.*

get ❷ VERB
to change from one state to another • *People draw the curtains once it gets dark.*
become • *The wind became stronger.*
grow • *He grew to love his work.*
turn • *The leaves have turned golden-brown.*

get on VERB
to enjoy someone's company • *I get on very well with his wife.*
be compatible • *Mary and I are very compatible.*
hit it off (INFORMAL) • *They hit it off straight away.*

ghost NOUN
the spirit of a dead person • *the ghost of the drowned girl*
apparition • *She felt as if she were seeing a ghostly apparition.*
phantom • *She was relentlessly pursued by a grossly disfigured phantom.*
spectre • *The Tower is said to be haunted by the spectre of Anne Boleyn.*
spirit • *the spirits of our dead ancestors*

RELATED WORD
● ADJECTIVE: spectral

gidday or **g'day** INTERJECTION
(AUSTRALIAN AND NEW ZEALAND)
hello • *Gidday, mate!*
hello • *Hello, Trish. Glad you could make it.*
hi (INFORMAL) • *Hi, how are you doing?*
good morning (FORMAL) • *Good morning, class.*
good afternoon (FORMAL) • *Good afternoon, Miss Bates.*
good evening (FORMAL) • *Good evening, ladies and gentlemen!*

gift ❶ NOUN
something you give someone • *He showered her with gifts.*
bequest (FORMAL) • *They received a bequest of $310,000.*
bonsela (SOUTH AFRICAN) • *a generous bonsela*
contribution • *companies that make charitable contributions*
donation • *donations of food and clothing for victims of the hurricane*
legacy • *What about the legacy from your uncle?*
present • *This book would make a great Christmas present.*

gift ❷ NOUN
a natural skill or ability • *a gift for comedy*
ability • *It's obvious he has an exceptional ability.*
aptitude • *She realised she had an aptitude for writing.*
flair • *Tony found he had a real flair for design.*
talent • *Both her children have a talent for music.*

give ❶ VERB
to provide someone with something • *I gave her a CD.*
award • *The Mayor awarded him a medal.*

a
b
c
d
e
f
g
h
i
j
k
l
m
n
o
p
q
r
s
t
u
v
w
x
y
z

Can't find the word you're looking for? Try the index.

A
B
C
D
E
F
G
H
I
J
K
L
M
N
O
P
Q
R
S
T
U
V
W
X
Y
Z

deliver • *The Canadians plan to deliver more food to southern Somalia.*
donate • *Others donated second-hand clothes.*
grant • *Permission was granted a few weeks ago.*
hand • *Isabel handed me a glass of orange juice.*
present • *The Queen presented the prizes.*
provide • *The government was not in a position to provide them with food.*
supply • *a contract to supply radar equipment to the Philippines*

MORE SYNONYMS
● accord
● administer
● bestow
● confer

ANTONYM
● take

give ② VERB
to collapse or break under pressure • *My knees gave under me.*
buckle • *His left wrist buckled under the strain.*
cave in • *Half the ceiling caved in.*
collapse • *The roof supports had collapsed.*
give way • *He fell when a ledge gave way beneath him.*
yield • *The handle yielded to her grasp.*

give in VERB
to admit that you are defeated • *Juppe should not give in to the strikers.*
capitulate • *Cohen capitulated to virtually every demand.*
concede • *Mr Pyke is not prepared to concede defeat.*

submit • *Mrs Jones submitted to an operation on her right knee.*
succumb • *The Minister said his country would never succumb to pressure.*
surrender • *He surrendered to American troops.*
yield • *an enemy who had shown no desire to yield*

glad ADJECTIVE
happy about something • *They'll be glad to get away from it all.*
delighted • *Frank will be delighted to see you.*
happy • *Jacques is very happy that you are here.*
joyful • *a joyful reunion with his mother*
overjoyed • *Shelley was overjoyed to see me.*
pleased • *They're pleased to be going home.*

ANTONYM
● sorry

glance ① NOUN
a brief look at something • *The boys exchanged glances.*
glimpse • *They caught a glimpse of their hero.*
look • *Lucille took a last look in the mirror.*
peek • *Could I just have another quick peek at the bedroom?*
peep • *Would you take a peep out of the window?*

glance ② VERB
to look at something quickly • *He glanced at his watch.*
glimpse • *I soon glimpsed the doctor in his garden.*
look • *Bethan looked quickly at the elegant people around her.*
peek • *She had peeked at him*

through a crack in the wall.
peep • *Now and then she peeped to see if he was noticing her.*
scan • *She scanned the advertisement pages of the newspaper.*

glance ❸ VERB
to hit something quickly and bounce away • *My fist glanced off his jaw.*
bounce • *The ball bounced off the opposite post.*
brush • *She brushed her lips across Michael's cheek.*
skim • *pebbles skimming across the water*

MORE SYNONYMS
● rebound
● ricochet

glare ❶ VERB
to look angrily at someone • *Joe glared at his brother.*
frown • *She looked up to see Vic frowning at her.*
glower • *He glowered at me but said nothing.*
scowl • *Robert scowled, and slammed the door behind him.*

glare ❷ NOUN
an angry look • *The waiter lowered his eyes to avoid Harold's furious glare.*
frown • *There was a deep frown on the boy's face.*
scowl • *Chris met the remark with a scowl.*

glare ❸ NOUN
very bright light • *the glare of the headlights*
blaze • *There was a sudden blaze of light.*
glow • *the glow of the fire*

gloomy ❶ ADJECTIVE
feeling very sad • *They are gloomy about their chances of success.*
dejected • *Everyone has days when they feel dejected.*
down • *The old man sounded really down.*
glum • *What on earth are you looking so glum about?*
miserable • *She went to bed, miserable and depressed.*
sad • *You must feel sad about what's happened.*

MORE SYNONYMS
● blue
● despondent
● downhearted

ANTONYM
● cheerful

gloomy ❷ ADJECTIVE
dark and depressing • *a gloomy house on the edge of Phoenix Park*
dark • *The house looked dark and unwelcoming.*
dismal • *damp and dismal weather*
dreary • *the dreary, industrial city of Ludwigshafen*
dull • *It's always dull and raining.*

ANTONYM
● sunny

glory ❶ NOUN
fame and admiration that someone gets • *It was her moment of glory.*
fame • *The film earned him international fame.*
honour • *the honour of captaining one's country*
immortality • *Some people want to achieve immortality through their work.*
praise • *Holbrooke deserves full praise for his efforts.*

a b c d e f g h i j k l m n o p q r s t u v w x y z

Can't find the word you're looking for? Try the index.

prestige • *I'm not in this job for the prestige.*

MORE SYNONYMS
- acclaim
- eminence
- renown

ANTONYM
- disgrace

glory ❷ NOUN
something impressive or beautiful • *Spring arrived in all its glory.*
grandeur • *the grandeur of the country mansion*
magnificence • *the magnificence of the sunset*
majesty • *the majesty of Niagara Falls*
splendour • *the splendour of the palace of Versailles*

glory ❸ VERB
to enjoy something very much • *The workers were glorying in their new-found freedom.*
gloat • *Their rivals were gloating over their triumph.*
relish • *He relished the idea of getting some cash.*
revel • *a ruthless killer who revels in his job*

gloss NOUN
a bright shine on a surface • *aluminium foil with a high gloss surface*
brilliance • *ceramic tiles of great brilliance*
gleam • *the gleam of brass*
polish • *His boots had a high polish.*
sheen • *The carpet had a silvery sheen to it.*
shine • *This gel gives a beautiful shine to the hair.*

glossy ADJECTIVE
smooth and shiny • *The leaves were dark and glossy.*
bright • *Her eyes were bright with excitement.*
brilliant • *The woman had brilliant green eyes.*
polished • *a highly polished floor*
shiny • *a shiny new sports car*
sleek • *sleek black hair*

glow ❶ NOUN
a dull steady light • *the glow of the fire*
gleam • *the first gleam of dawn*
glimmer • *In the east there was the slightest glimmer of light.*
light • *the light of the evening sun*

glow ❷ VERB
to shine with a dull steady light • *A light glowed behind the curtains.*
gleam • *Lights gleamed in the deepening mist.*
glimmer • *A few stars still glimmered.*
shine • *Scattered lights shone on the horizon.*
smoulder • *A very small fire was smouldering in the grate.*

glue VERB
to stick things together • *Glue the two halves together.*
fix • *Fix the fabric to the roller.*
paste • *The children were busy pasting gold stars on a chart.*
seal • *He sealed the envelope and put on a stamp.*
stick • *I stuck the notice on the board.*

go ❶ VERB
to move or travel somewhere • *I went home at the weekend.*
advance • *Rebel forces are advancing on the capital.*

drive • *My husband and I drove to Liverpool to see my mum.*
fly • *He flew to Los Angeles.*
journey (FORMAL) • *They intended to journey up the Amazon.*
leave • *What time are you leaving?*
proceed (FORMAL) • *The taxi proceeded along a lonely road.*
set off • *He set off for the station.*
travel • *Students often travel hundreds of miles to get here.*

go ❷ VERB
to work properly • *stuck on the motorway with a car that won't go*
function • *All the instruments functioned properly.*
work • *The pump doesn't work and we have no running water.*

go ❸ NOUN
an attempt to do something • *I always wanted to have a go at waterskiing.*
attempt • *one of his rare attempts at humour*
shot (INFORMAL) • *a shot at winning a brand new car*
stab (INFORMAL) • *Several sports stars have had a stab at acting and singing.*
try • *After a few tries, Patrick had given up.*

goal NOUN
something that a person hopes to achieve • *The goal is to make as much money as possible.*
aim • *The aim of the festival is to raise awareness of this issue.*
end • *This is another policy designed to achieve the same end.*
intention • *He announced his intention of standing for parliament.*
object • *The object of the exercise is to raise money for charity.*
objective • *His objective was to play golf and win.*

purpose • *His purpose was to make a profit.*
target • *She failed to achieve her target of losing 20 pounds.*

gobble VERB
to eat food very quickly • *Pete gobbled all the beef stew.*
bolt • *Being under stress can cause you to bolt your food.*
devour • *She devoured two bars of chocolate.*
wolf • *Pitt wolfed down a peanut butter sandwich.*

good ❶ ADJECTIVE
pleasant, acceptable or satisfactory • *We had a really good time.*
▷ *see Word Study* **good**, *pages 681–2*

ANTONYM
● bad

good ❷ ADJECTIVE
skilful or successful • *I'm not very good at art.*
▷ *see Word Study* **good**, *pages 681–2*

ANTONYM
● incompetent

good ❸ ADJECTIVE
kind, thoughtful and loving • *You are so good to me.*
▷ *see Word Study* **good**, *pages 681–2*

ANTONYM
● unkind

goodwill NOUN
kindness and helpfulness towards other people • *I invited them to dinner as a gesture of goodwill.*
benevolence • *He chuckles often and radiates benevolence.*
favour • *in order to gain the favour of whoever is in power*
friendliness • *Visitors remarked on the friendliness of the people.*

a
b
c
d
e
f
g
h
i
j
k
l
m
n
o
p
q
r
s
t
u
v
w
x
y
z

Can't find the word you're looking for? Try the index.

friendship • *The two countries signed treaties of friendship.*

gossip NOUN

informal conversation about other people • *Don't you like a good gossip?*

dirt • *the latest dirt on the other candidates*

hearsay • *They have had only hearsay and rumour to go on.*

MORE SYNONYMS

● chitchat
● prattle
● scandal
● tittle-tattle

go through VERB

to experience an unpleasant event • *I was going through a very difficult time.*

endure • *He'd endured years of pain and sleepless nights.*

experience • *British business was experiencing a severe recession.*

undergo • *Magee underwent emergency surgery.*

grab VERB

to take hold of something roughly • *I grabbed him by the neck.*

clutch • *Michelle clutched my arm.*

grasp • *He grasped both my hands.*

seize • *She seized a carving fork and advanced in my direction.*

snatch • *Mick snatched the cards from Archie's hand.*

grace NOUN

an elegant way of moving • *He moved with the grace of a trained boxer.*

elegance • *She is elegance personified.*

poise • *Ballet classes are important for poise and grace.*

ANTONYM

● clumsiness

grade VERB

to arrange things according to quality • *The oil is tasted and graded according to quality.*

class • *They are officially classed as visitors.*

classify • *Rocks can be classified according to their origin.*

group • *The fact sheets are grouped into seven sections.*

rate • *He was rated as one of the country's top young players.*

sort • *The students are sorted into three ability groups.*

MORE SYNONYMS

● evaluate
● sequence

gradual ADJECTIVE

happening or changing slowly • *the gradual improvement in communications*

continuous • *Our policy is one of continuous improvement.*

progressive • *One symptom of the disease is progressive loss of memory*

slow • *The distribution of passports has been a slow process.*

steady • *a steady rise in sales*

ANTONYM

● sudden

grammar NOUN

GRAMMAR WORDS

active	plural
aspect	possessive
comparative	singular
passive	superlative
person	tense

grand ❶ ADJECTIVE

very impressive in size or appearance

• _a grand building in the centre of town_
imposing • _the imposing gates at the entrance to the estate_
impressive • _The old boat presented an impressive sight._
magnificent • _magnificent views over the San Fernando valley_
majestic • _a stupendous vista of majestic peaks_
monumental • _a monumental sculpture of a human face_
splendid • _a splendid Victorian mansion_

MORE SYNONYMS
- glorious
- grandiose
- palatial

grand ❷ ADJECTIVE (INFORMAL)
pleasant or enjoyable • _It was a grand day._
brilliant (INFORMAL) • _I've had a brilliant time._
great (INFORMAL) • _I had a great time at university._
marvellous (INFORMAL) • _It was a marvellous day and we were all so happy._
terrific (INFORMAL) • _Everybody there was having a terrific time._
wonderful • _It was a wonderful experience._

grant ❶ NOUN
a money award given for a particular purpose • _My application for a grant has been accepted._
allocation • _The aid allocation for that country is under review._
allowance • _She gets an allowance for looking after Lillian._
award • _a study award worth £2,000_
handout • _a cash handout of six thousand rupees_
subsidy • _state subsidies to public transport companies_

grant ❷ VERB
to allow someone to have something • _France has agreed to grant him political asylum._
allocate • _The budget allocated $7 billion for development programmes._
allow • _Children should be allowed the occasional treat._
award • _A High Court judge awarded him £6 million damages._
give • _We have been given permission to attend the meeting._
permit • _The doorman said he could not permit them entry to the film._

MORE SYNONYMS
- accord
- bestow

ANTONYM
- deny

grant ❸ VERB
to admit that something is true • _I grant that you had some justification for your actions._
accept • _I do not accept that there is a crisis in British science._
acknowledge • _He acknowledged that he had been partly to blame._
admit • _I admit that I do make mistakes._
allow • _He allows that capitalist development may result in social inequality._
concede • _Bess finally conceded that Nancy was right._

ANTONYM
- deny

grasp ❶ VERB
to hold something firmly • _He grasped both my hands._
clutch • _I staggered and had to clutch at a chair for support._
grab • _I grabbed him by the neck._
grip • _She gripped the rope._

a
b
c
d
e
f
g
h
i
j
k
l
m
n
o
p
q
r
s
t
u
v
w
x
y
z

Can't find the word you're looking for? Try the index.

hold • He held the pistol tightly in his right hand.
seize • He seized my arm to hold me back.
snatch • I snatched at a hanging branch and pulled myself up.

grasp ❷ VERB
to understand an idea • The Government has not yet grasped the seriousness of the crisis.
absorb • He only absorbed about half the information we gave him.
appreciate • She never really appreciated the bitterness of the conflict.
assimilate • My mind could only assimilate one concept at a time.
realize • People don't realize how serious this recession has been.
take in • She listens to the explanation, but you can see she's not taking it in.
understand • They are too young to understand what is going on.

grasp ❸ NOUN
a firm hold • She slipped her hand from his grasp.
clasp • He gripped my hand in a strong clasp.
embrace • He held her in a passionate embrace.
grip • His strong hand eased the bag from her grip.
hold • He released his hold on the camera.

grasp ❹ NOUN
a person's understanding of something • They have a good grasp of foreign languages.
awareness • The children demonstrated their awareness of green issues.
comprehension (FORMAL) • This was utterly beyond her comprehension.

grip • He has lost his grip on reality.
knowledge • She has a good knowledge of these processes.
understanding • a basic understanding of computers

grateful ADJECTIVE
pleased and wanting to thank someone • I am grateful to you for your help.
appreciative • We have been very appreciative of their support.
indebted • I am deeply indebted to him for his help.
thankful • I'm just thankful that I've got a job.

ANTONYM
● ungrateful

gratitude NOUN
the feeling of being grateful • I wish to express my gratitude to Kathy Davis for her help.
appreciation • their appreciation of his efforts
recognition • an honour given in recognition of his help to the college
thanks • They accepted their certificates with words of thanks.

ANTONYM
● ingratitude

grave ❶ NOUN
a place where a corpse is buried • They visited her grave twice a year.
mausoleum • the great mausoleum at the top of the hill
pit • The bodies were buried in a shallow pit.
sepulchre • Death holds him in his sepulchre.
tomb • the tomb of the Unknown Soldier

Can't find the word you're looking for? Try the index.

RELATED WORD
● ADJECTIVE: sepulchral

grave ② ADJECTIVE (FORMAL)
very serious • *The situation in his country is very grave.*
acute • *The report has caused acute embarrassment to the government.*
critical • *Its finances are in a critical state.*
heavy (INFORMAL) • *Things were just starting to get heavy when the police arrived.*
serious • *The government faces very serious difficulties.*
sober • *a room filled with sad, sober faces*
solemn • *His solemn little face broke into smiles.*
sombre • *His expression became increasingly sombre.*

graze ① VERB
to slightly injure your skin • *He fell heavily and grazed his left arm.*
scrape • *She stumbled and fell, scraping her palms and knees.*
scratch • *The branches scratched my hands and face.*
skin • *He fell and skinned both his knees.*

graze ② NOUN
a slight injury to your skin • *He just has a slight graze.*
abrasion (FORMAL) • *He had severe abrasions to his right cheek.*
scratch • *She had scratches to her face.*

great ① ADJECTIVE
very large in size • *great columns of ice*
▷ see Word Study **great**, page 683

ANTONYM
● small

great ② ADJECTIVE
important or famous • *the great novels of the nineteenth century*
▷ see Word Study **great**, page 683

great ③ ADJECTIVE
very good • *I thought it was a great idea.*
▷ see Word Study **great**, page 683

ANTONYM
● terrible

greedy ADJECTIVE
wanting more than you need
• *greedy bosses who award themselves huge pay rises*
materialistic • *During the 1980s Britain became a very materialistic society.*
snoep (SOUTH AFRICAN; INFORMAL) • *a bunch of snoep businessmen*

MORE SYNONYMS
● acquisitive
● avaricious
● grasping
● voracious

green ADJECTIVE
concerned with environmental issues • *Children and adolescents are now aware of green issues.*
conservationist • *a chorus of protest from conservationist groups*
ecological • *shared interest in ecological issues*

MORE SYNONYMS
● eco-friendly
● environmentally friendly
● non-polluting
● ozone-friendly

RELATED WORD
● ADJECTIVE: verdant

a
b
c
d
e
f
g
h
i
j
k
l
m
n
o
p
q
r
s
t
u
v
w
x
y
z

Can't find the word you're looking for? Try the index.

A
B
C
D
E
F
G
H
I
J
K
L
M
N
O
P
Q
R
S
T
U
V
W
X
Y
Z

SHADES OF GREEN

apple green	khaki
avocado	lime
bottle-green	Lincoln green
chartreuse	olive
eau de nil	pea green
emerald	pistachio
grass-green	sage
jade	sea green

greet VERB

to say hello to someone when they
arrive • *The president was greeted
by local political leaders.*
meet • *A nurse met me at the
entrance.*
receive (FORMAL) • *250 guests
were received by the bride and
bridegroom.*
welcome • *She was there to
welcome him home.*

MORE SYNONYMS

● hail
● salute

grey NOUN OR ADJECTIVE

SHADES OF GREY

ash	silver
charcoal	silvery
gunmetal	slate
hoary	steel grey
leaden	stone
pewter	taupe
platinum	whitish

grief NOUN

a feeling of extreme sadness
• *a huge outpouring of national grief*
distress • *the intense distress they
were causing my family*
heartache • *She has suffered more
heartache than anyone deserves.*
misery • *All that money brought
nothing but misery.*
sadness • *It is with a mixture of*

sadness and joy that I say farewell.
sorrow • *a time of great sorrow*
unhappiness • *There was a lot of
unhappiness in my adolescence.*

MORE SYNONYMS

● anguish
● dejection
● heartbreak
● woe

ANTONYM

● happiness

grieve ❶ VERB

to feel extremely sad • *He still
grieves for his wife.*
lament • *All who knew Spender
will lament his death.*
mourn • *The whole nation mourns
the death of their great leader.*

grieve ❷ VERB

to make someone feel extremely
sad • *It grieved Elaine to be
separated from her son.*
distress • *It distresses me that the
President has not tackled crime.*
pain • *It pains me to think of you
struggling all alone.*
sadden • *The cruelty in the world
saddens me.*
upset • *The news upset me.*

ANTONYM

● cheer

grim ADJECTIVE

looking very serious • *Her face was
grim.*
grave • *Mrs Williams was looking
very grave.*
severe • *He leaned towards me, a
severe expression on his face.*
solemn • *What a solemn-faced kid
he had been.*
stern • *Michael gave the dog a
stern look.*

grip ❶ NOUN
a firm hold on something • *His strong hand eased the bag from her grip.*
clasp • *With one last clasp of his hand, she left him.*
grasp • *The spade slipped from her grasp and fell to the ground.*
hold • *He released his hold on the camera.*

grip ❷ NOUN
someone's control over something • *The president maintains an iron grip on his country.*
clutches • *She fell into the clutches of the wrong sort of person.*
control • *The port area is under the control of rebel forces.*
influence • *Alexandra fell under the influence of Grigori Rasputin.*
power • *I was really in the power of my mother.*

grip ❸ VERB
to hold something firmly • *Alison gripped the steering wheel and stared straight ahead.*
clutch • *Michelle clutched my arm.*
grasp • *He grasped both my hands.*
hold • *He was struggling to hold on to the rope.*

ground NOUN
the surface of the earth • *We slid down the roof and dropped to the ground.*
dirt • *They sat on the dirt in the shade of a tree.*
earth • *The road winds for miles through parched earth.*
land • *800 acres of agricultural land*
soil • *In Southern India the soil is fertile.*
terrain • *Farms give way to hilly terrain.*

grounds ❶ PLURAL NOUN
the land surrounding a building • *the grounds of the university*
estate • *Lord Wyville's estate in Yorkshire*
gardens • *an elegant Regency house set in beautiful gardens*
land • *Their home is on his father's land.*

grounds ❷ PLURAL NOUN
the reason for doing or thinking something • *Owen was against it on the grounds of expense.*
basis • *Could you tell me on what basis the fee is calculated?*
cause • *No one had cause to get angry or unpleasant.*
excuse • *There's no excuse for behaviour like that.*
justification • *There was no justification for what I was doing.*
reason • *Who would have a reason to want to kill her?*

MORE SYNONYMS
- foundation
- pretext
- rationale

group ❶ NOUN
a number of people or things • *a group of football supporters*
band • *a band of rebels*
bunch • *They're a nice bunch of lads.*
collection • *a collection of essays from foreign affairs experts*
crowd • *A small crowd of onlookers has gathered.*
gang • *Gangs of teenagers hang out in shop doorways.*
pack • *a pack of cards*
party • *a party of sightseers*
set • *Different sets of people often use the same buildings.*

A
B
C
D
E
F
G
H
I
J
K
L
M
N
O
P
Q
R
S
T
U
V
W
X
Y
Z

MORE SYNONYMS
- aggregation
- assemblage
- coterie

group ❷ VERB
to link people or things together
• *Their responses are grouped into 11 categories.*
arrange • *He started to arrange the books in piles.*
class • *They are officially classed as visitors.*
classify • *Rocks can be classified according to their origin.*
organize • *I was organizing the vast array of junk we had collected.*
sort • *The students are sorted into three ability groups.*

MORE SYNONYMS
- assort
- marshal

grow ❶ VERB
to increase in size or amount
• *Bacteria grow more quickly once food is contaminated.*
develop • *These clashes could develop into open warfare.*
expand • *Will the universe continue to expand forever?*
increase • *Industrial output increased by 2%.*
multiply • *Her husband multiplied his demands on her time.*

ANTONYM
- shrink

grow ❷ VERB
to be alive or exist • *Trees and bushes grew down to the water's edge.*
flourish • *The plant flourishes in slightly harsher climates.*
germinate • *Heat will encourage seeds to germinate.*

sprout • *It only takes a few days for beans to sprout.*

MORE SYNONYMS
- shoot
- spring up

grow ❸ VERB
to pass gradually into a particular state • *I grew a little afraid of the guy next door.*
become • *The wind became stronger.*
get • *The boys were getting bored.*
turn • *In October it turned cold.*

growth NOUN
the act of getting bigger • *the growth of the fishing industry*
development • *What are your plans for the development of your company?*
enlargement • *the enlargement of the European Union*
expansion • *a new period of economic expansion*
increase • *a sharp increase in the number of homeless people*

grumble ❶ VERB
to complain in a bad-tempered way • *"This is very inconvenient," he grumbled.*
carp • *the man whom other actors love to carp about*
complain • *They complained about the high cost of visiting Europe.*
groan • *parents groaning about the price of college tuition*
moan • *moaning about the weather*
mutter • *She could hear the old woman muttering about young people.*
whine • *children who whine that they are bored*
whinge • *All she ever does is whinge.*

Can't find the word you're looking for? Try the index.

grumble ❷ NOUN
a bad-tempered complaint
• *I didn't hear any grumbles from anyone at the time.*
complaint • *I get nothing but complaints about my cooking.*
moan • *Sometimes it helps to have a good old moan.*
murmur • *She paid without a murmur.*
objection • *If you have any objections, please raise them now.*
protest • *Despite our protests, they went ahead with the plan.*
whinge • *It's depressing listening to everybody's whinges.*

grumpy ADJECTIVE
bad-tempered and annoyed
• *a grumpy old man*
irritable • *He had missed his dinner and grew irritable.*
sulky • *She still looked like a sulky teenager.*
sullen • *Several leading players have maintained a sullen silence.*
surly • *They were surly, sometimes downright rude to me.*

MORE SYNONYMS
- bad-tempered
- cantankerous
- ill-tempered

guarantee ❶ NOUN
something that makes another thing certain • *The package offered a guarantee of job security.*
assurance • *a written assurance that he would start work at once*
pledge • *a pledge of support from the Ministry of Culture*
promise • *I'd made him a promise that I'd write a book for him.*
undertaking • *She gave an undertaking not to repeat the allegations.*

word • *He simply cannot be trusted to keep his word.*

guarantee ❷ VERB
to make it certain that something will happen • *Reports of this kind are guaranteed to cause anxiety.*
ensure • *We need to ensure that every student has basic literacy skills.*
pledge • *Both sides pledged that a nuclear war would never be fought.*
promise • *He promised that the rich would not get preferential treatment.*

guard ❶ VERB
to protect someone • *Police were guarding his home yesterday.*
defend • *He and his friends defended themselves against racist thugs.*
protect • *What can women do to protect themselves from heart disease?*
safeguard • *measures to safeguard their forces from chemical weapons*
shelter • *A neighbour sheltered the boy for seven days.*
shield • *She had shielded him from the terrible truth.*
watch over • *two policewomen to watch over him*

guard ❷ VERB
to stop someone making trouble or escaping • *The soldiers had been guarding paramilitary prisoners.*
patrol • *Prison officers continued to patrol the grounds.*
police • *It is extremely difficult to police the border.*
supervise • *Only two staff were supervising over 100 prisoners.*

guard ❸ NOUN
someone who guards people or places • *The prisoners overpowered their guards and locked them in a cell.*

a b c d e f g h i j k l m n o p q r s t u v w x y z

Can't find the word you're looking for? Try the index.

A
B
C
D
E
G
H
I
J
K
L
M
N
O
P
Q
R
S
T
U
V
W
X
Y
Z

sentry • *We can sneak past the sentries.*
warden • *The siege began when the prisoners seized three wardens.*

MORE SYNONYMS
- sentinel
- warder
- watchman

guess ❶ VERB
to form an idea or opinion about something • *Wood guessed that he was a very successful banker.*
estimate • *It's difficult to estimate how much money is involved.*
imagine • *"Was he meeting someone?" "I imagine so."*
reckon • *Toni reckoned that it must be about three o'clock.*
speculate • *The reader can speculate what will happen next.*
suppose • *I supposed you would have a meal somewhere.*
suspect • *I suspect they were right.*
think • *Nora thought he was seventeen years old.*

MORE SYNONYMS
- conjecture
- hazard
- surmise

guess ❷ NOUN
an attempt to give the right answer • *My guess is that the answer will be negative.*
feeling • *My feeling is that everything will come right for us.*
reckoning • *By my reckoning, 50% of the team will be available.*
speculation • *speculations about the future of the universe*

MORE SYNONYMS
- conjecture
- hypothesis

guide ❶ VERB
to lead someone somewhere • *He took Elliott by the arm and guided him out.*
accompany • *We accompanied Joe to the magazine's midtown offices.*
direct • *Officials directed him to the wrong airport.*
escort • *I escorted him to the door.*
lead • *The nurse led me to a large room.*

MORE SYNONYMS
- conduct
- convoy
- shepherd
- usher

guide ❷ VERB
to influence someone • *He should have let his instinct guide him.*
counsel (FORMAL) • *Green was counselled not to talk to reporters.*
govern • *Our thinking is as much governed by habit as by behaviour.*
influence • *My dad influenced me to do electronics.*

guilty ❶ ADJECTIVE
having done something wrong • *They were found guilty of murder.*
convicted • *a convicted drug dealer*
criminal • *He had a criminal record for petty theft.*

MORE SYNONYMS
- blameworthy
- culpable
- felonious

ANTONYM
- innocent

guilty ❷ ADJECTIVE
unhappy because you have done something bad • *When she saw me she looked guilty.*

Can't find the word you're looking for? Try the index.

ashamed • *Zumel said he was not ashamed of what he had done.*
regretful • *Surprisingly, she didn't feel regretful about her actions.*
remorseful (FORMAL) • *He felt remorseful for what he had done.*
sorry • *She was very sorry about all the trouble she'd caused.*

MORE SYNONYMS
- conscience-stricken
- contrite
- shamefaced

gullible ADJECTIVE
easily tricked • *I'm so gullible I would have believed him.*
naive • *It would be naive to believe Mr Gonzalez's statement.*
trusting • *She has an open, trusting nature.*

MORE SYNONYMS
- credulous
- unsuspecting

ANTONYM
- suspicious

gush VERB
to flow in large quantities • *Piping-hot water gushed out.*
flow • *Tears flowed down his cheeks.*
pour • *Blood was pouring from his broken nose.*
spurt • *a fountain that spurts water nine stories high*
stream • *water streaming from the pipes*

MORE SYNONYMS
- cascade
- issue
- jet

a b c d e f g h i j k l m n o p q r s t u v w x y z

Hh

habit ❶ NOUN
something that is done regularly
• *his habit of smiling at everyone he saw*
convention • *It's just a social convention that men don't wear skirts.*
custom • *an ancient Japanese custom*
practice • *the practice of clocking in at work*
routine • *my daily routine*
tradition • *a family tradition at Christmas*

habit ❷ NOUN
an addiction to something • *her cocaine habit*
addiction • *his addiction to gambling*
dependence • *the effects of drug dependence*

habitat NOUN
the natural home of a plant or animal • *the habitat of the spotted owl*
environment • *a safe environment for marine mammals*
territory • *a bird's territory*

hackneyed ADJECTIVE
used too often to be meaningful
• *hackneyed postcard snaps of lochs and glens*
banal • *banal lyrics*
clichéd • *clichéd slogans*
stale • *Her relationship with Mark has become stale.*
tired • *a tired excuse*

trite • *The film is teeming with trite ideas.*

MORE SYNONYMS
- run-of-the-mill
- threadbare
- timeworn

ANTONYM
- original

hail ❶ NOUN
a lot of things falling together
• *a hail of bullets*
barrage • *a barrage of angry questions*
bombardment • *the sound of heavy aerial bombardment*
shower • *a shower of rose petals*
storm • *The announcement provoked a storm of protest.*
volley • *A volley of shots rang out.*

hail ❷ VERB
to attract someone's attention
• *He hailed me from across the street.*
call • *He called me over the Tannoy.*
signal to • *The lollipop lady signalled to me to stop.*
wave down • *I ran on to the road and waved down a taxi.*

halt ❶ VERB
to come or bring to a stop • *She held her hand out to halt him.*
draw up • *The car drew up outside the house.*
pull up • *The cab pulled up, and the driver jumped out.*

Can't find the word you're looking for? Try the index.

stop • *The event literally stopped the traffic.*

halt ❷ VERB

to bring something to an end • *Production was halted.*

cease • *A small number of firms have ceased trading.*

check • *We have managed to check the spread of terrorism.*

curb • *efforts to curb the spread of nuclear weapons*

cut short • *They had to cut short a holiday abroad.*

end • *They decided to end the ceasefire.*

terminate • *His contract has been terminated.*

ANTONYM

● begin

halt ❸ NOUN

an interruption or end to something • *He brought the car to a halt.*

close • *Their 18-month marriage was brought to a close.*

end • *The war came to an end.*

pause • *There was a pause before he replied.*

standstill • *The country was brought to a standstill by strikes.*

stop • *He slowed the car almost to a stop.*

stoppage • *Air and ground crew are staging a 24-hour stoppage today.*

MORE SYNONYMS

● impasse
● termination

hamper VERB

to make movement or progress difficult for someone • *I was hampered by a lack of information.*

frustrate • *His attempt was frustrated by the weather.*

hinder • *A thigh injury hindered her mobility.*

impede • *Their work was being impeded by shortages of supplies.*

obstruct • *charged with obstructing the course of justice*

restrict • *Her life is restricted by asthma.*

MORE SYNONYMS

● encumber
● fetter

hand down VERB

to pass from one generation to another • *Recipes are handed down from mother to daughter.*

bequeath • *He bequeathed all his silver to his children.*

give • *a typewriter given to me by my father*

pass down • *an heirloom passed down from generation to generation*

pass on • *My parents passed on their love of classical music to me.*

MORE SYNONYMS

● bestow
● will

handicap ❶ NOUN

a physical or mental disability • *He learnt to overcome his handicap.*

defect • *a rare birth defect*

disability • *children with learning disabilities*

handicap ❷ NOUN

something that makes progress difficult • *Being a foreigner was not a handicap.*

barrier • *Taxes are the most obvious barrier to free trade.*

disadvantage • *the disadvantage of unemployment*

drawback • *The flat's only drawback was that it was too small.*

a
b
c
d
e
f
g
h
i
j
k
l
m
n
o
p
q
r
s
t
u
v
w
x
y
z

Can't find the word you're looking for? Try the index.

hindrance • *She was a help rather than a hindrance to my work.*
impediment • *an impediment to economic development*
obstacle • *the main obstacle to the deal*

handicap ❸ VERB
to make something difficult for someone • *Greater levels of stress may seriously handicap some students.*
burden • *We decided not to burden him with the news.*
hamper • *I was hampered by a lack of information.*
hinder • *A thigh injury hindered her mobility.*
impede • *Fallen rocks impeded the progress of the rescue workers.*
restrict • *laws to restrict foreign imports*

handle ❶ NOUN
the part of an object by which it is held • *a broom handle*
grip • *He fitted new grips to his golf clubs.*
hilt • *the hilt of the small, sharp knife*

handle ❷ VERB
to hold or move with the hands • *Wear rubber gloves when handling cat litter.*
feel • *The doctor felt his arm.*
finger • *He fingered the few coins in his pocket.*
grasp • *Grasp the end firmly.*
hold • *Hold it by the edge.*
touch • *She touched his hand reassuringly.*

handle ❸ VERB
to deal or control with something • *She handled the travel arrangements.*
administer • *The project is*

administered by the World Bank.
conduct • *This is no way to conduct a business.*
deal with • *The matter has been dealt with by the school.*
manage • *Within two years he was managing the store.*
supervise • *I supervise the packing of all mail orders.*
take care of • *He took care of the catering arrangements.*

handsome ❶ ADJECTIVE
very attractive in appearance • *a handsome man*
attractive • *an attractive young woman*
good-looking • *good-looking actors*

ANTONYM
● ugly

handsome ❷ ADJECTIVE
large and generous • *a handsome profit*
ample • *ample space for a good-sized kitchen*
considerable • *his considerable wealth*
generous • *a generous gift*
liberal • *a liberal donation*
plentiful • *a plentiful supply of vegetables*
sizable or **sizeable** • *He inherited the house and a sizeable chunk of land.*

ANTONYM
● small

handy ❶ ADJECTIVE
conveniently near • *Keep a pencil and paper handy.*
at hand • *Having the right equipment at hand will be enormously useful.*
at your fingertips • *Firms need*

information at their fingertips.
close • *a secluded area close to her home*
convenient • *Martin drove along until he found a convenient parking space.*
nearby • *He tossed the match into a nearby wastepaper bin.*
on hand • *Experts are on hand to offer advice.*

handy ❷ ADJECTIVE
easy to handle or use • *handy hints on looking after indoor plants*
convenient • *a convenient way of paying*
easy to use • *This ice cream maker is cheap and easy to use.*
helpful • *helpful instructions*
neat • *It had been such a neat, clever plan.*
practical • *the most practical way of preventing crime*
useful • *useful information*

hang ❶ VERB
to be attached at the top with the lower part free • *His jacket hung from a hook behind the door.*
dangle • *A gold bracelet dangled from his left wrist.*
droop • *Pale wilting roses drooped from a vase.*

hang ❷ VERB
to fasten something to another thing by its top • *She came out of the house to hang clothes on the line.*
attach • *He attached the picture to the wall with a nail.*
drape • *He draped the coat round his shoulders.*
fasten • *stirrups fastened to the saddle*
fix • *He fixed a pirate flag to the mast.*

suspend • *The TV is suspended from the ceiling on brackets.*

happen VERB
to take place • *The accident happened on Wednesday.*
come about • *It came about almost by accident.*
follow • *He was arrested in the confusion which followed.*
occur • *The crash occurred on a sharp bend.*
result • *Ignore the early warnings and illness could result.*
take place • *The festival took place last September.*

MORE SYNONYMS
- ensue
- materialize

happiness NOUN
a feeling of great pleasure • *Money can't buy happiness.*
delight • *To my delight, it worked perfectly.*
ecstasy • *a state of almost religious ecstasy*
elation • *His supporters reacted to the news with elation.*
joy • *tears of joy*
pleasure • *Everybody takes pleasure in eating.*
satisfaction • *job satisfaction*

MORE SYNONYMS
- exuberance
- felicity
- merriment

ANTONYM
- sadness

happy ❶ ADJECTIVE
feeling or causing joy • *a happy atmosphere*
▷ *see Word Study* **happy**, *page 684*

Can't find the word you're looking for? Try the index.

ANTONYM
- sad

happy ❷ ADJECTIVE
fortunate or lucky • *a happy coincidence*
▷ see Word Study **happy**, page 684

ANTONYM
- unlucky

hard ❶ ADJECTIVE
firm, solid, or rigid • *a hard piece of cheese*
firm • *a firm mattress*
rigid • *rigid plastic containers*
solid • *solid rock*
stiff • *stiff metal wires*
strong • *It has a strong casing which won't crack or chip.*
tough • *dark brown beans with a rather tough outer skin*

ANTONYM
- soft

hard ❷ ADJECTIVE
requiring a lot of effort • *hard work*
arduous • *a long, arduous journey*
exhausting • *It's a pretty exhausting job.*
laborious • *Keeping the garden tidy can be a laborious task.*
rigorous • *rigorous military training*
strenuous • *Avoid strenuous exercise in the evening.*
tough • *Change is often tough to deal with.*

ANTONYM
- easy

hard ❸ ADJECTIVE
difficult to understand • *That's a very hard question.*
baffling • *a baffling remark*
complex • *a complex problem*
complicated • *a complicated system of voting*

difficult • *It was a very difficult decision to make.*
puzzling • *Some of this book is rather puzzling.*

ANTONYM
- simple

harden VERB
to make or become stiff or firm • *Give the cardboard two coats of varnish to harden it.*
bake • *The soil had been baked solid by the heatwave.*
cake • *The blood had begun to cake and turn brown.*
freeze • *The lake freezes in winter.*
set • *Lower the heat and allow the omelette to set.*
stiffen • *paper that had been stiffened with paste*

MORE SYNONYMS
- anneal
- solidify

ANTONYM
- soften

hardly ADVERB
almost not or not quite • *I could hardly believe what I was seeing.*
barely • *His voice was barely audible.*
just • *Her hand was just visible under her coat.*
only just • *For centuries farmers there have only just managed to survive.*
scarcely • *He could scarcely breathe.*

hardship NOUN
difficult circumstances • *Many people are suffering economic hardship.*
adversity • *They manage to enjoy life despite adversity.*

Can't find the word you're looking for? Try the index.

destitution • *a life of poverty and destitution*
difficulty • *Many new golf clubs are in serious financial difficulty.*
misfortune • *She seemed to enjoy the misfortunes of others.*
want • *They were fighting for freedom of speech and freedom from want.*

MORE SYNONYMS
- oppression
- privation
- tribulation

harm ❶ VERB
to injure someone or damage something • *The hijackers seemed anxious not to harm anyone.*
abuse • *Animals are still being exploited and abused.*
damage • *He damaged his knee during training.*
hurt • *He fell and hurt his back.*
ill-treat • *They thought he had been ill-treating his wife.*
ruin • *My wife was ruining her health through worry.*
wound • *The bomb killed six people and wounded another five.*

harm ❷ NOUN
injury or damage • *All dogs are capable of doing harm to human beings.*
abuse • *The abuse of animals is inexcusable.*
damage • *The bomb caused extensive damage.*
hurt • *an evil desire to cause hurt and damage*
injury • *The two other passengers escaped serious injury.*

harmful ADJECTIVE
having a bad effect on something • *Whilst most stress is harmful, some is beneficial.*

damaging • *damaging allegations about his personal life*
destructive • *the awesome destructive power of nuclear weapons*
detrimental • *levels of radioactivity which are detrimental to public health*
hurtful • *Her comments can only be hurtful to the family.*
pernicious • *The pernicious influence of secret societies.*

MORE SYNONYMS
- baleful
- baneful
- deleterious
- injurious

ANTONYM
- harmless

harmless ADJECTIVE
safe to use or be near • *This experiment was harmless to the animals.*
innocuous • *Both mushrooms look innocuous but are in fact deadly.*
nontoxic • *a cheap and nontoxic method of cleaning up our water*
not dangerous • *The tests are not dangerous to the environment.*
safe • *The doll is safe for children.*

ANTONYM
- harmful

harsh ADJECTIVE
severe, difficult, and unpleasant • *harsh weather conditions*
austere • *The life of the troops was still comparatively austere.*
cruel • *an unusually cruel winter*
hard • *He had a hard life.*
ruthless • *the ruthless treatment of staff*
severe • *My boss gave me a severe reprimand.*

a
b
c
d
e
f
g
h
i
j
k
l
m
n
o
p
q
r
s
t
u
v
w
x
y
z

Can't find the word you're looking for? Try the index.

A
B
C
D
E
F
G
H
I
J
K
L
M
N
O
P
Q
R
S
T
U
V
W
X
Y
Z

stern • *a stern warning*

MORE SYNONYMS
- Draconian
- Spartan

ANTONYM
- mild

hassle ❶ NOUN (INFORMAL)
something that is difficult or
causes trouble • *It's not worth the
hassle.*
bother • *I buy sliced bread - it's
less bother.*
effort • *This chore is well worth the
effort.*
inconvenience • *the expense and
inconvenience of having central
heating installed*
trouble • *You've caused us a lot of
trouble.*
upheaval • *Moving house is always
a big upheaval.*

hassle ❷ VERB (INFORMAL)
to annoy someone by nagging or
making demands • *My husband
started hassling me.*
badger • *They kept badgering me
to go back.*
bother • *Go away and don't bother
me about all that just now.*
go on at • *She's always going on at
me to have a baby.*
harass • *We are routinely harassed
by the police.*
nag • *She had stopped nagging him
about his drinking.*
pester • *the creep who's been
pestering you to go out with him*

hasty ADJECTIVE
done or happening suddenly and
quickly • *The signs of their hasty
departure could be seen everywhere.*
brisk • *a brisk walk*
hurried • *a hurried breakfast*

prompt • *It is not too late, but
prompt action is needed.*
rapid • *a rapid retreat*
swift • *my swift departure*

hate ❶ VERB
to have a strong dislike for
something or someone • *Most
people hate him, but they don't care
to say so.*
abhor • *He abhorred violence.*
be sick of • *We're sick of being
ripped off.*
despise • *A lot of people despise
and loathe what I do.*
detest • *Jean detested being
photographed.*
dislike • *those who dislike change*
loathe • *a play universally loathed
by the critics*

ANTONYM
- love

hate ❷ NOUN
a strong dislike • *a violent bully,
destructive and full of hate*
animosity • *The animosity between
the two men grew.*
aversion • *I've always had an
aversion to being part of a group.*
dislike • *Consider what your likes
and dislikes are about your job.*
hatred • *her hatred of authority*
hostility • *He looked at her with
open hostility.*
loathing • *Critics are united in
their unmitigated loathing of the
band.*

MORE SYNONYMS
- animus
- detestation
- enmity
- odium

ANTONYM
- love

Can't find the word you're looking for? Try the index.

hateful ADJECTIVE
extremely unpleasant • *It was a hateful thing to say.*
abhorrent • *Discrimination is abhorrent to my council and our staff.*
despicable • *a despicable crime*
horrible • *a horrible little boy*
loathsome • *the loathsome spectacle we were obliged to witness*
obnoxious • *He was a most obnoxious character. No-one liked him.*
offensive • *an offensive remark*

hatred NOUN
an extremely strong feeling of dislike • *He has been accused of inciting racial hatred.*
animosity • *The animosity between the two men grew.*
antipathy • *public antipathy towards scientists*
aversion • *my aversion to housework*
dislike • *his dislike of modern buildings*
hate • *These people are so full of hate.*
revulsion • *They expressed their revulsion at his violent death.*

ANTONYM
● love

haughty ADJECTIVE
showing excessive pride • *He spoke in a haughty tone.*
arrogant • *an air of arrogant indifference*
conceited • *They had grown too conceited and pleased with themselves.*
disdainful • *She cast a disdainful glance at me.*
proud • *She was said to be proud and arrogant.*
snobbish • *They had a snobbish*

dislike for their intellectual inferiors.
stuck-up (INFORMAL) • *She was a famous actress, but she wasn't a bit stuck-up.*

ANTONYM
● humble

have ❶ VERB
to own something • *We have two tickets for the concert.*
hold • *He does not hold a firearm certificate.*
keep • *We keep chickens.*
own • *His father owns a local pub.*
possess • *He is said to possess a fortune.*

have ❷ VERB
to experience something • *He had a marvellous time.*
endure • *The company endured heavy losses.*
enjoy • *The average German will enjoy 40 days' paid holiday this year.*
experience • *Widows seem to experience more distress than do widowers.*
feel • *I felt a sharp pain in my shoulder.*
sustain • *He had sustained a cut on his left eyebrow.*
undergo • *He recently underwent brain surgery.*

head ❶ NOUN
a person's mind and mental abilities • *I don't have a head for business.*
aptitude • *an aptitude for accountancy*
brain • *If you stop using your brain you'll go stale.*
common sense • *Use your common sense.*
intelligence • *Try to use your intelligence to solve the puzzle -*

a
b
c
d
e
f
g
h
i
j
k
l
m
n
o
p
q
r
s
t
u
v
w
x
y
z

don't just guess.
mind • *I'm trying to clear my mind of all this.*
wits • *She has used her wits to get where she is today.*

MORE SYNONYMS
- intellect
- rationality

head ② NOUN
the top, front, or start of something • *the head of the queue*
beginning • *the beginning of this chapter*
front • *Stand at the front of the line.*
source • *the source of this great river*
start • *Go back to the start of this section.*
top • *the top of the stairs*

ANTONYM
- tail

head ③ NOUN
the person in charge of something • *heads of government*
boss • *the boss of the new company*
chief • *the President's chief of security*
director • *the director of the intensive care unit*
leader • *the leader of the Conservative Party*
manager • *the manager of our division*
president • *the president of the medical commission*
principal • *the principal of the school*

head ④ VERB
to be in charge of something • *He heads the department.*
be in charge of • *She's in charge of the overseas division.*

control • *He controls the largest fast food empire in the world.*
direct • *Christopher will direct day-to-day operations.*
lead • *leading a campaign to save the rainforest*
manage • *Within two years he was managing the store.*
run • *Each teacher will run a different workshop.*

health ① NOUN
the condition of your body
• *Smoking is bad for your health.*
condition • *He remains in a critical condition in hospital.*
constitution • *He must have an extremely strong constitution.*
shape • *He was still in better shape than many younger men.*

health ② NOUN
a state in which a person is feeling well. • *In hospital they nursed me back to health.*
fitness • *He has fitness problems.*
good condition • *He is in great condition for a man of 56.*
wellbeing • *Singing can create a sense of wellbeing.*

ANTONYM
- illness

healthy ① ADJECTIVE
having good health • *She was a very healthy child.*
active • *an active lifestyle*
fit • *A short, physically fit man of 61.*
in good shape (INFORMAL) • *I kept myself in good shape by swimming.*
robust • *a robust and vibrant young man*
strong • *a strong constitution*
well • *I'm not very well today.*

ANTONYM
- ill

Can't find the word you're looking for? Try the index.

healthy ❷ ADJECTIVE
producing good health • *a healthy diet*
beneficial • *Wine in moderation is beneficial to health.*
bracing • *a bracing walk*
good for you • *Regular, moderate exercise is good for you.*
nourishing • *sensible, nourishing food*
nutritious • *a hot, nutritious meal*
wholesome • *fresh, wholesome ingredients*

MORE SYNONYMS
● invigorating
● salubrious
● salutary

ANTONYM
● unhealthy

heap ❶ NOUN
a pile of things • *a heap of rubble*
hoard • *a hoard of silver and jewels*
mass • *a mass of flowers*
mound • *The bulldozers piled up huge mounds of dirt.*
pile • *a pile of betting slips*
stack • *stacks of books on the bedside table*

heap ❷ VERB
to pile things up • *She heaped vegetables onto his plate.*
pile • *He was piling clothes into the suitcase.*
stack • *They stacked up pillows behind his back.*

heaps PLURAL NOUN (INFORMAL)
plenty of something • *heaps of cash*
loads (INFORMAL) • *I've got loads of money.*
lots (INFORMAL) • *lots of fun*
plenty • *We've got plenty of time for a drink.*
stacks • *stacks of magazines*

tons (INFORMAL) • *I've got tons of work to do.*

hear ❶ VERB
to listen to something • *I heard the sound of gunfire.*
catch • *I don't believe I caught your name.*
eavesdrop • *The government illegally eavesdropped on his phone conversations.*
heed • *Few at the conference heeded his warning.*
listen in • *Secret agents listened in on his phone calls.*
listen to • *He spent his time listening to the radio.*
overhear • *I overheard two doctors discussing my case.*

hear ❷ VERB
to learn about something • *I heard that he was forced to resign.*
ascertain • *They had ascertained that he was not a spy.*
discover • *She discovered that they'd escaped.*
find out • *As soon as we found this out, we closed the ward.*
gather • *I gather the report is critical of the judge.*
learn • *She wasn't surprised to learn that he was involved.*
understand • *I understand that she's just taken early retirement.*

heat ❶ NOUN
the quality of being warm or hot • *the heat of the sun*
high temperature • *The suffering caused by the high temperature has been great.*
warmth • *the warmth of the sand between her toes*

ANTONYM
● cold

a
b
c
d
e
f
g
h
i
j
k
l
m
n
o
p
q
r
s
t
u
v
w
x
y
z

Can't find the word you're looking for? Try the index.

RELATED WORD
- ADJECTIVE: thermal

heat ❷ NOUN
a state of strong emotion • *in the heat of the election campaign*
excitement • *in a state of great excitement*
fervour • *religious fervour*
intensity • *the intensity of feeling about this issue*
passion • *He spoke with great passion.*
vehemence • *I was surprised by the vehemence of his criticism.*

heat ❸ VERB
to raise the temperature of something • *Heat the oil in a frying pan.*
reheat • *Reheat the soup to a gentle simmer.*
warm up • *Just before serving, warm up the tomato sauce.*

ANTONYM
- cool

heathen NOUN (OLD-FASHIONED)
someone who does not believe in an established religion • *She called us all heathens and hypocrites.*
pagan • *the sky-god of the ancient pagans*
unbeliever • *punishing unbelievers and traitors*

MORE SYNONYMS
- idolater
- infidel

ANTONYM
- believer

heaven ❶ NOUN
the place where good people are believed to go when they die • *She told them their mother was now in heaven.*

next world • *He said, "We will see each other again in the next world."*
paradise • *They believed they would go to paradise if they died in battle.*

MORE SYNONYMS
- Elysium (*Greek myth*)
- happy hunting ground (*Native American legend*)
- nirvana (*Buddhism, Hinduism*)
- Valhalla (*Norse myth*)
- Zion (*Christianity*)

ANTONYM
- hell

heaven ❷ NOUN
a place or situation liked very much • *I was in cinematic heaven.*
bliss • *a scene of domestic bliss*
ecstasy • *the ecstasy of being in love*
paradise • *The Algarve is a golfer's paradise.*
rapture • *the sheer rapture of listening to Bach's music*

heavy ❶ ADJECTIVE
great in weight or force • *a heavy frying pan*
bulky • *a bulky grey sweater*
massive • *a massive blue whale*

ANTONYM
- light

heavy ❷ ADJECTIVE
serious or important • *a heavy speech*
deep • *a period of deep personal crisis*
grave • *the grave crisis facing the country*
profound • *Anna's patriotism was profound.*
serious • *It was a question which deserved serious consideration.*

Can't find the word you're looking for? Try the index.

A B C D E F G H I J K L M N O P Q R S T U V W X Y Z

solemn • *a simple, solemn ceremony*
weighty • *Surely such weighty matters merit a higher level of debate.*

ANTONYM
- trivial

heed ❶ VERB
to pay attention to someone's advice • *Few at the conference heeded his warning.*
follow • *If you are not going to follow my advice, we are both wasting our time.*
listen to • *They won't listen to my advice.*
pay attention to • *The food industry is now paying attention to young consumers.*
take notice of • *We want the government to take notice of what we think.*

heed ❷ NOUN
careful attention • *He pays too much heed to her.*
attention • *He never paid much attention to his audience.*
notice • *So do they take any notice of public opinion?*

hell ❶ NOUN
the place where souls of evil people are believed to go after death • *Milton's Satan would rather "reign in Hell, than serve in Heaven".*
abyss • *Satan rules over the dark abyss.*
inferno • *an inferno described in loving detail by Dante*

MORE SYNONYMS
- fire and brimstone
- Gehenna (*New Testament, Judaism*)
- Hades (*Greek myth*)
- hellfire

- Tartarus (*Greek myth*)
- underworld

ANTONYM
- heaven

hell ❷ NOUN (INFORMAL)
an unpleasant situation or place • *Bullies can make your life hell.*
agony • *the agony of divorce*
anguish • *the anguish of families unable to trace relatives who've disappeared*
misery • *All that money brought nothing but sadness and misery.*
nightmare • *The years in prison were a nightmare.*
ordeal • *the painful ordeal of the last year*

hello INTERJECTION
a greeting • *I popped my head in to say hello.*
gidday (AUSTRALIAN AND NEW ZEALAND) • *Gidday, mate! How you doing?*
hi (INFORMAL) • *She smiled and said, "Hi".*
how do you do? (FORMAL) • *"How do you do, Mrs Brown?" Sam said, holding out his hand.*
good morning (FORMAL) • *Good morning, everyone.*
good afternoon (FORMAL) • *Good afternoon. Won't you sit down?*
good evening (FORMAL) • *Good evening, and welcome!*

ANTONYM
- goodbye

help ❶ VERB
to make something easier or better for someone • *He began to help with the chores.*
aid • *a software system to aid managers*
assist • *information to assist you*

a
b
c
d
e
f
g
h
i
j
k
l
m
n
o
p
q
r
s
t
u
v
w
x
y
z

Can't find the word you're looking for? Try the index.

lend a hand • *I'd be glad to lend a hand.*
support • *He thanked everyone who had supported the strike.*

A B C D E F G H I J K L M N O P Q R S T U V W X Y Z

help ❷ NOUN
assistance or support • *The books were not much help.*
advice • *He has given me lots of good advice in my time here.*
aid • *millions of dollars of aid*
assistance • *I would be grateful for any assistance.*
guidance • *the reports which were produced under his guidance*
helping hand • *Most mums would be grateful for a helping hand.*
support • *Only 60 clubs pledged their support for the scheme.*

helper NOUN
a person who gives assistance • *There is an adult helper for every two children.*
aide • *a presidential aide*
assistant • *a research assistant*
deputy • *I can't make it so I'll send my deputy.*
henchman • *Adolf Eichmann, Hitler's notorious henchman*
right-hand man • *He was the perfect right-hand man for the president.*
supporter • *He is a strong supporter of the plan.*

helpful ❶ ADJECTIVE
giving assistance or advice • *The staff in the office are very helpful.*
accommodating • *Lindi seemed a nice, accomodating girl.*
cooperative • *I made every effort to be cooperative.*
kind • *I must thank you for being so kind to me.*
supportive • *Her boss was very supportive.*

ANTONYM
- unhelpful

helpful ❷ ADJECTIVE
making a situation better • *Having the right equipment will be enormously helpful.*
advantageous • *an advantageous arrangement*
beneficial • *beneficial changes in the tax system*
constructive • *constructive criticism*
profitable • *a profitable exchange of ideas*
useful • *useful information*

helpless ADJECTIVE
weak or unable to cope • *a helpless baby*
defenceless • *a savage attack on a defenceless girl*
powerless • *He was powerless to help.*
unprotected • *She felt unprotected and defenseless.*
vulnerable • *the most vulnerable members of society*
weak • *taking ruthless advantage of a weak old man*

hesitant ADJECTIVE
uncertain about something • *At first he was hesitant to accept the role.*
diffident • *John was as outgoing as Helen was diffident.*
doubtful • *I was very doubtful about the chances for success.*
reluctant • *She was reluctant to get involved.*
unsure • *He made her feel awkward and unsure of herself.*
wavering • *wavering voters*

MORE SYNONYMS
- irresolute
- vacillating

hesitate VERB

to pause or show uncertainty • *She hesitated before replying.*
dither • *We're still dithering over whether to marry.*
pause • *The crowd paused for a minute, wondering what to do next.*
waver • *Louise never wavered in her determination to take up the post.*

hide ❶ VERB

to put something where it cannot be seen • *She hid her face in her hands.*
cache • *He has £289 million cached away.*
conceal • *The hat concealed her hair.*
secrete • *She secreted the gun in the kitchen cabinet.*
stash (INFORMAL) • *He had stashed money away in a secret offshore account.*

hide ❷ NOUN

the skin of a large animal • *the process of tanning hides*
pelt • *a bed covered with beaver pelts*
skin • *a leopard-skin coat*

high ❶ ADJECTIVE

tall or a long way above the ground • *a high tower*
▷ see Word Study **high**, page 685

ANTONYM
● low

high ❷ ADJECTIVE

great in degree, quantity, or intensity • *There is a high risk of heart disease.*
▷ see Word Study **high**, page 685

ANTONYM
● low

hill NOUN

TYPES OF HILL

brae (SCOTTISH)	dune
down	elevation
fell	knoll
foothill	kopje (S. AFRICAN)
height	mound
hillock	prominence
hummock	tor

hinder VERB

to get in the way of someone or something • *A thigh injury hindered her mobility.*
block • *The President is blocking the release of the two men.*
check • *We have managed to check the spread of terrorism.*
delay • *Various problems have delayed producton.*
frustrate • *They have frustrated his efforts to gain a work permit.*
hamper • *I was hampered by a lack of information.*
impede • *Fallen rocks are impeding the progress of rescue workers.*

MORE SYNONYMS
● encumber
● stymie

hint ❶ NOUN

an indirect suggestion • *He gave a strong hint that there would be a referendum sooner rather than later.*
clue • *How a man shaves may be a telling clue to his age.*
indication • *He gave no indication that he was ready to compromise.*
intimation • *I did not have any intimation that he was going to resign.*
suggestion • *We reject any suggestion that the law needs amending.*

hint ❷ NOUN

a helpful piece of advice • *I hope to get some fashion hints.*
advice • *Don't be afraid to ask for advice.*

a
b
c
d
e
f
g
h
i
j
k
l
m
n
o
p
q
r
s
t
u
v
w
x
y
z

Can't find the word you're looking for? Try the index.

pointer • *Here are a few pointers to help you make your choice.*
suggestion • *Can I give you a few suggestions?*
tip • *tips for busy managers*

hint ❸ VERB

to suggest something indirectly • *Criticism is hinted at but never made explicit.*
imply • *The report implied that his death was inevitable.*
indicate • *She has indicated that she may resign.*
insinuate • *an article which insinuated that he was lying*
intimate • *He intimated that he was contemplating a shake-up of the company.*
suggest • *Are you suggesting that I need to lose some weight?*

hire ❶ VERB

to pay money to use something • *She hired the car for three days.*
charter • *They chartered a jet to fly her home.*
lease • *He went to Toronto, where he leased an apartment.*
rent • *She rents a house with three other girls.*

hire ❷ VERB

to employ the services of someone • *The staff have been hired on short-term contracts.*
appoint • *The Prime Minister has appointed a civilian as defence minister.*
commission • *You can commission her to paint something especially for you.*
employ • *They employed me as a nanny.*
engage • *We engaged the services of a recognized engineer.*
sign up • *He persuaded the company to sign her up.*

hit ❶ VERB

to strike someone or something forcefully • *Both men had been hit with baseball bats.*
▷ *see Word Study **hit**, pages 686–7*

hit ❷ VERB

to collide with something • *The car had apparently hit a traffic sign.*
bang into • *She fell after another skier banged into her.*
bump • *The boat bumped against something.*
collide with • *He almost collided with Daisy.*
meet head-on • *Their cars met head-on down a narrow alleyway.*
run into • *The mail train ran into a derailed goods train at 75mph.*
smash into • *The car plunged down a cliff and smashed into a tree.*

hit ❸ NOUN

the action of hitting something • *Give it a good hard hit with the hammer.*
blow • *He went to hospital after a blow to the face.*
knock • *a painful knock on the knee*
rap • *There was a rap on the door.*
slap • *She reached forward and gave him a slap.*
smack • *a smack with a ruler*
stroke • *six strokes of the cane*

hoard ❶ VERB

to store for future use • *People have begun to hoard food and petrol.*
save • *Save some fuel in case of emergencies.*
stockpile • *People are stockpiling food for the coming winter.*
store • *It's perfect for storing eggs or vegetables.*

Can't find the word you're looking for? Try the index.

hoard ② NOUN

a store of things • *a hoard of silver and jewels*

cache • *a cache of weapons and explosives*

fund • *a scholarship fund for engineering students*

reserve • *the world's oil reserves*

stockpile • *stockpiles of nuclear warheads*

store • *I have a store of food and water here.*

supply • *food supplies*

hoarse ADJECTIVE

rough and unclear • *Nick's voice was hoarse with screaming.*

croaky • *He sounds a bit croaky today.*

gruff • *his gruff Scottish growl*

husky • *Her deep husky voice was her trademark.*

rasping • *Both men sang in a deep rasping tone.*

ANTONYM
● clear

hobby NOUN

an enjoyable activity pursued in your spare time • *My hobbies are music and photography.*

diversion • *Finger painting is very messy but an excellent diversion.*

leisure activity • *America's top leisure activity is watching television.*

leisure pursuit • *His main leisure pursuit is hill walking.*

pastime • *His favourite pastime is golf.*

hold ① VERB

to carry or support something • *Hold the baby while I load the car.*

carry • *He was carrying a briefcase.*

clasp • *She clasped the children to her.*

clutch • *He was clutching a photograph.*

embrace • *The couple in the corridor were embracing each other.*

grasp • *He grasped both my hands.*

grip • *They gripped the rope tightly.*

hold ② NOUN

power or control over someone or something • *The party has a considerable hold over its own leader.*

control • *He will have to give up his control of the company.*

dominance • *the gang's dominance of the London underworld*

sway • *ideas that held sway for centuries*

hold ③ NOUN

the act or a way of holding something • *He grabbed the rope and got a hold on it.*

grasp • *His hand was taken in a warm, firm grasp.*

grip • *His strong hand eased the bag from her grip.*

hole ① NOUN

an opening or hollow in something • *The builders had cut holes into the stone.*

gap • *The wind was tearing through gaps in the window frames.*

hollow • *Water gathers in a hollow and forms a pond.*

opening • *He squeezed through a narrow opening in the fence.*

pit • *He lost his footing and began to slide into the pit.*

split • *The seat has a few small splits around the corners.*

tear • *I peered through a tear in the van's curtains.*

hole ② NOUN

a weakness in a theory or argument • *There are some holes in that theory.*

a b c d e f g **h** i j k l m n o p q r s t u v w x y z

Can't find the word you're looking for? Try the index.

defect • *A defect in the aircraft caused the crash.*
error • *NASA discovered an error in its calculations.*
fault • *There is a fault in the computer program.*
flaw • *Almost all of these studies have serious flaws.*
loophole • *They exploited a loophole in the law.*

hole ❸ NOUN (INFORMAL)
a difficult situation • *He admitted that the government was in a hole.*
fix (INFORMAL) • *This will put homeowners in a fix.*
hot water (INFORMAL) • *They have already been in hot water over high prices this year.*
mess • *the many reasons why the economy is in such a mess*
predicament • *the once great club's current predicament*
tight spot • *This was one tight spot he couldn't get out of.*

holiday NOUN
time spent away from home for enjoyment • *I'm exhausted - I really need a holiday.*
break • *They are currently taking a short break in Spain.*
leave • *Why don't you take a few days' leave?*
recess • *Parliament returns today after its summer recess.*
time off • *He took time off to go sailing with wife.*
vacation • *We went on vacation to Puerto Rico.*

holy ❶ ADJECTIVE
relating to God or a particular religion • *All Christian holy places were closed for a day in protest.*
blessed • *Blessed are the peacemakers, for they shall be called the children of God.*
consecrated • *the consecrated bread from the Eucharist*
hallowed • *hallowed ground*
sacred • *sacred music*
sacrosanct • *For him the Sabbath was sacrosanct.*
venerated • *Jerusalem is Christianity's most venerated place.*

holy ❷ ADJECTIVE
religious and leading a good life • *In the East, holy men have always had long hair.*
devout • *She is a devout Catholic.*
pious • *He was brought up by pious female relatives.*
religious • *They are both very religious.*
saintly • *his saintly mother*
virtuous • *a virtuous family man*

MORE SYNONYMS
● god-fearing
● godly

ANTONYM
● wicked

home ❶ NOUN
the building in which someone lives • *They stayed at home and watched TV.*
abode • *a luxurious abode*
dwelling • *One thousand new dwellings are planned for the area.*
house • *our new house*
residence • *the Royal Family's private residence*

home ❷ ADJECTIVE
involving your own country • *the home news pages of this newspaper*
domestic • *over 100 domestic flights a day to 15 UK destinations*
internal • *The government stepped up internal security.*
national • *major national and international issues*

Can't find the word you're looking for? Try the index.

A B C D E F G H I J K L M N O P Q R S T U V W X Y Z

native • *He was glad to be back on his native soil.*

ANTONYM
- foreign

homely ADJECTIVE
simple, ordinary and comfortable • *The room was small and homely.*
comfortable • *A home should be warm and comfortable.*
cosy • *Guests can relax in the cosy bar.*
modest • *the modest home of a family who lived off the land*
simple • *They celebrated mass in a simple chapel.*
welcoming • *The restaurant is small and very welcoming.*

ANTONYM
- grand

honest ADJECTIVE
truthful and trustworthy • *He is a very honest, decent man.*
law-abiding • *law-abiding citizens*
reputable • *a reputable car dealer*
trustworthy • *He is a trustworthy and level-headed leader.*
truthful • *She could not give him a truthful answer.*
virtuous • *a virtuous family man*

ANTONYM
- dishonest

honour ❶ NOUN
personal integrity • *I can no longer serve with honour in your government.*
decency • *No-one had the decency to tell me to my face.*
goodness • *He retains a faith in human goodness.*
honesty • *His reputation for honesty and integrity is second to none.*

integrity • *He was praised for his fairness and high integrity.*

ANTONYM
- dishonour

honour ❷ NOUN
an award or mark of respect • *He was showered with honours - among them an Oscar.*
accolade • *the ultimate international accolade, the Nobel Peace prize*
commendation • *The officer received a commendation for brave conduct.*
homage • *films that pay homage to our literary heritage*
praise • *He had won consistently high praise for his theatre work.*
recognition • *At last, her father's work has received popular recognition.*
tribute • *He paid tribute to the organizing committee.*

MORE SYNONYMS
- acclaim
- kudos

honour ❸ VERB
to give someone special praise • *He was honoured by the French government with the Legion d'Honneur.*
commemorate • *a plaque commemorating the servicemen who died*
commend • *I commended her for that action.*
decorate • *He was decorated for his gallantry by the General.*
glorify • *My philosophy of life is to glorify God in all I do.*
praise • *He praised their excellent work.*

a
b
c
d
e
f
g
h
i
j
k
l
m
n
o
p
q
r
s
t
u
v
w
x
y
z

Can't find the word you're looking for? Try the index.

A
B
C
D
E
F
G
H
I
J
K
L
M
N
O
P
Q
R
S
T
U
V
W
X
Y
Z

hooligan NOUN

a destructive and violent young person • *English football hooligans*

delinquent • *a nine-year-old delinquent*

hoon (AUSTRALIAN AND NEW ZEALAND; INFORMAL) • *the rocks hurled by hoons*

lout • *He was attacked by stone-throwing louts.*

tough • *Residents may be too terrified of local toughs to protest.*

vandal • *The Scout hut was burnt down by vandals.*

yob (BRITISH AND AUSTRALIAN; SLANG) • *drunken yobs chanting football songs*

hope NOUN

a wish or feeling of desire and expectation • *There was little hope of recovery.*

ambition • *His ambition is to sail around the world.*

dream • *his dream of becoming a pilot*

expectation • *The hotel was being renovated in expectation of a tourist boom.*

hopeless ❶ ADJECTIVE

certain to fail or be unsuccessful • *Our situation is hopeless.*

forlorn • *the forlorn hope of finding a better life*

futile • *their futile attempts to avoid publicity*

impossible • *The tax is impossible to administer.*

pointless • *a pointless exercise that would only waste more time*

useless • *She knew it was useless to protest.*

vain • *a vain attempt to sign a goalkeeper*

hopeless ❷ ADJECTIVE

bad or inadequate • *I don't drive and the buses are hopeless.*

inadequate • *The problem lies with inadequate staffing.*

pathetic • *the pathetic state of the rail network*

poor • *The flat was in a poor state of repair.*

useless (INFORMAL) • *My husband is useless around the house.*

horrible ❶ ADJECTIVE

disagreeable or unpleasant • *a horrible little boy*

awful • *I had an awful time.*

disagreeable • *a disagreeable odour*

horrid • *My parents are horrid to each other.*

mean • *Why are you always so mean to me?*

nasty • *This divorce could turn nasty.*

unpleasant • *He's a very unpleasant little man.*

horrible ❷ ADJECTIVE

causing shock, fear, or disgust • *horrible crimes*

appalling • *They have been living under the most appalling conditions.*

dreadful • *She told me the dreadful news.*

grim • *a grim discovery*

gruesome • *gruesome murders*

terrifying • *a terrifying experience*

horrify VERB

to cause to feel horror or shock • *a crime trend that will horrify parents*

appal • *I was appalled by her behaviour.*

disgust • *He disgusted everyone with his boorish behaviour.*

dismay • *He was deeply dismayed by the decision.*

Can't find the word you're looking for? Try the index.

outrage • *Human rights campaigners were outraged by the execution.*
shock • *Pictures of emaciated prisoners shocked the world.*
sicken • *What he saw at the accident sickened him.*

horror ❶ NOUN

a strong feeling of alarm or disgust • *He gazed in horror at the knife.*
alarm • *She sat up in alarm.*
dread • *She thought with dread of the cold winter to come.*
fear • *I stood there crying and shaking with fear.*
fright • *He uttered a shriek and jumped with fright.*
panic • *He felt a sudden rush of panic at the thought.*
terror • *She shook with terror.*

horror ❷ NOUN

a strong fear of something • *his horror of death*
abhorrence • *their abhorrence of racism*
aversion • *Many people have a natural aversion to insects.*
disgust • *I threw the book aside in disgust.*
hatred • *My hatred for him is intense.*
loathing • *She looked at him with loathing.*
revulsion • *They expressed their revulsion at his violent death.*

MORE SYNONYMS

● abomination
● odium
● repugnance

horse NOUN

an animal kept for riding • *a fall from a horse*
brumby (AUSTRALIAN AND NEW

ZEALAND) • *There's a mob of about 30 brumbies up there.*
equine • *the history and uses of equines*
moke (AUSTRALIAN AND NEW ZEALAND; SLANG) • *a tired old moke*
nag (INFORMAL) • *He unhitched his sorry-looking nag from a nearby post.*
pony • *Peter trotted about on the fat pony he had been given.*

MORE SYNONYMS

● mount
● steed

RELATED WORDS

● ADJECTIVES: equestrian, equine, horsey
● NOUN: equitation
● MALE: stallion
● FEMALE: mare
● YOUNG: foal, colt, filly

hostile ADJECTIVE

unfriendly, aggressive, and unpleasant • *The Governor faced hostile crowds.*
antagonistic • *They were nearly all antagonistic to the idea.*
belligerent • *a belligerent war of words between India and Pakistan*
malevolent • *He fixed our photographer with a malevolent stare.*
unkind • *All last summer he'd been unkind to her.*

ANTONYM

● friendly

hostility NOUN

aggressive or unfriendly behaviour towards someone or something • *hostility to Black and ethnic groups*
animosity • *The animosity between the two men grew.*
antagonism • *a history of antagonism between the two sides*

a
b
c
d
e
f
g
h
i
j
k
l
m
n
o
p
q
r
s
t
u
v
w
x
y
z

Can't find the word you're looking for? Try the index.

A
B
C
D
E
F
G
H
I
J
K
L
M
N
O
P
Q
R
S
T
U
V
W
X
Y
Z

hatred • *her lifelong hatred of authority*
ill will • *He didn't bear anyone any ill will.*
malice • *There was no malice in her voice.*
resentment • *There is growing resentment against newcomers.*

MORE SYNONYMS
- animus
- detestation
- enmity

ANTONYM
- friendship

hot ❶ ADJECTIVE
having a high temperature • *a hot climate*
boiling • *It's boiling in here.*
heated • *a heated swimming pool*
scalding • *Her son was burned by scalding tea.*
scorching • *It was a scorching hot day.*
warm • *a warm, dry summer*

ANTONYM
- cold

hot ❷ ADJECTIVE
very spicy • *a hot, aromatic Thai red curry*
peppery • *a rich, peppery extra virgin olive oil*
spicy • *a spicy Cajun sauce*

ANTONYM
- bland

house NOUN
a building where a person or family lives • *They live in a large house with eight rooms.*
abode • *I went round the streets and found his new abode.*
building • *Their flat was on the first floor of the building.*

dwelling • *One thousand new dwellings are planned for the area.*
home • *One in four people are without adequate homes.*
residence • *the Royal Family's private residence*

hug ❶ VERB
to hold someone close to you • *Lynn and I hugged each other.*
clasp • *She clasped the children to her.*
cuddle • *They used to kiss and cuddle in front of everyone.*
embrace • *The couple in the corridor were embracing each other.*
squeeze • *He kissed her on the cheek and squeezed her tight.*

hug ❷ NOUN
the act of holding someone close to you • *She gave him a hug.*
clinch (SLANG) • *They were caught in a clinch when her parents returned home.*
embrace • *a young couple locked in an embrace*

huge ADJECTIVE
extremely large in amount, size, or degree • *a huge crowd*
colossal • *a colossal waste of money*
enormous • *The main bedroom is enormous.*
giant • *a giant statue*
immense • *He wielded immense power.*
massive • *a massive surge in popularity*
vast • *this vast area of northern Canada*

MORE SYNONYMS
- gargantuan
- prodigious

ANTONYM
- tiny

Can't find the word you're looking for? Try the index.

hui NOUN (NEW ZEALAND)
a meeting • *He arranged a hui which called together a broad span of Maori tribes.*
assembly • *an assembly of prizewinning journalists*
conference • *a conference attended by 280 delegates*
congress • *a congress of coal miners*
convention • *the annual convention of the Society of Professional Journalists*
gathering • *the annual gathering of the South Pacific Forum*
meeting • *Can we have a meeting to discuss that?*
rally • *They held a rally to mark International Human Rights Day.*

humane ADJECTIVE
showing kindness and sympathy towards others • *a more just and humane society*
benevolent • *a most benevolent employer*
caring • *a very caring boy*
charitable • *charitable work*
compassionate • *a deeply compassionate man*
kind • *She is warmhearted and kind.*
merciful • *a merciful God*
thoughtful • *a very thoughtful gesture*

MORE SYNONYMS
● altruistic
● humanitarian

humble ❶ ADJECTIVE
not vain or boastful • *He gave a great performance, but he was very humble.*
meek • *He was a meek, mild-mannered fellow.*
modest • *He's modest, as well as being a great player.*

unassuming • *She has a gentle, unassuming manner.*

ANTONYM
● haughty

humble ❷ ADJECTIVE
ordinary or unimportant • *A splash of wine will transform a humble casserole.*
lowly • *He was irked by his lowly status.*
modest • *his modest beginnings*
ordinary • *It was just an ordinary weekend.*
simple • *a simple dinner of rice and beans*

humble ❸ VERB
to make someone feel humiliated • *the little car company that humbled the industry giants*
disgrace • *I have disgraced the family's name.*
humiliate • *His teacher continually humiliates him in maths lessons.*

humid ADJECTIVE
damp and hot • *a hot, humid Italian summer*
clammy • *My shirt was clammy with sweat.*
muggy • *The weather was muggy and overcast.*
steamy • *The air was hot and steamy from the heat of a hundred bodies.*
sticky • *four hot, sticky days in the middle of August*

humiliate VERB
to hurt someone's pride • *He enjoyed humiliating me.*
disgrace • *I have disgraced my family.*
embarrass • *It embarrassed him that he had no idea of what was going on.*
humble • *The champion was humbled by the unseeded qualifier.*

a b c d e f **h** i j k l m n o p q r s t u v w x y z

Can't find the word you're looking for? Try the index.

A
B
C
D
E
F
G
H
I
J
K
L
M
N
O
P
Q
R
S
T
U
V
W
X
Y
Z

put down • *I know that I do put people down occasionally.*
shame • *Her son's affair had shamed her.*

humour ❶ NOUN
something which is thought to be funny • *The film's humour contains a serious message.*
comedy • *his career in comedy*
wit • *She was known for her biting wit.*

MORE SYNONYMS
● drollery
● jocularity

humour ❷ NOUN
the mood someone is in • *He hasn't been in a good humour lately.*
frame of mind • *Clearly, she was not in the right frame of mind to continue.*
mood • *Lily was in one of her aggressive moods.*
spirits • *He was in very low spirits.*
temper • *Lee stormed off the field in a furious temper.*

humour ❸ VERB
to please someone so that they will not become upset • *I nodded, partly to humour him.*
flatter • *I knew she was just flattering me.*
indulge • *He did not agree with indulging children.*
mollify • *The investigation was undertaken primarily to mollify pressure groups.*
pander to • *politicians who pander to big business*

hungry ADJECTIVE
wanting to eat • *I didn't have any lunch, so I'm really hungry.*
famished • *Isn't dinner ready? I'm famished.*

ravenous • *a pack of ravenous animals*
starving • *starving refugees*

hurry ❶ VERB
to move or do something as quickly as possible • *She hurried through the empty streets.*
dash • *He dashed upstairs.*
fly • *I must fly or I'll miss my train.*
get a move on (INFORMAL) • *Get a move on because my car's on a double yellow line.*
rush • *I've got to rush. I've got a meeting in a few minutes.*
scurry • *Reporters scurried to find telephones.*

hurry ❷ VERB
to make something happen more quickly • *his attempt to hurry the process of independence*
accelerate • *They must now accelerate the development of their new car.*
hasten • *This will hasten the closure of small pubs.*
quicken • *He quickened his pace a little.*
speed up • *an effort to speed up the negotiations*

ANTONYM
● slow down

hurt ❶ VERB
to cause someone to feel pain • *I didn't mean to hurt her.*
harm • *The hijackers seemed anxious not to harm anyone.*
injure • *motorists who kill, maim, and injure*
wound • *The bomb killed six people and wounded another five.*

hurt ❷ VERB
to upset someone or something • *What you said really hurt me.*

Can't find the word you're looking for? Try the index.

distress • *I did not want to frighten or distress the horse.*
sadden • *He is saddened that they did not win anything.*
upset • *I'm sorry if I've upset you.*
wound • *My relatives have wounded me in the past.*

hurt ❸ ADJECTIVE

upset or offended • *He felt hurt by all the lies.*
aggrieved • *He felt aggrieved at what happened.*
offended • *He was offended at being left out.*
upset • *I'm upset by your attitude.*
wounded • *I think she feels desperately wounded and unloved.*

MORE SYNONYMS

● piqued
● rueful

hygiene NOUN

the principles and practice of health and cleanliness • *Be extra careful about personal hygiene.*
cleanliness • *Many of the beaches fail to meet minimum standards of cleanliness.*
sanitation • *the hazards of contaminated water and poor sanitation*

hypnotize VERB

to put someone into a state in which they seem to be asleep but can respond to suggestions • *She will hypnotize you and will stop you from smoking.*
put in a trance • *A stage hypnotist put her in a trance.*
put to sleep • *First the hypnotist will put you to sleep.*

MORE SYNONYMS

● entrance
● mesmerize

hysterical ❶ ADJECTIVE

in a state of uncontrolled excitement or panic • *Calm down. Don't get hysterical.*
frantic • *A bird had been locked in and was by now quite frantic.*
frenzied • *her frenzied attempts to get free*
overwrought • *One overwrought man had to be restrained by friends.*
raving • *He looked at her as if she were a raving lunatic.*

hysterical ❷ ADJECTIVE

(INFORMAL)
extremely funny • *His stand-up routine was hysterical.*
comical • *Her expression is almost comical.*
hilarious • *He had a fund of hilarious jokes on the subject.*

a
b
c
d
e
f
g
h
i
j
k
l
m
n
o
p
q
r
s
t
u
v
w
x
y
z

Ii

idea ① NOUN
a plan or suggestion for something
• *She said she'd had a brilliant idea.*
plan • *I have a cunning plan.*
recommendation • *a range of recommendations for change*
scheme • *a proposed scheme*
solution • *He came up with a solution to the problem.*
suggestion • *Do you have a better suggestion?*

MORE SYNONYMS
● hypothesis
● theory

idea ② NOUN
an opinion or belief about something • *old-fashioned ideas about women*
belief • *my religious beliefs*
conviction • *a firm conviction that things have improved*
impression • *your first impressions of college*
notion • *I have a notion of what he is like.*
opinion • *a favourable opinion of our neighbours*
view • *Make your views known to local politicians.*

idea ③ NOUN
what you know about something
• *They had no idea where they were.*
clue • *I don't have a clue what you mean.*
guess • *My guess is he went east.*

hint • *He gave no hint about where he was.*
inkling • *We had an inkling that something was happening.*
notion • *I have a notion how it is done.*
suspicion • *I have a strong suspicion they are lying.*

ideal ① NOUN
a principle or idea you try to achieve • *I don't live up to my ideal of myself.*
principle • *acts that go against your principles*
standard • *My father has high moral standards.*
value • *the values of liberty and equality*

ideal ② NOUN
the best example of something
• *She remains his feminine ideal.*
epitome • *The hotel was the epitome of luxury.*
example • *He was held up as an example of courage.*
model • *a model of good manners*
paragon • *You are not a paragon of virtue.*
prototype • *He was the prototype of a strong leader.*
standard • *the standard by which we are compared*

MORE SYNONYMS
● archetype
● criterion
● paradigm

Can't find the word you're looking for? Try the index.

ideal ❸ ADJECTIVE

being the best example of
something • *the ideal person for the
job*
classic • *a classic example of
hypocrisy*
complete • *She is the complete
athlete.*
consummate • *a consummate
politician*
model • *She is a model pupil.*
perfect • *He is the perfect husband
for her.*
supreme • *a supreme method of
cooking vegetables*

identify ❶ VERB

to recognize or name someone or
something • *I tried to identify her
perfume.*
diagnose • *This illness is easily
diagnosed.*
label • *Poisonous substances
should be labelled as such.*
name • *The victims of the fire have
been named.*
pinpoint • *They could not pinpoint
the cause of death.*
place • *The man was familiar, but I
couldn't place him.*
recognize • *a man I recognized as
Luke's father*

identify ❷, identify with
VERB

to understand someone's feelings
• *I can't identify with the characters.*
associate with • *I associate myself
with the green movement.*
empathize with • *I empathize
with the people who live here.*
feel for • *I pitied and felt for him.*
relate to • *We have difficulty
relating to each other.*
respond to • *She responded to his
pain.*

idiot NOUN

a stupid person • *You're an idiot!*
fool • *He'd been a fool to get
involved.*
galah (AUSTRALIAN; INFORMAL)
• *sounding like an illiterate galah*
imbecile • *I don't want to deal
with these imbeciles.*
moron • *I think that Gordon is a
moron.*
oaf • *You clumsy oaf!*
twit (INFORMAL) • *I feel such a twit.*

idiotic ADJECTIVE

extremely foolish or silly • *an
idiotic thing to do*
crazy • *You were crazy to leave
then.*
daft (INFORMAL) • *He's not so daft
as to listen to them.*
dumb (INFORMAL) • *I've met a lot of
dumb people.*
foolish • *It is foolish to risk injury.*
senseless • *acts of senseless
violence*
stupid • *stupid ideas*

MORE SYNONYMS
- foolhardy
- insane
- moronic

idle ADJECTIVE

doing nothing • *a popular
occupation for idle, wealthy young
women*
jobless • *One in four people are
now jobless.*
redundant • *redundant workers*
unemployed • *jobs for the
unemployed*

MORE SYNONYMS
- inactive
- stationary

ANTONYM
- busy

a
b
c
d
e
f
g
h
i
j
k
l
m
n
o
p
q
r
s
t
u
v
w
x
y
z

Can't find the word you're looking for? Try the index.

A B C D E F G H I J K L M N O P Q R S T U V W X Y Z

ignorant ❶ ADJECTIVE

not knowing about something
• He was completely ignorant of the rules.
inexperienced • I am inexperienced at decorating.
innocent • He is innocent about the harm he is doing.
oblivious • John appeared oblivious to his surroundings.
unaware • She was unaware that she was being filmed.
unconscious • He was unconscious of his failure.

ignorant ❷ ADJECTIVE

not knowledgeable about things
• People are afraid to appear ignorant.
green • The new boy is very green and immature.
naive • a shy, naive man
unaware • Young children are fairly unaware.

MORE SYNONYMS

● uneducated
● unlearned
● untutored

ignore VERB

to take no notice of someone or something • Her husband ignored her.
blank (SLANG) • The crowd blanked her for the first four numbers.
discount • They simply discounted his feelings.
disregard • He disregarded his father's advice.
neglect • They never neglect their duties.
overlook • a fact that we all tend to overlook

ill ADJECTIVE

unhealthy or sick • Payne was seriously ill with pneumonia.
ailing • The President is said to be ailing.
poorly (BRITISH; INFORMAL) • Julie is still poorly.
queasy • I feel queasy on boats.
sick • He's very sick and he needs treatment.
unhealthy • an unhealthy-looking fellow
unwell • She felt unwell back at the office.

MORE SYNONYMS

● indisposed
● infirm
● under the weather

ANTONYM

● healthy

illegal ADJECTIVE

forbidden by the law • an illegal organization
banned • banned substances
criminal • a criminal offence
illicit • illicit drugs
outlawed • a place where hunting is outlawed
prohibited • a country where alcohol is prohibited
unlawful • unlawful acts

MORE SYNONYMS

● proscribed
● unauthorized
● wrongful

ANTONYM

● legal

illness NOUN

a particular disease • a mystery illness
affliction • a severe mental affliction
ailment • common ailments
complaint • a skin complaint
disease • He has been cured of the disease.

Can't find the word you're looking for? Try the index.

disorder • *a rare nervous disorder*
lurgy (BRITISH, AUSTRALIAN AND NEW ZEALAND; INFORMAL) • *It's only a matter of days before Joan gets the lurgy as well.*
sickness • *radiation sickness*

illusion ❶ NOUN
a thing that you think you can see • *Painters create the illusion of space.*
hallucination • *Perhaps the footprint was a hallucination.*
mirage • *I began to see mirages.*
semblance • *A semblance of normality has been restored.*

MORE SYNONYMS
- chimera
- phantasm

illusion ❷ NOUN
a false belief • *Their hopes proved to be an illusion.*
delusion • *I was under the delusion that I could win.*
fallacy • *It's a fallacy that the rich are generous.*
fancy • *childhood fancies*
misconception • *There are many misconceptions about school.*

imaginary ADJECTIVE
existing in your mind but not in real life • *an imaginary friend*
fictional • *a fictional character*
fictitious • *a fictitious illness*
hypothetical • *a hypothetical situation*
ideal • *in an ideal world*
illusory • *Freedom is illusory.*
invented • *distorted or invented stories*
mythological • *mythological creatures*

ANTONYM
- real

imagination NOUN
the ability to form new ideas • *a girl who lacks imagination*
creativity • *She paints with great creativity.*
ingenuity • *the ingenuity of engineers*
inventiveness • *the artistic inventiveness of Mozart*
originality • *a composer of great originality*
vision • *a leader with vision*

imagine ❶ VERB
to have an idea of something • *He could not imagine a more peaceful scene.*
conceive • *I can't even conceive of that much money.*
envisage • *I envisage them staying together.*
fantasize • *I fantasized about writing music.*
picture • *I tried to picture the place.*
visualize • *He could not visualize her as old.*

imagine ❷ VERB
to believe that something is the case • *I imagine you're talking about my brother.*
assume • *Don't assume we are similar.*
believe • *I believe you have my pen.*
gather • *I gather that his mother was Scottish.*
guess (INFORMAL) • *I guess he's right.*
suppose • *He supposed I would be back at school.*
suspect • *Susan suspected that things would get worse.*

MORE SYNONYMS
- fancy
- surmise

a b c d e f g h i j k l m n o p q r s t u v w x y z

Can't find the word you're looking for? Try the index.

A B C D E F G H I J K L M N O P Q R S T U V W X Y Z

imitate VERB
to copy someone or something
• She imitated her parents.
ape • She is aping her sister's style.
copy • I used to copy everything my big brother did.
emulate • Sons are expected to emulate their fathers.
impersonate • He could impersonate all the other students.
mimic • He mimicked her accent.
simulate • a machine which simulates natural sounds

MORE SYNONYMS
- mirror
- mock
- parody

immediate ❶ ADJECTIVE
happening or done without delay
• My immediate reaction was fear.
instant • He took an instant dislike to Mark.
instantaneous • The applause was instantaneous.

immediate ❷ ADJECTIVE
most closely connected to you
• my immediate family
close • I have a few close friends.
direct • your direct descendants
near • near relatives

immediately ❶ ADVERB
right away • Ingrid answered Peter's letter immediately.
at once • You must come at once.
directly • He will be there directly.
instantly • She'd been knocked down in the street and died almost instantly.
now • Get out, now!
promptly • The telephone was answered promptly.
right away • You'd better tell them right away.

straightaway • I'd like to see you straightaway.

MORE SYNONYMS
- forthwith
- posthaste

immediately ❷ ADVERB
very near in time or position
• immediately behind the house
closely • He rushed out, closely followed by Kemp.
directly • James stopped directly under the window.
right • He stood right behind me.

immense ADJECTIVE
very large or huge • an immense cloud of smoke
colossal • a colossal waste of money
enormous • The main bedroom is enormous.
giant • a giant oak table
gigantic • a gigantic task
huge • Several painters were working on a huge piece of canvas.
massive • a massive cruise liner
vast • a vast expanse of water

ANTONYM
- tiny

imminent ADJECTIVE
going to happen very soon • my sister's imminent arrival
close • My birthday is quite close.
coming • the coming dawn
forthcoming • their forthcoming marriage
impending • impending doom
looming • My exams are looming.
near • in the near future

immune ADJECTIVE
not subject to or affected by something • He seems immune to pressure.
exempt • She is exempt from blame.

free • *He was not completely free of guilt.*
protected • *He is protected from the law.*
resistant • *crops that are resistant to disease*
safe • *I was safe from punishment.*
unaffected • *She is unaffected by the sight of blood.*

MORE SYNONYMS
- insusceptible
- invulnerable

impatient ❶ ADJECTIVE
easily annoyed • *You are too impatient with others.*
brusque • *a brusque manner*
curt • *He had spoken in a very curt tone of voice.*
irritable • *Brian was nervous and irritable with her.*

MORE SYNONYMS
- intolerant
- snappy

ANTONYM
- patient

impatient ❷ ADJECTIVE
eager to do something • *He was impatient to leave.*
eager • *Children are eager to learn.*
restless • *The kids were bored and restless.*

impede VERB
to make someone's or something's progress difficult • *Fallen rocks are impeding the progress of rescue workers.*
block • *The country has been trying to block these imports.*
delay • *Various set-backs delayed production.*
disrupt • *The drought has severely disrupted agricultural production.*

get in the way • *She had a job which never got in the way of her hobbies.*
hamper • *The bad weather hampered rescue operations.*
hinder • *The investigation was hindered by the loss of vital documents.*
obstruct • *The authorities are obstructing the inquiry.*

imperfect ADJECTIVE
having faults or problems • *We live in an imperfect world.*
broken • *broken toys*
damaged • *damaged goods*
defective • *defective eyesight*
faulty • *a car with faulty brakes*
flawed • *a flawed character*

MORE SYNONYMS
- deficient
- impaired
- rudimentary

ANTONYM
- perfect

impersonal ADJECTIVE
not concerned with people and their feelings • *I found him strangely distant and impersonal.*
aloof • *His manner was aloof.*
cold • *Sharon was very cold with me.*
detached • *He felt emotionally detached from the victims.*
formal • *Business relationships are usually formal.*
neutral • *He told me the news in a neutral manner.*
remote • *She was beautiful but remote.*

MORE SYNONYMS
- bureaucratic
- businesslike
- dispassionate

a
b
c
d
e
f
g
h
i
j
k
l
m
n
o
p
q
r
s
t
u
v
w
x
y
z

implore VERB

to beg someone to do something
• *"Tell me what to do!" she implored him.*
beg • *I begged him to come with me.*
beseech (LITERARY) • *I beseech you to show him mercy.*
plead with • *The lady pleaded with her daughter to come home.*

important ❶ ADJECTIVE

necessary or significant • *Her sons are the most important thing to her.*
momentous • *the momentous decision to go to war*
serious • *a serious matter*
significant • *a significant discovery*
weighty • *We discussed weighty matters.*

MORE SYNONYMS
- salient
- seminal

ANTONYM
- unimportant

important ❷ ADJECTIVE

having great influence or power
• *the most important person in the country*
eminent • *an eminent scientist*
foremost • *a foremost expert in American history*
influential • *one of the most influential books ever written*
leading • *a leading nation in world politics*
notable • *notable celebrities*
powerful • *large, powerful countries*

MORE SYNONYMS
- pre-eminent
- prominent

impose ❶ VERB

to force something on someone
• *Fines were imposed on the culprits.*
dictate • *The policy is dictated from the top.*
enforce • *It is a difficult law to enforce.*
inflict • *Inflicting punishment to stop crime is not the answer.*
levy • *a tax levied on imported goods*
ordain • *the task of trying to ordain parliamentary behaviour*

impose ❷, impose on VERB

to take advantage of someone
• *I should stop imposing on your hospitality.*
abuse • *They abused my hospitality by eating everything.*
take advantage of • *He took advantage of her generosity.*
use • *She's just using you.*

impossible ADJECTIVE

unable to happen or be believed
• *You shouldn't promise impossible things.*
absurd • *absurd claims to have met big stars*
hopeless • *a hopeless task*
inconceivable • *It's inconceivable that people can still be living in those conditions.*
ludicrous • *his ludicrous plan to build a house*
out of the question • *Is a pay increase out of the question?*
unthinkable • *The idea of splitting up is unthinkable.*

MORE SYNONYMS
- outrageous
- unattainable
- unworkable

ANTONYM
- possible

impression ❶ NOUN

the way someone or something seems to you • *your first*

impressions of college
feeling • *the feeling that she was wasting her life*
hunch • *Was your hunch right or wrong?*
idea • *I had my own ideas about what had happened.*
notion • *I have a notion of what he is like.*
sense • *She has the sense that she was in trouble.*

impression ❷, make an impression VERB
to have a strong effect on people • *He certainly made an impression on his teachers.*
cause a stir • *News of her death caused a stir.*
influence • *You can't do anything to influence him.*
make an impact • *Events can make an impact on our lives.*

impressionable ADJECTIVE
easy to influence • *impressionable teenagers*
gullible • *I'm so gullible I'd have believed him.*
open • *an open, trusting nature*
receptive • *moulding their young, receptive minds*
sensitive • *Ouija boards can be dangerous, especially to sensitive people.*
susceptible • *Children can be susceptible to advertisements.*
vulnerable • *vulnerable old people*

MORE SYNONYMS
● ingenuous
● suggestible

impressive ADJECTIVE
tending to impress • *an impressive achievement*
awesome • *awesome mountains,*
deserts and lakes
exciting • *He tells the most exciting stories.*
grand • *a grand old building*
powerful • *a powerful image*
stirring • *stirring music*
striking • *her striking personality*

MORE SYNONYMS
● dramatic
● moving

imprison VERB
to lock someone up • *He was imprisoned for murder.*
confine • *Keep your dog confined to the house.*
detain • *They'll be detained and charged.*
incarcerate • *Prisoners were incarcerated in terrible conditions.*
jail • *An innocent man was jailed.*
lock up • *You people should be locked up!*
send to prison • *The judge sent him to prison for life.*

MORE SYNONYMS
● constrain
● immure
● intern

ANTONYM
● free

improbable ADJECTIVE
unlikely or unbelievable • *improbable stories*
doubtful • *It was doubtful if they would arrive on time.*
dubious • *dubious evidence*
far-fetched • *This all sounds a bit far-fetched.*
implausible • *a film with an implausible ending*
unbelievable • *an unbelievable storyline*
unlikely • *It is unlikely that he is alive.*

a
b
c
d
e
f
g
h
i
j
k
l
m
n
o
p
q
r
s
t
u
v
w
x
y
z

Can't find the word you're looking for? Try the index.

A B C D E F G H I J K L M N O P Q R S T U V W X Y Z

ANTONYM
- probable

improve VERB
to get or make better • *He improved their house.*
advance • *Medical technology has advanced.*
better • *They tried to better their working conditions.*
enhance • *Good jewellery enhances your outfits.*
look up (INFORMAL) • *Things are looking up for me now.*
progress • *Jack's condition is progressing well.*
upgrade • *You'll have to upgrade your image.*

MORE SYNONYMS
- ameliorate
- develop
- reform

ANTONYM
- worsen

improvement NOUN
the fact or process of getting better • *dramatic improvements in conditions*
advance • *the advances in air safety since the 1970s*
development • *monitoring her language development*
enhancement • *the enhancement of the human condition*
progress • *The doctors are pleased with her progress.*
upturn • *an upturn in the economy*

impudence NOUN
disrespectful talk or behaviour towards someone • *Have you ever heard such impudence?*
audacity • *He had the audacity to speak up.*
boldness • *I was amazed at her boldness towards him.*

cheek (INFORMAL) • *I can't believe he had the cheek to complain.*
chutzpah (AMERICAN; INFORMAL) • *He had the chutzpah to ask us to leave.*
gall • *the most presumptuous question any interviewer has ever had the gall to ask*
impertinence • *His words sounded like impertinence.*
insolence • *I got punished for insolence.*
nerve • *You've got a nerve coming round here after what you've done.*

inability NOUN
a lack of ability to do something • *an inability to concentrate*
impotence • *a sense of impotence in the situation*
inadequacy • *my inadequacy as a gardener*
incompetence • *the incompetence of government officials*
ineptitude • *political ineptitude*

ANTONYM
- ability

inadequate ❶ ADJECTIVE
not enough in quantity • *Supplies of medicine are inadequate.*
insufficient • *insufficient evidence to justify criminal proceedings*
lacking • *Why was military intelligence so lacking?*
poor • *poor wages*
scarce • *the region's scarce supplies of water*
short • *Deliveries are unreliable and food is short.*

ANTONYM
- adequate

inadequate ❷ ADJECTIVE
not good enough • *She felt painfully inadequate in the crisis.*

Can't find the word you're looking for? Try the index.

deficient • *He made me feel deficient as a mother.*
incapable • *He lost his job for being incapable.*
incompetent • *the power to sack incompetent teachers*
inept • *He was inept and lacked the intelligence to govern.*
pathetic • *She made some pathetic excuse.*
useless • *I'm useless around the house.*

inappropriate NOUN
not suitable for a purpose or occasion • *This behaviour is inappropriate.*
improper • *the improper use of resources*
incongruous • *an incongruous assortment of clothes*
unfit • *houses that are unfit for living in*
unseemly • *He thought crying was unseemly.*
unsuitable • *food that is unsuitable for children*
untimely • *their unjustified and untimely interference*

ANTONYM
● appropriate

incentive NOUN
something that encourages you to do something • *the incentive to work*
bait • *He added some bait to make the agreement sweeter.*
encouragement • *She didn't get much encouragement to do anything.*
inducement • *Are gangster films an inducement to crime?*
motivation • *Money is my motivation.*
stimulus • *He needed all the stimulus he could get.*

MORE SYNONYMS
● lure
● motive
● spur

incident NOUN
an event • *Little incidents can shape our lives.*
circumstance • *This is a fortunate circumstance.*
episode • *I'm glad this episode is over.*
event • *recent events in Europe*
happening • *the latest happenings in sport*
occasion • *I remember that occasion fondly.*
occurrence • *Nancy wondered about the strange occurrence.*

incite VERB
to excite someone into doing something • *The campaigners incited a riot.*
agitate for • *Workers agitated for better conditions.*
goad • *He tried to goad me into a response.*
instigate • *The violence was instigated by a few people.*
provoke • *I provoked him into doing something stupid.*
whip up • *an attempt to whip up public hostility to the president*

include VERB
to have as a part • *A British breakfast always includes sausages.*
contain • *This sheet contains a list of names.*
cover • *The books covers many topics.*
embrace • *a small county embracing two cities*
encompass • *classes which encompass a wide range of activities*
incorporate • *The new cars incorporate many improvements.*

a
b
c
d
e
f
g
h
i
j
k
l
m
n
o
p
q
r
s
t
u
v
w
x
y
z

Can't find the word you're looking for? Try the index.

involve • *a high-energy workout which involves nearly every muscle*

ANTONYM
- exclude

income NOUN
the money someone or something earns • *families on low incomes*
earnings • *his earnings as an accountant*
pay • *We complained about our pay.*
profits • *The bank made profits of millions of dollars.*
salary • *The lawyer was paid a good salary.*
takings • *The shop had huge takings that week.*
wages • *His wages have gone up.*

MORE SYNONYMS
- proceeds
- receipts
- revenue

incomparable ADJECTIVE
too good to be compared with anything else • *an area of incomparable beauty*
inimitable • *his inimitable style*
peerless (LITERARY) • *He gave a peerless performance.*
superlative • *The hotel has superlative views.*
supreme • *the supreme piece of writing about the war*
unparalleled • *unparalleled happiness*
unrivalled • *an unrivalled knowledge of music*

MORE SYNONYMS
- matchless
- unequalled

incompetent ADJECTIVE
lacking the ability to do something properly • *You are incompetent, and you know it.*
bungling • *a bungling amateur*
cowboy (BRITISH; INFORMAL) • *cowboy builders*
incapable • *an incapable leader*
inept • *an inept performance*
unable • *He felt unable to handle the situation.*
useless • *I felt useless and a failure.*

MORE SYNONYMS
- ineffectual
- inexpert
- unskilful

ANTONYM
- competent

incomplete ADJECTIVE
not finished or whole • *an incomplete book*
deficient • *a deficient diet*
half-pie (NEW ZEALAND; INFORMAL) • *His report was half-pie.*
insufficient • *insufficient information*
partial • *The concert was a partial success.*

MORE SYNONYMS
- imperfect
- undeveloped
- unfinished

ANTONYM
- complete

increase ❶ VERB
to make or become larger in amount • *The population continues to increase.*
enlarge • *They are trying to enlarge their customer base.*
expand • *We will expand the size of the picture.*
extend • *She plans to extend her stay.*

Can't find the word you're looking for? Try the index.

grow • *The sound grew in volume.*
multiply • *viruses which can multiply rapidly in the human body*
swell • *His anger swelled within him.*

MORE SYNONYMS
- augment
- escalate

ANTONYM
- decrease

increase ❷ NOUN
a rise in the amount of something • *a pay increase*
gain • *a gain in speed*
growth • *the growth of unemployment*
increment • *tiny increments of movement*
rise • *a rise in prices*
upsurge • *an upsurge of interest in books*

ANTONYM
- decrease

incredible ❶ ADJECTIVE
totally amazing • *a champion with incredible skill*
amazing • *an amazing success*
astonishing • *an astonishing piece of good luck*
astounding • *an astounding discovery*
extraordinary • *extraordinary beauty*
marvellous • *a marvellous thing to do*
sensational (INFORMAL) • *a sensational performance*

incredible ❷ ADJECTIVE
impossible to believe • *the incredible stories of some children*
absurd • *absurd ideas*

far-fetched • *This all sounds very far-fetched to me.*
improbable • *highly improbable claims*
unbelievable • *The film has an unbelievable plot.*
unimaginable • *unimaginable wealth*
unthinkable • *It's unthinkable that Tom forgot your birthday.*

MORE SYNONYMS
- implausible
- inconceivable
- preposterous

indecent ADJECTIVE
shocking or rude • *indecent lyrics*
crude • *crude pictures*
dirty • *dirty jokes*
improper • *improper behaviour*
lewd • *lewd comments*
rude • *a rude gesture*
vulgar • *vulgar language*

independent ❶ ADJECTIVE
separate from other people or things • *an independent political party*
autonomous • *an autonomous country*
free • *Do we have a free press?*
separate • *We live separate lives.*
unrelated • *two unrelated incidents*

independent ❷ ADJECTIVE
not needing other people's help • *a fiercely independent woman*
individualistic • *individualistic behaviour*
liberated • *a genuinely liberated woman*
self-sufficient • *I am quite self-sufficient.*
unaided • *She raised her children unaided.*

a b c d e f g h **i** j k l m n o p q r s t u v w x y z

Can't find the word you're looking for? Try the index.

A B C D E F G H I J K L M N O P Q R S T U V W X Y Z

indicate VERB
to show something • *a gesture which indicates his relief*
denote • *Messy writing denotes a messy mind.*
reveal • *His diary revealed his disturbed state of mind.*
show • *I would like to show my appreciation.*
signal • *Ted signalled that everything was all right.*
signify • *A white flag signifies surrender.*

MORE SYNONYMS
- imply
- manifest
- point to

indication NOUN
a sign of something • *He gave no indication that he had heard me.*
clue • *Did she give any clue as to how she was feeling?*
hint • *The Minister gave a strong hint that he intended to resign.*
sign • *Your blood will be checked for any sign of kidney failure.*
signal • *They saw the visit as an important signal of support.*
suggestion • *There is no suggestion that the two sides are any closer to agreeing.*
warning • *a warning of impending doom*

ANOTHER SYNONYM
- intimation

indirect ADJECTIVE
not done or going directly but by another way • *the indirect effects of smoking*
meandering • *the meandering course of the river*
oblique • *oblique threats*
rambling • *In a rambling answer, he denied the charge.*
roundabout • *a roundabout way of getting information*
tortuous • *a tortuous path*
wandering • *a wandering route through the woods*

ANTONYM
- direct

individual ❶ ADJECTIVE
relating to separate people or things • *individual dishes of trifle*
discrete (FORMAL) • *breaking down the job into discrete steps*
independent • *two independent studies*
separate • *Use separate chopping boards for different foods.*
single • *every single house in the street*

individual ❷ ADJECTIVE
different and unusual • *Develop your own individual writing style.*
characteristic • *a characteristic feature*
distinctive • *His voice was very distinctive.*
idiosyncratic • *a highly idiosyncratic personality*
original • *a chef with an original touch*
personal • *his own personal method of playing*
special • *her own special way of doing things*
unique • *Each person's signature is unique.*

individual ❸ NOUN
a person, different from any other person • *the rights of the individual*
character • *a remarkable character*
party • *Who is the guilty party?*
person • *One person died and*

Can't find the word you're looking for? Try the index.

several others were injured.
soul • *He's a jolly soul.*

ANOTHER SYNONYM
● personage

industrious ADJECTIVE
tending to work hard • *industrious groups of students*
busy • *an exceptionally busy man*
conscientious • *Sherry was slow but conscientious.*
diligent • *Williams was diligent in the writing of letters.*
hard-working • *an exceptionally disciplined and hard-working young man*
tireless • *a tireless and willing worker*

ANTONYM
● lazy

inefficient ADJECTIVE
badly organized and slow
• *an inefficient government*
disorganized • *My boss is completely disorganized.*
incapable • *If he fails he will be considered incapable.*
incompetent • *an incompetent officer*
inept • *an inept use of power*
sloppy • *sloppy management*

MORE SYNONYMS
● ineffectual
● inexpert
● slipshod

ANTONYM
● efficient

inexperienced ADJECTIVE
lacking experience of a situation or activity • *inexperienced drivers*
green (INFORMAL) • *He was a young lad, and very green.*
new • *a new mother*

raw • *raw talent*
unaccustomed • *Kate is unaccustomed to being on TV.*

ANTONYM
● experienced

infect VERB
to cause disease in something
• *One mosquito can infect many people.*
affect • *Neil has been affected by the virus.*
blight • *trees blighted by pollution*
contaminate • *These substances can contaminate fish.*
taint • *blood that had been tainted with HIV*

infectious ADJECTIVE
spreading from one person to another • *infectious diseases*
catching • *There is no suggestion that multiple sclerosis is catching.*
contagious • *a highly contagious disease of the lungs*
spreading • *The spreading virus is threatening the population.*

MORE SYNONYMS
● communicable
● virulent

inferior ❶ ADJECTIVE
having a lower position than something or someone else
• *Women were given inferior status.*
lesser • *the work of lesser writers*
lower • *lower animals*
minor • *a minor celebrity*
secondary • *He was relegated to a secondary position.*
second-class • *second-class citizens*
subordinate • *His subordinate officers followed his example.*

a
b
c
d
e
f
g
h
i
j
k
l
m
n
o
p
q
r
s
t
u
v
w
x
y
z

Can't find the word you're looking for? Try the index.

ANTONYM
- superior

inferior ❷ ADJECTIVE
of low quality • *inferior quality cassette tapes*
mediocre • *mediocre music*
poor • *a poor standard of service*
second-class • *a second-class education*
second-rate • *second-rate restaurants*
shoddy • *Customers no longer tolerate shoddy goods.*

ANTONYM
- superior

inferior ❸ NOUN
a person in a lower position than another • *You must still be polite to your inferiors.*
junior • *the office junior*
menial • *menials in poorly paid jobs*
subordinate • *All her subordinates adored her.*
underling • *Every underling feared him.*

ANTONYM
- superior

infinite ADJECTIVE
without any limit or end • *an infinite number of possibilities*
boundless • *boundless energy*
eternal • *the secret of eternal youth*
everlasting • *our everlasting friendship*
inexhaustible • *an inexhaustible supply of ideas*
perpetual • *a perpetual source of worry*
untold • *untold wealth*

MORE SYNONYMS
- bottomless

- interminable
- limitless

influence ❶ NOUN
power over other people • *He has quite a lot of influence.*
authority • *You have no authority over me.*
control • *Teachers have a lot of control over students.*
importance • *a politician of great importance*
power • *a position of power*
sway • *My mother holds sway at home.*

MORE SYNONYMS
- ascendancy
- domination

influence ❷ NOUN
an effect that someone or something has • *under the influence of alcohol*
effect • *Your age has an effect on your views.*
hold • *He is losing his hold on the public.*
magnetism • *a man of great personal magnetism*
spell • *under the spell of one of his teachers*
weight • *the weight of the law*

influence ❸ VERB
to have an effect on someone or something • *I never try to influence my children.*
affect • *He will not let personal preference affect his choice.*
control • *I can't control him.*
direct • *I don't need you directing my life.*
guide • *Let your instinct guide you.*
manipulate • *I hate the way he manipulates people.*
sway • *efforts to sway voters*

Can't find the word you're looking for? Try the index.

inform VERB

to tell someone about something
• *Please inform me of your progress.*
advise (FORMAL) • *I can advise you of his whereabouts.*
enlighten • *a history lesson which enlightens you*
notify • *Ann was notified of her sister's illness.*
tell • *Tell me what is going on.*

MORE SYNONYMS

● apprise
● communicate

inform on VERB

to tell the police about someone who has committed a crime
• *Somebody must have informed on the thieves.*
betray • *They betrayed their associates to the police.*
denounce • *He was denounced as a dangerous rebel.*
grass on (BRITISH; SLANG) • *He grassed on the members of his own gang.*
tell on (INFORMAL) • *It's all right, I won't tell on you.*

informal ADJECTIVE

relaxed and casual • *His manner was informal and relaxed.*
casual • *a casual attitude towards money*
colloquial • *colloquial language*
easy • *easy conversation*
familiar • *John was too familiar towards his teacher.*
natural • *Beth was friendly and natural with us.*
relaxed • *a relaxed atmosphere in class*

ANTONYM

● formal

information NOUN

the details you know about something • *Pat would not give any information about Sarah.*
data • *The survey provided valuable data.*
drum (AUSTRALIAN; INFORMAL)
• *I don't have the drum on this yet.*
facts • *Pass on all the facts to the police.*
material • *highly secret material*
news • *We have news of your brother.*
notice • *advance notice of the event*
word • *I received word that the guests had arrived.*

ingredient NOUN

a thing that something is made from • *Place all the ingredients in a pan.*
component • *the components of hamburgers*
constituent • *the main constituent of fish oil*
element • *the various elements in a picture*

inhabit VERB

to live in a place • *the people who inhabit these islands*
dwell • *the people who dwell in the forest*
live • *She has lived here for ten years.*
lodge • *Some people lodged permanently in the hallway.*
occupy • *Forty tenants occupy the block.*
populate • *a swamp populated by huge birds*
reside (FORMAL) • *He resides in the country.*

inhabitant NOUN

someone who lives in a place • *an inhabitant of Norway*

a b c d e f g h i j k l m n o p q r s t u v w x y z

Can't find the word you're looking for? Try the index.

citizen • *American citizens*
inmate • *prison inmates*
native • *Dr Brown is a native of New Zealand.*
occupant • *the previous occupant of the house*
resident • *the residents of the retirement home*

inheritance NOUN

something that is passed on • *The house would be his son's inheritance.*
bequest • *His aunt left a bequest for him in her will.*
heritage • *This building is part of our heritage.*
legacy • *His politeness was the legacy of his upbringing.*

injure VERB

to damage part of someone's body • *A bomb exploded, injuring five people.*
harm • *The hijackers did not harm anyone.*
hurt • *He hurt his back in an accident.*
maim • *Mines in rice paddies maim and kill civilians.*
wound • *wounded by shrapnel*

injury NOUN

damage to part of the body • *He sustained serious injuries in the accident.*
damage • *brain damage*
harm • *Dogs can do harm to human beings.*
wound • *a head wound*

injustice NOUN

unfairness and lack of justice • *the injustice of the system*
bias • *He shows bias against women.*
discrimination • *racial discrimination*
inequality • *people concerned about social inequality*
prejudice • *prejudice against workers over 45*
unfairness • *the unfairness of the decision*
wrong • *I intend to right past wrongs.*

ANTONYM
● justice

innocence NOUN

inexperience of evil or unpleasant things • *the innocence of babies*
gullibility • *I'm paying for my gullibility back then.*
inexperience • *their inexperience of the real world*
naivety • *There was a youthful naivety to his honesty.*
simplicity • *She prayed with childlike simplicity.*

MORE SYNONYMS
● artlessness
● ingenuousness
● unworldliness

innocent ❶ ADJECTIVE

not guilty of a crime • *the arrest of innocent suspects*
blameless • *I have led a blameless life.*
clear • *He was clear of blame for the accident.*
not guilty • *Both men were found not guilty.*

ANTONYM
● guilty

innocent ❷ ADJECTIVE

without experience of evil or unpleasant things • *They seem so young and innocent.*
childlike • *childlike trust*
guileless • *Her eyes were as guileless as a doll's.*

Can't find the word you're looking for? Try the index.

naive • *I was young and naive when I left home.*
pure • *She had led a pure life.*
spotless • *a spotless, pure child*
virginal • *a shy, virginal princess*

MORE SYNONYMS
- artless
- ingenuous
- unworldly

insane ADJECTIVE
mad • *Some people can't take the pressure and go insane.*
crazy • *If I sat home and worried, I'd go crazy.*
deranged • *a deranged man who shot 14 people in the main square*
mad • *She was afraid of going mad.*
mentally ill • *a patient who is mentally ill*
out of your mind • *I wonder if I'm going out of my mind.*
unhinged • *an experience which left her completely unhinged*

insert VERB
to put something into something else • *He inserted the key into the lock.*
enter • *Enter your name in the box.*
implant • *a device implanted in the arm*
introduce • *Scientists introduced new genes into mice.*
place • *Cover the casserole tightly and place in the oven.*
put • *She put a coin in the slot.*
set • *diamonds set in gold*

inside ADJECTIVE
surrounded by the main part and often hidden • *We booked an inside cabin.*
inner • *the inner ear*
innermost • *the innermost parts of the galaxy*

interior • *a car with plenty of interior space*
internal • *your internal organs*

ANTONYM
- outside

insides PLURAL NOUN (INFORMAL)
the parts inside your body • *My insides ached from eating too much.*
entrails • *chicken entrails*
guts • *fish guts*
innards • *the innards of a human body*
internal organs • *damage to internal organs*

MORE SYNONYMS
- viscera
- vitals

insignificant ADJECTIVE
small and unimportant • *a small, insignificant village*
irrelevant • *irrelevant details*
little • *It seems such a little thing to get upset over.*
minor • *Western officials say the problem is minor.*
petty • *Rows can start over petty things.*
trifling • *These difficulties may seem trifling to you.*
trivial • *He tried to wave aside these issues as trivial matters.*
unimportant • *The age difference seemed unimportant.*

ANOTHER SYNONYM
- inconsequential

ANTONYM
- significant

insincere ADJECTIVE
saying things you do not mean • *A lot of actors are insincere.*
deceitful • *deceitful and misleading remarks*

Can't find the word you're looking for? Try the index.

dishonest • *dishonest salespeople*
false • *a false confession*
two-faced • *the most two-faced politicians in the world*

ANTONYM
- sincere

insist VERB

to demand something forcefully • *My family insisted I should not give in.*
demand • *The teacher demanded an explanation.*
press • *She is pressing for improvements to education.*
urge • *We urge vigorous action be taken immediately.*

inspect VERB

to examine something carefully • *the right to inspect company files*
check • *Check each item for obvious flaws.*
examine • *He examined her passport and stamped it.*
eye • *We eyed each other thoughtfully.*
investigate • *Police are investigating the scene of the crime.*
scan • *The officer scanned the room.*
survey • *He surveyed the ruins of the building.*

MORE SYNONYMS
- audit
- scrutinize
- vet

instant ❶ NOUN

a short period of time • *The pain disappeared in an instant.*
flash • *It was all over in a flash.*
minute • *I'll see you in a minute.*
moment • *In a moment he was gone.*
second • *Seconds later, firemen reached his door.*

split second • *Her gaze met Michael's for a split second.*
trice • *She was back in a trice.*

instant ❷ ADJECTIVE

immediate and without delay • *He had taken an instant dislike to her.*
immediate • *We need an immediate reply.*
instantaneous • *an explosion resulting in the instantaneous deaths of all crew members*
prompt • *Prompt action is needed.*

instinct NOUN

a natural tendency to do something • *My first instinct was to protect myself.*
feeling • *You seem to have a feeling for drawing.*
impulse • *Peter resisted an impulse to smile.*
intuition • *You should trust your intuition.*
sixth sense • *Some sixth sense told him to keep going.*
urge • *He fought the urge to panic.*

instruct ❶ VERB

to tell someone to do something • *They have instructed solicitors to sue.*
command • *He commanded his troops to attack.*
direct • *They have been directed to give attention to this problem.*
order • *Williams ordered him to leave.*
tell • *A passer-by told him to move his car.*

ANTONYM
- forbid

instruct ❷ VERB

to teach someone about a subject or skill • *He instructs therapists in relaxation techniques.*

coach • *He coached me in French.*
educate • *We need to educate people about the destructive effects of alcohol.*
school • *She's been schooling her kids herself.*
teach • *She taught children French.*
train • *We train them in a range of building techniques.*
tutor • *He was tutoring her in the stringed instruments.*

insufficient ADJECTIVE
not enough for a particular purpose • *insufficient information*
deficient • *a deficient diet*
inadequate • *The problem lies with inadequate staffing.*
lacking • *My confidence is lacking.*
scant • *Gareth paid scant attention to what was going on.*
short • *She was short of breath.*

ANTONYM
- sufficient

insult ❶ VERB
to offend someone by being rude to them • *I did not mean to insult you.*
abuse • *footballers abusing referees*
affront • *He pretended to be affronted by what I said.*
offend • *I had no intention of offending the community.*
put down • *They seemed to delight in putting me down.*
slag (BRITISH; INFORMAL) • *He's always slagging me in front of his mates.*
slight • *They felt slighted by not being consulted.*
snub • *He snubbed her in public and made her feel foolish.*

ANTONYM
- compliment

insult ❷ NOUN
a rude remark that offends someone • *The two men exchanged insults.*
abuse • *Raft hurled verbal abuse at his co-star.*
affront • *She took my words as a personal affront.*
offence • *I meant no offence to Mr Hardy.*
slight • *She is very sensitive to slights.*
snub • *This was a deliberate snub to me.*

ANTONYM
- compliment

intelligence NOUN
the ability to understand and learn things • *students of high intelligence*
cleverness • *Her cleverness gets in the way of her emotions.*
comprehension • *an idea beyond human comprehension*
intellect • *Lucy's lack of intellect disappointed her father.*
perception • *You have brilliant perception and insight.*
sense • *They have the sense to seek help.*
understanding • *I've got no sense, no understanding.*
wit • *He had the wit to see this was a good idea.*

MORE SYNONYMS
- acumen
- capacity
- nous

intelligent ADJECTIVE
able to understand and learn things • *Dolphins are an intelligent species.*
acute • *His relaxed exterior hides a very acute mind.*

a
b
c
d
e
f
g
h
i
j
k
l
m
n
o
p
q
r
s
t
u
v
w
x
y
z

A B C D E F G H I J K L M N O P Q R S T U V W X Y Z

brainy (INFORMAL) • *I don't consider myself brainy.*
bright • *an exceptionally bright child*
clever • *a clever girl*
quick • *His quick mind soon grasped the situation.*
sharp • *a very sharp intellect*
smart • *He thinks he's as smart as Sarah.*

ANTONYM
● stupid

intend ❶ VERB
to decide or plan to do something • *She intended to move back to Cape Town.*
aim • *We aim to raise funds for charity.*
be determined • *Kate was determined to enjoy the day.*
mean • *I didn't mean any harm.*
plan • *He planned to leave Adelaide on Monday.*
propose • *Where do you propose building such a huge thing?*
resolve • *She resolved to report the matter.*

intend ❷ VERB
to mean for a certain use • *a book intended for serious students*
aim • *children's games aimed at developing quickness*
design • *The house had been designed for a large family.*
earmark • *That money was earmarked for house repairs.*
mean • *I was not meant for domestic life.*

intense ❶ ADJECTIVE
very great in strength or amount • *intense heat*
acute • *an acute shortage of accommodation*
deep • *He felt a deep sense of relief.*

extreme • *Proceed with extreme caution.*
fierce • *There was fierce competition for the job.*
great • *Dawes felt a great pain and weakness.*
powerful • *I had a powerful urge to scream at him.*
profound • *The book had a profound effect in the USA.*
severe • *I had severe problems.*

intense ❷ ADJECTIVE
tending to have strong feelings • *He was dark-haired and intense.*
ardent • *one of his most ardent supporters*
earnest • *Ella was a pious, earnest woman.*
fervent • *a fervent admirer of Beethoven's music*
fierce • *fierce loyalty to his friends*
impassioned • *He made an impassioned appeal for peace.*
passionate • *He is very passionate about the project.*
vehement • *a vehement critic of the plan*

intention NOUN
a plan to do something • *He announced his intention of retiring.*
aim • *The aim of this book is to inform you.*
goal • *The goal is to raise a lot of money.*
idea • *I bought books with the idea of reading them.*
object • *It was his object in life to find the island.*
objective • *His objective was to play golf and win.*
purpose • *He did not know the purpose of Vincent's visit.*

interest ❶ NOUN
a feeling of wanting to know about

something • *I have a great interest in that period of history.*
attention • *The book attracted considerable attention.*
fascination • *a lifelong fascination with the sea*
concern • *How it happened is of little concern to me.*
curiosity • *His reply satisfied our curiosity.*

interest ❷ NOUN
a hobby • *He has a wide range of sporting interests.*
activity • *I enjoy outdoor activities like canoeing and climbing.*
hobby • *My hobbies are football, photography and tennis.*
pastime • *His favourite pastime is golf.*
pursuit • *his favourite childhood pursuits*

interest ❸ VERB
to attract someone's attention and curiosity • *This part of the book interests me most.*
appeal • *The bright colours seem to appeal to children.*
captivate • *this author's ability to captivate young minds*
fascinate • *Politics fascinated my father.*
intrigue • *The situation intrigued him.*
stimulate • *Bill was stimulated by the challenge.*

ANTONYM
● bore

interesting ADJECTIVE
making you want to know, learn or hear more • *an interesting hobby*
absorbing • *an absorbing conversation*
compelling • *compelling drama*

entertaining • *a cheerful and entertaining companion*
gripping • *a gripping story*
intriguing • *the intriguing character of the author*
stimulating • *My trip to India had been stimulating.*

ANTONYM
● boring

interfere ❶ VERB
to try to influence a situation • *Stop interfering and leave me alone.*
butt in • *I butted in where I didn't belong.*
intervene • *Soldiers don't like civilians intervening in their affairs.*
intrude • *I don't want to intrude on your meeting.*
meddle • *Scientists should not meddle in such matters.*
tamper • *the price we pay for tampering with the environment*

interfere ❷ VERB
to have a damaging effect on a situation • *His problems interfered with his work.*
conflict • *an evening that conflicted with my work schedule*
disrupt • *Strikes disrupted air traffic in Italy.*
hinder • *A thigh injury hindered her movement.*
impede • *Fallen rocks impeded the progress of the rescue workers.*
inhibit • *factors which inhibit growth*
obstruct • *Lack of funds obstructed our progress.*

interrogate VERB
to question someone thoroughly • *I interrogated everyone even slightly involved.*

a
b
c
d
e
f
g
h
i
j
k
l
m
n
o
p
q
r
s
t
u
v
w
x
y
z

Can't find the word you're looking for? Try the index.

A
B
C
D
E
F
G
H
I
J
K
L
M
N
O
P
Q
R
S
T
U
V
W
X
Y
Z

examine • *Lawyers examined the witnesses.*
grill (INFORMAL) • *Jenkins kept telling police who grilled him: "I didn't kill her."*
question • *He was questioned by police.*
quiz • *She quizzed me quite closely for a while.*

MORE SYNONYMS
● cross-examine
● cross-question

interrupt ❶ VERB
to start talking when someone else is talking • *He tried to speak, but she interrupted him.*
butt in • *Mirella butted in without a greeting.*
heckle • *It is easy to heckle from the safety of the audience.*

interrupt ❷ VERB
to stop a process or activity for a time • *The match was interrupted by rain.*
break • *allowing passengers to break their journey with a stay in Fiji*
discontinue • *Do not discontinue the treatment without seeing your doctor.*
suspend • *Relief convoys will be suspended until the fighting stops.*

interval NOUN
a period of time between two moments or dates • *There was a long interval of silence.*
break • *a short break from work*
gap • *the gap between school terms*
hiatus • *There was a momentary hiatus in the sounds.*
interlude • *It was a happy interlude in the Kents' life.*
intermission • *There will be a short intermission between acts.*

pause • *a pause between two periods of intense activity*

intervene VERB
to step in to prevent conflict • *I relied on them to intervene if anything happened.*
arbitrate • *A committee was set up to arbitrate in the dispute.*
mediate • *efforts to mediate between the two communities*

introduction ❶ NOUN
the act of presenting someone or something new • *the introduction of a single European currency*
establishment • *the establishment of a democratic system*
inauguration • *the inauguration of the President*
initiation • *your initiation into adulthood*
institution • *the institution of new laws*
launch • *the launch of this popular author's new book*

introduction ❷ NOUN
a piece of writing at the beginning of a book • *The book contains a new introduction by the author.*
foreword • *I am happy to write the foreword to this collection.*
preface • *I read through the preface quickly.*
prologue • *the General Prologue to The Canterbury Tales*

intrude VERB
to disturb someone or something • *I don't want to intrude on your parents.*
butt in • *I butted in where I didn't belong.*
encroach • *Does your work encroach on your private life?*

Can't find the word you're looking for? Try the index.

infringe • *She promised not to infringe on his space.*
interrupt • *Georgina interrupted his thoughts.*
trespass • *I don't like to trespass on your time.*
violate • *These men were violating her family's privacy.*

invade VERB
to enter a country by force • *The allies invaded the Italian mainland at Anzio.*
attack • *Government planes attacked the town.*
enter • *The Taleban entered western Kabul.*
occupy • *Soldiers occupied the town within a few minutes.*
violate • *A helicopter violated Greek territory yesterday.*

invent ❶ VERB
to be the first person to think of a device • *He invented the first electric clock.*
coin • *Lanier coined the term 'virtual reality'.*
come up with (INFORMAL) • *He came up with a gadget to relieve hayfever.*
conceive • *He conceived the first portable computer.*
create • *The company decided to create a new perfume.*
formulate • *He formulated his plan for escape.*
originate • *the designer who originated platform shoes*

MORE SYNONYMS
● design
● devise
● improvise

invent ❷ VERB
to make up a story or excuse

• *I tried to invent a plausible excuse.*
concoct • *A newspaper concocted an imaginary interview.*
fabricate • *The evidence against them was fabricated.*
make up • *Donna was known for making up stories about herself.*
manufacture • *The children manufactured an elaborate tale.*

investigate VERB
to find out all the facts about something • *Police are still investigating the incidents.*
examine • *I have examined all the possible alternatives.*
explore • *a book which explores the history of technology*
probe • *He probed into her private life.*
research • *I'm researching for an article on New England.*
sift • *I sifted the evidence for conclusions.*
study • *Experts are studying the security in the building.*

invincible ADJECTIVE
unable to be defeated • *When Woods is on form he is invincible.*
impregnable • *an impregnable fortress*
indomitable • *the indomitable spirit of the Polish people*
unbeatable • *a performance record that is unbeatable*

MORE SYNONYMS
● indestructible
● insurmountable
● unassailable

invisible ADJECTIVE
unable to be seen • *His face was invisible beneath his hat.*
concealed • *a concealed weapon*

a
b
c
d
e
f
g
h
i
j
k
l
m
n
o
p
q
r
s
t
u
v
w
x
y
z

Can't find the word you're looking for? Try the index.

A B C D E F G H I J K L M N O P Q R S T U V W X Y Z

disguised • *a disguised panel in the wall*
hidden • *a hidden camera*
inconspicuous • *She tried to make herself inconspicuous.*
unseen • *His work was guided by an unseen hand.*

MORE SYNONYMS
● imperceptible
● indiscernible

ANTONYM
● visible

involve VERB
to have as a necessary part • *Running a kitchen involves a great deal of discipline.*
incorporate • *The program incorporates a range of activities.*
require • *Caring for a baby requires special skills.*
take in • *This study takes in a number of areas.*

MORE SYNONYMS
● entail
● necessitate

irrational ADJECTIVE
not based on logical reasons • *irrational fears*
absurd • *It was an absurd over-reaction.*
crazy • *crazy ideas*
illogical • *his completely illogical arguments*
nonsensical • *Such an idea sounds paradoxical, if not downright nonsensical.*
unsound • *The thinking is good-hearted, but muddled and unsound.*

MORE SYNONYMS
● silly
● unreasoning

irregular ❶ ADJECTIVE
not smooth or even • *an irregular surface*
asymmetrical • *She has asymmetrical features.*
bumpy • *bumpy roads*
jagged • *jagged fragments of stained glass*
lopsided • *his lopsided smile*
ragged • *the ragged edges of a tear*
uneven • *uneven teeth*

ANTONYM
● regular

irregular ❷ ADJECTIVE
not forming a regular pattern • *He worked irregular hours.*
erratic • *a planet with an erratic orbit*
haphazard • *a haphazard system*
occasional • *occasional rain showers*
patchy • *Her career has been patchy.*
random • *The stock market is random and unpredictable.*
variable • *a variable rate of interest*

MORE SYNONYMS
● fitful
● sporadic

ANTONYM
● regular

irresponsible ADJECTIVE
not concerned with the consequences of your actions • *an irresponsible attitude*
careless • *a careless driver*
reckless • *reckless spending*
thoughtless • *a thoughtless remark*
wild • *a night of wild abandon*

ANTONYM
● responsible

irritable ADJECTIVE
easily annoyed • *Nicol was unusually tense and irritable.*
bad-tempered • *You're very bad-tempered today.*
cantankerous • *a cantankerous old man*
petulant • *He was like a petulant child.*
ratty (BRITISH AND NEW ZEALAND; INFORMAL) • *There's no need to get ratty.*

MORE SYNONYMS
● irascible
● tetchy

irritate VERB
to annoy someone • *Their attitude irritates me.*
anger • *This article angered me.*
annoy • *It just annoyed me to hear him going on.*
bother • *Nothing bothers me.*
exasperate • *Bertha was exasperated by the delay.*
needle (INFORMAL) • *If her remark needled him, he didn't show it.*
ruffle • *He doesn't get ruffled by anything.*

MORE SYNONYMS
● gall
● provoke

issue ❶ NOUN
a subject that people are talking about • *important issues of the day*
concern • *Political concerns continue to dominate the news.*
matter • *He touched on many matters in his speech.*
problem • *the energy problem*
question • *The whole question of aid is a tricky one.*
subject • *the president's views on the subject*

topic • *the main topic for discussion*

issue ❷ NOUN
a particular edition of a newspaper or magazine • *the latest issue of the Lancet*
copy • *a copy of 'USA Today'*
edition • *There's an article about the film in next month's edition.*
instalment • *a magazine published in monthly instalments*

issue ❸ VERB
to make a formal statement • *They have issued a statement denying the allegations.*
deliver • *He delivered a speech to his fellow union members.*
give • *The minister gave a warning that war should be avoided at all costs.*
make • *He says he was depressed when he made the statement.*
pronounce • *The authorities took time to pronounce their verdicts.*
read out • *She read out an announcement outside the court.*
release • *The police are not releasing any more details about the attack.*

ANTONYM
● withdraw

issue ❹ VERB
to give something officially • *Staff will be issued with badges.*
equip • *plans to equip the reserve army with guns*
furnish (FORMAL) • *They will furnish you with the necessary items.*
give out • *The prizes were given out by a local dignitary.*
provide • *The government was unable to provide them with food.*
supply • *an agreement not to supply these countries with chemical weapons*

a
b
c
d
e
f
g
h
i
j
k
l
m
n
o
p
q
r
s
t
u
v
w
x
y
z

Can't find the word you're looking for? Try the index.

item ❶ NOUN
one of a collection or list of things
• *an item on the agenda*
article • *articles of clothing*
matter • *He dealt with a variety of matters.*
point • *Many of the points in the report are correct.*
thing • *Big things are paid for by the government.*

item ❷ NOUN
a newspaper or magazine article
• *There was an item in the paper about him.*
article • *a short article in one of the papers*
feature • *The magazine contained a special feature on the project.*
notice • *notices in today's national newspapers*
piece • *I disagree with your recent piece about Australia.*
report • *a film report on the scandal*

A
B
C
D
E
F
G
H
I
J
K
L
M
N
O
P
Q
R
S
T
U
V
W
X
Y
Z

Can't find the word you're looking for? Try the index.

Jj

a b c d e f g h i j k l m n o p q r s t u v w x y z

jagged ADJECTIVE
sharp and spiky • *jagged black cliffs*
barbed • *barbed wire*
craggy • *craggy mountains*
rough • *the rough surface of the rock*
serrated • *a serrated knife*

ANTONYM
smooth

jail ❶ NOUN
a place where prisoners are held • *sentenced to 18 months in jail*
nick (BRITISH, AUSTRALIAN AND NEW ZEALAND; SLANG) • *He spent seven years in the nick.*
prison • *his release from prison*

MORE SYNONYMS
● lockup
● penal institution
● penitentiary

jail ❷ VERB
to put in prison • *He was jailed for twenty years.*
detain • *Police can detain a suspect for 48 hours.*
imprison • *imprisoned for 18 months on charges of theft*
incarcerate • *They have been incarcerated as political prisoners.*

jam ❶ NOUN
a crowded mass of people or things • *stuck in a jam on the motorway*
crowd • *elbowing his way through the crowd*

crush • *We got separated in the crush.*
mass • *a mass of excited fans*
mob • *a growing mob of demonstrators*
multitude • *surrounded by a noisy multitude*
throng • *An official pushed through the throng.*

jam ❷ NOUN
a difficult situation • *We're in a real jam now.*
dilemma • *faced with a dilemma*
fix (INFORMAL) • *a difficult economic fix*
hole (SLANG) • *He admitted that the government was in a hole.*
plight • *the plight of the Third World countries*
predicament • *a way out of our predicament*
quandary • *We're in a quandary over our holiday plans.*
trouble • *You are in serious trouble.*

jam ❸ VERB
to push something somewhere roughly • *He jammed his hat on to his head.*
cram • *He crammed the bank notes into his pocket.*
force • *I forced the key into the ignition.*
ram • *He rammed the muzzle of the gun against my forehead.*
stuff • *She stuffed the newspaper into a litter bin.*

Can't find the word you're looking for? Try the index.

jam ④ VERB
to become stuck • *The second time he fired, his gun jammed.*
stall • *The engine stalled.*
stick • *She tried to open the window but it was stuck.*

jealous ADJECTIVE
wanting to have something which someone else has • *She was jealous of his success.*
envious • *envious of the attention his brother was getting*
resentful • *resentful of her husband's hobby*

MORE SYNONYMS
● covetous
● emulous

job ① NOUN
the work someone does to earn money • *I'm still looking for a job.*
employment • *unable to find employment*
occupation • *his occupation as a carpenter*
position • *He's leaving to take up a position abroad.*
post • *She has resigned her post as his assistant.*
profession • *She chose nursing as her profession.*
trade • *her trade as a jeweller*

job ② NOUN
a duty or responsibility • *It's your job to find out what's going on.*
concern • *The technical aspects are the concern of the engineers.*
duty • *I consider it my duty to write and thank you.*
function • *an important function to fill*
responsibility • *It's not my responsibility to look after your mother.*

role • *Our role is to keep the peace.*
task • *She had the task of breaking the bad news.*

join ① VERB
to become a member of something • *He joined the Army five years ago.*
enlist • *He was 18 when he enlisted in the US Navy.*
enrol • *She has enrolled in an acting class.*
sign up • *I've signed up as a member.*

ANTONYM
● resign

join ② VERB
to fasten two things together • *two sticks joined together by a chain*
attach • *The gadget can be attached to any surface.*
connect • *two rooms connected by a passage*
couple • *an engine coupled to a gearbox*
fasten • *a wooden bench fastened to the floor*
link • *tree houses linked by ropes*
tie • *He tied the dog to a post by its leash.*

MORE SYNONYMS
● append
● knit
● splice

ANTONYM
● separate

joke ① NOUN
something that makes people laugh • *I heard a great joke today.*
gag (INFORMAL) • *a gag about unscrupulous lawyers*
jest • *It was only intended as a jest.*
lark • *They just did it for a lark.*

Can't find the word you're looking for? Try the index.

A
B
C
D
E
F
G
H
I
J
K
L
M
N
O
P
Q
R
S
T
U
V
W
X
Y
Z

prank • *an end-of-term prank*
quip • *a famous quip by Groucho Marx*
wisecrack (INFORMAL) • *She was tempted to make a wisecrack.*
witticism • *laughing at each other's witticisms*

MORE SYNONYMS
- jape
- sally

joke ② VERB
to say something funny • *She was always joking about her appearance.*
banter • *He played trick shots and bantered with the crowd.*
chaff • *They chaffed us about our chances of winning.*
jest • *drinking and jesting with his cronies*
kid (INFORMAL) • *Don't worry, I'm only kidding.*
quip • *"You'll have to go on a diet," he quipped.*
tease • *"You must be in love," she teased.*

journey ① NOUN
the act of travelling from one place to another • *the journey from Paris to Bordeaux*
excursion • *The trip includes an excursion to Zermatt.*
expedition • *an expedition to the South Pole*
passage • *a 10-hour passage from Swansea*
tour • *a two-month tour of Europe*
trek • *a trek through the Gobi desert*
trip • *a business trip*
voyage • *the first space shuttle voyage*

journey ② VERB
to travel from one place to another

• *In 1935, she journeyed through Turkey and Africa.*
go • *We went from Glasgow to London in six hours.*
proceed • *proceeding along the road in the wrong direction*
tour • *He toured China in 1993.*
travel • *Gran travelled down by train.*
trek • *trekking through the jungle*
voyage • *They voyaged as far as Spain.*

joy NOUN
great happiness • *Her face shone with joy.*
bliss • *an expression of pure bliss*
delight • *He let out a yell of delight.*
ecstasy • *Her eyes closed in ecstasy.*
elation • *He felt a surge of elation at the news.*
rapture • *His speech was received with rapture.*

MORE SYNONYMS
- exaltation
- exultation
- felicity

ANTONYM
- misery

joyful ADJECTIVE
extremely happy • *a joyful smile*
delighted • *I'm delighted to be here.*
elated • *the elated faces of the freed hostages*
jubilant • *the jubilant crowds*
over the moon (INFORMAL) • *I was over the moon to hear about your promotion.*

MORE SYNONYMS
- cock-a-hoop
- enraptured

a b c d e f g h i j k l m n o p q r s t u v w x y z

judge | 320

judge ❶ NOUN

the person in charge of a law court
• *The judge awarded him £2000 in damages.*
beak (BRITISH; SLANG) • *a third appearance before the beak*
justice • *his appointment as a Justice of the High Court*
magistrate • *defendants appearing before a magistrate*

RELATED WORD

● ADJECTIVE: judicial

judge ❷ NOUN

someone who picks the winner or keeps control of a competition
• *A panel of judges are selecting the finalists.*
referee • *The referee awarded a free kick against Rourke.*
umpire • *the umpire's decision*

judge ❸ VERB

to form an opinion about someone or something • *Don't judge people by their looks.*
appraise • *The teachers are appraised by an official.*
assess • *It is too early to assess the impact of the change.*
consider • *We consider him to be dangerous.*
estimate • *The cost of the damage is estimated at over a million dollars.*
evaluate • *a test to evaluate a candidate's potential*
rate • *The film was rated a hit.*

judge ❹ VERB

to pick the winner or keep control in a competition • *Entrants will be judged in two age categories.*
referee • *He has refereed in two World Cups.*
umpire • *He umpired baseball games.*

MORE SYNONYMS

● adjudge
● adjudicate

judgment NOUN

an opinion or decision based on evidence • *It's hard to form a judgment without all the facts.*
appraisal • *a calm appraisal of the situation*
assessment • *my own personal assessment of our position*
conclusion • *I've come to the conclusion that she knows what she's talking about.*
opinion • *Seek a medical opinion before you travel.*
ruling • *a High Court ruling*
verdict • *The doctor's verdict was that he was entirely healthy.*
view • *In my view, things aren't going to get any better.*

jump ❶ VERB

to leap up or over something
• *I jumped over the fence.*
bound • *He bounded up the steps.*
clear • *The horse cleared the gate by inches.*
hurdle • *He crossed the lawn and hurdled the fence.*
leap • *He had leapt from a window and escaped.*
spring • *The lion roared once and sprang.*
vault • *Ned vaulted over a fallen tree.*

jump ❷ VERB

to increase suddenly • *Sales jumped by 25% last year.*
escalate • *Costs escalated dramatically.*
increase • *Trading has increased by 20% this month.*
rise • *Unemployment is rising rapidly.*
surge • *The party's share of the vote surged from 10% to 17%.*

A B C D E F G H I J K L M N O P Q R S T U V W X Y Z

Can't find the word you're looking for? Try the index.

jump ❸ NOUN
a leap into the air • *the longest ever jump by a man*
bound • *With one bound Jack was free.*
leap • *Smith took the gold medal with a leap of 2.37 metres.*
vault • *She regained the record with a vault of 3.80 metres.*

junior ADJECTIVE
having a relatively low position compared to others • *a junior minister*
inferior • *inferior status*
lesser • *He resigned to take a lesser position and a cut in wages.*
lower • *the lower ranks of council officers*
subordinate • *sixty of his subordinate officers*

ANTONYM
● senior

junk NOUN
old articles that people usually throw away • *What are you going to do with all that junk?*
clutter • *She likes her worktops to be clear of clutter.*
odds and ends • *My handbag's full of useless odds and ends.*
refuse • *a weekly collection of refuse*
rubbish • *They piled most of their rubbish into skips.*
scrap • *a small yard containing a heap of scrap*
trash • *cluttered with trash*

justice ❶ NOUN
fairness in the way that people are treated • *He wants freedom, justice and equality.*
equity • *Income should be distributed with some sense of equity.*
fairness • *concern about the fairness of the election campaign*
impartiality • *a system lacking impartiality*

ANTONYM
● injustice

justice ❷ NOUN
the person in charge of a law court • *his appointment as a Justice of the High Court*
judge • *The judge awarded him £2000 in damages.*
magistrate • *defendants appearing before a magistrate*

justify VERB
to show that something is reasonable or necessary • *How can you justify what you've done?*
defend • *Her conduct is hard to defend.*
excuse • *That still doesn't excuse his behaviour.*
explain • *She left a note explaining her actions.*
vindicate • *Ministers are confident their decision will be vindicated.*
warrant • *These allegations warrant an investigation.*

a
b
c
d
e
f
g
h
i
j
k
l
m
n
o
p
q
r
s
t
u
v
w
x
y
z

Kk

kai NOUN (NEW ZEALAND; INFORMAL)
food • *I'm starving - let's have some kai.*
food • *Enjoy your food.*
grub (INFORMAL) • *Get yourself some grub.*
provisions • *enough provisions for two weeks*
rations • *The soldiers sampled the officers' rations.*
tucker (AUSTRALIAN AND NEW ZEALAND; INFORMAL) • *I haven't had any decent tucker for days.*

MORE SYNONYMS
- sustenance (FORMAL)
- victuals

keen ❶ ADJECTIVE
showing eagerness and enthusiasm for something • *a keen amateur photographer*
ardent • *one of his most ardent supporters*
avid • *an avid reader*
eager • *We're eager to have another baby.*
enthusiastic • *Tom was very enthusiastic about the place.*
fond of • *Are you fond of Chinese cuisine?*
into (INFORMAL) • *I'm really into football.*

keen ❷ ADJECTIVE
quick to notice or understand things • *a keen intellect*
astute • *an astute judge of character*
brilliant • *She had a brilliant mind.*
perceptive • *a perceptive gaze*
quick • *His quick mind soon grasped the situation.*
shrewd • *Her questions showed a shrewd perception.*

keep ❶ VERB
to have and look after something • *His father keeps a small shop.*
care for • *vintage cars lovingly cared for by their owners*
maintain • *The house costs a fortune to maintain.*
preserve • *the need to preserve the rainforests*

keep ❷ VERB
to store something • *She kept her money under the mattress.*
deposit • *You are advised to deposit your valuables in the hotel safe.*
hold • *Our stock is held in a warehouse.*
store • *Store the cookies in an airtight tin.*

keep ❸ VERB
to do what you said you would do • *I always keep my promises.*
carry out • *He carried out his threat.*
fulfil • *He fulfilled all his responsibilities.*
honour • *The two sides have agreed to honour a new ceasefire.*

kidnap VERB
to take someone away by force

• *Four tourists have been kidnapped by rebels.*
abduct • *people claiming to have been abducted by aliens*
capture • *The guerrillas shot down one plane and captured the pilot.*
seize • *hostages seized by terrorists*

kill VERB

to make someone or something die • *The earthquake killed 62 people.*
assassinate • *the plot to assassinate Martin Luther King*
butcher • *The guards butchered hundreds of prisoners.*
destroy • *The jockey was unhurt but his horse had to be destroyed.*
execute • *He was executed for treason.*
exterminate • *an effort to exterminate all the rats*
massacre • *300 civilians have been massacred by the rebels.*
murder • *the widow of the murdered leader*
slaughter • *Whales are being slaughtered for commercial gain.*
slay • *a painting of Saint George slaying the dragon*

MORE SYNONYMS

● annihilate
● dispatch

kin PLURAL NOUN

the people who are related to you • *She has gone to live with her husband's kin.*
family • *There's a history of heart disease in our family.*
kindred • *his loyalty to his friends and kindred*
people • *She was reunited with her people.*
relations • *I was staying with relations in Atlanta.*

relatives • *On Sundays his relatives come to visit.*

kind ❶ NOUN

a particular type of person or thing • *I don't like that kind of film.*
brand • *his favourite brand of whisky*
breed • *a rare breed of cattle*
category • *Cereal bars are the fastest-growing category of breakfast products.*
class • *a better class of restaurant*
classification • *the cost of coverage for different classifications of motorcycle*
genre • *a writer who does not confine himself to one particular genre*
grade • *an improved grade of fertilizer*
sort • *a dozen trees of various sorts*
species • *a rare species of moth*
type • *What type of guns were they?*
variety • *a new variety of rose*

kind ❷ ADJECTIVE

considerate towards other people • *Thank you for being so kind to me.*
benevolent • *a very benevolent employer*
benign • *a benign ruler*
charitable • *a charitable nature*
compassionate • *My father was a deeply compassionate man.*
considerate • *a caring and considerate husband*
good • *a good man driven to a desperate act*
humane • *the humane treatment of prisoners*
kind-hearted • *Mark was kind-hearted, generous, and loved life.*
kindly • *a kindly old man*
thoughtful • *a thoughtful gesture*
unselfish • *his generous and unselfish attitude towards others*

a
b
c
d
e
f
g
h
i
j
k
l
m
n
o
p
q
r
s
t
u
v
w
x
y
z

Can't find the word you're looking for? Try the index.

A
B
C
D
E
F
G
H
I
J
K
L
M
N
O
P
Q
R
S
T
U
V
W
X
Y
Z

MORE SYNONYMS
- lenient
- philanthropic

ANTONYM
- cruel

kindness NOUN
the quality of being considerate towards other people • *Everyone has treated me with great kindness.*
benevolence • *an act of selfless benevolence*
charity • *Ms Rubens writes with warmth and charity.*
compassion • *He showed no compassion to his victim.*
gentleness • *the gentleness with which she treated her mother*
humanity • *Her speech showed great maturity and humanity.*

MORE SYNONYMS
- kindliness
- magnanimity
- philanthropy
- tenderness

ANTONYM
- cruelty

king NOUN
a man who is the head of a royal family • *the king and queen of Spain*
monarch • *the coronation of the new monarch*
sovereign • *the first British sovereign to visit the country*

RELATED WORDS
- ADJECTIVES: royal, regal,
- monarchical

know ❶ VERB
to understand or be aware of something • *I don't know anything about cars.*
apprehend • *It is impossible to apprehend the whole painting at once.*
be aware of • *Smokers are aware of the risks they run.*
comprehend • *They do not comprehend the nature of the problem.*
perceive • *the world as we perceive it*
see • *Don't you see what he's up to?*
understand • *too young to understand what was happening*

know ❷ VERB
to be familiar with a person or thing • *I believe you two already know each other.*
be acquainted with • *Are you acquainted with my husband?*
be familiar with • *I am familiar with his work.*
recognize • *She recognized him at once.*

knowledge NOUN
all you know about something • *She had no knowledge of French.*
education • *a man with little education*
learning • *people of great learning*
scholarship • *a lifetime of scholarship*
wisdom • *a source of wisdom and knowledge*

Can't find the word you're looking for? Try the index.

Ll

label ❶ NOUN
a piece of paper or plastic attached to something for information • *He peered at the label on the bottle.*
sticker • *She's got a disabled sticker on her car.*
tag • *a name tag*
ticket • *a price ticket*

label ❷ VERB
to put a label on something • *The produce was labelled 'Made in China'.*
flag • *Flag the pages which need corrections.*
sticker • *products stickered at a special price*
tag • *The pigeon was tagged with a numbered band.*

labour ❶ NOUN
very hard work • *the labour of weeding and digging*
effort • *legs aching with the effort of the climb*
exertion • *She felt dizzy with the exertion of walking.*
industry • *At last his industry was rewarded.*
toil • *their day's toil in the fields*
work • *All our work is starting to pay off.*

labour ❷ NOUN
the workforce of a country or industry • *unskilled labour*
employees • *Only a third of all employees are union members.*
workers • *Thousands of workers have been laid off.*
workforce • *a country where half the workforce is unemployed*

labour ❸ VERB
to work very hard • *peasants labouring in the fields*
slave • *We've been slaving half the night to finish this.*
toil • *workers toiling in wretched conditions*
work • *He works twelve hours a day.*

ANTONYM
- relax

lack ❶ NOUN
the shortage or absence of something which is needed • *a lack of funds*
absence • *an absence of evidence*
deficiency • *tests for vitamin deficiency*
scarcity • *a scarcity of water*
shortage • *a food shortage*
want • *becoming weak from want of rest*

MORE SYNONYMS
- dearth
- insufficiency
- scantiness

ANTONYM
- abundance

lack ❷ VERB
to be without something that is needed • *She lacks confidence.*
be deficient in • *Your diet is deficient in vitamins.*

a b c d e f g h i j k l m n o p q r s t u v w x y z

Can't find the word you're looking for? Try the index.

be short of • *I'm short of cash.*
miss • *Your jacket is missing a button.*

lag VERB

to make slower progress than other
people or things • *He is now lagging
10 points behind the champion.*
fall behind • *The city is falling
behind in attracting tourists.*
trail • *The Communist party is
trailing badly in the opinion polls.*

lake NOUN

TYPES OF LAKE

lagoon	mere
loch (SCOTTISH)	reservoir
lough (IRISH)	tarn

lame ❶ ADJECTIVE

unable to walk properly because of
an injured leg • *She was lame in
one leg.*
crippled • *a woman crippled by
arthritis*
hobbling • *a hobbling old man*
limping • *limping from a
hamstring injury*

lame ❷ ADJECTIVE

weak or unconvincing • *a lame
excuse*
feeble • *his feeble attempt at humour*
flimsy • *MPs condemned his
evidence as flimsy.*
pathetic • *a pathetic attempt at
humour*
poor • *a poor effort*
unconvincing • *an unconvincing
argument*
weak • *a weak performance*

lament ❶ VERB

to express sorrow or regret over
something • *She lamented the
death of her brother.*
grieve • *grieving over his dead wife
and son*

mourn • *We mourned the loss of
our home.*
wail • *a mother wailing for her lost
child*
weep • *She wept for her lost love.*

MORE SYNONYMS

● bemoan
● bewail

lament ❷ NOUN

something you say to express
sorrow or regret • *a lament for a
vanished age*
moan • *a moan of sorrow*
wail • *wails of grief*

MORE SYNONYMS

● lamentation
● plaint

land ❶ NOUN

an area of ground which someone
owns • *a dispute over land*
estate • *a shooting party on his
estate in Yorkshire*
grounds • *the palace grounds*
property • *travellers who camped
on his property*

land ❷ NOUN

a region or country • *America is the
land of opportunity.*
country • *the boundary between
the two countries*
nation • *the nation's financial crisis*
province • *The Algarve is
Portugal's southernmost province.*
region • *the region of Tuscany*
territory • *the disputed territory of
Kashmir*

land ❸ VERB

to arrive on the ground after flying
or sailing • *We landed in New York
around noon.*
alight • *A thrush alighted on a
nearby branch.*

Can't find the word you're looking for? Try the index.

dock • *The ship docked in Le Havre.*
touch down • *The plane touched down in Barbados.*

language ❶ NOUN
the system of words people use to communicate • *She speaks four languages.*
dialect • *the Cantonese dialect*
idiom • *the Gaelic idiom*
jargon • *scientific jargon*
lingo (INFORMAL) • *I don't speak the lingo.*
tongue • *The French feel passionately about their native tongue.*
vernacular • *an Indian vernacular derived from Sanskrit*
vocabulary • *a new word in the German vocabulary*

MORE SYNONYMS
- argot
- cant
- lingua franca
- patois

language ❷ NOUN
the style in which you speak or write • *He explained the process in plain language.*
phrasing • *The phrasing of this report is confusing.*
style • *a simple writing style*
wording • *The wording of the contract was ambiguous.*

MORE SYNONYMS
- phraseology
- terminology

large ADJECTIVE
of a greater size or amount than usual • *a large room*
big • *Her husband was a big man.*
colossal • *a colossal task*
enormous • *an enormous house*
giant • *a giant bird*
gigantic • *a gigantic spider*

great • *a great hall as long as a church*
huge • *huge profits*
immense • *an immense chamber*
massive • *a massive ship*
vast • *a vast desert*

MORE SYNONYMS
- gargantuan
- sizable *or* sizeable

ANTONYM
- small

last ❶ ADJECTIVE
the most recent • *last year*
latest • *his latest thriller*
most recent • *her most recent film*
preceding • *The bank's turnover had risen during the preceding year.*
previous • *his previous marriage*

ANTONYM
- first

last ❷ ADJECTIVE
happening or remaining after all the others of its kind • *the last three chapters of the book*
closing • *the closing years of this century*
concluding • *the concluding scene of the film*
final • *This is your final chance.*
ultimate • *the ultimate result of the move*

ANTONYM
- first

last ❸ VERB
to continue to exist or happen • *The film lasted for two and a half hours.*
carry on • *Our marriage can't carry on like this.*
continue • *The exhibition continues till 25 November.*

a b c d e f g h i j k l m n o p q r s t u v w x y z

Can't find the word you're looking for? Try the index.

endure • *Somehow their friendship endures.*
persist • *The problem persists.*
remain • *The building remains to this day.*
survive • *companies which survived after the recession*

late ❶ ADJECTIVE

after the expected time • *The train was late.*
behind • *I've got behind with my payments.*
behind time • *Hurry up. We're behind time already.*
belated • *a belated birthday card*
delayed • *The kick-off was delayed by 10 minutes.*
last-minute • *buying some last-minute Christmas presents*
overdue • *The birth is two weeks overdue.*

MORE SYNONYMS
- behindhand
- tardy
- unpunctual

ANTONYM
- early

late ❷ ADJECTIVE

dead, especially recently • *my late husband*
dead • *He has been dead for a year now.*
deceased • *his recently deceased mother*
departed • *memories of departed friends*

MORE SYNONYMS
- defunct
- perished

laugh ❶ VERB

to make a noise which shows you are amused or happy • *You never laugh at my jokes.*
▷ see Word Study **laugh**, page 688

laugh ❷ NOUN

the noise you make when amused or happy • *She has a very infectious laugh.*
chortle • *"That's what you think," he said with a chortle.*
chuckle • *We had a quiet chuckle at his mistake.*
giggle • *She gave a nervous giggle.*
guffaw • *He let out a huge guffaw of amusement.*
snigger • *barely able to stifle a snigger*
titter • *A titter went round the room.*

law ❶ NOUN

a country's system of rules • *The use of this drug is against the law.*
charter • *a citizen's charter for France*
code • *a code of conduct*
constitution • *proposed changes to the constitution*

RELATED WORDS
- ADJECTIVES: legal, judicial

law ❷ NOUN

one of the rules of a country • *The anti-stalking law was introduced in 1990.*
act • *A new act has been passed by Parliament.*
code • *a code designed to protect the rights of children*
decree • *a decree lifting sanctions against China*
regulation • *regulations outlawing child labour*
rule • *a rule that was imposed in 1962*
statute • *a practice regulated by statute*

MORE SYNONYMS
- edict
- ordinance

A B C D E F G H I J K **L** M N O P Q R S T U V W X Y Z

Can't find the word you're looking for? Try the index.

lawyer NOUN
someone who advises people about the law • *I'm discussing the matter with my lawyers.*
advocate • *A public advocate will be appointed to represent you.*
attorney • *a prosecuting attorney*
barrister • *The author is a practising barrister.*
counsel • *His counsel advised him to appeal against the verdict.*
solicitor • *She took advice from a solicitor.*

lay ❶ VERB
to put something somewhere • *Lay a sheet of newspaper on the floor.*
place • *She placed a mug of coffee in front of him.*
put • *He put the photograph on the desk.*
set • *He set his briefcase on the floor.*
set down • *I set the glasses down on the table.*
settle • *He settled his coat over my shoulders.*
spread • *She spread a towel over the sand and lay down.*

lay ❷ VERB
to arrange or set something out • *A man came to lay the carpet.*
arrange • *He started to arrange the books in piles.*
set out • *The flower garden was set out with large beds of roses.*

layer NOUN
something that covers a surface or comes between two other things • *A fresh layer of snow covered the street.*
blanket • *a blanket of fog*
coat • *a coat of paint*
coating • *a crisp chocolate coating*
covering • *a thin covering of dust*
film • *a film of plastic*

sheet • *a sheet of ice*
stratum • *the correct geological stratum*

layout NOUN
the way in which something is arranged • *the layout of the garden*
arrangement • *the arrangement of a room*
design • *the design of the museum*
format • *the format of the book*
plan • *a detailed plan of the house*

laze VERB
to relax and do no work • *We spent a few days lazing around by the pool.*
idle • *We spent hours idling in one of the cafés.*
loaf • *loafing around the house all day*
lounge • *They lounged in the shade.*

ANTONYM
● work

lazy ADJECTIVE
not willing to work • *a lazy and incompetent employee*
idle • *an idle young layabout*
slack • *Many workers have simply become too slack.*

MORE SYNONYMS
● good-for-nothing
● indolent
● shiftless
● slothful
● workshy

ANTONYM
● industrious

lead ❶ VERB
to guide or take someone somewhere • *She led him into the house.*
conduct • *He asked if he might conduct us to the ball.*

a
b
c
d
e
f
g
h
i
j
k
l
m
n
o
p
q
r
s
t
u
v
w
x
y
z

Can't find the word you're looking for? Try the index.

A
B
C
D
E
F
G
H
I
J
K
L
M
N
O
P
Q
R
S
T
U
V
W
X
Y
Z

escort • *They were escorted by police to their plane.*
guide • *He took me by the arm and guided me out.*
steer • *Nick steered them towards the door.*
usher • *I ushered him into the office.*

lead ❷ VERB

to be in charge of • *He led the country between 1949 and 1984.*
command • *the general who commanded the troops*
direct • *He will direct day-to-day operations.*
govern • *his ability to govern the country*
head • *Who heads the firm?*
manage • *I manage a small team of workers.*
supervise • *He supervised more than 400 volunteers.*

lead ❸ NOUN

a clue which may help solve a crime • *The police are following up several leads.*
clue • *a vital clue to the killer's identity*
indication • *All the indications suggest that he is the murderer.*
trace • *No traces of violence were found on the body.*

leader NOUN

the person in charge of something • *the leader of the Republican Party*
boss (INFORMAL) • *Who's the boss around here?*
captain • *the captain of the team*
chief • *the chief of police*
commander • *a commander in the Royal Navy*
director • *the director of the film*
head • *Heads of government met in New York.*

principal • *the principal of the school*
ringleader • *the ringleader of the gang*

ANTONYM
● follower

leading ADJECTIVE

particularly important, respected, or advanced • *a leading industrial nation*
chief • *one of his chief rivals*
eminent • *an eminent surgeon*
key • *the key witness at the trial*
major • *Exercise has a major part to play in preventing disease.*
main • *one of the main tourist areas of Amsterdam*
principal • *one of the principal figures in politics today*
prominent • *a prominent member of the Law Society*
top • *a top model*

MORE SYNONYMS
● foremost
● pre-eminent

lead to VERB

to cause something to happen • *Smoking leads to heart disease and cancer.*
cause • *Knocks can cause damage to the spine.*
contribute to • *injuries which contributed to his death*
produce • *The drug produces side effects.*

MORE SYNONYMS
● bring on
● conduce to
● result in

leaflet NOUN

a piece of paper with information about a subject • *Protesters were handing out leaflets in the street.*

Can't find the word you're looking for? Try the index.

booklet • *a booklet about mortgage rates*
brochure • *a travel brochure*
circular • *A circular was sent out to shareholders.*
pamphlet • *an anti-vivisection pamphlet*

MORE SYNONYMS
- handbill
- mailshot

leak ❶ VERB
to escape from a container or other object • *The gas had leaked from a cylinder.*
escape • *A vent was opened to let some air escape.*
ooze • *Blood was oozing from the wound.*
seep • *Radioactive water has seeped into underground reservoirs.*
spill • *70,000 tonnes of oil spilled from the tanker.*

leak ❷ NOUN
a hole which lets gas or liquid escape • *Have you plugged the leaks?*
chink • *A mist rose from the chinks in the pavement.*
crack • *The lava oozed through cracks in the rock.*
fissure • *Water trickled out of fissures in the limestone.*
hole • *The sea was flowing in through the hole in the ship's hull.*
puncture • *My tyre has a slow puncture.*

leap ❶ VERB
to jump a great distance or height • *The deer leapt into the air.*
bounce • *She bounced up and down on the spot, looking for attention.*
bound • *The dog came bounding up the stairs.*

jump • *I jumped over the fence.*
spring • *He sprang to his feet.*
vault • *He could easily vault the wall.*

leap ❷ NOUN
a jump of great distance or height • *a leap of 2.37 metres*
jump • *the longest jumps by a man and a woman*
bound • *With one bound, Jack was free.*
spring • *The cheetah gave a great spring into the air.*

learn ❶ VERB
to gain knowledge by studying or training • *I am trying to learn French.*
grasp • *The basics of the language are easy to grasp.*
master • *He's having trouble mastering the piano.*
pick up • *You'll soon pick up enough German to get by.*

learn ❷ VERB
to find out about something • *On learning who she was, I asked to meet her.*
ascertain • *They had ascertained that he was not a spy.*
determine • *calculations to determine the rate of tax*
discover • *She discovered that they'd escaped.*
find out • *As soon as we found this out, we closed the ward.*
gather • *I gather the report is critical of the judge.*
hear • *I heard he had moved away.*
understand • *I understand that she's just taken early retirement.*

learned ADJECTIVE
having gained a lot of knowledge by studying • *a very learned man*

Can't find the word you're looking for? Try the index.

A B C D E F G H I J K L M N O P Q R S T U V W X Y Z

academic • *I feel intimidated by academic people.*
erudite • *a witty and erudite leader*
intellectual • *an artistic and intellectual couple*
literate • *a literate and educated readership*
scholarly • *a scholarly researcher*

MORE SYNONYMS
● lettered
● well-read

least ADJECTIVE

as small or few as possible • *Stick to foods with the least fat.*
fewest • *Which product has the fewest calories?*
lowest • *the lowest temperatures on record for this time of year*
minimum • *the minimum height for a policeman*
slightest • *He showed only the slightest hint of emotion.*
smallest • *the smallest measurable unit of light*

ANTONYM
● most

leave ❶ VERB

to go away from a person or place • *He is not allowed to leave the country.*
abandon • *He claimed that his parents had abandoned him.*
depart • *A number of staff departed during his time as director.*
desert • *Medical staff have deserted the city's main hospital.*
forsake • *I would never forsake my children.*
go • *Let me know when you're ready to go.*
quit • *He quit his job as an office boy.*
withdraw • *Troops withdrew from the country last month.*

MORE SYNONYMS
● abscond
● decamp

leave ❷ NOUN

a period of time off work • *Why don't you take a few days' leave?*
holiday • *I still have several days' holiday to take.*
time off • *He took time off to go sailing with his wife.*
vacation • *We went on vacation to Puerto Rico.*

MORE SYNONYMS
● furlough
● sabbatical

lecture ❶ NOUN

a formal talk about a particular subject • *In his lecture he covered several topics.*
address • *an address to the American people*
discourse • *a lengthy discourse on market strategy*
presentation • *a business presentation*
sermon • *his first sermon as a bishop*
speech • *He delivered his speech in French.*
talk • *a brief talk on the history of the site*

MORE SYNONYMS
● exposition
● oration

lecture ❷ NOUN

a talk intended to tell someone off • *The police gave us a stern lecture on safety.*
reprimand • *He has been given a severe reprimand.*
scolding • *given a scolding for offending his opponents*
ticking-off (INFORMAL) • *We were*

given a ticking-off for running in the corridors.
warning • *He was given a severe warning from the referee.*

lecture ❸ VERB
to teach by giving formal talks to audiences • *She has lectured all over the world.*
give a talk • *He set about campaigning, giving talks and fund-raising.*
speak • *He's been invited to speak at the Democratic Convention.*
talk • *Today, I plan to talk about the issues of education and nursery care.*
teach • *She has taught at the university for 34 years.*

left-wing ADJECTIVE
believing in socialist policies • *a left-wing demonstration*
leftist • *three leftist guerrilla groups*
liberal • *a politician with liberal views*
radical • *a radical feminist*
socialist • *Europe's last socialist state*

legacy NOUN
property someone leaves you when they die • *He left his sons a generous legacy.*
bequest • *He made a bequest to his favourite charity.*
estate • *documents concerning the estate*
heirloom • *a family heirloom*
inheritance • *She was worried she'd lose her inheritance to her stepmother.*

legal ❶ ADJECTIVE
relating to the law • *the Dutch legal system*
forensic • *the forensic skill of a*

good barrister
judicial • *a judicial review*
judiciary • *various levels of the judiciary system*

legal ❷ ADJECTIVE
allowed by the law • *The strike was perfectly legal.*
authorized • *an authorized procedure*
lawful • *What I did was lawful and proper.*
legitimate • *a legitimate business*
permissible • *the current permissible levels of pesticide in food*
rightful • *the rightful owner of the property*
valid • *a valid passport*

MORE SYNONYMS
● constitutional
● licit
● sanctioned

ANTONYM
● illegal

leisure NOUN
time when you can relax • *There wasn't a lot of time for leisure.*
free time • *He played piano in his free time.*
recreation • *Saturday afternoons are for recreation.*
relaxation • *Make time for a bit of relaxation.*
time off • *I haven't had any time off all day.*

ANTONYM
● work

leisurely ADJECTIVE
unhurried or calm • *a leisurely walk along the beach*
comfortable • *going at a comfortable speed*
easy • *an easy pace*

a
b
c
d
e
f
g
h
i
j
k
l
m
n
o
p
q
r
s
t
u
v
w
x
y
z

Can't find the word you're looking for? Try the index.

A
B
C
D
E
F
G
H
I
J
K
L
M
N
O
P
Q
R
S
T
U
V
W
X
Y
Z

gentle • *His movements were gentle and deliberate.*
relaxed • *a relaxed meal*
unhurried • *an unhurried way of life*

ANTONYM
● hasty

lekker ADJECTIVE (SOUTH AFRICAN; SLANG)
pleasant or tasty • *We had a really lekker meal.*
delectable • *delectable chocolates*
delicious • *a wide selection of delicious desserts*
luscious • *luscious fruit*
pleasant • *a pleasant dinner*
tasty • *Try this tasty dish for supper.*

length ❶ NOUN
the distance from one end of something to the other • *The fish was about a metre in length.*
distance • *Work out the distance of the journey.*
extent • *the extent of the rain forest*
span • *a butterfly with a two-inch wing span*

length ❷ NOUN
the amount of time something lasts for • *The film is over two hours in length.*
duration • *The duration of the course is one year.*
period • *for a limited period only*
space • *A dramatic change takes place in the space of a few minutes.*
span • *The batteries have a life span of six hours.*
term • *a 12-month term of service*

lengthen VERB
to make something longer • *The runway had to be lengthened.*
extend • *They have extended the deadline.*

make longer • *You can make your hair longer by using extensions.*
prolong • *a move which will prolong the strike*
stretch • *Take care not to stretch the fabric.*

MORE SYNONYMS
● elongate
● protract

ANTONYM
● shorten

lessen VERB
to decrease in size or amount • *changes to their diet that would lessen the risk of disease*
abate • *The storm gradually abated.*
decrease • *Population growth is decreasing by 1.4% each year.*
diminish • *The threat of war has diminished.*
dwindle • *his dwindling authority*
lower • *The Central Bank has lowered interest rates.*
minimize • *attempts to minimize the risk of developing cancer*
reduce • *Gradually reduce the dosage.*
shrink • *The forests have shrunk to half their size.*

MORE SYNONYMS
● de-escalate
● downsize

ANTONYM
● increase

lesson NOUN
a period of time for being taught • *Johanna took piano lessons.*
class • *I go to dance classes.*
coaching • *He needs extra coaching in maths.*
lecture • *a series of lectures on art*

Can't find the word you're looking for? Try the index.

period • *We get six periods of French a week.*
tutoring • *a growing demand for private tutoring*

let ❶ VERB
to allow someone to do something • *The authorities won't let her leave the country.*
allow • *I pleaded to be allowed to go.*
give permission • *Who gave you permission to come here?*
permit • *Permit me to express my opinion.*
sanction • *He may now be ready to sanction the use of force.*

ANTONYM
● forbid

let ❷ VERB
to let someone use your property for money • *She always lets her house for the summer.*
hire out • *The machines are hired out to farmers.*
lease • *She plans to lease the building to students.*
rent • *He rents rooms to backpackers.*

level ❶ ADJECTIVE
completely flat • *a plateau of level ground*
flat • *Cricket should be played on a totally flat field.*
horizontal • *Every horizontal surface was covered with plants.*

ANTONYM
● uneven

level ❷ VERB
to make something flat • *We levelled the ground.*
flatten • *Flatten the dough and cut it into four pieces.*

plane • *planing the surface of the wood*
smooth • *He smoothed his hair.*

level ❸ NOUN
a point on a scale which measures something • *Crime levels have started to decline.*
grade • *the lowest grade of staff*
rank • *He rose to the rank of captain.*
stage • *an early stage of development*
standard • *a decent standard of living*
status • *We were reduced to the status of animals.*

lie ❶ VERB
to rest somewhere horizontally • *The injured man was lying on his back.*
loll • *He was lolling on the sofa.*
lounge • *We lounged on the beach all day.*
recline • *She reclined on the couch.*
sprawl • *They sprawled in a lawn chair, snoozing.*

MORE SYNONYMS
● be prostrate
● be recumbent
● be supine
● repose

lie ❷ VERB
to say something that is not true • *She always lies about her age.*
fib • *He fibbed when she asked him where he'd been.*
perjure oneself • *All of the witnesses perjured themselves.*
tell a lie • *He could never tell a lie or do anything devious.*

MORE SYNONYMS
● dissimulate
● equivocate
● forswear oneself
● prevaricate

a
b
c
d
e
f
g
h
i
j
k
l
m
n
o
p
q
r
s
t
u
v
w
x
y
z

Can't find the word you're looking for? Try the index.

lie ❸ NOUN
something you say which is not true • *His whole story was a lie.*
deceit • *the deceits of political leaders*
fabrication • *She described the magazine interview as "a complete fabrication".*
falsehood • *He accused them of spreading falsehoods about him.*
fib • *I caught him out in another fib.*
fiction • *His account of events is a complete fiction.*

life NOUN
the time during which you are alive • *a long and active life*
existence • *a very miserable existence*
life span • *This species of snake has a life span of up to 25 years.*
lifetime • *a lifetime devoted to service for others*
time • *If I had my time again, I would do things differently.*

RELATED WORDS
● ADJECTIVES: animate, vital

lift ❶ VERB
to move something to a higher position • *straining to lift heavy weights*
elevate • *a mechanism to elevate the platform*
hoist • *I hoisted my rucksack on to my shoulder.*
pick up • *Anthony picked up his case from the floor.*
raise • *He raised his hand to wave.*

ANTONYM
● lower

lift ❷ VERB
to remove something such as a ban or law • *the decision to lift sanctions against Iran*

cancel • *The government has cancelled the state of emergency.*
end • *pressure to end the embargo*
relax • *an attempt to persuade the US Congress to relax the law*
remove • *an amendment to remove the ban on divorce*

MORE SYNONYMS
● rescind
● revoke

light ❶ NOUN
brightness that enables you to see things • *Cracks of light filtered through the shutters.*
brightness • *the brightness of the full moon*
brilliance • *the brilliance of the noonday sun*
glare • *shading his eyes from the glare*
glow • *the red glow of the dying fire*
illumination • *The only illumination came from a small window.*
radiance • *The bedside lamp cast a soft radiance over her face.*

MORE SYNONYMS
● incandescence
● luminescence
● luminosity
● phosphorescence

ANTONYM
● dark

RELATED WORD
● PREFIX: photo-

light ❷ ADJECTIVE
pale in colour • *a light blue shirt*
bleached • *bleached pine tables*
blonde or **blond** • *blonde hair*
fair • *to protect my fair skin*
pale • *dressed in pale pink*
pastel • *delicate pastel shades*

Can't find the word you're looking for? Try the index.

ANTONYM
- dark

light ❸ ADJECTIVE
not weighing much • *working out with light weights*
flimsy • *a flimsy cardboard box*
lightweight • *They will carry lightweight skis on their backs.*
portable • *a portable television*
slight • *She is small and slight.*

ANTONYM
- heavy

light ❹ VERB
to make a place bright • *The room was lit by a single candle.*
brighten • *The late afternoon sun brightened the room.*
illuminate • *No streetlights illuminated the road.*
light up • *Fireworks lit up the sky.*

ANTONYM
- darken

light ❺ VERB
to make a fire start burning • *It's time to light the barbecue.*
ignite • *A stray spark ignited the fireworks.*
kindle • *I kindled a fire in the stove.*

ANTONYM
- extinguish

like ❶ PREPOSITION
similar to • *He looks just like my father.*
akin • *She looked at me with something akin to hatred.*
analogous • *a process analogous to the curing of tobacco*
parallel • *Our situation is parallel to yours.*
similar • *a taste similar to that of celery*

ANTONYM
- unlike

like ❷ VERB
to find someone or something pleasant • *I really like this music.*
adore (INFORMAL) • *All her employees adored her.*
appreciate • *I know you appreciate good food.*
be fond of • *Are you fond of Chinese cuisine?*
be keen on • *I'm not very keen on sport.*
be partial to • *I'm partial to men with dark hair.*
enjoy • *Most children enjoy cartoons.*
go for • *What kind of man do you go for?*
have a soft spot for • *I've always had a soft spot for him.*
have a weakness for • *I have a weakness for slushy romantic novels.*
love • *She loves reading.*
relish • *He relished the idea of proving me wrong.*
revel in • *She appears to revel in being unpopular.*

ANTONYM
- dislike

likely ADJECTIVE
having a good chance of happening • *It seems likely that he will come back.*
anticipated • *the anticipated result*
expected • *the expected response*
liable • *He is liable to be a nuisance.*
possible • *It's quite possible that I'm wrong.*
probable • *the probable outcome*

ANTONYM
- unlikely

Can't find the word you're looking for? Try the index.

A B C D E F G H I J K L M N O P Q R S T U V W X Y Z

limit ❶ NOUN

a point beyond which something cannot go • *the speed limit*
bounds • *the bounds of good taste*
deadline • *We finished the job within the deadline.*
maximum • *He was given two years in prison, the maximum allowed for the charges.*
ultimate • *This hotel is the ultimate in luxury.*
utmost • *His skills were tested to the utmost.*

limit ❷ VERB

to prevent something from going any further • *Limit yourself to six units of alcohol a week.*
confine • *Damage was confined to a small portion of the building.*
curb • *measures to curb inflation*
fix • *The mortgage rate is fixed at 8.5%.*
ration • *I'm rationing myself to ten cigarettes a day.*
restrict • *The patient was restricted to a meagre diet.*

MORE SYNONYMS

- circumscribe
- delimit
- demarcate
- straiten

limp ADJECTIVE

not stiff or firm • *a limp lettuce leaf*
drooping • *the drooping branches of a birch*
flabby • *a flabby stomach*
floppy • *She fondled the dog's floppy ears.*
slack • *his slack belly*
soft • *a soft dough*

MORE SYNONYMS

- flaccid
- pliable

ANTONYM

- stiff

line ❶ NOUN

a long thin mark on something • *Draw a line down the centre of the page.*
rule • *He drew a rule under the last name.*
score • *There was a long score on the car's bonnet.*
streak • *dark streaks on the surface of the moon*
stripe • *a green jogging suit with white stripes down the sides*

line ❷ NOUN

a row of people or things • *a line of spectators*
column • *a column of figures*
file • *A file of mourners walked behind the coffin.*
queue • *a long queue of angry motorists*
rank • *ranks of police in riot gear*
row • *a row of pretty little cottages*

line ❸ NOUN

the route along which something moves • *the line of flight*
course • *the course of the river*
path • *The lava annihilates everything in its path.*
route • *the most direct route*
track • *a railway track*
trajectory • *the trajectory of the missile*

link ❶ NOUN

a connection between two things • *the link between sunbathing and skin cancer*
affiliation • *He has no affiliation with any political party.*
association • *the association between the two companies*

Can't find the word you're looking for? Try the index.

attachment • *Mother and child form a close attachment.*
bond • *The experience created a bond between us.*
connection • *He has denied any connection to the bombing.*
relationship • *the relationship between humans and their environment*
tie • *She has ties with this town.*

MORE SYNONYMS
- affinity
- liaison

link ❷ VERB
to connect two things • *tree houses linked by ropes*
attach • *Attach the curtains to the rods with hooks.*
connect • *two rooms connected by a passage*
couple • *The engine is coupled to a gearbox.*
fasten • *a wooden bench fastened to the floor*
join • *the skin which joins the eye to the eyelid*
tie • *He tied the dog to the tree by its lead.*

ANTONYM
- separate

liquid ❶ NOUN
a substance which is not solid and can be poured • *Drink plenty of liquids for the next few days.*
fluid • *The fluid can be removed with a syringe.*
liquor • *Pour the liquor off into the pan.*
solution • *a solution of honey and vinegar*

liquid ❷ ADJECTIVE
in the form of a liquid • *wash in warm water with liquid detergent*

fluid • *a fluid fertiliser*
molten • *molten metal*
runny • *a dessertspoon of runny honey*

list ❶ NOUN
a set of things written down one below the other • *There were six names on the list.*
catalogue • *a chronological catalogue of the Beatles' songs*
directory • *a telephone directory*
index • *The book includes a comprehensive subject index.*
inventory • *an inventory of stolen goods*
listing • *a listing of all the schools in the area*
record • *Keep a record of everything you eat and drink.*
register • *a register of births, deaths and marriages*

list ❷ VERB
to set things down in a list • *All the ingredients are listed on the label.*
catalogue • *I was cataloguing my video collection.*
index • *Most of the archive has been indexed.*
record • *400 species of fungi have been recorded.*
register • *a registered charity*

MORE SYNONYMS
- enumerate
- itemize
- tabulate

listen VERB
to hear and pay attention to something • *I'll repeat that for those of you who weren't listening.*
attend • *Close your books and attend to me.*
hark • *Hark! I hear the sound of footsteps.*

a
b
c
d
e
f
g
h
i
j
k
l
m
n
o
p
q
r
s
t
u
v
w
x
y
z

Can't find the word you're looking for? Try the index.

hear • *Will you hear me saying my lines?*
pay attention • *Pay attention or you won't know what to do.*

little ❶ ADJECTIVE
small in size or amount • *a little old lady*
▷ see Word Study **little**, page 689

ANTONYM
● large

little ❷ NOUN
a small amount or degree • *We offered her plenty to eat, but she would only take a little.*
▷ see Word Study **little**

live ❶ VERB
to have your home somewhere • *She has lived here for 20 years.*
dwell • *the people who dwell in the forest*
inhabit • *the fish that inhabit the coral reefs*
reside • *He used to reside in England.*
stay (SCOTTISH AND SOUTH AFRICAN) • *We've stayed in this house since we got married.*

live ❷ VERB
to be alive • *He will not live much longer.*
be alive • *You are lucky to be alive.*
exist • *the chances of finding life existing on Mars*

live ❸ ADJECTIVE
not dead or artificial • *a live spider*
alive • *It is unlikely that he is still alive.*
animate • *an animate object*
living • *living tissue*

lively ADJECTIVE
full of life and enthusiasm • *a lively personality*

active • *an active youngster*
animated • *an animated discussion*
energetic • *She gave an energetic performance.*
perky • *He wasn't quite as perky as usual.*
sparkling • *I was enjoying a sparkling conversation.*
sprightly • *a sprightly old man*
vivacious • *She is vivacious and charming.*

ANTONYM
● dull

load ❶ NOUN
something being carried • *This truck can carry a load of up to 10 tons.*
cargo • *The boat was carrying its usual cargo of bananas.*
consignment • *The first consignment of food has been sent.*
freight • *Most of the freight was carried by rail.*
shipment • *a shipment of weapons*

load ❷ VERB
to put a lot of things on or into • *The trucks were loaded with blankets and supplies.*
fill • *The van was filled with crates.*
pack • *helicopters packed with medical supplies*
pile • *Her trolley was piled with groceries.*
stack • *stalls stacked with wares*

loan ❶ NOUN
a sum of money that you borrow • *a small business loan*
advance • *She was paid a $100,000 advance on her next novel.*
credit • *He can't get credit to buy the equipment.*
mortgage • *I took out a second mortgage on the house.*

Can't find the word you're looking for? Try the index.

loan ❷ VERB
to lend something to someone
• *He loaned us the painting for our exhibition.*
advance • *I advanced him some money till we got home.*
lend • *Will you lend me your jacket?*

local ❶ ADJECTIVE
belonging to the area where you live • *This is a local shop for local people.*
community • *the revival of family and community life*
district • *the district council*
neighbourhood • *a neighbourhood watch scheme*
parish • *the parish priest*
regional • *the regional elections*

local ❷ NOUN
a person who lives in a particular area • *That's what the locals call the place.*
inhabitant • *the inhabitants of Glasgow*
native • *She is proud to be a native of Sydney.*
resident • *a protest by residents of the village*

locate VERB
to find out where someone or something is • *We have been unable to locate him.*
find • *They can't find it on the map.*
pinpoint • *Computers pinpointed where the shells came from.*
track down • *She has spent years trying to track down her parents.*

located ADJECTIVE
existing or standing in a particular place • *The restaurant is located near the cathedral.*
placed • *The hotel is wonderfully placed right in the city centre.*

sited • *a castle romantically sited on a river estuary*
situated • *His hotel is situated in a lovely place.*

location NOUN
a place or position • *a house with a beautiful location*
place • *the place where the temple used to stand*
point • *a popular meeting point for tourists*
position • *The ship radioed its position to the coastguard.*
site • *the site of the murder*
situation • *The hotel has a superb isolated location.*
spot • *Can you show me the spot where it happened?*
whereabouts • *His exact whereabouts are still not known.*

MORE SYNONYMS
● locale
● locus

lock ❶ VERB
to close and fasten something with a key • *Are you sure you locked the door?*
latch • *He latched the gate.*
padlock • *The box has been padlocked shut.*

ANTONYM
● unlock

lock ❷ NOUN
a device used to fasten something • *The lock had been burst open.*
latch • *A key clicked in the latch of the front door.*
padlock • *He put a padlock on the door of his flat.*

logical ❶ ADJECTIVE
using logic to work something out • *a logical argument*

a
b
c
d
e
f
g
h
i
j
k
l
m
n
o
p
q
r
s
t
u
v
w
x
y
z

Can't find the word you're looking for? Try the index.

consistent • *a consistent and well-presented theory*
rational • *a rational analysis*
reasoned • *a reasoned discussion*
sound • *His reasoning is sound, but he has missed the point.*
valid • *Both sides put forward valid points.*

MORE SYNONYMS
- cogent
- coherent

ANTONYM
- illogical

logical ❷ ADJECTIVE
sensible in the circumstances
• *a logical deduction*
judicious • *the judicious use of military force*
obvious • *I jumped to the obvious conclusion.*
plausible • *a plausible explanation*
reasonable • *a reasonable course of action*
sensible • *the sensible thing to do*
wise • *a wise decision*

ANTONYM
- illogical

lonely ❶ ADJECTIVE
unhappy because of being alone
• *She's lonely and just wants to talk.*
alone • *scared of being alone in the house*
forlorn • *He looked a forlorn figure as he left the pitch.*
forsaken • *a forsaken and bitter man*
lonesome • *I'm lonesome without you.*

lonely ❷ ADJECTIVE
isolated and not visited by many people • *a lonely hillside*
deserted • *a deserted farmhouse*
desolate • *a desolate place*

isolated • *Many of the villages are in isolated areas.*
remote • *a remote outpost*
secluded • *a secluded area close to her home*
uninhabited • *an uninhabited island*

MORE SYNONYMS
- godforsaken
- out-of-the-way
- unfrequented

long ❶ ADJECTIVE
continuing for a great amount of time • *a long interval when no-one spoke*
▷ see Word Study **long**, page 690

ANTONYM
- short

long ❷ ADJECTIVE
great in length or distance • *a long line of people*
▷ see Word Study **long**, page 690

ANTONYM
- short

long ❸ VERB
to want something very much
• *He longed for a cigarette.*
ache • *She still ached for her dead husband.*
covet • *She coveted his job.*
crave • *I crave approval.*
hunger • *Jules hungered for adventure.*
lust • *She lusted after a designer kitchen.*
pine • *I pine for the countryside.*
yearn • *He yearned for freedom.*

longing NOUN
a strong wish for something
• *her longing to return home*
craving • *a craving for sugar*
desire • *her desire for a child of her own*

Can't find the word you're looking for? Try the index.

hankering · *a hankering to be an actress*
hunger · *a hunger for success*
thirst · *a thirst for adventure*
yearning · *a yearning to be part of a normal family*

look ❶ VERB
to turn your eyes towards something and see it · *She looked at me with something like hatred.*
▷ see Word Study **look**, pages 691–2

look ❷ VERB
to appear or seem to be · *the desire to look attractive*
appear · *He appeared intoxicated.*
look like · *You look like you need a good night's sleep.*
seem · *She seemed tense.*
seem to be · *They seem to be lacking in enthusiasm.*

look ❸ NOUN
the action of turning your eyes towards something · *Lucy took a last look in the mirror.*
gaze · *her concentrated gaze*
glance · *a cursory glance*
glimpse · *a fleeting glimpse*
peek · *Give me a peek at his letter.*

look ❹ NOUN
the way someone or something appears · *He had the look of a desperate man.*
air · *a nonchalant air*
appearance · *He was fastidious about his appearance.*
bearing · *a man of military bearing*
expression · *I saw his puzzled expression.*
face · *Why are you all wearing such long faces?*
semblance · *a semblance of normality*

look after VERB
to take care of someone or something · *Will you look after my cats when I go on holiday?*
care for · *vintage cars lovingly cared for by their owners*
mind · *Jim will mind the shop while I'm away.*
nurse · *My mother nursed him while he was ill.*
take care of · *I'll take care of the house for you.*
tend · *He tended his flower beds.*
watch · *My mother will watch the kids while we're out.*

lookalike NOUN
a person who looks like someone else · *an Elvis lookalike*
dead ringer (INFORMAL) · *a dead ringer for his brother*
double · *He's the exact double of his father at that age.*
spitting image (INFORMAL) · *She is the spitting image of me.*

look for VERB
to try to find a person or thing · *I'm looking for my son.*
forage · *foraging for food*
hunt · *Police are hunting for clues.*
search · *Rescue teams are searching for the missing crew members.*
seek · *They have had to seek work as labourers.*

loose ❶ ADJECTIVE
not firmly held or fixed · *a loose tooth*
free · *She broke her fall with her free hand.*
unsecured · *corridors blocked by unsecured objects*
wobbly · *a wobbly bridge*

ANTONYM
● secure

a
b
c
d
e
f
g
h
i
j
k
l
m
n
o
p
q
r
s
t
u
v
w
x
y
z

Can't find the word you're looking for? Try the index.

A
B
C
D
E
F
G
H
I
J
K
L
M
N
O
P
Q
R
S
T
U
V
W
X
Y
Z

loose ❷ ADJECTIVE
not fitting closely • *Wear loose clothes for comfort.*
baggy • *a baggy black jumper*
slack • *Those trousers are very slack on you.*
sloppy • *wearing a sloppy t-shirt, jeans and trainers*

ANTONYM
● tight

loosen VERB
to make something looser • *He loosened his tie.*
slacken • *We slackened the guy-ropes.*
undo • *She began to undo the tiny buttons.*
untie • *He untied his shoes and slipped them off.*

ANTONYM
● tighten

loot ❶ VERB
to steal from a place during a riot or battle • *Gangs began breaking windows and looting shops.*
pillage • *The bandits pillaged the church.*
plunder • *They plundered and burned the town.*
raid • *Rustlers have raided a village in the region.*
ransack • *The three raiders ransacked the house.*

loot ❷ NOUN
stolen or illegal money or goods • *The loot was never recovered.*
booty • *They divided the booty between them.*
haul • *the biggest haul of cannabis ever seized*
plunder • *pirates in search of easy plunder*
spoils • *the spoils of war*

swag (SLANG) • *The thieves carried the swag off in a stolen car.*

lose ❶ VERB
to be unable to find • *I've lost my keys.*
drop • *She's dropped a contact lens.*
mislay • *I seem to have mislaid my glasses.*
misplace • *Somehow my suitcase was misplaced.*

ANTONYM
● find

lose ❷ VERB
to be beaten • *We lost the match.*
be beaten • *He was soundly beaten in the election.*
be defeated • *They were defeated in the final.*

ANTONYM
● win

lost ❶ ADJECTIVE
not knowing where you are • *I think we're lost.*
adrift • *two men adrift on a raft in the middle of the sea*
astray • *a man astray*
off-course • *After a while I realized I was completely off-course.*

lost ❷ ADJECTIVE
unable to be found • *a mother wailing for her lost child*
mislaid • *searching for his mislaid keys*
misplaced • *I've found your misplaced glasses.*
missing • *a missing person*
vanished • *unable to contact the vanished convoy*

lot ❶, a lot or lots NOUN
a large amount of something • *Remember to drink lots of water.*

abundance • *an abundance of food*
a great deal • *I've spent a great deal of time on this project.*
masses (INFORMAL) • *There were masses of flowers at her funeral.*
piles (INFORMAL) • *He's got piles of money.*
plenty • *We've got plenty of time.*
quantities • *She drank quantities of hot, sweet tea.*
scores • *There were scores of witnesses.*

lot ❷ NOUN
an amount or number • *We've just sacked one lot of builders.*
batch • *a batch of cookies*
bunch (INFORMAL) • *My neighbours are a noisy bunch.*
crowd • *They're a real crowd of villains.*
group • *a small group of football supporters*
quantity • *a quantity of water*
set • *a set of photographs*

loud ❶ ADJECTIVE
having a high level of sound • *a loud explosion*
blaring • *a blaring television*
deafening • *a deafening roar*
noisy • *a noisy old car*
resounding • *a resounding slap*
strident • *her strident voice*
thunderous • *thunderous applause from the crowd*

MORE SYNONYMS
● clamorous
● sonorous
● stentorian

ANTONYM
● quiet

loud ❷ ADJECTIVE
too brightly coloured • *a loud tie*

flamboyant • *a flamboyant outfit*
flashy • *flashy clothes*
garish • *a garish three-piece suite*
gaudy • *a gaudy purple-and-orange hat*
lurid • *She painted her toenails a lurid pink.*

ANTONYM
● dull

lovable ADJECTIVE
easy to love • *His vulnerability makes him very lovable.*
adorable • *an adorable black kitten*
charming • *a charming young Frenchman*
enchanting • *He was an enchanting baby.*
endearing • *one of his most endearing qualities*
sweet • *a sweet little girl*

MORE SYNONYMS
● captivating
● engaging
● winsome

ANTONYM
● hateful

love ❶ VERB
to feel strong affection for someone • *I loved my husband very much.*
adore • *She adored her parents.*
cherish • *He genuinely loved and cherished her.*
worship • *She had worshipped him from afar for years.*

MORE SYNONYMS
● be in love with
● dote on
● hold dear
● idolize

ANTONYM
● hate

a
b
c
d
e
f
g
h
i
j
k
l
m
n
o
p
q
r
s
t
u
v
w
x
y
z

Can't find the word you're looking for? Try the index.

A
B
C
D
E
F
G
H
I
J
K
L
M
N
O
P
Q
R
S
T
U
V
W
X
Y
Z

love ❷ VERB

to like something very much
• *We both love fishing.*
appreciate • *I know you appreciate good food.*
enjoy • *Do you enjoy opera?*
like • *I've always liked horror films.*
relish • *I relish the challenge of dangerous sports.*

MORE SYNONYMS

● delight in
● have a weakness for
● take pleasure in

ANTONYM

● hate

love ❸ NOUN

a strong feeling of affection
• *a mother's love for her children*
adoration • *He had been used to female adoration all his life.*
affection • *She thought of him with great affection.*
ardour • *an attempt to rekindle their lost ardour*
devotion • *At first she was flattered by his devotion.*
infatuation • *consumed with infatuation for her*
passion • *the object of her passion*

ANTONYM

● hatred

love ❹ NOUN

a strong liking for something
• *her love of animals*
devotion • *his devotion to literature*
fondness • *a fondness for good wine*
liking • *my liking for classical music*
weakness • *He had a weakness for cats.*

MORE SYNONYMS

● partiality
● penchant

ANTONYM

● hatred

lovely ADJECTIVE

very attractive and pleasant • *You look lovely.*
attractive • *Polperro is an attractive harbour village.*
beautiful • *She's a very beautiful woman.*
delightful • *a delightful garden*
enjoyable • *I've had a very enjoyable time.*
pleasant • *a pleasant little apartment*
pretty • *a pretty room overlooking a beautiful garden*

ANTONYM

● horrible

loving ADJECTIVE

feeling or showing love • *a loving husband and father*
affectionate • *openly affectionate with each other*
devoted • *a devoted couple*
doting • *a doting father*
fond • *She gave him a fond smile.*
tender • *Her voice was tender.*
warm • *a warm and loving mother*

MORE SYNONYMS

● demonstrative
● solicitous
● warm-hearted

ANTONYM

● cold

low ❶ ADJECTIVE

short or not far above the ground
• *The sun was low in the sky.*
little • *a little table*
short • *a short flight of steps*
small • *a small stool*
squat • *squat stone houses*

Can't find the word you're looking for? Try the index.

stunted · *stunted trees*
sunken · *a sunken garden*

ANTONYM
● high

low ❷ ADJECTIVE
small in degree or quantity · *low prices*
minimal · *minimal expenditure*
modest · *a modest rate of unemployment*
poor · *working for poor wages*
reduced · *reduced customer demand*
scant · *scant stocks of fish*
small · *produced in small numbers*

ANTONYM
● high

low ❸ ADJECTIVE
not considered respectable · *a man of low birth*
common · *She might be a little common, but at least she wasn't boring.*
contemptible · *He mixes with the most contemptible people in society.*
despicable · *a despicable wretch*
disreputable · *the company of disreputable women*
lowly · *his lowly status*
vulgar · *She considers herself to be above the vulgar rabble.*

lower ❶ VERB
to move something downwards · *They lowered the coffin into the grave.*
drop · *He dropped his plate into the sink.*
let down · *They let the barrier down.*
take down · *The pilot took the helicopter down.*

ANTONYM
● raise

lower ❷ VERB
to make something less in amount · *a commitment to lower taxes*
cut · *The first priority is to cut costs.*
decrease · *The government plans to decrease interest rates.*
diminish · *to diminish the prestige of the monarchy*
lessen · *a diet that would lessen the risk of disease*
minimize · *attempts to minimize the risk of cancer*
reduce · *Gradually reduce the dosage.*
slash · *We're slashing our prices.*

ANTONYM
● increase

loyal ADJECTIVE
firm in your friendship or support · *a loyal friend*
constant · *I've lost my best friend and constant companion.*
dependable · *a cheerful, dependable mate*
faithful · *She remained faithful to her husband.*
staunch · *a staunch supporter*
true · *a true friend*
trusty · *a trusty ally*

MORE SYNONYMS
● steadfast
● true-hearted
● unswerving
● unwavering

ANTONYM
● treacherous

luck NOUN
something that happens by chance · *It was just luck that we happened to meet.*
accident · *It came about almost by accident.*
chance · *We only met by chance.*

Can't find the word you're looking for? Try the index.

a
b
c
d
e
f
g
h
i
j
k
l
m
n
o
p
q
r
s
t
u
v
w
x
y
z

A
B
C
D
E
F
G
H
I
J
K
L
M
N
O
P
Q
R
S
T
U
V
W
X
Y
Z

destiny • *Is it destiny that brings people together?*
fate • *a simple twist of fate*
fortune • *smiled on by fortune*

MORE SYNONYMS
● fortuity
● predestination

lucky ❶ ADJECTIVE
having a lot of good luck • *He had always been lucky at cards.*
blessed • *being blessed with good looks*
charmed • *She seems to have a charmed life.*
fortunate • *He was extremely fortunate to survive.*

ANTONYM
● unlucky

lucky ❷ ADJECTIVE
happening by chance with good consequences • *a lucky break*
fortuitous • *a fortuitous combination of circumstances*
fortunate • *a fortunate accident*
opportune • *I had arrived at an opportune moment.*
timely • *his timely intervention*

MORE SYNONYMS
● adventitious
● propitious
● providential

ANTONYM
● unlucky

lump ❶ NOUN
a solid piece of something • *a big lump of dough*
ball • *a ball of clay*
cake • *a cake of soap*
chunk • *a chunk of bread*
hunk • *a hunk of beef*

piece • *a piece of cake*
wedge • *a wedge of cheese*

lump ❷ NOUN
a bump on the surface of something • *I've got a big lump on my head.*
bulge • *My purse made a bulge in my pocket.*
bump • *a bump in the road*
hump • *a hump on his back*
swelling • *a swelling over one eye*

MORE SYNONYMS
● protrusion
● protuberance
● tumescence

lure ❶ VERB
to attract someone somewhere or into doing something • *We are being lured into a trap.*
attract • *Warm weather attracts the fish close to the shore.*
beckon • *The mermaids beckoned the sailors towards the rocks.*
draw • *What drew him to the area was its proximity to London.*
entice • *Retailers will do anything to entice shoppers through their doors.*
tempt • *trying to tempt American tourists back to Britain*

lure ❷ NOUN
something that you find very attractive • *the lure of rural life*
attraction • *the attraction of living on the waterfront*
bait • *using cheap bread and milk as a bait to get people into the shop*
magnet • *The park is a magnet for health freaks.*
pull • *feel the pull of the past*
temptation • *the many temptations to which they will be exposed*

Can't find the word you're looking for? Try the index.

lustful ADJECTIVE
feeling or showing strong sexual
desire • *lustful thoughts*
carnal • *carnal desires*
lecherous • *a lecherous old man*
lewd • *his arrest for lewd behaviour*

MORE SYNONYMS
● lascivious
● libidinous
● wanton

luxurious ADJECTIVE
expensive and full of luxury
• *a luxurious lifestyle*
de luxe • *de luxe cars*
lavish • *a lavish party*
opulent • *an opulent office*
plush (INFORMAL) • *a plush hotel*
sumptuous • *a sumptuous feast*

ANTONYM
● plain

luxury ❶ NOUN
comfort in expensive surroundings
• *a life of luxury*
affluence • *the trappings of
affluence*
opulence • *the sheer opulence of
her new life*
sumptuousness • *The hotel lobby
was sumptuousness itself.*

luxury ❷ NOUN
something enjoyable which you do
not have often • *Telephones are still
a luxury in poor countries.*
extra • *The car is a basic model
with no extras.*

extravagance • *Eating out is an
extravagance.*
indulgence • *This car is one of my
few indulgences.*
treat • *I only eat cakes as a treat.*

lying ❶ NOUN
the action of telling lies • *I've had
enough of your lying.*
deceit • *the deceits of political leaders*
dishonesty • *deliberate dishonesty*
fabrication • *His story is pure
fabrication.*
fibbing • *Her fibbing eventually got
her into trouble.*
perjury • *This witness has
committed perjury.*

MORE SYNONYMS
● dissimulation
● duplicity
● mendacity

lying ❷ ADJECTIVE
telling lies • *The man is just a lying
cheat.*
deceitful • *deceitful and
misleading remarks*
dishonest • *a dishonest account of
events*
false • *a false confession*
untruthful • *She unwittingly gave
untruthful answers.*

MORE SYNONYMS
● dissembling
● mendacious

ANTONYM
● honest

Mm

machine NOUN
a piece of equipment • *a machine to pump water out of mines*
apparatus • *an apparatus for use in fires*
appliance • *electrical appliances*
contraption • *a strange contraption called the General Gordon Gas Bath*
device • *a timer device for a bomb*
instrument • *navigation instruments*
mechanism • *the locking mechanism*

mad ❶ ADJECTIVE
mentally ill • *She was afraid of going mad.*
barmy (SLANG) • *Bill used to say I was barmy.*
batty (SLANG) • *some batty uncle of theirs*
crazy (INFORMAL) • *If I worried about all this stuff, I'd go crazy.*
deranged • *after a deranged man shot 14 people*
insane • *Her father is insane.*
loony (SLANG) • *She's as loony as her brother!*

ANTONYM
● sane

mad ❷ ADJECTIVE
very foolish or unwise • *He'd be mad to refuse.*
barmy (SLANG) • *a barmy idea*
crazy (INFORMAL) • *People thought they were crazy to try it.*
daft (INFORMAL) • *That's a daft question.*
foolhardy • *Some described the act as foolhardy.*
foolish • *It would be foolish to raise hopes unnecessarily.*
stupid • *It would be stupid to pretend otherwise.*

mad ❸ ADJECTIVE (INFORMAL)
angry about something • *They both got mad at me for interfering.*
angry • *She was angry at her husband.*
enraged • *I got more and more enraged at my father.*
fuming • *Mrs Vine was still fuming.*
furious • *He is furious at the way his wife has been treated.*
incensed • *Mum was incensed at his lack of compassion.*
infuriated • *He knew how infuriated this would make me.*
irate • *Bob was very irate, shouting and screaming about the flight delay.*
livid (INFORMAL) • *I am absolutely livid about it.*

magic NOUN
a special power • *They believe in magic.*
sorcery • *the use of sorcery to combat evil influences*
witchcraft • *people who practise witchcraft*

MORE SYNONYMS
● necromancy
● occultism

Can't find the word you're looking for? Try the index.

magical ADJECTIVE
wonderful and exciting • *Paris is a magical city.*
bewitching • *bewitching brown eyes*
enchanting • *an enchanting child*

MORE SYNONYMS
- entrancing
- spellbinding

main ADJECTIVE
most important • *the main reason*
cardinal • *one of the cardinal rules of movie reviewing*
chief • *one of his chief rivals*
foremost • *one of the foremost scholars on ancient Indian culture*
leading • *a leading industrial nation*
major • *one of the major causes of cancer*
predominant • *Her predominant emotion was confusion.*
primary • *the primary source of water in the region*
prime • *the prime suspect*
principal • *the principal source of sodium in our diets*

mainly ADVERB
true in most cases • *The staff were mainly Russian.*
chiefly • *He painted chiefly portraits.*
generally • *It is generally true that the darker the fruit the higher its iron content.*
largely • *The early studies were done on men, largely by male researchers.*
mostly • *Cars are mostly metal.*
predominantly • *Business is conducted predominantly by phone.*
primarily • *The body is made up primarily of bone, muscle, and fat.*
principally • *This is principally because the market is weak.*

MORE SYNONYMS
- for the most part
- in general
- on the whole

major ADJECTIVE
very important or serious • *a major problem*
critical • *a critical factor*
crucial • *He took the crucial decisions himself.*
leading • *a leading industrial nation*
outstanding • *an outstanding contribution*
significant • *Her upbringing had a significant effect on her relationships.*

ANTONYM
- minor

majority NOUN
more than half • *The majority of our cheeses are made with pasteurized milk.*
best part • *for the best part of 24 hours*
better part • *I spent the better part of £100 on her.*
bulk • *the bulk of the world's great poetry*
mass • *the mass of the population*
most • *Most of the book is completely true.*

MORE SYNONYMS
- lion's share
- preponderance

make ❶ VERB
to construct something • *Sheila makes all her own clothes.*
assemble • *Workers were assembling planes.*
build • *Workers at the site build the F-16 jet fighter.*
construct • *the campaign to construct a temple on the site*

a
b
c
d
e
f
g
h
i
j
k
l
m
n
o
p
q
r
s
t
u
v
w
x
y
z

Can't find the word you're looking for? Try the index.

create • *It's great for a radio producer to create a show like this.*
fabricate • *All the tools are fabricated from high quality steel.*
fashion • *Stone Age settlers fashioned necklaces from sheep's teeth.*
form • *a figure formed from clay*
manufacture • *They manufacture plastics.*
produce • *We try to produce items that are the basics of a stylish wardrobe.*

make ❷ VERB

to force someone to do something • *Mary made him clean up the plate.*
compel • *legislation to compel cyclists to wear a helmet*
drive • *Jealousy drives people to murder.*
force • *A back injury forced her to withdraw from the competition.*
oblige • *Finally I was obliged to abandon the car.*

MORE SYNONYMS
- coerce
- impel

make ❸ NOUN

a particular type • *a certain make of wristwatch*
brand • *a brand of cigarette*
model • *To keep the cost down, opt for a basic model.*

make up ❶ VERB

to form the parts of something • *Women police officers make up 13% of the police force.*
compose • *The force would be composed of troops from NATO countries.*
comprise • *a crowd comprised of the wives and children of scientists*

constitute • *Hindus constitute 83% of India's population.*
form • *Cereals form the staple diet.*

make up ❷ VERB

to invent a story • *It's very unkind of you to make up stories about him.*
concoct • *The prisoner concocted the story to get a lighter sentence.*
fabricate • *Officers fabricated evidence against them.*
invent • *I must invent something I can tell my mother.*

MORE SYNONYMS
- formulate
- manufacture

making ❶ NOUN

the act of creating something • *the making of this movie*
assembly • *the assembly of an explosive device*
building • *The building of the airport continues.*
construction • *boat construction*
creation • *the creation of large parks and forests*
fabrication • *the design and fabrication of the space shuttle*
manufacture • *the manufacture of nuclear weapons*
production • *These proteins stimulate the production of blood cells.*

making ❷, in the making ADJECTIVE

about to become something • *a captain in the making*
budding • *a budding author*
emergent • *an emergent state*
potential • *a potential champion*
up-and-coming • *an up-and-coming golfer*

male ADJECTIVE

relating to men • *a deep male voice*

Can't find the word you're looking for? Try the index.

A B C D E F G H I J K L **M** N O P Q R S T U V W X Y Z

manly • *He was the ideal of manly beauty.*
masculine • *masculine characteristics like facial hair*

ANTONYM
- female

malicious ADJECTIVE
having the intention of hurting someone • *She described the charges as malicious.*
cruel • *Children can be so cruel.*
malevolent (FORMAL) • *She gave me a malevolent stare.*
mean • *Someone's played a mean trick on you.*
spiteful • *spiteful telephone calls*
vicious • *a vicious attack on an innocent man's character*

MORE SYNONYMS
- malignant
- rancorous (FORMAL)

man ❶ NOUN
an adult male human being • *a young man*
bloke (BRITISH, AUSTRALIAN AND NEW ZEALAND; INFORMAL) • *a really nice bloke*
chap (INFORMAL) • *I am a very lucky chap.*
gentleman • *It seems this gentleman was waiting for the doctor.*
guy (INFORMAL) • *a guy from Manchester*
male • *A high proportion of crime is perpetrated by young males.*

ANTONYM
- woman

man ❷ NOUN
people in general • *All men are equal.*
humanity • *He has rendered a great service to humanity.*

human race • *Can the human race carry on expanding?*
mankind • *the evolution of mankind*

MORE SYNONYMS
- Homo sapiens
- humankind

mana NOUN (NEW ZEALAND)
the authority and influence of an important person • *a leader of great mana*
authority • *figures of authority*
influence • *He denies using any political influence.*
power • *positions of great power*
standing • *The Prime Minister's standing was high in the US.*
stature • *his stature as the world's greatest cellist*
status • *the status of a national hero*

ANOTHER SYNONYM
- sway (LITERARY)

manage ❶ VERB
to succeed in doing something • *We managed to find somewhere to sit.*
cope with • *how my mother coped with bringing up three children*
succeed in • *We have succeeded in persuading cinemas to show the video.*

manage ❷ VERB
to be in charge of something • *Within two years he was managing the store.*
be in charge of • *Who's in charge of the canteen?*
command • *Who would command the troops in the event of war?*
control • *He now controls the largest retail development empire in southern California.*

a
b
c
d
e
f
g
h
i
j
k
l
m
n
o
p
q
r
s
t
u
v
w
x
y
z

Can't find the word you're looking for? Try the index.

direct • *Christopher will direct day-to-day operations.*
run • *Is this any way to run a country?*

management ❶ NOUN

the act of running an organization • *The zoo needed better management.*
control • *The restructuring involves Mr Ronson giving up control of the company.*
direction • *Organizations need clear direction.*
running • *the day-to-day running of the clinic*

management ❷ NOUN

the people who run an organization • *The management is doing its best.*
administration • *They would like the college administration to exert more control.*
board • *a recommendation which he wants to put before the board*
bosses (INFORMAL) • *a dispute between workers and bosses*
directors • *the board of directors of a local bank*
employers • *Employers are said to be considering the demand.*

manager NOUN

a person in charge of running an organization • *the manager of Daiwa's New York branch*
boss (INFORMAL) • *He cannot stand his boss.*
director • *the financial director of Braun UK*
executive • *an advertising executive*

manifest ADJECTIVE (FORMAL)

obvious or easily seen • *the manifest failure of the policy*

blatant • *a blatant attempt to spread the blame*
clear • *a clear case of homicide*
conspicuous • *Politics has changed in a conspicuous way.*
glaring • *a glaring example of fraud*
obvious • *an obvious injustice*
patent • *This was patent nonsense.*
plain • *He's made it plain that he wants to be involved.*

manner ❶ NOUN

the way that you do something • *She smiled again in a friendly manner.*
fashion • *another drug that works in a similar fashion*
mode • *He switched automatically into interview mode.*
style • *Kenny's writing style*
way • *He had a strange way of talking.*

manner ❷ NOUN

the way that someone behaves • *his kind manner*
bearing • *his military bearing*
behaviour • *her anti-social behaviour*
conduct • *principles of civilized conduct*
demeanour • *a cheerful demeanour*

MORE SYNONYMS
● comportment
● deportment

manoeuvre ❶ VERB

to move something skilfully • *It took expertise to manoeuvre the boat so close to the shore.*
guide • *He took Elliott by the arm and guided him out.*
navigate • *He attempted to navigate his way through the crowds.*

A
B
C
D
E
F
G
H
I
J
K
L
M
N
O
P
Q
R
S
T
U
V
W
X
Y
Z

Can't find the word you're looking for? Try the index.

negotiate • *I negotiated my way out of the airport.*
steer • *I steered him towards the door.*

manoeuvre ❷ NOUN
a clever action • *manoeuvres to block the electoral process*
dodge • *a tax dodge*
ploy • *a cynical marketing ploy*
ruse • *This was a ruse to divide them.*
tactic • *The tactic paid off.*

MORE SYNONYMS
● machination
● stratagem
● subterfuge

manufacture ❶ VERB
to make goods in a factory • *Several models are being manufactured here.*
assemble • *a factory where they assemble tractors*
fabricate • *a plant which fabricates aeroplane components*
make • *making cars at two plants in Europe*
mass-produce • *the invention of machinery to mass-produce footwear*
produce • *The company produced computer parts.*
process • *The material will be processed into plastic pellets.*

manufacture ❷ NOUN
the making of goods in a factory • *the manufacture of nuclear weapons*
assembly • *the assembly of cars by robots*
fabrication • *the design and fabrication of the shuttle*
making • *the steps that go into the making of a book*
mass production • *the mass production of baby food*
production • *We need to maintain*

the production of cars at last year's level.

many ❶ ADJECTIVE
a large number • *Among his many hobbies was the breeding of fine horses.*
countless • *She brought joy to countless people.*
innumerable • *He has invented innumerable excuses.*
myriad • *the myriad other tasks we are trying to perform*
numerous • *Sex crimes were just as numerous as they are today.*
umpteen (INFORMAL) • *He has produced umpteen books.*

MORE SYNONYMS
● multifarious
● multitudinous

ANTONYM
● few

many ❷ PRONOUN
a large number of people or things • *in many of these neighbourhoods*
a lot • *A lot of people would agree with you.*
a mass • *a mass of books and papers*
a multitude • *for a multitude of reasons*
large numbers • *Large numbers of people stayed away.*
lots (INFORMAL) • *lots of strange new animals*
plenty • *plenty of vegetables*
scores • *Scores of people were injured.*

ANTONYM
● few

mark ❶ NOUN
a small stain • *I can't get this mark off the curtain.*
▷ see Word Study **mark**, page 693

a
b
c
d
e
f
g
h
i
j
k
l
m
n
o
p
q
r
s
t
u
v
w
x
y
z

mark ❷ VERB

to stain something • *to stop the pen ink from marking her shirt*
smudge • *Her face was smudged with dirt.*
stain • *His clothing was stained with mud.*
streak • *Rain had begun to streak the window-panes.*

market NOUN

a place to buy or sell things • *the fish market at Billingsgate*
bazaar • *an Eastern bazaar*
fair • *a craft fair*

marriage NOUN

the relationship between a husband and wife • *six years of marriage*
matrimony (FORMAL) • *the bonds of matrimony*
wedlock (FORMAL) • *a child conceived out of wedlock*

RELATED WORDS

- ADJECTIVES: conjugal, connubial,
- marital, nuptial

marsh NOUN

TYPES OF MARSH

bog	quagmire
fen	quicksands
mire	saltmarsh
morass	slough
mudflats	swamp

marvellous ADJECTIVE

wonderful or excellent • *a marvellous actor*
brilliant • *a brilliant performance*
excellent • *She does an excellent job as Bill's secretary.*
first-rate • *The meal was absolutely first-rate.*
magnificent • *She was magnificent as Lady Macbeth.*

remarkable • *a remarkable achievement*
splendid • *splendid photographs*
superb • *a superb novel*
wonderful • *It's wonderful to see you.*

ANTONYM

- terrible

mass ❶ NOUN

a large number or amount • *a mass of papers*
crowd • *A huge crowd of people gathered in the square.*
heap • *a heap of bricks*
load • *a load of kids*
throng • *A shout went up from the throng of spectators.*
lump • *a lump of clay*
mob • *a growing mob of demonstrators*
pile • *a pile of sand*

mass ❷ ADJECTIVE

involving a large number of people • *mass unemployment*
general • *We are trying to raise general awareness about this issue.*
popular • *popular anger at the decision*
universal • *universal health care*
widespread • *widespread support for the proposals*

mass ❸ VERB

to gather together in a large group • *Police began to mass at the shipyard.*
assemble • *Thousands of people assembled in the stadium.*
congregate • *Youngsters congregate here in the evenings.*
gather • *In the evenings, we gathered round the fireplace.*
group • *The children grouped together under the trees.*

Can't find the word you're looking for? Try the index.

A B C D E F G H I J K L **M** N O P Q R S T U V W X Y Z

master ❶ NOUN
a male schoolteacher • *a retired maths master*
instructor • *a college instructor*
teacher • *her chemistry teacher*
tutor • *an adult education tutor in German*

master ❷ VERB
to learn how to do something • *She found it easy to master the typewriter.*
become proficient in • *He quickly became proficient in the language.*
get the hang of (INFORMAL) • *It's a bit tricky till you get the hang of it.*
grasp • *It took him a while to grasp the basics of the process.*
learn • *He enjoyed learning new skills.*

match ❶ NOUN
an organized game • *a football match*
competition • *a surfing competition*
contest • *one of the best contests in recent boxing history*
game • *England's first game of the new season*

match ❷ VERB
to be similar to • *The shoes matched her dress.*
agree • *Their statements do not agree.*
correspond • *The two maps correspond closely.*
fit • *The punishment must always fit the crime.*
go with • *The curtains didn't go with the carpet.*
suit • *the best package to suit your needs*
tally • *The figures didn't seem to tally.*

MORE SYNONYMS
- accord
- harmonize

material ❶ NOUN
any type of cloth • *the thick material of her skirt*
cloth • *a piece of cloth*
fabric • *silk and other delicate fabrics*

material ❷ NOUN
a solid substance • *the materials to make red dye*
matter • *waste matter from industries*
stuff • *the stuff from which the universe is made*
substance • *a crumbly black substance*

matter ❶ NOUN
something that you have to deal with • *business matters*
affair • *The funeral was a sad affair.*
business • *This whole business has upset me.*
issue • *a major political issue*
question • *the difficult question of unemployment*
situation • *The situation is now under control.*
subject • *a difficult subject on which to reach a compromise*

matter ❷ NOUN
any substance • *The atom is the smallest divisible particle of matter.*
material • *a conducting material such as metal*
stuff • *a dress made from some flimsy stuff*
substance • *a poisonous substance*

matter ❸ VERB
to be important • *It does not matter how long their hair is.*

a b c d e f g h i j k l m n o p q r s t u v w x y z

Can't find the word you're looking for? Try the index.

be of consequence • *Their
choice of partner is of no
consequence to anyone but
themselves.*
count • *It's as if my opinions just
don't count.*
make a difference • *Exercise
makes all the difference.*

mature ❶ VERB
to become fully developed
• *Children mature earlier these days.*
come of age • *The money was
held in trust until he came of age.*
grow up • *She grew up in Tokyo.*
reach adulthood • *She died
before reaching adulthood.*

mature ❷ ADJECTIVE
fully developed • *He's very mature
for his age.*
adult • *a pair of adult birds*
full-grown • *a full-grown male
orang-utan*
fully-fledged • *He has developed
into a fully-fledged adult.*
grown • *a grown man*
grown-up • *They have two grown-
up children.*

maximum ❶ ADJECTIVE
being the most that is possible
• *the maximum recommended intake*
top • *a top speed of 200 mph*
utmost • *a question of the utmost
importance*

ANTONYM
● minimum

maximum ❷ NOUN
the most that is possible
• *a maximum of fifty men*
ceiling • *an agreement to put a
ceiling on salaries*
height • *when emigration was at
its height*
most • *The most he'll make is a*

hundred pounds.
upper limit • *the need to put an
upper limit on spending*
utmost • *He did his utmost to
make her agree.*

ANTONYM
● minimum

maybe ADVERB
it is possible that • *Maybe I should
have done a bit more.*
conceivably • *The mission could
conceivably be accomplished within
a week.*
it could be • *It could be that's why
he refused.*
perhaps • *Perhaps, in time, she'll
understand.*
possibly • *Television is possibly to
blame for this.*

MORE SYNONYMS
● mayhap
● peradventure
● perchance

meagre ADJECTIVE
very small and inadequate • *his
meagre pension*
inadequate • *inadequate portions*
measly (INFORMAL) • *The average
British bathroom measures a measly
3.5 square metres.*
paltry • *a paltry fine of £150*
scant • *She berated the police for
paying scant attention to the theft.*
sparse • *sparse vegetation*

MORE SYNONYMS
● exiguous
● insubstantial
● scanty
● skimpy

meal NOUN
an occasion when people eat • *She
sat next to him throughout the meal.*

banquet • *a state banquet at Buckingham Palace*
dinner • *a series of official dinners*
feast • *the wedding feast*
kai (AUSTRALIAN AND NEW ZEALAND; INFORMAL) • *a cheap kai in a local restaurant*

MORE SYNONYMS
- repast
- spread

mean ❶ VERB
to convey a message • *The red signal means that you can shoot.*
denote • *Red eyes denote strain and fatigue.*
indicate • *Today's vote indicates a change in policy.*
signify • *Becoming a father signified that he was now an adult.*

mean ❷ VERB
to intend to do something • *I meant to phone you, but didn't have time.*
aim • *I aim to arrive early.*
intend • *She intended to move back to France.*
plan • *They plan to marry in the summer.*

mean ❸ ADJECTIVE
unwilling to spend money • *Don't be mean with the tip.*
miserly • *He is miserly with both his time and his money.*
snoep (SOUTH AFRICAN; INFORMAL) • *Have you ever met anyone as snoep as him?*
tight (INFORMAL) • *He was so tight that he wouldn't even spend three roubles.*

MORE SYNONYMS
- parsimonious
- penny-pinching
- stingy
- tight-fisted

ANTONYM
- generous

meaning NOUN
the idea expressed by something • *the meaning of this dream*
drift • *Grace was beginning to get his drift.*
gist • *I could not get the gist of their conversation.*
message • *the message of the film*
significance • *The President's visit is loaded with symbolic significance.*

MORE SYNONYMS
- connotation
- import

measure ❶ VERB
to check the size of something • *We measured how tall he was.*
gauge • *He gauged the wind at over 30 knots.*
survey • *geological experts who surveyed the cliffs*

MORE SYNONYMS
- calibrate
- quantify

measure ❷ NOUN
an amount of something • *There has been a measure of agreement.*
amount • *a certain amount of disappointment*
degree • *a degree of success*
portion • *I have spent a considerable portion of my life here.*
proportion • *A large proportion of my time was spent abroad.*

measure ❸ NOUN
an action in order to achieve something • *Tough measures are needed to maintain order.*
expedient • *I reduced my spending by the simple expedient of destroying my credit card.*

a b c d e f g h i j k l **m** n o p q r s t u v w x y z

Can't find the word you're looking for? Try the index.

A
B
C
D
E
F
G
H
I
J
K
L
M
N
O
P
Q
R
S
T
U
V
W
X
Y
Z

manoeuvre • *manoeuvres to block the electoral process*
means • *The move is a means to fight crime.*
procedure • *safety procedures*
step • *steps to discourage drink-driving*

medicine NOUN
something you take to make you better • *They prevent the food and medicine from reaching Iraq.*
drug • *Three new drugs recently became available.*
medication • *some medication for her ulcers*
muti (SOUTH AFRICAN; INFORMAL) • *muti for treating a fever*
remedy • *At the moment we are trying a herbal remedy.*

medium ❶ ADJECTIVE
average in size • *He was of medium height.*
average • *a ginger tomcat of average size*
medium-sized • *a medium-sized saucepan*
middling • *Small and middling flats have increased in price much more than luxury ones.*

medium ❷ NOUN
a means of communication • *the medium of television*
channel • *through diplomatic channels*
vehicle • *The play seemed an ideal vehicle for his music.*

MORE SYNONYMS
● agency
● instrument

meek ADJECTIVE
quiet and timid • *a meek, mild-mannered fellow*
deferential • *the traditional*

requirement for Asian women to be deferential to men
docile • *docile, obedient children*
mild • *a mild man*
submissive • *Most doctors want their patients to be submissive.*
timid • *a timid child*
unassuming • *He's very polite and unassuming.*

MORE SYNONYMS
● acquiescent
● compliant
● mild-mannered

ANTONYM
● bold

meet ❶ VERB
to be in the same place as someone • *I met her quite by chance.*
bump into (INFORMAL) • *I bumped into a friend of yours today.*
come across • *where I came across a group of noisy children*
come upon • *We turned the corner and came upon a group of hikers.*
encounter • *the most gifted child he had ever encountered*
run across • *We ran across some old friends.*
run into • *You'll never guess who I ran into the other day.*

meet ❷ VERB
to gather in a group • *We meet for lunch once a week.*
assemble • *a convenient place for students to assemble between classes*
congregate • *Youngsters love to congregate here in the evening.*
convene • *Senior officials convened in October.*
gather • *We all gathered in the boardroom.*
get together • *the last time we all got together*

meet ❸ VERB
to fulfil a need • *services intended to meet the needs of the elderly*
answer • *Would communism answer their needs?*
fulfil • *All the requirements were fulfilled.*
satisfy • *Candidates must satisfy the general conditions for admission.*

meeting ❶ NOUN
an event at which people come together for a purpose • *a business meeting*
audience • *an audience with the Pope*
conference • *a conference on education*
congress • *a medical congress*
convention • *the annual convention of the World Boxing Council*
gathering • *a social gathering*
get-together (INFORMAL) • *a get-together I had at my home*
reunion • *a family reunion*

MORE SYNONYMS
● conclave
● convocation

meeting ❷ NOUN
an occasion when you meet someone • *a chance meeting*
assignation (LITERARY) • *She had an assignation with her boyfriend.*
encounter • *a remarkable encounter with a group of soldiers*
rendezvous • *Baxter arranged a six o'clock rendezvous.*
tryst • *a lovers' tryst*

melodramatic ADJECTIVE
behaving in an exaggerated way • *Don't you think you're being rather melodramatic?*

histrionic • *She let out a histrionic groan.*
sensational • *sensational tabloid newspaper reports*
theatrical • *In a theatrical gesture Glass clamped his hand over his eyes.*

melt ❶ VERB
to become liquid • *The snow had melted.*
dissolve • *Heat gently until the sugar dissolves.*
thaw • *It's so cold the snow doesn't get a chance to thaw.*

MORE SYNONYMS
● deliquesce
● liquefy

melt ❷ VERB
to disappear • *Her inhibitions melted.*
disappear • *The immediate threat has disappeared.*
disperse • *The crowd dispersed peacefully.*
dissolve • *His new-found optimism dissolved.*
evaporate • *My anger evaporated.*
vanish • *All her fears suddenly vanished.*

memorable ADJECTIVE
likely to be remembered • *a memorable victory*
catchy • *a catchy tune*
historic • *a historic meeting*
notable • *with a few notable exceptions*
striking • *the most striking feature of those statistics*
unforgettable • *an unforgettable experience*

memory NOUN
the ability to remember • *Every detail is fresh in my memory.*
recall • *a man blessed with total recall*

a
b
c
d
e
f
g
h
i
j
k
l
m
n
o
p
q
r
s
t
u
v
w
x
y
z

Can't find the word you're looking for? Try the index.

remembrance (FORMAL)
• *My remembrance of the incident is somewhat hazy.*

MORE SYNONYMS
- recollection
- retention

mend VERB
to repair something broken
• *I should have had the catch mended.*
darn • *a woman darning socks*
fix • *If something is broken, we get it fixed.*
patch • *They patched the barn roof.*
renovate • *The couple spent thousands renovating the house.*
repair • *to get her car repaired*
restore • *experts who specialize in restoring ancient parchments*

mention ❶ VERB
to talk about something briefly
• *I may not have mentioned it to her.*
allude to • *She alluded to his absence in vague terms.*
bring up • *Why are you bringing it up now?*
broach • *I broached the subject of her early life.*
hint • *The President hinted that he might make some changes.*
intimate • *He did intimate that he is seeking legal action.*
refer to • *In his speech, he referred to a recent trip to Canada.*
touch on • *The film touches on these issues, but only superficially.*
touch upon • *I'd like to touch upon a more serious question now.*

mention ❷ NOUN
a brief comment about something
• *There was no mention of elections.*
allusion • *She made an allusion to the events in Los Angeles.*

reference • *He made no reference to any agreement.*

merciful ❶ ADJECTIVE
showing kindness • *He is merciful and sympathetic to others.*
compassionate • *a deeply compassionate man*
humane • *the desire for a more humane society*
kind • *She is warm-hearted and kind to everyone.*

ANTONYM
- merciless

merciful ❷ ADJECTIVE
showing forgiveness • *We can only hope the court is merciful.*
forgiving • *I don't think people are in a very forgiving mood.*
lenient • *He believes the government is already lenient with drug traffickers.*

ANTONYM
- merciless

merciless ADJECTIVE
showing no kindness or forgiveness • *the merciless efficiency of a modern police state*
callous • *his callous disregard for human life*
cruel • *Children can be so cruel.*
heartless • *I couldn't believe they were so heartless.*
implacable • *a powerful and implacable enemy*
ruthless • *his ruthless treatment of employees*

MORE SYNONYMS
- hard-hearted
- pitiless
- unforgiving

ANTONYM
- merciful

Can't find the word you're looking for? Try the index.

A B C D E F G H I J K L **M** N O P Q R S T U V W X Y Z

mercy ❶ NOUN
the quality of kindness • *He showed no mercy.*
compassion • *his compassion for a helpless woman*
kindness • *He was treated with kindness by numerous officials.*
pity • *She saw no pity in their faces.*

MORE SYNONYMS
● benevolence
● charity

mercy ❷ NOUN
the quality of forgiveness • *He threw himself upon the mercy of the court.*
forgiveness • *He fell to his knees begging for forgiveness.*
leniency • *He said he would show no leniency towards them.*

MORE SYNONYMS
● clemency
● forbearance

merit ❶ NOUN
worth or value • *Box-office success mattered more than artistic merit.*
excellence • *the top US award for excellence in journalism*
value • *The value of this work experience should not be underestimated.*
virtue • *There is little virtue in such an approach.*
worth • *people who had already proved their worth to their companies*

merit ❷ NOUN
a good quality that something has • *Whatever its merits, their work would never be used.*
advantage • *The great advantage of home-grown oranges is their flavour.*
asset • *Her leadership qualities were her greatest asset.*
strength • *The book's strength lay in its depiction of modern-day Tokyo.*
strong point • *Science was never my strong point at school.*
virtue • *Its other great virtue is its hard-wearing quality.*

merit ❸ VERB
to deserve something • *Such ideas merit careful consideration.*
be entitled to • *She is entitled to feel proud.*
be worthy of • *The bank might think you're worthy of a loan.*
deserve • *He deserves a rest.*
earn • *Companies must earn a reputation for honesty.*
warrant • *no evidence to warrant a murder investigation*

mess ❶ NOUN
a state of untidiness • *I'll clear up the mess later.*
chaos • *Their concerts often ended in chaos.*
disarray • *He found the room in disarray.*
disorder • *Inside all was disorder.*

mess ❷ NOUN
a situation that is full of problems • *the reasons why the economy is in such a mess*
fix (INFORMAL) • *The government has really got itself into a fix.*
jam (INFORMAL) • *They were in a real jam.*
muddle • *Our finances are in a muddle.*
turmoil • *Her marriage was in turmoil.*

mess ❸, mess up VERB
to spoil something • *He had messed up his career.*
botch up • *I hate having builders botch up repairs on my house.*

Can't find the word you're looking for? Try the index.

A
B
C
D
E
F
G
H
I
J
K
L
M
N
O
P
Q
R
S
T
U
V
W
X
Y
Z

bungle • *Two prisoners bungled an escape bid.*
make a hash of (INFORMAL) • *The government made a total hash of things.*
muck up (SLANG) • *He always seemed to muck everything up.*

message ❶ NOUN
a piece of information for someone • *He left a message on her answerphone.*
bulletin • *a news bulletin*
communication • *The ambassador brought a communication from the President.*
despatch or **dispatch** • *this dispatch from our West Africa correspondent*
memo • *office memos*
memorandum • *a memorandum from the Ministry of Defence*
note • *I'll have to leave a note for Karen.*
word • *There is no word from the authorities on the reported attack.*

MORE SYNONYMS
● communiqué
● missive

message ❷ NOUN
the idea conveyed by something • *the story's anti-drugs message*
meaning • *while we discussed the meaning of the play*
moral • *the moral of the story*
point • *My point is that I'm not going to change.*
theme • *The book's central theme is power.*

messenger NOUN
someone who carries a message • *There will be a messenger at the airport to collect the photographs.*
courier • *a motorcycle courier*

envoy • *an envoy to the King*
runner • *a bookie's runner*

MORE SYNONYMS
● emissary
● go-between
● herald

method NOUN
a way of doing something • *the traditional method of making wine*
approach • *different approaches to gathering information*
mode • *the capitalist mode of production*
procedure • *He did not follow the correct procedure.*
technique • *the techniques of modern agriculture*
way • *a way of making new friends*

middle ❶ NOUN
the part furthest from the edges • *in the middle of the room*
centre • *the centre of the table*
halfway point • *Postle was third fastest at the halfway point.*
midst • *a house in the midst of huge trees*

MORE SYNONYMS
● midpoint
● midsection

middle ❷ ADJECTIVE
furthest from the edges • *the middle house*
central • *central London*
halfway • *a point halfway between the two posts*

mild ❶ ADJECTIVE
not strong or powerful • *a mild shampoo*
insipid • *It tasted bland and insipid.*
weak • *weak beer*

ANTONYM
● strong

Can't find the word you're looking for? Try the index.

mild ❷ ADJECTIVE
gentle and good-tempered
• *a mild man*
gentle • *her gentle nature*
meek • *a meek, mild-mannered fellow*
placid • *a placid child who rarely cried*

MORE SYNONYMS
● easy-going
● equable
● pacific
● peaceable

mild ❸ ADJECTIVE
warmer than usual • *The area is famous for its mild winter climate.*
balmy • *balmy summer evenings*
temperate • *a temperate climate*

mind ❶ NOUN
your ability to think • *You have a very suspicious mind.*
brain • *Once you stop using your brain you soon go stale.*
head • *I can't get that song out of my head.*
imagination • *Africa was alive in my imagination.*
intellect • *good health and a lively intellect*
psyche • *disturbing elements of the human psyche*

RELATED WORD
● ADJECTIVE: mental

mind ❷ VERB
to be annoyed by something
• *I don't mind what you do.*
be bothered • *I'm not bothered if he has another child.*
care • *young men who did not care whether they lived or died*
object • *I don't object to his smoking.*

mind ❸ VERB
to look after something • *My mother is minding the shop.*
keep an eye on • *She asked me to keep an eye on the children.*
look after • *I looked after the dogs while she was away.*
take care of • *There was no one else to take care of the children.*
watch • *She bought the tickets while I watched the cases.*

minimum ADJECTIVE
being the least possible • *the minimum height for a policeman*
least possible • *I try to cause the least amount of trouble possible.*
minimal • *The aim is to incur minimal expense.*

ANTONYM
● maximum

minor ADJECTIVE
less important • *a minor injury*
lesser • *They pleaded guilty to lesser charges.*
petty • *petty crime*
secondary • *matters of secondary importance*
slight • *We have a slight problem.*
trifling • *Outside California these difficulties may seem trifling.*
trivial • *trivial details*

ANTONYM
● major

minute ❶ NOUN
a short period of time • *I'll be with you in just a minute.*
flash • *It was all over in a flash.*
instant • *For an instant, Catherine was tempted to flee.*
moment • *Stop for one moment and think about what you're doing!*
second • *Just a second. I'm coming.*
trice • *I'll be back in a trice.*

a
b
c
d
e
f
g
h
i
j
k
l
m
n
o
p
q
r
s
t
u
v
w
x
y
z

Can't find the word you're looking for? Try the index.

minute ❷ ADJECTIVE

extremely small • *Only a minute amount is needed.*

microscopic • *microscopic fibres*

negligible • *They are convinced the strike will have a negligible impact.*

slender • *We won the vote by a slender majority.*

small • *small particles of dust*

tiny • *a tiny fraction of US production*

MORE SYNONYMS

● diminutive
● minuscule

ANTONYM

● vast

miracle NOUN

a surprising and fortunate event • *the Italian economic miracle*

marvel • *a marvel of high technology*

wonder • *the wonders of science*

miserable ❶ ADJECTIVE

very unhappy • *a job which made me miserable*

dejected • *Everyone has days when they feel dejected.*

depressed • *He seemed somewhat depressed.*

down • *Try to support each other when one of you is feeling down.*

downcast • *After his defeat Mr Rabin looked downcast.*

low • *"I didn't ask for this job," he tells friends when he is low.*

melancholy • *It was in these hours that he felt most melancholy.*

mournful • *He looked mournful, even near to tears.*

sad • *It left me feeling sad and empty.*

unhappy • *She is desperately unhappy.*

wretched • *I feel really confused and wretched.*

MORE SYNONYMS

● disconsolate
● sorrowful

ANTONYM

● cheerful

miserable ❷ ADJECTIVE

causing unhappiness • *a miserable little flat*

gloomy • *Officials say the outlook for next year is gloomy.*

pathetic • *a pathetic sight*

sorry • *The fires have left the industry in a sorry state.*

wretched • *He died in wretched poverty.*

misery NOUN

great unhappiness • *All that money brought nothing but misery.*

depression • *He's been suffering from depression.*

despair • *feelings of despair*

grief • *her grief at her husband's suicide*

melancholy • *with an air of melancholy*

sadness • *with a mixture of sadness and joy*

sorrow • *a time of great sorrow*

unhappiness • *There was a lot of unhappiness in my adolescence.*

woe • *a tale of woe*

ANTONYM

● joy

misfortune NOUN

an unfortunate event • *I had the misfortune to fall off my bike.*

adversity • *times of adversity*

bad luck • *He has had his share of bad luck.*

Can't find the word you're looking for? Try the index.

A B C D E F G H I J K L **M** N O P Q R S T U V W X Y Z

misrepresent VERB
to give a false account of something • *Keynes deliberately misrepresented the views of his opponents.*
distort • *The minister said his remarks had been distorted by the press.*
falsify • *falsifying personal details on his CV*
twist • *You're twisting my words.*

miss ❶ VERB
to fail to notice • *It's on the second floor. You can't miss it.*
fail to notice • *He failed to notice that the lights had turned red.*
mistake • *There's no mistaking her sincerity.*
overlook • *a fact that we all tend to overlook*

miss ❷ VERB
to feel the loss of • *The boys miss their father.*
long for • *Steve longed for the good old days.*
pine for • *Make sure your pet won't pine for you while you're away.*
yearn for • *He yearned for his freedom.*

mistake ❶ NOUN
something that is wrong • *spelling mistakes*
blunder • *It had been a monumental blunder to give him the assignment.*
error • *a mathematical error*
gaffe • *a social gaffe*
oversight • *By an unfortunate oversight, full instructions do not come with the product.*
slip • *There must be no slips.*

MORE SYNONYMS
● inaccuracy
● miscalculation

mistake ❷ VERB
to think one thing is another thing • *I mistook him for the owner of the house.*
confuse with • *I can't see how anyone could confuse you with your brother!*
misinterpret as • *She misinterpreted his remarks as a threat.*
mix up with • *People often mix me up with other actors.*
take for • *She had taken him for a journalist.*

mistreat VERB
to treat someone badly • *She had been mistreated by men in the past.*
abuse • *parents who abuse their children*
ill-treat • *They thought Mr Smith had been ill-treating his wife.*

mix VERB
to combine things • *Mix the ingredients together slowly.*
amalgamate • *a need to amalgamate the two companies*
blend • *Blend the butter with the sugar.*
combine • *Combine the flour with 3 tablespoons of water.*
merge • *how to merge the graphic with text*
mingle • *the mingled smell of flowers and cigar smoke*

MORE SYNONYMS
● intermingle
● interweave

mixture NOUN
a combination of things • *a sticky mixture of flour and water*
alloy • *an alloy of copper and tin*
amalgamation • *an amalgamation of two organizations*

a
b
c
d
e
f
g
h
i
j
k
l
m
n
o
p
q
r
s
t
u
v
w
x
y
z

Can't find the word you're looking for? Try the index.

blend • *a blend of wine and sparkling water*
combination • *a fantastic combination of colours*
compound • *a compound of water, sugar, vitamins and enzymes*
fusion • *fusions of jazz and pop*
medley • *We communicated in a medley of foreign words and gestures.*

MORE SYNONYMS
- amalgam
- composite
- conglomeration
- mix

mix up VERB
to confuse two things • *People often mix us up.*
confuse • *Great care is taken to avoid confusing the two projects.*
muddle • *Critics have begun to muddle the two names.*

mix-up NOUN
a mistake in something planned • *a mix-up with the bookings*
mistake • *There must be some mistake.*
misunderstanding • *Ensure that there is no misunderstanding about the instructions.*
muddle • *There's been a muddle about whose responsibility it is.*

moan ❶ VERB
to make a low sound • *Laura moaned in her sleep.*
groan • *He began to groan with pain.*
grunt • *The driver grunted, convinced that Michael was crazy.*

moan ❷ VERB
to complain about something • *Carol is always moaning about her husband.*

complain • *People always complain that the big banks are unfriendly.*
groan • *His parents were beginning to groan about the price of college tuition.*
grumble • *A tourist grumbled that the waiter spoke too much Spanish.*
whine • *They come to me to whine about their troubles.*
whinge (INFORMAL) • *Stop whingeing and get on with it.*

MORE SYNONYMS
- bleat
- carp

moan ❸ NOUN
a low sound • *She let out a faint moan.*
groan • *a groan of disappointment*
grunt • *grunts of disapproval*

mock ❶ VERB
to make fun of someone • *Don't mock me.*
deride (FORMAL) • *Other countries are derided for selling arms to the enemy.*
laugh at • *I thought they were laughing at me because I was ugly.*
make fun of • *Don't make fun of me.*
poke fun at • *She poked fun at people's shortcomings.*
ridicule • *Mr Goss ridiculed that suggestion.*
scoff at • *Some people may scoff at the idea that animals communicate.*

mock ❷ ADJECTIVE
not genuine • *mock surprise*
artificial • *artificial limbs*
bogus • *their bogus insurance claim*
counterfeit • *counterfeit money*
dummy • *dummy weapons*
fake • *a fake fur*

Can't find the word you're looking for? Try the index.

false • *false teeth*
feigned • *with feigned indifference*
imitation • *imitation leather*
phoney or **phony** (INFORMAL) • *a phoney excuse*
pretended • *with pretended zeal*
sham • *sham marriages*

MORE SYNONYMS
- ersatz
- pseudo

mockery NOUN
the act of mocking someone
• *Was there a glint of mockery in his eyes?*
derision • *shouts of derision*
jeering • *there was a chorus of jeering, whistles and laughter*
ridicule • *Davis was subjected to public ridicule.*

model ❶ NOUN
a copy of something • *an architect's model of a wooden house*
dummy • *a tailor's dummy*
replica • *a replica of the Statue of Liberty*
representation • *a representation of a human figure*

MORE SYNONYMS
- facsimile
- mock-up

model ❷ NOUN
a perfect example of something
• *The essay is a model of clarity.*
epitome • *the epitome of good taste*
example • *He is an example to the younger lads.*
ideal • *the Japanese ideal of beauty*
paragon • *a paragon of virtue*

MORE SYNONYMS
- archetype
- exemplar

model ❸ VERB
to make something into a shape
• *clay modelled into the shape of a bear*
carve • *One of the prisoners had carved a wooden chess set.*
fashion • *Stone Age settlers fashioned necklaces from sheep's teeth.*
form • *figures formed from modelling clay*
mould • *We moulded a chair out of mud.*
sculpt • *An artist sculpted a full-size replica of her head.*
shape • *Shape each half into a loaf.*

moderate ❶ ADJECTIVE
neither too much nor too little
• *moderate exercise*
average • *I was only average academically.*
fair • *Reimar had a fair command of English.*
medium • *a medium size*
middling • *The Beatles enjoyed only middling success until 1963.*
reasonable • *reasonable force*

moderate ❷ VERB
to become or make less extreme
• *They are hoping he can be persuaded to moderate his views.*
abate • *The storm had abated.*
curb • *You must curb your extravagant tastes.*
ease • *Tensions had eased.*
relax • *Rules have been relaxed recently.*
soften • *to soften the blow of steep price rises*
temper • *He had to learn to temper his enthusiasm.*
tone down • *He toned down his statements after the meeting.*

modern ❶ ADJECTIVE
relating to the present time
• *modern society*

a
b
c
d
e
f
g
h
i
j
k
l
m
n
o
p
q
r
s
t
u
v
w
x
y
z

Can't find the word you're looking for? Try the index.

contemporary • *contemporary music*
current • *the current situation*
present • *the government's present economic difficulties*
present-day • *Even by present-day standards these were large aircraft.*
recent • *in recent years*

modern ❷ ADJECTIVE
new and involving the latest ideas • *modern technology*
latest • *the latest fashions*
new • *new methods of treating cancer*
up-to-date • *Germany's most up-to-date electric power station*
up-to-the-minute • *up-to-the-minute information*

ANTONYM
● old-fashioned

modest ❶ ADJECTIVE
small in size or amount • *a modest improvement*
limited • *They may only have a limited amount of time.*
middling • *The Beatles enjoyed only middling success until 1963.*
moderate • *moderate exercise*
small • *a relatively small problem*

modest ❷ ADJECTIVE
not boastful • *Lord Carrington is modest about his achievements.*
humble • *He gave a great performance, but he was very humble.*
unassuming • *She has a gentle, unassuming manner.*

MORE SYNONYMS
● self-effacing
● unpretentious

ANTONYM
● conceited

moment ❶ NOUN
a short period of time • *He paused for a moment.*
instant • *The pain disappeared in an instant.*
minute • *See you in a minute.*
second • *Seconds later, firemen reached the door.*
split second • *Her gaze met Michael's for a split second.*

MORE SYNONYMS
● flash
● trice

moment ❷ NOUN
a point in time • *At that moment, the doorbell rang.*
instant • *At that instant the museum was plunged into darkness.*
point • *At this point Diana arrived.*
time • *It seemed like a good time to tell her.*

money NOUN
coins or banknotes • *I needed to earn some money.*
capital • *Companies are having difficulty in raising capital.*
cash • *We were desperately short of cash.*
dosh (BRITISH, AUSTRALIAN AND NEW ZEALAND) • *They'll have the dosh to pay for a new sign.*
dough (INFORMAL) • *He worked hard for his dough.*
funds • *The concert will raise funds for research into AIDS.*

RELATED WORD
● ADJECTIVE: pecuniary

mood NOUN
a state of mind • *She was in a really cheerful mood.*
frame of mind • *Lewis was not in the right frame of mind to continue.*

Can't find the word you're looking for? Try the index.

humour • *Could that have been the source of his good humour?*
spirits • *A bit of exercise will help lift his spirits.*
state of mind • *I want you to get into a whole new state of mind.*
temper • *I was in a bad temper last night.*

moody ❶ ADJECTIVE
depressed or unhappy • *Tony, despite his charm, could sulk and be moody.*
irritable • *He had missed his dinner, and grew irritable.*
morose • *She was morose and reticent.*
sulky • *a sulky adolescent*
sullen • *a sullen and resentful workforce*

MORE SYNONYMS
● huffy
● ill-tempered
● testy
● tetchy

moody ❷ ADJECTIVE
liable to change your mood • *David's mother was unstable and moody.*
temperamental • *He is very temperamental.*
volatile • *He has a volatile temper.*

MORE SYNONYMS
● capricious
● mercurial

more ADJECTIVE
greater than something else • *I've got more chips than you.*
added • *For added protection choose lipsticks with a sun screen.*
additional • *The US is sending additional troops to the region.*
extra • *Extra staff have been taken on.*

further • *There are likely to be further delays.*

ANTONYM
● less

motivate VERB
to cause a particular behaviour • *What motivates athletes to take drugs?*
drive • *Jealousy drives people to murder.*
inspire • *What inspired you to change your name?*
lead • *His abhorrence of racism led him to write the book.*
move • *It was punk that first moved him to join a band.*
prompt • *Japan's recession has prompted consumers to cut back on buying cars.*
provoke • *The destruction of the mosque has provoked much anger.*

mountain NOUN

TYPES OF MOUNTAIN	
alp	mount
ben (SCOTTISH)	peak
elevation	precipice
height	range

move ❶ VERB
to change position • *The train began to move.*
▷ see Word Study **move**, pages 694-5

move ❷ VERB
to change residence • *She had often considered moving to London.*
migrate • *Peasants have migrated to the cities.*
move house • *They move house fairly frequently.*
relocate • *if the company was to relocate*

Can't find the word you're looking for? Try the index.

a
b
c
d
e
f
g
h
i
j
k
l
m
n
o
p
q
r
s
t
u
v
w
x
y
z

A
B
C
D
E
F
G
H
I
J
K
L
M
N
O
P
Q
R
S
T
U
V
W
X
Y
Z

move ❸ VERB
to cause a deep emotion • *Her story moved us to tears.*
affect • *Her loss still clearly affects him.*
touch • *Her enthusiasm touched me.*

movement ❶ NOUN
a change of position • *They monitor the movement of the fish going up river.*
flow • *the frantic flow of cars and buses along the street*
motion • *the wind from the car's motion*

movement ❷ NOUN
a group of people with similar aims • *the peace movement*
campaign • *the campaign against public smoking*
faction • *the leaders of the country's warring factions*
group • *members of an environmental group*
organization • *the International Labour Organization*

moving ADJECTIVE
causing deep emotion • *It was a moving moment.*
affecting • *one of the most affecting scenes in the film*
emotional • *an emotional reunion*
poignant • *a poignant love story*
stirring • *a stirring speech*
touching • *the touching tale of a wife who stood by husband she loved*

muddle ❶ NOUN
a state of disorder • *Our finances are in a muddle.*
chaos • *Their concerts often ended in chaos.*
confusion • *There was confusion when a man fired shots.*

disarray • *He found the room in disarray.*
disorder • *Inside all was disorder.*
disorganization • *a state of complete disorganization*
jumble • *a meaningless jumble of words*
mess • *the reasons why the economy is in such a mess*
tangle • *a tangle of wires*

muddle ❷ VERB
to mix things up • *One or two critics have begun to muddle the two names.*
confuse • *Great care is taken to avoid confusing the two projects.*
jumble • *a number of animals whose remains were jumbled together*
mix up • *People often mix us up.*

multiply VERB
to increase in number • *The trip wore on and the hazards multiplied.*
increase • *The population continues to increase.*
proliferate • *Computerized databases are proliferating fast.*
spread • *Cholera is not spreading as quickly as it did in the past.*

mumble VERB
to speak quietly • *He mumbled a few words.*
murmur • *He murmured something to the professor.*
mutter • *He sat there muttering to himself.*

murder ❶ NOUN
the act of killing someone • *after being found guilty of murder*
assassination • *the assassination of John F. Kennedy*
homicide • *the scene of the homicide*

Can't find the word you're looking for? Try the index.

killing • *a brutal killing*
manslaughter • *She was found guilty of manslaughter.*
slaughter • *the imperial army's slaughter of Chinese civilians*
slaying (LITERARY) • *a trail of motiveless slayings*

murder ❷ VERB

to kill someone • *a thriller about two men who murder a third*
assassinate • *Robert Kennedy was assassinated in 1968.*
kill • *a man who killed his wife*
slaughter • *Thirty-four people were slaughtered while queueing up to cast their votes.*
slay (LITERARY) • *gang leader slain in drive-by shooting*
take the life of • *He admitted to taking the lives of at least 35 more women.*

mysterious ❶ ADJECTIVE

strange and not well understood • *He died in mysterious circumstances.*
arcane (FORMAL) • *the arcane world of high finance*
baffling • *a baffling array of wires*

cryptic • *My father's notes are more cryptic here.*
enigmatic • *one of Orson Welles's most enigmatic films*
mystifying • *I find your attitude rather mystifying.*

MORE SYNONYMS

● abstruse
● obscure
● recondite

mysterious ❷ ADJECTIVE

secretive about something • *Stop being so mysterious.*
furtive • *with a furtive glance over her shoulder*
secretive • *the secretive world of spying*

mystery NOUN

something that is not understood • *the mystery surrounding his death*
conundrum • *this theological conundrum*
enigma • *Iran remains an enigma for the outside world.*
puzzle • *"Women are a puzzle," he said.*
riddle • *the answer to the riddle of why it was never finished*

a
b
c
d
e
f
g
h
i
j
k
l
m
n
o
p
q
r
s
t
u
v
w
x
y
z

Nn

A
B
C
D
E
F
G
H
I
J
K
L
M
N
O
P
Q
R
S
T
U
V
W
X
Y
Z

naked ❶ ADJECTIVE
not wearing any clothes • *a naked man diving into the sea*
bare • *her bare feet*
nude • *nude bathing*
stark-naked • *She didn't seem to notice I was stark-naked.*
unclothed • *an unclothed male body*
undressed • *She couldn't remember getting undressed.*

ANTONYM
● clothed

naked ❷ ADJECTIVE
openly displayed or shown • *naked aggression*
blatant • *evidence of blatant discrimination*
evident • *the party's evident dislike of the president*
manifest • *his manifest enthusiasm*
open • *open opposition to the government*
unmistakable • *with unmistakable amusement in his eyes*

MORE SYNONYMS
● overt
● patent
● stark

ANTONYM
● secret

name ❶ NOUN
a word that identifies a person or thing • *My name is Joe.*

designation • *a level four alert, a designation reserved for very serious incidents*
epithet • *the common epithet for the Buddha*
nickname • *He's heard your nickname is Codfish.*
term • *I don't know the medical term for it.*
title • *Your actual title would be business manager.*

MORE SYNONYMS
● appellation
● denomination
● sobriquet

RELATED WORD
● ADJECTIVE: nominal

name ❷ NOUN
the opinion people have about someone • *to protect Janet's good name*
character • *a series of personal attacks on my character*
reputation • *I know Chris has a bad reputation.*

name ❸ VERB
to give a name to someone or something • *a little girl named Betsy*
baptize • *She could be baptized Margaret.*
call • *in a town called Fishingport*
christen • *He wanted to christen his son Arthur Albert.*
dub • *a girl cruelly dubbed "the Worm"*

Can't find the word you're looking for? Try the index.

style • *a character who styled himself the Memory Man*
term • *He had been termed a temporary employee.*

narrow ADJECTIVE
having a small distance from side to side • *a narrow stream*
fine • *the fine hairs on her arms*
slender • *long slender legs*
slim • *a slim volume of Auden's poems*
thin • *a thin layer of clay*

ANTONYM
● wide

narrow-minded ADJECTIVE
unwilling to consider new ideas or other people's opinions • *their own narrow-minded view of the world*
biased • *a biased view*
bigoted • *bigoted opinions*
insular • *those insular British travellers*
opinionated • *the most opinionated rubbish I have read*
prejudiced • *a whole host of prejudiced and xenophobic ideas*

MORE SYNONYMS
● parochial
● reactionary

ANTONYM
● tolerant

nasty ADJECTIVE
very unpleasant • *a nasty taste*
disagreeable • *a disagreeable experience*
disgusting • *the most disgusting behaviour*
foul • *They produce a foul smell of rotten eggs.*
horrible • *I've got a horrible feeling about this one.*
repellent • *the most repellent*

human being I have ever met
unpleasant • *some unpleasant surprises*
vile • *All the food is vile.*

ANTONYM
● pleasant

natural ❶ ADJECTIVE
normal and to be expected • *the natural reaction to a failed marriage*
common • *It is a common response.*
everyday • *the everyday drudgery of work*
normal • *Biting is normal for puppies when they are teething.*
ordinary • *The cottage looks quite ordinary from the road.*
typical • *typical symptoms of stress*
usual • *It was not usual for the women to accompany them.*

ANTONYM
● unnatural

natural ❷ ADJECTIVE
not trying to pretend • *He was so natural with the children.*
candid • *rather candid about her marriage*
frank • *an unusually frank interview*
genuine • *He always seems so genuine.*
real • *She came across as a real person.*
unaffected • *She sang with unaffected simplicity.*

MORE SYNONYMS
● artless
● ingenuous

ANTONYM
● false

natural ❸ ADJECTIVE
existing from birth and not learned • *I never had much natural rhythm.*

Can't find the word you're looking for? Try the index.

a b c d e f g h i j k l m n o p q r s t u v w x y z

inborn • *an inborn sense of optimism*
inherent • *the inherent goodness of people*
innate • *the innate conservatism of his predecessor*
instinctive • *an instinctive distrust of authority*
intuitive • *an intuitive understanding of the market*
native • *He relies on his native wit to get him through.*

MORE SYNONYMS
● immanent
● indigenous

nature NOUN
someone's character • *It's not in my nature to sit still.*
character • *the funny side of his character*
make-up • *Compromise was never part of his make-up.*
personality • *his dominating personality*

naughty ❶ ADJECTIVE
tending to behave badly • *a naughty little boy*
bad • *the bad behaviour of their teenage children*
disobedient • *Lucy was similarly disobedient.*
impish • *an impish sense of humour*
mischievous • *a mischievous child*
wayward • *He tried to control his wayward son.*

ANTONYM
● well-behaved

naughty ❷ ADJECTIVE
rude or indecent • *a programme all about naughty words*
bawdy • *a series of bawdy jokes*
lewd • *his arrest for lewd behaviour*

obscene • *making obscene gestures to the crowd*
vulgar • *The lyrics were vulgar.*

MORE SYNONYMS
● ribald
● risqué
● smutty

near ❶ PREPOSITION
not far from • *He drew his chair nearer the fire.*
adjacent to • *a garden and maze adjacent to the castle*
alongside • *the huts set up alongside the river*
close to • *We parked close to the pavement.*
next to • *I realised someone was standing next to me.*
not far from • *a car park not far from the entrance*

near ❷ ADJECTIVE
not far away in distance • *A beautiful woman is near.*
adjacent • *an adjacent room*
adjoining • *A phone rang in an adjoining office.*
close • *a close neighbour*
nearby • *the nearby village*

ANTONYM
● far

near ❸ ADJECTIVE
not far away in time • *The time of judgment is near.*
approaching • *the approaching deadline*
forthcoming • *the forthcoming football season*
imminent • *He is in imminent danger.*
looming • *The students are panicking due to the looming exams.*
nigh • *The end of the world is nigh.*
upcoming • *the upcoming elections*

Can't find the word you're looking for? Try the index.

nearly ADVERB
not completely but almost
• *The beach was nearly empty.*
almost • *Over the past decade their wages have almost doubled.*
as good as • *The World Championship is as good as over.*
just about • *We are just about finished with this section.*
practically • *The house was practically a wreck.*
virtually • *Their country is virtually bankrupt.*

neat ❶ ADJECTIVE
having everything arranged in a tidy way • *The house was clean and neat.*
orderly • *an orderly office*
smart • *a smart navy blue suit*
spruce • *Mundo was looking spruce in a suit.*
tidy • *He always kept his bedroom tidy.*
trim • *a street of trim little villas*

ANTONYM
● untidy

neat ❷ ADJECTIVE
not mixed with anything else
• *a small glass of neat vodka*
pure • *a carton of pure orange juice*
straight • *calling for a straight whisky*

MORE SYNONYMS
● undiluted
● unmixed

necessary ❶ ADJECTIVE
needed so that something can happen • *Make the necessary arrangements.*
essential • *It is essential that you visit a dentist.*
imperative • *It is imperative we end up with a win.*

indispensable • *Jordan is an indispensable part of the peace process.*
required • *That book is required reading.*
vital • *Bone marrow is vital for producing blood cells.*

MORE SYNONYMS
● de rigueur
● requisite

ANTONYM
● unnecessary

necessary ❷ ADJECTIVE
(FORMAL)
certain to happen or exist
• *a necessary consequence of war*
certain • *one certain outcome of the conference*
inevitable • *She now accepts that a divorce is inevitable.*
inexorable • *The growth in travel has been inexorable.*
unavoidable • *The union knows that job losses are unavoidable.*

need VERB
to believe you must have or do something • *You need some fresh air.*
demand • *The children demand her attention.*
require • *If you require further information, please telephone.*
want • *I want a drink.*

neglect ❶ VERB
to fail to look after someone or something • *unhappy and neglected children*
ignore • *They see the government ignoring poor people.*
overlook • *Pensioners feel they are being overlooked.*
turn your back on • *Do not turn your back on the unemployed.*

a
b
c
d
e
f
g
h
i
j
k
l
m
n
o
p
q
r
s
t
u
v
w
x
y
z

Can't find the word you're looking for? Try the index.

neglect ❷ VERB (FORMAL)
to fail to do something • *He had neglected to give her his address.*
fail • *I was shattered and I failed to tell her about the good bits.*
forget • *She forgot to lock her door.*
omit • *He omitted to mention his connection with the company.*

neglect ❸ NOUN
lack of care • *Most of her plants died from neglect.*
disregard • *a callous disregard for his victims*
indifference • *Indifference to patients is rare in America.*
unconcern • *the government's unconcern for the environment*

nervous ADJECTIVE
worried about something • *She had been nervous before the match.*
anxious • *I was very anxious about her safety.*
apprehensive • *Their families are apprehensive about the trip.*
edgy • *I was edgy and tired.*
jittery (INFORMAL) • *She still feels jittery when she visits her sister.*
jumpy • *The Italians are getting jumpy after drawing against the Swiss.*
tense • *too tense to sleep*
toey (AUSTRALIAN AND NEW ZEALAND; SLANG) • *Dad's getting a bit toey.*
uptight (INFORMAL) • *an uptight British couple*
worried • *I was worried about you.*

ANTONYM
● calm

neutral ADJECTIVE
not supporting either side • *We stayed neutral during the war.*
disinterested • *a disinterested observer*

dispassionate • *a full and dispassionate account*
impartial • *How can he give impartial advice?*
nonaligned • *the Arab and nonaligned countries*

MORE SYNONYMS
● even-handed
● nonpartisan
● unbiased
● unprejudiced

ANTONYM
● biased

never ADVERB
at no time at all • *I never said I was leaving.*
at no time • *At no time did he see the helicopter.*
not ever • *The problem won't ever go away.*

new ADJECTIVE
recently created or discovered • *a new hotel*
▷ see Word Study **new**, page 696

ANTONYM
● old

news NOUN
information about things that have happened • *news about the civil war*
bulletin • *the main evening bulletin*
disclosure • *disclosures about his private life*
dispatch • *the latest dispatches from the war zone*
information • *up-to-date information on weather*
intelligence • *military intelligence from behind Iraqi lines*
latest (INFORMAL) • *the latest on the bomb explosion*

Can't find the word you're looking for? Try the index.

tidings (FORMAL) • *the bearer of bad tidings*
word • *There is no word about casualties.*

next ❶ ADJECTIVE
coming immediately after something else • *Their next child was a girl.*
ensuing • *the ensuing years of violence*
following • *The following day I went to work as usual.*
subsequent • *As subsequent events showed, he was wrong.*
succeeding • *succeeding generations of students*

next ❷ ADVERB
coming immediately after something else • *Steve arrived next.*
afterwards • *I felt dizzy afterwards and had to sit down.*
subsequently • *She was subsequently married to his cousin.*

next ❸ ADJECTIVE
in a position nearest to something • *in the next room*
adjacent • *I pulled into the adjacent driveway.*
adjoining • *in adjoining streets*
closest • *Britain's closest neighbours*
nearest • *the nearest Italian restaurant*
neighbouring • *Liberians fleeing to neighbouring countries*

nice ADJECTIVE
attractive or enjoyable • *Did you have a nice time, dear?*
▷ see Word Study **nice**, page 697

no INTERJECTION
not at all • *"Any problems?" - "No, everything's fine."*
absolutely not • *"Did they consult you?" -" Absolutely not."*

certainly not • *"Perhaps it would be better if I withdrew." - "Certainly not!"*
definitely not • *"Are you going to the party?" - "Definitely not."*
not at all • *"You're not upset, are you?" - "Not at all."*
of course not • *"I'd like to talk to the lads, if you don't mind." - "Of course not, Chief."*

ANTONYM
● yes

noble ❶ ADJECTIVE
deserving admiration because of honesty, bravery and unselfishness • *a good and noble thing to do*
generous • *It reflects his generous nature.*
honourable • *His colleagues were honourable people.*
magnanimous • *Miss Balding is magnanimous in victory.*
upright • *a very upright, trustworthy man*
virtuous • *the virtuous Mrs Friendall*
worthy • *less worthy members of our profession*

ANTONYM
● ignoble

noble ❷ NOUN
someone from the highest social rank • *The Scottish nobles were united.*
aristocrat • *All his sisters had married German aristocrats.*
lord • *They assumed that Amy was a snob because her father was a lord.*
nobleman • *a Spanish nobleman*
peer • *He was made a life peer in 1981.*

ANTONYM
● peasant

a
b
c
d
e
f
g
h
i
j
k
l
m
n
o
p
q
r
s
t
u
v
w
x
y
z

Can't find the word you're looking for? Try the index.

noise NOUN

a loud or unpleasant sound • *He is making an awful noise.*
commotion • *There was a commotion in the corridor.*
din • *He'd never heard a din like it.*
hubbub • *the hubbub of Paris in the 1880s*
pandemonium • *There was pandemonium in the classroom.*
racket • *There was a terrible racket going on.*
row • *Whatever is that row?*
uproar • *The courtroom was in an uproar.*

MORE SYNONYMS

- clamour
- rumpus
- tumult

ANTONYM

- silence

noisy ADJECTIVE

making a lot of noise • *a noisy audience of schoolchildren*
deafening • *a deafening roar*
loud • *The disco music was a little too loud.*
piercing • *her piercing laugh*
strident • *the strident vocals of Joy Malcolm*
tumultuous • *He took the field to tumultuous applause.*
vociferous • *vociferous support from the Scottish fans*

MORE SYNONYMS

- clamorous
- riotous
- uproarious

ANTONYM

- quiet

nominate VERB

to suggest someone for a position

• *The party refused to nominate him as its candidate.*
name • *He'll be naming a new captain.*
propose • *Cliff was proposed as chairman.*
recommend • *He recommended him as his successor at Boston.*
select • *no prospect of being selected to stand for Parliament*
submit • *Mr Heath submitted a list of 200 names.*
suggest • *Some commentators have suggested Clark for the job.*

nonsense NOUN

foolish words or behaviour • *I say the allegations are complete nonsense.*
bull (SLANG) • *They're teaching our kids a load of bull.*
drivel • *mindless drivel aimed at Middle America*
garbage (INFORMAL) • *One source claimed the rumours were complete garbage.*
inanity • *the burbling inanities of the tabloids*
rot • *She is talking complete rot.*
rubbish • *complete and utter rubbish*
waffle (BRITISH; INFORMAL) • *He writes smug, sanctimonious waffle.*

normal ADJECTIVE

usual and ordinary • *my normal routine*
average • *What's your average day like?*
conventional • *conventional tastes*
habitual • *their country of habitual residence*
ordinary • *It was just an ordinary weekend.*
regular • *It looks like a regular cigarette.*
routine • *a routine medical check*
standard • *standard practice*

Can't find the word you're looking for? Try the index.

typical • *A typical day begins at 8.30.*
usual • *She did not collect him at the usual time.*

ANTONYM
● unusual

nosy ADJECTIVE
trying to find out about other people's business • *nosy neighbours watching us through the curtains*
curious • *surrounded by a group of curious villagers*
eavesdropping • *We don't want to be overheard by eavesdropping servants.*
inquisitive • *Bears are naturally inquisitive creatures.*
prying • *I hid it away, safe from prying eyes.*

note ❶ NOUN
a short letter • *I wrote him a note asking him to come round.*
communication (FORMAL) • *a communication from the President*
letter • *I have received a letter from a friend.*
memo • *a leaked memo to managers*
memorandum • *A memorandum has been sent to the members of the board.*
message • *He sent his mate round with a message for me.*
reminder • *We keep getting reminders from the garage to pay our bill.*

MORE SYNONYMS
● epistle
● missive (OLD-FASHIONED)

note ❷ NOUN
a written record that helps you remember something • *I made a note of his address.*

account • *Keep an account of all your outgoings.*
jotting • *Carry a notebook with you for your jottings.*
record • *Keep a record of all payments.*
register • *She kept a register of each child's progress.*

note ❸ NOUN
an atmosphere, feeling, or quality • *I detected a note of bitterness in his voice.*
hint • *Was there was a hint of irony in that remark?*
tone • *He laughed again, this time with a cold, sharp tone.*
touch • *There is an unmistakable touch of pathos in his last film.*
trace • *He wrote on the subject without a trace of sensationalism.*

note ❹ VERB
to become aware of or mention a fact • *I noted that the rain had stopped.*
mention • *I mentioned in passing that I liked her dress.*
notice • *Contact the police if you notice anything suspicious.*
observe (FORMAL) • *Hooke observed a reddish spot on the surface of the planet.*
perceive • *He perceived a certain tension between them.*
register • *The sound was so familiar that she didn't register it.*
remark • *Everyone has remarked what a lovely lady she is.*
see • *A lot of people saw what was happening but did nothing.*

notice ❶ VERB
to become aware of something • *Then I noticed Billy wasn't laughing.*
detect • *He detects signs of growing support for his plan.*

a b c d e f g h i j k l m **n** o p q r s t u v w x y z

Can't find the word you're looking for? Try the index.

discern • *I did not discern any change in attitudes.*
note • *I noted that the rain had stopped.*
observe • *I've observed how hard he had to work.*
perceive • *gradually perceiving the possibilities*
see • *I saw that the lobby was swarming with police.*
spot • *Allen spotted me on the other side of the dance floor.*

notice ❷ NOUN

a written announcement • *a handwritten notice in the window*
advertisement • *one advertisement in a local paper*
bill • *students posting bills near the campus for a demo*
poster • *a poster advertising a charity concert*
sign • *a hand-written cardboard sign hung round his neck*

notice ❸ NOUN

warning that something is going to happen • *She was transferred without notice.*
advance warning • *advance warning of the attack*
intimation • *He has given no intimation of an intention to resign.*
notification • *Official notification is expected to arrive today.*
warning • *I was sacked without warning.*

noticeable ADJECTIVE

obvious and easy to see
• *a noticeable improvement*
conspicuous • *a conspicuous lack of sympathy*
evident • *He ate with evident enjoyment.*
obvious • *There are obvious dangers.*

perceptible • *Germany is showing a perceptible improvement.*
unmistakable • *a growing but unmistakable impatience*

MORE SYNONYMS

● manifest
● salient

notify VERB

to officially inform someone of something • *The skipper notified the coastguard of the tragedy.*
advise (FORMAL) • *I think it best that I advise you of my decision first.*
inform • *They would inform him of any progress they made.*
tell • *He told me I was on a final warning.*
warn • *They warned him of the dangers.*

notorious ADJECTIVE

well-known for something bad
• *The district was notorious for violent crime.*
disreputable • *a low and disreputable character*
infamous • *an industry infamous for late payment of debts*
scandalous • *her scandalous affair with the president*

now ADVERB

at the present time or moment
• *I need to talk to him now.*
at once • *I really must go at once.*
currently • *The vaccines are currently being tested.*
immediately • *Please come immediately.*
nowadays • *I don't see much of Tony nowadays.*
right now • *Stop that noise right now!*
straightaway • *I think you should see a doctor straightaway.*

Can't find the word you're looking for? Try the index.

A B C D E F G H I J K L M N O P Q R S T U V W X Y Z

without delay • *We'll come round without delay.*

nuisance NOUN
someone or something that is annoying • *Sorry to be a nuisance.*
annoyance • *Snoring can be an annoyance.*
bother • *Most men hate the bother of shaving.*
hassle (INFORMAL) • *Writing out a cheque is a hassle.*
inconvenience • *the inconvenience of a rail strike*
irritation • *He describes the tourists as "an irritation".*
pain (INFORMAL) • *She found dressing up for the occasion a real pain.*
pest • *I didn't want to be a cry baby or a pest.*

MORE SYNONYMS
- plague
- vexation

numb ❶ ADJECTIVE
unable to feel anything • *Your right arm goes numb.*
dead • *Hillier suffered a dead leg playing for the reserves.*
frozen • *a frozen shoulder*
insensitive • *The brain itself is insensitive to pain.*
paralysed • *He has been left with a paralysed arm.*

MORE SYNONYMS
- benumbed
- insensible

numb ❷ VERB
to make you unable to feel anything • *The cold numbed my fingers.*
dull • *morphine to dull the pain*

freeze • *an epidural to freeze the hip area*
paralyse • *people paralysed by illness or injury*
stun • *the gun used to stun the animals*

MORE SYNONYMS
- benumb
- deaden
- immobilize

number ❶ NOUN
a word or symbol used for counting • *Pick a number between one and ten.*
digit • *a six-digit password*
figure • *a figure between a hundred and a thousand*
numeral • *Roman numerals*

MORE SYNONYMS
- character
- integer

number ❷ NOUN
a quantity of things or people • *Adrian has introduced me to a large number of people.*
collection • *a huge collection of books about Keats*
crowd • *a huge crowd of supporters*
horde • *a horde of drunken villagers*
multitude • *Bands can play to multitudes of fans.*

numerous ADJECTIVE
existing or happening in large numbers • *on numerous occasions*
lots of • *I've got lots of photos of the kids.*
many • *I have met Imran many times.*
several • *He is fluent in several languages.*

a
b
c
d
e
f
g
h
i
j
k
l
m
n
o
p
q
r
s
t
u
v
w
x
y
z

Can't find the word you're looking for? Try the index.

Oo

oaf NOUN
a clumsy or aggressive person
• *You drunken oaf!*
brute • *Custer was an idiot and a brute.*
lout • *a drunken lout*

oath NOUN
a formal promise • *He took an oath of loyalty to the government.*
pledge • *The meeting ended with a pledge to step up cooperation.*
promise • *If you make a promise, you should keep it.*
vow • *I made a silent vow to be more careful.*

obedient ADJECTIVE
tending to do what you are told
• *He was always very obedient to his parents.*
law-abiding • *law-abiding citizens*
submissive • *Most doctors want their patients to be submissive.*
subservient • *her willingness to be subservient to her children*

MORE SYNONYMS
● biddable
● compliant

ANTONYM
● disobedient

obey VERB
to do what you are told • *Most people obey the law.*
abide by • *They have got to abide by the rules.*
adhere to • *All members adhere to a strict code of practice.*
comply with • *The army will comply with the ceasefire.*
follow • *Take care to follow the instructions carefully.*
observe • *forcing motorists to observe speed restrictions*

ANTONYM
● disobey

object ❶ NOUN
anything solid and non-living
• *everyday objects such as wooden spoons*
article • *household articles*
thing • *What's that thing in the middle of the fountain?*

object ❷ NOUN
an aim or purpose • *The object of the exercise is to raise money for the charity.*
aim • *The aim of the festival is to increase awareness of Hindu culture.*
goal • *The goal is to raise as much money as possible.*
idea • *The idea is to give children the freedom to explore.*
intention • *It is my intention to remain in my position.*
objective • *His objective was to win.*
purpose • *What is the purpose of your visit?*

object ❸ VERB
to express disapproval • *A lot of people will object to the book.*

Can't find the word you're looking for? Try the index.

oppose • *Many parents oppose bilingual education in schools.*
protest • *He picked up the cat before Rosa could protest.*

MORE SYNONYMS
● demur
● expostulate

ANTONYM
● approve

objection NOUN
disapproval of something • *despite objections by the White House*
opposition • *Opposition to this plan has come from the media.*
protest • *protests against the government*

ANTONYM
● support

obscene ADJECTIVE
indecent and likely to upset people • *obscene pictures*
bawdy • *a bawdy song*
blue • *a blue movie*
dirty • *a dirty book*
filthy • *a filthy joke*
indecent • *an indecent suggestion*
lewd • *lewd comments*
pornographic • *a pornographic magazine*

MORE SYNONYMS
● ribald
● salacious
● smutty

obscure ❶ ADJECTIVE
known by only a few people • *an obscure Mongolian dialect*
little-known • *a little-known Austrian composer*
unknown • *an unknown writer*

ANTONYM
● famous

obscure ❷ ADJECTIVE
difficult to understand • *The news was shrouded in obscure language.*
arcane • *the arcane world of contemporary classical music*
cryptic • *cryptic comments*
opaque • *the opaque language of the inspector's reports*

MORE SYNONYMS
● abstruse
● esoteric
● recondite

ANTONYM
● simple

obscure ❸ VERB
to make something difficult to see • *His view was obscured by trees.*
cloak • *a land permanently cloaked in mist*
cloud • *Perhaps anger had clouded his vision.*
conceal • *The hat concealed her hair.*
hide • *The compound was hidden by trees and shrubs.*
mask • *A thick grey cloud masked the sun.*
screen • *Most of the road was screened by a block of flats.*
shroud • *Mist shrouded the outline of Buckingham Palace.*

ANTONYM
● expose

observant ADJECTIVE
good at noticing things • *Painting makes you really observant of things.*
attentive • *the attentive audience*
perceptive • *a perceptive remark*
vigilant • *He warned the public to be vigilant.*
watchful • *Keep a watchful eye on babies and toddlers.*

a b c d e f g h i j k l m n **o** p q r s t u v w x y z

MORE SYNONYMS
- eagle-eyed
- sharp-eyed

A
B
C
D
E
F
G
H
I
J
K
L
M
N
O
P
Q
R
S
T
U
V
W
X
Y
Z

observe ❶ VERB
to watch something carefully • *He has spent years observing their behaviour.*
monitor • *I have been monitoring his progress carefully.*
scrutinize • *She scrutinized his features to see if he was telling the truth.*
study • *Debbie studied her friend's face for a moment.*
survey • *He surveys American politics from an interesting standpoint.*
view • *You can view the lesson from the gallery.*
watch • *A man was watching him from across the square.*

observe ❷ VERB
to notice something • *I observed a number of strange phenomena.*
discover • *They discovered that they were being watched.*
note • *People noted how much care she took over her work.*
notice • *Contact the police if you notice anything unusual.*
see • *I saw a man coming towards me.*
spot • *Moments later, smoke was spotted coming out of the kitchen.*
witness • *Anyone who witnessed the attack should call the police.*

observe ❸ VERB
to make a comment about something • *"You've had your hair cut," he observed.*
comment • *Stuart commented that this was true.*
mention • *I mentioned that I didn't like contemporary music.*

remark • *"Some people have more money than sense," he remarked.*
say • *She said that I looked tired.*
state • *He stated that this was, indeed, the case.*

obsession NOUN
a compulsion to think about something • *her obsession with Christopher*
complex • *I have never had a complex about my height.*
fixation • *the country's fixation on the war*
mania • *a mania for horror films*
preoccupation • *today's preoccupation with royal misdeeds*
thing (INFORMAL) • *He's got this thing about ties.*

obstacle NOUN
something which makes it difficult to go forward • *a large obstacle to improving housing conditions*
barrier • *Taxes are the most obvious barrier to free trade.*
difficulty • *the difficulties ahead*
hindrance • *The higher rates have been a hindrance to economic recovery.*
hurdle • *the first hurdle for many women returning to work*
impediment • *There was no legal impediment to the marriage.*
obstruction • *an obstruction in the road*

MORE SYNONYMS
- bar
- stumbling block

obstinate ADJECTIVE
unwilling to change your mind • *He is obstinate and will not give up.*
dogged • *his dogged insistence on their rights*

headstrong • *He's young and very headstrong.*
inflexible • *His opponents viewed him as dogmatic and inflexible.*
intractable • *He protested but Wright was intractable.*
stubborn • *a stubborn character who is used to getting his own way*
wilful • *a wilful child*

MORE SYNONYMS
- intransigent
- recalcitrant
- refractory

ANTONYM
- flexible

obstruct VERB
to block a road or path • *Lorries obstructed the road.*
bar • *He stood there, barring her way.*
block • *Some students blocked the highway.*
choke • *The roads are choked with cars.*
clog • *The traffic clogged the Thames bridges.*

obtain VERB
to get something • *He tried to obtain a false passport*
acquire • *I recently acquired a beautiful old lamp.*
get • *trying to get enough food to live*
get hold of • *It's hard to get hold of guns.*
get your hands on (INFORMAL) • *reading everything she could get her hands on*
procure (FORMAL) • *It became hard to procure fuel.*
secure (FORMAL) • *continuing their efforts to secure a ceasefire*

obvious ADJECTIVE
easy to see or understand • *an obvious injustice*

apparent • *It was apparent that he had lost interest.*
blatant • *a blatant foul*
clear • *a clear breach of the rules*
evident • *His love of nature is evident in his paintings.*
overt • *parents who showed us no overt affection*
palpable • *The tension between them is palpable.*
plain • *It was plain to him that I was having a nervous breakdown.*
self-evident • *The implications for this country are self-evident.*

MORE SYNONYMS
- conspicuous
- manifest
- patent

occasion ❶ NOUN
an important event • *The launch of a ship was a big occasion.*
affair • *The visit was to be a purely private affair.*
event • *A new book by Grass is always an event.*

occasion ❷ NOUN
an opportunity to do something • *an important occasion for setting out government policy*
chance • *the chance to practise medicine in British hospitals*
opportunity • *I had an opportunity to go to New York.*
time • *This was no time to make a speech.*

occasion ❸ VERB (FORMAL)
to cause something • *damage occasioned by fire*
bring about • *the only way to bring about peace*
give rise to • *The judge's decision gave rise to practical problems.*
induce • *an economic crisis induced*

a
b
c
d
e
f
g
h
i
j
k
l
m
n
o
p
q
r
s
t
u
v
w
x
y
z

Can't find the word you're looking for? Try the index.

by high oil prices
produce • *The drug is known to produce side-effects in women.*
prompt • *The demonstration prompted fears of more violence.*
provoke • *The incident has provoked outrage in Okinawa.*

occasional ADJECTIVE

happening sometimes • *an occasional outing*
intermittent • *after three hours of intermittent rain*
odd • *at odd moments*
periodic • *periodic bouts of illness*
sporadic • *a year of sporadic fighting*

ANTONYM
● frequent

occur ❶ VERB

to happen or exist • *The disease occurs throughout Africa.*
appear • *a test to reveal infection before symptoms appear*
arise • *A problem may arise later in pregnancy.*
be present • *This vitamin is present in breast milk.*
exist • *A conflict of interest may exist in such situations.*
happen • *The accident happened close to Martha's Vineyard.*
take place • *Elections will take place on the second of November.*

occur ❷ VERB

to come into your mind • *It didn't occur to me to check.*
cross your mind • *The possibility of failure did cross my mind.*
dawn on • *It dawned on me that I shouldn't give up without a fight.*
strike • *A thought struck her.*

odd ADJECTIVE

strange or unusual • *an odd coincidence*

bizarre • *his bizarre behaviour*
curious • *a curious mixture of the ancient and modern*
funny • *There's something funny about him.*
peculiar • *Rachel thought it tasted peculiar.*
queer (OLD-FASHIONED) • *There's something a bit queer going on.*
singular (FORMAL) • *Where he got that singular notion I just can't think.*
strange • *Then a strange thing happened.*
weird • *That first day was weird.*

ANTONYM
● ordinary

offend VERB

to upset or embarrass someone • *He says he had no intention of offending the community.*
affront • *He pretended to be affronted, but inwardly he was pleased.*
insult • *Buchanan says he was insulted by the judge's remarks.*
outrage • *Many people have been outraged by what was said.*

ANTONYM
● please

offensive ADJECTIVE

rude and upsetting • *offensive behaviour*
abusive • *abusive language*
insulting • *an insulting remark*
objectionable • *I find your tone highly objectionable.*

offer ❶ VERB

to ask if someone wants something • *Rhys offered him an apple.*
hold out • *I held out my ticket for him to check.*

Can't find the word you're looking for? Try the index.

tender • *She has tendered her resignation.*

MORE SYNONYMS
- extend
- proffer
- submit

offer ❷ NOUN

something that someone offers you • *He had refused several excellent job offers.*
proposition • *I made her a proposition.*
tender • *a tender for a public contract*

official ❶ ADJECTIVE

approved by someone in authority • *the official figures*
authorized • *the authorized biography*
certified • *a certified accountant*
formal • *No formal announcement has been made.*
licensed • *a licensed doctor*

ANTONYM
- unofficial

official ❷ NOUN

someone in authority • *a senior UN official*
executive • *a senior bank executive*
officer • *a local authority education officer*
representative • *trade union representatives*

MORE SYNONYMS
- bureaucrat
- functionary

often ADVERB

happening many times • *They often spent Christmas at Prescott Hill.*
frequently • *He was frequently depressed.*

repeatedly • *Both men have repeatedly denied the allegations.*

okay or OK ADJECTIVE (INFORMAL)

acceptable or satisfactory • *Is it okay if I come by myself?*
acceptable • *It is becoming more acceptable for women to drink.*
all right • *if it's all right with you*

old ❶ ADJECTIVE

having lived for a long time • *an old lady*
▷ see Word Study old, page 698

ANTONYM
- young

old ❷ ADJECTIVE

in the past • *my old art teacher*
▷ see Word Study old, page 698

ANTONYM
- new

old-fashioned ADJECTIVE

no longer fashionable • *old-fashioned shoes*
antiquated • *an antiquated system*
archaic • *archaic practices such as these*
dated • *Some of the language sounds quite dated.*
obsolete • *So much equipment becomes obsolete almost as soon as it's made.*
outdated • *outdated attitudes*
outmoded • *toiling in outmoded factories*
out of date • *a make of car that is now out of date*
passé • *Punk is passé.*

MORE SYNONYMS
- behind the times
- obsolescent
- old-time

a
b
c
d
e
f
g
h
i
j
k
l
m
n
o
p
q
r
s
t
u
v
w
x
y
z

Can't find the word you're looking for? Try the index.

A
B
C
D
E
F
G
H
I
J
K
L
M
N
O
P
Q
R
S
T
U
V
W
X
Y
Z

ANTONYM
- fashionable

omen NOUN
a sign of what will happen • *Her appearance at this moment is an omen of disaster.*
sign • *people who look to the skies for signs*
warning • *a warning of trouble to come*

MORE SYNONYMS
- augury
- portent

ominous ADJECTIVE
suggesting that something bad will happen • *an ominous silence*
sinister • *a sinister message*
threatening • *a threatening sky*

MORE SYNONYMS
- inauspicious
- portentous
- unpropitious

omit VERB
to not include something • *Omit the salt in this recipe.*
exclude • *Women felt excluded from the workplace.*
leave out • *The Spaniard has been left out of the team.*
miss out • *What about Sally? You've missed her out!*
skip • *It is all too easy to skip meals.*

only ❶ ADVERB
involving one person or thing
• *Only Keith knows whether he will continue.*
just • *It's not just a financial matter.*
merely • *Watson was far from being merely a furniture expert.*
purely • *a racing machine, designed purely for speed*
simply • *Most of the damage was*

simply because of fallen trees.
solely • *decisions based solely upon what we see in magazines*

only ❷ ADJECTIVE
having no other examples • *their only hit single*
one • *My one aim is to look after the horses well.*
sole • *Our sole intention is to reunite her with her baby.*

open ❶ VERB
to cause something not to be closed • *She opened the door.*
uncover • *When the seedlings sprout, uncover the tray.*
undo • *I managed secretly to undo a corner of the parcel.*
unlock • *She unlocked the case.*

MORE SYNONYMS
- unfasten
- unseal

ANTONYM
- shut

open ❷ ADJECTIVE
not closed • *an open box of chocolates*
ajar • *He left the door ajar.*
uncovered • *The uncovered bucket in the corner stank.*
undone • *pictures of him with his shirt undone*
unlocked • *an unlocked room*

MORE SYNONYMS
- unfastened
- unsealed

ANTONYM
- shut

open ❸ ADJECTIVE
not trying to deceive someone
• *He had always been open with her.*
candid • *I haven't been completely*

candid with him.
frank • *My client has been less than frank with me.*
honest • *He had been honest with her and she had tricked him!*

opening ❶ ADJECTIVE
coming first • *the opening day of the season*
first • *the first night of the play*
inaugural • *his inaugural address*
initial • *the aim of this initial meeting*
introductory • *an introductory offer*

opening ❷ NOUN
the first part of something • *the opening of the film*
beginning • *the beginning of the book*
commencement (FORMAL) • *at the commencement of the course*
start • *four years after the start of the Great War*

ANTONYM
● conclusion

opening ❸ NOUN
a hole or gap • *a narrow opening in the fence*
chink • *a chink in the wall*
cleft • *a narrow cleft in the rocks*
crack • *Kathryn had seen him through a crack in the curtains.*
gap • *the wind tearing through gaps in the window frames*
hole • *a hole in the wall*
slot • *a slot in which to insert a coin*
space • *a half-inch space between the curtains*
vent • *Steam escaped from the vent at the front of the machine.*

MORE SYNONYMS
● aperture
● fissure
● orifice

opinion NOUN
a belief or view • *I wasn't asking for your opinion.*
assessment • *What is your assessment of the situation?*
belief • *his religious beliefs*
estimation • *He has gone down considerably in my estimation.*
judgment • *In your judgment, what has changed?*
point of view • *Thanks for your point of view, John.*
view • *Make your views known to your local MP.*
viewpoint • *to include as many viewpoints as possible*

oppose VERB
to disagree with something
• *protesters opposing planned nuclear tests*
fight against • *a lifetime fighting against racism*
resist • *They resisted our attempts to modernize.*
speak out against • *He spoke out strongly against some of the radical ideas.*

MORE SYNONYMS
● take a stand against
● take issue with

ANTONYM
● support

opposite ❶ ADJECTIVE
completely different to something
• *I take the opposite view to you.*
conflicting • *three powers with conflicting interests*
contrary • *He has a contrary opinion to mine.*
contrasting • *two men with completely contrasting backgrounds*
opposed • *This was a straight conflict of directly opposed aims.*

a
b
c
d
e
f
g
h
i
j
k
l
m
n
o
p
q
r
s
t
u
v
w
x
y
z

A
B
C
D
E
F
G
H
I
J
K
L
M
N
O
P
Q
R
S
T
U
V
W
X
Y
Z

reverse • *The wrong attitude will have exactly the reverse effect.*

MORE SYNONYMS
- antithetical
- diametrically opposed

opposite ❷ NOUN
a completely different person or thing • *He was the complete opposite of Raymond.*
antithesis (FORMAL) • *The antithesis of the Middle Eastern buyer is the Japanese.*
contrary • *I'm not a feminist, quite the contrary.*
converse • *Don't you think that the converse might also be possible?*
reverse • *This didn't upset him at all, in fact quite the reverse.*

MORE SYNONYMS
- inverse
- obverse

opposition NOUN
disagreement about something • *Much of the opposition to this plan has come from the media.*
disapproval • *His action had been greeted with almost universal disapproval.*
hostility • *There is hostility to this method among traditionalists.*
resistance • *Initially I met resistance from my own family.*

ANTONYM
- support

oppressed ADJECTIVE
treated cruelly or unfairly • *a member of an oppressed minority*
abused • *those who work with abused children*
downtrodden • *the downtrodden, bored housewife*

MORE SYNONYMS
- enslaved
- tyrannized

oppression NOUN
cruel or unfair treatment • *the oppression of black people throughout history*
persecution • *the persecution of minorities*
tyranny • *The 1930s was a decade of tyranny in Europe.*

MORE SYNONYMS
- subjection
- subjugation

optimistic ADJECTIVE
hopeful about the future • *an optimistic mood*
buoyant • *She was in a buoyant mood.*
confident • *I am confident that everything will come out right in time.*
hopeful • *I am hopeful this misunderstanding will be rectified.*
positive • *a positive frame of mind*
sanguine • *They have begun to take a more sanguine view.*

ANTONYM
- pessimistic

oral ADJECTIVE
spoken rather than written • *oral history*
spoken • *the spoken word*
verbal • *a verbal agreement*

orange NOUN or ADJECTIVE

SHADES OF ORANGE	
amber	ochre
apricot	peach
carrot	tangerine

ordeal NOUN
a difficult and unpleasant

Can't find the word you're looking for? Try the index.

experience • *the ordeal of being arrested*
hardship • *One of the worst hardships is having so little time.*
nightmare • *Taking my son Peter to a restaurant was a nightmare.*
torture • *Waiting for the result was torture.*
trial • *the trials of adolescence*
tribulation (FORMAL) • *the trials and tribulations of everyday life*

order ❶ NOUN
a command by someone in authority • *I don't take orders from him any more.*
command • *The tanker failed to respond to a command to stop.*
decree • *He issued a decree ordering all armed groups to disband.*
dictate • *to ensure that the dictates of the Party are followed*
directive • *a new EU directive*
instruction • *MPs defied a party instruction to vote against the Bill.*

order ❷ NOUN
a well-organized situation • *the wish to impose order upon confusion*
harmony • *the ordered harmony of the universe*
regularity • *the chessboard regularity of their fields*
symmetry • *the beauty and symmetry of a snowflake*

ANTONYM
● disorder

order ❸ VERB
to tell someone to do something • *He ordered his men to stop firing.*
command • *He commanded his troops to attack.*
decree • *the rule that decreed no alcohol on the premises*

direct • *a court order directing the group to leave the land*
instruct • *The family has instructed solicitors to sue Thomson.*
ordain • *Nehru ordained that socialism should rule.*

ANTONYM
● forbid

orderly ADJECTIVE
well-organized or well-arranged • *Their vehicles were parked in orderly rows.*
neat • *She put her wet clothes in a neat pile in the corner.*
regular • *regular rows of wooden huts*
tidy • *a tidy desk*

ANTONYM
● disorderly

ordinary ADJECTIVE
not special or different • *an ordinary day*
conventional • *a respectable married woman with conventional opinions*
normal • *He lives a normal life.*
regular • *the regular barman*
routine • *a routine procedure*
standard • *It was standard practice.*
usual • *all the usual inner-city problems*

MORE SYNONYMS
● run-of-the-mill
● unexceptional
● unremarkable

ANTONYM
● special

organization ❶ NOUN
a group or business • *charitable organizations*
association • *research associations*

a
b
c
d
e
f
g
h
i
j
k
l
m
n
o
p
q
r
s
t
u
v
w
x
y
z

Can't find the word you're looking for? Try the index.

body • *the Chairman of the policemen's representative body*
company • *the Ford Motor Company*
confederation • *the Confederation of Indian Industry*
group • *an environmental group*
institution • *financial institutions*
outfit (INFORMAL) • *We are a professional outfit.*

organization ❷ NOUN
the planning and arranging of something • *He was involved in the organization of conferences and seminars.*
organizing • *His duties involved the organizing of transport.*
planning • *The trip needs careful planning.*
structuring • *improvements in the structuring of courses*

organize VERB
to plan and arrange something • *Organizing a wedding takes time.*
arrange • *The bank can arrange a loan for students.*
establish • *How do you establish a workable system?*
jack up (NEW ZEALAND; INFORMAL) • *to jack up a demonstration*
plan • *A team meeting was planned for last night.*
set up • *This tribunal was set up by the government.*

origin ❶ NOUN
the beginning or cause of something • *the origins of the custom*
derivation • *The derivation of its name is obscure.*
root • *His sense of guilt had its roots in his childhood.*
source • *the source of the problem*

MORE SYNONYMS
- genesis
- provenance

origin ❷ NOUN
someone's family background • *She was of Swedish origin.*
ancestry • *Noel can trace her ancestry to the 11th century.*
descent • *All the contributors were of African descent.*
extraction • *a Malaysian citizen of Australian extraction*
lineage • *a respectable family of ancient lineage*
stock • *people of Mediterranean stock*

original ❶ ADJECTIVE
being the first example of something • *the original owner of the cottage*
first • *Her first reaction was disgust.*
initial • *His initial response was to disbelieve her.*

original ❷ ADJECTIVE
imaginative and clever • *a stunningly original idea*
fresh • *These designers are full of fresh ideas.*
new • *These proposals aren't new.*
novel • *a novel way of losing weight*

MORE SYNONYMS
- innovative
- innovatory

ANTONYM
- unoriginal

ornament NOUN
an object that you display • *a shelf containing ornaments*
adornment • *a building without any adornments*
bauble • *a Christmas tree*

Can't find the word you're looking for? Try the index.

decorated with coloured baubles
decoration • *The only wall decorations are candles.*
knick-knack • *Her flat is spilling over with knick-knacks.*
trinket • *She sold trinkets to tourists.*

ostentatious ADJECTIVE

intended to impress people with appearances • *an ostentatious lifestyle*
extravagant • *They make extravagant shows of generosity.*
flamboyant • *flamboyant clothes*
flashy • *a flashy sports car*
grandiose • *the grandiose building which housed the mayor's offices*
pretentious • *This pub was smaller and less pretentious.*
showy • *large, showy flowers*

outbreak NOUN

a sudden occurrence of something • *the outbreak of war*
eruption • *this sudden eruption of violence*
explosion • *the global explosion of interest in rugby*

outdo VERB

to do something better than another person • *She would love to outdo her sister Manuela.*
go one better than • *You always have to go one better than anyone else.*
outshine • *Jesse has begun to outshine me in sports.*
surpass • *determined to surpass the achievements of his older brothers*
top • *How are you going to top that?*

MORE SYNONYMS
- best
- eclipse

outlook ❷ NOUN
the future prospects of something
• *The economic outlook is one of rising unemployment.*
future • *a conference on the country's political future*
prospects • *a detailed review of the company's prospects*

out of date ADJECTIVE
no longer useful • *The information is already out of date.*
antiquated • *an antiquated system*
archaic • *archaic practices such as these*
obsolete • *So much equipment becomes obsolete almost as soon as it's made.*
old-fashioned • *old-fashioned shoes*
outdated • *outdated attitudes*
outmoded • *toiling in outmoded factories*

ANTONYM
● modern

outside ❶ NOUN
the outer part of something • *The moth was on the outside of the glass.*
exterior • *the exterior of the building*
facade • *the refurbishing of the cathedral's facade*
face • *the face of the watch*
surface • *the surface of the road*

ANTONYM
● inside

outside ❷ ADJECTIVE
not inside • *an outside toilet*
exterior • *the oven's exterior surfaces*
external • *the external walls*
outdoor • *outdoor activities*
outer • *the outer suburbs of the city*

outward • *with no outward sign of injury*
surface • *Its total surface area was seven thousand square feet.*

ANTONYM
● inside

outskirts PLURAL NOUN
the edges of an area • *the outskirts of New York*
edge • *We were on a hill, right on the edge of town.*
perimeter • *the perimeter of the airport*
periphery • *countries on the periphery of Europe*

MORE SYNONYMS
● environs
● purlieus

outspan VERB (SOUTH AFRICAN)
to relax • *Let's take a break and just outspan for a while.*
laze • *Fred lazed in an easy chair.*
relax • *I ought to relax and stop worrying.*
rest • *He rested for a while before starting work again.*
take it easy • *Try to take it easy for a week or two.*

outstanding ❶ ADJECTIVE
extremely good • *an outstanding tennis player*
brilliant • *a brilliant performance*
excellent • *the recording quality is excellent.*
exceptional • *children with exceptional ability*
first-class • *first-class service*
first-rate • *The show was first-rate.*
great • *great cultural achievements*
superb • *a superb 18-hole golf course*

Can't find the word you're looking for? Try the index.

A
B
C
D
E
F
G
H
I
J
K
L
M
N
O
P
Q
R
S
T
U
V
W
X
Y
Z

outstanding ② ADJECTIVE

still owed • *The total debt outstanding is $70 billion.*
due • *They sent me £100 and advised me that no further payment was due.*
overdue • *pay overdue salaries*
owing • *There is still some money owing for the rent.*
payable • *The amount payable is £175.*
unpaid • *a pile of unpaid bills*

over ① PREPOSITION

more than a particular amount • *It cost over a million dollars.*
above • *speeds above 50 mph*
exceeding • *a budget exceeding $700 million a year*
in excess of • *a fortune in excess of 150 million pounds*
more than • *The airport had been closed for more than a year.*

RELATED WORDS

● PREFIXES: hyper-, super-, supra-,
● sur-

over ② ADJECTIVE

completely finished • *I am glad it's all over.*
at an end • *The matter is now at an end.*
complete • *The work of restoring the farmhouse is complete.*
done • *When her deal is done, the client emerges with her purchase.*
finished • *once the season's finished*
gone • *Any chance of winning was now gone.*
past • *The time for loyalty is past.*
up • *when the six weeks were up*

overcome VERB

to manage to deal with something • *Molly had overcome her fear of flying.*

conquer • *He has never conquered his addiction to smoking.*
get the better of • *She didn't allow her emotions to get the better of her.*
master • *His genius alone has mastered every crisis.*
surmount • *I realized I had to surmount the language barrier.*
triumph over • *a symbol of good triumphing over evil*
vanquish (LITERARY) • *the man who helped vanquish Napoleon*

overlook VERB

to ignore or fail to notice something • *We tend to overlook warning signals about our health.*
disregard • *The police must not be allowed to disregard human rights.*
forget • *She never forgets his birthday.*
ignore • *For years her talents were ignored by the film industry.*
miss • *His searching eye never missed a detail.*
neglect • *She never neglects her duties.*
turn a blind eye to • *Are teachers turning a blind eye to these issues?*

overrule VERB

to reject a decision officially • *The Court of Appeal overruled this decision.*
overturn • *when the Russian parliament overturned his decision*
reverse • *They will not reverse the decision to increase prices.*

MORE SYNONYMS

● countermand
● override

oversee VERB

to make sure a job is done properly

a
b
c
d
e
f
g
h
i
j
k
l
m
n
o
p
q
r
s
t
u
v
w
x
y
z

Can't find the word you're looking for? Try the index.

• Get a supervisor to oversee the work.
be in charge of • *She is in charge of day-to-day operations.*
coordinate • *Government officials have been sent to coordinate the relief effort.*
direct • *his coolness in directing the rescue of the hostages*
manage • *Within two years, he was managing the project.*
preside • *Mr Brown will be presiding over the day's events.*
supervise • *He supervises the vineyards.*

overthrow VERB

to remove someone from power by force • *The government was overthrown in a military coup.*
bring down • *They brought down the government by withdrawing their support.*
depose • *He fled to Hawaii after being deposed as president.*
oust • *His opponents tried to oust him with a vote of no confidence.*
topple • *the revolution which toppled the regime*

overturn ❶ VERB

to knock something over • *Alex jumped up so violently that he overturned his glass.*
capsize • *I didn't count on his capsizing the raft.*
knock down • *Isabel rose so abruptly that she knocked down her chair.*
knock over • *Emma knocked over the box of cornflakes.*
tip over • *He tipped the table over in front of him.*
topple • *Winds and rain toppled trees and electricity lines.*
upset • *Don't upset the piles of sheets under the box.*

MORE SYNONYMS
● upend
● upturn

overturn ❷ VERB

to reject a decision officially • *when the Russian parliament overturned his decision*
overrule • *The Court of Appeal overruled this decision.*
reverse • *They will not reverse the decision to increase prices.*

MORE SYNONYMS
● countermand
● override

overweight ADJECTIVE

too fat, and therefore unhealthy • *Being overweight increases your risk of heart problems.*
fat • *I could eat what I liked without getting fat.*
hefty • *She was quite a hefty woman.*
obese • *Obese people tend to have higher blood pressure than lean people.*
stout • *a stout man with grey hair*

MORE SYNONYMS
● corpulent
● rotund

own ❶ ADJECTIVE

belonging to a particular person or thing • *She stayed in her own house.*
personal • *That's my personal opinion.*
private • *76 bedrooms, all with private bathrooms*

own ❷ VERB

to have something that belongs to you • *His father owns a local pub.*
have • *They have a house in France.*
keep • *His father kept a village shop.*

Can't find the word you're looking for? Try the index.

A B C D E F G H I J K L M N O P Q R S T U V W X Y Z

possess • *I would give her everything I possess.*

own ❸, on your own
ADVERB
without other people • *I work best on my own.*
alone • *She lives alone.*
by oneself • *I didn't know if I could raise a child by myself.*
independently • *several people working independently*
unaided • *She brought us up completely unaided.*

owner NOUN
the person to whom something belongs • *the owner of the store*
possessor • *the proud possessor of a truly incredible voice*
proprietor • *the proprietor of a local restaurant*

a
b
c
d
e
f
g
h
i
j
k
l
m
n
o
p
q
r
s
t
u
v
w
x
y
z

Can't find the word you're looking for? Try the index.

Pp

pacify VERB

to calm down someone who is angry • *She shrieked again, refusing to be pacified.*

appease • *The offer has not appeased separatists.*

calm • *A business lunch helped calm her nerves.*

mollify • *The investigation was undertaken to mollify pressure groups.*

placate • *He went aboard to placate the angry passengers.*

soothe • *She took him in her arms and soothed him.*

MORE SYNONYMS

- assuage
- propitiate

pain ➊ NOUN

an unpleasant feeling of physical hurt • *I felt a sharp pain in my lower back.*

ache • *Poor posture can cause neck aches.*

discomfort • *Steve had some discomfort but no real pain.*

irritation • *These oils may cause irritation to sensitive skin.*

soreness • *The soreness lasted for about six weeks.*

trouble • *back trouble*

twinge • *He felt a slight twinge in his hamstring.*

pain ➋ NOUN

a feeling of deep unhappiness • *the pain of rejection*

agony • *the agony of divorce*

anguish • *Mark looked at him in anguish.*

distress • *Jealousy causes distress and painful emotions.*

grief • *The grief soon gave way to anger.*

misery • *All that money brought nothing but sadness and misery.*

painful ➊ ADJECTIVE

causing emotional pain • *painful memories*

distressing • *one of the most distressing episodes in his life*

grievous • *Their loss would be a grievous blow to our industry.*

saddening • *a saddening experience*

unpleasant • *an unpleasant truth*

painful ➋ ADJECTIVE

causing physical pain • *a painful knock on the knee*

aching • *his aching joints*

excruciating • *an excruciating headache*

sore • *a sore throat*

tender • *My leg is very tender and sore.*

pale ADJECTIVE

rather white or without much colour • *Migrating birds filled the pale sky.*

ashen • *He fell back, shocked, his face ashen.*

colourless • *a colourless liquid*

faded • *a girl in faded jeans*

Can't find the word you're looking for? Try the index.

sallow • *His face was sallow and shiny with sweat.*
wan • *He looked wan and tired.*
white • *He turned white and began to stammer.*

panic ❶ NOUN
a very strong feeling of fear or anxiety • *The earthquake caused panic among the population.*
alarm • *She sat up in alarm.*
dismay • *She discovered to her dismay that she was pregnant.*
fear • *my fear of the dark*
fright • *To hide my fright I asked a question.*
hysteria • *mass hysteria*
terror • *She shook with terror.*

panic ❷ VERB
to become afraid or anxious • *Guests panicked when the bomb exploded.*
become hysterical • *Miss Brady became hysterical when he produced the gun.*
go to pieces • *England went to pieces when they conceded a goal.*
lose your nerve • *They lost their nerve and pulled out of the deal.*

parade NOUN
a line of people moving as a display • *A military parade marched through the streets.*
cavalcade • *a cavalcade of limousines and police motorcycles*
march • *Organizers expect 300,000 protesters to join the march.*
pageant • *a traditional Christmas pageant*
procession • *religious processions*
tattoo • *the world-famous Edinburgh military tattoo*

paragraph NOUN

> **PARTS OF A PARAGRAPH**
>
> clause   sentence
> phrase   word

paralyse VERB
to make someone lose feeling and movement • *Her sister had been paralysed in a road accident.*
cripple • *He heaved his crippled leg into an easier position.*
disable • *He was disabled by polio.*

parent NOUN
your father or your mother • *I told my parents I was moving out.*
father • *Her father was furious.*
mother • *the mother of two girls*
old (AUSTRALIAN AND NEW ZEALAND; INFORMAL) • *a visit to the olds*
patriarch • *a domineering patriarch*

parody NOUN
an amusing imitation of someone else's style • *a parody of an American sitcom*
imitation • *I can do a pretty good imitation of him.*
satire • *a sharp satire on the American political process*
spoof (INFORMAL) • *a spoof on Hollywood life*
takeoff (INFORMAL) • *She did a brilliant takeoff of the Queen.*

MORE SYNONYMS
● lampoon
● skit

part ❶ NOUN
a piece or section of something • *I like that part of Edinburgh.*
bit • *a bit of paper*
fraction • *a fraction of a second*
fragment • *fragments of glass*
piece • *a piece of cheese*

a
b
c
d
e
f
g
h
i
j
k
l
m
n
o
p
q
r
s
t
u
v
w
x
y
z

Can't find the word you're looking for? Try the index.

portion • *Damage was confined to a small portion of the castle.*
section • *a large orchestra, with a vast percussion section*

part ❷ NOUN

a person's involvement in something • *He tried to conceal his part in the accident.*
capacity • *He has served the club in many capacities.*
duty • *My duty is to look after the animals.*
function • *Their main function is to raise capital for industry.*
involvement • *You have no proof of my involvement in anything.*
role • *the drug's role in preventing infection*

part ❸, take part in VERB

to do something with other people • *Thousands took part in the demonstrations.*
be instrumental in • *He was instrumental in tracking down the killers.*
be involved in • *My grandparents were involved in the Methodist church.*
have a hand in • *He had a hand in three of the goals.*
join in • *I hope that everyone will be able to join in the fun.*
participate in • *They expected him to participate in the ceremony.*
play a part in • *He continued to play a part in drug operations from prison.*

participate VERB

to take part in an activity • *Over half the population participate in sport.*
be involved in • *HMS Cardiff was also involved in the exercise.*
engage in • *They have refused to engage in all-party talks.*
enter into • *We entered into discussions with them weeks ago.*
join in • *Their rivals refused to join in any price war.*
take part • *The oldest car taking part was built in 1907.*

particular ❶ ADJECTIVE

relating to only one thing or person • *That particular place is dangerous.*
distinct • *The book is divided into two distinct parts.*
exact • *Do you think I could get the exact thing I want?*
express • *I bought the camera for the express purpose of taking railway photographs.*
peculiar • *This is not a problem peculiar to London.*
precise • *the precise location of the ship*
specific • *There are several specific problems to be dealt with.*

particular ❷ ADJECTIVE

especially great or intense • *Pay particular attention to the forehead.*
exceptional • *children with exceptional ability*
marked • *a marked increase in crime in the area*
notable • *Two other notable events took place last week.*
singular • *It was a goal of singular brilliance.*
special • *a special occasion*
uncommon • *Both are blessed with an uncommon ability to fix things.*

MORE SYNONYMS

- especial
- noteworthy

particular ❸ ADJECTIVE

not easily satisfied • *Ted was very particular about the colours he used.*

Can't find the word you're looking for? Try the index.

choosy (INFORMAL) • *Skiers should be choosy about the insurance policy they buy.*

exacting • *exacting standards of craftsmanship*

fastidious • *He was fastidious about his appearance.*

fussy • *She is very fussy about her food.*

meticulous • *meticulous attention to detail*

partly ADVERB

to some extent but not completely • *This is partly my fault.*

in part (FORMAL) • *The levels of blood glucose depend in part on what you eat.*

in some measure (FORMAL) • *Power is in some measure an act of will.*

partially • *Jo is partially sighted.*

to some degree • *These statements are, to some degree, correct.*

to some extent • *Her concern is, to some extent, understandable.*

partner ❶ NOUN

either member of a couple in a relationship • *My partner moved in with me last year.*

husband • *Are husbands and wives included in the invitation?*

wife • *His wife is a lawyer.*

mate • *She has found her ideal mate.*

spouse • *Anything left to your spouse is free from inheritance tax.*

partner ❷ NOUN

the person someone is doing something with • *my tennis partner*

companion • *her travelling companion*

team-mate • *his team-mate at Ferrari*

part of speech NOUN

PARTS OF SPEECH	
adjective	preposition
adverb	pronoun
conjunction	reflexive verb
noun	verb
plural noun	

party ❶ NOUN

a social event where people enjoy themselves • *Most teenagers like to go to parties.*

celebration • *a New Year's Eve celebration*

function • *a charity function at the hotel*

gathering • *a gathering of friends and relatives*

get-together (INFORMAL) • *a family get-together*

hooley or **hoolie** (NEW ZEALAND, SCOTS AND IRISH) • *a hooley down on the beach*

reception • *a wedding reception*

party ❷ NOUN

an organization for people with the same political beliefs • *his resignation as party leader*

alliance • *The two parties have agreed to form an electoral alliance.*

clique • *the clique attached to Prime Minister*

coalition • *a coalition of right-wing and religious factions*

faction • *the party's small pro-European faction*

grouping • *two main political groupings pressing for independence*

party ❸ NOUN

a group who are doing something together • *a research party of scientists*

band • *a small but dedicated band of supporters*

a b c d e f g h i j k l m n o **p** q r s t u v w x y z

Can't find the word you're looking for? Try the index.

crew • *a ship's crew*
gang • *a gang of criminals*
squad • *the West Indies squad to tour Australia*
team • *Each consultant has a team of doctors under him.*
unit • *the health services research unit*

pass ❶ VERB

to exceed or go past something • *He gave a triumphant wave as he passed the winning post.*
exceed • *The demand for places at some schools exceeds the supply.*
go beyond • *Did your relationship go beyond a close friendship?*
outdo • *The Colombian fans outdid the home supporters in fervour.*
outstrip • *Demand continues to outstrip supply.*
overtake • *Britain's lottery will this year overtake Japan's as the world's biggest.*
surpass • *He was determined to surpass the achievements of his brothers.*

pass ❷ VERB

to be successful in a test • *Wendy has just passed her driving test.*
get through • *I got through my banking exams last year.*
graduate • *He graduated in engineering.*
qualify • *I qualified as a doctor.*
succeed • *the skills and qualities needed to succeed*

ANTONYM
● fail

pass ❸ NOUN

a document that allows you to go somewhere • *Don't let any cars onto the land unless they've got a pass.*

identification • *Passport control asked me if I had any further identification.*
passport • *You should take your passport with you when changing money.*
ticket • *I'm not going to renew my season ticket.*

passage ❶ NOUN

a space that connects two places • *He cleared a passage for himself through the crammed streets.*
channel • *a drainage channel*
course • *the river's twisting course*
path • *A group of reporters blocked the path.*
road • *the road between Jerusalem and Bethlehem*
route • *the most direct route to the town centre*
way • *This is the way in.*

passage ❷ NOUN

a narrow space that connects one place with another • *up some stairs and along a narrow passage towards a door*
aisle • *the frozen food aisle*
corridor • *They sat crowded together in the hospital corridor.*
hall • *The lights were on in the hall and in the bedroom.*
lobby • *the cramped pitch-dark lobby*

passage ❸ NOUN

a section of a book or piece of music • *a passage from the Bible*
excerpt • *an excerpt from her speech*
extract • *an extract from his new book*
quotation • *a favourite quotation from St Augustine*
section • *a section from the first movement of Beethoven's Eroica symphony*

Can't find the word you're looking for? Try the index.

passion ❶ NOUN
a strong feeling of physical
attraction • *the passion had gone
from their relationship*
desire • *sexual desire*
infatuation • *Daisy's infatuation
with the doctor*
love • *our love for each other*
lust • *He is obsessed by his lust for
her.*

passion ❷ NOUN
any strong emotion • *He spoke
with great passion.*
emotion • *Her voice trembled with
emotion.*
excitement • *I was in a state of
great excitement.*
fire • *His speeches were full of fire.*
intensity • *His intensity alarmed me.*
warmth • *He greeted us both with
warmth and affection.*
zeal • *his zeal for teaching*

passionate ADJECTIVE
expressing very strong feelings
about something • *I'm a
passionate believer in public art.*
ardent • *ardent supporters of
capital punishment*
emotional • *an emotional farewell*
heartfelt • *My heartfelt sympathy
goes out to all the relatives.*
impassioned • *He made an
impassioned appeal for peace.*
intense • *intense hatred*
strong • *Many viewers have strong
opinions about violence on TV.*

passive ADJECTIVE
submissive or not playing an active
part • *His passive attitude made
things easier for me.*
docile • *docile, obedient children*
receptive • *The voters had seemed
receptive to his ideas.*
resigned • *She was already

resigned to losing her home.*
submissive • *Most doctors want
their patients to be submissive.*

MORE SYNONYMS
- acquiescent
- compliant
- inactive
- quiescent

past ❶, the past NOUN
the period of time before the
present • *We would like to put the
past behind us.*
antiquity • *famous monuments of
classical antiquity*
days gone by • *This brings back
memories of days gone by.*
former times • *In former times he
would have been clapped in irons.*
long ago • *The old men told stories
of long ago.*

past ❷ ADJECTIVE
happening or existing before the
present • *details of his past activities*
ancient • *ancient history*
bygone • *a bygone era*
former • *Remember him as he was
in his former years.*
olden • *We were talking about the
olden days on his farm.*
previous • *She has a teenage
daughter from a previous marriage.*

MORE SYNONYMS
- erstwhile
- quondam

ANTONYM
- future

past ❸ PREPOSITION
situated on the other side of
somewhere • *It's just past the
church there.*
beyond • *Beyond the garden was a
small orchard.*

a
b
c
d
e
f
g
h
i
j
k
l
m
n
o
p
q
r
s
t
u
v
w
x
y
z

Can't find the word you're looking for? Try the index.

by • *He walked by her house every day.*

over • *He lived in the house over the road.*

pastime NOUN

a hobby or something done for pleasure • *His favourite pastime is snooker.*

activity • *activities range from canoeing to birdwatching*

diversion • *Finger painting is very messy but an excellent diversion.*

hobby • *My hobbies are squash and swimming.*

recreation • *Saturday afternoon is for recreation and outings.*

path ❶ NOUN

a strip of ground for people to walk on • *We followed the paths along the clifftops.*

footpath • *It is accessible only by footpath.*

pathway • *a pathway leading towards the nearby river*

towpath • *He took a cycle trip along a canal towpath.*

track • *We set off over a rough mountain track.*

trail • *He was following a broad trail through the trees.*

way • *the Pennine Way*

path ❷ NOUN

the space ahead of someone as they move along • *A group of reporters stood in his path.*

course • *obstacles blocking our course*

direction • *St Andrews was 10 miles in the opposite direction.*

passage • *Two men elbowed a passage through the shoppers.*

route • *All escape routes were blocked by armed police.*

way • *Get out of my way!*

pathetic ❶ ADJECTIVE

causing someone to feel pity • *She now looked small, shrunken, and pathetic.*

heartbreaking • *a heartbreaking succession of miscarriages*

sad • *He seemed a rather sad figure.*

MORE SYNONYMS

● pitiable
● plaintive

pathetic ❷ ADJECTIVE

very poor or unsuccessful
• *pathetic excuses*

feeble • *This is a particularly feeble argument.*

lamentable • *a lamentable display by the league leaders*

pitiful • *They are paid pitiful wages.*

poor • *The flat was in a poor state of repair.*

sorry • *Their oil industry is in a sorry state.*

patience NOUN

the ability to stay calm in a difficult situation • *It was exacting work and required all his patience.*

calmness • *calmness under pressure*

composure • *He regained his composure and went on to win the match.*

cool (SLANG) • *The big Irishman was on the verge of losing his cool.*

restraint • *They behaved with more restraint than I'd expected.*

tolerance • *a low tolerance of errors*

MORE SYNONYMS

● equanimity
● forbearance
● imperturbability

Can't find the word you're looking for? Try the index.

A B C D E F G H I J K L M N O **P** Q R S T U V W X Y Z

patient ❶ ADJECTIVE
staying calm in a difficult situation
• *Please be patient - your cheque will arrive.*
calm • *She is usually a calm and diplomatic woman.*
composed • *a composed and charming manner*
long-suffering • *long-suffering train commuters*
philosophical • *He is philosophical about the defeat.*
serene • *She looks dreamily into the distance, serene, calm and happy.*

ANTONYM
● impatient

patient ❷ NOUN
a person receiving medical treatment • *patients who wish to change their doctor*
case • *He is a suitable case for treatment.*
invalid • *elderly invalids*
sick person • *a ward full of very sick people*
sufferer • *asthma sufferers*

pattern ❶ NOUN
a decorative design of repeated shapes • *red and purple thread stitched into a pattern of flames*
design • *tableware decorated with a blackberry design*
motif • *a rose motif*

pattern ❷ NOUN
a diagram or shape used as a guide for making something • *sewing patterns*
design • *They drew up the design for the house in a week.*
diagram • *Follow the diagram on page 20.*
plan • *a plan of the garden*
stencil • *flower stencils*

template • *Make a paper template of the seat of the chair.*

pause ❶ VERB
to stop doing something for a short time • *On leaving, she paused for a moment at the door.*
break • *They broke for lunch.*
delay • *Various problems delayed the launch.*
halt • *Striking workers halted production at the plant.*
rest • *He rested briefly before pressing on.*
take a break • *He needs to take a break from work.*
wait • *I waited to see how she responded.*

pause ❷ NOUN
a short period when activity stops
• *There was a pause while the barmaid set down two plates.*
break • *Do you want to have a little break?*
halt • *Agricultural production was brought to a halt.*
interruption • *The sudden interruption stopped her in mid-flow.*
interval • *I had a drink during the interval.*
rest • *I think he's due for a rest now.*
stoppage • *Miners have voted for a one-day stoppage next month.*

MORE SYNONYMS
● caesura
● entr'acte

pay ❶ VERB
to give money to someone to settle a debt • *You can pay by credit card.*
compensate • *Farmers could be compensated for their loss of subsidies.*
honour • *The bank refused to honour the cheque.*
settle • *I settled the bill for our drinks.*

Can't find the word you're looking for? Try the index.

a b c d e f g h i j k l m n o **p** q r s t u v w x y z

A
B
C
D
E
F
G
H
I
J
K
L
M
N
O
P
Q
R
S
T
U
V
W
X
Y
Z

MORE SYNONYMS
- recompense
- reimburse
- remunerate

pay ❷ VERB
to give someone a benefit • *It pays to be honest.*
be advantageous • *It is easy to imagine cases where cheating is advantageous.*
be worthwhile • *He believed the operation had been worthwhile.*

pay ❸ NOUN
money paid to someone for work done • *their complaints about pay and conditions*
earnings • *his earnings as an accountant*
fee • *solicitors' fees*
income • *a modest income*
payment • *a redundancy payment*
salary • *The lawyer was paid a good salary.*
wages • *His wages have gone up.*

MORE SYNONYMS
- emolument
- recompense
- reimbursement
- remuneration
- stipend

payment NOUN
an amount of money that is paid to someone • *mortgage payments*
advance • *She was paid a £100,000 advance for her next two novels.*
deposit • *A $50 deposit is required when ordering.*
instalment • *The first instalment is payable on application.*
premium • *higher insurance premiums*
remittance • *Please make your*

remittance payable in sterling.

peace ❶ NOUN
a state of undisturbed calm and quiet • *They left me in peace to recover from the funeral.*
calm • *the rural calm of Grand Rapids, Michigan*
quiet • *He wants some peace and quiet before his match.*
silence • *They stood in silence.*
stillness • *An explosion shattered the stillness of the night air.*
tranquillity • *The hotel is a haven of tranquillity.*

MORE SYNONYMS
- quietude
- repose

peace ❷ NOUN
freedom from war • *The people do not believe that the leaders want peace.*
armistice • *the armistice between North Korea and the United Nations*
cessation of hostilities • *a resolution calling for an immediate cessation of hostilities*
truce • *an uneasy truce between the two sides*

ANTONYM
- war

peaceful ADJECTIVE
quiet and calm • *a peaceful house in the heart of the countryside*
calm • *a calm spot amid the bustle of the city*
placid • *the placid waters of Lake Erie*
quiet • *The street was unnaturally quiet.*
serene • *a beautiful, serene park*
still • *In the room it was very still.*
tranquil • *the tranquil paradise of his native Antigua*

Can't find the word you're looking for? Try the index.

peak ❶ NOUN

the point at which something is at its greatest or best • *the peak of the morning rush hour*

climax • *The tournament is building up to a dramatic climax.*

culmination • *The marriage was the culmination of an eight-month romance.*

high point • *The high point of this trip was a day at the races.*

zenith • *His career is now at its zenith.*

MORE SYNONYMS

- acme
- apogee
- ne plus ultra

peak ❷ NOUN

the pointed top of a mountain • *snow-covered peaks*

brow • *He overtook a car as he approached the brow of a hill.*

crest • *Burns was clear over the crest of the hill.*

pinnacle • *He plunged 25 metres from a rocky pinnacle.*

summit • *the first man to reach the summit of Mount Everest*

top • *the top of Mount Sinai*

MORE SYNONYMS

- aiguille
- apex

peak ❸ VERB

to reach the highest point or greatest level • *His career peaked during the 1970s.*

be at its height • *when trade union power was at its height*

climax • *a tour that climaxed with a three-night stint at Wembley Arena*

come to a head • *The siege came to a head with the death of a marshal.*

culminate • *The celebration of the centenary will culminate with a dinner.*

reach its highest point • *The stockmarket reached its highest point since the 1987 crash.*

peculiar ❶ ADJECTIVE

strange and perhaps unpleasant • *a very peculiar sense of humour*

bizarre • *bizarre behaviour*

curious • *a curious mixture of the ancient and modern*

funny • *Children get some funny ideas sometimes.*

odd • *Something odd began to happen.*

queer • *There's something queer going on.*

strange • *There was something strange about the flickering blue light.*

weird • *It must be weird to be so rich.*

peculiar ❷ ADJECTIVE

associated with one particular person or thing • *He has his own peculiar way of doing things.*

distinctive • *She has a very distinctive laugh.*

distinguishing • *Does he have any distinguishing features?*

individual • *all part of her very individual personality*

personal • *cultivating their own personal style*

special • *Everyone has their own special problems or fears.*

unique • *a feature unique to humans*

ANOTHER SYNONYM

- idiosyncratic

peek ❶ VERB

to have a quick look at something

a
b
c
d
e
f
g
h
i
j
k
l
m
n
o
p
q
r
s
t
u
v
w
x
y
z

Can't find the word you're looking for? Try the index.

A
B
C
D
E
F
G
H
I
J
K
L
M
N
O
P
Q
R
S
T
U
V
W
X
Y
Z

• *She peeked at him through a crack in the wall.*
glance • *He glanced at his watch.*
peep • *Children came to peep at him round the doorway.*
snatch a glimpse • *Spectators lined the route to snatch a glimpse of the Queen.*
sneak a look • *We sneaked a look at his diary.*

peek ❷ NOUN
a quick look at something • *He took his first peek at the new course yesterday.*
glance • *Trevor and I exchanged a glance.*
glimpse • *Some people had waited all day to catch a glimpse of her.*
look • *She took a last look in the mirror.*
peep • *He took a peep at his watch.*

pent-up ADJECTIVE
held back for a long time without release • *She had a lot of pent-up anger to release.*
inhibited • *inhibited sexuality*
repressed • *repressed hostility*
suppressed • *Deep sleep allowed suppressed anxieties to surface.*

people ❶ PLURAL NOUN
men, women, and children • *Millions of people have lost their homes.*
human beings • *The disease can be transmitted to human beings.*
humanity • *crimes against humanity*
humans • *millions of years before humans appeared on earth*
mankind • *the evolution of mankind*

people ❷ PLURAL NOUN
all the men, women, and children of a particular place • *It's a triumph*

for the American people.
citizens • *the citizens of New York City*
inhabitants • *the inhabitants of Hong Kong*
population • *Africa's rapidly rising population*
public • *the British public*

perceptive ADJECTIVE
good at noticing or realizing things • *a perceptive account of the poet's life*
acute • *His relaxed exterior hides an extremely acute mind.*
astute • *He made a series of astute business decisions.*
aware • *They are politically very aware.*
penetrating • *He never stopped asking penetrating questions.*
sharp • *He has a sharp eye and an excellent memory.*

MORE SYNONYMS
- insightful
- percipient
- perspicacious

perfect ❶ ADJECTIVE
of the highest standard and without fault • *His English was perfect.*
expert • *There is a great deal to learn from his expert approach.*
faultless • *faultless technique*
flawless • *her flawless complexion*
masterly • *a masterly performance*
polished • *polished promotional skills*
skilled • *a skilled repair job*

ANTONYM
- imperfect

perfect ❷ ADJECTIVE
complete or absolute • *They have a perfect right to say so.*

Can't find the word you're looking for? Try the index.

absolute • *absolute nonsense*
complete • *The resignation came as a complete surprise.*
consummate • *He acted the part with consummate skill.*
sheer • *an act of sheer desperation*
unmitigated • *Last year's crop was an unmitigated disaster.*
utter • *utter nonsense*

perfect ❸ VERB
to make something as good as it can be • *The technique was perfected during the 1960s.*
hone • *a chance to hone their skills*
improve • *Their French has improved enormously.*
polish • *He spent time polishing the script.*
refine • *Surgical techniques are constantly being refined.*

perform ❶ VERB
to carry out a task or action • *people who have performed acts of bravery*
carry out • *Police believe the attacks were carried out by nationalists.*
complete • *He completed the test in record time.*
do • *He crashed trying to do a tricky manoeuvre.*
execute • *The landing was skilfully executed.*
fulfil • *Fulfil the tasks you have been allocated.*

perform ❷ VERB
to act, dance, or play music in public • *students performing Shakespeare's Macbeth*
act • *acting in Tarantino's films*
do • *I've always wanted to do a one-man show on Broadway.*
play • *His ambition is to play the part of Dracula.*

present • *The company is presenting a new production of 'Hamlet'.*
put on • *The band are hoping to put on a UK show.*
stage • *The group staged their first play in the late 1970s.*

perhaps ADVERB
maybe • *Perhaps you're right.*
conceivably • *The mission could conceivably be accomplished in a week.*
it could be • *It could be he's upset at what you said.*
maybe • *Maybe she is in love.*
possibly • *Do you think that he could possibly be right?*

period NOUN
a particular length of time • *a period of a few months*
interval • *a long interval when no-one spoke*
spell • *a long spell of dry weather*
stretch • *an 18-month stretch in the army*
term • *a 5-year prison term*
time • *At 15 he left home for a short time.*
while • *I haven't seen him for a long while.*

permanent ADJECTIVE
lasting for ever or present all the time • *a permanent solution to the problem*
abiding • *one of his abiding interests*
constant • *Inflation is a constant threat.*
enduring • *an enduring friendship*
eternal • *the quest for eternal youth*
lasting • *We are well on our way to a lasting peace.*
perpetual • *a perpetual source of worry*

a
b
c
d
e
f
g
h
i
j
k
l
m
n
o
p
q
r
s
t
u
v
w
x
y
z

Can't find the word you're looking for? Try the index.

A
B
C
D
E
F
G
H
I
J
K
L
M
N
O
P
Q
R
S
T
U
V
W
X
Y
Z

MORE SYNONYMS
- immutable
- imperishable
- steadfast

ANTONYM
- temporary

permission NOUN
authorization to do something • *He asked permission to leave the room.*
approval • *The plan will require official approval.*
assent • *He requires the assent of parliament.*
authorization • *his request for authorization to use military force*
consent • *Can she be examined without my consent?*
go-ahead • *The government gave the go-ahead for five major road schemes.*
licence • *He has given me licence to do the job as I see fit.*

ANTONYM
- ban

permit ❶ VERB
to allow something or make it possible • *The guards permitted me to bring my camera.*
allow • *Smoking will not be allowed.*
authorize • *They are expected to authorize the use of military force.*
enable • *The test should enable doctors to detect the disease early.*
give the green light to • *He has been given the green light to resume training.*
grant • *Permission was granted a few weeks ago.*
sanction • *The chairman will not sanction a big-money signing.*

ANTONYM
- ban

permit ❷ NOUN
an official document allowing someone to do something • *a work permit*
authorization • *We didn't have authorization to go.*
licence • *a driving licence*
pass • *a rail pass*
passport • *My passport expires next year.*
permission • *Permission for the march has not been granted.*
warrant • *Police issued a warrant for his arrest.*

persecute VERB
to treat someone with continual cruelty and unfairness • *The Communists began by brutally persecuting the Church.*
hound • *He has been hounded by the press.*
ill-treat • *They thought Mr Smith had been ill-treating his wife.*
oppress • *Minorities here have been oppressed for generations.*
pick on • *She was repeatedly picked on by the manager.*
torment • *They were tormented by other pupils.*
torture • *He would not torture her further by trying to argue with her.*

person NOUN
a man, woman, or child • *The amount of sleep we need varies from person to person.*
human • *the common ancestor of humans and the great apes*
human being • *This protein occurs naturally in human beings.*
individual • *the rights and responsibilities of the individual*
living soul • *The nearest living soul was 20 miles away.*
soul • *a tiny village of only 100 souls*

personal ADJECTIVE
belonging to a particular person or thing • *personal belongings*
individual • *Divide the vegetables among four individual dishes.*
own • *My wife decided I should have my own shop.*
particular • *his own particular style of preaching*
peculiar • *her own peculiar talents*
private • *my private life*
special • *Every person will have his or her own special problems.*

personality ❶ NOUN
a person's character and nature • *She has such a kind, friendly personality.*
character • *a negative side to his character*
identity • *our own sense of cultural identity*
individuality • *People should be free to express their individuality.*
make-up • *There was some fundamental flaw in his make-up.*
nature • *She trusted people. That was her nature.*
psyche • *disturbing elements of the human psyche*

personality ❷ NOUN
a famous person in entertainment or sport • *television personalities*
big name • *the big names in French cinema*
celebrity • *Hollywood celebrities*
famous name • *a famous name from Inter Milan's past*
household name • *The TV series that made him a household name.*
star • *film stars*

persuade VERB
to make someone do something by reason or charm • *He persuaded the company to sign her up.*

bring round (INFORMAL) • *We will do what we can to bring them round to our point of view.*
coax • *She coaxed Bobby into talking about himself.*
induce • *I would do anything to induce them to stay.*
sway • *Don't ever be swayed by fashion.*
talk into • *He talked me into marrying him.*
win over • *By the end of the day he had won over the crowd.*

MORE SYNONYMS
● impel
● inveigle

perverted ADJECTIVE
practising abnormal and unacceptable behaviour • *She has been a victim of perverted phone calls and letters.*
depraved • *the work of depraved and evil criminals*
deviant • *Not all drug abusers produce deviant offspring.*
immoral • *those who think that birth control is immoral*
unhealthy • *His interest developed into an unhealthy obsession.*

MORE SYNONYMS
● debauched
● vitiated

pessimistic ADJECTIVE
believing that bad things will happen • *a pessimistic view of life*
despondent • *despondent about their children's future*
gloomy • *a gloomy view of the future*
glum • *They are not entirely glum about the car industry's prospects.*
hopeless • *Even able pupils feel hopeless about job prospects.*

a
b
c
d
e
f
g
h
i
j
k
l
m
n
o
p
q
r
s
t
u
v
w
x
y
z

Can't find the word you're looking for? Try the index.

ANTONYM
- optimistic

pest ❶ NOUN
an insect or animal that damages
crops or livestock • *10% of the crop
was lost to a pest called corn
rootworm.*
bane • *The bane of farmers across
the country is the badger.*
blight • *potato blight*
scourge • *This parasitic mite is the
scourge of honey bees.*

pest ❷ NOUN
an annoying person • *I didn't want
to be a cry baby or a pest.*
bane • *Student journalists were the
bane of my life.*
bore • *I don't enjoy his company.
He's a bore and a fool.*
nuisance • *He could be a bit of a
nuisance when he was drunk.*
pain (INFORMAL) • *She's been a real
pain recently.*
pain in the neck (INFORMAL) • *I've
always been a pain in the neck to
publishers.*

pester VERB
to bother someone continually
• *He gets fed up with people
pestering him for money.*
annoy • *She kept on annoying me.*
badger • *She badgered her doctor
time and again.*
bother • *We are playing a trick on
a man who keeps bothering me.*
bug (INFORMAL) • *Stop bugging
me.*
drive someone up the wall
(SLANG) • *I sang in the bath and
drove my sister up the wall.*
get on someone's nerves
(INFORMAL) • *I was beginning to get
on her nerves.*

MORE SYNONYMS
- bedevil
- chivvy

petty ❶ ADJECTIVE
small and unimportant • *endless
rules and petty regulations*
insignificant • *In 1949, Bonn was
a small, insignificant city.*
measly (INFORMAL) • *The average
bathroom measures a measly 3.5
square metres.*
trifling • *The sums involved are
trifling.*
trivial • *trivial details*
unimportant • *It was an
unimportant job, and paid very little*

petty ❷ ADJECTIVE
selfish and small-minded • *I think
that attitude is a bit petty.*
cheap • *politicians making cheap
political points*
mean • *I'd feel mean saying no.*
small-minded • *their small-
minded preoccupation with making
money*

phoney ADJECTIVE (INFORMAL)
false and intended to deceive
• *a phoney accent*
bogus • *a bogus insurance claim*
counterfeit • *counterfeit currency*
fake • *fake certificates*
false • *a false name and address*
forged • *forged documents*
sham • *a sham marriage*

MORE SYNONYMS
- feigned
- spurious

ANTONYM
- genuine

pick ❶ VERB
to choose something • *He picked ten
people to interview for six sales jobs.*

choose • *There are several options to choose from.*
decide upon • *He decided upon a career in publishing.*
hand-pick • *He was hand-picked for his job by the Admiral.*
opt for • *I think we should opt for a more cautious approach.*
select • *the party's policy of selecting candidates*
settle on • *I finally settled on an Audi TT roadster.*

pick ❷ VERB
to remove a flower or fruit with your fingers • *He helps his mother pick fruit.*
gather • *We spent the afternoon gathering berries.*
harvest • *Many farmers are refusing to harvest the cane.*
pluck • *I plucked a lemon from the tree.*

pick ❸ NOUN
the best • *the pick of the country's young athletes*
elite • *the elite of women's tennis*
flower • *the flower of Polish manhood*
pride • *the hovercraft, once the pride of British maritime engineering*

pick on VERB
to criticize someone unfairly or treat them unkindly • *Bullies pick on younger children.*
bait • *He delighted in baiting his mother.*
tease • *He teased me mercilessly about going to Hollywood.*
torment • *They were tormented by other pupils.*

picture ❶ NOUN
a drawing, painting, or photograph • *It's got a picture of me on the cover.*

drawing • *She did a drawing of me.*
illustration • *Tolkien's illustrations for The Hobbit*
painting • *his collection of Impressionist paintings*
photograph • *He wants to take some photographs of the house.*
portrait • *Velazquez's portrait of Pope Innocent X*
sketch • *pencil sketches*

RELATED WORD
 ADJECTIVE: pictorial

picture ❷ VERB
to imagine something clearly • *He pictured her with long black hair.*
conceive of • *I can't conceive of doing work that doesn't interest me.*
imagine • *It's difficult to imagine anything coming between them.*
see • *A good idea, but can you see Taylor trying it?*
visualize • *He could not visualize her as old.*

MORE SYNONYMS
 envision
 see in the mind's eye

piece ❶ NOUN
a portion or part of something • *a piece of cheese*
bit • *a bit of paper*
chunk • *He was accused of stealing a tin of pineapple chunks.*
fragment • *There were fragments of cork in the wine.*
part • *The engine has got only three moving parts.*
portion • *Damage was confined to a small portion of the castle.*
slice • *a slice of bread*

piece ❷ NOUN
something that has been written, created, or composed • *his piece on fox hunting*

Can't find the word you're looking for? Try the index.

a b c d e f g h i j k l m n o **p** q r s t u v w x y z

article • *a newspaper article*
composition • *Schubert's piano compositions*
creation • *the fashion designer's latest creations*
study • *Leonardo's studies of horsemen*
work • *In my opinion, this is Rembrandt's greatest work.*

piece together VERB
to assemble things or parts to make something complete
• *Doctors painstakingly pieced together the broken bones.*
assemble • *He is assembling evidence concerning a murder.*
join • *Join all the sections together.*
mend • *I should have had it mended, but never got round to it.*
patch together • *A hasty deal was patched together.*
repair • *the cost of repairing earthquake damage*
restore • *The trust is playing a leading part in restoring old cinemas.*

pierce VERB
to make a hole in something with a sharp instrument • *Pierce the potato with a fork.*
bore • *tunnels bored into the foundations of the building*
drill • *I drilled five holes at equal distance.*
lance • *It's a painful experience having the boil lanced.*
penetrate • *The Earth's atmosphere was penetrated by a meteor.*
puncture • *The bullet punctured the skull.*

pig NOUN
a farm animal kept for meat • *the number of pigs at the trough*
hog • *He's as fat as a hog.*

piggy (INFORMAL) • *These two piggies are going to market!*
porker • *a 30kg Vietnamese potbellied porker*
swine • *herds of oxen, sheep and swine*

RELATED WORDS
● ADJECTIVE: porcine
● MALE: boar
● FEMALE: sow
● YOUNG: piglet
● COLLECTIVE NOUN: litter
● HABITATION: sty

pile ❶ NOUN
a quantity of things lying one on top of another • *a pile of books*
heap • *a compost heap*
hoard • *a hoard of jewels*
mound • *The bulldozers piled up huge mounds of dirt.*
mountain • *They have mountains of coffee to sell.*
stack • *a stack of magazines on the table*

pile ❷ NOUN
the raised fibres of a soft surface • *the carpet's thick pile*
down • *The whole plant is covered with fine down.*
fur • *This creature's fur is short and dense.*
nap • *The cotton is lightly brushed to heighten the nap.*

pile ❸ VERB
to put things one on top of another • *A few newspapers were piled on the table.*
heap • *She heaped more carrots onto his plate.*
hoard • *They've begun to hoard petrol and food.*
stack • *They are stacked neatly in piles of three.*

Can't find the word you're looking for? Try the index.

pink NOUN OR ADJECTIVE

SHADES OF PINK	
coral	rose
flesh	salmon
fuchsia	shell pink
oyster pink	shocking pink

pit NOUN
a large hole in something • *He lost his footing and began to slide into the pit.*
chasm • *The coach plunged down the chasm.*
hole • *The builders had cut holes into the soft stone.*
pothole • *She was seriously injured when she fell 90 feet down a pothole.*

pity ❶ VERB
to feel sorry for someone • *I don't know whether to hate or pity him.*
feel for • *She cried on the phone and I really felt for her.*
feel sorry for • *This is my biggest win but I don't feel sorry for the bookies.*
sympathize with • *I sympathize with you for your loss.*

pity ❷ NOUN
sympathy for other people's suffering • *She saw no pity in their faces.*
charity • *They showed a lack of charity and understanding to her.*
compassion • *his compassion for a helpless woman*
kindness • *He was treated with kindness by numerous officials.*
mercy • *Neither side showed any mercy.*
sympathy • *We expressed our sympathy for his loss.*
understanding • *We would like to thank them for their patience and understanding.*

MORE SYNONYMS
● clemency
● forbearance

pity ❸ NOUN
a regrettable fact • *It's a pity they can't all have the same opportunities.*
crime (INFORMAL) • *It would be a crime to travel to Australia and not stop in Sydney.*
crying shame • *It would be a crying shame to split up a winning partnership.*
shame • *It's a shame it had to close.*

place ❶ NOUN
any point or area • *The pain is always in the same place.*
area • *a picnic area*
location • *The first thing he looked at was his office's location.*
point • *The pain originated from a point in his right thigh.*
position • *the ship's position*
site • *a bat sanctuary with special nesting sites*
spot • *the island's top tourist spots*

place ❷, take place VERB
to happen • *The meeting took place on Thursday.*
come about • *That came about when we went to Glastonbury last year.*
go on • *This has been going on for around a year.*
happen • *We cannot say for sure what will happen.*
occur • *The crash occurred when the crew shut down the wrong engine.*

place ❸ VERB
to put something somewhere • *Chairs were placed in rows for the parents.*

a
b
c
d
e
f
g
h
i
j
k
l
m
n
o
p
q
r
s
t
u
v
w
x
y
z

Can't find the word you're looking for? Try the index.

deposit • *Imagine if you were suddenly deposited on a desert island.*

locate • *the best city in which to locate a business*

plant • *So far no one has admitted to planting the bomb.*

position • *plants which are carefully positioned in the alcove*

put • *She put the photograph on her desk.*

situate • *The hotel is situated next to the railway station.*

plain ❶ ADJECTIVE

very simple in style with no decoration • *It was a plain, grey stone house.*

austere • *The church was austere and simple.*

bare • *bare wooden floors*

spartan • *her spartan home in a tiny village*

stark • *a stark white, characterless fireplace*

ANTONYM
● fancy

plain ❷ ADJECTIVE

obvious and easy to recognize or understand • *It was plain to him that I was having a nervous breakdown.*

clear • *The book is clear and readable.*

comprehensible • *a comprehensible manual*

distinct • *a distinct smell of burning coal*

evident • *His footprints were clearly evident in the heavy dust.*

obvious • *an obvious injustice*

unmistakable • *His voice was unmistakable.*

plain ❸ NOUN

TYPES OF PLAIN

flat	mesa
flatland	plateau
grassland	prairie
llano	savannah
lowland	steppe

plan ❶ NOUN

a way thought out to do something • *a plan to amalgamate the two parties*

method • *He did it by his usual method.*

proposal • *The proposals need careful study.*

scheme • *The scheme was an abject failure.*

strategy • *What should our marketing strategy achieve?*

system • *the advantages of the new system over the old one*

plan ❷ NOUN

a detailed diagram of something • *a detailed plan of the prison*

blueprint • *a blueprint for a new bathroom*

diagram • *a circuit diagram*

layout • *He tried to recall the layout of the farmhouse.*

scale drawing • *scale drawings of locomotives*

plan ❸ VERB

to decide in detail what is to be done • *when we plan road construction*

arrange • *We arranged a social event once a year.*

design • *He approached me to design the restaurant.*

devise • *We devised a plan.*

draft • *The legislation was drafted by the committee.*

formulate • *He formulated his plan for escape.*

A B C D E F G H I J K L M N O P Q R S T U V W X Y Z

Can't find the word you're looking for? Try the index.

play ① VERB

to take part in games or use toys
• *Polly was playing with her teddy bear.*

amuse oneself • *He amused himself by rollerskating round the building.*

entertain oneself • *I used to entertain myself by building model planes.*

frolic • *Tourists sunbathe and frolic in the ocean.*

have fun • *having fun with your friends*

play ② VERB

to take part in a sport or game
• *Alain was playing cards with his friends.*

compete • *Eight entrants competed for the prize.*

participate • *Sixteen teams participated in the tournament.*

take on • *Scotland take on South Africa at Murrayfield.*

take part • *The teams taking part are cricket's bitterest enemies.*

vie with • *Arsenal are vying with Leeds for second spot in the league.*

play ③ NOUN

a piece of drama performed on stage, radio, or television
• *Chekhov's best play*

comedy • *a romantic comedy*

drama • *He also wrote radio dramas and film scripts.*

pantomime • *He regularly performs in Christmas pantomimes.*

show • *a one-woman show*

tragedy • *Shakespeare's tragedies*

plead VERB

to beg someone for something
• *She pleaded with her daughter to come home.*

appeal • *The United Nations appealed for aid from the international community.*

ask • *I've asked you time and again not to do that.*

beg • *We are not going to beg for help any more.*

beseech (LITERARY) • *She beseeched him to show mercy.*

implore • *Opposition leaders implored the president to break the deadlock.*

pleasant ① ADJECTIVE

enjoyable or attractive • *I've got a pleasant little flat.*

agreeable • *workers in more agreeable and better paid occupations*

delightful • *It was the most delightful garden I'd ever seen.*

enjoyable • *an enjoyable meal*

lekker (SOUTH AFRICAN; SLANG) • *a lekker little town*

lovely • *He had a lovely voice.*

nice • *It's nice to be here together again.*

pleasurable • *He found sailing more pleasurable than skiing.*

ANTONYM
● unpleasant

pleasant ② ADJECTIVE

friendly or charming • *an extremely pleasant and obliging man*

affable • *He is an affable and approachable man.*

amiable • *She had been surprised at how amiable and polite he had seemed.*

charming • *He can be charming to his friends.*

friendly • *She has a friendly relationship with her customers.*

likable or **likeable** • *He's an immensely likable man.*

nice • *He's a nice fellow, very quiet and courteous.*

a
b
c
d
e
f
g
h
i
j
k
l
m
n
o
p
q
r
s
t
u
v
w
x
y
z

Can't find the word you're looking for? Try the index.

please VERB

to give pleasure to • *I was tidying my bedroom to please mum.*
amuse • *The thought seemed to amuse him.*
charm • *He charmed all of us.*
delight • *music that has delighted audiences all over the world*
entertain • *Children's TV not only entertains but also teaches.*

pleased ADJECTIVE

happy or satisfied • *I'm pleased with the way things have been going.*
contented • *She had a contented smile on her face.*
delighted • *I know he will be delighted to see you.*
glad • *I'm glad he changed his mind in the end.*
happy • *She's a confident and happy child.*
satisfied • *satisfied customers*

pleasure NOUN

a feeling of happiness and satisfaction • *Everybody takes pleasure in eating.*
amusement • *Her impersonations provided great amusement.*
enjoyment • *her enjoyment of the countryside*
happiness • *My happiness helped to erase the bad memories.*
joy • *tears of joy*
satisfaction • *job satisfaction*

plentiful ADJECTIVE

existing in large amounts • *a plentiful supply*
abundant • *Birds are abundant in the tall vegetation.*
ample • *The design created ample space for a large kitchen.*

bountiful • *a bountiful harvest of fruits and vegetables*
copious • *He attended the lectures and took copious notes.*
infinite • *an infinite variety of landscapes*

MORE SYNONYMS
● lavish
● profuse

ANTONYM
● scarce

plenty NOUN

a lot of something • *There's plenty to go round.*
enough • *Have you had enough?*
great deal • *I've spent a great deal of time on this project.*
heaps (INFORMAL) • *You have heaps of time.*
lots (INFORMAL) • *He has made lots of amendments to the script.*
plethora • *a plethora of new products*

plot ❶ NOUN

a secret plan made by a group of people • *the plot to assassinate Martin Luther King*
conspiracy • *a conspiracy to steal nuclear missiles*
intrigue • *political intrigues*
plan • *a secret government plan to build a nuclear waste dump*
scheme • *an elaborate scheme to dupe the police*

MORE SYNONYMS
● cabal
● machination
● stratagem

plot ❷ NOUN

the story of a novel or play • *The film has a ludicrously complicated plot.*

Can't find the word you're looking for? Try the index.

narrative • *a fast-moving narrative*
scenario • *The movie's scenario is nonsensical.*
story • *I doubt the appeal of cinematic sex without a story.*
story line • *It sounds like a typical story line from a soap opera.*

plot ❸ VERB
to plan something secretly with others • *Prosecutors allege the defendants plotted to overthrow the government.*
conspire • *The countries had secretly conspired to acquire nuclear weapons.*
hatch • *He hatched a plot to murder his wife.*
plan • *I suspect they are secretly planning to raise taxes.*
scheme • *He claimed that they were scheming against him.*

MORE SYNONYMS
● cabal
● collude
● machinate

plug ❶ NOUN
a small, round object for blocking a hole • *She put the plug in the sink and filled it with water.*
bung • *Remove the bung from the barrel.*
cork • *the sound of popping champagne corks*
stopper • *a bottle sealed with a cork stopper*

plug ❷ VERB
to block a hole with something • *working to plug a major oil leak*
block • *When the shrimp farm is built it will block the stream.*
fill • *Fill small holes with wood filler.*

seal • *She filled the containers and sealed them with a cork.*

plump ADJECTIVE
rather fat • *a plump, fresh-faced young woman*
beefy (INFORMAL) • *beefy bodyguards*
burly • *burly shipyard workers*
chubby • *I was quite chubby as a child.*
fat • *I could eat what I liked without getting fat.*
stout • *He was a tall, stout man of sixty.*
tubby • *He's a bit on the tubby side.*

point ❶ NOUN
the purpose or meaning something has • *Cutting costs is not the point of the exercise.*
aim • *The aim of this book is to inform you.*
goal • *The goal is to raise a lot of money.*
intention • *It was never my intention to injure anyone.*
object • *It was his object in life to find the island.*
purpose • *He did not know the purpose of Vincent's visit.*

point ❷ NOUN
a quality or feature • *Tact was never her strong point.*
attribute • *Cruelty is a regrettable attribute of human behaviour.*
characteristic • *their physical characteristics*
feature • *They're one of my best features.*
quality • *mature people with leadership qualities*
side • *the dark side of his character*
trait • *Creativity is a human trait.*

a b c d e f g h i j k l m n o **p** q r s t u v w x y z

Can't find the word you're looking for? Try the index.

point ❸ NOUN
the thin sharp end of something
• *the point of a needle*
nib • *the nib of my pen*
prong • *the prongs of a fork*
tip • *the tip of my scissors*

poison NOUN
a substance that can kill people or
animals • *Mercury is a known poison.*
toxin • *the liver's ability to break
down toxins*
venom • *the cobra's deadly venom*

RELATED WORD
● ADJECTIVE: toxic

poisonous ADJECTIVE
containing something that causes
death or illness • *a large cloud of
poisonous gas*
noxious • *Many household
products give off noxious fumes.*
toxic • *The cost of cleaning up toxic
waste.*
venomous • *The adder is Britain's
only venomous snake.*

poke ❶ VERB
to jab or prod someone or
something • *She poked a fork into
the turkey skin.*
dig • *His companions were digging
him in the ribs.*
elbow • *As I tried to get past him
he elbowed me in the face.*
jab • *Somebody jabbed an umbrella
into his leg.*
nudge • *She nudged me awake
after I dozed off.*
prod • *He prodded Murray with the
shotgun.*
stab • *He stabbed at Frank with his
forefinger.*

poke ❷ NOUN
a jab or prod • *She gave Richard a
playful poke.*

dig • *She silenced him with a sharp
dig in the small of the back.*
jab • *a quick jab of the brakes*
nudge • *She slipped her arm under
his and gave him a nudge.*
prod • *He gave the donkey a mighty
prod in the backside.*

polish ❶ VERB
to make smooth and shiny by
rubbing • *He polished his shoes
every morning.*
buff • *He was already buffing the
car's hubs.*
shine • *Let him dust and shine the
furniture.*
wax • *a Sunday morning spent
washing and waxing the car*

polish ❷ VERB
to improve a skill or technique
• *Polish up your writing skills.*
brush up • *She spent the summer
brushing up on her driving.*
improve • *I want to improve my
golf game.*
perfect • *We perfected a hand-
signal system.*
refine • *Surgical techniques are
constantly being refined.*

polish ❸ NOUN
elegance or refinement • *The opera
lacks the polish of his later work.*
class (INFORMAL) • *For sheer class,
Mark Waugh is the best batsman of
the World Cup.*
elegance • *The furniture combined
practicality with elegance.*
finesse • *It's good but it lacks the
finesse of vintage champagne.*
grace • *Ballet classes are important
for learning poise and grace.*
refinement • *a girl who possessed
both dignity and refinement*
style • *Paris, you have to admit,
has style.*

Can't find the word you're looking for? Try the index.

MORE SYNONYMS
- politesse
- suavity
- urbanity

polite ❶ ADJECTIVE

having good manners • *It's not polite to point at people.*
civil • *I have to force myself to be civil to him.*
courteous • *Her reply was courteous but firm.*
respectful • *Their children are always respectful to their elders.*
well-behaved • *well-behaved little girls*
well-mannered • *a very pleasant and well-mannered student*

ANTONYM
- rude

polite ❷ ADJECTIVE

cultivated or refined • *Certain words are not acceptable in polite society.*
cultured • *He is immensely cultured and well-read.*
genteel • *two ladies with genteel manners and voices*
refined • *His speech and manner are very refined.*
sophisticated • *Recently her tastes have become more sophisticated.*
urbane • *She describes him as charming and urbane.*

politeness NOUN

the quality of being civil to someone • *She listened to him but only out of politeness.*
civility • *Handle customers with tact and civility.*
courtesy • *He did not even have the courtesy to reply to my fax.*
decency • *He should have had the decency to inform me.*

etiquette • *the rules of diplomatic etiquette*

pollute VERB

to contaminate with something harmful • *Heavy industry pollutes our rivers with noxious chemicals.*
contaminate • *Have any fish been contaminated in the Arctic Ocean?*
infect • *a virus which is spread mainly by infected blood*
poison • *Drilling operations have poisoned the Nile delta.*
taint • *blood tainted with the hepatitis viruses*

MORE SYNONYMS
- adulterate
- befoul
- smirch

pompous ADJECTIVE

behaving in a way that is too serious and self-important • *a pompous man with a high opinion of his own capabilities*
arrogant • *an air of arrogant indifference*
grandiose • *grandiose plans which never got off the ground*
ostentatious • *an ostentatious wedding reception*
pretentious • *His response was full of pretentious nonsense.*
puffed up • *He is puffed up with own importance.*

MORE SYNONYMS
- pontifical
- portentous
- vainglorious

ponder VERB

to think about something deeply • *I'm continually pondering how to improve the team.*
brood • *I guess everyone broods over things once in a while.*

a b c d e f g h i j k l m n o **p** q r s t u v w x y z

Can't find the word you're looking for? Try the index.

A
B
C
D
E
F
G
H
I
J
K
L
M
N
O
P
Q
R
S
T
U
V
W
X
Y
Z

consider • *You have to consider the feelings of those around you.*
contemplate • *He lay in bed contemplating his future.*
mull over • *I'll leave you alone here so you can mull it over.*
reflect • *I reflected on the child's future.*
think • *I have often thought about this problem.*

poor ❶ ADJECTIVE
having little money • *They see the government ignoring poor people.*
broke (INFORMAL) • *He was broke when I married him.*
destitute • *destitute people living on the streets*
hard up (INFORMAL) • *Her parents were very hard up.*
impoverished • *one of the most impoverished suburbs of Rio de Janeiro*
penniless • *a penniless refugee*
poverty-stricken • *a teacher of poverty-stricken kids*

ANTONYM
● rich

poor ❷ ADJECTIVE
of a low quality or standard • *He was a poor actor.*
feeble • *a feeble attempt to save Figo's shot*
inferior • *The cassettes were of inferior quality.*
mediocre • *His school record was mediocre.*
second-rate • *Passengers are fed up using a second-rate service.*
shoddy • *shoddy goods*
unsatisfactory • *questions to which he received unsatisfactory answers*

popular ❶ ADJECTIVE
liked or approved of by a lot of

people • *These delicious pastries will be very popular.*
fashionable • *fashionable wine bars*
favourite • *Britain's favourite soap opera*
in demand • *He was much in demand as a lecturer.*
in favour • *He is now back in favour with the manager.*
sought-after • *one of the most sought-after new names in Hollywood*
well-liked • *She was very sociable and well-liked by the other students.*

ANTONYM
● unpopular

popular ❷ ADJECTIVE
involving or intended for ordinary people • *the popular press*
common • *Much of the countryside has fallen out of common ownership and into private hands.*
conventional • *a respectable married woman with conventional opinions*
general • *general awareness about bullying*
universal • *universal health care*

portion NOUN
a part or amount of something • *I have spent a considerable portion of my life here.*
bit • *I missed the first bit of the meeting.*
chunk • *Cut the melon into chunks.*
helping • *She gave them extra helpings of ice-cream.*
part • *A large part of his earnings went on repaying the loan.*
piece • *Do you want another piece?*
segment • *the middle segment of his journey*
serving • *Each serving contains 240 calories.*

Can't find the word you're looking for? Try the index.

pose ① VERB

to ask a question • *When I finally posed the question, "Why?" he merely shrugged.*

ask • *I wasn't the only one asking questions.*

put • *Some workers may be afraid to put questions publicly.*

submit • *Passengers are invited to submit questions.*

MORE SYNONYMS

- posit
- propound

pose ② VERB

to pretend to be someone else • *The team posed as drug dealers to trap the ringleaders.*

impersonate • *He was once jailed for impersonating a policeman.*

masquerade as • *He masqueraded as a doctor and fooled everyone.*

pass oneself off as • *He frequently passed himself off as a lawyer.*

pretend to be • *We spent the afternoon pretending to be foreign tourists.*

posh ① ADJECTIVE (INFORMAL)

smart, fashionable and expensive • *a posh hotel*

classy (INFORMAL) • *expensive cars with classy brand names*

elegant • *an elegant society ball*

exclusive • *a member of Britain's most exclusive club*

fashionable • *fashionable restaurants*

smart • *smart London dinner parties*

stylish • *stylish décor*

up-market • *an up-market agency aimed at professional people*

posh ② ADJECTIVE

upper-class • *He sounded very posh on the phone.*

aristocratic • *a wealthy, aristocratic family*

genteel • *two ladies with genteel manners and voices*

upper-class • *upper-class speech*

MORE SYNONYMS

- blue-blooded
- patrician (FORMAL)

ANTONYM

- common

position ① NOUN

the place where someone or something is • *The ship's name and position were reported to the coastguard.*

location • *She knew the exact location of their headquarters.*

place • *The pain is always in the same place.*

point • *The pain originated from a point in his right thigh.*

whereabouts • *Finding his whereabouts proved surprisingly easy.*

position ② VERB

to put something somewhere • *Position trailing plants near the edges.*

arrange • *Arrange the books in neat piles.*

lay out • *Grace laid out the knives and forks at the table.*

locate • *the best city in which to locate a business*

place • *Chairs were placed in rows for the parents.*

put • *She put the photograph on her desk.*

positive ① ADJECTIVE

completely sure about something • *I was positive he'd known about that money.*

a
b
c
d
e
f
g
h
i
j
k
l
m
n
o
p
q
r
s
t
u
v
w
x
y
z

Can't find the word you're looking for? Try the index.

certain • *It wasn't a balloon - I'm certain about that.*
confident • *My Ryan is confident of success.*
convinced • *He was convinced that I was part of the problem.*
sure • *It is impossible to be sure about the value of the land.*

positive ❷ ADJECTIVE
providing definite proof of the truth or identity of something • *positive evidence*
clear • *a clear case of mistaken identity*
clear-cut • *The issue is not so clear-cut.*
conclusive • *Research on the matter is far from conclusive.*
concrete • *He had no concrete evidence.*
firm • *There is no firm evidence to prove this.*

MORE SYNONYMS
● incontrovertible
● indisputable
● unequivocal

positive ❸ ADJECTIVE
tending to emphasize what is good • *I anticipate a positive response.*
constructive • *We welcome constructive criticism.*
helpful • *Camilla's helpful comments*

ANTONYM
● negative

possess ❶ VERB
to have something as a quality • *He possesses both stamina and great technique.*
be blessed with • *She was blessed with a photographic memory.*
be born with • *Mozart was born with perfect pitch.*

enjoy • *I have always enjoyed good health.*
have • *They have talent in abundance.*

possess ❷ VERB
to own something • *He was said to possess a huge fortune.*
acquire • *I have acquired a new car.*
control • *He now controls the entire company.*
hold • *He does not hold a firearm certificate.*
occupy • *US forces now occupy part of the country.*
seize • *Troops have seized the airport and railway terminals.*
take over • *They plan to take over another airline.*

possession NOUN
ownership of something • *How did this picture come into your possession?*
control • *The restructuring involves his giving up control of the firm.*
custody • *She will have custody of their two children.*
ownership • *the growth of home ownership*
tenure • *his 28-year tenure of the house*

possessions PLURAL NOUN
the things owned by someone • *People had lost all their possessions.*
assets • *The group had assets worth over 10 million dollars.*
belongings • *He was identified only by his personal belongings.*
effects • *His daughters were collecting his effects.*
estate • *She left her entire estate to a charity.*
property • *the rightful owner of the property*

Can't find the word you're looking for? Try the index.

things • *She told him to take all his things and not to return.*

possibility NOUN
something that might be true or might happen • *the possibility of a ban*
chance • *There's no chance of that happening.*
hope • *We had absolutely no hope of raising the money.*
likelihood • *the likelihood of infection*
odds • *What are the odds of that happening?*
prospect • *There is little prospect of peace.*
risk • *It reduces the risk of heart disease.*

possible ① ADJECTIVE
likely to happen or able to be done • *I am grateful to the staff for making this work possible.*
attainable • *I always thought promotion was attainable.*
feasible • *Whether such cooperation is feasible is a matter of doubt.*
practicable • *It was not reasonably practicable for Mr Tyler to attend.*
viable • *commercially viable products*
workable • *This isn't a workable solution in most cases.*

ANTONYM
● impossible

possible ② ADJECTIVE
likely or capable of being true or correct • *It's possible there's an explanation for all this.*
conceivable • *It is just conceivable that a survivor might be found.*
imaginable • *a place of no imaginable strategic value*
likely • *Experts say a "yes" vote is still the likely outcome.*
potential • *the channel's potential audience*

postpone VERB
to put off to a later time • *The visit has been postponed until tomorrow.*
adjourn • *The proceedings have been adjourned until next week.*
defer • *Customers often defer payments for as long as possible.*
delay • *I wanted to delay my departure until June.*
put back • *The news conference has been put back a couple of hours.*
put off • *The Association has put off the event until October.*
shelve • *Sadly, the project has now been shelved.*

potential ① ADJECTIVE
possible but not yet actual • *potential sources of finance*
likely • *A draw is the likely outcome.*
possible • *Her family is discussing a possible move to America.*
probable • *A bomb was the accident's most probable cause.*

potential ② NOUN
ability to achieve future success • *Denmark recognized the potential of wind energy early.*
ability • *You have the ability to become a good pianist.*
aptitude • *more aptitude for academic work than the others*
capability • *We experience differences in mental capability depending on the time of day.*
capacity • *people's creative capacities*
power • *the power of speech*
wherewithal • *She didn't have the financial wherewithal to do it.*

a
b
c
d
e
f
g
h
i
j
k
l
m
n
o
p
q
r
s
t
u
v
w
x
y
z

A
B
C
D
E
F
G
H
I
J
K
L
M
N
O
P
Q
R
S
T
U
V
W
X
Y
Z

pour VERB

to flow quickly and in large quantities • *Blood was pouring from his broken nose.*

course • *The tears coursed down her cheeks.*

flow • *compressor stations that keep that gas flowing*

gush • *Piping-hot water gushed out.*

run • *Water was running down the walls.*

spout • *a fountain that spouts water 40 feet into the air*

stream • *She came in, rain streaming from her clothes and hair.*

poverty NOUN

the state of being very poor • *Garvey died in loneliness and poverty.*

destitution • *refugees living in destitution*

hardship • *Many people are suffering economic hardship.*

insolvency • *Several companies are on the brink of insolvency.*

want • *We are fighting for freedom from want.*

MORE SYNONYMS

● indigence
● penury
● privation

power ❶ NOUN

control over people and activities • *a position of great power and influence*

ascendancy • *The extremists in the party are gaining ascendancy.*

control • *He has been forced to give up control over the company.*

dominion • *They truly believe they have dominion over us.*

sovereignty • *the resumption of Chinese sovereignty over Hong Kong in 1997*

supremacy • *The party has re-established its supremacy.*

power ❷ NOUN

authority to do something • *The police have the power of arrest.*

authority • *The judge had no authority to order a second trial.*

authorization • *I don't have the authorization to make such a decision.*

licence • *He has given me licence to do the job as I see fit.*

privilege • *the ancient powers and privileges of parliament*

right • *the right to vote*

power ❸ NOUN

physical strength • *Power and bulk are vital to success in rugby.*

brawn • *He's got plenty of brains as well as brawn.*

might • *The might of the army could prove a decisive factor.*

strength • *He threw it forward with all his strength.*

vigour • *His body lacks the vigour of a normal two-year-old.*

powerful ❶ ADJECTIVE

able to control people and events • *Russia and India, two large, powerful countries*

commanding • *We're in a more commanding position than we've been in for ages.*

dominant • *He was a dominant figure in the Italian film industry.*

influential • *He had been influential in shaping economic policy.*

powerful ❷ ADJECTIVE

physically strong • *It's such a big powerful dog.*

mighty • *a mighty young athlete*

strapping • *He was a bricklayer – a big, strapping fellow.*
strong • *I'm not strong enough to carry him.*
sturdy • *The camera was mounted on a sturdy tripod.*
vigorous • *He was a vigorous, handsome young man.*

ANTONYM
● weak

powerful ❸ ADJECTIVE
having a strong effect • *a powerful argument*
compelling • *a compelling reason to leave*
convincing • *convincing evidence*
effective • *Antibiotics are effective against this organism.*
forceful • *forceful action to stop the suffering*
persuasive • *Mr. Knight made a persuasive case for removing the tax.*
telling • *He spoke reasonably, carefully, and with telling effect.*

powerless ADJECTIVE
unable to control or influence events • *I was powerless to save her.*
helpless • *Many people felt helpless against the violence.*
impotent • *The West is impotent to influence the Balkan war.*
incapable • *He is incapable as a manager.*

practical ❶ ADJECTIVE
involving experience rather than theory • *practical suggestions for healthy eating*
applied • *plans to put more money into applied research*
pragmatic • *a pragmatic approach to the problems of Latin America*

practical ❷ ADJECTIVE
likely to be effective • *The clothes are*

lightweight and practical for holidays.
functional • *The design is functional but stylish.*
sensible • *sensible footwear*

ANTONYM
● impractical

practical ❸ ADJECTIVE
able to deal effectively with problems • *the practical common sense essential in management*
accomplished • *an accomplished cook*
experienced • *a team packed with experienced professionals*
proficient • *A great number of them are proficient in foreign languages.*
seasoned • *The author is a seasoned academic.*
skilled • *amateur but highly skilled observers of wildlife*
veteran • *a veteran broadcaster*

practice ❶ NOUN
something that people do regularly • *a public inquiry into bank practices*
custom • *I have tried to adapt to local customs.*
habit • *a survey on eating habits*
method • *her usual method of getting through the traffic*
routine • *We had to change our daily routine and lifestyle.*
way • *a return to the old ways of doing things*

practice ❷ NOUN
regular training or exercise • *I need more practice.*
drill • *The teacher ran them through the drill again.*
exercise • *Lack of exercise can lead to feelings of exhaustion.*
preparation • *Behind any successful event lie months of preparation.*

a
b
c
d
e
f
g
h
i
j
k
l
m
n
o
p
q
r
s
t
u
v
w
x
y
z

Can't find the word you're looking for? Try the index.

rehearsal • *rehearsals for a concert tour*
training • *her busy training schedule*

practise ❶ VERB
to do something repeatedly so as to gain skill • *Lauren practises the piano every day.*
polish • *They just need to polish their technique.*
rehearse • *She was in her room rehearsing her lines.*
train • *He was training for the new season.*

practise ❷ VERB
to take part in the activities of a religion, craft, or custom • *Acupuncture has been practised in China for thousands of years.*
do • *I used to do karate.*
follow • *Do you follow any particular religion?*
observe • *American forces are observing Christmas quietly.*

praise ❶ VERB
to express strong approval of someone • *Many others praised Sanford for taking a strong stand.*
admire • *All those who knew him will admire him for his work.*
applaud • *He should be applauded for his courage.*
approve • *Not everyone approves of the festival.*
congratulate • *I must congratulate the organizers for a well run event.*
pay tribute to • *He paid tribute to his captain.*

MORE SYNONYMS
● acclaim
● eulogize
● extol
● laud

ANTONYM
● criticize

praise ❷ NOUN
something said or written to show approval • *She is full of praise for the range of services available.*
accolade • *the ultimate international accolade, the Nobel Peace Prize*
approval • *an obsessive drive to gain her mother's approval*
commendation • *They received a commendation from the Royal Society of Arts.*
congratulation • *I offered her my congratulations.*
tribute • *We marched past in tribute to our fallen comrades.*

MORE SYNONYMS
● encomium
● eulogy
● panegyric

ANTONYM
● criticism

precaution NOUN
an action intended to prevent something from happening • *It's still worth taking precautions against accidents.*
insurance • *Farmers grew a mixture of crops as an insurance against crop failure.*
preventative measure • *a preventative measure against heart disease*
protection • *protection against damage to buildings*
provision • *People need to make decent provision for their old age.*
safeguard • *legislation that offers safeguards against discrimination*

A
B
C
D
E
F
G
H
I
J
K
L
M
N
O
P
Q
R
S
T
U
V
W
X
Y
Z

precious ADJECTIVE

of great value and importance
• *precious jewels*
expensive • *an expensive new coat*
invaluable • *I was to gain
invaluable experience over that year.*
priceless • *his priceless collection
of Chinese art*
prized • *These shells were very
highly prized by the Indians.*
valuable • *valuable books*

ANTONYM
● worthless

precise ADJECTIVE

exact and accurate • *We may never
know the precise details.*
accurate • *an accurate description
of his attackers*
actual • *The actual number of
victims is higher than statistics
suggest.*
correct • *This information was
correct at the time of going to press.*
exact • *The exact number of protest
calls has not been revealed.*
particular • *a very particular
account of events*
specific • *I asked him to be more
specific.*
very • *Those were his very words.*

ANTONYM
● vague

predicament NOUN

a difficult situation • *The decision
will leave her in a peculiar
predicament.*
fix (INFORMAL) • *The government
has really got itself into a fix.*
hot water (INFORMAL) • *His antics
keep landing him in hot water with
officials.*
jam (INFORMAL) • *We are in a real
jam now.*

scrape (INFORMAL) • *He's had his
fair share of scrapes with the law.*
tight spot • *This was one tight spot
he couldn't get out of.*

predict VERB

to say that something will happen
in the future • *The opinion polls are
predicting a very close contest.*
forecast • *He forecasts that house
prices will rise by 5% this year.*
foresee • *He did not foresee any
problems.*
foretell • *prophets who have
foretold the end of the world*
prophesy • *She prophesied a bad
ending for the expedition.*

MORE SYNONYMS
● forebode
● portend
● presage
● prognosticate
● soothsay

prediction NOUN

something that is forecast in
advance • *He was unwilling to make
a prediction for the coming year.*
forecast • *a forecast of heavy
weather to come*
prophecy • *the interpreters of
Biblical prophecy*

prefer VERB

to like one thing more than
another thing • *Does he prefer a
particular sort of music?*
be partial to • *I'm quite partial to
mussels.*
favour • *Both sides favour a
diplomatic solution.*
go for • *They went for a more up-
market approach.*
incline towards • *The majority
are inclined towards a forgiving
attitude.*

a
b
c
d
e
f
g
h
i
j
k
l
m
n
o
p
q
r
s
t
u
v
w
x
y
z

like better • *I like the flat shoes better.*

prefix NOUN

PREFIXES

ante-	multi-
anti-	neo-
auto-	non-
bi-	over-
centi-	poly-
co-	post-
contra-	pre-
de-	pro-
demi-	pseudo-
dis-	re-
ex-	self-
extra-	semi-
hyper-	step-
in-	sub-
inter-	super-
intra-	tele-
mega-	trans-
micro-	tri-
mid-	ultra-
milli-	un-
mini-	under-
mono-	vice-

prejudice ❶ NOUN

an unreasonable or unfair dislike or preference • *prejudice against workers over 45*
bias • *Bias against women permeates every level of the judicial system.*
partiality • *She is criticized for her one-sidedness and partiality.*
preconception • *preconceptions about the sort of people who did computing*

prejudice ❷ NOUN

intolerance towards certain people or groups • *racial prejudice*
bigotry • *religious bigotry*
chauvinism • *the growth of Russian chauvinism*

discrimination • *sex discrimination*
racism • *the fight to rid sport of racism*
sexism • *sexism in the workplace*

premonition NOUN

a feeling that something unpleasant is going to happen • *He had a premonition that he would die.*
foreboding • *His triumph was overshadowed by an uneasy sense of foreboding.*
funny feeling (INFORMAL) • *I have a funny feeling something unpleasant is about to happen.*
omen • *Her appearance at this moment is an omen of disaster.*
sign • *a sign of impending doom*

MORE SYNONYMS

- portent
- presage
- presentiment

preoccupied ADJECTIVE

totally involved with something or deep in thought • *I am preoccupied with my tennis career.*
absorbed • *They were completely absorbed in each other.*
engrossed • *Tom didn't notice because he was too engrossed in his work.*
immersed • *He's becoming really immersed in his studies.*
oblivious • *When he was in his car he was totally oblivious to everybody else.*
wrapped up • *She's wrapped up in her new career.*

present ❶ ADJECTIVE

being at a place or event • *He had been present at the birth of his son.*
at hand • *Having the right equipment at hand will be very useful.*

here • *He was here a minute ago.*
in attendance • *Police and several fire engines are in attendance.*
there • *The group of old buildings is still there today.*
to hand • *I haven't got the instructions to hand.*

ANTONYM
● absent

present ❷ NOUN
something given to someone
• *a birthday present*
bonsela (SOUTH AFRICAN) • *your kind bonsela to the hospital*
donation • *Employees make regular donations to charity.*
gift • *a Christmas gift*
offering • *Hindus kill turtles ritually as an offering to their gods.*

present ❸ VERB
to give something to someone
• *The Mayor presented the prizes.*
award • *For his dedication he was awarded a medal of merit.*
bestow • *The Queen bestowed on him a knighthood.*
donate • *He frequently donates large sums to charity.*
give • *She gave me a pen for my birthday.*
grant • *France has agreed to grant him political asylum.*
hand out • *One of my jobs was to hand out the prizes.*

press ❶ VERB
to apply force or weight to something • *Press the blue button.*
compress • *Poor posture compresses the body's organs.*
crush • *Peel and crush the garlic.*
mash • *Mash the bananas with a fork.*
push • *She pushed the door open.*

squeeze • *He squeezed her arm reassuringly.*

press ❷ VERB
to try hard to persuade someone to do something • *Trade Unions are pressing him to stand firm.*
beg • *I begged him to come back with me.*
implore • *"Tell me what to do!" she implored him.*
petition • *All the attempts to petition the government failed.*
plead • *I pleaded to be allowed to go.*
pressurize • *He thought she was trying to pressurize him.*
urge • *He had urged her to come to Ireland.*

MORE SYNONYMS
● entreat
● exhort
● importune

pretend VERB
to claim or give the appearance of something untrue • *Sometimes the boy pretended to be asleep.*
counterfeit • *the coins he is alleged to have counterfeited*
fake • *He faked his own death last year.*
falsify • *He was charged with falsifying business records.*
feign • *The striker was accused of feigning injury.*
pass oneself off as • *She tried to pass herself off as an actress.*

pretentious ADJECTIVE
making unjustified claims to importance • *Many critics thought her work and ideas pretentious and empty.*
affected • *She passed along with an affected air and a disdainful look.*

a
b
c
d
e
f
g
h
i
j
k
l
m
n
o
P
q
r
s
t
u
v
w
x
y
z

Can't find the word you're looking for? Try the index.

A B C D E F G H I J K L M N O **P** Q R S T U V W X Y Z

conceited • *I thought him conceited and arrogant.*
ostentatious • *an ostentatious wedding reception*
pompous • *He's pompous and has a high opinion of his own capabilities.*
snobbish • *a snobbish dislike for their intellectual inferiors*

MORE SYNONYMS
- bombastic
- grandiloquent
- magniloquent
- vainglorious

pretty ❶ ADJECTIVE
attractive in a delicate way • *She's a very charming and very pretty girl.*
attractive • *She has a round attractive face.*
beautiful • *a beautiful child*
cute • *a cute little baby*
lovely • *his lovely wife*

pretty ❷ ADVERB (INFORMAL)
quite or rather • *He spoke pretty good English.*
fairly • *Both ships are fairly new.*
kind of (INFORMAL) • *I was kind of embarrassed about it.*
quite • *It was quite hard.*
rather • *She's rather vain.*

prevent VERB
to stop something from happening • *the most practical way of preventing crime*
avert • *A fresh tragedy was narrowly averted yesterday.*
foil • *The plot was foiled by policemen.*
hinder • *Research is hindered by lack of cash.*
impede • *Fallen rocks are impeding the progress of the rescue workers.*
stop • *a new diplomatic initiative to try to stop the war*
thwart • *Her ambition to become an artist was thwarted by failing eyesight.*

previous ADJECTIVE
happening or existing before something else • *the previous year*
earlier • *His earlier works include impressive still lifes.*
former • *a former president of Mexico*
one-time • *the country's one-time military rulers*
past • *a return to the turbulence of past centuries*
preceding • *This is examined in detail in the preceding chapter.*
prior • *I can't make it. I have a prior engagement.*

price ❶ NOUN
the amount of money paid for something • *a sharp increase in the price of petrol*
amount • *I was asked to pay the full amount.*
charge • *an annual management charge of 1.25%*
cost • *the cost of a loaf of bread*
fee • *the annual membership fee*
figure • *A figure of £2000 was mentioned.*
value • *The company's market value rose to 5.5 billion dollars.*

price ❷ VERB
to fix the price or value of something • *I just can't imagine why it has been priced at this level.*
cost • *We hope it won't cost too much.*
estimate • *His personal riches were estimated at $368 million.*
put a price on • *The company has refused to put a price on its bid.*
value • *I had my jewellery valued for insurance purposes.*

Can't find the word you're looking for? Try the index.

pride ❶ NOUN

a feeling of satisfaction about your
achievements • *We take pride in
offering you the highest standards.*
delight • *Haig took obvious delight
in proving his critics wrong.*
pleasure • *Our first win gave me
great pleasure.*
satisfaction • *His success was a
great source of satisfaction to him.*

pride ❷ NOUN

an excessively high opinion of
yourself • *His pride may still be his
downfall.*
arrogance • *He has a swaggering
arrogance.*
conceit • *He knew, without
conceit, that he was considered
a genius.*
egotism • *typical showbiz egotism*
smugness • *a trace of smugness in
his voice*
snobbery • *intellectual snobbery*
vanity • *her vanity about her long
hair*

MORE SYNONYMS

- haughtiness
- hauteur
- hubris
- superciliousness

ANTONYM

- humility

priest NOUN

TYPES OF PRIEST

guru (*Hinduism, Sikhism*)
high priest *or* high priestess
imam (*Muslim*)
lama (*Buddhism*)
minister (*Christianity*)
priest
rabbi (*Judaism*)
shaman *or* medicine man

prim ADJECTIVE

behaving very correctly and easily
shocked by anything rude • *We
tend to assume the Victorians were
very prim and proper.*
proper • *He was very pompous and
proper.*
prudish • *I'm not prudish but I
think those photos are obscene.*
puritanical • *He has a puritanical
attitude towards sex.*
strait-laced • *He very strait-laced
and narrow-minded.*

prime ❶ ADJECTIVE

main or most important • *a prime
cause of brain damage*
chief • *The job went to one of his
chief rivals.*
leading • *a leading industrial
nation*
main • *the city's main tourist area*
principal • *our principal source of
foreign exchange earnings*

prime ❷ ADJECTIVE

of the best quality • *prime beef*
best • *He'll have the best care.*
choice • *our choicest chocolates*
first-rate • *He's a first-rate officer.*
select • *With that historic win he
now joins a select band of golfers.*
superior • *superior coffee beans*

primitive ADJECTIVE

very simple or basic • *a very small
primitive cottage*
crude • *crude stone carvings*
rough • *a rough wooden table*
rude • *He constructed a rude cabin
for himself.*
rudimentary • *The bomb was
rudimentary but lethal.*
simple • *a simple shelter*

principal ADJECTIVE

main or most important • *Their*

A
B
C
D
E
F
G
H
I
J
K
L
M
N
O
P
Q
R
S
T
U
V
W
X
Y
Z

principal concern is that of winning the election.
chief • *his chief reason for withdrawing*
first • *The first duty of this government is to tackle poverty.*
foremost • *one of the world's foremost scholars of classical poetry*
main • *What are the main differences between them?*
major • *the major factor in her decision*
primary • *the primary cause of his problems*
prime • *Police will see me as the prime suspect!*

principle ❶ NOUN
a set of moral rules guiding personal conduct • *a woman of principle*
conscience • *the law on freedom of conscience and religious organizations*
integrity • *He has always been a man of integrity.*
morals • *public morals*
scruples • *a man with no moral scruples*
sense of duty • *He did it out of a sense of duty to his men.*

principle ❷ NOUN
a general rule or scientific law • *the basic principles of Marxism*
axiom • *the long-held axiom that education leads to higher income*
canon • *the canons of political economy*
doctrine • *Christian doctrine*
fundamental • *the fundamentals of astronomy*
law • *the laws of motion*

MORE SYNONYMS
● dictum
● precept
● verity

printing NOUN

PRINTING WORDS

bold print	lower case
character	roman
fount *or* font	typesize
italics	typeface

prison NOUN
a building where criminals are kept in captivity • *a high-security prison*
dungeon • *The castle's dungeons haven't been used for years.*
jail • *Three prisoners escaped from the jail.*
nick (BRITISH, AUSTRALIAN AND NEW ZEALAND; SLANG) • *I was banged up in the nick for six months.*
penal institution • *Thirty years in a penal institution is indeed a harsh penalty.*

prisoner NOUN
someone kept in prison or captivity • *top-security prisoners*
captive • *the difficulties of spending four months as a captive*
convict • *convicts serving life sentences*
hostage • *negotiations to release the hostages*

private ❶ ADJECTIVE
for few people rather than people in general • *a private bathroom*
exclusive • *Many of our cheeses are exclusive to our shops in Britain.*
individual • *Divide the vegetables among four individual dishes.*
personal • *It's for my own personal use.*
special • *her own special problems*

private ❷ ADJECTIVE
taking place among a small number of people • *He was buried in a private ceremony.*

Can't find the word you're looking for? Try the index.

clandestine • *He had a clandestine meeting with his lover.*
confidential • *confidential information about her private life*
secret • *a secret love affair*

ANTONYM
● public

prize ❶ NOUN
a reward given to the winner of something • *He won first prize at the Leeds Piano Competition.*
accolade • *the ultimate international accolade, the Nobel Peace Prize*
award • *the Booker Prize, Britain's top award for fiction*
honour • *He was showered with honours – among them an Oscar.*
trophy • *They haven't won a trophy since 1991.*

prize ❷ ADJECTIVE
of the highest quality or standard • *a prize bull*
award-winning • *an award-winning restaurant*
first-rate • *a first-rate thriller writer*
outstanding • *an outstanding horse*
top • *Holland's top striker*

prize ❸ VERB
to value highly • *These ornaments are prized by collectors.*
cherish • *We cherish our independence.*
esteem • *one of Europe's most esteemed awards*
treasure • *She treasures her memories of those joyous days.*
value • *I value the work he gives me.*

probability NOUN
the likelihood of something

happening • *the probability of a serious earthquake*
chances • *The chances of success for the product are good.*
likelihood • *the likelihood of infection*
odds • *The odds are that you are going to fail.*
prospect • *the prospect for peace in Rwanda*

probable ADJECTIVE
likely to be true or to happen • *a misunderstanding about the probable cost*
apparent • *There is no apparent reason for the crime.*
feasible • *Whether this is feasible is a matter of doubt.*
likely • *Further delays are likely.*
on the cards • *A promotion is definitely on the cards for you.*
plausible • *a plausible explanation*

MORE SYNONYMS
● credible
● ostensible
● verisimilar

ANTONYM
● improbable

probably ADVERB
in all likelihood • *The wedding's probably going to be in late August.*
doubtless • *He will doubtless try to change my mind.*
in all probability • *Victory will, in all probability, earn France the title.*
likely • *The entire surplus will most likely be handed over.*
presumably • *The spear is presumably the murder weapon.*

problem ❶ NOUN
an unsatisfactory situation causing difficulties • *the economic problems of the inner city*

a
b
c
d
e
f
g
h
i
j
k
l
m
n
o
p
q
r
s
t
u
v
w
x
y
z

Can't find the word you're looking for? Try the index.

difficulty • *This company is facing great difficulties.*
predicament • *the once great club's current predicament*
quandary • *We're in a quandary over our holiday plans.*
trouble • *I had trouble parking this morning.*

problem ❷ NOUN

a puzzle that needs to be solved
• *a mathematical problem*
conundrum • *an apparently insoluble conundrum*
puzzle • *The data has presented astronomers with a puzzle.*
riddle • *the riddle of the birth of the universe*

procedure NOUN

the correct or usual way of doing something • *He did not follow the correct procedure in applying for a visa.*
method • *new teaching methods*
policy • *It is our policy to prosecute shoplifters.*
practice • *a public inquiry into bank practices*
process • *the production process*
strategy • *a strategy for controlling malaria*
system • *an efficient filing system*

proceed ❶ VERB

to start doing or continue to do something • *I had no idea how to proceed.*
begin • *He stood up and began to move about the room.*
carry on • *"Can I start with a couple of questions?" - "Carry on."*
continue • *I need some advice before I can continue with this task.*
get under way • *The court case got under way last autumn.*
go on • *Go on with your work.*

start • *I started to follow him up the stairs.*

ANTONYM
● cease

proceed ❷ VERB (FORMAL)

to move in a particular direction
• *She proceeded along the hallway.*
advance • *I advanced slowly, one step at a time.*
continue • *He continued rapidly up the path.*
go on • *They went on through the forest.*
make your way • *He made his way to the marketplace.*
progress • *He progressed slowly along the coast in an easterly direction.*
travel • *You can travel to Helsinki tomorrow.*

process ❶ NOUN

a method of doing or producing something • *The building process was spread over three years.*
course of action • *It is important that we take the right course of action.*
means • *The move is a means to fight crime.*
method • *new teaching methods*
procedure • *the correct procedure for applying for a visa*
system • *an efficient filing system*

process ❷ VERB

to deal with or treat something
• *Your application is being processed.*
deal with • *the way that banks deal with complaints*
dispose of • *They disposed of the problem quickly.*
handle • *She didn't know how to handle the problem.*
take care of • *They left it to me to try and take care of the problem.*

Can't find the word you're looking for? Try the index.

A B C D E F G H I J K L M N O P Q R S T U V W X Y Z

produce ❶ VERB
to make something • *a white wine produced mainly from black grapes*
construct • *an inner frame constructed from timber*
create • *It was created from odds and ends.*
invent • *He invented the first electric clock.*
make • *One of my jobs was to make the tea.*
manufacture • *They manufacture plastics.*

produce ❷ VERB
to bring out something so it can be seen or discussed • *To hire a car you must produce a driving licence.*
advance • *Many new theories have been advanced recently.*
bring forward • *We will bring forward new proposals for legislation.*
bring to light • *new evidence brought to light by the police*
put forward • *He has put forward new peace proposals.*

product NOUN
something that is made to be sold • *Many household products give off noxious fumes.*
commodity • *basic commodities such as bread and milk*
goods • *imported goods*
merchandise • *The club sells a wide range of merchandise.*
produce • *locally grown produce*

productive ❶ ADJECTIVE
producing a large number of things • *Training makes workers highly productive.*
fertile • *a product of his fertile imagination*
fruitful • *a landscape that was fruitful and lush*

prolific • *She is a prolific writer of novels and short stories.*

MORE SYNONYMS
- fecund
- generative

ANTONYM
- unproductive

productive ❷ ADJECTIVE
bringing favourable results • *I'm hopeful the talks will be productive.*
constructive • *constructive criticism*
useful • *We made some progress during a useful exchange.*
valuable • *The experience was very valuable.*
worthwhile • *It had been a worthwhile discussion.*

ANTONYM
- unproductive

profession NOUN
a job that requires advanced education or training • *Harper was a teacher by profession.*
business • *May I ask you what business you're in?*
career • *a career in journalism*
occupation • *her new occupation as an author*

proficient ADJECTIVE
able to do something well • *They tend to be proficient in foreign languages.*
able • *an able young rider*
accomplished • *an accomplished fundraiser*
adept • *an adept guitar player*
capable • *a very capable speaker*
competent • *a competent civil servant*
efficient • *a team of efficient workers*

Can't find the word you're looking for? Try the index.

skilful • *He is skilful at managing people.*
skilled • *a network of amateur but highly skilled observers of wildlife*

ANTONYM
● incompetent

profit ❶ NOUN
money gained in business or trade • *The bank made pre-tax profits of $3.5 million.*
earnings • *his earnings as an accountant*
proceeds • *The proceeds from the concert will go to charity.*
revenue • *tax revenues*
surplus • *Japan's trade surplus*
takings • *the pub's weekly takings*

ANTONYM
● loss

profit ❷ VERB
to gain or benefit from something • *They profited shamefully at the expense of my family.*
capitalize on • *The rebels are trying to capitalize on the public's discontent.*
exploit • *They are trying to exploit the troubles to their advantage.*
make the most of • *Happiness is the ability to make the most of what you have.*
take advantage of • *She took advantage of him even after their divorce.*

programme ❶ NOUN
a planned series of events • *a programme of official engagements*
agenda • *This is sure to be an item on the agenda again next week.*
schedule • *We both have such hectic schedules.*

timetable • *We've finally managed to agree on a timetable for formal talks.*

programme ❷ NOUN
a broadcast on radio or television • *local news programmes*
broadcast • *a broadcast by the President*
show • *my favourite TV show*

progress ❶ NOUN
improvement or development • *progress in the fight against cancer*
advance • *dramatic advances in road safety*
breakthrough • *a breakthrough in their research*
headway • *The police are making little headway in the investigation.*
improvement • *considerable room for improvement in facilities for patients*

progress ❷ VERB
to become more advanced or skilful • *His reading is progressing well.*
advance • *Japan has advanced from a rural society to an industrial power.*
blossom • *In just a few years it has blossomed into an international event.*
develop • *workshops designed to develop acting skills*
improve • *Their French has improved enormously.*

prohibit VERB
to forbid something or make it illegal • *a law which prohibited trading on Sundays*
ban • *The country will ban smoking in all offices this year.*
forbid • *The country's constitution forbids the military use of nuclear energy.*

Can't find the word you're looking for? Try the index.

outlaw • *In 1975 gambling was outlawed.*
prevent • *Residents may be prevented from leaving the islands.*

ANTONYM
- allow

prominent ❶ ADJECTIVE
important • *the children of very prominent or successful parents*
eminent • *an eminent scientist*
famous • *England's most famous modern artist*
important • *an important figure in the media*
notable • *the notable linguist, Henriette Walter*
noted • *a noted Hebrew scholar*
renowned • *Sir William Crookes, the renowned chemist*
well-known • *He liked to surround himself with well-known people.*

prominent ❷ ADJECTIVE
very noticeable, or sticking out a long way • *a prominent feature of the landscape*
conspicuous • *a conspicuous landmark*
eye-catching • *I outlined it in black to make it more eye-catching.*
jutting • *a jutting chin*
noticeable • *Squeezing spots only makes them more noticeable.*
obvious • *His cultural roots are most obvious in his poetry.*
pronounced • *The exhibition has a pronounced Scottish theme.*
striking • *a striking aspect of these statistics*

MORE SYNONYMS
- blatant
- salient

promiscuous ADJECTIVE
having many casual sexual relationships • *a promiscuous teenager*
loose • *If you wear a short skirt in here you're considered a loose woman.*
wanton • *A woman with many sexual partners is still considered wanton.*

MORE SYNONYMS
- libertine
- licentious
- of easy virtue

promise ❶ VERB
to say that you will definitely do or not do something • *I promise not to be back too late.*
assure • *She assured me that she would deal with the problem.*
give your word • *He had given us his word he would join the club.*
guarantee • *Most countries guarantee the right to free education.*
pledge • *They have pledged to support the opposition.*
vow • *I vowed that someday I would return to live in Europe.*

promise ❷ VERB
to show signs of • *This promised to be a very long night.*
hint at • *One finding hints at support for this theory.*
indicate • *His early work indicates talent.*
show signs of • *Already she shows signs of beauty.*

MORE SYNONYMS
- augur
- bespeak
- betoken
- bid fair

Can't find the word you're looking for? Try the index.

promise ❸ NOUN

an undertaking to do or not do something • *If you make a promise, you should keep it.*

assurance • *He gave written assurance that he would start work at once.*

guarantee • *They can give no guarantee that they will fulfil their obligations.*

pledge • *a pledge to step up cooperation between the two countries*

undertaking • *an undertaking that he would be a responsible parent*

vow • *I kept my marriage vows.*

promote ❶ VERB

to encourage the progress or success of something • *All attempts to promote a ceasefire have failed.*

back • *She backed the new initiative enthusiastically.*

support • *He thanked everyone who had supported the strike.*

promote ❷ VERB

to encourage the sale of a product by advertising • *She's in Europe promoting her new film.*

advertise • *She is contracted to advertise their beauty products.*

plug (INFORMAL) • *He was on the show to plug his latest film.*

publicize • *I was publicizing the film in London.*

promote ❸ VERB

to raise someone to a higher rank or position • *He has been promoted twice in two years.*

elevate • *He was elevated to the post of Prime Minister.*

upgrade • *He was upgraded to supervisor.*

prompt ❶ VERB

to make someone decide to do something • *Falling rates of pay have prompted consumers to stop buying new cars.*

cause • *What caused you to change your mind?*

induce • *Many teachers were induced to take early retirement.*

inspire • *These herbs will inspire you to try out all sorts of dishes.*

motivate • *How do you motivate people to work hard?*

spur • *Is it the money that spurs these firefighters to risk their lives?*

prompt ❷ VERB

to encourage someone to say something • *"What was that you were saying about a guided tour?" he prompted her.*

coax • *"Tell us what happened next," he coaxed me.*

remind • *"You stopped in the middle of your story," I reminded mother.*

prompt ❸ ADVERB

exactly at the time mentioned • *The invitation specifies eight o'clock prompt.*

exactly • *He arrived at exactly five o'clock.*

on the dot • *At nine o'clock on the dot, they have breakfast.*

precisely • *The meeting began at precisely 4.00 pm.*

sharp • *She planned to get up at 8.00 sharp.*

prompt ❹ ADJECTIVE

done without any delay • *a serious condition which needs prompt treatment*

immediate • *These incidents had an immediate effect.*

instant • *He took an instant dislike to this woman.*

Can't find the word you're looking for? Try the index.

instantaneous • *This would result in his instantaneous dismissal.*
quick • *hoping for a quick end to the dispute*
rapid • *their rapid response to the situation*
swift • *make a swift decision*

prone ❶ ADJECTIVE
having a tendency to be affected by or do something • *She is prone to depression.*
disposed • *I might have been disposed to like him in other circumstances.*
given • *I am not very given to emotional displays.*
inclined • *Nobody felt inclined to argue with Smith.*
liable • *equipment that is liable to break*
susceptible • *She's very susceptible to colds and flu.*

prone ❷ ADJECTIVE
lying flat and face downwards • *We were lying prone on the grass.*
face down • *He was lying face down on his bed.*
prostrate • *The injured jockey lay prostrate on the ground.*

proof NOUN
evidence that confirms that something is true or exists • *You have to have proof of residence in the state of Texas.*
confirmation • *further confirmation that house prices are no longer falling*
evidence • *To date there is no evidence to support this theory.*
testimony • *His testimony was an important element of the prosecution case.*
verification • *verification of her story*

MORE SYNONYMS
- authentication
- certification
- corroboration
- substantiation

proper ❶ ADJECTIVE
correct or most suitable • *the proper course of action*
appropriate • *a smart outfit appropriate to the job*
apt • *an apt title for the book*
correct • *the correct way to do things*
fitting • *His address was a fitting end to a bitter campaign.*
right • *He's the right man for the job.*
suitable • *She had no other dress suitable for the occasion.*

ANTONYM
- improper

proper ❷ ADJECTIVE
accepted or conventional • *She wanted a proper wedding.*
accepted • *the accepted way of doing things*
conventional • *conventional surgical methods*
orthodox • *orthodox police methods*

property ❶ NOUN
the things that belong to someone • *her personal property*
assets • *The company has assets of 3.5 billion francs.*
belongings • *I collected my belongings and left.*
effects • *After the funeral he sorted his father's personal effects.*
estate • *His estate was valued at $150,000.*
possessions • *People had lost their homes and all their possessions.*

a
b
c
d
e
f
g
h
i
j
k
l
m
n
o
p
q
r
s
t
u
v
w
x
y
z

Can't find the word you're looking for? Try the index.

property ➋ NOUN

a characteristic or quality • *Mint has powerful healing properties.*
attribute • *a normal attribute of human behaviour*
characteristic • *their physical characteristics*
feature • *a feature of the local culture*
hallmark • *The killing had the hallmarks of a professional assassination.*
quality • *mature people with leadership qualities*
trait • *Creativity is a human trait.*

proportion NOUN

part of an amount or group • *a tiny proportion of the population*
percentage • *It has a high percentage of protein.*
quota • *Britain's fishing quota has been cut.*
segment • *a fast-growing segment of the market*
share • *I pay a share of the phone and gas bills.*

prospect NOUN

expectation or something anticipated • *There was no prospect of going home.*
expectation • *The hotel was being renovated in expectation of a tourist boom.*
hope • *There is little hope of improvement now.*
outlook • *Officials say the outlook for next year is gloomy.*
promise • *New Year brought the promise of better things to come.*

protect VERB

to prevent someone or something from being harmed • *Cash dispensers are protected by thick steel and glass.*

defend • *I had to defend myself against the attack.*
guard • *Soldiers guarded homes near the airport.*
safeguard • *action to safeguard the ozone layer*
shelter • *a wooden house, sheltered by a low pointed roof*
shield • *He shielded his head from the sun with a newspaper.*

protection NOUN

something that protects • *a diet believed to offer protection against some cancers*
barrier • *a flood barrier*
buffer • *Keep savings as a buffer against unexpected cash needs.*
cover • *air cover for ground operations*
safeguard • *a safeguard against weeds*
shelter • *an air-raid shelter*

protest ➊ VERB

to disagree with someone or object to something • *She protested that she was a patriot, not a traitor.*
complain • *People always complain that the big banks are unhelpful.*
disagree • *I disagree with the drug laws in general.*
disapprove • *Her mother disapproved of her working in a pub.*
object • *We objected strongly but were outvoted.*
oppose • *Many parents oppose bilingual education in schools.*

MORE SYNONYMS

- demur
- expostulate
- remonstrate

protest ➋ NOUN

a strong objection • *The council has*

Can't find the word you're looking for? Try the index.

ignored their protests by backing the scheme.

complaint • the way that banks deal with complaints

objection • I questioned the logic of his objections.

outcry • The incident caused an international outcry.

proud ADJECTIVE
feeling pleasure or satisfaction
• I was proud of our players today.

gratified • He was gratified by the audience's response.

honoured • I am honoured to work with her.

pleased • I was pleased to call him my friend.

prove VERB
to provide evidence that something is definitely true
• History will prove him to have been right all along.

ascertain • They had ascertained that he was not a spy.

confirm • X-rays confirmed that he had not broken any bones.

demonstrate • You have to demonstrate that you are reliable.

establish • The autopsy established the cause of death.

verify • I can verify that it takes about thirty seconds.

MORE SYNONYMS
- authenticate
- corroborate
- evince
- substantiate

ANTONYM
- disprove

provide VERB
to make something available to someone • I'll be glad to provide a copy of this.

contribute • NATO agreed to contribute troops and equipment.

equip • proposals to equip all officers with body armour

furnish • They'll be able to furnish you with the rest of the details.

outfit • They outfitted him with artificial legs.

supply • the blood vessels supplying oxygen to the brain

provoke ❶ VERB
to try to make someone angry
• I didn't want to do anything to provoke him.

anger • It's important not to anger her.

annoy • You're just trying to annoy me.

enrage • He enraged the government by going back on the agreement.

goad • My little brother was always goading me.

insult • I didn't mean to insult you.

irritate • If you go on irritating that dog, it'll bite you.

tease • I'm sorry, I shouldn't tease you like that.

provoke ❷ VERB
to cause an unpleasant reaction
• His comments have provoked a shocked reaction.

cause • These policies are likely to cause problems.

evoke • The programme has evoked a storm of protest.

produce • The decision produced a furious reaction among fans.

prompt • The allegations prompted an indignant response from the accused.

rouse • This roused a feeling of rebellion in him.

set off • The arrival of the supply

a
b
c
d
e
f
g
h
i
j
k
l
m
n
o
p
q
r
s
t
u
v
w
x
y
z

Can't find the word you're looking for? Try the index.

van set off a minor riot among
waiting villagers.
spark off • *a political crisis sparked
off by religious violence*

pry VERB
to try to find out about someone
else's private business • *We do not
want people prying into our
business.*
interfere • *I wish everyone would
stop interfering and just leave me
alone.*
intrude • *The press were intruding
into my personal life.*
poke your nose in (INFORMAL)
• *Who asked you to poke your nose
in?*
poke your nose into (INFORMAL)
• *strangers who poke their noses into
our affairs*
snoop (INFORMAL) • *He was
snooping around Kim's hotel room.*

pub NOUN
a place where alcoholic drinks are
served • *He goes to the pub most
nights.*
bar (BRITISH) • *He works in a bar.*
boozer (BRITISH, AUSTRALIAN AND
NEW ZEALAND; INFORMAL) • *the
local boozer*
inn • *a village inn*
lounge • *the hotel lounge*
public house • *a robbery at a
public house in New Milton*
saloon • *a Wild West saloon*
tavern • *an old country tavern*

public ❶ NOUN
people in general • *the public's
confidence in the government*
masses • *a quest to bring the
Internet to the masses*
nation • *The President spoke to the
nation.*
people • *the will of the people*

populace • *a large proportion of
the populace*
society • *a menace to society*

public ❷ ADJECTIVE
relating to people in general
• *public support for the idea*
civic • *a sense of civic pride*
general • *The project should raise
general awareness about bullying.*
popular • *Popular anger has been
expressed in demonstrations.*
universal • *the universal outrage
at the deaths*

public ❸ ADJECTIVE
provided for everyone to use or
open to anyone • *public transport*
communal • *a communal dining
room*
community • *a village community
centre*
open to the public • *Part of the
castle is now open to the public.*
universal • *universal health care*

ANTONYM
● private

publicity NOUN
information or advertisements
about an item or event
• *government publicity campaigns*
advertising • *tobacco advertising
in women's magazines*
plug (INFORMAL) • *The whole
interview was an unashamed plug
for her new book.*
promotion • *They've spent a lot of
money on advertising and
promotion.*

publicize VERB
to advertise something or make it
widely known • *The author
appeared on TV to publicize her
book.*
advertise • *The product has been*

Can't find the word you're looking for? Try the index.

much advertised in specialist magazines.
plug (INFORMAL) • *another celebrity plugging their latest book*
promote • *a tour to promote his second solo album*

publish VERB
to make a piece of writing available for reading • *We publish a range of titles.*
bring out • *The newspapers all brought out special editions.*
print • *a letter printed in the Times yesterday*
put out • *a statement put out by the Iraqi news agency*

puke VERB (INFORMAL)
to vomit • *They got drunk and puked.*
be sick • *She got up and was sick in the handbasin.*
chunder (AUSTRALIAN AND NEW ZEALAND; SLANG) • *the time you chundered in the taxi*
spew (INFORMAL) • *He's really drunk. I hope he doesn't start spewing.*
throw up (INFORMAL) • *She threw up after reading reports of the trial.*
vomit • *Anything containing cow's milk made him vomit.*

pull ❶ VERB
to draw an object towards you • *a wooden plough pulled by oxen*
drag • *He dragged his chair towards the table.*
draw • *He drew his chair nearer the fire.*
haul • *A crane was used to haul the car out of the stream.*
tow • *They threatened to tow away my van.*
tug • *She kicked him, tugging his thick hair.*

yank • *She yanked open the drawer.*

ANTONYM
● push

pull ❷ NOUN
the attraction or influence of something • *The pull of Mexico was too strong.*
attraction • *The attraction of Hollywood began to pall.*
lure • *The lure of rural life is as strong as ever.*
magnetism • *the sheer magnetism of his presence*

punctual ADJECTIVE
arriving or leaving at the correct time • *The most punctual airline last year was Swissair.*
in good time • *It is now 5am and we are in good time.*
on time • *I'm generally early or on time for an appointment.*
prompt • *We expect you to be prompt for all your classes.*

punctuation NOUN

PUNCTUATION MARKS	
apostrophe	dash
asterisk	exclamation mark
bracket	full stop
bullet point	hyphen
colon	question mark
comma	semicolon

punish VERB
to make someone suffer a penalty for some misbehaviour • *I got punished for insolence.*
discipline • *He was disciplined by his company but not dismissed.*
penalize • *Bad teaching is not penalized in a formal way.*
rap someone's knuckles • *The company got its knuckles rapped for this advertisement.*

A
B
C
D
E
F
G
H
I
J
K
L
M
N
O
P
Q
R
S
T
U
V
W
X
Y
Z

sentence • *He has admitted the charge and will be sentenced later.*
throw the book at • *The football authorities seem certain to throw the book at him.*

punishment NOUN
a penalty for a crime or offence • *The punishment must always fit the crime.*
penalty • *One of those arrested could face the death penalty.*
retribution • *He didn't want any further involvement for fear of retribution.*

MORE SYNONYMS
● chastening
● chastisement
● just deserts

puny ADJECTIVE
very small and weak • *He's always been a puny lad.*
feeble • *He was old and feeble.*
frail • *She lay in bed looking frail.*
sickly • *He has been a sickly child.*
skinny • *a skinny little boy*
weak • *His arms and legs were weak.*

pupil NOUN
a student taught at a school • *She is a model pupil.*
scholar (SOUTH AFRICAN) • *a bunch of rowdy scholars*
schoolboy or **schoolgirl** • *a group of ten-year-old schoolboys*
schoolchild • *The bus was packed with schoolchildren.*
student • *The students are sorted into three ability groups.*

pure ❶ ADJECTIVE
clean and free from harmful substances • *The water is pure enough to drink.*
clean • *Tiled kitchen floors are easy*

to keep clean.
germ-free • *chlorine gas used to keep water germ-free*
pasteurized • *The milk is pasteurized to kill bacteria.*
spotless • *She kept the kitchen spotless.*
sterilized • *sterilized surgical equipment*

MORE SYNONYMS
● unadulterated
● unblemished
● uncontaminated
● unpolluted
● untainted

ANTONYM
● impure

pure ❷ ADJECTIVE
complete and total • *a matter of pure luck*
absolute • *You're talking absolute nonsense.*
complete • *complete and utter rubbish*
outright • *an outright rejection of the deal*
sheer • *acts of sheer desperation*
unmitigated • *Last year's crop was an unmitigated disaster.*
utter • *This, of course, is utter nonsense.*

purple NOUN or ADJECTIVE

SHADES OF PURPLE	
amethyst	lilac
aubergine	magenta
gentian	mauve
heather	mulberry
heliotrope	plum
indigo	puce
lavender	royal purple

purpose ❶ NOUN
the reason for something • *What*

is the purpose of this meeting?
aim • *the aim of the policy*
function • *Their main function is to raise capital for industry.*
intention • *The intention of the scheme is to encourage faster sales.*
object • *the object of the exercise*
point • *I don't see the point of it.*
reason • *What is the real reason for the delay?*

purpose ②, on purpose
ADVERB
deliberately • *Did you do that on purpose?*
by design • *The pair met often – at first by chance but later by design.*
deliberately • *It looks as if the fire was started deliberately.*
intentionally • *I've never hurt anyone intentionally.*
knowingly • *He said that he'd never knowingly taken illegal drugs.*
purposely • *They are purposely withholding information.*

push ① VERB
to apply force to something in order to move it • *She pushed the door open.*
press • *He pressed his back against the door.*
ram • *He rammed the key into the lock.*
shove • *He shoved her aside.*
thrust • *They thrust him into the back of the jeep.*

ANTONYM
● pull

push ② VERB
to persuade someone into doing something • *His mother pushed him into auditioning for a part.*
encourage • *She encouraged me to stick to the diet.*

persuade • *They persuaded him to moderate his views.*
press • *Trade unions are pressing him to stand firm.*
urge • *He had urged her to come to Ireland.*

pushy ADJECTIVE (INFORMAL)
unpleasantly forceful and determined • *a confident and pushy young woman*
aggressive • *a very aggressive business executive*
ambitious • *You have to be ambitious to make it in this business.*
assertive • *Women have become more assertive over the last ten years.*
bossy • *She remembers being a rather bossy little girl.*
forceful • *Sarah is notorious for her forceful and quarrelsome nature.*
obtrusive • *"You are rude and obtrusive, Mr Smith," said Tommy.*

put ① VERB
to place something somewhere
• *She put the photograph on the desk.*
deposit • *On his way out he deposited a glass in front of me.*
lay • *Lay a sheet of newspaper on the floor.*
place • *He placed it in the inside pocket of his jacket.*
position • *Plants were carefully positioned in the alcove.*
rest • *He rested his arms on the back of the chair.*

put ② VERB
to express something • *I think you put that very well.*
phrase • *I would have phrased it quite differently.*

a
b
c
d
e
f
g
h
i
j
k
l
m
n
o
p
q
r
s
t
u
v
w
x
y
z

Can't find the word you're looking for? Try the index.

word • *You misinterpreted his letter, or else he worded it poorly.*

put down ❶ VERB

to criticize someone and make them appear foolish • *Racist jokes come from wanting to put down other people.*
belittle • *She's always belittling her husband in public.*
criticize • *She rarely criticized any of her children.*
find fault • *I wish you wouldn't find fault with me in front of the kids.*
humiliate • *His teacher continually humiliates him.*

put down ❷ VERB

to kill an animal that is ill or dangerous • *Magistrates ordered the dog to be put down immediately.*
destroy • *The horse had to be destroyed.*
kill • *Animals should be killed humanely.*
put out of its misery • *The bird was so badly injured I decided to put it out of its misery.*
put to sleep • *Take the dog to the vet's and have her put to sleep.*

put off VERB

to delay something • *Ministers have put off making a decision until next month.*
defer • *Customers often defer payment for as long as possible.*
delay • *She wants to delay the wedding.*
postpone • *The visit has been postponed indefinitely.*
put back • *The news conference has been put back a couple of hours.*
put on ice • *The decision has been put on ice until October.*

reschedule • *Since I'll be away, I'd like to reschedule the meeting.*

put up with VERB

to tolerate something disagreeable • *They won't put up with a return to the bad old days.*
abide • *I can't abide arrogant people.*
bear • *He can't bear to talk about it.*
stand • *She cannot stand her boss.*
stand for • *We won't stand for it any more.*
stomach • *He could not stomach violence.*
tolerate • *She can no longer tolerate the position she is in.*

MORE SYNONYMS

● brook
● countenance

puzzle ❶ VERB

to perplex and confuse • *There was something about her that puzzled me.*
baffle • *An apple tree producing square fruit is baffling experts.*
bewilder • *His silence bewildered her.*
confuse • *German politics surprised and confused him.*
mystify • *The audience were mystified by the plot.*
stump • *I was stumped by an unexpected question.*

MORE SYNONYMS

● confound
● flummox
● nonplus
● perplex

puzzle ❷ NOUN

a game or question that requires a lot of thought to solve • *a crossword puzzle*

Can't find the word you're looking for? Try the index.

brain-teaser (INFORMAL)
• *It took me ages to solve that brain-teaser.*
conundrum • *It was a conundrum with no solution.*

poser • *Here is a little poser for you.*
problem • *a mathematical problem*
riddle • *See if you can answer this riddle.*

Qq

qualification ❶ NOUN
a skill or achievement • *His qualifications are impressive.*
ability • *a man of considerable abilities*
accomplishment • *Carl was proud of his son's accomplishments.*
achievement • *the highest academic achievement*
capability • *Her capabilities were not fully appreciated.*
quality • *Colley's leadership qualities*
skill • *a skill you can use*

MORE SYNONYMS
● attribute
● endowment

qualification ❷ NOUN
something added to make a statement less strong • *The argument is not true without qualification.*
condition • *You can make any conditions you like.*
exception • *a major exception to this general argument*
modification • *to consider modifications to his proposal*
reservation • *men whose work I admire without reservation*

qualify VERB
to pass the tests necessary for an activity • *I qualified as a doctor 30 years ago.*
get certified • *They wanted to get certified as divers.*

become licensed • *You can only become licensed by doing an accredited course.*
gain qualifications • *the opportunity to gain medical qualifications*
graduate • *She graduated as a physiotherapist in 1960.*

quality ❶ NOUN
the measure of how good something is • *The quality of food very poor.*
calibre • *a man of your calibre*
distinction • *a chef of great distinction*
grade • *high grade meat and poultry*
merit • *a work of real merit*
value • *He set a high value upon their friendship.*
worth • *a person's true worth*

quality ❷ NOUN
a characteristic of something • *These qualities are essential for success.*
aspect • *every aspect of our lives*
characteristic • *their physical characteristics*
feature • *the most striking feature of his work*
mark • *the mark of a great composer*
property • *the magnetic propertie. of iron*
trait • *the young Ms Rankine's personality traits*

Can't find the word you're looking for? Try the index.

MORE SYNONYMS
- attribute
- peculiarity

quantity ❶ NOUN
an amount you can measure or count • *a large quantity of alcohol*
amount • *a small amount of mayonnaise*
number • *There are a limited number of seats available.*
part • *the greater part of his wealth*
sum • *a large sum of money*

MORE SYNONYMS
- portion
- quota

quantity ❷ NOUN
the amount of something that there is • *emphasis on quality rather than quantity*
extent • *the extent of the damage*
measure • *The government has had a fair measure of success.*
size • *He gauged the size of the audience.*
volume • *the sheer volume of traffic and accidents*

MORE SYNONYMS
- bulk
- expanse
- magnitude

quarrel ❶ NOUN
an angry argument • *I had a terrible quarrel with my brother.*
argument • *an argument about money*
disagreement • *My instructor and I had a brief disagreement.*
dispute • *Brand eavesdropped on the petty dispute.*
feud • *a two-year feud between neighbours*
fight • *It was a silly fight about where we parked the car.*

row • *Maxine and I had a terrible row.*
squabble • *minor squabbles about phone bills*

MORE SYNONYMS
- altercation
- fracas
- fray

quarrel ❷ VERB
to have an angry argument • *My brother quarrelled with my father.*
argue • *They were still arguing later.*
bicker • *They bickered endlessly over procedure.*
clash • *She had clashed with Doyle in the past.*
fall out (INFORMAL) • *Mum and I used to fall out a lot.*
fight • *The couple often fought with their son.*
row • *He had rowed with his girlfriend.*
squabble • *The children were squabbling over the remote control.*

queasy ADJECTIVE
feeling slightly sick • *He already felt queasy.*
ill • *I was feeling ill.*
nauseous • *The medication may make you feel nauseous.*
queer • *Twenty minutes later, he began to feel queer.*
sick • *The very thought of food made him feel sick.*
unwell • *He felt unwell this afternoon.*

query ❶ NOUN
a question • *If you have any queries, please contact us.*
inquiry • *I'll be happy to answer all your inquiries, if I can.*
question • *The President refused to*

Can't find the word you're looking for? Try the index.

a
b
c
d
e
f
g
h
i
j
k
l
m
n
o
p
q
r
s
t
u
v
w
x
y
z

answer further questions on the subject.

ANTONYM
- response

query ② VERB
to question something because it seems wrong • *No one queried my decision.*
challenge • *The move was challenged by two countries.*
dispute • *He disputed the allegations.*
object to • *A lot of people objected to the plan.*
question • *It never occurred to me to question the doctor's decisions.*

question ① NOUN
a problem that needs to be discussed • *Can we get back to the question of the car?*
issue • *What is your view on this issue?*
motion • *The conference is now debating the motion.*
point • *There is another point to consider.*
subject • *He raised the subject of money.*
topic • *the topic of where to go on holiday*

question ② VERB
to ask someone questions • *A man is being questioned by police.*
examine • *Lawyers examined the witnesses.*
interrogate • *I interrogated everyone even slightly involved.*
probe • *tabloid journalists probing us for details*
quiz • *She quizzed me quite closely for a while.*

MORE SYNONYMS
- cross-examine

- interview
- investigate

ANTONYM
- answer

question ③ VERB
to express doubts about something • *He never stopped questioning his own beliefs.*
challenge • *Rose convincingly challenged the story.*
dispute • *Nobody disputed that Davey was clever.*
distrust • *I distrusted my ability to keep quiet.*
doubt • *Nobody doubted his sincerity.*
query • *No one queried my decision.*
suspect • *Do we suspect the motives of our friends?*

quick ① ADJECTIVE
moving with great speed • *You'll have to be quick to catch the flight.*
brisk • *a brisk walk*
fast • *a very fast driver*
hasty • *He spoke in a hasty, nervous way.*
rapid • *a rapid rise through the company*
speedy • *a speedy recovery*
swift • *She is as swift as an arrow.*

MORE SYNONYMS
- express
- fleet
- headlong

ANTONYM
- slow

quick ② ADJECTIVE
lasting only a short time • *a quick chat*
brief • *a brief meeting*
cursory • *a cursory glance inside the van*

Can't find the word you're looking for? Try the index.

hasty • *a hasty meal of bread and soup*
hurried • *He ate a hurried breakfast.*
perfunctory • *With a perfunctory smile, she walked past Jessica.*

ANTONYM
- long

quick ❸ ADJECTIVE
happening without any delay • *a quick response*
hasty • *This is no hasty decision.*
prompt • *Prompt action is needed.*
sudden • *this week's sudden cold snap*

quickly ADVERB
with great speed • *Stop me if I'm speaking too quickly.*
fast • *How fast were you driving?*
hastily • *sheltering in hastily erected tents*
hurriedly • *students hurriedly taking notes*
rapidly • *moving rapidly across the field*
speedily • *She speedily recovered herself.*
swiftly • *They had to act swiftly to save him.*

ANTONYM
- slowly

quiet ❶ ADJECTIVE
making very little noise • *The children were quiet and contented.*
hushed • *Tales were exchanged in hushed tones.*
inaudible • *a tiny, almost inaudible squeak*
low • *I spoke in a low voice to Sullivan.*
silent • *He could speak no English and was silent.*
soft • *There was some soft music playing.*

MORE SYNONYMS
- noiseless
- soundless

ANTONYM
- noisy

quiet ❷ ADJECTIVE
peaceful and calm • *a quiet evening at home*
calm • *The city seems relatively calm today.*
mild • *The night was mild.*
peaceful • *a peaceful old house*
restful • *a restful scene*
serene • *the beautiful, serene park*
tranquil • *a tranquil lake*

MORE SYNONYMS
- motionless
- placid
- untroubled

quiet ❸ NOUN
silence or lack of noise • *The teacher called for quiet.*
calmness • *the calmness of this area*
peace • *I enjoy peace and quiet.*
serenity • *the peace and serenity of a tropical sunset*
silence • *There was a silence around the table.*
stillness • *the stillness of the summer night*
tranquillity • *the tranquillity of village life*

ANTONYM
- noise

quit VERB
to leave a place or stop doing something • *Leigh quit his job as a salesman.*
discontinue • *Do not discontinue the treatment without seeing your doctor.*

Can't find the word you're looking for? Try the index.

a b c d e f g h i j k l m n o p q r s t u v w x y z

A
B
C
D
E
F
G
H
I
J
K
L
M
N
O
Q
R
S
T
U
V
W
X
Y
Z

give up • *She gave up smoking last year.*
leave • *He left school with no qualifications.*
resign • *Scott resigned from the firm.*
retire • *Littlejohn was forced to retire from the race.*
stop • *I stopped working last year to have a baby.*

MORE SYNONYMS
- abandon
- cease

quite ❶ ADVERB
fairly but not very • *He is quite old.*
fairly • *Both ships are fairly new.*
moderately • *a moderately attractive man*
rather • *I made some rather bad mistakes.*
reasonably • *I can dance reasonably well.*
somewhat • *He's somewhat deaf.*

quite ❷ ADVERB
completely and totally • *Jane lay quite still.*

absolutely • *I absolutely refuse to get married.*
completely • *something completely different*
entirely • *an entirely new approach*
fully • *He has still not fully recovered.*
perfectly • *They are perfectly safe to eat.*
totally • *The fire totally destroyed the house.*

MORE SYNONYMS
- precisely
- wholly

quote VERB
to repeat the exact words someone has said • *She quoted a great line from Shakespeare.*
cite • *She cites a favourite poem by George Herbert.*
extract • *This material has been extracted from the handbook.*
recite • *They recited poetry to one another.*
repeat • *Could you repeat the whole interview word for word?*

Can't find the word you're looking for? Try the index.

Rr

race ❶ NOUN
a group of human beings with
similar physical characteristics
• *Discrimination on the grounds of
race is illegal.*
ethnic group • *Ethnic group and
nationality are often different.*
nation • *a mature and cultured
nation*
people • *an address to the
American people*

race ❷ VERB
to move very quickly • *When school
was over, Kate raced home.*
dash • *He dashed upstairs.*
fly • *I must fly or I'll miss my train.*
hurry • *They hurried down the street.*
run • *The gunmen escaped by
running into the woods.*
speed • *speeding along as fast as I
could*
tear • *The door flew open and she
tore into the room.*

racket ❶ NOUN
a lot of noise • *The racket went on
past midnight.*
clamour • *She could hear a
clamour in the road.*
commotion • *He heard a
commotion outside.*
din • *make themselves heard over
the din of the crowd*
hubbub • *His voice was drowned
out by the hubbub of the fans.*
noise • *There was too much noise
in the room.*

row • *"Whatever is that row?" she
demanded.*
rumpus • *There was such a
rumpus, she had to shout to make
herself heard.*

MORE SYNONYMS
● cacophony
● tumult

racket ❷ NOUN
an illegal way of making money
• *a drugs racket*
enterprise • *a money-laundering
enterprise*
fraud • *tax frauds*
scheme • *a quick money-making
scheme*

rage ❶ NOUN
a feeling of very strong anger
• *trembling with rage*
anger • *She felt deep anger at what
he had said.*
frenzy • *Their behaviour drove her
into a frenzy.*
fury • *Her face was distorted with
fury and pain.*
wrath • *He incurred the wrath of
the referee.*

rage ❷ VERB
to be angry or speak angrily about
something • *He was raging at their
lack of response.*
be furious • *He is furious at the
way his wife has been treated.*
fume • *I was still fuming over her
remark.*

Can't find the word you're looking for? Try the index.

A
B
C
D
E
F
G
H
I
J
K
L
M
N
O
P
Q
R
S
T
U
V
W
X
Y
Z

lose your temper • *They had never seen me lose my temper before.*

rave • *She cried and raved for weeks.*

storm • *"It's a disaster", he stormed.*

rage ❸ VERB

to continue with great force • *The fire raged out of control.*

be at its height • *when the storm was at its height*

rampage • *a mob rampaging through the town*

storm • *armies storming across the continent*

surge • *The flood surged through the village.*

raid ❶ VERB

to attack something by force • *Soldiers raided the capital.*

assault • *Their stronghold was assaulted by pirates.*

attack • *We are being attacked!*

break into • *No-one saw them break into the warehouse.*

invade • *The invading army took all their food supplies.*

plunder • *plundering the homes of the inhabitants*

MORE SYNONYMS

● pillage
● rifle
● sack

raid ❷ NOUN

an attack on something • *a bank raid*

attack • *a surprise attack on the house*

break-in • *The break-in occurred last night.*

foray • *Guerrillas made forays into the territory.*

MORE SYNONYMS

● incursion
● sortie

rain ❶ NOUN

water falling from the clouds • *A spot of rain fell on her hand.*

deluge • *homes damaged in the deluge*

downpour • *A two-day downpour swelled water levels.*

drizzle • *The drizzle had stopped and the sun was shining.*

rainfall • *four years of below average rainfall*

showers • *bright spells followed by scattered showers*

rain ❷ VERB

to fall from the sky in drops • *It rained the whole weekend.*

drizzle • *It was starting to drizzle when I left.*

pour • *We drove all the way in pouring rain.*

teem • *It teemed the entire day.*

raise ❶ VERB

to make something higher • *a drive to raise standards of literacy*

elevate • *Emotional stress can elevate blood pressure.*

heave • *He heaved his crippled leg into an easier position.*

hoist • *He climbed on the roof to hoist the flag.*

lift • *She lifted the last of her drink to her lips.*

ANTONYM

● lower

raise ❷ VERB

to look after children until they are grown up • *the house where she was raised*

bring up • *She brought up four children single-handed.*

Can't find the word you're looking for? Try the index.

nurture • *the best way to nurture a child to adulthood*
rear • *He reared his sister's family as well as his own.*

raise ❸ VERB
to mention or suggest something • *He had raised no objections at the time.*
advance • *Some important ideas were advanced at the conference.*
bring up • *I hesitate to bring up this matter with you, but I have no choice.*
broach • *Eventually I broached the subject of her early life.*
introduce • *always willing to introduce a new topic*
moot • *The project was first mooted last year.*
suggest • *one possibility that might be suggested*

ramble ❶ NOUN
a long walk in the countryside • *They went for a ramble through the woods.*
excursion • *They organized an excursion into the hills.*
hike • *a long hike along the valley floor*
stroll • *The next day we took a stroll along the river bank.*
walk • *We often go for walks in the country.*

ramble ❷ VERB
to go for a long walk • *freedom to ramble across the moors*
amble • *ambling along a country lane*
stray • *You mustn't stray across the border.*
stroll • *whistling as he strolled along the road*
walk • *We finished the evening by walking along the beach.*

wander • *He loved to wander in the woods.*

MORE SYNONYMS
● perambulate
● rove

ramble ❸ VERB
to talk in a confused way • *He started rambling and repeating himself.*
babble • *She babbled on and on about the visitors.*
chatter • *I was so nervous that I chattered away like an idiot.*

rampage ❶ VERB
to rush about angrily or violently • *children rampaging round the garden*
go berserk • *The crowd went berserk at the sight of him.*
rage • *His shop was stormed by a raging mob.*
run amok • *He was arrested after running amok with a gun.*
run riot • *The prisoners ran riot after the announcement.*

rampage ❷, on the rampage ADJECTIVE
rushing about in a wild and violent way • *a bull on the rampage*
amok • *The gunman ran amok and killed several people.*
berserk • *The fans went berserk and mobbed the stage.*
wild • *They just went wild after he left.*

random ❶ ADJECTIVE
not based on a definite plan • *random violence against innocent victims*
aimless • *after several hours of aimless searching*
arbitrary • *Arbitrary arrests and detention without trial were common.*

a
b
c
d
e
f
g
h
i
j
k
l
m
n
o
p
q
r
s
t
u
v
w
x
y
z

Can't find the word you're looking for? Try the index.

A
B
C
D
E
F
G
H
I
J
K
L
M
N
O
P
Q
R
S
T
U
V
W
X
Y
Z

haphazard • *He had never seen such a haphazard approach to writing.*
indiscriminate • *the indiscriminate use of fertilisers*
spot • *picked up in a spot check*

MORE SYNONYMS
- desultory
- fortuitous
- unpremeditated

random ❷, at random
ADVERB
without any definite plan • *chosen at random*
aimlessly • *wandering around aimlessly for hours*
arbitrarily • *The questions were chosen quite arbitrarily.*
haphazardly • *The books were stacked haphazardly on the shelves.*
indiscriminately • *This disease strikes indiscriminately.*
randomly • *a randomly selected sample*

MORE SYNONYMS
- adventitiously
- unsystematically
- willy-nilly

range ❶ NOUN
the maximum limits of something • *Tactical nuclear weapons have shorter ranges.*
bounds • *the bounds of good taste*
extent • *the full extent of my knowledge*
field • *The subject covers a very wide field.*
limits • *outside the city limits*
province • *This doesn't fall within our province.*
scope • *He promised to widen the scope of their activities.*

range ❷ NOUN
a number of different things of the

same kind • *a wide range of colours*
assortment • *There was a good assortment to choose from.*
class • *Cars in this class are expensive*
gamut • *I experienced the whole gamut of emotions.*
selection • *a wide selection of delicious meals*
series • *a completely new model series*
variety • *The shop stocks a variety of local craft products.*

range ❸ VERB
to vary between two extremes • *goods ranging between the everyday and the exotic*
extend • *The reclaimed land extends from here to the river.*
go • *Their sizes go from very small to enormous.*
run • *Accommodation runs from log cabins to high-standard hotels.*
stretch • *with interests that stretched from chemicals to sugar*
vary • *The cycle of sunspots varies between 8 to 15 years.*

rank ❶ NOUN
someone's level in a group • *He rose to the rank of captain.*
class • *relationships between social classes*
echelon • *the upper echelons of society*
grade • *Staff turnover is high among the junior grades.*
level • *various levels of the judiciary system*
standing • *a woman of wealth and social standing*
station • *a humble station in life*
status • *promoted to the status of foreman*

rank ❷ NOUN
a row of people or things • *ranks of*

Can't find the word you're looking for? Try the index.

police in riot gear
column • *a column of figures*
file • *They walked in single file to the top.*
line • *He waited in a line of slow-moving vehicles.*
row • *She lived in the middle of a row of pretty cottages.*

rank ❸ ADJECTIVE

complete and absolute • *It was rank stupidity to go there alone.*
absolute • *not intended for absolute beginners*
complete • *her complete ignorance*
downright • *That was just downright rudeness.*
sheer • *his sheer stupidity*
unmitigated • *an unmitigated villain*
utter • *his utter disregard for other people*

MORE SYNONYMS

- arrant
- egregious

rare ADJECTIVE

not common or frequent • *a rare species of bird*
exceptional • *in exceptional circumstances*
few • *Genuine friends are few.*
scarce • *Jobs are becoming increasingly scarce.*
sparse • *Information about the tests is sparse.*
sporadic • *occurring at only sporadic intervals*
uncommon • *The disease is uncommon in younger women.*
unusual • *an unusual variety but a very attractive one*

ANTONYM

- common

rash ❶ ADJECTIVE

acting in a hasty and foolish way
• *It would be rash to act on such flimsy evidence.*
foolhardy • *Some described his behaviour as foolhardy.*
hasty • *This is no hasty decision.*
impetuous • *As usual, he reacted in a heated and impetuous way.*
impulsive • *He is too impulsive to take this responsibility.*
reckless • *his reckless driving*

MORE SYNONYMS

- heedless
- injudicious
- unthinking

rash ❷ NOUN

an irritated area on your skin
• *I noticed a rash on my leg.*
eruption • *an unpleasant skin eruption*
outbreak • *an outbreak of blisters around his mouth*

rash ❸ NOUN

a large number of events happening together • *a rash of strikes*
epidemic • *A victim of the recent epidemic of shootings.*
flood • *a flood of complaints about the programme*
plague • *Last year there was a plague of burglaries.*
spate • *a spate of attacks on horses*
wave • *the current wave of violent attacks*

rate ❶ NOUN

the speed or frequency of something • *appearing at the rate of one a week*
frequency • *She phoned with increasing frequency.*
pace • *at an accelerated pace*

a
b
c
d
e
f
g
h
i
j
k
l
m
n
o
p
q
r
s
t
u
v
w
x
y
z

Can't find the word you're looking for? Try the index.

speed • *moving at the speed of light*
tempo • *They wanted to speed up the tempo of change.*
velocity • *changes in wind velocity*

rate ❷ NOUN
the cost or charge for something
• *phone calls at cheap rates*
charge • *An annual charge will be made for this service.*
cost • *a low-cost mortgage*
fee • *The work will be invoiced at the usual fee.*
price • *falling share prices*
tariff • *How much you pay depends on your tariff.*

rate ❸ VERB
to give an opinion of someone's qualities • *He was rated as one of the best.*
appraise • *She gave me an appraising glance.*
class • *classed as one of the top ten athletes*
consider • *I considered myself to be quite good at maths.*
count • *That would be counted as wrong.*
rank • *The hotel was ranked as one of the world's best.*
regard • *a highly regarded member of staff*

MORE SYNONYMS
● adjudge
● esteem
● evaluate

rather ADVERB
to a certain extent • *We got along rather well.*
fairly • *Both ships are fairly new.*
pretty (INFORMAL) • *I'm pretty tired now.*
quite • *The cottage looks quite ordinary from the road.*

relatively • *I think I'm relatively easy to get on with.*
slightly • *slightly startled by his sudden appearance*
somewhat • *He said, somewhat unconvincingly, that he would pay.*

rational ADJECTIVE
using reason rather than emotion
• *to arrive at a rational conclusion*
enlightened • *enlightened companies who take a pragmatic view*
logical • *There must be a logical explanation for it.*
reasonable • *a perfectly reasonable decision*
sensible • *The sensible thing is to leave them alone.*

rave ❶ VERB
to talk in an uncontrolled way • *He started raving about being treated badly.*
babble • *She babbled on and on about her plans.*
rage • *He was raging at their lack of response.*
rant • *She started ranting about her boss's attitude.*

rave ❷ VERB (INFORMAL)
to be enthusiastic about something • *She raved about the facilities there.*
be wild about (INFORMAL) • *He was just wild about the play.*
enthuse • *She enthused about the local architecture.*
gush • *"It was brilliant," he gushed.*

reach ❶ VERB
to arrive somewhere • *He did not stop until he reached the door.*
arrive at • *to arrive at an erroneous conclusion*
attain • *She worked hard to attain a state of calm.*

A B C D E F G H I J K L M N O P Q R S T U V W X Y Z

get as far as • *If we get as far as the coast we will be quite satisfied.*
get to • *You must get to the end before noon.*
make • *They didn't think they would make the summit.*

reach ❷ VERB
to extend as far as something
• *Her cloak reached to the ground.*
extend to • *The boundaries extend to the edge of the lake.*
go as far as • *Try to make the ball go as far as the trees.*
touch • *I could touch both walls with my arms extended.*

reach ❸ VERB
to arrive at a certain stage or level
• *Unemployment has reached record levels.*
arrive at • *They planted a flag when they arrived at the top.*
attain • *He was close to attaining his personal best.*
climb to • *Attendance climbed to a record level this year.*
fall to • *Profits are expected to fall to their lowest level.*
rise to • *She rose rapidly to the top of her profession.*

reaction ❶ NOUN
a person's response to something
• *Reaction to the visit was mixed.*
acknowledgment • *She made no acknowledgment of my question.*
answer • *In answer to speculation in the press, she declared her interest.*
feedback • *Continue to ask for feedback on your work.*
response • *in response to a request from the members*

reaction ❷ NOUN
a response to something

unpopular • *a reaction against religious leaders*
backlash • *the male backlash against feminism*
counterbalance • *an organization set up as a counterbalance to the official group*

read ❶ VERB
to look at something written
• *I love to read in bed.*
glance at • *He just glanced briefly at the article.*
look at • *She was looking at the evening paper.*
pore over • *poring over a dictionary*
scan • *There's only time to scan through it quickly.*
study • *I'll study the text more closely later.*

read ❷ VERB
to understand what someone means • *as if he could read her thoughts*
comprehend • *Her expression was difficult to comprehend.*
decipher • *She was still no closer to deciphering the code.*
interpret • *You have to interpret their gestures, too.*

ready ❶ ADJECTIVE
prepared for action or use • *The plums are ready to eat now.*
organized • *Everything is organized for the party tomorrow.*
prepared • *He was prepared for a tough fight.*
primed • *The other side is primed for battle.*
ripe • *Are those strawberries ripe yet?*
set • *We'll be set to go in five minutes.*

a
b
c
d
e
f
g
h
i
j
k
l
m
n
o
p
q
r
s
t
u
v
w
x
y
z

Can't find the word you're looking for? Try the index.

ready ➋ ADJECTIVE
willing to do something • *She was always ready to give interviews.*
agreeable • *We can go ahead if you are agreeable.*
eager • *Children are eager to learn.*
happy • *always happy to help*
keen • *He wasn't keen to get involved.*
willing • *questions which they were not willing to answer*

MORE SYNONYMS
● minded
● predisposed

ready ➌ ADJECTIVE
easily produced or obtained • *ready cash*
accessible • *The system should be accessible to everyone.*
available • *Food is available round the clock.*
convenient • *a convenient excuse*
handy • *Keep a pencil and paper handy.*

real ➊ ADJECTIVE
actually existing and not imagined • *You're dealing with real life now.*
actual • *She was the actual basis for the leading character.*
authentic • *containing authentic details of what happened*
concrete • *I don't have any concrete evidence.*
factual • *a factual account*
genuine • *His worries about the future were genuine ones.*
legitimate • *These are legitimate concerns.*
tangible • *I cannot see any tangible benefits in these changes.*
true • *the true story of his life*

ANTONYM
● imaginary

real ➋ ADJECTIVE
genuine and not imitation • *Is that a real gun?*
authentic • *an authentic French recipe*
bona fide • *We are happy to donate to bona fide charities.*
dinkum (AUSTRALIAN AND NEW ZEALAND; INFORMAL) • *a place which serves dinkum Aussie tucker*
genuine • *It's a genuine Rembrandt, all right.*
honest • *It was an honest attempt to set things right.*
sincere • *His remorse was completely sincere, not just an act.*
rightful • *the rightful heir to the throne*
true • *He is a true believer in human rights.*
unaffected • *her genuine and unaffected sympathy for the victims*

ANTONYM
● fake

realistic ➊ ADJECTIVE
accepting the true situation • *It's only realistic to admit that things will go wrong.*
down-to-earth • *We welcomed her down-to-earth approach.*
level-headed • *a sensible, level-headed approach*
matter-of-fact • *He sounded matter-of-fact and unemotional.*
practical • *a highly practical attitude to life*
sensible • *I'm trying to persuade you to be more sensible.*
sober • *a more sober assessment of the situation*

realistic ➋ ADJECTIVE
true to real life • *His novels are more realistic than his short stories.*

Can't find the word you're looking for? Try the index.

authentic • *They have to look authentic.*
faithful • *faithful copies of old household items*
lifelike • *almost as lifelike as a photograph*
true • *It gave a true picture of how things were.*

MORE SYNONYMS
● naturalistic
● representational
● vérité

reality NOUN
something that is true and not imagined • *Fiction and reality were increasingly blurred.*
authenticity • *The film's authenticity impressed the critics.*
fact • *No-one knew how much of what he said was fact.*
realism • *His stories had an edge of realism.*
truth • *I must tell you the truth about this situation.*

realize VERB
to become aware of something • *People don't realize how serious it is.*
appreciate • *He appreciates the difficulties we face.*
comprehend • *They do not comprehend the nature of the problem.*
grasp • *She still couldn't grasp what had really happened.*
recognize • *Of course I recognize that evil exists.*
understand • *I didn't understand what he meant until later.*

really ➊ ADVERB
very or certainly • *I've had a really good time.*
absolutely • *feeling absolutely exhausted*

certainly • *I am certainly getting tired of hearing about it.*
extremely • *My mobile phone is extremely useful.*
remarkably • *They have been remarkably successful.*
terribly • *I'm terribly sorry to bother you.*
truly • *a truly splendid man*
very • *learning very quickly*

really ➋ ADVERB
in actual fact • *He didn't really love her.*
actually • *I pretended I was interested, but I was actually half asleep.*
in fact • *It sounds simple, but in fact it's very difficult.*
in reality • *He came across as streetwise, but in reality he was not.*
truly • *I truly never minded caring for Rusty.*

reason ➊ NOUN
the cause of something that happens • *for a multitude of reasons*
cause • *The true cause of the accident may never be known.*
grounds • *some grounds for optimism*
incentive • *There is no incentive to adopt these measures.*
motive • *Police have ruled out robbery as a motive.*
purpose • *the purpose of their visit*

reason ➋ NOUN
the ability to think • *a conflict between emotion and reason*
intellect • *good health and a lively intellect*
judgment • *His judgment was impaired.*
rationality • *We live in an era of rationality.*

a
b
c
d
e
f
g
h
i
j
k
l
m
n
o
p
q
r
s
t
u
v
w
x
y
z

Can't find the word you're looking for? Try the index.

reasoning • *a lack of sound reasoning and logic*
sense • *He should have had more sense.*

reason ❸ VERB

to try to persuade someone of something • *It's better to reason with them than to use force.*
bring round (INFORMAL) • *We'll try to bring you round to our point of view.*
persuade • *I had to persuade him of the advantages.*
win over • *They still hoped to win him over to their way of thinking.*

reasonable ❶ ADJECTIVE

fair and sensible • *a reasonable sort of chap*
fair • *You can be sure she will be fair with you.*
moderate • *an easygoing man of very moderate views*
rational • *Please try to be rational about this.*
sane • *No sane person wishes to see a war.*
sensible • *She was a sensible girl and did not panic.*
sober • *We are now more sober and realistic.*
steady • *a politician who was steady almost to the point of being boring*
wise • *You're a wise old man: tell me what to do.*

MORE SYNONYMS

● judicious
● plausible

reasonable ❷ ADJECTIVE

based on good reasoning • *It seems reasonable to expect rapid urban growth.*
justifiable. • *Our violence was*

justifiable on the grounds of political necessity.
legitimate • *That's a perfectly legitimate fear.*
logical • *There was a logical explanation.*
sensible • *a sensible solution*
sound • *sound advice*
understandable • *His unhappiness was understandable.*

reasonable ❸ ADJECTIVE

not too expensive • *His fees were quite reasonable.*
cheap • *She said she'd share a flat if I could find somewhere cheap enough.*
competitive • *homes offered for sale at competitive prices*
fair • *It's a fair price for a car like that.*
inexpensive • *an inexpensive divorce settlement*
low • *The low prices and friendly service made for a pleasant evening.*
modest • *a modest charge*

reassure VERB

to make someone feel less worried • *She reassured me that everything was fine.*
bolster • *measures intended to bolster morale*
cheer up • *I wrote it just to cheer myself up.*
comfort • *He tried to comfort her as far as he could.*
encourage • *Investors were encouraged by the news.*

MORE SYNONYMS

● buoy up
● hearten
● inspirit

rebel VERB

to fight against authority and

accepted values • *I rebelled against everything when I was young.*
defy • *It was the first time she had defied her mother.*
mutiny • *Sailors mutinied against their officers.*
resist • *activists convicted of resisting apartheid*
revolt • *The islanders revolted against the prince.*

rebellion NOUN
an organized opposition to authority • *the ruthless suppression of the rebellion*
insurrection • *They were plotting to stage an armed insurrection.*
mutiny • *convicted of mutiny and high treason*
revolt • *The revolt ended in failure.*
revolution • *after the French Revolution*
uprising • *Isolated attacks turned into a full-scale uprising.*

receive ❶ VERB
to accept something from someone • *Did they receive my letter?*
accept • *They accepted the parcel gratefully.*
be given • *We were all given presents.*
get • *She got some lovely things.*
pick up • *He picked up an award for his performance.*
take • *Will you take this parcel for your neighbour?*

receive ❷ VERB
to experience something • *We received a very warm welcome.*
encounter • *He encountered some unexpected opposition.*
suffer • *He suffered some bangs and bumps.*
sustain • *She had sustained a cut*

on her arm.
undergo • *You may have to undergo a bit of teasing.*

receive ❸ VERB
to welcome visitors • *You must be there to receive your guests.*
entertain • *She loved to entertain friends at home.*
greet • *They greeted the visitors at the door.*
meet • *I'll come down to meet you.*
take in • *The country took in many refugees.*
welcome • *Several people came by to welcome me.*

recent ADJECTIVE
happening a short time ago • *his most recent acquisition*
current • *a sound knowledge of current affairs*
fresh • *fresh footprints in the snow*
new • *the subject of a new film*
present-day • *Even by present-day standards these were large aircraft.*
up-to-date • *the most up-to-date computers*

MORE SYNONYMS
● contemporary
● latter-day

recession NOUN
a decline in economic conditions • *companies which survived after the recession*
decline • *signs of economic decline*
depression • *the Great Depression of the 1930s*
downturn • *due to a sharp downturn in the industry*
slump • *Many jobs were lost during the slump.*

reckon ❶ VERB (INFORMAL)
to think or believe something is

a
b
c
d
e
f
g
h
i
j
k
l
m
n
o
p
q
r
s
t
u
v
w
x
y
z

Can't find the word you're looking for? Try the index.

the case • *I reckon he's still fond of her.*

assume • *If mistakes occurred, they were assumed to be my fault.*

believe (FORMAL) • *"You've never heard of him?" "I don't believe so."*

consider • *Barbara considers that people who sell these birds are acting illegally.*

judge • *I would judge that my earnings are considerably below those of my sister.*

suppose • *I suppose I'd better do some homework.*

think • *I think there should be a ban on tobacco advertising.*

MORE SYNONYMS

- deem (FORMAL)
- hold to be
- surmise (FORMAL)

reckon ❷ VERB

to calculate an amount • *The figure is now reckoned to be 15%.*

calculate • *We calculate that the average size farm in the county is 65 acres.*

count • *The years before their arrival in prison are not counted as part of their sentence.*

estimate • *Analysts estimate its current popularity at around ten per cent.*

figure out • *I roughly figured out the total.*

work out • *It is proving hard to work out the value of their assets.*

recognize ❶ VERB

to know who or what someone or something is • *I recognized him at once.*

identify • *She tried to identify the perfume.*

know • *You'd know him if you saw him again.*

place • *He couldn't place my voice immediately.*

spot • *I spotted the house quite easily.*

recognize ❷ VERB

to accept or acknowledge something • *He was recognized as an outstanding pilot.*

acknowledge • *Her great bravery was acknowledged.*

appreciate • *In time you'll appreciate his good points.*

honour • *achievements honoured with the Nobel Prize*

salute • *We salute your great courage.*

reconstruct ❶ VERB

to rebuild something that has been damaged • *The city centre has been completely reconstructed.*

rebuild • *The task of rebuilding would be very expensive.*

recreate • *They try to recreate the atmosphere of former times.*

regenerate • *the ability to regenerate damaged tissues*

renovate • *The hotel was being renovated.*

restore • *experts who specialize in restoring old furniture*

MORE SYNONYMS

- reassemble
- remodel

reconstruct ❷ VERB

to build up from small details • *The police reconstructed the scene of the crime.*

build up • *They built up an image of him from several different descriptions.*

deduce • *The date can be deduced from other documents.*

piece together • *It was easy to*

piece together the shattered
fragments.

ecord ❶ NOUN

a stored account of something
• medical records
account • The company keeps
detailed accounts.
archives • Earlier issues are stored
in the archives.
file • the right to inspect company
files
journal • He kept a journal while
he was travelling.
minute • Did you read the minutes
of the last meeting?
register • a register of births,
deaths and marriages

ecord ❷ NOUN

what someone has done in the
past • You will be rejected if you
have a criminal record.
background • His background was
in engineering.
career • His career spoke for itself.
curriculum vitae • I must update
my curriculum vitae.
track record (INFORMAL) • Her
track record as a teacher was
impeccable.

ecord ❸ VERB

to note and store information
• Her diary records her daily life in
detail.
document • All these facts have
been well documented.
enter • All the names are entered in
this book.
log • They log everyone who comes
in or out.
note • I must note your birthday.
register • We registered his birth
straight away.
write down • If I don't write it
down, I'll forget it.

recover ❶ VERB

to get better again • He has still not
fully recovered.
convalesce • those convalescing
from illness or surgery
get better • He never really got
better again.
get well • Get well soon!
improve • The condition of your
hair will soon improve.
recuperate • recuperating from a
serious injury
revive • Business soon revived once
he came back.

recover ❷ VERB

to get something back again
• They took legal action to recover
the money.
get back • We got everything back
after the burglary.
recapture • trying to recapture the
atmosphere of our holiday
recoup • trying to recoup their
losses
regain • It took him a while to
regain his composure.
retrieve • I retrieved my bag from
the back seat.

recovery ❶ NOUN

the act of getting better again • He
made a remarkable recovery after his
illness.
healing • Adams claims that
humour is an integral part of
healing.
improvement • Germany is
showing a perceptible improvement.
recuperation • great powers of
recuperation
revival • little chance of a revival of
interest

MORE SYNONYMS

● convalescence
● rally

a
b
c
d
e
f
g
h
i
j
k
l
m
n
o
p
q
r
s
t
u
v
w
x
y
z

Can't find the word you're looking for? Try the index.

recovery ❷ NOUN

the act of getting something back
• *a reward for the recovery of the painting*

recapture • *An offensive was launched for the recapture of the airbase.*

reclamation • *the reclamation of dry land from the marshes*

restoration • *She owed the restoration of her sight to this remarkable technique.*

retrieval • *electronic storage and retrieval systems*

recruit ❶ VERB

to persuade people to join a group
• *He helped to recruit volunteers.*

draft • *drafted into the armed forces*

enlist • *I had to enlist the help of six people to move it.*

enrol • *She enrolled me on her evening course.*

muster • *trying to muster support for the movement*

recruit ❷ NOUN

someone who has recently joined a group • *the latest batch of recruits*

beginner • *The course is suitable for beginners.*

convert • *a recent convert to their religion*

novice • *I'm a novice at these things.*

trainee • *My first job was as a graduate trainee with a bank.*

MORE SYNONYMS
● neophyte
● proselyte
● tyro

red NOUN or **ADJECTIVE**

RELATED WORDS
● ADJECTIVES: rubicund, ruddy

SHADES OF RED	
burgundy	fuchsia
cardinal	magenta
carmine	maroon
cerise	poppy
cherry	raspberry
claret	ruby
crimson	scarlet
cyclamen	strawberry
flame	vermilion

reduce ❶ VERB

to make something smaller in size or amount • *Gradually reduce the dosage.*

curtail • *His powers will be severely curtailed.*

cut • *The first priority is to cut costs.*

cut down • *Try to cut down your coffee consumption.*

decrease • *The government plans to decrease interest rates.*

diminish • *to diminish the prestige of the monarchy*

lessen • *a diet that would lessen the risk of disease*

lower • *a commitment to lower taxes*

shorten • *taking steps to shorten queues*

ANTONYM
● increase

reduce ❷ VERB

to bring to a weaker or inferior state • *The village was reduced to rubble.*

degrade • *I wouldn't degrade myself by going out with him.*

demote • *The Soviet team have been demoted to second place.*

downgrade • *The female role has been downgraded in the drive for equality.*

drive • *an old woman driven to shoplifting to survive*

Can't find the word you're looking for? Try the index.

force • *The men were so hungry they were forced to eat grass.*

refer ❶ VERB
to mention something • *In his speech, he referred to a recent trip to Canada.*
allude • *She alluded to his absence in vague terms.*
bring up • *Why are you bringing that up now?*
cite • *She cites a favourite poem by George Herbert.*
mention • *She did not mention her mother's illness.*

refer ❷ VERB
to look at to find something out • *I had to refer to the manual.*
consult • *He had to consult a dictionary.*
look up • *I looked up your file to get your address.*

refined ❶ ADJECTIVE
polite and well-mannered • *His speech and manner are very refined.*
civilized • *the demands of civilized behaviour*
genteel • *two ladies with genteel manners and voices*
gentlemanly • *Sopwith behaved in his usual gentlemanly manner.*
ladylike • *They are models of ladylike decorum.*
polite • *polite and correct behaviour*

ANTONYM
● common

refined ❷ ADJECTIVE
processed to remove impurities • *refined sugar*
distilled • *distilled water*
filtered • *two pints of spring or filtered water*
processed • *a diet high in*

processed foods
pure • *crisp pure air*
purified • *freshly purified drinking water*

reform ❶ NOUN
a major change or improvement • *radical economic reforms*
amendment • *an amendment to remove the ban on divorce*
correction • *a correction of social injustice*
improvement • *She is pressing for improvements to education.*
rehabilitation • *the rehabilitation of young offenders*

MORE SYNONYMS
● amelioration
● betterment
● rectification

reform ❷ VERB
to make major changes or improvements to something • *his plans to reform the economy*
amend • *They want to amend the current system.*
better • *industrial action to better their working conditions*
correct • *keen to correct injustices*
rectify • *measures suggested to rectify the financial situation*
rehabilitate • *a loan for Bulgaria to rehabilitate its railway system*

MORE SYNONYMS
● ameliorate
● emend
● revolutionize

refresh VERB
to make you feel more energetic • *A glass of fruit juice will refresh you.*
brace • *a bracing walk*
enliven • *Music can enliven the spirit.*

a
b
c
d
e
f
g
h
i
j
k
l
m
n
o
p
q
r
s
t
u
v
w
x
y
z

Can't find the word you're looking for? Try the index.

rejuvenate • *He was told that the Italian climate would rejuvenate him.*

revive • *The cold water revived me a bit.*

stimulate • *a toner to stimulate the skin*

MORE SYNONYMS
- freshen
- invigorate
- revitalize
- revivify

refuge NOUN

a place where you go for safety • *a mountain refuge*

asylum • *political asylum*

harbour • *Patches of gorse were a great harbour for foxes.*

haven • *The island is a haven for international criminals.*

sanctuary • *a sanctuary from the outside world*

shelter • *an underground shelter*

refuse ❶ VERB

to say you will not do something • *He refused to speculate about the contents of the letter.*

abstain • *people who abstain from eating meat*

decline • *He declined to comment on the story.*

withhold • *Financial aid for Britain has been withheld.*

refuse ❷ VERB

to say you will not allow or accept something • *He offered me a drink, which I refused.*

decline • *He declined their invitation.*

reject • *The court rejected their petition.*

spurn • *You spurned his last offer.*

turn down • *He has turned down the job.*

ANTONYM
- accept

refuse ❸ NOUN

rubbish or waste • *a weekly collection of refuse*

garbage • *rotting piles of garbage*

junk (INFORMAL) • *What are you going to do with all that junk?*

litter • *If you see litter in the corridor, pick it up.*

rubbish • *They had piled most of their rubbish into yellow skips.*

trash • *I forgot to take out the trash.*

waste • *a law that regulates the disposal of waste*

regard ❶ VERB

to have particular views about someone or something • *I regard creativity as a gift.*

consider • *I consider activities such as jogging a waste of time.*

judge • *This may or may not be judged as reasonable.*

look on • *A lot of people looked on him as a healer.*

see • *I don't see it as my duty to take sides.*

think of • *We all thought of him as a father.*

view • *They view the United States as a land of opportunity.*

regard ❷ VERB (LITERARY)

to look at someone in a particular way • *She regarded him curiously for a moment.*

contemplate • *He contemplated her in silence.*

eye • *We eyed each other thoughtfully.*

gaze • *gazing at herself in the mirror*

look • *She looked at him earnestly.*

Can't find the word you're looking for? Try the index.

scrutinize • *She scrutinized his features to see if he was to be trusted.*

watch • *Chris watched him sipping his brandy.*

region NOUN

a large area of land • *a remote mountainous region of Afghanistan*

area • *The area is renowned for its cuisine.*

district • *I drove around the business district.*

land • *a land permanently cloaked in mist*

locality • *All other factories in the locality went on strike.*

quarter • *We wandered through the Chinese quarter.*

sector • *the northeast sector of Bosnia*

territory • *the disputed territory of Kashmir*

tract • *They cleared large tracts of forest.*

zone • *a different time zone*

regret ❶ VERB

to be sorry something has happened • *I gave in to him, and I have regretted it ever since.*

be sorry • *I'm sorry you feel that way about it.*

grieve • *grieving over the death of his wife*

lament • *We lament the loss of a fine novelist.*

mourn • *to mourn the loss of a loved one*

repent • *He repents his past sins.*

MORE SYNONYMS
- bemoan
- bewail
- rue

regret ❷ NOUN

the feeling of being sorry about something • *He expressed regret that he had caused any offence.*

grief • *his guilt and grief over the failed relationship*

pang of conscience • *He need not feel any pangs of conscience over his decision.*

penitence • *an abject display of penitence*

remorse • *He expressed remorse over his own foolishness.*

repentance • *an apparent lack of genuine repentance*

sorrow • *I feel real sorrow that my dad did this.*

MORE SYNONYMS
- compunction
- contrition
- ruefulness
- self-reproach

regular ❶ ADJECTIVE

even or equally spaced • *soft music with a regular beat*

consistent • *a consistent heart-rate*

constant • *a constant temperature*

even • *an even level of sound*

periodic • *Periodic checks are carried out.*

rhythmic • *the rhythmic beating of the drum*

steady • *a steady pace*

uniform • *The Earth rotates on its axis at a uniform rate.*

ANTONYM
- irregular

regular ❷ ADJECTIVE

usual or normal • *I was filling in for the regular bartender.*

customary • *her customary place at the table*

everyday • *part of everyday life*

a b c d e f g h i j k l m n o p q r s t u v w x y z

Can't find the word you're looking for? Try the index.

A B C D E F G H I J K L M N O P Q R S T U V W X Y Z

habitual • *habitual practices*
normal • *a normal day*
ordinary • *It was just an ordinary weekend.*
routine • *a routine knee operation*
typical • *My typical day begins at 8.30.*
usual • *In a usual week I watch about 15 hours of television.*

reject VERB

to refuse to accept or agree to something • *We reject any suggestion that the law needs amending.*
decline • *They declined his proposal.*
deny • *He denied our offer of assistance.*
rebuff • *She rebuffed his advances.*
refuse • *He offered me a drink, which I refused.*
renounce • *She renounced her parents' religion.*
say no to • *Just say no to drugs.*
spurn • *He spurned the advice of management consultants.*
turn down • *She turned down his offer of marriage.*

MORE SYNONYMS
● disallow
● repudiate

ANTONYM
● accept

rejoice VERB

to be very happy about something • *Today we can rejoice in our success.*
be overjoyed • *I was overjoyed to see him.*
celebrate • *We should celebrate our victory.*
delight • *He delighted in her success.*
glory • *glorying in the achievement of his troops*

MORE SYNONYMS
● exult
● revel

relation ❶ NOUN

a connection between two things • *This theory bears no relation to reality.*
bearing • *Diet has an important bearing on your general health.*
bond • *the bond between a mother and child*
connection • *a possible connection between BSE and human disease*
correlation • *the correlation between unemployment and crime*
link • *a link between obesity and heart problems*
relationship • *the relationship between success and effort*

relation ❷ NOUN

a member of your family • *I was staying with relations in Atlanta.*
kin • *She has gone to live with her husband's kin.*
kinsman • *the prince who murdered his father and kinsmen*
kinswoman • *She was a kinswoman of the Duke of Portland.*
relative • *Get a relative to look after the children.*

relationship ❶ NOUN

the way people act towards each other • *He has a friendly relationship with his customers.*
affinity • *the natural affinity between the female members of the community*
association • *the association between the two countries*
bond • *The experience created a bond between us.*
connection • *He felt a personal connection with her.*
rapport • *He has a terrific rapport with kids.*

Can't find the word you're looking for? Try the index.

relationship ❷ NOUN

a close friendship, especially a sexual one • *I found myself in a relationship I couldn't handle.*
affair • *an affair with a married man*
liaison • *Nobody knew of their brief liaison.*

relationship ❸ NOUN

the connection between two things • *the relationship between humans and their environment*
connection • *the connection between age and ill-health*
correlation • *the correlation between unemployment and crime*
link • *the link between smoking and lung cancer*
parallel • *the parallel between painting and music*

relax VERB

to be calm and become less worried • *I never have any time to relax.*
laze • *I'm just going to laze around and do nothing.*
rest • *Try to rest as much as you can.*
take it easy • *the chance to just take it easy for a week or two*
unwind • *It helps them to unwind after a busy day at work.*

relaxed ❶ ADJECTIVE

calm and not worried or tense • *As soon as I made the decision, I felt more relaxed.*
at ease • *It is essential to feel at ease with your therapist.*
calm • *Diane felt calm and unafraid as she entered the courtroom.*
comfortable • *He liked me and I felt comfortable with him.*
cool • *He was marvellously cool, smiling as if nothing had happened.*

easy • *By then I was feeling a little easier about the situation.*
serene • *that serene smile of his*
unflustered • *He has a calm, unflustered temperament.*

ANTONYM
● tense

relaxed ❷ ADJECTIVE

calm and peaceful • *The atmosphere at lunch was relaxed.*
calm • *The city appears relatively calm today.*
casual • *We have a very casual relationhip.*
comfortable • *a comfortable silence*
informal • *an informal occasion*
peaceful • *Sundays are usually quiet and peaceful in our house.*

ANTONYM
● tense

release ❶ VERB

to set someone or something free • *negotiations to release the hostages*
deliver • *I thank God for delivering me from that pain.*
discharge • *He may be discharged from hospital today.*
extricate • *They managed to extricate the survivors from the wreckage.*
free • *Israeli is set to free more Lebanese prisoners.*
let go • *They held him for three hours and then let him go.*
liberate • *liberated under the terms of the amnesty*
set free • *birds set free into the wild*

MORE SYNONYMS
● emancipate
● manumit
● unfetter

a
b
c
d
e
f
g
h
i
j
k
l
m
n
o
p
q
r
s
t
u
v
w
x
y
z

Can't find the word you're looking for? Try the index.

release ❷ VERB

to make something available • *The new album is released next week.*

issue • *He has issued a press statement.*

launch • *The company has just launched a new range of products.*

publish • *His latest book will be published in May.*

put out • *putting out a series of novels by Nobel prize winners*

release ❸ NOUN

the setting free of someone or something • *his release from prison*

discharge • *a discharge from the army*

emancipation • *the emancipation of slaves in the 19th century*

freedom • *Hinckley campaigned for his freedom.*

liberation • *their liberation from a Nazi concentration camp*

liberty • *her television appearances pleading for his liberty*

MORE SYNONYMS

- deliverance
- manumission

relentless ADJECTIVE

never stopping or becoming less intense • *The pressure was relentless.*

incessant • *incessant rain*

nonstop • *nonstop background music*

persistent • *in the face of persistent criticism*

sustained • *a sustained attack*

unrelenting • *unrelenting protests*

unremitting • *the unremitting demands of duty*

relevant ADJECTIVE

connected with what is being discussed • *We have passed on all relevant information.*

applicable • *These fees are not applicable to mortgages in Scotland.*

apposite • *He could not think of anything apposite to say.*

appropriate • *The name seemed very appropriate.*

apt • *an apt comment*

pertinent • *She had asked some pertinent questions.*

MORE SYNONYMS

- appurtenant
- germane
- material

ANTONYM

- irrelevant

reliable ADJECTIVE

able to be trusted • *You have to demonstrate that you are reliable.*

dependable • *dependable information*

faithful • *a faithful friend*

safe • *It's all right, you're in safe hands.*

sound • *sound advice*

staunch • *a staunch supporter*

sure • *a sure sign of rain*

true • *a true account*

trustworthy • *a trustworthy and level-headed leader*

ANTONYM

- unreliable

religion NOUN

RELIGIONS

animism	Rastafarianism
Baha'ism	shamanism
Buddhism	Shinto
Christianity	Sikhism
Confucianism	Taoism
Hinduism	Zen
Islam	Zoroastrianism *or*
Jainism	Zoroastrism
Judaism	

Can't find the word you're looking for? Try the index.

religious ❶ ADJECTIVE
connected with religion • *religious worship*
devotional • *an altar covered with devotional pictures*
divine • *a request for divine guidance*
doctrinal • *their doctrinal differences*
holy • *To Tibetans, this is a holy place.*
sacred • *Bach's sacred music*
scriptural • *scriptural and theological references*
spiritual • *We've got no spiritual values.*
theological • *theological studies*

religious ❷ ADJECTIVE
having a strong belief in a god or gods • *They are both very religious.*
devout • *She is a devout Catholic.*
God-fearing • *They brought up their children to be God-fearing Christians.*
godly • *a learned and godly preacher*
pious • *He was brought up by pious female relatives.*
righteous • *struggling to be righteous and chaste*

reluctant ADJECTIVE
unwilling to do something • *He was reluctant to ask for help.*
averse • *I'm not averse to going along with the idea.*
disinclined • *He was disinclined to talk about himself.*
hesitant • *His advisers are hesitant to let the United States enter the conflict.*
loath • *The finance minister is loath to cut income tax.*
slow • *The world community has been slow to respond to the crisis.*

unwilling • *For months I had been unwilling to go through with it.*

ANTONYM
● eager

remain ❶ VERB
to stay somewhere • *You'll have to remain in hospital for the time being.*
be left • *He was left in the car.*
linger • *I lingered for a few days until he arrived.*
stay behind • *I was told to stay behind after the class.*
wait • *Wait here until I come back.*

remain ❷ VERB
to stay the same • *The men remained silent.*
continue • *This state of affairs cannot continue.*
endure • *Somehow their friendship endures.*
go on • *The debate goes on.*
last • *Nothing lasts forever.*
stay • *They could stay afloat without swimming.*
survive • *companies which survived after the recession*

remainder NOUN
the part that is left of something • *He gulped down the remainder of his coffee.*
balance • *pay the balance on delivery*
last • *He finished off the last of the wine.*
others • *She took one and put the others back.*
remnants • *The remnants of the force were fleeing.*
remains • *tidying up the remains of their picnic*
rest • *I'm going to throw a party, then invest the rest of the money.*

a
b
c
d
e
f
g
h
i
j
k
l
m
n
o
p
q
r
s
t
u
v
w
x
y
z

Can't find the word you're looking for? Try the index.

A
B
C
D
E
F
G
H
I
J
K
L
M
N
O
P
Q
R
S
T
U
V
W
X
Y
Z

remains PLURAL NOUN

the parts of something left over
• *the remains of an ancient mosque*
debris • *screws, bolts and other debris from a scrapyard*
dregs • *Colum drained the dregs from his cup.*
leftovers • *Refrigerate any leftovers.*
relics • *a museum of war relics*
remnants • *Beneath the present church were remnants of Roman flooring.*
residue • *Discard the milky residue left behind.*
scraps • *the scraps from the dinner table*
vestiges • *an attempt to destroy the last vestiges of evidence*

MORE SYNONYMS

- detritus
- leavings

remark ❶ VERB

to mention or comment on something • *She had remarked on the boy's improvement.*
comment • *So far, he has not commented on these reports.*
mention • *I mentioned that I didn't like jazz.*
observe • *"You're very pale," he observed.*
say • *"Well done," he said.*
state • *We stated that he had resigned.*

remark ❷ NOUN

something you say • *a vulgar remark*
comment • *his abrasive wit and caustic comments*
observation • *a few general observations*
statement • *That statement puzzled me.*
utterance • *admirers who hung on her every utterance*

word • *No-one had an unkind word to say about him.*

remember VERB

to bring to mind something from the past • *I do not remember the exact words.*
call to mind • *He invited the congregation to call to mind their sins.*
recall • *He tried to recall the layout of the farmhouse.*
recognize • *I don't recognize that name.*
retain • *information which can be retained in the memory*

MORE SYNONYMS

- recollect
- reminisce

ANTONYM

- forget

remind VERB

to make someone remember something • *He reminds me of myself at that age.*
bring back to • *Talking about the accident brought it all back to me.*
jog someone's memory • *See if this picture helps jog your memory.*
make someone remember • *Your article made me remember my own traumas.*
put in mind • *His eagerness to please put her in mind of a puppy.*
refresh someone's memory • *I read through the list to refresh my memory.*

remote ❶ ADJECTIVE

far off in distance • *a remote farm in the hills*
distant • *in that distant land*
far-off • *start a new life in a far-off country*
inaccessible • *people living in inaccessible parts of the country*

Can't find the word you're looking for? Try the index.

isolated • *Many of the refugee villages are in isolated areas.*
lonely • *It felt like the loneliest place in the world.*
outlying • *Tourists can visit outlying areas by jeep.*

remote ② ADJECTIVE
far away in time • *It dates from the remote past.*
distant • *a glimpse into the more distant future*
far-off • *She has entirely forgotten those far-off days*

remote ③ ADJECTIVE
not wanting to be friendly • *She looked beautiful, but at the same time so remote.*
aloof • *He seemed aloof, standing watching the others.*
cold • *What a cold, unfeeling woman she was.*
detached • *He tries to remain emotionally detached from the prisoners.*
distant • *He is courteous but distant.*
reserved • *She's quite a reserved person.*
withdrawn • *Her husband had become withdrawn and moody.*

remote ④ ADJECTIVE
not very great • *The chances of his surviving are pretty remote.*
poor • *The odds of it happening again are very poor.*
slender • *There is a slender possibility that the plan might work.*
slight • *Is there even a slight hope that she might change her mind?*
slim • *There's still a slim chance that he may become Prime Minister.*
small • *There was still a small possibility that he might phone.*

remove VERB
to take something off or away • *I removed the splinter from her finger.*
delete • *He deleted files from the computer system.*
detach • *Detach and keep the bottom part of the form.*
eject • *He was ejected from the restaurant.*
eliminate • *Eliminate dairy products from your diet.*
erase • *She had erased the message.*
extract • *She is having a tooth extracted today.*
get rid of • *to get rid of raw sewage by pumping it out to sea*
take away • *She took away the tray.*
take off • *I won't take my coat off, I'm not staying.*
take out • *Take that dog out of here.*
withdraw • *She withdrew her hand from Roger's.*

MORE SYNONYMS
- efface
- excise
- expunge

renew VERB
to begin something again • *Syria renewed diplomatic relations with Egypt.*
begin again • *The audience began the slow handclap again.*
recommence • *He recommenced work on his novel.*
re-establish • *He had re-established his close friendship with Anthony.*
reopen • *It is feared that this issue could re-open the controversy.*
resume • *Rebels have refused to resume peace talks.*

Can't find the word you're looking for? Try the index.

renounce VERB (FORMAL)
to reject something or give it up
• *She renounced terrorism.*
disown • *The comments were later disowned by an official spokesman.*
give up • *He did not want to give up his right to the title.*
reject • *children who reject their parents' political and religious beliefs*
relinquish • *He does not intend to relinquish power.*

ANOTHER SYNONYM
● eschew (FORMAL)

renovate VERB
to repair an old building or machine • *They spent thousands renovating the house.*
do up • *his father's obsession with doing up old cars*
modernize • *plans to modernize the refinery*
recondition • *The company specializes in reconditioning photocopiers.*
refurbish • *This hotel has been completely refurbished.*
repair • *He has repaired the roof to make the house more windproof.*
restore • *The old town square has been beautifully restored.*
revamp • *plans to revamp the airport*

repair ❶ NOUN
something you do to mend something that is damaged • *The landlord carried out the repairs himself.*
darn • *a sock with a big darn in it*
mend • *Spray the area with paint to make the mend invisible.*
patch • *jackets with patches on the elbows*
restoration • *the restoration of a war-damaged building*

repair ❷ VERB
to mend something that is damaged • *The money will be used to repair faulty equipment.*
fix • *If something is broken, get it fixed.*
mend • *They mended it without charge.*
patch • *They patched the barn roof*
patch up • *Patch up those holes.*
renovate • *They spent thousands renovating the house.*
restore • *experts who specialize in restoring ancient parchments*

repay VERB
to give back money which is owed
• *It will take me years to repay the loan*
pay back • *I'll pay you back that money tomorrow.*
refund • *Any extra that you have paid will be refunded to you.*
settle up • *If we owe you anything we can settle up when you come.*

MORE SYNONYMS
● make restitution
● recompense
● reimburse
● remunerate
● square

repeat VERB
to say or write something again
• *Since you didn't listen, I'll repeat that.*
echo • *"Are you frightened?" "Frightened?" she echoed. "Of what?*
reiterate • *The lawyer could only reiterate what he had said before.*
say again • *"I'm sorry," she said again.*

MORE SYNONYMS
● iterate
● recapitulate
● restate

Can't find the word you're looking for? Try the index.

repel ❶ VERB
to horrify and disgust • *The thought of spiders repels me.*
disgust • *He disgusted everyone with his boorish behaviour.*
offend • *viewers who are easily offended*
revolt • *The smell revolted him.*
sicken • *What he saw there sickened him.*

ANTONYM
● attract

repel ❷ VERB
to fight and drive back enemy forces • *troops along the border ready to repel an enemy attack*
drive off • *They drove the guerrillas off with infantry and air strikes.*
repulse • *Cavalry and artillery were sent to repulse the enemy forces.*
resist • *The tribe resisted the Spanish invaders.*

replace VERB
to take the place of something else • *the man who replaced him as England skipper*
succeed • *He was succeeded by his son.*
supersede • *Horses were superseded by cars.*
supplant • *Anger supplanted all other feelings.*
take over from • *the man taking over from Mr Berry as chairman*
take the place of • *Debit cards are taking the place of cash and cheques.*

replacement NOUN
a person or thing that takes the place of another • *He has nominated Adams as his replacement.*
proxy • *They must nominate a proxy to vote on their behalf.*

stand-in • *He was a stand-in for my regular doctor.*
substitute • *an artificial substitute for silk*
successor • *He recommended him as his successor.*
surrogate • *They had expected me to be a surrogate for my sister.*

reply ❶ VERB
to give someone an answer • *He did not even have the courtesy to reply to my fax.*
answer • *He avoided answering the question.*
counter • *"It's not that simple," he countered in a firm voice.*
respond • *"Mind your manners, lady!" I responded.*
retort • *"Nobody asked you," he retorted.*
return • *"I can manage," she returned coldly.*

MORE SYNONYMS
● reciprocate
● rejoin
● riposte

reply ❷ NOUN
an answer given to someone • *There was a trace of irony in his reply.*
answer • *She could not give him a truthful answer.*
response • *His response was brusque.*
retort • *His sharp retort clearly made an impact.*

MORE SYNONYMS
● rejoinder
● riposte

report ❶ VERB
to tell about or give an official account of something • *He reported the theft to the police.*

a
b
c
d
e
f
g
h
i
j
k
l
m
n
o
p
q
r
s
t
u
v
w
x
y
z

Can't find the word you're looking for? Try the index.

cover • *The US news media will cover the trial closely.*
describe • *His condition was described as "improving".*
inform of • *Inform the police of any suspicious activity.*
notify • *The skipper notified the coastguard of the tragedy.*
state • *The police stated that he had been arrested.*

report ❷ NOUN
an account of an event or situation • *reports of serious human rights violations*
account • *a dishonest account of events*
description • *a detailed description of the match*
statement • *a deliberately misleading statement*

represent ❶ VERB
to stand for something else • *This rune represents wealth and plenty.*
mean • *This tarot card means the death of your present situation.*
stand for • *The olive branch stands for peace.*
symbolize • *a scene which symbolizes the movie's message*

MORE SYNONYMS
● betoken
● equate with

represent ❷ VERB
to describe something in a particular way • *The popular press tends to represent him as a hero.*
depict • *Children's books usually depict farm animals as lovable.*
describe • *She was always described as an intellectual.*
picture • *In the American press she*

was pictured as a heroine.
portray • *She was portrayed as a heartless, terrible woman.*
show • *He was shown as an intelligent and courageous man.*

representative ❶ NOUN
a person who acts on behalf of another or others • *Employees from each department elect a representative.*
agent • *You are buying direct, rather than through an agent.*
delegate • *a union delegate*
deputy • *I can't make it so I'll send my deputy.*
proxy • *They must nominate a proxy to vote on their behalf.*
spokesman • *the party's education spokesman*
spokeswoman • *a spokeswoman for her generation*

representative ❷ ADJECTIVE
typical of the group to which it belongs • *fairly representative groups of adults*
characteristic • *a characteristic feature*
illustrative • *an illustrative example*
typical • *a typical Italian menu*

MORE SYNONYMS
● archetypal
● emblematic
● indicative

reputation NOUN
the opinion that people have of a person or thing • *The college has a good reputation.*
character • *a man of good character*
name • *I have disgraced the family's name.*
renown • *a singer of great renown*

Can't find the word you're looking for? Try the index.

repute • *a writer and scholar of some repute*
standing • *This has done nothing to improve his standing.*
stature • *his stature as the world's greatest cellist*

request ❶ VERB
to ask for something politely or formally • *She requested that the door be left open.*
ask • *The government is being asked to consider the plan.*
beg • *May I beg a favour of you?*
seek • *You should seek a medical opinion.*

MORE SYNONYMS
● entreat
● solicit

request ❷ NOUN
the action of asking for something politely or formally • *France had agreed to his request for political asylum.*
appeal • *an appeal for witnesses to come forward*
application • *Their application was vetoed.*
call • *calls to decrease income tax*
plea • *his plea for help in solving the killing*

MORE SYNONYMS
● entreaty
● petition

require ❶ VERB
to need something • *A baby requires warmth and security.*
demand • *The task of reconstruction would demand patience and hard work.*
depend on • *I depend on this money to survive.*
be in need of • *The house was in need of modernization.*
need • *He desperately needed money.*
want (INFORMAL) • *The windows wanted cleaning.*

require ❷ VERB
to say that someone must do something • *The rules require employers to provide safety training.*
compel • *legislation that would compel cyclists to wear a helmet*
demand • *This letter demands an immediate reply.*
direct • *a court order directing the group to leave the area*
instruct • *They have instructed their solicitor to sue for compensation.*
oblige • *This decree obliges unions to delay strikes.*
order • *The court ordered him to pay the sum in full.*

requirement NOUN
something that you must have or do • *The products met all legal requirements.*
demand • *the demands and challenges of his new job*
essential • *the basic essentials for bachelor life*
necessity • *food and other daily necessities*
need • *special nutritional needs*
specification • *These companies will have to meet new European specifications.*

MORE SYNONYMS
● prerequisite (FORMAL)
● stipulation (FORMAL)

research ❶ NOUN
the act of studying and finding out about something • *funds for research into AIDS*
analysis • *They collected blood samples for laboratory analysis.*

a
b
c
d
e
f
g
h
i
j
k
l
m
n
o
p
q
r
s
t
u
v
w
x
y
z

Can't find the word you're looking for? Try the index.

A B C D E F G H I J K L M N O P Q R S T U V W X Y Z

examination • *a framework for the examination of these topics*
exploration • *an exploration of classical myths*
investigation • *Further investigation was hindered by the loss of all documentation.*
study • *The study demonstrated a link between obesity and heart problems.*

research ❷ VERB
to study and find out about something • *I'm researching for an article on New England.*
analyse • *We haven't had time to analyse those samples yet.*
examine • *The spacecraft will examine how solar wind affects Earth's magnetic field.*
explore • *I would probably be wise to explore the matter further.*
investigate • *Gas officials are investigating the cause of the explosion.*
study • *She's been studying chimpanzees for thirty years.*

resemblance NOUN
a similarity between two things • *I can see a resemblance between you.*
analogy • *the analogy between racism and homophobia*
correspondence • *There's little correspondence between our lifestyles.*
likeness • *These myths have a startling likeness to one another.*
parallel • *There were parallels between the two murders.*
similarity • *similarities between mother and son*

MORE SYNONYMS
- comparability
- parity
- semblance
- similitude

resemble VERB
to be similar to something else • *Venison resembles beef in flavour.*
bear a resemblance to • *She bears a resemblance to Marilyn Monroe.*
be like • *The ground is like concrete.*
be similar to • *The gun was similar to an air pistol.*
look like • *He looks like his father.*
parallel • *His fate paralleled that of his predecessor.*
take after • *You take after your grandmother.*

resent VERB
to feel bitter and angry about something • *I resent the slur on my integrity.*
be angry about • *I was angry at the way he spoke to me.*
be offended by • *She was offended by his comments.*
dislike • *I dislike his patronizing attitude.*
object to • *I object to being treated like an idiot.*
take offence at • *She took offence at the implied criticism.*

resentful ADJECTIVE
bitter about something that has happened • *a sullen and resentful workforce*
aggrieved • *He is still aggrieved at the size of the fine.*
angry • *I was angry that I wasn't consulted.*
bitter • *a forsaken and bitter man*
embittered • *He had grown into an embittered, hardened adult.*
huffy • *He's so huffy if he doesn't get his own way.*
indignant • *They were indignant that they had not been consulted.*

Can't find the word you're looking for? Try the index.

offended • *He was offended at being left out.*

MORE SYNONYMS
- in high dudgeon
- peeved
- piqued

resentment NOUN

a feeling of anger and bitterness
• *There is growing resentment against newcomers.*
anger • *Perhaps anger had clouded his vision.*
animosity • *The animosity between the two men grew.*
bitterness • *I feel bitterness towards the person who knocked me down.*
grudge • *It was an accident and I bear no grudges.*
huff • *She went off in a huff.*
indignation • *He could hardly contain his indignation.*
rancour • *There was no trace of envy or rancour in her face.*

MORE SYNONYMS
- pique
- umbrage

reserve ❶ VERB

to keep for a particular person or purpose • *Hotel rooms have been reserved for us.*
hoard • *They've begun to hoard food and petrol.*
hold • *The information is held in a database.*
keep • *Grate the lemon zest and keep it for later.*
put by • *She had enough put by for her fare.*
save • *Save me a seat.*
set aside • *funds set aside for education*
stockpile • *People are stockpiling food for the coming winter.*

store • *potatoes stored for sale out of season*

reserve ❷ NOUN

a supply kept for future use
• *a drain on the cash reserves*
cache • *a cache of weapons and explosives*
fund • *a pension fund*
hoard • *a hoard of food and petrol*
stock • *stocks of paper and ink*
stockpile • *stockpiles of chemical weapons*
store • *a secret store of sweets*
supply • *food supplies*

resign ❶ VERB

to leave a job • *Scott resigned from the firm.*
abdicate • *The King abdicated to marry an American divorcee.*
hand in your notice • *I handed in my notice on Friday.*
leave • *I am leaving to become a teacher.*
quit • *He quit his job as an office boy.*
step down (INFORMAL) • *He headed the government until he stepped down in 1990.*

resign ❷, resign oneself
VERB

to accept an unpleasant situation
• *She had resigned herself to losing her home.*
accept • *You've got to accept the fact that he's left you.*
bow • *He bowed to the inevitable and allowed her to go.*
reconcile oneself • *She had reconciled herself to never seeing him again.*

resist VERB

to refuse to accept something and try to prevent it • *They resisted our attempts to modernize.*

a
b
c
d
e
f
g
h
i
j
k
l
m
n
o
p
q
r
s
t
u
v
w
x
y
z

Can't find the word you're looking for? Try the index.

defy • *arrested for defying the ban on street trading*
fight • *He vigorously fought the proposal.*
oppose • *Many parents oppose bilingual education in schools.*
refuse • *The patient has the right to refuse treatment.*
struggle against • *nations struggling against Communist takeovers*

ANTONYM
○ accept

resolve ❶ VERB
to decide firmly to do something
• *She resolved to report the matter.*
decide • *She decided to quit smoking.*
determine • *He determined to rescue his two countrymen.*
intend • *I intended to teach him a lesson he wouldn't forget.*
make up your mind • *Once he made up his mind to do it, there was no stopping him.*

resolve ❷ VERB
to find a solution to a problem
• *We must find a way to resolve these problems.*
clear up • *The confusion was soon cleared up.*
find a solution to • *the ability to find an effective solution to the crisis*
overcome • *Find a way to overcome your difficulties.*
solve • *These reforms did not solve the problem of unemployment.*
sort out • *The two countries have sorted out their trade dispute.*
work out • *It seems like a nightmare, but I'm sure we can work it out.*

resolve ❸ NOUN
absolute determination • *He doesn't weaken in his resolve.*

determination • *the expression of fierce determination on her face*
resolution • *"I'm going on a diet," she said with sudden resolution.*
tenacity • *Hard work and sheer tenacity are crucial to career success.*

MORE SYNONYMS
○ doggedness
○ single-mindedness
○ willpower

respect ❶ VERB
to have a good opinion of someone
• *I want him to respect me as a career woman.*
admire • *I admire him for his honesty.*
have a good opinion of • *Nobody seems to have a good opinion of him.*
have a high opinion of • *He had a very high opinion of Neil.*
honour • *the Scout's promise to honour God and the Queen*
look up to • *He looks up to his dad.*
think highly of • *His boss thinks very highly of him.*
venerate • *My father venerated General Eisenhower.*

MORE SYNONYMS
○ esteem
○ revere
○ reverence
○ set store by

ANTONYM
○ disrespect

respect ❷ NOUN
a good opinion of someone • *We have no respect for him at all.*
admiration • *I have always had the greatest admiration for him.*
esteem • *We have to win the trust and esteem of our clients.*
regard • *I hold him in high regard.*

Can't find the word you're looking for? Try the index.

reverence • *We did it out of reverence for the dead.*

ANTONYM
● disrespect

respectable ❶ ADJECTIVE
considered to be acceptable and correct • *respectable families*
decent • *They married after a decent interval.*
good • *He comes from a good family.*
honourable • *His colleagues were honourable people.*
proper • *It was not proper for women to go on the stage.*
reputable • *a reputable firm*
upright • *an upright and trustworthy man*
worthy • *worthy citizens*

respectable ❷ ADJECTIVE
adequate or reasonable • *a respectable rate of economic growth*
appreciable • *making appreciable progress*
considerable • *a considerable amount*
decent • *a decent standard of living*
fair • *She had a fair command of English.*
reasonable • *He couldn't make a reasonable living from his writing.*

responsibility ❶ NOUN
the duty to deal with or take care of something • *The garden is your responsibility.*
duty • *My duty is to look after the animals.*
obligation • *You have an obligation to help him.*
onus • *The onus was on him to make sure he didn't fail.*

responsibility ❷ NOUN
the blame for something which has happened • *We must all accept responsibility for our mistakes.*
blame • *I'm not going to take the blame for this.*
fault • *This is all your fault.*
guilt • *He was not completely free of guilt.*
liability • *He admitted liability for the crash.*

MORE SYNONYMS
● accountability
● culpability

responsible ❶ ADJECTIVE
being the person in charge of something • *The Cabinet is collectively responsible for policy.*
in charge • *I wish someone else was in charge of this inquiry.*
in control • *Who is in control of the operation?*

responsible ❷ ADJECTIVE
being to blame for something • *I hold you responsible for this mess.*
at fault • *I was not at fault as my vehicle was stationary.*
guilty • *I still maintain that I am not guilty.*
to blame • *Television is possibly to blame for this.*

responsible ❸ ADJECTIVE
sensible and dependable • *He had to show that he would be a responsible parent.*
dependable • *a dependable, trustworthy teacher*
level-headed • *a sensible, level-headed approach*
reliable • *You have to demonstrate that you are reliable.*
sensible • *She's a sensible girl, if a bit headstrong.*
sound • *sound advice*
trustworthy • *He is a trustworthy leader.*

Can't find the word you're looking for? Try the index.

ANTONYM
- irresponsible

rest ❶ NOUN

the remaining parts of something
• *Take what you want and leave the rest.*
balance • *You pay half now and the balance on delivery.*
others • *She took one and put the others back.*
remainder • *He gulped down the remainder of his coffee.*
surplus • *Coat with seasoned flour, shaking off the surplus.*

rest ❷ NOUN

a period when you relax and do nothing • *I'll start again after a rest.*
break • *He needs to take a break from work.*
holiday • *I could really do with a holiday.*
leisure • *We get no leisure, no time off, no overtime pay.*
relaxation • *Make time for a bit of relaxation.*
respite • *a respite from the rush of everyday life*

rest ❸ VERB

to relax and do nothing for a while
• *He rested briefly before going on.*
have a break • *Paul felt he had to have a break.*
idle • *He sat idling in his room.*
laze • *lazing on the beach*
put your feet up • *Nobody's home, so I can put my feet up for a while.*
relax • *Guests can relax in the cosy bar.*
sit down • *I'll have to sit down for a minute.*
take it easy • *the chance to just take it easy for a couple of weeks*

restless ADJECTIVE

unable to sit still or relax • *She had been restless and irritable all day.*
edgy • *She was nervous and edgy, still chain-smoking.*
fidgety • *bored, fidgety youngsters*
fretful • *The whole family was fretful and argumentative.*
jumpy • *If she can't smoke she gets jumpy and irritable.*
on edge • *She's been on edge for weeks.*
unsettled • *The staff were unsettled and demoralized.*

restore ❶ VERB

to cause something to return to its previous state • *He was anxious to restore his reputation.*
re-establish • *an attempt to re-establish diplomatic relations*
reinstate • *the failure to reinstate the ceasefire*
reintroduce • *the plan to reintroduce wolves to the Highlands*
return • *their attempts to return the country to an agrarian economy*

restore ❷ VERB

to clean and repair something
• *experts who specialize in restoring ancient parchments*
fix up • *It took us months to fix this house up.*
mend • *They finally got round to mending the roof.*
rebuild • *plans to rebuild the opera house*
reconstruct • *reconstructing paintings by old masters*
refurbish • *The city is refurbishing the cathedral's facade.*
renovate • *The hotel was being renovated in expectation of a tourist boom.*
repair • *The money will be used to repair faulty equipment.*

Can't find the word you're looking for? Try the index.

MORE SYNONYMS
- recondition
- retouch

restrain VERB
to hold someone or something back • *He had to be restrained by his friends.*
contain • *He could hardly contain his rage.*
control • *She tried to control her excitement.*
curb • *You must curb your extravagant tastes.*
hamper • *I was hampered by a lack of information.*
hinder • *Research is hindered by lack of cash.*
hold back • *He could no longer hold back his laughter.*
inhibit • *factors which inhibit growth*

MORE SYNONYMS
- constrain
- rein
- straiten

restrict VERB
to limit the movement or actions of someone or something • *laws to restrict foreign imports*
confine • *Keep your dog confined to the house.*
contain • *The curfew had contained the violence.*
hamper • *I was hampered by a lack of information.*
handicap • *handicapped by the terms of the contract*
impede • *Their work was being impeded by shortages of supplies.*
inhibit • *factors which inhibit growth*
limit • *He limited payments on the country's foreign debt.*
restrain • *the need to restrain wage rises*

MORE SYNONYMS
- circumscribe
- demarcate
- straiten

restriction NOUN
a rule or situation that limits what you can do • *a speed restriction*
constraint • *financial constraints*
control • *a call for stricter gun control*
curb • *support for a curb on migration from neighbouring countries*
limitation • *A slipped disc causes severe limitation of movement.*
regulation • *regulations outlawing child labour*
restraint • *new restraints on trade unions*
stipulation • *The only dress stipulation was "no jeans".*

result ❶ NOUN
the situation that is caused by something • *the result of lengthy deliberation*
consequence • *This could have disastrous consequences for industry.*
effect • *the intended effect of the revised guidelines*
outcome • *The ultimate outcome will be different.*
product • *the product of five years' work*
upshot • *The upshot is that our employees are all unhappy.*

result ❷ VERB
to be caused by something • *The crash resulted from a defect in the aircraft.*
arise • *the publicity that arises from incidents of this kind*
derive • *Poor health often derives from poverty.*

a
b
c
d
e
f
g
h
i
j
k
l
m
n
o
p
q
r
s
t
u
v
w
x
y
z

Can't find the word you're looking for? Try the index.

develop • *a determination which has developed from his new-found confidence*

ensue • *If the system collapses, chaos will ensue.*

follow • *the consequences which followed his release from prison*

happen • *What will happen if the test proves positive?*

stem • *Her hatred of cars stems from her mother's death in a crash.*

result in VERB

to cause something to happen • *50% of road accidents result in head injuries.*

bring about • *The Suez crisis brought about petrol rationing.*

cause • *The play caused a stir here.*

lead to • *brain damage which leads to paralysis*

retaliate VERB

to do something to someone in return for what they did • *The militia said it would retaliate against any attacks.*

get back at • *a desire to get back at our enemies*

get even with (INFORMAL) • *He wanted to get even with his former employers.*

get your own back (INFORMAL) • *the opportunity to get your own back on your husband*

hit back • *In this article he hits back at his critics.*

pay someone back • *I'll pay him back for what he's done.*

take revenge • *taking revenge for his father's murder*

retreat ❶ VERB

to move away from someone or something • *damage inflicted by the rebels as they retreated from the town*

back away • *He put up his hands in protest and began to back away.*

back off • *I stood up for myself and they backed off.*

draw back • *They drew back in fear.*

pull back • *Their forces have pulled back in all areas.*

withdraw • *Troops withdrew from the country last month.*

ANTONYM
● advance

retreat ❷ NOUN

the action of moving away from someone or something • *the long retreat from Moscow*

departure • *the departure of all foreign forces from the country*

evacuation • *the evacuation of British troops from Dunkirk*

flight • *my panicked flight from London*

withdrawal • *French withdrawal from Algeria*

ANTONYM
● advance

retreat ❸ NOUN

a quiet place you can go to • *He spent the day hidden away in his country retreat.*

haven • *The hotel is a haven of tranquillity.*

refuge • *a refuge from the harsh realities of the world*

sanctuary • *a sanctuary located on an island*

return ❶ VERB

to go back to a place • *The plane failed to return at the scheduled time.*

come back • *He said he'd come back later.*

go back • *I love going back home.*

Can't find the word you're looking for? Try the index.

reappear • *He reappeared two nights later.*
turn back • *We've come too far now to turn back.*

return ❷ VERB
to give something back • *They guarantee to return your original investment.*
give back • *He is refusing to give the dog back.*
pay back • *You have to pay back the loan, plus an arrangement fee.*
refund • *The company will refund the full cost.*
repay • *I can afford to repay the loan.*

MORE SYNONYMS
- recompense
- reimburse

reveal ❶ VERB
to tell people about something • *They were not ready to reveal any of the details.*
announce • *She was planning to announce her engagement.*
disclose • *He will not disclose the name of his patient.*
divulge • *I do not want to divulge where the village is.*
get off your chest (INFORMAL) • *I feel it's done me good to get it off my chest.*
let on • *She never let on that anything was wrong.*

reveal ❷ VERB
to uncover something that is hidden • *The carpet was removed to reveal the original pine floor.*
bring to light • *The truth is unlikely to be brought to light.*
lay bare • *His real motives were laid bare.*
uncover • *Auditors said they had uncovered evidence of fraud.*

unearth • *Quarry workers have unearthed the skeleton of a mammoth.*
unveil • *The statue will be unveiled next week.*

revenge ❶ NOUN
vengeance for wrongs or injury received • *acts of revenge*
reprisal • *Witnesses are unwilling to testify through fear of reprisals.*
retaliation • *The attack was in retaliation for his murder.*
retribution • *They did not want their names used for fear of retribution.*
vengeance • *He swore vengeance on everyone involved in the murder.*

revenge ❷ VERB
to take vengeance on someone • *to revenge himself on the press*
avenge • *He was trying to avenge the death of his friend.*
get even • *I'm going to get even with you for this.*
get your own back (INFORMAL) • *I simply want to get my own back on him.*
hit back • *He hit back at those who criticized him.*
pay someone back • *Some day I'll pay you back for this.*
retaliate • *I was sorely tempted to retaliate.*

reverse ❶ VERB
to change into something different or contrary • *They won't reverse the decision to increase prices.*
change • *They should change the law to make this practice illegal.*
invalidate • *A contract signed now might be invalidated at a future date.*
overrule • *In 1998 the Court of Appeal overruled the decision.*

a
b
c
d
e
f
g
h
i
j
k
l
m
n
o
p
q
r
s
t
u
v
w
x
y
z

A B C D E F G H I J K L M N O P Q R S T U V W X Y Z

overturn • *When the parliament overturned his decision, he backed down.*

retract • *He was asked to retract his comments but refused.*

MORE SYNONYMS
- countermand
- negate
- rescind
- revoke

reverse ❷ NOUN

the opposite of what has just been said or done • *The reverse seldom applies.*

contrary • *I'm not a feminist, quite the contrary.*

converse • *In fact, the converse is true.*

opposite • *When I told him to do something he always did the opposite.*

review ❶ NOUN

a critical assessment of a book or performance • *We've never had a good review in the music press.*

commentary • *He'll be writing a weekly commentary on American culture.*

criticism • *literary criticism*

notice • *Richards's solo work received good notices.*

review ❷ NOUN

a general survey or report • *a review of safety procedures*

analysis • *an analysis of American trade policy*

examination • *an examination of the top 250 companies*

report • *the committee's annual report*

study • *a recent study of treatments for back pain*

survey • *a survey of 250 businessmen*

revise VERB

to alter or correct something • *The second edition was completely revised.*

amend • *They voted unanimously to amend the constitution.*

correct • *time spent correcting his students' work*

edit • *We have the right to edit this book once it's finished.*

revamp • *It is time to revamp the system.*

update • *He was back in the office, updating the work schedule.*

revive VERB

to make or become lively or active again • *an attempt to revive the Russian economy*

rally • *Markets began to rally worldwide.*

resuscitate • *a bid to resuscitate the weekly magazine*

MORE SYNONYMS
- invigorate
- reanimate
- rekindle
- revitalize

reward NOUN

something given in return for a service • *As a reward for good behaviour, treat your child to a new toy.*

bonus • *We don't get a Christmas bonus any more.*

bounty • *They paid bounties to people to give up their weapons.*

payment • *Players now expect payment for interviews.*

prize • *He won first prize.*

rhythm NOUN

a regular movement or beat • *His body twists and sways to the rhythm.*

beat • *the thumping beat of rock music*
pulse • *the repetitive pulse of the drum beat*
tempo • *Elgar supplied his works with precise indications of tempo.*
time • *A reel is in four-four time.*

rich ❶ ADJECTIVE
having a lot of money and possessions • *You're going to be a very rich man.*
affluent • *an affluent neighbourhood*
loaded (SLANG) • *Of course he can afford it. He's loaded.*
opulent • *his opulent lifestyle*
prosperous • *the youngest son of a relatively prosperous family*
wealthy • *a wealthy international businessman*
well off • *My grandparents were quite well off.*

ANTONYM
● poor

rich ❷ ADJECTIVE
abundant in something • *Bananas are rich in vitamin A.*
abundant • *the Earth's most abundant natural resources*
fertile • *a fertile imagination*
plentiful • *a plentiful supply of vegetables*

MORE SYNONYMS
● copious
● fecund
● plenteous

rid, get rid of VERB
to remove or destroy something • *a senior manager who wanted to get rid of him*
dispose of • *He disposed of the murder weapon.*
dump • *We dumped our bags at the hotel.*

eject • *Officials used guard dogs to eject the protestors.*
jettison • *The crew jettisoned excess fuel.*
remove • *Most of her fears had been removed.*
weed out • *We must weed these people out as soon as possible.*

ridiculous ADJECTIVE
very foolish • *It is ridiculous to suggest we are having a romance.*
absurd • *absurd claims to have met big stars*
laughable • *He claims the allegations are "laughable".*
ludicrous • *It's a completely ludicrous idea.*
preposterous • *their preposterous claim that they had unearthed a plot*

right ❶ ADJECTIVE
in accordance with the facts • *That clock never tells the right time.*
accurate • *an accurate record of events*
correct • *The correct answers can be found at the bottom of the page.*
exact • *That clock never tells the exact time.*
factual • *His version of events is not strictly factual.*
genuine • *a genuine eyewitness account*
precise • *Officials did not give precise figures.*
strict • *He has never been a playboy in the strict sense of the word.*
true • *The true cost often differs from that.*
valid • *Your point is a valid one.*

MORE SYNONYMS
● spot-on
● unerring
● veracious

a
b
c
d
e
f
g
h
i
j
k
l
m
n
o
p
q
r
s
t
u
v
w
x
y
z

Can't find the word you're looking for? Try the index.

ANTONYM
- wrong

right ❷ ADJECTIVE

most suitable • *The time is right for our escape.*

acceptable • *This was beyond the bounds of acceptable behaviour.*

appropriate • *an appropriate outfit for the occasion*

desirable • *This goal is neither achievable nor desirable.*

done • *It just isn't done to behave like that in public.*

fit • *a subject which is not fit for discussion*

fitting • *a fitting end to an exciting match*

okay or **OK** (INFORMAL) • *Is it okay if I bring a friend with me?*

proper • *It was not thought proper for a woman to appear on the stage.*

seemly • *the rules of civility and seemly conduct*

suitable • *the most suitable man for the job*

right ❸ NOUN

what is just and fair • *At least he knew right from wrong.*

fairness • *a decision based not on fairness but on expediency*

equity • *Income should be distributed with some sense of equity.*

honour • *His whole life was dominated by his sense of honour.*

integrity • *They always strove to maintain a high level of integrity.*

justice • *He has no sense of justice or fair play.*

legality • *They are expected to observe the principles of legality.*

morality • *standards of morality and justice in society*

virtue • *Virtue is not confined to the Christian world.*

MORE SYNONYMS
- lawfulness
- rectitude
- righteousness
- uprightness

right-wing ADJECTIVE

believing in capitalist policies • *some right-wing politicians*

conservative • *the conservative manifesto*

reactionary • *reactionary army people*

Tory (BRITISH) • *a senior Tory peer*

rigid ❶ ADJECTIVE

unchangeable and often considered severe • *Hospital routines for nurses are very rigid.*

fixed • *fixed laws*

inflexible • *Workers said the system was too inflexible.*

set • *They have very set ideas about how to achieve this.*

strict • *a strict diet*

stringent • *stringent rules*

rigid ❷ ADJECTIVE

not easy to bend • *rigid plastic containers*

firm • *a firm platform*

hard • *Something cold and hard pressed into his back.*

solid • *The concrete will stay as solid as a rock.*

stiff • *Her fingers were stiff with cold.*

ANTONYM
- flexible

ring ❶ VERB

to make a loud clear sound • *He heard the school bell ring.*

chime • *The clock chimed three o'clock.*

clang • *A little later the church bell clanged.*

peal • *Church bells pealed at the stroke of midnight.*
resonate • *a strap hung with bells and resonating gongs*
toll • *The pilgrims tolled the bell.*

ring ➋ NOUN

an object or group of things in the shape of a circle • *a ring of blue smoke*
band • *a black arm-band*
circle • *Cut out four circles of pastry.*
hoop • *a steel hoop*
loop • *a loop of garden hose*
round • *small fresh rounds of goats' cheese*

ring ➌ NOUN

a group of people involved in an illegal activity • *a drug-trafficking ring*
band • *a small band of plotters*
cell • *a cell of neo-Nazis*
clique • *A small clique of people is trying to take over the party.*
syndicate • *a major crime syndicate*

riot ➊ NOUN

a disturbance made by an unruly mob • *a prison riot*
anarchy • *a decade of civil war and anarchy*
disorder • *mass public disorder*
disturbance • *Three fans were injured in a violent disturbance outside a pub.*
mob violence • *last week's mob violence in Bucharest*
strife • *communal strife in Los Angeles*

riot ➋ VERB

to take part in a riot • *They rioted in protest against the Government.*
go on the rampage • *Rock fans went on the rampage after a concert.*

rampage • *A curfew was imposed as gangs rampaged through the streets.*
run riot • *hooligans running riot in the streets*
take to the streets • *Workers and students took to the streets in protest.*

rise ➊ VERB

to move upwards • *Wilson watched the smoke rise from his cigar.*
ascend • *He held her hand as they ascended the steps.*
climb • *We climbed up the steps on to the bridge.*
go up • *He went up the ladder quickly.*
move up • *They moved up to second place after their win.*

rise ➋ VERB

to increase • *House prices are expected to rise this year.*
go up • *Life expectancy has gone up from 50 to 58.*
grow • *The Chinese economy continues to grow.*
increase • *the decision to increase prices*
intensify • *The conflict is bound to intensify.*
mount • *For several hours the tension mounted.*

ANTONYM
● fall

rise ➌ NOUN

an increase in something • *a rise in prices*
improvement • *a major improvement in standards*
increase • *a substantial increase in workload*
upsurge • *an upsurge of interest in books*

a
b
c
d
e
f
g
h
i
j
k
l
m
n
o
p
q
r
s
t
u
v
w
x
y
z

ANTONYM
- fall

risk ❶ NOUN
a chance that something
unpleasant might happen • *That's
a risk I'm happy to take.*
danger • *the dangers of smoking*
gamble • *Booking a holiday can be
a gamble.*
peril • *the perils of starring in a TV
commercial*
pitfall • *the pitfalls of working
abroad*

risk ❷ VERB
to do something knowing that
something unpleasant might
happen • *If he doesn't play, he risks
losing his place in the team.*
chance • *No assassin would
chance a shot from amongst that
crowd.*
dare • *Few people dared go
anywhere on foot.*
gamble • *gambling his life savings
on the stock market*
jeopardize • *The talks may still be
jeopardized by disputes.*
put in jeopardy • *A series of
setbacks have put the whole project
in jeopardy.*

rival ❶ NOUN
the person someone is competing
with • *He is well ahead of his
nearest rival.*
adversary • *political adversaries*
antagonist • *Greece's key rival and
chief antagonist, Turkey*
challenger • *his only challenger for
the presidency*
opponent • *He's a tough opponent
but I'm too good for him.*

rival ❷ VERB
to be the equal or near equal of

• *As a holiday destination, South
Africa rivals Kenya for weather.*
be a match for • *On our day we
are a match for anyone.*
equal • *The victory equalled
Portugal's best in history.*
match • *I think we matched them
in every department.*

river NOUN

TYPES OF RIVER

beck	rivulet
brook	stream
burn (SCOTTISH)	tributary
creek	watercourse
estuary	waterway

road NOUN
a route used by travellers and
vehicles • *There was very little
traffic on the roads.*
motorway • *Britain's first
motorway, the M1*
route • *the most direct route to the
town centre*
street • *He walked briskly down
the street.*
track • *a rough mountain track*

rob VERB
to take something from a person
illegally • *He was beaten senseless
and robbed of all his money.*
burgle • *He admitted that he was
trying to burgle the surgery.*
con (INFORMAL) • *The businessman
had conned him of $10,000.*
defraud • *charges of conspiracy to
defraud the government*
loot • *thugs who have looted
shops*
steal from • *trying to steal from a
woman in the street*
swindle • *two executives who
swindled their employer*

Can't find the word you're looking for? Try the index.

A B C D E F G H I J K L M N O P Q **R** S T U V W X Y Z

romantic ADJECTIVE
connected with sexual love • *a romantic relationship*
amorous • *The object of his amorous intentions is Wendy.*
loving • *a loving husband*
passionate • *a passionate love affair*
tender • *They embraced and kissed. It was a tender moment.*

room ❶ NOUN
a separate section in a building • *You can stay in my spare room.*
chamber • *the council chamber*
office • *I'm in the office at the end of the corridor.*

room ❷ NOUN
unoccupied space • *There wasn't enough room for his gear.*
capacity • *a seating capacity of 17,000*
elbow room • *There wasn't too much elbow room in the cockpit.*
space • *the high cost of office space*

rot ❶ VERB
to become rotten • *The grain started rotting in the silos.*
decay • *The bodies buried in the fine ash slowly decayed.*
decompose • *The debris slowly decomposes into compost.*
fester • *The wound is festering and gangrene has set in.*
spoil • *Fats spoil by becoming rancid.*

RELATED WORD
● ADJECTIVE: putrid

rot ❷ NOUN
the condition that affects things when they rot • *The timber frame was not protected against rot.*
decay • *tooth decay*
deterioration • *gum deterioration*
mould • *He scraped the mould off the cheese.*

MORE SYNONYMS
● putrefaction
● putrescence

rotten ❶ ADJECTIVE
decayed and no longer of use • *The front bay window is rotten.*
bad • *That milk in the fridge is bad.*
decayed • *teeth so decayed they need to be pulled*
decomposed • *The body was too badly decomposed to be identified at once.*
mouldy • *mouldy bread*
sour • *sour milk*

rotten ❷ ADJECTIVE (INFORMAL)
of very poor quality • *It's a rotten idea.*
inferior • *overpriced and inferior products*
lousy (SLANG) • *The menu is limited and the food is lousy.*
poor • *The wine was very poor.*
unsatisfactory • *if you have obtained unsatisfactory goods or services*

rough ❶ ADJECTIVE
uneven and not smooth • *My bicycle bumped along the rough ground.*
bumpy • *bumpy cobbled streets*
craggy • *craggy mountains*
rocky • *a bleak and rocky shore*
rugged • *a remote and rugged plateau*
uneven • *The ball bobbled awkwardly on the uneven surface.*

ANTONYM
● smooth

rough ❷ ADJECTIVE
difficult or unpleasant • *Teachers have been given a rough time.*
difficult • *It's been a difficult month for us.*
hard • *I've had a hard life.*

a b c d e f g h i j k l m n o p q **r** s t u v w x y z

Can't find the word you're looking for? Try the index.

tough • *She had a pretty tough childhood.*
unpleasant • *The last few weeks here have been very unpleasant.*

rough ❸ ADJECTIVE
only approximately correct • *At a rough guess it is five times more profitable.*
approximate • *The times are approximate only.*
estimated • *There are an estimated 90,000 gangsters in the country.*
sketchy • *a sketchy account of the incident*
vague • *She could only give a vague description of the intruder.*

MORE SYNONYMS
● imprecise
● inexact

round ❶ ADJECTIVE
shaped like a ball or a circle • *She has a round attractive face.*
circular • *a circular hole twelve feet wide*
cylindrical • *a cylindrical container*
rounded • *a low rounded hill*
spherical • *gold spherical earrings*

round ❷ NOUN
one of a series of events • *After round three, two Americans shared the lead.*
lap • *the last lap of the race*
period • *the second period of extra time*
session • *The World Champion was ahead after the first two sessions.*
stage • *the second stage of the Tour de France*

route NOUN
a way from one place to another • *the direct route to the town centre*

channel • *a safe channel avoiding the reefs*
course • *The ship was on a course that followed the coastline.*
itinerary • *The next place on our itinerary was Silistra.*
path • *We followed the path along the clifftops.*
road • *The coastal road is longer, but more scenic.*
way • *I'm afraid I can't remember the way.*

routine ❶ ADJECTIVE
ordinary, and done regularly • *a series of routine medical tests*
everyday • *an everyday occurrence*
normal • *The hospital claimed they were following their normal procedure.*
ordinary • *It was just an ordinary weekend for us.*
regular • *one of the regular checks we carry out*
standard • *It was standard practice for untrained clerks to do this work.*
typical • *This was a fairly typical morning scene in our house.*
usual • *The usual methods were not effective.*

routine ❷ NOUN
the usual way or order someone does things • *The players had to change their daily routine.*
order • *Babies respond well to order in their daily lives.*
pattern • *All three attacks followed the same pattern.*
practice • *a public inquiry into bank practices*
procedure • *The White House said there would be no change in procedure.*
programme • *It is best to follow some sort of structured programme.*

Can't find the word you're looking for? Try the index.

499 | rude

schedule • *He has been forced to adjust his schedule.*
system • *an efficient filing system*

row ❶ NOUN
several things arranged in a line • *He was greeted by a row of glum faces.*
bank • *a bank of video screens*
column • *a column of figures*
line • *a sparse line of spectators*
queue • *a queue of shoppers*
rank • *a rank of taxis*

row ❷ NOUN
a serious disagreement • *This could provoke a major diplomatic row with France.*
altercation • *He had an altercation with the umpire.*
argument • *an argument about money*
quarrel • *I had a terrible quarrel with my brother.*
squabble • *There have been minor squabbles about phone bills.*

rowdy ADJECTIVE
rough and noisy • *He complained to the police about rowdy neighbours.*
boisterous • *Most of the children were noisy and boisterous.*
noisy • *My neighbours are a noisy bunch.*
unruly • *a mother accompanied by her ghastly unruly child*
wild • *They loved fast cars and wild parties.*

MORE SYNONYMS
● obstreperous
● uproarious

royal ADJECTIVE
concerning a king or a queen or their family • *the royal yacht*
imperial • *the Imperial palace in Tokyo*

regal • *Never has she looked more regal.*
sovereign • *the Queen's sovereign authority*

rubbish ❶ NOUN
unwanted things or waste material • *tons of rubbish waiting to be dumped*
garbage • *I found all kinds of garbage left behind by the tide.*
litter • *fines for dropping litter*
refuse • *The Council made a weekly collection of refuse.*
trash • *The yards are overgrown and covered with trash.*
waste • *the safe disposal of toxic waste*

rubbish ❷ NOUN
foolish words or speech • *Don't talk rubbish!*
drivel • *mindless drivel*
garbage • *I personally think this is complete garbage.*
hot air (INFORMAL) • *His justification was just hot air.*
nonsense • *all that poetic nonsense about love*
rot • *What a load of pompous rot!*

rude ❶ ADJECTIVE
not polite • *He is rude to her friends.*
disrespectful • *They shouldn't treat their mother in this disrespectful way.*
impertinent • *I don't like being asked impertinent questions.*
impudent • *his rude and impudent behaviour*
insolent • *a defiant, almost insolent look*

MORE SYNONYMS
● churlish
● discourteous
● peremptory

a b c d e f g h i j k l m n o p q r s t u v w x y z

Can't find the word you're looking for? Try the index.

A
B
C
D
E
F
G
H
I
J
K
L
M
N
O
P
Q
R
S
T
U
V
W
X
Y
Z

ANTONYM
- polite

rude ❷ ADJECTIVE
unexpected and unpleasant • *a rude awakening*
abrupt • *The recession brought an abrupt end to his happiness.*
unpleasant • *an unpleasant surprise*
violent • *violent mood swings*

ruin ❶ VERB
to destroy or spoil something • *The crops have been ruined.*
break • *He's broken all his toys.*
damage • *This could damage our chances of winning.*
destroy • *a recipe for destroying the economy*
devastate • *A fire had devastated large parts of the castle.*
impair • *The flavour is impaired by overcooking.*
mar • *The celebrations were marred by violence.*
mess up • *He's messed up his whole career.*
spoil • *Don't let a stupid mistake spoil your life.*
undo • *He intends to undo everything I have fought for.*
wreck • *He wrecked the garden.*

ruin ❷ NOUN
the state of being destroyed or spoiled • *The vineyards were falling into ruin.*
decay • *The house fell into a state of decay.*
destruction • *the destruction caused by the rioters*
devastation • *A bomb brought chaos and devastation to the city centre yesterday.*
disrepair • *Many of the buildings had fallen into disrepair.*

downfall • *His lack of experience led to his downfall.*
fall • *the fall of the Roman empire*

ruin ❸ NOUN
the remaining parts of a severely damaged thing • *the burnt-out ruins of houses*
remains • *the remains of an ancient mosque*
shell • *the shells of burned buildings*
wreck • *We thought of buying the house as a wreck and doing it up.*

rule ❶ NOUN
a statement of what is allowed • *This was against the rules.*
decree • *a decree lifting sanctions against China*
guideline • *Are there strict guidelines for animal experimentation?*
law • *inflexible moral laws*
order • *He was sacked for disobeying orders.*
regulation • *new safety regulations*

MORE SYNONYMS
- dictum
- ordinance
- precept

rule ❷, as a rule ADVERB
usually or generally • *As a rule, I eat my meals in front of the TV.*
generally • *It is generally true that the darker the fruit the higher its iron content.*
mainly • *Mainly I work alone.*
normally • *Normally, the transport system carries 50,000 passengers a day.*
on the whole • *Their wines are, on the whole, of a very high standard.*
usually • *She is usually a calm and diplomatic woman.*

Can't find the word you're looking for? Try the index.

a
b
c
d
e
f
g
h
i
j
k
l
m
n
o
p
q
r
s
t
u
v
w
x
y
z

rule ❸ VERB

to govern people • *For four centuries, he says, foreigners have ruled Angola.*

administer • *calls for the UN to administer the country until the election*

be in power • *They were in power for eighteen years.*

govern • *The citizens are thankful they are not governed by a dictator.*

lead • *He led the country between 1949 and 1984.*

reign • *Henry II reigned from 1154 to 1189.*

ruler NOUN

a person who rules or commands • *He was a weak-willed and indecisive ruler.*

commander • *He is commander of the US Fifth Fleet.*

governor • *He was governor of the province in the late 1970s.*

head of state • *the heads of state of all the countries in the European Union*

leader • *the leader of the German Social Democratic Party*

monarch • *the coronation of the new monarch*

sovereign • *the first British sovereign to set foot on Spanish soil*

rumour NOUN

a story which may or may not be true • *persistent rumours of quarrels within the movement*

gossip • *We spent the first hour exchanging gossip.*

hearsay • *Much of what was reported to them was hearsay.*

whisper • *I've heard a whisper that the Bishop intends to leave.*

word • *What's the latest word from Washington?*

run ❶ VERB

to move on foot at a rapid pace • *I excused myself and ran back to the telephone.*

bolt • *The pig rose, squealing, and bolted.*

gallop • *The horses galloped away.*

jog • *He could scarcely jog around the block that first day.*

sprint • *She sprinted the car.*

run ❷ VERB

to manage • *He ran a small hotel.*

administer • *the authorities who administer the island*

be in charge of • *He is in charge of public safety.*

control • *He now controls a large retail development empire.*

direct • *Christopher will direct day-to-day operations.*

look after • *I look after his finances for him.*

manage • *Within two years he was managing the store.*

rush ❶ VERB

to move fast or do something quickly • *Someone rushed out of the building.*

dash • *She dashed in from the garden.*

fly • *I must fly or I'll miss my train.*

gush • *Piping-hot water gushed out.*

hasten • *One of them hastened towards me.*

hurry • *She had to hurry home to look after her son.*

race • *He raced across town to her house.*

run • *I excused myself and ran to the door.*

scurry • *Reporters scurried to get to the phones.*

shoot • *The car shot out of a junction and smashed into them.*

Can't find the word you're looking for? Try the index.

A B C D E F G H I J K L M N O P Q R S T U V W X Y Z

rush ❷ VERB

to force into immediate action without sufficient preparation • *Ministers won't be rushed into a response.*

hurry • *I don't want to hurry you.*

hustle • *You won't hustle me into making a commitment.*

press • *attempting to press me into making a statement*

pressurize • *Do not be pressurized into making your decision immediately.*

push • *Don't be pushed into signing anything.*

rush ❸ NOUN

a state of hurrying • *the rush not to be late for school*

bustle • *the bustle of modern life*

dash • *a 160-mile dash to the hospital*

hurry • *Eric left the house in a hurry.*

race • *a race to get the work finished before the deadline*

scramble • *the scramble to get a seat on the early morning flight*

stampede • *There was a stampede for the exit.*

Can't find the word you're looking for? Try the index.

Ss

sack ❶ VERB (INFORMAL)
to dismiss from a job • *sacked for punching his boss*
discharge • *discharged from the army*
dismiss • *the power to dismiss employees*
fire (INFORMAL) • *He was fired for poor timekeeping.*

sack ❷, the sack NOUN (INFORMAL)
dismissal from a job • *He got the sack after three months.*
discharge • *He plans to appeal his discharge.*
dismissal • *the case for his dismissal*
termination of employment • *wrongful termination of employment*

sacrifice ❶ VERB
to give something up • *She sacrificed her family life for her career.*
forego • *If we forego our summer holiday we can afford a car.*
forfeit • *The company is forfeiting safety for the sake of profit.*
give up • *I gave up my job to be with you.*
surrender • *We have surrendered our political authority for economic gain.*

sacrifice ❷ NOUN
the action of giving something up • *He was willing to make any sacrifice for peace.*
renunciation • *religious principles of renunciation and dedication*
self-denial • *an unprecedented act of self-denial*

sad ❶ ADJECTIVE
feeling unhappy about something • *The loss of our friendship makes me sad.*
blue • *I don't know why I'm feeling so blue today.*
dejected • *Everyone has days when they feel dejected.*
depressed • *She's depressed about this whole situation.*
dismal • *What are you all looking so dismal about?*
down • *The old man sounded really down.*
downcast • *a downcast expression*
glum • *a row of glum faces*
gloomy • *Don't look so gloomy, Mr Todd. I'll do my best for you.*
grief-stricken • *comforting the grief-stricken relatives*
low • *He used to listen when I was feeling low.*
melancholy • *melancholy thoughts*
mournful • *the mournful expression on his face*
unhappy • *I hate to see you so unhappy.*
wistful • *I found myself feeling wistful at the memory of him.*

Can't find the word you're looking for? Try the index.

A
B
C
D
E
F
G
H
I
J
K
L
M
N
O
P
Q
R
S
T
U
V
W
X
Y
Z

MORE SYNONYMS
- disconsolate
- doleful
- heavy-hearted
- low-spirited
- lugubrious
- woebegone

ANTONYM
- happy

sad ❷ ADJECTIVE
making you feel unhappy • *a sad song*
depressing • *a depressing film*
dismal • *a dark, dismal day*
gloomy • *a gloomy tale of a poor orphan*
harrowing • *a harrowing documentary about drug addicts*
heart-rending • *heart-rending pictures of the victims*
melancholy • *the melancholy music used throughout the film*
mournful • *a mournful ballad*
moving • *a deeply moving account of her life*
pathetic • *the pathetic sight of oil-covered sea birds*
poignant • *a poignant love story*
tragic • *his tragic death*
upsetting • *I'm afraid I have some upsetting news for you.*

sadness NOUN
the feeling of being unhappy • *I said goodbye with a mixture of sadness and joy.*
dejection • *a feeling of dejection and despair*
depression • *plunged into the deepest depression*
despondency • *Deep despondency set in again.*
melancholy • *Dean had shaken off his melancholy.*
unhappiness • *His unhappiness*

shows in his face.

MORE SYNONYMS
- cheerlessness
- dolefulness
- dolour

ANTONYM
- happiness

safe ❶ ADJECTIVE
not causing harm or danger • *This is not a safe place for a woman on her own.*
harmless • *harmless substances*
innocuous • *Both mushrooms look innocuous but are in fact deadly.*
wholesome • *fresh, wholesome ingredients*

ANTONYM
- dangerous

safe ❷ ADJECTIVE
not in any danger • *I felt warm and safe with him.*
all right • *I'll be all right on my own.*
in safe hands • *It's all right, you're in safe hands.*
okay or **OK** (INFORMAL) • *Could you check that the baby's okay?*
out of danger • *We were not out of danger yet.*
out of harm's way • *I'm keeping him well out of harm's way.*
protected • *Keep the plants dry and protected from frost.*
safe and sound • *I'm hoping he will come home safe and sound.*
secure • *I would like to feel financially secure.*

safeguard ❶ VERB
to protect something
• *international action to safeguard the ozone layer*
defend • *his courage in defending*

Can't find the word you're looking for? Try the index.

religious and civil rights
guard • *He closely guarded her identity.*
look after • *People tend to look after their own property.*
preserve • *We need to preserve the forest.*
protect • *What can we do to protect ourselves against heart disease?*
save • *This machine could help save babies from cot death.*
shield • *They moved to shield their children from adverse publicity.*

safeguard ② NOUN
something that protects people or things • *adequate safeguards for civil liberties*
barrier • *a barrier against the outside world*
cover • *Airlines are required to provide cover against such incidents.*
defence • *The immune system is our main defence against disease.*
protection • *Innocence is no protection from the evils in our society.*

safety NOUN
the state of being safe from harm or danger • *I was very anxious about her safety.*
immunity • *natural immunity to the disease*
protection • *protection from harmful rays*
security • *a false sense of security*

ANTONYM
● danger

salty ADJECTIVE
tasting of or containing salt • *a good rasher of salty bacon*
brak (SOUTH AFRICAN) • *the brak shallow water near the dam wall*

briny • *the flow of the briny water*
salted • *8 ounces of slightly salted butter*

same ADJECTIVE
exactly like one another • *The two words sound the same but have different spellings.*
alike • *No two families are alike.*
equal • *Mix equal quantities of soy sauce and rice vinegar.*
equivalent • *One unit is roughly equivalent to a glass of wine.*
identical • *Nearly all the houses were identical.*
indistinguishable • *symptoms indistinguishable from those of AIDS*

ANTONYM
● different

sanction ① VERB
to officially approve of or allow something • *He is ready to sanction the use of force.*
allow • *I cannot be seen to allow violence on school premises.*
approve • *The parliament has approved a programme of economic reforms.*
authorize • *We are willing to authorize a police raid.*
back • *persuading the government to back the plan*
endorse • *policies endorsed by the voting public*
permit • *Will he let the court's decision stand and permit the execution?*
support • *The party is under pressure to support the ban.*

ANTONYM
● veto

sanction ② NOUN
official approval of something • *The king could not enact the law*

a
b
c
d
e
f
g
h
i
j
k
l
m
n
o
p
q
r
s
t
u
v
w
x
y
z

Can't find the word you're looking for? Try the index.

without the sanction of parliament.
approval • *The chairman has given his approval.*
authorization • *You will need the authorization of a parent or guardian.*
backing • *He said the president had the backing of his government.*
blessing • *With the blessing of the White House, the group is meeting to identify more budget cuts.*
permission • *Finally she gave permission for him to marry.*
support • *The prime minister gave his support to the reforms.*

MORE SYNONYMS
- assent
- mandate
- ratification (FORMAL)

sanctions NOUN
penalties for countries which break the law • *The United States is considering imposing sanctions against the regime.*
ban • *After four years, he lifted the ban.*
boycott • *the lifting of the economic boycott against the country*
embargo • *They called on the government to lift its embargo on trade with the country.*
penalties • *legally binding penalties against treaty violators*

sane ❶ ADJECTIVE
having a normal healthy mind • *This was not the act of a sane person.*
lucid • *She was lucid right up until her death.*
normal • *the question of what constitutes normal behaviour*
rational • *He seemed perfectly rational to me.*

MORE SYNONYMS
- compos mentis
- of sound mind

ANTONYM
- mad

sane ❷ ADJECTIVE
showing good sense • *a sane and practical policy*
judicious • *the judicious use of military force*
level-headed • *a sensible, level-headed approach*
rational • *a rational analysis*
reasonable • *a reasonable course of action*
sensible • *the sensible thing to do*
sound • *sound advice*

sarcastic ADJECTIVE
saying the opposite of what you mean to make fun of someone • *A sarcastic remark was on the tip of her tongue.*
caustic • *his abrasive wit and caustic comments*
ironic • *an ironic remark*
sardonic • *a sardonic sense of humour*
satirical • *a satirical TV show*

MORE SYNONYMS
- derisive
- mordacious
- mordant

satisfactory ADJECTIVE
acceptable or adequate • *a satisfactory explanation*
acceptable • *The air pollution exceeds acceptable levels.*
adequate • *One in four people are without adequate homes.*
all right • *The meal was all right, but nothing special.*
good enough • *He's not good enough for you.*

Can't find the word you're looking for? Try the index.

passable • *She speaks passable French.*

sufficient • *One teaspoon of sugar should be sufficient.*

ANTONYM
- unsatisfactory

satisfied ADJECTIVE
happy because you have got what you want • *We are not satisfied with these results.*

content • *I'm perfectly content where I am.*

contented • *She led a quiet, contented life.*

happy • *I'm not happy with the situation.*

pleased • *He seemed pleased with the arrangement.*

ANTONYM
- disappointed

satisfy ❶ VERB
to give someone as much of something as they want • *a solution which I hope will satisfy everyone*

gratify • *He was gratified by the audience's response.*

indulge • *I don't believe in indulging children.*

please • *Our prime objective is to please our customers.*

MORE SYNONYMS
- assuage
- mollify
- pander to
- sate
- satiate
- slake

satisfy ❷ VERB
to convince someone of something • *He had to satisfy the doctors that he was fit to play.*

convince • *trying to convince the public that its product is safe*

persuade • *I had to persuade him of the advantages.*

put someone's mind at rest • *He has done his best to put my mind at rest.*

reassure • *I tried to reassure them, but they knew I was lying.*

satisfy ❸ VERB
to fulfil a requirement • *Candidates must satisfy the conditions for admission.*

fulfil • *All the minimum requirements were fulfilled.*

meet • *The current arrangements are inadequate to meet their needs.*

savage ❶ ADJECTIVE
cruel and violent • *a savage attack*

barbarous • *the barbarous customs of earlier times*

barbaric • *a particularly barbaric act of violence*

brutal • *a very brutal murder*

cruel • *the cruel practice of bullfighting*

ferocious • *the most ferocious violence ever seen on the streets of London*

inhuman • *the inhuman slaughter of these beautiful creatures*

vicious • *a vicious blow to the head*

violent • *violent crimes*

savage ❷ NOUN
a violent and uncivilized person • *They really are a bunch of savages.*

barbarian • *Our maths teacher was a complete barbarian.*

beast • *You beast! Let me go!*

brute • *He was a brute and he deserved his fate.*

lout • *a drunken lout*

monster • *These men were total monsters.*

a
b
c
d
e
f
g
h
i
j
k
l
m
n
o
p
q
r
s
t
u
v
w
x
y
z

Can't find the word you're looking for? Try the index.

A
B
C
D
E
F
G
H
I
J
K
L
M
N
O
P
Q
R
S
T
U
V
W
X
Y
Z

savage ❸ VERB
to attack and bite someone • *He was savaged to death by the animal.*
attack • *A lion attacked him when he was a child.*
bite • *Every year thousands of children are bitten by dogs.*
maul • *The dog went berserk and mauled one of the girls.*

save ❶ VERB
to rescue someone or something • *He saved my life.*
come to someone's rescue • *His uncle came to his rescue.*
deliver • *I thanked God for delivering me from the pain.*
redeem • *to redeem souls from purgatory*
rescue • *rescued from the flames*
salvage • *salvaging equipment from the wreckage*

save ❷ VERB
to keep someone or something safe • *a new machine which could save babies from cot death*
keep safe • *to keep my home safe from germs*
preserve • *preserving old buildings*
protect • *What can we do to protect ourselves from heart disease?*
safeguard • *measures to safeguard the ozone layer*

save ❸ VERB
to keep something for later use • *They are saving for a house.*
hoard • *They've begun to hoard food and petrol.*
keep • *Grate the lemon zest and keep it for later.*
put by • *He's putting his money by in a deposit account.*
reserve • *Drain the fruit and reserve the juice.*
set aside • *£130 million would be*

set aside for repairs to schools.

MORE SYNONYMS
- economize
- husband
- retrench

ANTONYM
- waste

say ❶ VERB
to speak words • *She said they were very impressed.*
▷ see Word Study **say**, pages 699–702

say ❷ NOUN
a chance to express your opinion • *voters who want a say in the matter*
voice • *Parents are given a voice in decision-making.*
vote • *Every employee felt he had a vote in the company's future.*

saying NOUN
a well-known sentence or phrase • *the saying, "charity begins at home"*
adage • *the old adage, "the show must go on"*
axiom • *the long-held axiom that education leads to higher income*
maxim • *I believe in the maxim, "If it ain't broke, don't fix it".*
proverb • *an old Chinese proverb*

MORE SYNONYMS
- aphorism
- apophthegm
- dictum
- saw

scarce ADJECTIVE
rare or uncommon • *Jobs are becoming increasingly scarce.*
few • *Our options are few.*
rare • *Puffins are now rare in this country.*
uncommon • *an extreme but by n means uncommon case*

Can't find the word you're looking for? Try the index.

unusual • *To be appreciated as a parent is quite unusual.*

ANTONYM
- common

scare ❶ VERB
to frighten someone • *You're scaring me.*
alarm • *We could not see what had alarmed him.*
frighten • *He knew that Soli was trying to frighten him.*
give someone a fright • *The snake moved and gave everyone a fright.*
intimidate • *Jones had set out to intimidate and dominate Paul.*
startle • *Sorry, I didn't mean to startle you.*
terrify • *Flying terrifies him.*
terrorize • *pensioners terrorized by anonymous phone calls*
unnerve • *We were unnerved by the total silence.*

scare ❷ NOUN
a short period of feeling very frightened • *We got a bit of a scare.*
fright • *the last time I had a real fright*
shock • *It gave me quite a shock to see his face on the screen.*
start • *The sudden noise gave me quite a start.*

scare ❸ NOUN
a situation where people worry about something • *Despite the health scare there are no plans to withdraw the drug.*
alert • *a security alert*
hysteria • *Everyone was getting carried away by the hysteria.*
panic • *the panic over GM foods*

scary ADJECTIVE (INFORMAL)
frightening • *Prison is going to be a scary thing for him.*
alarming • *an alarming report on the rise of street crime*
chilling • *a chilling account of the accident*
creepy (INFORMAL) • *places that are really creepy at night*
eerie • *the eerie dark path*
frightening • *a very frightening experience*
hair-raising • *a hair-raising encounter with a wild boar*
spooky • *The whole place has a slightly spooky atmosphere.*
terrifying • *I find it terrifying to be surrounded by a crowd of people.*
unnerving • *It is very unnerving to find out that someone you know is carrying the virus.*

scatter VERB
to throw or drop things all over an area • *She scattered the petals over the grave.*
shower • *The bomb exploded, showering shrapnel over a wide area.*
sow • *Sow the seeds in a warm place.*
sprinkle • *Sprinkle a tablespoon of sugar over the fruit.*
throw about • *They started throwing food about.*

MORE SYNONYMS
- broadcast
- disseminate
- strew

ANTONYM
- gather

scene ❶ NOUN
a picture or view of something • *a village scene*
landscape • *Arizona's desert landscape*
panorama • *a panorama of fertile valleys*

Can't find the word you're looking for? Try the index.

a b c d e f g h i j k l m n o p q r s t u v w x y z

view • *a view of the lake*

MORE SYNONYMS
● outlook
● vista

scene ❷ NOUN

the place where something
happens • *the scene of the crime*
location • *filmed in an exotic
location*
place • *Can you show me the place
where the attack happened?*
setting • *Rome is the perfect
setting for romance.*
site • *the site of the battle*
spot • *the ideal spot for a picnic*

scene ❸ NOUN

an area of activity • *the music scene*
arena • *the political arena*
business • *the potential to
revolutionize the publishing business*
environment • *the Japanese
business environment*
world • *the fashion world*

scenery NOUN

the things you see in the
countryside • *drive slowly down the
lane enjoying the scenery*
landscape • *Arizona's desert
landscape*
panorama • *admiring the distant
mountain panorama*
surroundings • *a holiday home in
beautiful surroundings*
terrain • *The terrain changed from
arable land to desert.*
view • *The view from our window
was spectacular.*

MORE SYNONYMS
● outlook
● vista

scold VERB

to tell someone off • *She scolded*

her daughter for being cheeky.
chide • *Cross chided himself for
worrying.*
lecture • *My mother always used
to lecture me about not eating
properly.*
rebuke • *I turned to him and
sharply rebuked him.*
reprimand • *reprimanded for
talking in the corridor*
tell off (INFORMAL) • *The teacher
really told her off.*
tick off (INFORMAL) • *ticked off for
being late*

MORE SYNONYMS
● berate
● castigate
● reprove
● upbraid

scorn ❶ NOUN

great contempt felt for something
• *The proposal was greeted with
scorn.*
contempt • *I treated this remark
with the contempt it deserved.*
derision • *shouts of derision*
disdain • *Janet looked at him with
disdain.*
mockery • *his mockery of all things
English*

scorn ❷ VERB

to treat with great contempt
• *Eleanor scorns the work of others.*
despise • *She secretly despises him.*
disdain • *He disdained politicians.*
look down on • *I wasn't successful
so they looked down on me.*
slight • *He felt slighted by this
treatment.*

MORE SYNONYMS
● be above
● contemn
● hold in contempt

A B C D E F G H I J K L M N O P Q R S T U V W X Y Z

scornful ADJECTIVE
showing contempt for something
• He is deeply scornful of his rivals.
contemptuous • She gave a contemptuous little laugh.
disdainful • He is disdainful of politicians.
scathing • He made some scathing comments about the design.
sneering • a sneering tone
supercilious • His manner is supercilious and arrogant.
withering • Her mother gave her a withering look.

scrape ❶ VERB
to rub a rough or sharp object against something • We had to scrape the frost from the windscreen.
graze • He had grazed his knees a little.
scour • Scour the pans.
scratch • The branches scratched my face and hands.
scuff • scuffed shoes
skin • I found that I had skinned my knuckles.

scrape ❷ VERB
to make a harsh noise by rubbing
• his shoes scraping across the ground
grate • His chair grated as he got to his feet.
grind • Blocks of ice ground against each other.
rasp • The blade rasped over his skin.
scratch • He scraped his knife over the worktop.

scream ❶ VERB
to shout or cry in a high-pitched voice • If he says that again, I shall scream.
cry • a crying baby
howl • He howled like a wounded animal.

screech • "Get me some water!" I screeched.
shout • I shouted at mother to get the police.
shriek • She shrieked and leapt from the bed.
squeal • Jennifer squealed with delight.
yell • I pushed him away, yelling abuse.

scream ❷ NOUN
a loud, high-pitched cry • Hilda let out a scream.
cry • a cry of horror
howl • a howl of rage
screech • The figure gave a screech.
shriek • a shriek of joy
squeal • the squeal of piglets
yell • Something brushed Bob's face and he let out a yell.

scrounge VERB (INFORMAL)
to get something by asking rather than working for it • He's always scrounging lifts.
beg • They managed to beg a lift from a passing fisherman.
bludge (AUSTRALIAN AND NEW ZEALAND; INFORMAL) • They've come here to bludge food and money.
cadge • Can I cadge a cigarette?
sponge (INFORMAL) • I got tired of him sponging off me and threw him out.

scruffy ADJECTIVE
dirty and untidy • four scruffy youths
ragged • a ragged band of men
seedy • his seedy clothes
shabby • a shabby, tall man with dark eyes
tatty • a tatty old cardigan
unkempt • His hair was unkempt and filthy.

a
b
c
d
e
f
g
h
i
j
k
l
m
n
o
p
q
r
s
t
u
v
w
x
y
z

Can't find the word you're looking for? Try the index.

MORE SYNONYMS
- disreputable
- slovenly
- ungroomed

ANTONYM
- smart

scrutinize VERB
to examine something very carefully • She scrutinized his features.
examine • He examined her passport.
inspect • Cut the fruit in half and inspect the pips.
pore over • We spent hours poring over the files.
scan • She kept scanning the crowd for Paul.
search • Her eyes searched his face.
study • Debbie studied the document for a moment.

scungy ADJECTIVE (AUSTRALIAN AND NEW ZEALAND; SLANG)
dirty • living in some scungy flat on the outskirts of town
dirty • He was wearing a dirty old mac.
filthy • This flat is so filthy I can't possibly stay here.
foul • foul polluted water
seedy • a seedy hotel
sleazy • sleazy bars
sordid • sordid little rooms
squalid • a squalid bedsit

search ❶ VERB
to look for something • The security forces are searching for the missing men.
comb • Police combed the woods for the murder weapon.
forage • foraging for food
fossick (AUSTRALIAN AND NEW ZEALAND) • to help Gaston fossick

for food around the hut
hunt • hunting for a job
look • He's looking for a way out of this situation.
scour • They had scoured the intervening miles of moorland.
seek • the man he had been seeking for weeks
sift • sifting through the wreckage for clues

search ❷ NOUN
the action of looking for something • Police will resume the search today.
hunt • the hunt for my lost boy
quest • his quest to find true love

secret ADJECTIVE
known about by only a few people • a secret location
closet (INFORMAL) • a closet Fascist
confidential • a confidential report
covert • She gave him a covert glance.
furtive • furtive meetings
hidden • a hidden camera
undercover • undercover FBI agents
underground • the underground communist movement

MORE SYNONYMS
- cloak-and-dagger
- conspiratorial
- undisclosed

RELATED WORD
- ADJECTIVE: cryptic

secretive ADJECTIVE
hiding your feelings and intentions • Jake was very secretive about his family affairs.
cagey (INFORMAL) • He is cagey about what he was paid for the business.
reserved • He was unemotional and reserved.

reticent • *She is very reticent about her achievements.*

MORE SYNONYMS
- tight-lipped
- uncommunicative
- unforthcoming

section NOUN
one of the parts into which something is divided • *this section of the motorway*
division • *the company's sales division*
instalment • *Payment can be made in instalments.*
part • *the upper part of the body*
piece • *The equipment was taken down the shaft in pieces.*
portion • *I had learnt a portion of the Koran.*
segment • *the third segment of the journey*

secure ❶ VERB (FORMAL)
to manage to get something • *His achievements helped him to secure the job.*
acquire • *General Motors recently acquired a 50% stake in the company.*
gain • *Hard work may not be enough to gain a place at university.*
get • *I got a job at the sawmill.*
obtain • *He tried to obtain a false passport.*
procure (FORMAL) • *trying to procure the release of the hostages*

secure ❷ VERB
to make something safe • *We need to secure the building against attack.*
fortify • *British soldiers are working to fortify the airbase.*
make impregnable • *Their intention was to make the old fort impregnable.*
make safe • *Crime Prevention*

Officers will suggest ways to make your home safe.
strengthen • *In the 14th century they strengthened this wall against raiders.*

secure ❸ VERB
to fasten or attach something firmly • *The frames are secured by rails to the wall.*
attach • *The gadget can be attached to any vertical surface.*
bind • *Bind the ends of the cord together with thread.*
fasten • *Her long hair was fastened by an elastic band.*
fix • *He fixed a bayonet to the end of his rifle.*
lock • *Are you sure you locked the front door?*
moor • *She moored her barge on the river bank.*
tie up • *They dismounted and tied up their horses.*

ANTONYM
- release

secure ❹ ADJECTIVE
tightly locked or well protected • *Make sure your home is as secure as possible.*
fortified • *The door is fortified against flooding.*
impregnable • *The old castle was completely impregnable against raids.*
protected • *the right of women to be protected from sexual harassment*
safe • *We want to go to a football match knowing we are safe from hooliganism.*
shielded • *The company is shielded from takeover attempts.*

secure ❺ ADJECTIVE
firmly fixed in place • *Shelves are*

a
b
c
d
e
f
g
h
i
j
k
l
m
n
o
p
q
r
s
t
u
v
w
x
y
z

only as secure as their fixings.
fastened • Make sure the safety belt is fastened.
firm • If you have to climb up, use a firm platform.
fixed • Check the holder is fixed in its place on the wall.
locked • Leave doors and windows locked.
solid • I yanked on the bracket to see if it was solid.
stable • The structure must be stable.
tight • He kept a tight hold of her arm.

secure ❻ ADJECTIVE
feeling safe and happy • She felt secure when she was with him.
confident • In time he became more confident.
protected • It's good to have a place in which you feel protected and loved.
reassured • I feel much more reassured when I've been for a health check.
relaxed • There are very few people he feels relaxed with.
safe • He kissed me and I felt warm and safe.

ANTONYM
● insecure

see ❶ VERB
to look at or notice something • Did you see what happened?
behold • She looked into his eyes and beheld madness.
discern • We could just discern the outline of the island.
glimpse • She glimpsed the man's face briefly.
look • She turned to look at him.
notice • She noticed a bird sitting on the roof.

observe • He observed a reddish spot on the planet's surface.
perceive • Infants start to perceive objects at a very early age.
sight • A fleet of French ships was sighted.
spot • I think he spotted me but didn't want to be seen.

MORE SYNONYMS
● catch sight of
● descry
● espy

see ❷ VERB
to realize or understand something • I see what you mean.
appreciate • He appreciates the difficulties.
comprehend • They do not comprehend the nature of the problem.
follow • Do you follow what I'm saying?
get • You don't seem to get the point.
grasp • They have not grasped the seriousness of the crisis.
realize • They realized too late that they were wrong.
understand • I'm not sure I understand.

see ❸ VERB
to find something out • I'll see what's happening outside.
ascertain • Ascertain what services your bank provides.
determine • The investigation will determine what really happened.
discover • Try to discover what you are good at.
find out • Watch the next episode to find out what happens.

seek ❶ VERB
to try to find something • The

police were still seeking information.
be after • *At last I found what I was after.*
hunt • *Police are hunting for clues.*
look for • *I'm looking for a lost child.*
search for • *searching for answers*

seek ❷ VERB
to try to do something • *De Gaulle sought to reunite the country.*
aim • *We aim to raise funds for charity.*
aspire to • *He aspired to work in music journalism.*
attempt • *He was forever attempting to arrange deals.*
endeavour • *They are endeavouring to protect trade union rights.*
strive • *The school strives to treat pupils as individuals.*
try • *We are trying to bring about a better world.*

seem VERB
to appear to be • *He seemed such a quiet man.*
appear • *She appeared intoxicated.*
give the impression • *He gave the impression of being the perfect husband.*
look • *The cottage looks quite ordinary from the road.*
look like • *You look like a nice guy.*

seize ❶ VERB
to grab something firmly • *He seized the phone.*
grab • *I grabbed him by the neck.*
grasp • *He grasped both my hands.*
snatch • *Mick snatched the cards from Archie's hand.*

seize ❷ VERB
to take control of something
• *Rebels have seized the airport.*

annex • *the plan to invade and annex Kuwait*
appropriate • *The land was appropriated by Communists.*
confiscate • *The police confiscated weapons and ammunition.*
hijack • *Almost 250 trucks were hijacked.*
impound • *The ship was impounded under the terms of the trade embargo.*

MORE SYNONYMS
● commandeer
● take possession of

select ❶ VERB
to choose something • *They selected only the brightest pupils.*
choose • *Houston was chosen as the site for the conference.*
decide on • *I'm still trying to decide on an outfit for the wedding.*
opt for • *You may wish to opt for one method straight away.*
pick • *He had picked ten people to interview for the jobs.*
settle on • *I finally settled on the estate car because it was so roomy.*
single out • *His boss has singled him out for a special mission.*
take • *"I'll take the grilled tuna,"* she told the waiter.

select ❷ ADJECTIVE
of good quality • *a select band of top-ranking sportsmen*
choice • *We use only the choicest ingredients.*
exclusive • *Britain's most exclusive club*
first-class • *a first-class hotel*
first-rate • *The first-rate cast includes many famous names.*
hand-picked • *a hand-picked series of timeless classics*
prime • *one of the City's prime*

a
b
c
d
e
f
g
h
i
j
k
l
m
n
o
p
q
r
s
t
u
v
w
x
y
z

Can't find the word you're looking for? Try the index.

sites, with a view of several historic buildings
special • *a special group of government officials*
superior • *a superior range of products*

selfish ADJECTIVE
caring only about yourself • *his greedy and selfish behaviour*
egoistic or **egoistical** • *egoistic motives*
egotistic or **egotistical** • *an intensely egotistic streak*
greedy • *greedy bosses awarding themselves big rises*
self-centred • *He was self-centred, but he wasn't cruel.*

MORE SYNONYMS
- self-interested
- self-seeking
- ungenerous

sell ❶ VERB
to let someone have something in return for money • *I just sold my car.*
deal in • *They deal in antiques.*
hawk • *vendors hawking trinkets*
peddle • *arrested for peddling drugs*
trade in • *They trade in spices and all kinds of grain.*

ANTONYM
- buy

sell ❷ VERB
to have available for people to buy • *a little shop that sells teapots*
deal in • *a business dealing in honey*
stock • *The shop stocks a variety of local craft products.*
trade in • *a company that trades in sporting memorabilia*

ANTONYM
- buy

send ❶ VERB
to arrange for something to be delivered • *He sent a basket of fruit and a card.*
dispatch • *He dispatched a telegram of congratulation.*
forward • *A letter was forwarded from the clinic.*
remit • *Many immigrants regularly remit money to their families.*

send ❷ VERB
to transmit a signal or message • *The pilot was trying to send a distress signal.*
broadcast • *to broadcast a message to a whole group of people at once*
transmit • *the most efficient way to transmit data*

senior ADJECTIVE
the highest and most important in an organization • *senior jobs*
best • *These officers have traditionally taken the best jobs.*
better • *Well-qualified women are now attaining better positions.*
high-ranking • *a high-ranking officer in the medical corps*
superior • *negotiations between crew members and their superior officers*

ANTONYM
- junior

sense ❶ NOUN
a feeling you have about something • *an overwhelming sense of guilt*
consciousness • *a consciousness of tension*
feeling • *It gave me a feeling of satisfaction.*

Can't find the word you're looking for? Try the index.

impression • *The music creates an impression of menace.*

sense ❷ NOUN
the ability to think and behave sensibly • *He had the good sense to call me at once.*
brains (INFORMAL) • *At least I had the brains to keep quiet.*
common sense • *completely lacking in common sense*
intelligence • *He didn't have the intelligence to understand what was happening.*
judgment • *I respect his judgment.*
reason • *a conflict between emotion and reason*
wisdom • *the wisdom that comes of old age*

MORE SYNONYMS
- nous
- sagacity
- wit *or* wits

sense ❸ VERB
to become aware of something • *She sensed he wasn't telling her the whole story.*
be aware of • *He was aware of her anger.*
feel • *Suddenly, I felt a presence behind me.*
get the impression • *I get the impression he's lying.*
have a hunch • *Lowe had a hunch he was on to something.*
realize • *We realized something was wrong.*

sensible ADJECTIVE
showing good sense and judgment • *a sensible, level-headed approach*
down-to-earth • *the most down-to-earth person I've ever met*
judicious • *the judicious use of military force*

practical • *practical suggestions*
prudent • *It is prudent to start any exercise programme gradually.*
rational • *a rational decision*
sound • *sound advice*
wise • *a wise move*

ANTONYM
- foolish

sensitive ADJECTIVE
easily upset about something • *He was sensitive about his height.*
easily offended • *I am not a feminist, nor am I easily offended.*
easily upset • *He remained deeply neurotic and easily upset.*
thin-skinned • *I'm too thin-skinned - I want everyone to like me.*
touchy • *She is very touchy about her weight.*

sentimental ADJECTIVE
expressing exaggerated sadness or tenderness • *sentimental love stories*
maudlin • *Jimmy turned maudlin after three drinks.*
mushy (INFORMAL) • *I go completely mushy when I see a baby.*
nostalgic • *nostalgic for the good old days*
sloppy (INFORMAL) • *I hate sloppy romantic films.*
slushy (INFORMAL) • *slushy ballads*

MORE SYNONYMS
- dewy-eyed
- mawkish
- overemotional

separate ❶ ADJECTIVE
not connected to something else • *The question muddles up two separate issues.*
detached • *a detached house*
disconnected • *sequences of disconnected events*

Can't find the word you're looking for? Try the index.

A
B
C
D
E
F
G
H
I
J
K
L
M
N
O
P
Q
R
S
T
U
V
W
X
Y
Z

discrete • *two discrete sets of nerves*
divorced • *speculative theories divorced from reality*
isolated • *He lives as if isolated from the rest of the world.*
unconnected • *The two murders are unconnected.*

ANTONYM
● connected

separate ❷ VERB
to end a connection between people or things • *Police moved in to separate the two groups.*
detach • *Three of the carriages on the train became detached.*
disconnect • *Make sure supply plugs are disconnected from the mains.*
divide • *This was a ruse to divide them.*

MORE SYNONYMS
● bifurcate
● sunder
● uncouple

ANTONYM
● connect

separate ❸ VERB
to end a relationship or marriage • *Her parents separated when she was very young.*
break up • *She hadn't used his name since they broke up.*
divorce • *We divorced ten years ago.*
part • *He is parting from his Swedish-born wife Eva.*
split up • *I split up with my boyfriend last year.*

sequence ❶ NOUN
a number of events coming one after another • *an unbroken*

sequence of victories
chain • *the chain of events leading to the assassination*
course • *a course of injections*
cycle • *the cycle of birth, growth, decay, and death*
progression • *The story of American freedom is anything but a linear progression.*
series • *a series of explosions*
string • *a string of burglaries*
succession • *He took a succession of jobs that stood him in good stead.*

sequence ❷ NOUN
a particular order in which things are arranged • *the colour sequence: yellow, orange, purple, blue*
arrangement • *a simple arrangement of coloured tiles*
order • *Music shops should arrange their recordings in alphabetical order.*
pattern • *a systematic pattern of behaviour*
progression • *the natural progression of the seasons*
structure • *The bricks had been arranged in a regular structure.*

series NOUN
a number of things coming one after the other • *a series of loud explosions*
chain • *a bizarre chain of events*
run • *The England skipper is haunted by a run of low scores.*
sequence • *a sequence of novels*
string • *a string of burglaries*
succession • *He had a succession of jobs.*

serious ❶ ADJECTIVE
very bad and worrying • *They survived their serious injuries.*
acute • *an acute attack of appendicitis*

Can't find the word you're looking for? Try the index.

alarming • *the alarming increase in drug abuse*
bad • *a bad bout of flu*
critical • *He remains in a critical condition in hospital.*
dangerous • *His wound proved more dangerous than it seemed at first.*
extreme • *the most extreme case doctors have ever seen*
grave • *We are all in grave danger.*
grievous • *grievous wounds*
grim • *Our situation is grim indeed.*
intense • *Intense fighting has broken out in the capital.*
precarious • *He is in a very precarious position.*
severe • *a severe shortage of drinking water*
worrying • *It is a worrying situation.*

serious ❷ ADJECTIVE
important and deserving careful thought • *I regard this as a serious matter.*
crucial • *Negotiations were at a crucial stage.*
deep • *This novel raises deep questions about the nature of faith.*
difficult • *The government faces even more difficult problems.*
far-reaching • *His actions will have far-reaching consequences.*
grave • *a grave situation*
important • *We've got more important things to worry about now.*
momentous • *the momentous decision to go to war*
pressing • *a pressing problem*
profound • *a man who thinks about the more profound issues of life*
significant • *the most significant question of all*

urgent • *He is not equipped to deal with an urgent situation like this.*
weighty • *a weighty problem*

ANTONYM
● funny

serious ❸ ADJECTIVE
sincere about something • *I was not quite sure whether he was serious.*
earnest • *It is my earnest hope that we can work things out.*
genuine • *a genuine offer*
heartfelt • *a full and heartfelt apology*
honest • *He looked at me in honest surprise.*
in earnest • *I can never tell if he is in earnest or not.*
resolute • *He was resolute about his ideals.*
resolved • *They are quite resolved about their decision.*
sincere • *He's sincere in his views.*

serious ❹ ADJECTIVE
quiet and not laughing much • *He's quite a serious person.*
earnest • *She looked up at me with an earnest expression.*
grave • *He was looking unusually grave.*
humourless • *a dour, humourless Scotsman*
pensive • *We're both in a pensive mood today.*
sober • *sad, sober faces*
solemn • *His solemn little face broke into a smile.*
staid • *bored with her marriage to a staid country doctor*
stern • *a stern headmaster feared by all the pupils*

set ❶ NOUN
a group of things that belong together • *a set of tools*

a b c d e f g h i j k l m n o p q r **s** t u v w x y z

Can't find the word you're looking for? Try the index.

batch • *the latest batch of recruits*
kit • *I forgot my gym kit.*
outfit • *She was wearing a brand new outfit.*
series • *a series of books covering the history of aviation*

MORE SYNONYMS
- assemblage
- compendium
- ensemble

set ❷ VERB
to put or place something somewhere • *He set his case down on the floor.*
deposit • *Imagine if you were suddenly deposited on a desert island.*
lay • *Lay a sheet of newspaper on the floor.*
locate • *The restaurant is located near the cathedral.*
place • *She placed a mug of coffee in front of him.*
position • *Plants were carefully positioned in the alcove.*
put • *He put the photograph on the desk.*
rest • *He rested one of his crutches against the rail.*
stick • *Just stick your bag down anywhere.*

set ❸ ADJECTIVE
fixed and not varying • *a set charge*
arranged • *We arrived at the arranged time.*
established • *the established order*
firm • *a firm booking*
fixed • *a fixed rate of interest*
predetermined • *His destiny was predetermined from the moment of his birth.*
scheduled • *The plane failed to return at the scheduled time.*

set on ADJECTIVE
determined to do something • *She was set on going to the States.*
bent • *He's bent on suicide.*
determined • *His enemies are determined to ruin him.*
intent • *an actress who was intent on making a comeback*

settle ❶ VERB
to put an end to an argument or problem • *The dispute has been settled.*
clear up • *Eventually the confusion was cleared up.*
decide • *None of the cases had been decided.*
dispose of • *the way in which you disposed of that problem*
put an end to • *I just want to put and end to this situation.*
reconcile • *urging the two parties to reconcile their differences*
resolve • *They hoped the crisis could be resolved peacefully.*
straighten out • *doing their best to straighten out this confusion*

settle ❷ VERB
to decide or arrange something • *Let's settle where we're going tonight.*
agree • *We haven't agreed a date yet.*
arrange • *Have you arranged our next appointment?*
decide on • *They decided on an evening to meet.*
determine • *The final wording had not yet been determined.*
fix • *He's going to fix a time when I can see him.*

settle ❸ VERB
to make your home in a place • *refugees settling in Britain*
make your home • *those who had*

made their homes in China
move to • *His family moved to New Zealand when he was 12.*
people • *The plateau was peopled by nomadic tribes.*
populate • *The island was populated by Native Americans.*

MORE SYNONYMS
- colonize
- put down roots
- take up residence

set up VERB
to make arrangements for something • *setting up a system of communication*
arrange • *We have arranged a series of interviews.*
establish • *We have established links with industry and commerce.*
install • *I'm having cable installed next week.*
institute • *to institute better levels of quality control*
organize • *a two-day meeting organized by the UN*

several ADJECTIVE
indicating a small number • *several boxes filled with albums*
assorted • *overnight stops in assorted hotels*
some • *some cheers from the gallery*
sundry • *He has won sundry music awards.*
various • *a dozen trees of various sorts*

severe ❶ ADJECTIVE
extremely bad or unpleasant • *severe cash flow problems*
acute • *an acute economic crisis*
critical • *if the situation becomes critical*
deep • *We will be in deep trouble if*

this goes on.
dire • *This would have dire consequences for domestic peace.*
extreme • *people living in extreme poverty*
grave • *He said the situation was very grave.*
intense • *A number of people collapsed in the intense heat.*
serious • *The government faces very serious difficulties.*
terrible • *terrible injuries*

ANTONYM
- mild

severe ❷ ADJECTIVE
stern and harsh • *This was a dreadful crime and a severe sentence is necessary.*
disapproving • *Janet gave him a disapproving look.*
grim • *Her expression was grim and unpleasant.*
hard • *His father was a hard man.*
harsh • *the cold, harsh cruelty of her husband*
stern • *He said stern measures would be taken.*
strict • *My parents were very strict.*

sexy ADJECTIVE
sexually attractive or exciting • *a sexy voice*
erotic • *an erotic film*
seductive • *I love dressing up to look seductive.*
sensual • *a wide, sensual mouth*
sensuous • *his sensuous young mistress*
voluptuous • *a voluptuous figure*

shabby ❶ ADJECTIVE
ragged and worn in appearance • *a shabby overcoat*
dilapidated • *a dilapidated old building*

a
b
c
d
e
f
g
h
i
j
k
l
m
n
o
p
q
r
s
t
u
v
w
x
y
z

Can't find the word you're looking for? Try the index.

ragged • *dressed in a ragged coat*
scruffy • *a scruffy basement flat in London*
seedy • *his seedy clothes*
tatty • *a tatty old cardigan*
threadbare • *a square of threadbare carpet*
worn • *a worn corduroy jacket*

MORE SYNONYMS
- down at heel
- run-down
- the worse for wear

shabby ❷ ADJECTIVE
behaving meanly and unfairly • *shabby treatment*
contemptible • *contemptible behaviour*
despicable • *a despicable thing to do*
dirty • *That was a dirty trick.*
mean • *It was mean of you to hurt her like that.*
rotten (INFORMAL) • *That's a rotten thing to say!*

MORE SYNONYMS
- dishonourable
- ignoble
- scurvy

shake ❶ VERB
to move something from side to side or up and down • *You have to shake the bottle before use.*
agitate • *Gently agitate the water.*
brandish • *He appeared brandishing a knife.*
flourish • *He flourished his glass to make the point.*
wave • *The crowd were waving flags and cheering.*

shake ❷ VERB
to move from side to side or up and down • *The whole building shook with the force of the blast.*

jolt • *The train jolted again.*
quake • *The whole mountain quaked.*
quiver • *Her bottom lip began to quiver.*
shiver • *shivering with fear*
shudder • *Elaine shuddered with cold.*
tremble • *The leaves trembled in the breeze.*
vibrate • *The engine began to vibrate alarmingly.*

MORE SYNONYMS
- joggle
- oscillate

shake ❸ VERB
to shock and upset someone • *The news shook me quite a bit.*
distress • *Her death had profoundly distressed me.*
disturb • *dreams so vivid that they disturb me for days*
rattle (INFORMAL) • *He was obviously rattled by events.*
shock • *Pictures of emaciated prisoners shocked the world.*
unnerve • *unnerved by the sight*
upset • *I was too upset to speak.*

MORE SYNONYMS
- discompose
- traumatize

shaky ADJECTIVE
weak and unsteady • *threatening an already shaky economy*
rickety • *Mona climbed the rickety wooden stairway.*
tottering • *the baby's first tottering steps*
trembling • *She held out one frail, trembling hand.*
unstable • *an unstable lamp on top of an old tea-chest*
unsteady • *His voice was unsteady.*

Can't find the word you're looking for? Try the index.

wobbly • *I'm sorry, this table's a bit wobbly.*

shame ❶ NOUN
a feeling of guilt or embarrassment • *She felt a deep sense of shame.*
embarrassment • *He turned red with embarrassment.*
humiliation • *the humiliation of discussing her husband's affair*
ignominy • *the ignominy of being made redundant*

MORE SYNONYMS
● abashment
● loss of face
● mortification

shame ❷ NOUN
something that makes people lose respect for you • *I don't want to bring shame on the family.*
discredit • *It was to his discredit that he did nothing.*
disgrace • *He had to resign in disgrace.*
dishonour • *his sense of dishonour at his brother's conduct*
scandal • *They often abandoned their children because of fear of scandal.*

shame ❸ VERB
to make someone feel ashamed • *Her son's affair had shamed her.*
disgrace • *I have disgraced my country.*
embarrass • *It embarrassed him that he had no idea of what was going on.*
humiliate • *His teacher continually humiliates him in maths lessons.*

MORE SYNONYMS
● abash
● mortify

shameless ADJECTIVE
behaving badly without showing any shame • *shameless dishonesty*
barefaced • *a barefaced lie*
brazen • *a brazen theft*
flagrant • *a flagrant violation of the law*
unabashed • *an unabashed egotist*
unashamed • *blatant, unashamed hypocrisy*
wanton • *a wanton woman*

shape ❶ NOUN
the outline of something • *a round shape*
contours • *the contours of the mountains*
figure • *a trim figure*
form • *the form of the human body*
lines • *The belt spoilt the lines of her long dress.*
outline • *the dim outline of a small boat*

shape ❷ VERB
to make something in a particular form • *Shape the dough into a loaf.*
fashion • *buttons fashioned from bone*
form • *The polymer is formed into a thin sheet.*
make • *gold made into wedding rings*
model • *She began modelling animals from clay.*
mould • *Mould the cheese into small ovals.*

share ❶ VERB
to divide something between two or more people • *We shared a bottle of champagne.*
divide • *The prize money was divided between the two winners.*
split • *We split the bill between us.*

share ❷ NOUN
a portion of something • *a share of the profits*

Can't find the word you're looking for? Try the index.

A
B
C
D
E
F
G
H
I
J
K
L
M
N
O
P
Q
R
S
T
U
V
W
X
Y
Z

allotment • *a daily allotment of three ounces of bread*
portion • *his portion of the inheritance*
quota • *a quota of four tickets per person*
ration • *their daily ration of water*

sharp ❶ ADJECTIVE
having a fine cutting edge or point • *a sharp knife*
jagged • *jagged rocks*
keen • *a keen edge*
pointed • *pointed teeth*
razor-sharp • *the razor-sharp blade*

ANTONYM
● blunt

sharp ❷ ADJECTIVE
quick to notice or understand things • *a sharp intellect*
alert • *She is alert and sprightly despite her 85 years.*
astute • *He made a series of astute business decisions.*
bright • *an exceptionally bright child*
observant • *an observant eye*
perceptive • *a perceptive gaze*
quick • *His quick mind soon grasped the situation.*
quick-witted • *He is very alert and quick-witted.*

sharp ❸ ADJECTIVE
sudden and significant • *a sharp rise in prices*
abrupt • *Her idyllic world came to an abrupt end when her parents died.*
marked • *a marked increase in crimes against property*
sudden • *a sudden change in course*

sheer ❶ ADJECTIVE
complete and total • *acts of sheer desperation*

absolute • *I think it's absolute nonsense.*
complete • *He shook his head in complete bewilderment.*
pure • *To have an uninterrupted night's sleep was pure bliss.*
total • *This is total madness!*
unqualified • *It has been an unqualified disaster.*
utter • *a look of utter confusion*

MORE SYNONYMS
● unadulterated
● unalloyed
● unmitigated (FORMAL)

sheer ❷ ADJECTIVE
vertical • *There was a sheer drop just outside my window.*
perpendicular • *the perpendicular wall of sandstone*
steep • *a narrow valley with steep sides*
vertical • *The climber inched up a vertical wall of rock.*

sheer ❸ ADJECTIVE
very light and delicate • *sheer black tights*
delicate • *delicate fabric*
fine • *a fine, pale grey material*
lightweight • *lightweight materials with Lycra*
thin • *the thin silk of her blouse*

ANTONYM
● thick

shelter ❶ NOUN
a place providing protection • *a bus shelter*
hostel • *She spent two years living in a hostel.*
refuge • *a mountain refuge*
sanctuary • *His church became a sanctuary for people fleeing the civil war.*

Can't find the word you're looking for? Try the index.

shelter ❷ NOUN

protection from bad weather or
danger • *the hut where they were
given food and shelter*
asylum • *refugees who sought
political asylum*
cover • *They ran for cover from the
storm.*
harbour • *Patches of gorse were a
great harbour for foxes.*
haven • *The island is a haven for
international criminals.*
protection • *Riot shields acted as
protection against the attack.*
refuge • *They took refuge in an old
barn.*
safety • *the safety of one's own
home*
sanctuary • *Some of them sought
sanctuary in the church.*

shelter ❸ VERB

to stay somewhere in order to be
safe • *a man sheltering in a
doorway*
hide • *They hid behind a tree.*
huddle • *She huddled inside the
porch.*
take cover • *Shoppers took cover
behind cars as the shots rang out.*

shelter ❹ VERB

to hide or protect someone
• *A neighbour sheltered the boy for
seven days.*
harbour • *He was accused of
harbouring terrorist suspects.*
hide • *They hid me until the coast
was clear.*
protect • *A purple headscarf
protected her against the wind.*
shield • *He shielded his head from
the sun with a sack.*

shine VERB

to give out a bright light • *The sun
is shining.*

beam • *The spotlight beamed down
on the stage.*
gleam • *The moonlight gleamed on
the water.*
glow • *The lantern glowed softly in
the darkness.*
radiate • *the amount of light
radiated by an ordinary light bulb*
shimmer • *The lake shimmered in
the sunlight.*
sparkle • *Diamonds sparkled on
her wrists.*

shining ADJECTIVE

giving out or reflecting light
• *shining stainless steel tables*
bright • *a bright star*
brilliant • *brilliant sunshine*
gleaming • *gleaming headlights*
luminous • *the luminous dial on
the clock*
radiant • *He saw a figure
surrounded by a radiant light.*
shimmering • *a shimmering gold
fabric*
sparkling • *elegant cutlery and
sparkling crystal*

MORE SYNONYMS

● effulgent
● incandescent

shock ❶ NOUN

a sudden upsetting experience
• *The extent of the damage came as
a shock.*
blow • *It was a terrible blow when
he was made redundant.*
bombshell • *His departure was a
bombshell for the team.*
distress • *She wanted to save her
mother all the distress she could.*
trauma • *the trauma of losing a
parent*

shock ❷ VERB

to make you feel upset • *I was*

a b c d e f g h i j k l m n o p q r s t u v w x y z

shocked by his appearance.
numb • *numbed by suffering and terror*
paralyse • *He stood paralysed with horror.*
shake • *The news of her death has shaken us all.*
stagger • *The judge said he was staggered by the defendant's callousness.*
stun • *Audiences were stunned by the film's violent ending.*
traumatize • *My wife was traumatized by the experience.*

shock ❸ VERB
to offend because of being rude or immoral • *She is very easily shocked.*
appal • *I was appalled by her rudeness.*
disgust • *He disgusted everyone with his boorish behaviour.*
offend • *Many people are offended by strong swearwords.*
outrage • *They were outraged by his racist comments.*

MORE SYNONYMS
● nauseate
● scandalize

shop NOUN
a place where things are sold • *I had to race round the shops.*
boutique • *He owns a jewellery boutique.*
market • *He sold fruit on a small market stall.*
store • *Within two years he was managing the store.*
supermarket • *Most of us do our food shopping in the supermarket.*

MORE SYNONYMS
● emporium
● hypermarket
● mart

shore NOUN

TYPES OF SHORE	
bank	sands
beach	seaboard
coast	seashore
foreshore	shingle
front	strand
lakeside	waterside

short ❶ ADJECTIVE
not lasting very long • *a short break*
▷ *see Word Study* **short**, *page 703*

ANTONYM
● long

short ❷ ADJECTIVE
small in height • *a short, elderly man*
▷ *see Word Study* **short**, *page 703*

ANTONYM
● tall

short ❸ ADJECTIVE
not using many words • *a short speech*
▷ *see Word Study* **short**, *page 703*

MORE SYNONYMS
● abridged
● laconic
● pithy

shortage NOUN
a lack of something • *a shortage of funds*
dearth • *the dearth of good fiction by English authors*
deficiency • *tests for vitamin deficiency*
lack • *I was hampered by a lack of information.*
scarcity • *a scarcity of water*
shortfall • *a shortfall in income*
want • *a want of manners and charm*

A
B
C
D
E
F
G
H
I
J
K
L
M
N
O
P
Q
R
S
T
U
V
W
X
Y
Z

MORE SYNONYMS
- insufficiency
- paucity

ANTONYM
- abundance

shorten VERB
to make something shorter
• *Smoking can shorten your life.*
abbreviate • *He abbreviated his name to Alec.*
cut • *The film was cut to two hours.*
trim • *I need to get my hair trimmed.*

MORE SYNONYMS
- abridge
- downsize
- truncate

ANTONYM
- lengthen

shout ❶ NOUN
a loud call or cry • *I heard a distant shout.*
bellow • *a bellow of rage*
cry • *She gave a cry of horror.*
roar • *a roar of approval*
scream • *screams of terror*
yell • *He let out a yell of delight.*

shout ❷ VERB
to call or cry out loudly • *He shouted something to his brother.*
bawl • *Laura and Peter were bawling at each other.*
bellow • *He bellowed orders down the phone.*
call • *He could hear them calling his name.*
cry • *"You're under arrest!" he cried.*
roar • *"I'll kill you for that!" he roared.*
scream • *screaming at them to get out of my house*
yell • *She pushed him away, yelling abuse.*

show ❶ NOUN
to prove something • *Tests show that smoking can cause cancer.*
demonstrate • *The study demonstrated a link between obesity and heart problems.*
prove • *History will prove him to be right.*

show ❷ VERB
to do something in order to teach someone else • *I'll show you how to set the video timer.*
demonstrate • *She demonstrated how to make ice cream.*
instruct • *He instructed us on how to give first aid.*
teach • *She taught me how to ride.*

show ❸ VERB
to display a quality or characteristic
• *Her sketches showed artistic promise.*
demonstrate • *He has demonstrated his ability.*
display • *He displayed remarkable courage.*
indicate • *Her choice of words indicated her real feelings.*
manifest • *Fear can manifest itself in many ways.*
reveal • *His reaction revealed a lack of self-confidence.*

MORE SYNONYMS
- evince
- testify to

show ❹ NOUN
a public exhibition • *a fashion show*
display • *a gymnastics display*
exhibition • *an art exhibition*
presentation • *Julie's successful presentation to the board*

show ❺ NOUN
a display of a feeling or quality
• *a show of affection*

a
b
c
d
e
f
g
h
i
j
k
l
m
n
o
p
q
r
s
t
u
v
w
x
y
z

Can't find the word you're looking for? Try the index.

A B C D E F G H I J K L M N O P Q R S T U V W X Y Z

air • *an air of indifference*
display • *a display of remorse*
pose • *a pose of injured innocence*
pretence • *They have given up all pretence of neutrality.*
semblance • *trying to maintain a semblance of order*

shrewd ADJECTIVE
showing intelligence and good judgment • *a shrewd businessman*
astute • *an astute judge of character*
canny • *He was far too canny to give himself away.*
crafty • *He is a clever man and a crafty politician.*
perceptive • *a perceptive analysis of the situation*
sharp • *He is very sharp, and a quick thinker.*
smart • *a very smart move*

MORE SYNONYMS
● perspicacious
● sagacious

shrill ADJECTIVE
high-pitched and piercing • *the shrill whistle of the engine*
penetrating • *a penetrating voice*
piercing • *a piercing squawk*
sharp • *the sharp cry of a vixen*

shrink VERB
to become smaller • *All my jumpers have shrunk in the wash.*
contract • *The ribcage expands and contracts as you breathe.*
diminish • *The threat of nuclear war has diminished.*
dwindle • *The factory's workforce has dwindled from 4000 to 200.*
get smaller • *Electronic systems are getting smaller.*
narrow • *The gap between the two parties has narrowed.*

ANTONYM
● grow

shut ❶ VERB
to close something • *Someone had forgotten to shut the door.*
close • *If you are cold, close the window.*
fasten • *He fastened the diamond clasp of the necklace.*
slam • *He slammed the gate shut behind him.*

ANTONYM
● open

shut ❷ ADJECTIVE
closed or fastened • *A smell of burning came from behind the shut door.*
closed • *All the exits were closed.*
fastened • *The pockets are fastened with buttons.*
sealed • *a sealed envelope*

ANTONYM
● open

shy ADJECTIVE
nervous in the company of other people • *a shy, quiet-spoken girl*
bashful • *Offstage, he is bashful and awkward.*
retiring • *He was the quiet, retiring type.*
self-conscious • *I felt a bit self-conscious in my swimming costume.*
timid • *a timid little boy*

MORE SYNONYMS
● diffident
● self-effacing

ANTONYM
● bold

sick ❶ ADJECTIVE
unwell or ill • *a ward full of very sick people*

ailing • *She tenderly nursed her ailing mother.*
poorly (INFORMAL) • *I called Julie and she's still poorly.*
under par (INFORMAL) • *The flu has left me feeling under par.*
under the weather • *Are you still a bit under the weather?*
unwell • *She had been unwell for some time.*

ANTONYM
● well

sick ❷ ADJECTIVE
feeling as if you are going to vomit • *The very thought of food made him sick.*
ill • *The smell of curry always makes me ill.*
nauseous • *These drugs may make you feel nauseous.*
queasy • *The motion of the ship was already making him queasy.*

sick ❸, sick of ADJECTIVE
(INFORMAL)
tired of something • *I'm sick of your complaints.*
bored • *I'm getting bored with the whole business.*
fed up • *He is fed up with this country.*
tired • *I am tired of this music.*
weary • *She was weary of being alone.*

side ❶ NOUN
the edge of something • *Her head hung over the side of the bed.*
edge • *She fell over the edge of the balcony.*
verge • *He parked on the verge of the road.*

RELATED WORD
● ADJECTIVE: lateral

side ❷ NOUN
one of two groups involved in a dispute or contest • *Both sides began to prepare for battle.*
camp • *Most of his supporters had now defected to the opposite camp.*
faction • *leaders of the warring factions*
party • *the candidates for the three main parties*
team • *Both teams played well.*

side with VERB
to support someone in an argument • *Louise always sided with her sister.*
agree with • *She's bound to agree with her husband.*
stand up for • *I was the one who always stood up for my mother.*
support • *a fellow prisoner who supported her*
take the part of • *Why do you always take his part?*

sight ❶ NOUN
the ability to see • *My sight is so bad now that I can't read any more.*
eyesight • *He suffered from weak eyesight.*
visibility • *Visibility was very poor.*
vision • *It can cause blindness or serious loss of vision.*

RELATED WORDS
● ADJECTIVES: optical, visual

sight ❷ NOUN
something you see • *It was a ghastly sight.*
display • *These flowers make a colourful display in spring.*
scene • *a bizarre scene*
spectacle • *an impressive spectacle*

sight ❸ VERB
to see something or someone • *He had been sighted in Cairo.*

a
b
c
d
e
f
g
h
i
j
k
l
m
n
o
p
q
r
s
t
u
v
w
x
y
z

Can't find the word you're looking for? Try the index.

A
B
C
D
E
F
G
H
I
J
K
L
M
N
O
P
Q
R
S
T
U
V
W
X
Y
Z

see • *I saw a deer in the woods today.*
spot • *I drove round till I spotted her.*

sign ❶ NOUN
a mark or symbol • *The negative number is preceded by a minus sign.*
character • *the characters used in the hallmarking system*
emblem • *a small yellow hammer-and-sickle emblem*
logo • *the company's logo*
mark • *Put a tick mark against the statements you agree with.*
symbol • *the chemical symbol for mercury*

sign ❷ NOUN
a notice put up to give a warning or information • *a sign saying that the highway was closed*
board • *He studied the destination board on the front of the bus.*
notice • *a notice saying "no entry"*
placard • *The protesters sang songs and waved placards.*

sign ❸ NOUN
evidence of something • *the first signs of recovery*
clue • *the only real clue that something was wrong*
evidence • *there has been no evidence of criminal activity*
hint • *He showed only the slightest hint of emotion.*
indication • *All the indications suggest that he is the murderer.*
symptom • *typical symptoms of stress*
token • *a token of goodwill*
trace • *No traces of violence were found on the body.*

signal ❶ NOUN
something which is intended to give a message • *a distress signal*
beacon • *an emergency beacon*

cue • *He gave me my cue to speak.*
gesture • *She made a menacing gesture with her fist.*
sign • *They gave him the thumbs-up sign.*

signal ❷ VERB
to make a sign as a message to someone • *He was frantically signalling to her to shut up.*
beckon • *I beckoned her over.*
gesticulate • *He was gesticulating at a hole in the ground.*
gesture • *I gestured towards the house, and he went in.*
motion • *He motioned to her to go behind the screen.*
nod • *They nodded goodnight to the security man.*
sign • *She signed to me to come near.*
wave • *He waved the servants out of the tent.*

significant ADJECTIVE
large or important • *This drug seems to have a significant effect on the disease.*
considerable (FORMAL) • *Doing it properly makes considerable demands on our time.*
important • *The strike represents an important challenge to the government.*
impressive • *an impressive achievement*
marked • *a marked increase in crimes against property*
notable • *With a few notable exceptions, doctors are a pretty sensible lot.*
pronounced • *The exhibition has a pronounced Scottish theme.*
striking • *The most striking feature of these statistics is the rate of growth.*

Can't find the word you're looking for? Try the index.

ANTONYM
- insignificant

silence ❶ NOUN
an absence of sound • *There was a momentary silence.*
calm • *He liked the calm of the evening.*
hush • *A hush fell over the crowd.*
lull • *a lull in the conversation*
peace • *I love the peace of the countryside.*
quiet • *The quiet of the flat was very soothing.*
stillness • *An explosion shattered the stillness of the night air.*

ANTONYM
- noise

silence ❷ NOUN
an inability or refusal to talk • *breaking his silence for the first time about the affair*
dumbness • *a woman traumatized into dumbness*
muteness • *He retreated into stubborn muteness.*
reticence • *Fran didn't seem to notice my reticence.*
speechlessness • *He was shy to the point of speechlessness.*

MORE SYNONYMS
- taciturnity
- uncommunicativeness
- voicelessness

silence ❸ VERB
to make someone or something quiet • *The shock silenced her completely.*
deaden • *We hung up curtains to try and deaden the noise.*
gag • *I gagged him with a towel.*
muffle • *You can muffle the sound with absorbent material.*
quiet • *A look from her husband quieted her at once.*
quieten • *She tried to quieten her breathing.*
stifle • *He put his hand to his mouth to stifle a giggle.*
still • *He raised a hand to still Alex's protest.*
suppress • *She barely suppressed a gasp.*

silent ❶ ADJECTIVE
not saying anything • *The class fell silent as the teacher entered.*
dumb • *We were all struck dumb for a moment.*
mute • *a mute look of appeal*
speechless • *speechless with rage*
taciturn • *a taciturn man with a solemn expression*
wordless • *They exchanged a wordless look of understanding.*

MORE SYNONYMS
- tongue-tied
- uncommunicative

silent ❷ ADJECTIVE
making no noise • *The room was silent except for the ticking of the clock.*
hushed • *the vast, hushed space of the cathedral*
quiet • *a quiet engine*
soundless • *My bare feet were soundless on the carpet.*
still • *The room was suddenly still.*

ANTONYM
- noisy

silly ADJECTIVE
foolish or ridiculous • *I know it's silly to get so upset.*
absurd • *He found fashion absurd.*
daft • *That's a daft question.*
foolish • *It is foolish to risk injury.*
idiotic • *What an idiotic thing to say!*

a
b
c
d
e
f
g
h
i
j
k
l
m
n
o
p
q
r
s
t
u
v
w
x
y
z

Can't find the word you're looking for? Try the index.

inane • *He stood there with an inane grin on his face.*
ridiculous • *a ridiculous suggestion*
stupid • *a stupid mistake*

MORE SYNONYMS
- asinine
- fatuous
- puerile
- witless

similar ADJECTIVE
like something else • *an accident similar to Hakkinen's*
alike • *You two are very alike.*
analogous • *a ritual analogous to those of primitive tribal cultures*
comparable • *paying the same wages for work of comparable value*
like • *They're as like as two peas in a pod.*
uniform • *droplets of uniform size*

ANTONYM
- different

similarity NOUN
the quality of being like something else • *the similarity of our backgrounds*
analogy • *the analogy between racism and homophobia*
likeness • *These myths have a startling likeness to one another.*
resemblance • *I could see the resemblance to his grandfather.*
sameness • *He grew bored by the sameness of the speeches.*

MORE SYNONYMS
- comparability
- congruence
- similitude

ANTONYM
- different

simple ❶ ADJECTIVE
easy to understand or do • *a simple task*
easy • *This ice cream maker is cheap and easy to use.*
elementary • *elementary computer skills*
straightforward • *It was a straightforward question.*
uncomplicated • *an uncomplicated story*
understandable • *He writes in a clear, understandable style.*

ANTONYM
- complicated

simple ❷ ADJECTIVE
plain in style • *a simple but stylish outfit*
classic • *classic designs which will fit in anywhere*
clean • *the clean lines of Shaker furniture*
plain • *Her dress was plain but hung well on her.*
severe • *hair scraped back in a severe style*

ANTONYM
- elaborate

simplify VERB
to make something easier to do or understand • *measures intended to simplify the procedure*
make simpler • *restructuring the tax system to make it simpler*
streamline • *an effort to cut costs and streamline operations*

sin ❶ NOUN
wicked and immoral behaviour • *preaching against sin*
crime • *a life of crime*
evil • *You can't stop all the evil in the world.*
offence • *an offence which can*

Can't find the word you're looking for? Try the index.

carry the death penalty
wickedness • *a sign of human wickedness*
wrong • *I intend to right that wrong.*

MORE SYNONYMS
- iniquity
- misdeed
- transgression
- trespass

sin ❷ VERB
to do something wicked and immoral • *I admit that I have sinned.*
do wrong • *They have done wrong and they know it.*

sincere ADJECTIVE
saying things that you really mean • *my sincere apologies*
genuine • *a display of genuine emotion*
heartfelt • *heartfelt sympathy*
real • *the real affection between them*
wholehearted • *a wholehearted and genuine response*

ANTONYM
- insincere

single ❶ ADJECTIVE
only one and no more • *A single shot was fired.*
lone • *A lone policeman guarded the doors.*
one • *I just had one drink.*
only • *My only regret is that I never knew him.*
sole • *the sole survivor of the accident*
solitary • *There is not one solitary scrap of evidence.*

single ❷ ADJECTIVE
not married • *I'm surprised you're still single.*

unattached • *I only know two or three unattached men.*
unmarried • *an unmarried mother*

single ❸ ADJECTIVE
for one person only • *a single room*
individual • *an individual portion*
separate • *separate beds*

singular ADJECTIVE (FORMAL)
unusual and remarkable • *a smile of singular sweetness*
exceptional • *children with exceptional ability*
extraordinary • *The task requires extraordinary patience and endurance.*
rare • *a leader of rare strength and instinct*
remarkable • *a remarkable achievement*
uncommon • *She read Cecilia's letter with uncommon interest.*
unique • *a woman of unique talent and determination*
unusual • *He had an unusual aptitude for mathematics.*

sinister ADJECTIVE
seeming harmful or evil • *There was something cold and sinister about him.*
evil • *an evil smile*
forbidding • *a huge, forbidding building*
menacing • *His dark eyebrows gave him a menacing look.*
ominous • *A dark and ominous figure stood in the doorway.*
threatening • *his threatening appearance*

MORE SYNONYMS
- baleful
- bodeful
- disquieting

a
b
c
d
e
f
g
h
i
j
k
l
m
n
o
p
q
r
s
t
u
v
w
x
y
z

Can't find the word you're looking for? Try the index.

A
B
C
D
E
F
G
H
I
J
K
L
M
N
O
P
Q
R
S
T
U
V
W
X
Y
Z

situation NOUN
what is happening • *a serious situation*
case • *a clear case of mistaken identity*
circumstances • *I wish we could have met in happier circumstances.*
plight • *the plight of Third World countries*
scenario • *a nightmare scenario*
state of affairs • *This state of affairs cannot continue.*

size ❶ NOUN
how big or small something is • *the size of the audience*
dimensions • *He considered the dimensions of the problem.*
extent • *the extent of the damage*
proportions • *In the tropics, plants grow to huge proportions.*

size ❷ NOUN
the fact of something being very large • *the sheer size of Australia*
bulk • *Despite his bulk, he moved gracefully.*
immensity • *The immensity of the universe is impossible to grasp.*

MORE SYNONYMS
● magnitude
● vastness

skilful ADJECTIVE
able to do something very well • *the country's most skilful politician*
able • *a very able businessman*
accomplished • *an accomplished pianist*
adept • *an adept diplomat*
competent • *a competent and careful driver*
expert • *He is expert at handling complex negotiations.*
masterly • *a masterly performance*

proficient • *proficient with computers*
skilled • *a skilled wine maker*

MORE SYNONYMS
● adroit
● dexterous

ANTONYM
● incompetent

skill NOUN
the ability to do something well • *This task requires great skill.*
ability • *a man of considerable abilities*
competence • *his high professional competence*
dexterity • *Reid's dexterity on the guitar*
expertise • *the expertise to deal with these problems*
facility • *a facility for languages*
knack • *the knack of getting on with people*
proficiency • *basic proficiency in English*

skilled ADJECTIVE
having the knowledge to do something well • *skilled workers, such as plumbers*
able • *an able craftsman*
accomplished • *an accomplished pianist*
competent • *a competent and careful driver*
experienced • *lawyers who are experienced in these matters*
expert • *It takes an expert eye to see the symptoms.*
masterly • *the artist's masterly use of colour*
professional • *professional people like doctors and engineers*
proficient • *He is proficient in several foreign languages.*

skilful • *the artist's skilful use of light and shade*
trained • *Our workforce is highly trained.*

ANTONYM
- incompetent

skinny ADJECTIVE
extremely thin • *a skinny little boy*
bony • *a long bony finger*
emaciated • *television pictures of emaciated prisoners*
lean • *a tall, lean figure*
scrawny • *the vulture's scrawny neck*
thin • *He is small and very thin with white skin.*
underfed • *Kate still looks pale and underfed.*
undernourished • *undernourished children*

ANTONYM
- plump

slander ❶ NOUN
something untrue and malicious said about someone • *He is now suing the company for slander.*
libel • *defendants seeking damages for libel*
scandal • *She loves spreading scandal.*
slur • *a vicious slur on his character*
smear • *He called the allegation "an evil smear".*

MORE SYNONYMS
- aspersion
- calumny
- defamation
- obloquy

slander ❷ VERB
to say untrue and malicious things about someone • *He has been charged with slandering the Prime Minister.*

libel • *The newspaper which libelled him had to pay compensation.*
malign • *He claims he is being unfairly maligned.*
smear • *an attempt to smear their manager*

MORE SYNONYMS
- calumniate
- defame
- traduce
- vilify

slang NOUN

SOME SLANG WORDS	
babe	hols
bug	hot
celeb	jammy
chill	manky
cool	minging
fave	minted
fit	pants
gimp	snazzy
goss	tidy
grass on	24/7
gross	wicked

sleep ❶ NOUN
the natural state of rest in which you are unconscious • *They were exhausted from lack of sleep.*
doze • *I had a doze after lunch.*
hibernation • *Many animals go into hibernation during the winter.*
kip (BRITISH; SLANG) • *Mason went home for a couple of hours' kip.*
nap • *I might take a nap for a while.*
slumber • *He had fallen into exhausted slumber.*
snooze (INFORMAL) • *a little snooze after dinner*

MORE SYNONYMS
- dormancy
- repose
- siesta

a
b
c
d
e
f
g
h
i
j
k
l
m
n
o
p
q
r
s
t
u
v
w
x
y
z

Can't find the word you're looking for? Try the index.

A
B
C
D
E
F
G
H
I
J
K
L
M
N
O
P
Q
R
S
T
U
V
W
X
Y
Z

sleep ❷ VERB

to rest in a natural state of unconsciousness • *The baby slept during the car journey.*
doze • *He dozed in an armchair.*
hibernate • *Dormice hibernate from October to May.*
kip (BRITISH; SLANG) • *He kipped on my sofa last night.*
slumber • *The girls were slumbering peacefully.*
snooze (INFORMAL) • *Mark snoozed in front of the television.*
take a nap • *Try to take a nap every afternoon.*

sleepy ❶ ADJECTIVE

tired and ready to go to sleep • *Do you feel sleepy during the day?*
drowsy • *This medicine may make you feel drowsy.*
lethargic • *He felt too lethargic to get dressed.*
sluggish • *I was still feeling sluggish after my nap.*

MORE SYNONYMS
● somnolent
● torpid

sleepy ❷ ADJECTIVE

not having much activity or excitement • *a sleepy little village*
dull • *a dull town*
quiet • *a quiet rural backwater*

slender ❶ ADJECTIVE

attractively thin • *a tall, slender woman*
lean • *Like most athletes, she was lean and muscular.*
slight • *She is small and slight.*
slim • *Jean is pretty, with a slim build.*

MORE SYNONYMS
● svelte
● sylphlike
● willowy

slender ❷ ADJECTIVE

small in amount or degree • *He won, but only by a slender majority.*
faint • *They now have only a faint chance of survival.*
remote • *a remote possibility*
slight • *There is a slight improvement in his condition.*
slim • *a slim hope*
small • *a small chance of success*

MORE SYNONYMS
● inconsiderable
● tenuous

slight ADJECTIVE

small in amount or degree • *a slight dent*
insignificant • *an insignificant amount*
minor • *a minor inconvenience*
negligible • *The strike will have a negligible impact.*
small • *It only makes a small difference.*
trivial • *trivial details*

MORE SYNONYMS
● paltry
● scanty

ANTONYM
● large

slip ❶ VERB

to go somewhere quickly and quietly • *Amy slipped downstairs and out of the house.*
creep • *I crept up to my room.*
sneak • *Sometimes he would sneak out to see me.*
steal • *They can steal away at night to join us.*

slip ❷ NOUN

a small mistake • *There must be no slips.*
blunder • *an embarrassing blunder*

Can't find the word you're looking for? Try the index.

error • *a tactical error*
mistake • *Many people are anxious about making mistakes in grammar.*

MORE SYNONYMS
- faux pas
- imprudence
- indiscretion

slogan NOUN
a short easily-remembered phrase • *a poster with the slogan, "Your country needs you"*
jingle • *a catchy advertising jingle*
motto • *"Who Dares Wins" is the motto of the Special Air Service.*

slope ❶ NOUN
a flat surface with one end higher than the other • *The street is on a slope.*
gradient • *a steep gradient*
incline • *The car was unable to negotiate the incline.*
ramp • *There is a ramp allowing access for wheelchairs.*

MORE SYNONYMS
- declination
- declivity
- inclination

slope ❷ VERB
to be at an angle • *The bank sloped sharply down to the river.*
fall • *The road fell steeply.*
rise • *The climb is arduous, rising steeply through thick bush.*
slant • *His handwriting slanted to the left.*

slow ❶ ADJECTIVE
moving or happening with little speed • *slow, regular breathing*
gradual • *Losing weight is a gradual process.*
leisurely • *He walked at a leisurely pace.*

lingering • *He died a lingering death in hospital.*
ponderous • *His steps were heavy and ponderous.*
sluggish • *a sluggish stream*
unhurried • *She rose with unhurried grace.*

ANTONYM
- fast

slow ❷ ADJECTIVE
not very clever • *He got hit in the head and he's been a bit slow ever since.*
dense • *He's not a bad man, just a bit dense.*
dim • *He is rather dim.*
dumb (INFORMAL) • *too dumb to realise what was going on*
obtuse • *It should be obvious even to the most obtuse person.*
stupid • *He can't help being a bit stupid.*
thick • *I can't believe I've been so thick.*

slow (down) VERB
to go or cause to go more slowly • *The car slowed and then stopped.*
check • *attempts to check the spread of AIDS*
decelerate • *He decelerated when he saw the warning sign.*

slowly ADVERB
not quickly or hurriedly • *He turned and began to walk away slowly.*
by degrees • *By degrees, the tension passed out of him.*
gradually • *Their friendship gradually deepened.*
unhurriedly • *The islanders drift along unhurriedly from day to day.*

ANTONYM
- quickly

a
b
c
d
e
f
g
h
i
j
k
l
m
n
o
p
q
r
s
t
u
v
w
x
y
z

Can't find the word you're looking for? Try the index.

sly ADJECTIVE

cunning and deceptive • *She is devious, sly and manipulative.*
crafty • *a crafty villain*
cunning • *Some of these kids can be very cunning.*
devious • *an extremely dangerous, evil and devious man*
scheming • *You're a scheming little rat, aren't you?*
underhand • *underhand tactics*
wily • *a wily politician*

small ❶ ADJECTIVE

not large in size, number or amount • *a small child*
▷ see Word Study **small**, page 704

small ❷ ADJECTIVE

not important or significant
• *small changes*
▷ see Word Study **small**, page 704

smart ❶ ADJECTIVE

clean and neat in appearance
• *a smart navy blue outfit*
chic • *chic Parisian women*
elegant • *Patricia looked beautiful and elegant, as always.*
neat • *a neat grey flannel suit*
spruce • *Chris was looking spruce in his uniform.*
stylish • *stylish white shoes*

MORE SYNONYMS

- modish
- natty
- snappy

ANTONYM

- scruffy

smart ❷ ADJECTIVE

clever and intelligent • *a smart idea*
astute • *a series of astute business decisions*
bright • *She is not very bright.*

canny • *He was far too canny to give himself away.*
clever • *Nobody disputed that Davey was clever.*
ingenious • *an ingenious plan*
intelligent • *Dolphins are an intelligent species.*
shrewd • *a shrewd businessman*

ANTONYM

- dumb

smell ❶ NOUN

the quality of something which you sense through your nose
• *a smell of dark wood*
aroma • *the aroma of fresh bread*
fragrance • *the fragrance of his cologne*
odour • *a disagreeable odour*
perfume • *enjoying the perfume of the lemon trees*
pong (BRITISH AND AUSTRALIAN; INFORMAL) • *What's that horrible pong?*
reek • *the reek of whisky*
scent • *flowers chosen for their scent*
stench • *a foul stench*
stink • *the stink of stale beer on his breath*

MORE SYNONYMS

- bouquet
- fetor
- malodour

smell ❷ VERB

to have an unpleasant smell
• *Do my feet smell?*
pong (BRITISH AND AUSTRALIAN; INFORMAL) • *She said he ponged a bit.*
reek • *The whole house reeks of cigar smoke.*
stink • *His breath stinks of garlic.*

Can't find the word you're looking for? Try the index.

smell ❸ VERB
to become aware of the smell of
something • *I could smell liquor on
his breath.*
scent • *The dog had scented
something in the bushes.*
sniff • *He opened his window and
sniffed the air.*

smelly ADJECTIVE
having a strong unpleasant smell
• *smelly socks*
foul • *His breath was foul.*
reeking • *poisoning the air with
their reeking cigars*
stinking • *piles of stinking rubbish*

MORE SYNONYMS
● fetid
● malodorous
● noisome

ANTONYM
● fragrant

smile ❶ VERB
to move the corners of your mouth
upwards because you are pleased
• *When he saw me, he smiled and
waved.*
beam • *She beamed at him in
delight.*
grin • *He grinned broadly.*
smirk • *The two men looked at me,
nudged each other and smirked.*

smile ❷ NOUN
the expression you have when you
smile • *She gave me a big smile.*
beam • *a strange beam of
satisfaction on his face*
grin • *She looked at me with a
sheepish grin.*
smirk • *a smirk of triumph*

smooth ADJECTIVE
not rough or bumpy • *a smooth
wooden surface*

glassy • *glassy green pebbles*
glossy • *glossy dark fur*
polished • *He slipped on the
polished floor.*
silky • *The sauce should be silky in
texture.*
sleek • *her sleek, waist-length hair*

ANTONYM
● rough

smug ADJECTIVE
pleased with yourself • *They looked
at each other in smug satisfaction.*
complacent • *an aggravating,
complacent little smile*
conceited • *They had grown too
conceited and pleased with
themselves.*
self-satisfied • *a self-satisfied
little snob*
superior • *He stood there looking
superior.*

snag NOUN
a small problem or disadvantage
• *The snag was that he had no
transport.*
catch • *It sounds too good to be
true - what's the catch?*
difficulty • *The only difficulty may
be the price.*
disadvantage • *The disadvantage
is that this plant needs frequent
watering.*
drawback • *The flat's only
drawback was its size.*
problem • *The only problem about
living here is the tourists.*

MORE SYNONYMS
● downside
● stumbling block

sneak ❶ VERB
to go somewhere quietly
• *Sometimes he would sneak out to
see me.*

a
b
c
d
e
f
g
h
i
j
k
l
m
n
o
p
q
r
s
t
u
v
w
x
y
z

Can't find the word you're looking for? Try the index.

lurk • *I saw someone lurking outside.*
sidle • *He sidled into the bar, trying to look inconspicuous.*
slip • *Amy slipped downstairs and out of the house.*
steal • *They can steal out and join us later.*

MORE SYNONYMS
- skulk
- slink

sneak ❷ VERB
to put or take something somewhere secretly • *I sneaked the books out of the library.*
slip • *He slipped me a note.*
smuggle • *We smuggled a camera into the concert.*
spirit • *treasures spirited away to foreign museums*

sneaky ADJECTIVE
doing things secretly or being done secretly • *He only won by using sneaky tactics.*
crafty • *the crafty methods used by salesmen to get people to sign up*
deceitful • *They claimed the government had been deceitful.*
devious • *He was devious, saying one thing to me and another to her.*
dishonest • *It would be dishonest to mislead people in that way.*
mean • *That was a mean trick.*
slippery • *She's a slippery customer, and should be watched.*
sly • *He's a sly old beggar.*
untrustworthy • *His opponents say he's untrustworthy.*

snooper NOUN
a person who interferes in other people's business • *a tabloid snooper*
meddler • *a meddler in the affairs of state*

stickybeak (AUSTRALIAN AND NEW ZEALAND; INFORMAL) • *She's just an old stickybeak.*

MORE SYNONYMS
- busybody
- nosy parker

soak VERB
to make something very wet • *The water had soaked his jacket.*
bathe • *Bathe the infected area in a salt solution.*
permeate • *The water had permeated the stone.*
steep • *green beans steeped in olive oil*
wet • *Wet the hair and work the shampoo through it.*

MORE SYNONYMS
- douse
- drench
- saturate

sociable ADJECTIVE
enjoying the company of other people • *She's usually outgoing and sociable.*
friendly • *The people here are very friendly.*
gregarious • *I'm not a gregarious person.*
outgoing • *He was shy and she was very outgoing.*

MORE SYNONYMS
- companionable
- convivial

society ❶ NOUN
the people in a particular country or region • *a major problem in society*
civilization • *an ancient civilization*
culture • *people from different cultures*

Can't find the word you're looking for? Try the index.

society ❷ NOUN
an organization for people with the same interest or aim • *the school debating society*
association • *the Football Association*
circle • *a local painting circle*
club • *He was at the youth club.*
fellowship • *the Visual Arts Fellowship*
group • *an environmental group*
guild • *the Screen Writers' Guild*
institute • *the Women's Institute*
league • *the World Muslim League*
organization • *student organizations*
union • *the International Astronomical Union*

soft ❶ ADJECTIVE
not hard, stiff or firm • *a soft bed*
flexible • *a flexible material*
pliable • *a pliable dough*
squashy • *a squashy tomato*
supple • *supple leather*
yielding • *yielding cushions*

MORE SYNONYMS
● bendable
● ductile
● gelatinous
● malleable
● tensile

ANTONYM
● hard

soft ❷ ADJECTIVE
quiet and not harsh • *a soft tapping at my door*
gentle • *a gentle voice*
low • *She spoke in a low whisper.*
mellow • *mellow background music*
muted • *Their loud conversation became muted.*
quiet • *He always spoke in a quiet tone to which everyone listened.*
subdued • *His voice was more subdued than usual.*

MORE SYNONYMS
● dulcet
● mellifluous

soft ❸ ADJECTIVE
not bright • *The bedside lamp cast a soft radiance over her face.*
dim • *The light was dim and eerie.*
faint • *The stars cast a faint light.*
light • *The walls were painted a light yellow.*
mellow • *Their colour schemes tend towards rich, mellow shades.*
pale • *dressed in pale pink*
pastel • *delicate pastel hues*
subdued • *subdued lighting*

ANTONYM
● bright

soil ❶ NOUN
the surface of the earth • *The soil is reasonably moist after the rain.*
clay • *a thin layer of clay*
dirt • *The bulldozers piled up huge mounds of dirt.*
earth • *a huge pile of earth*
ground • *a hole in the ground*

soil ❷ VERB
to make something dirty • *He looked at her as though her words might soil him.*
dirty • *He was afraid the dog's hairs might dirty the seats.*
foul • *The cage was fouled with droppings.*
pollute • *chemicals which pollute rivers*
smear • *The pillow was smeared with makeup.*
spatter • *Her dress was spattered with mud.*
stain • *Some foods can stain the teeth.*

Can't find the word you're looking for? Try the index.

MORE SYNONYMS
- befoul
- begrime
- besmirch
- defile
- smirch
- sully

ANTONYM
- clean

solemn ADJECTIVE
not cheerful or humorous • *a taciturn man with a solemn expression*
earnest • *Ella was a pious, earnest woman.*
grave • *He was looking unusually grave.*
serious • *She looked at me with big, serious eyes.*
sober • *sad, sober faces*
staid • *He is boring, old fashioned and staid.*

solid ❶ ADJECTIVE
hard and firm • *a block of solid wax*
firm • *a firm mattress*
hard • *The snow was hard and slippery.*

solid ❷ ADJECTIVE
not likely to fall down • *a solid structure*
stable • *stable foundations*
strong • *a strong fence*
sturdy • *The camera was mounted on a sturdy tripod.*
substantial • *The posts are made of concrete and are fairly substantial.*

solitude NOUN
the state of being alone • *He went to the cottage for a few days of solitude.*
isolation • *the isolation he endured while in captivity*
loneliness • *I have a fear of loneliness.*

privacy • *the privacy of my own room*
seclusion • *She lived in seclusion with her husband.*

solve VERB
to find the answer to a problem or question • *attempts to solve the mystery*
clear up • *During dinner the confusion was cleared up.*
crack • *He finally managed to crack the code.*
decipher • *trying to decipher the symbols on the stone tablets*
get to the bottom of • *The police wanted to get to the bottom of the case.*
resolve • *Scientists hope this will finally resolve the mystery.*
work out • *I've worked out where I'm going wrong.*

sometimes ADVERB
now and then • *Her voice was so low she was sometimes mistaken for a man.*
at times • *She can be a little common at times.*
every now and then • *He checks up on me every now and then.*
every so often • *Every so often he does something silly.*
from time to time • *I go back to see my mum from time to time.*
now and again • *I enjoy a day out now and again.*
now and then • *These people like a laugh now and then.*
occasionally • *I know that I do put people down occasionally.*
once in a while • *It does you good to get out once in a while.*

soon ADVERB
in a very short time • *You'll be hearing from us very soon.*

Can't find the word you're looking for? Try the index.

A B C D E F G H I J K L M N O P Q R S T U V W X Y Z

any minute now • *Any minute now she's going to start crying.*
before long • *Interest rates will come down before long.*
in a minute • *I'll be with you in a minute.*
in the near future • *The controversy is unlikely to be resolved in the near future.*
presently • *I'll deal with you presently.*
shortly • *The trial will begin shortly.*

ANTONYM
● later

sophisticated ❶ ADJECTIVE
having refined tastes • *a charming, sophisticated companion*
cosmopolitan • *The family are rich and extremely cosmopolitan.*
cultivated • *an elegant and cultivated woman*
cultured • *He is immensely cultured and well-read.*
refined • *a woman of refined tastes*
urbane • *a polished, urbane manner*

sophisticated ❷ ADJECTIVE
advanced and complicated • *a sophisticated piece of equipment*
advanced • *the most advanced optical telescope in the world*
complex • *complex machines*
complicated • *a complicated voting system*
elaborate • *an elaborate design*
intricate • *intricate controls*
refined • *a more refined engine*

ANTONYM
● simple

sore ADJECTIVE
causing pain and discomfort • *a sore throat*
inflamed • *Her eyes were red and inflamed.*

painful • *a painful knock on the knee*
raw • *Her hands were rubbed raw by the rope.*
sensitive • *the pain of sensitive teeth*
smarting • *My eyes were smarting from the smoke.*
tender • *My stomach feels very tender.*

sorrow ❶ NOUN
deep sadness or regret • *a time of great sorrow*
grief • *Their grief soon gave way to anger.*
heartache • *suffering the heartache of a divorce*
melancholy • *She has an air of melancholy.*
misery • *All his money brought him nothing but misery.*
mourning • *The period of mourning may be long.*
pain • *My heart is full of pain.*
regret • *She accepted his resignation with regret.*
sadness • *It is with a mixture of sadness and joy that I say farewell.*
unhappiness • *I had a lot of unhappiness in my adolescence.*
woe (FORMAL) • *a tale of woe*

ANTONYM
● joy

sorrow ❷ NOUN
things that cause deep sadness and regret • *the joys and sorrows of family life*
heartache • *all the heartaches of parenthood*
hardship • *One of the worst hardships is having so little time with my family.*
misfortune • *She seems to enjoy the misfortunes of others.*
trouble • *She told me all her troubles.*

a
b
c
d
e
f
g
h
i
j
k
l
m
n
o
p
q
r
s
t
u
v
w
x
y
z

Can't find the word you're looking for? Try the index.

woe (WRITTEN) • *He did not tell his friends about his woes.*
worry • *a life with no worries*

MORE SYNONYMS
- affliction
- tribulation (FORMAL)

ANTONYM
- joy

sorry ❶ ADJECTIVE
feeling sadness or regret • *I'm terribly sorry to bother you.*
apologetic • *"I'm afraid I can't help," she said with an apologetic smile.*
penitent • *He sat silent and penitent in a corner.*
regretful • *Now I'm totally regretful that I did it.*
remorseful • *He was genuinely remorseful.*
repentant • *repentant sinners*

MORE SYNONYMS
- conscience-stricken
- contrite
- guilt-ridden
- shamefaced

sorry ❷ ADJECTIVE
feeling sympathy for someone • *I was sorry to hear about your husband's death.*
moved • *I'm moved by what you say.*
sympathetic • *She gave me a sympathetic glance.*

sorry ❸ ADJECTIVE
in a bad condition • *He was in a pretty sorry state when we found him.*
deplorable • *living in deplorable conditions*
miserable • *a miserable existence*
pathetic • *the pathetic sight of oil-*

covered sea birds
pitiful • *a pitiful creature*
poor • *the poor condition of the pitch*
sad • *a sad state of affairs*
wretched • *the wretched victims of war*

MORE SYNONYMS
- piteous
- pitiable

sort ❶ NOUN
one of the different kinds of something • *a dozen trees of various sorts*
brand • *his favourite brand of whisky*
category • *The topics were divided into six categories.*
class • *a better class of restaurant*
group • *Weathermen classify clouds into several different groups.*
kind • *different kinds of roses*
make • *a certain make of car*
species • *400 species of fungi have been recorded.*
style • *Several styles of hat were available.*
type • *What type of dog should we get?*
variety • *many varieties of birds*

MORE SYNONYMS
- ilk
- stamp

sort ❷ VERB
to arrange things into different kinds • *He sorted the material into three folders.*
arrange • *Arrange the books in neat piles.*
categorize • *ways to categorize information*
classify • *Rocks can be classified according to their mode of origin.*

Can't find the word you're looking for? Try the index.

A B C D E F G H I J K L M N O P Q R S T U V W X Y Z

divide • *The subjects were divided into four groups.*
grade • *musical pieces graded according to difficulty*
group • *The fact sheet is grouped into seven sections.*
separate • *His work can be separated into three main categories.*

sound ❶ NOUN
something that can be heard • *the sound of gunfire*
din • *make themselves heard over the din of the crowd*
hubbub • *the hubbub of excited conversation*
noise • *the noise of bombs and guns*
racket • *the racket of drills and electric saws*
tone • *the clear tone of the bell*

ANTONYM
● silence

RELATED WORDS
● ADJECTIVES: acoustic, sonic

sound ❷ VERB
to produce or cause to produce a noise • *A young man sounded the bell.*
blow • *A guard was blowing his whistle.*
chime • *He heard the doorbell chime.*
clang • *The church bell clanged.*
peal • *Church bells pealed at the stroke of midnight.*
ring • *She heard the school bell ringing.*
set off • *Any escape sets off the alarm.*
toll • *The pilgrims tolled the bell.*

sound ❸ ADJECTIVE
healthy, or in good condition • *His body was still sound.*
all right • *Does the roof seem all right?*

fine • *She told me her heart was perfectly fine.*
fit • *Exercise is the first step to a fit body.*
healthy • *His once healthy mind was deteriorating.*
in good condition • *The timbers were all in good condition.*
intact • *The boat did not appear damaged and its equipment seemed intact.*
robust • *He is in robust health for a man of his age.*

sound ❹ ADJECTIVE
reliable and sensible • *a sound financial proposition*
down-to-earth • *Their ideas seem very down-to-earth.*
good • *Give me one good reason why I should tell you.*
reasonable • *a perfectly reasonable decision*
reliable • *It's difficult to give a reliable estimate.*
sensible • *sensible advice*
solid • *good solid information*
valid • *Both sides made some valid points.*

sour ❶ ADJECTIVE
having a sharp taste • *The stewed apple was sour even with sugar added.*
acid • *The wine had an acid taste.*
bitter • *a bitter drink*
pungent • *a pungent sauce*
sharp • *a clean, sharp flavour*
tart • *the tart qualities of citrus fruit*

MORE SYNONYMS
● acerbic
● acetic

ANTONYM
● sweet

Can't find the word you're looking for? Try the index.

sour 2 ADJECTIVE

unpleasant in taste because no longer fresh • *This cream's gone sour.*
curdled • *curdled milk*
off • *This meat's gone off.*
rancid • *rancid butter*

sour 3 ADJECTIVE

bad-tempered and unfriendly • *a sour expression*
disagreeable • *a shallow, disagreeable man*
embittered • *an embittered old lady*
jaundiced • *a jaundiced attitude*
tart • *a tart reply*

MORE SYNONYMS
- churlish
- peevish
- waspish

source NOUN

the place where something comes from • *the source of his confidence*
beginning • *the beginning of all the trouble*
cause • *the cause of the problem*
derivation • *The derivation of the name is obscure.*
origin • *the origin of life*
originator • *the originator of the theory*

MORE SYNONYMS
- fount
- fountainhead
- wellspring

souvenir NOUN

something you keep as a reminder • *a souvenir of our holiday*
keepsake • *a cherished keepsake*
memento • *a memento of the occasion*
relic • *the threadbare teddy bear, a relic of childhood*

reminder • *a permanent reminder of this historic event*

space 1 NOUN

an area which is empty or available • *a car with plenty of interior space*
accommodation • *We have accommodation for six people.*
capacity • *the capacity of the airliner*
room • *no room to manoeuvre*

RELATED WORD
- ADJECTIVE: spatial

space 2 NOUN

the gap between two things • *the space between the two tables*
blank • *I've left a blank here for your signature.*
distance • *the distance between the island and the mainland*
gap • *The wind was tearing through gaps in the window frames.*
interval • *the intervals between the trees*

space 3 NOUN

a period of time • *two incidents in the space of a week*
interval • *a long interval of silence*
period • *for a limited period only*
span • *The batteries have a life span of six hours.*
time • *At 15 he left home for a short time.*
while • *Sit down for a while.*

spacious ADJECTIVE

having or providing a lot of space • *a spacious lounge*
ample • *the city's ample car parks*
broad • *a broad expanse of green lawn*
expansive • *an expansive play area*
extensive • *The palace stands in extensive grounds.*

Can't find the word you're looking for? Try the index.

huge • *a huge apartment overlooking the park*
large • *a large detached house*
vast • *a vast chamber*

MORE SYNONYMS
- capacious
- commodious
- roomy
- sizable *or* sizeable

spare ❶ ADJECTIVE
in addition to what is needed
• *Luckily I had a spare pair of glasses.*
extra • *Allow yourself some extra time in case of emergencies.*
free • *I'll do it as soon as I get some free time.*
superfluous • *I got rid of all my superfluous belongings.*
surplus • *They sell their surplus produce.*

MORE SYNONYMS
- leftover
- supernumerary

spare ❷ VERB
to make something available • *Can you spare some money for a cup of tea?*
afford • *It's all I can afford to give you.*
give • *It's good of you to give me some of your time.*
let someone have • *I can let you have some milk and sugar.*

spare ❸ VERB
to save someone from an unpleasant experience • *I wanted to spare her that suffering.*
let off (INFORMAL) • *I'll let you off this time.*
pardon • *Relatives had begged authorities to pardon him.*
relieve from • *a machine which relieves you of the drudgery of housework*
save from • *I was trying to save you from unnecessary worry.*

sparkle VERB
to shine with small bright points of light • *Diamonds sparkled on her wrists.*
gleam • *sunlight gleaming on the water*
glisten • *The wall glistened with frost.*
glitter • *A million stars glittered in the black sky.*
shimmer • *In the distance the lake shimmered.*
twinkle • *The old man's eyes twinkled.*

MORE SYNONYMS
- coruscate
- scintillate

speak VERB
to use your voice to say words
• *She turned to look at the person who was speaking.*
▷ see Word Study **say**, pages 699–702

special ❶ ADJECTIVE
more important or better than others of its kind • *You are very special to me.*
exceptional • *children with exceptional ability*
important • *This is an important occasion.*
significant • *of significant importance*
unique • *a unique talent*

ANTONYM
- ordinary

special ❷ ADJECTIVE
relating to one person or group in particular • *the special needs of the chronically sick*

Can't find the word you're looking for? Try the index.

A
B
C
D
E
F
G
H
I
J
K
L
M
N
O
P
Q
R
S
T
U
V
W
X
Y
Z

characteristic • *a characteristic feature*
distinctive • *the distinctive smell of chlorine*
individual • *Each family needs individual attention.*
particular • *Fatigue is a particular problem for women.*
peculiar • *This is not a problem peculiar to London.*
specific • *the specific needs of the elderly*

ANTONYM
- general

specify VERB
to state or describe something precisely • *Specify which size and colour you want.*
be specific about • *She was never very specific about her date of birth.*
indicate • *Please indicate your preference below.*
name • *The victims of the fire have been named.*
spell out • *He spelled out the reasons why he was leaving.*
state • *Please state your name.*
stipulate • *His duties were stipulated in the contract.*

spectator NOUN
a person who watches something • *Spectators lined the route.*
bystander • *an innocent bystander*
eyewitness • *Eyewitnesses say the police opened fire in the crowd.*
observer • *a disinterested observer*
onlooker • *A small crowd of onlookers was there to greet her.*
witness • *There were scores of witnesses.*

speech NOUN
a formal talk given to an audience • *He delivered his speech in French.*

address • *an address to the American people*
discourse • *a lengthy discourse on strategy*
lecture • *a series of lectures on art*
talk • *a talk on Celtic mythology*

MORE SYNONYMS
- disquisition
- harangue
- homily
- oration

speed ❶ NOUN
the rate at which something moves or happens • *a top speed of 200 mph*
haste • *the old saying "more haste, less speed"*
hurry • *the hurry and excitement of the city*
momentum • *This campaign is gaining momentum.*
pace • *He walked at a leisurely pace.*
rapidity • *My moods alternate with alarming rapidity.*
swiftness • *Time is passing with incredible swiftness.*
velocity • *the velocity of light*

speed ❷ VERB
to move quickly • *The pair sped off when the police arrived.*
career • *His car careered into a river.*
flash • *The bus flashed past me.*
gallop • *galloping along the corridor*
race • *He raced across town.*
rush • *He rushed off, closely followed by Kemp.*
tear • *Miranda tore off down the road.*

spin VERB
to turn quickly around a central

point • *as the earth spins on its axis*
pirouette • *She pirouetted in front of the mirror.*
revolve • *The satellite revolves around the planet.*
rotate • *rotating propellers*
turn • *a turning wheel*
whirl • *The fallen leaves whirled around.*

spirit ❶ NOUN
the part of you that is not physical
• *His spirit had left his body.*
life force • *the life force of all animate things*
soul • *praying for the soul of her dead husband*

spirit ❷ NOUN
a ghost or supernatural being • *a protection against evil spirits*
apparition • *an apparition of her dead son*
ghost • *the premise that ghosts exist*
phantom • *People claimed to have seen the phantom.*
spectre • *a spectre from the other world*
sprite • *a water sprite*

spirit ❸ NOUN
liveliness and energy • *They played with spirit.*
animation • *They both spoke with animation.*
energy • *At 80 her energy is amazing.*
enthusiasm • *They seem to be lacking in enthusiasm.*
fire • *His performance was full of fire.*
force • *She expressed her feelings with some force.*
vigour • *We resumed the attack with renewed vigour.*
zest • *He threw himself into the project with typical zest.*

MORE SYNONYMS
● brio
● mettle

spite ❶, in spite of
PREPOSITION
even though something is the case
• *In spite of all the gossip, Virginia stayed behind.*
despite • *They manage to enjoy life despite adversity.*
even though • *They did it even though I warned them not to.*
notwithstanding
• *Notwithstanding his age, Sikorski had an important job.*
regardless of • *He led from the front, regardless of the danger.*
though • *I enjoy painting, though I am not very good at it.*

spite ❷ NOUN
a desire to hurt someone • *He just did it out of spite.*
ill will • *He didn't bear anyone any ill will.*
malevolence • *a streak of malevolence*
malice • *There was no malice in her voice.*
spitefulness • *petty spitefulness*
venom • *His wit had a touch of venom about it.*

MORE SYNONYMS
● malignity
● rancour

spiteful ADJECTIVE
saying or doing nasty things to hurt people • *a stream of spiteful telephone calls*
bitchy (INFORMAL) • *It's not just women who are bitchy.*
catty (INFORMAL) • *She's always making catty remarks.*

a b c d e f g h i j k l m n o p q r **s** t u v w x y z

A B C D E F G H I J K L M N O P Q R **S** T U V W X Y Z

cruel • *They gave him a cruel nickname.*
malevolent • *a malevolent stare*
malicious • *spreading malicious gossip*
nasty • *What nasty little snobs you all are.*
snide • *He made a snide comment about her weight.*
venomous • *a venomous attack*
vindictive • *How can you be so vindictive?*

splendid ❶ ADJECTIVE
very good indeed • *I've had a splendid time.*
cracking (BRITISH, AUSTRALIAN AND NEW ZEALAND; INFORMAL) • *It's a cracking script.*
excellent • *The recording quality is excellent.*
fantastic (INFORMAL) • *a fantastic combination of colours*
fine • *a fine little fellow*
glorious • *a glorious career*
great (INFORMAL) • *a great bunch of guys*
marvellous • *a marvellous thing to do*
wonderful • *a wonderful movie*

splendid ❷ ADJECTIVE
beautiful and impressive • *a splendid old mansion*
gorgeous • *a gorgeous Renaissance building*
grand • *a grand hotel*
imposing • *imposing wrought-iron gates*
impressive • *an impressive spectacle*
magnificent • *magnificent views across the valley*
superb • *The hotel has a superb isolated location.*

split ❶ VERB
to divide into two or more parts

• *The ship split in two.*
diverge • *Their paths began to diverge.*
fork • *Ahead of us, the road forked.*
part • *For a moment the clouds parted.*
separate • *Fluff the rice with a fork to separate the grains.*

MORE SYNONYMS
● bifurcate
● cleave
● disunite

split ❷ VERB
to have a crack or tear • *His trousers split.*
burst • *A water pipe has burst.*
come apart • *My jacket's coming apart at the seams.*
crack • *A gas main cracked.*
rip • *I felt the paper rip as we pulled in opposite directions.*

split ❸ NOUN
a crack or tear in something • *There's a split in my mattress.*
crack • *The larvae burrow into cracks in the floor.*
fissure • *Water trickled out of fissures in the limestone.*
rip • *the rip in her new dress*
tear • *the ragged edges of a tear*

split ❹ NOUN
a division between two things • *the split between rugby league and rugby union*
breach • *a serious breach in relations between the two countries*
breakup • *the breakup of the Soviet Union in 1991*
divergence • *a divergence between France and its allies*
division • *the conventional division between 'art' and 'life'*

Can't find the word you're looking for? Try the index.

rift • *There is a rift between us and the rest of the family.*
schism • *the schism which divided the Christian world*

spoil ❶ VERB

to damage or destroy something
• *Don't let it spoil your holiday.*
damage • *This could damage our chances of winning.*
destroy • *His criticism has destroyed my confidence.*
harm • *This product harms the environment.*
impair • *The flavour is impaired by overcooking.*
mar • *The celebrations were marred by violence.*
mess up • *He's messed up his life.*
ruin • *My wife was ruining her health through worry.*
wreck • *the injuries which nearly wrecked his career*

spoil ❷ VERB

to give someone everything they want • *Grandparents often spoil their grandchildren.*
cosset • *We did not cosset our children.*
indulge • *a heavily indulged youngest daughter*
pamper • *pampered pets*

MORE SYNONYMS

● coddle
● mollycoddle
● overindulge

spoilsport NOUN

a person who spoils other people's fun • *They made me feel like a spoilsport for saying no.*
misery (BRITISH; INFORMAL)
• *the miseries in the government*
wowser (AUSTRALIAN; SLANG)
• *a small group of wowsers*

spooky ADJECTIVE

eerie and frightening • *The whole place had a slightly spooky atmosphere.*
creepy (INFORMAL) • *a place that is really creepy at night*
eerie • *The wind made eerie noises in the trees.*
frightening • *Whenever I fall asleep, I see these frightening faces.*
ghostly • *The moon shed a ghostly light on the fields.*
haunted • *a haunted house*
supernatural • *The blade glowed with a supernatural light.*
scary • *a scary ruined castle*
uncanny • *The strange, uncanny feeling was creeping all over me.*

spot ❶ NOUN

a small round mark on something
• *a navy blue dress with white spots*
blemish • *A small blemish spoiled the surface.*
blot • *an ink blot*
blotch • *His face was covered in red blotches.*
mark • *a little red mark on my neck*
smudge • *There was a dark smudge on his forehead.*
speck • *a speck of dirt*

spot ❷ NOUN

a location or place • *an out-of-the-way spot*
location • *The hotel is in a superb isolated location.*
place • *Jerusalem is Christianity's most venerated place.*
point • *the point where the river had burst its banks*
position • *She moved the body to a position where it would not be seen.*
scene • *He left a note at the scene of the crime.*

a b c d e f g h i j k l m n o p q r s t u v w x y z

Can't find the word you're looking for? Try the index.

A
B
C
D
E
F
G
H
I
J
K
L
M
N
O
P
Q
R
S
T
U
V
W
X
Y
Z

site • *plans to construct a temple on the site*

spot ❸ VERB

to see or notice something • *Her drama teacher spotted her ability.*

catch sight of • *I caught sight of an ad in the paper.*

detect • *The test should enable doctors to detect the disease early.*

discern • *I did not discern any change.*

observe • *Can you observe any difference?*

see • *I can see a resemblance between you.*

sight • *A fleet of French ships was sighted.*

MORE SYNONYMS

● descry
● espy

spread ❶ VERB

to open out or extend over an area • *He spread his coat over the bed.*

extend • *The new territory would extend over one-fifth of Canada's land mass.*

fan out • *She spun, and her dress's full skirt fanned out in a circle.*

open • *She opened her arms and gave me a big hug.*

sprawl • *The recreation area sprawls over 900 acres.*

unfold • *When the bird lifts off, its wings unfold to a six-foot span.*

unfurl • *We began to unfurl the sails.*

unroll • *I unrolled my sleeping bag.*

spread ❷ VERB

to put a thin layer on a surface • *Spread the bread with the cream cheese.*

apply • *Apply the preparation evenly over the wood's surface.*

coat • *Coat the fish with the paste.*

cover • *I covered the table with a cloth.*

overlay • *The floor was overlaid with rugs.*

plaster • *She plastered herself in sun lotion.*

smear • *Smear a little oil over the inside of the bowl.*

smother • *He likes to smother his bread with butter.*

spread ❸ VERB

to reach or affect more people gradually • *The sense of fear is spreading in the neighbourhood.*

circulate • *Rumours were circulating that the project was to be abandoned.*

grow • *Opposition grew and the government agreed to negotiate.*

expand • *The industry is looking for opportunities to expand into other countries.*

increase • *The population continues to increase.*

proliferate • *the free Internet services that are proliferating across the world*

travel • *News of his work travelled all the way to Asia.*

spread ❹ NOUN

the extent or growth of something • *the gradual spread of information*

diffusion • *the development and diffusion of ideas*

expansion • *the rapid expansion of private health insurance*

extent • *the growing extent of the problem*

growth • *the growth of nationalism*

increase • *an increase of violence along the border*

progression • *This drug slows the progression of HIV.*

Can't find the word you're looking for? Try the index.

proliferation • *the proliferation of nuclear weapons*
upsurge • *the upsurge in interest in these books*

squabble ❶ VERB
to quarrel about something trivial
• *Mum and Dad squabble all the time.*
argue • *They went on arguing all the way down the road.*
bicker • *The two women bickered constantly.*
fall out • *Mum and I used to fall out a lot.*
feud • *feuding neighbours*
fight • *Mostly, they fight about paying bills.*
quarrel • *At one point we quarrelled over something silly.*
row • *They rowed all the time.*
wrangle • *The two sides spend their time wrangling over procedural problems.*

squabble ❷ NOUN
a quarrel • *There have been minor squabbles about phone bills.*
altercation • *an altercation with the referee*
argument • *a heated argument*
barney (BRITISH, AUSTRALIAN AND NEW ZEALAND; INFORMAL) • *We had such a barney that we nearly split up.*
disagreement • *My instructor and I had a brief disagreement.*
dispute • *a dispute between the two countries over farm subsidies*
fight • *He had a big fight with his dad that night.*
quarrel • *I had a terrible quarrel with my brother.*
row • *A man had been stabbed to death in a family row.*
tiff • *She was walking home after a tiff with her boyfriend.*

staff NOUN
the people who work for an organization • *She made little effort to socialize with other staff.*
employees • *a temporary employee*
personnel • *An announcement was made to all personnel.*
team • *The team worked well under his direction.*
workers • *weekend and night-shift workers*
workforce • *a sullen and resentful workforce*

stage ❶ NOUN
a part of a process • *the closing stages of the race*
lap • *The first lap was clocked at under a minute.*
period • *We went through a period of unprecedented change.*
phase • *a passing phase*
point • *a critical point in the campaign*
step • *the next step in the process*

stage ❷ VERB
to organize something • *Workers have staged a number of one-day strikes.*
arrange • *We're arranging a surprise party for her.*
engineer • *He was the one who engineered the merger.*
mount • *a security operation mounted by the army*
orchestrate • *a carefully orchestrated campaign*
organize • *a two-day meeting organized by the UN*

stain ❶ NOUN
a mark on something • *grass stains*
blot • *an ink blot*
mark • *I can't get this mark to come off.*

Can't find the word you're looking for? Try the index.

a b c d e f g h i j k l m n o p q r s t u v w x y z

spot • *brown spots on the skin caused by the sun*

stain ② VERB

to make a mark on something • *Some foods can stain the teeth.*
dirty • *Sheets can be reused until they are damaged or dirtied.*
mark • *the places where Steve's boots had marked the wood*
soil • *a soiled white apron*
spot • *her coat was spotted with blood*

MORE SYNONYMS

- discolour
- smirch

stale ADJECTIVE

no longer fresh • *a lump of stale bread*
flat • *flat beer*
old • *mouldy old cheese*
sour • *sour milk*
stagnant • *stagnant water*

MORE SYNONYMS

- fusty
- musty

ANTONYM

- fresh

standard ① NOUN

a particular level of quality or achievement • *There will be new standards of hospital cleanliness.*
calibre • *the high calibre of these researchers*
criterion • *The most important criterion for entry is excellence in your chosen field.*
guideline • *The accord lays down guidelines for the conduct of government agents.*
level • *The exercises are marked according to their level of difficulty.*

norm • *the commonly accepted norms of democracy*
quality • *Everyone can improve their quality of life.*
requirement • *These products meet all legal requirements.*

standard ② ADJECTIVE

usual, normal, and correct • *It was standard practice for them to consult the parents.*
accepted • *It is accepted wisdom that the state of your body impacts on your state of mind.*
correct • *the correct way to produce a crop of tomato plants*
customary • *It is customary to offer a drink or a snack to guests.*
normal • *Some shops were closed, but that's quite normal for a Thursday.*
orthodox • *orthodox police methods*
regular • *This product looks and tastes like regular lemonade.*
usual • *It is usual to tip waiters.*

standards PLURAL NOUN

moral principles of behaviour • *My father has always had high moral standards.*
ethics • *the difference between our personal and social ethics*
ideals • *The party has drifted too far from its socialist ideals.*
morals • *Western ideas and morals*
principles • *He refused to do anything that went against his principles.*
rules • *They were expected to adhere to the rules of the convent.*
scruples • *a man with no moral scruples*
values • *the values of liberty and equality*

star NOUN

a famous person • *a film star*

Can't find the word you're looking for? Try the index.

celebrity • *A host of celebrities attended the premiere.*
idol • *the city's greatest soccer idol*
luminary (LITERARY) • *The event attracted such pop luminaries as Madonna.*

stare VERB
to look at something for a long time • *He stared at the floor, lost in meditation.*
gaze • *gazing at herself in the mirror*
look • *He looked at her with open hostility.*
ogle • *ogling the girls as they went past*

MORE SYNONYMS
● gawp
● goggle

start ❶ VERB
to begin to take place • *School starts again next week.*
arise • *A conflict is likely to arise.*
begin • *A typical day begins at 8.30.*
come into being • *The festival came into being in 1986.*
come into existence • *a club that came into existence only 30 years ago*
commence • *The academic year commences at the beginning of October.*
get under way • *The game got under way.*
originate • *The disease originated in Africa.*

ANTONYM
● finish

start ❷ VERB
to begin to do something • *Susie started to cry.*
begin • *He began to groan with pain.*
commence • *The hunter*

commenced to skin the animal.*
embark upon • *He's embarking on a new career as a writer.*
proceed • *He proceeded to get drunk.*
set about • *How do you set about getting a mortgage?*

ANTONYM
● stop

start ❸ VERB
to cause something to begin • *a good time to start a business*
begin • *The US is prepared to begin talks immediately.*
create • *Criticism will only create feelings of failure.*
establish • *The school was established in 1899.*
found • *Baden-Powell founded the Boy Scouts in 1908.*
get going • *I've worked hard to get this business going.*
inaugurate (FORMAL) • *the company which inaugurated the first scheduled international flight*
initiate • *They wanted to initiate a discussion.*
instigate • *The violence was instigated by a few people.*
institute • *We have instituted a number of measures.*
introduce • *The government has introduced other money-saving schemes.*
launch • *The police have launched an investigation into the incident.*
open • *We opened the srvice with a hymn.*
pioneer • *the man who invented and pioneered DNA testing*
set in motion • *Several changes have already been set in motion.*
set up • *A committee was set up to arbitrate in the dispute.*

a
b
c
d
e
f
g
h
i
j
k
l
m
n
o
p
q
r
s
t
u
v
w
x
y
z

Can't find the word you're looking for? Try the index.

trigger • *Nuts can trigger an allergic reaction in some people.*

ANTONYM
- stop

start ➍ NOUN

the beginning of something • *His career had an auspicious start.*
beginning • *the beginning of all the trouble*
birth • *the birth of modern art*
commencement • *Applicants should be at least 16 before the commencement of the course.*
dawn • *the dawn of a new age*
foundation • *the foundation of the National Organization for Women*
inauguration • *the inauguration of new exam standards*
inception (FORMAL) • *Since its inception the company has produced 53 different aircraft designs.*
initiation • *There was a year between initiation and completion.*
onset • *the onset of puberty*
opening • *the opening of the trial*
outset • *There were lots of problems from the outset.*

ANTONYM
- finish

state ➊ NOUN

the condition or circumstances of something • *the pathetic state of the rail network*
circumstances • *He's in desperate circumstances.*
condition • *He remains in a critical condition in hospital.*
plight • *the plight of Third World countries*
position • *We are in a privileged position.*
predicament • *the once great club's current predicament*

shape • *Her finances were in terrible shape.*
situation • *a precarious situation*

state ➋ NOUN

a country • *the state of Denmark*
country • *a country where alcohol is prohibited*
kingdom • *The kingdom's power declined.*
land • *in that distant land*
nation • *a leading nation in world politics*
republic • *In 1918, Austria became a republic.*

MORE SYNONYMS
- body politic
- commonwealth
- federation

state ➌ VERB

to say something, especially in a formal way • *Please state your occupation.*
affirm • *a speech in which he affirmed his policies*
articulate • *an attempt to articulate his feelings*
assert • *He asserted his innocence.*
declare • *He declared that he would fight on.*
express • *He expressed regret that he had caused any offence.*
say • *The police said he had no connection with the security forces.*
specify • *Please specify your preferences below.*

MORE SYNONYMS
- aver
- expound
- propound

statement NOUN

a short written or spoken piece giving information • *He was depressed when he made that statement.*

Can't find the word you're looking for? Try the index.

account • *He gave a detailed account of what happened that night.*

announcement • *He made his announcement after talks with the President.*

bulletin • *A bulletin was released announcing the decision.*

declaration • *a public declaration of support*

explanation • *They have given no public explanation for his dismissal.*

proclamation • *The proclamation of independence was broadcast over the radio.*

report • *A press report said that at least six people had died.*

testimony • *His testimony was an important part of the prosecution case.*

status NOUN

a person's social position • *the status of children in society*

position • *a privileged position*

prestige • *to diminish the prestige of the monarchy*

rank • *He was stripped of his rank.*

standing • *This has done nothing to improve his standing.*

stay VERB

to remain somewhere • *She stayed in bed till noon.*

hang around (INFORMAL) • *I can't hang around here all day.*

linger • *I lingered on for a few days until he arrived.*

loiter • *We loitered around looking in shop windows.*

remain • *You'll have to remain in hospital for the time being.*

tarry • *The shop's aim is to persuade you to tarry and spend.*

wait • *I'll wait here till you come back.*

steadfast ADJECTIVE

refusing to change or give up • *He remained steadfast in his belief.*

constant • *He has been her constant companion for the last four months.*

faithful • *this party's most faithful voters*

firm • *He held a firm belief in the afterlife.*

immovable • *On one issue, however, she was immovable.*

resolute • *a decisive and resolute international leader*

staunch • *a staunch supporter of these proposals*

steady • *He was firm and steady, unlike many men she knew.*

unshakeable • *his unshakeable belief in the project*

steady ❶ ADJECTIVE

continuing without interruptions • *a steady rise in profits*

consistent • *consistent support*

constant • *under constant pressure*

continuous • *Japanese-style programmes of continuous improvement*

even • *an even level of sound*

nonstop • *nonstop background music*

regular • *a regular beat*

uninterrupted • *28 years of uninterrupted growth*

steady ❷ ADJECTIVE

not shaky or wobbling • *O'Brien held out a steady hand.*

firm • *Make sure the tree is securely mounted on a firm base.*

secure • *Check joints are secure and the wood is sound.*

stable • *stable foundations*

steady ❸ VERB

to prevent something from shaking

Can't find the word you're looking for? Try the index.

a
b
c
d
e
f
g
h
i
j
k
l
m
n
o
p
q
r
s
t
u
v
w
x
y
z

or wobbling • *Two men were steadying a ladder.*
brace • *the old timbers which braced the roof*
secure • *The frames are secured by horizontal rails.*
stabilize • *gyros which stabilize the platform*
support • *Thick wooden posts support the ceiling.*

steal ❶ VERB
to take something without permission • *He was accused of stealing a tin of pineapple chunks.*
appropriate • *Several other companies have appropriated the idea.*
nick (BRITISH, AUSTRALIAN AND NEW ZEALAND; SLANG) • *I nicked that money from the till.*
pilfer • *Staff were pilfering behind the bar.*
pinch (INFORMAL) • *Someone's pinched my wallet.*
swipe (SLANG) • *Did you just swipe that book?*
take • *The burglars took anything they could carry.*

MORE SYNONYMS
- embezzle
- filch
- misappropriate
- purloin
- thieve

steal ❷ VERB
to move somewhere quietly and secretly • *They can steal out and join us later.*
creep • *We crept away under cover of darkness.*
slip • *I wanted to duck down and slip past but they saw me.*
sneak • *Sometimes he would sneak out to see me.*

tiptoe • *She slipped out of bed and tiptoed to the window.*

steep ❶ ADJECTIVE
rising sharply and abruptly • *a steep hill*
sheer • *a sheer drop*
vertical • *The slope was almost vertical.*

ANTONYM
- gradual

steep ❷ ADJECTIVE
larger than is reasonable • *steep prices*
excessive • *excessive charges*
extortionate • *an extortionate rate of interest*
high • *high loan rates*
unreasonable • *unreasonable interest charges*

MORE SYNONYMS
- exorbitant
- overpriced

steep ❸ VERB
to soak something in a liquid • *green beans steeped in olive oil*
immerse • *Immerse the gammon in cold water to remove the salt.*
marinate • *Marinate the chicken for at least four hours.*
soak • *Soak the beans overnight.*

sterile ❶ ADJECTIVE
free from germs • *Protect the cut with a sterile dressing.*
antiseptic • *an antiseptic hospital room*
germ-free • *Keep your working surfaces germ-free.*
sterilized • *a sterilized laboratory*

sterile ❷ ADJECTIVE
unable to produce • *He found out he was sterile.*
barren • *a barren mare*

Can't find the word you're looking for? Try the index.

unproductive • *70 million acres of unproductive land*

MORE SYNONYMS
- infecund
- unfruitful

ANTONYM
- fertile

stick ❶ NOUN
a long, thin piece of wood • *crowds armed with sticks and stones*
bat • *a baseball bat*
cane • *He wore a grey suit and leaned heavily on his cane.*
mace • *a statue of a king holding a golden mace*
pole • *He reached up with a hooked pole to roll down the shutter.*
rod • *a witch-doctor's rod*
truncheon • *a policeman's truncheon*
twig • *the sound of a twig breaking underfoot*
wand • *You can't wave a magic wand and make everything okay.*

stick ❷ VERB
to thrust something somewhere • *They stuck a needle in my back.*
dig • *She dug her spoon into the moussaka.*
insert • *He inserted the key into the lock.*
jab • *A needle was jabbed into my arm.*
poke • *He poked his finger into the hole.*
push • *She pushed her thumb into his eye.*
put • *Just put it through my letter-box when you're finished with it.*
ram • *He rammed the jacket under the seat.*
shove • *We shoved a copy of the newsletter beneath their door.*

stuff • *I stuffed my hands in my pockets.*
thrust • *A small aerial thrust up from the grass verge.*

stick ❸ VERB
to attach • *Stick down any loose bits of flooring.*
attach • *We attach labels to things before we file them away.*
bond • *Strips of wood are bonded together.*
fix • *Fix the photo to the card using double-sided tape.*
fuse • *The scientists fused immune cells with cancer cells.*
glue • *Glue the fabric around the window.*
paste • *The children were busy pasting stars on to a chart.*

stick ❹ VERB
to become attached • *The soil stuck to my boots.*
adhere • *Small particles adhere to the seed.*
bond • *Diamond does not bond well with other materials.*
cling • *His sodden trousers were clinging to his shins.*
fuse • *The flakes fuse together and produce ice crystals.*

stick ❺ VERB
to jam or become jammed • *The dagger stuck tightly in the silver scabbard.*
catch • *His jacket buttons caught in the net.*
jam • *Every few moments the machinery became jammed.*
lodge • *The car has a bullet lodged in the passenger door.*
snag • *The fishermen said their nets kept snagging on underwater objects.*

Can't find the word you're looking for? Try the index.

sticky ADJECTIVE
covered with a substance that
sticks to other things • *She thrust
her hand into the sticky mess.*
adhesive • *adhesive tape*
tacky • *covered with a tacky resin*

MORE SYNONYMS
- glutinous
- viscid
- viscous

stiff ❶ ADJECTIVE
firm and not easily bent • *stiff
metal wires*
firm • *a firm mattress*
hard • *the hard wooden floor*
rigid • *a rigid plastic container*
solid • *a block of solid wax*
taut • *He lifted the wire until it was
taut.*

ANTONYM
- limp

stiff ❷ ADJECTIVE
not friendly or relaxed • *the rather
stiff and formal surroundings of the
Palace*
cold • *Sharon was very cold with me.*
forced • *a forced smile*
formal • *His voice was grave and
formal.*
stilted • *Our conversation was
stilted and polite.*
unnatural • *a strained and
unnatural atmosphere*
wooden • *a wooden performance*

MORE SYNONYMS
- constrained
- prim
- standoffish

stiff ❸ ADJECTIVE
difficult or severe • *a stiff exam*
arduous • *an arduous undertaking*
difficult • *a difficult job*

exacting • *exacting standards*
formidable • *a formidable task*
hard • *a hard day's work*
rigorous • *rigorous military training*
tough • *a tough challenge*

still ADJECTIVE
not moving • *The air was still.*
calm • *the calm waters of the
harbour*
inert • *He covered the inert body
with a blanket.*
motionless • *He stood there,
motionless.*
stationary • *The train was
stationary for 90 minutes.*
tranquil • *a tranquil lake*

stink ❶ VERB
to smell very bad • *His breath
stinks of garlic.*
pong (BRITISH AND AUSTRALIAN;
INFORMAL) • *She said he ponged a
bit.*
reek • *The whole house reeks of
cigar smoke.*

stink ❷ NOUN
a very bad smell • *the stink of stale
beer on his breath*
pong (BRITISH AND AUSTRALIAN;
INFORMAL) • *What's that horrible
pong?*
stench • *a foul stench*

MORE SYNONYMS
- fetor
- malodour

stock ❶ NOUN
shares bought in an investment
company • *the buying of stocks*
bonds • *the recent sharp decline in
bond prices*
investments • *Earn a rate of
return of 8% on your investments.*
shares • *He was keen to buy shares
in the company.*

Can't find the word you're looking for? Try the index.

A B C D E F G H I J K L M N O P Q R S T U V W X Y Z

stock ❷ NOUN

the total amount of goods for sale in a shop • *The shop withdrew a quantity of stock from sale.*
goods • *Are all your goods on display?*
merchandise (FORMAL) • *25% off selected merchandise*

stock ❸ NOUN

a supply of something • *Troops have seized a large stock of weapons.*
reserve • *65% of the world's oil reserves*
reservoir • *the body's short-term reservoir of energy*
stockpile • *treaties to cut stockpiles of chemical weapons*
store • *my secret store of chocolate biscuits*
supply • *What happens when food supplies run low?*

stock ❹ NOUN

an animal or person's ancestors • *We are both from working-class stock.*
ancestry • *a family who can trace their ancestry back to the sixteenth century*
descent • *All the contributors were of African descent.*
extraction • *Her father was of Italian extraction.*
lineage • *a respectable family of ancient lineage*
parentage • *She's a Londoner of mixed parentage.*
origin • *people of Asian origin*

stock ❺ VERB

to keep a supply of goods to sell • *The shop stocks a wide range of paint.*
deal in • *They deal in kitchen equipment.*
sell • *It sells everything from hair ribbons to oriental rugs.*
supply • *We supply office furniture and accessories.*
trade in • *He had been trading in antique furniture for 25 years.*

stock ❻ ADJECTIVE

commonly used • *National security is the stock excuse for government secrecy.*
hackneyed • *It may be an old hackneyed phrase, but it's true.*
overused • *an overused catch phrase*
routine • *We've tried all the routine methods of persuasion.*
standard • *the standard ending for a formal letter*
stereotyped • *stereotyped ideas about women*
typical • *the typical questions journalists ask celebrities*
usual • *He came out with all the usual excuses.*

stockpile ❶ VERB

to store large quantities of something • *People are stockpiling food for the winter.*
accumulate • *Some people get rich by accumulating wealth very gradually.*
amass • *It is best not to enquire how he amassed his fortune.*
collect • *Two young girls were collecting firewood.*
gather • *We gathered enough wood to last the night.*
hoard • *They've begun to hoard food and petrol.*
save • *Scraps of material were saved for quilts.*
stash (INFORMAL) • *He had stashed money in an offshore account.*
store up • *Investors were storing up cash in anticipation of disaster.*

a
b
c
d
e
f
g
h
i
j
k
l
m
n
o
p
q
r
s
t
u
v
w
x
y
z

Can't find the word you're looking for? Try the index.

A
B
C
D
E
F
G
H
I
J
K
L
M
N
O
P
Q
R
S
T
U
V
W
X
Y
Z

stockpile ➋ NOUN
a large store of something
• *stockpiles of fuel*
arsenal • *a formidable arsenal of guns and landmines*
cache • *a cache of weapons and explosives*
hoard • *a hoard of silver and jewels worth $40m*
reserve • *The country's reserves of food are running low.*
stash (INFORMAL) • *her mother's stash of sleeping pills*
stock • *Stocks of ammunition were being used up.*
store • *his secret store of sweets*

stocky ADJECTIVE
short but solid-looking • *a stocky, middle-aged man*
chunky • *the chunky South African tennis player*
solid • *a solid build*
sturdy • *a short, sturdy woman in her early sixties*

MORE SYNONYMS
• stubby
• thickset

stomach NOUN
the front part of the body below the waist • *Breathe out and flatten your stomach.*
belly • *the enormous belly of the Italian foreign minister*
paunch • *Nicholson surveyed his spreading paunch.*
puku (NEW ZEALAND) • *a pain in my puku*
tummy (INFORMAL) • *I'd like a flatter tummy, but then who doesn't?*

stop ➊ VERB
to cease doing something • *I stopped working last year to have a baby.*

cease • *A small number of firms have ceased trading.*
cut out (INFORMAL) • *Will you cut out that racket?*
desist • *boycotting Norwegian products until they desist from whaling*
discontinue • *Do not discontinue the treatment without seeing your doctor.*
end • *public pressure to end the embargo*
quit • *He's trying to quit smoking.*

ANTONYM
• start

stop ➋ VERB
to come to an end • *He prayed for the blizzard to stop.*
cease • *At one o'clock the rain ceased.*
come to an end • *An hour later, the meeting came to an end.*
conclude • *The evening concluded with dinner and speeches.*
end • *The talks ended in disagreement.*
finish • *The teaching day finishes at around 4 pm.*
halt • *Discussions have halted again.*

ANTONYM
• start

stop ➌ VERB
to prevent something • *measures to stop the trade in ivory*
arrest • *trying to arrest the bleeding*
check • *a policy to check fast population growth*
prevent • *the most practical way of preventing crime*

MORE SYNONYMS
• forestall
• nip something in the bud

store ❶ NOUN
a supply kept for future use • I have a store of food and water here.
cache • a cache of weapons and explosives
fund • an extraordinary fund of energy
hoard • a hoard of supplies
reserve • the world's oil reserves
reservoir • the body's short-term reservoir of energy
stock • stocks of paper and ink
stockpile • stockpiles of nuclear warheads
supply • food supplies

store ❷ NOUN
a place where things are kept • a grain store
depot • a government arms depot
storeroom • a storeroom filled with furniture
warehouse • a carpet warehouse

MORE SYNONYMS
- depository
- repository
- storehouse

store ❸ VERB
to keep something for future use • The information can be stored in a computer.
hoard • They've begun to hoard food and petrol.
keep • Grate the lemon zest and keep it for later.
save • His allotment of gas had to be saved for emergencies.
stash (INFORMAL) • He had stashed money away in a secret offshore account.
stockpile • People are stockpiling food for the coming winter.

story NOUN
a tale told or written to entertain

people • a poignant love story
account • a true account
anecdote • her store of theatrical anecdotes
legend • an old Scottish legend
narrative • a fast-moving narrative
tale • a fairy tale
yarn • a children's yarn about giants

straight ❶ ADJECTIVE
upright or level • Keep your arms straight.
erect • The upper back and neck are held in an erect position.
even • to ensure an even hem
horizontal • a horizontal line
level • a completely level base
perpendicular • Position your body perpendicular with the slope.
upright • He sat upright in his chair.
vertical • Keep the spine vertical.

ANTONYM
- crooked

straight ❷ ADJECTIVE
honest, frank and direct • They wouldn't give me a straight answer.
blunt • She is blunt about her personal life.
candid • I haven't been completely candid with you.
forthright • a forthright reply
frank • a frank discussion
honest • Please be honest with me.
outright • This was outright rejection.
plain • plain talking
point-blank • a point-blank refusal

straightforward ❶
ADJECTIVE
easy and involving no problems • The question seemed straightforward enough.

a
b
c
d
e
f
g
h
i
j
k
l
m
n
o
p
q
r
s
t
u
v
w
x
y
z

A
B
C
D
E
F
G
H
I
J
K
L
M
N
O
P
Q
R
S
T
U
V
W
X
Y
Z

basic • *The film's story is pretty basic.*
easy • *The shower is easy to install.*
elementary • *elementary computer skills*
routine • *a fairly routine procedure*
simple • *simple advice on filling in your tax form*
uncomplicated • *good British cooking with its uncomplicated, natural flavours*

ANTONYM
● complicated

straightforward ❷
ADJECTIVE
honest, open, and frank • *I liked his straightforward, intelligent manner.*
candid • *I haven't been completely candid with you.*
direct • *He avoided giving a direct answer.*
forthright • *He was known for his forthright manner.*
frank • *They had a frank discussion about the issue.*
honest • *I was totally honest about what I was doing.*
open • *He had always been open with her.*
plain • *I believe in plain talking.*
straight • *He never gives a straight answer to a straight question.*

ANTONYM
● devious

strain ❶ NOUN
worry and nervous tension • *the stresses and strains of a busy career*
anxiety • *Her voice was full of anxiety.*
pressure • *the pressure of work*
stress • *the stress of exams*
tension • *Laughing relieves tension and stress.*

strain ❷ VERB
to make something do more than it is able to do • *You'll strain your eyes reading in this light.*
overwork • *Too much food will overwork your digestive system.*
tax • *He is beginning to tax my patience.*

MORE SYNONYMS
● overexert
● overtax
● push to the limit

strange ❶ ADJECTIVE
unusual or unexpected • *A strange thing happened.*
abnormal • *an abnormal fear of spiders*
bizarre • *a bizarre scene*
curious • *a curious mixture of ancient and modern*
extraordinary • *an extraordinary occurrence*
funny • *a funny feeling*
odd • *There was something odd about her.*
peculiar • *It tasted very peculiar.*
queer • *I think there's something a bit queer going on.*
uncommon • *A 15-year lifespan is not uncommon for a dog.*
weird • *He's a really weird guy.*

MORE SYNONYMS
● out-of-the-way
● outré
● unaccountable

strange ❷ ADJECTIVE
new or unfamiliar • *alone in a strange country*
alien • *transplanted into an alien culture*
exotic • *filmed in an exotic location*
foreign • *This was a foreign country, so unlike his own.*

new • *I'm always open to new experiences.*
novel • *a novel idea*
unfamiliar • *visiting an unfamiliar city*

strength ➊ NOUN
physical energy and power • *an astonishing display of physical strength*
brawn • *He's got plenty of brains as well as brawn.*
might • *the full might of the army*
muscle • *demonstrating both muscle and skill*
stamina • *The race requires a lot of stamina.*

MORE SYNONYMS
- brawniness
- lustiness
- sinew

ANTONYM
- weakness

strength ➋ NOUN
the degree of intensity • *an indication of the strength of feeling among parents*
force • *the force of his argument*
intensity • *the intensity of their emotions*
potency • *the extraordinary potency of his personality*
power • *the overwhelming power of love*
vehemence • *I was surprised by the vehemence of his criticism.*
vigour • *We resumed the attack with renewed vigour.*

ANTONYM
- weakness

strengthen ➊ VERB
to give something more power • *This move will strengthen his political standing.*

consolidate • *to consolidate an already dominant position*
encourage • *encouraged by the shouts of their supporters*
harden • *evidence which hardens suspicions about their involvement*
stiffen • *This only stiffened his resolve to quit.*
toughen • *new laws to toughen police powers*

MORE SYNONYMS
- fortify
- hearten
- invigorate

ANTONYM
- weaken

strengthen ➋ VERB
to support the structure of something • *The builders had to strengthen the joists with timber.*
bolster • *steel beams used to bolster the roof*
brace • *tottering pillars braced by scaffolding*
fortify • *citadels fortified by high stone walls*
reinforce • *They had to reinforce the walls with exterior beams.*
support • *the thick wooden posts that supported the ceiling*

ANTONYM
- weaken

stress ➊ NOUN
worry and nervous tension • *the stresses and strains of a busy career*
anxiety • *Her voice was full of anxiety.*
hassle (INFORMAL) • *I don't think it's worth the money or the hassle.*
pressure • *I felt the pressure of being the first woman in the job.*
strain • *She was tired and under great strain.*

Can't find the word you're looking for? Try the index.

A
B
C
D
E
F
G
H
I
J
K
L
M
N
O
P
Q
R
S
T
U
V
W
X
Y
Z

tension • *Laughing relieves tension.*
worry • *It was a time of worry for us.*

stress ❷ VERB
to emphasize something • *The leaders have stressed their commitment to the talks.*
accentuate • *make-up which accentuates your best features*
emphasize • *He flourished his glass to emphasize the point.*
repeat • *We are not, I repeat not, in the negotiating process.*
underline • *The report underlined his concern about falling standards.*

MORE SYNONYMS
● belabour
● dwell on
● point up
● underscore

stretch ❶ VERB
to extend over an area or time • *an artificial reef stretching the length of the coast*
continue • *The road continued into the distance.*
cover • *The oil slick covered a total area of seven miles.*
extend • *The caves extend for some 18 kilometres.*
go on • *The dispute looks set to go on into the new year.*
hang • *The branches hang right down to the ground.*
last • *His difficulties are likely to last well beyond childhood.*
reach • *a caravan park which reached from one end of the bay to the other*
spread • *The estuary spreads as far as the eye can see.*

stretch ❷ VERB
to reach out with part of your body

• *She arched her back and stretched herself.*
extend • *Stand straight with your arms extended at your sides.*
reach • *He reached up for an overhanging branch.*
straighten • *Point your toes and straighten both legs slowly.*

ANTONYM
● bend

stretch ❸ NOUN
an area of land or water • *It's a very dangerous stretch of road.*
area • *extensive mountainous areas of Europe and South America*
expanse • *a huge expanse of grassland*
extent • *a vast extent of fertile country*
sweep • *The ground fell away in a broad sweep down the river.*
tract • *They cleared large tracts of forest for farming.*

stretch ❹ NOUN
a period of time • *He would study for eight hour stretches.*
period • *a long period of time*
run • *The show will transfer to the West End, after a month's run in Birmingham.*
space • *They've come a long way in a short space of time.*
spell • *a long spell of dry weather*
stint • *He is coming home after a five-year stint abroad.*
term • *She worked the full term of her pregnancy.*
time • *doing very little exercise for several weeks at a time*

strict ❶ ADJECTIVE
very firm in demanding obedience • *My parents were very strict.*
authoritarian • *He has an*

authoritarian approach to parenthood.
firm • *the guiding hand of a firm father figure*
rigid • *a rigid hospital routine*
rigorous • *rigorous military training*
stern • *Her mother was stern and hard to please.*
stringent • *stringent rules*

strict ❷ ADJECTIVE
precise and accurate • *He has never been a playboy in the strict sense of the word.*
accurate • *an accurate record of events*
exact • *I do not remember the exact words.*
meticulous • *meticulous attention to detail*
particular • *very particular dietary requirements*
precise • *precise instructions*
true • *a true account*

strive VERB
to make a great effort to achieve something • *He strives hard to keep himself fit.*
attempt • *He attempted to smile, but found it difficult.*
do your best • *I'll do my best to find out.*
do your utmost • *She was certain he would do his utmost to help her.*
endeavour (FORMAL) • *They are endeavouring to protect trade union rights.*
make an effort • *He made no effort to hide his disappointment.*
seek • *We have never sought to impose our views.*
try • *He tried to block her advancement in the Party.*

strong ❶ ADJECTIVE
having powerful muscles
• *a strong, robust man*
▷ see Word Study **strong**, pages 705–6

ANTONYM
● weak

strong ❷ ADJECTIVE
able to withstand rough treatment
• *a strong casing, which won't crack or chip*
▷ see Word Study **strong**, pages 705–6

ANTONYM
● fragile

strong ❸ ADJECTIVE
great in degree or intensity • *Despite strong opposition, she was victorious.*
▷ see Word Study **strong**

ANTONYM
● faint

structure ❶ NOUN
the way something is made or organized • *the structure of this molecule*
arrangement • *an intricate arrangement of treadles, rods and cranks*
construction • *The chairs were light in construction but very strong.*
design • *The shoes were of good design and good quality.*
make-up • *the chemical make-up of the oceans and atmosphere*
organization • *the organization of the economy*

MORE SYNONYMS
● configuration
● conformation

structure ❷ NOUN
something that has been built
• *The museum is an impressive structure.*

a
b
c
d
e
f
g
h
i
j
k
l
m
n
o
p
q
r
s
t
u
v
w
x
y
z

Can't find the word you're looking for? Try the index.

A
B
C
D
E
F
G
H
I
J
K
L
M
N
O
P
Q
R
S
T
U
V
W
X
Y
Z

building • *an ugly modern building*
construction • *an impressive steel and glass construction*
edifice • *historic edifices in the area*

struggle ❶ VERB

to try hard to do something • *They had to struggle to make ends meet.*
strain • *straining to lift heavy weights*
strive • *He strives hard to keep himself fit.*
toil • *toiling to make up for lost time*
work • *I had to work hard for everything I've got.*

struggle ❷ NOUN

something that is hard to achieve • *Life became a struggle for survival.*
effort • *It was an effort to finish in time.*
labour • *weary from their labours*
toil • *another day of toil and strife*
work • *It's been hard work, but rewarding.*

stubborn ADJECTIVE

determined not to change or give in • *a stubborn character who is used to getting his own way*
dogged • *his dogged insistence on his rights*
inflexible • *His opponents viewed him as dogmatic and inflexible.*
obstinate • *a wicked and obstinate child*
tenacious • *a tenacious and persistent interviewer*
wilful • *a headstrong and wilful young lady*

MORE SYNONYMS

● intractable
● obdurate
● recalcitrant
● refractory

stuck-up ADJECTIVE (INFORMAL)

proud and conceited • *She was famous, but she wasn't a bit stuck-up.*
arrogant • *He was so arrogant, he never even said hello to me.*
conceited • *He's a very conceited young man.*
disdainful • *She cast a disdainful glance at me.*
haughty • *She looks haughty, but when you get to know her, she's very friendly.*
proud • *He's too proud to use public transport.*
snobbish • *I'd expected her to be snobbish, but she was warm and welcoming.*

study ❶ VERB

to spend time learning about something • *He is studying History and Economics.*
learn • *I'm learning French.*
read up • *She spent a year reading up on farming techniques.*
swot (BRITISH, AUSTRALIAN AND NEW ZEALAND; INFORMAL) • *swotting for their finals*

study ❷ VERB

to look at something carefully • *He studied the map in silence.*
contemplate • *He contemplated his hands, frowning.*
examine • *He examined her passport and stamped it.*
pore over • *We spent hours poring over travel brochures.*

MORE SYNONYMS

● peruse
● scrutinize

study ❸ NOUN

the activity of learning about a subject • *the serious study of medieval architecture*

Can't find the word you're looking for? Try the index.

lessons • *He was lagging behind in his lessons.*
research • *funds for research into AIDS*
school work • *She buried herself in school work.*
swotting (BRITISH, AUSTRALIAN AND NEW ZEALAND; INFORMAL) • *She put her success down to last-minute swotting.*

stuff ❶ NOUN
a substance or group of things • *"That's my stuff," he said, pointing to a bag.*
apparatus • *all the apparatus you'll need for the job*
belongings • *I collected my belongings and left.*
equipment • *outdoor playing equipment*
gear • *fishing gear*
kit • *I forgot my gym kit.*
material • *organic material*
substance • *The substance that's causing problems comes from barley.*
tackle • *Martin kept his fishing tackle in his room.*
things • *Sara told him to take all his things and not to return.*

MORE SYNONYMS
● paraphernalia
● trappings

stuff ❷ VERB
to push something somewhere quickly and roughly • *He stuffed the newspapers into a litter bin.*
cram • *I crammed her hat into a waste-basket.*
force • *I forced the key into the ignition.*
jam • *Pete jammed his hands into his pockets.*
push • *Someone had pushed a tissue into the keyhole.*
ram • *He rammed his clothes into a drawer.*
shove • *We shoved a newsletter beneath their door.*
squeeze • *I squeezed everything into my rucksack.*
thrust • *She thrust a stack of photos into my hands.*

stuff ❸ VERB
to fill something with a substance or objects • *He stood there, stuffing his mouth with popcorn.*
cram • *I crammed my bag full of clothes and set off.*
fill • *I filled the box with polystyrene chips.*
load • *They loaded all their equipment into backpacks.*
pack • *a lorry packed with explosives*

stuffy ❶ ADJECTIVE
formal and old-fashioned • *his lack of stuffy formality*
dull • *They are nice people but rather dull.*
formal • *an austere and formal family*
old-fashioned • *She was condemned as an old-fashioned prude.*
staid • *He is boring, old-fashioned and staid.*
strait-laced • *She is very strait-laced and narrow-minded.*

MORE SYNONYMS
● fusty
● old-fogeyish
● priggish
● stodgy

stuffy ❷ ADJECTIVE
not containing enough fresh air • *It was hot and stuffy in the classroom.*

a
b
c
d
e
f
g
h
i
j
k
l
m
n
o
p
q
r
s
t
u
v
w
x
y
z

Can't find the word you're looking for? Try the index.

A B C D E F G H I J K L M N O P Q R S T U V W X Y Z

close • *The atmosphere was close.*
heavy • *The air was heavy, moist and sultry.*
muggy • *It was muggy and overcast.*
oppressive • *The little room was windowless and oppressive.*
stale • *A layer of smoke hung in the stale air.*
stifling • *the stifling heat of the room*

MORE SYNONYMS
- fetid
- frowsty
- sultry
- unventilated

stupid ADJECTIVE
lacking intelligence or good judgment • *How could I have been so stupid?*
absurd • *absurd ideas*
daft (INFORMAL) • *That's a daft question.*
dim • *He is rather dim.*
foolish • *It is foolish to risk injury.*
idiotic • *What an idiotic thing to say!*
inane • *She's always asking inane questions.*
obtuse • *It should be obvious even to the most obtuse person.*
thick • *I must have seemed incredibly thick.*

MORE SYNONYMS
- asinine
- crass
- cretinous
- fatuous
- imbecilic
- moronic

ANTONYM
- clever

stupidity NOUN
lack of intelligence or good

judgment • *I was astonished by his stupidity.*
absurdity • *the absurdity of the suggestion*
folly • *the danger and folly of taking drugs*
foolishness • *He expressed remorse over his own foolishness.*
inanity • *The inanity of the conversation.*
silliness • *He sounded quite exasperated by my silliness.*

MORE SYNONYMS
- asininity
- fatuity
- imbecility
- obtuseness

sturdy ADJECTIVE
strong and unlikely to be damaged • *The camera was mounted on a sturdy tripod.*
durable • *Fine china is surprisingly durable.*
hardy • *He looked like a farmer, round-faced and hardy.*
robust • *very robust, simply-designed machinery*
solid • *The car feels very solid.*
substantial • *Jack had put on weight – he seemed more substantial.*
stout • *a stout oak door*
strong • *a strong casing which won't crack or chip*
well-built • *Mitchell is well-built and of medium height.*

ANTONYM
- fragile

style ❶ NOUN
the way in which something is done • *a dictatorial management style*
approach • *his blunt approach*

Can't find the word you're looking for? Try the index.

manner • *a satire in the manner of Dickens*
method • *a new method of education*
mode • *a cheap and convenient mode of transport*
technique • *his driving technique*
way • *He had a strange way of talking.*

style ❷ NOUN
smartness and elegance • *She has not lost her grace and style.*
chic • *French designer chic*
elegance • *Princess Grace's understated elegance*
flair • *dressed with typical Italian flair*
sophistication • *to add a touch of sophistication to any wardrobe*
taste • *impeccable taste*

MORE SYNONYMS
● élan
● panache
● savoir-faire

subdue VERB
to bring people under control by force • *The government have not been able to subdue the rebels.*
crush • *ruthless measures to crush the revolt*
defeat • *an important role in defeating the rebellion*
overcome • *working to overcome the enemy forces*
overpower • *The police eventually overpowered him.*
quell • *tough new measures to quell the disturbances*
vanquish • *his vanquished foe*

subject ❶ NOUN
the thing or person being discussed • *They exchanged views on a wide range of subjects.*

issue • *an issue that had worried him for some time*
matter • *I don't want to discuss the matter.*
object • *the object of much heated discussion*
point • *There is another point to consider.*
question • *the difficult question of unemployment*
theme • *The book's central theme is power.*
topic • *The weather is a constant topic of conversation.*

subject ❷ VERB
to make someone experience something • *He was subjected to constant interruptions.*
expose • *people exposed to high levels of radiation*
put through • *My husband put me through hell.*
submit • *The old woman was submitted to a terrifying ordeal.*

submit ❶ VERB
to accept or agree to something unwillingly • *I submitted to their requests.*
agree • *Management has agreed to the union's conditions.*
bow • *Some shops are bowing to consumer pressure and stocking the product.*
capitulate • *He capitulated to their ultimatum.*
comply • *The commander said his army would comply with the ceasefire.*
give in • *Officials say they won't give in to the workers' demands.*
surrender • *We'll never surrender to these terrorists.*
yield • *She yielded to her mother's nagging and took the child to a specialist.*

a
b
c
d
e
f
g
h
i
j
k
l
m
n
o
p
q
r
s
t
u
v
w
x
y
z

Can't find the word you're looking for? Try the index.

A
B
C
D
E
F
G
H
I
J
K
L
M
N
O
P
Q
R
S
T
U
V
W
X
Y
Z

ANTONYM
● resist

submit ❷ VERB

to formally present a document or proposal • *They submitted their reports to the Chancellor.*
hand in • *I'm supposed to hand in my dissertation on Friday.*
present • *The group intends to present this petition to the parliament.*
propose • *He has proposed a bill to abolish the House of Commons.*
put forward • *He has put forward new peace proposals.*
send in • *Applicants are asked to send in a CV and covering letter.*
table • *They've tabled a motion criticizing the Government for its actions.*
tender • *She tendered her resignation.*

ANTONYM
● withdraw

substance NOUN

a solid, powder, liquid or gas • *Poisonous substances should be labelled as such.*
element • *a chart of the chemical elements*
fabric • *Condensation will rot the fabric of the building.*
material • *an armchair of some resilient plastic material*
stuff • *the stuff from which the universe is made*

substitute ❶ VERB

to use one thing in place of another • *You can substitute honey for the sugar.*
exchange • *exchanging one set of problems for another*
interchange • *Meat can be interchanged with pulses as a source of protein.*
replace • *We dug up the concrete and replaced it with grass.*
swap • *Some hostages were swapped for convicted prisoners.*
switch • *They switched the tags on the cables.*

substitute ❷ NOUN

something used in place of another thing • *an artificial substitute for silk*
deputy • *I can't make it so I'll send my deputy.*
proxy • *They must nominate a proxy to vote on their behalf.*
replacement • *He has nominated Adams as his replacement.*
representative • *Employees from each department elect a representative.*
surrogate • *They had expected me to be a surrogate for my sister.*

MORE SYNONYMS
● locum
● locum tenens
● makeshift
● stopgap

subtract VERB

to take one number away from another • *If you subtract 3 from 5 you get 2.*
deduct • *Marks will be deducted for spelling mistakes.*
take away • *Take away the number you first thought of.*
take from • *Take the 5% discount from the total amount due.*

ANTONYM
● add

succeed ❶ VERB

to achieve the result you intend • *To succeed, you must learn to overcome obstacles.*

be successful • *We must help our clubs to be successful in Europe.*
do well • *Their team did well.*
flourish • *The business flourished.*
make it (INFORMAL) • *It is hard for an English actress to make it in Hollywood.*
prosper • *His team have always prospered in cup competitions.*
thrive • *The company has thrived by selling cheap, simple products.*
triumph • *a symbol of good triumphing over evil*
work • *The plan worked.*

ANTONYM
● fail

succeed ❷ VERB
to be the next person to have someone's job • *David is almost certain to succeed him as chairman.*
replace • *the man who replaced him as England skipper*
take over from • *Last year he took over from Bauman as chief executive.*

success ❶ NOUN
the achievement of a goal, fame, or wealth • *Do you believe that work is the key to success?*
celebrity • *I never expected this kind of celebrity when I was writing my novel.*
eminence • *a pilot who achieved eminence in the aeronautical world*
fame • *her rise to fame as a dramatist*
prosperity • *the country's economic prosperity*
triumph • *last year's Republican triumph in the elections*
victory • *Union leaders are heading for victory in their battle over workplace rights.*
wealth • *His hard work brought him wealth and respect.*

MORE SYNONYMS
● ascendancy (FORMAL)
● coup

ANTONYM
● failure

success ❷ NOUN
a person or thing achieving popularity or greatness • *Everyone who knows her says she will be a huge success.*
celebrity • *At the age of 12, Dan is already a celebrity.*
hit • *The song became a massive hit.*
sensation • *the film that turned her into an overnight sensation*
star • *I always knew she would be a star.*
triumph • *a triumph of modern surgery*
winner • *Selling was my game and I intended to be a winner.*

ANTONYM
● failure

successful ADJECTIVE
having achieved what you intended to do • *Mr Singh was a highly successful salesman.*
flourishing • *a flourishing business*
lucrative • *a lucrative career*
profitable • *a profitable exchange of ideas*
rewarding • *a rewarding investment*
thriving • *a thriving housebuilding industry*
top • *a top model*

sudden ADJECTIVE
happening quickly and unexpectedly • *a sudden cry*
abrupt • *Her idyllic world came to an abrupt end when her parents died.*

a
b
c
d
e
f
g
h
i
j
k
l
m
n
o
p
q
r
s
t
u
v
w
x
y
z

Can't find the word you're looking for? Try the index.

A B C D E F G H I J K L M N O P Q R S T U V W X Y Z

hasty • *his hasty departure*
quick • *I had to make a quick decision.*
swift • *a swift blow to the stomach*
unexpected • *His death was totally unexpected.*

ANTONYM
● gradual

suffer VERB
to be affected by pain or something unpleasant • *I knew he was suffering some discomfort.*
bear • *He bore his trials with dignity and grace.*
endure • *The writer endured a harsh life.*
experience • *Widows seem to experience more distress than do widowers.*
go through • *I wouldn't like to go through that again.*
sustain • *He had sustained massive facial injuries.*
undergo • *He had to undergo a body search.*

sufficient ADJECTIVE
being enough for a purpose • *He had sufficient time to prepare his speech.*
adequate • *an adequate income*
ample • *an ample supply of petrol*
enough • *enough cash to live on*

ANTONYM
● insufficient

suffix NOUN

SUFFIXES

-less   -logy *or* -ology
-like   -ness

suggest ❶ VERB
to mention something as a possibility or recommendation

• *Clive suggested going out for tea.*
advise • *I advise you to keep quiet.*
advocate • *Mr Jones advocates longer school days.*
propose • *And where do you propose building such a huge thing?*
recommend • *I have no qualms about recommending this approach.*

suggest ❷ VERB
to hint that something is the case • *Reports suggested the factory would close.*
hint • *The President hinted that he might make some changes.*
imply • *The tone of the report implied that his death was inevitable.*
indicate • *She has indicated that she may resign.*
insinuate • *an article which insinuated that he was lying*
intimate • *He did intimate that he is seeking legal action.*

suggestion ❶ NOUN
an idea mentioned as a possibility • *practical suggestions*
plan • *The government is being asked to consider the plan.*
proposal • *the proposal to do away with nuclear weapons*
proposition • *a business proposition*
recommendation • *a range of recommendations for change*

suggestion ❷ NOUN
a slight indication of something • *a suggestion of dishonesty*
hint • *He showed only the slightest hint of emotion.*
indication • *He gave no indication of remorse.*
insinuation • *The insinuation is that I have something to hide.*
intimation • *He did not give any intimation that he was going to resign.*

Can't find the word you're looking for? Try the index.

trace • *No traces of violence were found on the body.*

suit VERB

to be acceptable • *They will only move if it suits them.*

be acceptable to • *The name chosen had to be acceptable to everyone.*

do • *A holiday at home will do me just fine.*

please • *I'll leave when it pleases me and not before.*

satisfy • *Nothing you can do will satisfy him.*

suitable ADJECTIVE

right or acceptable for a particular purpose • *Conditions were not suitable for life to flourish.*

acceptable • *a mutually acceptable new contract*

appropriate • *an appropriate outfit for the occasion*

apt • *an apt name*

fit • *the suggestion that she is not a fit mother*

fitting • *a fitting background for her beauty*

proper • *It was not thought proper for a woman to be on stage.*

right • *He always said just the right thing.*

satisfactory • *a satisfactory arrangement*

MORE SYNONYMS

- apposite
- befitting
- pertinent
- seemly

ANTONYM

- unsuitable

sulky ADJECTIVE

showing annoyance by being silent and moody • *a sulky adolescent*

huffy • *What are you being so huffy about?*

moody • *Her husband had become withdrawn and moody.*

petulant • *He's just being childish and petulant.*

resentful • *a resentful workforce*

sullen • *He lapsed into a sullen silence.*

summary NOUN

a short account of something's main points • *a summary of the report*

outline • *an outline of the proposal*

review • *a film review*

rundown • *Here's a rundown of the options.*

summing-up • *The judge concluded his summing-up.*

synopsis • *a brief synopsis of the book*

MORE SYNONYMS

- abridgment
- digest
- précis
- recapitulation
- résumé

sum up VERB

to describe briefly • *He summed up his weekend in one word: "Disastrous".*

recapitulate • *Let's just recapitulate the essential points.*

summarize • *The article can be summarized in three sentences.*

superb ADJECTIVE

very good indeed • *With superb skill, he managed to make a perfect landing.*

breathtaking • *The house has breathtaking views.*

excellent • *You've done an excellent job.*

a
b
c
d
e
f
g
h
i
j
k
l
m
n
o
p
q
r
s
t
u
v
w
x
y
z

Can't find the word you're looking for? Try the index.

A
B
C
D
E
F
G
H
I
J
K
L
M
N
O
P
Q
R
S
T
U
V
W
X
Y
Z

exquisite • *His photography is exquisite.*
magnificent • *a magnificent country house*
marvellous • *She is a marvellous cook.*
outstanding • *an outstanding performance*
splendid • *a splendid Victorian mansion*
superior • *a superior blend of the finest coffee beans*
unrivalled • *He has an unrivalled knowledge of British politics.*
wonderful • *The sun setting over the mountains was a wonderful sight.*

ANOTHER SYNONYM
● superlative

superior ❶ ADJECTIVE
better than other similar things
• *superior coffee beans*
better • *I'd like to move to a better area.*
choice • *the choicest cuts of meat*
de luxe • *a de luxe model*
exceptional • *children with exceptional ability*
first-rate • *a first-rate thriller*
surpassing • *her surpassing achievements*
unrivalled • *colour printing of unrivalled quality*

ANTONYM
● inferior

superior ❷ ADJECTIVE
showing pride and self-importance
• *He stood there looking superior.*
condescending • *I'm fed up with your condescending attitude.*
disdainful • *She passed along with a disdainful look.*
haughty • *He spoke in a haughty tone.*

lofty • *lofty disdain*
patronizing • *his patronizing attitude to the homeless*
snobbish • *a snobbish dislike for their intellectual inferiors*
stuck-up (INFORMAL) • *She was a famous actress, but she wasn't a bit stuck-up.*
supercilious • *His manner is supercilious and arrogant.*

superior ❸ NOUN
a person in a higher position than you • *his immediate superior*
boss (INFORMAL) • *Her boss was very supportive.*
manager • *His plans found favour with his manager.*
senior • *He was described by his seniors as a model officer.*
supervisor • *Each student has a supervisor.*

ANTONYM
● inferior

supervise VERB
to oversee a person or activity • *He supervised more than 400 volunteers.*
be in charge of • *He is in charge of the whole project.*
direct • *Christopher will direct day-to-day operations.*
have charge of • *He has charge of a three-acre estate.*
keep an eye on • *I told you to keep an eye on the children.*
manage • *I manage a small team of workers.*
oversee • *an architect to oversee the work*
run • *Each teacher will run a different workshop.*

MORE SYNONYMS
● preside over
● superintend

Can't find the word you're looking for? Try the index.

supplement ❶ VERB

to add to something to improve it • *I suggest supplementing your diet with vitamin A.*

add to • *A good bathroom adds to the value of any house.*

augment • *a way to augment the family income*

complement • *an in-work benefit that complements earnings*

reinforce • *measures which will reinforce their current strengths*

top up • *compulsory contributions to top up pension schemes*

supplement ❷ NOUN

something added to something else • *a supplement to their basic pension*

addition • *an addition to the existing system*

appendix • *The report includes a six-page appendix.*

complement • *The photographs are a perfect complement to the text.*

extra • *an optional extra*

supplies PLURAL NOUN

food or equipment for a particular purpose • *I had only two pints of water in my emergency supplies.*

equipment • *vital medical equipment*

provisions • *provisions for two weeks*

rations • *Aid officials said food rations had been distributed.*

stores • *an important part of a ship's stores*

supply ❶ VERB

to provide someone with something • *an agreement not to supply chemical weapons*

equip • *plans for equipping the island with water*

furnish • *They'll be able to furnish you with the details.*

give • *We'll give you all the information you need.*

provide • *They'll provide all the equipment.*

MORE SYNONYMS

● endow
● purvey

supply ❷ NOUN

an amount of something available for use • *a plentiful supply of vegetables*

cache • *a cache of weapons and explosives*

fund • *an extraordinary fund of energy*

hoard • *a hoard of food and petrol*

reserve • *The Gulf has 65% of the world's oil reserves.*

stock • *stocks of paper and ink*

stockpile • *stockpiles of chemical weapons*

store • *I have a store of food and water here.*

support ❶ VERB

to agree with someone's ideas or aims • *We supported his political campaign.*

back • *a new witness to back his claim*

champion • *He passionately championed the cause.*

defend • *He defended all of Clarence's decisions, right or wrong.*

promote • *He continued to promote the idea of Scottish autonomy.*

second • *The Prime Minister seconded the call for discipline.*

side with • *accused of siding with terrorists*

uphold • *We uphold the capitalist free economy.*

a
b
c
d
e
f
g
h
i
j
k
l
m
n
o
p
q
r
s
t
u
v
w
x
y
z

Can't find the word you're looking for? Try the index.

ANTONYM
- oppose

support ② VERB
to help someone in difficulties
• *Try to support each other when one of you is feeling down.*
encourage • *When things aren't going well, he encourages me.*
help • *He'd do anything to help a friend.*

support ❸ VERB
to hold something up from underneath • *Thick wooden posts support the ceiling.*
bolster • *steel beams used to bolster the roof*
brace • *The roll-over bar braces the car's structure.*
hold up • *Her legs wouldn't hold her up.*
prop up • *Use sticks to prop the plants up.*
reinforce • *They had to reinforce the walls with exterior beams.*

MORE SYNONYMS
- buttress
- shore up

support ❹ NOUN
an object that holds something up
• *the metal supports which hold up the canvas*
brace • *He will have to wear a neck brace for several days.*
foundation • *the foundation on which the bridge was built*
pillar • *the pillars supporting the roof*
post • *The device is fixed to a post.*
prop • *a structural part such as a beam or prop*

MORE SYNONYMS
- abutment
- stanchion

Can't find the word you're looking for? Try the index.

supporter NOUN
a person who agrees with or helps someone • *He is a strong supporter of the plan.*
adherent • *Communism was gaining adherents in Latin America.*
advocate • *a strong advocate of free market policies*
ally • *a close political ally*
champion • *a champion of women's causes*
fan • *fans of this football club*
follower • *followers of the Dalai Lama*
sponsor • *the first sponsor of Buddhism in Japan*

MORE SYNONYMS
- patron
- protagonist

suppose VERB
to think that something is probably the case • *Where do you suppose he has gone?*
assume • *I assume you have permission to be here?*
believe • *We believe them to be hidden somewhere in the area.*
expect • *I don't expect you've had much experience in the job yet.*
guess • *I guess you're right.*
imagine • *We tend to imagine that the Victorians were prim and proper.*
presume • *I presume you're here on business.*
think • *Do you think she was embarrassed?*

MORE SYNONYMS
- conjecture
- surmise (FORMAL)

supposed ❶ ADJECTIVE
planned, expected, or required to do something • *You're not supposed to leave a child on its own.*

expected • *You were expected to arrive much earlier than this.*

meant • *Parties are meant to be fun.*

obliged • *He is legally obliged to declare his interests.*

required • *Will I be required to come to every meeting?*

supposed ❷ ADJECTIVE

generally believed or thought to be the case • *What is his son supposed to have said?*

alleged • *The accused is alleged to have killed a man.*

assumed • *As usual, the mistakes were assumed to be my fault.*

believed • *He is believed to have died in 1117.*

meant • *They are meant to be one of the top teams in the world.*

presumed • *This area is presumed to be safe.*

reputed • *The monster is reputed to live in the deep waters of a Scottish loch.*

rumoured • *They are rumoured to be on the verge of splitting up.*

suppress ❶ VERB

to prevent people from doing something • *international attempts to suppress drug trafficking*

crush • *a plan to crush the uprising*

quash • *It may help to quash these rumours.*

quell • *The army moved in to quell the uprising.*

stamp out • *steps to stamp out bullying in schools*

stop • *measures to stop the trade in ivory*

suppress ❷ VERB

to stop yourself from expressing a feeling or reaction • *She barely suppressed a gasp.*

conceal • *Robert could not conceal his relief.*

contain • *He could hardly contain his rage.*

curb • *He curbed his temper.*

repress • *people who repress their emotions*

restrain • *unable to restrain her anger*

smother • *I smothered a chuckle.*

stifle • *Miller stifled a yawn and looked at his watch.*

supreme ADJECTIVE

of the highest degree or rank • *They conspired to seize supreme power.*

chief • *his chief rival*

foremost • *the world's foremost scientists*

greatest • *the city's greatest soccer idol*

highest • *the highest academic achievement*

leading • *the world's leading basketball players*

paramount • *a factor of paramount importance*

pre-eminent • *a pre-eminent political figure*

principal • *the principal reason*

top • *the president's top military advisers*

ultimate • *the ultimate international accolade, the Nobel Prize*

sure ❶ ADJECTIVE

having no doubts • *She was no longer sure how she felt about him.*

certain • *certain of getting a place on the team*

clear • *He is not clear on how he will go about it.*

convinced • *He is convinced it's your fault.*

a b c d e f g h i j k l m n o p q r **s** t u v w x y z

Can't find the word you're looking for? Try the index.

definite • *a definite answer*
positive • *I'm positive it will happen.*
satisfied • *We must be satisfied that the treatment is safe.*

ANTONYM
● unsure

sure ➋ ADJECTIVE
reliable or definite • *a sure sign that something is wrong*
definite • *a definite advantage*
dependable • *dependable information*
foolproof • *a foolproof system*
infallible • *an infallible eye for detail*
reliable • *a reliable source*
trustworthy • *trustworthy reports*
undeniable • *a sad but undeniable fact*

surprise ➊ NOUN
something unexpected • *The resignation came as a complete surprise.*
bombshell • *His departure was a bombshell for the team.*
jolt • *Henderson was jolted by the news.*
revelation • *Degas's work had been a revelation to her.*
shock • *I got a shock when I saw her.*
start • *You gave me quite a start.*

surprise ➋ NOUN
the feeling caused by something unexpected • *an exclamation of surprise*
amazement • *He stared in baffled amazement.*
astonishment • *"What?" Meg asked in astonishment.*
incredulity • *The announcement has been met with incredulity.*

wonder • *Cross shook his head in wonder.*

surprise ➌ VERB
to give someone a feeling of surprise • *I was surprised by the vehemence of his criticism.*
amaze • *Most of the cast were amazed by the play's success.*
astonish • *I was astonished to discover his true age.*
astound • *He was astounded at the result.*
stagger • *I was staggered by his reaction.*
stun • *Audiences were stunned by the film's tragic end.*
take aback • *Derek was taken aback when a man answered the phone.*

MORE SYNONYMS
● flabbergast
● nonplus

surrender ➊ VERB
to agree that the other side has won • *We'll never surrender to the terrorists.*
capitulate • *They had no choice but to capitulate.*
give in • *She gave in to him on everything.*
submit • *I refuse to submit to their demands.*
succumb • *The Minister said his country would never succumb to pressure.*
yield • *The government had to yield to local opinion.*

surrender ➋ VERB
to give something up to someone else • *We have surrendered our political authority for economic gain.*
cede • *After the war, Spain ceded the island to America.*

Can't find the word you're looking for? Try the index.

give up • *She is loath to give up her hard-earned liberty.*
relinquish • *He does not intend to relinquish power.*
renounce • *He renounced his claim to the throne.*
yield • *He was obliged to yield territory to France.*

surrender ❸ NOUN
a situation in which one side gives in to the other • *unconditional surrender*
capitulation • *the German capitulation at the end of the First World War*
submission • *The army intends to starve the city into submission.*

surround VERB
to be all around a person or thing • *He was surrounded by bodyguards.*
encircle • *A forty-foot-high concrete wall encircles the jail.*
enclose • *The land was enclosed by a fence.*
encompass • *the largest lake in Canada wholly encompassed by a town*
envelop • *The rich smell of the forest enveloped us.*
hem in • *a valley hemmed in by mountains*

surroundings PLURAL NOUN
the area and environment around a person or place • *He felt a longing for familiar surroundings.*
background • *a fitting background for her beauty*
environment • *a safe environment for marine mammals*
location • *filmed in an exotic location*
neighbourhood • *living in an affluent neighbourhood*
setting • *Rome is the perfect setting for romance.*

MORE SYNONYMS
- environs
- milieu

survive VERB
to live or exist in spite of difficulties • *companies which survived after the recession*
endure • *Somehow their friendship endures.*
last • *Nothing lasts forever.*
live • *having lived through the 1930s depression*
outlive • *They have outlived the horror of the war.*
pull through • *He should pull through okay.*

suspect ❶ VERB
to think something is likely • *I suspect they are secretly planning to raise taxes.*
believe • *Police believe the attacks were carried out by nationalists.*
feel • *I somehow feel he was involved.*
guess • *As you probably guessed, I don't like him much.*
suppose • *The problem is more complex than he supposes.*

suspect ❷ VERB
to have doubts about something • *He suspected her motives.*
distrust • *I don't have any particular reason to distrust them.*
doubt • *Do you doubt my word?*
mistrust • *He mistrusts all journalists.*

suspect ❸ ADJECTIVE
not to be trusted • *a rather suspect holy man*
dodgy (BRITISH, AUSTRALIAN AND NEW ZEALAND; INFORMAL) • *a dodgy car dealer*

a
b
c
d
e
f
g
h
i
j
k
l
m
n
o
p
q
r
s
t
u
v
w
x
y
z

Can't find the word you're looking for? Try the index.

doubtful • *These details are of doubtful origin.*
dubious • *dubious practices*
fishy (INFORMAL) • *There's something very fishy about it.*
questionable • *the questionable motives of politicians*

suspicion ➊ NOUN

a feeling of mistrust • *I was always regarded with suspicion because of my background.*
distrust • *an instinctive distrust of authority*
doubt • *I have my doubts about his ability to govern.*
misgiving • *His first words filled us with misgiving.*
mistrust • *a deep mistrust of banks*
scepticism • *The report has been greeted with scepticism.*

MORE SYNONYMS

- dubiety
- qualm

suspicion ➋ NOUN

a feeling that something is true • *I have a strong suspicion they are lying.*
hunch • *Lowe had a hunch he was on to something.*
idea • *I had an idea that he joined the army later.*
impression • *I get the impression he's hiding something.*

suspicious ➊ ADJECTIVE

feeling distrustful of someone or something • *He was rightly suspicious of their motives.*
apprehensive • *She was apprehensive of strangers.*
distrustful • *Voters are deeply distrustful of all politicians.*
doubtful • *At first I was doubtful about their authenticity.*

sceptical • *Other archaeologists are sceptical about his findings.*
wary • *Many people are wary of lawyers.*

suspicious ➋ ADJECTIVE

causing feelings of distrust • *suspicious circumstances*
dodgy (BRITISH, AUSTRALIAN AND NEW ZEALAND; INFORMAL) • *He was a bit of a dodgy character.*
doubtful • *selling something of doubtful quality*
dubious • *This claim seems to us rather dubious.*
fishy (INFORMAL) • *There's something fishy going on here.*
funny • *There's something funny about him.*
questionable • *the questionable motives of politicians*
shady (INFORMAL) • *shady deals*
suspect • *The whole affair has been highly suspect.*

swap VERB

to replace one thing for another • *Some hostages were swapped for convicted prisoners.*
barter • *bartering wheat for cotton and timber*
exchange • *exchanging one set of problems for another*
interchange • *Meat can be interchanged with pulses as a source of protein.*
switch • *They switched the tags on the cables.*
trade • *They traded land for goods and money.*

sweet ➊ ADJECTIVE

containing a lot of sugar • *a mug of sweet tea*
cloying • *a cloying apricot chutney*
sugary • *a sugary meringue pie*

Can't find the word you're looking for? Try the index.

sweetened • *sweetened shortcrust pastry*

ANTONYM
- sour

sweet ❷ ADJECTIVE
having a pleasant smell • *the sweet smell of roses*
aromatic • *a plant with aromatic leaves*
fragrant • *fragrant clover*
perfumed • *perfumed soaps*
sweet-smelling • *cottage gardens filled with sweet-smelling flowers and herbs*

sweet ❸ ADJECTIVE
pleasant-sounding and tuneful • *the sweet sounds of children's singing*
harmonious • *harmonious sounds*
mellow • *mellow background music*
melodious • *The melodious tones of the organ echoed around the great cathedral.*
musical • *He had a soft, musical voice.*
tuneful • *The band were noted for their tuneful backing vocals.*

MORE SYNONYMS
- dulcet
- euphonious

sweet ❹ NOUN
a sweet-tasting thing such as a toffee • *His sack was full of packets of sweets.*
candy (AMERICAN) • *We were sick after eating some syrupy candies she had made.*
confectionery • *The company specializes in selling confectionery from all over the world.*
lolly (AUSTRALIAN AND NEW ZEALAND) • *Avoid feeding him too many lollies.*
sweetie • *She presented him with a jar of his favourite sweeties as a thank-you.*

swerve VERB
to change direction suddenly to avoid hitting something • *He swerved to avoid a truck.*
swing • *The car swung off the road.*
turn • *He turned sharply to the left.*
veer • *The vehicle veered out of control.*

swift ADJECTIVE
happening or moving very quickly • *make a swift decision*
brisk • *walking at a brisk pace*
express • *a special express service*
fast • *The question is how fast the process will be.*
hurried • *a hurried breakfast*
prompt • *Prompt action is needed.*
quick • *The country has been developing at a very quick pace.*
rapid • *Will the Tunnel provide more rapid transport than ferries?*
speedy • *We wish Bill a speedy recovery.*

ANTONYM
- slow

symbol NOUN
a design or idea used to represent something • *the chemical symbol for mercury*
emblem • *His badge bore a small yellow hammer-and-sickle emblem.*
figure • *the figure of a five-pointed star*
logo • *the company's logo*
mark • *a mark of identification*
representation • *This rune is a representation of a spearhead.*
sign • *a multiplication sign*

a b c d e f g h i j k l m n o p q r **s** t u v w x y z

Can't find the word you're looking for? Try the index.

A B C D E F G H I J K L M N O P Q R S T U V W X Y Z

token • *He gave her a ring as a token of his love.*

sympathy NOUN

kindness and understanding towards someone in trouble • *My heartfelt sympathy goes out to all the relatives.*

compassion • *I was impressed by the compassion he showed for a helpless old woman.*

empathy • *They displayed an admirable understanding of the crime and empathy with the victim.*

pity • *He showed no pity for his victims.*

tenderness • *She smiled, politely, rather than with tenderness.*

understanding • *I'd like to thank you for your patience and understanding.*

system NOUN

an organized way of doing or arranging something • *the advantages of the new system over the old one*

arrangement • *an intricate arrangement of treadles, rods and cranks*

method • *the methods employed in the study*

procedure • *This is now the standard procedure.*

routine • *his daily routine*

structure • *the structure of local government*

technique • *a new technique for processing sound*

MORE SYNONYMS

● methodology
● modus operandi

Tt

tact NOUN
the ability not to offend people
• *He has handled the affair with
great tact.*
delicacy • *Both countries are
behaving with rare delicacy.*
diplomacy • *It took all Minnelli's
diplomacy to get him to return.*
discretion • *I appreciate your
discretion.*
sensitivity • *The police treated the
victims with great sensitivity.*

tactful ADJECTIVE
showing tact • *Sorry, that wasn't a
very tactful question.*
diplomatic • *She is very direct. I
tend to be more diplomatic.*
discreet • *They were gossipy and
not always discreet.*
sensitive • *his sensitive handling of
the situation*

ANTONYM
• tactless

take ❶ VERB
to require something • *He takes
three hours to get ready.*
demand • *The task of rebuilding
would demand much patience.*
require • *The race requires a lot of
stamina.*

take ❷ VERB
to carry something • *I'll take these
papers home and read them.*
bear (FORMAL) • *They bore the
hardwood box into the kitchen.*

bring • *He poured a brandy for
Dena and brought it to her.*
carry • *She carried the shopping
from the car.*
convey (FORMAL) • *The minibus
conveyed us to the city centre.*
ferry • *A plane arrives to ferry
guests to the island.*
fetch • *Sylvia fetched a towel from
the bathroom.*
transport • *They use tankers to
transport the oil to Los Angeles.*

take ❸ VERB
to lead someone somewhere • *She
took me to a Mexican restaurant.*
bring • *Come to my party and bring
a girl with you.*
conduct (FORMAL) • *He asked if he
might conduct us to the ball.*
escort • *I escorted him to the door.*
guide • *a young Egyptologist who
guided us through the tombs*
lead • *She confessed to the killing
and led police to his remains.*
usher • *I ushered him into the
office.*

take care of ❶ VERB
to look after someone or
something • *There was no-one to
take care of the children.*
care for • *They hired a nurse to
care for her.*
look after • *I love looking after the
children.*
mind • *Jim will mind the shop while
I'm away.*

Can't find the word you're looking for? Try the index.

nurse • *All the years he was sick, my mother had nursed him.*
protect • *He vowed to protect her all the days of her life.*
tend • *He tends the flower beds that he has planted.*
watch • *Are parents expected to watch their children 24 hours a day?*

ANTONYM
● neglect

take care of ❷ VERB
to deal with a problem, task, or situation • *"Do you need clean sheets?" "No, Mrs May took care of that."*
attend to • *We have business to attend to first.*
cope with • *A new system has been designed to cope with the increased demand.*
deal with • *the way that building societies deal with complaints*
handle • *She handled the president's travel arrangements during the campaign.*
manage • *He expects me to manage all the household expenses on very little.*
see to • *While Frank saw to the luggage, Sara took the children home.*

take in ❶ VERB
to deceive someone • *He was a real charmer who totally took me in.*
con (INFORMAL) • *The British public has been conned by the government.*
deceive • *He has deceived us all.*
dupe • *Some offenders dupe the psychologists who assess them.*
fool • *Art dealers fool a lot of people.*
mislead • *It appears we were misled by a professional con artist.*

trick • *He'll be upset when he finds out how you tricked him.*

take in ❷ VERB
to understand something • *She seemed to take in all he said.*
absorb • *It will take time for us to absorb the news.*
appreciate • *She never really appreciated the bitterness of the conflict.*
assimilate • *My mind could only assimilate one of these ideas at a time.*
comprehend • *He failed to comprehend the significance of this remark.*
digest • *They need time to digest the information they have learned.*
get • *You just don't get what I'm saying, do you?*
grasp • *The Government has not yet grasped the seriousness of the crisis.*
understand • *They are too young to understand what is going on.*

talent NOUN
a natural ability • *Both her children have a talent for music.*
ability • *Her drama teacher spotted her ability.*
aptitude • *Alan has no aptitude for music.*
capacity • *people's creative capacities*
flair • *a dentist with a flair for invention*
genius • *his genius for chess*
gift • *a gift for teaching*
knack • *He's got the knack of getting people to listen.*

talk ❶ VERB
to say things • *They were talking about American food.*
▷ see Word Study **say**, pages 699–702

talk ❷ NOUN

a conversation • *We had a long talk about her father.*
chat • *I had a chat with him.*
chatter • *idle chatter*
conversation • *We had a long conversation.*

talk ❸ NOUN

an informal speech • *a talk about AIDS*
address • *an address to the American people*
discourse • *a lengthy discourse on strategy*
lecture • *a series of lectures*
sermon • *a church sermon*
speech • *He delivered his speech in French.*

MORE SYNONYMS

- disquisition
- oration

talkative ADJECTIVE

talking a lot • *His eyes grew bright and he suddenly became very talkative.*
chatty • *She's quite a chatty person.*
communicative • *She has become a lot more communicative.*
long-winded • *I hope I'm not being too long-winded.*

tall ADJECTIVE

higher than average • *tall buildings*
high • *a high wall*
lanky • *He was six foot four, all lanky and leggy.*
lofty • *lofty ceilings*
soaring • *the soaring spires of churches like St Peter's*
towering • *towering cliffs of black granite*

ANTONYM

- short

tangle ❶ NOUN

a mass of long things knotted together • *a tangle of wires*
jumble • *a jumble of twisted tubes*
knot • *Her hair was full of knots.*
mass • *a flailing mass of arms and legs*
mat • *the thick mat of sandy hair on his chest*
muddle • *The back of the tapestry was a muddle of threads.*
web • *a thick web of fibres*

tangle ❷ VERB

to twist together or catch someone or something • *Dolphins can get tangled in fishing nets and drown.*
catch • *a fly caught in a spider's web*
jumble • *The wires were all jumbled together and tied in a knot.*
knot • *The kite strings had got knotted together.*
twist • *Her hands began to twist the handles of the bag.*

task NOUN

a job that you have to do • *Walker had the task of breaking the bad news.*
assignment • *written assignments and practical tests*
chore • *household chores*
duty • *I carried out my duties conscientiously.*
job • *He was given the job of tending the fire.*
mission • *Salisbury sent him on a diplomatic mission to North America.*
undertaking • *Organizing the show has been a massive undertaking.*

taste ❶ NOUN

the flavour of something • *I like the taste of wine.*

a b c d e f g h i j k l m n o p q r s **t** u v w x y z

Can't find the word you're looking for? Try the index.

flavour • *a crumbly texture with a strong flavour*
tang • *the tang of lemon*

taste ❷ NOUN
a small amount of food or drink • *He swirled the brandy around before taking another small taste.*
bite • *Chew each mouthful fully before the next bite.*
mouthful • *She gulped down a mouthful of coffee.*
sip • *a sip of wine*

taste ❸ NOUN
a liking for something • *a taste for adventure*
appetite • *his appetite for success*
fondness • *I've always had a fondness for jewels.*
liking • *She had a liking for good clothes.*
penchant (FORMAL) • *He had a penchant for playing jokes on people.*

MORE SYNONYMS
● partiality
● predilection

tasteless ❶ ADJECTIVE
having little flavour • *The fish was mushy and tasteless.*
bland • *It tasted bland, like warmed cardboard.*
insipid • *a rather insipid meal*

ANTONYM
● tasty

tasteless ❷ ADJECTIVE
vulgar and unattractive • *a house crammed with tasteless ornaments*
flashy • *a flashy sports car*
garish • *garish bright red boots*
gaudy • *her gaudy floral hat*
tacky (INFORMAL) • *tacky holiday souvenirs*
tawdry • *a tawdry seaside town*

vulgar • *a very vulgar house*

ANTONYM
● tasteful

tasty ADJECTIVE
having a pleasant flavour • *The food was very tasty.*
appetizing • *a choice of appetizing dishes*
delicious • *a wide selection of delicious desserts*
lekker (SOUTH AFRICAN; SLANG) • *a lekker meal*
luscious • *luscious fruit*
palatable • *some very palatable wines*

MORE SYNONYMS
● flavourful
● flavoursome

ANTONYM
● tasteless

tax ❶ NOUN
money paid to the government • *the tax on new cars*
duty • *customs duties*
excise • *These products are excused VAT and excise.*
levy (FORMAL) • *an annual motorway levy on all drivers*
tariff • *America wants to eliminate tariffs on items such as electronics.*

tax ❷ VERB
to make heavy demands on someone • *They must be told not to tax your patience.*
drain • *conflicts that drain your energy*
exhaust • *She has exhausted my sympathy.*
sap • *The illness sapped his strength.*
strain • *The volume of flights is straining the air traffic control system.*

Can't find the word you're looking for? Try the index.

A B C D E F G H I J K L M N O P Q R S T U V W X Y Z

stretch • *The drought there is stretching American resources to their limits.*

teach VERB

to instruct someone how to do something • *She taught Julie to read.*
coach • *He coached the basketball team.*
drill • *He drills the choir to a high standard.*
educate • *He was educated at Haslingden Grammar School.*
instruct • *He instructed family members in nursing techniques.*
school • *He had been schooled to take over the family business.*
train • *They train teachers in counselling skills.*
tutor • *She was tutored at home by her parents.*

teacher NOUN

someone who teaches something • *a geography teacher*
coach • *her drama coach*
don • *a Cambridge don*
guru • *a religious guru*
instructor • *a driving instructor*
lecturer • *a lecturer in law*
master • *a retired maths master*
mistress • *like a school mistress presiding over an exam*
professor • *a professor of economics*
tutor • *He surprised his tutors by failing the exam.*

MORE SYNONYMS

● educator
● pedagogue

team ❶ NOUN

a group of people • *the football team*
band • *a band of rebels*

crew • *the ship's crew*
gang • *a gang of workmen*
group • *The students work in groups.*
side • *Italy were definitely the better side.*
squad • *the England under-21 squad*
troupe • *troupes of travelling actors*

team ❷ VERB

to work together • *A friend suggested that we team up for a working holiday.*
collaborate • *The two men met and agreed to collaborate.*
cooperate • *They would cooperate in raising their child.*
join forces • *The groups joined forces to fight against the ban.*
link up • *the first time the two armies have linked up*
pair up • *Men and teenage girls pair up to dance.*
unite • *The two parties have been trying to unite.*
work together • *We have always wanted to work together.*

tear ❶ NOUN

a hole in something • *I peered through a tear in the curtains.*
hole • *the hole in my shoe*
ladder • *There was a ladder in her tights.*
rip • *the rip in her new dress*
rupture • *a rupture in the valve*
scratch • *I pointed to a number of scratches in the tile floor.*
split • *the split in his trousers*

tear ❷ VERB

to make a hole in something • *She nearly tore my overcoat.*
ladder • *after she laddered her tights*

a
b
c
d
e
f
g
h
i
j
k
l
m
n
o
p
q
r
s
t
u
v
w
x
y
z

Can't find the word you're looking for? Try the index.

rip • *I tried not to rip the paper.*
rupture • *a ruptured appendix*
scratch • *Knives will scratch the worktop.*
shred • *They may be shredding documents.*
split • *I'd split my trousers.*

MORE SYNONYMS
- rend
- sunder

tear ❸ VERB
to go somewhere in a hurry • *He tore through busy streets in a high-speed chase.*
charge • *He charged through the door.*
dart • *Ingrid darted across the deserted street.*
dash • *He dashed upstairs.*
fly • *She flew to their bedsides when they were ill.*
race • *He raced across town.*
shoot • *Another car shot out of a junction.*
speed • *A low shot sped past Lukic.*
zoom • *We zoomed through the gallery.*

MORE SYNONYMS
- bolt
- career

tease VERB
to make fun of someone • *He used to tease me about wanting to act.*
make fun of • *The kids at school made fun of me and my Cockney accent.*
mock • *Don't mock me!*
needle (INFORMAL) • *He used to enjoy needling people.*
taunt • *Other youths taunted him about his clothes.*

tell ❶ VERB
to let someone know something

• *They told us the dreadful news.*
inform • *My daughter informed me that she was pregnant.*
notify • *We have notified the police.*

MORE SYNONYMS
- acquaint
- apprise

tell ❷ VERB
to give someone an order • *A passer-by told the driver to move his car.*
command • *He commanded his troops to attack.*
direct (FORMAL) • *They have been directed to give special attention to the problem.*
instruct • *The family has instructed solicitors to sue the company.*
order • *He ordered his men to cease firing.*

MORE SYNONYMS
- call upon
- enjoin

tell ❸ VERB
to judge something correctly • *I could tell he was scared.*
discern • *It was hard to discern why this was happening.*
see • *I could see she was lonely.*

temporary ADJECTIVE
lasting a short time • *a temporary loss of memory*
ephemeral • *a reminder that earthly pleasures are ephemeral*
fleeting • *a fleeting glimpse*
interim • *an interim measure*
momentary • *a momentary lapse*
passing • *a passing phase*
provisional • *a provisional coalition government*
transient • *Modelling is a transient career.*
transitory • *the transitory nature of political success*

MORE SYNONYMS
- impermanent
- short-lived

ANTONYM
- permanent

tempt VERB
to persuade someone to do something • *Children not attending schools may be tempted into crime.*
entice • *She resisted attempts to entice her into politics.*
lure • *The company aims to lure smokers back to cigarettes.*
seduce • *We are seduced into buying all these items.*

tend ❶ VERB
to happen usually or often • *I tend to forget things.*
be apt • *She was apt to raise her voice.*
be inclined • *He was inclined to self-pity.*
be liable • *equipment that is liable to break*
be prone • *We know males are more prone to violence.*
have a tendency • *Shetland jumpers have a tendency to be annoyingly itchy.*

tend ❷ VERB
to look after someone or something • *the way we tend our cattle*
care for • *They hired a nurse to care for her.*
look after • *I love looking after the children.*
nurse • *In hospital they nursed me back to health.*
take care of • *There was no one else to take care of the animals.*

tendency NOUN
behaviour that happens very often

• *a tendency to be critical*
inclination • *his artistic inclinations*
leaning • *their socialist leanings*
propensity • *his propensity for violence*

MORE SYNONYMS
- predisposition
- proclivity
- proneness

tender ❶ ADJECTIVE
showing gentle and caring feelings • *tender, loving care*
affectionate • *She gave him an affectionate smile.*
caring • *He is a lovely boy, and very caring.*
compassionate • *a deeply compassionate film*
gentle • *Michael's voice was gentle and consoling.*
kind • *She is warmhearted and kind to everyone and everything.*
loving • *He was a most loving husband and father.*
sensitive • *He was always so sensitive.*
warm • *She was a very warm person.*

ANTONYM
- tough

tender ❷ ADJECTIVE
painful and sore • *My tummy felt very tender.*
aching • *The weary holidaymakers soothed their aching feet in the sea.*
bruised • *bruised legs*
inflamed • *Her eyes were inflamed.*
painful • *Her glands were swollen and painful.*
raw • *the drag of the rope against the raw flesh of my shoulders*
sensitive • *Ouch! I'm sorry, my lip*

a b c d e f g h i j k l m n o p q r s **t** u v w x y z

Can't find the word you're looking for? Try the index.

A B C D E F G H I J K L M N O P Q R S **T** U V W X Y Z

is still a bit sensitive.
sore • *My chest is still sore from the surgery.*

tender ❸ VERB

to offer something such as an apology or resignation • *She tendered her resignation.*
hand in • *All the opposition members have handed in their resignation.*
offer • *May I offer my sincere condolences?*

tender ❹ NOUN

a proposal to provide something at a price • *Builders will be asked to submit a tender for the work.*
bid • *Sydney's successful bid for the 2000 Olympic Games*
estimate • *The firm is preparing an estimate for the work.*
package • *We opted for the package submitted by the existing service provider.*
submission • *A written submission has to be prepared.*

tense ❶ ADJECTIVE

nervous and unable to relax • *Never had she seen him so tense.*
anxious • *She had become very anxious and alarmed.*
edgy • *She was nervous and edgy, still chain-smoking.*
jittery (INFORMAL) • *Investors have become jittery about the country's economy.*
jumpy • *I told myself not to be so jumpy.*
nervous • *It has made me very nervous about going out.*
uptight (INFORMAL) • *Penny never got uptight about exams.*

ANTONYM
● calm

tense ❷ ADJECTIVE

causing anxiety • *the tense atmosphere at the talks*
anxious • *They had to wait ten anxious days.*
nerve-racking • *It was more nerve-racking than taking a World Cup penalty.*
stressful • *a stressful job*

tense ❸ ADJECTIVE

having tight muscles • *She lay, eyes shut, body tense.*
rigid • *Andrew went rigid whenever he saw a dog.*
strained • *His shoulders were strained with effort.*
taut • *when muscles are taut or cold*
tight • *It is better to stretch the tight muscles first.*

ANTONYM
● relaxed

term ❶ NOUN

a fixed period of time • *a 12 month term of service*
period • *for a limited period only*
session • *The parliamentary session ends on October 4th.*
spell • *a six-month spell of practical experience*
stretch • *He did an 18-month stretch in prison.*
time • *He served the time of his contract and then left the company.*

MORE SYNONYMS
● duration
● incumbency

term ❷ NOUN

a name or word for a particular thing • *the medical term for a heart attack*
designation • *Level Four Alert is a designation reserved for very serious incidents.*

Can't find the word you're looking for? Try the index.

expression • *She used some remarkably coarse expressions.*
name • *The correct name for this condition is bovine spongiform encephalopathy.*
word • *The word ginseng comes from the Chinese "Shen-seng".*

terms PLURAL NOUN

conditions that have been agreed • *the terms of the merger agreement*
conditions • *They may be breaching the conditions of their contract.*
provisions • *the provisions of the Amsterdam treaty*
proviso • *He left me the house with the proviso that it had to stay in the family.*
stipulations • *He left, violating the stipulations of his parole.*

terrible ❶ ADJECTIVE

serious and unpleasant • *a terrible illness*
appalling • *an appalling headache*
awful • *an awful crime*
desperate • *a desperate situation*
dreadful • *a dreadful mistake*
frightful (OLD-FASHIONED) • *He got himself into a frightful muddle.*
horrendous • *horrendous injuries*
horrible • *a horrible mess*
horrid (OLD-FASHIONED) • *What a horrid smell!*
rotten • *What rotten luck!*

terrible ❷ ADJECTIVE

of very poor quality • *Paddy's terrible haircut*
abysmal • *The standard of play was abysmal.*
appalling • *Her singing is appalling.*
awful • *Jeans look awful on me.*
dire • *Most of the poems were dire.*
dreadful • *My financial situation*

is dreadful.
horrible • *a horrible meal*
rotten • *I think it's a rotten idea.*

ANTONYM
● excellent

territory NOUN

the land that a person or country controls • *gangs fighting to defend their territories*
area • *They claim that the entire area belongs to Syria.*
country • *He is an ambassador to a foreign country.*
district • *Stick to your own district and stay out of ours.*
domain • *He surveyed his domain from the roof of the castle.*
dominion • *men who ruled their dominions with ruthless efficiency*
land • *New mines were discovered on what had been Apache land.*
province • *debates about the political future of their province*
state • *This state remains suspended from the Commonwealth.*

test ❶ VERB

to find out what something is like • *travelling to Holland to test a British-built boat*
assess • *The test was to assess aptitude rather than academic achievement.*
check • *It's worth checking each item for obvious flaws.*
try • *Howard wanted me to try the wine.*
try out • *London Transport hopes to try out the system in September.*

test ❷ NOUN

an attempt to test something • *the banning of nuclear tests*
assessment • *He was remanded for assessment by doctors.*

a b c d e f g h i j k l m n o p q r s **t** u v w x y z

check • *regular checks on his blood pressure*
trial • *clinical trials*

texture NOUN

the way that something feels • *Her skin is pale, the texture of fine wax.*
consistency • *Mix the dough to the right consistency.*
feel • *Linen raincoats have a crisp, papery feel.*

theft NOUN

the crime of stealing • *the theft of classified documents*
robbery • *The man was serving a sentence for robbery.*
stealing • *She was jailed for six months for stealing.*
thieving • *an ex-con who says he's given up thieving*

MORE SYNONYMS
○ larceny
○ pilfering

theory NOUN

an idea that explains something • *Darwin's theory of evolution*
conjecture • *That was a conjecture, not a fact.*
hypothesis • *Different hypotheses have been put forward.*
supposition • *As with many such suppositions, no one had ever tested it.*
surmise (FORMAL) • *His surmise proved correct.*

therefore ADVERB

as a result • *Muscles need lots of fuel and therefore burn lots of calories.*
as a result • *I slept in, and, as a result, I was late for work.*
consequently • *He's more experienced, and consequently earns a higher salary.*

for that reason • *I'd never met my in-laws before. For that reason, I was a little nervous.*
hence (FORMAL) • *These products are all natural, and hence, better for you.*
so • *I was worried about her, so I phoned to check how she was.*
thus • *His men were getting tired, and thus, careless.*

thesaurus NOUN

PARTS OF A DICTIONARY OR THESAURUS

antonym	homophone
definition	pronunciation
entry	root word
example	synonym
homonym	word derivation

thick ❶ ADJECTIVE

measuring a large distance from side to side • *a thick stone wall*
fat • *a fat book*
wide • *a desk that was almost as wide as the room*

ANTONYM
○ thin

thick ❷ ADJECTIVE

containing little water • *thick soup*
clotted • *clotted cream*
concentrated • *a glass of concentrated orange juice*
condensed • *tins of condensed milk*

ANTONYM
○ watery

thick ❸ ADJECTIVE

grouped closely together • *thick dark hair*
bristling • *a bristling moustache*
dense • *a large dense forest*
lush • *the lush green meadows*

Can't find the word you're looking for? Try the index.

A B C D E F G H I J K L M N O P Q R S **T** U V W X Y Z

luxuriant • *the luxuriant foliage of Young Island*

ANTONYM
- sparse

thicken VERB
to become thicker • *The clouds thickened.*
clot • *The patient's blood refused to clot.*
condense • *Water vapour condenses to form clouds.*
congeal • *The blood had started to congeal.*
set • *as the jelly starts to set*

MORE SYNONYMS
- coagulate
- jell

ANTONYM
- thin

thief NOUN
someone who steals something
• *a car thief*
burglar • *Burglars broke into their home.*
crook (INFORMAL) • *a petty crook*
mugger (INFORMAL) • *after being threatened by a mugger*
pickpocket • *a gang of pickpockets*
robber • *armed robbers*
shoplifter • *a persistent shoplifter*

MORE SYNONYMS
- housebreaker
- pilferer

thin ❶ ADJECTIVE
measuring a small distance from side to side • *The material was too thin.*
fine • *the fine hairs on her arms*
narrow • *a narrow strip of land*
slim • *a slim volume of verse*

ANTONYM
- thick

thin ❷ ADJECTIVE
not carrying a lot of fat • *a tall, thin man with grey hair*
▷ *see Word Study thin, page 707*

ANTONYM
- fat

thin ❸ ADJECTIVE
containing a lot of water • *thin soup*
dilute or **diluted** • *a dilute solution of bleach*
runny • *a runny soft cheese*
watery • *watery beer*
weak • *a cup of weak tea*

ANTONYM
- thick

thing NOUN
a physical object • *What's that thing doing here?*
article • *household articles*
object • *everyday objects such as wooden spoons*

things PLURAL NOUN
someone's clothes or belongings
• *Sara told him to take all his things with him.*
belongings • *He was identified only by his personal belongings.*
effects • *His daughters were collecting his effects.*
gear • *They helped us put our gear back into the van.*
possessions • *People had lost all their possessions.*
stuff • *Where have you put all your stuff?*

think ❶ VERB
to consider something • *Let's think what we can do next.*
consider • *The government is being asked to consider the plan.*

a b c d e f g h i j k l m n o p q r s **t** u v w x y z

A
B
C
D
E
F
G
H
I
J
K
L
M
N
O
P
Q
R
S
T
U
V
W
X
Y
Z

contemplate • *He cried as he contemplated his future.*
deliberate • *She deliberated over the decision for a good few years.*
meditate • *He meditated on the problem.*
mull over • *I'll leave you alone so you can mull it over.*
muse (LITERARY) • *Many of the papers muse on the fate of the President.*
ponder • *I'm continually pondering how to improve the team.*
reflect • *I reflected on the child's future.*

MORE SYNONYMS
- cogitate
- ruminate

think ❷ VERB
to believe something • *I think she has a secret boyfriend.*
believe • *Experts believe that the drought will be extensive.*
consider • *He considers that this is the worst recession this century.*
deem (FORMAL) • *Many people have ideas that their society deems to be dangerous.*
hold • *The theory holds that minor events are the trigger for larger events.*
imagine • *I imagine he was just showing off.*
judge • *He judged that this was the moment to say what had to be said.*
reckon • *Toni reckoned that it must be about three o'clock.*

thorough ADJECTIVE
careful and complete • *a thorough examination*
complete • *a complete overhaul of the engine*
comprehensive • *a comprehensive guide to the region*

exhaustive • *exhaustive enquiries*
full • *Mr Primakov gave a full account of his meeting with the President.*
intensive • *four weeks of intensive study*
meticulous • *A happy wedding day requires meticulous planning.*
painstaking • *a painstaking search*
scrupulous • *Observe scrupulous hygiene when preparing and cooking food.*

MORE SYNONYMS
- all-embracing
- in-depth

thought ❶ NOUN
an idea or opinion • *his thoughts on love*
idea • *his ideas about democracy*
notion • *We each have a notion of what kind of person we'd like to be.*
opinion • *most of those who expressed an opinion*
view • *Make your views known to your MP.*

thought ❷ NOUN
the activity of thinking • *After much thought I decided to end my marriage.*
consideration • *There should be careful consideration of the BBC's future role.*
contemplation • *He was lost in contemplation of the landscape.*
deliberation • *the result of lengthy deliberation*
meditation • *He stared at the floor, lost in meditation.*
reflection • *after days of reflection*
thinking • *This is definitely a time for decisive action and quick thinking.*

Can't find the word you're looking for? Try the index.

MORE SYNONYMS
- cogitation
- introspection
- rumination

thoughtful ❶ ADJECTIVE
quiet and serious • *He was looking very thoughtful.*
contemplative • *a quiet, contemplative sort of chap*
pensive • *He looked unusually pensive before the start.*
reflective • *I walked on in a reflective mood.*

MORE SYNONYMS
- introspective
- meditative
- ruminative

thoughtful ❷ ADJECTIVE
showing consideration for others • *a thoughtful and caring man*
attentive • *an attentive husband*
caring • *a caring son*
considerate • *the most considerate man I've ever known*
kind • *She is warmhearted and kind to everyone.*

MORE SYNONYMS
- solicitous
- unselfish

ANTONYM
- thoughtless

thoughtless ADJECTIVE
showing a lack of consideration • *It was thoughtless of her to mention it.*
insensitive • *My husband is very insensitive about my problem.*
tactless • *a tactless remark*

MORE SYNONYMS
- inconsiderate
- undiplomatic

ANTONYM
- thoughtful

threat ❶ NOUN
a statement that someone will harm you • *death threats*
menace • *demanding money with menaces*
threatening remark • *He was overheard making threatening remarks to the couple.*

threat ❷ NOUN
something that seems likely to harm you • *the threat of tropical storms*
hazard • *a health hazard*
menace • *a menace to the public*
risk • *a fire risk*

threaten ❶ VERB
to promise to do something bad • *He threatened her with a knife.*
make threats to • *all the threats he'd made to harm her*
menace • *She's being menaced by her sister's latest boyfriend.*

threaten ❷ VERB
to be likely to cause harm • *The newcomers threaten the livelihood of the workers.*
endanger • *Toxic waste could endanger lives.*
jeopardize • *He has jeopardized the future of his government.*
put at risk • *If they have the virus, they are putting patients at risk.*
put in jeopardy • *A series of setbacks have put the whole project in jeopardy.*

thrifty ADJECTIVE
careful not to waste money or resources • *Britain become a nation of thrifty consumers and bargain hunters.*
careful • *He's very careful with his money.*

a
b
c
d
e
f
g
h
i
j
k
l
m
n
o
p
q
r
s
t
u
v
w
x
y
z

Can't find the word you're looking for? Try the index.

economical • *a very economical way to travel*
frugal • *a frugal lifestyle*
prudent • *the need for a much more prudent use of energy*

thrill ❶ NOUN
a feeling of excitement • *the thrill of waking up on Christmas morning*
high (INFORMAL) • *the high of a win over New Zealand*
kick (INFORMAL) • *I got a kick out of seeing my name in print.*

thrill ❷ VERB
to cause a feeling of excitement • *It thrilled me to see her looking so happy.*
excite • *I only take on work that excites me.*
give a kick (INFORMAL) • *It gave me a kick to actually meet her.*

thrive VERB
to be successful • *His company continues to thrive.*
do well • *Connie did well at school.*
flourish • *Racism and crime still flourish in the ghetto.*
prosper • *His team have always prospered in cup competitions.*

throw VERB
to make something move through the air • *throwing a tennis ball against a wall*
cast • *He cast the stone away.*
chuck (INFORMAL) • *He chucked the paper in the bin.*
fling • *Peter flung his shoes into the corner.*
hurl • *Groups of angry youths hurled stones at police.*
lob • *Thugs lobbed a grenade into the crowd.*
pitch • *Simon pitched the empty bottle into the lake.*

sling • *He took off his anorak and slung it into the back seat.*
toss • *She tossed her suitcase onto one of the beds.*

thug NOUN
a very violent person • *a gang of armed thugs*
bandit • *terrorist acts carried out by bandits*
hooligan • *severe measures against soccer hooligans*
tough • *The neighbourhood toughs beat them both up.*
tsotsi (SOUTH AFRICAN) • *Many are too terrified of local tsotsis to protest.*

tidy ❶ ADJECTIVE
arranged in an orderly way • *a tidy desk*
neat • *She put her clothes in a neat pile.*
orderly • *a beautiful, clean and orderly city*

MORE SYNONYMS
● shipshape
● spick-and-span

ANTONYM
● untidy

tidy ❷ VERB
to make something neat • *He tidied his garage.*
spruce up • *Many buildings have been spruced up.*
straighten • *straightening cushions and organizing magazines*

ANTONYM
● mess up

tie ❶ VERB
to fasten something • *They tied the ends of the bag securely.*
bind • *Bind the ends of the cord together with thread.*
fasten • *instructions on how to*

fasten the strap to the box
knot • *He knotted the laces securely together.*
lash • *The shelter is built by lashing poles together.*
rope • *I roped myself to the chimney.*
secure • *He secured the canvas straps as tight as they would go.*
tether • *tethering his horse to a tree*
truss • *She trussed him quickly with a stolen bandage.*

ANTONYM
● untie

tie ❷ VERB
to have the same score • *Rafferty tied with Nobilo.*
be level • *At the end of 90 minutes the teams were level.*
draw • *Holland and Ireland drew 1-1.*

tie ❸ NOUN
a connection with something • *I had very close ties with the family.*
affiliation • *They asked her what her political affiliations were.*
affinity • *He has a close affinity with the landscape.*
bond • *The experience created a special bond between us.*
connection • *The police say he had no connection with the security forces.*
relationship • *family relationships*

tight ❶ ADJECTIVE
fitting closely • *The shoes are too tight.*
constricted • *His throat began to feel swollen and constricted.*
cramped • *families living in cramped conditions*
snug • *a snug black T-shirt*

ANTONYM
● loose

tight ❷ ADJECTIVE
firmly fastened • *a tight knot*
firm • *He managed to get a firm grip of it.*
secure • *Check joints are secure and the wood is sound.*

tight ❸ ADJECTIVE
not slack or relaxed • *Pull the elastic tight.*
rigid • *I went rigid with shock.*
taut • *The clothes line is pulled taut and secured.*
tense • *A bath can relax tense muscles.*

ANTONYM
● slack

tilt ❶ VERB
to raise one end of something • *Leonard tilted his chair back on two legs.*
incline • *Jack inclined his head.*
lean • *Lean the plants against a wall.*
slant • *The floor slanted down to the window.*
slope • *The bank sloped down sharply to the river.*
tip • *She had to tip her head back to see him.*

MORE SYNONYMS
● cant
● list

tilt ❷ NOUN
a raised position • *the tilt of the earth's axis*
angle • *The boat is now leaning at a 30 degree angle.*
gradient • *a gradient of 1 in 3*
incline • *at the edge of a steep incline*

a
b
c
d
e
f
g
h
i
j
k
l
m
n
o
p
q
r
s
t
u
v
w
x
y
z

Can't find the word you're looking for? Try the index.

A
B
C
D
E
F
G
H
I
J
K
L
M
N
O
P
Q
R
S
T
U
V
W
X
Y
Z

slant • *The house is on a slant.*
slope • *The street must have been on a slope.*

MORE SYNONYMS
● camber
● list
● pitch

time ❶ NOUN

a particular period • *I enjoyed my time in Durham.*
interval • *a long interval of silence*
period • *a period of calm*
spell • *a brief spell teaching*
stretch • *an 18-month stretch in the army*
while • *They walked on in silence for a while.*

RELATED WORD
● ADJECTIVE: temporal

time ❷ VERB

to plan when something will happen • *We had timed our visit for March 7.*
schedule • *The space shuttle had been scheduled to blast off at 04:38.*
set • *A court hearing has been set for December 16.*

timid ADJECTIVE

lacking courage or confidence • *a timid child*
bashful • *Offstage, he is bashful and awkward.*
cowardly • *I was too cowardly to complain.*
diffident • *Helen was diffident and reserved.*
nervous • *a very nervous woman*
shy • *a shy, quiet-spoken girl*

MORE SYNONYMS
● faint-hearted
● pusillanimous
● timorous

ANTONYM
● bold

tiny ADJECTIVE

very small • *The living room is tiny.*
diminutive • *a diminutive figure standing at the entrance*
microscopic • *a microscopic amount of the substance*
miniature • *He looked like a miniature version of his brother.*
minute • *Only a minute amount is needed.*
negligible • *The pay that the soldiers received was negligible.*
wee (SCOTTISH) • *a wee boy*

MORE SYNONYMS
● infinitesimal
● Lilliputian

ANTONYM
● huge

tire VERB

to use a lot of energy • *If driving tires you, take the train.*
drain • *My emotional turmoil had drained me.*
exhaust • *Walking in deep snow had totally exhausted him.*
fatigue • *He is easily fatigued.*

MORE SYNONYMS
● enervate
● wear out
● weary

tired ADJECTIVE

having little energy • *She was too tired to take a shower.*
drained • *as United stalked off, stunned and drained*
drowsy • *He felt pleasantly drowsy.*
exhausted • *She was too exhausted and distressed to talk.*
fatigued • *Winter weather can leave you feeling fatigued.*

Can't find the word you're looking for? Try the index.

sleepy • *I was beginning to feel sleepy.*
tuckered out (AUSTRALIAN AND NEW ZEALAND; INFORMAL) • *You must be tuckered out after that bus trip.*
weary • *a weary traveller*
worn out • *He's just worn out after the drive.*

together ❶ ADVERB
with other people • *We went on long bicycle rides together.*
collectively • *The Cabinet is collectively responsible for policy.*
en masse • *The people marched en masse.*
in unison • *Michael and the landlady nodded in unison.*
jointly • *an agency jointly run by New York and New Jersey*
shoulder to shoulder • *They could fight shoulder to shoulder against a common enemy.*
side by side • *areas where different nationalities live side by side*

together ❷ ADVERB
at the same time • *Three horses crossed the finish line together.*
as one • *The 40,000 crowd rose as one.*
at once • *You can't do two things at once.*
concurrently • *There were three races running concurrently.*
simultaneously • *The two guns fired almost simultaneously.*
with one accord • *With one accord they turned and walked back.*

tolerable ❶ ADJECTIVE
able to be tolerated • *The pain was tolerable.*
acceptable • *a mutually acceptable new contract*

bearable • *A cool breeze made the heat bearable.*

ANTONYM
● unbearable

tolerable ❷ ADJECTIVE
fairly satisfactory • *a tolerable salary*
acceptable • *We've made an acceptable start.*
adequate • *The level of service was adequate.*
okay or **OK** (INFORMAL) • *For a fashionable restaurant like this the prices are okay.*
passable • *Ms Campbell speaks passable French.*
reasonable • *able to make a reasonable living from his writing*
so-so (INFORMAL) • *Their lunch was only so-so.*

tolerant ADJECTIVE
accepting of different views and behaviour • *more tolerant attitudes to unmarried couples having children*
broad-minded • *a very fair and broad-minded man*
liberal • *She is known to have liberal views on divorce.*
open-minded • *I am very open-minded about that question.*
understanding • *Fortunately for John, he had an understanding wife.*

MORE SYNONYMS
● forbearing
● latitudinarian

ANTONYM
● narrow-minded

tolerate ❶ VERB
to accept something you disagree with • *We will not tolerate such behaviour.*

Can't find the word you're looking for? Try the index.

A
B
C
D
E
F
G
H
I
J
K
L
M
N
O
P
Q
R
S
T
U
V
W
X
Y
Z

accept • *Urban dwellers often accept noise as part of city life.*
put up with • *You're late again and I won't put up with it.*

tolerate ② VERB
to accept something unpleasant • *She can no longer tolerate the position that she's in.*
bear • *He can't bear to talk about it.*
endure • *unable to endure the pain*
stand • *He can't stand me smoking.*

tomb NOUN
a burial chamber • *Carter discovered Tutankhamun's tomb.*
grave • *They used to visit her grave twice a year.*
mausoleum • *the elaborate mausoleums of the Paris cemetery*
sarcophagus • *an Egyptian sarcophagus*
sepulchre (LITERARY) • *the ornate lid of the sepulchre*
vault • *the family vault*

too ① ADVERB
also or as well • *You were there too.*
as well • *She published historical novels as well.*
besides • *You get to take lots of samples home as well.*
in addition • *There are, in addition, other objections to the plan.*
into the bargain • *The machine can play CDs into the bargain.*
likewise • *She sat down and he did likewise.*
moreover • *He didn't know, and moreover, he didn't care.*

too ② ADVERB
more than a desirable or acceptable amount • *You've had too many late nights.*

excessively • *He had an excessively protective mother.*
over- • *I didn't want to seem over-eager.*
overly • *Most people consider him to be overly ambitious.*
unduly • *She's unduly concerned with what people think of her.*
unreasonably • *These prices seem unreasonably high to me.*

tool NOUN
a hand-held instrument for doing a job • *The best tool for the purpose is a pair of shears.*
implement • *knives and other useful implements*
instrument • *instruments for cleaning and polishing teeth*
utensil • *cooking utensils*

top ① NOUN
the highest part of something • *I waited at the top of the stairs.*
apex • *at the very apex of the pyramid*
brow • *the brow of the hill*
crest • *the crest of the wave*
crown • *the crown of the head*
culmination • *the culmination of his career*
head • *A different name was placed at the head of the chart.*
height • *at the height of his success*
high point • *the high point of his movie career*
peak • *at the peak of the morning rush hour*
pinnacle • *the pinnacle of sporting achievement*
ridge • *He died after falling from a ridge on Mount Snowdon.*
summit • *the summit of the mountain*
zenith (LITERARY) • *His career is now at its zenith.*

Can't find the word you're looking for? Try the index.

MORE SYNONYMS
- acme
- apex
- apogee

ANTONYM
- bottom

top ❷ NOUN
the lid of a container • *a bottle top*
cap • *She unscrewed the cap of her water bottle.*
lid • *the lid of the jar*
stopper • *a scent bottle with a stopper in blue frosted glass*

top ❸ ADJECTIVE
being the best of its kind • *He was the top student in physics.*
best • *the best pupil of his year*
chief • *one of the world's chief nuclear scientists*
elite • *the elite troops of the presidential bodyguard*
foremost • *the foremost urban painter of his age*
head • *He was head boy when he was at school.*
highest • *He achieved one of the highest positions in the land.*
lead • *She has landed the lead role in a major film.*
leading • *a leading member of the community*
pre-eminent • *a pre-eminent political figure*
premier • *the country's premier theatre company*
prime • *The store will be built in a prime location.*
principal • *the principal singer with the Royal Opera House*

top ❹ VERB
to be greater than something • *The temperature topped 90 degrees.*
cap • *He capped his display with two fine goals.*
exceed • *Its research budget exceeds $700 million a year.*
go beyond • *This goes beyond anything I've ever attempted before.*
outstrip • *Demand is outstripping supply.*
surpass • *He has surpassed the record of nine wins in one season.*

top ❺ VERB
to be better than someone or something • *You'll never manage to top that story.*
beat • *Nothing beats a nice, long bath at the end of a day.*
better • *As an account of adolescence, this novel cannot be bettered.*
eclipse • *Nothing is going to eclipse winning the Olympic title.*
improve • *We need to improve on our performance against France.*
outdo • *Both sides are trying to outdo each other.*
surpass • *He was determined to surpass the achievements of his brothers.*

total ❶ NOUN
several things added together • *The companies have a total of 1776 employees.*
aggregate • *three successive defeats by an aggregate of 12 goals*
sum • *the sum of all the angles*
whole • *taken as a percentage of the whole*

total ❷ ADJECTIVE
complete in all its parts • *a total failure*
absolute • *absolute beginners*
complete • *a complete mess*
out-and-out • *an out-and-out lie*
outright • *an outright rejection of the deal*

a
b
c
d
e
f
g
h
i
j
k
l
m
n
o
p
q
r
s
t
u
v
w
x
y
z

Can't find the word you're looking for? Try the index.

unconditional • *unconditional surrender*
undivided • *You have my undivided attention.*
unmitigated • *an unmitigated failure*
unqualified • *an unqualified success*
utter • *utter nonsense*

MORE SYNONYMS
● all-out
● thoroughgoing

total ❸ VERB
to reach the sum of • *Their debts totalled over 300,000 dollars.*
add up to • *Profits can add up to millions of dollars.*
amount to • *Spending on sports-related items amounted to £9.75 billion.*
come to • *That comes to over a thousand pounds.*

touch ❶ VERB
to put your hand on something • *Don't touch that dial.*
feel • *The doctor felt his head.*
finger • *He fingered the few coins in his pocket.*
handle • *Wear rubber gloves when handling cat litter.*

touch ❷ VERB
to come into contact with • *Annie lowered her legs until her feet touched the floor.*
brush • *Something brushed against her leg.*
graze • *A bullet had grazed his arm.*
meet • *when the wheels meet the ground*

RELATED WORD
● ADJECTIVE: tactile

touch ❸ VERB
to emotionally affect someone • *I was touched by his kindness.*
affect • *Jazza was badly affected by his divorce.*
move • *These stories surprised and moved me.*
stir • *She stirred something very deep in me.*

touching ADJECTIVE
causing sadness or sympathy • *a touching tale*
affecting (LITERARY) • *an affecting memorial to Countess Rachel*
moving • *It was a moving moment for Marianne.*
poignant • *a poignant love story*

touchy ADJECTIVE
easily upset • *She is very touchy about her past.*
easily offended • *viewers who are easily offended*
sensitive • *Young people are very sensitive about their appearance.*
toey (AUSTRALIAN AND NEW ZEALAND; SLANG) • *Don't be so toey.*

MORE SYNONYMS
● oversensitive
● thin-skinned

tough ❶ ADJECTIVE
able to put up with hardship • *She is tough and ambitious.*
hardened • *hardened criminals*
hardy • *a hardy race of pioneers*
resilient • *a good soldier, calm and resilient*
robust • *Perhaps men are more robust than women?*
rugged • *Rugged individualism forged America's frontier society.*
strong • *Eventually I felt strong enough to look at him.*

Can't find the word you're looking for? Try the index.

tough ❷ ADJECTIVE
difficult to break or damage
• beans with a rather tough outer skin
durable • Fine bone china is both strong and durable.
hard-wearing • hard-wearing cotton shirts
leathery • leathery skin
resilient • an armchair of some resilient plastic material
robust • very robust machinery
rugged • You need a rugged, four-wheel drive vehicle.
solid • The car feels very solid.
strong • a strong casing, which won't crack or chip
sturdy • The camera was mounted on a sturdy tripod.

ANTONYM
● fragile

tough ❸ ADJECTIVE
full of hardship • She had a pretty tough childhood.
arduous • an arduous journey
difficult • We're living in difficult times.
exacting • an exacting task
hard • a hard life

ANTONYM
● easy

trace ❶ VERB
to look for and find something
• Police are trying to trace the owner.
locate • We've simply been unable to locate him.
track down • She had spent years trying to track down her parents.

trace ❷ NOUN
a sign of something • No trace of his father had been found.
evidence • He'd seen no evidence of fraud.

hint • I saw no hint of irony on her face.
indication • He gave no indication of remorse.
record • There's no record of any marriage or children.
sign • Sally waited for any sign of illness.
suggestion • a faint suggestion of a tan
whiff • Not a whiff of scandal has ever tainted his private life.

trace ❸ NOUN
a small amount of something
• to write without a trace of sensationalism
dash • a story with a dash of mystery
drop • a drop of sherry
remnant • Beneath the present church were remnants of Roman flooring.
suspicion • large blooms of white with a suspicion of pale pink
tinge • Could there have been a slight tinge of envy in Eva's voice?
touch • a touch of flu
vestige • the last vestige of a UN force that once numbered 30,000

MORE SYNONYMS
● iota
● jot
● soupçon

trade ❶ NOUN
the buying and selling of goods
• foreign trade
business • a career in business
commerce • They have made their fortunes from industry and commerce.

RELATED WORD
● ADJECTIVE: mercantile

trade ❷ NOUN
the kind of work someone does

a b c d e f g h i j k l m n o p q r s **t** u v w x y z

• He learnt his trade as a diver in the North Sea.
business • the music business
line • Are you in the publishing line too?
line of work • In my line of work I often get home too late for dinner.
occupation • her new occupation as an author
profession • Harper was a teacher by profession.

trade ❸ VERB

to buy and sell goods • They had years of experience of trading with the West.
deal • They deal in antiques.
do business • the different people who did business with me
traffic • those who traffic in illegal drugs

trader NOUN

someone who trades in goods • a timber trader
broker • a financial broker
dealer • dealers in commodities
merchant • a wine merchant

tradition NOUN

a long-standing custom • the rich traditions of Afro-Cuban music
convention • It's just a social convention that men don't wear skirts.
custom • an ancient Japanese custom

traditional ADJECTIVE

existing for a long time • her traditional Indian dress
conventional • conventional family planning methods
established • the established church

ANTONYM
● unconventional

tragic ADJECTIVE

very sad • a tragic accident
distressing • distressing news
heartbreaking • a heartbreaking succession of miscarriages
heart-rending • heart-rending pictures of refugees

train VERB

to teach someone how to do something • We train them in bricklaying and other building techniques.
coach • He coached the basketball team.
drill • He drills the choir to a high standard.
educate • I was educated at the local grammar school.
instruct • All their members are instructed in first aid.
school • He has been schooled to take over the family business.
teach • This is something they teach us to do in our first year.
tutor • She decided to tutor her children at home.

transform VERB

to change something completely • This technology has transformed our society.
alter • New curtains can completely alter the look of a room.
change • alchemists attempting to change base metals into gold
convert • They have converted the church into a restaurant.
reform • He was totally reformed by this experience.
revolutionize • a device which will revolutionize the way you cook

transparent ADJECTIVE

able to be seen through • a sheet of transparent plastic
clear • a clear glass panel

A B C D E F G H I J K L M N O P Q R S T U V W X Y Z

Can't find the word you're looking for? Try the index.

crystalline (LITERARY) • *crystalline lakes*
sheer • *a sheer black shirt*
translucent • *translucent corrugated plastic*

MORE SYNONYMS
- diaphanous
- see-through

ANTONYM
- opaque

transport ❶ NOUN
the moving of goods and people • *The prices quoted include transport costs.*
removal • *the furniture removal business*
shipment • *transported to the docks for shipment overseas*
transportation • *the transportation of refugees*

transport ❷ VERB
to move people or goods somewhere • *They use tankers to transport the oil to Los Angeles.*
carry • *The ship could carry seventy passengers.*
convey (FORMAL) • *a branch line to convey fish direct to Billingsgate*
ship • *the food being shipped to Iraq*
transfer • *She was transferred to another hospital.*

trap ❶ NOUN
a device for catching animals • *a rabbit trap*
net • *a fishing net*
snare • *a snare for catching birds*

trap ❷ VERB
to catch animals • *The locals were encouraged to trap and kill the birds.*
catch • *an animal caught in a trap*
corner • *like a cornered rat*
snare • *He'd snared a rabbit earlier*

in the day.

trap ❸ VERB
to trick someone • *Were you trying to trap her into making some admission?*
dupe • *a plot to dupe stamp collectors into buying fake rarities*
trick • *His family tricked him into going to Pakistan.*

MORE SYNONYMS
- ensnare
- entrap

trash ❶ NOUN
waste material • *He picks up your trash on Mondays.*
garbage • *rotting piles of garbage*
refuse • *a weekly collection of refuse*
rubbish • *They had piled most of their rubbish into yellow skips.*
waste • *a law that regulates the disposal of waste*

trash ❷ NOUN
something of poor quality • *Don't read that awful trash.*
garbage (INFORMAL) • *He spends his time watching garbage on TV.*
rubbish • *He described her book as absolute rubbish.*

travel VERB
to make a journey somewhere • *You had better travel to Helsinki tomorrow.*
go • *We went to Rome.*
journey (FORMAL) • *He intended to journey up the Amazon.*
make your way • *He made his way home at last.*
take a trip • *We intend to take a trip there sometime.*

MORE SYNONYMS
- proceed
- voyage

a
b
c
d
e
f
g
h
i
j
k
l
m
n
o
p
q
r
s
t
u
v
w
x
y
z

Can't find the word you're looking for? Try the index.

treacherous ❶ ADJECTIVE
likely to betray someone • *He denounced the party's treacherous leaders.*
disloyal • *disloyal Cabinet colleagues*
faithless • *an oppressive father and faithless husband*
unfaithful • *his unfaithful wife*
untrustworthy • *Jordan has tried to brand his opponents as untrustworthy.*

MORE SYNONYMS
● perfidious
● traitorous

ANTONYM
● loyal

treacherous ❷ ADJECTIVE
dangerous or unreliable • *treacherous mountain roads*
dangerous • *a dangerous stretch of road*
hazardous • *hazardous seas*
perilous (LITERARY) • *The roads grew even steeper and more perilous.*

treasure VERB
to consider something very precious • *He treasures his friendship with her.*
cherish • *The previous owners had cherished the house.*
hold dear • *forced to renounce everything he held most dear*
prize • *one of the gallery's most prized possessions*
value • *if you value your health*

MORE SYNONYMS
● revere
● venerate

treat ❶ VERB
to behave towards someone • *Artie treated most women with indifference.*
act towards • *the way you act towards other people*
behave towards • *He always behaved towards me with great kindness.*
deal with • *in dealing with suicidal youngsters*

treat ❷ VERB
to give someone medical care • *the doctor who treated her*
care for • *They hired a nurse to care for her.*
nurse • *All the years he was sick my mother had nursed him.*

trendy ADJECTIVE (INFORMAL)
fashionable • *a trendy night club*
fashionable • *a very fashionable place to go on holiday*
in (SLANG) • *what's in and what's not*
in fashion • *Calf-length skirts are in fashion this season.*
in vogue • *African art is in vogue at the moment.*
latest • *the latest thing in camera technology*
stylish • *This city has got a lot more stylish in recent years.*

tribute NOUN
something that shows admiration • *Police paid tribute to her courage.*
accolade (FORMAL) • *To play for your country is the ultimate accolade.*
compliment • *We consider it a compliment to be called "conservative".*
honour • *Only two writers are granted the honour of a solo display.*
praise • *That is high praise indeed.*
testimony • *a testimony to her dedication*

Can't find the word you're looking for? Try the index.

trick ❶ NOUN
something that deceives someone
• *We are playing a trick on a man who keeps bothering me.*
con (INFORMAL) • *Slimming snacks that offer miraculous weight loss are a con.*
deception • *the victim of a cruel deception*
hoax • *a bomb hoax*
ploy • *a cynical marketing ploy*
ruse • *This was a ruse to divide them.*

MORE SYNONYMS
- stratagem
- subterfuge

trick ❷ VERB
to deceive someone • *They tricked me into giving them all my money.*
con (INFORMAL) • *We have been conned for 20 years.*
deceive • *He deceived me into thinking the money was his.*
dupe • *I was duped into letting them in.*
fool • *They tried to fool you into coming after us.*
take in (INFORMAL) • *I wasn't taken in for a minute.*

MORE SYNONYMS
- hoax
- hoodwink

tricky ADJECTIVE
difficult to do or to deal with • *This could be a very tricky problem.*
complex • *the whole complex issue of crime and punishment*
complicated • *a complicated operation*
delicate • *This brings us to the delicate question of his future.*
difficult • *It was a difficult decision to make.*

hard • *That's a hard question to answer.*
problematic • *It's a very problematic piece to play.*
puzzling • *a puzzling case to solve*
sensitive • *The death penalty is a very sensitive issue.*

trip ❶ NOUN
a journey to a place • *a business trip*
excursion • *a coach excursion to Trondheim*
jaunt • *a jaunt in the car*
journey • *the journey to Bordeaux*
outing • *a school outing*
voyage • *Columbus's voyage to the West Indies*

trip ❷ VERB
to fall over • *I tripped on the stairs.*
fall over • *Plenty of top skiers fell over.*
lose your footing • *He lost his footing and slid into the water.*
stumble • *He stumbled and almost fell.*

triumph ❶ NOUN
a great success • *The championships proved to be a personal triumph for the coach.*
success • *The jewellery was a great success.*
victory • *a victory for common sense*

MORE SYNONYMS
- coup
- feather in your cap
- tour de force

ANTONYM
- failure

triumph ❷ VERB
to be successful • *a symbol of good triumphing over evil*

Can't find the word you're looking for? Try the index.

a
b
c
d
e
f
g
h
i
j
k
l
m
n
o
p
q
r
s
t
u
v
w
x
y
z

come out on top (INFORMAL)
• *The only way to come out on top is to adopt a different approach.*
prevail • *I do hope he will prevail over the rebels.*
succeed • *if they can succeed in America*
win • *The top four teams all won.*

ANTONYM
● fail

trivial ADJECTIVE
not important • *She doesn't concern herself with such trivial details.*
insignificant • *The dangers are insignificant compared with those of smoking.*
minor • *a minor inconvenience*
negligible • *The strike will have a negligible impact.*
paltry • *They had no interest in paltry domestic concerns.*
petty • *I wouldn't indulge in such petty schoolboy pranks.*
slight • *It's only a slight problem.*
trifling • *The sums involved were trifling.*
unimportant • *Too much time is spent discussing unimportant matters.*

MORE SYNONYMS
● frivolous
● inconsequential

ANTONYM
● important

trouble ❶ NOUN
a difficulty or problem • *financial troubles*
bother • *Vince is having a spot of bother with the law.*
difficulty • *economic difficulties*
hassle (INFORMAL) • *We had loads of hassles trying to find somewhere to rehearse.*

problem • *The main problem is unemployment.*

trouble ❷ VERB
to make someone feel worried
• *He was troubled by the lifestyle of his son.*
agitate • *The thought agitates her.*
bother • *Is something bothering you?*
disturb • *dreams so vivid that they disturb me for days*
worry • *I didn't want to worry you.*

trouble ❸ VERB
to cause someone inconvenience
• *Can I trouble you for some milk?*
bother • *I don't know why he bothers me with this kind of rubbish.*
disturb • *a room where you won't be disturbed*
impose upon • *I was afraid you'd feel we were imposing on you.*
inconvenience • *He promised to be quick so as not to inconvenience them further.*
put out • *I've always put myself out for others.*

true ❶ ADJECTIVE
not invented • *The film is based on a true story.*
accurate • *an accurate assessment of the situation*
correct • *a correct diagnosis*
factual • *any comparison that is not strictly factual*

ANTONYM
● inaccurate

true ❷ ADJECTIVE
real or genuine • *She was a true friend.*
authentic • *authentic Italian food*
bona fide • *We are happy to donate to bona fide charities.*
genuine • *There was a risk of*

Can't find the word you're looking for? Try the index.

A
B
C
D
E
F
G
H
I
J
K
L
M
N
O
P
Q
R
S
T
U
V
W
X
Y
Z

genuine refugees being returned to Vietnam.

real • No, it wasn't a dream. It was real.

ANTONYM
● false

trust VERB
to believe that someone will do something • The president can't be trusted.
count on • I can always count on you to cheer me up.
depend on • You can depend on me.
have confidence in • We have the utmost confidence in your abilities.
have faith in • I have no faith in him any more.
place your trust in • I would never place my trust in one so young.
rely upon • I know I can rely on you to sort it out.

trusty ADJECTIVE
considered to be reliable • a trusty member of the crew
dependable • a dependable and steady worker
faithful • his faithful black Labrador
firm • Betty became a firm friend of the family.
reliable • the problem of finding reliable staff
solid • one of my most solid supporters
staunch • He proved himself a staunch ally.
true • a true friend
trustworthy • trying to find a trustworthy adviser

truth NOUN
the facts about something

• Marcel is keen to get to the truth of what happened.
fact • How much was fact and how much fancy no one knew.
reality • Fiction and reality were increasingly blurred.

RELATED WORDS
● ADJECTIVES: veritable, veracious

try ❶ VERB
to make an effort to do something • I tried hard to persuade him to stay.
attempt • They are accused of attempting to murder British soldiers.
endeavour (FORMAL) • I will endeavour to arrange it.
make an attempt • He made three attempts to break the record.
make an effort • He made no effort to hide his disappointment.
seek • We have never sought to impose our views.
strive • The school strives to treat pupils as individuals.

try ❷ VERB
to test the quality of something • Howard wanted me to try the wine.
check out • We went to the club to check it out.
sample • We sampled a selection of different bottled waters.
test • The drug was tested on rats.
try out • London Transport hopes to try out the system in September.

try ❸ NOUN
an attempt to do something • After a few tries he pressed the right button.
attempt • a deliberate attempt to destabilize the defence
effort • his efforts to improve
endeavour (FORMAL) • His first endeavours in the field were wedding films.

a
b
c
d
e
f
g
h
i
j
k
l
m
n
o
p
q
r
s
t
u
v
w
x
y
z

A
B
C
D
E
F
G
H
I
J
K
L
M
N
O
P
Q
R
S
T
U
V
W
X
Y
Z

go (INFORMAL) • *She won on her first go.*
shot (INFORMAL) • *I have had a shot at professional cricket.*

tubby ADJECTIVE
rather fat • *He's a bit on the tubby side.*
chubby • *She was very chubby as a child.*
fat • *He was short and fat.*
overweight • *Being overweight is bad for your health.*
plump • *a plump, good-natured little woman*
podgy • *Eddie is a little podgy round the middle.*
portly • *a portly gentleman*
stout • *His wife was a small, stout lady.*

tug ❶ VERB
to give something a quick, hard pull • *A little boy tugged at her skirt excitedly.*
drag • *He grabbed my ankle and dragged me back.*
draw • *She took his hand and drew him along.*
haul • *I gripped his wrist and hauled him up.*
heave • *They heaved the last bag into the van.*
jerk • *He jerked his hand out of mine angrily.*
pluck • *The beggar plucked at her sleeve as she passed.*
pull • *She pulled down the hem of her skirt over her knees.*
wrench • *The horse wrenched its head free.*
yank • *He grabbed my arm and yanked me out of the car.*

tug ❷ NOUN
a quick, hard pull • *He felt a tug at his arm.*

heave • *With a mighty heave, she pulled herself away from him.*
jerk • *He gave a sudden jerk of the reins.*
pull • *Give the cord three sharp pulls.*
wrench • *He lowered the flag with a quick wrench.*
yank • *He gave the phone a savage yank.*

tune NOUN
a series of musical notes • *She was humming a merry little tune.*
melody • *a beautiful melody*
strains • *She could hear the tinny strains of a chamber orchestra.*

MORE SYNONYMS
● air
● theme

turn ❶ VERB
to change the direction or position of something • *She had turned the bedside chair to face the door.*
rotate • *Take each foot in both your hands and rotate it.*
spin • *He spun the wheel sharply and made a U-turn.*
swivel • *She swivelled her chair round.*
twirl • *Bonnie twirled her empty glass in her fingers.*
twist • *She twisted her head sideways.*

turn ❷ VERB
to become or make something different • *A hobby can be turned into a career.*
change • *She has now changed into a happy, self-confident woman.*
convert • *a table that converts into an ironing board*
mutate • *Overnight, the gossip begins to mutate into headlines.*

Can't find the word you're looking for? Try the index.

transform • *the speed at which your body transforms food into energy*

MORE SYNONYMS
- metamorphose
- transfigure
- transmute

turn ❸ NOUN
someone's right or duty to do something • *Tonight it's my turn to cook.*
chance • *All eligible people would get a chance to vote.*
go • *Whose go is it?*
opportunity • *Now is your opportunity to say what you've always wanted.*

twist ❶ VERB
to turn something round • *Her hands began to twist the handles of the bag.*
bend • *Bend the bar into a horseshoe.*
curl • *She sat with her legs curled under her.*
twine • *He had twined his chubby arms around Vincent's neck.*
weave • *He weaves his way through a crowd.*
wring • *after wringing the chicken's neck*

MORE SYNONYMS
- entwine
- wreathe

twist ❷ VERB
to bend into a new shape • *The car was left a mess of twisted metal.*
distort • *A painter may exaggerate or distort shapes and forms.*
mangle • *the mangled wreckage*
screw up • *Amy screwed up her face.*

MORE SYNONYMS
- contort
- warp

twist ❸ VERB
to injure a part of your body • *I've twisted my ankle.*
sprain • *He fell and sprained his wrist.*
wrench • *He had wrenched his back badly from the force of the fall.*

MORE SYNONYMS
- rick
- turn

two-faced ADJECTIVE
not honest in dealing with other people • *a two-faced, manipulative woman*
deceitful • *a deceitful, conniving liar*
dishonest • *He's been dishonest in his dealings with us both.*
disloyal • *I can't stand people who are disloyal.*
false • *He had been betrayed by his false friends.*
hypocritical • *a hypocritical and ambitious careerist*
insincere • *They are still widely seen as insincere and untrustworthy.*
treacherous • *He has been consistently treacherous to both sides.*

type NOUN
a group of things that have features in common • *There are various types of dog suitable as pets.*
brand • *his favourite brand of whisky*
breed • *a rare breed of cattle*
class • *a better class of restaurant*
group • *Weather forecasters classify clouds into several different groups.*

a
b
c
d
e
f
g
h
i
j
k
l
m
n
o
p
q
r
s
t
u
v
w
x
y
z

Can't find the word you're looking for? Try the index.

A
B
C
D
E
F
G
H
I
J
K
L
M
N
O
P
Q
R
S
T
U
V
W
X
Y
Z

kind • *I don't like that kind of film.*
make • *He'll only drive a certain make of car.*
sort • *a dozen trees of various sorts*
species • *a rare species of moth*
style • *Several styles of hat were available.*
variety • *Many varieties of birds live here.*

typical ADJECTIVE
having the usual characteristics of something • *a typical American child*
average • *The average adult man burns 1500 to 2000 calories per day.*
characteristic • *a characteristic feature of the landscape*
normal • *a normal day*

regular • *He describes himself as just a regular guy.*
representative • *fairly representative groups of adults*
standard • *It was standard practice in cases like this.*
stock • *He had a stock answer for all problems.*
usual • *a neighbourhood beset by all the usual inner-city problems*

MORE SYNONYMS
- archetypal
- archetypical
- stereotypical

ANTONYM
uncharacteristic

Can't find the word you're looking for? Try the index.

Uu

ugly ADJECTIVE
having a very unattractive
appearance • *She makes me feel
dowdy and ugly.*
plain • *a shy, plain girl with a pale
complexion*
unattractive • *painted in an
unattractive shade of green*
unsightly • *The view was spoiled
by some unsightly houses.*

MORE SYNONYMS
● unlovely
● unprepossessing

ANTONYM
● beautiful

ultimate ❶ ADJECTIVE
being the final one of a series • *It
is not possible to predict the ultimate
outcome.*
eventual • *Reunification is the
eventual aim.*
final • *the fifth and final day*
last • *This is his last chance to do
something useful.*

ultimate ❷ ADJECTIVE
the most important or powerful
• *the ultimate goal of any player*
greatest • *Our greatest aim was to
take the gold medal.*
paramount • *His paramount
ambition was to be an actor.*
supreme • *the supreme test of his
abilities*
utmost • *This has to be our utmost
priority.*

ultimate ❸ NOUN
the finest example of something
• *This hotel is the ultimate in luxury.*
epitome • *She was the epitome of
the successful businesswoman.*
extreme • *This was shyness taken
to the extreme.*
height • *the height of bad manners*
peak • *roses at the peak of
perfection*

unaware ADJECTIVE
not knowing about something
• *Many people are unaware of how
much they eat.*
ignorant • *They are completely
ignorant of the relevant facts.*
oblivious • *John appeared oblivious
to his surroundings.*
unconscious • *totally unconscious
of my presence*
unsuspecting • *The cars were then
sold to unsuspecting buyers.*

ANTONYM
● aware

unbearable ADJECTIVE
too unpleasant to be tolerated
• *Life was unbearable for the
remaining citizens.*
intolerable • *The heat and
humidity were intolerable.*
oppressive • *An oppressive
sadness weighed upon him.*
unacceptable • *She left her
husband because of his unacceptable
behaviour.*

Can't find the word you're looking for? Try the index.

MORE SYNONYMS
- insufferable
- unendurable

ANTONYM
- tolerable

unbelievable ❶ ADJECTIVE
extremely great or surprising • *He showed unbelievable courage.*
colossal • *There has been a colossal waste of public money.*
incredible • *You're always an incredible help on these occasions.*
stupendous • *It cost a stupendous amount of money.*

unbelievable ❷ ADJECTIVE
so unlikely it cannot be believed • *He came up with some unbelievable story.*
implausible • *a film with an implausible ending*
improbable • *highly improbable claims*
inconceivable • *It was inconceivable that he'd hurt anyone.*
incredible • *It seems incredible that anyone would want to do that.*
preposterous • *The whole idea was preposterous.*
unconvincing • *In response he was given the usual unconvincing excuses.*

ANTONYM
- believable

uncertain ❶ ADJECTIVE
not knowing what to do • *For a moment he looked uncertain as to how to respond.*
doubtful • *He was a bit doubtful about starting without her.*
dubious • *We were a bit dubious about it at first.*
unclear • *I'm unclear about where to go.*

undecided • *Even then she was still undecided about her future plans.*

MORE SYNONYMS
- irresolute
- vacillating

ANTONYM
- certain

uncertain ❷ ADJECTIVE
not definite • *facing an uncertain future*
ambiguous • *The wording of the contract was ambiguous.*
doubtful • *The outcome of the match is still doubtful.*
indefinite • *suspended for an indefinite period*
indeterminate • *a woman of indeterminate age*

MORE SYNONYMS
- conjectural
- undetermined

ANTONYM
- certain

unclear ADJECTIVE
confusing and not obvious • *It is unclear how much popular support they have.*
ambiguous • *in order to clarify the earlier ambiguous statement*
confused • *The situation remains confused, as no clear victor has emerged.*
vague • *The description was pretty vague.*

ANTONYM
- clear

uncomfortable ❶ ADJECTIVE
feeling or causing discomfort • *an uncomfortable bed*
awkward • *Its shape made it awkward to carry.*

Can't find the word you're looking for? Try the index.

cramped • *living in very cramped conditions*
disagreeable • *designed to make flying a less disagreeable experience*
ill-fitting • *Walking was difficult because of her ill-fitting shoes.*
painful • *a painful back injury*

ANTONYM
⬤ comfortable

uncomfortable ❷ ADJECTIVE
not relaxed or confident • *Talking about money made her uncomfortable.*
awkward • *Offstage, he is bashful and awkward.*
embarrassed • *an embarrassed silence*
ill at ease • *I always feel ill at ease in their company.*
self-conscious • *She was always self-conscious about her height.*
uneasy • *He looked uneasy and refused to answer any more questions.*

ANTONYM
⬤ comfortable

uncommon ❶ ADJECTIVE
not happening or seen often • *This type of cancer is uncommon among young women.*
exceptional • *These are exceptional circumstances.*
extraordinary • *an act of extraordinary generosity*
few • *Genuine friends are few.*
infrequent • *one of the infrequent visitors to the island*
out of the ordinary • *My story is nothing out of the ordinary.*
scarce • *places where jobs are scarce*
sparse • *Traffic is sparse on this stretch of road.*

rare • *a rare occurrence*
unusual • *an unusual sight these days*

ANOTHER SYNONYM
⬤ unprecedented

ANTONYM
⬤ common

uncommon ❷ ADJECTIVE
unusually great • *She had read Cecilia's last letter with uncommon interest.*
acute • *He has an acute dislike of children.*
exceptional • *a woman of exceptional beauty*
extraordinary • *a young player of extraordinary energy*
extreme • *regions suffering from extreme poverty*
great • *They share a great love of Bach's music.*
intense • *intense heat*
remarkable • *a musician of remarkable talent*

ANOTHER SYNONYM
⬤ unparalleled

unconscious ❶ ADJECTIVE
in a state similar to sleep • *By the time the ambulance arrived, he was unconscious.*
asleep • *They were fast asleep in their beds.*
senseless • *He was beaten senseless and robbed of all his money.*
stunned • *stunned by a blow to the head*

MORE SYNONYMS
⬤ comatose
⬤ insensible

ANTONYM
⬤ conscious

a
b
c
d
e
f
g
h
i
j
k
l
m
n
o
p
q
r
s
t
u
v
w
x
y
z

Can't find the word you're looking for? Try the index.

unconscious ❷ ADJECTIVE

not aware of what is happening
• *quite unconscious of their presence*
oblivious • *He seemed oblivious of his surroundings.*
unaware • *He was unaware of the chaos he was causing.*
unknowing • *unknowing accomplices in his crimes*
unsuspecting • *She was an unsuspecting victim of his deceit.*

ANTONYM
● aware

uncover ❶ VERB

to find something out • *Auditors said they had uncovered evidence of fraud.*
bring to light • *The truth is unlikely to be brought to light.*
expose • *His lies were exposed in court.*
reveal • *He will reveal the truth behind the scandal.*
show up • *His true character has been shown up for what it is.*
unearth • *a campaign to unearth supposed conspiracies*

uncover ❷ VERB

to remove the lid or cover from something • *When the seedlings sprout, uncover the tray.*
expose • *The wreck was exposed by the action of the tide.*
lay bare • *Layers of paint and flaking plaster were laid bare.*
open • *I opened a new jar of coffee.*
reveal • *His shirt was open, revealing a tattooed chest.*
unearth • *Quarry workers have unearthed the skeleton of a mammoth.*
unveil • *The statue will be unveiled next week.*
unwrap • *unwrapping Christmas presents*

under PREPOSITION

at a lower level than something • *a labyrinth of tunnels under the ground*
below • *The sun had already sunk below the horizon.*
beneath • *the frozen grass crunching beneath his feet*
underneath • *people trapped underneath the wreckage*

ANTONYM
● above

undergo VERB

to have something happen to you • *He had to undergo major surgery.*
be subjected to • *She was subjected to constant interruptions.*
endure • *The company endured heavy losses.*
experience • *They seem to experience more distress than the others.*
go through • *I wouldn't like to go through that again.*
suffer • *The peace process had suffered a serious setback.*

undermine VERB

to make something less secure or strong • *You're trying to undermine my confidence again.*
impair • *Their actions will impair France's national interests.*
sap • *I was afraid the illness had sapped my strength.*
subvert • *an attempt to subvert their culture from within*
weaken • *Her authority had been fatally weakened.*

ANTONYM
● strengthen

understand ❶ VERB

to know what someone means • *Do you understand what I'm saying?*

Can't find the word you're looking for? Try the index.

catch on (INFORMAL) • *I didn't catch on immediately to what he meant.*
comprehend • *Whenever she failed to comprehend, she just laughed.*
follow • *I don't follow you at all.*
get • *Did you get that joke?*
grasp • *He instantly grasped that they were talking about him.*
see • *"I see," she said at last.*
take in • *too much to take in at once*

understand ❷ VERB
to know why or how something is happening • *too young to understand what was going on*
appreciate • *You must appreciate how important this is.*
comprehend • *I just cannot comprehend your viewpoint.*
fathom • *His attitude was hard to fathom.*
grasp • *We immediately grasped the seriousness of the crisis.*
realize • *People just don't realize how serious it could be.*

MORE SYNONYMS
● conceive
● discern

understand ❸ VERB
to hear of something • *I understand she hasn't been well.*
believe • *She's coming back tomorrow, I believe.*
gather • *We gather the report is critical of the judge.*
hear • *I hear you've been having some problems.*
learn • *On learning who he was, I wanted to meet him.*

understanding ❶ NOUN
a knowledge of something • *a basic understanding of computers*

appreciation • *some appreciation of the problems of consumers*
comprehension • *completely beyond our comprehension*
grasp • *a good grasp of foreign languages*
knowledge • *I have no knowledge of his business affairs.*
perception • *Her questions showed a shrewd perception.*

understanding ❷ NOUN
an informal agreement • *There was an understanding between us.*
accord • *trying to reach an accord*
agreement • *A new defence agreement was signed last month.*
pact • *an electoral pact between the parties*

understanding ❸ ADJECTIVE
having a sympathetic nature • *Fortunately he had an understanding wife.*
compassionate • *a deeply compassionate man*
considerate • *They should be more considerate towards the prisoners.*
sensitive • *He was always sensitive and caring.*
sympathetic • *a sympathetic listener*

undertaking NOUN
a task which you have agreed to do • *Organizing the show has been a massive undertaking.*
affair • *It's going to be a tricky affair to arrange.*
business • *Livestock farming is an arduous and difficult business.*
endeavour • *an endeavour that was bound to end in failure*
enterprise • *a risky enterprise such as horse breeding*
job • *What made you decide to take this job on?*

a
b
c
d
e
f
g
h
i
j
k
l
m
n
o
p
q
r
s
t
u
v
w
x
y
z

Can't find the word you're looking for? Try the index.

operation • *the man in charge of the entire operation*
project • *I can't take responsibility for such a huge project.*
task • *a task I do not feel equipped to take on*
venture • *a venture that few were willing to invest in*

uneasy ADJECTIVE
worried that something may be wrong • *I was very uneasy about these developments.*
agitated • *She seemed agitated about something.*
anxious • *He admitted he was still anxious about the situation.*
nervous • *Consumers say they are nervous about their jobs.*
perturbed • *I am not too perturbed at this setback.*
worried • *If you're worried about it, just ask for more details.*

MORE SYNONYMS
● apprehensive
● discomposed
● restive

ANTONYM
● comfortable

unemployed ADJECTIVE
not having a job • *an unemployed mechanic*
idle • *He has been idle for almost a month.*
jobless • *One in four people are now jobless.*
redundant • *aid for the 30,000 redundant miners*

ANTONYM
● employed

uneven ❶ ADJECTIVE
having an unlevel or rough surface • *I tripped on an uneven pavement.*

bumpy • *bumpy cobbled streets*
not level • *It was hard to walk because the road was not level.*
not smooth • *The icing isn't smooth enough.*
rough • *She picked her way across the rough ground.*

ANTONYM
● level

uneven ❷ ADJECTIVE
not the same or consistent • *six lines of uneven length*
fluctuating • *a fluctuating temperature*
inconsistent • *Their performance was inconsistent over the whole season.*
irregular • *at irregular intervals*
patchy • *Her career has been patchy.*
variable • *The potassium content of food is very variable.*

ANTONYM
● even

unexpected ADJECTIVE
not considered likely to happen • *His death was completely unexpected.*
astonishing • *What an astonishing piece of good luck!*
chance • *a chance meeting*
surprising • *a most surprising turn of events*
unforeseen • *The show was cancelled due to unforeseen circumstances.*

MORE SYNONYMS
● fortuitous
● unanticipated
● unheralded

unfair ADJECTIVE
without right or justice • *It was*

Can't find the word you're looking for? Try the index.

unfair that he should suffer so much.
unjust • *an unjust decision*
wrong • *It would be wrong to allow the case to go any further.*
wrongful • *his claim for wrongful dismissal*

MORE SYNONYMS
- inequitable
- iniquitous

ANTONYM
- fair

unfaithful ADJECTIVE
not being faithful to your partner • *He was unfaithful to her for years.*
adulterous • *an adulterous relationship*
two-timing (INFORMAL) • *She called him a two-timing rat.*

ANTONYM
- faithful

unfamiliar ADJECTIVE
not having been seen or heard of before • *She grew many plants which were unfamiliar to me.*
alien • *transplanted into an alien culture*
exotic • *filmed in an exotic location*
foreign • *This was a foreign country, so unlike his own.*
new • *This was a new experience for me.*
novel • *having to cope with many novel situations*
strange • *All these faces were strange to me.*
unknown • *I'd discovered a writer quite unknown to me.*

unfriendly ADJECTIVE
not showing any warmth or kindness • *He can expect an unfriendly welcome.*
aloof • *His manner was aloof.*

antagonistic • *They were always antagonistic to newcomers.*
cold • *She was a cold, unfeeling woman.*
disagreeable • *He may be clever but he's most disagreeable.*
hostile • *The prisoner eyed him in hostile silence.*
unkind • *They're always unkind to newcomers.*

MORE SYNONYMS
- ill-disposed
- uncongenial

ANTONYM
- friendly

ungrateful ADJECTIVE
not appreciating the things you have • *the most miserable and ungrateful people on earth*
unappreciative • *He was unappreciative of our efforts.*
unthankful • *mercenary players and unthankful supporters*

ANTONYM
- grateful

unhappy ADJECTIVE
feeling sad or depressed • *He was a shy, sometimes unhappy man.*
depressed • *She's depressed about this whole situation.*
despondent • *After the interview John was despondent.*
down • *They felt really down after they spoke to him.*
miserable • *My job made me really miserable sometimes.*
sad • *I felt sad to leave our little house.*

MORE SYNONYMS
- crestfallen
- disconsolate
- sorrowful

a
b
c
d
e
f
g
h
i
j
k
l
m
n
o
p
q
r
s
u
v
w
x
y
z

Can't find the word you're looking for? Try the index.

ANTONYM
- happy

unhealthy ❶ ADJECTIVE
likely to cause illness • *an unhealthy lifestyle*
bad for you • *the argument that eating meat is bad for you*
harmful • *Try to avoid harmful habits like smoking.*
insanitary • *the insanitary conditions of slums*
noxious • *factories belching out noxious fumes*
unwholesome • *an epidemic originating from the unwholesome food they ate*

ANTONYM
- healthy

unhealthy ❷ ADJECTIVE
not well • *an unhealthy looking man with a bad complexion*
ailing • *The President is said to be ailing.*
crook (AUSTRALIAN AND NEW ZEALAND; INFORMAL) • *I'm sorry to hear you've been crook, mate.*
ill • *He didn't look at all ill when I last saw him.*
not well • *When I'm not well, she looks after me.*
poorly (BRITISH; INFORMAL) • *She's still poorly after that bout of pneumonia.*
sick • *He's very sick and he needs treatment.*
unwell • *an infection which could make you very unwell*

ANTONYM
- healthy

unimportant ADJECTIVE
having little significance or importance • *The difference in their ages seemed unimportant at the time.*

insignificant • *In 1949, Bonn was a small, insignificant city.*
minor • *a minor inconvenience*
paltry • *They had little interest in paltry domestic concerns.*
slight • *We have a slight problem.*
trivial • *She waved aside the trivial details.*

ANTONYM
- important

uninterested ADJECTIVE
not interested in something • *I'm completely uninterested in anything you have to say.*
apathetic • *apathetic about politics*
bored • *She looked bored with the whole performance.*
impassive • *He remained impassive while she ranted on.*
indifferent • *He is totally indifferent to our problems.*
nonchalant • *"Suit yourself," I said, trying to sound nonchalant.*
passive • *That passive attitude of his drives me mad.*
unconcerned • *She is unconcerned about anything except herself.*

ANTONYM
- interested

union ❶ NOUN
an organization of people or groups with mutual interests • *a trades union*
association • *a member of several different associations*
coalition • *governed by a coalition of three parties*
confederation • *a confederation of mini-states*
federation • *a federation of six separate agencies*
league • *the League of Nations*

Can't find the word you're looking for? Try the index.

A B C D E F G H I J K L M N O P Q R S T U V W X Y Z

union ❷ NOUN

the joining together of two or more things • *The majority voted for union with Russia.*
amalgamation • *an amalgamation of two organizations*
blend • *a blend of traditional charm and modern amenities*
combination • *the combination of science and art*
fusion • *fusions of jazz and pop*
mixture • *a mixture of nuts, raisins, and capers*

MORE SYNONYMS
- amalgam
- conjunction
- synthesis

unite VERB

to join together and act as a group • *We must unite to fight our common enemy.*
collaborate • *They all collaborated on the project.*
combine • *The companies have combined to form a multinational.*
join • *People of all kinds joined to make a dignified protest.*
join forces • *The two parties are joining forces.*
link up • *the first time the two armies have linked up*
merge • *The media group hopes to merge with its rival company.*
pull together • *The staff and management are pulling together to save the company.*
work together • *industry and government working together*

ANTONYM
- divide

universal ADJECTIVE

relating to everyone or to the whole universe • *These programmes have a universal appeal.*
common • *The common view is that it is a good thing.*
general • *This project should raise general awareness about the problem.*
unlimited • *destruction on an unlimited scale*
widespread • *Food shortages are widespread.*
worldwide • *the fear of a worldwide epidemic*

MORE SYNONYMS
- catholic
- omnipresent
- overarching

unkind ADJECTIVE

lacking in kindness and consideration • *It's very unkind to describe her in those terms.*
cruel • *Children can be so cruel.*
malicious • *spreading malicious gossip*
mean • *I'd feel mean saying no.*
nasty • *What nasty little snobs you are!*
spiteful • *How can you say such spiteful things about us?*
thoughtless • *a small minority of thoughtless and inconsiderate people*

ANTONYM
- kind

unknown ADJECTIVE

not familiar or famous • *He was an unknown writer at that time.*
humble • *He started out as a humble fisherman.*
obscure • *an obscure Greek composer*
unfamiliar • *There were several unfamiliar names on the list.*
unsung • *among the unsung heroes of our time*

a
b
c
d
e
f
g
h
i
j
k
l
m
n
o
p
q
r
s
u
v
w
x
y
z

ANTONYM
- famous

unlike PREPOSITION
different from • *She was unlike him in every way.*
different from • *I've always felt different from most people.*
dissimilar to • *a cultural background not dissimilar to our own*
distinct from • *Their cuisines are quite distinct from each other.*
divergent from (FORMAL) • *That viewpoint is not much divergent from that of his predecessor.*
far from • *His politics are not all that far from mine.*

ANTONYM
- like

unlikely ADJECTIVE
probably not true or likely to happen • *a military coup seems unlikely*
implausible • *a film with an implausible ending*
incredible • *an incredible pack of lies*
unbelievable • *I know it sounds unbelievable, but I wasn't there that day.*
unconvincing • *He came up with a very unconvincing excuse.*

ANTONYM
- likely

unlucky ADJECTIVE
having bad luck • *He was unlucky not to score during the first half.*
cursed • *the most cursed family in history*
hapless • *a hapless victim of chance*
luckless • *the luckless parents of a difficult child*

unfortunate • *Some unfortunate person nearby could be injured.*
wretched • *wretched people who had to sell or starve*

ANTONYM
- lucky

unnecessary ADJECTIVE
completely needless • *He frowns upon unnecessary expense.*
needless • *causing needless panic*
pointless • *pointless meetings*
uncalled-for • *uncalled-for rudeness*

ANTONYM
- necessary

unpleasant ❶ ADJECTIVE
causing feelings of discomfort or dislike • *It has a very unpleasant smell.*
bad • *I have some bad news.*
disagreeable • *a disagreeable experience*
distasteful • *I find her gossip distasteful.*
nasty • *This divorce could turn nasty.*
repulsive • *repulsive fat white slugs*
unpalatable • *Only then did I learn the unpalatable truth.*

ANTONYM
- pleasant

unpleasant ❷ ADJECTIVE
rude or unfriendly • *a thoroughly unpleasant person*
disagreeable • *He may be clever, but he's a very disagreeable man.*
horrid • *I must have been a horrid little girl.*
objectionable • *His tone was highly objectionable.*
obnoxious • *Clarissa's obnoxious brother James*

Can't find the word you're looking for? Try the index.

rude • *He was frequently rude to waiters and servants.*
unfriendly • *spoken in a rather unfriendly voice*

ANTONYM
○ pleasant

unpopular ADJECTIVE
disliked by most people • *an unpopular idea*
detested • *The rebels toppled the detested dictator.*
disliked • *one of the most disliked choices on offer*
shunned • *the shunned former minister*
undesirable • *all sorts of undesirable effects on health*

ANTONYM
○ popular

unpredictable ADJECTIVE
unable to be foreseen • *Britain's notoriously unpredictable weather*
chance • *A chance meeting can change your life.*
doubtful • *The outcome remains doubtful.*
hit and miss (INFORMAL)
• *Farming can be a very hit and miss affair.*
unforeseeable • *unforeseeable weather conditions*

ANTONYM
○ predictable

unsatisfactory ADJECTIVE
not good enough • *His work was judged unsatisfactory.*
disappointing • *The results were disappointing.*
inadequate • *The problem goes far beyond inadequate staffing.*
mediocre • *a mediocre string of performances*

poor • *Her school record was poor at first.*
unacceptable • *The quality of his work was unacceptable.*

ANTONYM
○ satisfactory

unsteady ADJECTIVE
not held or fixed securely and likely to fall over • *a slightly unsteady item of furniture*
precarious • *The beds are precarious-looking hammocks strung from the walls.*
rickety • *She stood on a rickety old table.*
shaky • *He climbed up the shaky ladder to the scaffold.*
tottering • *a tottering pile of bricks*
unsafe • *That bridge looks decidedly unsafe to me.*
unstable • *funds used to demolish dangerously unstable buildings*
wobbly • *cat-scratched upholstery and wobbly chairs*

ANTONYM
○ steady

unsuitable ADJECTIVE
not appropriate for a purpose • *Her shoes were unsuitable for walking any distance.*
improper • *an improper diet*
inappropriate • *inappropriate use of the Internet*
unacceptable • *using completely unacceptable language*
unfit • *unfit for human habitation*

MORE SYNONYMS
○ inapposite
○ unseemly

ANTONYM
○ suitable

a
b
c
d
e
f
g
h
i
j
k
l
m
n
o
p
q
r
s
u
v
w
x
y
z

Can't find the word you're looking for? Try the index.

untidy ADJECTIVE

not neatly arranged • *The place quickly became untidy.*

bedraggled • *My hair was a bedraggled mess.*

chaotic • *the chaotic mess of papers on his desk*

cluttered • *There was no space on the cluttered worktop.*

jumbled • *We moved our supplies into a jumbled heap.*

messy • *She was a good, if messy, cook.*

unkempt • *the unkempt grass in front of the house*

MORE SYNONYMS

- disordered
- shambolic

ANTONYM

- tidy

untrue ADJECTIVE

not true • *The allegations were completely untrue.*

erroneous • *an erroneous description*

false • *He gave a false name and address.*

fictitious • *the source of the fictitious rumours*

inaccurate • *the passing on of inaccurate or misleading information*

incorrect • *an incorrect account of the sequence of events*

misleading • *It would be misleading to say we were friends.*

mistaken • *I had a mistaken idea of what had happened.*

ANTONYM

- true

unusual ADJECTIVE

not occurring very often • *many rare and unusual plants*

curious • *a curious mixture of ancient and modern*

exceptional • *exceptional circumstances*

extraordinary • *What an extraordinary thing to happen!*

rare • *one of the rarest species in the world*

uncommon • *It's a very uncommon surname.*

unconventional • *produced by an unconventional technique*

MORE SYNONYMS

- atypical
- unwonted

ANTONYM

- common

unwell ADJECTIVE

ill or sick • *He felt unwell and had to go home early.*

ailing • *The President is said to be ailing.*

crook (AUSTRALIAN AND NEW ZEALAND; INFORMAL) • *I'm sorry to hear you've been crook, mate.*

ill • *Payne was seriously ill with pneumonia.*

poorly (BRITISH; INFORMAL) • *Julie is still poorly after her bout of flu.*

queasy • *I always feel queasy on boats.*

sick • *He's very sick and he needs treatment.*

MORE SYNONYMS

- indisposed
- under the weather

ANTONYM

- well

unwilling ADJECTIVE

not wanting to do something • *an unwilling participant in school politics*

averse • *I'm not averse to going*

Can't find the word you're looking for? Try the index.

A B C D E F G H I J K L M N O P Q R S T U V W X Y Z

along with the suggestion.
grudging • *a grudging acceptance of the situation*
loath • *She is loath to give up her hard-earned liberty.*
reluctant • *They were reluctant to get involved at first.*

ANTONYM
- willing

unwise ADJECTIVE
foolish or not sensible • *It would be unwise to expect too much of her.*
daft • *You'd be daft to get on the wrong side of him.*
foolish • *It was foolish to risk injury like that.*
idiotic • *What an idiotic thing to do!*
irresponsible • *irresponsible plans for tax cuts*
rash • *Don't panic or do anything rash.*
senseless • *It would be senseless to try and stop him now.*
silly • *You're not going to go and do something silly, are you?*
stupid • *I've had enough of your stupid suggestions.*

MORE SYNONYMS
- imprudent
- injudicious

ANTONYM
- wise

upkeep NOUN
the process and cost of maintaining something • *The money will be used for the upkeep of the grounds.*
keep • *He does not contribute towards his keep.*
maintenance • *the regular maintenance of government buildings*
overheads • *We must cut our*

overheads or we shall have to close.
preservation • *the preservation of historical sites*
running • *The running of the house took up all her time.*

upset ❶ ADJECTIVE
feeling unhappy about something • *She was very upset when she heard the news.*
agitated • *in an excited and agitated state*
distressed • *The animals were distressed by the noise.*
frantic • *frantic with worry*
hurt • *I was very hurt when they refused.*
troubled • *He sounded deeply troubled.*
unhappy • *The divorce made him very unhappy.*

upset ❷ VERB
to make someone worried or unhappy • *The whole incident upset me terribly.*
agitate • *The thought agitates her.*
bother • *Don't let his manner bother you.*
distress • *The whole thing really distressed him.*
disturb • *These dreams disturb me for days afterwards.*
grieve • *deeply grieved by their suffering*
ruffle • *She doesn't get ruffled by anything.*

MORE SYNONYMS
- discompose
- faze
- perturb

upset ❸ VERB
to turn something over accidentally • *Don't upset that pile of papers.*

a
b
c
d
e
f
g
h
i
j
k
l
m
n
o
p
q
r
s
t
u
v
w
x
y
z

Can't find the word you're looking for? Try the index.

capsize • *He capsized the boat through his carelessness.*
knock over • *The kitten knocked over the vase.*
overturn • *She overturned her glass of wine as she stood up.*
spill • *The waiter spilled the drinks all over the table.*

urge ❶ NOUN

a strong wish to do something • *stifling the urge to scream*
compulsion • *a compulsion to write*
desire • *I had a strong desire to help and care for people.*
drive • *a demonic drive to succeed*
impulse • *Peter resisted an impulse to smile.*
longing • *his longing to return home*
wish • *She had a genuine wish to make amends.*

urge ❷ VERB

to try hard to persuade someone • *He urged the government to change the law.*
beg • *I begged him to leave me alone.*
beseech • *Her eyes beseeched him to show mercy.*
implore • *He left early, although they implored him to stay.*
plead • *kneeling on the floor pleading for mercy*
press • *The unions are pressing him to stand firm.*

MORE SYNONYMS
- entreat
- exhort
- solicit

urgent ADJECTIVE

needing to be dealt with quickly • *an urgent need for food and water*

compelling • *There are compelling reasons to act swiftly.*
immediate • *The immediate problem is transportation.*
imperative • *It is imperative we end up with a win.*
pressing • *one of our most pressing problems*

use ❶ VERB

to perform a task with something • *Use a sharp knife to trim the edges.*
apply • *The company applies this technology to solve practical problems.*
employ • *the methods employed in the study*
operate • *Can you operate a fax machine?*
utilize • *The body utilizes many different minerals.*

MORE SYNONYMS
- avail oneself of
- ply

use ❷ NOUN

the act of using something • *the use of force*
application • *Her theory was put into practical application.*
employment • *the employment of completely new methods*
operation • *the operation of the computer mouse*
usage • *Parts of the motor wore out because of constant usage.*

use ❸ NOUN

the purpose for which something is utilized • *of no practical use whatsoever*
end • *The police force was manipulated for political ends.*
object • *the object of the exercise*
point • *I don't see the point of a thing like that.*

Can't find the word you're looking for? Try the index.

purpose • *It is wrong to use it for military purposes.*

useful ADJECTIVE
something which helps or makes things easier • *a great deal of useful information*
beneficial • *It may be beneficial to study the relevant guidelines.*
effective • *Antibiotics are effective against this organism.*
helpful • *a number of helpful booklets*
practical • *practical suggestions for healthy eating*
valuable • *Here are a few valuable tips to help you to succeed.*
worthwhile • *a worthwhile source of income*

ANTONYM
● useless

useless ADJECTIVE
not suitable or useful • *We realized that our money was useless here.*
futile • *It would be futile to make any further attempts.*
impractical • *A tripod is impractical when following animals on the move.*
unproductive • *increasingly unproductive land*
unsuitable • *This tool is completely unsuitable for use with metal.*
worthless • *The old skills are worthless now.*

MORE SYNONYMS
● disadvantageous
● ineffectual
● unavailing

ANTONYM
● useful

usual ADJECTIVE
done or happening most often • *sitting at his usual table*
accustomed • *She acted with her accustomed shrewdness.*
common • *the commonest cause of death*
customary • *It's customary to offer guests a drink.*
habitual • *He soon recovered his habitual geniality.*
normal • *That's quite normal for a Friday.*
regular • *samples from one of their regular suppliers*
standard • *It was standard practice to put them outside.*

utter ADJECTIVE
complete or total • *scenes of utter chaos*
absolute • *This is absolute madness!*
complete • *a complete mess*
consummate • *a consummate professional*
out-and-out • *an out-and-out lie*
outright • *an outright rejection of the deal*
perfect • *a perfect stranger*
pure • *She did it out of pure malice.*
sheer • *an act of sheer stupidity*
thorough • *She is a thorough snob.*
total • *a total failure*

MORE SYNONYMS
● unconditional
● unmitigated
● unqualified

a
b
c
d
e
f
g
h
i
j
k
l
m
n
o
p
q
r
s
u
v
w
x
y
z

Can't find the word you're looking for? Try the index.

Vv

vague ADJECTIVE
not clearly expressed or clearly visible • *vague promises about raising standards*
hazy • *Many details remain hazy.*
indefinite • *at some indefinite time in the future*
indistinct • *The lettering was worn and indistinct.*
loose • *a loose translation*
uncertain • *Students are facing an uncertain future.*
unclear • *The proposals were sketchy and unclear.*

MORE SYNONYMS
- ill-defined
- indeterminate
- nebulous

ANTONYM
- definite

vain ❶ ADJECTIVE
very proud of your looks or qualities • *I think he is shallow and vain.*
conceited • *They had grown too conceited and pleased with themselves.*
egotistical • *an egotistical show-off*
ostentatious • *He was generous with his money without being ostentatious.*
proud • *She was said to be proud and arrogant.*
stuck-up (INFORMAL) • *She was a famous actress, but she wasn't a bit stuck-up.*

MORE SYNONYMS
- narcissistic
- overweening
- swaggering

vain ❷ ADJECTIVE
not successful in achieving what was intended • *He made a vain effort to cheer her up.*
abortive • *the abortive coup attempt*
fruitless • *It was a fruitless search.*
futile • *their futile attempts to avoid publicity*
unproductive • *an unproductive strategy*
useless • *a useless punishment which fails to stop crime*

ANTONYM
- successful

vain ❸, in vain ADJECTIVE
unsuccessful in achieving what was intended • *Her complaints were in vain.*
fruitless • *Four years of negotiation were fruitless.*
to no avail • *His protests were to no avail.*
unsuccessful • *Previous attempts have been unsuccessful.*
wasted • *Their efforts were wasted.*

valley NOUN

TYPES OF VALLEY	
canyon	dale
chasm	defile
coomb	dell
cwm (WELSH)	depression

Can't find the word you're looking for? Try the index.

dingle	gully
glen	hollow
gorge	ravine
gulch	strath (Scottish)

valuable ❶ ADJECTIVE

having great importance or usefulness • *The experience was very valuable.*

beneficial • *Using computers has a beneficial effect on learning.*

helpful • *a number of helpful booklets*

important • *Her sons are the most important thing in her life.*

prized • *one of the gallery's most prized possessions*

useful • *a mine of useful information*

worthwhile • *a worthwhile source of income*

MORE SYNONYMS

- cherished
- esteemed
- treasured

ANTONYM

- useless

valuable ❷ ADJECTIVE

worth a lot of money • *valuable old books*

costly • *a small and costly bottle of scent*

expensive • *exclusive, expensive possessions*

precious • *rings set with precious jewels*

ANTONYM

- worthless

valuables PLURAL NOUN

the things you own that cost a lot of money • *Leave your valuables in the hotel safe.*

heirlooms • *family heirlooms*

treasures • *The house was full of art treasures.*

value ❶ NOUN

the importance or usefulness of something • *Studies are needed to see if these therapies have any value.*

advantage • *the great advantage of this method*

benefit • *They see no benefit in educating these children.*

effectiveness • *the effectiveness of the new system*

importance • *They have always placed great importance on live performances.*

merit • *the artistic merit of their work*

use • *This is of no use to anyone.*

usefulness • *the usefulness of the Internet in disseminating new ideas*

virtue • *the great virtue of modern technology*

worth • *This system has already proved its worth.*

value ❷ NOUN

the amount of money that something is worth • *The value of his house has risen by more than 100%.*

cost • *the cost of a loaf of bread*

market price • *buying shares at the current market price*

price • *a sharp increase in the price of petrol*

selling price • *the average selling price of a new home*

worth • *He sold the car for less than half its worth.*

value ❸ VERB

to appreciate something and think it is important • *Do you value your friends enough?*

appreciate • *I would appreciate your advice.*

a
b
c
d
e
f
g
h
i
j
k
l
m
n
o
p
q
r
s
t
u
v
w
x
y
z

Can't find the word you're looking for? Try the index.

cherish • *Cherish every moment you have with your children.*
have a high opinion of • *Your boss seems to have a high opinion of you.*
prize • *These items are prized by collectors.*
rate highly • *He is an excellent keeper and I rate him highly.*
respect • *I respect his talent as a pianist.*
treasure • *memories I will treasure for the rest of my life*

value ❹ VERB
to decide how much money something is worth • *I have had my jewellery valued for insurance purposes.*
appraise • *He was called in to appraise and sell the cottage.*
assess • *Experts are now assessing the cost of the restoration.*
cost • *an operation costed at around $649m*
estimate • *a personal fortune estimated at more than $400m*
evaluate • *The company needs to evaluate the cost of leasing the building.*
price • *The property was priced at less than £1m.*

vanish ❶ VERB
to disappear • *The moon vanished behind a cloud.*
become invisible • *The plane became invisible in the clouds.*
be lost to view • *They watched the ship until it was lost to view.*
disappear • *The aircraft disappeared off the radar.*
fade • *We watched the harbour fade into the mist.*
recede • *Gradually Luke receded into the distance.*

ANTONYM
● appear

vanish ❷ VERB
to cease to exist • *Dinosaurs vanished from the earth millions of years ago.*
become extinct • *Without help, these animals will become extinct.*
cease • *At one o'clock the rain ceased.*
cease to exist • *Without trees, the world as we know it would cease to exist.*
die out • *Britain's bear population died out about 2,000 years ago.*
dissolve • *The crowds dissolved and we were alone.*
evaporate • *All my pleasure evaporated when I saw him.*
fade away • *Her black mood faded away.*
go away • *All she wanted was for the pain to go away.*
melt away • *All my cares melted away.*
pass • *Breathe deeply and the panic attack will pass.*

vanquish VERB
to defeat someone completely • *a happy ending in which the hero vanquishes the monsters*
beat • *the team that beat us in the finals*
conquer • *a great warrior who conquers the enemies of his people*
crush • *their bid to crush the rebels*
defeat • *His guerrillas defeated the colonial army in 1954.*
overcome • *They overcame the opposition to win the cup.*
rout • *the battle at which the Norman army routed the English*
trounce • *Australia trounced France by 60 points to 4.*

A B C D E F G H I J K L M N O P Q R S T U V W X Y Z

Can't find the word you're looking for? Try the index.

variation NOUN
a change from the normal or usual pattern • *a variation of the same route*
alteration • *some alterations in your diet*
change • *a change of attitude*
departure • *Her new novel is a departure from her previous work.*
deviation • *Deviation from the norm is not tolerated.*
difference • *a noticeable difference in his behaviour*
diversion • *a welcome diversion from the daily grind*

variety ❶ NOUN
a number of different kinds of things • *a wide variety of readers*
array • *an attractive array of bright colours*
assortment • *an assortment of pets*
collection • *a huge collection of books*
medley • *a medley of vegetables*
mixture • *a mixture of sweets*
range • *a range of sun-care products*

MORE SYNONYMS
- cross section
- miscellany
- multiplicity

variety ❷ NOUN
a particular type of something • *a new variety of celery*
category • *There are three broad categories of soil.*
class • *several classes of butterflies*
kind • *different kinds of roses*
sort • *several articles of this sort*
strain • *a new strain of the virus*
type • *What type of guns were they?*

various ADJECTIVE
of several different types • *trees of various sorts*
assorted • *swimsuits in assorted colours*
different • *different brands of drinks*
disparate • *the disparate cultures of India*
diverse • *Society is more diverse than ever before.*
miscellaneous • *a hoard of miscellaneous junk*
sundry • *sundry journalists and lawyers*

MORE SYNONYMS
- heterogeneous
- manifold

vary ❶ VERB
to change to something different • *weather patterns vary greatly*
alter • *During the course of a day the light alters constantly.*
alternate • *My moods alternate with alarming rapidity.*
change • *My feelings haven't changed.*
fluctuate • *Weight may fluctuate markedly.*

vary ❷ VERB
to introduce changes in something • *Vary your routes as much as possible.*
alternate • *Alternate the chunks of fish with chunks of vegetable.*
diversify • *They decided to diversify their products.*
modify • *The government refuses to modify its position.*

MORE SYNONYMS
- permutate
- reorder

vast ADJECTIVE
extremely large • *farmers who own vast stretches of land*

a
b
c
d
e
f
g
h
i
j
k
l
m
n
o
p
q
r
s
t
u
v
w
x
y
z

Can't find the word you're looking for? Try the index.

colossal • *a colossal statue*
enormous • *The main bedroom is enormous.*
giant • *a giant meteorite heading for the earth*
gigantic • *a gigantic shopping mall*
great • *a great hall as long as a church*
huge • *a huge crowd*
immense • *an immense castle*
massive • *a massive theme park*

ANTONYM
● tiny

verdict NOUN

a decision or opinion on something
• *The doctor's verdict was that he was fine.*
conclusion • *I've come to the conclusion that she's lying.*
decision • *The editor's decision is final.*
finding • *The court announced its findings.*
judgment • *My judgment is that things are going to get worse.*
opinion • *a medical opinion*

very ADVERB

to a great degree • *very bad dreams*
deeply • *I was deeply sorry to hear about your loss.*
extremely • *My mobile phone is extremely useful.*
greatly • *I was greatly relieved when he finally arrived.*
highly • *Mr Singh was a highly successful salesman.*
really • *I know her really well.*
terribly • *I'm terribly sorry to bother you.*

MORE SYNONYMS
● exceedingly
● profoundly
● remarkably

veto ❶ VERB

to forbid something • *Treasury officials vetoed the plans.*
ban • *The authorities have banned the advertisement.*
forbid • *Most airlines forbid the use of mobile phones on their planes.*
prohibit • *The government intends to prohibit all trade with the country.*

veto ❷ NOUN

the act of forbidding or power to forbid something • *Dr. Baker has the power of veto.*
ban • *the arms ban on the Bosnian government*
prohibition • *a prohibition on nuclear testing*

victory NOUN

a success in a battle or competition • *his 15th consecutive victory in a doubles final*
laurels • *a former British champion took the laurels in this event*
success • *league and cup successes*
superiority • *United Nations air forces won air superiority.*
triumph • *last year's Republican triumph in the elections*
win • *eight wins in nine games*

ANTONYM
● defeat

view ❶ NOUN

a personal opinion • *his political views*
attitude • *other people's attitudes towards you*
belief • *people's beliefs about crime*
conviction • *a firm conviction that things have improved*
feeling • *It is my feeling that Klein is right.*
opinion • *a favourable opinion of our neighbours*

point of view • *an unusual point of view on the subject*

view ❷ NOUN
the things you can see from a particular place • *There was a beautiful view from the window.*
aspect • *the Yorkshire hills which give the cottage a lovely aspect*
landscape • *Arizona's desert landscape*
panorama • *a panorama of fertile valleys*
perspective • *the aerial perspective of St Paul's Cathedral*
scene • *Wright surveyed the scene from his chosen seat.*
spectacle • *a sweeping spectacle of rugged peaks*

MORE SYNONYMS
- outlook
- prospect
- vista

view ❸ VERB
to think of something in a particular way • *They viewed me with contempt.*
consider • *We consider them to be our friends.*
deem (FORMAL) • *His ideas were deemed unacceptable.*
judge • *His work was judged unsatisfactory.*
regard • *They regard the tax as unfair.*

viewpoint NOUN
an attitude towards something • *We all have our own personal viewpoints.*
attitude • *other people's attitudes towards you*
belief • *people's beliefs about crime*
conviction • *a very personal, political conviction*

feeling • *What are your feelings on this matter?*
opinion • *a favourable opinion of our neighbours*
point of view • *an unusual point of view on the subject*

violence ❶ NOUN
behaviour which is intended to hurt people • *Twenty people were killed in the violence.*
bloodshed • *The government must avoid further bloodshed.*
brutality • *the brutality of the war in Vietnam*
cruelty • *Human beings are capable of such cruelty to each other.*
force • *If you use any force, I shall inform the police.*
savagery • *acts of vicious savagery*
terrorism • *political terrorism in the 19th century*

violence ❷ NOUN
force and energy • *Amy spoke with sudden violence.*
fervour • *views he had put forward with fervour*
force • *She expressed her feelings with some force.*
harshness • *the harshness of her words*
intensity • *His voice hoarsened with intensity.*
severity • *the severity of her scoldings*
vehemence • *Tweed was taken aback by her vehemence.*

violent ❶ ADJECTIVE
intending to hurt or kill people • *violent criminals*
bloodthirsty • *a bloodthirsty monster*
brutal • *a brutal crime*
cruel • *He is cruel towards animals.*
murderous • *a murderous bank-robber*

a
b
c
d
e
f
g
h
i
j
k
l
m
n
o
p
q
r
s
t
u
v
w
x
y
z

Can't find the word you're looking for? Try the index.

savage • *savage warriors*
vicious • *He was a cruel and vicious man.*

ANTONYM
- gentle

violent ❷ ADJECTIVE
happening unexpectedly and with great force • *violent storms*
powerful • *He was caught by a powerful blow.*
raging • *a raging flood*
rough • *A wooden ship sank in rough seas.*
strong • *strong winds and rain*
turbulent • *the turbulent events of the century*
wild • *the wild gales sweeping up from the channel*

MORE SYNONYMS
- tempestuous
- tumultuous

violent ❸ ADJECTIVE
said, felt, or done with great force • *the violent reaction to his plans*
acute • *pain which grew more and more acute*
furious • *a furious row*
intense • *a look of intense dislike*
powerful • *a powerful backlash against the government*
severe • *a severe emotional shock*
strong • *strong words*

MORE SYNONYMS
- forcible
- passionate
- vehement

virtue ❶ NOUN
the quality of doing what is morally right • *He is a paragon of virtue.*
goodness • *He has faith in human goodness.*
integrity • *He was praised for his*

fairness and integrity.
morality • *standards of morality and justice in society*

MORE SYNONYMS
- probity
- rectitude
- righteousness

virtue ❷ NOUN
an advantage something has • *the virtue of neatness*
advantage • *the advantages of the new system*
asset • *The one asset the job provided was contacts.*
attribute • *a player with every attribute you could want*
merit • *the merits of various football teams*
plus (INFORMAL) • *The nutrients in milk have pluses and minuses.*
strength • *the strengths and weaknesses of our position*

virtue ❸, by virtue of PREPOSITION
because of • *The article stuck in my mind by virtue of one detail.*
as a result of • *People will feel better as a result of their efforts.*
because of • *She was promoted because of her experience.*
by dint of • *He succeeds by dint of hard work.*
on account of • *The city is popular with tourists on account of its many museums.*
thanks to • *Thanks to recent research, new treatments are available.*

visible ❶ ADJECTIVE
able to be seen • *The warning lights were clearly visible.*
clear • *the clearest pictures ever of Pluto*

Can't find the word you're looking for? Try the index.

conspicuous • *He felt more conspicuous than he'd have liked.*
distinguishable • *colours just distinguishable in the dark*
in sight • *There wasn't another vehicle in sight.*
observable • *the observable part of the Universe*
perceptible • *Daniel gave a barely perceptible nod.*

ANTONYM
- invisible

visible ❷ ADJECTIVE
noticeable or evident • *There was little visible excitement.*
apparent • *There is no apparent reason for the crime.*
evident • *He ate with evident enjoyment.*
manifest • *his manifest enthusiasm*
noticeable • *subtle but noticeable changes*
obvious • *There are obvious dangers.*
plain • *It is plain a mistake has been made.*

MORE SYNONYMS
- conspicuous
- discernible
- patent

vision ❶ NOUN
a mental picture in which you imagine things • *my vision of the future*
conception • *my conception of a garden*
daydream • *He learned to escape into daydreams.*
dream • *his dream of becoming a pilot*
fantasy • *fantasies of romance and true love*

ideal • *your ideal of a holiday*
image • *an image in your mind of what you are looking for*

vision ❷ NOUN
the ability to imagine future developments • *a total lack of vision and imagination*
foresight • *They had the foresight to invest in technology.*
imagination • *He had the imagination to foresee dangers.*
insight • *the development of insight and understanding*
intuition • *Her intuition told her something was wrong.*

vision ❸ NOUN
an experience in which you see things others cannot • *She was convinced her visions were real.*
apparition • *One of the women was the apparition he had seen.*
hallucination • *The drug can cause hallucinations.*
illusion • *Perhaps the footprint was an illusion.*
mirage • *The girl was a mirage, created by his troubled mind.*
phantom • *People claimed to have seen the phantom.*
spectre • *a spectre from the other world*

MORE SYNONYMS
- chimera
- phantasm
- wraith

visit ❶ VERB
to go to see and spend time with someone • *He wanted to visit his brother in Sydney.*
call on • *Don't hesitate to call on me.*
go to see • *I'll go to see him in the hospital.*

a
b
c
d
e
f
g
h
i
j
k
l
m
n
o
p
q
r
s
t
u
v
w
x
y
z

Can't find the word you're looking for? Try the index.

A
B
C
D
E
F
G
H
I
J
K
L
M
N
O
P
Q
R
S
T
U
V
W
X
Y
Z

look up • *She looked up friends she had not seen for a while.*

visit ➋ NOUN
a trip to see a person or place • *Helen had recently paid him a visit.*
call • *He decided to pay a call on Tommy.*
stay • *An experienced guide is provided during your stay.*
stop • *The last stop in Mr Cook's tour was Paris.*

vital ➊ ADJECTIVE
necessary or very important • *a blockade which cut off vital fuel supplies*
central • *He is central to the whole project.*
critical • *This decision will be critical to our future.*
crucial • *the man who played a crucial role in the negotiations*
essential • *It is essential that you see a doctor soon.*
important • *the most important piece of evidence in the case*
indispensable • *an indispensable piece of equipment*
necessary • *the skills necessary for survival*
pivotal • *He played a pivotal role in the match.*

vital ➋ ADJECTIVE
energetic and full of life • *Old age has diminished a once vital person.*
active • *an active youngster*
dynamic • *a dynamic and exciting place*
energetic • *She became a shadow of her happy, energetic self.*
lively • *a beautiful, lively young girl*
spirited • *the spirited heroine of this film*
sprightly • *a sprightly old man*

vivacious • *She is vivacious and charming.*

vomit VERB
to have food and drink come back up through the mouth • *Any product made from milk made him vomit.*
be sick • *She was sick in the handbasin.*
bring up • *Certain foods are difficult to bring up.*
chunder (AUSTRALIAN AND NEW ZEALAND; SLANG) • *the time you chundered in the taxi*
heave • *He gasped and heaved and vomited again.*
puke (INFORMAL) • *They got drunk and puked out of the window.*
regurgitate • *swallowing and regurgitating large quantities of water*

vote ➊ NOUN
a decision made by allowing people to state their preference • *Do you think we should have a vote on that?*
ballot • *The result of the ballot will be known soon.*
plebiscite (FORMAL) • *A plebiscite made Hitler the Chancellor.*
polls • *In 1945, Churchill was defeated at the polls.*
referendum • *Estonia planned to hold a referendum on independence.*

vote ➋ VERB
to indicate a choice or opinion • *It seems that many people would vote for the opposition.*
cast a vote • *90% of those who cast a vote*
go to the polls • *Voters are due to go to the polls on Sunday.*
opt • *The mass of Spaniards opted for democracy.*

Can't find the word you're looking for? Try the index.

return • *Members will be asked to return a vote for or against the motion.*

vote ❸ VERB
to suggest that something should happen • *I vote that we all go to Holland.*
propose • *I propose that we all try to get some sleep.*
recommend • *I recommend that he be sent home early.*
suggest • *I suggest we go round the table and introduce ourselves.*

vulgar ❶ ADJECTIVE
socially unacceptable or offensive • *vulgar language*
coarse • *coarse humour*
crude • *crude pictures*
dirty • *dirty jokes*
indecent • *an indecent suggestion*
rude • *a rude gesture*
uncouth • *that oafish, uncouth person*

MORE SYNONYMS
● improper
● ribald
● unrefined

ANTONYM
● refined

vulgar ❷ ADJECTIVE
showing a lack of taste or quality • *I think it's a very vulgar house.*
common • *She could be a little common at times.*
flashy • *flashy clothes*
gaudy • *a gaudy purple-and-orange hat*
tasteless • *a house with tasteless decor*
tawdry • *a tawdry seaside town*

ANTONYM
● sophisticated

vulnerable ADJECTIVE
weak and without protection • *vulnerable old people*
exposed • *The west coast is very exposed to Atlantic winds.*
sensitive • *Most people are highly sensitive to criticism.*
susceptible • *an area that is susceptible to attack*
weak • *He spoke up for the weak and defenceless.*

MORE SYNONYMS
● assailable
● defenceless
● unprotected

a
b
c
d
e
f
g
h
i
j
k
l
m
n
o
p
q
r
s
t
u
v
w
x
y
z

Can't find the word you're looking for? Try the index.

Ww

wait ❶ VERB
to spend time before something
happens • *Wait until we get there.*
linger • *I lingered on for a few days
until he arrived.*
pause • *The crowd paused for a
minute, wondering what to do next.*
remain • *You'll have to remain in
hospital for the time being.*
stand by • *Ships are standing by to
evacuate the people.*
stay • *Stay here while I go for
help.*

wait ❷ NOUN
a period of time before something
happens • *They faced a three-hour
wait before they could leave.*
delay • *The accident caused some
delay.*
interval • *a long interval when no-
one spoke*
pause • *There was a pause before
he replied.*

wake VERB
to make or become conscious
again after sleep • *It was still dark
when he woke.*
awake • *We were awoken by the
doorbell.*
come to • *When she came to she
found it was raining.*
rouse • *We roused him at seven so
he would be on time.*
stir • *She shook him and he started
to stir.*
waken • *wakened by the thunder*

walk ❶ VERB
to go on foot • *I walked slowly
along the road.*
▷ see Word Study **walk**, pages 708–
709

walk ❷ NOUN
a journey made by walking • *We'll
have a quick walk while it's fine.*
hike • *a long hike in the country*
march • *a day's march north of
their objective*
ramble • *They went for a ramble
through the woods.*
stroll • *After dinner we took a stroll
around the city.*
trek • *He's on a trek across the
Antarctic.*

MORE SYNONYMS
● constitutional
● perambulation
● saunter

walk ❸ NOUN
the way someone moves when
walking • *Despite his gangling walk
he was a good dancer.*
carriage • *her regal carriage*
gait • *an awkward gait*
pace • *moving at a brisk pace down
the road*
stride • *He lengthened his stride to
catch up with her.*

wander VERB
to move about in a casual way
• *They wandered aimlessly around
the village.*

Can't find the word you're looking for? Try the index.

cruise • *A police car cruised by.*
drift • *The balloon drifted slowly over the countryside.*
ramble • *freedom to ramble across the moors*
range • *They range widely in search of food.*
roam • *Barefoot children roamed the streets.*
stroll • *We strolled down the street, looking at the shops.*

want ❶ VERB
to feel a desire for something
• *I want a red car for a change.*
covet • *He coveted his boss's job.*
crave • *Sometimes she still craved chocolate.*
desire • *He could make them do whatever he desired.*
wish • *I don't wish to know that.*

want ❷ VERB
to need something • *My hair wants cutting.*
be deficient in • *Their diet was deficient in vitamins.*
demand • *The task of reconstruction demanded much sacrifice.*
lack • *training to give him the skills he lacked*
need • *My car needs servicing.*
require • *He knows exactly what is required of him.*

want ❸ NOUN
a lack of something • *becoming weak from want of rest*
absence • *a complete absence of evidence*
deficiency • *They did blood tests for signs of vitamin deficiency.*
lack • *He got the job in spite of his lack of experience.*
scarcity • *an increasing scarcity of water*

shortage • *A shortage of funds is holding them back.*

MORE SYNONYMS
● dearth
● insufficiency
● paucity

ANTONYM
● abundance

war ❶ NOUN
a period of armed conflict between countries • *The war dragged on for five years.*
combat • *men who died in combat*
conflict • *The conflict is bound to intensify.*
fighting • *He was killed in the fighting which followed the treaty.*
hostilities • *in case hostilities break out*
strife • *The country was torn with strife.*
warfare • *chemical warfare*

ANTONYM
● peace

RELATED WORDS
● ADJECTIVES: belligerent, martial

war ❷ VERB
to fight against something • *The two countries had been warring with each other for years.*
battle • *Thousands of people battled with the police.*
clash • *The two armies clashed at first light.*
combat • *measures to combat smuggling*
fight • *The tribe fought with its rivals.*

warm ❶ ADJECTIVE
having some heat but not hot
• *a warm spring day*
balmy • *balmy summer evenings*
heated • *a heated swimming pool*

a
b
c
d
e
f
g
h
i
j
k
l
m
n
o
p
q
r
s
t
u
v
w
x
y
z

Can't find the word you're looking for? Try the index.

lukewarm • *Heat the milk until lukewarm.*
pleasant • *After a chilly morning, the afternoon was very pleasant.*
tepid • *a bath full of tepid water*

ANTONYM
- cold

warm ➋ ADJECTIVE
friendly and affectionate • *a warm and likable personality*
affectionate • *with an affectionate glance at her children*
amiable • *He was very amiable company.*
cordial • *We were given a most cordial welcome.*
friendly • *All her colleagues were very friendly.*
genial • *a warm-hearted friend and genial host*
loving • *He is a loving husband and father.*

ANTONYM
- unfriendly

warm ➌ VERB
to heat something gently • *The sun came out and warmed his back.*
heat • *Heat the bread in the oven.*
heat up • *The fire soon heated up the room.*
melt • *He melted the butter in a small pan.*
thaw • *Always thaw pastry thoroughly.*
warm up • *You must begin gently to warm up the muscles.*

ANTONYM
- cool

warn VERB
to give advance notice of something unpleasant • *I warned him about those loose tiles.*

alert • *The siren alerted them to the danger.*
caution • *Their reaction cautioned him against any further attempts.*
forewarn • *We were forewarned of what to expect.*
notify • *The weather forecast notified them of the coming storm.*

MORE SYNONYMS
- admonish
- apprise

warning NOUN
something that tells people of possible danger • *advance warning of the attack*
alarm • *They heard the fire alarm and ran to safety.*
alert • *a security alert*
caution • *a note of caution*
notice • *three months' notice*
premonition • *He had a premonition of bad news.*

MORE SYNONYMS
- augury
- caveat
- presage

wary ADJECTIVE
showing lack of trust in something • *She was wary of marriage.*
cautious • *His experience has made him cautious.*
distrustful • *Voters are deeply distrustful of all politicians.*
guarded • *The boy gave him a guarded look.*
suspicious • *He was rightly suspicious of their motives.*
vigilant • *He warned the public to be vigilant.*

MORE SYNONYMS
- chary
- circumspect
- heedful

Can't find the word you're looking for? Try the index.

wash ❶ VERB
to clean something with water
• *He got a job washing dishes.*
bathe • *She bathed her blistered feet.*
cleanse • *the correct way to cleanse the skin*
launder • *freshly laundered shirts*
rinse • *Rinse several times in clear water.*
scrub • *I was scrubbing the bathroom floor.*
shampoo • *You must shampoo your hair first.*

wash ❷ VERB
to carry something by the force of water • *washed ashore by the waves*
carry off • *The debris was carried off on the tide.*
erode • *Exposed soil is quickly eroded by wind and rain.*
sweep away • *The floods swept away the houses by the river.*

waste ❶ VERB
to use too much of something unnecessarily • *I wouldn't waste my money on something like that.*
fritter away • *He just fritters his time away.*
squander • *He had squandered his chances of winning.*
throw away • *You're throwing away a good opportunity.*

ANTONYM
● save

waste ❷ NOUN
using something excessively or unnecessarily • *What a complete waste of money!*
extravagance • *widespread tales of his extravagance*
misuse • *This project is a misuse of public funds.*

squandering • *a squandering of his valuable time*

MORE SYNONYMS
● dissipation
● misapplication
● prodigality

waste ❸ ADJECTIVE
not needed or wanted • *waste paper*
leftover • *leftover pieces of fabric*
superfluous • *She got rid of many superfluous belongings.*
unused • *spoiled or unused ballot papers*

wasteful ADJECTIVE
using something in a careless or extravagant way • *wasteful duplication of effort*
extravagant • *an extravagant lifestyle*
uneconomical • *the uneconomical duplication of jobs*

MORE SYNONYMS
● improvident
● profligate
● spendthrift

ANTONYM
● thrifty

watch ❶ NOUN
a period of time when a guard is kept on something • *Keep a close watch on the prisoners.*
observation • *In hospital she'll be under observation night and day.*
supervision • *A toddler requires close supervision.*
surveillance • *kept under constant surveillance*

MORE SYNONYMS
● vigilance
● watchfulness

a
b
c
d
e
f
g
h
i
j
k
l
m
n
o
p
q
r
s
t
u
w
x
y
z

Can't find the word you're looking for? Try the index.

watch ② VERB

to look at something for some time
• *I don't watch television very often.*
gaze at • *gazing at herself in the mirror*
look at • *They looked closely at the insects.*
observe • *Researchers observed the behaviour of small children.*
pay attention • *Pay attention or you won't know what to do.*
see • *We went to see the semi-finals.*
view • *The police have viewed the video recording of the incident.*

watch ③ VERB

to look after something • *You must watch the baby carefully.*
guard • *They were guarded the whole time they were there.*
look after • *I looked after her cat while she was away.*
mind • *Can you mind the store for a couple of hours?*
take care of • *Can you take care of the kids while I get my hair done?*

watch out VERB

to be careful or alert for something
• *You have to watch out for snakes in the swamp.*
be alert • *The bank is alert to the danger.*
be watchful • *Be watchful for any warning signs.*
keep your eyes open • *They kept their eyes open for any troublemakers.*
look out • *What are the symptoms to look out for?*

waterfall NOUN

TYPES OF WATERFALL

cascade	chute
cataract	fall

linn (SCOTTISH)	torrent
rapids	white water

wave ① VERB

to move or flap to and fro • *The doctor waved a piece of paper at him.*
brandish • *He appeared brandishing a knife.*
flap • *He flapped his hand at me to be quiet.*
flourish • *He flourished his glass to emphasize the point.*
flutter • *a fluttering white lace handkerchief*
shake • *Shake the rugs well to air them.*

MORE SYNONYMS
- oscillate
- undulate

wave ② NOUN

a ridge of water on the surface of the sea • *the sound of the waves breaking on the shore*
breaker • *The foaming breakers crashed on to the beach.*
ripple • *gentle ripples on the surface of the lake*
swell • *We bobbed gently on the swell of the incoming tide.*

wave ③ NOUN

an increase in a type of activity
• *the crime wave*
flood • *a flood of complaints about the programme*
movement • *a growing movement towards democracy*
rush • *He felt a sudden rush of panic at the thought.*
surge • *the recent surge in inflation*
trend • *This is a growing trend.*
upsurge • *There was an upsurge of business confidence after the war.*

way ① NOUN

a manner of doing something • *an*

A B C D E F G H I J K L M N O P Q R S T U V W X Y Z

excellent way of cooking meat

approach • *different approaches to gathering information*

manner • *in a friendly manner*

means • *The move is a means to fight crime.*

method • *using the latest teaching methods*

procedure • *He failed to follow the correct procedure when applying for a visa.*

technique • *The tests were performed using a new technique.*

way ❷ NOUN

the customs or behaviour of a person or group • *Their ways are certainly different.*

conduct • *People judged him by his social skills and conduct.*

custom • *an ancient Japanese custom*

manner • *His manner was rather abrupt.*

practice • *a public enquiry into bank practices*

style • *Behaving like that isn't his style.*

MORE SYNONYMS
- idiosyncrasy
- wont

way ❸ NOUN

a route taken to a particular place • *I can't remember the way.*

channel • *a safe channel avoiding the reefs*

course • *The ship was on a course that followed the coastline.*

lane • *the busiest shipping lanes in the world*

path • *The lava annihilates everything in its path.*

road • *the road into the village*

route • *the most direct route to the town centre*

645 | **weak**

weak ❶ ADJECTIVE

lacking in strength • *She had a weak heart.*

delicate • *She was physically delicate and mentally unstable.*

faint • *Feeling faint is one of the symptoms of angina.*

feeble • *old and feeble and unable to walk far*

frail • *in frail health*

puny • *He was puny as a child but grew up to be a top athlete.*

sickly • *a sickly baby with no resistance to illness*

wasted • *muscles which were wasted through lack of use*

MORE SYNONYMS
- debilitated
- decrepit
- enervated
- infirm

ANTONYM
- strong

weak ❷ ADJECTIVE

likely to break or fail • *a weak economy*

deficient • *The plane had a deficient landing system.*

faulty • *The money will be used to repair faulty equipment.*

inadequate • *inadequate safety measures*

weak ❸ ADJECTIVE

easily influenced by other people • *He was a weak man who wouldn't stick his neck out.*

powerless • *a powerless ruler governed by his advisers*

spineless • *bureaucrats and spineless politicians*

MORE SYNONYMS
- indecisive
- irresolute

Can't find the word you're looking for? Try the index.

A
B
C
D
E
F
G
H
I
J
K
L
M
N
O
P
Q
R
S
T
U
V
W
X
Y
Z

ANTONYM
- resolute

weaken VERB

to make or become less strong
• *His authority was weakened by their actions.*
diminish • *to diminish the prestige of the monarchy*
fail • *His strength began to fail after a few hours.*
flag • *Her enthusiasm was in no way flagging.*
lessen • *The drugs lessen the risk of an epidemic.*
reduce • *Reduced consumer demand caused the company to collapse.*
sap • *I was afraid the illness had sapped my strength.*
undermine • *They were accused of trying to undermine the government.*
wane • *His interest in sport began to wane.*

MORE SYNONYMS
- debilitate
- enervate
- mitigate

ANTONYM
- strengthen

weakness ❶ NOUN

a lack of physical or moral strength
• *His extreme weakness caused him to collapse.*
defect • *a serious character defect*
flaw • *His main flaw is his bad temper.*
fragility • *They are at risk because of the fragility of their bones.*
frailty • *the triumph of will over human frailty*
imperfection • *He concedes that there are imperfections in the system.*
vulnerability • *the extreme*

vulnerability of the young chicks

MORE SYNONYMS
- Achilles' heel
- debility
- infirmity

ANTONYM
- strength

weakness ❷ NOUN

a great liking for something
• *a weakness for chocolate*
fondness • *a fondness for good wine*
liking • *a liking for tripe and onions*
passion • *His other great passion was his motorbike.*
penchant • *a stylish woman with a penchant for dark glasses*

MORE SYNONYMS
- partiality
- predilection

ANTONYM
- dislike

wealth ❶ NOUN

a large amount of money
• *Economic reform brought them wealth.*
affluence • *the trappings of affluence*
fortune • *He made a fortune in the property boom.*
means • *a person of means*
money • *All that money brought nothing but sadness and misery.*
prosperity • *Japan's economic prosperity*
riches • *His Olympic medal brought him fame and riches.*
substance • *run by local men of substance*

wealth ❷ NOUN

a lot of something • *a wealth of information*

Can't find the word you're looking for? Try the index.

abundance • *This area has an abundance of safe beaches.*
bounty • *autumn's bounty of fruits and berries*
plenty • *He grew up in a time of plenty.*
store • *She dipped into her store of theatrical anecdotes.*

MORE SYNONYMS
- copiousness
- cornucopia
- plenitude
- profusion

ANTONYM
- shortage

wealthy ADJECTIVE
having plenty of money • *She came from a very wealthy background.*
affluent • *living in an affluent neighbourhood*
comfortable • *from a stable, comfortable family*
opulent • *Most of the cash went on supporting his opulent lifestyle.*
prosperous • *The place looks more prosperous than ever.*
rich • *I'm going to be very rich one day.*
well-to-do • *a rather well-to-do family in the shipping business*

ANTONYM
- poor

wear ❶ VERB
to be dressed in something • *He was wearing a brown uniform.*
be clothed in • *She was clothed in a flowered dress.*
be dressed in • *The women were dressed in their finest attire.*
don • *The police responded by donning riot gear.*
have on • *I had my new shoes on that night.*

put on • *He had to put on his glasses to read the paper.*
sport (INFORMAL) • *sporting a red tie*

wear ❷ VERB
to become worse in condition with use or age • *The old stone steps were worn in the middle.*
corrode • *The underground pipes were badly corroded.*
erode • *Exposed rock is quickly eroded by wind and rain.*
fray • *fraying edges on the stair carpet*
rub • *The inscription had been rubbed smooth by generations of hands.*
wash away • *The topsoil had been washed away by the incessant rain.*

MORE SYNONYMS
- abrade
- deteriorate

wear ❸ NOUN
the type of use which causes something to be damaged • *The tyres showed signs of wear.*
corrosion • *Zinc is used to protect other metals from corrosion.*
deterioration • *The building is already showing signs of deterioration.*
erosion • *erosion of the river valleys*
use • *The carpet must be able to cope with heavy use.*

MORE SYNONYMS
- abrasion
- attrition

wear out VERB
to make someone tired • *The past few days have really worn me out.*
exhaust • *The long working day exhausted him.*
tire • *If driving tires you, take the train.*

a
b
c
d
e
f
g
h
i
j
k
l
m
n
o
p
q
r
s
t
u
v
w
x
y
z

Can't find the word you're looking for? Try the index.

weary • *wearied by the constant demands on his time*

weary ADJECTIVE
very tired • *She sank to the ground, too weary to walk another step.*
drained • *He's always completely drained after a performance.*
exhausted • *She was too exhausted and upset to talk.*
fatigued • *Winter weather can leave you feeling fatigued.*
tired • *He was too tired even to take a shower.*
tuckered out (AUSTRALIAN AND NEW ZEALAND; INFORMAL) • *You must be tuckered out after that bus trip.*
worn out • *He's just worn out after the long drive.*

weather NOUN

TYPES OF WEATHER

cloud	heatwave
drought	ice
frost	lightning
hail	sunshine
haze	thaw

WORDS USED TO DESCRIBE THE WEATHER

balmy	humid
blustery	icy
breezy	mild
clammy	misty
clear	muggy
close	overcast
cloudy	rainy
cold	showery
drizzly	snowy
dry	stormy
dull	sultry
fine	sunny
foggy	thundery
hot	wet

WORDS FOR RAIN AND SNOW

drizzle	sleet
rain	slush
shower	snow

WORDS FOR STORM

blizzard	squall
hailstorm	storm
snowstorm	tempest

WORDS FOR WIND

breeze	squall
cyclone	tornado
gale	typhoon
gust	whirlwind
hurricane	wind

WORDS FOR FOG

fog	haze
haar	mist

weird ADJECTIVE
strange or odd • *I had such a weird dream last night.*
bizarre • *his bizarre behaviour*
curious • *What a curious thing to say!*
extraordinary • *an extraordinary occurrence*
funny • *There's something funny about him.*
odd • *an odd coincidence*
singular (FORMAL) • *I can't think where you got such a singular notion.*
strange • *Didn't you notice anything strange about her?*
peculiar • *It tasted very peculiar.*
queer • *I think there's something queer going on here.*

ANTONYM
● ordinary

weirdo NOUN (INFORMAL)
a person who behaves in a strange

way • *All the other kids thought I was a weirdo.*
crank (INFORMAL) • *He kept quiet in case people thought he was a crank.*
eccentric • *a local eccentric who wears shorts all year round*
freak (INFORMAL) • *Barry's always been looked on as a bit of a freak.*
loony (SLANG) • *I realize I must sound like a complete loony.*
nut (SLANG) • *There's some nut out there with a gun.*
nutter (BRITISH; SLANG) • *She was being stalked by a real nutter.*

well ❶ ADVERB
in a satisfactory way • *The interview went well.*
satisfactorily • *The system should work satisfactorily.*
smoothly • *So far, the operation is going smoothly.*
splendidly • *They have behaved splendidly.*
successfully • *The changeover is working successfully.*

well ❷ ADVERB
with skill and ability • *He draws well.*
ably • *He was ably assisted by the other members of staff.*
admirably • *dealing admirably with a difficult situation*
adequately • *He speaks French very adequately.*
competently • *They handled the situation very competently.*
effectively • *In the first half he operated effectively in defence.*
efficiently • *He works efficiently and accurately.*
expertly • *Shopkeepers expertly rolled spices up in bay leaves.*
professionally • *These tickets have been forged very professionally.*
skilfully • *He skilfully exploited his company's strengths.*

MORE SYNONYMS
● adeptly
● proficiently

ANTONYM
● badly

well ❸ ADVERB
fully and with thoroughness • *They should be well washed and well dried.*
amply • *I was amply rewarded for my trouble.*
closely • *He studied the documents closely.*
completely • *Make sure you defrost it completely.*
fully • *The new system is now fully under way.*
highly • *one of the most highly regarded authors*
meticulously • *He had planned his trip meticulously.*
rigorously • *Their duties have not been performed as rigorously as they might have been.*
thoroughly • *Add the oil and mix thoroughly.*

well ❹ ADVERB
in a kind way • *He treats his employees well.*
compassionately • *He always acted compassionately towards her.*
considerately • *I expect people to deal with me considerately and fairly.*
favourably • *companies who treat men more favourably than women*
humanely • *They treat their livestock humanely.*
kindly • *Children are capable of behaving kindly.*

a
b
c
d
e
f
g
h
i
j
k
l
m
n
o
p
q
r
s
t
u
v
w
x
y
z

Can't find the word you're looking for? Try the index.

with consideration • *He was treated with consideration and kindness.*

well ❺ ADJECTIVE
having good health • *I'm not very well today.*
blooming • *She felt confident, blooming, and attractive.*
fit • *He keeps himself really fit.*
healthy • *Most people want to be healthy and happy.*
in good condition • *He's in good condition for his age.*
in good health • *He seemed to be in good health and spirits.*
robust • *He's never been a very robust child.*
sound • *a sound body*
strong • *Eat well and you'll soon be strong again.*

MORE SYNONYMS
● able-bodied
● hale
● in fine fettle

ANTONYM
● sick

wet ❶ ADJECTIVE
covered in liquid • *Don't get your feet wet.*
damp • *Her hair was still damp.*
drenched • *getting drenched by icy water*
moist • *The soil is reasonably moist after the September rain.*
saturated • *The filter has been saturated with oil.*
soaked • *soaked to the skin*
sodden • *We took off our sodden clothes.*
waterlogged • *The game was called off because the pitch was waterlogged.*

ANTONYM
● dry

wet ❷ ADJECTIVE
in rainy weather conditions • *It was a miserable wet day.*
humid • *hot and humid weather conditions*
misty • *The air was cold and misty.*
rainy • *The rainy season starts in December.*
showery • *The day had been showery with sunny intervals.*

ANTONYM
● dry

wet ❸ VERB
to put liquid on to something • *Wet the edges and stick them together.*
dampen • *You must dampen the laundry before you iron it.*
irrigate • *irrigated by a system of interconnected canals*
moisten • *Take a sip of water to moisten your throat.*
soak • *The water had soaked his jacket and shirt.*
spray • *It can spray the whole field in half an hour.*
water • *We have to water the plants when the weather is dry.*

MORE SYNONYMS
● drench
● humidify
● saturate

ANTONYM
● dry

whim NOUN
a sudden fancy for something • *We decided to go more or less on a whim.*
craze • *the latest fitness craze*
fad (INFORMAL) • *just a passing fad*
fancy • *I had a fancy for some strawberries.*

Can't find the word you're looking for? Try the index.

impulse • *He resisted the impulse to buy a new one.*
urge • *He had an urge to open a shop of his own.*

MORE SYNONYMS
- caprice
- vagary
- whimsy

white NOUN OR ADJECTIVE

SHADES OF WHITE

cream	off-white
ecru	oyster white
ivory	pearl
magnolia	snow-white

whole ❶ ADJECTIVE
indicating all of something • *We spent the whole summer abroad.*
complete • *The list filled a complete page.*
entire • *There are only ten in the entire country.*
full • *a full week's notice*
total • *The evening was a total fiasco.*
uncut • *the uncut version of the film*
undivided • *He has my undivided loyalty.*

whole ❷ NOUN
the full amount of something • *the whole of Asia*
aggregate • *the aggregate of the individual scores*
all • *All is not lost.*
everything • *Everything that happened is my fault.*
lot • *He lost the lot within five minutes.*
sum total • *The small room contained the sum total of their possessions.*
total • *The eventual total was far higher.*

wicked ❶ ADJECTIVE
very bad or evil • *That was a wicked thing to do.*
atrocious • *He had committed atrocious crimes against the refugees.*
bad • *Please forgive our bad behaviour.*
depraved • *the work of depraved criminals*
evil • *the country's most evil terrorists*
sinful • *"This is a sinful world," he said.*
vicious • *He was a cruel and vicious man.*

MORE SYNONYMS
- egregious
- iniquitous
- nefarious

wicked ❷ ADJECTIVE
mischievous in an amusing or attractive way • *She always felt wicked when eating chocolate.*
impish • *an impish sense of humour*
mischievous • *like a mischievous child*
naughty • *little boys using naughty words*

wide ❶ ADJECTIVE
measuring a large distance from side to side • *It should be wide enough to give plenty of working space.*
▷ see Word Study **wide**, page 710

ANTONYM
- narrow

wide ❷ ADJECTIVE
extensive in scope • *a wide range of colours*
▷ see Word Study **wide**, page 710

a
b
c
d
e
f
g
h
i
j
k
l
m
n
o
p
q
r
s
t
u
v
w
x
y
z

Can't find the word you're looking for? Try the index.

A B C D E F G H I J K L M N O P Q R S T U V W X Y Z

ANTONYM
- narrow

wide ❸ ADVERB
as far as possible • *Open wide!*
▷ see Word Study **wide**, page 710

widespread ADJECTIVE
existing over a large area • *Food shortages are widespread.*
broad • *The agreement won broad support among the people.*
common • *the common view that treatment is ineffective*
extensive • *The bomb caused extensive damage.*
pervasive • *the pervasive influence of the army in national life*
prevalent • *Smoking is becoming more prevalent among girls.*
rife • *Bribery and corruption were rife in the industry.*

wild ❶ ADJECTIVE
not cultivated or domesticated
• *a meadow of wild flowers*
fierce • *Fierce hyenas scavenged for food after the kill.*
free • *stunning pictures of wild and free animals*
natural • *In the natural state this animal is not ferocious.*
uncultivated • *developed from an uncultivated type of grass*
undomesticated • *These cats lived wild and were completely undomesticated.*
untamed • *the untamed horses of the Camargue*
warrigal (AUSTRALIAN; LITERARY)
• *a warrigal mare*

wild ❷ ADJECTIVE
in stormy conditions • *They were not deterred by the wild weather.*
howling • *a howling gale*
raging • *The trip involved crossing*

a raging torrent.
rough • *The two ships collided in rough seas.*
stormy • *a dark and stormy night*
violent • *That night they were hit by a violent storm.*

wild ❸ ADJECTIVE
without control or restraint • *wild with excitement*
boisterous • *Most of the children were noisy and boisterous.*
rowdy • *The television coverage revealed their rowdy behaviour.*
turbulent • *five turbulent years of rows and reconciliations*
uncontrolled • *His uncontrolled behaviour disturbed the entire group.*
wayward • *wayward children with a history of emotional problems*

MORE SYNONYMS
- disorderly
- riotous
- uproarious

will ❶ VERB
to leave something to someone when you die • *He had willed his fortune to his daughter.*
bequeath • *She bequeathed her collection to the local museum.*
leave • *Everything was left to the housekeeper.*
pass on • *He passed on much of his estate to his eldest son.*

will ❷ NOUN
the strong determination to achieve something • *the will to win*
determination • *Determination has always been a part of his make-up.*
purpose • *They are enthusiastic and have a sense of purpose.*
resolution • *He began to form a resolution to clear his name.*

Can't find the word you're looking for? Try the index.

resolve • *This will strengthen the public's resolve.*
willpower • *succeeding by sheer willpower*

will ❸ NOUN
what someone wants • *the will of the people*
choice • *It's your choice.*
inclination • *She showed no inclination to go.*
mind • *You can go if you have a mind to do so.*
volition • *a product of our volition*
wish • *done against my wishes*

RELATED WORD
● ADJECTIVE: voluntary

willing ADJECTIVE
ready and eager to do something
• *a willing helper*
agreeable • *We can go ahead if you are agreeable.*
eager • *Children are eager to learn.*
game (INFORMAL) • *He still had new ideas and was game to try them.*
happy • *That's a risk I'm happy to take.*
prepared • *I'm not prepared to take orders from her.*
ready • *ready to die for their beliefs*

MORE SYNONYMS
● amenable
● compliant
● desirous

ANTONYM
● unwilling

win ❶ VERB
to defeat your opponents • *The top four teams all won.*
be victorious • *Despite the strong opposition she was victorious.*
come first • *They unexpectedly came first this year.*

prevail • *the votes he must win in order to prevail*
succeed • *the skills and qualities needed to succeed*
triumph • *a symbol of good triumphing over evil*

ANTONYM
● lose

win ❷ VERB
to succeed in obtaining something
• *moves to win the support of the poor*
achieve • *We have achieved our objective.*
attain • *He's half-way to attaining his pilot's licence.*
gain • *After three weeks the hostages finally gained their freedom.*
get • *My entry got a commendation this year.*
secure • *Her achievements helped secure her the job.*

win ❸ NOUN
a victory in a contest • *a run of seven games without a win*
success • *his success in the Monaco Grand Prix*
triumph • *their World Cup triumph*
victory • *the 3-1 victory over Switzerland*

ANTONYM
● defeat

winner NOUN
a person who wins something
• *The winners will be notified by post.*
champion • *a former Olympic champion*
conqueror • *This time they easily overcame their former conquerors.*
victor • *He emerged as the victor by the second day.*

a b c d e f g h i j k l m n o p q r s t u v **w** x y z

Can't find the word you're looking for? Try the index.

ANTONYM
- loser

wisdom NOUN
judgment used to make sensible decisions • *the wisdom that comes from experience*
discernment • *Her keen discernment made her an excellent collector.*
insight • *a man of considerable insight and diplomatic skills*
judgment • *He respected our judgment on this matter.*
knowledge • *the quest for scientific knowledge*
reason • *a conflict between emotion and reason*

MORE SYNONYMS
- astuteness
- erudition
- sagacity

ANTONYM
- foolishness

RELATED WORD
- ADJECTIVE: sagacious

wise ADJECTIVE
able to make use of experience and judgment • *a wise old man*
informed • *an informed guess at his wealth*
judicious • *the judicious use of military force*
perceptive • *the words of a perceptive political commentator*
rational • *You must look at both sides before you can reach a rational decision.*
sensible • *The sensible thing is to leave them alone.*
shrewd • *a shrewd deduction about what was going on*

ANTONYM
- foolish

wish ❶ NOUN
a desire for something • *She was sincere in her wish to make amends.*
desire • *her desire for a child of her own*
hankering • *She had always had a hankering to be an actress.*
hunger • *a hunger for success*
longing • *He felt a longing for familiar surroundings.*
urge • *He had an urge to open a shop of his own.*
want • *Supermarkets respond to the wants of their customers.*

wish ❷ VERB
to want something • *We wished to return.*
desire • *He was bored and desired to go home.*
hunger • *She hungered for adventure.*
long • *I'm longing for the holidays.*
thirst • *thirsting for knowledge*
want • *people who know exactly what they want in life*
yearn • *The younger ones yearned to be part of a normal family.*

withdraw ❶ VERB
to take something out • *He withdrew some money from the bank.*
draw out • *I'll have to draw out some of my savings.*
extract • *She extracted another dress from the wardrobe.*
remove • *I removed the splinter from her finger.*
take out • *There was a fee for taking out money from the account.*

withdraw ❷ VERB
to back out of an activity • *They withdrew from the conference.*
back out • *He backed out of the agreement.*

Can't find the word you're looking for? Try the index.

leave • *Davis left the game to go to hospital.*
pull out • *The general pulled out of the talks after two days.*
retire • *The jury retired three hours ago.*
retreat • *retreating from the harsh realities of life*

MORE SYNONYMS
- disengage
- secede

wither ❶ VERB
to become weaker and fade away • *Will the company flourish or wither?*
decline • *The church's influence has declined.*
fade • *Prospects for peace have already started to fade.*

wither ❷ VERB
to shrivel up and die • *Crops withered under the sun.*
droop • *plants drooping in the heat*
shrivel • *They watched their crops shrivel and die in the drought.*
wilt • *The roses wilted the day after she bought them.*

witness ❶ NOUN
someone who has seen something happen • *The police appealed for witnesses to come forward.*
bystander • *Seven other innocent bystanders were injured.*
eyewitness • *Eyewitnesses say the soldiers opened fire on the crowd.*
observer • *A casual observer would not have noticed them.*
onlooker • *a small crowd of onlookers*
spectator • *carried out in full view of spectators*

witness ❷ VERB
to see something happening • *Anyone who witnessed the attack should call the police.*
be present at • *Many men are now present at the birth of their children.*
observe • *We observed them setting up the machine gun.*
see • *I saw him do it.*
watch • *She had watched them drinking heavily before the accident.*

witty ADJECTIVE
amusing in a clever way • *He's so witty I could listen to him for hours.*
amusing • *He provided an irreverent and amusing commentary to the film.*
brilliant • *a brilliant after-dinner speaker*
clever • *He raised some smiles with several clever lines.*
funny • *a film packed with incredibly funny dialogue*
humorous • *a satirical and humorous parody*
sparkling • *He's famous for his sparkling conversation.*

woman NOUN
an adult female human being • *women over 75 years old*
dame (SLANG) • *Who does that dame think she is?*
female • *The average young female is fairly affluent.*
girl • *a night out with the girls*
lady • *Your table is ready, ladies, so please come through.*
lass • *a lass from the country*
sheila (AUSTRALIAN AND NEW ZEALAND; INFORMAL) • *his role as a sheila in his own play*
vrou (SOUTH AFRICAN) • *Have you met his vrou yet?*

ANTONYM
- man

A
B
C
D
E
F
G
H
I
J
K
L
M
N
O
P
Q
R
S
T
U
V
W
X
Y
Z

wonder ❶ VERB

to think about something with curiosity • *I wondered what that noise was.*
ask oneself • *You have to ask yourself what this really means.*
ponder • *pondering how to improve the team*
puzzle • *Researchers continue to puzzle over the origins of the disease.*
speculate • *He refused to speculate about the contents of the letter.*

wonder ❷ VERB

to be surprised and amazed • *He wondered at her anger.*
be amazed • *Most of the cast were amazed by the play's success.*
be astonished • *I was astonished to discover his true age.*
boggle • *The mind boggles at what might be in store for us.*
marvel • *We marvelled at her endless energy.*

wonder ❸ NOUN

something that amazes people • *one of the wonders of nature*
marvel • *a marvel of high technology*
miracle • *It's a miracle no one was killed.*
phenomenon • *a well-known geographical phenomenon*
spectacle • *a spectacle not to be missed*

wonderful ❶ ADJECTIVE

extremely good • *It's wonderful to see you.*
excellent • *The recording quality is excellent.*
great (INFORMAL) • *a great bunch of guys*
marvellous • *What a marvellous time we had!*

superb • *The hotel has a superb isolated location.*
tremendous • *I thought it was a tremendous book.*

wonderful ❷ ADJECTIVE

very impressive • *The sunset was a truly wonderful sight.*
amazing • *containing some amazing special effects*
astounding • *The results are quite astounding.*
incredible • *The intensity of colour was incredible.*
magnificent • *magnificent views across the valley*
remarkable • *It was a remarkable achievement to complete the course.*

MORE SYNONYMS

● phenomenal
● wondrous

word ❶ NOUN

RELATED WORDS

● ADJECTIVES: lexical, verbal

PARTS OF A WORD	
capital letter	phoneme
consonant	prefix
grapheme	suffix
letter	syllable

word ❷ NOUN

a remark • *I'd like to say a word of thanks to everyone who helped me.*
comment • *He left without any further comment.*
remark • *Apart from that one remark, he stayed quiet all evening.*
statement • *Verity issued a brief statement to the press.*
utterance • *a crowd of admirers who hung on his every utterance*

word ❸ NOUN

a brief conversation • *James, could*

Can't find the word you're looking for? Try the index.

I have a quick word with you?

chat • *We need to have a chat about the arrangements some time.*
conversation • *He recalled his brief conversation with the Queen.*
discussion • *We had a very short discussion about what to do.*
talk • *I bumped into him yesterday and we had a quick talk.*

word ❹ NOUN

a message • *Since then we've had no word from them.*

announcement • *There has been no formal announcement from either government.*
bulletin • *A spokesperson said no bulletin would be issued.*
communication • *The ambassador brought a communication from the President.*
information • *They will issue written information in due course.*
intelligence • *He wanted to pass this intelligence on to her.*
message • *Did he leave any message for me?*
news • *Is there any news from the embassy?*

word ❺ NOUN

a promise or guarantee • *He gave me his word that he would be there.*

assurance • *Do I have your assurance that you'll take responsibility?*
oath • *She gave her solemn oath not to tell anyone.*
pledge • *He gave his personal pledge that he would help.*
promise • *I'll support you - you have my promise on that.*
word of honour • *I want your word of honour that you'll respect my anonymity.*

work ❶ VERB

to do the tasks required of you • *I had to work twelve hours a day.*

labour • *peasants labouring in the fields*
slave • *slaving over a hot stove*
slog away • *They are still slogging away at algebra.*
toil • *Workers toiled long hours in the mills.*

ANTONYM
- laze

work ❷ NOUN

someone's job • *She's trying to find work.*

business • *We have business to attend to first.*
craft • *He learned his craft from an expert.*
employment • *unable to find employment*
job • *I got a job at the sawmill.*
livelihood • *fishermen who depend on the seas for their livelihood*
occupation • *Please state your occupation.*
profession • *a dentist by profession*

MORE SYNONYMS
- calling
- métier
- pursuit

work ❸ NOUN

the tasks that have to be done • *Sometimes he had to take work home.*

assignment • *written assignments and practical tests*
chore • *We share the household chores.*
duty • *My duty is to look after the animals.*
job • *It turned out to be a bigger job than expected.*

a
b
c
d
e
f
g
h
i
j
k
l
m
n
o
p
q
r
s
t
u
v
w
x
y
z

Can't find the word you're looking for? Try the index.

task • *catching up with administrative tasks*
yakka (AUSTRALIAN AND NEW ZEALAND; INFORMAL) • *a decade of hard yakka on the land*

worker NOUN

a person who works • *seeking a reliable research worker*
craftsman • *furniture made by a local craftsman*
employee • *Many of its employees are women.*
labourer • *a farm labourer*
workman • *Workmen are building a steel fence.*

MORE SYNONYMS

● artisan
● hand
● proletarian

work out ❶ VERB

to find the solution to something • *It took us some time to work out what was happening.*
calculate • *First, calculate your monthly living expenses.*
figure out • *You don't need to be a detective to figure that one out.*
resolve • *They hoped the crisis could be quickly resolved.*
solve • *We'll solve the case ourselves and surprise everyone.*

work out ❷ VERB

to happen in a certain way • *Things didn't work out that way after all.*
develop • *Wait and see how the situation develops.*
go • *Did it all go well?*
happen • *Things don't happen the way you want them to.*
turn out • *Sometimes life doesn't turn out as we expect.*

worn-out ❶ ADJECTIVE

no longer usable because of

extreme wear • *a worn-out pair of shoes*
broken-down • *Broken-down cars lined the road.*
tattered • *tattered clothes*
threadbare • *a square of threadbare carpet*
worn • *Worn tyres cost lives.*

worn-out ❷ ADJECTIVE

extremely tired • *You must be worn-out after the journey.*
exhausted • *too exhausted to do any more*
fatigued • *Winter weather can leave you feeling fatigued.*
prostrate • *He lay prostrate with exhaustion.*
tired • *I need to rest because I'm tired.*
weary • *a weary traveller*

worried ADJECTIVE

being anxious about something • *His parents were worried about his lack of progress.*
anxious • *I was very anxious about her safety.*
bothered • *I'm not bothered about it at all.*
concerned • *a phone call from a concerned neighbour*
nervous • *Consumers say they are nervous about their jobs.*
troubled • *He was troubled by the lifestyle of his son.*
uneasy • *an uneasy feeling that everything was going wrong*

MORE SYNONYMS

● overwrought
● perturbed
● unquiet

ANTONYM

● unconcerned

worry ❶ VERB

to feel anxious about something

Can't find the word you're looking for? Try the index.

• Don't worry, it's bound to arrive soon.

be anxious *• They admitted they were still anxious about the situation.*

brood *• constantly brooding about her family*

feel uneasy *• I felt very uneasy at the lack of response.*

fret *• You mustn't fret about someone else's problems.*

worry ❷ VERB
to disturb someone with a problem *• I didn't want to worry the boys with this.*

bother *• I hate to bother you again so soon.*

hassle (INFORMAL) *• Then my boss started hassling me.*

pester *• I wish they'd stop pestering me for an answer.*

plague *• I'm not going to plague you with more questions.*

trouble *• Don't trouble me while I'm working.*

MORE SYNONYMS
● harry
● importune
● perturb

worry ❸ NOUN
a feeling of anxiety *• a major source of worry*

anxiety *• anxieties about money*

apprehension *• real anger and apprehension about the future*

concern *• growing concern for the environment*

fear *• His fears might be groundless.*

misgiving *• She had some misgivings about what she was about to do.*

unease *• a deep sense of unease about the coming interview*

worsen VERB
to become more difficult *• My relationship with my mother worsened.*

decline *• Hourly output declined in the third quarter.*

degenerate *• The whole tone of the campaign began to degenerate.*

deteriorate *• The weather conditions are deteriorating.*

go downhill (INFORMAL) *• Things have gone steadily downhill since he left.*

ANTONYM
● improve

worship ❶ VERB
to praise and revere something *• People go to church to pray and worship their god.*

glorify *• The monks devoted their days to glorifying God.*

honour *• the Scout's promise to honour God*

praise *• She asked the church to praise God.*

pray to *• They prayed to their gods to bring them rain.*

venerate *• the most venerated religious figure in the country*

MORE SYNONYMS
● deify
● exalt
● revere

ANTONYM
● dishonour

worship ❷ VERB
to love and admire someone *• She had worshipped him from afar for years.*

adore *• an adoring husband*

idolize *• She idolized her father as she was growing up.*

love *• He genuinely loved and cherished her.*

a b c d e f g h i j k l m n o p q r s t u v w x y z

ANTONYM
- despise

worship ❸ NOUN
a feeling of love and admiration for something • *the worship of the ancient Roman gods*
admiration • *Her eyes widened in admiration.*
adoration • *He had been used to female adoration all his life.*
adulation • *The book was received with adulation by the critics.*
devotion • *flattered by his devotion*
homage • *The emperor received the homage of every prince.*
praise • *singing hymns in praise of their god*

MORE SYNONYMS
- deification
- exaltation

PLACES OF WORSHIP

altar
basilica (*Christianity*)
cathedral (*Christianity*)
chapel (*Christianity*)
church (*Christianity*)
gurdwara (*Sikhism*)
meeting house (*Quakerism*)
mosque (*Muslim*)
pagoda (*Hinduism, Buddhism*)
shrine
synagogue (*Judaism*)
tabernacle (*Judaism, Christianity*)

worthless ADJECTIVE
having no real value or worth • *a worthless piece of junk*
meaningless • *their sense of a meaningless existence*
paltry • *a paltry amount*
poor • *a poor reward for his effort*
trifling • *We were paid a trifling sum.*
trivial • *She would go to the doctor for any trivial complaint.*
useless • *I felt useless and a failure.*
valueless • *commercially valueless trees*

MORE SYNONYMS
- negligible
- nugatory

ANTONYM
- valuable

write VERB
to record something in writing • *Write your name and address on a postcard and send it to us.*
inscribe • *Their names were inscribed on the front of the pillar.*
record • *Her letters record the domestic and social details of her life.*
take down • *notes taken down in shorthand*

writing NOUN

TYPES OF WRITING

autobiography	myth
ballad	narrative
biography	non-fiction
column	novel
dissertation	obituary
editorial	parable
epitaph	play
essay	poem
fable	report
feature	review
fiction	rhyme
legend	riddle
letter	script
lyric	story
memoir	thesis

STYLES USED IN WRITING

alliteration	narrative
cliché	parody
idiom	pun
metaphor	satire

Can't find the word you're looking for? Try the index.

FEATURES OF WRITING

character	plot
dialogue	setting
imagery	subplot
motif	theme

wrong ❶ ADJECTIVE
not correct or truthful • *That was the wrong answer.*
false • *We don't know if the information is true or false.*
faulty • *His diagnosis was faulty from the outset.*
incorrect • *a decision based on figures which were incorrect*
mistaken • *a mistaken view of the situation*
unsound • *The thinking is good-hearted, but muddled and unsound.*
untrue • *The remarks were completely untrue.*

MORE SYNONYMS
● erroneous
● fallacious

ANTONYM
● right

wrong ❷ ADJECTIVE
morally unacceptable • *It's wrong to hurt people.*
bad • *I may be a thief but I'm not a bad person.*

crooked • *crooked business deals*
evil • *the country's most evil terrorists*
illegal • *It is illegal to intercept radio messages.*
immoral • *Many would consider such practices immoral.*
unfair • *It was unfair that he should suffer so much.*
unjust • *unjust treatment*

MORE SYNONYMS
● felonious
● iniquitous
● reprehensible
● under-the-table
● unethical

ANTONYM
● right

wrong ❸ NOUN
an unjust action • *the wrongs of our society*
abuse • *controversy over human rights abuses*
crime • *crimes against humanity*
grievance • *He had a deep sense of grievance.*
injustice • *A great injustice had been done to him in the past.*
sin • *He admitted the many sins of his youth.*

a
b
c
d
e
f
g
h
i
j
k
l
m
n
o
p
q
r
s
t
u
v
w
x
y
z

Yy

yellow NOUN OR ADJECTIVE

SHADES OF YELLOW

amber	lemon
canary yellow	mustard
champagne	primrose
citrus yellow	saffron
daffodil	sand
gold	straw

yes INTERJECTION
an expression used to agree with something or say it is true • *"Are you a friend of his?" "Yes."*
aye (SCOTTISH; INFORMAL) • *"Can I borrow this?" "Aye, but I want it back."*
okay • *"Will we leave now?" "Okay, if you like."*
sure • *"Can I come too?" "Sure."*
ya (SOUTH AFRICAN) • *"Are you a runaway?" "Ya," the child replied.*
yeah (INFORMAL) • *Yeah, I think we've met once.*

ANTONYM
● no

yokel NOUN
a person who lives in the country • *a bunch of those yokels*
bushie or **bushy** (AUSTRALIAN AND NEW ZEALAND; INFORMAL) • *"I'm a bit of a bushie at heart," she said.*
countryman • *They are true old-fashioned countrymen.*
peasant • *In rural Mexico a peasant is rarely without his machete.*

young ❶ ADJECTIVE
not yet mature • *young people*
adolescent • *He spent his adolescent years playing guitar.*
immature • *an immature female whale*
infant • *his infant daughter*
junior • *a junior member of the family*
juvenile • *a juvenile delinquent*
little • *What were you like when you were little?*
youthful • *the youthful stars of the film*

ANTONYM
● old

young ❷ PLURAL NOUN
the babies an animal has • *The hen may not be able to feed its young.*
babies • *animals making nests for their babies*
brood • *a hungry brood of fledglings*
family • *a family of weasels*
litter • *a litter of pups*
little ones • *a family of elephants with their little ones*
offspring • *female rats' offspring*

Zz

zero NOUN
nothing or the number o • *I will now count from zero to ten.*
nil • *They beat Argentina one-nil.*

nothing • *Some weeks I earn nothing.*
nought • *How many noughts are there in a million?*

a
b
c
d
e
f
g
h
i
j
k
l
m
n
o
p
q
r
s
t
u
v
w
x
y
z

WORD STUDIES

BAD is such a commonly-used word that it has come to lose much of its effectiveness. Depending on the sense and context of what you are saying, there are many other much more expressive words that can be used instead.

1 If you would like to describe something as having a harmful effect, you could try:
extremely **damaging** • **destructive** effect • **detrimental** impact • **harmful** effects • **unhealthy** lifestyle • **unpleasant** side-effects

2 If you would like to describe something that has made someone feel upset or uneasy, you could try:
distressing images • **disturbing** news • **grim** time • **painful** memories • **traumatic** period • **unsettling** atmosphere • **upsetting** experience

3 If you would like to describe something that has, or is causing physical pain, you could try:
acute attack • **agonizing** death • **excruciating** pain • **intense** cramps • **painful** back • **serious** knee problems • **severe** stomach pains • **terrible** migraine

4 If you would like to describe something or someone that lacks skill, you could try:
incompetent managers • **inept** performance • **poor** judge • **useless** at ...

5 If you would like to describe poor quality, you could try:
defective products • **deficient** diet • **faulty** goods • **imperfect** work • **inadequate** work conditions • **inferior** quality • **pathetic** excuse • **poor** housing • **sorry** state of affairs • **unsatisfactory** service

6 If you would like to describe something or someone with an evil character, you could try:
morally corrupt court • **criminal** actions • **depraved** criminals • **evil** man • **immoral** act • **sinful** act • **villainous** characters • **wicked** stepmother • something **wrong**

7 If you're talking or writing about food, you could try:
mouldy cheese • This meat's **gone off** • **rancid** butter • **rotten** eggs • **sour** milk

8 If you're talking about language, you could try:
obscene lyrics • **offensive** language • **rude** words • **vulgar** expression

BADLY, like **BAD**, can be avoided in favour of less commonly-used and more expressive alternatives.

1 If you would like to describe something that has been or is being done in an inferior way, you could try:
   inadequately trained • **ineptly** run • **poorly** organized • **shoddily** built • **unsatisfactorily** regulated

2 If you would like to describe someone who has been seriously hurt or affected, you could try:
   deeply hurt • **desperately** unhappy • **gravely** ill • **seriously** injured

3 If you would like to describe someone who has been treated in a cruel way, you could try:
   brutally assaulted • **callously** treated • **cruelly** tormented • **savagely** beaten • **viciously** struck

There are a number of alternatives for the word **BEST** which will make your writing more interesting.

1 **If you would like to describe something as being of the highest standard, you could try:**
the **finest** wines • **first-rate** performance • **foremost** painter • **greatest** film • Britain's **leading** actors • England's **outstanding** tennis players • **pre-eminent** pop act • London's **principal** publishing houses • **superlative** products • **supreme** achievement • **top** athletes

2 **If you would like to describe something as the most desirable thing, you could try:**
correct thing • **most desirable** outcome • **most fitting** location • **right** person

3 **If you would like to describe something as the best or most preferred of its kind, you could try:**
the **cream** of Scottish artists • the **elite** of the sporting world • the **finest** wine • the **pick** of the crop

BETTER

Like best, the word **BETTER** can be replaced with a number of alternatives to add variety and interest to your written and spoken English.

1 **If you want to describe something as being of higher quality or worth, you could try:**
no **finer** place • **much grander** house • **greater** prize • **higher-quality** service • **much nicer** room • **preferable** to • far **superior** to yours • **surpassing** quality • **worthier** cause

2 **If you want to describe someone as having greater skill, you could use:**
the **greater** writer • **more advanced** skiers • **more expert** at some things • **more skilful** player • **more talented** than he is

3 **If you want to describe someone as having improved health, you could say:**
now I'm **cured** • a lot **fitter** • **fully recovered** • much **healthier** • definitely **improving** • **on the mend** now (*informal*) • she's **recovering** • getting **stronger** • feeling **well** again

BIG

A cautionary tale: a teacher was trying to get her class to substitute more interesting words for very commonly-used ones in their writing. She noticed that one boy had described a castle as "big" in his essay, and asked him to write the sentence again in a more creative way. He came back with the following: "I saw a castle which was big, and when I say big, I mean big."

1 **If you would like to describe something that is large in size, you could try:**
colossal statue • **enormous** building • **gigantic** creature • **great** commotion • **huge** cake • **immense** task • **large** map • **massive** display • **significant** difference • **vast** stadium

2 **If you would like to describe an intense issue or problem, you could try:**
grave crisis • **momentous** decision • **serious** disadvantage • **urgent** need • **weighty** problem

3 **If you would like to describe someone or their actions as generous, you could try:**
gracious host • **benevolent** ruler • **kind-hearted** stranger • **noble** gesture • **heroic** deed • **unselfish** act

4 **If you would like to emphasize something or someone's importance, you could try:**
eminent politician • **important** influence • **influential** figure • **leading** screenwriters • **major** role • **powerful** businessman • **principal** guest • **prominent** jazz musician • **significant** investor

5 **If you would like to describe someone or something that is grown-up, you could try:**
elder sibling • **full-grown** animal • **mature** tree • **grown** man

There are lots of more descriptive words which you can use instead of **BREAK**, if you want to give additional information about how something breaks.

1 **If something hard cracks, or you crack it, it becomes slightly damaged, with lines appearing on its surface:**
A gas main had **cracked** under my garden.
To get at the coconut flesh, **crack** the shell with a hammer.

2 **If something fractures, or you fracture it, it gets a slight crack in it:**
One strut had **fractured** and had to be repaired.
You've **fractured** a rib.

3 **If something snaps, or you snap it, it breaks suddenly, with a sharp cracking noise:**
A twig **snapped** under his foot.
She gripped the pipe in both hands, trying to **snap** it in half.

4 **If something splits, or you split it, it breaks into two or more parts:**
In the gale, the ship **split** in two.
We **split** the boards down the middle.

5 **If something splinters, or you splinter it, it breaks into thin, sharp pieces:**
The ruler **splintered** into pieces.
The stone hit the glass, **splintering** it.

6 **If something fragments, or is fragmented, it breaks or** separates into small parts:
The rock began to **fragment** and crumble.

7 **If something crumbles, or you crumble it, it breaks into many small pieces:**
Under the pressure, the flint **crumbled** into fragments.
Crumble the cheese into a bowl.

8 **If something shatters, it breaks into many small pieces:**
safety glass won't **shatter** if it's hit

9 **If something disintegrates, it breaks into many pieces and is destroyed:**
The car's windscreen **disintegrated** with the impact of the crash.

10 **If you smash something, or it smashes, it breaks into many small pieces, often because it has been hit or dropped:**
Someone had **smashed** a bottle.
Two glasses fell off the table and **smashed** into pieces.

11 **If you wreck or demolish something, you completely destroy it:**
The storm **wrecked** the bridge.
The hurricane **demolished** houses across the area.

Depending on which sense of **CALL** you are thinking of, there are a number of words which you can substitute for it to make your language more interesting.

1 If you are talking about giving someone or something a name, you could try:
christen his first-born son Arthur • **designated** an "area of natural beauty" • the man **dubbed** "the world's greatest living explorer" • they **named** their child

2 If you are describing something as being a particular way, you could try:
I **consider** myself • I'm not what you'd **describe** as • do you **judge** this • He **referred to** her as • widely **regarded** as • **termed** as political • people will **think** us

3 If you are talking about bringing a group of things or people together, you could try:
they **assembled** the group • **convened** a council • **gathered** together **muster** an army • **summoned** to a meeting

4 If you are talking about someone saying something loudly, you could try:
he **announced** • she **cried** • she **cried out** • he **shouted** to me • **yelled** over to us

5 If you are talking about sending for someone, you could try:
please **fetch** • **sent** for • I was **summoned**

6 If you are talking about using the telephone, you could try:
Contact us immediately • **phone** me • I'll **ring** you • please **telephone**

7 If you are talking about paying someone a visit, you could try:
drop in (informal) • **pop in** (informal) • **stop by**

CLOSE

CLOSE is another over-used word. Depending on whether you are talking about people or things which are close in distance or in time, the closeness of personal relationships, a closeness in resemblance between two things, or you are referring to a description or translation, you can use various other words as substitutes.

1 If you would like to describe something that is CLOSE in distance, you could try:
at hand • adjacent buildings • adjoining stall • keep something handy • quite near • nearby shop • neighbouring table

2 If you would like to describe people who have a CLOSE relationship, you could try:
attached to one another • dear companion • deeply devoted couple • too familiar • very friendly • intimate friends • loving relationship

3 If you would like to describe something which is going to happen soon, you could try:
My birthday is approaching • the time is at hand • is coming • a deal is imminent • impending disaster • the day is near

4 If you would like to describe people or things that have a resemblance, you could try:
distinct resemblance • marked similarity • pronounced similarities to • strong resemblance

5 If you are talking about a description or translation, you could try:
accurate description • exact translation • faithful rendition • literal interpretation • precise detail • strict account

There are a number of alternative words which you can use instead of **CRY**, if you want to say a little more about how someone cries.

1 **If you weep, you cry. This is quite a literary word:**
The woman began to **weep** uncontrollably.

2 **If you whimper, you make a low, unhappy sound as if you are about to cry:**
He huddled in a corner, **whimpering** with fear.

3 **If you sob, you cry in a noisy way, with short breaths:**
Her sister broke down and began to **sob** into her handkerchief.

4 **If you blubber, you cry noisily and in an unattractive way:**
To our surprise, he began to **blubber** like a child.

5 **If you howl or wail, you cry with a long, loud noise:**
The baby was **howling** in the next room.
A mother **wailing** for her lost child.

6 **If you bawl, you cry very loudly:**
One of the toddlers was **bawling**.

There are many useful alternatives for the word **CUT**. Different words can be used instead, depending on what it is that is being cut, what is being used to do the cutting, and how deep or extensive the cutting is.

1 **If you nick something, you make a small cut on its surface:**
He **nicked** his chin while he was shaving.

2 **If you score something, you cut a line or lines on its surface:**
Lightly **score** the surface of the steaks with a cook's knife.

3 **If you pierce something with a sharp object, or a sharp object pierces it, the object goes through it and makes a hole in it:**
Pierce the skin of the potato with a fork.
One bullet had **pierced** his lung.

4 **If something penetrates an object, it goes inside it or passes through it:**
a spider with fangs big enough to **penetrate** the skin

5 **If you slit something, you make a long narrow cut in it:**
He began to **slit** open each envelope.

6 **If you gash or slash something, you make a long, deep cut in it:**
He **gashed** his leg on the barbed wire.
She threatened to **slash** her wrists.

7 **If you clip something, you cut small pieces from it in order to shape it:**
I saw an old man out **clipping** his hedge.

8 **If you trim something, you cut off small amounts of it to make it look neater:**
I have my hair **trimmed** every eight weeks.

9 **If you pare something, you cut off its skin or outer layer:**
She was sitting **paring** her nails with a pair of clippers.

10 **If you prune a tree or bush, you cut off some of its branches:**
Apple trees can be **pruned** once they've lost their leaves.

11 **If you mow grass, you cut it with a lawnmower:**
He **mowed** the lawn and did various other chores.

12 **If you snip something, you cut it with scissors or shears:**
The hairdresser **snipped** off my split ends.

13 If you **split** or **divide** something, you cut it into two or more parts:
Split the planks down the middle.
Divide the pastry into four equal parts.

14 If you **sever** something, you cut it off or cut right through it:
He severed the tendon of his thumb in an industrial accident.

15 If you **saw** something, you cut it with a saw:
Your father is sawing wood in the garden.

16 If you **hack** something, you cut it using rough strokes:
Matthew desperately hacked through the straps.

17 If you **slice** something, you cut it into thin pieces:
I sliced the beef into thin strips.

18 If you **chop** something, you cut it into pieces with strong downward movements of a knife or axe:
You will need to chop the onions very finely.

19 If you **carve** an object, you make it by cutting it out of a substance such as wood or stone:
He carves these figures from pine.

20 If you **carve** meat, you cut slices from it:
Andrew began to carve the roast.

21 If you **hew** stone or wood, you cut it, perhaps with an axe. This is an old-fashioned word:
He felled, peeled and hewed his own timber.

22 If you **hew** something out of stone or wood, you make it by cutting it from stone or wood:
medieval monasteries hewn out of the rockface

23 If you **lop** something off, you cut it off with one quick stroke:
Somebody has lopped the heads off our tulips.

24 If you **dock** an animal's tail, you cut it off:
I think it is cruel to dock the tail of any animal.

Word Studies

There are a number of more descriptive words which you can use instead of the basic **EAT**, to say something about the way in which a person eats.

1 **If you consume something, you eat it. This is a formal word:**
Andrew would **consume** nearly a pound of cheese a day.

2 **When an animal feeds, or feeds on something, it eats:**
After a few days the caterpillars stopped **feeding**.
Slugs **feed on** decaying plant material.

3 **If you swallow something, you make it go from your mouth into your stomach:**
Snakes **swallow** their prey whole.

4 **If you snack, you eat things between meals:**
Instead of **snacking** on crisps and chocolate, eat fruit.

5 **If you chew something, you break it up with your teeth so that it is easier to swallow:**
I pulled out a filling while I was **chewing** a toffee.

6 **If you nibble food, you eat it by biting very small pieces of it, perhaps because you are not very hungry:**
She **nibbled** at a piece of dry toast.

7 **If you munch food, you eat it by chewing it slowly, thoroughly, and rather noisily:**
Luke **munched** his sandwiches appreciatively.

8 **If you stuff yourself, you eat a lot of food:**
They'd **stuffed** themselves with sweets before dinner.

9 **If you gobble, guzzle, wolf (down), or scoff food, you eat it quickly and greedily. Guzzle, wolf (down), and scoff are all informal words:**
Pete **gobbled** all the stew before anyone else arrived.
women who **guzzle** chocolate whenever they are unhappy
I was back in the changing room **wolfing** sandwiches.
She bought a hot dog from a stand and **wolfed** it down.
You greedy so-and-so! You've **scoffed** the lot!

10 **If you devour something, you eat it quickly and eagerly:**
She **devoured** half an apple pie.

Word Studies

END is a commonly over-used word. Depending on your context, you can use the following substitutes to add variety and interest to your writing.

1   If you would like to describe the **END** of a period of time, you could try:
    by the **close** of last year • **ending** of a great era • the **expiry** of his period • nearing its **finish**

2   If you would like to describe the **END** of an event, you could try:
    the dramatic **climax** • the **close**
    • the **conclusion** of
    • the remarkable **culmination**
    • tragic **ending** • grand **finale**
    • a disappointing **finish**

3   If you would like to describe the furthest-away part of something, you could try:
    the **boundaries** of the paths
    • beyond the **bounds** • the **edge** of the cliff • the western **extremity** • official city **limits** • beyond the forest **margin**

4   If you would like to describe the point of something long or sharp, you could try:
    the southernmost **point** • the **tip**

5   If you would like to describe a leftover piece of something, you could try:
    a cigarette **butt** • trimmings and **leftovers** • **remnants** of fabric
    • **scraps** of spare material
    • a ticket **stub** • The **stump** of his left arm

6   If you would like to describe the purpose of doing something, you could try:
    united by a common **aim**
    • working towards the same **goal**
    • real **intentions** • the stated **object** • the **objective** of • the true **purpose** • business **reasons**

Some words used to describe a person who is overweight can be more hurtful or insulting than others. There are also words to describe varying degrees of being overweight.

1 **Someone who is overweight weighs more than is considered healthy. However, you can be just a little overweight as well as very overweight:**
Since having my baby, I feel slightly **overweight**.

2 **If you say someone is podgy, you mean that they are slightly FAT. This is an informal word:**
Eddie's getting a little **podgy** round the middle.

3 **If you describe someone as fleshy, you mean that they are slightly too FAT:**
He was well-built, but too **fleshy** to be an imposing figure.

4 **A chubby, tubby or stout person is rather FAT:**
I was greeted by a small, **chubby** man.
He had been a short, **tubby** child who was taunted about his weight.
a tall, **stout** man with gray hair

5 **If you describe someone as obese, you mean that they are fatter than overweight, perhaps to the point of being unhealthy:**
Obese people tend to have higher blood pressure than lean people.

6 **You can use the word plump to describe someone who is rather fat or rounded, usually when you think this is a good quality:**
Maria was a pretty little thing, small and **plump** with a mass of dark curls.

7 **If you describe a woman's figure as rounded or curvy you mean that it is attractive because it is well-developed and not too thin:**
a beautiful woman with blue eyes and a full, **rounded** figure
she's very **curvy**

8 **A roly-poly person is pleasantly FAT and round. This is an informal word:**
a short, **roly-poly** little woman with laughing eyes

9 **If you describe a woman as buxom, you mean that she looks healthy and attractive and has a rounded body and big breasts:**
Melissa was a tall, **buxom** blonde.

10 **A portly person is rather fat. This word is mostly used to describe men:**
a **portly**, middle-aged man

Like bad, the word **GOOD** is used in so many ways to describe so many things that it has lost a great deal of its effectiveness. A wide range of alternatives is available to you for every context in which you might be tempted to use **GOOD**; try to vary your language and vocabulary by choosing these instead.

1 **If you would like to describe something that is of** GOOD **quality, you could try:**
acceptable standard • **awesome** special effects *(slang)* • **excellent** meal • **fine** wines • **first-class** game • **first-rate** service • **great** book • **satisfactory** quality • **splendid** hotel • **super** recipe *(informal)* • **superb** selection

2 **If you would like to describe a** GOOD **experience, you could try:**
agreeable evening • **delightful** few hours • **enjoyable** trip • **lovely** time in Paris • **pleasant** stay • **satisfactory** season

3 **If you would like to describe something that has a beneficial effect, you could try:**
advantageous changes • **beneficial** effects • **favourable** conditions • **positive** results

4 **If you would like to describe someone or something that is morally virtuous, you could try:**
commendable character • **decent** person • **ethical** stance • **honest** citizens • **honourable** person • morally **righteous** people • morally **upright** • **virtuous** life • **worthy** causes

5 **If you would like to describe a kind and thoughtful person or action, you could try:**
kindly and **benevolent** • too **charitable** • He's **considerate** to his sisters • **generous** and selfless nature • a **gracious** and genial host • a **humane** and caring woman • it's very **kind** of you • **kind-hearted** colleagues • a **kindly** soul • an **obliging** fellow • **thoughtful** of him to offer

6 **If you would like to describe someone who is skilled at something, you could try:**
able student • an **accomplished** pianist • **adept** at manipulating the press • very **capable** nanny • very **clever** at raising money • careful and **competent** worker • **efficient** manager • **expert** cyclists • **first-rate** teacher • **proficient** driver • **skilled** carpenter • most **talented** musicians

7 **If you would like to describe someone's behaviour, you could try:**
disciplined behaviour • meek and **docile** child • a **dutiful** wife and three **obedient** children • **orderly** behaviour • polite and **well-behaved**

8 If you would like to describe any kind of GOOD advice, you could try:

thoughtful and **constructive** input • **helpful** suggestions • **sound** advice • **practical** guidelines • **useful** tips

9 If you would like to describe a GOOD idea, you could try:

judicious approach • **practical** solution • **prudent** strategy for economic recovery • a **sensible** way • a **wise** plan

10 If you would like to describe a GOOD price, sum of money, amount or quantity, you could try:

ample supply • a **considerable** income • **fair** bit over the asking price • a **large** profit • **reasonable** number • **substantial** amount

11 If you would like to describe a person's mood, you could try:

buoyant spirits • **cheerful** nature • **genial** mood • **happy** disposition • **optimistic** frame of mind • **sunny** mood

There are a number of ways in which the word **GREAT** can be used, depending on what you are referring to. But why not make your language more interesting and use one of the following instead?

1 **If you would like to describe something that is GREAT in size, you could try:**
a **big** house • a **colossal** tomb • a **huge** marquee • **large** pile of logs • an **enormous** hall • **extensive** range of stock • **gigantic** theme park • an **immense** building • **stupendous** sum of money • **tremendous** challenge • a **vast** area

2 **If you would like to describe something that is GREAT in degree, you could try:**
a **high** degree of risk • **excessive** speeds • **extravagant** claims • **extreme** violence • **tremendous** strength

3 **If you would like to describe something that is GREAT in importance, you could try:**
one of our **chief** problems • an **important** question • our **main** competitor • **major** issue in the next election • a **momentous** occasion • Our **principal** aim • a **serious** deficiency in the system • a **significant** step towards peace

4 **If you would like to describe someone or something that is famous, you could try:**
the **celebrated** author • a **distinguished** baritone • **eminent** French scientists • the **famed** Australian actor • a **famous** artist • the world's most **illustrious** ballerinas • a **notable** chess player • Scotland's most **prominent** historian • the **renowned** heart surgeon

5 **If you would like to describe someone's skill, you could try:**
an **excellent** maths teacher • suitable only for **expert** skiers • a **masterly** display • an **outstanding** cricketer • the most **skilful** snooker player • a **skilled** boxer • a **superb** goalkeeper • a **superlative** thriller writer • a **talented** management team

6 **If you would like to describe the quality of something or someone, you could try:**
a **beaut** place to live (*Australian, New Zealand*) • good food and **fine** wines • **excellent** pasta sauce • **superb** works of art • **fantastic** firework display (*informal*) • their **first-rate** service • **marvellous** rooftop restaurant (*informal*) • **outstanding** works of art • **superb** staircase made from oak • a **terrific** party • You've done a **tremendous** job • a **wonderful** time

HAPPY

HAPPY is another over-used word. You can vary your language by choosing one of the alternatives shown here.

Word Studies

1 **If you would like to describe someone or something as displaying a cheerful nature or mood, you could try:**
a **cheerful** disposition • a **cheery** face • You're very **chirpy** today (*informal*) • a **jolly** fat man • a **merry** laugh • her **unfailingly** sunny nature

2 **If you would like to describe something that causes joy, you could try:**
the **agreeable** task • **blissful** marriage • truly **festive** occasion • a **gratifying** relationship • a **joyful** event • the **joyous** news • a **pleasurable** memory

3 **If you would like to describe someone who is willing to do something, you could try:**
She was **content** just to sit • always **glad** to be of service • **pleased** to take you there myself • I'd be **prepared** to talk • He's **ready** to help anyone • I'm **willing** to wait

4 **If you would like to describe a feeling of joy at something, you could try:**
delighted with their new home • I was **ecstatic** to see Marianne again • **elated** that she had won • He is understandably **euphoric** • **glad** to be back • a **joyful** pride in his work • They were **jubilant** over their election victory • **overjoyed** to be reunited • We're very **pleased** • I'm just **thrilled** • The team are **over the moon** with this result (*informal*)

5 **If you would like to describe something as lucky, you could try:**
an **auspicious** start • a **convenient** outcome • a **favourable** result • a very **fortunate** situation • a **lucky** chance • hardly an **opportune** moment • his **timely** arrival

Word Studies

HIGH is another word which has a number of meanings. Depending on just what you are describing as **HIGH**, you have a whole range of substitutes to choose from to give your writing some added variety and expressiveness.

1 **If you are describing a building, ceiling or mountain, you could try:**
an apartment in an **elevated** position • **lofty** towers and spires • a **soaring** spire • the **steep** hill • **tall** walls • **towering** red sandstone cliffs

2 **If you are describing a HIGH amount or HIGH degree of something, you could try:**
state of **acute** anxiety • driving at **excessive** speed • drinking **extraordinary** quantities • under **extreme** pressure • a **great** level of interest • **severe** penalties

3 **If you are describing the cost or price of something, you could try:**
costly premiums • too **dear** • **expensive** prices • charges are very **steep** (informal)

4 **If you are describing the wind, you could try:**
blustery breezes • **extreme** wind and cold • thunder and **squally** winds • **strong** gusts • **violent** gales

5 **If you are describing someone or something important, you could try:**
chief position in the company • most **eminent** scientists • an **important** post • in **exalted** circles • an **influential** place • a **leading** figure • the **most** powerful • her **pre-eminent** position • **prominent** political figures • their **superior** status

6 **If you are describing a voice or a sound, you could try:**
high-pitched cry • a **penetrating** whistle • a **piercing** note • **shrill** scream • **soprano** voice

7 **If you are describing a person's spirits, you could try:**
in **buoyant** spirits • in such **cheerful** spirits • that **elated** feeling • an **exhilarated** frame of mind • his **exuberant** moods • I felt **joyful** • in a very **merry** mood

The word **HIT** is often over-used. There are a number of more descriptive words which you can use to give additional information about the way in which something is **HIT**, or how hard it is **HIT**.

1 If you **strike** someone or something, you HIT them deliberately. This is a formal word:
She stepped forward and **struck** him across the mouth.

2 If you **tap** something, you HIT it with a quick light blow or series of blows:
Tap the egg gently with a teaspoon to crack the shell.

3 If you **rap** something, or **rap on** it, you HIT it with a series of quick blows:
rapping the glass with the knuckles of his right hand
He **rapped on** the door with his cane.

4 If you **slap** or **smack** someone, you hit them with the palm of your hand:
I **slapped** him hard across the face.
She **smacked** the child on the side of the head.

5 If you **knock** someone or something, you HIT it roughly, especially so that it falls or moves:
She accidentally **knocked** the tin off the shelf.

6 If you **beat** something, you HIT it hard, usually several times or continuously for a period of time:
a circle of men **beating** drums

7 If you **swat** something such as an insect, you HIT it with a quick, swinging movement using your hand or a flat object:
Every time a fly came near, I **swatted** it with a newspaper.

8 If you **hammer** something, you HIT it hard several times to make a noise:
We had to **hammer** the door and shout to attract their attention.

9 If you **pound** something, you HIT it with great force, usually loudly and repeatedly:
He **pounded** the table with both fists.

10 If you **batter** someone or something, you HIT them very hard, using your fists or a heavy object:
He **battered** her round the head with a club.

11 If you **bang** something, you HIT it hard, making a loud noise:
We **banged** on the door and shouted to be let out.

12 If you **belt** someone, you HIT them very hard. This is an informal word:
She drew back her fist and **belted** him right in the stomach.

13 If you **bash** someone or something, you HIT them hard. This is an informal word:
The chef was **bashed** over the head with a bottle.

14 If you **whack** someone or something, you HIT them hard. This is an informal word:
Someone **whacked** me with a baseball bat.

15 If you **wallop** someone or something, you HIT them very hard, often causing a dull sound. This is an informal word:
Once, she **walloped** me over the head with a frying pan.

16 If you **thump** someone or something, you HIT them hard, usually with your fist:
I'm warning you, if you don't shut up, I'll **thump** you.

There are a number of more interesting or creative words you can use in place of the basic verb **LAUGH**, if you want to say something about the way in which a person laughs.

1   **If you chuckle, you laugh quietly:**
I **chuckled** to myself at the look on his face.

2   **If you chortle, you laugh in a pleased or amused way:**
He sat there **chortling** at my predicament.

3   **If you snigger, you laugh in a quiet, sly way, perhaps at something rude or unkind:**
two schoolboys who were telling dirty jokes and **sniggering**

4   **If you giggle, you laugh in a high-pitched way, because you are amused, nervous or embarrassed. This word is often used of children or girls:**
They followed me around, **giggling** every time I spoke.

5   **If you titter, you give a short, nervous laugh, often at something rude or because you are embarrassed:**
The audience began to **titter** as he came on dressed in drag.

6   **If you cackle, you laugh in a loud, harsh and unpleasant way, often at something bad which happens to someone else:**
The old woman **cackled** in glee.

7   **If you guffaw, howl, or roar, you laugh very loudly because you think something is very funny:**
They **guffawed** at me as I walked past.
The crowd **howled** at his antics.
He threw back his head and **roared** at this witticism.

Depending on what you are describing, you can choose from any of the following alternatives instead of the over-used word **LITTLE**.

1 If you are describing an object or the physical size of something, you could try:
dainty sandwiches and cakes • **dwarf** tulips • a **mini** laptop • **miniature** toy boats • **minute** particles of soil • **pygmy** goats • a **skimpy** bikini • a **small** table • **tiny** pieces • a **wee** bit of cake

2 If you are describing someone's height, you could try:
dainty Japanese girl • his **diminutive** stature • **petite** women • too **short** • a short, **squat** figure • a **tiny** woman • a **wee** guy

3 If you are describing the quantity of something, you could try:
hardly any work • **not much** difference • **meagre** pay increase • **measly** ration of food • a **paltry** salary • He paid **scant** attention

4 If you are describing someone's age, you could try:
my **baby** sister • her **infant** son • two **small** kids • a **young** child

5 If you are describing the duration of an action or event, you could try:
a **brief** pause • a **fleeting** glimpse • a **hasty** peek • a **momentary** lapse • a **quick** smile • a **short** break

6 If you are describing the importance of something, you could try:
an **insignificant** detail • a **minor** squabble • Their **influence** is negligible • **petty** complaints • a **trifling** problem • **trivial** matters • an **unimportant** event

7 If you are describing a small amount of something, you could try:
a **bit** of peace • a **dash** of bravado • a **fragment** of skin tissue • with just a **hint** of coriander • a **small amount** of cash • a **spot** of milk • a **touch** of irritation • a **trace** of blood

Try to vary your language by using one of these substitutes for **LONG**.

1 If you are talking about the physical extent of something: an **elongated** body • an **extensive** list • **lengthy** queues

2 If you are talking about the duration of something: an **extended** period
• an **interminable** debate

• a **lengthy** delay • **lingering** death • a **long-drawn-out** war
• a **prolonged** labour is dangerous for both mother and child
• **protracted** negotiations over pay rises • writing music is a **slow** process • a **sustained** run of bad luck

Word Studies

All of the following words mean to **LOOK**, but each one has an extra shade of meaning which makes it a more expressive substitute for the word look in particular situations or contexts.

1 If you glance, peek, or peep at something, you LOOK at it quickly, and often secretly:
He **glanced** at his watch as she spoke.
She **peeked** at him through the curtains.
He **peeped** at me to see if I was watching him.

2 If you scan something written or printed, you LOOK at it quickly:
She **scanned** the advertisement pages of the newspapers.

3 If you eye or regard someone or something, you LOOK at them carefully:
The waiters **eyed** him with suspicion.
He **regarded** me curiously.

4 If you gaze or stare at someone or something, you LOOK at them steadily for a long time, for example because you find them interesting or because you are thinking about something else. Staring is often thought to be rude, but gazing is not:
She sat **gazing** into the fire for a long time.
They **stared** silently into each other's eyes.

5 If you observe or watch someone or something, you LOOK at them for a period of time to see what they are doing or what is happening:
A man was **observing** him from across the square.
I hate people **watching** me while I eat.

6 If you survey or view someone or something, you LOOK at the whole of them carefully:
He stood up and **surveyed** the crowd.
The mourners filed past to **view** the body.

7 If you examine, scrutinize, or study something, you LOOK at it very carefully, often to find out information from it:
He **examined** all the evidence.
He **scrutinized** her passport and stamped it.
We **studied** the menu for several minutes.

8 If you glare, glower, or scowl at someone, you stare at them angrily:
He **glared** resentfully at me.
She stood **glowering** at me with her arms crossed.
She **scowled** at the two men as they came into the room.

9 If you **peer** or **squint** at something, you try to see it more clearly by narrowing or screwing up your eyes as you LOOK at it:
He was **peering** at me through the keyhole.
She **squinted** at the blackboard, trying to read what was on it.

10 If you **gape** at someone or something, you LOOK at them in surprise, usually with your mouth open:
She was **gaping** at the wreckage, lost for words.

11 If you **goggle** at someone or something, you LOOK at them with your eyes wide open, usually because you are surprised by them:
He **goggled** at me in disbelief.

12 If you **ogle** someone, you LOOK at them in a way that makes it very obvious that you find them attractive:
I hate the way he **ogles** every woman who goes by.

MARK is rather a vague word. Depending on what you are referring to, there are a number of more interesting synonyms which you can use in its place.

1 **If you would like to describe a stain, you could try:**
   an ink **blot** • a **line** of dirt • a lipstick **smudge** • a grease **spot** • a **stain** • a **streak** of mud

2 **If you would like to describe a damaged area, you could try:**
   slight **blemishes** • purple **blotches** • cuts and **bruises** • a tiny **dent** • little **nicks** on his chin • a jagged **scar** • a long **scratch**

3 **If you would like to describe a written or printed symbol, you could try:**
   with Chinese **characters** • the company's **emblem** • the Papal **insignia** • a multiplication **sign** • date **stamp** on the front • a flag bearing the **symbol**

4 **If you would like to describe a characteristic of something, you could try:**
   the essential **attributes** • a defining **characteristic** • fundamental **features** • the hallmark • a **measure** • a **symptom** • a common **trait**

5 **If you would like to describe something that is an indication of something else, you could try:**
   a **gesture** of goodwill • an **indication** of his regard • a **sign** of respect • a **symbol** of mourning • a **token** of our friendship

MOVE is not a very expressive word. If you can use a more descriptive substitute to say something about the way in which a person or thing moves, it will give your writing variety and interest.

1 **When a person crawls, they MOVE forwards on their hands and knees:**
As he tried to **crawl** away, he was kicked in the head.

2 **When an insect crawls somewhere, it MOVES there quite slowly:**
I watched the moth **crawl** up the outside of the lampshade.

3 **If a person or animal creeps somewhere, they MOVE quietly and slowly:**
I tried to **creep** upstairs without being heard.

4 **To inch somewhere means to MOVE there very carefully and slowly:**
He began to **inch** along the ledge.

5 **If you edge somewhere, you MOVE very slowly in that direction:**
He **edged** closer to the telephone.

6 **If a person or animal slithers somewhere, they MOVE by sliding along the ground in an uneven way:**
Robert lost his footing and **slithered** down the bank.
The snake **slithered** into the water.

7 **If you wriggle somewhere, for example through a small gap, you MOVE there by twisting and turning your body:**
I **wriggled** through a gap in the fence.

8 **When people or small animals scamper or scuttle somewhere, they MOVE there quickly with small, light steps:**
The children got off the bus and **scampered** into the playground.
The crabs **scuttled** along the muddy bank.

9 **When people or small animals scurry somewhere, they MOVE there quickly and hurriedly, often because they are frightened:**
The attack began, sending residents **scurrying** for cover.

10 **If you hurry, race, or rush somewhere, you go there as quickly as you can:**
Claire **hurried** along the road.
He **raced** across town to the hospital.
A schoolgirl **rushed** into a burning building to save a baby.

11 **If you hasten somewhere, you hurry there. This is a literary word:**
He **hastened** along the corridor to Grace's room.

12 If you **hare off** somewhere, you go there very quickly. This is an informal British word:
She **hared off** to ring the doctor.

13 If you **dash**, **dart**, or **shoot** somewhere, you run or go there quickly and suddenly:
She jumped up and **dashed** out of the room.
The girl turned and **darted** away through the trees.
They had almost reached the boat when a figure **shot** past them.

14 If you say that someone or something **flies** in a particular direction, you are emphasizing that they MOVE there with a lot of speed and force:
I **flew** downstairs to answer the door.

15 If you **sprint**, you run as fast as you can over a short distance:
The sergeant **sprinted** to the car.

16 If you **gallop**, you run somewhere very quickly:
They were **galloping** round the garden playing football.

17 When you run, you MOVE quickly because you are in a hurry to get somewhere:
I excused myself and **ran** back to the telephone.

18 If you **jog**, you run slowly:
She **jogged** off in the direction he had indicated.

19 If you **tear** somewhere, you MOVE there very quickly, often in an uncontrolled or dangerous way:
Without looking to the left or right, he **tore** off down the road.

20 If a person or animal **bolts**, they suddenly start to run very fast, often because something has frightened them:
I made some excuse and **bolted** towards the exit.

21 If a group of animals or people **stampede**, they run in a wild, uncontrolled way:
The crowd **stampeded** out of the hall.

Depending on the sense of **NEW** which you mean, there are a number of alternatives which you can use to vary your writing and make it more interesting.

1   **If you would like to describe something that has not been used or owned before, you could try:**
    a **brand new** car • a **fresh** page • **unused** wedding dresses

2   **If you would like to describe something that is unfamiliar, you could try:**
    a completely **different** idea • a **novel** way • an **original** idea • a **strange** country • the **unaccustomed** experience • visiting **unfamiliar** places • completely **unknown**

3   **If you would like to describe something that has been recently discovered or created, you could try:**
    the company's most **advanced** drugs • the **current** gossip • **fresh** footprints • **ground-breaking** discovery • all the **latest** films • **ultra-modern** shopping mall • most **recent** novel • **up-to-date** computers • **up-to-the-minute** information

NICE

When you are writing or talking and you are going to use the word **NICE**, try to think of a more descriptive and interesting word instead. Here are some ideas for words and phrases that you might use to describe different aspects of people and things.

1 **If you are describing someone's appearance, you could try:**
an **attractive** young lady • looking very **beautiful** • a very **cute** girl • he was **dishy** • Her son is good-looking • he's really **gorgeous** • a very **handsome** young man • a **lovely** woman • You look very **pretty**

2 **If you are describing an object, place or view, you could try:**
beautiful little antique shop • **charming** little fishing village • **delightful** place • **lovely** old English garden • a **pretty** room

3 **If you are describing an item of clothing, you could try:**
chic designer frock • very **elegant** dress • a **fetching** outfit • a **smart** navy-blue suit • such **stylish** clothes

4 **If you are describing an event or occasion, you could try:**
very **agreeable** • a **delightful** time • much more **enjoyable** • such a **fantastic** party • a **lovely** holiday • a very **pleasant** experience • the **pleasurable** sensation

5 **If you are describing someone's personality, you could try:**
very **amiable** man • very **considerate** towards his sisters • very **friendly** to strangers • unfailingly **good-natured** • **kind** to everyone • a **kindly** old man • an immensely **likeable** chap • a very **thoughtful** gesture

6 **If you are describing food or drink, you could try:**
An **appetizing** smell • some **delectable** raspberries • food here is **delicious** • **luscious** peaches • **mouthwatering** dessert • serving **tasty** dishes

7 **If you are describing the weather, you could try:**
a **beautiful** morning • the weather is **fine** • a **glorious** day

8 **If you are describing a room, flat or house, you could try:**
a **comfortable** home • a **cosy** parlour • a **homely** atmosphere • a very **relaxing** room

Depending on the sense of **OLD** which you mean, there are a number of alternatives which you can use to vary your writing and make it more interesting.

1 If you are describing someone who has lived for a long time, you could try:
an **aged** parent • her **ancient** grandparents • an **elderly** man • a **venerable** father-figure

2 If you are describing something in the past, you could try:
relics of **ancient** cultures • rituals of a **bygone** civilization • an **earlier** marriage • those **early** days • his **ex**-wife • a **former** lover • in **olden** times • **one-time** president • **past** grievances • **previous** tenants • **prior** criminal convictions • those **remote** days

3 If you are describing something that is out of date, you could try:
antiquated teaching methods • **archaic** practices • very much **behind the times** • sounds quite dated • These computers are **obsolete** • an **old-fashioned** style • **outdated** attitudes • working with **outmoded** equipment • a make of car that is now **out of date** • That kind of music is **passé**

There are a number of more interesting or creative words you can use in place of the basic verbs **SAY**, speak, and talk, if you want to describe the way in which a person says something.

1 **If you mention something, you SAY something about it, usually briefly:**
He never **mentioned** that he was married.

2 **If you observe that something is the case, you make a comment about it, especially when it is something you have noticed or thought about a lot:**
"He's a very loyal friend," Daniel **observed**.

3 **If you announce something, you tell people about it publicly or officially:**
"We're engaged!" she **announced**.

4 **If someone asserts a fact or belief, they state it firmly:**
"The facts are clear," the Prime Minister **asserted**.

5 **If you declare that something is true, you SAY that it is true in a firm, deliberate way:**
"I'm absolutely thrilled with the result," he **declared**.

6 **If you put in a remark, you interrupt someone or add to what they have said with the remark:**
"Not that it's any of your business," Helen **put in**.

7 **When people chat, they talk to each other in a friendly and informal way:**
We were just **chatting** in the corridor.

8 **If you converse with someone, you talk to them. This is a formal word:**
They were **conversing** in German.

9 **When people natter, they talk casually for a long time about unimportant things:**
Susan and her friend were still **nattering** when I left.

10 **If you gossip with someone, you talk informally, especially about other people or events:**
We sat and **gossiped** well into the evening.

11 If you **explain** something, you give details about it so that it can be understood:

"We weren't married at that point," she **explained**.

12 If you **ask** something, you SAY it in the form of a question because you want to know the answer:

"How is Frank?" he **asked**.

13 If you **inquire** about something, you ask for information about it. This is a formal word:

"Is something wrong?" he **inquired**.

14 To **query** or **question** means to ask a question:

"Can I help you?" the assistant **queried**.

"What if something goes wrong?" he **questioned** anxiously.

15 When you **answer** or **reply** to someone who has just spoken, you SAY something back to them:

"When are you leaving?" she asked.

"Tomorrow," he **answered**.

"That's a nice outfit," he commented. "Thanks," she **replied**.

16 When you **respond** to something that has been said, you react to it by saying something yourself:

"Are you well enough to carry on?"

"Of course," she **responded** scornfully.

17 To **retort** means to reply angrily to someone. This is a formal word:

"I don't agree," James said.

"Who cares what you think?" she **retorted**.

18 If someone **babbles**, they talk in a confused or excited way:

"I'm so excited I don't know what I'm doing," she **babbled**.

19 If you **chatter**, you talk quickly and excitedly about things which are not important:

Everyone was **chattering** away in different languages.

20 If you **gabble**, you SAY things so quickly that it is difficult for people to understand you:

Marcello sat on his knee and **gabbled** excitedly.

21 If you prattle, you talk a great deal about something unimportant:
She was **prattling** on about this guy she had met the night before.

22 If someone rambles, they talk but do not make much sense because they keep going off the subject:
an old man who **rambled** about his feud with his neighbours

23 If someone breathes something, they SAY it very quietly. This is a literary word:
"Oh, thank God you're here," he **breathed**.

24 When you whisper, you SAY something very quietly, using your breath rather than your throat:
"Keep your voice down," I **whispered**.

25 If you grunt something, you SAY it in a low voice, often because you are annoyed or not interested:
"Rubbish," I **grunted**, "You just didn't try hard enough."

26 If you mumble, you speak very quietly and not at all clearly, so that your words are hard to make out:
"I didn't know I was meant to do it," she **mumbled**.

27 If you murmur something, you speak very quietly, so that not many people can hear you:
"How convenient," I **murmured**.

28 If you mutter, you speak very quietly, often because you are complaining about something:
"Oh great," he **muttered**, "That's all I need."

29 If you croak something, you SAY it in a low, rough voice:
"Water!" he **croaked**.

30 If you hiss something, you SAY it forcefully in a whisper:
"Stay here and don't make a sound," he **hissed**.

31 If you rasp something, you SAY it in a harsh, unpleasant voice:
"Get into the car," he **rasped**.

32 When someone growls something, they SAY it in a low, rough, and angry voice:
"I ought to kill you for this," Sharpe **growled**.

33 If you snap at someone, you speak to them in a sharp, unfriendly way:
"Of course you can't have it," he **snapped**.

34 If you groan or moan something, you SAY it in a low voice, usually because you are unhappy or in pain:
"My leg - I think it's broken," Eric **groaned**.
"I can't stand it any longer," she **moaned**.

SHORT

Some words used to describe a person who is **SHORT** can be more hurtful or insulting than others.

1 **A little or small person is not large in physical size:**
   She was too **little** to reach the books on the top shelf.
   She is **small** for her age.

2 **A diminutive person is very small:**
   a **diminutive** figure standing at the entrance

3 **A tiny person is extremely small:**
   Though she was **tiny**, she had a loud voice.

4 **If you describe a woman as petite, you are politely saying that she is small and not fat. This is a complimentary word:**
   a **petite** blonde woman

5 **If you describe someone as dumpy, you mean they are SHORT and fat. This is an uncomplimentary word:**
   a **dumpy** woman in a baggy tracksuit

6 **If you describe someone as squat, you mean that they are SHORT and thick, usually in an unattractive way:**
   Eddie was a short, **squat** fellow in his mid-forties.

SMALL

Depending on the sense of **SMALL** which you mean, there are a number of alternatives which you can use to vary your writing and make it more interesting.

1 **If you are describing an object or the physical size of something, you could try:**
We sat around a **little** table
• a **miniature** camera • a pair of **minuscule** shorts • Only a **minute** amount is needed
• The living room is **tiny**

2 **If you are describing an area, you could try:**
only a **little** distance from the station • squeeze through a **narrow** space • a **restricted** habitat

3 **If you are describing the size of a person, you could try:**
a **diminutive** figure • a **dumpy** woman • too **little** to reach
• **petite** blonde woman • a **short**, squat fellow • she was **tiny**

4 **If you are describing someone's age, you could try:**
my **baby** sister • an **infant** prodigy
• when you were **little** • a **young** child

5 **If you are describing a business, you could try:**
humble corner shop • The company started from **modest** beginnings • a **small-scale** cheese industry • an **unpretentious** restaurant

6 **If you are describing the importance of something, you could try:**
a seemingly **inconsequential** event
• an **insignificant** village in the hills • such a fuss over such a **little** thing • a **minor** detail
• The impact of the strike will be **negligible** • over the most **petty** things • It will only make a **slight** difference • These are **trifling** objections • bogged down in **trivial** details • a comparatively **unimportant** event

STRONG is an over-used word. Depending on what you are referring to, there are many substitutes which you can use in its place to add variety and interest to your writing.

1 **If you are describing a person who has powerful muscles, you could try:**
He was tall and **athletic**
• a **brawny** young rugby player
• a big, **burly** man • a **powerful** bodybuilder • she was lean and **muscular** • a big, **strapping** fellow • a fit, **well-built** runner

2 **If you are describing a person who is in good physical condition, you could try:**
She is positively **blooming** with health • It won't be long till you're **fit** again • a **healthy** child • He's **in good condition** • a **robust** child • in **sound** physical condition

3 **If you are describing a person who is confident and courageous, you could try:**
be **brave** for the children's sake
• a **courageous** leader • a **plucky** schoolgirl • You've always been **resilient** • feisty, **self-confident** women • You have to be **tough**

4 **If you are describing an object that is able to withstand rough treatment, you could try:**
made of **durable** plastic
• **hard-wearing** cotton overalls
• a **heavy-duty** canvas bag
• **reinforced** concrete supports

• a camera mounted on a **sturdy** tripod • a **substantial** boat with a powerful rigging • a **tough** vehicle designed for all terrains • You need a **well-built** fence all round the garden

5 **If you are describing feelings which are great in degree or intensity, you could try:**
acute feelings of self-consciousness
• an **ardent** admirer • a **deep** resentment • my **fervent** hope
• He inspires **fierce** loyalty • an **intense** dislike • a **keen** interest in football • a **passionate** believer
• his **profound** distrust • His announcement sparked off **vehement** criticism • His plans met with **violent** hostility • his **zealous** religious beliefs

6 **If you are describing an argument which is convincing or supported by a lot of evidence, you could try:**
a **compelling** case • a **convincing** theory • some **effective** arguments against • **persuasive** reasons justifying the move • a **sound** case for using organically-grown produce
• the most **telling** condemnation of the system

7 **If you are describing a very noticeable smell, you could try:** an **overpowering** aftershave
- a **powerful** smell of ammonia
- the **pungent** aroma of oregano

8 **If you are describing food or drink that has a powerful flavour, you could try:** a **hot** curry • the **overpowering** taste of chillies • a **piquant** sauce • a liqueur with a **powerful** aniseed flavour • I love the **sharp** taste of pickles • Avoid **spicy** foods and alcohol

9 **If you are describing a person's accent as being very noticeable, you could try:** a **distinct** American drawl
- a **marked** West country accent
- his **noticeable** southern accent
- **unmistakeable** Latin accent

10 **If you are describing very bright colours, you could try:** She always dresses in **bold** colours • **bright** reds and blues • **Brilliant** jewel colours • **glaring** red Chanel dress • shirts with **loud** patterns

Some words which you might use to describe someone who is **THIN** are complimentary, some are neutral, and others are definitely uncomplimentary.

1   **A slender person is attractively THIN and graceful:**
    a tall, **slender** lady in a straw hat

2   **A slim person has an attractively THIN and well-shaped body:**
    a pretty, **slim** girl with blue eyes

3   **A slight person has a fairly THIN and delicate-looking body:**
    He is a **slight**, bespectacled, intellectual figure.

4   **A light person does not weigh very much:**
    You need to be **light** to be a dancer.

5   **Someone who is spare is tall and not at all fat. This is a literary word:**
    She was thin and **spare**, with a sharp, intelligent face.

6   **If you describe someone as lean, you mean that they are THIN but look strong and healthy:**
    Like most athletes, she was **lean** and muscular.

7   **If you say someone is lanky, you mean that they are tall and THIN and move rather awkwardly:**
    He had grown into a **lanky** teenager.

8   **A skinny person is extremely THIN, in a way that you find unattractive. This is an informal word:**
    I don't think these **skinny** supermodels are at all sexy.

9   **If you say a person is scraggy or scrawny, you mean that they look unattractive because they are so THIN:**
    a **scraggy**, shrill, neurotic woman
    a **scrawny** child of fifteen

10 **Someone who is bony has very little flesh covering their bones:**
    a **bony** old woman dressed in black

11 **If someone is underweight, they are too THIN and therefore not healthy:**
    Nearly a third of the girls were severely **underweight**.

12 **A person or animal that is emaciated is very THIN and weak from illness or lack of food:**
    horrific television pictures of **emaciated** prisoners

Word Studies

There are a number of more interesting or creative words you can use in place of the basic verb **WALK**, if you want to say something about the way in which a person walks.

1 **If you step in a particular direction, you move your foot in that direction:**
   I **stepped** carefully over the piles of rubbish.

2 **If you tread in a particular way, you WALK in that way. This is rather a literary word:**
   She **trod** carefully across the grass.

3 **If you amble or stroll, you WALK in a slow, relaxed way:**
   We **ambled** along the beach hand in hand.
   They **strolled** down the High Street, looking in shop windows.

4 **If you tiptoe, you WALK very quietly without putting your heels on the ground, so as not to be heard:**
   She slipped out of bed and **tiptoed** to the window.

5 **If you wander, you WALK around in a casual way, often without intending to go anywhere in particular:**
   Khachi was **wandering** aimlessly about in the garden.

6 **If you saunter, you WALK in a slow, casual way:**
   He was **sauntering** along as if he had all the time in the world.

7 **If you toddle, you WALK unsteadily, with short quick steps. This word is most often used of babies or small children:**
   My daughter **toddles** around after me wherever I go.

8 **If you mince, you WALK with quick, small steps in a put-on, effeminate way:**
   drag artists **mincing** around the stage in tight dresses and high heels

9 **If you pace, you WALK up and down a small area, usually because you are anxious or impatient:**
   As he waited, he **paced** nervously around the room.

10 **If you stride, you WALK with quick, long steps:**
   He turned abruptly and **strode** off down the corridor.

WALK

11 If you march, you WALK quickly and in a determined way, perhaps because you are angry:
She **marched** into the office and demanded to see the manager.

12 If you stamp, you put your feet down very hard when you WALK, usually because you are angry:
"I'm leaving!" he shouted as he **stamped** out of the room.

13 If you flounce, you WALK quickly and with exaggerated movements, in a way that shows you are annoyed or upset about something:
She **flounced** out of the room in a huff.

14 If you stalk, you WALK in a stiff, proud, or angry way:
He **stalked** out of the meeting, slamming the door.

15 If you lurch, you WALK with sudden, jerky movements:
He **lurched** around the room as if he was drunk.

16 If you reel, you WALK about in an unsteady way as if you are going to fall:
He lost his balance and **reeled** back.

17 If you stumble, you trip while you are walking and almost fall:
I **stumbled** into the phone box and dialled 999.

18 If you stagger or totter, you WALK very unsteadily, often because you are ill or drunk:
He **staggered** home from the pub every night.
I had to **totter** around on crutches for six weeks.

19 If you hike or ramble, you WALK some distance in the countryside for pleasure:
They **hiked** along a remote trail.
a relaxing holiday spent **rambling** over the fells

20 If you trek, you make a journey across difficult country by walking:
This year we're going **trekking** in Nepal.

21 You can also use trek to describe someone walking rather slowly and unwillingly, usually because they are tired:
We **trekked** all round the shops looking for white shoes.

22 If you plod, tramp, or trudge, you WALK slowly, with heavy steps, often because you are tired:
He **plodded** about after me, looking bored.
They spent all day **tramping** through the snow.
We had to **trudge** all the way back up the hill.

There are a number of ways in which the word **WIDE** can be used, depending on what you are referring to. But you can make your language more interesting by using one of the following instead.

1 **If you would like to describe something measuring a large distance from side to side, you could try:**
a large woman with an **ample** bosom • ridiculously **baggy** trousers • His shoulders were **broad** • an **expansive** play area • The grounds were more **extensive** • a **full** skirt • an **immense** body of water • in **large** rivers and lakes • I like **roomy** jackets • a **spacious** kitchen • long **sweeping** curve • **vast** stretches of land • a **voluminous** trench coat

2 **If you would like to describe the extent to which something is opened or extended, you could try:**
He opened the map out **completely** so that we could see • She extended the aerial **fully** • His mouth was **fully open** in astonishment • Spread it **right out** to the edges

3 **If you would like to describe something that is extensive in scope, you could try:**
ample scope here for the imagination • **broad** range of issues • very **catholic** tastes in music • an **encyclopedic** knowledge of the subject • treatment of the topic is **exhaustive** • **comprehensive** guide • **extensive** press coverage • introduce **far-ranging** reforms • **immense** range of holiday activities • an **inclusive** survey • **large** selection of goods • **vast** range of products • **wide-ranging** but simple

SUBJECT LISTS

Contents

Art

abstract
acrylic
charcoal
collage
collection
colour
crosshatch
dimension
display
easel
exhibition
foreground
frieze

gallery
highlight
illusion
impasto
kiln
landscape
palette
pastel
perspective
portrait
sketch
spectrum

Design and food technology

aesthetic
brief
carbohydrate
component
design
diet
evaluation
fabric
fibre
flour
flow chart
hygiene
ingredient
innovation
knife
knives
linen

machine
manufacture
mineral
natural
nutrition
polyester
portfolio
presentation
production
protein
recipe
sew
specification
tension
textile
vitamin

English literature

Poetry

accented
alliteration
allusion
apostrophe
assonance
atmosphere
ballad
caesura
chorus
clause
clerihew
cliché
comparison
conjunction
connotation
consonant
couplet
dialogue
direct speech
effect
figurative
figure of speech
function
genre
haiku
hexameter
iambic foot
iambic pentameter
iambic rhythm
imagery
intention
limerick
metaphor
meter
monosyllable
monosyllabic
myth

narration
narrator
octave
ode
onomatopoeia
onomatopoeiac
pentameter
personification
playwright
poetic licence
quatrain
refrain
repetition
resolution
rhyme
rhyming couplet
rhythm
scanning
scene
sentimentality
sestet
simile
soliloquy
sonnet
stanza
stressed
structure
subordinate
syllable
synonym
tetrameter
tone
unaccented syllable
unstressed syllable
vocabulary
vowel

PROSE

advertise
advertisement
author
character
comma
exclamation
expectation
exposition
first person
flat character
grammar
impersonal narrator
introduction
intrusive narrator
irony
ironic
limited point of view

narrator
narrative voice
omniscient point of view
pamphlet
paragraph
plot
plural
prefix
preposition
punctuation
round character
second person
story
suffix
tabloid
third person
trait

Subject Lists

GEOGRAPHY

ECONOMIC WORLD

arable farming
chemical fertiliser
commercial farming
factory farms
farming subsidies
fungicide
heavy industry
herbicide
human development index
life expectancy
light industry

migrant workers
mixed farming
natural resources
nonrenewable resources
organic farming
pastoral farming
renewable resources
shanty settlement
shifting cultivation
subsistence farming

ENVIRONMENTAL WORLD

biosphere
herbivore

organism
photosynthesis

GEOMORPHOLOGICAL PROCESSES

abrasion
alluvium
atmospheric depression
attrition
beach nourishment
biological weathering
chemical weathering
coastal flooding
confluence
corrasion
corrosion
deposition
drainage basin
erosion
flood plain

freeze-thaw
global warming
hurricane
igneous rock
metamorphic rock
metamorphosis
physical weathering
reefs
sedimentary rock
storm surge
typhoon
waterfall
wave-cut notch
wave-cut platform
weathering

THE PHYSICAL WORLD

acid lava
basic lava
composite volcano
compressional plate boundary
crater
destructive boundary
epicentre
lava

magma
Richter scale
seismograph
shield volcano
tectonic plates
tensional plate boundary
tsunami

POPULATION

conurbation
counter urbanisation
depopulation
dot map
internal migration

international migration
population density
population distribution
population pyramids
rural urban fringe

WEATHER AND CLIMATE

acid rain
altitude
anemometer
atmosphere
Beaufort scale
climate
condensation
convectional rainfall
deforestation
depression
drought
equatorial regions
evaporation
fossil fuels
frontal rain
greenhouse effect
hydrology
infiltration
isobar

isotherm
latitude
leeward side
meteorologist
millibars
ocean current
pollution
precipitation
rain gauge
relief rainfall
ultraviolet radiation
vegetation
water cycle
water table
water vapour
weather forecasters
windward side
wind speed

Subject Lists

HISTORY

agriculture
agricultural
bias
castle
cathedral
Catholic
chronology
chronological
citizen
civilisation
colony
colonisation
conflict
constitution
constitutional
contradict
contradiction
current
defence
disease
document
dynasty
economy
economical
emigration

government
immigrant
imperial
imperialism
independence
invasion
motive
parliament
politics
political
priest
propaganda
Protestant
rebel
rebellion
reign
religious
republic
revolt
revolution
siege
source
trade
traitor

INFORMATION AND COMMUNICATION TECHNOLOGY

binary
byte
cable
cartridge
CD-ROM
computer
connect
connection
cursor
data
database
delete
disk
document
electronic
graphic
hardware
icon
input
interactive
interface

internet
justify
keyboard
megabyte
memory
modem
module
monitor
multimedia
network
output
password
preview
processor
program
scanner
sensor
server
software
spreadsheet
virus

Subject Lists

INVESTIGATING WORDS

anomalous results
annotation
bias
classification
classify
control
controlling variables
data
database
data search
dependent/independent variables
evaluate
evaluation
evidence
evidence of reaction
fair testing
insufficient data
line of best fit
predicting
prediction
quadrat sampling

qualitative data
qualitative observations
quantitative observations
reliability of results
reliable data
reliable evidence
repeat reading
sample
sample size
sampling
scientific method
secondary sources
sequence of events
spreadsheet
strength of evidence
sufficient data
survey
technique
theory
trial measurements
validity of conclusions

MATHEMATICS

ALGEBRA

▷ Formulae

area	perimeter
base	pi
circumference	radius
equation	subject
formulae	substitution
height	variable
hypotenuse	volume

▷ Graphs

constant	mapping
coordinates	one-dimensional
function	origin
gradient	parabola
graph	slope
horizontal	straight line
integers	two-dimensional
intersection	vertical
linear	

▷ Linear Equations

index	solution
inequality	simplify
inverse	

▷ Simultaneous Equations

linear	solving
sequence	unknown

Numbers

▷ Estimation and Approximation

omit   significant figure

▷ Fractions

cancel   numerator
denominator   proper fractions

▷ Indices

base number   powers
index notation   raise to a power

▷ Mental arithmetic

cube   expression
cuboid   measures
decimals   ratio

▷ Ratios and proportions

actual   proportional
enlarge   reduce
equivalent   scale
initial

▷ Using your calculator

addition   multiplication
amount   negative
area of a circle   operations
calculate   percentage
cube root   positive
digit   power
divide   reciprocal
division   recurring
estimate   root
fraction   square
guess   square root
minus   subtraction
multiply

SHAPE, SPACE, AND MEASUREMENTS

▷ Circles

perpendicular
quadrilateral
subtends

supplementary
symmetry

▷ Construction

pair of compasses
construction
diagonal
midpoint
polygon
protractor

radius
regular hexagon
regular pentagon
regular polygon
rhombus
vertex

▷ Lines and Angles

acute angle
adjacent angle
bisect
complementary angle
corresponding angle
degrees
interior angles

intersect
obtuse angle
parallel
reflex angle
right angle
supplementary angle

▷ Loci

circle
equidistant
locus

loci
parallel lines

▷ Measures

abbreviation
accuracy
axis
capacity
compound
constant
conversion
cube

cuboid
cylinder
diameter
estimate
formula
imperial
kilogram
kilometre

Subject Lists

length
litre
metre
parallelogram
prism

radius
trapezium
tonne
weight

▷ Polygons

decagon
exterior angle
heptagon
hexagon
nonagon

octagon
pentagon
polygon
regular polygon
triangle

▷ Quadrilaterals

adjacent

isosceles

▷ Solids

hexagon
isometric
octagon
parallelogram

pentagon
rectangle
rhombus
square

▷ Transformation geometry

congruent shapes
order of rotation
reflection
rotation

similar
transformation
translation

▷ Triangles

equilateral
exterior

scalene

HANDLING DATA

▷ Collecting data

continuous data
cumulative frequency
data
frequency
frequency distribution table
grouped data

mean *or* arithmetic data
median
mode
range
tally
tally table

▷ Interpreting data

bar chart *or* graph
census
cumulative frequency graph
cumulative graph
frequency polygon
histogram

hypothesis
pie chart *or* graph
quartile
questionnaire
survey

▷ Probability

a certain chance
chance
equally likely
even
event
favourable
fifty-fifty

impossible
likelihood scale
likely
outcome
probability scale
unlikely outcome

Music

choir
chord
chromatic
composition
conductor
crotchet
dynamics
instrument
instrumental
interval
lyric
major
melody
minim
minor
musician
octave

orchestra
orchestral
ostinato
percussion
pitch
quaver
rhythm
scale
score
semibreve
synchronise
syncopation
tempo
ternary
timbre
triad
vocal

Physical education

active
activity
agile
agility
athletic
athlete
biceps
exercise
field
gym
gymnastics
hamstring
injury

league
medicine
mobile
mobility
muscle
personal
pitch
qualify
relay
squad
tactic
tournament
triceps

PHYSICAL, SOCIAL AND HEALTH EDUCATION

able
ability
achieve
achievement
addict
addiction
approve
approval
communication
control
dependant
dependency
discipline
discussion
effort
emotion
emotional
encourage
encouragement
gender
generous
generosity
involve
involvement
prefer
preference
pressure
racism
racist
reality
relationship
represent
representative
reward
sanction
sexism
sexist
stereotype

Subject Lists

Religious Education

baptism
Bible
biblical
Buddhist
Buddhism
burial
celebrate
celebration
ceremony
Christian
commandment
commitment
creation
disciple
faith
festival
funeral
Hindu
Hinduism
hymn
immoral
immorality
Islam
Israel
Judaism
Jewish

marriage
miracle
moral
morality
Muslim
parable
pilgrim
pilgrimage
pray
prayer
prejudice
prophet
religious
religion
shrine
sign
Sikh
Sikhism
special
spirit
spiritual
symbol
synagogue
temple
wedding
worship

SCIENCE

LIFE PROCESSES AND LIVING THINGS

▷ Breathing

artery
bronchus
cilia
diaphragm
diffusion
emphysema
exhalation
exhale
haemoglobin
inhalation
inhale

lung cancer
lungs
mucus
nicotine
respiratory centre
respire
ribcage
tar
trachea
vein
ventilation

▷ Cell activity

anabolism
cell membrane
cell wall
cells
cellular respiration
cellulose
cytoplasm
excretion
growth
joules
magnification
movement

multicellular
nucleus
nutrition
organ
protoplasm
reproduction
sensitivity
skin
tissue
unicellular
variable

▷ Circulatory system

blood vessel
coronary heart disease
heart
hypertension
oxygenated blood

plasma
red blood cells
stroke
white blood cells

Subject Lists

▷ Classification

abdomen
amphibian
association
characteristics
class
classification
classify
confidence
correlation
database
environmental
family

identification
invertebrate
kingdom
leg
limb
mammal
phylum
reptile
segment
shell
taxonomic group
vertebrate

▷ Human nutrition

absorption
anaemia
anorexia
bulimia
carbohydrate
catabolism
chemical digestion
deficiency of vitamins
digestion
defecation
enzymes

food
intestine
kwashiorkor
mechanical digestion
metabolism
obesity
propulsion
protein
take in or absorb
transport or translocation
villus

▷ Human reproduction

adolescence
amniotic sac
baby
cervix
ejaculation
fallopian tube
foetus or fetus
gestation
hereditary
inherited
mammary glands
menopause
menstruation

national data
oviduct
ovulation
placenta
puberty
scrotum
semen
sexual intercourse
testis
umbilical cord
uterus
vagina

▷ Inheritance

addiction	hybrid
breed	meiosis
chromosome	mitosis
clone	mutation
data set	ovum
embryo	purebred
family tree	selective breeding
fertilisation	sex cells
gametes	sperm
gene	variation
genetically modified	variety
genetic information	zygote

▷ Microbes and disease

antibiotic	infectious disease
anti-microbial	inoculation
bacteria	measles
bronchitis	meningitis
chickenpox	mumps
cholera	pathogen
common cold	pneumonia
diphtheria	salmonella *or* salmonellosis
epidemic	tonsillitis
food poisoning	tuberculosis
fungi	vaccination
German measles *or* rubella	virus
glandular fever	viruses
immunisation	whooping cough
immunity	yellow fever
infection	

▷ Movement

antagonistic muscles	ligament
endoskeleton	plaster cast
exoskeleton	synovial joint
fracture	tendon
joint	

Subject Lists

▷ Plant nutrition and growth

chloroplast
compete
competition
fungicide
herbicide
insecticide
iodine solution
pesticide

pigment
soda lime
sodium bicarbonate
sodium hydroxide
toxin
weedkillers
yield

▷ Plant reproduction

adapted feature
anther
calyx
carpel
chemical reaction
chlorophyll
clone
complete flower
corolla
cotyledon
filament
fruit

incomplete flower
metabolism
ovary
ovule
perfect flower
petal
pistil
pollen
pollination
stamen
stigma
vegetative

▷ Plant respiration

aerobic respiration
anaerobic respiration
combustion
glucose *or* sugar

lactic acid
lime water
oxidation reaction

▷ The solar system and beyond

asteroid
eclipse
orbit

planet
rotate
satellite

▷ Sound and hearing

alternative explanation	pitch
dynamics	temporary deafness
frequency amplitude	volume
loudness	wave
noise pollution	

▷ Variation

continuous variation	family tree
discontinuous variation	

LIVING THINGS AND THEIR ENVIRONMENT

▷ Adaptation

biosphere	nocturnal
hibernation	photosynthesis
individual	phototropism
migration	transpiration

▷ Competition

carrying capacity	natural selection
community	population
consumer	population density
ecosystem	population size
environment	predator
evolution	producer
extinct	species
habitat	variation

▷ Environmental chemistry

air and water quality	ozone depletion
catalytic converter	vegetation cover

Subject Lists

▷ Feeding relationships

availability of oxygen
autotrophic
carnivore
climatic
conifer
dormant
ecological pyramid
environmental conditions
fern
food chain
food web

herbivore
insulation
light intensity
mineral
omnivore
pesticide
prey
pyramid of numbers
stress
temperature sensor
transect

MATERIALS AND THEIR PROPERTIES

▷ Acids and alkalis

acid
acid rain
alkali
base
caustic
corrosive
equation
harmful

hazard
hydrochloric acid
indicator
neutralisation
pH-scale
react
risk

▷ Chemical changes

anode
calcium carbonate
carbon
carbon dioxide
cathode
decompose
endothermic
exothermic
generalisation
hydrogen
line graph
methane

oxidation
oxidising agent
monomer
polymer
polymerisation
product
reactant
reducing agent
reduction
respiration
word equation
zinc

▷ Geological changes

aligned
chemical weathering
crystal
erupt
fossil
granite
igneous rock
iron rich
lava
limestone
magma
metamorphic rock
millennia
millions of years

obsidian
onion skin peeling
physical weathering
porosity
porous
pumice
relative density
rock cycle
sandstone
sedimentary layer
sedimentary rock
sedimentation
shale
volcanic ash

▷ Light

image
opaque
reflection

refraction
spectrum
transparent

▷ Metals and non-metals

brittle
combustion reaction
copper carbonate
copper nitrate
copper sulfate
displacement reaction
electrical conductivity
lustre
magnesium nitrate
magnesium sulfate
malleable
metal oxide

nature
order of reactivity
potassium nitrate
react
reactivity
reactivity series
resonant
salt
thermal conductivity
visible change
zinc chloride

▷ Physical changes

affect
alloy
attracted
boiling point
calcium chloride
chromatography
composition
conduction
conductor
contraction
convection
density
distillation
effect
expansion
filtration
gas pressure
heat (as energy)
insoluble

insulator
interpret
kinetic energy
melting point
mingling
miscible
mixing
mixture
model
particle
pure
radiation
saturated solution
sodium carbonate
solubility
solute
solvent
vibration

PHYSICAL PROCESSES

▷ Electric currents and circuits

ammeter
ampere
battery
bulb *or* lamp
closed circuit
connecting wire
conventional current
electric current

electromotive force (EMF)
energy transfer
open circuit
parallel circuit
power supply
series circuit
switch

▷ Energy and electricity

chemical energy
conservation
dissipation
dynamo
electrical energy
electric generator

heat and light
movement as kinetic energy
position as potential energy
power station
sound

▷ Forces and motion

acceleration
accuracy
activity
air resistance
area
balanced forces
constant speed
counterbalance
distance
drag
energy
friction
force
fuel
gravitational attraction

hydraulic
lever
mass
moment
pivot
pneumatic
power
precision
pressure
principle of moments
resistance
revolve
speed
turning effect
upthrust

▷ Magnetism and its effects

coil
core
electromagnet
magnetic field
magnetic field line
magnetic material
non-magnetic material
north pole
permanent magnet

precision
qualitative and quantitative
    observation
range
relay
repeat
solenoid
South pole
temporary magnet

Subject Lists

▷ Static electricity

atom
chlorine
compound
electron
element
formula
molecule
negatively charged object
neutral object

neutron
positively charged object
products of reaction
proton
sodium
sodium chloride
state
symbol

a great deal → a **lot** or **lots**
a great distance → far
a long way → far
a lot → many
a mass → many
a multitude → many
abandon → cancel
abandon → leave
abandon → quit
abandoned → derelict
abash → shame
abashed → embarrassed
abashment → shame
abate → decrease
abate → ease
abate → fall
abate → lessen
abate → moderate
abatement → decrease
abbreviate → shorten
abdicate → resign
abduct → kidnap
abhor → dislike
abhor → hate
abhorrence → horror
abhorrent → hateful
abide → bear
abide → put up with
abide by → obey
abiding → permanent
ability → capacity
ability → gift
ability → potential
ability → qualification
ability → skill
ability → talent
abjure → deny
able → capable
able → expert
able → proficient
able → skilful
able → skilled
able-bodied → well
ably → well
abnormal → strange
abode → home
abode → house
abomination → horror
abortive → futile

abortive → vain
about → almost
above → over
abrade → wear
abrasion → graze
abrasion → wear
abridge → cut
abridge → shorten
abridged → short
abridgment → summary
abrogate → cancel
abrupt → rude
abrupt → sharp
abrupt → sudden
abscond → escape
abscond → leave
absence → lack
absence → want
absolute → complete
absolute → final
absolute → perfect
absolute → pure
absolute → rank
absolute → sheer
absolute → total
absolute → utter
absolutely → exactly
absolutely → quite
absolutely → really
absolutely not → no
absolution → forgiveness
absolve → clear
absolve → forgive
absorb → busy
absorb → fascinate
absorb → grasp
absorb → take in
absorbed → preoccupied
absorbing → interesting
abstain → decline
abstain → refuse
abstruse → mysterious
abstruse → obscure
absurd → impossible
absurd → incredible
absurd → irrational
absurd → ridiculous
absurd → silly
absurd → stupid

absurdity → stupidity
abundance → a **lot** or **lots**
abundance → wealth
abundant → ample
abundant → generous
abundant → plentiful
abundant → rich
abuse → **impose** on
abuse → harm
abuse → insult
abuse → mistreat
abuse → wrong
abused → oppressed
abusive → offensive
abutment → support
abysmal → awful
abysmal → terrible
abyss → hell
academic → learned
accelerate → hurry
accelerated → fast
accent → emphasis
accent → emphasize
accentuate → emphasize
accentuate → stress
accept → **resign** oneself
accept → admit
accept → assume
accept → believe
accept → grant
accept → receive
accept → tolerate
acceptable → adequate
acceptable → all right
acceptable → correct
acceptable → okay
acceptable → right
acceptable → satisfactory
acceptable → suitable
acceptable → tolerable
accepted → general
accepted → proper
accepted → standard
access → entrance
accessible → available
accessible → ready
accessory → attachment
accessory → extra
accessory → fitting

accident → chance
accident → crash
accident → luck
accident-prone → clumsy
accidental → casual
acclaim → credit
acclaim → glory
acclaim → honour
acclaim → praise
accolade → honour
accolade → praise
accolade → prize
accolade → tribute
accommodating → helpful
accommodation → space
accompany → guide
accomplish → achieve
accomplish → carry out
accomplish → fulfil
accomplished → able
accomplished → capable
accomplished → practical
accomplished → proficient
accomplished → skilful
accomplished → skilled
accomplishment → achievement
accomplishment → act
accomplishment → action
accomplishment → qualification
accord → agree
accord → give
accord → grant
accord → match
accord → understanding
accordant → compatible
account → bill
account → note
account → record
account → report
account → statement
account → story
accountability → blame
accountability → responsibility

accoutrements → equipment
accumulate → collect
accumulate → concentrate
accumulate → gather
accumulate → stockpile
accurate → correct
accurate → exact
accurate → faithful
accurate → precise
accurate → right
accurate → strict
accurate → true
accurately → exactly
accuse → blame
accustomed → usual
ace → expert
acerbic → sour
acetic → sour
ache → long
ache → pain
ache for → be dying for
ache for → desire
achieve → accomplish
achieve → carry out
achieve → fulfil
achieve → gain
achieve → win
achievement → act
achievement → action
achievement → qualification
Achilles' heel → weakness
aching → painful
aching → tender
acid → bitter
acid → sour
acknowledge → accept
acknowledge → admit
acknowledge → confess
acknowledge → grant
acknowledge → recognize
acknowledgment → confession
acknowledgment → reaction

acme → extreme
acme → peak
acme → top
acquaint → tell
acquaintance → contact
acquainted with → aware of
acquainted with → familiar
acquiescent → meek
acquiescent → passive
acquire → buy
acquire → earn
acquire → gain
acquire → get
acquire → obtain
acquire → possess
acquire → secure
acquisitive → greedy
acquit → clear
acquit yourself → conduct yourself
acquittal → forgiveness
acrid → bitter
acrimonious → bitter
act → appear
act → behave
act → conduct yourself
act → law
act → perform
act against → counteract
act on → affect
act out → act
act towards → treat
action → activity
action → case
action → fight
active → alive
active → appear
active → busy
active → healthy
active → lively
active → vital
activist → fanatic
activity → action
activity → bustle
activity → excitement
activity → exercise
activity → interest
activity → pastime

actual → precise
actual → real
actually → really
acumen → intelligence
acute → bright
acute → brilliant
acute → extreme
acute → grave
acute → intelligent
acute → intense
acute → perceptive
acute → serious
acute → severe
acute → uncommon
acute → violent
ad → advertisement
adage → saying
adamant → firm
adapt → fit
adaptable → flexible
adapted → accustomed
add to → augment
add to → enlarge
add to → extend
add to → supplement
add up → add
add up → count
add up to → total
added → extra
added → more
addendum → addition
addiction → habit
addition → extra
addition → supplement
additional → extra
additional → more
address → lecture
address → speech
address → talk
adept → capable
adept → expert
adept → proficient
adept → skilful
adeptly → well
adequate → acceptable
adequate → all right
adequate → decent
adequate → satisfactory
adequate → sufficient

adequate → tolerable
adequately → well
adhere → stick
adhere to → obey
adherent → fan
adherent → follower
adherent → supporter
adhesive → sticky
adjacent → near
adjacent → next
adjacent to → beside
adjacent to → near
adjoin → add
adjoining → near
adjoining → next
adjourn → postpone
adjudge → judge
adjudge → rate
adjudicate → judge
adjunct → addition
adjust → adapt
adjustment → correction
administer → control
administer → give
administer → handle
administer → rule
administer → run
administration → bureaucracy
administration → management
admirable → fine
admirably → well
admiration → approval
admiration → esteem
admiration → respect
admiration → worship
admire → appreciate
admire → approve
admire → praise
admire → respect
admirer → fan
admission → confession
admission → entrance
admit → confess
admit → grant
admonish → warn
ado → fuss
adolescent → young

adorable → lovable
adoration → love
adoration → worship
adore → like
adore → love
adore → worship
adored → beloved
adoring → fond
adorn → decorate
adornment → ornament
adrift → lost
adroit → expert
adroit → skilful
adulation → flattery
adulation → worship
adult → mature
adulterate → pollute
adulterous → unfaithful
adumbrate → outline
advance → develop
advance → early
advance → gain
advance → go
advance → improve
advance → improvement
advance → loan
advance → payment
advance → proceed
advance → produce
advance → progress
advance → raise
advance warning → notice
advanced → sophisticated
advantage → beauty
advantage → benefit
advantage → merit
advantage → value
advantage → virtue
advantageous → beneficial
advantageous → favourable
advantageous → helpful
advent → appearance
adventitious → lucky
adventitiously → at random
adventure → excitement

Index

Index

astound → surprise
astounding → amazing
astounding → incredible
astounding → wonderful
astray → lost
astringent → bitter
astute → acute
astute → bright
astute → clever
astute → keen
astute → perceptive
astute → sharp
astute → shrewd
astute → smart
astuteness → wisdom
asylum → refuge
asylum → shelter
asymmetrical → irregular
at a loss → confused
at an end → over
at ease → comfortable
at ease → relaxed
at fault → responsible
at hand → available
at hand → handy
at hand → present
at home → comfortable
at large → free
at last → finally
at liberty → free
at no time → never
at odds → different
at once → immediately
at once → now
at once → together
at sea → confused
at someone's disposal →
 available
at the last moment →
 finally
at times → sometimes
at variance → different
at your fingertips →
 handy
atone → compensate
atonement →
 compensation
atrocious → dreadful
atrocious → wicked

attach → add
attach → connect
attach → fasten
attach → fix
attach → hang
attach → join
attach → link
attach → secure
attach → stick
attachment → affection
attachment →
 association
attachment → bond
attachment → fitting
attachment → friendship
attachment → link
attack → bomb
attack → invade
attack → raid
attack → savage
attain → acquire
attain → earn
attain → gain
attain → reach
attain → win
attainable → possible
attempt → aim
attempt → effort
attempt → go
attempt → seek
attempt → strive
attempt → try
attend → frequent
attend → listen
attend to → deal
attend to → take care of
attention → care
attention →
 consideration
attention → heed
attention → interest
attentive → alert
attentive → observant
attentive → thoughtful
attest → declare
attire → clothes
attire → dress
attitude → conduct
attitude → outlook

attitude → view
attitude → viewpoint
attorney → lawyer
attract → appeal
attract → lure
attraction → beauty
attraction → charm
attraction → lure
attraction → pull
attractive → beautiful
attractive → cute
attractive → handsome
attractive → lovely
attractive → pretty
attractiveness → beauty
attribute → characteristic
attribute → feature
attribute → point
attribute → property
attribute → qualification
attribute → quality
attribute → virtue
attrition → wear
atypical → unusual
au courant → aware
audacious → bold
audacious → daring
audacity → cheek
audacity → daring
audacity → impudence
audibly → aloud
audience → meeting
audit → inspect
augment → add
augment → build
augment → enlarge
augment → extend
augment → increase
augment → supplement
augur → promise
augury → omen
augury → warning
auspicious → favourable
austere → harsh
austere → plain
authentic → actual
authentic → exact
authentic → genuine
authentic → real

authentic → realistic
authentic → true
authenticate → confirm
authenticate → prove
authentication → proof
authenticity → reality
authoritarian → bossy
authoritarian → strict
authority → control
authority → expert
authority → influence
authority → mana
authority → power
authorization → approval
authorization →
  permission
authorization → permit
authorization → power
authorization → sanction
authorize → allow
authorize → approve
authorize → permit
authorize → sanction
authorized → legal
authorized → official
automated → automatic
automobile → car
autonomous →
  independent
auxiliary → extra
avail oneself of → use
available → ready
avaricious → greedy
avenge → revenge
aver → declare
aver → state
average → all right
average → common
average → medium
average → moderate
average → normal
average → typical
averse → reluctant
averse → unwilling
averse to → against
aversion → dislike
aversion → hate
aversion → hatred
aversion → horror

avert → prevent
avid → ardent
avid → eager
avid → enthusiastic
avid → keen
avoid → abstain
avoid → dodge
avoid → escape
avow → declare
avowal → declaration
awake → wake
award → give
award → grant
award → present
award → prize
award-winning → prize
aware → perceptive
aware of → familiar
awareness → grasp
away → absent
awe → fear
awesome → impressive
awful → dreadful
awful → horrible
awful → terrible
awkward → clumsy
awkward → embarrassed
awkward →
  uncomfortable
awkwardness →
  clumsiness
awkwardness →
  embarrassment
axiom → principle
axiom → saying
aye → yes
élan → energy
élan → style
babalas → drunk
babble → ramble
babble → rave
babies → young
baby → child
bacchic → drunk
back → advocate
back → finance
back → gamble
back → promote
back → sanction

back → support
back away → retreat
back off → retreat
back out → withdraw
background → foil
background → record
background →
  surroundings
backing → blessing
backing → sanction
backlash → reaction
backside → bottom
bad → evil
bad → naughty
bad → rotten
bad → serious
bad → unpleasant
bad → wicked
bad → wrong
bad for you → unhealthy
bad luck → misfortune
bad-tempered → grumpy
bad-tempered → irritable
badger → hassle
badger → pester
badness → evil
baffle → confuse
baffle → puzzle
baffled → confused
baffling → confusing
baffling → hard
baffling → mysterious
baggy → full
baggy → loose
bailiwick → field
bairn → baby
bairn → child
bait → incentive
bait → lure
bait → pick on
bake → cook
bake → harden
balance → compensate
balance → difference
balance → remainder
balance → rest
baleful → harmful
baleful → sinister
ball → lump

be careful → beware
be cautious → beware
be clothed in → wear
be compatible → get on
be composed of → **consist** of
be concerned → care
be defeated → fail
be defeated → lose
be deficient in → lack
be deficient in → want
be determined → intend
be determined by → depend
be dressed in → wear
be dubious → doubt
be engrossed in → concentrate
be entitled to → deserve
be entitled to → merit
be envious → envy
be equal to → equal
be familiar with → know
be fond of → like
be frightened → fear
be full of → crawl
be furious → rage
be given → receive
be in charge of → administer
be in charge of → control
be in charge of → head
be in charge of → manage
be in charge of → oversee
be in charge of → run
be in charge of → supervise
be in contact → communicate
be in love with → love
be in need of → require
be in power → rule
be in touch → communicate
be in vain → fail
be inclined → tend
be incompatible → conflict
be instrumental in → take **part** in

be interested → care
be invented → appear
be involved in → participate
be involved in → take **part** in
be jealous → envy
be keen on → like
be left → remain
be level → tie
be liable → tend
be like → resemble
be lost to view → disappear
be lost to view → vanish
be made up of → **consist** of
be of consequence → matter
be of the same opinion → agree
be offended by → resent
be on fire → burn
be on the surface → float
be opposite → face
be over → cease
be overjoyed → rejoice
be overrun → crawl
be partial to → like
be partial to → prefer
be present → occur
be present at → witness
be prone → tend
be prostrate → lie
be recumbent → lie
be related → correspond
be relevant to → concern
be scared → fear
be sceptical → doubt
be short of → lack
be sick → puke
be sick → vomit
be sick of → hate
be similar to → resemble
be sorry → regret
be specific about → specify
be subject to → depend
be subjected to → undergo

be successful → succeed
be sufficient → do
be supine → lie
be unfaithful → betray
be unsuccessful → fail
be victorious → win
be wary → beware
be watchful → watch out
be wild about → rave
be worthwhile → pay
be worthy of → deserve
be worthy of → merit
beach → coast
beacon → signal
bead → blob
bead → drip
bead → drop
beak → judge
beam → shine
beam → smile
bear → bring
bear → carry
bear → put up with
bear → suffer
bear → take
bear → tolerate
bear a resemblance to → resemble
bear in mind → consider
bear on → concern
bear out → confirm
bearable → tolerable
bearing → appearance
bearing → look
bearing → manner
bearing → relation
beast → animal
beast → savage
beat → bang
beat → club
beat → defeat
beat → rhythm
beat → top
beat → vanquish
beaut → excellent
beautiful → fine
beautiful → lovely
beautiful → pretty
beautify → decorate

Index

because of → by **virtue** of
beckon → lure
beckon → signal
become → get
become → grow
become available → appear
become aware → find
become extinct → vanish
become hysterical → panic
become invisible → vanish
become licensed → qualify
become proficient in → master
bed → base
bed → bottom
bedeck → decorate
bedevil → pester
bedraggled → untidy
beefy → plump
befitting → suitable
before → in **front**
before long → soon
beforehand → early
beforehand → first
befoul → pollute
befoul → soil
beg → appeal
beg → ask
beg → implore
beg → plead
beg → press
beg → request
beg → scrounge
beg → urge
beg someone's pardon → apologize
beggary → poverty
begin → proceed
begin → start
begin again → renew
beginner → recruit
beginning → head
beginning → opening
beginning → source

beginning → start
begrime → soil
begrudge → envy
begrudging → bitter
beguile → charm
beguile → deceive
beguile → fascinate
behave → conduct yourself
behave towards → treat
behaviour → conduct
behaviour → manner
behest → command
behind → bottom
behind → late
behind the times → old-fashioned
behind time → late
behindhand → late
behold → see
belabour → stress
belated → late
belief → confidence
belief → faith
belief → idea
belief → opinion
belief → view
belief → viewpoint
believe → assume
believe → consider
believe → expect
believe → feel
believe → imagine
believe → reckon
believe → suppose
believe → suspect
believe → think
believe → understand
believed → supposed
believer → follower
belittle → put down
belligerent → aggressive
belligerent → hostile
bellow → shout
belly → stomach
belong → fit
belongings → possessions
belongings → property

belongings → stuff
belongings → things
beloved → dear
below → under
bemoan → complain
bemoan → lament
bemoan → regret
bemuse → confuse
bench → court
bend → curve
bend → fold
bend → twist
bend down → crouch
bendable → soft
beneath → below
beneath → under
beneficent → benevolent
beneficial → favourable
beneficial → healthy
beneficial → helpful
beneficial → useful
beneficial → valuable
benefit → advantage
benefit → beauty
benefit → blessing
benefit → gain
benefit → value
benevolence → generosity
benevolence → goodwill
benevolence → kindness
benevolence → mercy
benevolent → compassionate
benevolent → humane
benevolent → kind
benign → benevolent
benign → gentle
benign → kind
bent → crooked
bent → set on
bent on → determined
benumb → numb
benumbed → numb
bequeath → hand down
bequeath → will
bequest → gift
bequest → inheritance
bequest → legacy

Index

bored → uninterested
boring → dreary
boring → dull
boring → flat
boss → chief
boss → employer
boss → head
boss → leader
boss → manager
boss → superior
bosses → management
bossy → pushy
botch up → mess
bother → agitate
bother → annoy
bother → concern
bother → distress
bother → disturb
bother → fuss
bother → hassle
bother → irritate
bother → nuisance
bother → pester
bother → trouble
bother → upset
bother → worry
bothered → anxious
bothered → worried
bottom → base
bottomless → deep
bottomless → infinite
bounce → glance
bounce → leap
bound → bounce
bound → jump
bound → leap
boundary → border
boundary → edge
boundary → extreme
boundless → infinite
bounds → border
bounds → limit
bounds → range
bountiful → plentiful
bounty → abundance
bounty → generosity
bounty → reward
bounty → wealth
bouquet → bunch

bouquet → fragrance
bouquet → smell
bourgeois → conventional
bout → event
bout → fight
boutique → shop
bovine → cow
bow → **resign** oneself
bow → bend
bow → submit
box → case
boycott → sanctions
brace → refresh
brace → steady
brace → strengthen
brace → support
bracing → healthy
brag → boast
bragger → braggart
bragging → boastful
brain → genius
brain → head
brain → mind
brain-teaser → puzzle
brains → genius
brains → sense
brainy → bright
brainy → brilliant
brainy → clever
brainy → intelligent
brak → dog
brak → salty
brake → curb
brand → kind
brand → make
brand → sort
brand → type
brandish → flourish
brandish → shake
brandish → wave
brash → bold
brash → cocky
brave → bold
brave → daring
bravery → courage
bravery → daring
brawl → fight
brawn → power
brawn → strength

brawniness → strength
brazen → bold
brazen → shameless
breach → break
breach → division
breach → split
break → burst
break → crack
break → dash
break → disobey
break → gap
break → holiday
break → interrupt
break → interval
break → pause
break → rest
break → ruin
break free → escape
break into → raid
break out → escape
break up → disintegrate
break up → separate
break your promise →
  betray
break-in → raid
breakable → fragile
breakdown → failure
breaker → wave
breakfast → eat
breakneck → furious
breakthrough → advance
breakthrough → progress
breakup → split
breathing → alive
breathtaking → superb
breed → kind
breed → type
bribe → bait
bribe → corrupt
bribery → corruption
brick → block
brief → concise
brief → quick
bright → acute
bright → bold
bright → brilliant
bright → cheerful
bright → clever
bright → colourful

bump into → meet
bumpy → irregular
bumpy → rough
bumpy → uneven
bunch → band
bunch → group
bunch → lot
bundle → bunch
bung → plug
bungle → botch
bungle → mess
bungling → incompetent
buoy up → reassure
buoyant → cheerful
buoyant → optimistic
burble → babble
burden → handicap
bureaucrat → official
bureaucratic →
  impersonal
burglar → thief
burgle → rob
burly → plump
burrow → dig
burst → broken
burst → explode
burst → flash
burst → split
bush → country
bushie → yokel
bushy → yokel
business → affair
business → company
business → concern
business → enterprise
business → event
business → firm
business → matter
business → profession
business → scene
business → trade
business → undertaking
business → work
businesslike → efficient
businesslike →
  impersonal
bustle → activity
bustle → fuss
bustle → rush

busy → active
busy → industrious
busybody → snooper
but → except
butcher → kill
butt in → interfere
butt in → interrupt
butt in → intrude
buttocks → bottom
buttress → support
buy off → corrupt
buyer → customer
by → past
by degrees → slowly
by design → on **purpose**
by dint of → by **virtue** of
by oneself → on your **own**
bygone → former
bygone → past
bystander → spectator
bystander → witness
Byzantine → complicated
cabal → plot
cache → hide
cache → hoard
cache → reserve
cache → stockpile
cache → store
cache → supply
cacophony → racket
cadence → beat
cadge → scrounge
caesura → pause
cagey → secretive
cajole → coax
cake → harden
cake → lump
calamitous → fatal
calamity → blow
calamity → disaster
calculate → count
calculate → reckon
calculate → work out
calculated → deliberate
calculating → devious
calculation → count
calibrate → measure
calibre → quality
calibre → standard

call → cry
call → hail
call → name
call → request
call → shout
call → visit
call for → demand
call off → cancel
call on → visit
call to mind → remember
call upon → appeal
call upon → tell
calling → work
callous → cruel
callous → merciless
callousness → cruelty
calm → cool
calm → ease
calm → pacify
calm → patient
calm → peace
calm → peaceful
calm → quiet
calm → relaxed
calm → silence
calm → still
calmness → calm
calmness → patience
calmness → quiet
calumniate → slander
calumny → slander
camaraderie → fellowship
camber → tilt
camp → base
camp → side
campaign → agitate
campaign → movement
cancel → delete
cancel → lift
cancel out → compensate
candid → direct
candid → frank
candid → natural
candid → open
candid → straight
candid → straightforward
candy → sweet
cane → stick
canine → dog

Index

categorize → classify
categorize → sort
category → class
category → kind
category → sort
category → variety
catholic → universal
cattle → cow
catty → spiteful
cause → bring
cause → bring about
cause → create
cause → factor
cause → grounds
cause → lead to
cause → prompt
cause → provoke
cause → reason
cause → result in
cause → source
cause a stir → make an impression
caustic → sarcastic
caution → advise
caution → care
caution → warn
caution → warning
cautious → careful
cautious → deliberate
cautious → wary
cavalcade → parade
cavalier → careless
cave in → give
caveat → warning
cavilling → critical
cease → disappear
cease → end
cease → fail
cease → halt
cease → quit
cease → stop
cease → vanish
cease to exist → vanish
cede → surrender
ceiling → maximum
celebrate → commemorate
celebrate → rejoice
celebrated → famous

celebration → party
celebrity → personality
celebrity → star
celebrity → success
cell → ring
censorious → abusive
censorious → critical
censure → abuse
censure → accuse
censure → attack
censure → condemn
censure → criticism
censure → criticize
censure → disapproval
censure → fault
central → basic
central → crucial
central → middle
central → vital
centre → base
centre → focus
centre → middle
certain → confident
certain → definite
certain → necessary
certain → positive
certain → sure
certainly → really
certainly not → no
certainty → fact
certification → proof
certified → official
certify → declare
cessation of hostilities → peace
chaff → joke
chagrin → embarrassment
chagrined → ashamed
chain → sequence
chain → series
challenge → contest
challenge → dare
challenge → dispute
challenge → query
challenge → question
challenger → competitor
challenger → rival
challenging → formidable
chamber → compartment

chamber → room
champ → chew
champion → advocate
champion → back
champion → defender
champion → support
champion → supporter
champion → winner
championship → competition
chance → accidental
chance → casual
chance → fate
chance → gamble
chance → luck
chance → occasion
chance → possibility
chance → risk
chance → turn
chance → unexpected
chance → unpredictable
chances → probability
change → adapt
change → affect
change → exchange
change → reverse
change → transform
change → turn
change → variation
change → vary
channel → medium
channel → passage
channel → route
channel → way
chaos → confusion
chaos → disorder
chaos → mess
chaos → muddle
chaotic → confused
chaotic → untidy
chap → man
char → burn
character → eccentric
character → figure
character → individual
character → name
character → nature
character → number
character → personality

Index

collapse → downfall
collapse → faint
collapse → fall
collapse → give
colleague → assistant
colleague → associate
collect → assemble
collect → concentrate
collect → gather
collect → stockpile
collected → calm
collected → cool
collection → body
collection → group
collection → number
collection → variety
collectively → together
collide → bump
collide → crash
collide with → hit
collision → crash
colloquial → informal
colloquium → conference
collude → plot
colonize → settle
colossal → enormous
colossal → huge
colossal → immense
colossal → large
colossal → unbelievable
colossal → vast
colour → blush
colourless → pale
column → feature
column → line
column → rank
column → row
comatose → unconscious
comb → search
combat → conflict
combat → fight
combat → war
combination → blend
combination → cross
combination → mixture
combination → union
combine → blend
combine → mix
combine → unite

combo → band
combustion → fire
come about → happen
come about → take **place**
come across → discover
come across → find
come across → meet
come after → follow
come apart → split
come back → return
come between → divide
come first → win
come into being →
   appear
come into being → start
come into existence →
   appear
come into existence →
   start
come into view → appear
come of age → mature
come on → flourish
come out → appear
come out on top →
   triumph
come to → cost
come to → total
come to → wake
come to a decision →
   decide
come to a head → peak
come to an end → cease
come to an end → stop
come to grief → fail
come to someone's
   rescue → save
come together →
   assemble
come up with → invent
come upon → meet
come with → accompany
comedy → humour
comedy → play
comely → attractive
comfort → reassure
comfortable → cosy
comfortable → easy
comfortable → homely
comfortable → leisurely

comfortable → relaxed
comfortable → wealthy
comic → funny
comical → funny
comical → hysterical
coming → appearance
coming → future
coming → imminent
command → administer
command → control
command → direction
command → exact
command → instruct
command → lead
command → manage
command → order
command → tell
commandeer → seize
commander → leader
commander → ruler
commanding → powerful
commemorate →
   celebrate
commemorate → honour
commence → begin
commence → start
commencement →
   beginning
commencement →
   opening
commencement → start
commend → advise
commend → honour
commendation → credit
commendation → honour
commendation → praise
comment → observe
comment → remark
comment → word
commentary → review
commerce → business
commerce → finance
commerce → trade
commercial →
   advertisement
commercial → economic
commission → employ
commission → hire
committed → fervent

committee → council
commodious → spacious
commodity → product
common → everyday
common → frequent
common → general
common → low
common → natural
common → popular
common → universal
common → usual
common → vulgar
common → widespread
common sense → sense
common sense → sense
commonplace → common
commonwealth → state
commotion → bustle
commotion → excitement
commotion → fuss
commotion → noise
commotion → racket
communal → public
communicable →
  infectious
communicate → convey
communicate → express
communicate → inform
communicate with →
  contact
communication →
  contact
communication →
  message
communication → note
communication → word
communicative →
  talkative
communiqué → message
community → colony
community → company
community → local
community → public
compact → agreement
compact → bond
companion → friend
companion → partner
companionable →
  friendly

companionable →
  sociable
companionship →
  company
companionship →
  fellowship
company → association
company → band
company → body
company → business
company → enterprise
company → firm
company → organization
comparability →
  resemblance
comparability →
  similarity
comparable → similar
compassion → kindness
compassion → mercy
compassion → pity
compassion → sympathy
compassionate →
  benevolent
compassionate → gentle
compassionate →
  humane
compassionate → kind
compassionate →
  merciful
compassionate → tender
compassionate →
  understanding
compassionately → well
compel → drive
compel → force
compel → make
compel → require
compelling → interesting
compelling → powerful
compelling → urgent
compendium → set
compensate → pay
compete → play
competence → ability
competence → skill
competent → able
competent → capable
competent → efficient

competent → proficient
competent → skilful
competent → skilled
competently → well
competition →
  competitor
competition → contest
competition → event
competition → match
competitive →
  reasonable
competitor → candidate
complacent → smug
complain → grumble
complain → moan
complain → protest
complaint → disorder
complaint → grumble
complaint → illness
complaint → protest
complement → augment
complement → blend
complement → foil
complement →
  supplement
complete → absolute
complete → accomplish
complete → achieve
complete → finish
complete → ideal
complete → over
complete → perfect
complete → perform
complete → pure
complete → rank
complete → sheer
complete → thorough
complete → total
complete → utter
complete → whole
completely → quite
completely → well
completion → finish
complex → complicated
complex → elaborate
complex → hard
complex → obsession
complex → sophisticated
complex → tricky

compliant → agreeable
compliant → meek
compliant → obedient
compliant → passive
compliant → willing
complicated → complex
complicated → confusing
complicated → elaborate
complicated → hard
complicated → sophisticated
complicated → tricky
complication → difficulty
compliment → flatter
compliment → tribute
complimentary → free
comply → follow
comply → submit
comply with → obey
component → attachment
component → fitting
component → ingredient
comportment → conduct
comportment → manner
compos mentis → sane
compose → create
compose → form
compose → make up
composed → calm
composed → cool
composed → patient
composite → combination
composite → mixture
composition → piece
composure → patience
compound → blend
compound → mixture
comprehend → know
comprehend → read
comprehend → realize
comprehend → see
comprehend → take in
comprehend → understand
comprehensible → plain
comprehension → grasp
comprehension → intelligence
comprehension → understanding

comprehensive → broad
comprehensive → extensive
comprehensive → full
comprehensive → general
comprehensive → thorough
compress → press
compressed → firm
comprise → **consist** of
comprise → contain
comprise → make up
compromise → endanger
compulsion → force
compulsion → urge
compunction → regret
computation → count
compute → count
comrade → companion
comradely → friendly
con → cheat
con → deceive
con → dupe
con → fool
con → rob
con → take in
con → trick
conceal → cover
conceal → hide
conceal → obscure
conceal → suppress
concealed → invisible
concede → give in
concede → grant
conceit → pride
conceited → boastful
conceited → cocky
conceited → haughty
conceited → pretentious
conceited → smug
conceited → stuck-up
conceited → vain
conceivable → possible
conceivably → maybe
conceivably → perhaps
conceive → imagine
conceive → invent
conceive → understand
conceive of → picture

concentrate → centre
concentrate → essence
concentrate → focus
concentrated → thick
conception → vision
concern → anxiety
concern → bother
concern → business
concern → care
concern → consideration
concern → enterprise
concern → interest
concern → issue
concern → job
concern → worry
concerned → anxious
concerned → worried
concerning → about
conclave → council
conclave → meeting
conclude → complete
conclude → end
conclude → finish
conclude → gather
conclude → stop
concluding → final
concluding → last
conclusion → decision
conclusion → finish
conclusion → judgment
conclusion → verdict
conclusive → convincing
conclusive → final
conclusive → positive
concoct → invent
concoct → make up
concourse → company
concrete → positive
concrete → real
concur → agree
concur with → accept
concurrently → together
condemn → censure
condemn → criticize
condemn → disapprove
condemnation → censure
condemnation → disapproval
condemned → doomed

conservative →
 conventional
conservative → right-
 wing
consider → contemplate
consider → feel
consider → judge
consider → ponder
consider → rate
consider → reckon
consider → regard
consider → think
consider → view
considerable → extensive
considerable →
 handsome
considerable →
 respectable
considerable → significant
considerably → far
considerate →
 accommodating
considerate → kind
considerate → thoughtful
considerate →
 understanding
considerately → well
consideration → aspect
consideration → factor
consideration → thought
consignment → load
consistency → texture
consistent → compatible
consistent → logical
consistent → regular
consistent → steady
consolation → comfort
console → comfort
consolidate → strengthen
consonant → compatible
consort → associate
conspicuous → bold
conspicuous → clear
conspicuous → evident
conspicuous → manifest
conspicuous → noticeable
conspicuous → obvious
conspicuous → prominent
conspicuous → visible

conspiracy → plot
conspiratorial → secret
conspire → plot
constant → continual
constant → continuous
constant → devoted
constant → even
constant → loyal
constant → permanent
constant → regular
constant → steadfast
constant → steady
consternation → alarm
constituent → ingredient
constitute → form
constitute → make up
constitution → health
constitution → law
constitutional → legal
constitutional → walk
constrain → imprison
constrain → restrain
constrained → stiff
constraint → restriction
constricted → tight
construct → assemble
construct → build
construct → fashion
construct → make
construct → produce
construction → making
construction → structure
constructive → helpful
constructive → positive
constructive → productive
consult → refer
consultant → adviser
consultation → discussion
consume → drain
consume → exhaust
consumer → customer
consummate → complete
consummate → ideal
consummate → perfect
consummate → utter
contagious → infectious
contain → curb
contain → include
contain → restrain

contain → restrict
contain → suppress
container → box
container → case
contaminate → infect
contaminate → pollute
contemn → scorn
contemplate → consider
contemplate → ponder
contemplate → regard
contemplate → study
contemplate → think
contemplation →
 consideration
contemplation → thought
contemplative →
 thoughtful
contemporary → current
contemporary → modern
contemporary → recent
contempt → scorn
contemptible → low
contemptible → shabby
contemptuous → scornful
contend → compete
contender → candidate
content → satisfied
contented → comfortable
contented → pleased
contented → satisfied
contention → competition
contest → compete
contest → competition
contest → dispute
contest → event
contest → game
contest → match
contestant → competitor
continual → constant
continual → frequent
continually → always
continue → extend
continue → last
continue → proceed
continue → remain
continue → stretch
continued → continuous
continuous → constant
continuous → continual

continuous → gradual
continuous → steady
contort → twist
contours → form
contours → outline
contours → shape
contract → agreement
contract → bond
contract → develop
contract → diminish
contract → shrink
contradict → clash
contradict → deny
contradict → dispute
contraption → machine
contrary → opposite
contrary → reverse
contrast → compare
contrast → difference
contrast → foil
contrasting → different
contrasting → opposite
contravene → break
contravene → disobey
contravention → breach
contribute → provide
contribute to → lead to
contribution → gift
contrite → guilty
contrite → sorry
contrition → regret
control → administer
control → check
control → command
control → contain
control → curb
control → determine
control → direct
control → direction
control → grip
control → head
control → hold
control → influence
control → manage
control → management
control → possess
control → possession
control → power
control → restrain

control → restriction
control → run
controvert → argue
contusion → bump
conundrum → mystery
conundrum → problem
conurbation → city
convalesce → recover
convalescence → recovery
convene → assemble
convene → gather
convene → meet
convenient → handy
convenient → ready
convention → conference
convention → custom
convention → gathering
convention → habit
convention → hui
convention → meeting
convention → tradition
conventional → conservative
conventional → formal
conventional → normal
conventional → ordinary
conventional → popular
conventional → proper
conventional → traditional
conversation → chat
conversation → discussion
conversation → talk
conversation → word
conversational → colloquial
converse → opposite
converse → reverse
convert → adapt
convert → change
convert → recruit
convert → transform
convert → turn
convey → bear
convey → bring
convey → carry
convey → communicate

convey → take
convey → transport
convict → prisoner
convicted → guilty
conviction → belief
conviction → idea
conviction → view
conviction → viewpoint
convince → satisfy
convinced → certain
convinced → confident
convinced → positive
convinced → sure
convincing → powerful
convivial → friendly
convivial → sociable
convocation → conference
convocation → council
convocation → meeting
convoluted → complex
convoluted → complicated
convoy → guide
cool → apathetic
cool → calm
cool → patience
cool → relaxed
cool off → cool
cooperate → team
cooperative → helpful
coordinate → oversee
cope with → deal
cope with → endure
cope with → manage
cope with → take care of
copious → abundant
copious → plentiful
copious → rich
copiousness → wealth
copy → fake
copy → imitate
copy → issue
cordial → friendly
cordial → warm
core → basis
core → centre
core → essence
cork → plug

corner → bend
corner → trap
cornucopia → abundance
cornucopia → wealth
corporation → body
corporation → business
corporation → company
corporation → firm
corpse → body
corpulent → overweight
correct → accurate
correct → appropriate
correct → fitting
correct → fix
correct → formal
correct → precise
correct → proper
correct → reform
correct → revise
correct → right
correct → standard
correct → true
correction → reform
correlate → correspond
correlation → connection
correlation → relation
correlation → relationship
correspond → communicate
correspond → fit
correspond → match
correspondence → connection
correspondence → resemblance
corridor → passage
corroborate → confirm
corroborate → prove
corroboration → proof
corrode → eat away
corrode → erode
corrode → wear
corrosion → wear
corrupt → criminal
corrupt → crooked
corrupt → dirty
corrupt → dishonest
corruption → dishonesty
coruscate → sparkle

cosmopolitan → sophisticated
cosset → spoil
cost → charge
cost → price
cost → rate
cost → value
cost-effective → economical
costly → dear
costly → expensive
costly → valuable
costume → clothes
costume → dress
cosy → comfortable
cosy → homely
coterie → company
coterie → group
couch → express
counsel → advice
counsel → advise
counsel → guide
counsel → lawyer
count → calculate
count → matter
count → rate
count → reckon
count on → depend
count on → trust
count up → add
countenance → expression
countenance → face
countenance → put up with
counter → foil
counter → reply
counteract → compensate
counterbalance → compensate
counterbalance → counteract
counterbalance → reaction
counterfeit → copy
counterfeit → fake
counterfeit → mock
counterfeit → phoney
counterfeit → pretend

countermand → cancel
countermand → overrule
countermand → overturn
countermand → reverse
countervail → compensate
countervail → counteract
countless → many
country → land
country → state
country → territory
countryman → yokel
countryside → country
coup → success
coup → triumph
couple → associate
couple → attach
couple → connect
couple → join
couple → link
coupling → connection
courage → bravery
courage → daring
courageous → bold
courageous → brave
courier → messenger
course → direction
course → line
course → passage
course → path
course → pour
course → route
course → sequence
course → way
course of action → process
courteous → polite
courteousness → courtesy
courtesy → favour
courtesy → politeness
cove → bay
covenant → agreement
covenant → bond
cover → defence
cover → defend
cover → include
cover → protection
cover → report

crooked → wrong
crop up → appear
cross → angry
cross out → delete
cross section → variety
cross your mind → occur
cross-examine →
  interrogate
cross-examine →
  question
cross-question →
  interrogate
crouch → bend
crow → boast
crow → brag
crowd → band
crowd → bunch
crowd → company
crowd → group
crowd → jam
crowd → lot
crowd → mass
crowd → number
crowing → boastful
crown → top
crucial → critical
crucial → essential
crucial → major
crucial → serious
crucial → vital
crude → indecent
crude → primitive
crude → vulgar
cruel → harsh
cruel → malicious
cruel → merciless
cruel → savage
cruel → spiteful
cruel → unkind
cruel → violent
cruelty → violence
cruise → wander
crumb → bit
crumble → crush
crumble → disintegrate
crumple → crush
crumple → fold
crunch → chew
crusade → campaign

crush → crumple
crush → dash
crush → defeat
crush → jam
crush → press
crush → subdue
crush → suppress
crush → vanquish
crux → essence
cry → bay
cry → scream
cry → shout
crying shame → pity
cryptic → mysterious
cryptic → obscure
crystalline → clear
crystalline → transparent
cuddle → hug
cue → signal
culminate → peak
culmination → finish
culmination → peak
culmination → top
culpability → blame
culpability →
  responsibility
culpable → criminal
culpable → guilty
culprit → criminal
cultivate → breed
cultivated → educated
cultivated → sophisticated
culture → background
culture → society
cultured → civilized
cultured → educated
cultured → polite
cultured → sophisticated
cunning → crafty
cunning → sly
curb → check
curb → contain
curb → halt
curb → limit
curb → moderate
curb → restrain
curb → restriction
curb → suppress
curdled → sour

cure → correct
curiosity → interest
curious → bizarre
curious → nosy
curious → odd
curious → peculiar
curious → strange
curious → unusual
curious → weird
curl → coil
curl → twist
current → fashionable
current → flow
current → modern
current → recent
currently → now
curriculum → course
curriculum vitae →
  record
curse → abuse
cursed → unlucky
cursory → casual
cursory → quick
curt → abrupt
curt → impatient
curtail → decrease
curtail → reduce
curtailment → decrease
curve → bend
custody → possession
custom → convention
custom → habit
custom → practice
custom → tradition
custom → way
customary → conventional
customary → regular
customary → standard
customary → usual
cut → carve
cut → chop
cut → lower
cut → reduce
cut → shorten
cut back → cut
cut down → decrease
cut down → reduce
cut out → eliminate
cut out → stop

Index

Index

decency → politeness
decent → respectable
deception → con
deception → fraud
deception → trick
decide → conclude
decide → determine
decide → resolve
decide → settle
decide on → select
decide on → settle
decide upon → pick
decided → definite
deciding → critical
decipher → crack
decipher → read
decipher → solve
decision → verdict
decisive → critical
decisive → crucial
deck → decorate
declaration →
  announcement
declaration → statement
declare → state
declination → slope
decline → decrease
decline → drop
decline → fail
decline → fall
decline → recession
decline → refuse
decline → reject
decline → wither
decline → worsen
declivity → slope
decompose → rot
decomposed → rotten
decorate → honour
decorated → fancy
decoration → ornament
decorous → fitting
decorum → ceremony
decoy → bait
decrease → abate
decrease → cut
decrease → decline
decrease → diminish
decrease → drop

decrease → fall
decrease → lessen
decrease → lower
decrease → reduce
decree → command
decree → law
decree → order
decree → rule
decrepit → weak
dedicate → bless
dedicated → devoted
deduce → conclude
deduce → reconstruct
deduct → subtract
deduction → conclusion
deed → achievement
deed → act
deed → action
deem → consider
deem → feel
deem → reckon
deem → think
deem → view
deep → extreme
deep → far
deep → heavy
deep → intense
deep → serious
deep → severe
deeply → very
defamation → slander
defame → slander
defeat → beat
defeat → failure
defeat → foil
defeat → subdue
defeat → vanquish
defect → fault
defect → flaw
defect → handicap
defect → hole
defect → weakness
defective → faulty
defective → imperfect
defence → safeguard
defenceless → helpless
defenceless → vulnerable
defend → champion
defend → guard

defend → justify
defend → protect
defend → safeguard
defend → support
defender → champion
defer → delay
defer → postpone
defer → put off
deferential → meek
deficiency → defect
deficiency → failure
deficiency → fault
deficiency → lack
deficiency → shortage
deficiency → want
deficient → imperfect
deficient → inadequate
deficient → incomplete
deficient → insufficient
deficient → weak
deficit → deficiency
defile → soil
define → describe
define → explain
definite → certain
definite → clear
definite → final
definite → sure
definitely → certainly
definitely not → no
definition → explanation
definitive → final
deformed → crooked
defraud → cheat
defraud → con
defraud → rob
defunct → dead
defunct → late
defy → challenge
defy → dare
defy → disobey
defy → rebel
defy → resist
degenerate → worsen
degrade → reduce
degree → extent
degree → measure
dehumidify → dry
dehydrate → dry

depose → overthrow
deposit → dump
deposit → keep
deposit → payment
deposit → place
deposit → put
deposit → set
depository → store
depot → store
deprave → corrupt
depraved → evil
depraved → perverted
depraved → wicked
depravity → evil
depreciate → fall
depressed → down
depressed → miserable
depressed → sad
depressed → unhappy
depressing → sad
depression → crash
depression → misery
depression → recession
depression → sadness
deprivation → deficiency
depth → extreme
depths → bottom
deputy → helper
deputy → representative
deputy → substitute
deranged → insane
deranged → mad
deride → belittle
deride → make **fun** of
deride → mock
derision → abuse
derision → contempt
derision → mockery
derision → scorn
derisive → sarcastic
derivation → origin
derivation → source
derive → base
derive → result
derogatory → critical
descend → drop
descendants → family
descent → origin
descent → stock

describe → explain
describe → report
describe → represent
description → explanation
description → report
descry → find
descry → see
descry → spot
desert → abandon
desert → barren
desert → leave
deserted → empty
deserted → lonely
deserve → merit
desiccate → dry
design → intend
design → invent
design → layout
design → pattern
design → plan
design → structure
designate → class
designation → name
designation → term
designed → calculated
desirable → right
desire → longing
desire → passion
desire → urge
desire → want
desire → wish
desirous → willing
desist → abstain
desist → stop
desist from → cease
desolate → barren
desolate → lonely
despair → misery
despatch → message
desperate → terrible
despicable → hateful
despicable → low
despicable → shabby
despise → hate
despise → scorn
despite → in **spite** of
despondency → despair
despondency → disappointment

despondency → sadness
despondent → disappointed
despondent → down
despondent → gloomy
despondent → pessimistic
despondent → unhappy
destiny → fate
destiny → luck
destitute → poor
destitution → hardship
destitution → poverty
destroy → bomb
destroy → dash
destroy → eat away
destroy → erode
destroy → kill
destroy → put down
destroy → ruin
destroy → spoil
destruction → ruin
destructive → deadly
destructive → harmful
desultory → random
detach → remove
detach → separate
detached → alone
detached → distant
detached → impersonal
detached → remote
detached → separate
detail → describe
detailed → elaborate
detailed → full
detain → imprison
detain → jail
detect → discern
detect → find
detect → notice
detect → spot
deter → discourage
deteriorate → erode
deteriorate → wear
deteriorate → worsen
deterioration → rot
deterioration → wear
determinant → factor
determination → drive
determination → resolve

Index

discernment → wisdom
discharge → drain
discharge → dump
discharge → fire
discharge → free
discharge → release
discharge → sack
discharge → the **sack**
disciple → follower
discipline → field
discipline → punish
disclaim → deny
disclose → reveal
disclosure → news
discolour → fade
discolour → stain
discomfit → embarrass
discomfited →
  embarrassed
discomfiture →
  embarrassment
discomfort → pain
discompose → agitate
discompose → shake
discompose → upset
discomposed → uneasy
disconcert → embarrass
disconnect → separate
disconnected → separate
disconsolate → miserable
disconsolate → sad
disconsolate → unhappy
discontinue → cease
discontinue → interrupt
discontinue → quit
discontinue → stop
discord → conflict
discount → ignore
discourse → discussion
discourse → lecture
discourse → speech
discourse → talk
discourteous → rude
discover → determine
discover → find
discover → hear
discover → learn
discover → observe
discover → see

discredit → disgrace
discredit → disprove
discredit → shame
discreditable →
  disgraceful
discreet → tactful
discrepancy → difference
discrete → different
discrete → individual
discrete → separate
discretion → freedom
discretion → tact
discretionary → flexible
discriminate →
  distinguish
discriminating → acute
discriminating → fussy
discrimination →
  injustice
discrimination →
  prejudice
discussion → conference
discussion → word
disdain → contempt
disdain → scorn
disdainful → haughty
disdainful → scornful
disdainful → stuck-up
disdainful → superior
disease → disorder
disease → illness
disenchanted →
  disappointed
disenchantment →
  disappointment
disengage → withdraw
disfigured → deformed
disgrace → humble
disgrace → humiliate
disgrace → shame
disguised → invisible
disgust → horrify
disgust → horror
disgust → repel
disgust → shock
disgusting → nasty
dishearten → discourage
disheartened →
  disappointed

dishonest → corrupt
dishonest → crooked
dishonest → dubious
dishonest → insincere
dishonest → lying
dishonest → sneaky
dishonest → two-faced
dishonesty → corruption
dishonesty → lying
dishonour → disgrace
dishonour → shame
dishonourable → crooked
dishonourable →
  disgraceful
dishonourable → shabby
disillusioned →
  disappointed
disillusionment →
  disappointment
disinclined → reluctant
disintegrate → erode
disinterested → fair
disinterested → neutral
dislike → animosity
dislike → disapprove
dislike → hate
dislike → hatred
dislike → resent
disliked → unpopular
disloyal → false
disloyal → treacherous
disloyal → two-faced
dismal → drab
dismal → gloomy
dismal → sad
dismay → horrify
dismay → panic
dismiss → banish
dismiss → discharge
dismiss → fire
dismiss → sack
dismissal → discharge
dismissal → the **sack**
disobedient → naughty
disobeyed → broken
disorder → confusion
disorder → illness
disorder → mess
disorder → muddle

disorder → riot
disordered → confused
disordered → untidy
disorderly → wild
disorganization → confusion
disorganization → muddle
disorganized → confused
disorganized → inefficient
disorientated → dazed
disown → renounce
disparage → belittle
disparage → criticize
disparagement → criticism
disparaging → abusive
disparaging → critical
disparate → different
disparate → various
disparity → difference
disparity → gap
dispassionate → cool
dispassionate → fair
dispassionate → impersonal
dispassionate → neutral
dispatch → kill
dispatch → message
dispatch → news
dispatch → send
dispel → banish
dispense → administer
dispense → distribute
dispense with → dispose of
disperse → distribute
disperse → melt
dispirited → down
display → flourish
display → show
display → sight
displease → annoy
displeasure → annoyance
dispose of → discard
dispose of → dump
dispose of → get **rid** of
dispose of → process
dispose of → settle

disposed → prone
disposition → character
disproportionate → excessive
dispute → argument
dispute → challenge
dispute → contest
dispute → disagree
dispute → disagreement
dispute → fight
dispute → quarrel
dispute → query
dispute → question
dispute → squabble
disqualification → ban
disqualify → ban
disquiet → concern
disquieting → sinister
disquisition → speech
disquisition → talk
disregard → contempt
disregard → ignore
disregard → neglect
disregard → overlook
disrepair → ruin
disreputable → low
disreputable → notorious
disreputable → scruffy
disrespect → contempt
disrespectful → rude
disrupt → disturb
disrupt → impede
disrupt → interfere
dissembling → lying
disseminate → circulate
disseminate → communicate
disseminate → scatter
dissent → disagree
dissent → disagreement
dissimilar → different
dissimilar to → unlike
dissimulate → lie
dissimulation → lying
dissipation → excess
dissipation → waste
dissolve → eat away
dissolve → melt
dissolve → vanish

dissuade → discourage
distance → length
distance → space
distant → cold
distant → far
distant → foreign
distant → remote
distaste → dislike
distasteful → unpleasant
distend → enlarge
distilled → refined
distinct → different
distinct → particular
distinct → plain
distinct from → unlike
distinction → difference
distinction → quality
distinctive → characteristic
distinctive → individual
distinctive → peculiar
distinctive → special
distinguishable → visible
distinguished → famous
distinguishing → characteristic
distinguishing → peculiar
distort → cloud
distort → colour
distort → misrepresent
distort → twist
distorted → crooked
distorted → deformed
distorted → garbled
distracted → absent-minded
distraction → escape
distress → agitate
distress → alarm
distress → concern
distress → disturb
distress → grief
distress → grieve
distress → hurt
distress → pain
distress → shake
distress → shock
distress → upset
distress signal → alarm

Index

down at heel → shabby
down-to-earth → realistic
down-to-earth → sensible
down-to-earth → sound
downcast → disappointed
downcast → miserable
downcast → sad
downfall → collapse
downfall → failure
downfall → ruin
downgrade → belittle
downgrade → reduce
downhearted → gloomy
downpour → flood
downpour → rain
downright → absolute
downright → rank
downside → disadvantage
downside → snag
downsize → cut
downsize → lessen
downsize → shorten
downstairs → down
downtrodden → oppressed
downturn → decline
downturn → recession
downwards → down
doze → sleep
drab → dreary
drab → dull
Draconian → harsh
draft → design
draft → plan
draft → recruit
drag → annoyance
drag → draw
drag → pull
drag → tug
dragoon → bully
drain → dry
drain → empty
drain → exhaust
drain → tax
drain → tire
drained → tired
drained → weary
drama → play

dramatic → exciting
dramatic → impressive
drape → hang
drastic → extreme
draw → attract
draw → drag
draw → earn
draw → extract
draw → lure
draw → pull
draw → tie
draw → tug
draw away → distract
draw back → retreat
draw off → drain
draw out → withdraw
draw up → design
draw up → form
draw up → halt
drawback → catch
drawback → disadvantage
drawback → fault
drawback → handicap
drawback → snag
drawing → picture
dread → fear
dread → horror
dreadful → awful
dreadful → horrible
dreadful → terrible
dream → daydream
dream → hope
dream → vision
dreary → drab
dreary → gloomy
dregs → remains
drench → soak
drench → wet
drenched → wet
dress → clothes
dribble → drip
dribble → drop
dried-up → dry
drift → float
drift → flow
drift → meaning
drift → wander
drill → pierce
drill → practice

drill → teach
drill → train
drink → alcohol
drip → drop
drive → blow
drive → chase
drive → energy
drive → force
drive → go
drive → make
drive → motivate
drive → reduce
drive → urge
drive into → crash
drive off → repel
drive someone up the wall → pester
drivel → garbage
drivel → nonsense
drivel → rubbish
drizzle → rain
droll → funny
drollery → humour
droop → hang
droop → wither
drooping → limp
drop → ball
drop → blob
drop → dash
drop → decline
drop → decrease
drop → deposit
drop → drip
drop → dump
drop → fall
drop → lose
drop → lower
drop → trace
drop out of sight → disappear
droplet → blob
droplet → drip
droplet → drop
drown → flood
drowsy → sleepy
drowsy → tired
drug → medicine
drum → advice
drum → information

embrace → grasp
embrace → hold
embrace → hug
embrace → include
emend → correct
emend → reform
emendation → correction
emerge → appear
emergence →
appearance
emergent → in the
  making
eminence → fame
eminence → glory
eminence → success
eminent → important
eminent → leading
eminent → prominent
emissary → messenger
emit → discharge
emolument → pay
emotion → feeling
emotion → passion
emotional → moving
emotional → passionate
empathize with →
  identify with
empathy → sympathy
emphasize → feature
emphasize → stress
employ → busy
employ → hire
employ → use
employed → busy
employee → worker
employees → labour
employees → staff
employer → boss
employers →
  management
employment → job
employment → use
employment → work
emporium → shop
empty → bare
empty → barren
empty → blank
empty → discharge
empty → drain

empty → fond
emulate → copy
emulate → imitate
emulous → jealous
en masse → together
enable → permit
enamoured → crazy
enchant → charm
enchant → delight
enchant → entrance
enchant → fascinate
enchanting → lovable
enchanting → magical
encircle → enclose
encircle → surround
enclose → surround
encomium → praise
encompass → include
encompass → surround
encounter → experience
encounter → meet
encounter → meeting
encounter → receive
encourage → back
encourage → push
encourage → reassure
encourage → strengthen
encourage → support
encouragement →
  incentive
encroach → intrude
encumber → hamper
encumber → hinder
end → back
end → cease
end → complete
end → conclude
end → conclusion
end → extreme
end → finish
end → goal
end → halt
end → lift
end → stop
end → use
end result → effect
endanger → threaten
endearing → lovable
endeavour → attempt

endeavour → enterprise
endeavour → seek
endeavour → strive
endeavour → try
endeavour → undertaking
ending → conclusion
ending → finish
endless → continual
endorse → advocate
endorse → approve
endorse → back
endorse → confirm
endorse → defend
endorse → sanction
endorsement → approval
endow → equip
endow → supply
endowment →
  qualification
endure → bear
endure → continue
endure → go through
endure → have
endure → last
endure → remain
endure → suffer
endure → survive
endure → tolerate
endure → undergo
enduring → permanent
energetic → active
energetic → alive
energetic → lively
energetic → vital
energy → activity
energy → drive
energy → effort
energy → spirit
enervate → tire
enervate → weaken
enervated → faint
enervated → weak
enforce → impose
engage → book
engage → busy
engage → employ
engage → hire
engage in → participate
engaged → active

exclamation → cry
exclude → ban
exclude → boycott
exclude → forbid
exclude → omit
exclusive → posh
exclusive → private
exclusive → select
excoriate → criticize
excruciating → painful
excursion → drive
excursion → journey
excursion → ramble
excursion → trip
excuse → defence
excuse → forgive
excuse → grounds
excuse → justify
excuse yourself → decline
excused → exempt
execute → accomplish
execute → administer
execute → carry out
execute → conduct
execute → do
execute → kill
execute → perform
executive → manager
executive → official
exemplar → example
exemplar → model
exempt → immune
exemption → freedom
exercise → practice
exertion → effort
exertion → exercise
exertion → labour
exhaust → drain
exhaust → tax
exhaust → tire
exhaust → wear out
exhausted → tired
exhausted → weary
exhausted → worn-out
exhausting → hard
exhaustive → full
exhaustive → thorough
exhibit → bear

exhibition → fair
exhibition → show
exhilarating → exciting
exhort → press
exhort → urge
exiguous → meagre
exile → banish
exist → live
exist → occur
existence → life
exoneration → forgiveness
exorbitant → excessive
exorbitant → expensive
exorbitant → steep
exotic → foreign
exotic → strange
exotic → unfamiliar
expand → bulge
expand → elaborate
expand → enlarge
expand → extend
expand → grow
expand → increase
expand → spread
expand on → enlarge on
expanse → amount
expanse → area
expanse → extent
expanse → quantity
expanse → stretch
expansion → growth
expansion → spread
expansive → broad
expansive → extensive
expansive → spacious
expect → figure
expect → suppose
expectation → hope
expectation → prospect
expected → likely
expected → supposed
expedient → measure
expedition → journey
expel → banish
expel → chase
expel → discharge
expense → cost
expensive → dear

expensive → precious
expensive → valuable
experience → endure
experience → event
experience → feel
experience → go through
experience → have
experience → suffer
experience → undergo
experienced → expert
experienced → practical
experienced → skilled
expert → able
expert → experienced
expert → fundi
expert → perfect
expert → skilful
expert → skilled
expertise → ability
expertise → experience
expertise → skill
expertly → well
expire → die
explain → justify
explanation → defence
explanation → excuse
explanation → statement
explicit → blunt
explicit → clear
explode → burst
explode → fire
exploit → achievement
exploit → action
exploit → profit
exploitation → abuse
exploration → research
explore → investigate
explore → research
explosion → bang
explosion → outbreak
explosive → bomb
expose → betray
expose → subject
expose → uncover
exposed → bare
exposed → vulnerable
exposition → explanation
exposition → lecture
expostulate → argue

expostulate → object
expostulate → protest
expound → explain
expound → state
express → convey
express → particular
express → quick
express → state
express → swift
express regret →
  apologize
expression → look
expression → term
expulsion → discharge
expunge → remove
exquisite → beautiful
exquisite → superb
extend → build
extend → enlarge
extend → expand
extend → increase
extend → lengthen
extend → offer
extend → range
extend → spread
extend → stretch
extend to → reach
extended → continuous
extensive → broad
extensive → full
extensive → spacious
extensive → widespread
extent → area
extent → length
extent → quantity
extent → range
extent → size
extent → spread
extent → stretch
exterior → face
exterior → front
exterior → outside
exterminate → kill
external → outside
extinct → dead
extol → praise
extortion → corruption
extortionate → steep
extra → excess

extra → luxury
extra → more
extra → spare
extra → supplement
extract → essence
extract → exact
extract → passage
extract → quote
extract → remove
extract → withdraw
extraction → origin
extraction → stock
extraordinary → bizarre
extraordinary → curious
extraordinary →
  exceptional
extraordinary →
  incredible
extraordinary → singular
extraordinary → strange
extraordinary →
  uncommon
extraordinary → unusual
extraordinary → weird
extravagance → excess
extravagance → luxury
extravagance → waste
extravagant → extreme
extravagant → fancy
extravagant →
  ostentatious
extravagant → wasteful
extreme → acute
extreme → deep
extreme → drastic
extreme → intense
extreme → serious
extreme → severe
extreme → ultimate
extreme → uncommon
extremely → really
extremely → very
extremist → fanatic
extricate → release
exuberance → happiness
exude → emit
exult → rejoice
exultation → joy
eye → inspect

eye → regard
eye-catching →
  prominent
eyesight → sight
eyewitness → spectator
eyewitness → witness
fabric → cloth
fabric → material
fabric → substance
fabricate → build
fabricate → invent
fabricate → make
fabricate → make up
fabricate → manufacture
fabrication → lie
fabrication → lying
fabrication → making
fabrication →
  manufacture
facade → outside
face → brave
face → expression
face → front
face → look
face → outside
face down → prone
facility → capacity
facility → skill
facsimile → copy
facsimile → model
fact → reality
fact → truth
faction → movement
faction → party
faction → side
factor → aspect
factor → consideration
facts → information
factual → real
factual → right
factual → true
fad → craze
fad → fashion
fad → whim
faddish → fussy
fade → die out
fade → disappear
fade → vanish
fade → wither

fade away → die
fade away → vanish
fade out → die
faded → faint
faded → pale
fail → collapse
fail → neglect
fail → weaken
fail to notice → miss
fail to remember →
 forget
failing → defect
failing → fault
failure → collapse
failure → crash
faint → dim
faint → slender
faint → soft
faint → weak
faint-hearted → cowardly
faint-hearted → timid
fair → acceptable
fair → all right
fair → beautiful
fair → festival
fair → light
fair → market
fair → moderate
fair → reasonable
fair → respectable
fairly → pretty
fairly → quite
fairly → rather
fairness → justice
fairness → right
faith → belief
faith → confidence
faithful → accurate
faithful → devoted
faithful → exact
faithful → loyal
faithful → realistic
faithful → reliable
faithful → steadfast
faithful → trusty
faithfully → exactly
faithless → treacherous
fake → copy
fake → false

fake → fraud
fake → mock
fake → phoney
fake → pretend
fall → decline
fall → descend
fall → downfall
fall → drop
fall → ruin
fall → slope
fall apart → disintegrate
fall behind → lag
fall down → collapse
fall ill → develop
fall out → argue
fall out → quarrel
fall out → squabble
fall over → trip
fall through → fail
fall to → reach
fall to pieces →
 disintegrate
fallacious → faulty
fallacious → wrong
fallacy → illusion
false → deceptive
false → fake
false → insincere
false → lying
false → mock
false → phoney
false → two-faced
false → untrue
false → wrong
falsehood → lie
falsify → misrepresent
falsify → pretend
fame → glory
fame → success
familiar → accustomed
familiar → informal
familiar with → aware of
family → kin
family → young
famished → hungry
famous → prominent
famous name →
 personality
fan → follower

fan → supporter
fan out → spread
fanatical → crazy
fancy → desire
fancy → elaborate
fancy → illusion
fancy → imagine
fancy → whim
fantasize → daydream
fantasize → imagine
fantastic → splendid
fantasy → daydream
fantasy → dream
fantasy → vision
far → distant
far from → unlike
far-fetched →
 improbable
far-fetched → incredible
far-flung → distant
far-off → distant
far-off → remote
far-reaching → extensive
far-reaching → serious
faraway → distant
fare → do
fare → food
farmer → cocky
fascinate → appeal
fascinate → entrance
fascinate → interest
fascination → charm
fascination → interest
fashion → craze
fashion → form
fashion → make
fashion → manner
fashion → model
fashion → shape
fashionable → current
fashionable → popular
fashionable → posh
fashionable → trendy
fast → express
fast → quick
fast → quickly
fast → swift
fasten → attach
fasten → bond

Index

felonious → criminal
felonious → guilty
felonious → wrong
felony → crime
female → woman
feminine → female
fence → barrier
fence off → enclose
feral → fierce
ferocious → fierce
ferocious → savage
ferret out → find
ferry → take
fertile → creative
fertile → productive
fertile → rich
fervent → ardent
fervent → eager
fervent → enthusiastic
fervent → fanatical
fervent → intense
fervour → enthusiasm
fervour → feeling
fervour → heat
fervour → violence
fester → rot
festival → celebration
festival → fair
festivity → celebration
festoon → decorate
fetch → get
fetch → take
fetching → attractive
fete → fair
fete → festival
fetid → smelly
fetid → stuffy
fetor → smell
fetor → stink
fetter → hamper
feud → argue
feud → argument
feud → dispute
feud → quarrel
feud → squabble
feverish → excited
few → rare
few → scarce
few → uncommon

fewest → least
fiasco → failure
fiat → command
fib → lie
fibbing → lying
fickle → changeable
fiction → lie
fictional → imaginary
fictitious → false
fictitious → imaginary
fictitious → untrue
fiddle → fidget
fidget → fuss
fidgety → restless
field → range
fierce → furious
fierce → intense
fierce → wild
fight → argue
fight → argument
fight → clash
fight → compete
fight → contest
fight → quarrel
fight → resist
fight → squabble
fight → war
fight against → oppose
fight for → champion
fight for breath → gasp
fight shy of → avoid
fighting → conflict
fighting → war
figure → body
figure → build
figure → number
figure → outline
figure → price
figure → shape
figure → symbol
figure out → reckon
figure out → work out
filch → steal
file → line
file → rank
file → record
fill → load
fill → plug
fill → stuff

fill in → brief
fill out → expand
filled → full
film → layer
filtered → refined
filth → dirt
filthy → dirty
filthy → obscene
filthy → scungy
final → last
final → ultimate
finale → finish
finalize → finish
finance → fund
financial → economic
find → discover
find → locate
find a solution to → resolve
find fault → complain
find fault → put down
find fault with → criticize
find out → determine
find out → discover
find out → hear
find out → learn
find out → see
find unacceptable → disapprove
finding → decision
finding → verdict
fine → beautiful
fine → excellent
fine → narrow
fine → sheer
fine → sound
fine → splendid
fine → thin
fine point → detail
finesse → polish
finger → feel
finger → handle
finger → touch
finicky → fussy
finish → cease
finish → complete
finish → conclude
finish → conclusion
finish → end

Index

force → strength
force → stuff
force → violence
forced → stiff
forceful → powerful
forceful → pushy
forcible → violent
ford → cross
forebear → ancestor
forebode → predict
foreboding → premonition
forecast → expect
forecast → predict
forecast → prediction
forefather → ancestor
forego → sacrifice
foreground → emphasize
foreign → strange
foreign → unfamiliar
foremost → chief
foremost → first
foremost → important
foremost → leading
foremost → main
foremost → principal
foremost → supreme
foremost → top
forensic → legal
foresee → expect
foresee → predict
foresight → vision
forestall → frustrate
forestall → stop
foretell → predict
forethought → care
forethought → caution
forever → always
forewarn → alert
forewarn → warn
foreword → introduction
forfeit → sacrifice
forged → false
forged → phoney
forgery → copy
forgery → fake
forgery → fraud
forget → neglect
forget → overlook
forgetful → absent-

minded
forgive → excuse
forgiveness → mercy
forgiving → merciful
forgo → abstain
fork → split
forlorn → futile
forlorn → hopeless
forlorn → lonely
form → body
form → build
form → condition
form → design
form → figure
form → make
form → make up
form → model
form → outline
form → shape
formal → impersonal
formal → official
formal → stiff
formal → stuffy
formality → ceremony
format → layout
former → past
former → previous
former times → the **past**
formerly → before
formidable → stiff
formulate → create
formulate → invent
formulate → make up
formulate → plan
forsake → abandon
forsake → leave
forsaken → lonely
forswear oneself → lie
forthcoming → future
forthcoming → imminent
forthcoming → near
forthright → blunt
forthright → direct
forthright → straight
forthright →
straightforward
forthwith → immediately
fortification → barrier
fortification → fort

fortified → secure
fortify → secure
fortify → strengthen
fortitude → bravery
fortress → fort
fortuitous → casual
fortuitous → lucky
fortuitous → random
fortuitous → unexpected
fortuity → luck
fortunate → lucky
fortune → chance
fortune → fate
fortune → luck
fortune → wealth
forum → conference
forward → bold
forward → send
fossick → search
foster → encourage
foul → disgusting
foul → nasty
foul → scungy
foul → smelly
foul → soil
found → base
found → start
foundation → base
foundation → fund
foundation → grounds
foundation → start
foundation → support
founder → collapse
fount → source
fountainhead → source
foxy → cunning
fracas → quarrel
fraction → part
fractious → cross
fracture → crack
fractured → broken
fragility → weakness
fragment → bit
fragment → disintegrate
fragment → part
fragment → piece
fragmented → broken
fragrance → smell
fragrant → sweet

frail → fragile
frail → puny
frail → weak
frailty → weakness
frame → body
frame → build
frame of mind → humour
frame of mind → mood
frangible → fragile
frank → blunt
frank → candid
frank → direct
frank → natural
frank → open
frank → straight
frank → straightforward
frantic → furious
frantic → hysterical
frantic → upset
fraternity → association
fraternize → associate
fraud → con
fraud → corruption
fraud → fake
fraud → racket
fraudulence → dishonesty
fraudulent → corrupt
fraudulent → crooked
fraudulent → deceptive
fraudulent → dishonest
fray → quarrel
fray → wear
freak → curiosity
freak → weirdo
free → available
free → discharge
free → immune
free → independent
free → loose
free → release
free → spare
free → wild
free time → leisure
freedom → release
freeze → cool
freeze → harden
freeze → numb
freezing → cold

freight → load
frenetic → furious
frenzied → furious
frenzied → hysterical
frenzy → rage
frequency → rate
frequent → continual
frequently → often
fresh → original
fresh → recent
freshen → refresh
fret → fuss
fret → worry
fretful → cross
fretful → restless
friction → conflict
friend → china
friend → companion
friendliness → goodwill
friendly → cosy
friendly → favourable
friendly → pleasant
friendly → sociable
friendly → warm
friendship → goodwill
fright → alarm
fright → fear
fright → horror
fright → panic
fright → scare
frighten → alarm
frighten → scare
frightened → afraid
frightening → scary
frightening → spooky
frightful → awful
frightful → dreadful
frightful → terrible
frigid → cold
frigid → frozen
fringe → border
fringe → edge
fritter away → waste
frivolous → trivial
frock → dress
frolic → play
from time to time → sometimes
front → face

front → head
frontage → front
frontier → border
froth → boil
froth → foam
frown → glare
frown on → disapprove
frowsty → stuffy
frozen → numb
frugal → economical
frugal → thrifty
frugality → economy
fruit → effect
fruitful → fertile
fruitful → productive
fruitless → in vain
fruitless → vain
frustrate → dash
frustrate → foil
frustrate → hamper
frustrate → hinder
fry → cook
fulfil → accomplish
fulfil → achieve
fulfil → carry out
fulfil → keep
fulfil → meet
fulfil → perform
fulfil → satisfy
full → abundant
full → busy
full → complete
full → crowded
full → thorough
full → whole
full of life → alive
full-grown → mature
fully → quite
fully → well
fully-fledged → mature
fume → rage
fuming → furious
fuming → mad
fun → entertainment
function → act
function → behave
function → go
function → job
function → part

function → party
function → purpose
functional → practical
functionary → official
fund → bank
fund → finance
fund → hoard
fund → reserve
fund → store
fund → supply
fundamental → basic
fundamental → basis
fundamental → essential
fundamental → principle
fundamentals → essentials
funds → money
funny → odd
funny → peculiar
funny → strange
funny → suspicious
funny → weird
funny → witty
funny feeling → premonition
fur → coat
fur → pile
furious → angry
furious → mad
furious → violent
furlough → leave
furnish → issue
furnish → provide
furnish → supply
furore → excitement
further → benefit
further → encourage
further → extra
further → more
furthermore → also
furtive → mysterious
furtive → secret
fury → anger
fury → frenzy
fury → rage
fuse → bond
fuse → combine
fuse → stick
fusion → blend

fusion → mixture
fusion → union
fuss → bustle
fussy → elaborate
fussy → particular
fusty → stale
fusty → stuffy
futile → hopeless
futile → useless
futile → vain
future → outlook
fuzzy → dim
gabble → babble
gaffe → mistake
gaffer → employer
gag → joke
gag → silence
gaggle → bunch
gain → acquire
gain → advance
gain → benefit
gain → increase
gain → secure
gain → win
gain qualifications → qualify
gainsay → deny
gait → walk
gala → celebration
gala → festival
galah → idiot
gall → cheek
gall → impudence
gall → irritate
gallantry → bravery
gallantry → courtesy
gallop → run
gallop → speed
gamble → risk
game → agreeable
game → contest
game → match
game → willing
gamut → range
gang → band
gang → bunch
gang → group
gang → party
gang → team

gap → breach
gap → hole
gap → interval
gap → opening
gap → space
garb → clothes
garb → dress
garbage → nonsense
garbage → refuse
garbage → rubbish
garbage → trash
gardens → grounds
gargantuan → huge
gargantuan → large
garish → flashy
garish → gaudy
garish → loud
garish → tasteless
garments → clothes
gash → cut
gate → entrance
gate → entry
gather → assemble
gather → collect
gather → concentrate
gather → crowd
gather → hear
gather → imagine
gather → learn
gather → mass
gather → meet
gather → pick
gather → stockpile
gather → understand
gathering → function
gathering → hui
gathering → meeting
gathering → party
gauche → clumsy
gaudy → loud
gaudy → tasteless
gaudy → vulgar
gauge → measure
gauzy → fine
gawky → clumsy
gawp → stare
gaze → look
gaze → regard
gaze → stare

gaze at → watch
gear → clothes
gear → equipment
gear → stuff
gear → things
Gehenna → hell
gelatinous → soft
general → broad
general → common
general → mass
general → popular
general → public
general → universal
generally → as a **rule**
generally → mainly
generally → on **average**
generate → bring about
generate → cause
generative → fertile
generative → productive
generic → general
generous → handsome
generous → noble
genesis → origin
genial → cheery
genial → friendly
genial → warm
genius → talent
genre → class
genre → kind
genteel → polite
genteel → posh
genteel → refined
gentle → leisurely
gentle → mild
gentle → soft
gentle → tender
gentleman → man
gentlemanly → refined
gentleness → kindness
genuine → actual
genuine → authentic
genuine → dinkum
genuine → natural
genuine → real
genuine → right
genuine → serious
genuine → sincere
genuine → true

germ-free → pure
germ-free → sterile
germane → appropriate
germane → relevant
germinate → grow
gesticulate → signal
gesture → signal
get → acquire
get → develop
get → earn
get → extract
get → grow
get → obtain
get → receive
get → secure
get → see
get → take in
get → understand
get → win
get a move on → hurry
get across → convey
get as far as → reach
get away → escape
get back → recover
get back at → retaliate
get better → recover
get certified → qualify
get even → revenge
get even with → retaliate
get going → start
get hold of → contact
get hold of → obtain
get in the way → impede
get in touch with →
    contact
get off your chest →
    reveal
get on → do
get on someone's
    nerves → annoy
get on someone's
    nerves → bother
get on someone's
    nerves → pester
get out of → dodge
get rid of → dispose of
get rid of → dump
get rid of → eliminate
get rid of → remove

get smaller → shrink
get the better of →
    overcome
get the hang of → master
get the impression →
    sense
get through → pass
get to → acquire
get to the bottom of →
    solve
get together → meet
get under way → proceed
get under way → start
get well → recover
get your hands on →
    obtain
get your own back →
    retaliate
get your own back →
    revenge
get-together → gathering
get-together → meeting
get-together → party
ghastly → awful
ghastly → dreadful
ghost → spirit
ghostly → spooky
giant → huge
giant → immense
giant → large
giant → vast
gibberish → garbage
gidday → hello
giddy → dizzy
giddy → faint
gift → blessing
gift → capacity
gift → present
gift → talent
gigantic → colossal
gigantic → enormous
gigantic → immense
gigantic → large
gigantic → vast
giggle → laugh
girl → female
girl → woman
girlish → female
gist → meaning

Index

grave → deep
grave → grim
grave → heavy
grave → serious
grave → severe
grave → solemn
grave → tomb
graze → scrape
graze → touch
great → acute
great → brilliant
great → deep
great → excellent
great → extensive
great → extreme
great → grand
great → intense
great → large
great → outstanding
great → splendid
great → uncommon
great → vast
great → wonderful
great deal → plenty
greatest → foremost
greatest → supreme
greatest → ultimate
greatly → very
greedy → selfish
green → field
green → ignorant
green → inexperienced
greet → receive
gregarious → sociable
grenade → bomb
grey → dim
grey → drab
grief → misery
grief → pain
grief → regret
grief → sorrow
grief-stricken → sad
grievance → complaint
grievance → wrong
grieve → distress
grieve → lament
grieve → regret
grieve → upset
grievous → painful

grievous → serious
grill → cook
grill → interrogate
grim → horrible
grim → serious
grim → severe
grime → dirt
grimy → dirty
grin → smile
grind → scrape
grip → clasp
grip → grasp
grip → handle
grip → hold
gripping → interesting
grit → courage
groan → grumble
groan → moan
grog → alcohol
gross → disgusting
ground → base
ground → bottom
ground → earth
ground → soil
grounds → argument
grounds → cause
grounds → land
grounds → reason
group → arrange
group → association
group → band
group → bunch
group → category
group → class
group → club
group → collection
group → company
group → grade
group → lot
group → mass
group → movement
group → organization
group → society
group → sort
group → team
group → type
grouping → party
grouse → complain
grow → develop

grow → expand
grow → get
grow → increase
grow → rise
grow → spread
grow up → mature
grown → mature
grown-up → adult
grown-up → mature
growth → gain
growth → increase
growth → spread
grub → kai
grubby → dirty
grudge → resentment
grudging → unwilling
gruesome → horrible
gruff → hoarse
grumble → complain
grumble → complaint
grumble → moan
grumpy → cross
grunt → moan
guarantee → bond
guarantee → ensure
guarantee → promise
guaranteed → certain
guaranteed → definite
guard → defend
guard → protect
guard → safeguard
guard → watch
guard against → beware
guarded → cautious
guarded → wary
guardian → champion
guess → assume
guess → estimate
guess → figure
guess → idea
guess → imagine
guess → suppose
guess → suspect
guffaw → laugh
guidance → advice
guidance → direction
guidance → help
guide → direct
guide → ease

Index

hard → tricky
hard up → poor
hard-bitten → callous
hard-hearted → merciless
hard-wearing → tough
hard-working → industrious
harden → strengthen
hardened → tough
hardhearted → callous
hardly → barely
hardship → difficulty
hardship → ordeal
hardship → poverty
hardship → sorrow
hardworking → active
hardy → sturdy
hardy → tough
hark → listen
harm → abuse
harm → damage
harm → hurt
harm → injure
harm → injury
harm → spoil
harmful → unhealthy
harmless → safe
harmonious → compatible
harmonious → sweet
harmonize → blend
harmonize → match
harmony → order
harrowing → sad
harry → worry
harsh → drastic
harsh → severe
harshness → violence
harvest → pick
hassle → annoy
hassle → difficulty
hassle → nuisance
hassle → stress
hassle → trouble
hassle → worry
haste → speed
hasten → dash
hasten → hurry
hasten → rush
hastily → fast

hastily → quickly
hasty → quick
hasty → rash
hasty → sudden
hatch → plot
hate → dislike
hate → hatred
hatred → animosity
hatred → dislike
hatred → hate
hatred → horror
hatred → hostility
haughtiness → pride
haughty → stuck-up
haughty → superior
haul → drag
haul → draw
haul → loot
haul → pull
haul → tug
haunt → frequent
haunted → spooky
hauteur → pride
have → bear
have → experience
have → own
have → possess
have a break → rest
have a go → attack
have a good opinion of → respect
have a hand in → take part in
have a high opinion of → respect
have a high opinion of → value
have a hunch → sense
have a meal → eat
have a soft spot for → like
have a tendency → tend
have a weakness for → like
have a weakness for → love
have a yen for → fancy
have an accident → crash
have charge of → supervise

have confidence in → trust
have faith in → trust
have fun → play
have on → wear
have power over → control
haven → refuge
haven → retreat
haven → shelter
having a liking for → fond
hawk → sell
hazard → danger
hazard → gamble
hazard → guess
hazard → threat
hazardous → dangerous
hazardous → treacherous
haze → cloud
hazy → dim
hazy → vague
head → boss
head → chief
head → command
head → foam
head → lead
head → leader
head → mind
head → top
head of state → ruler
headlong → quick
headquarters → base
headstrong → obstinate
headway → progress
heal → cure
healing → recovery
healthy → beneficial
healthy → fit
healthy → sound
healthy → well
heap → bunch
heap → mass
heap → pile
heaps → plenty
hear → gather
hear → learn
hear → listen
hear → understand
hearsay → gossip

Index

hostility → hate
hostility → opposition
hot air → rubbish
hot water → hole
hot water → predicament
hound → chase
hound → follow
hound → persecute
house → accommodate
house → accommodation
house → company
house → home
housebreaker → thief
household name →
  personality
housing →
  accommodation
hover → float
how do you do? → hello
howl → bay
howl → scream
howling → wild
hub → centre
hub → focus
hubbub → noise
hubbub → racket
hubbub → sound
hubris → pride
huddle → shelter
hue → colour
huff → resentment
huffy → moody
huffy → resentful
huffy → sulky
hug → clasp
huge → colossal
huge → enormous
huge → immense
huge → large
huge → spacious
huge → vast
human → person
human being → individual
human being → person
human beings → people
human race → man
humane → benevolent
humane →
  compassionate

humane → gentle
humane → kind
humane → merciful
humanely → well
humanitarian →
  compassionate
humanitarian → humane
humanity → kindness
humanity → man
humanity → people
humankind → man
humans → people
humble → humiliate
humble → modest
humble → unknown
humdrum → boring
humdrum → dreary
humdrum → dull
humid → damp
humid → wet
humidify → wet
humidity → damp
humiliate → degrade
humiliate → embarrass
humiliate → humble
humiliate → put down
humiliate → shame
humiliated → ashamed
humiliated →
  embarrassed
humiliation →
  embarrassment
humiliation → shame
humorous → funny
humorous → witty
humour → mood
humourless → serious
hump → bulge
hump → bump
hump → lump
hunch → impression
hunch → suspicion
hunger → long
hunger → longing
hunger → wish
hunger for → be **dying**
  for
hungry → eager
hunk → beauty

hunk → lump
hunt → chase
hunt → fossick
hunt → look for
hunt → search
hunt → seek
hurdle → barrier
hurdle → difficulty
hurdle → jump
hurdle → obstacle
hurl → dash
hurl → throw
hurried → fast
hurried → hasty
hurried → quick
hurried → swift
hurriedly → fast
hurriedly → quickly
hurrry → rush
hurry → accelerate
hurry → bustle
hurry → fly
hurry → race
hurry → rush
hurry → speed
hurt → abuse
hurt → damage
hurt → harm
hurt → injure
hurt → upset
hurtful → harmful
hurtle into → crash
husband → partner
husband → save
hush → silence
hushed → quiet
hushed → silent
husky → hoarse
hustle → rush
hygienic → clean
hypermarket → shop
hypocritical → two-faced
hypothesis → guess
hypothesis → idea
hypothesis → theory
hypothetical → imaginary
hysteria → frenzy
hysteria → panic
hysteria → scare

icy → cold
icy → frozen
idea → impression
idea → intention
idea → object
idea → suspicion
idea → thought
ideal → cause
ideal → example
ideal → imaginary
ideal → model
ideal → vision
ideals → standards
identical → alike
identical → equal
identical → even
identical → same
identification → pass
identify → associate
identify → recognize
identity → personality
ideology → belief
idiom → expression
idiom → language
idiomatic → colloquial
idiosyncrasy → attribute
idiosyncrasy →
    characteristic
idiosyncrasy → way
idiosyncratic →
    characteristic
idiosyncratic → individual
idiosyncratic → peculiar
idiot → fool
idiotic → silly
idiotic → stupid
idiotic → unwise
idle → laze
idle → lazy
idle → rest
idle → unemployed
idol → favourite
idol → star
idolater → heathen
idolize → love
idolize → worship
ignite → light
ignoble → shabby
ignominy → shame

ignoramus → fool
ignorant → unaware
ignore → exclude
ignore → neglect
ignore → overlook
ilk → sort
ill → crook
ill → evil
ill → queasy
ill → sick
ill → unhealthy
ill → unwell
ill at ease →
    uncomfortable
ill will → animosity
ill will → hostility
ill will → spite
ill-defined → dim
ill-defined → vague
ill-disposed → unfriendly
ill-fated → doomed
ill-fitting → uncomfortable
ill-tempered → grumpy
ill-tempered → moody
ill-treat → harm
ill-treat → mistreat
ill-treat → persecute
ill-treatment → abuse
illegal → criminal
illegal → crooked
illegal → wrong
illicit → criminal
illicit → illegal
illness → disorder
illogical → absurd
illogical → irrational
illuminate → light
illuminated → bright
illumination → light
illusion → vision
illusory → deceptive
illusory → imaginary
illustrate → explain
illustration → case
illustration → example
illustration → picture
illustrative →
    representative
illustrious → famous

image → appearance
image → vision
imaginable → believable
imaginable → possible
imagination → mind
imagination → vision
imaginative → creative
imagine → assume
imagine → expect
imagine → guess
imagine → picture
imagine → suppose
imagine → think
imbecile → idiot
imbecilic → stupid
imbecility → stupidity
imbibe → drink
imitate → copy
imitation → copy
imitation → fake
imitation → mock
imitation → parody
immaculate → clean
immanent → natural
immature → childish
immature → young
immediate → direct
immediate → instant
immediate → prompt
immediate → urgent
immediately → now
immense → colossal
immense → enormous
immense → huge
immense → large
immense → vast
immensity → size
immerse → busy
immerse → steep
immersed → preoccupied
imminent → near
immobilize → numb
immoderate → excessive
immoderate → fanatical
immoral → perverted
immoral → wrong
immorality → evil
immortal → eternal
immortality → glory

immovable → steadfast
immune → exempt
immunity → freedom
immunity → safety
immure → confine
immure → imprison
immutable → constant
immutable → permanent
impact → force
impair → cripple
impair → ruin
impair → spoil
impair → undermine
impaired → imperfect
impart → communicate
impart → convey
impartial → fair
impartial → neutral
impartiality → justice
impasse → halt
impassioned → fervent
impassioned → intense
impassioned → passionate
impassive → blank
impassive → calm
impassive → uninterested
impeach → accuse
impeccable → clean
impede → delay
impede → hamper
impede → handicap
impede → hinder
impede → interfere
impede → prevent
impede → restrict
impediment → barrier
impediment → difficulty
impediment → handicap
impediment → obstacle
impel → force
impel → make
impel → persuade
impending → future
impending → imminent
imperative → necessary
imperative → urgent
imperceptible → invisible
imperfect → faulty

imperfect → incomplete
imperfection → defect
imperfection → fault
imperfection → flaw
imperfection → weakness
imperial → royal
imperious → bossy
imperishable → permanent
impermanent → temporary
impersonate → imitate
impersonate → pose
impertinence → impudence
impertinent → cheeky
impertinent → rude
imperturbability → patience
imperturbable → calm
imperturbable → cool
impetuous → rash
impinge on → affect
impish → naughty
impish → wicked
implacable → merciless
implant → insert
implausible → improbable
implausible → incredible
implausible → unbelievable
implausible → unlikely
implement → carry out
implement → conduct
implement → gadget
implement → tool
implore → appeal
implore → ask
implore → beg
implore → plead
implore → press
implore → urge
imply → hint
imply → indicate
imply → suggest
import → meaning
importance → emphasis

importance → influence
importance → value
important → prominent
important → serious
important → significant
important → special
important → valuable
important → vital
importune → beg
importune → press
importune → worry
impose → administer
impose → exact
impose upon → trouble
imposing → grand
imposing → splendid
impossible → hopeless
imposter → fraud
impotence → inability
impotent → powerless
impound → seize
impoverished → poor
impractical → useless
imprecise → faulty
imprecise → rough
impregnable → invincible
impregnable → secure
impression → idea
impression → sense
impression → suspicion
impressive → grand
impressive → significant
impressive → splendid
imprimatur → approval
imprison → confine
imprison → jail
improbable → incredible
improbable → unbelievable
improper → inappropriate
improper → indecent
improper → unsuitable
improper → vulgar
improve → correct
improve → perfect
improve → polish
improve → progress
improve → recover
improve on → top

Index

intact → complete
intact → sound
integer → number
integrate → combine
integrity → character
integrity → honour
integrity → principle
integrity → right
integrity → virtue
intellect → genius
intellect → head
intellect → intelligence
intellect → mind
intellect → reason
intellectual → educated
intellectual → learned
intelligence → head
intelligence → news
intelligence → sense
intelligence → word
intelligent → bright
intelligent → brilliant
intelligent → clever
intelligent → smart
intemperance → excess
intend → aim
intend → mean
intend → resolve
intended → calculated
intense → acute
intense → ardent
intense → colourful
intense → deep
intense → extreme
intense → fierce
intense → furious
intense → passionate
intense → serious
intense → severe
intense → uncommon
intense → violent
intensify → build
intensify → rise
intensity → heat
intensity → passion
intensity → strength
intensity → violence
intensive → thorough
intent → set on

intent on → determined
intention → aim
intention → goal
intention → object
intention → point
intention → purpose
intentional → deliberate
intentionally → on
    purpose
interchange → change
interchange → exchange
interchange → substitute
interchange → swap
interest → activity
interest → appeal
interest → curiosity
interest → enthusiasm
interested → curious
interesting → colourful
interfere → pry
interim → temporary
interior → inside
interlude → break
interlude → gap
interlude → interval
interminable → constant
interminable → continual
interminable → infinite
intermingle → mix
intermission → interval
intermittent → occasional
intern → confine
intern → imprison
internal → home
internal → inside
internal organs → insides
interpose → comment
interpret → read
interrogate → ask
interrogate → question
interrupt → intrude
interruption → delay
interruption → pause
intersect → cross
interstice → crack
interval → break
interval → gap
interval → pause
interval → period

interval → space
interval → time
interval → wait
intervene → interfere
interview → appointment
interview → question
interweave → mix
intimate → cosy
intimate → hint
intimate → mention
intimate → suggest
intimation → hint
intimation → indication
intimation → notice
intimation → suggestion
intimidate → bully
intimidate → frighten
intimidate → scare
intimidating → formidable
intimidating →
    frightening
into → keen
into the bargain → also
into the bargain → too
intolerable → unbearable
intolerant → impatient
intoxicated → drunk
intoxicating → exciting
intractable → difficult
intractable → obstinate
intractable → stubborn
intransigent → obstinate
intrepid → bold
intrepid → brave
intrepid → daring
intrepidity → courage
intrepidity → daring
intricate → complex
intricate → complicated
intricate → elaborate
intricate → fancy
intricate → sophisticated
intrigue → fascinate
intrigue → interest
intrigue → plot
intriguing → interesting
introduce → insert
introduce → raise
introduce → start

jiggle → fidget
jilt → abandon
jingle → slogan
jittery → nervous
jittery → tense
job → appointment
job → duty
job → function
job → task
job → undertaking
job → work
jobless → idle
jobless → unemployed
jocular → funny
jocularity → humour
jog → run
jog someone's memory → remind
joggle → shake
join → attach
join → connect
join → fasten
join → link
join → piece together
join → unite
join forces → cooperate
join forces → team
join forces → unite
join in → participate
join in → take part in
jointly → together
jolly → bright
jolly → cheerful
jolly → cheery
jolt → blow
jolt → bump
jolt → shake
jolt → surprise
jot → bit
jot → trace
jotting → note
journal → record
journey → drive
journey → go
journey → travel
journey → trip
jovial → cheery
joy → delight
joy → ecstasy

joy → happiness
joy → pleasure
joyful → glad
jubilant → joyful
judge → conclude
judge → consider
judge → feel
judge → justice
judge → reckon
judge → regard
judge → think
judge → view
judgment → belief
judgment → common sense
judgment → conclusion
judgment → decision
judgment → opinion
judgment → reason
judgment → sense
judgment → verdict
judgment → wisdom
judicial → legal
judiciary → legal
judicious → logical
judicious → reasonable
judicious → sane
judicious → sensible
judicious → wise
jumble → muddle
jumble → tangle
jumbled → garbled
jumbled → untidy
jump → bounce
jump → dive
jump → leap
jumpy → nervous
jumpy → restless
jumpy → tense
junction → connection
junior → inferior
junior → young
junk → garbage
junk → refuse
jurisdiction → control
just → barely
just → exactly
just → hardly
just → only

just about → nearly
just deserts → punishment
justice → judge
justice → right
justifiable. → reasonable
justification → cause
justification → defence
justification → excuse
justification → grounds
justify → defend
justify → deserve
jut out → extend
jutting → prominent
juvenile → child
juvenile → childish
juvenile → frivolous
juvenile → young
juxtapose → compare
kai → food
kai → meal
kaleidoscopic → colourful
keen → acute
keen → ardent
keen → astute
keen → eager
keen → enthusiastic
keen → fierce
keen → fine
keen → ready
keen → sharp
keenness → enthusiasm
keep → breed
keep → have
keep → own
keep → reserve
keep → save
keep → store
keep → upkeep
keep an eye on → mind
keep an eye on → supervise
keep on → continue
keep out → exclude
keep safe → save
keep your eyes open → watch out
keepsake → souvenir
kernel → essence

Index

lapse → error
larceny → theft
large → broad
large → extensive
large → spacious
large numbers → many
largely → mainly
lark → joke
lascivious → lustful
lash → tie
lass → woman
last → continue
last → endure
last → final
last → remain
last → remainder
last → stretch
last → survive
last → ultimate
last-minute → late
lasting → permanent
lastly → finally
latch → catch
latch → lock
late → dead
later → after
later → future
latest → fashionable
latest → last
latest → modern
latest → news
latest → trendy
lather → foam
latitude → freedom
latitudinarian → tolerant
latter-day → recent
laud → praise
laugh at → make **fun** of
laugh at → mock
laughable → ridiculous
launch → fire
launch → introduction
launch → release
launch → start
launder → wash
laundered → clean
laurels → victory
lavish → generous
lavish → luxurious

lavish → plentiful
law → principle
law → rule
law court → court
law-abiding → honest
law-abiding → obedient
lawbreaker → criminal
lawful → legal
lawfulness → right
lawsuit → case
lay → deposit
lay → put
lay → set
lay bare → reveal
lay bare → uncover
lay out → position
layer → coating
layout → form
layout → plan
laze → outspan
laze → relax
laze → rest
lead → bring
lead → command
lead → direct
lead → drive
lead → guide
lead → head
lead → motivate
lead → rule
lead → take
lead → top
lead to → cause
lead to → create
lead to → result in
leaden → cloudy
leaden → dull
leader → boss
leader → chief
leader → head
leader → ruler
leadership → direction
leading → first
leading → foremost
leading → important
leading → in **front**
leading → main
leading → major
leading → prime

leading → supreme
leading → top
league → association
league → fellowship
league → society
league → union
lean → bend
lean → skinny
lean → slender
lean → tilt
leaning → tendency
leap → dive
leap → jump
learn → discover
learn → find
learn → gather
learn → hear
learn → master
learn → study
learn → understand
learned → educated
learner → beginner
learning → knowledge
lease → hire
lease → let
least possible →
  minimum
leathery → tough
leave → abandon
leave → blessing
leave → deposit
leave → flee
leave → go
leave → holiday
leave → quit
leave → resign
leave → will
leave → withdraw
leave behind → abandon
leave in the lurch →
  abandon
leave out → exclude
leave out → omit
leavings → remains
lecherous → lustful
lecture → lesson
lecture → scold
lecture → speech
lecture → talk

Index

lecturer → teacher
leeway → freedom
leftist → left-wing
leftover → spare
leftover → waste
leftovers → remains
legacy → gift
legacy → inheritance
legal → formal
legality → right
legend → story
legendary → famous
legitimate → fair
legitimate → legal
legitimate → real
legitimate → reasonable
leisure → ease
leisure → rest
leisure activity → hobby
leisure pursuit → hobby
leisurely → easy
leisurely → slow
lekker → pleasant
lekker → tasty
lend → loan
lend a hand → help
lengthen → enlarge
leniency → mercy
lenient → gentle
lenient → kind
lenient → merciful
lessen → abate
lessen → decrease
lessen → diminish
lessen → lower
lessen → reduce
lessen → weaken
lessening → decrease
lesser → inferior
lesser → junior
lesser → minor
lessons → study
let → allow
let down → disappointed
let down → lower
let go → discharge
let go → release
let in → admit
let off → spare

let on → reveal
let someone have →
  spare
lethal → deadly
lethal → fatal
lethargic → sleepy
letter → note
lettered → learned
level → balance
level → even
level → extent
level → flat
level → rank
level → standard
level → straight
level-headed → cool
level-headed → realistic
level-headed →
  responsible
level-headed → sane
level-headedness →
  common sense
levelled → flat
levy → charge
levy → duty
levy → impose
levy → tax
lewd → indecent
lewd → lustful
lewd → naughty
lewd → obscene
liability → blame
liability → fault
liability → responsibility
liable → likely
liable → prone
liaison → affair
liaison → association
liaison → link
liaison → relationship
libel → slander
liberal → generous
liberal → handsome
liberal → left-wing
liberal → tolerant
liberality → generosity
liberate → discharge
liberate → free
liberate → release

liberated → free
liberated → independent
liberation → release
libertine → promiscuous
liberty → freedom
liberty → release
libidinous → lustful
licence → freedom
licence → permission
licence → permit
licence → power
licensed → official
licentious → promiscuous
licit → legal
lid → top
lie on the surface → float
life → energy
life force → spirit
life span → life
lifelike → realistic
lifetime → life
lift → raise
light → easy
light → fair
light → glow
light → soft
light up → light
light-headed → dazed
light-headed → dizzy
light-headed → faint
light-hearted → bright
light-hearted → cheerful
lightweight → fine
lightweight → light
lightweight → sheer
likable → pleasant
like → enjoy
like → love
like → similar
like better → prefer
likeable → pleasant
likelihood → chance
likelihood → possibility
likelihood → probability
likely → believable
likely → possible
likely → potential
likely → probable
likely → probably

likeness → copy
likeness → resemblance
likeness → similarity
likewise → too
liking → affection
liking → attachment
liking → love
liking → taste
liking → weakness
Lilliputian → tiny
lily-livered → cowardly
limber → agile
limit → confine
limit → curb
limit → extreme
limit → restrict
limitation → curb
limitation → restriction
limited → modest
limitless → countless
limitless → infinite
limits → border
limits → range
limpid → clear
limping → lame
line → border
line → course
line → rank
line → row
line → trade
line of work → trade
lineage → origin
lineage → stock
lineaments → face
lines → shape
linger → remain
linger → stay
linger → wait
lingering → slow
lingo → language
lingua franca → language
link → associate
link → attach
link → bond
link → connect
link → connection
link → join
link → relation
link → relationship

link up → team
link up → unite
lion's share → majority
lionized → famous
lip → edge
liquefy → melt
liquor → alcohol
liquor → liquid
lissom → agile
lissom → flexible
lissome → agile
lissome → flexible
list → tilt
listen in → hear
listen to → hear
listen to → heed
listing → list
literate → learned
lithe → agile
lithe → flexible
litter → garbage
litter → refuse
litter → rubbish
litter → young
little → insignificant
little → low
little → young
little ones → young
little-known → obscure
live → inhabit
live → survive
live on → endure
livelihood → work
liveliness → activity
lively → active
lively → alive
lively → bright
lively → busy
lively → colourful
lively → vital
livid → furious
livid → mad
living → alive
living → live
living soul → person
load → bunch
load → burden
load → mass
load → stuff

loaded → full
loaded → rich
loads → heaps
loaf → laze
loam → earth
loath → reluctant
loath → unwilling
loathe → dislike
loathe → hate
loathing → dislike
loathing → hate
loathing → horror
loathsome → hateful
lob → throw
lobby → passage
locale → location
locality → area
locality → region
locate → find
locate → place
locate → position
locate → set
locate → trace
location → place
location → position
location → scene
location → spot
location → surroundings
lock → fasten
lock → secure
lock up → imprison
locked → secure
lockup → jail
locum → substitute
locum tenens →
    substitute
locus → location
lodge → inhabit
lodge → stick
lodgings →
    accommodation
lofty → superior
lofty → tall
log → record
logic → argument
logical → rational
logical → reasonable
logo → sign
logo → symbol

Index

mass → jam
mass → majority
mass → tangle
mass production → manufacture
mass-produce → manufacture
massacre → kill
masses → a **lot** or lots
masses → public
massive → colossal
massive → enormous
massive → heavy
massive → huge
massive → immense
massive → large
massive → vast
master → beat
master → expert
master → fundi
master → genius
master → learn
master → overcome
master → teacher
masterly → expert
masterly → perfect
masterly → skilful
masterly → skilled
mastermind → genius
mastery → command
mastery → control
masticate → chew
mat → tangle
match → agree
match → blend
match → contest
match → correspond
match → equal
match → fit
match → game
match → rival
matchless → incomparable
mate → china
mate → companion
mate → friend
mate → partner
material → cloth
material → information

material → matter
material → relevant
material → stuff
material → substance
materialistic → greedy
materialize → come
materialize → happen
matrimony → marriage
matter → affair
matter → business
matter → count
matter → event
matter → issue
matter → item
matter → material
matter → subject
matter-of-fact → realistic
mature → develop
maudlin → corny
maudlin → sentimental
maul → savage
mausoleum → grave
mausoleum → tomb
mawkish → corny
mawkish → sentimental
maxim → saying
maximum → full
maximum → limit
maybe → perhaps
mayhap → maybe
métier → work
meadow → field
meagre → few
mean → horrible
mean → intend
mean → malicious
mean → petty
mean → represent
mean → shabby
mean → sneaky
mean → unkind
meandering → indirect
meaning → message
meaningless → empty
meaningless → worthless
means → measure
means → process
means → way
means → wealth

meant → supposed
measly → meagre
measly → petty
measure → extent
measure → quantity
measured → deliberate
measureless → countless
mechanical → automatic
mechanism → machine
meddle → interfere
meddler → snooper
mediate → intervene
medical → examination
medication → drug
medication → medicine
medicine → cure
medicine → drug
mediocre → inferior
mediocre → poor
mediocre → unsatisfactory
meditate → consider
meditate → deliberate
meditate → think
meditation → thought
meditative → thoughtful
medium → moderate
medium-sized → medium
medley → mixture
medley → variety
meek → gentle
meek → humble
meek → mild
meet → experience
meet → greet
meet → receive
meet → satisfy
meet → touch
meet head-on → hit
meeting → appointment
meeting → conference
meeting → convention
meeting → gathering
meeting → hui
melancholy → down
melancholy → miserable
melancholy → misery
melancholy → sad
melancholy → sadness
melancholy → sorrow

miniature → tiny
minimal → low
minimal → minimum
minimize → belittle
minimize → lessen
minimize → lower
minimum → least
minor → child
minor → inferior
minor → insignificant
minor → slight
minor → trivial
minor → unimportant
minus → disadvantage
minuscule → minute
minute → instant
minute → moment
minute → record
minute → tiny
miracle → wonder
mirage → illusion
mirage → vision
mirror → imitate
misapplication → waste
misappropriate → steal
miscalculate → err
miscalculation → mistake
miscarriage → failure
miscellaneous → various
miscellany → variety
mischievous → naughty
mischievous → wicked
misconception → illusion
misdeed → crime
misdeed → sin
misdemeanour → crime
miserable → down
miserable → gloomy
miserable → sorry
miserable → unhappy
miserly → mean
misery → evil
misery → grief
misery → hell
misery → pain
misery → sorrow
misery → spoilsport
misfortune → blow
misfortune → disaster

misfortune → hardship
misfortune → sorrow
misgiving → anxiety
misgiving → doubt
misgiving → suspicion
misgiving → worry
misinterpret as → mistake
mislaid → lost
mislay → lose
mislead → con
mislead → deceive
mislead → fool
mislead → take in
misleading → deceptive
misleading → untrue
misplace → lose
misplaced → lost
miss → lack
miss → overlook
miss out → omit
missile → bomb
missing → absent
missing → lost
mission → task
missive → message
missive → note
mist → cloud
mistake → confuse
mistake → error
mistake → miss
mistake → mix-up
mistake → slip
mistaken → false
mistaken → untrue
mistaken → wrong
mistress → teacher
mistrust → suspect
mistrust → suspicion
misty → wet
misunderstanding → mix-up
misuse → waste
mitigate → weaken
mix → associate
mix → blend
mix → combination
mix → combine
mix → mixture

mix up → confuse
mix up → muddle
mix up with → mistake
mixture → blend
mixture → combination
mixture → cross
mixture → union
mixture → variety
moan → complain
moan → grumble
moan → lament
mob → crowd
mob → jam
mob → mass
mob violence → riot
mock → imitate
mock → make **fun** of
mock → tease
mock-up → model
mockery → scorn
mode → fashion
mode → manner
mode → method
mode → style
model → design
model → example
model → ideal
model → make
model → shape
moderate → change
moderate → modest
moderate → reasonable
moderately → quite
modernize → renovate
modest → homely
modest → humble
modest → low
modest → reasonable
modification → change
modification → qualification
modify → adapt
modify → change
modify → vary
modish → smart
modus operandi → system
moggie → cat
moggy → cat

moist → damp
moist → wet
moisten → wet
moisture → damp
moke → horse
mollify → calm
mollify → humour
mollify → pacify
mollycoddle → spoil
molten → liquid
moment → instant
moment → minute
momentary → brief
momentary → temporary
momentous → critical
momentous → crucial
momentous → important
momentous → serious
momentum → speed
monarch → king
monarch → ruler
monetary → economic
monetary → financial
money → financial
money → wealth
money-making → economic
mongrel → dog
monitor → observe
monotonous → boring
monotonous → dreary
monotonous → dull
monotonous → flat
monotony → boredom
monster → savage
monumental → grand
mood → humour
moody → sulky
moor → secure
moot → raise
moral → message
morality → right
morality → virtue
morals → principle
morals → standards
mordacious → sarcastic
mordant → sarcastic
more → extra
more than → over

moreover → also
moreover → too
moron → fool
moron → idiot
moronic → idiotic
moronic → stupid
morose → down
morose → moody
mortal → deadly
mortal → fatal
mortal → individual
mortgage → loan
mortification → embarrassment
mortification → shame
mortified → ashamed
mortified → embarrassed
mortify → embarrass
mortify → shame
most → majority
most → maximum
most important → foremost
most recent → last
mostly → mainly
mother → parent
motif → pattern
motion → movement
motion → question
motion → signal
motionless → quiet
motionless → still
motivate → drive
motivate → prompt
motivation → cause
motivation → drive
motivation → incentive
motive → cause
motive → incentive
motive → reason
motor → automobile
motor → car
motorway → road
motto → slogan
mould → fashion
mould → model
mould → rot
mould → shape
mouldy → rotten

mound → heap
mound → pile
mount → climb
mount → horse
mount → rise
mount → stage
mountain → pile
mourn → grieve
mourn → lament
mourn → regret
mournful → miserable
mournful → sad
mourning → sorrow
mouthful → taste
mouthwatering → delicious
move → draw
move → motivate
move → touch
move house → move
move to → settle
move up → rise
moved → sorry
movement → campaign
movement → cause
movement → wave
moving → impressive
moving → sad
moving → touching
much → far
muck → dirt
muck up → mess
mucky → dirty
mud → dirt
muddle → cloud
muddle → disorder
muddle → mess
muddle → mix up
muddle → mix-up
muddle → tangle
muddle up → confuse
muddled → confused
muddy → cloudy
muddy → dirty
muffle → silence
mug → face
mugger → thief
muggy → humid
muggy → stuffy

mull over → consider
mull over → deliberate
mull over → ponder
mull over → think
multicoloured → colourful
multifarious → many
multiplicity → variety
multiply → breed
multiply → grow
multiply → increase
multitude → bunch
multitude → crowd
multitude → jam
multitude → number
multitudinous → countless
multitudinous → many
munch → chew
mundane → everyday
municipality → city
munificence → generosity
munificent → generous
murder → kill
murderous → fierce
murderous → violent
murk → dark
murkiness → dark
murky → cloudy
murky → dark
murky → dim
murky → dull
murmur → grumble
murmur → mumble
muscle → strength
muse → consider
muse → think
muse on → contemplate
mushy → sentimental
musical → sweet
muster → gather
muster → recruit
musty → stale
mutable → changeable
mutate → change
mutate → turn
mutation → change
mute → dumb
mute → silent
muted → dull

muted → faint
muted → soft
muteness → silence
muti → medicine
mutiny → rebel
mutiny → rebellion
mutt → dog
mutter → grumble
mutter → mumble
myriad → countless
myriad → many
mysterious → funny
mystify → confuse
mystify → puzzle
mystifying → mysterious
mythological → imaginary
nadir → extreme
nag → hassle
nag → horse
nagging → continual
naive → fond
naive → gullible
naive → ignorant
naive → innocent
naivety → innocence
naked → bare
name → celebrity
name → identify
name → nominate
name → reputation
name → specify
name → term
naming → appointment
nap → pile
nap → sleep
narcissism → conceit
narcissistic → conceited
narcissistic → vain
narcotic → drug
narrative → plot
narrative → story
narrow → shrink
narrow → thin
nasty → disagreeable
nasty → horrible
nasty → spiteful
nasty → unkind
nasty → unpleasant
nation → land

nation → public
nation → race
nation → state
national → home
native → home
native → inhabitant
native → local
native → natural
natter → chat
natty → smart
natural → automatic
natural → informal
natural → wild
naturalistic → realistic
nature → character
nature → essence
nature → personality
naughty → wicked
nausea → disgust
nauseate → disgust
nauseate → shock
nauseating → disgusting
nauseous → crook
nauseous → queasy
nauseous → sick
navigate → manoeuvre
ne plus ultra → peak
ne'er-do-well → failure
near → beside
near → immediate
near → imminent
near at hand → near
nearby → handy
nearby → near
nearest → next
nearly → about
nearly → almost
neat → handy
neat → orderly
neat → smart
neat → tidy
nebulous → vague
necessary → basic
necessary → vital
necessitate → demand
necessitate → involve
necessities → essentials
necessity → requirement
neck and neck → even

Index

not liable → exempt
not many → few
not quite → almost
not smooth → uneven
not well → unhealthy
not working → dead
notable → important
notable → memorable
notable → particular
notable → prominent
notable → significant
note → comment
note → entry
note → message
note → notice
note → observe
note → record
noted → famous
noted → prominent
noteworthy → particular
nothing → zero
notice → advertisement
notice → discern
notice → heed
notice → information
notice → item
notice → note
notice → observe
notice → review
notice → see
notice → sign
notice → warning
noticeable → conspicuous
noticeable → evident
noticeable → prominent
noticeable → visible
notification → notice
notify → advise
notify → alert
notify → inform
notify → report
notify → tell
notify → warn
notion → idea
notion → impression
notion → thought
notwithstanding → despite
notwithstanding → in
  spite of

nought → zero
nourishing → healthy
nourishment → food
nous → intelligence
nous → sense
novel → original
novel → strange
novel → unfamiliar
novelty → curiosity
novice → beginner
novice → recruit
now → immediately
now and again →
  sometimes
now and then →
  sometimes
nowadays → now
noxious → poisonous
noxious → unhealthy
nude → bare
nude → naked
nudge → poke
nugatory → worthless
nuisance → annoyance
nuisance → bother
nuisance → pest
nullify → foil
nullify → frustrate
numb → frozen
numb → shock
numbed → dazed
number → figure
number → quantity
numeral → figure
numeral → number
numerous → many
nurse → look after
nurse → take care of
nurse → tend
nurse → treat
nurture → breed
nurture → raise
nut → weirdo
nutritious → healthy
nutter → weirdo
oaf → idiot
oath → word
obdurate → firm
obdurate → stubborn

obese → overweight
obey → follow
object → article
object → disagree
object → goal
object → intention
object → mind
object → point
object → protest
object → purpose
object → subject
object → thing
object → use
object to → query
object to → resent
objection → complaint
objection → disagreement
objection → grumble
objection → protest
objectionable →
  disagreeable
objectionable → offensive
objectionable →
  unpleasant
objective → aim
objective → goal
objective → intention
objective → object
obligate → force
obligation → bond
obligation → duty
obligation → responsibility
obligatory → compulsory
oblige → force
oblige → make
oblige → require
obliged → supposed
obliging →
  accommodating
obliging → good
oblique → indirect
obliterate → blot out
obliterate → destroy
obliteration → destruction
oblivious → ignorant
oblivious → preoccupied
oblivious → unaware
oblivious → unconscious
obloquy → slander

obnoxious → disagreeable
obnoxious → disgusting
obnoxious → hateful
obnoxious → unpleasant
obscene → crude
obscene → naughty
obscure → blot out
obscure → cover
obscure → dim
obscure → mysterious
obscure → unknown
obsequiousness →
 flattery
observable → visible
observance → ceremony
observant → alert
observant → sharp
observation → comment
observation → remark
observation → watch
observe → comment
observe → discern
observe → follow
observe → note
observe → notice
observe → obey
observe → practise
observe → remark
observe → see
observe → spot
observe → watch
observe → witness
observer → spectator
observer → witness
obsessed → crazy
obsession → complex
obsessive → fanatical
obsolescent → old-
 fashioned
obsolete → old-fashioned
obsolete → out of date
obstacle → barrier
obstacle → difficulty
obstacle → handicap
obstinate → stubborn
obstreperous → difficult
obstreperous → rowdy
obstruct → bar
obstruct → block

obstruct → close
obstruct → delay
obstruct → hamper
obstruct → impede
obstruct → interfere
obstruction → barrier
obstruction → blockage
obstruction → delay
obstruction → obstacle
obtain → acquire
obtain → buy
obtain → earn
obtain → extract
obtain → gain
obtain → get
obtain → secure
obtrusive → pushy
obtuse → dim
obtuse → dumb
obtuse → slow
obtuse → stupid
obtuseness → stupidity
obverse → opposite
obvious → clear
obvious → conspicuous
obvious → evident
obvious → logical
obvious → manifest
obvious → noticeable
obvious → plain
obvious → prominent
obvious → visible
occasion → bring
occasion → case
occasion → chance
occasion → create
occasion → incident
occasional → irregular
occasionally →
 sometimes
occultism → magic
occupant → inhabitant
occupation → job
occupation → profession
occupation → trade
occupation → work
occupied → active
occupied → busy
occupy → busy

occupy → inhabit
occupy → invade
occupy → possess
occur → come
occur → happen
occur → take **place**
occurrence → case
occurrence → incident
odd → bizarre
odd → curious
odd → extraordinary
odd → funny
odd → occasional
odd → peculiar
odd → strange
odd → weird
oddity → curiosity
odds → chance
odds → possibility
odds → probability
odds and ends → junk
odium → hate
odium → horror
odour → smell
of course not → no
of easy virtue →
 promiscuous
of sound mind → sane
off → sour
off-course → lost
offence → breach
offence → crime
offence → insult
offence → sin
offend → insult
offend → repel
offend → shock
offended → hurt
offended → resentful
offender → criminal
offensive → abusive
offensive → attack
offensive → hateful
offer → tender
offering → present
offhand → careless
offhand → casual
office → department
office → room

officer → official
official → formal
officialdom → bureaucracy
offset → compensate
offset → counteract
offspring → child
offspring → young
ogle → stare
OK → all right
OK → correct
OK → right
OK → safe
OK → tolerable
okay → all right
okay → correct
okay → right
okay → safe
okay → tolerable
okay → yes
old → former
old → parent
old → stale
old hat → corny
old-fashioned → out of date
old-fashioned → stuffy
old-fogeyish → stuffy
old-time → old-fashioned
olden → past
omen → premonition
ominous → sinister
omit → exclude
omit → fail
omit → forget
omit → neglect
omnipresent → universal
on → about
on account of → because
on account of → by **virtue** of
on edge → restless
on guard → alert
on hand → handy
on the cards → probable
on the dot → exactly
on the dot → prompt
on the whole → as a **rule**
on the whole → mainly

on time → punctual
once in a while → sometimes
once more → again
one → only
one → single
one-eyed → biased
one-sided → biased
one-sidedness → favouritism
one-time → previous
onerous → formidable
ongoing → current
onlooker → spectator
onlooker → witness
only → single
only just → hardly
onset → beginning
onset → start
onslaught → attack
onus → responsibility
ooze → leak
opaque → cloudy
opaque → obscure
open → bare
open → candid
open → flexible
open → frank
open → impressionable
open → naked
open → spread
open → start
open → straightforward
open → uncover
open to the public → public
open-handed → generous
open-handedness → generosity
open-minded → tolerant
opening → beginning
opening → breach
opening → chance
opening → first
opening → gap
opening → hole
opening → start
operate → act
operate → behave

operate → drive
operate → function
operate → use
operation → action
operation → campaign
operation → enterprise
operation → undertaking
operation → use
opine → comment
opinion → advice
opinion → belief
opinion → feeling
opinion → idea
opinion → judgment
opinion → thought
opinion → verdict
opinion → view
opinion → viewpoint
opinionated → narrow-minded
opponent → competitor
opponent → enemy
opponent → rival
opportune → favourable
opportune → lucky
opportunity → chance
opportunity → occasion
opportunity → turn
oppose → contest
oppose → disagree
oppose → object
oppose → protest
oppose → resist
opposed → different
opposed → opposite
opposite → reverse
opposition → competition
opposition → competitor
opposition → conflict
opposition → disagreement
opposition → objection
oppress → bully
oppress → persecute
oppression → abuse
oppression → hardship
oppressive → stuffy
oppressive → unbearable
oppressor → bully

Index

passionate → ardent
passionate → crazy
passionate → enthusiastic
passionate → fanatical
passionate → fervent
passionate → intense
passionate → romantic
passionate → violent
passive → apathetic
passive → uninterested
passport → pass
passport → permit
past → former
past → over
past → previous
paste → bond
paste → glue
paste → stick
pastel → light
pastel → soft
pasteurized → pure
pastime → activity
pastime → hobby
pastime → interest
pasture → field
patch → mend
patch → repair
patch together → piece
  together
patch up → fix
patch up → repair
patchy → irregular
patchy → uneven
patent → clear
patent → conspicuous
patent → evident
patent → manifest
patent → naked
patent → obvious
patent → visible
path → course
path → direction
path → line
path → passage
path → route
path → way
pathetic → hopeless
pathetic → inadequate
pathetic → lame

pathetic → miserable
pathetic → sad
pathetic → sorry
pathway → path
patois → language
patriarch → parent
patrician → posh
patrol → guard
patron → customer
patron → supporter
patronize → frequent
patronizing → superior
pattern → design
pattern → routine
pattern → sequence
paucity → shortage
paucity → want
paunch → stomach
pause → break
pause → gap
pause → halt
pause → hesitate
pause → interval
pause → wait
pay → income
pay attention → listen
pay attention → watch
pay attention to → heed
pay back → repay
pay back → return
pay for → buy
pay for → finance
pay for → fund
pay someone back →
  retaliate
pay someone back →
  revenge
pay tribute to →
  commemorate
pay tribute to → praise
payable → outstanding
payment → charge
payment → compensation
payment → cost
payment → pay
payment → reward
peace → calm
peace → quiet
peace → silence

peaceable → mild
peaceful → quiet
peaceful → relaxed
peacefulness → calm
peak → top
peak → ultimate
peal → ring
peal → sound
peasant → yokel
peculiar → bizarre
peculiar → characteristic
peculiar → curious
peculiar → funny
peculiar → odd
peculiar → particular
peculiar → personal
peculiar → special
peculiar → strange
peculiar → weird
peculiarity → attribute
peculiarity →
  characteristic
peculiarity → quality
pecuniary → financial
pedagogue → teacher
peddle → sell
pedestal → base
peek → glance
peek → look
peep → glance
peep → peek
peer → noble
peerless → incomparable
peeved → resentful
peevish → cross
peevish → sour
pellet → ball
pellucid → clear
pelt → coat
pelt → hide
penal institution → jail
penal institution →
  prison
penalize → punish
penalties → sanctions
penalty → cost
penalty → punishment
penchant → love
penchant → taste

perspective → attitude
perspective → outlook
perspective → view
perspicacious → acute
perspicacious → perceptive
perspicacious → shrewd
persuade → coax
persuade → convince
persuade → push
persuade → reason
persuade → satisfy
persuasion → faith
persuasive → convincing
persuasive → powerful
pert → bold
pertain to → concern
pertinent → relevant
pertinent → suitable
perturb → agitate
perturb → concern
perturb → upset
perturb → worry
perturbation → anxiety
perturbed → uneasy
perturbed → worried
peruse → examine
peruse → study
pervasive → extensive
pervasive → widespread
pervert → corrupt
pessimistic → down
pest → annoyance
pest → nuisance
pester → hassle
pester → worry
pet → favourite
peter out → die
petition → appeal
petition → beg
petition → press
petition → request
petrified → frightened
petty → insignificant
petty → minor
petty → trivial
petulant → irritable
petulant → sulky
phantasm → illusion

phantasm → vision
phantom → ghost
phantom → spirit
phantom → vision
phase → stage
phenomenal → exceptional
phenomenal → wonderful
phenomenon → wonder
philanthropic → benevolent
philanthropic → kind
philanthropy → kindness
philosophical → patient
phobia → complex
phoney → fake
phoney → mock
phony → fake
phony → mock
phosphorescence → light
photograph → picture
phrase → express
phrase → expression
phrase → put
phraseology → language
phrasing → language
physiognomy → face
physique → body
physique → build
physique → figure
pick → choose
pick → favourite
pick → select
pick on → bully
pick on → persecute
pick out → distinguish
pick up → acquire
pick up → develop
pick up → learn
pick up → lift
pick up → receive
pickpocket → thief
picnic → eat
picture → imagine
picture → represent
piece → article
piece → bit
piece → block
piece → feature

piece → item
piece → lump
piece → part
piece → portion
piece → section
piece together → reconstruct
piercing → noisy
piercing → shrill
pigeonhole → classify
piggy → pig
pigment → colour
pigmentation → colour
pile → bunch
pile → heap
pile → load
pile → mass
pile-up → crash
piles → a **lot** or lots
pilfer → steal
pilferer → thief
pilfering → theft
pillage → loot
pillage → raid
pillar → support
pilot → drive
pinch → dash
pinch → emergency
pinch → steal
pine → long
pine for → be **dying** for
pine for → miss
pinnacle → extreme
pinnacle → peak
pinnacle → top
pinpoint → identify
pinpoint → locate
pioneer → start
pious → holy
pious → religious
pipe dream → daydream
pipe dream → dream
pique → anger
pique → resentment
piqued → hurt
piqued → resentful
pirouette → spin
pit → abyss
pit → grave

Index

pit → hole
pitch → throw
pitch → tilt
piteous → sorry
pitfall → difficulty
pitfall → risk
pithy → concise
pithy → short
pitiable → pathetic
pitiable → sorry
pitiful → pathetic
pitiful → sorry
pitiless → merciless
pity → mercy
pity → sympathy
pivotal → critical
pivotal → crucial
pivotal → vital
placard → sign
placate → calm
placate → pacify
place → appointment
place → deposit
place → fit
place → identify
place → insert
place → lay
place → location
place → position
place → put
place → recognize
place → scene
place → set
place → spot
place your trust in →
   trust
placed → located
placid → gentle
placid → mild
placid → peaceful
placid → quiet
plague → annoy
plague → nuisance
plague → rash
plague → worry
plain → blank
plain → clear
plain → common
plain → evident

plain → frank
plain → manifest
plain → obvious
plain → simple
plain → straight
plain → straightforward
plain → ugly
plain → visible
plaint → lament
plaintive → pathetic
plan → aim
plan → arrange
plan → contemplate
plan → course
plan → design
plan → idea
plan → intend
plan → layout
plan → mean
plan → organize
plan → pattern
plan → plot
plan → suggestion
plane → level
planet → earth
planned → calculated
planning → organization
plant → factory
plant → place
plaster → spread
plausible → believable
plausible → convincing
plausible → logical
plausible → probable
plausible → reasonable
play → act
play → appear
play → perform
play a part → appear
play a part in → take **part**
   in
play a trick on → dupe
play the part of → act
play up → emphasize
player → figure
plea → appeal
plea → defence
plea → request
plead → appeal

plead → ask
plead → beg
plead → press
plead → urge
plead with → implore
pleasant → agreeable
pleasant → lekker
pleasant → lovely
pleasant → warm
please → appeal
please → delight
please → entertain
please → satisfy
please → suit
pleased → glad
pleased → proud
pleased → satisfied
pleasing → beautiful
pleasurable → agreeable
pleasurable → pleasant
pleasure → delight
pleasure →
   entertainment
pleasure → fun
pleasure → happiness
pleasure → pride
pleat → fold
plebiscite → vote
pledge → bond
pledge → guarantee
pledge → oath
pledge → promise
pledge → word
plenitude → wealth
plenteous → rich
plentiful → abundant
plentiful → generous
plentiful → handsome
plentiful → rich
plenty → a **lot** or lots
plenty → abundance
plenty → heaps
plenty → many
plenty → wealth
plenty of → ample
plethora → abundance
plethora → excess
plethora → plenty
pliable → flexible

pliable → limp
pliable → soft
pliant → flexible
plight → jam
plight → situation
plight → state
plough into → crash
ploy → manoeuvre
ploy → trick
pluck → bravery
pluck → courage
pluck → pick
pluck → tug
plucky → brave
plug → advertise
plug → advertisement
plug → block
plug → promote
plug → publicity
plug → publicize
plummet → decline
plummet → descend
plummet → drop
plummet → fall
plump → tubby
plunder → loot
plunder → raid
plunge → fall
plus → virtue
plush → luxurious
ply → use
poach → cook
podgy → tubby
poignant → moving
poignant → sad
poignant → touching
point → aspect
point → consideration
point → detail
point → item
point → location
point → message
point → moment
point → place
point → position
point → purpose
point → question
point → spot
point → stage

point → subject
point → use
point of view → attitude
point of view → feeling
point of view → opinion
point of view → view
point of view → viewpoint
point out → comment
point to → indicate
point up → stress
point-blank → straight
pointed → sharp
pointer → hint
pointless → hopeless
pointless → unnecessary
poise → grace
poison → pollute
poke → dig
poke → stick
poke fun at → mock
poke your nose in → pry
poke your nose into →
  pry
pole → bar
pole → stick
police → guard
policy → course
policy → procedure
polish → finish
polish → gloss
polish → perfect
polish → practise
polished → glossy
polished → perfect
polished → smooth
polite → refined
politeness → courtesy
politesse → polish
polls → vote
pollute → soil
pomp → ceremony
pompous → pretentious
ponder → consider
ponder → contemplate
ponder → deliberate
ponder → think
ponder → wonder
ponderous → slow
pong → smell

pong → stink
pontifical → pompous
pony → horse
pooch → dog
pool → fund
poor → deficient
poor → hopeless
poor → inadequate
poor → inferior
poor → lame
poor → low
poor → pathetic
poor → remote
poor → rotten
poor → sorry
poor → unsatisfactory
poor → worthless
poorly → crook
poorly → ill
poorly → sick
poorly → unhealthy
poorly → unwell
poorly lit → dim
populace → public
popular → common
popular → fashionable
popular → mass
popular → public
populate → inhabit
populate → settle
population → people
pore over → read
pore over → scrutinize
pore over → study
porker → pig
pornographic → dirty
pornographic → obscene
portable → light
portend → predict
portent → omen
portent → premonition
portentous → ominous
portentous → pompous
portion → measure
portion → part
portion → piece
portion → quantity
portion → section
portion → share

Index

Index

protected → safe
protected → secure
protection → defence
protection → precaution
protection → safeguard
protection → safety
protection → shelter
protector → champion
protest → agitate
protest → complaint
protest → grumble
protest → object
protest → objection
protestation → claim
protestation → declaration
protocol → ceremony
protocol → convention
prototype → example
prototype → ideal
protract → lengthen
protrude → bulge
protrude → extend
protrusion → bulge
protrusion → lump
protuberance → bump
protuberance → lump
proud → haughty
proud → stuck-up
proud → vain
prove → confirm
prove → show
prove false → disprove
provenance → origin
provender → food
proverb → saying
provide → equip
provide → give
provide → issue
provide → supply
providence → fate
providential → lucky
province → field
province → land
province → range
province → territory
provision → condition
provision → precaution
provisional → temporary

provisions → food
provisions → kai
provisions → supplies
provisions → terms
proviso → condition
proviso → terms
provoke → bring about
provoke → cause
provoke → excite
provoke → incite
provoke → irritate
provoke → motivate
provoke → occasion
proxy → replacement
proxy → representative
proxy → substitute
prudence → caution
prudence → common sense
prudence → economy
prudent → careful
prudent → cautious
prudent → economical
prudent → sensible
prudent → thrifty
prudish → prim
prying → nosy
pseudo → mock
pseudo- → fake
pseudo- → false
psyche → mind
psyche → personality
psychedelic → colourful
public → people
public house → pub
publication → book
publicize → advertise
publicize → promote
publish → release
puerile → childish
puerile → frivolous
puerile → silly
puff → gasp
puffed up → pompous
pugnacious → aggressive
puke → vomit
puku → stomach
pull → attract
pull → draw

pull → lure
pull → tug
pull back → retreat
pull out → extract
pull out → withdraw
pull through → survive
pull together → cooperate
pull together → unite
pull up → halt
pulse → rhythm
pump → drain
punch-drunk → dazed
punctilious → careful
puncture → burst
puncture → leak
puncture → pierce
pungent → sour
puny → weak
purchase → buy
purchaser → customer
pure → absolute
pure → innocent
pure → neat
pure → refined
pure → sheer
pure → utter
purely → only
purified → clean
purified → refined
puritanical → prim
purlieus → outskirts
purloin → steal
purpose → function
purpose → goal
purpose → intention
purpose → object
purpose → point
purpose → reason
purpose → use
purpose → will
purposeful → determined
purposely → on **purpose**
pursue → chase
pursue → follow
pursuit → activity
pursuit → interest
pursuit → work
purvey → supply

Index

question → contest
question → dispute
question → doubt
question → interrogate
question → issue
question → matter
question → query
question → subject
questionable → doubtful
questionable → dubious
questionable → suspect
questionable → suspicious
queue → line
queue → row
quick → acute
quick → astute
quick → brief
quick → intelligent
quick → keen
quick → prompt
quick → sharp
quick → sudden
quick → swift
quick-witted → clever
quick-witted → sharp
quicken → accelerate
quicken → hurry
quickly → fast
quiescent → passive
quiet → calm
quiet → easy
quiet → peace
quiet → peaceful
quiet → silence
quiet → silent
quiet → sleepy
quiet → soft
quieten → calm
quieten → silence
quietude → peace
quintessence → essence
quip → joke
quirk → characteristic
quirky → eccentric
quit → leave
quit → resign
quit → stop

quite → exactly
quite → pretty
quite → rather
quiver → shake
quiz → ask
quiz → interrogate
quiz → question
quondam → past
quota → proportion
quota → quantity
quota → share
quotation → passage
quote → estimate
rabid → fanatical
race → dash
race → fly
race → rush
race → speed
race → tear
racism → prejudice
racket → noise
racket → sound
radiance → light
radiant → bright
radiant → brilliant
radiant → shining
radiate → emit
radiate → shine
radical → drastic
radical → extreme
radical → left-wing
rage → anger
rage → frenzy
rage → rampage
rage → rave
ragged → irregular
ragged → scruffy
ragged → shabby
raging → furious
raging → violent
raging → wild
raid → attack
raid → loot
rail → bar
raiment → clothes
raiment → dress
rainfall → rain
rainy → wet
raise → breed

raise → collect
raise → lift
rally → gathering
rally → hui
rally → recovery
rally → revive
ram → drive
ram → jam
ram → push
ram → stick
ram → stuff
ramble → walk
ramble → wander
rambling → indirect
ramp → slope
rampage → rage
rampage → riot
rampart → barrier
rancid → sour
rancorous → bitter
rancorous → malicious
rancour → resentment
rancour → spite
random → absent-minded
random → accidental
random → irregular
randomly → at random
range → area
range → choice
range → variety
range → wander
rank → class
rank → classify
rank → level
rank → line
rank → rate
rank → row
rank → status
ransack → loot
rant → rave
rap → blame
rap → hit
rap someone's knuckles → punish
rapid → fast
rapid → hasty
rapid → prompt
rapid → quick

rapid → swift
rapidity → speed
rapidly → fast
rapidly → quickly
rapport → relationship
rapture → delight
rapture → ecstasy
rapture → heaven
rapture → joy
rare → exceptional
rare → scarce
rare → singular
rare → uncommon
rare → unusual
raring to go → eager
rarity → curiosity
rash → unwise
rasp → scrape
rasping → hoarse
rate → class
rate → consider
rate → cost
rate → count
rate → grade
rate → judge
rate highly → appreciate
rate highly → value
rather → pretty
rather → quite
ratification → approval
ratification → sanction
ration → limit
ration → share
rational → logical
rational → reasonable
rational → sane
rational → sensible
rational → wise
rationale → grounds
rationality → head
rationality → reason
rationalize → cut
rations → kai
rations → supplies
rattle → shake
ratty → irritable
rave → rage
ravenous → hungry
raving → hysterical

raw → cold
raw → inexperienced
raw → sore
raw → tender
raze → destroy
razor-sharp → sharp
résumé → outline
résumé → summary
re-establish → renew
re-establish → restore
reach → contact
reach → extend
reach → stretch
reach a decision → decide
reach adulthood → mature
reach its highest point → peak
reactionary → conservative
reactionary → narrow-minded
reactionary → right-wing
read out → issue
reading → extract
ready → agreeable
ready → fluent
ready → willing
real → authentic
real → genuine
real → natural
real → sincere
real → true
realism → reality
realistic → actual
reality → fact
reality → truth
realize → accomplish
realize → appreciate
realize → discover
realize → find
realize → fulfil
realize → grasp
realize → see
realize → sense
realize → understand
really → very
reanimate → revive

reap → earn
reap → gain
reappear → return
rear → back
rear → bottom
rear → breed
rear → raise
reason → argue
reason → cause
reason → excuse
reason → grounds
reason → purpose
reason → sense
reason → wisdom
reasonable → cheap
reasonable → decent
reasonable → logical
reasonable → moderate
reasonable → rational
reasonable → respectable
reasonable → sane
reasonable → sound
reasonable → tolerable
reasonably → quite
reasoned → logical
reasoning → argument
reasoning → reason
reassemble → reconstruct
reassure → comfort
reassure → encourage
reassure → satisfy
reassured → secure
rebound → bounce
rebound → glance
rebuff → reject
rebuild → reconstruct
rebuild → restore
rebuke → scold
rebut → deny
recalcitrant → obstinate
recalcitrant → stubborn
recall → memory
recall → remember
recapitulate → repeat
recapitulate → sum up
recapitulation → summary
recapture → recover
recapture → recovery

refreshing → cool
refreshment → food
refrigerate → cool
refuge → retreat
refuge → shelter
refund → compensate
refund → repay
refund → return
refurbish → renovate
refurbish → restore
refuse → decline
refuse → deny
refuse → garbage
refuse → junk
refuse → reject
refuse → resist
refuse → rubbish
refuse → trash
refute → deny
refute → disprove
regain → recover
regal → royal
regard → admiration
regard → esteem
regard → rate
regard → respect
regard → view
regard as → consider
regarding → about
regardless of → despite
regardless of → in **spite** of
regenerate → reconstruct
region → area
region → land
regional → local
register → list
register → note
register → record
regret → disappointment
regret → sorrow
regretful → guilty
regretful → sorry
regular → average
regular → constant
regular → continual
regular → conventional
regular → even
regular → formal

regular → normal
regular → orderly
regular → ordinary
regular → routine
regular → standard
regular → steady
regular → typical
regular → usual
regularity → order
regulation → law
regulation → restriction
regulation → rule
regulations → bureaucracy
regurgitate → vomit
rehabilitate → reform
rehabilitation → reform
rehearsal → practice
rehearse → practise
reheat → heat
reign → rule
reimburse → compensate
reimburse → pay
reimburse → repay
reimburse → return
reimbursement → compensation
reimbursement → pay
rein → restrain
reinforce → augment
reinforce → strengthen
reinforce → supplement
reinforce → support
reinstate → restore
reintroduce → restore
reiterate → repeat
reject → boycott
reject → deny
reject → refuse
reject → renounce
rejoice → celebrate
rejoin → reply
rejoinder → answer
rejoinder → reply
rejuvenate → refresh
rekindle → revive
relate → connect
relate to → **identify** with
relating to → about

relation → bond
relation → connection
relations → family
relations → kin
relationship → affair
relationship → association
relationship → connection
relationship → link
relationship → relation
relationship → tie
relative → relation
relatively → rather
relatives → family
relatives → kin
relax → calm
relax → ease
relax → lift
relax → moderate
relax → outspan
relax → rest
relaxation → ease
relaxation → leisure
relaxation → rest
relaxed → calm
relaxed → casual
relaxed → comfortable
relaxed → cool
relaxed → cosy
relaxed → easy
relaxed → informal
relaxed → leisurely
relaxed → secure
relaxing → comfortable
release → discharge
release → emit
release → free
release → freedom
release → issue
relentless → constant
relentless → fierce
reliable → responsible
reliable → sound
reliable → sure
reliable → trusty
reliance → confidence
relic → souvenir
relics → remains
relief → comfort
relief → escape

relieve → ease
relieve from → spare
religion → faith
religious → holy
relinquish → renounce
relinquish → surrender
relish → enjoy
relish → enthusiasm
relish → glory
relish → like
relish → love
relocate → move
reluctant → hesitant
reluctant → unwilling
rely on → depend
rely on → expect
rely upon → trust
remain → continue
remain → endure
remain → last
remain → stay
remain → wait
remainder → difference
remainder → rest
remains → body
remains → remainder
remains → ruin
remark → comment
remark → expression
remark → note
remark → observe
remark → word
remarkable →
 exceptional
remarkable → marvellous
remarkable → singular
remarkable →
 uncommon
remarkable → wonderful
remarkably → really
remarkably → very
remedy → correct
remedy → cure
remedy → medicine
remembrance →
 memory
remind → prompt
reminder → note
reminder → souvenir

reminisce → remember
remission → forgiveness
remit → function
remit → send
remittance → payment
remnant → trace
remnants → remainder
remnants → remains
remodel → reconstruct
remonstrate → argue
remonstrate → protest
remorse → regret
remorseful → guilty
remorseful → sorry
remote → distant
remote → far
remote → impersonal
remote → lonely
remote → slender
removal → transport
remove → banish
remove → eliminate
remove → extract
remove → get **rid** of
remove → lift
remove → withdraw
remunerate →
 compensate
remunerate → pay
remunerate → repay
remuneration →
 compensation
remuneration → pay
remunerative →
 economic
rend → tear
rendezvous →
 appointment
rendezvous → meeting
renounce → abstain
renounce → deny
renounce → reject
renounce → surrender
renovate → decorate
renovate → mend
renovate → reconstruct
renovate → repair
renovate → restore
renown → fame

renown → glory
renown → reputation
renowned → famous
renowned → prominent
rent → hire
rent → let
renunciation → sacrifice
reopen → renew
reorder → vary
repair → fix
repair → mend
repair → piece together
repair → renovate
repair → restore
reparation →
 compensation
repast → meal
repay → compensate
repay → return
repeal → cancel
repeat → quote
repeat → stress
repeated → continual
repeated → frequent
repeatedly → often
repel → disgust
repellent → disgusting
repellent → nasty
repent → regret
repentance → regret
repentant → sorry
repetitious → boring
replace → change
replace → substitute
replace → succeed
replacement →
 substitute
replica → copy
replica → model
replication → copy
reply → answer
report → announcement
report → feature
report → item
report → review
report → statement
repose → lie
repose → peace
repose → sleep

repository → container
repository → store
reprehensible → wrong
representation → model
representation → symbol
representational → realistic
representative → official
representative → substitute
representative → typical
repress → contain
repress → suppress
repressed → pent-up
reprimand → caution
reprimand → lecture
reprimand → scold
reprisal → revenge
reproach → censure
reproduce → breed
reproduce → copy
reproduction → copy
reproduction → fake
reprove → scold
republic → state
repudiate → deny
repudiate → reject
repugnance → horror
repugnant → disgusting
repulse → repel
repulsion → disgust
repulsive → unpleasant
reputable → honest
reputable → respectable
reputation → fame
reputation → name
repute → reputation
reputed → supposed
request → appeal
require → demand
require → expect
require → involve
require → need
require → take
require → want
required → compulsory
required → necessary
required → supposed
requirement → condition

requirement → standard
requisite → compulsory
requisite → condition
requisite → necessary
reschedule → put off
rescind → abolish
rescind → cancel
rescind → lift
rescind → reverse
rescue → save
research → investigate
research → study
resemblance → similarity
resent → envy
resentful → bitter
resentful → jealous
resentful → sulky
resentment → animosity
resentment → envy
resentment → hostility
reservation → qualification
reserve → bank
reserve → book
reserve → fund
reserve → hoard
reserve → save
reserve → stock
reserve → stockpile
reserve → store
reserve → supply
reserved → cold
reserved → distant
reserved → remote
reserved → secretive
reservoir → bank
reservoir → fund
reservoir → stock
reservoir → store
reside → inhabit
reside → live
residence → home
residence → house
resident → inhabitant
resident → local
residue → remains
resign → quit
resigned → passive
resilient → tough

resist → oppose
resist → rebel
resist → repel
resistance → defence
resistance → opposition
resistant → immune
resolute → determined
resolute → firm
resolute → serious
resolute → steadfast
resolution → decision
resolution → determination
resolution → resolve
resolution → will
resolve → decide
resolve → determination
resolve → determine
resolve → intend
resolve → settle
resolve → solve
resolve → will
resolve → work out
resolved → serious
resonant → deep
resonate → ring
resounding → loud
respect → admiration
respect → admire
respect → appreciate
respect → approval
respect → approve
respect → consider
respect → consideration
respect → detail
respect → esteem
respect → value
respectable → decent
respectful → polite
respite → break
respite → rest
resplendent → bright
respond → answer
respond → reply
respond to → **identify** with
response → answer
response → reaction
response → reply

riddle → mystery
riddle → problem
riddle → puzzle
ride → drive
ridge → top
ridicule → make **fun** of
ridicule → mock
ridicule → mockery
ridiculous → absurd
ridiculous → crazy
ridiculous → daft
ridiculous → silly
rife → widespread
rifle → raid
rift → breach
rift → fissure
rift → split
right → accurate
right → correct
right → fitting
right → immediately
right → power
right → proper
right → suitable
right away → immediately
right now → now
right-hand man → assistant
right-hand man → helper
righteous → religious
righteousness → right
righteousness → virtue
rightful → legal
rightful → real
righting → correction
rigid → firm
rigid → hard
rigid → stiff
rigid → strict
rigid → tense
rigid → tight
rigorous → hard
rigorous → stiff
rigorous → strict
rigorously → well
rim → border
rim → edge
ring → sound
ringleader → leader

rinse → wash
riotous → noisy
riotous → wild
rip → split
rip → tear
rip off → cheat
ripe → ready
riposte → answer
riposte → reply
ripple → wave
rise → gain
rise → increase
rise → jump
rise → slope
rise to → reach
risible → funny
risk → danger
risk → dare
risk → endanger
risk → gamble
risk → possibility
risk → threat
risky → dangerous
risqué → dirty
risqué → naughty
rite → ceremony
ritual → ceremony
ritual → custom
rival → competitor
rivalry → competition
road → passage
road → route
road → way
roam → wander
roar → shout
roast → cook
robber → thief
robbery → theft
robe → dress
robot → automatic
robust → fit
robust → healthy
robust → sound
robust → sturdy
robust → tough
robust → well
rocket → bomb
rocket → explode
rocky → rough

rod → bar
rod → stick
rogue → crook
role → duty
role → function
role → job
role → part
roll → flow
romance → affair
room → capacity
room → space
rooms → flat
roomy → spacious
root → cause
root → origin
rope → tie
rot → eat away
rot → nonsense
rot → rubbish
rotate → spin
rotate → turn
rotten → shabby
rotten → terrible
rotund → overweight
rough → approximate
rough → broad
rough → crude
rough → jagged
rough → primitive
rough → uneven
rough → violent
rough → wild
roughly → about
round → ring
round off → conclude
round up → gather
roundabout → indirect
rounded → blunt
rounded → round
rouse → excite
rouse → provoke
rouse → wake
rousing → exciting
rout → defeat
rout → vanquish
route → course
route → direction
route → line
route → passage

sad → sorry
sad → unhappy
sadden → distress
sadden → grieve
sadden → hurt
saddened → disappointed
saddening → painful
sadistic → cruel
sadness → grief
sadness → misery
sadness → sorrow
safe → harmless
safe → immune
safe → reliable
safe → secure
safe and sound → safe
safeguard → defence
safeguard → defend
safeguard → guard
safeguard → precaution
safeguard → protect
safeguard → protection
safeguard → save
safety → shelter
sagacious → clever
sagacious → shrewd
sagacity → sense
sagacity → wisdom
sagging → flabby
sail → fly
saintly → holy
salacious → dirty
salacious → obscene
salary → income
salary → pay
salient → important
salient → noticeable
salient → prominent
sallow → pale
sally → joke
saloon → pub
salted → salty
salubrious → healthy
salutary → healthy
salute → greet
salute → recognize
salvage → save
sameness → similarity
sample → example

sample → try
sanction → allow
sanction → approval
sanction → approve
sanction → blessing
sanction → let
sanction → permit
sanctioned → legal
sanctuary → refuge
sanctuary → retreat
sanctuary → shelter
sands → beach
sane → reasonable
sanguine → optimistic
sanitation → hygiene
sap → drain
sap → tax
sap → undermine
sap → weaken
sarcophagus → tomb
sardonic → sarcastic
sate → satisfy
satiate → satisfy
satire → parody
satirical → sarcastic
satirize → make **fun** of
satisfaction → comfort
satisfaction → delight
satisfaction → happiness
satisfaction → pleasure
satisfaction → pride
satisfactorily → well
satisfactory → acceptable
satisfactory → adequate
satisfactory → decent
satisfactory → suitable
satisfied → certain
satisfied → confident
satisfied → pleased
satisfied → sure
satisfy → convince
satisfy → fulfil
satisfy → meet
satisfy → suit
saturate → soak
saturate → wet
saturated → full
saturated → wet
saucy → bold

saunter → walk
savage → violent
savagery → cruelty
savagery → violence
save → but
save → except
save → hoard
save → reserve
save → safeguard
save → stockpile
save → store
save from → spare
saving → cut
savoir-faire → style
saw → saying
say → choice
say → comment
say → observe
say → remark
say → state
say again → repeat
say no to → reject
say sorry → apologize
scalding → hot
scale → climb
scale → extent
scale drawing → plan
scan → glance
scan → inspect
scan → read
scan → scrutinize
scandal → disgrace
scandal → gossip
scandal → shame
scandal → slander
scandalize → shock
scandalous → disgraceful
scandalous → notorious
scant → insufficient
scant → low
scant → meagre
scantiness → lack
scanty → few
scanty → meagre
scanty → slight
scarce → few
scarce → inadequate
scarce → rare
scarce → uncommon

sensible → rational
sensible → realistic
sensible → reasonable
sensible → responsible
sensible → sane
sensible → sound
sensible → wise
sensitive → fine
sensitive → impressionable
sensitive → sore
sensitive → tactful
sensitive → tender
sensitive → touchy
sensitive → tricky
sensitive → understanding
sensitive → vulnerable
sensitivity → tact
sensual → sexy
sensuous → sexy
sentence → condemn
sentence → punish
sentiment → feeling
sentimental → corny
sentinel → guard
sentry → guard
separate → alone
separate → different
separate → divide
separate → independent
separate → individual
separate → single
separate → sort
separate → split
separation → division
sepulchre → grave
sepulchre → tomb
sequence → grade
sequence → series
serendipitous → casual
serene → cool
serene → patient
serene → peaceful
serene → quiet
serene → relaxed
serenity → calm
serenity → quiet
series → range

series → sequence
series → set
serious → acute
serious → critical
serious → deep
serious → grave
serious → heavy
serious → important
serious → severe
serious → solemn
sermon → lecture
sermon → talk
serrated → jagged
serve as → form
service → ceremony
service → favour
serviceable → convenient
serving → portion
session → round
session → term
set → bunch
set → category
set → class
set → firm
set → group
set → harden
set → insert
set → lay
set → lot
set → ready
set → rigid
set → thicken
set → time
set about → begin
set about → start
set against one another → divide
set aside → allow
set aside → reserve
set aside → save
set at liberty → free
set back → delay
set down → lay
set free → discharge
set free → release
set in motion → start
set loose → free
set off → explode
set off → fire

set off → flatter
set off → go
set off → provoke
set off → sound
set out → lay
set someone back → cost
set store by → respect
set up → organize
set up → start
set upon → attack
setback → blow
setback → delay
setback → disappointment
setting → scene
setting → surroundings
settle → confirm
settle → determine
settle → lay
settle → pay
settle on → choose
settle on → pick
settle on → select
settle up → repay
settled → definite
settlement → agreement
settlement → colony
several → numerous
severe → acute
severe → drastic
severe → extreme
severe → grim
severe → harsh
severe → intense
severe → serious
severe → simple
severe → violent
severity → violence
sexism → prejudice
shabby → scruffy
shade → colour
shade → cover
shadow → blot out
shadowy → dark
shadowy → dim
shady → corrupt
shady → crooked
shady → suspicious
shaft → bar

shake → disturb
shake → shock
shake → wave
shaky → unsteady
sham → fake
sham → mock
sham → phoney
shambolic → untidy
shame → disgrace
shame → embarrass
shame → embarrassment
shame → humiliate
shame → pity
shamefaced → guilty
shamefaced → sorry
shameful → disgraceful
shampoo → wash
shape → body
shape → build
shape → condition
shape → design
shape → determine
shape → fashion
shape → figure
shape → form
shape → health
shape → model
shape → outline
shape → state
share → proportion
share out → distribute
shares → stock
shark → crook
sharp → acute
sharp → astute
sharp → bitter
sharp → bright
sharp → brilliant
sharp → intelligent
sharp → perceptive
sharp → prompt
sharp → shrewd
sharp → shrill
sharp → sour
sharp-eyed → observant
shatter → dash
shattered → broken
shed → discard
sheen → gloss

sheepish → ashamed
sheepish → embarrassed
sheer → absolute
sheer → fine
sheer → perfect
sheer → pure
sheer → rank
sheer → steep
sheer → transparent
sheer → utter
sheet → layer
sheila → female
sheila → woman
shell → bomb
shell → ruin
shelter → accommodate
shelter → defend
shelter → guard
shelter → protect
shelter → protection
shelter → refuge
shelve → delay
shelve → postpone
shepherd → guide
shield → defend
shield → guard
shield → protect
shield → safeguard
shield → shelter
shielded → secure
shiftless → lazy
shimmer → shine
shimmer → sparkle
shimmering → shining
shine → finish
shine → gloss
shine → glow
shine → polish
shiny → glossy
ship → transport
shipment → load
shipment → transport
shipshape → tidy
shirk → avoid
shirk → dodge
shiver → shake
shock → amaze
shock → amazement
shock → blow

shock → horrify
shock → scare
shock → shake
shock → surprise
shocking → disgraceful
shoddy → inferior
shoddy → poor
shoot → fire
shoot → grow
shoot → rush
shoot → tear
shoot up → explode
shoplifter → thief
shopper → customer
shore → bank
shore → beach
shore → coast
shore up → support
short → abrupt
short → brief
short → concise
short → deficient
short → inadequate
short → insufficient
short → low
short-lived → temporary
shortage → lack
shortage → want
shortcoming → defect
shortcoming → failure
shorten → reduce
shortfall → shortage
shortly → soon
shot → attempt
shot → go
shot → try
shoulder → assume
shoulder → bear
shoulder to shoulder → together
shout → call
shout → cry
shout → scream
shove → push
shove → stick
shove → stuff
show → betray
show → expose
show → fair

show → front
show → indicate
show → play
show → programme
show → represent
show signs of → promise
show up → appear
show up → come
show up → expose
show up → uncover
show-off → braggart
shower → hail
shower → scatter
showers → rain
showery → wet
showy → flashy
showy → gaudy
showy → ostentatious
shred → tear
shrewd → acute
shrewd → astute
shrewd → clever
shrewd → keen
shrewd → smart
shrewd → wise
shriek → scream
shrink → cower
shrink → decrease
shrink → diminish
shrink → flinch
shrink → lessen
shrinkage → decline
shrivel → burn
shrivel → wither
shroud → obscure
shudder → shake
shun → avoid
shunned → unpopular
shut → close
shut up → confine
shy → timid
sick → crook
sick → ill
sick → queasy
sick → unhealthy
sick → unwell
sick person → patient
sicken → disgust
sicken → horrify

sicken → repel
sickening → disgusting
sickly → puny
sickly → weak
sickness → illness
side → aspect
side → bank
side → face
side → point
side → team
side by side → together
side with → support
sidestep → avoid
sidestep → dodge
sidetrack → distract
sidle → edge
sidle → sneak
siesta → sleep
sift → investigate
sift → search
sight → see
sight → spot
sign → indication
sign → notice
sign → omen
sign → premonition
sign → signal
sign → symbol
sign → trace
sign up → hire
sign up → join
signal → famous
signal → indicate
signal → indication
signal to → hail
significance → meaning
significant → important
significant → major
significant → serious
significant → special
signify → count
signify → indicate
signify → mean
silence → peace
silence → quiet
silent → dumb
silent → quiet
silhouette → figure
silhouette → outline

silky → smooth
silliness → stupidity
silly → daft
silly → foolish
silly → frivolous
silly → irrational
silly → unwise
similar → alike
similar → like
similarity → resemblance
similarly → alike
similitude → resemblance
similitude → similarity
simple → crude
simple → easy
simple → homely
simple → humble
simple → primitive
simple → straightforward
simplicity → ease
simplicity → innocence
simply → only
simulate → copy
simulate → fake
simulate → imitate
simulated → false
simultaneously → together
sin → evil
sin → wrong
since → because
sincere → dinkum
sincere → real
sincere → serious
sinew → strength
sinful → evil
sinful → wicked
sinfulness → evil
singe → burn
single → alone
single → individual
single out → favour
single out → select
single-minded → determined
single-mindedness → determination
single-mindedness → resolve

Index

solid → stocky
solid → sturdy
solid → tough
solid → trusty
solidify → harden
solitary → single
solution → idea
solution → liquid
solve → crack
solve → resolve
solve → work out
sombre → drab
sombre → dull
sombre → grave
some → several
somewhat → quite
somewhat → rather
somnolent → sleepy
sonorous → deep
sonorous → loud
sookie → cowardly
sooner → before
soothe → calm
soothe → comfort
soothe → pacify
soothsay → predict
sophisticated → polite
sophistication → style
sorcery → magic
sordid → scungy
sore → painful
sore → tender
soreness → pain
sorrow → distress
sorrow → evil
sorrow → grief
sorrow → misery
sorrow → regret
sorrowful → miserable
sorrowful → unhappy
sorry → ashamed
sorry → guilty
sorry → miserable
sorry → pathetic
sort → arrange
sort → category
sort → class
sort → classify
sort → form

sort → grade
sort → group
sort → kind
sort → type
sort → variety
sort out → resolve
sortie → raid
sought-after → popular
soul → essence
soul → individual
soul → person
soul → spirit
soul mate → friend
sound → bay
sound → logical
sound → reasonable
sound → reliable
sound → responsible
sound → sane
sound → sensible
sound → well
soundless → quiet
soundless → silent
soupçon → trace
sour → bitter
sour → rotten
sour → stale
source → cause
source → head
source → origin
sovereign → king
sovereign → royal
sovereign → ruler
sovereignty → power
sow → scatter
space → capacity
space → gap
space → length
space → opening
space → room
space → stretch
spacious → broad
spacious → extensive
span → cross
span → length
span → space
spare → extra
spark off → provoke
sparkle → flash

sparkle → shine
sparkling → brilliant
sparkling → lively
sparkling → shining
sparkling → witty
sparse → few
sparse → meagre
sparse → rare
sparse → uncommon
Spartan → harsh
spartan → bare
spartan → plain
spate → burst
spate → flood
spate → rash
spatter → soil
speak → lecture
speak out against → oppose
special → different
special → exceptional
special → individual
special → particular
special → peculiar
special → personal
special → private
special → select
specialist → expert
specialist → fundi
speciality → field
species → breed
species → kind
species → sort
species → type
specific → particular
specific → precise
specific → special
specification → requirement
specify → state
specimen → example
specious → deceptive
speck → bit
speck → spot
spectacle → sight
spectacle → view
spectacle → wonder
spectator → witness
spectre → ghost

Index

spectre → spirit
spectre → vision
speculate → guess
speculate → wonder
speculation → guess
speech → lecture
speech → talk
speechless → dumb
speechless → silent
speechlessness →
  silence
speed → fly
speed → race
speed → rate
speed → tear
speed up → accelerate
speed up → hurry
speedily → quickly
speedy → fast
speedy → quick
speedy → swift
spell → influence
spell → period
spell → stretch
spell → term
spell → time
spell out → specify
spellbind → entrance
spellbind → fascinate
spellbinding → magical
spendthrift → wasteful
spew → puke
sphere → ball
spherical → round
spheroid → ball
spick-and-span → tidy
spicy → hot
spill → leak
spill → upset
spin → drive
spin → turn
spineless → cowardly
spineless → weak
spiral → coil
spirit → energy
spirit → essence
spirit → ghost
spirit → sneak
spirited → energetic

spirited → vital
spirits → alcohol
spirits → humour
spirits → mood
spiritual → religious
spiteful → malicious
spiteful → unkind
spitefulness → spite
spitting image →
  lookalike
splash → dash
splash → drip
spleen → anger
splendid → fine
splendid → first-rate
splendid → grand
splendid → marvellous
splendid → superb
splendidly → well
splendour → glory
splenetic → cross
splice → join
split → breach
split → burst
split → divide
split → division
split → fissure
split → hole
split → share
split → tear
split second → instant
split second → moment
split up → divide
split up → separate
spoil → rot
spoil → ruin
spoils → loot
spoken → oral
spokesman →
  representative
spokeswoman →
  representative
sponge → clean
sponge → scrounge
sponsor → supporter
spoof → parody
spooky → creepy
spooky → scary
sporadic → irregular

sporadic → occasional
sporadic → rare
sport → wear
spot → discern
spot → location
spot → notice
spot → observe
spot → place
spot → random
spot → recognize
spot → scene
spot → see
spot → sight
spot → stain
spotless → clean
spotless → innocent
spotless → pure
spotlight → feature
spouse → partner
spout → pour
sprain → twist
sprawl → lie
sprawl → spread
spray → bunch
spray → wet
spread → circulate
spread → communicate
spread → distribute
spread → lay
spread → meal
spread → multiply
spread → stretch
spreading → infectious
sprightly → active
sprightly → agile
sprightly → lively
sprightly → vital
spring → develop
spring → jump
spring → leap
spring up → grow
sprinkle → scatter
sprinkling → dash
sprint → dash
sprint → run
sprite → spirit
sprout → grow
spruce → neat
spruce → smart

spruce up → tidy
spur → drive
spur → incentive
spur → prompt
spurious → false
spurious → phoney
spuriousness → fraud
spurn → boycott
spurn → refuse
spurn → reject
spurt → gush
squabble → argue
squabble → argument
squabble → clash
squabble → disagreement
squabble → fight
squabble → quarrel
squabble → row
squad → party
squad → team
squalid → scungy
squander → waste
squandering → waste
square → agree
square → repay
squash → crush
squashy → soft
squat → crouch
squat → low
squeal → scream
squeeze → clasp
squeeze → cram
squeeze → ease
squeeze → hug
squeeze → press
squeeze → stuff
squirm → fidget
stab → attempt
stab → effort
stab → go
stab → poke
stabilize → balance
stabilize → steady
stable → constant
stable → secure
stable → solid
stable → steady
stack → heap
stack → load

stack → pile
stacks → heaps
stage → level
stage → perform
stage → round
stagger → amaze
stagger → shock
stagger → surprise
staggering → amazing
stagnant → stale
staid → conventional
staid → serious
staid → solemn
staid → stuffy
stain → colour
stain → mark
stain → soil
stake → gamble
stale → boring
stale → corny
stale → hackneyed
stale → stuffy
stalk → follow
stall → jam
stamina → strength
stamp → sort
stamp out → crush
stamp out → eliminate
stamp out → suppress
stampede → charge
stampede → dash
stampede → rush
stance → attitude
stanchion → support
stand → base
stand → endure
stand → put up with
stand → tolerate
stand by → wait
stand for → allow
stand for → put up with
stand for → represent
stand up for → side with
stand up to → brave
stand-in → replacement
standard → average
standard → common
standard → conventional
standard → ideal

standard → level
standard → normal
standard → ordinary
standard → routine
standard → stock
standard → typical
standard → usual
standing → mana
standing → rank
standing → reputation
standing → status
standoffish → cold
standoffish → distant
standoffish → stiff
standstill → halt
star → celebrity
star → feature
star → personality
star → success
stark → naked
stark → plain
stark-naked → naked
start → begin
start → beginning
start → flinch
start → head
start → opening
start → proceed
start → scare
start → surprise
starter → beginner
startle → alarm
startle → frighten
startle → scare
startled → frightened
startling → amazing
starving → hungry
stash → hide
stash → stockpile
stash → store
state → condition
state → country
state → declare
state → observe
state → remark
state → report
state → specify
state → territory
state of affairs → situation

stockpile → bank
stockpile → gather
stockpile → hoard
stockpile → reserve
stockpile → stock
stockpile → store
stockpile → supply
stodgy → stuffy
stomach → bear
stomach → put up with
stony → cold
stoop → bend
stop → block
stop → cease
stop → check
stop → end
stop → halt
stop → prevent
stop → quit
stop → suppress
stop → visit
stop working → fail
stopgap → substitute
stoppage → blockage
stoppage → halt
stoppage → pause
stopper → plug
stopper → top
store → bank
store → collection
store → fund
store → hoard
store → keep
store → reserve
store → shop
store → stock
store → stockpile
store → supply
store → wealth
store up → stockpile
storehouse → store
storeroom → store
stores → supplies
storm → attack
storm → charge
storm → hail
storm → rage
stormy → wild
story → article

story → feature
story → plot
story line → plot
stout → overweight
stout → plump
stout → sturdy
stout → tubby
straight → direct
straight → neat
straight → straightforward
straightaway →
  immediately
straightaway → now
straighten → stretch
straighten → tidy
straighten out → settle
straightforward → blunt
straightforward → candid
straightforward → direct
straightforward → easy
straightforward → frank
straightforward → simple
strain → bother
strain → breed
strain → burden
strain → difficulty
strain → stress
strain → struggle
strain → tax
strain → variety
strained → tense
strains → tune
strait-laced → prim
strait-laced → stuffy
straiten → limit
straiten → restrain
straiten → restrict
straits → distress
strand → beach
strand → coast
strange → bizarre
strange → curious
strange → eccentric
strange → extraordinary
strange → funny
strange → odd
strange → peculiar
strange → unfamiliar
strange → weird

strapping → powerful
stratagem → manoeuvre
stratagem → plot
stratagem → trick
strategy → plan
strategy → procedure
stratum → layer
stray → ramble
streak → line
streak → mark
stream → flood
stream → flow
stream → gush
stream → pour
streamline → simplify
street → road
strength → character
strength → energy
strength → force
strength → merit
strength → power
strength → virtue
strengthen → build
strengthen → encourage
strengthen → secure
strenuous → hard
stress → beat
stress → burden
stress → care
stress → emphasize
stress → strain
stressful → tense
stretch → extend
stretch → lengthen
stretch → period
stretch → range
stretch → tax
stretch → term
stretch → time
strew → scatter
strict → accurate
strict → faithful
strict → right
strict → rigid
strict → severe
stricture → criticism
stride → walk
strident → loud
strident → noisy

Index

Index

submit → give in
submit → nominate
submit → offer
submit → pose
submit → subject
submit → surrender
subordinate → inferior
subordinate → junior
subsequent → next
subsequently → after
subsequently → next
subservient → obedient
subside → abate
subside → decrease
subside → fall
subsidize → fund
subsidy → grant
subsistence → food
substance → essence
substance → material
substance → matter
substance → stuff
substance → wealth
substantial → solid
substantial → sturdy
substantiate → confirm
substantiate → prove
substantiation → proof
substitute → change
substitute → replacement
subterfuge → manoeuvre
subterfuge → trick
subtle → fine
subvert → undermine
succeed → flourish
succeed → follow
succeed → pass
succeed → replace
succeed → triumph
succeed → win
succeed in → manage
succeeding → next
success → triumph
success → victory
success → win
successfully → well
succession → sequence
succession → series
successor → replacement

succinct → concise
succumb → develop
succumb → give in
succumb → surrender
sudden → abrupt
sudden → quick
sudden → sharp
suffer → bear
suffer → endure
suffer → feel
suffer → receive
suffer → undergo
sufferer → patient
suffering → distress
suffice → do
sufficient → adequate
sufficient → ample
sufficient → satisfactory
sugary → sweet
suggest → advise
suggest → hint
suggest → nominate
suggest → raise
suggest → vote
suggestible →
  impressionable
suggestion → advice
suggestion → hint
suggestion → idea
suggestion → indication
suggestion → trace
suit → blend
suit → flatter
suit → match
suitable → appropriate
suitable → favourable
suitable → fitting
suitable → proper
suitable → right
sulky → grumpy
sulky → moody
sullen → grumpy
sullen → moody
sullen → sulky
sully → soil
sultry → stuffy
sum → count
sum → quantity
sum → total

sum total → whole
summarize → outline
summarize → sum up
summary → outline
summing-up → summary
summit → peak
summit → top
sumptuous → luxurious
sumptuousness → luxury
sunder → separate
sunder → tear
sundry → several
sundry → various
sunken → low
sunny → cheery
sup → drink
superabundance →
  excess
superb → brilliant
superb → excellent
superb → first-rate
superb → marvellous
superb → outstanding
superb → splendid
superb → wonderful
supercilious → scornful
supercilious → superior
superciliousness → pride
superfluity → excess
superfluous → excess
superfluous → spare
superfluous → waste
superintend → supervise
superintendence →
  control
superior → prime
superior → select
superior → senior
superior → smug
superior → superb
superiority → advantage
superiority → victory
superlative → first-rate
superlative →
  incomparable
superlative → superb
supermarket → shop
supernatural → spooky
supernumerary → spare

Index

theme → message
theme → subject
theme → tune
theological → religious
theory → idea
there → present
thick → broad
thick → dim
thick → dumb
thick → slow
thick → stupid
thickset → stocky
thief → crook
thieve → steal
thieving → theft
thin → narrow
thin → sheer
thin → skinny
thin-skinned → sensitive
thin-skinned → touchy
thing → article
thing → complex
thing → item
thing → object
thing → obsession
things → possessions
things → stuff
think → assume
think → consider
think → expect
think → feel
think → guess
think → ponder
think → reckon
think → suppose
think about → consider
think about →
  contemplate
think highly of → approve
think highly of → respect
think of → contemplate
think of → regard
thinking → thought
thirst → longing
thirst → wish
thorny → difficult
thorough → absolute
thorough → careful
thorough → complete

thorough → full
thorough → utter
thoroughgoing → total
thoroughly → well
though → but
though → in **spite** of
thought → consideration
thoughtful → good
thoughtful → humane
thoughtful → kind
thoughtless →
  irresponsible
thoughtless → unkind
thrash → beat
threadbare → hackneyed
threadbare → shabby
threadbare → worn-out
threat → danger
threaten → endanger
threatening → ominous
threatening → sinister
threatening remark →
  threat
thrift → economy
thrifty → economical
thrill → delight
thrill → excite
thrill → excitement
thrilled → excited
thrilling → exciting
thrive → flourish
thrive → succeed
thriving → successful
throng → crowd
throng → jam
throng → mass
throw about → scatter
throw away → discard
throw away → dispose of
throw away → dump
throw away → waste
throw down the
  gauntlet → dare
throw out → discard
throw out → dump
throw the book at →
  punish
throw up → puke
thrust → dig

thrust → drive
thrust → push
thrust → stick
thrust → stuff
thud → bump
thumbnail sketch →
  outline
thump → bang
thump → blow
thump → bump
thunderous → loud
thus → therefore
thwart → block
thwart → dash
thwart → foil
thwart → frustrate
thwart → prevent
tick off → caution
tick off → scold
ticket → label
ticket → pass
ticking-off → lecture
tide → current
tide → flow
tidings → news
tidy → neat
tidy → orderly
tie → association
tie → attach
tie → bond
tie → fasten
tie → join
tie → link
tie up → secure
tiff → disagreement
tiff → squabble
tight → mean
tight → secure
tight → tense
tight spot → hole
tight spot → predicament
tight-fisted → mean
tight-lipped → secretive
tightly → fast
till → dig
time → beat
time → chance
time → life
time → moment

tumultuous → furious
tumultuous → noisy
tumultuous → violent
tuneful → sweet
tunnel → dig
turbulent → violent
turbulent → wild
turf → earth
turmoil → disorder
turmoil → mess
turn → bend
turn → curve
turn → get
turn → grow
turn → spin
turn → swerve
turn → twist
turn a blind eye to → excuse
turn a blind eye to → overlook
turn aside → distract
turn back → return
turn down → decline
turn down → refuse
turn down → reject
turn out → work out
turn red → blush
turn scarlet → blush
turn under → fold
turn up → appear
turn up → come
turn up → find
turn your back on → neglect
turn your stomach → disgust
tutor → adviser
tutor → instruct
tutor → master
tutor → teach
tutor → teacher
tutor → train
tutoring → lesson
twice → double
twig → stick
twin → double
twine → coil
twine → twist

twinge → pain
twinkle → flash
twinkle → sparkle
twirl → turn
twist → bend
twist → coil
twist → misrepresent
twist → tangle
twist → turn
twisted → crooked
twit → idiot
twitch → fidget
two-faced → insincere
two-timing → unfaithful
twofold → double
type → breed
type → category
type → class
type → form
type → kind
type → sort
type → variety
typical → average
typical → characteristic
typical → natural
typical → normal
typical → regular
typical → representative
typical → routine
typical → stock
typically → on **average**
tyrannical → absolute
tyrannized → oppressed
tyranny → oppression
tyro → recruit
ultimate → extreme
ultimate → final
ultimate → last
ultimate → limit
ultimate → supreme
umbrage → resentment
umpire → judge
umpteen → many
unabashed → shameless
unable → incompetent
unacceptable → unbearable
unacceptable → unsatisfactory

unacceptable → unsuitable
unaccountable → strange
unaccustomed → inexperienced
unadulterated → pure
unadulterated → sheer
unadventurous → conventional
unaffected → immune
unaffected → natural
unaffected → real
unaided → independent
unaided → on your **own**
unanticipated → abrupt
unanticipated → unexpected
unappreciative → ungrateful
unapproachable → distant
unashamed → shameless
unassailable → invincible
unassuming → humble
unassuming → meek
unassuming → modest
unattached → single
unattainable → impossible
unattractive → ugly
unauthorized → illegal
unavailing → useless
unavoidable → necessary
unaware → ignorant
unaware → unconscious
unbeatable → invincible
unbelievable → improbable
unbelievable → incredible
unbelievable → unlikely
unbeliever → heathen
unbiased → fair
unbiased → neutral
unblemished → pure
unbroken → flat
uncalled-for → unnecessary

Index

Index

Index